Fodor's 2010

COSTA RICA

Fodor's Travel Publications New York, Toronto, London, Sydney, Auckland

www.fodors.com

Be a Fodor's Correspondent

Share your trip with Fodor's

Our latest guidebook to Costa Rica—now in full color—owes its success to travelers like you. Throughout, you'll find photographs submitted by members of Fodors.com to our "Show Us Your . . . Costa Rica" photo contest. Facing this page is a our grand prize–winning photograph of tree frogs, taken by Monica Richards. Stumbling upon hundreds of these little guys near a watering hole in one of Bosque del Cabo's gardens was one of the highlights of her trip to the Osa Peninsula.

We are especially proud of this color edition. No other guide to Costa Rica is as up to date or has as much practical planning information, along with hundreds of color photographs and illustrated maps. We've also included "Word of Mouth" quotes from travelers who shared their experiences with others on our forums. If you're inspired and can plan a better trip because of this guide, we've done our job.

We invite you to join the travel conversation: Your opinion matters to us and to your fellow travelers. Come to Fodors.com to plan your trip, share an experience, ask a question, submit a photograph, post a review, or write a trip report. Tell our editors about your trip. They want to know what went well and how we can make this guide even better. Share your opinions at our feedback center at fodors.com/feedback, or email us at editors@fodors.com with the subject line "Costa Rica Editor." You might find your comments published in a future Fodor's guide. We look forward to hearing from you.

Happy Traveling!

Tim Jarrell, Publisher

FODOR'S COSTA RICA 2010

Editor: Margaret Kelly

Editorial Contributors: Joanna Cantor, Katie Hamlin, Alexis Kelly, Laura Kidder
Writers: Leland Baxter-Neal, David Dudenhoefer, Gillian Gillers, Liz Goodwin, Heidi Johanson, Dorothy MacKinnon, Holly Sonneland, Mark Sullivan, Jeffrey Van Fleet

Production Editor: Carrie Parker
Maps & Illustrations: David Lindroth, Mark Stroud, *cartographers;* Bob Blake, Rebecca Baer, *map editors*; William Wu, *information graphics*
Design: Fabrizio La Rocca, *creative director*; Guido Caroti, Siobhan O'Hare, *art directors*; Tina Malaney, Chie Ushio, Ann McBride, Jessica Walsh, *designers*; Melanie Marin, *senior picture editor*
Cover Photo: (Man Rappelling): Randy Faris/Corbis
Production Manager: Amanda Bullock

COPYRIGHT

ISBN 978-1-4000-0847-6

ISSN 1522-6131

SPECIAL SALES

This book is available at special discounts for bulk purchases for sales promotions or premiums. Special editions, including personalized covers, excerpts of existing books, and corporate imprints, can be created in large quantities for special needs. For more information, write to Special Markets/Premium Sales, 1745 Broadway, MD 6-2, New York, New York 10019, or e-mail specialmarkets@randomhouse.com.

AN IMPORTANT TIP & AN INVITATION

Although all prices, opening times, and other details in this book are based on information supplied to us at press time, changes occur all the time in the travel world, and Fodor's cannot accept responsibility for facts that become outdated or for inadvertent errors or omissions. So **always confirm information when it matters,** especially if you're making a detour to visit a specific place. Your experiences—positive and negative—matter to us. If we have missed or misstated something, **please write to us.** We follow up on all suggestions. Contact the Costa Rica editor at editors@fodors.com or c/o Fodor's at 1745 Broadway, New York, NY 10019.

PRINTED IN SINGAPORE

10 9 8 7 6 5 4 3 2 1

CONTENTS

Fodor's Features

MAPS

ABOUT THIS BOOK

Our Ratings

Sometimes you find terrific travel experiences and sometimes they just find you. But usually the burden is on you to select the right combination of experiences. That's where our ratings come in.

As travelers we've all discovered a place so wonderful that its worthiness is obvious. And sometimes that place is so experiential that superlatives don't do it justice: you just have to be there to know. These sights, properties, and experiences get our highest rating, **Fodor's Choice,** indicated by orange stars throughout this book.

Black stars highlight sights and properties we deem **Highly Recommended,** places that our writers, editors, and readers praise again and again for consistency and excellence.

By default, there's another category: any place we include in this book is by definition worth your time, unless we say otherwise. And we will.

Disagree with any of our choices? Care to nominate a place or suggest that we rate one more highly? Visit our feedback center at www.fodors.com/feedback.

Budget Well

Hotel and restaurant price categories from ¢ to $$$$ are defined in the opening pages of each chapter. For attractions, we always give standard adult admission fees; reductions are usually available for children, students, and senior citizens. Want to pay with plastic? **AE, D, DC, MC, V** following restaurant and hotel listings indicate whether American Express, Discover, Diners Club, MasterCard, and Visa are accepted.

Restaurants

Unless we state otherwise, restaurants are open for lunch and dinner daily. We mention dress only when there's a specific requirement and reservations only when they're essential or not accepted—it's always best to book ahead.

Hotels

Hotels have private bath, phone, TV, and air-conditioning and operate on the European Plan (aka EP, meaning without meals), unless we specify that they use the Continental Plan (CP, with a Continental breakfast), Breakfast Plan (BP, with a full breakfast), or Modified American Plan (MAP, with breakfast and dinner), or are all-inclusive (AI, including all meals and most activities). We always list facilities but not whether you'll be charged an extra fee to use them, so when pricing accommodations, find out what's included.

Listings
- ★ Fodor's Choice
- ★ Highly recommended
- ✉ Physical address
- ✥ Directions or Map Coordinates
- Mailing address
- ☎ Telephone
- Fax
- On the Web
- E-mail
- Admission fee
- ⊙ Open/closed times
- Ⓜ Metro stations
- Credit cards

Hotels & Restaurants
- Hotel
- Number of rooms
- Facilities
- Meal plans
- ✕ Restaurant
- Reservations
- Smoking
- BYOB
- Hotel with restaurant that warrants a visit

Outdoors
- Golf
- Camping

Other
- Family-friendly
- ⇨ See also
- Branch address
- ☞ Take note

1

Experience Costa Rica

WHAT'S WHERE

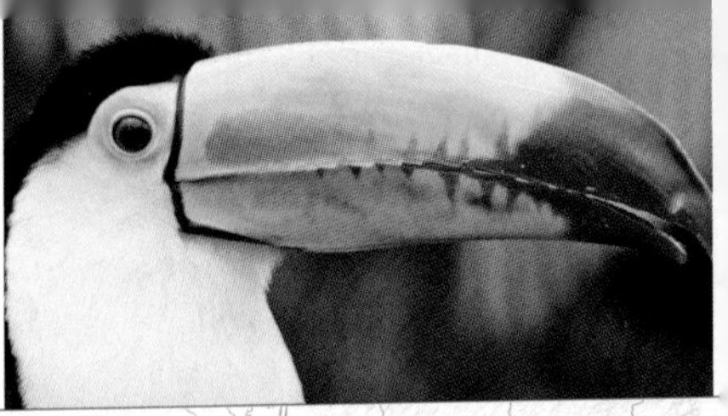

3 San José. Do you know the way to San José? You will soon enough. Almost everyone passes through on their way to the beach or the mountains. This capital city isn't much to look at, but it has great restaurants and nightlife, and fascinating museums dedicated to gold and jade.

4 The Central Valley. You won't want to linger long in the Central Valley, as it lacks any of the country's big-name attractions. But there are quite a few day-trip possibilities, including exploring mountain villages, rafting through white-water rapids, and gaping into the mouths of some of the country's most accessible active volcanoes.

5 The Northern Plains. The Northern Plains attract those who don't like sitting still. After zipping along cables through the misty jungle of Monteverde Cloud Forest, windsurfing on glittering Lake Arenal, or watching the nightly fireworks of Arenal Volcano, you can reward yourself with a dip in the bubbly waters of Tabacón Hot Springs.

6 The North Pacific. If you came for beaches, the Northern Pacific is for you. Each has a unique personality: Flamingo's endless stretch of sand draws sun worshippers;

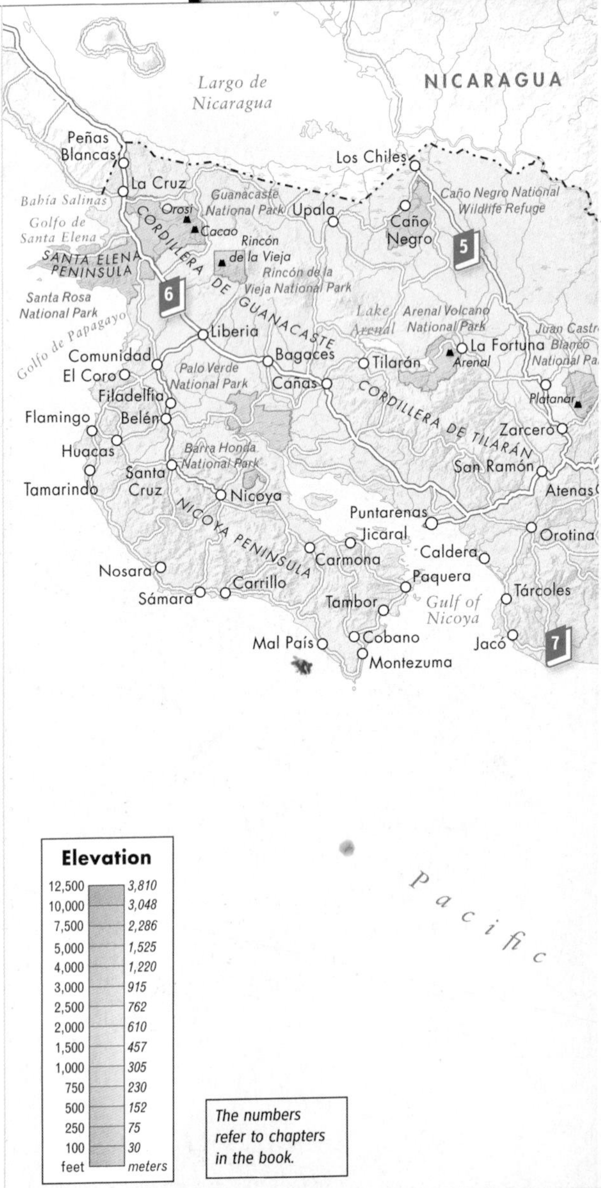

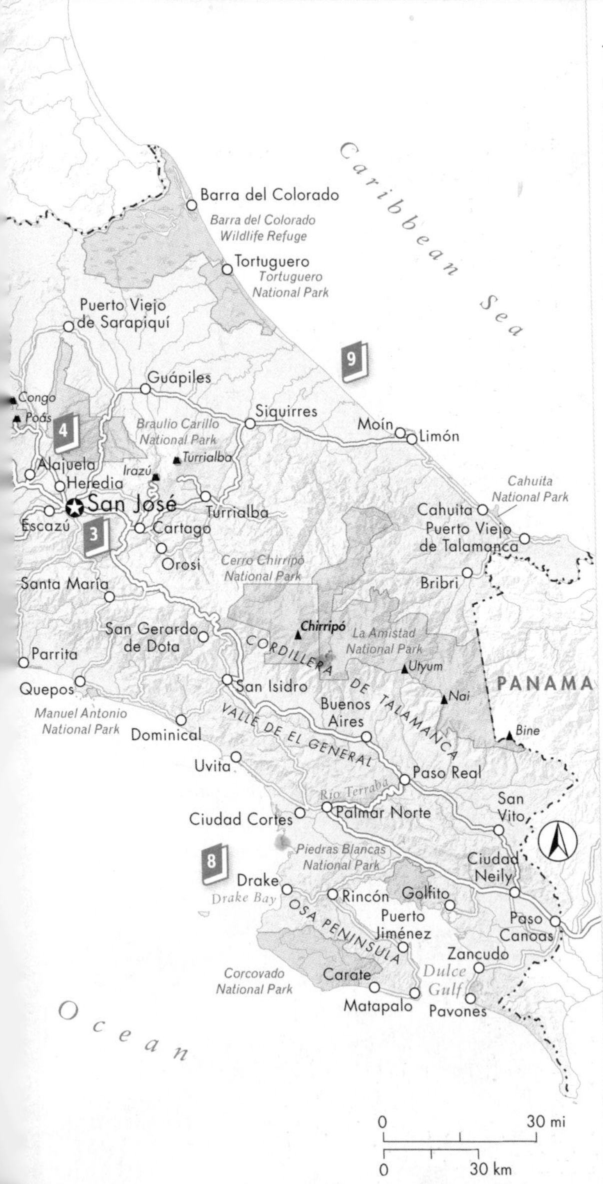

Tamarindo's nightlife is legendary; Avellanas's strong swells challenge surfers; Ostional's nesting sea turtles bring nature lovers; and the Papagayo Peninsula's all-inclusive resorts provide every creature comfort.

7 The Central Pacific. The area's not just for spring-breakers (although it helps in funky surf towns like Jacó). Drive down the coast to the cluster of small hotels and restaurants at Manuel Antonio. The national park, on a peninsula jutting into the ocean, has the easiest wildlife-viewing on the planet.

8 The South Pacific. Also known as "the Amazon of Costa Rica," rustic lodges in the Osa Peninsula sit on the edge of the country's wildest region. Hikes reveal toucans and scarlet macaws in the treetops, and boating trips often include swimming with whales and dolphins.

9 The Caribbean. Despite its name, Costa Rica's Caribbean isn't known for white-sand beaches or crystal-blue waters. Come here for the spirited music, tasty food, and the chance to mix with the Afro-Caribbean population. The coast also attracts turtle-watchers, as four different kinds nest at Tortuguero National Park.

COSTA RICA PLANNER

When to Go

The sunniest, driest season in most of the country occurs from roughly mid-December through April, which is the busiest tourist season. Afternoon showers kick in by May and last through November most everywhere, with a brief dry season in June and July. Costa Rica promotes the rainy season as the "green season," touting lush vegetation, smaller crowds, and lower prices. Showers interrupt your afternoon beach time, and remote roads can be washed out during the worst of the rains.

Temperatures generally range between 20°C (70°F) and 30°C (85°F). It's the humidity, not the heat, that causes you discomfort, especially in the dense forest of the Caribbean coast, the northern lowlands, and the Osa Peninsula. The arid North Pacific is Costa Rica's hottest region, with temperatures frequently exceeding 33°C (90°F) in the dry season.

One final point: we typically hear, "I didn't realize the rain forest would be so . . . *rainy.*" Well, you heard it here: it rains often and heartily in the rain forest. The dense foliage and elaborate root systems rely on there being frequent showers year-round.

Getting Here

San José's Aeropuerto Internacional Juan Santamaría is in the center of the country, so it's especially convenient for destinations in the Central Valley and along the Central Pacific. The closest destinations are less than an hour away. The only other international gateway is Liberia's Aeropuerto Internacional Daniel Oduber Quirós in the western part of the country. Flying here makes sense if you're planning to spend most of your time in Guanacaste or on the Nicoya Peninsula.

A relatively small number of travelers arrive in Costa Rica by road, especially with the difficulties taking rental cars between countries. Long-distance buses travel directly to San José from the larger cities in Nicaragua and Panama, but these are arduous journeys. The Managua–to–San José route takes between 8 and 10 hours.

Getting Around

To save time, many people take domestic flights to their ultimate destination. SANSA flies to various destinations from its hubs in San José's Aeropuerto Internacional Juan Santamaría and Liberia's Aeropuerto Internacional Daniel Oduber Quirós. Nature Air flies out of San José's domestic airport, tiny Aeropuerto Tobias Bolaños. Both offer flights to resort areas, especially those near the beaches. Regional airports are very small, often with a one-room terminal and a staff that arrives at about the same time as the plane.

Costa Rican towns are connected by regular bus service. Buses between major destinations have comfortable seats and air-conditioning. If you have to transfer along the way, you may get a converted school bus cooled only by the tropical breezes. If you're traveling a long distance, make sure to request a *directo* (express) bus. Otherwise you may stop in every small town along the way.

The country's recently improved highway system means renting a car is a great way to get around. You can travel on your own schedule, stopping where you like. Larger airports have rental desks; at smaller airports a representative will meet you and drive you to the nearby office.

1

Festivals and Celebrations

Every day is a patron saint's day somewhere in Costa Rica, and unless you spend all your time ensconced in a resort, you'll probably see a sign for some community's annual *festejo patronal* (patron-saint festival), in homage to its namesake and protector. A loud firecracker explosion rouses participants at dawn to kick off the festivities.

The festivals mirror Costa Rica: devoutly Catholic but increasingly secularized, with bingo games, rickety carnival rides—a certain amount of luck and prayer is in order here—horse parades, and amateurish bullfights (the bull is not killed in Costa Rica). The Imperial—Costa Rica's most popular brand of beer—flows copiously. But it is still a religious tradition, and an important part of the day is a Mass and parade where the saint's figure is carried through the streets.

New Year's Day *(Año Nuevo)* is a time that most Costa Ricans spend with family and friends. Mid-January brings the **Santa Cruz Fiestas** *(Fiestas de Santa Cruz)*, with bullfights, rodeo, folk dancing and marimba music. **Día de la Candelaria,** to honor the famed virgin, is celebrated on February 2.

Holy Week, or Semana Santa, lasting from Palm Sunday through Easter Sunday, is a huge celebration in Costa Rica, especially on Good Friday, when there are religious processions all over the country. Not a thing is open Thursday and Friday. Good luck making reservations during this time. **Día de Juan Santamaría** on April 11 is a public holiday commemorating Costa Rica's national hero. **Día del Trabajo,** on May 1, is Costa Rica's Labor Day.

Day of the Virgin of the Angels *(Día de la Virgen de los Angeles)*, on August 2, celebrates Costa Rica's patron saint with religious processions from San José to the Basilica de Nuestra Señora de Los Angeles in Cartago. **Independence Day** *(Día de la Independencia)* is celebrated on September 15 with lantern-lighted parades the night before and marching bands throughout the country.

Immaculate Conception *(Inmaculada Concepción de la Virgen María)*, on December 8, is observed with Masses to honor the Virgin Mary. The celebration of **Christmas** *(Navidad)* goes on throughout December, and extends into the last week of the month, with year-end festivals including bullfights around San José.

Money Matters

The local currency is known as the *colón*. You may want to get a small amount of *colónes* before your trip to pay for meals or taxi rides once you arrive. However, there are currency exchange booths in the international arrivals terminal of San José's Aeropuerto Internacional Juan Santamaría. The airport also has an automatic teller machine that dispenses both dollars and colónes, but it's hidden away in the stairway of the parking garage. Any employee can point you in the right direction.

Most ATMs—or ATHs, as they are most often called here—are linked to both the Cirrus and the Plus networks, so they can be used by holders of most U.S.-issued debit and credit cards. Make sure before you leave that your PIN has four numbers, as most machines don't accept longer ones.

Credit cards are accepted by almost all businesses catering to tourists. Because businesses are charged a hefty fee for credit-card purchases, some will add a small surcharge or impose a minimum purchase amount if you use plastic. It's always a good idea to ask beforehand.

COSTA RICA TOP ATTRACTIONS

Arenal Volcano

(A) Costa Rica has half a dozen active volcanoes, but none put on a show like the Arenal Volcano. During the day you're likely to see smoke billowing from the crater. This doesn't compare with what you'll see at night, when orangey red lava oozes down the perfectly shaped cone. If you're very lucky, the clouds will part long enough for you to spot glowing rocks shooting into the air.

Selvatura Park

(B) Soaring over the treetops on a zip line is a thrilling experience. But canopy tours aren't just for adrenaline junkies. Many rain forests have hanging bridges and elevated platforms to give you a bird's-eye view of the rain forest. Many of the best, like Selvetura, are around Monteverde Cloud Forest Biological Reserve and the Santa Elena Reserve, but others are clustered around Lake Arenal and Manuel Antonio.

Manuel Antonio National Park

(C) Some of the country's most thrilling views can be seen from the trails through Manuel Antonio National Park. As you emerge from the rain forest, don't be surprised to find yourself alone on a palm-shaded beach. Make sure to look up—three types of monkey make their home in the canopy, and on a good day you might see them all.

Corcovado National Park

(D) Birdwatchers come to this vast and pristine rain forsest with hopes of catching a glimpes of the endangered harpy eagle. It's notoriously difficult to see, but other feathered friends—like the scarlet macaw, the orange-bellied trogon, and the golden-hooded tanager—practically pose for pictures. No need to head off into the rain forest with your binoculars; dozens of hummingbirds are likely to dart around you as you relax by the pool.

Playa Carrillo

(E) This long, picturesque beach, backed by a line of swaying palms and protective cliffs, is certainly one of the most beautiful streches of sand in the country. Perfect for swimming, snorkeling, or just walking, the beach isn't marred by a single building. Visit on a weekday and it's possible that you may have the entire shore to yourself.

Turrialba

(G) Heavy rainfall, steep mountains, and rocky terrain make this region a magnet for white-water rafting enthusiasts, and there's a river to match anyone's level of expertise. Not far from San José, the Central Valley has outfitters who offer everything from easy day trips to challenging multiday excursions. Many of these companies congregate around the community of Turrialba, the country's white-water capital and close to the Rio Pacuare and Rio Reventazón.

Nicoya Peninsula

(F) Popular with the sun-and-fun crowd, the peninsula still has a yet-to-be-discovered feel. Maybe that's because its sandy shores are never covered with a checkerboard of beach blankets. Drive a few miles in any direction and you can find one all to yourself. But civilization isn't far away, some of the country's best restaurants are within reach.

Monteverde Cloud Forest Biological Reserve

(H) The roads leading here are terrible, but you won't mind a bit once you see the mist-covered reserve. Because of the constant moisture, this private park is unbelievably lush. It's gorgeous during the day, but many prefer to take a night hike, when you can see colorful birds asleep in the branches, hairy tarantulas in search of prey, and nocturnal mammals like the wide-eyed kinkajoo.

FAQS

Do I need any special documents to get into the country?

Aside from a passport that's valid for at least one month after date of entry, you don't need anything else to enter the country. You'll be given a 30-day tourist visa as you pass through immigration. You're no longer required to have your passport with you at all times during your trip, but make sure to carry a photocopy.

How difficult is it to travel around the country?

It's extremely easy. Thanks to the domestic airlines, getting to your ultimate destination takes far less time than just a few years ago; almost every worthwhile spot is within an hour of San José. Long-distance buses and vans are usually very comfortable, so don't overlook these as a way to get to far-flung destinations. Renting a car is a great way to get around, because you're not tied to somebody else's schedule. The roads are well marked, the signs are easy to read, and the traffic is pretty light outside of urban areas. It's good to have a detailed map if you're driving in rural areas, as it's easy to miss a turn.

Are the roads as bad as they say?

Yes and no. You'll still find potholes the size of bathtubs on the road leading to Monteverde Cloud Forest Biological Reserve, and the gravel roads on the Nicoya Peninsula are often so grooved by the rain that they feel like an endless series of speed bumps. But many of the roads, including the Pan-American Highway that runs the length of the country, have been markedly improved. The most dramatic improvements have been made near the resort area of Lake Arenal. Repairs to the road between Nuevo Arenal and La Fortuna have cut your travel time almost in half. During and immediately after the summer rainy season is the worst time for driving. The constant deluge takes its toll on the pavement.

Should I rent a four-wheel-drive vehicle?

Probably so. If your trip will take you mostly to the beaches, you won't necessarily need a 4WD vehicle. If you're headed to more mountainous areas, such as any destination in the Northern Plains, you'll definitely want one. But even on the most badly maintained roads through the mountains you'll see locals getting around just fine in their beat-up sedans. There's usually only a minor difference in the cost, so there's no reason not to go for the 4WD.

Should I get insurance on the rental car?

Even if your own insurance covers rental cars, go ahead and take full insurance. The cost is often less than $10 a day. For that you get the peace of mind of knowing that you're not going to be hassled for a scratch on the fender or a crack in the windshield. One traveler reported returning a rental car with a front bumper completely detached, and because he had full insurance the clerk just smiled and wished him a good trip home.

Should I consider a package tour?

If you're terrified of traveling on your own, sign up for a tour. But Costa Rica is such an easy place to get around that there's really no need. Part of the fun is the exploring—finding a secluded beach, hiking down to a hidden waterfall, discovering a great craft shop—and that's just not going to happen on a tour. If you're more comfortable with a package tour, pick one with a specific focus, like bird-watching or boating, so that you're less likely to get a generic tour.

Do I need a local guide?

Guides are a great idea for the first-time visitor in search of wildlife. A good guide will know where to find the animals, and will bring along a telescope so that you can get an up-close look at that sloth high in the trees or the howler monkeys across the clearing. After the first day, however, you'll probably grab your binoculars and head out on your own. It's much more gratifying to tell the folks back home that you discovered that banded anteater all by yourself.

Will I have trouble if I don't speak Spanish?

No problemo. Most people in businesses catering to tourists speak at least a little English. If you encounter someone who doesn't speak English, they'll probably point you to a coworker who does. Even if you're in a far-flung destination, locals will go out of their way to find somebody who speaks your language.

Can I drink the water?

Costa Rica is the only Central American country where you don't have to get stressed out about drinking the water. The water is potable in all but the most remote regions. That said, many people don't like the taste of the tap water and prefer bottled water.

Are there any worries about the food?

None whatsoever. Even the humblest roadside establishment is likely to be scrupulously clean. If you have any doubts about a place, just move on to the next one. There's no problem enjoying fruit, cheese, bread, or other local products sold from the stands set up along the roads.

Do I need to get any shots?

You probably don't have to get any vaccinations or take any special medications. The U.S. Centers for Disease Control and Prevention warn that there is some concern about malaria, especially in remote areas along the Caribbean coast. If you plan to spend any amount of time there, you may want to talk with your doctors about antimalarial medications well before your trip.

Should I bring any medications?

The only thing we recommend is using an insect repellent containing the active ingredient DEET. Ordinary repellents, even those labeled "extra strength," aren't going to do the trick against the mosquitoes of the tropics. To find a repellent with DEET, your best bet is a sporting goods store rather than your local drugstore. A formulation with 10% to 25% DEET will be fine; those with more are likely to irritate your skin.

Can I use my ATM card?

Most ATMs are on both the Cirrus and Plus networks, so they accept debit and credit cards issued by U.S. banks. Some might accept cards with just the MasterCard or just the Visa logo; if that's the case, try a machine at a different bank. Know the exchange rate before you use an ATM for the first time so that you know about how much local currency you want to withdraw.

Do most places take credit cards?

Almost all tourist-oriented businesses accept credit cards. You may encounter smaller restaurants and hotels that don't accept them at all, but these are pretty rare. Some businesses don't like to accept credit cards because their banks charge them exorbitant fees for credit-card transactions. They will usually relent and charge you a small fee for the privilege.

COSTA RICA TODAY

Government

Costa Rica is a democratic republic whose structure will be very familiar to any citizen of the United States. The 1949 constitution divides the government into independent executive, legislative, and judicial branches. All citizens are guaranteed equality before the law, the right to own property, freedom of speech, and freedom of religion.

In 1969, the constitution was amended to ban a president from serving more than one term. In 2003, the ban was reversed, allowing Nobel Peace Prize laureate Oscar Arias Sánchez to run for a second term. In 2006, he was reelected in a tight and highly contested election, running on a platform of promoting free trade. He took office on May 8, 2006. Since then he has spent a lot of political capital pushing through his pro-business platform.

The country is famous for lacking an army, which was abolished when the constitution was ratified in 1949. The country's stable government and economy have made this possible, even as its neighbors were embroiled in civil war. The country does maintain a small national guard.

Economy

By the mid-1980s, Costa Rica had diversified its economy beyond agriculture and tourism was bringing in more money than its three major cash crops: coffee, bananas, and pineapples. High-tech companies such as Intel and Motorola and pharmaceutical companies like Proctor and Gamble and GlaxoSmithKline opened plants and service centers in Costa Rica, providing well-paid jobs for educated professionals.

In 2007, there were huge demonstrations in the streets of San José before a vote on the proposed Central American Free Trade Agreement. Opponents of the plan, which would liberalize trade between Costa Rica, its neighbors, and the United States, said it would spell disaster for the country's agricultural industry. Voters narrowly approved the plan in November.

The economy continues to bedevil Costa Rica. Although economic growth continues to rise, it still has a 5% trade deficit and annual inflation of about 9%. But unemployment has dropped in recent years to just over 5%, comparable to that of the United States.

Tourism

Today Costa Rica faces the challenge of conserving its natural resources while still permitting modern development. The government has been unable or unwilling to control illegal logging, an industry that threatens to destroy the country's old-growth forests. Urban sprawl in the communities surrounding San José and the development of megaresorts along the Pacific coast threaten forests, wildlife, and the slow pace of life that makes Costa Rica so desirable.

Although tourism injects much-needed foreign cash into the economy, the government has not fully decided the best way to promote its natural wonders. The buzzwords now are not just ecotourism and sustainable development, but also adventure tourism and extreme sports. The two sides do not always see eye to eye.

Religion

Because it was a Spanish colony, Costa Rica continues to have a close relationship to the Catholic Church. Catholicism was made the country's official religion in the country's constitution. Because of this, priests are the only type of religious leader authorized to perform civil marriages. (Others require the assistance of a legal official.)

More than 90% of Costa Ricans consider themselves Catholics. But even among this group, most people do not have a strong identification with the church or with its teachings. The live-and-let-live attitude of most Costa Ricans does not mesh well with religious doctrine. That's also probably why the evangelical churches that have made inroads in neighboring countries have not succeeded here.

Although every village has a church on its main square, it's usually hopping once a year—when the town's patron saint is honored. These are times for food, music, and dancing in the streets. If the celebrations lack much religious fervor—well, that's Costa Rica for you.

Sports

Like everyone else on this soccer-mad isthmus, Costa Ricans take their game seriously and can get nasty when it comes to their national team; U.S. players reported being pelted with batteries and bags of urine during one game. When the national team returned after humiliating losses in the 2006 World Cup, an angry crowd met them at the airport chanting "dog" at the coach.

On the national level, the big local rivalry ("derby" in soccer parlance) is between LD Alajuelense and Deportivo Saprissa (La Monstruo Morado, or "The Purple Monster"). Each has won the Costa Rican championship 24 times, which makes the rivalry particularly intense. You can tell how important the sport is when you fly into the country. As your plane flies across the Central Valley, you'll notice that every village, no matter how small, has a soccer field. When not being used for sports, they often double as pastures for horses.

Cash Crops

If nearby Honduras was the original "Banana Republic," 19th-century Costa Rica was a "Coffee Republic." Coffee remains inexorably entwined with the country, with economists paying close attention to world prices and kids in rural areas still taking class time off to help with the harvest.

The irony is that it's hard to get a decent cup of the stuff here. True to economic realities of developing countries, the high-quality product gets exported, with the inferior coffee staying behind for the local market. (The same is true of bananas, Costa Rica's other signature agricultural product.) The best places to get a cup of high-quality Costa Rican coffee are upscale restaurants and hotels. Owners understand foreign tastes and have export-quality coffee on hand. Gift shops sell the superior product as well.

The Central Valley is where you'll find many of the coffee plantations. You'll recognize them immediately by the rows of brilliant green plants covered in red berries. Because many of these plants are sensitive to light, they are often shaded by tall trees or even by canopies of fabric. Tours of the plantations are a great way to get to know the local cash crop.

In recent years, the producers of coffee have focused on quality rather than quantity. That's why bananas are now the top agricultural export, followed by pineapples. Both grow in sunny lowland areas, which are abundant on both the Atlantic and Pacific coasts. These crops are treated with just as much care as coffee. You're likely to see bunches of bananas wrapped in plastic bags—while still on the tree. This prevents blemishes that make them less appealing to foreign consumers.

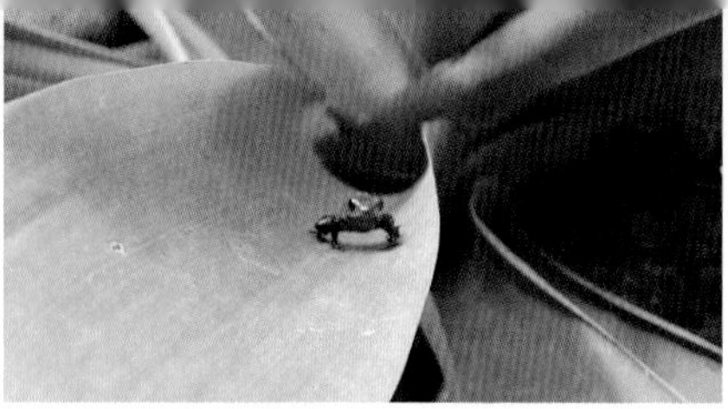

ECOTOURISM, COSTA RICA STYLE

Perhaps more than anyone else, two men who wrote a field guide about tropical birds were responsible for the ecotourism movement in Costa Rica.

According to Carlos Manuel Rodríguez, the country's former minister for environment and energy, "When *A Guide to the Birds of Costa Rica* by F. Gary Stiles and Alexander Skutch was published in the late 1980s, the government noticed that it was bringing birdwatchers here," he told a reporter for *The Guardian*, a London newspaper. "From then on, a national tourism plan was developed."

The country's leaders, seeing so many of its primary growth forests being felled at an alarming rate by loggers and farmers, established its national park system in 1970. But it wasn't until nearly two decades later, when *A Guide to the Birds of Costa Rica* was published, that they realized that the land they had set aside could help transform the tiny country's economy.

Of the 1.5 million people who travel each year to Costa Rica, many are bird-watchers who come in search of the keel-billed toucan, the scarlet-rumped tanager, or any of the 850 other species of birds. Other travelers are in search of animals, such as two types of sloths, three types of anteater, and four species of monkey, all of them surprisingly easy to spot in the country's national parks and private reserves.

But other people come to Costa Rica to go white-water rafting on the rivers, soar through the treetops attached to zip lines, or take a spin in a motorboat. And many people combine a little bit of everything into their itineraries.

Which raises a couple of questions: Is the person coming to see the wildlife practicing ecotourism? Is the adventure traveler? And exactly what is the definition of ecotourism, anyway?

Defining Ecotourism

The word ecotourism is believed to have been coined by Mexican environmentalist Héctor Ceballos-Lascuráin in 1983. According to Ceballos-Lascuráin, ecotourism "involves traveling to relatively undisturbed natural areas with the specific object of studying, admiring and enjoying the scenery and its wild plants and animals."

His original definition seemed a bit too general, so in 1993 he amended it with a line that stressed that "ecotourism is environmentally responsible travel."

Ceballos-Lascuráin said he is pleased that ecotourism has gained such acceptance around the world. But he is also concerned that the term has been "variously abused and misused in many places."

The trouble, he said, is a misunderstanding about what is meant by the term ecotourism. In Costa Rica, for example, it has been used to describe everything from hiking through the rain forest to rumbling over the hillsides in all-terrain vehicles, and from paddling in a kayak to dancing to disco music on a diesel-powered yacht.

"I am sad to see," Ceballos-Lascuráin told a reporter for EcoClub, "that 'ecotourism' is seen mainly as adventure tourism and carrying out extreme sports in a more or less natural environment, with little concern for conservation or sustainable development issues."

That is not to say that adventure sports can't be part of a green vacation. It all depends what impact they have on the environment and the local community.

Going Green

Over the past decade, the concept of ecotourism has made a strong impression on the average traveler. Many people now realize that mass tourism can be damaging to environmentally sensitive places like Costa Rica but that much can be done to alleviate the negative effects. At the same time, *ecotourism* has become a marketing term used to attract customers who have the best intentions. But is there really such a thing as an eco-friendly car-rental company or a green airline?

In addition to giving travelers the chance to observe and learn about wildlife, ecotourism should accomplish three things: refrain from damaging the environment, strengthen conservation efforts, and improve the lives of local people.

The last part might seem a bit beside the point, but environmentalists point out that much of the deforestation in Costa Rica and other countries is by poor people trying to eke out a living through sustenance farming. Providing them with other ways to make a living is the best way to prevent this.

What can you do? Make sure the hotel you choose is eco-friendly. A great place to start is the Costa Rican Tourism Board (🌐*www.turismo-sostenible.co.cr*). It has a rating system for hotels and lodges called the Certification for Sustainable Tourism. The Costa Rica–based Rainforest Alliance (🌐*www.rainforest-alliance.org*) has a convenient searchable database of sustainable lodges. The International Ecotourism Society (🌐*www.ecotourism.org*) has a database of tour companies, hotels, and other travel services that are committed to sustainable practices.

Other Things You Can Do

What else can help? Make sure your tour company follows sustainable policies, including contributing to conservation efforts, hiring and training locals for most jobs, educating visitors about the local ecology and culture, and taking steps to mitigate negative impacts on the environment.

Here are a few other things you can do:

- Use locally owned lodges, car-rental agencies, or tour companies. Eat in local restaurants, shop in local markets, and attend local events. Enrich your experience and support the community by hiring local guides.
- Stray from the beaten path—by visiting areas where few tourists go, you can avoid adding to the stress on hot spots and enjoy a more authentic Costa Rican experience.
- Support conservation by paying entrance fees to parks and protected sites and contributing to local environmental groups.
- Don't be overly aggressive if you bargain for souvenirs, and don't shortchange local people on payments or tips for services.

The point here is that you can't assume that companies have environmentally friendly practices, even if they have pictures of animals on their Web site or terms like eco-lodge in their name. Do business only with companies that promote sustainable tourism, and you'll be helping to preserve this country's natural wonders for future generations.

WEDDINGS AND HONEYMOONS

Ever dreamed of getting married on a sandy beach shaded by palm trees? Many people who envision such a scene immediately think of the Caribbean. But Costa Rica is fast becoming a favored destination for tropical nuptials.

One reason is that compared with the complicated procedures in many other destinations, getting married in Costa Rica is fairly easy. There are no residency restrictions or blood-test requirements. At least a month in advance, couples of the opposite sex who are over 18 should provide their local wedding planner with a copy of their birth certificates and passports so they can be submitted to the local authorities.

Things are a bit more complicated if there was a previous marriage. The couple needs to provide documentation that the marriage was terminated. Divorce papers must be translated into Spanish and notarized. There's one archaic law still on the books: a woman who has been previously married must wait at least 10 months after her divorce or provide a medical statement attesting to not being pregnant (presumably with her ex-husband's child); a man has no waiting period.

The Big Day

Judges, attorneys, and Catholic priests have legal authority to certify a marriage in Costa Rica. (Most foreign couples avoid the latter because a Catholic wedding requires months of preparation.) The official ceremony is very simple, but couples are free to add their own vows or anything else they would like. The officiant will register the marriage with the civil registry and the couple's embassy.

At the wedding, the couple needs to have at least two witnesses who are not family members. Many couples choose their best man and maid of honor. If necessary, the wedding planner can provide witnesses.

The license itself takes three months to issue and is sent to the couple's home address. For an extra fee couples can ask for the process to be expedited. Virtually all Western countries recognize the legality of a Costa Rican marriage.

Beautiful Backdrops

Although Costa Rica offers no shortage of impressive backdrops for a ceremony, the Central Pacific coast sees the most tourist weddings and honeymoons. May and June are the most popular months, but many people choose January or February because you are virtually guaranteed sunny skies. Manuel Antonio's Makanda by the Sea, La Mariposa, Si Como No, and Punta Leona's Villa Caletas are among the many lodgings here with events staffs well versed in planning ceremonies and tending to the legalities.

There are many details to attend to: flowers, music, and photography. Most large hotels have on-staff wedding planners to walk you through the process. Couples can also hire their own wedding planner, which is often less expensive. Either way, wedding planners will likely have a wide range of services available, and couples can pick and choose.

Honeymoons

As far as honeymoons go, there's no place in Costa Rica that is inappropriate. Although honeymoons on the beach, especially along the Northern Pacific and Central Pacific coasts, are popular, many couples opt for treks to the mountains or the rain forests. Dozens of newlyweds choose offbeat adventures, such as spotting sea turtles along the Caribbean coast or swimming with pilot whales off the Osa Peninsula.

KIDS AND FAMILIES

With so much to keep them interested and occupied, Costa Rica is a blast with kids. What makes it so much fun is that the activities here are things the whole family can do together: discovering a waterfall in a rain forest, snorkeling with sea turtles, or white-water rafting down a roaring river. There are also activities for kids that will allow parents time to stroll hand-in-hand down a deserted beach.

Choosing a Destination

Basing yourself in one place for several days is a great idea. Climbing into the car every day or two not only makes the kids miserable, but means that the best part of the day is spent traveling. The good news is that there are many destinations where you could stay for a week and still not do and see everything.

Headed to the beach? Remember that for families, not all beaches are created equal. Choose a destination with a range of activities. Manuel Antonio, on the Central Pacific coast, is your best bet. The proximity to the national park is the main selling point, but you're also close to other nature preserves. As for activities, there's everything from snorkeling and surfing lessons to kayaking excursions to zip-line adventures. And the range of kid-friendly restaurants is unmatched anywhere in the country. On the Nicoya Peninsula, Playas del Coco and Playa Tamarindo have a decent amount of activities for the small fry.

Santa Elena, the closest town to Monteverde Cloud Forest Biological Reserve, is another great base. There are several nature preserves in the area, and they offer both day and night hikes. If skies are cloudy—as they often are—there are indoor attractions like the display of slithering snakes. The town is compact and walkable, and has many eateries with children's menus. La Fortuna, the gateway to the Lake Arenal area, has activities from waterfall hikes to canopy tours. The town itself isn't very attractive, so you'll want to choose a place nearby.

Believe it or not, the San José area is not a bad base. Activities like white-water rafting are nearby, and on rainy days you can visit the city's excellent museums dedicated to gold and jade. The hotels in the surrounding countryside are often a long drive from good restaurants. We prefer the hotels in the city, as dozens of restaurants line the pedestrian-only streets.

Kid-Friendly Activities

You can't beat the beach in Costa Rica. Avoid those without lifeguards, and take warning signs about rip currents very seriously. Snorkeling and surfing lessons are great for older kids, but stick with a licensed company rather than that enthusiastic young person who approaches you on the beach.

Canopy tours are good for kids of all ages. Ask the staff about how long a tour will take, because once you set out on a hike over a series of hanging bridges, you often have no choice but to continue on to the end. Zip lines are appropriate for older teens, but they should always be accompanied by an adult.

For the smallest of the small fry, the butterfly enclosures and hummingbird gardens that you find near most resort areas are wonderful diversions. Indoor activities, like the display of frogs at Santa Elena, fascinate youngsters. And don't avoid the easier hikes in the national parks. Seeing animals in the wild is likely to start a lifelong love of animals.

GREAT ITINERARIES

BEACHES, RAIN FORESTS, AND VOLCANOES

Day 1: Arrival

Arrive in San José (most arrivals are in the evening) and head straight to one of the small luxury hotels north of the city in the Central Valley. A favorite of ours is Finca Rosa Blanca, a fairy-tale retreat overlooking miles of coffee farms.

Logistics: Brace yourself for long lines at immigration if you arrive in the evening along with all the other large flights from North America. Try to get a seat near the front of the plane, and don't dawdle when disembarking.

Day 2: Poás Volcano and Tabacón Hot Springs

Volcán Poás, where you can peer over the edge of a crater, lies nearby. Fortify yourself with the fruits, jellies, and chocolates sold by vendors on the road up to the summit. A scenic drive takes you to the La Fortuna area. Drop your luggage at one of many fantastic hotels (Montaña de Fuego is our pick for fabulous volcano views), and go directly to Tabacón Hot Springs & Resort. Take a zip-line or hanging-bridges tour through the forest canopy and then pamper yourself with a spa treatment. Finish the day by sinking into a volcanically heated mineral bath with a cocktail at your side as the sun sets behind fiery Volcán Arenal.

Logistics: Get an early start to get the best views of Poás. Shuttle vans can get you to Arenal and have hotel-to-hotel service.

Day 3: Caño Negro Wildlife Refuge

Spend your entire day in the Caño Negro Wildlife Refuge, a lowland forest reserve replete with waterfowl near the Nicaraguan border.

Logistics: Book your trip the night before; tour operators in La Fortuna keep evening hours for exactly that reason. All transport will be included.

Day 4: Scenic Drive to the Central Pacific

Today's a traveling day—a chance to really see the country's famous landscape and infamous roads. (Believe us, they get a lot worse than this route.) A few hours' drive from Arenal takes you to fabled Manuel Antonio on the Central Pacific coast. Beyond-beautiful hotels are the norm here, and you have your choice of seaside villas or tree-shrouded jungle lodges. We like the hillside La Mariposa, which has commanding views.

Logistics: Hotel-to-hotel shuttle-van services can get you to Manuel Antonio. If you drive instead, start out as early as possible. You'll pass through two mountainous stretches (between La Fortuna and San Ramón, and between Atenas and the coast) that fog over by midafternoon.

Day 5: Manuel Antonio National Park

Manuel Antonio is Costa Rica's most famous national park for a reason: it has beaches, lush rain forest, mangrove swamps, and rocky coves with abundant marine life. You can—and should—spend an entire day exploring the park, home to capuchin monkeys, sloths, agoutis, and 200 species of birds. It's also one of two locales in the country where you'll see squirrel monkeys.

Logistics: Almost all Manuel Antonio hotels have transport to the park. If yours doesn't, taxis are plentiful and cheap.

Day 6: Beach Yourself

Days 1 through 5 were "on the go" days. Reward yourself today with lots of relaxation. Manuel Antonio means beaches, and there are several to choose from.

Manuel Antonio and neighboring Quepos mean restaurants, too, the best selection of any beach community in the country.

Logistics: Most everything you need here is strung along the 5-km (3-mi) road between Quepos and Manuel Antonio National Park. It's practically impossible to get lost.

Day 7: San José

A morning drive back to San José gives you time to spend the afternoon in the city. We like the cozy, classy Hotel Le Bergerac. Visit the Teatro Nacional, the capital's must-see sight, and save time for late-afternoon shopping. An evening dinner caps off your trip before you turn in early to get ready for tomorrow morning's departure.

Logistics: As the number of visitors to Costa Rica grows, so does the number of passengers using Aeropuerto Internacional Juan Santamaría. We recommend that you check in three hours before your flight. Better safe than sorry.

TIPS

- Aside from Day 2, it's entirely possible to do this route without a car.
- Hotels in the Central Valley and San José are used to booking visitors for their first and last nights in the country, and may allow you to leave items so you don't have to lug them around.
- Arenal lies equidistant between Liberia and San José, but we suggest flying into San José for this itinerary because road access to Arenal and from Manuel Antonio is better.
- Cloud cover makes volcano viewing the luck of the draw, and no one can negotiate with Mother Nature. Early mornings and dry season give you the best chances for seeing Arenal and Poás in action.
- Get as early a start as possible if you're driving. The mountain roads between San José and La Fortuna and between Manuel Antonio and San José can fog over by midafternoon.

GREAT ITINERARIES

MORE BEACHES, RAIN FORESTS, AND VOLCANOES

Day 1: Arrival

Most arrivals to Liberia, Costa Rica's second international airport, are in early afternoon. You can't go wrong with any North Pacific beach, but we like Playa Hermosa for its pivotal location, one that lets you use it as a base for visiting area attractions. Check out small, personal, breezy Hotel Playa Hermosa/Bosque del Mar, the perfect antidote to the megaresorts that lie not too far away.

Logistics: The big all-inclusives up here have their own minivans to whisk you in air-conditioned comfort from airport to resort. Smaller lodgings such as Hotel Playa Hermosa/Bosque del Mar can arrange to have transport waiting, with advance notice.

Day 2: Playa Hermosa

Morning is a great time to laze on the beach in this part of Costa Rica. The breezes are refreshingly cool and the sun hasn't started to beat down. After lunch, explore Playa Hermosa's metropolis, the small town of Playas del Coco. Quite frankly Coco is our least favorite beach up here. But we like the town for its little souvenir shops, restaurants, and local color.

Logistics: Taxis are the easiest way to travel between Playa Hermosa and Coco, about 10 minutes away. Have your hotel call one, and flag one down on the street in town when it's time to return.

Day 3: Rincón de la Vieja Volcano

The top of Rincón de la Vieja Volcano with its steaming, bubbling, oozing fumaroles lies about 90 minutes from Hermosa. Lather on the sunscreen and head for the Hacienda Guachipelín and its volcano-viewing hikes, canopy tours, rappelling, horseback riding, mountain biking, and river tubing. Cap off the day with a spa treatment, complete with thermal mud bath.

Logistics: If you don't have a rental car, book a private driver for the day, which can usually be arranged through your hotel.

Day 4: Golf or Diving

Golf is big up here. The 18-hole Garra de León course at the Paradisus Playa Conchal resort is about 45 minutes from Hermosa. The other popular, slightly pricey, sport here is scuba diving. Dive operators are based in nearby Playas del Coco or Playa Panamá. A daylong course gives you a taste of the deep.

Logistics: The resort will arrange transport to and from the golf course, and dive operators will pick you up from and return you to your hotel.

Day 5: Palo Verde National Park

We like the morning guided tours at Palo Verde National Park, one of the last remaining dry tropical forests in Central America. The Organization for Tropical Studies, which operates the biological station here, has terrific guides. Spend the afternoon observing nature in a more relaxed fashion with a float down the nearby Río Corobicí. (These are not the screaming rapids so famed in white-water circles.)

Logistics: This excursion is a bit roundabout, so this is the day your own vehicle would come in handiest. But you can also hire a private driver (arranged through your hotel). Bring water to drink: it gets hot here.

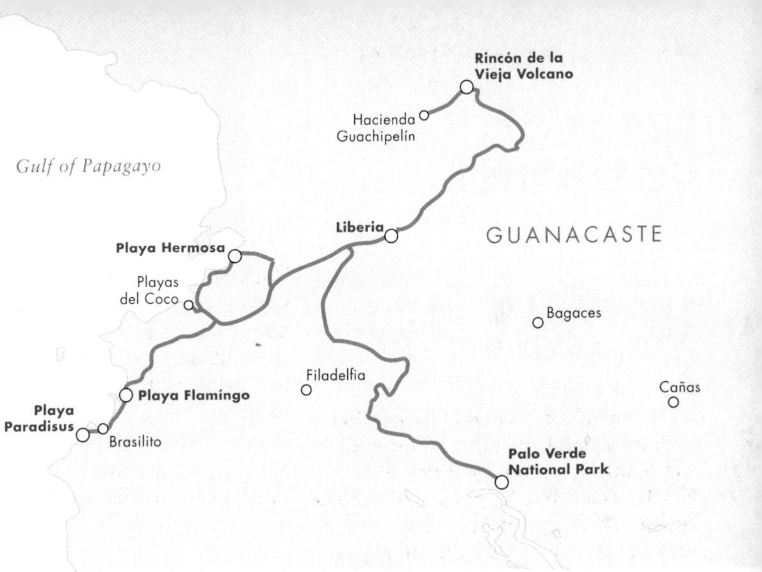

Day 6: Sailing

Make your final day a relaxing one with a few hours on the waves. Many sailboats operate from this section of coast. Our choice is the 52-foot *Samonique III*, which sails out of Playa Flamingo most afternoons at 2. A four-hour excursion includes sandwiches, appetizers, and an open bar. Legendary Pacific sunsets are tossed in at no extra charge.

Logistics: The *Samonique III* folks can arrange transport from hotel to boat and back again.

Day 7: Departure

Grab a last dip in the ocean this morning, because your flight departs from Liberia in the early afternoon.

Logistics: The advent of international flights to Liberia has fueled this region's meteoric rise to fame, but the airport's size has not kept pace with the number of passengers. Expansion is eventually on the way, but presently, lines can be long. Allow yourself plenty of time for check-in.

TIPS

- Fly into Liberia. Although it's logical to think "San José" when planning flights to Costa Rica, it makes no sense if you plan to spend your entire time in the North Pacific.
- A car is ideal for this itinerary, yet many area attractions and tour operators provide transport to and from area lodging if you aren't too far afield (one of the reasons we like Playa Hermosa).
- All-inclusive resorts do a good job of organizing local excursions with local operators, so if you're staying at one, take advantage of them.
- Getting from beach to beach often requires travel back inland. There is no real (i.e., navigable) coastal road.
- If ever there were a case for an off-season vacation, this is it. This driest, hottest part of the country gets very dry and hot from January through April. The rains green everything up, and frankly, we prefer the region during the low season after April.

THE PEOPLE OF COSTA RICA

Unlike many of its neighbors, Costa Rica never had a dominant indigenous population. When Christopher Columbus arrived in the early 16th century, he didn't encounter empires like those in present-day Mexico and Peru. Instead, a small contingent of Carib Indians rowed out in canoes to meet his ship. The heavy gold bands the indigenous peoples wore led to the land being called Costa Rica, or "Rich Coast."

On the mainland, the Spanish encountered disparate tribes like the Chorotega, Bribri, Cabecar, and Boruca peoples. Archeological evidence shows that they had lived in the region for thousands of years. But that would change with breathtaking speed. European diseases felled many of their members, and the brutality of slavery imposed by the colonial power drove most of those remaining into the mountains.

Some of these peoples still exist, although in relatively small communities. Several thousand Bribri, Kekoldi, and other peoples live in villages scattered around Talamanca, a mountainous region close to the border of Panama. Although many traditions have been lost over the years, some have managed to retain their own languages and religions. If you're interested in seeing the local culture, tour companies in the coastal communities of Limón and Puerto Viejo de Talamanca can arrange visits to these villages.

That isn't to say that there's no local culture. More than 90% of the country's residents are *mestizos*, or mixed-race descendants of the Spanish. But few people express any pride in their Spanish heritage. Perhaps that is because Spain had little interest in Costa Rica, the smallest and poorest of its Central American colonies. Instead, the people here created a unique culture that mixes parts of Europe, Latin America, and the Caribbean. There's a strong emphasis on education, and the 95% literacy rate is by far the highest in the region. There's a laid-back attitude toward life, typified by the common greeting of *pura vida*, which translates literally as "pure life" but means something between "no worries" and "don't sweat the small stuff."

It sounds like a cliché, but Costa Ricans are an incredibly welcoming people. Anyone who has visited other Central American cultures will be surprised at how Ticos seem genuinely happy to greet newcomers. If you ever find yourself lost in a town or village, you may find locals more than willing to not only point you in the right direction, but walk you all the way to your destination.

Others cultures have added their own spice to Costa Rica. On the Caribbean coast you'll find Afro-Caribbean peoples, descendants of Jamaicans who arrived in the late 19th century to build the railroad and remained to work on banana and cacao plantations. In the seaside town of Limón, cruise ships frequently call, and the passengers who hurry down the gangplank encounter steel-drum music, braided hair, and rickety houses painted every color of the rainbow. They may think that they have discovered the "real" Costa Rica, and they have, in a way. But they also have barely scratched the surface.

Understanding Biodiversity

WORD OF MOUTH

"I spotted this huge iguana measuring approx. 4 feet sunning along Playa Uvita; he allowed me to get within inches to take several pictures."

—photo by Justin Hubbell, Fodors.com member.

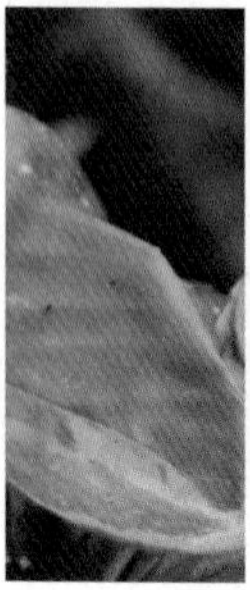

By Leland Baxter-Neal

Costa Rica's forests hold an array of flora and fauna so vast and diverse that scientists haven't even named thousands of the species found here. The country covers less than 0.03% of the Earth's surface, yet it contains nearly 5% of the planet's plant and animal species. Costa Rica has at least 9,000 plant species, including more than 1,200 types of orchids, some 2,000 kinds of butterflies, and 876 bird species.

Costa Rica acts as a natural land bridge between North and South America, so there is a lot of intercontinental exchange. But the country's flora and fauna add up to more than what has passed between the continents. Costa Rica's biological diversity is the result of its tropical location, its varied topography, and the many microclimates resulting from the combination of mountains, valleys, and lowlands. The isthmus also acts as a hospitable haven to many species that couldn't complete the journey from one hemisphere to the other. The rain forests of Costa Rica's Caribbean and southwestern lowlands are the most northerly home of such southern species as the crab-eating raccoon. The tropical dry forests of the northern Pacific slope are the southern limit for such North American species as the Virginia opossum. And then there are the dozens of northern bird species that spend their winter holidays here.

Research and planning go a long way in a place like Costa Rica. A short trip around the country can put you in one landscape after another, each with its own array of plants and animals. The country's renowned national park system holds examples of all of its major ecosystems, and some of its most impressive sights. In terms of activities, there's more interesting stuff to do here than could possibly ever fit into one vacation. But keep in mind that somewhere around three-fourths of the country has been urbanized or converted to agriculture, so if you want to see the spectacular nature that we describe in this book, you need to know where to go. In addition to this section on biodiversity, you'll find regional planning information, national park highlights, and a list of our favorite ecolodges at the front of each chapter.

DID YOU KNOW?

For some time, this area had been under serious threat from homesteading. In 1972, scientist George Powell and longtime residentWilford Guindon established Reserva Biológica Bosque Nuboso Monteverde (Monteverde Cloud Forest Preserve). In 2007, Costa Ricans voted it one of Costa Rica's Seven Wonders.

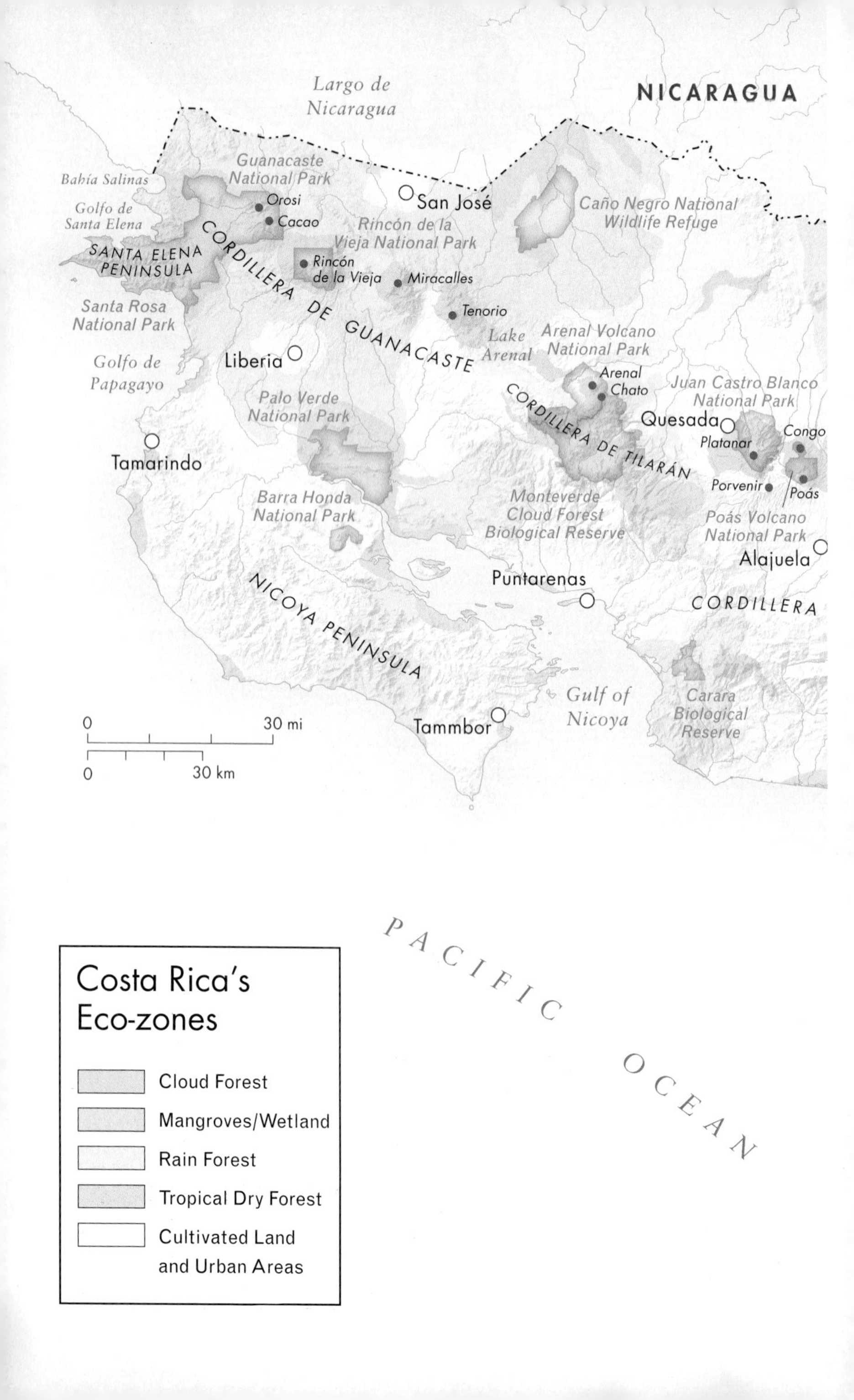

Largo de Nicaragua
NICARAGUA
Bahía Salinas
Golfo de Santa Elena
SANTA ELENA PENINSULA
Guanacaste National Park
Orosi
Cacao
San José
Caño Negro National Wildlife Refuge
Rincón de la Vieja National Park
Rincón de la Vieja
Miracalles
Tenorio
CORDILLERA DE GUANACASTE
Santa Rosa National Park
Golfo de Papagayo
Liberia
Lake Arenal
Arenal Volcano National Park
Arenal
Chato
Juan Castro Blanco National Park
Palo Verde National Park
CORDILLERA DE TILARÁN
Quesada
Platanar
Congo
Tamarindo
Porvenir
Poás
Barra Honda National Park
Monteverde Cloud Forest Biological Reserve
Poás Volcano National Park
Alajuela
Puntarenas
CORDILLERA
NICOYA PENINSULA
Gulf of Nicoya
Carara Biological Reserve
Tammbor
0
30 mi
0
30 km
PACIFIC OCEAN
Costa Rica's Eco-zones
Cloud Forest
Mangroves/Wetland
Rain Forest
Tropical Dry Forest
Cultivated Land and Urban Areas

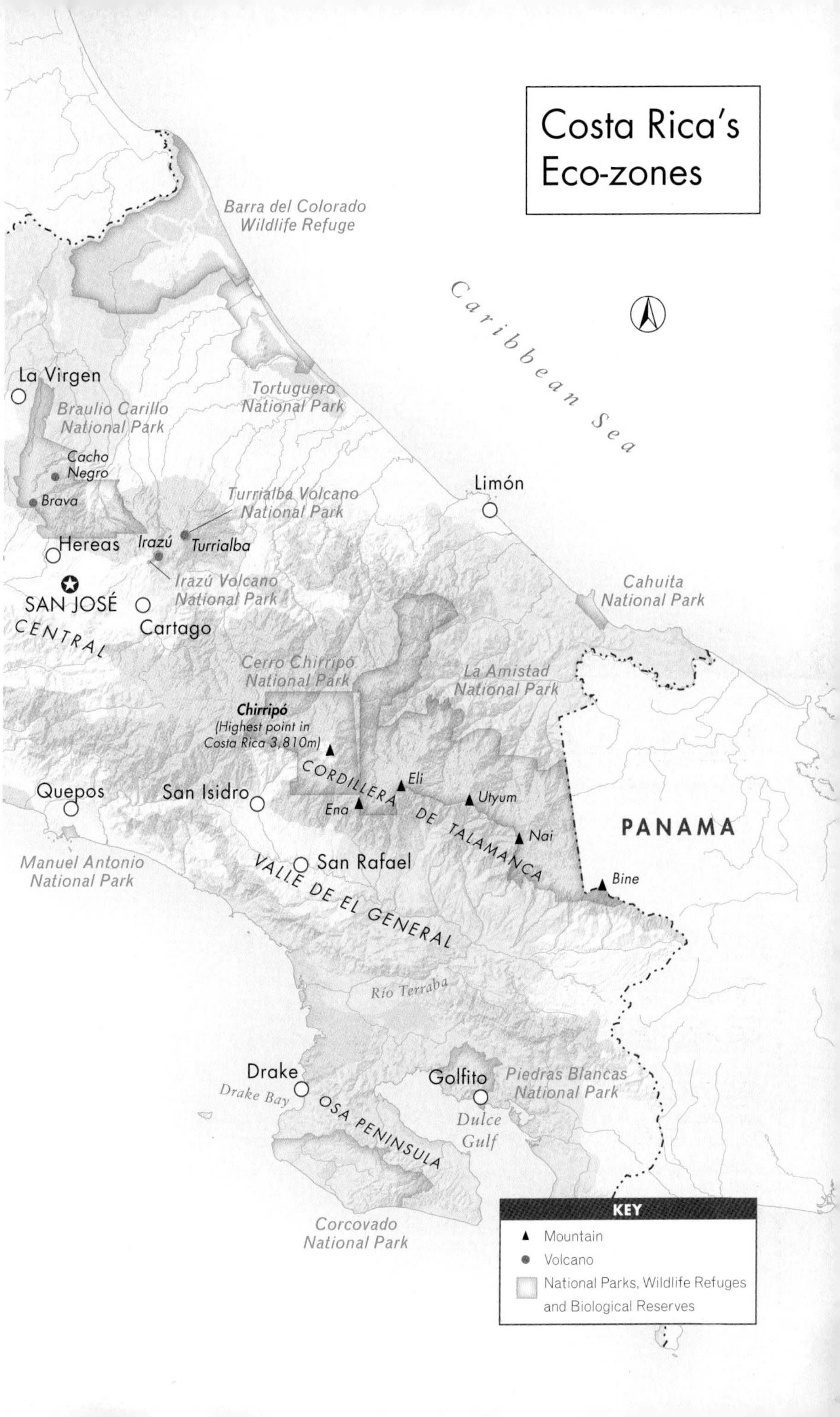

Costa Rica's Eco-zones
Barra del Colorado Wildlife Refuge
Caribbean Sea
La Virgen
Braulio Carillo National Park
Tortuguero National Park
Cacho Negro
Brava
Turrialba Volcano National Park
Limón
Hereas
Irazú
Turrialba
Irazú Volcano National Park
SAN JOSÉ
Cartago
CENTRAL
Cahuita National Park
Cerro Chirripó National Park
La Amistad National Park
Chirripó
(Highest point in Costa Rica 3,810m)
CORDILLERA DE TALAMANCA
Eli
Utyum
Ena
Nai
Bine
Quepos
San Isidro
PANAMA
San Rafael
Manuel Antonio National Park
VALLE DE EL GENERAL
Río Terraba
Drake
Drake Bay
Golfito
Piedras Blancas National Park
OSA PENINSULA
Dulce Gulf
Corcovado National Park
KEY
Mountain
Volcano
National Parks, Wildlife Refuges and Biological Reserves

RAIN FOREST

Warm and wet, Costa Rica's rain forest is the quintessential dripping, squawking, chirping, buzzing jungle. In this sultry landscape of green on green, birds flap and screech overhead and twigs snap under the steps of unseen creatures. All of the ingredients for life—water, sunlight, and more water—drench these areas.

WORD OF MOUTH

"We've been to Manuel Antonio during the first week of July, and it was very hot with afternoon rain each day. The rain didn't stop us from doing anything; we kind of expected it, so just did our tours early in the day."

—volcanogirl

The amount of rain in a rain forest is stunning. The enormous swath of forest in the Caribbean lowlands averages more than 4 meters (13 feet) of rain a year. Corcovado National Park, on the Osa Peninsula, can get 5.5 meters (18 feet).

The soaring canopy soaks up the lion's share of sunlight, seriously depriving the plants below. Underneath the highest trees are several distinct layers of growth. The understory is made up of smaller and younger trees, shaded, but also protected from harsh winds and rainfall. Shrubby species and even younger trees

stand farther below, and small plants, fungus, dead trees, and fallen leaves cover the constantly decomposing forest floor.

Light rarely passes through these layers and layers of growth. At the forest floor, plants lie poised, in a stasis of sorts, waiting for one of the giants above to fall and open a patch of sky. When this does happen, an incredible spectacle occurs as the waiting plants unveil an arsenal of evolutionary tricks. Vines twist out, looking for other trees to pull themselves up along, shoots explode from hidden bulbs, and ferns and lianas battle for height and access to the sun.

But as competitive as the jungle sounds, it is essentially a series of ecosystems based on interdependence and cooperation. Trees depend on the animals that eat their fruit to disperse their seeds. Fungi feed off the nutrients produced by the decomposing forest floor. From death comes life—an abundance of life.

Costa Rica's rain forests have suffered from agriculture and cattle farming, but they're still home to the majority of the nation's biodiversity, with more species per square mile than anywhere else.

ADVENTURE HIGHLIGHTS

- Novice birdwatchers can enroll in La Selva's Saturday morning bird-watching 101 class. It's taught by some of the finest naturalist in the country.
- Join the folks at Brisas del Nara, 20 mi outside of Manual Antonio, for an all-day horseback riding excursion through the protected Cerra Nara mountain zone. It ends with a swim in a natural pool with 350-foot waterfall.
- Stray way off the beaten path on a multiday hike through Corcovado National Park with tropical biologist Mike Boston from Osa Aventura.

FLORA

To enter into a Costa Rican rainforest is to be overwhelmed by the diversity and intensity of life. A single hectare contain almost 100 species of trees, and many of the more than 1,000 species of orchids are nested into their branches.

GUARIA MORADA

Almost every tree here plays host to lichens, woody vines called lianas, and rootless epiphytes, including the national flower, *guaria morada* (*Guarianthe skinneri*). Because this is an orchid species, you'll find it in several different shapes and colors: the flowers can be from pure white to deep magenta, and the base of its lip can range from yellow to white. There can be anywhere from 4 to 14 flowers per stem.

THE SILK COTTON TREE

The silk cotton tree (*Ceiba pentandra*), known locally as ceiba, is one of the most easily recognizable of the rain forest giants. Growing nearly 60 meters (200 feet) tall, it can be identified close to the ground by its tall, winding, and narrow roots, which act as buttresses to support the enormous trunk.

STRANGLER FIG

Aptly called *matapalo* in Spanish, meaning "tree killer," the strangler fig begins its life as an epiphyte, living high in the branches of another tree. Over several years, it slowly grows dangling roots to the forest floor that capture nutrients from the soil, thicken, and eventually meld onto the host tree. Eventually—it might take as long as 100 years—the strangler completely engulfs its host. In time the "strangled" tree decomposes and disintegrates, leaving the strangler fig—replete with branches, leaves, flowers, and fruit—standing hollow but victorious.

FALSE BIRD OF PARADISE

No avid photographer will return from Costa Rica without snapping a few shots of a heliconia, one of the most vibrant families of plants in the rain forest. This genus of flowering plant, containing between 100 and 200 species, includes the false bird of paradise (*Heliconia rostrata*), a dangling, impossibly colorful flower of alternating bulbous protrusions, colored red and tipped with green and yellow. Its vibrant colors and nectar make it a favorite for hummingbirds.

The Silk Cotton Tree

Guaria morada

Strangler Fig

False Bird of Paradise

2

FAUNA

Keep an eye out for three-wattled bellbirds, chestnut-mandibled toucans, or the Baird's tapir. A host of wild cats, include the jaguar, ocelot, jaguarundi, puma, and margay.

SCARLET MACAWS

Every bit the pirate's crimson parrot, these large and noisy birds mate for life, travel in pairs or large groups, and can often be found gathered in almond trees in low-elevation forests of the central and southern Pacific coast. Their cousin, the critically endangered great green macaw, travels across the Caribbean lowlands, following the ripening of the mountain almond.

HARPY EAGLE

The endangered harpy eagle, nearly extinct from Costa Rica, is the country's largest and most powerful raptor. It's named for the Greek spirits that carried the dead to the underworld of Hades, who are said to have the faces of humans but the bodies of eagles. Harpy eagles are huge—females are more than .6 meters (2 feet) in length and have a 1.8-meter (6-foot) wingspan. They hunt above the canopy, searching for large mammals or, occasionally, large birds like the macaw.

THREE-TOED OR TWO-TOED SLOTH

Through difficult for us to spot, the barely moving three-toed sloth and two-toed sloth are principal meals for the harpy eagle. This animal fur is a small self-sustaining ecosystem unto itself: because the forest is so wet and the sloth so inert, two species of blue-green algae thrive on its fur and provide it with needed camouflage. Nonparasitic insects also live here, feeding off the algae and keeping the growth under control.

MORPHO BUTTERFLY

The bright blue morpho butterfly bounces through the jungle like a small piece of sky on a string. The entire life cycle, from egg to death, is approximately 137 days, and the adult butterflies live for only about a month. Once they emerge from the cocoon, morphos have few predators thanks to the poisonous compounds that they retain from feeding habits back in their caterpillar days. In fact, the hairy brown tufts on the morpho caterpillar have been known to irritate human skin.

■ **TIP→The vibrantly colored red-eyed tree frog, like the white tent bat, sometimes rests on the underside of large jungle leaves; gently turn a few leaves over as you're hiking and take a peek. You might get lucky.**

Scarlet Macaw

Harpy Eagle

Three-toed-sloth

Blue Morpho

EXPERIENCING A RAIN FOREST

Photographing a spiderweb

For an ecosystem as diverse as the rain forest, it is fitting that there are a variety of ways to explore and experience it.

HIKING

Hiking or walking through any one of Costa Rica's numerous national parks is an easy way to fully experience the vibrancy of the life found there. And we can't say this too many times: guided hikes are the way to go for anyone who hopes to catch a glimpse of the more exotic and hard-to-find species or better understand the complexity of the surrounding ecosystems.

MOUNTAIN BIKING

During the dry season, some parks open up trails for mountain bikers. But once the rains begin, a bike trip can turn into a long slog through the mud. Before you rent a bike, ask about the conditions of the trails.

RAFTING

Gentle, slow-moving rivers beg to be explored by canoe or kayak. It's a wonderful way to experience the deep calm of the jungle, and stealthy enough to increase your chances of seeing wildlife. If you're more of a thrill seeker, choose from any of the white-water rafting tours that pass through rain forests.

CANOPY TOURS

Canopy tours are a wonderful way to get a bird's—or sloth's—view of the rain forest. Suspension bridges and zip lines, originally used for canopy research, offer a fantastic glimpse into the upper reaches of the forest. If you're not very mobile or don't feel like walking, go on a rain forest tram; it's like a small, slow-moving gondola that carries passengers gently through the jungle canopy.

TOP DESTINATIONS

Most of Costa Rica's rainforest can be found across the Caribbean lowlands and on the southern Pacific Coast.

LA SELVA

If anybody knows anything about the rain forest, it is the researchers at the La Selva biological station, situated in the midst of 3,900 acres of protected forest in the Caribbean lowlands. The station, run by the Organization for Tropical Studies, was founded by famed biologist Leslie Holdridge in 1954 and is one of the most important sites worldwide for research on tropical rain forest. The research station can sleep up to 80 people in dormitory-style rooms, and feed as many as 100 in the dining hall. More than 50 km (31 mi) of trails provide access to a variety of ecosystems. (See Chapter 5.)

MANUEL ANTONIO NATIONAL PARK

For a tame, up-close glimpse of the rain forest and some of its more photogenic inhabitants, Manuel Antonio National Park is a favorite. Located on the central Pacific coast, Manuel Antonio is one of Costa Rica's most visited—and smallest—national parks. Capuchin monkeys are used to humans to the point of practically ignoring them, unless a snack is poking out from an unattended backpack. The highly endangered squirrel monkeys are less bold, but can be seen at the park or from nearby hotels. Sloths are a common sight along the trail, as are a host of exotic birds and other creatures. But despite the apparent vibrancy of life found here, Manuel Antonio is isolated, with no biological bridges to other forests, and threatened by encroaching development. (See Chapter 7.)

Squirrel Monkey; danmike, Fodors.com member

A green and black poison frog, La Selva

CORCOVADO NATIONAL PARK

At the other end of the spectrum is Corcovado National Park, the remote, untamed jewel of Costa Rica's biodiversity crown. Covering one-third of the Osa Peninsula, Corcovado National Park holds about one-quarter of all tree species in Costa Rica and at least 140 identified species of mammals. Covering 172 square mi (445 square km), the park includes Central America's largest tract of lowland Pacific rain forest, including some old-growth areas. Corcovado is home to the largest concentration of jaguars left in the country, and the biggest population of scarlet macaw. There are at least 117 species of amphibians and reptiles, and more than 360 bird species. Ranger stations and campsites are available for the more adventurous, and luxurious eco-lodges surround the park for those who don't like to rough it. (See Chapter 8.)

VOLCANOES

As part of the Pacific Ring of Fire, the country has three volcanic mountain ranges: Guanacaste, Central, and Tilarán. There are around 300 volcanic points in Costa Rica, but only five have formed volcanoes that have erupted in recent memory: Turrialba, Irazu, Poás, Rincón de la Vieja, and Arenal.

WORD OF MOUTH

"I was at Arenal about 2 weeks ago. Had a great time but didn't see any red lava because the day I did the volcano park hike it was cloudy. However, I did hear the rumble and the boulders . . . It was a lot of fun."

—lbw14

Costa Rica's volcanoes are the result of friction between two enormous tectonic plates—the Cocos plate and the Caribbean plate. As these plates rub against each other, the friction partially melts rock, creating magma or lava. Magma is forced toward the surface, leaking through cracks or weak spots in the crust along with volcanic gas. In Rincón de la Vieja, lava and gas escapes through craters high on the volcano, as well as seeping up through the surrounding ground, creating bubbling mud pits, hot springs, and fumaroles.

The volcanic mountain ranges divide the country's Pacific and Caribbean slopes and are responsible for the differences in climate between each side. Rain-laden trade winds blowing westward can't pass over these ranges without shedding their precipitation and rising. This creates Guanacaste's rain shadow: the dry plains and tropical dry forest that lie leeward, or west of the mountains. The mountains block the rain-producing weather system and cast a "shadow" of dryness.

Costa Rica's volcanic lakes occur when there is no natural drainage from a crater. The chemicals, minerals, and gasses from below the Earth's crust infuse the water and vibrantly color it. Irazú's lake is neon green; the baby-blue lagoon in Poás is extremely acidic and gives off toxic sulfur clouds and massive amounts of carbon dioxide.

The surface ecology of a volcano varies. Rincón de la Vieja is skirted by Guanacaste's signature grasslands and tropical dry forest. Poás Volcano is blanketed with rain forest and tipped with cloud forest. Some of the country's best coffee is grown on the slopes of Poás.

ADVENTURE HIGHLIGHTS

- A hike through lush cloud forest will take you to the five magnificent waterfalls at La Paz Waterfall Gardens in Poás Volcano National Park.
- Anglers love the guapote, tilapia, and machaca pulled from in Lake Arenal.
- The Arenal area is the jumping off point for Class II–IV white-water rafting trips on the Blancas, Arenal, Toro, and San Carlos rivers.
- Take the tough hike to La Fortuna Waterfall, near Arenal. Swimming under the waterfall is a slice of paradise.

FLORA

The habitat and ecology of these geologic giants is influenced mostly by their surrounding ecology zones and elevation. Conditions around the crater of an active volcano are intensely harsh but some tougher species do manage to survive.

FERN

Contrary to popular stereotypes, ferns don't necessarily grow in shady, moist environments. The tongue fern (*Elaphoglossum lingua*) extends long, rubbery, tongue-shaped leaves and has evolved to grow around the lava rock and hardened ash. You'll find it around the top of the Poás Volcano. Farther down, you'll find other types of ferns adapted to friendlier conditions.

OAK

Forests in Costa Rica's higher mountain areas share some plant species with cloud forests. However, the plants here have adapted to live in cold temperatures and, if the volcano is active, in compacted ash. Surrounding the Botos Lagoon, on the south side of the principal Poás crater, is high-elevation cloud forest of oak (*Quercus costaricensis and Q. copeyensis*), small cedar (*Brunellia costaricensis*), and the flowering cyprus (*Escallonia poasana*)—trees that are typically crowded with epiphytes, bromeliads, and mosses.

MYRTLE

Myrtle (*Myrtaceae*), and other low-lying shrubs survive this environment thanks to their slow growth rate. Myrtle, poor man's umbrella (*Gunnera insignis*), papelillo (*Senecio oerstedianus*), and other shrubs and ferns cover the higher bluffs around Irazu's crater. Mistletoe (*Psittacanthus*) can be found near the major volcanoes in the Central Valley. These flowering plants are interesting because they attach to trees by haustoria, a special structure that penetrates the host plant and absorbs its water and nutrients. When the mistletoe dies, it leaves a mark on the tree, a woodrose or *rosa de palo*.

WILD BALSAM

Wild balsam, oak, and poor man's umbrella carpet the inactive cones around Rincón de la Vieja. Tropical dry forest species grow further down. Look for the guanacaste tree (*Enterolobium cyclocarpum*), Spanish cedar (*Cedrela odorata*), oak (*Q. oocarpa*), and the country's largest wild population of the guardia morada orchid, Costa Rica's national flower.

Ferns

Great Roble Oak

Wild Balsam aka Touch-me-not Balsam

Myrtle

2

FAUNA

Like the flora around a volcano, the wildlife diversity of this region is dictated by the ecology around the mountain. Also, the more humans there are, the fewer animals you'll see.

PUMA

In the Barva region, pumas (also called mountain lions and cougars) and even jaguars still stalk the more remote forests, searching for the tapir or an unlucky spider monkey. The puma is an excellent climber and can jump to branches 5 meters (16 feet) off the ground, essentially giving monkeys nowhere to hide. Pumas have never been hunted for their pelts, but are suffering from habitat destruction. In Costa Rica, they are rarely found outside of protected areas.

FIERY-THROATED HUMMINGBIRD

Birds are one of the most populous types of creature to live on the flanks of Poás and many more of Costa Rica's volcanoes. The fiery-throated hummingbird, the summer tanager, the sooty robin, and the emerald toucanet are among the 79 bird species that have been recorded at Poás. The fiery-throated hummingbird is recognizable by its forecrown, throat, and breast colors, as well as its bluish hump and blue-black tail.

NORTH AMERICAN PORCUPINE

The much drier region of Rincón de la Vieja has a distinctly different—and broader—set of animal inhabitants, including the North American porcupine and the agouti (a large, short-legged relative of the guinea pig). Pumas, ocelots, raccoons, and three species of monkeys (the howler, the white-faced capuchin, and the Central American spider monkey) are among the larger mammals. More than 300 bird species have been recorded there, including the collared aracari, the bare-necked umbrella bird, and the three-wattled bellbird.

NINE-BANDED ARMADILLO

Irazú is home to smaller creatures such as the nine-banded armadillo, the eastern cottontail, and the little spotted cat. The nine-banded armadillo has a long snout and fantastic sense of smell. It can hold its breath for up to six minutes. This helps it keep dirt out of its nostrils while digging. Under stressful conditions, a female armadillo can prolong her pregnancy for up to three years by delaying the implantation of the fertilized egg into the uterus wall.

Puma

North American Porcupine

Fiery-Throated Hummingbird

Nine-banded armadillo

EXPERIENCING THE VOLCANOES

Horseback riding in Arenal

The Guatuso people believed that the fire god lived inside the Arenal Volcano . . . and in 1968, the gods were not happy. After 500 years of dormancy, Arenal erupted savagely, burying three small villages and killing 87 people. Today, thousands live at its base in the thriving town of La Fortuna, which is literally in Arenal's shadow.

HIKING

Volcano tourism is a major draw for international visitors, but given the dangers at the active sites, activities at the top are limited. There are no zip lines across open craters, and there's no snorkeling in acidic volcano lakes. At the peak, activities are limited to viewing, hiking, and photography. But the otherworldly look and feel of these sights is reason enough to visit. On rare clear nights at Arenal, you can see lava spewing and flowing down the side of the mountain.

STANDING IN AWE

Volcanic activity is not, however, limited to a volcano's peak. The underground heat that fuels these giants also results in hot springs, bubbling mud pits, and geysers, among other geological wonders. Minerals from the dormant Tenorio Volcano create a fascinating effect in one of the rivers running down its side, the Rio Celeste, giving it a baby-blue tint. Arenal's reflection can be seen in pools of water heated by the same underground lava spewing from its peak.

HORSEBACK RIDING

Many of Costa Rica's volcanoes are the centerpieces to broad national parks. Depending on the park, the infrastructure can be outstanding or nonexistent. Arenal and Poás have good horseback-riding trails and outfitters.

TOP DESTINATIONS

Costa Rica's volcanoes are often the centerpieces of large national parks.

ARENAL VOLCANO

At 1,680 meters (5,512 feet), Arenal Volcano, rising on the northwestern plains of San Carlos, is every bit an awesome sight. Tall and perfectly conical, its sides are scarred by a history of violent eruptions and textured by decades of flowing lava. Located at the northern end of the Tilarán Mountain Range, northwest of the capital, it is Costa Rica's best-known volcano, its most active, and one of the 10 most active volcanoes in the world. Unfortunately, Arenal's peak is often shrouded from sight because of the gasses and steam that escape from the crater. One scary bit of research concluded that Arenal has a 400-year cycle of major eruptions, and the activity since the 1968 explosion is small in comparison with what it's capable of. (See Chapter 5.)

RINCÓN DE LA VIEJA

A mass of slopes, craters, and biodiversity that bridges the continental divide, Rincón de la Vieja is in Costa Rica's arid northwest. It's not the classic conical volcano, but rather a ridge made of a series of craters that include bare, rocky bowls with brilliantly colored lakes, and velvety cones covered in rain forest.

Gaudy Leaf Frog; Marco13, Fodors.com member.

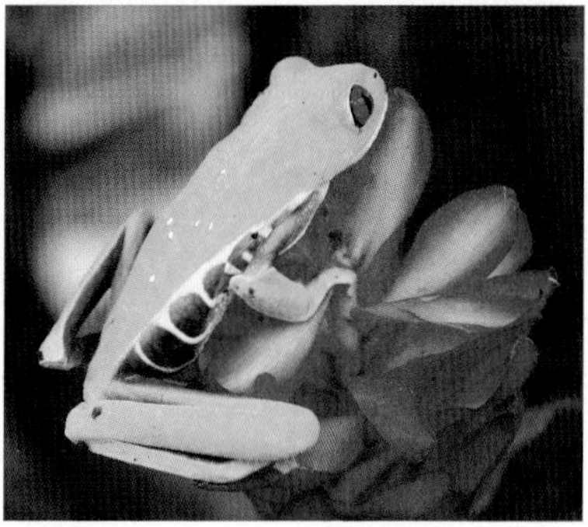

On the Road to Arenal; piper35w, Fodors.com member

Scientists believe Rincón de la Vieja was born of simultaneous volcanic activity at nine different eruption points. The Rincón de la Vieja National Park covers nearly 35,000 acres and is a wonderland of volcanic activity that includes bubbling mud pits, hot springs, and geysers, as well as refreshing lagoons and spectacular waterfalls. (See Chapter 6.)

POÁS VOLCANO

Poás Volcano is Costa Rica's most visited national park, in part because it is the closest active volcano to the capital of San José and the Aeropuerto Internacional Juan Santamaría. Located in the Cordillera Volcánica Central Mountain Range, Poás is topped by three craters, the tallest reaching 2,708 meters (8,885 feet) above sea level. Only the main cone has shown any volcanic eruptions in the last 200 years. You can get a good look at the crater from the viewing deck. (See Chapter 5.)

Note: A 6.2 earthquake struck only 10 km (6 mi) from Poás in January 2009, destroying two nearby villages and killing 23 people (at this writing, 7 people had still not been found). However, seismologists and geologists assured the public that it was not related to any volcanic activity at Poás.

CLOUD FOREST

The four mountain ranges that make up Costa Rica's own piece of the continental divide split the country into its Caribbean and Pacific regions. At these higher altitudes, temperatures cool, clouds settle, and rainfall increases. The forests found here are shrouded in mist and rich in biodiversity. Welcome to Costa Rica's famed cloud forests.

WORD OF MOUTH

"It's a magical place. I loved when the misty clouds started coming in . . . you can see why they call it a cloud forest! You'll hear birds and may spot a bit of wildlife if you go slowly and look carefully."
—Melissa5

Like its lowland rain forest cousins, cloud forests are packed with plant and animal species, thanks largely to their water-drenched conditions. There's an average of 5 meters (16 feet) of rainfall a year, but that number doubles when you factor in the amount of moisture gleaned from the clouds and fog that drift through every day. Like rain forests, giant hardwoods reaching as high as almost 60 meters (200 feet) set the ceiling for this ecology zone, while a variety of smaller trees, ferns, shrubs, and other plants fill the understories. Epiphytes flourish here, as do mosses, lichens, and

liverwort. These plants cling to passing moisture and capture it like sponges. As a result, cloud forests are constantly soaking wet even when there is no rain.

Because conditions in a cloud forest can be harsh, many of the tougher and more adaptable rain forest species make their home here. The relentless, heavy cloud cover can block sunlight even from the highest reaches of the forest, and deeper inside, light is rare. Photosynthesis and growth is slower, so the plants tend to be smaller with thicker trunks and stems. These unique conditions also produce an unusually high number of endemic and rare species.

The Monteverde Cloud Forest Preserve, one of the world's most famous protected cloud forests, shelters innumerable life-forms. There are more than 100 mammal species; 400 bird species, including at least 30 species of hummingbird; 500 plus species of butterfly; and more than 2,500 plant species, including 420 types of orchids. There are only a handful of protected cloud forests here and worldwide and this type of ecozone is increasingly threatened by human encroachment.

ADVENTURE HIGHLIGHTS

- Leave the car at home and travel on horseback to or from the Arenal Volcano area and Monteverde Cloud Forest. Contact Desafío Adventures, the only guides we recommend for this journey.
- Expert birder Marino Chacón of the Savage Hotel will give you an education on one of his daylong natural history hikes around San Gerardo de Dota cloud forest.
- Selvatura, right next to Monteverde, is the only canopy tour in the area with a zip line built entirely inside the cloud forest.

FLORA

A typical hectare (2½ acres) of rain forest might be home to nearly 100 species of trees. Contrast that with a mere 30 in the richest forests of North America.

ROBLE TREE

Majestic roble, or oak—principally the white oak (Quercus copeyensis) and black oak (*Quercus costarricensis*)—is the dominant tree of Costa Rica's cloud forests and grows to 60 meters (200 feet). The deciduous hardwood *cedro dulce*, or Spanish cedar (*Cedrela tonduzii*), is also a giant at 40 meters (147 feet). These two are joined by evergreens like the *jaúl*, or alder, and the *aguacatillo*, a name meaning "little avocado" that's given to a variety of trees from the *lauracea* family.

POOR MAN'S UMBRELLA

If you're caught in the rain, take cover under a poor man's umbrella (*Gunnera insignis* and *Gunnera talamancana*), whose broad and sturdy leaves sometime grow large enough to shelter an entire family. These shrubby plants love the dark, moist interior of the cloud forest.

EPIPHYTES

Epiphytes thrive in cloud and rain forests, thanks to all the moisture and nutrients in the air. The *stanhopea* orchid is interesting because of its clever pollination tricks. The blossoms' sweet smell attracts bees, but the flower's waxy surface is slippery so they slide down inside. As they slowly work their way out, they brush up against the flower's column and collect pollen. This pollen is then transferred to the sticky stigma of other flowers.

Bromeliads, another family of flowering plants, competes with epiphytes for space on the branches and trunks of the forest's trees. The spiraling leaves form catches for water, falling plant material, and insect excretion. These are mineral-rich little ponds for insects and amphibians, and drinking and bathing water for birds and other animals.

STAR ORCHID

The star orchid (*Epidendrum radicans*) is one of the few orchids that is not an epiphyte. It mimics in color and shape other nectar-filled flowers in order to attract butterflies who unwittingly become pollinators.

White Oak Tree

Poor Man's Umbrella

Epiphyte Stanhopea

Star Orchid

FAUNA

The resplendent quetzal, the blue-crowned motmot, the orange-bellied trogon, and the emerald toucanet are just some of the hundreds of species that can be logged in a cloud forest.

GLASS FROGS

One of the more bizarre amphibians is the transparent glass frog of the *Centrolenellu* genus, whose internal organs can be seen through its skin. It lives in trees and bushes and can often be heard at night near the rivers and streams. Cloud forests have fewer amphibian species than rain forests, but amphibian populations worldwide have plummeted in recent decades. No one knows the cause yet. Some blame acid rain and pesticides; others believe it is yet another sign of coming ecological disaster.

RESPLENDENT QUETZAL

Perhaps the most famed resident of Costa Rica's cloud forests is the illustrious resplendent quetzal. Every year, bird-watchers come to Costa Rica hoping to spot the green, red, and turquoise plumage of this elusive trogon. Considered a sacred creature by the Maya and the namesake of Guatemala's currency, the quetzal spends much of its time perched in its favorite tree, the *aguacatillo*.

COLLARED TROGON

The collared trogon and the orange-bellied trogon are in the same family as the quetzel. They all share square black-and-white tail plumage and bright orange or yellow chest feathers. The collared trogon perches very quietly and is easy to miss. Luckily, it doesn't fly far, so its flight is easy to follow.

COLLARED ARACARI

This big billed toucan can be recognized by its chalky-white upper mandible. Males and females look similar—black head, bright yellow under parts, and a red-tinted black band across the belly. You can see this bird in the Caribbean lowlands and less frequently in the Caribbean foothills. These are equal opportunity birds, with both sexes incubating the eggs and taking care of the toucan chicks. They also get help by the other adults in the flock.

Glass Frogs

Resplendent Quetzal

Collared Aracari

Collared Trogon

2

EXPERIENCING A CLOUD FOREST

Zipline tour in Selvature just outside of Monteverde Cloud Forest

You may need to get down and dirty—well, more like wet and muddy—to experience a cloud forest's natural wonders, but then, that's half the fun.

HIKING

Well-guided hikes through this eerie landscape make it easier to spot the less obvious features of this complex ecosystem. Compared with the barren tropical dry forest, and colorful rain forest, cloud forests don't easily offer up their secrets. Binoculars and a good guide will go a long way toward making your hike and wildlife spotting richer experiences.

BIRD-WATCHING

Bird-watching is rewarding in the cloud forest, where some of the most vibrant and peculiar of nature's winged creatures can be found. Rise early, enjoy some locally grown coffee, and check the aguacatillo trees for quetzals. If you opt to go without a guide, bring along waterproof binoculars and a good guidebook (we recommend *The Birds of Costa Rica*, by Richard Garrigues and Robert Dean) for spotting and identifying birds.

CANOPY TOURS

Canopy tours and suspended bridges run right through the upper reaches of the cloud forest—an ecosystem in its own right. Spot birds, monkeys, and exotic orchids from a viewpoint that was once nearly impossible to reach. Get even closer to butterflies, amphibians, snakes, and insects at various exhibits in the parks' research centers.

FISHING

If freshwater fishing in spectacular surroundings is right up your alley, check out the Savegre River, in the San Gerardo de Dota Valley. It's been stocked with wild rainbow trout since the 1950s.

2

TOP DESTINATIONS

Regardless of which cloud forest you visit, bring a raincoat and go with a guide if you want to see wildlife. You'll marvel at their ability to spot a sloth at a hundred paces.

MONTEVERDE CLOUD FOREST BIOLOGICAL RESERVE

Costa Rica's most famous cloud forest reserve is packed with an astonishing variety of life: 2,500 plant species, 400 species of birds, 500 types of butterflies, and more than 100 different mammals have been catalogued so far. The reserve reaches 1,535 meters (5,032 feet) above sea level, spans the Tilarán Mountain Range, and encompasses 9,885 acres of cloud forest and rain forest. There are 13 km (8 mi) of well-marked trails, zip-line tours, and suspended bridges for canopy viewing, bird tours, guided night walks, and a field research station with an amphibian aquarium. Allow a generous slice of time for leisurely hiking; longer hikes are made possible by some strategically placed overnight refuges along the way. (See Chapter 5.)

SAN GERARDO DE DOTA

One of Costa Rica's premier nature destinations, San Gerardo de Dota is a damp, epiphyte-laden forest of giant oak trees and an astonishing number of resplendent quetzels. Outdoor enthusiasts may never want to leave these parts—some of the country's best hiking is in this valley, and it's popular with bird-watchers. It's also great for horseback riding and trout fly-fishing. (See Chapter 8.)

Braulio Carrillo National Park

Banded Anteater; maddytem, Fodors.com member

BRAULIO CARRILLO NATIONAL PARK

Descending from the Cordillera Volcánica Central Mountain Range, the Braulio Carrillo National Park is an awesome, intimidating, and rugged landscape of dense cloud forest that stretches toward the rain forests of the Caribbean lowlands. The enormous park encompasses 117,580 acres of untamed jungle and is less than an hour's drive from San José. The country's principal east-bound highway cuts a path straight through it. Elusive (and endangered) jaguars and pumas are among the many animal species here, and scenic viewpoints are plentiful along the highway. A handful of trails, including the Los Niños Circular Trail and the Los Guarumos Trail, can be taken into the park's interior. (See Chapter 5.)

TROPICAL DRY FOREST

The most endangered biome in the world, these seasonal forests swing between two climate extremes—from drenching wet to bone dry. To survive, plants undergo a drastic physical transformation: forests burst into life during the rainy months, and are brown, leafless, and seemingly dead during the dry season.

WORD OF MOUTH

"I wouldn't be too concerned about that heat BECAUSE it is so dry . . . no humidity to speak of which can make things comfortable when you're in the shade. I've always visited Guanacaste in or around February and prefer it for that reason."

—joeschmo

For about half the year, northwestern Costa Rica is as wet as the rest of the country. The weather blows in from the Pacific and it can rain every day. During the dry season, from January to April, weather patterns change, winds shift, and the land becomes parched.

Tall deciduous hardwoods are the giants in this ecology zone, with spindly branches creating a seasonal canopy as high as 30 meters (100 feet). A thorny and rambling understory of smaller trees and bushes thrives thanks to the plentiful light permitted once the canopy falls to the forest floor. The challenges of the dry months

have forced plants to specialize. The hardwoods are solitary and diffuse, their seeds spread far and wide by animals and insects. Some even flower progressively through the dry season, depending on the plant species and the particular bees and birds that have evolved to pollinate them.

Dry season is perfect for bird- and animal-watching since the lack of foliage makes wildlife-spotting easy. Keep your eyes peeled for monkeys, parrots, lizards, coyotes, rabbits, snakes, and even jaguars.

There was once one great uninterrupted swath of dry forest that began in southern Mexico, rolled across Mesoamerica, and ended in northwest Costa Rica. Today, less than 2% of the Central American tropical dry forest remains, the majority of it in Costa Rica. But even here, the forest is fractured into biologically isolated islands, thanks to decades of logging and agriculture. The Guanacaste parks system has managed to corral off large chunks of land for preservation, and private and government efforts are under way to create biological corridors between isolated dry forests so that animals and plants can roam farther and deepen their gene pools, so critical to their survival.

ADVENTURE HIGHLIGHTS

- Adrenalin-spiked tours with Hacienda Guachipelín (just outside of Rincón de la Vieja National Park) include river tubing, rappelling, zip lines, and a tarzan swing.
- Let the knowledgeable folks from the Organization for Tropical Studies (OTS) take you on a guided bird-watching boat tour through Palo Verde National Park.
- Take the kids on a bird and monkey watching journey down the Rio Corobicí, in Palo Verde National Park.

FLORA

Among other types of flora, tropical forests are filled with deciduous hardwoods, such as mahogany (*Swietenia macrophylla*), black laurel (*Cordia gerascanthus*), ronrón (*Astronium graveolens*), and cocobolo (*Dalbergia retusa*). Much of the wood is highly prized, so many of these trees are facing extinction outside of national parks and protected areas.

GUANACASTE

Perhaps the most striking and easy-to-spot resident of Costa Rica's tropical dry forest is the guanacaste (*Enterolobium cyclocarpum*), an imposing tree with an enormous, spherical canopy that seems straight out of the African savanna. The guanacaste is the northwest province's namesake and Costa Rica's national tree. It's most easily identified standing alone in pastures. Without the competition of the forest, a pasture guanacaste sends massive branches out low from its trunk, creating an arching crown of foliage close to the ground. The ear-shaped seedpods are also a distinct marker; the hard seeds inside are popular with local artisan jewelers.

Guanacaste

FRANGIPANI TREE

The frangipani tree (*Plumeria rubra*) can grow up to 8 meters (26 feet) and has meaty pink, white, or yellow blossoms. The flowers are most fragrant at night to lure sphinx moths. Unfortunately for the moth, the blooms don't produce nectar. The plant simply dupes their pollinators into hopping from bloom to bloom and tree to tree in a fruitless search for food.

Frangipani; plumboy, Fodors.com member

GUMBO-LIMBO

Costa Ricans call the gumbo-limbo tree (*Bursera simaruba*) *indio desnudo* (naked Indian) because of its red, peeling bark. This tree is also found in Florida, and the wood has historically been used for making carousel horses in the United States.

Gumbo-limbo

CORNIZUELO

The spiky, cornizuelo (*Acacia collinsii*) is an intriguing resident of the lower levels because of its symbiotic relationship with ants. This small evergreen tree puts out large thorns that serve as a home for a certain ant species. In exchange for food and shelter, the ants provide the tree protection from other leaf-munching insects or vines. Sometimes the ants will even cut down encroaching vegetation on the forest floor, allowing the tree to thrive.

Cornizuelo

FAUNA

Tropical forests are literally crawling with life. Bark scorpions, giant cockroaches, and tarantulas scuttle along the forest floor, and the buzz from wasps and cicadas gives the air an almost electric feel. A careful eye may be able to pick out walking sticks frozen still among the twigs. The jaguar, and one if its favorite prey, the endangered tapir, also stalk these forests.

WHITE-FACED CAPUCHIN

Monkeys are common all over Costa Rica, and the dry forests are home to three species: the howler monkeys, with their leathery black faces and deep barking call, are the loudest of the forest's mammals; the white-faced capuchin travel in playful packs; and the endangered spider monkey require large, undisturbed tracts of forest for a healthy population to survive. This last group is in steep decline—another indicator of the overall health of this eco-region.

COYOTE

Nearly unique to the dry tropical forest is the coyote, which feeds on rodents, lizards, and an assortment of small mammals, as well as sea turtle eggs (when near the beach) and other improvised meals. Like the Virginia opossum and the white-tailed deer, the coyote is believed to have traveled south from North America through the once-interconnected tropical dry forest of Mesoamerica.

NEOTROPICAL RATTLESNAKE

The venomous neotropical rattlesnake and the exquisite painted wood turtle are among the reptiles that exclusively call this region home. Salvin's spiny pocket mouse, the eastern cottontail rabbit, and both the spotted and hooded skunk are also unique to Costa Rica's dry forests.

BLACK-HEADED TROGON

With an open canopy for much of the year, and plentiful ground rodents and reptiles, these forests are great hunting grounds for birds of prey like the roadside hawk and the spectacled owl. The white-throated magpie jay travels in noisy mobs, while the scissor-tailed flycatcher migrates from as far north as the southern United States. The rufous-naped wren builds its nest in the spiky acacia trees. The black-headed trogon, with its bright yellow breast, and the elegant trogon both nest exclusively in Costa Rica's tropical dry forest.

White-faced capuchin

Coyote

Black-headed Trogon

Neotropical Rattlesnake

EXPERIENCING A DRY TROPICAL FOREST

Rincón de la Vieja National Park

Many of Costa Rica's roads are rough at best, and tropical forests are often remote. We recommend hiring a 4WD for getting around.

HIKING

The absolute best way to experience these endangered woods is to strap on your hiking boots, grab a hat and lots of water, and get out and walk. Most of the dry forests are protected lands and found in Guanacaste's national parks. Some have road access, making it possible to drive through the park, but most are accessible only by hiking trails. During the rainy season, roads become mud pits and hiking trails are almost impassable, so it's best to visit during the dry season.

BIRD- AND WILDLIFE-WATCHING

Most people come to these areas for bird-watching and wildlife-spotting, but it's best done during the dry season, when all of the foliage drops from the trees. Bring a good bird or wildlife guide, binoculars, lots of water (we can't stress this enough), and plenty of patience. It's a good idea to find a watering hole and just hunker down and let the animals come to you. If you don't want to explore the forest alone, tours can be arranged through hotels, ranger stations, and private research centers inside the parks. In terms of bird and wildlife guides, we recommend *The Birds of Costa Rica* by Richard Garrigues and Robert Dean and *The Mammals of Costa Rica* by Mark Wainwright. If you'd like to know more about plants, pick up *Tropical Plants of Costa Rica* by Willow Zuchowski.

BIKING

Some parks allow biking, but again, this is certainly something you don't want to do during the rains. Contact the park that you'll be visiting ahead of time for trail and rental information.

2

TOP DESTINATIONS

Most of Costa Rica's remaining tropical dry forests are located in the northwest of the country, not too far from the Nicaragua border.

SANTA ROSA NATIONAL PARK

The largest piece of tropical dry forest under government protection in Central America spreads out over Santa Rosa National Park, about 35 km (22 mi) north of Guanacaste's capital, Liberia. The park, which covers 380 square km (146 square mi) also includes two beaches and coastal mangrove forest. Thanks to trails and equipped campsites, you can venture deep into the park. During the dry season, visibility is excellent and chances are good in terms of spotting some of the hundreds of bird and animal species there. Playa Nancite, Santa Rosa's northern beach, is also one of the world's most important and most protected beaches for the nesting of olive ridley sea turtles. They come ashore by the hundreds of thousands between May and October (during the rainy season when access to the beaches are difficult) in a phenomenon called the *arribada*. (See Chapter 6.)

GUANACASTE NATIONAL PARK

Santa Rosa bumps up against Guanacaste National Park, which is composed of some tropical dry forest and former

Hummingbird Nesting; reedjoella, Fodors.com member

farmland that's being regenerated to its natural state. The park is intended to serve as a much-needed biological corridor from Santa Rosa up to the cloud forests of the Orosi and Cacao volcanoes, to the east. Park infrastructure is generally lacking, though three biological stations offer some accommodations. (See Chapter 6.)

Canopy Tour at Rincón de la Vieja National Park

RINCÓN DE LA VIEJA NATIONAL PARK

More tropical dry forest can be found inside the Rincón de la Vieja National Park, ringing the base of the two volcanoes of this protected area—Santa María and Rincón de la Vieja. (See Chapter 6.)

PALO VERDE NATIONAL PARK

Farther south, Palo Verde National Park skirts the northeastern side of the Rio Tempisque, straddling some of the country's most spectacular wetlands and tropical dry forest. Thanks to these two very different ecology zones, Palo Verde is packed with very diverse bird, plant, and animal species—bird-watchers love this park. The Organization for Tropical Studies has a biological station at Palo Verde and offers tours and accommodations. Park guards also maintain a ranger station with rustic overnight accommodations. (See Chapter 6.)

WETLANDS & MANGROVES

Wetlands are any low-lying areas that are perpetually saturated with water. Their complex ecosystems support a variety of living things—both endemic species unique to the area and visitors who travel halfway around the hemisphere to get here. Here, land species have evolved to live much of their lives in water.

WORD OF MOUTH

"The wildlife viewing [in Tortuguero] just never stopped. Howler monkeys, all types of water birds, caimans and crocodiles, both species of toucans, spider monkeys, white faced capuchins, kingfishers and parrots . . . we thought we were in 7th heaven!" —colibri

One of the more common types of wetlands in Costa Rica is a floodplain, created when a river or stream regularly overflows its banks, either because of heavy rains or incoming ocean tides. Thanks to huge deposits of sediment that are left as the floodwaters recede, the ground is extremely fertile and plants thrive, as do the animals that feed here.

Mangroves are a particularly unique type of wetland and cover 1% of the country. They are found at the edges of tidal areas, such as ocean inlets, estuaries, and canals where salt water mixes with fresh.

Mangrove forests are made up of a small variety of plants, principally mangrove trees, but attract a huge variety of animals.

Mangrove trees are able to survive in this stressful habitat because they have developed the ability to cope with constant flooding, tolerate a lack of oxygen, and thrive in a mix of salt and fresh water thanks to uniquely adapted roots and leaves. The nutrient-rich sediment and mud that builds up around these trees and between their prop roots creates habitat for plankton, algae, crabs, oysters, and shrimp. These, in turn, attract larger and larger animals that come to feed, giving mangrove forests a remarkable level of biodiversity.

These thick coastal forests are protective barriers for inland ecosystems; they dissipate the force of storm winds and sudden surges in tides or floods triggered by coastal storms or tsunamis.

Sadly, coastal development is a big threat to mangroves. It is illegal to clear mangrove forests, but enforcement is weak, and builders of marinas, docks, and beachfront developments have been caught doing it. Wetlands are also threatened by the human encroachment and the diversion of water for agricultural use.

ADVENTURE HIGHLIGHTS

- Witness the awesome spectacle of nesting turtles at Tortuguero National Park. Turtle watching excursions require a certified guide and only take place between the February and November nesting season.
- Anglers can hook mackerel, tarpoon, snook, calba, and snapper in the canals and along the coast of Tortuguero and Barra Colorado.
- Take a mellow kayaking tour through mangrove estuary of Isla Damas, near Manuel Antonio. You'll probably see monkeys, crocodiles, and any number of birds.

FLORA

Wetland and mangrove plants share an ability to live in soggy conditions. However, not all wetland plants are able survive brackish water in the way coastal mangrove flora can.

WATER HYACINTH

The succulent, floating water hyacinth (*Eichornia crassipes*) is recognizable by its lavender-pink flowers that are sometimes bundled at 8 to 15 per single stalk. The stems rise from a bed of thick, floating green leaves, whereas the plant's feathery roots hang free in the still, fresh water. The water hyacinth is prolific and invasive; they've even been known to clog the canals of Tortguero.

Water Hyacinth

THORNY SENSITIVE PLANT

Aquatic grasses and herbs grow along the shallower edges of swamps and marshlands where they can take root underwater and still reach the air above. The curious dormilona, or thorny sensitive plant (*Mimosa pigra*) is another invasive wetland shrub and can be identified by the way its fernlike leaves wilt shyly to the touch, only to straighten out a little later.

Thorny sensitive plant

RED MANGROVE

Costa Rica has seven species of mangrove trees, including red mangrove (*Rhizophora mangle*), black mangrove (*Avicennia germinans*), the white mangrove (*Laguncularia racemosa*), and the more rare tea mangrove (*Pelliciera rhizophorae*). Red mangrove is easily identified by its tall arching prop roots that give it a firm foothold against wind and waves. The tidal land is also unstable, so all mangroves need a lot of root just to keep upright. As a result, many have more living matter underwater than above ground. They also depend on their prop roots for extra nutrients and oxygen; the red mangrove filters salt at its roots.

Red Mangrove

BLACK MANGROVE

The black mangrove can grow as tall as 12 meters (40 feet) and has adapted to survive in its habitat by excreting salt through special glands in its leaves. It grows on the banks above the high-tide line and has evolved to breathe through small roots it sends up vertically in case of flooding.

Black Mangrove

FAUNA

Though the diversity of plant life in mangrove swamps and wetlands is small compared with other ecozones, this habitat attracts an extremely wide variety of fauna.

RAINBOW PARROTFISH

Rainbow parrotfish, in addition to many other fish species, spend time as juveniles in mangrove areas, feeding in the relative safety of the roots until they're big enough to venture out into more open water. Parrotfish have a few unusual abilities: they are hermaphroditic and can change sex in response to population density; at night they wrap themselves in a protective mucus cocoon; and they eat coral and excrete a fine white sand. One parrotfish can create a ton of sand per year, which ultimately washes ashore. Think about it the next time you're lying on the beach.

Rainbow Parrotfish

CRAB-EATING RACCOON

Bigger creatures are attracted to these mangroves precisely because of the veritable buffet of sea snacks. The crab-eating raccoon will prowl the canopy of the mangrove forests as well as the floor, feeding on crabs and mollusks. The endangered American crocodile and the spectacled caiman can be found listing through waters or sunning themselves on the banks of mangrove habitat.

Crab-eating Raccoon

BLACK-CROWNED NIGHT HERON

Mangroves are critical nesting habitats for a number of birds, including the endangered mangrove hummingbird, the yellow-billed continga, the Amazon kingfisher, and the black-crowned night heron. Interestingly, black-crowned night herons don't distinguish between their own young and those from other nests, so they willingly brood strange chicks.

Black Crowned Night Heron

BLACK-BELLIED WHISTLING DUCK

Bird-watchers love the wide-open wetlands and marshes, with flocks of thousands of migrating and resident species. In these tropical floodplains pink-tinged roseate spoonbills will be found stalking the shallow water alongside the majestic great egret and the bizarre and endangered jabiru stork. Keep an eye out for the black-bellied whistling duck, which actually perches and nests in trees. These migrant ducks can also be found in some southern U.S. states.

Black-Bellied Whistling Duck

EXPERIENCING THE WETLANDS & MANGROVES

Paddling through Tortuguero at dawn; Thornton Cohen, Fodors.com member

Wildlife-viewing in general can be very rewarding in these areas, because a wide variety of creatures come together and share the habitat.

BIRD-WATCHING

The most populous and diverse of the creatures that live in and depend on wetlands and mangroves are birds, so bring some binoculars and your field guide and prepare to check off some species. For good photos, take a long lens and tripod, and get an early start—midday sun reflecting off the ubiquitous water can make your photos washed out or create some challenging reflections.

VIEWING PLATFORMS

Hiking can be more difficult in these areas because wetlands are by definition largely underwater. But some areas have elevated platforms that make for great up-close viewing of the interior parts of marshes and shallow lagoons.

BOATING

The best way to see Costa Rica's remaining mangrove forests is by boat—we recommend using a kayak or canoe. These vessels allow you to slip along canals and protected coastlines in near silence, increasing your chance of creeping up on many of the more impressive creatures that call this habitat home. A guided boat tour is also recommended—a good naturalist or biologist, or even a knowledgeable local, will know where creatures habitually hang out and will be able to distinguish between thick branches and a knotted boa at the top of a shore-side tree.

FISHING

Canals that are not part of protected areas can be ripe for fishing—another, tastier way to get a close-up look at some of the local fauna. Make sure to ask about what's biting, as well as local fishing regulations.

TOP DESTINATIONS

The Ramsar Convention on Wetlands is an intergovernmental treaty to provide a framework for the conservation of the world's wetlands. There are 11 Ramsar wetlands in Costa Rica: all are impressive but we've listed only our top three.

PALO VERDE NATIONAL PARK

Within the Palo Verde National Park is perhaps Costa Rica's best-known wetland—a system that includes shallow, permanent freshwater lagoons, marshes, mangroves, and woodlands that are seasonally flooded by the Tempisque River. A good portion of this 45,511-acre park is covered by tropical dry forest, as mentioned earlier. In fact, this park has 12 different habitats, creating one of the most diverse collections of life in the country. At least 55 aquatic plants and 150 tree species have been identified here, and the largest number of aquatic and wading birds in all of Mesoamerica can be found at Palo Verde wetlands. A total of 279 bird species have been recorded within the Palo Verde, so little surprise that it's listed by the Ramsar Convention as a wetland of international importance. The Organization of Tropical Studies maintains a research station at the park with limited accommodations but great views of the marshes, as well as extremely knowledgeable guides. (See Chapter 6.)

Tortuguero; StupFD, Fodors.com member

Alpha Howler Monkey; Liz Stuart, Fodors.com member

TORTUGUERO NATIONAL PARK

Ninety-nine percent of mangrove forests are found on Costa Rica's Pacific coast. But the best place to see some of the remaining 1% on the Caribbean side is Tortuguero National Park. Like Palo Verde, Tortuguero is home to a wide variety of life—11 distinct habitats in total, including extensive wetlands and mangrove forests. Beach-nesting turtles (*tortugas*) are the main attraction here, but the park is included in the Ramsar list of internationally important wetlands. Many of the species listed above can be spotted along the banks of Tortuguero's famous canals. (See Chapter 6.)

CAÑO NEGRO NATIONAL WILDLIFE REFUGE

A third Ramsar wetland is found in the Caño Negro National Wildlife Refuge, in the more remote northern plains close to the border with Nicaragua. Caño Negro has a seasonal lake that can cover as many as 1,975 acres and grow as deep as 3 meters (10 feet). The lake is actually a pool created by the Frio River that dries up to nearly nothing between February and May. The park also has marshes, semi-permanently flooded old-growth forest, and other wetland habitats. (See Chapter 5.)

SHORELINE

Costa Rica has a whopping 1,290-km-long (799-mi-long) coastline that varies from expansive beaches, tranquil bays, muddy estuaries, and rocky outcroppings. They're backed by mangrove, rain, transitional, and tropical-dry forests.

WORD OF MOUTH

"If you only have time for a quick, affordable little beach getaway, Flamingo Beach could be just what you are looking for. The sunsets in this area really are fantastic."

—Linda137

Each of Costa Rica's costal environments, as well as the currents and the wind, has it's own distinct impact on the ecology of the beach.

Costa Rica's sand beaches come in different shades and textures: pulverized black volcanic rock (Playa Negra), crushed white shells (Playa Conchal), finely ground white coral and quartz (Playa Carrillo), and gray rock sediment (many stretches along both coasts). These strips of sand may seem devoid of life, but they're actually ecological hotbeds, where mammals, birds, and amphibians, live, feed, or reproduce. The hardiest

of creatures can be found in the tidal pools that form on rockier beaches; keep an eye out for colorful fish, starfish, and sea urchins, all of which endure pounding waves, powerful tides, broiling sun, and predator attacks from the air, land, or sea.

By law, all of Costa Rica's beaches are public, but beaches near population centers get strewn with trash quite quickly. It's one of the great ironies of Costa Rica that a country renowned for its environmental achievements litters with such laissez-faire. Limited access tends to make for more scenic beaches. If you're worried about pollution, keep an eye out for Blue Flag beaches (see Chapter 6 for a complete list), an ecological rating system that evaluates water quality—both ocean and drinking water—trash cleanup, waste management, security, signage, and environmental education. Blue flags are awarded to communities, rather than to individual hotels, which feeds a sense of cooperation. In 2002, the competition was opened to inland communities. Out of 120 that applied, 88 communities—58 beaches and 30 inland towns—won flags at the 2009 ceremonies.

ADVENTURE HIGHLIGHTS

- From October 15 to February 15, Playa Grande sees throngs of leatherback turtles come ashore to nest. Sixty days later, the hatchlings will scramble towards the water.
- Gentle, consistent waves and lots of good surf schools makes Samara, on the northern Pacific coast, a good choice for first-timers hoping to catch a wave.
- Snorkeling is phenomenal near Cahuita's coral reef on the Caribbean coast. Watch out for colorful blue parrot fish, angelfish, sponges, and seaweeds.

FLORA

The plants along the coast play an important role in maintaining the dunes and preventing erosion in the face of heavy winds and other forces.

COCONUT PALMS

Coconut palm trees are the most distinctive plants in any tropical setting. No postcard photo of a white-sand beach would be complete without at least one palm tilting precariously over the shore. Palm trees (from the Arecaceae family) require a lot of sunlight and will, thanks to their strong root system, often grow at nearly horizontal angles to escape the shade of beachside forests. The coconut palm is also the proud parent of the world's largest seed—the delicious coconut—which can float long distances across the ocean, washing up on a foreign shore and sprouting a new tree from the sand.

Coconut Palms

MANZANILLO DE PLAYA

Steer clear of the poisonous manchineel, or *manzanillo de playa* (*Hippomane mancinella*), the most toxic tree in Costa Rica. Its fruit and bark secrete a white latex that's highly irritable to the touch and poisonous—even fatal—if ingested. Don't burn it either because the smoke can also cause allergic reactions. The tree can be identified by its small, yellowish apples and bright green leaves. It's found along the northern Pacific coast, stretches of the Nicoya Peninsula, the Central Pacific's Manuel Antonio National Park, and on the Osa Peninsula.

Manzaniillo de playa

SEAGRAPE

Seagrape (*Coccoloba uvifera*) and similar types of shrubby, ground-hugging vegetation grow closer to the water, around the edges of the beach. These plants play a part in keeping the beach stable and preventing erosion.

Seagrape

MANGROVE

Mangrove swamps are rich, murky forests that thrive in brackish waters up and down Costa Rica's coasts. They grow in what's known as the intertidal zone, the part of the coast that's above sea level at low tide and submerged at high tide. Mangrove trees (*rhizophora*) are just one of the species that live in these coastal swamps—you can recognize them by their stilt-roots, the long tendril-like roots that allow the tree to breathe even when it's partially submerged. These forests are vibrant and complex ecosystems in their own right and were explained earlier in this chapter.

Mangrove tree

FAUNA

Beaches are tough environments where few animals actually make their home. But as we all know, you don't have to live on the beach to enjoy it.

OLIVE RIDLEY TURTLE

At 34 to 45 kilos (75 to 100 lbs) the olive ridley (*Lepidochelys olivacea*) is the smallest of the five marine turtles that nest in Costa Rica. During mass nesting times (*arribada*), anywhere from tens to hundreds of thousands of females drag themselves ashore, gasping audibly, to lay their eggs. Between dusk and dawn, the prehistoric creatures crawl over the beach, sometimes even over one another, on their way between the ocean and their nests. People who are lucky enough to witness the event never forget it. Costa Rica's shores are also visited by the green turtle, the hawksbill, the loggerhead, and the leatherback turtle.

Olive Ridley Turtle

IGUANAS

A common sight on Costa Rica's sandy shores are iguanas. The green iguana (Iguana iguana) and the black spiny-tailed iguana, or black iguana (Ctenosaura simi), are often found sunning themselves on rocks or a few feet from the shade (and protection) of trees. Interestingly, green iguana has been known to lay eggs and share nests with American crocodiles and Spectacled Caimans.

Iguanas

PAINTED GHOST CRAB

These intriguingly named crabs are called "ghosts" because they move so quickly that they seem to disappear. They're also one of the few creatures that actually live full-time on the beach. Sun beats down, wind is strong, danger lurks everywhere, and there's little to no cover, but painted ghost crabs (*Ocypode cuadrata*) survive all this by burrowing deep under the sand where the temperature and humidity is more constant and there's safe protection from surface threats, like the black iguana.

Painted Ghost Crab

BROWN PELICAN

Brown pelicans fly in tight formation, dropping low over the sea and running parallel with the swells in search of shoals of fish. Browns are unique in that they're the only pelican species that plunge from the air to catch their food. After a successful dive, they have to guard against gulls, who will actually try to pluck the freshly caught fish from their pouch.

Brown Pelican

EXPERIENCING THE SHORELINE

Nesting Olive Ridley Turtles at Ostional Wildlife Refuge

Costa Rica's beaches have tons of activities. If you like getting wet, the ocean is bathwater warm and there are water-sports outfitters just about everywhere. There are also plenty of hammocks and cafés.

HORSEBACK RIDING

Horseback riding on the beach is great fun, but you can't do it everywhere. Many of the most popular beaches have outlawed it for health reasons, especially if it's where a lot of people swim.

SURFING

Costa Rica is a world-class surfing destination, and the Pacific coast in particular has enough surf spots to satisfy both pros and novices. You can arrange lessons in most beach towns. Surfing is an activity that involves a lot of floating, so it allows for plenty of wildlife-watching: keep a weather eye for jumping fish, sting rays, dolphins, and squads of brown pelicans.

TURTLE TOURS

Witnessing the nesting ritual of Costa Rica's visiting sea turtles is a truly unforgettable experience. Various organizations oversee the nesting beaches and arrange tours. The onslaught of mother turtles is most intense throughout the night, so setting out just before dawn is the best way to see and take pictures of the phenomenon in progress at first light.

⚠Take great care at beaches that drop off steeply as you enter the water. This is an indicator not only of large waves that crash straight onto the shore but also of strong currents.

TOP DESTINATIONS

Differences in the look of the sand, the quality of the waves, and the beauty of the backdrop all affect your beach experience. Costa Rica's beach scenes are wildly diverse, so a little planning can go a long way.

BALLENA NATIONAL MARINE PARK

This unique park is along one of the more remote stretches of coastline, on the southern end of the Central Pacific region, and encompasses several beaches. *Ballena*, which is Spanish for "whale," gets its name for a peculiar sandbar formation at Playa Uvita beach that goes straight out toward the ocean before splitting and curving in two directions, much like a whale's tale. (See Chapter 8.)

MANUEL ANTONIO NATIONAL PARK

On the northern end of the Pacific, Manuel Antonio National Park shelters some of the country's more precious beaches. A series of half-moon bays with sparkling sands are fronted by transitional forest—a combination of flora and fauna from the tropical dry forests farther north and the tropical rain forests that stretch south. Wildlife is abundant at Manuel Antonio, and the towering jungle at the beach's edge can give the area a wild and paradisiacal feel. (See Chapter 7.)

Montezuma; Justin Hubbell, Fodors.com member

Uvita Beach; Toronto Jeff, Fodors.com member

THE NICOYA PENINSULA

A succession of incredible beaches are scattered along this region of the Pacific coast, from Montezuma to Mal País, Sámara to Punta Guiones. Ostional, just north of Guiones, offers something none of the others can: the *arribada*. The beach is part of the Ostional Wildlife Refuge, granting an extra level of protection to the area. (See Chapter 6.)

THE CARIBBEAN

This coast has an entirely different feel from the Pacific. North of Limon, there are miles of undeveloped, protected beaches where green sea turtles come from July to October to lay eggs. There have also been sightings of the loggerhead, hawksbill, and leatherback turtles. The currents here are strong, so don't plan on swimming.

To the south of Limon, beaches are bordered by dense green vegetation all year long, and the quality of the sand can change dramatically as you wander from cove to cove. Some of the country's healthiest living coral reefs are offshore, so snorkeling is worthwhile. Beaches of note are Playa Negra, Playa Blanca, Playa Negro, and Punta Uva. (See Chapter 9.)

San José

WORD OF MOUTH

"Try staying in San José for a couple of days (the Hotel Don Carlos is a great bargain; the Grano de Oro is more upscale but still a good deal). . . . You can take a city tour: the Gold Museum, Plaza de la Cultura, Mercado, National Theater, and Jade Museum . . . the best the city has to offer."

—shillmac

WELCOME TO SAN JOSÉ

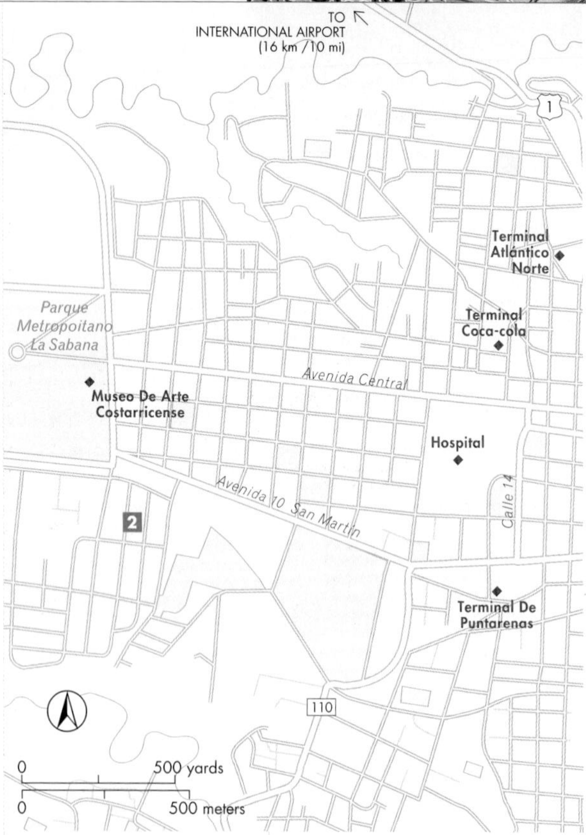

TOP REASONS TO GO

★ **Historic Barrios Amón and Otoya:** These northern neighborhoods abutting and sometimes overlapping downtown have quiet tree-lined streets and century-old houses turned trendy hotels and restaurants.

★ **Gold and Jade museums:** For a sense of indigenous Costa Rica, frequently forgotten during the nation's march to modernity, the country's two best museums are must-sees.

★ **Eating out:** After traveling around Costa Rica eating mostly rice and beans and chicken, you'll appreciate San José's varied restaurants.

★ **Shopping:** San José is the best place to stock up on both essentials and souvenirs. Look for folkloric crafts, ceramics, textiles, leather-and-wood rocking chairs, and, of course, coffee.

★ **Location, location, location:** From the capital's pivotal position you can be on a coffee tour, at the base of a giant volcano, or riding river rapids in just 30 minutes.

1 Downtown. This area holds San José's historic and commercial districts and many top attractions: the Museo del Jade (Jade Museum), Museo del Oro (Gold Museum), Mercado Central (Central Market), and Teatro Nacional (National Theater).

2 West of Downtown. The mostly residential neighborhoods here are anchored by large Parque Metropolitano La Sabana (La Sabana Park) and the Museo de Arte Costarricense (Museum of Costa Rican Art).

GETTING ORIENTED

The metropolitan area holds more than 1 million residents, but the city proper is small, with some 300,000 people living in its 44 square km (17 square mi). Most sights are concentrated in three downtown neighborhoods, La Soledad, La Merced, and El Carmen, named for their anchor churches. Borders are fuzzy: one barrio (neighborhood) flows into the next, districts overlap, and the city itself melts into its suburbs with nary a sign to denote where one community ends and another begins.

3 North of Downtown. Historic barrios Amón and Otoya and the Museo de los Niños (Children's Museum) are a few of the attractions to the north.

4 East of Downtown. Several good restaurants and hotels and the Universidad de Costa Rica (University of Costa Rica) are ensconced in the San Pedro suburb.

SAN JOSÉ PLANNER

When to Go

Although it sits just 9 degrees north of the equator, San José's altitude keeps the temperatures pleasant year-round, with highs of 26°C to 28°C (79°F to 83°F) and lows of 17°C to 19°C (65°F to 68°F). Early settlers put down roots here, attracted by moderate temperatures, rich volcanic soil, and long distance from pirates. The result is a capital that really does live up to its billing as "the city of eternal spring." December and January are the coolest, windiest months. In March and April the heat and dust pick up noticeably.

The first rains arrive in May and provide a welcome break in the temperatures. May through August the pattern is usually sunny mornings, brief afternoon showers, and clear, brisk evenings. September and October become waterlogged; it can rain nonstop for days at a time. Rains finally dissipate by mid- to late November as the transition to another dry season begins.

San José in a Day

If you have only a day to spend in San José, the must-see stops are the Teatro Nacional (National Theater)—we recommend the guided tour—and the Museo del Oro Precolombino (Precolumbian Gold Museum). That's easy to accomplish since they sit on the same block.

With more time, take in the Museo del Jade (Jade Museum) and Museo Nacional (National Museum). Or visit to the Museo para la Paz (Peace Museum). The Museo de los Niños (Children's Museum), north of downtown, is a kid-pleaser. (It's in a dicey part of the barrio El Carmen, more north of downtown than actually in downtown; take a taxi.)

Our Good Walk *(⇨ below)* gives you a taste of the city in just an hour.

Bypass San José?

OK. So San José isn't necessarily the Costa Rica you came to see. Those beaches and rain forests beckon, after all. If that is, indeed, the case, you can avoid the city altogether.

The international airport actually lies just outside the city of Alajuela, about 30 minutes northwest of the capital. Look for lodgings in Alajuela, San Antonio de Belén, Escazú, or Santa Ana—all within striking distance of the airport. Or head west. For information about lodgings near Aeropuerto Internacional Juan Santamaría, see Chapter 3.

Few international flights arrive in the morning, but they do exist, especially via Miami. Get here early, and you can head out of town immediately.

A third option is to join the growing number of visitors flying into Daniel Oduber International Airport in Liberia, where Costa Rica's northern and western reaches (including the north Pacific) are at your fingertips.

Day Trips from the Capital

The capital sits smack-dab in the middle of the country and in the middle of the fertile Central Valley. Although a day trip to either coast would be grueling—despite Costa Rica's small size, it takes longer than you think to get from place to place—you can easily pop out to the Central Valley's major sights and be back in the city in time for dinner. Several of these attractions provide pickup service in San José, some for a nominal additional cost. Alternatively, tour operators include many of these attractions on their itineraries.

FROM SAN JOSE BY CAR

TO	TRAVEL TIME	SEE PAGE
Basílica de los Ángeles	30 mins southeast	⇨p. 166
Butterfly Farm	45 mins west	⇨p. 149
Café Britt	30 mins north	⇨p. 164
Carara National Park	2 hrs southwest	⇨p. 364
Doka Coffee Estate	1 hr west	⇨p. 151
Guayabo National Monument	2 hrs southeast, 4WD necessary	⇨p. 176
INBioparque	10 mins north	⇨p. 156
Irazú Volcano	60 mins east	⇨p. 167
La Paz Waterfall Gardens	2 hrs north	⇨p. 242
Orosi Valley	60 mins southeast	⇨p. 169
Poás Volcano	60 mins northwest	⇨p. 190
Rain Forest Aerial Tram	45 mins north	⇨p. 532
River Rafting	2–2½ hrs southeast or north	⇨p. 178
Sarchí	60 mins northwest	⇨p. 197
Tortuga Island	3 hrs west	⇨p. 378
Tropical Bungee	60 mins west	⇨p. 196
World of Snakes	60 mins west	⇨p. 196
Zoo Ave	45 mins west	⇨p. 149

Play It Safe

San José is safer than other Latin American capitals. Violent crime is rare; the greatest threat you're likely to face is petty theft. Standard big-city precautions apply:

■ Exchange money only at banks. Street money changers slip counterfeit bills into their stash, or doctor their calculators to compute unfavorable rates. In the extreme, they might grab your cash and run off.

■ Select ATMs in well-lighted areas. Better still, use a bank's ATM during opening hours, when a guard will likely be present. Go with a buddy, and conceal cash immediately.

■ Use only licensed red taxis with yellow triangles on the front doors. The license plate of an official taxi begins with TSJ ("Taxi San José").

■ Park in guarded, well-lighted lots (about $1 an hour). If you must park on the street, make sure informal *guachimen* (watchmen) are present. Usually this is someone with a big stick who will expect payment of about $1 per hour. Do not leave anything valuable in your parked vehicle.

3

SAN JOSÉ PLANNER

Essentials

Currency Exchange BAC San José (✉ *Avda. 2, Cs. Central–1, Barrio El Carmen* ☎ *2295–9797*). **Banco Nacional** (✉ *Avda. 1, Cs. 2–4, Barrio La Merced* ☎ *2212–2000*). **Scotiabank** (✉ *Behind Teatro Nacional, Barrio La Soledad* ☎ *2521–5680*).

Medical Assistance Clínica Bíblica (✉ *Avda. 14, Cs. Central–1, Barrio El Pacífico* ☎ *2522–1000* 🌐 *www.clinicabiblica.com*). **Hospital La Católica** (✉ *Attached to San Antonio Church on C. Esquivel Bonilla, Guadalupe* ☎ *2246–3000* 🌐 www.hospitallacatolica.com).

Shuttle Companies Grayline (☎ *2232–3681* 🌐 *www.graylinecostarica.com*). **Interbus** (☎ *2283–5573* 🌐 *www.interbusonline.com*).

Taxis Alfaro (☎ *2221–8466*). **Coopetaxi** (☎ *2235–9966*). **San Jorge** (☎ *2221–3434*). **Taxis Unidos Aeropuerto** (☎ *2221–6865*).

Visitor Info Instituto Costarricense de Turismo *(ICT)* (✉ *C. 5, Avdas. Central–2, Barrio La Soledad* ☎ *2222–1090* 🌐 www.visitcostarica.com ✉ *Aeropuerto Juan Santamaría Alajuela* ☎ *2443–1535*).

Getting Here and Around

By Air: Aeropuerto Internacional Juan Santamaría (*16 km/10 mi northwest of downtown*) receives international flights and those of domestic airline SANSA. Domestic Nature Air flights use tiny, informal Aeropuerto Internacional Tobías Bolaños (*3 km/2 mi west of downtown*).

By Bus: The Gran Terminal del Caribe, Terminal Atlántico Norte, Terminal de Puntarenas, and so-called Terminal Coca-Cola (the former Coke bottling plant) bus stations are all in sketchy neighborhoods. Always take a taxi to and from them. Better: use air-conditioned minivan shuttles instead of buses to travel into and out of the capital.

City buses are cheap (30¢–50¢) and easy to use. For Paseo Colón and La Sabana, take buses marked SABANA-CEMENTERIO from stops at Avenida 2 between Calles 5 and 7 or Avenida 3 next to the post office. For Los Yoses and San Pedro, take the SAN PEDRO bus from Avenida Central between Calles 9 and 11.

By Car: Paved roads fan out from Paseo Colón west to Escazú and northwest to the airport and Heredia. For the Pacific coast, Guanacaste, and Nicaragua, take the Carretera Interamericana (Pan-American Highway; PAH) north (CA1). Calle 3 runs north into the highway to Guápiles, Limón, and the Atlantic coast through Braulio Carrillo National Park, with a turnoff to Sarapiquí. Follow Avenida Central or 2 east through San Pedro to enter the PAH south (CA2), which has a turnoff for Cartago, Volcán Irazú, and Turrialba before it heads over the mountains toward Panama.

Avoid driving in the city. Streets are narrow, rush hour (7–9 AM and 5–7 PM) traffic is horrible, and drivers can be reckless. What's more, San José and neighboring San Pedro enforce rigid weekday driving restrictions (6 AM–7 PM) for all private vehicles, including your rental car.

By Taxi: You can hail cabs on the street or call for one. All licensed cabs are red with a gold triangle on the front doors (though Taxis Unidos Aeropuerto—which goes to the airport—are orange). A 3-km (2-mi) ride costs around $3; tipping isn't customary. By law cabbies must use *marías* (meters) within the metropolitan area.

DID YOU KNOW?

In addition to the world's largest collection of American jade, San José's Museo del Jade has a risqué display of pre-Columbian ceramic fertility symbols—indicative of humankinds eternal preoccupation with sex.

ECO-LODGES IN SAN JOSÉ

Clean? Green? Pristine? San José is none of these, but even in Costa Rica's congested capital, you can count on a handful of pioneers who keep the environmental spirit alive.

The capital's few pockets of greenery are its parks, and, in this regard, the city does itself proud. The grandiose monuments so common in other Latin America countries are not very prominent. Small is the watchword in Costa Rica, so parks are places to enjoy mini eco-refuges rather than shrines to past heroes and glories. A trio of parks—Morazán, España, and Nacional—graces the area just northeast of downtown and provides a mostly contiguous several blocks of peace and quiet. The vast La Sabana park on San José's west side once served as the country's international airport. Its lush greenery and ample space for recreation get our vote as being one of the most pleasing uses of urban space. The capital's parks have one big downside: after dark, a small cast of unsavory characters replaces the throngs of daytrippers. Make a point to vacate city parks when the sun goes down.

GOOD PRACTICES

Use public transportation whenever possible. Buses travel everywhere in San José and suburbs, and taxis are relatively easy to find. In addition to reducing your carbon footprint, it also saves you the hassle of driving and parking in an already congested city.

Ask if your hotel recycles glass, plastic and aluminum. A few lodgings—and, unfortunately, "few" is the operative term here—do. Take advantage if you can.

Don't litter—the city has a burdensome trash problem—although you'll swear no one else here follows this advice. Dispose of your trash properly.

TOP ECO-LODGES IN SAN JOSÉ

To ensure that your hotel really is eco-friendly, do a bit of research or ask a few questions. Check on the property's lighting—does it use compact flourescent bulbs? What about sensors or timers? Is any form of alternative energy, like solar or wind power, employed? Are there low-flow faucets, showers, and toilets? What sort of recycling programs are in place for guests *and* staff? Answers to such questions give you a sense of whether a property is green or not. Below are a couple San José properties that do more than pay lip service to the environmental movement.

CLARION HOTEL AMÓN PLAZA

From its active in-hotel recycling program and its eco-friendly store that sells no products made from endangered woods, to its small garden that acquaints you with rainforest plant species and its liaison program with the community, the Amón Plaza is greener than most countryside hotels.

HOTEL RINCÓN DE SAN JOSÉ

Your hot water in this small Barrio Otoya hotel will be solar heated, and the place makes maximum use of natural lighting during the day in its public areas. The Rincón de San José uses only biodegradable products whenever possible, it also engages in an active recycling program. Even captured rainwater finds its way into your room's toilet basin.

HOTEL PRESIDENTE

Costa Rica's first "carbon neutral" hotel has taken major steps to reduce its carbon footprint. What is left over is offset by a tree-planting project the lodging supports. The Presidente has organized a small but growing consortium of San José hotels to take up recycling. All in all, not bad for a place located smack dab in the center of the city.

PEDESTRIANS ONLY

What's that old saying about good intentions and the road to hell? The government here is forever announcing some grandiose plan to make San José more livable and a bit less of an urban hell. Few, however, make it off the ground, mostly due to a chronic lack of funds. Two have come to fruition, though, and you will notice the benefit.

For years, the city government has been turning downtown streets into pedestrian-only malls. Some 34 blocks in the center city—sections of Avenidas Central and 4, and Calles 2, 3, and 17—now have *bulevar* (boulevard) status, with more on the drawing board. Thank the European Union for much of the funding.

Rigid weekday driving restrictions cover all of San José along and parts of neighboring San Pedro. The last digit of your license plate dictates the day of the week when you may not bring a car into the large restricted zone. The city still hosts far too many cars, but the 20% reduction in vehicles each weekday has made a noticeable difference.

By Jeffrey Van Fleet

The center of all that is Costa Rica probably won't be the center of your trip to Costa Rica. If you're like many visitors, you'll spend two nights in San José—tops. Most international flights arrive in the evening and leave in the morning, so you'll probably head out of town early on the first day, only to return the night before heading home. But consider giving the capital a chance.

Amid the noise and traffic, shady parks, well-maintained museums, lively plazas, terrific restaurants, and great hotels do exist. Further, the city makes a great base for day trips: from downtown it's a mere 30- to 40-minute drive to the tranquil countryside and myriad outdoor activities of the surrounding Central Valley.

You'd never know San José is as old as it is—given the complete absence of colonial architecture—but settlers migrating from then provincial capital Cartago founded the city in 1737. After independence in 1821, San José cemented its position as the new nation's capital after struggles and a brief civil war with fellow Central Valley cities Cartago, Alajuela, and Heredia. Revenues from the coffee and banana industries financed the construction of stately homes, theaters, and a trolley system (later abandoned and now visible only in old sepia photographs).

As recently as the mid-1900s San José was no larger than the present-day downtown area; old-timers remember the vast coffee and cane plantations that extended beyond its borders. The city began to mushroom only after World War II, when old buildings were razed to make room for concrete monstrosities. The sprawl eventually connected the capital with nearby cities.

New York or London it is not, but for the Tico living out in Tilarán, today's San José glitters every bit as much. It has attracted people from all over Costa Rica, yet it remains, in many ways, a collection of distinct neighborhoods where residents maintain friendly small-town ways. For you, this might mean the driver you're following will decide to abruptly stop his vehicle to buy a lottery ticket or chat with a friend on the street.

Or it might mean you have to navigate a maze of fruit-vendor stands on a crowded sidewalk. But this is part of what keeps San José a big small town.

No, you shouldn't sacrifice precious beach or rain forest time for a stay in San José. But the city is worth a day or two—as a way to ease into Costa Rica at the start of a visit or as a way of wrapping things up with a well-deserved dose of civilization.

EXPLORING

The Irish group U-2 could have written its song "Where the Streets Have No Name" about San José. Admittedly, some of its streets have names, but no one seems to know or use them. Streets in the center of the capital are laid out in a grid, with *avenidas* (avenues) running east and west, and *calles* (streets), north and south. Odd-number avenues increase in number north of Avenida Central; even-number avenues, south. Streets east of Calle Central have odd numbers; those to the west are even.

The farther you get from downtown, the scarcer street signs become. Costa Ricans rely instead on a charming and exasperating system of designating addresses by the distance from landmarks, as in "100 meters north and 50 meters west of the school." Another quirk: "100 meters" always refers to one city block, regardless of how long it actually is. Likewise, "200 meters" is two blocks, and so on. (As you can imagine, getting a pizza delivered here is quite a challenge.)

Historically, the reference point was the church, but these days it might be a bar, Burger King, or even a long-gone landmark: the eastern suburb of San Pedro uses the *higuerón,* a fig tree that was felled long ago but lives on in the hearts of Costa Ricans. Your best bet is to follow the time-honored practice of *ir y preguntar* (keep walking and keep asking).

DOWNTOWN

It's a trend seen the world over: businesses and residents flee city centers for the space, blissful quiet, and lower-priced real estate of the 'burbs. Although Costa Rica's capital is experiencing this phenomenon, downtown still remains the city's historic and vibrant (if noisy and congested) heart. Government offices have largely stayed put here, as have the most attractions. It's impossible to sightsee here without finding yourself downtown.

Boundaries are fuzzy. For example, the neighborhoods of El Carmen, La Merced, and La Soledad are anchored in downtown but sprawl outward from the center city. And, in an effort to seem trendier, several establishments in downtown's northern fringes prefer to say that they're in the more fashionable barrios of Amón or Otoya.

TOP ATTRACTIONS

6 Fodor's Choice ★ **Museo del Jade.** The Jade Museum has the world's largest collection of American jade—that's "American" in the hemispheric sense. Nearly all the items on display were produced in pre-Columbian times, and most of the jade (pronounced *hah*-day in Spanish) dates from 300 BC to AD 700. In the spectacular Jade Room, pieces are illuminated from behind so you can appreciate their translucency. A series of drawings explains how this extremely hard stone was cut using string saws with quartz-and-sand abrasive. Jade was sometimes used in jewelry designs, but it was most often carved into oblong pendants. The museum also has other pre-Columbian artifacts, such as polychrome vases and three-legged *metates* (small stone tables for grinding corn), and a gallery of modern art. The final room on the tour has a startling display of ceramic fertility symbols. A photo-filled, glossy, English-language guide to the museum sells for $15; the Spanish version is only $3. The museum is looking for a new home at this writing, with tentative plans to transfer the collection to an as-yet-unconstructed facility somewhere near the Plaza de la Democracia. A larger facility would allow all 5,000-plus pieces in the collection to be displayed. At present, you can see only about a quarter of them. The museum's location on the first floor of a tall office building gives it a downtown feel, even if it's at the northern edge of the city center. ✉ *INS building, Avda. 7, Cs. 9–11, Barrio Amón* ☎ *2287–6034* 🎫 *$7* ⏲ *Weekdays 8:30–3:30, Sat. 9–1.*

3 Fodor's Choice ★ **Museo del Oro Precolombino.** The dazzling, modern *Pre-Columbian Gold Museum*, in a three-story underground structure beneath the Plaza de la Cultura, contains Central America's largest collection of pre-Columbian gold jewelry—20,000 troy ounces in more than 1,600 individual pieces—all owned by the Banco Central and displayed attractively in low-lit, bilingual exhibits. Many pieces are in the form of frogs and eagles, two animals perceived by the region's early cultures to have great spiritual significance. All that glitters here is not gold: most spectacular are the varied shaman figurines, which represent the human connection to animal deities. One of the halls houses the Museo Numismática (Coin Museum; admission included with Gold Museum), a repository of historic coins and bills and other objects used as legal tender throughout the country's history. Rotating art exhibitions happen on another level of the complex. ✉ *Eastern end of Plaza de la Cultura, C. 5, Avdas. Central–2, Barrio La Soledad* ☎ *2243–4202* 🌐 *www.museosdelbancocentral.org* 🎫 *$7, $4 students* ⏲ *Daily 9:30–5.*

2 ★ **Teatro Nacional.** The National Theatre is enchanting. Chagrined that touring prima donna Adelina Patti bypassed San José in 1890 for lack of a suitable venue, wealthy coffee merchants raised import taxes and hired Belgian architects to design this building, lavish with cast iron and Italian marble. The theater was inaugurated in 1897 with a performance of Gounod's *Faust,* featuring an international cast. The sandstone exterior is marked by Italianate arched windows, marble columns with bronze capitals, and statues of strange bedfellows Ludwig van Beethoven (1770–1827) and 17th-century Spanish golden-age playwright Pedro Calderón de la Barca (1600–81). The Muses of Dance, Music, and Fame are silhouetted in front of an iron cupola.

The sumptuous neo-baroque interior sparkles, too. Given the provenance of the building funds, it's not surprising that frescoes on the stairway inside depict coffee and banana production. Note Italian painter Aleardo Villa's famous ceiling mural *Alegoría del Café y Banano* (*Allegory of Coffee and Bananas*), a joyful harvest scene that appeared on Costa Rica's old five-colón note. (The now-defunct bill is prized by collectors and by visitors as a souvenir, and is often sold by vendors in the plaza between the theater and the Gran Hotel Costa Rica next door.) French designer Alain Guilhot created the building's nighttime external illumination system. (He did the same for the Eiffel Tower.) The soft coppers, golds, and whites highlight the theater's exterior nightly from 6 PM to 5 AM.

You can see the theater's interior by attending one of the performances that take place several nights a week (tickets are reasonable); intermission gives you a chance to nose around. The theater prizes punctuality, one of the few institutions in this country to do so. Performances start on time. Stop at the *boletería* (box office) in the lobby and see what strikes your fancy. (Don't worry if you left your tuxedo or evening gown back home; as long as you don't show up for a performance wearing shorts, jeans, or a T-shirt, no one will care.)

For a nominal admission fee you can also move beyond the lobby on an informative guided daytime visit. Thirty-minute tours in English or Spanish are given at 9, 10, and 11 AM and 1, 2, and 3 PM. If you're downtown on a Tuesday between February and Christmas, take in one of the Teatro al Mediodía (Theater at Midday) performances that begin at 12:10 PM. It might be a chamber-music recital or a one-act play (in Spanish). Admission is $9. The theater is sometimes closed for rehearsals, so call before you go. ✉ *Plaza de la Cultura, Barrio La Soledad* ☎ *2221–1329* 🌐 *www.teatronacional.go.cr* 🎫 *$5* ⏲ *Mon.–Sat. 9–4.*

NEED A BREAK?

Duck into the Café del Teatro Nacional (✉ *Plaza de la Cultura, Barrio La Soledad* ☎ *2221–3262*), off the theater lobby, to sit at a marble table and sip a hazelnut mocha beneath frescoed ceilings. The frescoes are part of an allegory of seminude figures celebrating the 1897 opening of the theater. Coffee runs from $2 to $4, depending on how much alcohol or ice cream is added. Sandwiches and cakes are $3 to $5. The café keeps the same hours as the theater but is open only until curtain time on performance nights and during intermission.

WORTH NOTING

13 **Catedral Metropolitana.** Built in 1871, and completely refurbished in the late 1990s to repair earthquake damage, the neoclassical Metropolitan Cathedral, topped by a corrugated tin dome, isn't terribly interesting outside. But inside are patterned floor tiles, stained-glass windows depicting various saints and apostles, and framed polychrome bas-reliefs illustrating the 14 Stations of the Cross. This renovation did away with one small time-honored tradition: rather than purchase and light a votive candle, the faithful now deposit a 50-colón coin illuminating a bulb in a row of tiny electric candles.

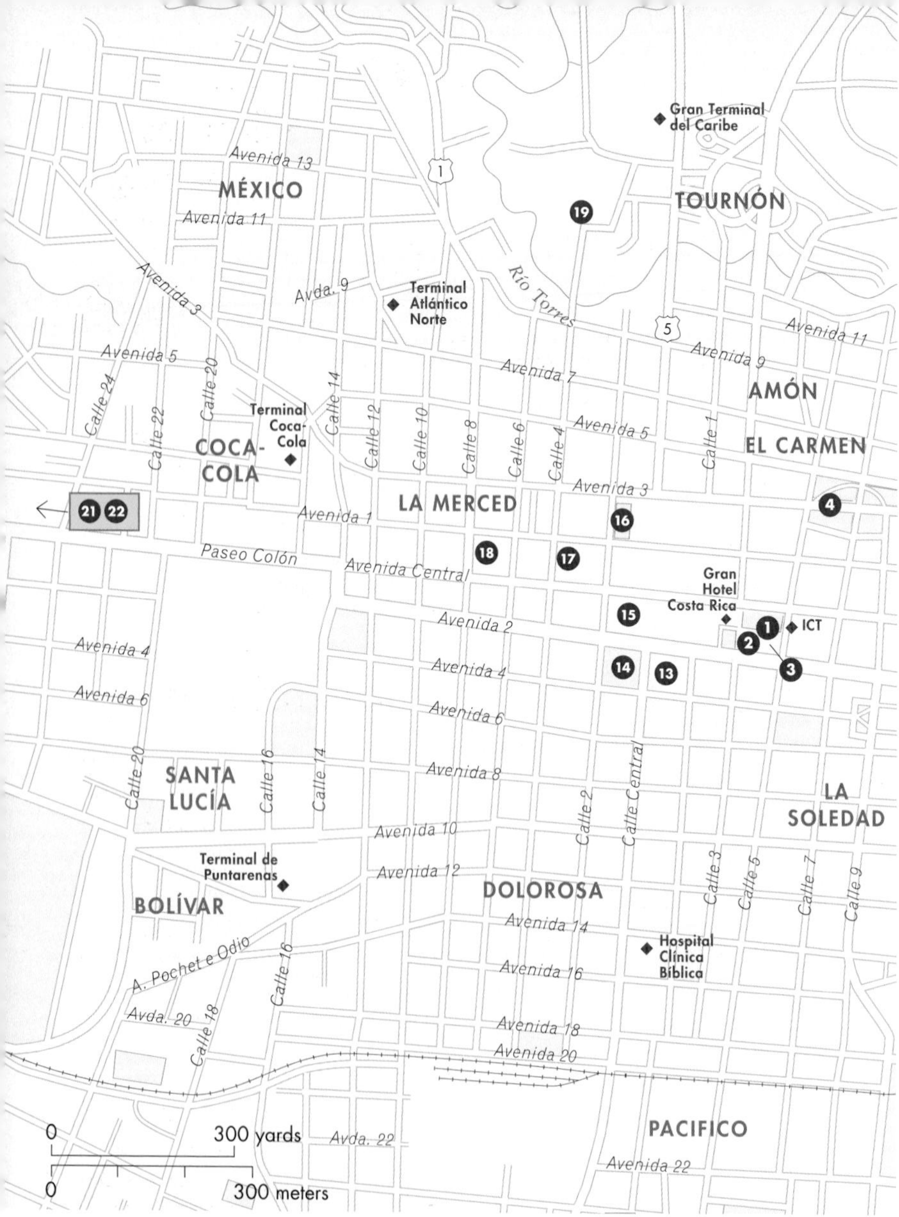

Downtown ▼

Catedral Metropolitana **13**
Centro Nacional de la Cultura **7**
Correos de Costa Rica **16**
Mercado Central **18**
Museo de Arte y Diseño Contemporáneo **8**
Museo del Jade **6**
Museo Nacional **10**
Museo del Oro Precolombino **3**
Museo para la Paz **12**
Parque Central **14**
Parque España **5**
Parque Morazán **4**
Parque Nacional **9**
Plaza de la Cultura **1**
Plaza de la Democracia **11**
Plaza del Banco Central **17**
Teatro Nacional **2**
Teatro Popular Melico Salazar **15**

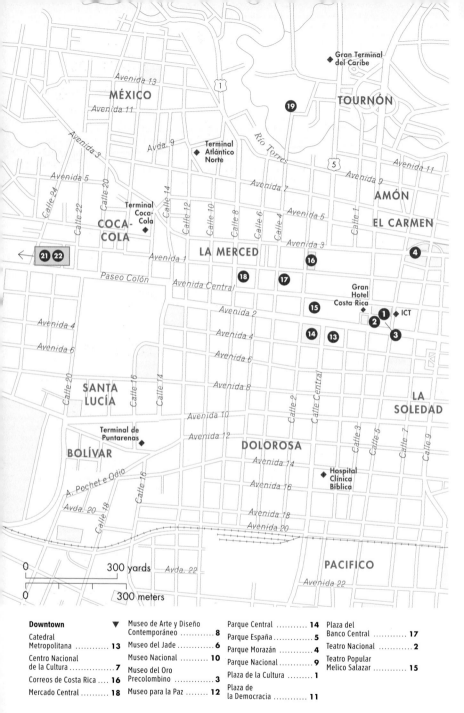

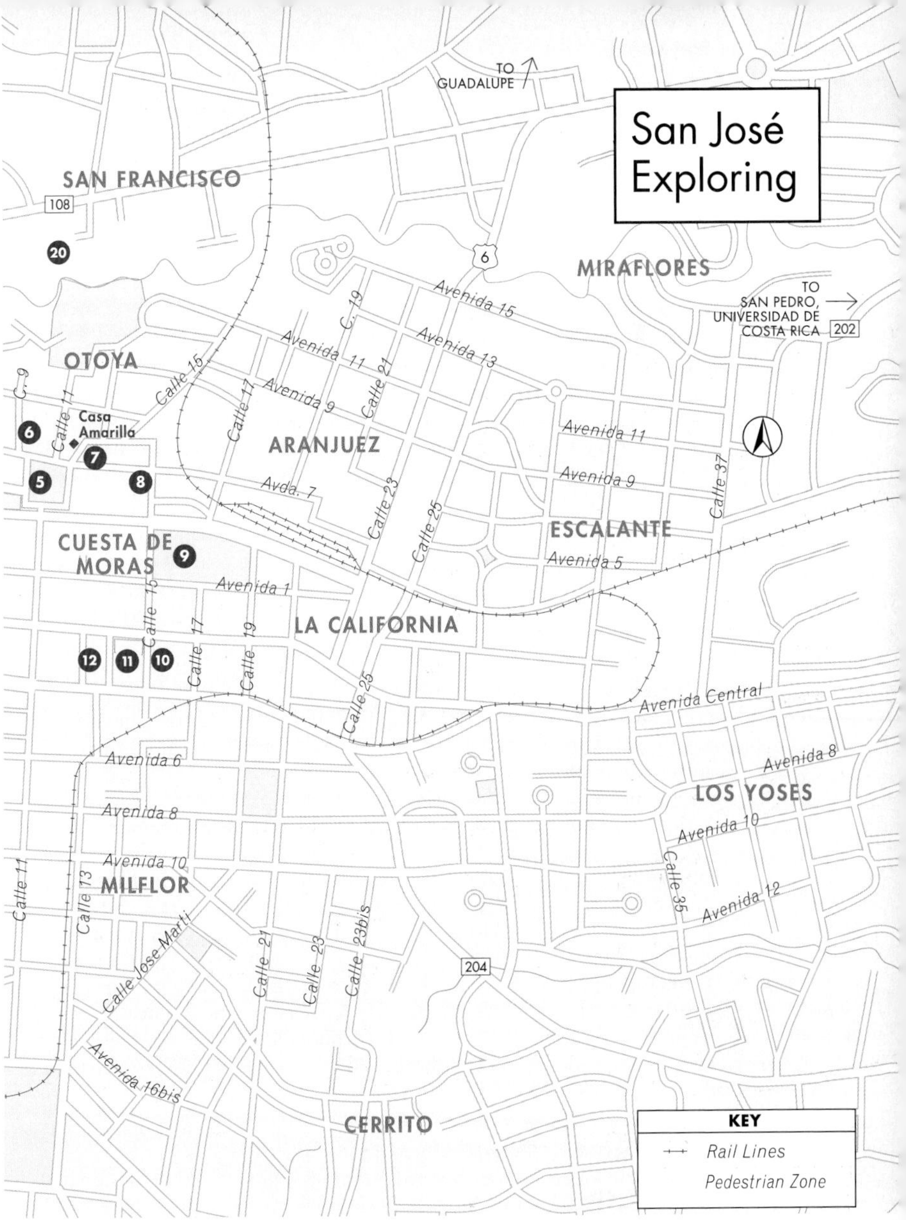

San José
Exploring
TO GUADALUPE
TO SAN PEDRO, UNIVERSIDAD DE COSTA RICA
202
108
6
204
SAN FRANCISCO
MIRAFLORES
OTOYA
ARANJUEZ
ESCALANTE
CUESTA DE MORAS
LA CALIFORNIA
LOS YOSES
MILFLOR
CERRITO
Casa Amarilla
Avenida 15
Avenida 13
Avenida 11
Avenida 9
Avda. 7
Avenida 5
Avenida 1
Avenida Central
Avenida 6
Avenida 8
Avenida 10
Avenida 12
Avenida 16bis
C. 9
C. 19
Calle 11
Calle 13
Calle 15
Calle 17
Calle 19
Calle 21
Calle 23
Calle 23bis
Calle 25
Calle 35
Calle 37
Calle Jose Martí
KEY
Rail Lines
Pedestrian Zone

The interior of the small Capilla del Santísimo (Chapel of the Host) on the cathedral's north side evokes ornate old Catholicism, much more so than the main sanctuary itself, and is a place for reflection and prayer. A marble statue of Pope John Paul II graces the garden on the building's north side. Masses are held throughout the day on Sunday starting at 7 AM, with one in English each Saturday at 4 PM, except the first Saturday of the month, when it starts at 3 PM. Thanks to a late-2008 restoration, the magnificent 1891 Belgian pipe organ fills the church with music once again. ✉ *C. Central, Avdas. 2–4, Barrio La Merced* ☎ *2221–3820* ⏲ *Weekdays 6–6, Sun. 6* AM*–9* PM.

DID YOU KNOW?

What's an old theater without its resident ghost? Patrons have claimed to see figures moving in the Teatro Nacional's second-floor paintings. Sightings were common during the theater's early days, although none have been reported in years.

7 **Centro Nacional de la Cultura.** Costa Rica cherishes its state enterprises. Here the government is your light and water utility, your phone company, your Internet service provider, your bank, your insurance agent, and your hospital. It is also your distillery, and this complex served as the headquarters of the Fábrica Nacional de Licores (FANAL, or National Liquor Factory) until 1981, when it moved to a modern facility west of Alajuela. In a heartwarming exception to the usual "tear it down" mentality so prevalent in San José, the Ministry of Culture converted the sloped-surface, double-block 1853 factory into the 14,000-square-meter *National Cultural Center,* with ministry offices, two theaters, and a museum. The metal **Teatro FANAL** (☎ *2222–2974*), once the fermentation area, now hosts frequent theater and music performances. The clay-brick **Teatro 1887** (☎ *2222–2974*) served as the factory's personnel office, and today dedicates itself to performances by the National Dance Company. What is now the theater's lobby was once the chemical testing lab. The stone-block storage depot next to the water towers at the southeast side of the complex became the Museo de Arte y Diseño Contemporáneo (⇨ *below*). A stone gate and sundial grace the entrance nearest the museum. The complex sits amid government offices, at the point where downtown's northern reaches fade into the more residential neighborhood of Barrio Otoya. ✉ *C. 13, Avdas. 3–5, Barrio Otoya* ☎ *2257–5524* ⏲ *Weekdays 8–5, Sat. 10–5.*

16 **Correos de Costa Rica** *(Central Post Office)*. The handsome, carved sea-green exterior of the post office, dating from 1917, is hard to miss among the bland buildings surrounding it. Collectors should stop at the second-floor **Museo Filatélico** (*Philatelic Museum* ☎ *2223–9766*) for its display of historic stamps. Early-20th-century telegraphs and telephones are also on display. The museum is open weekdays 8–5; admission is the purchase of a prepaid postcard sufficient for mailing to North America. Also of interest to philatelists is the office to the left as you face the stamp windows; it sells first-day issues. From the balcony you can see the loading of *apartados* (post-office boxes) going on below: Costa Ricans covet these hard-to-get boxes, as the city's lack of street addresses makes mail delivery a challenge. ✉ *C. 2, Avdas. 1–3,*

A GOOD WALK

This walk takes about an hour at a stroll. If you take a more leisurely approach, lingering at the parks or museums, it could take hours.

Everyone finds their way to the **Plaza de la Cultura**, a favorite meeting spot in the heart of the city, and it makes a good kick-off point for a walk. The ornate **Teatro Nacional** sits on the south side of the plaza. Pop in and buy a ticket for an evening performance, and/or grab a cup of coffee at the lobby café. The **Museo del Oro Precolombino** lies under the plaza. The gold collection could easily captivate you for an hour or two. From here, head two blocks north on Calle 5 to **Parque Morazán**, whose centerpiece Templo de Música is the symbol of the city. Traffic is particularly dangerous here, so take heed. The Edificio Metálico, a metal building that serves as a school, fronts the park's north side.

Continue just east of the park on Avenida 3 to the small **Parque España**, one of the city's most pleasant green spaces. The ornate building on the park's north side is the Andrew Carnegie–funded Casa Amarilla. At Avenida 7 is the modern Instituto Nacional Segoros (INS) building, whose ground-floor **Museo del Jade** has an extensive American jade collection. The Ministry of Culture complex, the **Centro Nacional de la Cultura**, fronts the park's east side. From Parque España, walk one long block east to the **Parque Nacional**. Two blocks south on Calle 17 is a pleasant pedestrian mall.

Pass the Asamblea Legislativa, where Costa Rica's congress meets, and come to the **Museo Nacional**. Loop around to the museum's west side to one of the higher levels on the Plaza de la Democracia, a great vantage point for sunsets. Avenida Central fronts the plaza's north side. Head back downhill, into the city center. The avenue becomes a lively pedestrian mall at Calle 9, and two blocks later you return to the Plaza de la Cultura.

Barrio La Merced ☎*2202–2900* 🌐*www.correos.go.cr* 🕑*Weekdays 7:30–5, Sat. 7:30–1.*

18 **Mercado Central** *(Central Market)*. This block-long melting pot is a warren of dark, narrow passages flanked by stalls packed with spices (some purported to have medicinal value), fish, fruit, flowers, pets, and wood and leather crafts. But the 1880 structure is a kinder, gentler introduction to a Central American market; there are no pigs or chickens or their accompanying smells to be found here. A few stands selling tourist souvenirs congregate near the entrances, but this is primarily a place where the average Costa Rican comes to shop. There are also dozens of cheap restaurants and snack stalls, including the country's first ice-cream vendor. Be warned: the concentration of shoppers makes this a hot spot for pickpockets, purse snatchers, and backpack slitters. Enter and exit at the southeast corner of the building (Avda. Central at C. 6). The green-and-white SALIDA signs direct you to other exits, but they spill onto slightly less–safe streets. Use the image of the Sacred Heart of Jesus, the market's patron and protector, near the center of the building, as your guide; it faces that safer corner by which you should exit. (Things probably weren't planned that way.) ✉*Bordered by Avdas.*

Central–1 and Cs. 6–8, Barrio La Merced ⏲*Mon.–Sat. 6–6.*

NEED A BREAK?

A slew of unnamed sodas—that's the Costa Rican term for a mom-and-pop eatery—populate the heart of the Mercado Central. Grab a quick bite while you shop. It's all very informal.

To sample the crème de la crème of locally made ice cream, head to Pop's. Mango is a favorite flavor. After a long walk on crowded sidewalks, it may be just what the doctor ordered. This chain is everywhere, and you'll find several outlets downtown. ✉***C. 3, Avdas. Central–2 Barrio La Soledad.***

CITY TOURS

Grayline Tours (☎*2220–2106* 🌐www.graylinecostarica.com) operates sightseeing and shopping tours. **Tico Walks** (☎*2283–8281*) gives two-and-a-half-hour guided walks of downtown. Show up in front of the Teatro Nacional at 10 AM, Tuesday, Thursday, Saturday, or Sunday.

8 **Museo de Arte y Diseño Contemporáneo.** This wonderfully minimalist space is perfect as the country's premier modern-art venue. The *Museum of Contemporary Art and Design*, or MADC as it's known around town, hosts changing exhibits by artists and designers from all over Latin America. You can arrange for a guided visit with a couple of days' notice. The museum occupies part of a government-office complex in that gray area where downtown San José transitions into residential neighborhoods. ✉*C. 15, Avdas. 3–5, Barrio Otoya* ☎*2257–7202* 🌐*www.madc.ac.cr* 🎟*$2, free Mon.* ⏲*Mon.–Sat. 10:30–5:30.*

10 **Museo Nacional.** In the mango-colored Bellavista Fortress, which dates from 1870, the National Museum gives you a quick and insightful lesson in English and Spanish on Costa Rican culture from pre-Columbian times to the present. Cases display pre-Columbian artifacts, period dress, colonial furniture, religious art, and photographs. Some of the country's foremost ethnographers and anthropologists are on the museum's staff. Outside are a veranda and a pleasant, manicured courtyard garden. A former army headquarters, this now-tranquil building saw fierce fighting during a 1931 army mutiny and the 1948 revolution, as the bullet holes pocking its turrets attest. But it was also here that three-time president José "Don Pepe" Figueres abolished the country's military in 1949. ✉*C. 17, between Avdas. Central and 2, Barrio La Soledad* ☎*2257–1433* 🌐*www.museocostarica.go.cr* 🎟*$4, $2 students* ⏲*Tues.–Sat. 8:30–4, Sun. 9–4:30.*

12 **Museo para la Paz.** Former president Oscar Arias won the 1987 Nobel Peace Prize for his tireless efforts to bring reconciliation to a war-torn Central America, and today he remains a vocal force for international peace and social justice. His Arias Foundation operates the Peace Museum, with bilingual exhibits documenting the isthmus's turbulent history and promoting the cause for peace. Messages from other Nobel laureates—the Dalai Lama, Lech Walesa, Rigoberta Menchú, Jimmy Carter, Al Gore, and Henry Kissinger among them—adorn one room. Begin your visit in the auditorium watching a 12-minute video in English, *The Dividends of Peace*. There's also an hour-long video that delves

TWO LAST NAMES

The immigration form you're given to fill out on your flight to Costa Rica has a space asking for your segunda apellido (second last name). We doubt you'll have one, but Costa Ricans all do.

If a Pedro Castillo marries an Ana Morales, and they have a son, Juan, his full legal name will consist of surnames from both his mother and his father: Juan Castillo Morales (although for the purposes of shorthand, he'll probably go by "Juan Castillo"). When Juan grows up and marries, his children will take his Castillo surname and his future wife's first surname. Juan's Morales name is lost to future generations.

Let's go back to our friends Ana and Pedro. Like most Costa Rican women, Ana likely decided to keep her own last names when she married, and not take Pedro's, a tradition that existed here long before liberated North American and European women adopted such customs. Of course, Ana might choose to call herself Ana Morales de Castillo ("of Castillo"), a convention usually seen only in aristocratic circles. If Ana outlives Pedro, she could choose to go by Ana Morales viuda de Castillo ("widow of Castillo"), a quaint tradition rarely seen these days.

into the topic. The museum usually doesn't appear to be open when you walk by. Call and let the attendant know you're coming. ✉ *Avda. 2 and C. 13, Barrio La Soledad* ☎ *2223–4664* 🌐 *www.arias.or.cr* *Free* ⏲ *Weekdays 8–noon and 1:30–4:30.*

14 **Parque Central.** At the city's nucleus, tree-planted Central Park is more plaza than park. A life-size bronze statue of a street sweeper (El Barrendero) cleans up some bronze litter; look also for Armonía (Harmony), a sculpture of three street musicians. In the center of the park is a spiderlike, ochre-color gazebo donated by former Nicaraguan dictator Anastasio Somoza. Several years ago a referendum was held to decide whether to demolish the despot's gift, but Ticos voted to preserve the bandstand for posterity. ✉ *Bordered by Avdas. 2–4 and Cs. 2–Central, Barrio La Merced.*

5 **Parque España.** One of our favorite spots is this shady little park. A bronze statue of Costa Rica's Spanish founder, Juan Vásquez de Coronado, overlooks an elevated fountain on its southwest corner; the opposite corner has a lovely tiled guardhouse. A bust of Queen Isabella of Castile stares at the yellow compound to the east of the park, the Centro Nacional de la Cultura. Just west of the park is a two-story, metal-sided school made in Belgium and shipped to Costa Rica in pieces more than a century ago. Local lore holds that the intended destination for the appropriately named Edificio Metálico (Metal Building) was really Chile, but that Costa Rica decided to keep the mistakenly shipped building components. The yellow colonial-style building to the east of the modern INS building is the 1912 Casa Amarilla, home of Costa Rica's Foreign Ministry (closed to the public.) The massive ceiba tree in front, planted by John F. Kennedy and the presidents of all the Central American nations in 1963, gives you an idea of how quickly things grow in the tropics. A garden around the corner on Calle 13 contains

a 2-meter-wide section of the Berlin Wall donated by Germany's foreign ministry after reunification. Ask the guard to let you into the garden if you want a closer look. ✉ *Bordered by Avdas. 7–3 and Cs. 11–17, Barrio El Carmen* ☎ *2257–7202.*

CAUTION

The ubiquitous TOURIST INFORMATION signs you see around downtown are really private travel agencies looking to sell you tours rather than provide unbiased information. The ICT (⇨ *Essentials, in the San José Planner, above*) is the official tourist office.

4 **Parque Morazán.** Anchored by the 1920 Templo de Música (Temple of Music), a neoclassic bandstand that has become the symbol of the city, downtown's largest park is somewhat barren, though the pink and golden trumpet trees on its northwest corner brighten things up when they bloom in the dry months. The park is named for Honduran general Francisco Morazán, whose dream for a united Central America failed in the 1830s. Avoid the park late at night, when a rough crowd and occasional muggers appear. ✉ *Avda. 3, Cs. 5–9, Barrio El Carmen.*

9 **Parque Nacional.** A bronze monument commemorating Central America's battles against American invader William Walker in 1856 forms the centerpiece of the large, leafy National Park. Five Amazons, representing the five nations of the isthmus, attack Walker, who shields his face from the onslaught. Costa Rica maintains the lead and shelters a veiled Nicaragua, the country most devastated by the war. Guatemala, Honduras, and El Salvador might dispute this version of events, but this is how Costa Rica chose to commission the work by French sculptor Louis Carrier Belleuse, a student of Rodin, in 1895. Bas-relief murals on the monument's pedestal depict key battles in the war against the Americans. ✉ *Bordered by Avdas. 1–3 and Cs. 15–19, Barrio La Soledad.*

1 **Plaza de la Cultura.** The crowds of people, vendors, and street entertainers at the Plaza de la Cultura—it's a favored spot for marimba bands, clowns, jugglers, and colorfully dressed South Americans playing Andean music—hide the fact that the expanse is really just a mass of concrete. The ornate Teatro Nacional dominates the plaza's southern half. Pop in and buy a ticket for an evening performance. The Museo del Oro Precolombino, with its highly visited exhibits of gold, lies under the plaza. The plaza's western edge is defined by the Gran Hotel Costa Rica, with its 24-hour Café 1930. ✉ *Bordered by Avdas. Central–2 and Cs. 3–5, Barrio La Soledad.*

11 **Plaza de la Democracia.** President Oscar Arias built this terraced open space west of the Museo Nacional to mark 100 years of democracy and to receive dignitaries during the 1989 hemispheric summit. The view west toward the dark-green Cerros de Escazú is nice in the morning and fabulous at sunset. Swarms of graffiti artists, who protested a free-trade agreement with the United States, trashed the plaza throughout 2007. After a 2008 remodeling and sprucing-up, it sparkles once again. Jewelry, T-shirts, and crafts from Costa Rica, Guatemala, and South America are sold in a string of stalls along the western edge. They are

Museo del Oro Precolumbino has the largest collection of pre-Columbian gold jewelry in Central America.

worth a stop. ✉ *Bordered by Avdas. Central–2 and Cs. 13–15, Barrio La Soledad.*

17 **Plaza del Banco Central.** An extension of Avenida Central, this plaza is popular with hawkers, money changers, and retired men, and can be a good place to get a shoe shine and listen to street musicians. Outside the western end of Costa Rica's modern federal-reserve bank building, don't miss *Presentes,* 10 sculpted, smaller-than-life figures of bedraggled *campesinos* (peasants). *La Chola,* a bronze 500-kg (1,100-lb) statue of a buxom rural woman, resides at sidewalk level on the small, shady plaza south of the bank. It's public art at its best. Beware: the money changers here are notorious for circulating counterfeit bills and using doctored calculators to shortchange unwitting tourists. Instead, change money at banks or through cash machines, where you get the best rate. ✉ *Bordered by Avdas. Central–1 and Cs. 2–4, Barrio La Merced.*

15 **Teatro Popular Melico Salazar.** Across Avenida 2 on the north side of Parque Central stands San José's second major performance hall (after the Teatro Nacional). The 1928 building is on the site of a 19th-century military barracks felled by an earthquake. The venue was later named for Costa Rican operatic tenor Manuel "Melico" Salazar (1887–1950). It was constructed specifically to provide a less highbrow alternative to the Teatro Nacional. But these days the Melico is plenty cultured, and provides the capital with a steady diet of music and dance performances. ✉ *Avda. 2 and C. 2, Barrio La Merced* ☎ *2233–5424* 🌐 *www.teatromelico.go.cr.*

NORTH AND EAST OF DOWNTOWN

Immediately northeast of downtown lie Barrio Amón and Barrio Otoya. Both neighborhoods are repositories of historic houses that have escaped the wrecking ball; many now serve as hotels, restaurants, galleries, and offices. (A few are even private residences.) Where these barrios begin and end depends on who's doing the talking. Locales on the fringes of the city center prefer to be associated with these "good neighborhoods" rather than with downtown. Barrio Escalante, to the east, isn't quite as gentrified but is fast becoming fashionable.

RAINY DAY TIPS

- Do outdoor sightseeing in the morning, before the afternoon rains arrive.
- Duck into museums—our top choices are the Gold and Jade museums.
- Do as Costa Ricans do and *tomar café* (take a coffee break).
- Don't wait until the evening rush hour (5–7 PM) to get a cab—empty ones are nearly nonexistent when it rains.

The sprawling suburb of San Pedro begins several blocks east of downtown San José. The town is home to the University of Costa Rica and all the intellect and cheap eats and nightlife that a student or student-wannabe could desire. But away from the heart of the university, San Pedro is awash in the consumerism of malls, fast-food restaurants, and car dealerships—although it manages to mix in stately districts such as the stylish Los Yoses for good measure. To get to San Pedro, take a $2 taxi ride from downtown and get off in front of Banco Nacional, just beyond the rotunda with the fountain at its center.

20 **Jardín de Mariposas Spyrogyra.** Spending an hour or two at this magical *Spyrogyra Butterfly Garden* is entertaining and educational for nature ★ lovers of all ages. Self-guided tours enlighten you on butterfly ecology and let you see the winged creatures close up. After an 18-minute video introduction, you're free to wander screened-in gardens along a numbered trail. Some 30 species of colorful butterflies flutter about, accompanied by six types of hummingbirds. Try to come when it's sunny, as butterflies are most active then. A small, moderately priced café borders the garden and serves sandwiches and Tico fare. ✉ *50 m east and 150 m south of main entrance to El Pueblo shopping center, Barrio Tournón* ☎ *2222–2937* 🌐 *www.butterflygardencr.com* 🎟 *$6, $3 children under 12* 🕑 *Daily 8–4.*

19 **Museo de los Niños.** San José's Children's Museum is in a former prison, and big kids may want to check it out just to marvel at the castlelike architecture and the old cells that have been preserved in an exhibit about life behind bars. Three halls in the complex are filled with eye-catching seasonal exhibits for kids, ranging in subject from local ecology to outer space. The exhibits are annotated in Spanish, but most are interactive, so language shouldn't be much of a problem. The museum's most popular resident is the Egyptian exhibit's sarcophagus; the mummy draws the "oohs" and "aahs." Officially, the complex is called the Centro Costarricense de Ciencia y Cultura (Costa Rican Center of Science and Culture), and that will be the sign that greets you on the front

CLOSE UP

Missing History

Blame it on the earthquakes. Costa Ricans are quick to attribute the scarcity of historic architecture in San José and around the country to a history of earth tremors. Indeed, major earthquakes have struck various locales around Costa Rica 10 times since the mid-18th century (6 times in the 20th century), felling untold numbers of historical structures.

But blame it on the wrecking ball, too, says architect Gabriela Sáenz, who works with the Ministry of Culture's Center for Research and Conservation of Cultural Patrimony. The tear-it-down approach really began to take its toll in the 1970s, an era when boxy, concrete buildings were in vogue around the world, Sáenz says. Costa Rica didn't establish its first school of architecture until 1972, staffed by faculty from Mexico, England, and Brazil. "It was hard for a real Costa Rican tradition to take hold," she explains. Mix that with a lack of government regulation and what Sáenz calls a typical Tico do-your-own-thing penchant, and the result is a city full of squat buildings.

The tide began to turn in 1995 with the passage of the Law of Historic and Architectural Patrimony. More than 300 historic structures in the country are currently protected under the legislation, and new buildings are added to the registry each year. But legal protection is no guarantee of funding necessary to actually restore a historic landmark.

You need to look hard, but San José really does have several diamonds in the rough. The National Theater and Central Post Office remain the two most visited examples of historic architecture in the capital. But the National Museum, the National Center of Culture, and several small hostelries and restaurants around town—especially in Barrios Amón and Otoya—are all modern transformations and restorations of structures with histories.

3

of the building. The Galería Nacional, adjoining the main building, is more popular with adults; it usually shows fine art by Costa Rican artists free of charge. Also adjoining the museum is the classical music venue Auditorio Nacional. Though just a short distance from downtown, the walk here takes you through a dodgy neighborhood. You'll definitely feel as though you've stepped out of the hustle and bustle of the center city. Take a taxi to and from. ✉ *North end of C. 4, Barrio El Carmen* ☎ *2258–4929* 🌐 *www.museocr.com* 🎫 *$2* ⏲ *Tues.–Fri. 8–4:30, weekends 9:30–5.*

NEED A BREAK?

We have to admit that Costa Rican baked goods tend toward the dry-as-dust end of the spectrum. But Italian-style bakery Giacomín (✉ *Next to Automercado, Los Yoses, San Pedro* ☎ *2234–2551* ✉ *C. 2, Avdas. 3–5, Barrio La Merced* ☎ *2221–5652*), near the University of Costa Rica, is an exception—it seems that a touch of liqueur added to the batter makes all the difference. Stand, European-style, at the downstairs espresso bar, or take your goodies to the tables and chairs on the upstairs balcony. Both branches close from noon to 2. You'll also find outlets in Escazú, Heredia, and Santa Ana out in the Central Valley.

CLOSE UP

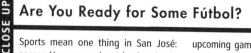

Are You Ready for Some Fútbol?

Sports mean one thing in San José: soccer. Very young boys (and a slowly increasing number of girls) kick around a ball—or some other object if no ball is available—in street pickup games, and they grow into fans passionate about their local team. But everyone puts aside regional differences when the reputation of Costa Rica's national team is on the line, as it is during the World Cup.

Consult the Spanish-language daily *La Nación* or ask at your hotel for details on upcoming games—you simply show up at the stadium box office. Prices range from $2 to $12. *Sombra numerado* (shaded seats) are the most expensive.

Professional soccer matches are usually played on Sunday morning or Wednesday night in either of two San José stadiums. The Estadio Ricardo Saprissa (next to the Clínica Integrada de Tibás) is home to Saprissa, the capital's beloved hometown team, and is in the northern suburb of Tibás.

WEST OF DOWNTOWN

Paseo Colón, one of San José's major boulevards, heads due west from downtown and leads to the vast La Sabana park, the city's largest parcel of green space. La Sabana anchors the even vaster west side of the city. A block or two off its exhaust-ridden avenues are quiet residential streets, and you'll find the U.S., Canadian, and British embassies here.

21 **Museo de Arte Costarricense.** A splendid collection of 19th- and 20th-century Costa Rican art, labeled in Spanish and English, is housed in 12 exhibition halls here. Be sure to visit the top-floor Salón Dorado to see the stucco, bronze-plate bas-relief mural depicting Costa Rican history, created by French sculptor Louis Feron. Guided tours are offered Tuesday–Friday 10–3. Wander into the sculpture garden in back and take in Jorge Jiménez's 7-meter-tall *Imagen Cósmica*, which depicts pre-Columbian traditions. The museum is undergoing restoration at this writing; check to see if it's operational before you visit. ✉ *C. 42 and Paseo Colón, Paseo Colón* ☎ *2222–7155* 🌐 *www.musarco.go.cr* 🎫 *$5, free Sun.* ⏲ *Tues.–Fri. 10–6, weekends 10–4.*

22 **Parque Metropolitano La Sabana.** Though it isn't centrally located, La Sabana (The Savannah) comes the closest of San José's green spaces to achieving the same function and spirit as New York's Central Park. A statue of 1930s president León Cortes greets you at the principal entrance at the west end of Paseo Colón. Behind the statue a 5-meter-tall menorah serves as a gathering place for San José's small Jewish community during Hanukkah. La Sabana was once San José's airport, and the whitewashed Museo de Arte Costarricense, just south of the Cortes statue, served as terminal and control tower.

The round Gimnasio Nacional (National Gymnasium) sits at the park's southeast corner and hosts sporting events and the occasional concert. At this writing a 40,000-seat stadium is under construction—a controversial gift from the government of China, which has decided to use its own construction workers rather than employ local people—near the park's northwest corner. In between are acres of space for soccer, basketball, tennis, swimming, jogging, picnicking, and kite flying. The park hums with activity on weekend days. You're welcome to join in the early-morning outdoor aerobics classes on Saturday and Sunday. A project is under way to replace many of the park's eucalyptus trees with more bird-friendly species native to Costa Rica.

A small building boom is taking place these days, with condos and office buildings going up around the perimeter of the park, another resemblance to New York's Central Park. (Because of building codes, "skyscraper" means a maximum of about 10 floors in earthquake-prone Costa Rica.) Like most of San José's green spaces, La Sabana should be avoided at night. ✉ *Bordered by C. 42, Avda. de las Américas, and Autopista Próspero Fernández, Paseo Colón.*

NEED A BREAK?

Costa Rica gave the world the so-called canopy tour, and you used to have to go pretty far afield to zip via cables through the treetops Tarzan-style. The metro area now counts two outlets of the Urban Canopy (✉ *Parque Metropolitano La Sabana, La Sabana* ☎ *2215–2544* ✉ *Parque del Este, near the Christ statue on the Sabanilla Highway, Sabanilla* 🎫 *$20* ⏲ *9–5*). The west-side branch in La Sabana park takes you over a series of eight cables, four bridges, and a rappel climb. On the far east side, the outlet in the Parque del Este contains a series of seven cables, with hiking trails for before or after offering ample birding opportunities.

WHERE TO EAT

Wherever you eat in San José, be it a small *soda* (informal eatery) or a sophisticated restaurant, dress is casual. Meals tend to be taken earlier than in other Latin American countries; few restaurants serve past 9 or 10 PM. Local cafés usually open for breakfast at 7 AM and remain open until 7 or 8 in the evening. Restaurants serving international cuisine are usually open from 11 AM to 9 PM. Some cafés that serve mainly San José office workers limit evening hours and close entirely on Sunday. Restaurants that do open on Sunday do a brisk business: it's the traditional family day out (and the maid's day off). ⚠ **Watch your things, no matter where you dine. Prowlers have been known to sneak into even the best restaurants, targeting purses slung over chair arms or placed under chairs.**

WHAT IT COSTS IN DOLLARS

	¢	$	$$	$$$	$$$$
Restaurants	under $5	$5–$10	$10–$15	$15–$25	over $25

Restaurant prices are per person for a main course at dinner.

DOWNTOWN

$$ ECLECTIC

✕ **Balcón de Europa.** With old sepia photos and a strolling guitarist who seems to have been working the room forever, Balcón de Europa transports you to the year of its inception, 1909. Pasta specialties such as

San José's ubiquitous red taxicabs.

the *plato mixto* (mixed plate with lasagna, tortellini, and ravioli) are so popular that they haven't changed much either. (Why tamper with success?) A new owner has, however, added French and Mediterranean dishes to the menu—try the blanquette of veal or the couscous. Among the lighter fare are a scrumptious hearts-of-palm salad or a sautéed corvina. Grab a table away from the door (i.e., from the noise of the bus stop across the street). FYI: old-timers refer to the place as Balcón de Franco; the late, legendary chef Franco Piatti was the restaurant's guiding light for years. ✉ *Avda. Central and C. 9, Barrio La Soledad* ☎ *2221–4841* ▭ *AE, D, DC, MC, V* ⊙ *No lunch weekends* ✥ *F3.*

$ CAFÉ ✕ **Café de la Posada.** The lack of alfresco dining in this tropical city is disappointing, but this café's covered terrace with tables fronting the Calle 17 pedestrian mall is a pleasant exception. The owners come from Argentina, and they know how to make a great cappuccino. Salads, quiches, and empanadas are specialties. The best bargains are the four rotating *platos del día* (daily specials), with entrée, salad, beverage, and dessert for $4. If you opt for dinner, make it an early one: the place closes at 7 on weeknights. ✉ *C. 17, Avdas. 2–4, Barrio La Soledad* ☎ *2258–1027* ▭ *AE, D, DC, MC, V* ⊙ *Closed Sun. No dinner Sat.* ✥ *H4.*

$$ CHINESE ✕ **Don Wang.** In a country where "Chinese cuisine" often means rice and vegetables bearing a suspicious resemblance to *gallo pinto* ("spotted rooster," a typical Costa Rican dish of black beans and rice), Don Wang's authenticity is a treat. Cantonese cuisine is the mainstay—the owner comes from that region of China—but these folks will Szechuan it up a bit if you ask. Mornings give way to the immensely popular dim sum, called *desayuno chino*, literally "Chinese breakfast." You can order dim sum all day, but the $5 specials last only until 11 AM. The

dining area is built around a stone garden and small waterfall. There's no television blaring here, a refreshing change from many Costa Rican restaurants. ✉ *C. 11, Avdas. 6–8, Barrio La Soledad* ☎ *2233–6484* ▭ *AE, D, DC, MC, V.* ✥ *G4.*

HAVE SOME SAUCE

Any self-respecting Tico home or restaurant keeps a bottle of **Salsa Lizano**, one of the country's signature food products, on hand. Its tang brightens up meat, vegetable, and rice dishes. Bottles of the stuff make great souvenirs, and you can buy them at **Más x Menos** (pronounced Más *por* Menos) supermarkets throughout the country. The main San José branch is at Avenida Central, between Calles 11 and 13.

$ COSTA RICAN ✗ **La Criollita.** Kick off your day with breakfast at this emerald-green restaurant. Mornings are the perfect time to snag one of the precious tables in the back garden, an unexpected refuge from noise and traffic. Breakfast platters come with eggs on the side: the *americano* has pancakes and toast; the *tico* comes with bread, fried bananas, and *natilla* (sour cream); and the huge *criollita* has ham or pork chops. Government workers from nearby offices start arriving late in the morning, and the lunchtime decibel level increases appreciably. (This is the one time of day we recommend avoiding the place.) Everyone filters out about 2 PM, and once again, you have a quiet place for coffee and dessert. ✉ *Avda. 7, Cs. 7–9, Barrio Amón* ☎ *2256–6511* ▭ *AE, D, DC, MC, V* ⏲ *Closed Sun. No dinner Sat.* ✥ *G3.*

$ COSTA RICAN ✗ **Mama's Place.** Mama's is a Costa Rican restaurant with a difference: the owners are Italian, so in addition to *corvina al ajillo* (sea bass sautéed with garlic) and other staple Tico fare, they serve homemade seafood chowder, traditional Italian pastas, and meat dishes with delicate wine sauces. The brightly decorated coffee shop opens onto busy Avenida 1; the more subdued dining room upstairs accommodates the overflow crowd. (You'll see former Chicago Bears football coach Mike Ditka's autographed picture up there.) At lunchtime it's usually packed with business types drawn to the delicious and inexpensive daily specials—choose from the rotating *platos del día* (daily specials) with pasta, meat, fish, or poultry—all to the accompaniment of ample focaccia. Mama's closes at 7 PM on weeknights. ✉ *Avda. 1, Cs. Central–2, Barrio El Carmen* ☎ *2223–2270 or 2256–5601* ▭ *AE, D, DC, MC, V* ⏲ *Closed Sun. No dinner Sat.* ✥ *E3.*

$ COSTA RICAN ✗ **Manolo's.** For any San José dweller, a mention of Manolo's brings their signature menu item *churros con chocolate* (fried dough with hot fudge sauce) to mind. But this 24-hour eatery is also known for its great sandwiches and espressos. Its location on the Avenida Central pedestrian thoroughfare and its outdoor tables allow for some of the city's best people-watching. Inside, however, the place feels more like a diner than a café, down to its plastic-coated menu and its promise of breakfast food at any hour. The owner always prepares a few Spanish favorites in addition to the typical Tico fare, such as *tortilla española* (a thick potato-and-onion omelet). ✉ *Avda. Central, Cs. Central–2, Barrio La Merced* ☎ *2221–2041* ▭ *AE, D, DC, MC, V* ✥ *E4.*

$ AMERICAN **News Café.** Pounce on one of the street-side tables if they're free. (They probably won't be available: a regular expat crowd holds court here.) The passing parade on Avenida Central is yours for the price of a cup of coffee. Breakfast and dinner fare is hearty, but the café is most popular at lunchtime and cocktail hour. You can get a Caesar salad and other American dishes here, including good burgers, sandwiches, and salads. The café is on the first floor of the 1960s landmark Hotel Presidente. *Avda. Central and C. 7, Barrio La Soledad 2222–3022 AE, D, DC, MC, V F4.*

$ COSTA RICAN **Nuestra Tierra.** But for the traffic zipping by on one of San José's busiest thoroughfares—and on that note, opt for a table on the side facing less busy Calle 15—you might think you're out in the rural Central Valley. Bunches of onions and peppers dangle from the ceiling, recalling a provincial Tico ranch. The generous homemade meals are delicious, and the incredibly friendly waitstaff, who epitomize Costa Rican hospitality and dress in folkloric clothing, prepare your coffee filtered through the traditional cloth *chorreador.* The place is open 24 hours, just in case *gallo pinto* (Costa Rican–style rice and beans) pangs hit at 3 AM. Some disparage the place as "too touristy." Perhaps it is, but it's also fun. *Avda. 2 and C. 15, Barrio La Soledad 2258–6500 No credit cards G4.*

¢ VEGETARIAN **Shakti.** The baskets of fruit and vegetables at the entrance and the wall of herbal teas, health-food books, and fresh herbs for sale by the register tell you you're in a vegetarian-friendly joint. The bright and airy macrobiotic restaurant—much homier than Vishnu, its major vegetarian competition—serves breakfast, lunch, and an early dinner, closing at 7 PM weekdays and 6 PM Saturday. Homemade bread, soy burgers, pita sandwiches (veggie or, for carnivorous dining companions, chicken), macrobiotic fruit shakes, and a hearty plato del día that comes with soup, green salad, and a fruit beverage fill out the menu. The *ensalada mixta* is a meal in itself, packed with root vegetables native to Costa Rica. *Avda. 8 and C. 13, Barrio La Soledad 2222–4475 Reservations not accepted MC, V Closed Sun. G5.*

$$$ ASIAN Fodor's Choice ★ **Tin Jo.** The colorful dining rooms of this converted house just southeast of downtown evoke Japan, India, China, Indonesia, or Thailand. In the Thai Room a 39-foot mural depicts a Buddhist temple. You can select from all of the above cuisines, with menus to match the varied dining areas. Start with a powerful Singapore sling (brandy and fruit juices) before trying such treats as *kaeng* (Thai shrimp and pineapple curry in coconut milk), *mu shu* (a beef, chicken, or vegetable stir-fry with crepes), samosas (stuffed Indian pastries), and sushi rolls. The vegetarian menu is extensive, too. Tin Jo stands out with always exceptional food, attention to detail, and attentive service that make it, hands down, the country's top Asian restaurant. *C. 11, Avdas. 6–8, Barrio La Soledad 2257–3622 or 2221–7605 AE, D, DC, MC, V G4.*

¢ VEGETARIAN **Vishnu.** HACIENDO UN NUEVO MUNDO, proudly proclaims the sign at the door. "Making a new world" might be a bit ambitious for a restaurant goal, but Vishnu takes its vegetarian offerings seriously. The dining area looks institutional—you'll sit at a sterile booth with Formica tables and gaze at posters of fruit on the walls—but the attraction is the inexpensive macrobiotic food. A yummy, good-value bet is usually the plato del día (soup, beverage, and dessert), but the menu also includes soy burgers, salads, fresh fruit juices, and a yogurt smoothie called *morir soñando* (literally, "to die dreaming"). ✉ *Avda. 1, west of C. 3, Barrio El Carmen* ☎ *2233–9976* ✍ *Reservations not accepted* ▭ *AE, D, DC, MC, V* ✥ *F3.*

NORTH AND EAST OF DOWNTOWN

$$ CAFÉ Fodor's Choice ★ ✕ **Café Mundo.** You could easily walk by this corner restaurant without noticing its tiny sign behind the foliage. The upstairs café serves meals on a porch, on a garden patio, or in two dining rooms. The soup of the day and fresh-baked bread start you out; main courses include shrimp in a vegetable cream sauce or *lomito en salsa de vino tinto* (tenderloin in a red-wine sauce). Save room for the best chocolate cake in town, drizzled with homemade blackberry sauce. Café Mundo is a popular, low-key gay hangout that draws a mixed gay-straight clientele. This is one of the few center-city restaurants with its own parking lot. ✉ *C. 15 and Avda. 9, Barrio Otoya* ☎ *2222–6190* ▭ *AE, D, DC, MC, V* ⏲ *Closed Sun. No lunch Sat.* ✥ *G2.*

$ ECLECTIC ✕ **Crokante.** Don't be surprised to see a lot of white coats here. The place is a lunch favorite of physicians from the large hospital down the street who come here for the filling, $6 *plato ejecutivo* lunch special. (Two of the three owners are doctors, too.) If you prefer to order off the menu, you'll find a good selection of steaks, pastas, and seafood. There's something reassuringly American about the main courses, but the appetizers (spicy hummus, breaded calamari, and mussels in mozzarella cheese) tread into a more experimental realm. The outdoor terrace overlooks a railroad track and busy street; you'll find inside dining to be quieter during the day. Evenings give way to more leisurely dining, with soft, live music on Friday and Saturday nights. ✉ *C. 15, Avda. 11, Barrio Otoya* ☎ *2258–1017* ▭ *AE, D, DC, MC, V* ⏲ *Closed Sun. No lunch Sat.* ✥ *H2.*

$$$ ECLECTIC ✕ **Jürgen's.** Jürgen's is a common haunt for *politicos*, and San José's elites meet to eat here. Decorated in gold and terra-cotta with leather and wood accents, the dining room of this contemporary restaurant feels more like a lounge than a fine restaurant. In fact, the classy bar, with a large selection of good wine and good cigars, is a prominent feature. The inventive menu, with such delicacies as medallions of roast duck and tuna fillet encrusted with sesame seeds, sets this place apart from the city's more traditional venues. ✉ *250 m north of the Subaru dealership, on Blvd. Barrio Dent, Barrio Dent* ☎ *2283–2239* ▭ *AE, D, DC, MC, V* ⏲ *Closed Sun. No lunch Sat.* ✥ *B5.*

$ ITALIAN ✕ **La Trattoria.** The green and gold here might make a Green Bay Packers fan feel right at home, but it's the excellent, reasonably priced homemade pasta dishes that make this popular lunch spot worth the stop. Begin your meal with fresh bread and any number of excellent antipasti, continuing on with your favorite pasta dish. And for dessert, who can resist tiramisu? ✉ *Behind Automercado, Barrio Dent, San Pedro* ☎ *2224–7065* ▭ *AE, D, DC, MC, V* ⏲ *Closed Sun.* ✥ *B5.*

$$$$ FRENCH ✕ **Le Chandelier.** San José doesn't get classier than this restaurant, where formal service and traditional sauce-heavy French dishes are part of the

experience. The dining room is elegant, with wicker chairs, a tile floor, and original paintings. The Swiss chef, Claude Dubuis, might start you off with saffron ravioli stuffed with ricotta cheese and walnuts. His main courses include such unique dishes as corvina in a *pejibaye* (peach palm) sauce, hearts of palm and veal chops glazed in a sweet port-wine sauce, and the more familiar *pato a la naranja* (duck à l'orange), or, for a tropical twist on that classic dish, *pato a la maracuyá* (duck in passion fruit). ✉ *50 m west and 100 m south of ICE building, San Pedro* ☎ *2225–3980* ▭ *AE, D, DC, MC, V* ⊙ *Closed Sun. No lunch Sat.* ✣ *C5.*

$$$ FRENCH Fodor's Choice ★ ✕ **L'Ile de France.** Long one of San José's most popular restaurants, L'Ile de France, in the Hotel Le Bergerac (yet technically a separate business) has dining in a tropical garden courtyard. The fairly traditional French menu has some interesting innovations. Start with the classic onion soup or with *pâté de lapin* (rabbit liver pâté); then sink your teeth into a pepper steak, broiled lamb with seasoned potatoes, or corvina in a spinach sauce. Save room for the profiteroles filled with vanilla ice cream and smothered in chocolate sauce. L'Ile de France blends exactly the right level of intimacy, grace, and style, giving it a slight edge over sophisticated Le Chandelier. ✉ *Hotel Le Bergerac; C. 35, Avdas. Central–2, 1st Los Yoses entrance, San Pedro* ☎ *2283–5812* ✍ *Reservations essential* ▭ *AE, D, DC, MC, V* ⊙ *Closed Sun. No lunch.* ✣ *B6.*

$ JAPANESE ✕ **Matsuri.** It's a bit off the beaten tourist path and it's in a shopping center, but this is one of the capital's best sushi joints. The chefs here have created 48 recipes for original rolls, sushi, and sashimi, using high-quality imported ingredients. Bento boxes serve as the weekday lunch specials. The oohing and aahing you hear upstairs is for the chefs performing at the teppanyaki grills to the delight and applause of patrons. ✉ *Plaza Cristal, 600 m south of Pop's ice-cream shop, Curridabat* ☎ *2280–5522* ▭ *AE, D, DC, MC, V* ✣ *H5.*

$$ ITALIAN ✕ **Pane e Vino.** Look closely at the extensive menu here: there are 40 varieties of the capital's best thin-crust pizza, and no one will rush you if you spend too much time pondering what you want. This lively two-level restaurant—it's a small chain, but this was the first location—rounds out its offerings with a complete selection of pastas. You can dine until midnight daily, except on Sunday, when you'll have to finish dinner by 10 PM. The Pizza Allessandre, topped with prosciutto, mozzarella, and olives, is the most popular dish, and for good reason. ✉ *50 m west and 15 m south of Más X Menos, San Pedro* ☎ *2280–2869* ▭ *AE, MC, V* ✣ *H2.*

$ MEDITERRANEAN ✕ **Pub Olio.** Although this combination pub and restaurant serves the full contingent of Mediterranean cuisine, we like to visit the place for drinks and Spanish-style *tapas* (appetizers). The century-old red-brick house with stained-glass windows draws everybody from tie-clad businessmen to university students who have money to spend on something more upscale than run-of-the-mill campus-area bars. Groups liven up the large front room—the quieter, smaller back rooms maintain a bit more romance. The staff hauls umbrella-covered tables out to the sidewalk on warm evenings. Olio is extremely proud that it offers a copy of its menu in Braille. ✉ *200 m north of Bagelmen's, Barrio Escalante* ☎ *2281–0541* ▭ *AE, D, DC, MC, V* ⊙ *Closed Sun. No lunch Sat.* ✣ *H5.*

WEST OF DOWNTOWN

$$$ SPANISH Fodor'sChoice ★ ✕ **Casa Luisa.** A big open window looking into the kitchen—where chef María Luisa Esparducer and her staff proudly show off their trade—is the first thing you encounter as you're shown to your table in this homey, upscale Catalan restaurant. The place is eclectic, with wood floors, arresting artwork, soft lighting, and flamenco music in the background. Start the meal with gazpacho or eggplant pâté, accompanied by a glass of top Spanish wine. The excellent main dishes include rosemary lamb chops, suckling pig, and rabbit in white wine sauce with truffles. Finish with a platter of nuts, dates, and figs drizzled with a wine sauce or the decadent *crema catalana* with a *brûlée* glaze. We give Casa Luisa the nod as the city's best Spanish restaurant for its combination of style and coziness. ✉ *400 m south and 40 m east of the Contraloría, Sabana Sur* ☎ *2296–1917* ▭ *AE, D, DC, MC, V* ⏲ *Closed Sun.* ✥ *A4.*

$$ MIDDLE EASTERN ✕ **Lubnan.** Negotiate the quirky wrought-iron-and-burlap revolving door at the entrance, and you've made it into one of San José's few Middle Eastern restaurants. The Lebanese owners serve a wide variety of dishes from their native region, so if you can't decide, the *mezza* serves two people and gives you a little bit of everything. For your own individual dish, try the juicy shish kebab *de cordero* (of lamb), or, if you're feeling especially adventurous, the raw ground-meat *kebbe naye* (with wheat meal) and *kafta naye* (without wheat meal). A hip bar in the back serves the same menu, but definitely eat out in the front restaurant Thursday night for the 9 PM belly-dancing show. ✉ *Paseo Colón, Cs. 22–24, Paseo Colón* ☎ *2257–6071* ▭ *AE, D, DC, MC, V* ⏲ *Closed Mon. No dinner Sun.* ✥ *B3.*

$$ PERUVIAN ★ ✕ **Machu Picchu.** A few travel posters and a fishnet holding crab and lobster shells are the only props used to evoke Peru, but no matter: the food is anything but plain, and the seafood is excellent at both the east- and west-side branches of this mainstay. The *pique especial de mariscos* (special seafood platter), big enough for two, presents you with shrimp, conch, and squid cooked four ways. The ceviche here is quite different from and better than that served in the rest of the country. A blazing Peruvian hot sauce served on the side adds zip to any dish, but be careful—apply it by the drop. Oh, and one more warning: the pisco sours go down very easily. ✉ *C. 32, 130 m north of KFC, Paseo Colón* ☎ *2222–7384* ✉ *150 m south of Ferretería El Mar, San Pedro* ☎ *2283–3679* ▭ *AE, D, DC, MC, V* ⏲ *Paseo Colón location closed Sun.* ✥ *A3.*

$$ ECLECTIC ✕ **Park Café.** Don't let appearances deceive you: the colonial-style house is only a decade old, but attention to architectural detail and antique furnishings make you think the building was transplanted from Antigua or Granada. An all-tapas menu makes up the fare here, with such tasty dishes as Thai-style tuna salad or red-snapper couscous. The menu varies from year to year, depending on what the owner has uncovered during his two-month European autumn buying trip. On that topic, owner Richard Neat is onetime proprietor of a two-star Michelin restaurant in London, and one of the few British chefs to achieve that distinction. Space is limited, making reservations a must. The January–April dry season takes the pressure off a bit, allowing seating to spill over from

the covered veranda to the open courtyard. ✉*100 m north of Rosti Pollos, Sabana Norte* ☎*2290–6324* ✍*Reservations essential* ▭*AE, MC, V* ⊗*Closed Sun. and Mon.* ✥*A4.*

¢ COSTA RICAN ✕ **Soda Tapia.** One of San José's most popular restaurants fronts the east side of La Sabana park. You can dine outdoors, but you'll have to contend with the traffic noise and the sight of the guard flagging cars in and out of the tiny parking lot. The place stays open until 2 AM, and around the clock on weekends. ✉*Sabana Este* ☎*2222–6734* ▭*AE, D, DC, MC, V* ✥*A4.*

WHERE TO STAY

San José has plenty of chains, including Best Western, Holiday Inn, Radisson, Quality Inn, Clarion, Meliá, and Barceló (the last two are Spanish chains). But it also has historic houses with traditional architecture that have been converted into small lodgings.

The historic houses are usually without concierge or pool and are found mainly in Barrios Amón and Otoya, and in the eastern suburb of San Pedro. The city also has a lower tier of lodgings with the simplicity (and prices) beloved of backpackers. Most smaller hotels don't have air-conditioning, but it rarely gets warm enough at this altitude to warrant it.

Many lodgings operate at near-full occupancy in high season (December through April). Reconfirm all reservations 24 hours in advance. If you're flying out early in the morning and prefer to stay near the airport, consider booking a hotel near Alajuela or San Antonio de Belén (⇨*See Chapter 4*).

WHAT IT COSTS IN DOLLARS

	¢	$	$$	$$$	$$$$
Hotels	under $50	$50–$75	$75–$150	$150–$250	over $250

Hotel prices are for two people in a standard double room in high season, excluding service and tax (16.4%).

DOWNTOWN

Staying in the downtown area allows you to travel around the city as most Ticos do: on foot. Stroll the parks, museums, and shops, and then retire to one of the many small or historic hotels with plenty of character.

$$–$$$ **Aurola Holiday Inn.** The upper floors of this veritable skyscraper in a city of low-lying buildings give you commanding vistas of the surrounding mountains—day views are the best, since San José doesn't glitter quite like New York at night. The good restaurant and casino are also on the top floor, making full use of their vantage points. Inside, however, you could just as well be in Ohio, as the interior decoration betrays no local influence. The high-ceiling lobby is modern and airy, with lots of shiny marble, and the place has all the facilities a business traveler's heart could desire. ■ **TIP→You'll get the hotel's best rates by reserving in advance via the local Costa Rican number or the hotel's own Web site, rather than the international Holiday Inn site.** **Pros:** business

facilities; central location. **Cons:** sameness of chain hotel; park across street dicey at night. ✉*Avda. 5 and C. 5, Barrio El Carmen* *Apdo. 7802–1000* ☎*2523–1260, 866/465–4329 in North America* *2255–1171* *www.aurola-holidayinn.com* *188 rooms, 12 suites* *In-room: safe, refrigerator, Wi-Fi. In-hotel: 2 restaurants, room service, bar, pool, gym, spa, laundry service, Internet terminal, parking (free), no-smoking rooms* *AE, D, DC, MC, V* *BP* *F3.*

3

$$ **Gran Hotel Costa Rica.** You cannot get more centrally located than the longtime grande dame of San José lodgings. It's a good deal for the money and the first choice of travelers who want to be where the action is (or want an in-house casino). A formal dining room and grand piano just off the lobby evoke the hotel's 1930s heyday. Rooms are large and bright, with small windows and tubs in the tiled baths. Even if you don't stay here, the arcaded Café 1930 that fronts the hotel is a pleasant stop for a bite any time of the day or night—it's open 24 hours. **TIP→Check the hotel's Internet site for frequent Web-only special rates.** **Pros:** central location; great people-watching from ground-floor café. **Cons:** some street noise; some rooms have thin walls. ✉*Avda. 2 and C. 3, Barrio La Soledad* *Apdo. 527–1000* ☎*2221–4000, 800/949–0592 in U.S.* *www.grandhotelcostarica.com* *104 rooms, 5 suites* *In-room: no a/c (some) safe, refrigerator, Wi-Fi. In-hotel: 3 restaurants, room service, bar, gym, laundry service, Internet terminal, parking (free), no-smoking rooms* *AE, D, DC, MC, V* *BP* *F3.*

$$ **Hotel Balmoral.** You're just as likely to hear Japanese spoken in the Balmoral's lobby as you are Spanish and English; the place is quite popular with Asian visitors. As with the Presidente across the street, you'll find all the standard amenities of a medium-price business-class hotel here, and, like the Presidente, the Balmoral draws a huge number of leisure travelers, too. But we prefer the Balmoral's dark wood and plush, older feel, as well as the bright, airy restaurant El Patio, which dishes up Costa Rican specialties amid two floors of greenery. **Pros:** central location; good restaurant. **Cons:** some street noise; some rooms showing their age. ✉*Avda. Central and C. 7, Barrio La Soledad* ☎*2222–5022, 800/691–4865 in North America* *www.balmoral.co.cr* *112 rooms, 8 suites* *In-room: safe, Wi-Fi. In-hotel: restaurant, bar, gym, laundry service, Internet terminal, parking (free)* *AE, D, DC, MC, V* *BP* *F4.*

$$ **Hotel Fleur de Lys.** Can a three-floor Victorian house with a brassy hot-pink-and-lavender exterior offer anything of interest beyond its front doors? Peek inside. The answer is a resounding yes. A quiet elegance that you'd never imagine lies inside this 80-year-old home, with garden restaurant and art gallery, on a block-long street that gets little traffic. Unsurprisingly, given the name of the place, rooms are tagged with names of flowers rather than numbers. We like the suites, which have raised bathtubs—two of them have whirlpool tubs as well—and dramatic glassed-in balcony entrances. Smoking is permitted in the hotel's common areas only. **Pros:** cozy rooms; close to sights. **Cons:** some noise from downstairs bar. ✉*C. 13 and Avdas. 2–6, Barrio La Soledad* *Apdo. 10736–1000* ☎*2223–1206* *www.hotelfleurdelys.com* *31 rooms, 6 suites* *In-room: no a/c, safe, Wi-Fi. In-hotel:*

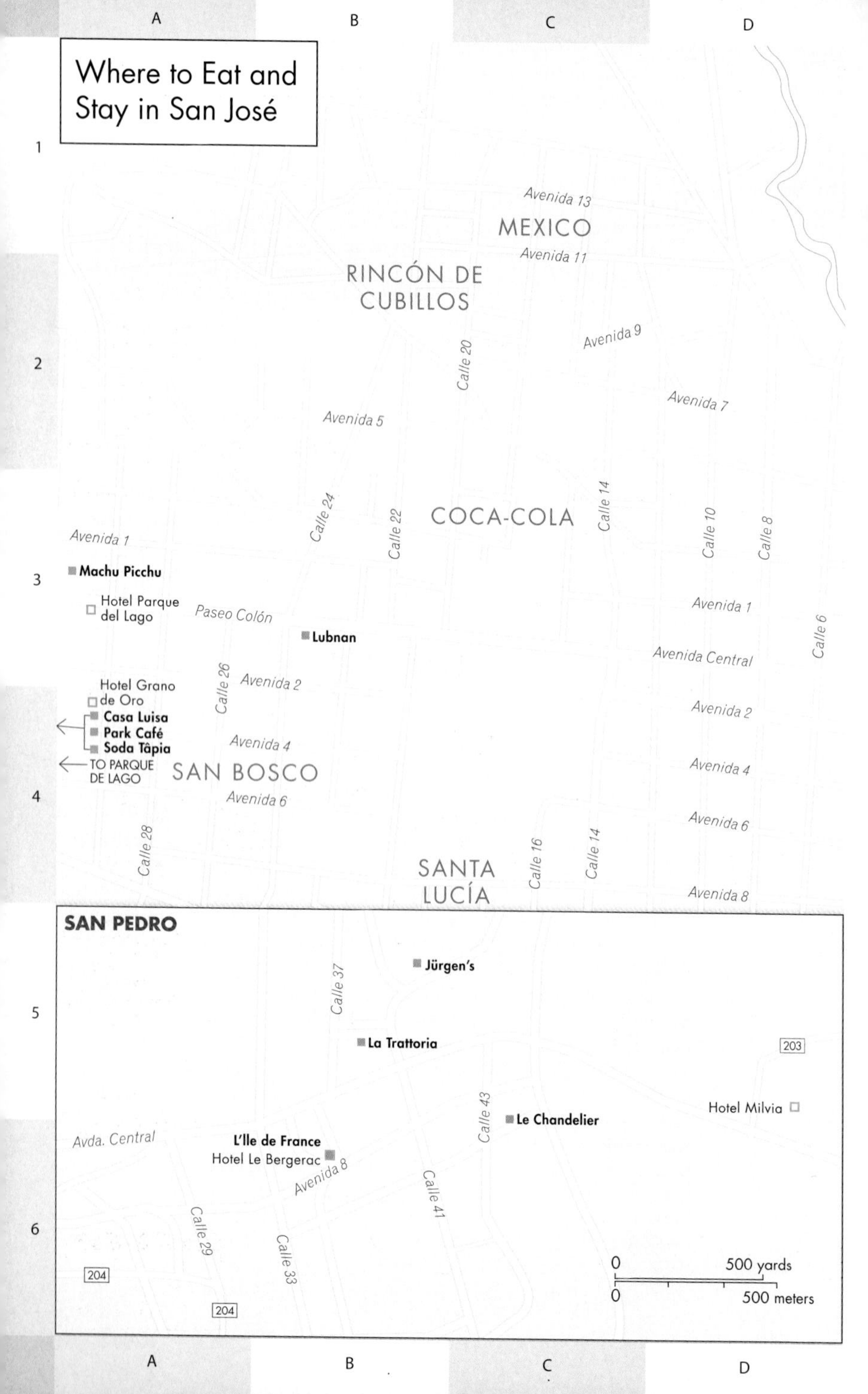

Where to Eat and Stay in San José
A
B
C
D
1
2
3
4
5
6
MEXICO
Avenida 13
Avenida 11
RINCÓN DE CUBILLOS
Avenida 9
Calle 20
Avenida 7
Avenida 5
COCA-COLA
Calle 24
Calle 22
Calle 14
Calle 10
Calle 8
Avenida 1
Machu Picchu
Hotel Parque del Lago
Paseo Colón
Lubnan
Avenida 1
Avenida Central
Calle 6
Hotel Grano de Oro
Casa Luisa
Park Café
Soda Tâpia
TO PARQUE DE LAGO
Calle 26
Avenida 2
Avenida 4
SAN BOSCO
Avenida 6
Avenida 2
Avenida 4
Avenida 6
Calle 28
SANTA LUCÍA
Calle 16
Calle 14
Avenida 8
SAN PEDRO
Jürgen's
Calle 37
La Trattoria
203
Hotel Milvia
Calle 43
Le Chandelier
Avda. Central
L'Ile de France
Hotel Le Bergerac
Avenida 8
Calle 41
Calle 29
Calle 33
204
204
0
500 yards
0
500 meters

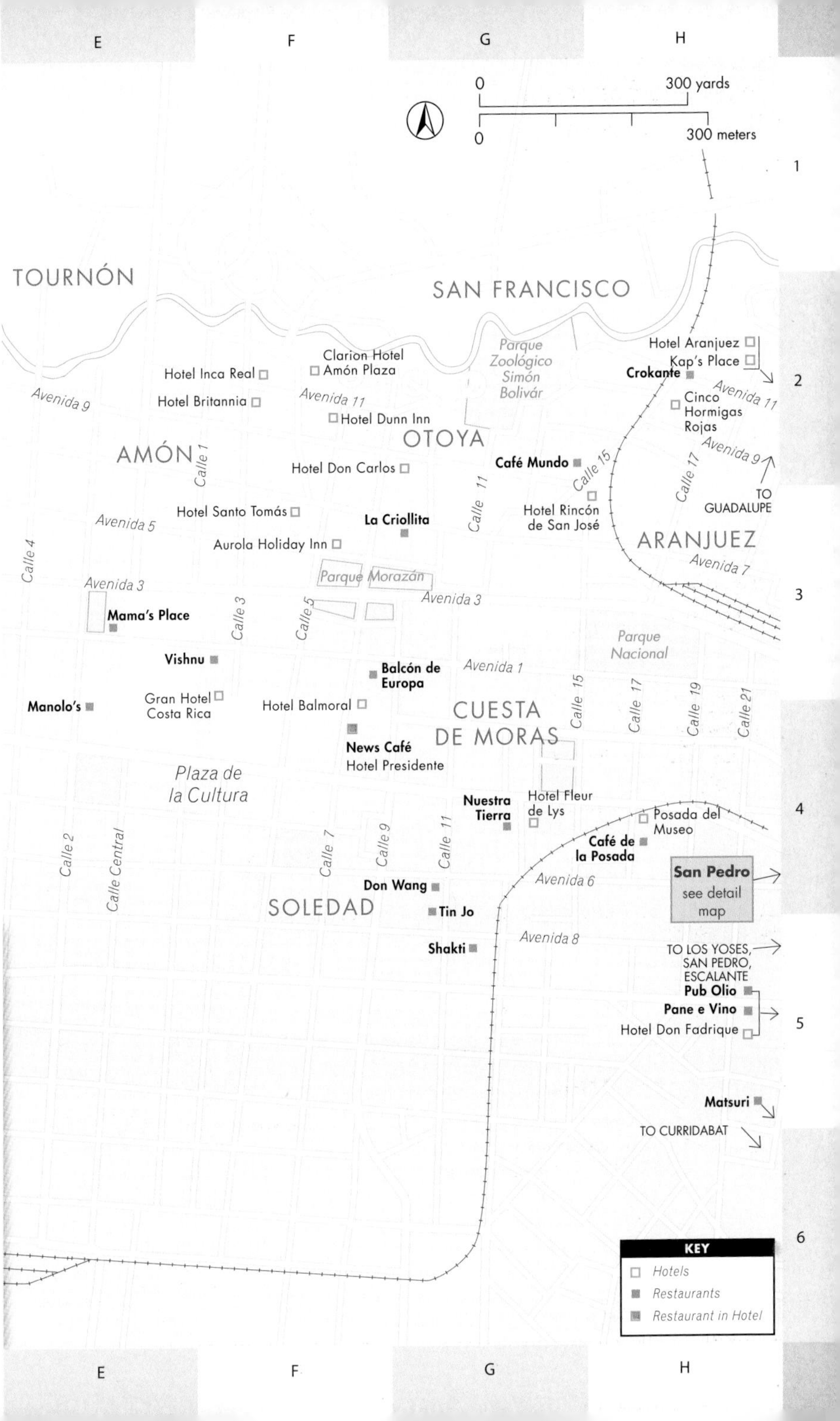
E
F
G
H
0
300 yards
0
300 meters
1
TOURNÓN
SAN FRANCISCO
Parque Zoológico Simón Bolívar
Hotel Aranjuez
Kap's Place
Crokante
Clarion Hotel Amón Plaza
Hotel Inca Real
2
Avenida 9
Hotel Britannia
Avenida 11
Hotel Dunn Inn
Avenida 11
Cinco Hormigas Rojas
OTOYA
Avenida 9
AMÓN
Calle 1
Hotel Don Carlos
Café Mundo
Calle 15
Calle 17
Calle 11
TO GUADALUPE
Hotel Santo Tomás
La Criollita
Hotel Rincón de San José
Avenida 5
Aurola Holiday Inn
ARANJUEZ
Calle 4
Avenida 7
Parque Morazán
Avenida 3
Avenida 3
3
Mama's Place
Calle 3
Calle 5
Parque Nacional
Vishnu
Balcón de Europa
Avenida 1
Manolo's
Gran Hotel Costa Rica
Hotel Balmoral
CUESTA DE MORAS
Calle 15
Calle 17
Calle 19
Calle 21
News Café
Hotel Presidente
Plaza de la Cultura
Nuestra Tierra
Hotel Fleur de Lys
4
Posada del Museo
Café de la Posada
Calle 2
Calle Central
Calle 7
Calle 9
Calle 11
Avenida 6
San Pedro see detail map
Don Wang
SOLEDAD
Tin Jo
Shakti
Avenida 8
TO LOS YOSES, SAN PEDRO, ESCALANTE
Pub Olio
Pane e Vino
5
Hotel Don Fadrique
Matsuri
TO CURRIDABAT
6
KEY
Hotels
Restaurants
Restaurant in Hotel
E
F
G
H

restaurant, bar, laundry service, Internet terminal, parking (free), no-smoking rooms ▭*AE, MC, V* |◎|*EP.* ✣*G4.*

$$ **Hotel Presidente.** The *presidente* referred to here is John F. Kennedy, who walked by during his 1963 visit as the hotel was under construction. You're looking at standard, medium-price, business-class accommodations here. Each of the comfortable rooms has one double and one single bed. The hotel draws a large contingent of business and leisure-travel guests. The rooftop terrace with hot tub has one of those secret great views of the city that no one knows about. **Pros:** central location; eco-friendly hotel. **Cons:** some street noise; some rooms have thin walls. ✉*Avda. Central and C. 7, Barrio La Soledad* *Apdo. 2922–1000* ☎*2222–3022* 🌐*www.hotel-presidente.com* *88 rooms, 12 suites* *In-room: safe, refrigerator, Wi-Fi. In-hotel: restaurant, room service, bar, gym, laundry service, Internet terminal, parking (free)* ▭*AE, D, DC, MC, V* |◎|*BP* ✣*F4.*

DONDE ESTA EL HO-JO?

We encourage you not to play it safe at a chain hotel. Most provide you with the exact sameness you'd find in Cleveland. Smaller hotels and their Tico hospitality (although many are owned by foreigners) are quintessentially Costa Rica.

$ **Posada del Museo.** This green, wooden, Victorian-style house (c. 1928) is a great place to stay if you're bound for San José's museums; hence the name. It's diagonally across the street from the Museo Nacional. Each room is different, but the friendly Argentine owners have maintained the original tiles, wooden double doors, and artfully painted ceilings throughout. The hallway on the second floor overlooks the two-story lobby from what the owners call their "Romeo and Juliet balcony." The Internet-ready data ports in each room are a rarity in a lodging of this size. **Pros:** cozy rooms; near museums. **Cons:** rush-hour train passes by; fronts busy street. ✉*Avda. 2 and C. 17, Barrio La Soledad* ☎*2258–1027* 🌐*www.hotelposadadelmuseo.com* *11 rooms, 3 suites* *In-room: no a/c. In-hotel: restaurant, laundry service, Internet terminal, parking (free)* ▭*AE, D, DC, MC, V* |◎|*BP* ✣*H4.*

NORTH AND EAST OF DOWNTOWN

Just north of downtown, old homes converted into small lodgings populate Barrios Amón and Otoya, two of the capital's most historic neighborhoods. Though we generally eschew the big hotel franchises, our favorite San José chain lodging is here.

The small properties just 10 minutes by cab east of downtown, toward the university, offer personalized service and lots of peace and quiet. Plenty of restaurants and bars are within easy reach.

¢–$ ★ **Cinco Hormigas Rojas.** The name of this whimsical little lodge translates as "five red ants." Behind the wall of vines that obscures it from the street is a wild garden—it's an unexpected urban bird-watching venue, and you'll get a guide to what you can see—leading to an interior space filled with original artwork. The largest room (the Hoja Dansante, or Dancing Leaf) overlooks the mini-jungle that is the front entrance. Color abounds, from the bright hues on the walls right down to the toilet seats. Sure enough, the resident owner is an artist—Mayra Güell turned the 80-year-old house she inherited from her grandmother into

DID YOU KNOW?

The auditorium floor in the Teatro Nacional was designed to be hoisted up to stage level by a manual winch so that it could also be used as a ballroom.

San José's most original B&B–cum–art gallery. She tosses in thoughtful touches such as a healthful boxed breakfast if you're heading out on an early-morning excursion, and coffee and tea 24/7. If you need everything just so and cherish the sameness and predictability of a chain hotel, look elsewhere, but if there's an artistic, bohemian bent to your personality, this is your place. **Pros:** friendly owner; artistic decor; bird-filled patio. **Cons:** small, dark rooms. ✉ *C. 15, between Avdas. 9–11, Barrio Otoya* ☎ *2255–3412* 🌐 *www.cincohormigasrojas.com* *4 rooms, 2 with bath* *In-room: no a/c (some), no phone, no TV (some), Wi-Fi. In-hotel: laundry service, Internet terminal, parking (paid)* ▭ *AE, MC, V* 🍴 *BP* ✥ *H2.*

$$–$$$ Fodor'sChoice ★ **Clarion Hotel Amón Plaza.** The mango-colored Amón Plaza achieves everything we like in a business-class hotel. It provides all the services and amenities you could need while transcending its chain status. Though large for a Barrio Amón lodging, the low-rise hotel doesn't overpower the surrounding neighborhood, and takes pride in the fact that each of its 80-plus rooms is slightly different. (One common feature: there's nothing mini about the minibars.) The price of the suites (but not the double rooms) includes all international calls and shuttle transport to anywhere in the metro area. Friday night sees cocktails and a buffet dinner at the hotel's open-air Cafetal de la Luz to the accompaniment of light music, but the café makes for a pleasant stop any time, any day, whether you stay here or not. **Pros:** business facilities; friendly staff; eco-friendly hotel. **Cons:** lacks intimate hospitality of a smaller hotel; some rooms showing their age; sits on steep street. ✉ *Avda. 11 and C. 3 Bis, Barrio Amón* ☎ *2523–4600, 877/424–6423 in North America* 🌐 *www.hotelamonplaza.com* *60 rooms, 27 suites* *In-room: safe, refrigerator, Wi-Fi. In-hotel: 2 restaurants, room service, bar, gym, spa, laundry service, Internet terminal, parking (free), no-smoking rooms* ▭ *AE, D, DC, MC, V* 🍴 *BP* ✥ *F2.*

¢–$ **Hotel Aranjuez.** Several 1940s-era houses with extensive gardens and lively common areas—where visitors swap travel advice—constitute this family-run bed-and-breakfast. Each room is different; some have private gardens or small sitting rooms. The Aranjuez is a short walk from most San José attractions and has discount tour services. The complimentary breakfast buffet is an amazing spread of eggs, pastries, tropical fruit, good Costa Rican coffee, and more, served on a marvelous, palm-shaded garden patio. And, a rarity in the heart of the city, this place walks the eco-walk, too, with solar-heating panels for hot water, composted gardens, and recycling. Luxurious it is not, but this is deservedly one of San José's most popular budget lodgings; reserve well in advance during the high season. Smoking isn't permitted in the hotel. ■ **TIP→** Be sure to confirm your reservation 48 hours before you arrive and, if possible, on the day of your arrival, giving an estimated arrival time. If you don't, you might find yourself without a room when you arrive, despite your reservation. You'll get a small discount if you pay in cash. **Pros:** good budget value; good place to meet other budget travelers. **Cons:** cumbersome reservations system; far from sights; very popular so difficult to procure space. ✉ *C. 19, Avdas. 11–13, Barrio Aranjuez* ☎ *2256–1825, 877/898–8663 in U.S.* 📠 *2223–3528* 🌐 *www.hotelaranjuez.com*

36 rooms, 31 with bath In-room: no a/c, safe, Wi-Fi (some). In-hotel: restaurant, laundry service, Internet terminal, parking (free), no-smoking rooms MC, V BP H2.

$$ **Hotel Britannia.** This mango-color home is the largest and most luxurious of the old Barrio Amón houses that now serve as lodgings. Technically, the Britannia is two houses in one: a stately old building with tile porch that has changed little since its construction in 1910 (except for the conversion of the old wine cellar into an intimate international restaurant) and a newer addition with slightly smaller, carpeted rooms. We like the deluxe rooms and junior suites in the original house: they're spacious—with high ceilings and windows on the street side—and worth the extra money, though street noise might be a problem if you're a light sleeper. All rooms are no-smoking. **Pros:** good value; cozy rooms. **Cons:** borders on sketchy neighborhood; some dark rooms. *C. 3 and Avda. 11, Barrio Amón Apdo. 3742–1000, San José 2223–6667, 800/263–2618 in North America www.hbritannia.com 19 rooms, 5 suites In-room: no a/c (some), safe, Wi-Fi. In-hotel: restaurant, room service, bar, laundry service, Internet terminal, no-smoking rooms AE, MC, V BP F2.*

$–$$ ★ **Hotel Don Carlos.** One of the city's first guesthouses (technically it's three houses), the Don Carlos has been in the same family for four generations. But the spirit of Carlos Bálser, the hotel's Liechtenstein-born founder—painter, geologist, archaeologist, and general jack-of-all-trades—lives on. Most rooms in the rambling old coffee-baron house have ceiling fans and big windows. Those in the Colonial Wing have a bit more personality, and several newer rooms on the third floor have views of the Irazú and Barva volcanoes. Orchids and pre-Columbian statues adorn the abundant public areas, and the 272-tile mural in the lobby depicts the history of San José. Even if you don't stay here—and this is an old favorite among Fodors.com forums users—the Don Carlos has arguably the best hotel gift shop in the country, well worth a stop. **Pros:** good value; good place to meet fellow travelers. **Cons:** some noise in interior rooms; some reports of long waits in restaurant. *C. 9 and Avda. 9, Barrio Amón Box 025216, Dept. 1686, Miami, FL 33102-5216 2221–6707, 866/675–9259 in North America www.doncarloshotel.com 33 rooms In-room: no a/c (some), safe, Wi-Fi. In-hotel: restaurant, room service, laundry service, Internet terminal, parking (free) AE, D, DC, MC, V BP G2.*

$$ **Hotel Don Fadrique.** This tranquil, family-run B&B on the outskirts of San José was named after Fadrique Gutiérrez, an illustrious great-uncle of the owners who constructed the Fortín in Heredia. A collection of original Costa Rican art decorates the lobby and rooms, most of which have hardwood floors, peach walls, and pastel bedspreads. Several carpeted rooms downstairs open onto lots of lush garden space. There is also an enclosed garden patio, and meals are served in an adjoining art gallery. Parking is free, but on the street, with a guard present 24/7. **Pros:** good value; friendly staff. **Cons:** far from sights. *C. 37 at Avda. 8, Los Yoses, San Pedro Apdo. 1754–2050, San Pedro 2225–8186 www.hoteldonfadrique.com 16 rooms In-room: no a/c, safe, Wi-Fi. In-hotel: restaurant, room service, laundry service, Internet terminal, no-smoking rooms AE, MC, V BP H5.*

$ **Hotel Dunn Inn.** Adjoining 1926 and 1933 houses fuse to create the cozy Barrio Amón experience at bargain prices. That said, the Dunn Inn is immensely popular, so reserve well in advance. Pinewood dominates in one section; brick in the other. Sun-filled rooms bear indigenous Bribri names. One room has a balcony, and a few do not have street-facing windows but look onto an interior courtyard. All have terra-cotta floors and little touches such as fresh flowers. The delightful, skylight-covered central patio serves as a bar and breakfast room. **Pros:** good value; friendly staff. **Cons:** difficult to get reservations; interior rooms catch noise from lobby and bar. ✉ *Avda. 11 at C. 5, Barrio Amón* ☎ *2222–3232, 888/360—9521 in North America* 🌐 *www.hoteldunninn.com* *26 rooms* *In-room: no a/c (some), safe, refrigerator, Wi-Fi. In-hotel: restaurant, bar, Internet terminal, parking (paid), no-smoking rooms* *AE, D, DC, MC, V* *EP* ✥ *F2.*

$ **Hotel Inca Real.** The Ecuadorian owners have constructed a modern Spanish colonial–style hotel that evokes South, rather than Central, America. Rooms congregate around a bright, skylight-covered, plant-filled central patio with wrought-iron gates around the second- and third-floor passageways. All rooms are ample in size. Those on the first floor are tiled; those on the second and third floors are carpeted. Some rooms have three beds, and all have back-friendly orthopedic mattresses. **Pros:** good value; comfy beds. **Cons:** borders on sketchy neighborhood; some noise from lobby. ✉ *Avda. 11, Cs. 3–5, Barrio Amón* ☎ *2223–8883* 🌐 *www.hotelincareal.com* *33 rooms* *In-room: safe, Wi-Fi. In-hotel: restaurant, bar, laundry service, Internet terminal, parking (free)* *V* *CP* ✥ *F2.*

$$ Fodor's Choice ★ **Hotel Le Bergerac.** Any other lodging of this caliber would be content to live off its reputation, and we'd never begrudge Le Bergerac if it did rest on its well-established laurels. But management is always tweaking and remodeling, and each time you return, you'll likely discover something new. (What *doesn't* change much is the rates.) The hotel occupies two former private homes and is furnished with antiques. All rooms have custom-made wood-and-stone dressers and writing tables; deluxe rooms have two beds, private garden terraces or balconies, and large bathrooms. The location on a steep hill might disorient you; you could walk upstairs to your room, fling open the terrace doors, expecting to walk out onto a balcony, and find instead a ground-level patio and mountain view. The in-hotel restaurant, L'Ile de France *(⇨ Where to Eat)*, is one of the city's best, so dinner reservations are essential, even for guests. Breakfast is served on a garden patio. As befits the name, on parle français. There are many small, upscale hotels in San José, but great service, attention to detail, and ample gardens set this place apart. Hands down, this is our favorite lodging in the city. **Pros:** top-notch service; cozy rooms; terrific restaurant. **Cons:** rooms on the small side; not near sights. ✉ *C. 35, Avdas. Central–2, 1st entrance to Los Yoses, San Pedro* *Apdo. 1107–1002, San José* ☎ *2234–7850* 🌐 *www.bergerachotel.com* *26 rooms* *In-room: no a/c, safe, Internet. In-hotel: restaurant, bar, laundry service, Internet terminal, parking (free), no-smoking rooms* *AE, D, DC, MC, V* *BP* ✥ *B6.*

"Our first full day in San Jose was full of wandering through the streets and markets. We happened upon this friendly artist who shared his paintings with us." —photo by Liz Stuart, Fodors.com member

$ **Hotel Milvia.** Apply the principles of feng shui to an old militia arms depository, and you get a charming B&B on a San Pedro backstreet. Manager Florencia Urbina belongs to a local art consortium called Bocaracá, whose motto is "Art in Society." She takes that maxim seriously: the group's lush tropical paintings adorn the lobby, breakfast salon, small bar, and common areas. Your room will be decorated with lovely hand-painted tiles and classic Tico furniture, and you pass through a Zen meditation garden each time you enter and exit the building. The Milvia is a great value, and makes for a charming, artsy retreat. Julia Roberts and Susan Sarandon are a couple of celebrities who've stayed here. **Pros:** good value; artistic decor. **Cons:** far from sights; even farther from airport. ✉ *100 m north and 100 m east of Centro Comercial Muñoz y Nanne, San Pedro* *Apdo. 1660–2050, San Pedro* ☎ *2225–4543 or 2283–9548* *2225–7801* *www.hotelmilvia.com* *9 rooms* *In-room: no a/c, safe, Wi-Fi. In-hotel: bar, laundry service, Internet terminal, parking (free), no-smoking rooms* *AE, D, DC, MC, V* *BP* *D5.*

$ **Hotel Rincón de San José.** Never mind that the interior looks more European than Latin American. (It was once called the Hotel Edelweiss, and everyone still refers to it by its old name.) This elegant little inn has comfortable guest quarters in a charming area near the Parque España. Rooms have carved doors, custom-made furniture, and small bathrooms. Most have hardwood window frames and floors; several have bathtubs. A 2008 expansion doubled the hotel's size, and though newer rooms echo the style of the older ones, they lack some of the hardwood accents. Complimentary breakfast is served in the garden courtyard, which doubles as a bar. The owners speak German and Dutch, in addition to the requisite English and Spanish. **Pros:** good value; friendly management; eco-friendly hotel. **Cons:** small rooms; rooms fronting street get some noise. ✉ *Avda. 9 and C. 15, Barrio Otoya* ☎ *2221–9702* 🌐 *www.hotelrincondesanjose.com* *42 rooms* *In-room: no a/c, safe, no TV (some), Wi-Fi. In-hotel: bar, laundry service, Internet terminal, parking (paid)* ▭ *AE, D, DC, MC, V* 🍴 *BP* ✣ *H3.*

$$ **Hotel Santo Tomás.** Don't be put off by the fact that the front of this century-old former coffee-plantation house butts up against the sidewalk on a busy street; close the front door behind you, and you'll find the lobby and rooms are set back away from the traffic noise. On the fringe of Barrio Amón, the hotel has spacious rooms with wood or tile floors and lots of deep, varnished-wood furnishings. Some of the tiled bathrooms have skylights. A bright breakfast room adjoins an interior patio, and if you keep traveling back into the interior of the building, you'll find a small outdoor pool, a rarity in a hotel of this size in the capital. The especially friendly, helpful staff makes this a real find. All rooms here are no-smoking. **Pros:** good value; friendly staff; central location. **Cons:** difficult parking; borders on sketchy neighborhood; small rooms. ✉ *Avda. 7, Cs. 3–5, Barrio Amón* ☎ *2255–0448, 877/446—0658 in North America* 🌐 *www.hotelsantotomas.com* *19 rooms* *In-room: no a/c, Wi-Fi. In-hotel: restaurant, bar, pool, gym, Internet terminal, parking (paid), no-smoking rooms* ▭ *MC, V* 🍴 *BP* ✣ *F3.*

¢–$ **Kap's Place.** This lodging literally sprawls: one of the three annexes is almost two blocks away from the main building. (And if you drive by too quickly, you'll likely miss that main building with its unassuming sign and white metal door.) Inside are bright, tropical rooms with lots of tile and wood; coffee and tea are brewing all the time in the reception area, and you can use the shared kitchen. You'll be asked to sign a two-page agreement when you register, attesting that you'll keep the noise down and won't bring unregistered guests to your room. The owners are committed to maintaining a family atmosphere here. **Pros:** good budget value; quiet. **Cons:** far from sights; small rooms; reception could be in another building. ✉ *C. 19 and Avdas. 11–13, 200 m west, 50 m north of Shell station, Barrio Aranjuez* ☎ *2221–1169 or 2257–0432* 📠 *2256–4850* 🌐 *www.kapsplace.com* *23 rooms, 18 with bath* *In-room: no a/c, no TV, Wi-Fi. In-hotel: Internet terminal, parking (paid), no-smoking rooms* ▭ *AE, D, DC, MC, V* 🍴 *EP* ✣ *H2.*

WEST OF DOWNTOWN

San José's vast west side contains only a smattering of lodgings, but among them is one of the city's best.

$$–$$$ Fodor's Choice ★ **Hotel Grano de Oro.** Two wooden houses—one dates from the turn of the 20th century, and the other from the 1950s—have been converted into one of the city's most charming inns, decorated throughout with old photos of the capital and paintings by local artists. Public areas have a glitzy elegance; head up to your room for the old coffee-plantation feel for which the hotel is known. Each room is different, and although you can't go wrong with any of them, the older house's rooms are the nicest, especially the Garden Suite, with hardwood floors, high ceilings, and

a private garden. The sumptuous restaurant, run by a French-trained chef, wraps around a lovely indoor patio and bromeliad-filled gardens, and has become one of the capital's premier dining venues. The hotel's sundeck has a view of both the city and the far-off volcanoes. The Grano de Oro is a consistent favorite with posters to Fodors.com forums. **Pros:** friendly management; top-notch service; superb restaurant. **Cons:** remodeling took away country feel in some areas; far from sights; need taxi to get here. ✉ *C. 30, Avdas. 2–4, Paseo Colón* ⓓ *1701 N.W. 97th Ave., SJO 36, Box 025216, Miami, FL 33102-5216* ☎ *2255–3322* 🌐 *www.hotelgranodeoro.com* ⇁ *40 rooms, 3 suites* ♿ *In-room: no a/c, safe, refrigerator, Wi-Fi. In-hotel: restaurant, bar, room service, laundry service, Internet terminal, Wi-Fi, parking (free), no-smoking rooms* ▭ *AE, D, DC, MC, V* ⊙ *EP* ⊕ *A4.*

$$–$$$ **Hotel Parque del Lago.** The management that brought you the South Pacific's Lapa Ríos (⇨ *See Cabo Matapalo in Chapter 7*), also runs things at this eco-conscious, west-side lodging. The business travelers who make up the bulk of the clientele are well served as much by the business services as by the recycling protocols and environmentally friendly soap. Rooms are a mix of sizes, but all have big windows, polished furniture, and armoires, in addition to ample closet space. **Pros:** good business facilities; friendly staff; eco-friendly hotel. **Cons:** far from sights; smallish rooms. ✉ *C. 40, Avda. 2, Paseo Colón* ☎ *2257–8787* 🌐 *www.parquedellago.com* ⇁ *33 rooms, 7 suites* ♿ *In-room: safe, refrigerator, Wi-Fi. In-hotel: restaurant, bar, gym, laundry service, Internet terminal, parking (free)* ▭ *AE, D, DC, MC, V* ⊙ *BP* ⊕ *A3.*

NIGHTLIFE AND THE ARTS

THE ARTS

The best source for theater, dance, film, and arts information is the "Viva" entertainment section of the Spanish-language daily *La Nación*. The paper also publishes the "Tiempo Libre" section each Friday, highlighting what's going on over the weekend. *San José Volando* is a free monthly magazine found in many upscale hotels and restaurants, and publishes features about what's going on around town. Listings in both publications are in Spanish but are easy to decipher.

The "Weekend" section of the English-language weekly The *Tico Times* lists information about arts and culture, much of it events of interest to the expatriate community. The paper comes out each Friday.

ART GALLERIES

San José's art galleries, public or private, museum or bohemian, keep daytime hours only, but all kick off a new show with an evening opening. They're free and open to the public, and they offer a chance to rub elbows with Costa Rica's art community (and to sip wine and munch on appetizers). Listings appear in *La Nación*'s "Viva" section. Your time in the capital might coincide with one of these by happenstance. (They're rarely announced in the paper more than a day or two in advance.) Look for the term *inauguración* (opening).

FILM

Dubbing of movies is rare; films are screened in their original language, usually English, and subtitled in Spanish. (Children's movies, however, *are* dubbed, although a multiplex cinema may offer some *hablada en inglés,* or screenings in English.) Plan to pay $5 for a ticket. Don't expect anything too avant-garde in most theaters; month-old Hollywood releases are the norm. Following trends seen elsewhere, theaters are fleeing downtown for the suburban malls.

Cine San Pedro (✉*Mall San Pedro, San Pedro* ☎*2283–5716*) is a 10-theater multiplex a short taxi ride from downtown. One of the few downtown theaters left, **Cine Variedades** (✉*C. 5, between Avdas. Central and 1, Barrio El Carmen* ☎*2222–6108*) shows mainstream Hollywood movies but has kept that old movie-palace feel. The **Sala Garbo** (✉*Avda. 2 and C. 28, Paseo Colón* ☎*2222–1034*) theater shows arty films, often in languages other than English with Spanish subtitles.

THEATER AND MUSIC

More than a dozen theater groups (many of which perform slapstick comedies) hold forth in smaller theaters around town. If your Spanish is up to it, call for a reservation. The curtain rises at 8 PM, Friday through Sunday, with some companies staging performances on Thursday night, too. If your Spanish isn't up to theater, there are plenty of dance and musical performances.

There are frequent dance performances and concerts in the **Teatro FANAL** and **Teatro 1887,** both in the **Centro Nacional de la Cultura** (✉*C. 13, Avdas. 3–5, Barrio Otoya* ☎*2257–5524*). The **Eugene O'Neill Theater** (✉*Centro Cultural Costarricense–Norteamericano, Avda. 1 and C. 37, Barrio Dent, San Pedro* ☎*2207–7554*) has chamber concerts and plays most weekend evenings. The cultural center is a great place to meet expatriate North Americans.

For six decades, the **Little Theatre Group** (☎*8355–1623* 🌐*www.littletheatregroup.org*) has presented English-language community-theater productions several times a year at various venues around town. The "Weekend" section of the English-language *The Tico Times* has listings.The **Teatro La Aduana** (✉*C. 25, Avda. 3, Barrio La California* ☎*2257–8305*) holds frequent dance and stage performances, and is home to the Compañía Nacional de Teatro (National Theater Company).

The baroque **Teatro Nacional** (✉*Plaza de la Cultura, Barrio La Soledad* ☎*2221–1329*) is the home of the excellent National Symphony Orchestra, which performs on Friday evening and Sunday morning between April and November. The theater also hosts visiting musical groups and dance companies. Tickets are $4–$40. San José's second-most popular theater, the **Teatro Popular Melico Salazar** (✉*Avda. 2, Cs. Central–2, Barrio La Merced* ☎*2233–5424*) has a full calendar of music and dance shows, as well as a few offbeat productions. Something goes on nearly every night of the week; tickets are $2–$20.

NIGHTLIFE

The metro area's hottest nightlife has migrated to the Central Valley suburbs of Escazú and Heredia these days. (⇨ *See Chapter 4.*) Both are about 20-minute taxi rides from downtown San José. The capital isn't devoid of places to go in the evening, however. It still contains plenty of bars, dance places, and restaurants and cafés where you can spend the evening. Take taxis to and from when you go. Most places will be happy to call you a cab—or, if there's a guard, he can hail you one—when it's time to call it a night.

BE AWARE

A few gems really do populate the downtown area, but several bars there double as prostitute pickup joints or are just boozy places where patrons go to pick fights. If you're downtown at night, drink at your hotel or one of the places we recommend, and don't wander directly south or west of Parque Central on foot.

Also avoid the Centro Comercial El Pueblo (usually known simply as El Pueblo), north of downtown. There have been problems with security at this entertainment and shopping complex.

AREAS

No one could accuse San José of having too few watering holes, but aside from the hotels there aren't many places to have a quiet drink, especially downtown. Barrios Amón and Otoya have little in the way of nightlife outside the occasional hotel bar.

The young and the restless hang out in the student-oriented places around the University of Costa Rica in the eastern suburb of San Pedro. The Calle de la Amargura (Street of Bitterness), named for the route Jesus took to the crucifixion, is much more secular than its name suggests and rocks loudly each night. (Nighttime robberies have occurred on "The Calle," so be wary.)

Don't write off every place around the university as rowdy. There are a few quiet bars and cafés where you can carry on a real conversation. Barrios La California and Escalante, an area anchored by the Santa Teresita church, amorphously connect central San José with San Pedro, and house some of the city's trendiest nightspots.

BARS

Intensely and proudly bohemian **Café Expresivo** (✉ *350 m east of church of Santa Teresita, Barrio Escalante* ☎ *2224–1202*) hosts poetry readings and acoustic guitar concerts and serves light pastas and sandwiches. **El Observatorio** (✉ *C. 23, across from Cine Magaly, Barrio La California* ☎ *2223–0725*) strikes an unusual balance between casual and formal: it's the kind of place where folks over 30 go to watch a soccer game but wear ties.

★ **Jazz Café San Pedro** (✉ *Avda. Central next to Banco Popular, San Pedro* ☎ *2253–8933* 🌐 *www.jazzcafecostarica.com*) draws big crowds, especially for live jazz on Tuesday and Wednesday nights. (Beware: the place gets very smoky.) The moniker "Jazz Café" used to suffice, but with the 2008 opening of a branch in the Central Valley suburb of Escazú, the location was added to the name. An older expat crowd hangs out at

3

Mac's American Bar (✉ *South side of La Sabana Park, next to the Tennis Club, Sabana Sur* ☎ *2234–3145*), which usually has the TV tuned to a sporting event. It gets our nod for serving the city's best burgers.

A refreshing change from the ubiquitous Imperial beer is what you'll find at **Stan's Irish Pub** (✉ *125 m west of Casa Presidencial, Zapote* ☎ *2253–4360*) which has Guinness on tap as well as an around-the-world selection of brews. Videos from the '60s, '70s, and '80s provide the backdrop at **Vyrus** (✉ *100 m west of Spoon, San Pedro* ☎ *2280–5890*). Inside is dark, couply, and kissy; the outdoor balcony is much more conducive to singing along with that Duran Duran song you haven't heard in ages.

CAFÉS AND RESTAURANTS

For a country so economically dependent on coffee, there's little evidence of a café culture here. Costa Ricans do observe coffee breaks religiously at home and at work, but outside a few places we list below, making a special trip somewhere to converse with friends over coffee isn't too common.

Café 1930 (✉ *Avda. 2 and C. 3, Barrio La Soledad* ☎ *2221–4011*), under the arcades at the entrance to the Gran Hotel Costa Rica, pulls 24-hour duty as a pleasant place for a drink or coffee. The highly recommended restaurant **Café Mundo** (✉ *C. 15 and Avda. 9, Barrio Otoya* ☎ *2222–6190*) is a quiet spot for a drink frequented by gay and bohemian crowds.

Near the university, **Fezcafé** (✉ *C. de la Amargura, San Pedro* ☎ *2280–6982*) is a quiet alternative to the rowdy nightlife nearby, at least until 8 PM on weeknights.

Walk by **Manolo's** (✉ *Avda. Central between Cs. Central and 2, Barrio La Merced* ☎ *2280–6982*) any hour of the night and a lively crowd is sure to be chatting over coffee and *churros con chocolate*. Smack-dab in the center of the campus nightlife, **Omar Khayyam** (✉ *C. de la Amargura, San Pedro* ☎ *2253–8455*) is a blissfully quiet refuge. Share a jug of wine and falafel or hummus with fried yuca on the covered patio.

Fill up on Spanish-style tapas at Mediterranean bar and restaurant **Pub Olio** (✉ *200 m north of Bagelmen's, Barrio Escalante* ☎ *2281–0541*). It draws a mix of professionals and older college students.

CASINOS

Ask about casino rules before you dive in and play: there are a few Costa Rican variations—for example, you don't get a bonus for blackjack, but you do for three of a kind or straights under local rules. (And yet some places boast that they play exactly like they do in Las Vegas.)

The term casino gets tossed around loosely in Costa Rica: a hotel can put a couple of video poker machines in its lobby and claim it operates a casino. The casino at the pink Hotel del Rey in Barrio El Carmen—arguably the city's most famous and definitely its most notorious gambling establishment—swarms with prostitutes. Avoid it.

A few of the city's larger hotels have casinos we do recommend, including the Clarion Amón Plaza, the Aurola Holiday Inn (the view from the casino is breathtaking), and the Gran Hotel Costa Rica. By law, casinos may open only from 6 PM to 2 AM.

DANCE CLUBS

San José's discos attract a *very* young crowd. Quite frankly, you'll feel ancient if you've passed 21. Live-music halls draw dancers of all ages, but most of these populate rougher neighborhoods on the city's south side and are best avoided.

For a dance-hall experience in a good neighborhood, we recommend the enormous **El Tobogán** (✉*200 m north and 100 m east of La República, Barrio Tournón* ☎*2223–8920*), an alternative to the postage stamp–size floors of most discos. Live Latin bands get everyone on their feet Friday and Saturday nights, and Sunday afternoon.

DANCE FEVER

Step into a San José nightclub and you might think Costa Ricans are born dancing. They aren't, but most learn to merengue, rumba (*bolero* here), mambo, cha-cha, and *swing* (called *cumbia* elsewhere) as children. Play catch-up at dance school **Merecumbé** (☎*2224–3531* 🌐*www.merecumbe.net*), which has 14 branches around Costa Rica. With a few days' notice you can arrange a private lesson with an English-speaking instructor. An hour or two is all you need to grasp the fundamentals of merengue and bolero, both of which are easy to master and work well with a variety of music—Latin and non-Latin—here and back home.

FOLKLORE

Noches Costarricenses (Costa Rican Nights) performances take place at **Pueblo Antiguo** (✣*3 km [2 mi] west of Hospital México, La Uruca* ☎*2257–4171*), a Tico version of Colonial Williamsburg (it depicts Costa Rica between 1880 and 1930) west of the city. The spectacle gets under way on Friday and Saturday nights from 6:30 to 9:30, with dinner and music and dance performances. The $50 price includes transportation to and from San José hotels and English-speaking guides. Arrange this through your hotel's front desk.

GAY AND LESBIAN

San José is reasonably open to gay and lesbian visitors, but given pronouncements of disapproval by city officials, you might want to temper your openness. Be discreet, and you'll be fine. The capital has a few bars, restaurants, and dance places patronized primarily by a gay and lesbian clientele, although all are welcome. Another tier of businesses, exemplified by the venerable Café Mundo, draws a mixed gay-straight clientele. The places we list have drawn crowds for years.

Al Despiste (✉*Across from Mudanzas Mundiales, Zapote* ☎*2234–5956*) is a gay bar that serves light bocas (appetizers) and has dance nights Wednesday–Sunday. **Club Oh!** (✉*C. 2, Avdas. 14–16A, Barrio El Pacífico* ☎*2248–1500*) is a mostly gay, techno-heavy disco with two dance floors and weekly drag shows. Take a taxi to and from here; the neighborhood's sketchy.

El Bochinche (✉*C. 11, Avdas. 10–12, Barrio La Soledad* ☎*2221–0500*) is a gay bar and dance club that doubles as a Mexican restaurant. A gay and lesbian crowd frequents **La Avispa** (✉*C. 1, Avdas. 8–10, Barrio La Soledad* ☎*2223–5343*), which has two dance floors with videos

Continued on page 124

LAST-MINUTE SOUVENIR SHOPPING

by Holly K. Sonneland

San José's markets can be crowded, but they're great fun for the savvy shopper. There are plenty of Costa Rican souvenirs for every pocketbook, and the city's bustling downtown is compact enough to make it easy to visit a few markets in a day ... or even an afternoon. It's a great way to explore the city and take care of last-minute gift shopping.

Some markets have a mishmash of items, whereas others are more specialized. Pick up cigars or peruse antiques in the back of the sleepy La Casona building downtown, or head over to the strip of covered traveler-friendly souvenir stands by Plaza de la Democracia to browse the artsy wares. Festive fake flora in glittery, tropical blue, green, and orange hues can be found at the permanent artisan bazaars.

For a lively experience, head to the gritty and labyrinthine Mercado Central edifice right on Avenida Central where you can jostle among working-class Ticos as you pick up an Imperial beer logo–emblazoned muscle T-shirt or a homemade herbal love potion. Keep a tight hold on your bag, and have fun practicing your spanish with the vendors.

GREAT GIFT IDEAS

Costa Rica's souvenirs pop with bright color and have that distinct, "*pura vida*" (pure life) flair.

COFFEE: The authentic modern-day Costa Rica souvenir, not to mention most appreciated back home. Load up on whole bean (*grano entero*), or, if you must get ground (*molido*), buy the "*puro*," otherwise it might have pre-added sugar. Café Britt is the country's most famous brand (¢2,500/lb).

COFFEE BREWERS: The original Costa Rican coffeemaker is called *el chorreador*. It's a simple wooden stand that's fitted with cloth sock-like filters. Finely ground coffee is dumped in the sock, and hot water is filtered into the mug beneath. Unadorned ones to sleek cherry wood cost around ¢1,700 and up. Don't forget to buy extra sock filters (¢250).

LOCAL LIBATIONS: If you don't have room for a six-pack, be sure to take home what is probably the world's best beer label, Imperial, on a stein or T-shirt (both ¢2,500). Or, snag a bottle of Costa Rica's signature sugarcane liquor, *guaro*, most commonly sold under the Cacique brand.

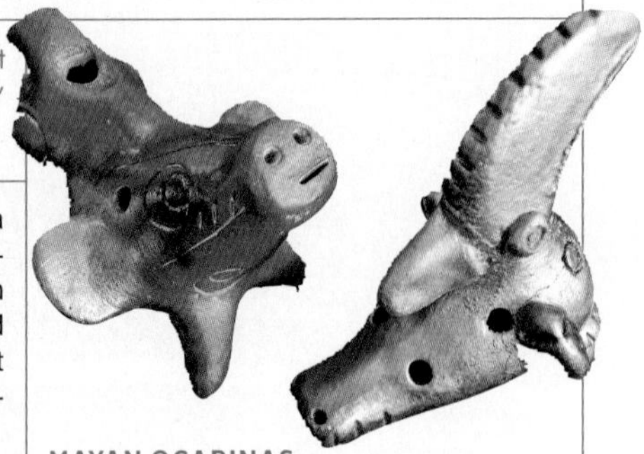

MAYAN OCARINAS
(¢2,500–¢7,000) Calling the ocarina two-faced would be an insult, but only because you wouldn't be giving it nearly enough credit. The Mayan resonant vessel flutes depict over a half-dozen animal faces when flipped around and were often given as gifts to travelers by the Chorotega indigenous group in northwestern Guanacaste.

HAMMOCKS: Swinging in one of these is the official posture of *pura vida*. Structured hammocks with wooden dowels on the ends (¢12,000 and up) are optimal, but dowel-less, cocoon-like hammocks (¢10,000 and up) are infinitely more compactable. Get a chair hammock (¢6,000) if you have limited hanging space back home.

OXCARTS: From the Sarchí region, the oxcart has become Costa Rica's most iconic craftsman artifact. Full-size ones can run a few hundred dollars, and many dealers can arrange to have them shipped for you. There's also a coffee table-size version (¢7,000) or, better yet, an oxcart napkin holder (¢1,500).

BRIBRÍ CEREMONIAL MASKS: The Bribrí people, from the central Caribbean and one of Costa Rica's last active indigenous groups, don these masks in their annual end-of-the-year festival, Dansa de los Diablitos (Dance of the Devils). It's an animistic production that depicts the avenging of the tribe for the decimation wrought by the conquistadors. Cheaper imitations abound, but Galería NAMU has the best—and most authentic—selection (¢65,000 to ¢100,000).

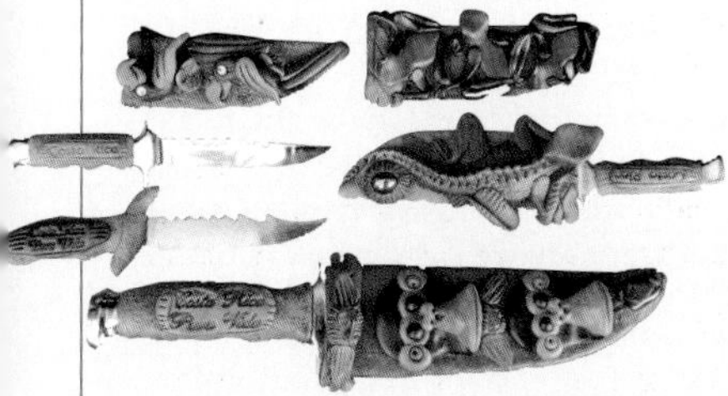

MACHETES: Knives and machetes are commonly used in the country's rural jungle areas and happily sold in leather slings to travelers (¢7,000). Also, knives (¢2,000–3,000) and other items, like frogs and butterflies made out of colored resin, might not be considered traditional but represent the Rastafarian side of the country. Be aware, weapons are not welcome in carry-on luggage on planes.

** All prices listed in colons*

JEWELRY: Go for oversized wooden hoop earrings (¢3,000), wire-wrought gold and silver baubles (¢3,500), or plaster-molded earrings adorned with toucans, frogs, and pineapples (¢1,500). Jewelry made from carved-out coco shells are popular, too.

TROPICAL WOODS AND PAPERS: Sleek mango-wood vases (¢8,250), inlaid rosewood cutting boards (¢8,000), and hand-painted rum rum wood mugs (¢3,850) are among the many elegant woodworks here. There's also scratch-and-sniff writing materials that would make Willy Wonka proud, with banana, mango, lemon, and coffee-scented (sorry, no schnozberry) stationery sets (¢3,700).

FOLKLORIC DRESSES AND SHIRTS: While they're often only pulled out on national holidays like Independence Day, a flounced dress (¢8,000 and up) or pinafore (¢5,000) might be just the kitschy gift you're looking for. Ranchero-style shirts (¢8,000) and straw hats (¢2,000) are also an option.

SAN JOSÉ MARKETS

San José's navigable city center, and its proximity to the airport, make it the perfect last-minute shopping spot.

MERCADO CENTRAL

This market is geared towards locals and has some of the lowest prices anywhere. Here you can visit flower and medicinal herb (of dubious medicinal properties) shops not found in other markets. ✉ Avenidas Central and 1, Calles 6 and 8 ⏲ Mon.–Sat. 8–6; Dec., open Sun.

LA CASONA

Souvenirs and tobacco products abound in this rambling, two-story building. At the far eastern end, go up the back stairs to the discount room, where regular items are discounted 25%–30%. Also upstairs is José "Chavo" Navarro's antique shop. ✉ Calle Central, between Avenidas Central and 1 ☎ 2222-7999 ⏲ 9:30–6.

GALERÍA NAMU

Almost inarguably the best—and, importantly, the only free-trade—store selling indigenous artwork and handcrafts. Owner Aisling French and her staff have developed extensive ties with the Costa Rica's few remaining

Shopping for coffee at Mercado Central.

tribal peoples, bringing their top-notch artisanship to the city. In particular, NAMU sells the highest quality Bribrí ceremonial masks in the country, and has recently developed ties with the Wounan tribe in Panama, who produce museum-quality chunga palm baskets. ✉ Avenida 7, between Calles 5 and 7 (across from Alliance Française) ☎ 2256-3412 ⏲ Mon.-Sat. 9-6:30.

PLAZA DE LA DEMOCRACIA

This strip of stands across the plaza from the National Museum is the most traveler-oriented market. Vendors also don't pay taxes here, so while some items (bulk coffee) are more expensive, others (choreadores) are actually cheaper than they are in Mercado Central. Hammocks are at the far north end, and Stand 82 has some of the best woodworks, along with Stands 25 and 66. Custom-made earrings are at Stand 40. ✉ Calle 13, between Avenidas Central and 2 ⏲ Daily, 8 until dusk.

ARTESANÍAS DEL SOL

This is a good place to get souvenirs, especially the popular piggy banks, basic pottery, and baskets, without the crowds. Christmas decorations are sold from September through December. ✉ 100 meters west of Plaza del Sol, Curridabat, eastern San José ☎ 2225-6800 ⏲ Daily, 8–6; Dec., daily, 8–8.

SHOPPING KNOW-HOW

Colorful clay piggy banks

MAKING A DEAL

Bargaining isn't the sport it is in other countries, and if Tico vendors do bargain, it's often only with travelers who expect it. Before you try to strike a deal, know that Ticos are not confrontational, and haggling, even if not ill-intended, will come off as rude.

Your best bet for getting a deal is to buy in bulk, or simply suggest you'll come back later and walk away. If the vendors really want to lower the price, they'll call you back. If you're buying a single item, you can ask a vendor to offer you a lower price once, at most twice, but don't push it further.

Costa Ricans are painfully polite and are particularly fond of terms of endearment, and it's worth it to indulge in the gentility when talking with market vendors. If you're comfortable enough with your Tico Spanish, or *pachuco*, use the terms in return. For example, Ticos employ a whole arsenal of royal-themed lingo: *rey* and *reina*, or king and queen, are ubiquitous forms of address, especially with middle-aged Ticos, although *reina* is more common than *rey*. You can easily use a "*Gracias, mi reina*," to the (female) vendor who's just given you a good price, but "*¿Cómo está mi rey?*" to a 20-something male vendor sounds a little strange. That being said, if you're a 20-something female shopper, be prepared to hear "*¿En cómo puedo servirle mi reina?*" literally, "How can I serve you my queen?" (said endearingly, not lecherously) from every other 50-year-old vendor whose stand you pass. *Regalar*, a verb that literally means "to gift," can be used to ask a vendor to hand you the item that you want to buy (*Puede regalarme esa bolsa verde, porfa?* I'll take that green bag, please?) or to cut you a deal (*Me la regala en tres mil?* Can you sell it to me for three thousand [colones]?)

Of course, if your Spanish is rusty, smiling always helps.

■ **TIP→ While most of the shops in these markets take credit cards, vendors will be more likely to cut you a deal if you pay in cash.**

PLAYING IT SAFE

Petty crime is on the rise in Costa Rica, but that shouldn't keep you from exploring the markets. It's important to note that what were once recommended precautions are now strongly advised. Keep cash in breast pockets and leave credit cards and important documents in the hotel. Also leave behind jewelry and fancy gear, especially cameras, that will make you stand out. (The lighting in the markets—all of them indoor—is very poor, and photos inevitably don't turn out anyway.) Most of the markets, like the rest of the city, are generally safe during the day but best avoided in the evening.

Ceremonial mask from Namu Gallery

and karaoke as well as a quieter upstairs bar with pool tables. The last Friday of each month is ladies' night.

GREAT VIEWS

Several miradores (lookout points) dot the mountains north and south of the city. **Ram Luna** (⊠*10 km [6 mi] south of San José, near Church of San Luis Tolosa, Aserrií* ☎*2230–3060*) in the far southern suburbs, is the most famous of these. You come here for the view—the lights of the Central Valley sparkle at your feet—and the music, more than the food. (Costa Rican fare is the staple here.) Make reservations if you plan to be here for Wednesday evening's folklore show.

SHOPPING

Although it might seem more "authentic" to buy your souvenirs at their out-country source, you can find everything in the city, a real bonus if you're pressed for time. If the capital has any real tourist shopping district, it's found loosely in the cluster of streets around Parque Morazán, just north of downtown, an area bounded roughly by avenidas 1 and 7 and calles 5 and 9. Stroll and search, because many other businesses congregate in the area as well.

The northeastern suburb of Moravia has a cluster of high-quality crafts and artisan shops—for good reason very popular with tour groups—in the three blocks heading north from the Colegio María Inmaculada. The street is two blocks behind the city's church.

MALLS

Old-timers lament the malling over of San José. Several huge enclosed centers anchor the metro area. These are complemented by dozens of smaller malls. Expect all the comforts of home—food courts and movie theaters included. **Mall San Pedro** (⊠*Rotonda de la Hispanidad, San Pedro* ☎*2283–7540*) sits in its namesake suburb, a short 10-minute taxi ride from downtown San José. The mammoth **Terramall** (⊠*Autopista Florencio del Castillo, Tres Ríos* ☎*2278–6970*) is the far eastern suburbs' prime shopping destination.

SPECIALTY STORES

BOOKS AND MAGAZINES

The New York Times, *The Wall Street Journal*, *The Miami Herald*, and *USA Today* arrive in San José the morning of publication, printed here and bound on bond paper. Find them at a select few outlets and shops in large hotels or at the airport.

With several locations around the metro area, **Casa de las Revistas** (⊠*C. 5, Avdas. 3–5, Barrio El Carmen* ☎*2256–5092*) has San José's best selection of magazines in English.

Librería Internacional (⊠*300 m west of Taco Bell, Barrio Dent* ☎*2253–9553*) is the city's largest bookstore. It evokes Borders or Barnes & Noble, though on a much smaller scale, and stocks English translations of Latin American literature as well as myriad coffee-table books on Costa Rica. The affable owners of **7th Street Books** (✉ *C. 7, Avdas. Central–1, Barrio La Soledad* ☎ *2256–8251*) make this store *the* place to stop in and see what's going on in the expat community. It has the city's best selection of books in English and is also strong on Latin America and tropical ecology. You can pick up *The Tico Times* here.

CRAFTS

The arts-and-crafts tradition in Costa Rica isn't as strong as in, say, Guatemala or Peru. At first glance you might be disenchanted with what you see in the run-of-the-mill souvenir shops. Keep your disappointment in check until you visit two of San José's outstanding purveyors of fine artisan work.

Fodor'sChoice ★ Downtown San José's must-stop shop is **Galería Namu** (✉ *Avda. 7, Cs. 5–7, behind Aurola Holiday Inn, Barrio Amón* ☎ *2256–3412* 🌐 *www.galerianamu.com*), which sells Costa Rican folkloric art and the best indigenous crafts in town. Its inventory brims with colorful creations by the Guaymí, Boruca, Bribri, Chorotega, Huetar, and Maleku peoples—all Costa Rican indigenous groups. You can also find exquisitely carved ivory-nut Tagua figurines and baskets made by Wounan Indians from Panama's Darién region and Tuno textiles from Honduras' Miskito coast. Take note of carved balsa masks, woven cotton blankets, and hand-painted ceramics.

The store looks expensive—and indeed, the sky's the limit in terms of prices—but if your budget is not so flush, say so: the good folks here can help you find something in the $10–$20 range that will make a more cherished souvenir of your trip than a *Pura Vida* T-shirt. As a bonus you'll get an information sheet describing your work's creator and art style. Namu has a reputation for fair prices for customers, and for fair pay to artists or artisans.

★ The staff and selection at **Kaltak Artesanías** (✉ *50 m north of Colegio María Inmaculada, Moravia* ☎ *2297–2736*) make it a real standout from all the Moravia shops. Walk in with some unformulated "I'm not sure what I want" notions, and the staff will help you find that perfect souvenir from among the selection of ceramics (Pefi and Osenbach designs, trademarks of two well-known artisans in the capital, are well represented), wood-and-leather rocking chairs, oxcarts of all sizes, orchids, and carvings from native *cocobolo* and *guápinol* woods and ash wood.

MUSIC

San José's music stores stock the Latin sounds of every artist from Chayanne to Shakira, but Costa Ricans take special pride in their hometown Latin-fusion group, the Grammy Award–winning Editus.

In addition to selling everything else imaginable, downtown department store **Universal** (✉ *Avda. Central, between Cs. Central and 1, Barrio El Carmen* ☎ *2222–2222*) stocks a good selection of Latin CDs in its first-floor music department.

SOUVENIRS

Hotel gift shop **Boutique Annemarie** (✉*Hotel Don Carlos, C. 9 and Avda. 9, Barrio Amón* ☎*2233–5343*) has a huge selection of popular souvenirs and CDs of Costa Rican musicians.

Some 100 souvenir vendors congregate in the block-long covered walkway known as the **Calle Nacional de Artesanía y Pintura** (✉*C. 13, Avdas. Central–2, western side of Plaza de la Democracia*), and offer some real bargains in hammocks, wood carvings, and clothing. Dozens of souvenir vendors set up shop on the two floors of **La Casona** (✉*C. 2, Avdas. Central–1, Barrio El Carmen* ☎*2222–7999*), in a rickety old downtown mansion. It's much like a flea market, and it's a fun place to browse.

LAST, LAST MINUTE BUYS

If you really didn't have time to shop, never fear. Aeropuerto Internacional Juan Santamaría has two noteworthy souvenir shops—**Britt Shop Costa Rica and Terra Verde**—for those last-minute purchases. Choose from various blends of coffee ($5 per pound) and such merchandise as hand-carved bowls and jewelry, aromatherapy candles, banana-paper stationery, and Costa Rica travel books—Fodor's included. (Merchandise selection is slightly different in each.) There's nary another store in the country carrying such a variety all in one place. The catch is that the airport shops charge U.S. prices.

La Ranita Dorada (✉*Avda. 1, between Cs. 9 and 11, Barrio El Carmen* ☎*2256–6808*) sells pretty standard souvenir fare—although it has quite a large selection of wood products—but the friendly staff, who happily take the time to give personalized service, make this place worth a stop.

Mercado Central (✉*Bordered by Avdas. Central–1 and Cs. 6–8, Barrio La Merced*) doesn't bill itself for souvenir shopping—the maze of passageways is where the average Costa Rican comes to stock up on day-to-day necessities—but a few stalls of interest to tourists congregate near the entrances. If you can't find it at **Mundo de Recuerdos** (✉*Across from Colegio María Inmaculada, Moravia* ☎*2240–8990*), it probably doesn't exist. Here's the largest of the Moravia shops with simply everything—at least of standard souvenir fare—you could ask for under one roof.

The museum-shop concept barely exists here, but the shop at the entrance of the **Museo del Oro Precolombino** (✉*C. 5, Avdas. Central–2, Barrio La Soledad* ☎*2243–4217*) is the exception. Look for a terrific selection of pre-Columbian-theme jewelry, art, exclusively designed T-shirts, coin- and bill-theme key chains, notebooks, and mouse pads.

The Central Valley

WORD OF MOUTH

"We happened upon this workshop (Taller Eloy Alfaro e Hijos) by accident because we had time to kill in Sarchi. It was one of the neatest experiences I've ever had in my visits to Costa Rica. They were in the process of constructing and decorating the world's largest oxcart for an exhibition in town. The family workshop runs completely on water, not electricity." —photo by jvcostarica, Fodors.com member

WELCOME TO THE CENTRAL VALLEY

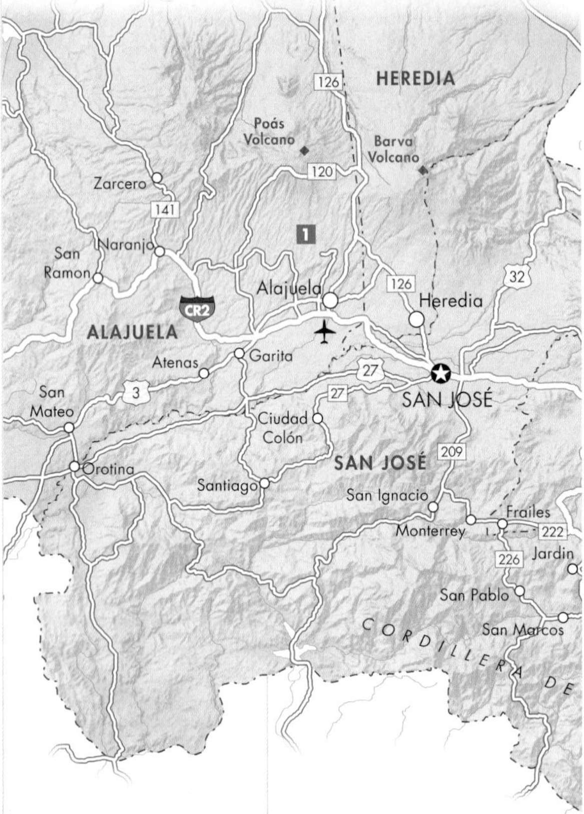

TOP REASONS TO GO

★ **Coffee:** Get up close and personal with harvesting and processing on coffee tours at two of the valley's many plantations: Café Britt and Doka Estate.

★ **The Orosi Valley:** Spectacular views and quiet, bucolic towns make this area a great day trip or overnight from San José.

★ **Rafting the Pacuare River:** Brave the rapids as you descend through tropical forest on one of the best rivers in Central America.

★ **The views:** Ascend the volcanic slopes that border the valley, meeting superb views almost anywhere you go.

★ **Avian adventures:** Flock to Tapantí National Park to see emerald toucanets, resplendent quetzals (if you're lucky), and nearly every species of Costa Rican hummingbird. Rancho Naturalista is the bird lovers' hotel of choice.

1 Areas north and west of San José. The areas north and west of San José are dominated by coffee farms and small valley towns whose beautiful hotels attract lots of tourists on their first and last nights in the country. Café Britt and Doka Estate are both here, as is the international airport, near Alajuela.

2 Cartago and Irazú Volcano. In the eastern Central Valley are Cartago and Irazú Volcano. Cartago is an older city than San José, with a couple of historic attractions. Irazú is Costa Rica's tallest volcano. On a clear day you can see both the Atlantic and Pacific oceans from its peak.

GETTING ORIENTED

The Central Valley is something of a misnomer, and its Spanish name, the *meseta central* (central plateau) isn't entirely accurate either. The two contiguous mountain ranges that run the length of the country—the Cordillera Central range (which includes Poás, Barva, Irazú, and Turrialba volcanoes) to the north and the Cordillera de Talamanca to the south—don't quite line up in the middle, leaving a trough between them. The "valley" floor is 914 to 1,524 meters (3,000 to 5,000 feet) above sea level. In the valley, your view toward the coasts is obstructed by the two mountain ranges. But from a hillside hotel, your view of San José and the valley can be spectacular.

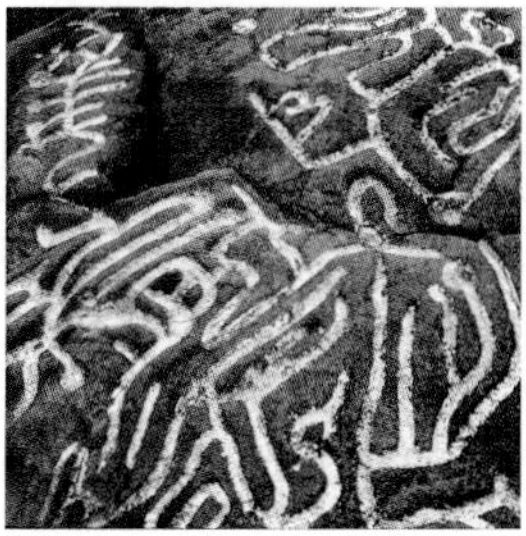

3 Turrialba. Rafting trips on the Pacuare and Reventazón are based in Turrialba, a bustling little town. The nearby Guayabo Ruins, of a city deserted in AD 1400, is Costa Rica's only significant archaeological site.

4 Orosi Valley. An often overlooked beauty is the Orosi Valley. The drive into the valley is simply gorgeous, and a tranquil way to spend a day. Birding destination Tapantí National Park is at the southern edge of the valley.

THE CENTRAL VALLEY PLANNER

How Much Time?

Central Valley is the Costa Rica of history and tradition, and many visitors overlook it. You could spend an entire week here without getting bored, but if you have only a week or two in Costa Rica, we recommend a maximum of two days before heading to rain forests and beaches in other parts of the country. Spending a day after you arrive, then another day or two before you fly out gives you a taste of the region, breaks up the travel time, and makes your last day interesting, rather than spent in transit back to San José. The drive between just about any two points in the Central Valley is two hours or less, so it's ideal for short trips. In a day you can explore the Orosi Valley and Cartago, raft the Pacuare River, or hop from the Butterfly Farm to a coffee plantation.

Word of Mouth

"Irazu does resemble a 'moonscape.' It is also very cold and breezy. The crater has emerald-green water. Pretty, but we were pretty much out of the car to see the crater, then back in to warm up!"

—MarciaM

Choosing a Place to Stay

Most international flights fly into Costa Rica in the evening and head out again early the next morning, meaning you likely have to stay your first and last nights in San José or nearby. Think of the Central Valley as "the nearby." For getting away from it all and still being close to the country's main airport, the lodgings around San José make splendid alternatives to staying in the city itself. It may pain you to tear yourself away from that beach villa or rain forest lodge, but you can still come back to something distinctive here on your last night in Costa Rica. Rustic *cabinas* (cottages), sprawling coffee plantations, nature lodges, and hilltop villas with expansive views are some of your options. The large chains are here as well, but the real gems are the so-called boutique hotels, many of which are family-run places and have unique designs that take advantage of exceptional countryside locations. Subtropical gardens are the norm, rather than the exception, and air-conditioning is usually not necessary.

Getting Around

The Central Valley has an extensive network of paved roads in relatively good shape, though this being Costa Rica, you can stumble upon gravel or dirt stretches when you least expect it. The Pan-American Highway runs roughly east–west through the valley and the center of San José. (It's numbered CA1 north and west and CA2 south and east of the capital.) Mountains ring the valley, so most trips to or from the lowlands require a drive up in elevation then back down. The bus network is good, but because sights tend to be spread out, it's less time-consuming to travel by car. The country's major airport is in Alajuela, so it's a perfect place to rent a vehicle. Consider taking taxis, too, if you'd rather leave the driving to someone else. They're plentiful, drivers know the roads (most of the time), and the prices are reasonable. Even several $10 taxi rides per day—and $10 gets you a reasonable distance—are cheaper than a rental car.

Faith and Folklore

The Central Valley wears its tradition, both religious and secular, on its collective sleeve. Costa Rica's biggest annual religious festival takes place in Cartago each August 2 and commemorates what tradition holds was a 1635 apparition of the Virgin Mary. It never captured the worldwide attention of Mexico's Guadalupe, France's Lourdes, or Portugal's Fatima, but no matter. The 1 million pilgrims who visit the site on that day alone are testament to its popularity here.

Nearby, at Ujarrás in the Orosi Valley, sit the ruins of the country's first church. Prayers to the Virgin Mary said here are reputed to have staved off pirate attacks—we have no other explanation—and numerous earthquakes. That second one is tougher to explain: this part of the valley has suffered its share of earth tremors throughout history.

Costa Ricans flee to the beach for Semana Santa, or Holy Week, in March or April, but the small community of San Joaquín, halfway between Alajuela and Heredia, makes a nice antidote to the beach crowds. The town holds some of the country's most impressive processions reenacting Jesus' trial and crucifixion.

Turning more pagan, Escazú holds the title of Costa Rica's spirit capital. Witches, mostly benevolent, but a few malevolent ones, too, are reputed to populate the community. You'd never know it from all the fast-food restaurants, car dealerships, and shopping malls you see as you pull into town. But old-timers high in the hills have hair-raising stories to tell about those proverbial things that go bump in the night.

Those hills above Escazú also host the annual Día del Boyero, or Oxcart Drivers' Day, the second Sunday in March. Oxen and carts parade to the church to be blessed by the priest. Those blessings must stick; oxcarts continue to be a favored mode of work transport throughout the Central Valley.

Dining and Lodging

WHAT IT COSTS IN DOLLARS

	¢	$	$$	$$$	$$$$
Restaurants	under $5	$5–$10	$10–$15	$15–$25	over $25
Hotels	under $50	$50–$75	$75–$150	$150–$250	over $250

Restaurant prices are per person for a main course at dinner. Hotel prices are for two people in a standard double room in high season, excluding service and tax (16.4%).

When to Go

Known for its "eternal spring," the Central Valley lacks the oppressive seasonal heat and rain of other parts of the country. Average highs are 24°C to 27°C (75°F to 80°F). Microclimates here are dictated by elevation: Cartago and the Irazú volcano perch at a higher elevation and are frequently more overcast and chillier than San José, especially at night. Heredia sits at about the same elevation as the capital, and enjoys a similar climate. The western valley slopes downward in elevation from San José, and you'll notice a slight warming by the time you get to Santa Ana, Alajuela, or San Antonio de Belén. The same goes for the Orosi Valley with its lower altitude. Turrialba sits lower still and represents a transition zone between the temperate Central Valley and balmy Caribbean coast. Afternoon downpours are common for an hour or two from mid-May to December (with a slight drop-off around July, but more prolonged rains in September and October), but the amount of rain is modest compared with the Caribbean coast and the southern Pacific. Don't rule out the rainy season—fewer travelers means you won't need reservations, rain is usually during afternoon siesta hours, and the valley is swathed in green after a few months of moisture. Holy Week (the week before Easter) and the last two weeks of the year are prime vacation times for Ticos, so reserve cars and hotel rooms in advance.

VOLCÁN IRAZÚ

The word Irazú is likely a corruption of Iztaru, a long-ago indigenous community whose name translated as "hill of thunder." The name is apt.

The volcano is considered active, but the gases and steam that billow from fumaroles on the northwestern slope are rarely visible from the peak above the crater lookouts. The mountain's first recorded eruption took place in 1723; the most recent was a series of eruptions that lasted from 1963 to 1965. Boulders and mud rained down on the countryside, damming rivers and causing serious floods, and the volcano dumped up to 20 inches of ash on sections of the Central Valley.

When conditions are clear, you can see the chartreuse lake inside the Cráter Principal. The stark moonscape of the summit contrasts markedly with the lush vegetation of Irazú's lower slopes, home to porcupines, armadillos, coyotes, and mountain hares. Listen for the low-pitched, throaty song of the *yigüirro*, or clay-colored thrush, Costa Rica's national bird. Its call is most pronounced just before the start of the rainy season.

BEST TIME TO GO

Early morning, especially in the January–April dry season, affords the best views, both of the craters and the surrounding countryside. Clouds move in by late morning. Wear warm, waterproof clothing if you get here that early: although rare, temperatures have dropped down close to freezing around dawn.

FUN FACT

Irazú has dumped a lot of ash over the centuries. The most recent eruptive period began on the day that John F. Kennedy arrived in Costa Rica in March 1963. The "ash storm" that ensued lasted on and off for two years.

VOLCANIC TIPS

A paved road leads all the way to the summit, where a small coffee shop sells hot beverages, and a persistent pair of coatis cruise the picnic tables for handouts. (Please resist the urge to feed them!) The road to the top climbs past vegetable fields, pastures, and native oak forests. You pass through the villages of Potrero Cerrado and San Juan de Chicuá before reaching the summit's bleak but beautiful main **crater**.

HIKING

Even before you get to the main entrance, check out the park's Prusia Sector, which has hiking trails that pass through majestic oak and pine forests and picnic areas. They're very popular with Tico families on weekends, so if you want the woods to yourself, come on a weekday. Trails in the park are well marked; avoid heading down any paths marked with PASO RESTRINGIDO ("passage restricted") signs.

BIRD WATCHING

The road to Irazú provides some of the best roadside birding opportunities in the country, especially on a week day when there isn't a constant parade of cars and buses heading up to the crater. Some of the most fruitful areas are on either side of the bridges you'll pass over. Reliable bird species that inhabit these roadsides are: acorn and hairy woodpeckers, the brilliant flame-throated warbler, and, buzzing around blossoms, the fiery-throated, green violet-ear, and (aptly named) volcano hummingbirds. Once past the main entrance, there are also plenty of opportunities to stop and bird roadside. Look for volcano juncos on the ground and slaty flowerpiercers visiting flowering shrubs.

TOP REASONS TO GO

THE VIEW

How many places in the world let you peer directly into the crater of an active volcano? Costa Rica offers you two: here at Irazú, and the Northern Plains' Volcán Poás. Poás's steaming cauldron is spookier, but Irazú's crater lake with colors that change according to the light is nonetheless impressive.

MORE VIEWS

"On a clear day, you can see forever," goes the old song from the musical of the same name. Irazú is one of the few places in Costa Rica that lets you glimpse both the Pacific and Atlantic (Caribbean) oceans at once. Clear is the key term here: clouds frequently obscure the view. Early morning gives you your best shot.

EASY TO GET TO

Irazú's proximity to San José and the entire eastern Central Valley makes it an easy half-day or day trip. Public transportation from the capital, frequently a cumbersome option to most of the country's national parks, is straightforward.

ECO-LODGES IN THE CENTRAL VALLEY

Suburbia oozes out with each passing year eating up once-idyllic Central Valley land, but it's still surprisingly easy to find vast undeveloped stretches, even in the metro area.

You'd never know it driving the highway west from San José through the valley of shopping malls and car dealerships, but Costa Rica's Central Valley is home to an ample amount of greenery. Two of the country's five active volcanoes (Irazú and Turrialba) loom here. Suburbia gives way to farmland in the hills far above Escazú and Santa Ana and make for tranquil day hikes. A terrific selection of country lodges populates the hills north of Alajuela and Heredia, and a stay in one of them is certain to give you that "so close (to the international airport) and yet so far" convenience. Tapantí National Park, in the far eastern sector of the valley, contains a real live cloud forest—it's not quite Monteverde, but it is far easier to get to—and Guayabo National Monument nearby is home to Costa Rica's only true archaeological ruins. The medium-size city of Turrialba has fast become the country's whitewater center. And the Orosi Valley defines pastoral tranquility.

GOOD PRACTICES

Make a point of getting out and meeting the local people here in the Central Valley. We'd argue that the tidy towns in this region are Costa Rica at its most "authentic," its most "Tico." Folks here still greet you with a hearty "Buenos días" each day. Respond in kind.

Consider taking public transportation in the Central Valley. Communities here are bunched close enough together to be well served by public buses and taxis can fill in the gaps. Plus, as development increases in the valley, managing your own vehicle here begins to resemble city driving.

TOP ECO-LODGES IN THE CENTRAL VALLEY

FINCA ROSA BLANCA COUNTRY INN, HEREDIA

The hotel on this eight-acre working coffee plantation just outside Heredia is one of just four properties in the country to have achieved the coveted "Five Leaves" status in the Certification for Sustainable Tourism. *(⇨ Certificate of Sustainable Tourism in Chapter 5).* In 2008, it also became Costa Rica's only lodging to receive a perfect score in this regard. In addition to all the amenities you'd expect from one of the Central Valley's most sumptuous accommodations, you can also take Finca Rosa Blanca's unique Sustainability Tour for a behind-the-scenes look at what a hotel can do to be more eco- and community-friendly. What other tour in Costa Rica lets you take in the workings of the laundry room, the solar panels, and the compost pile?

RANCHO NATURALISTA, TURRIALBA

Some 450 species of birds on the property—few lodgings can make such a claim, let alone one so close to the metropolitan area. But the fittingly named Rancho Naturalista near Turrialba has fast become the birding center of the Central Valley. From the bird checklist in the welcome packet in your room, to the resident professional birding guide, to the delightful deck where you can continue to birdwatch even after trekking around the grounds for the day, this is one of Costa Rica's premier locales for birdwatchers of all experience levels.

XANDARI RESORT HOTEL & SPA, ALAJUELA

Xandari is a favorite of honeymooners who might not be aware of its environmental stewardship. The 40-acre property in the hills above Alajuela maintains an active program of recycling and uses on-site, organically grown fruits and vegetables. The hotel is also turning back a portion of its coffee plantation to tree cover, which has been set aside as a nature reserve. Coffee is still cultivated on the remainder of the plantation and ends up in your morning cup, or as part of the coffee-scrub spa treatment.

COMMUNITY OUTREACH

A glance at high schools around the Central Valley reveals a growing number of outdoor eco-themed wall paintings, all part of an ever-growing annual Environmental Mural Contest. The name says it all: students from area schools compete each year to design and create original murals conveying environmental messages.

The works represent combined efforts of schools' art and biology departments, with students devoting an average of four months from the project's start to finish. Many of the murals measure 50 square meters, or around 540 square feet. The competition is designed to foster artistic skills, teamwork, and, of course, environmental awareness among students and faculty who take part.

The contest is directed by the non-profit FUNDECOR foundation, a local non-governmental organization whose objective is to put the brakes on deforestation and promote environmental consciousness. Local businesses support the effort, including a paint company that donates the materials.

THE CENTRAL VALLEY

Updated by Jeffrey Van Fleet

San José sits in a mile-high-ish mountain valley ringed by volcanoes whose ash has fertilized the soil and turned the region into Costa Rica's breadbasket. This is the land that coffee built, and the small cities of the Central Valley exhibit a tidiness and prosperity you don't see in the rest of the country.

For you, the visitor, the valley is chock-full of activities that will keep you occupied for a couple of days. There's no shortage of terrific lodgings out here—everything from family-run boutique hotels to the big international chains are yours for the night.

GETTING HERE

Although Aeropuerto Internacional Juan Santamaría is billed as San José's airport, it sits just outside the city of Alajuela. You can get taxis from the airport to any point in the Central Valley for $8 to $80. On your left, just before exiting the terminal, you'll see a counter where you can hire a taxi. Some hotels arrange pickup.

All points in the western Central Valley can be reached by car. For San Antonio de Belén, Heredia, Alajuela, and points north of San José, turn right at the west end of Paseo Colón onto the Pan-American Highway (Autopista General Cañas). All the attractions in the eastern Central Valley are accessible from San José by driving east on Avenidas 2, then Central, through San Pedro, then following signs from the intersection to Cartago. To get to the Orosi Valley, head straight through Cartago, turn right at the Basílica de Los Angeles, and follow the signs to Paraíso. The road through Cartago and Paraíso continues east to Turrialba.

Buses leave the international airport for Alajuela several times an hour; from Alajuela you can catch buses to Grecia, Sarchí, and San Ramón. Less frequent buses (one to three per hour) serve Heredia. For travel between the airports and Escazú, Cartago, or Turrialba, you have to change buses in San José, which usually means taking a taxi between bus terminals. All buses heading toward San José from Alajuela can drop you off at the airport, but you need to ask the driver when you board, and then remind him again as you draw near to the stop, "*Aeropuerto, por favor*" ("Airport, please").

GETTING AROUND

The best way to get around the Central Valley is by car. Most of the car-rental agencies in San José have offices at or near the airport in Alajuela. They will deliver vehicles to many of the hotels listed in this chapter, except those in Turrialba and the Orosi Valley.

Many visitors never consider taking a local bus to get around, but doing so puts you in close contact with locals—an experience you miss out on if you travel by taxi or tour bus. It's also cheap. If your Spanish and sense of direction are up to snuff and you have the time, give it a shot. Your hotel can help you get to the correct bus stop and a current schedule. Always opt for a taxi at night or when you're in a hurry.

All Central Valley towns have taxis, which usually wait for fares along the central parks. Taxis in Alajuela, Cartago, and Heredia can take you up to Poás, Irazú, and Barva volcanoes, but the trips are quite expensive (about $50). If you don't have a car, the only way to get to Tapantí National Park is to take a cab from Orosi (about $15 each way).

WEST OF SAN JOSÉ

As you drive north or west out of San José, the city's suburbs and industrial zones quickly give way to arable land, much of which is occupied by coffee farms. Within Costa Rica's coffee heartland are plenty of tranquil agricultural towns and two provincial capitals, Alajuela and Heredia. Both cities owe their relative prosperity to the coffee beans cultivated on the fertile lower slopes of the Poás and Barva volcanoes. The upper slopes, too cold for coffee crops, are dedicated to dairy cattle, strawberries, ferns, and flowers, making for markedly different and thoroughly enchanting landscapes along the periphery of the national parks. Because the hills above these small valley towns have some excellent restaurants and lodgings, rural overnights are a good alternative to staying in San José.

ESCAZÚ

5 km/3 mi southwest of San José.

Costa Rica's wealthiest community and the Central Valley's most prestigious address, Escazú nevertheless mixes glamour with tradition, BMWs with oxcarts, Louis Vuitton with burlap produce sacks. As you exit the highway and crest the first gentle hill, you might think you made a wrong turn and ended up in Southern California, but farther up you return to small-town Central America. Narrow roads wind their way up the steep slopes, past postage-stamp coffee fields and lengths of shoulder-to-shoulder, modest houses with tidy gardens and the occasional oxcart parked in the yard. Unfortunately, the area's stream of new developments and high-rises has steadily chipped away at the rural

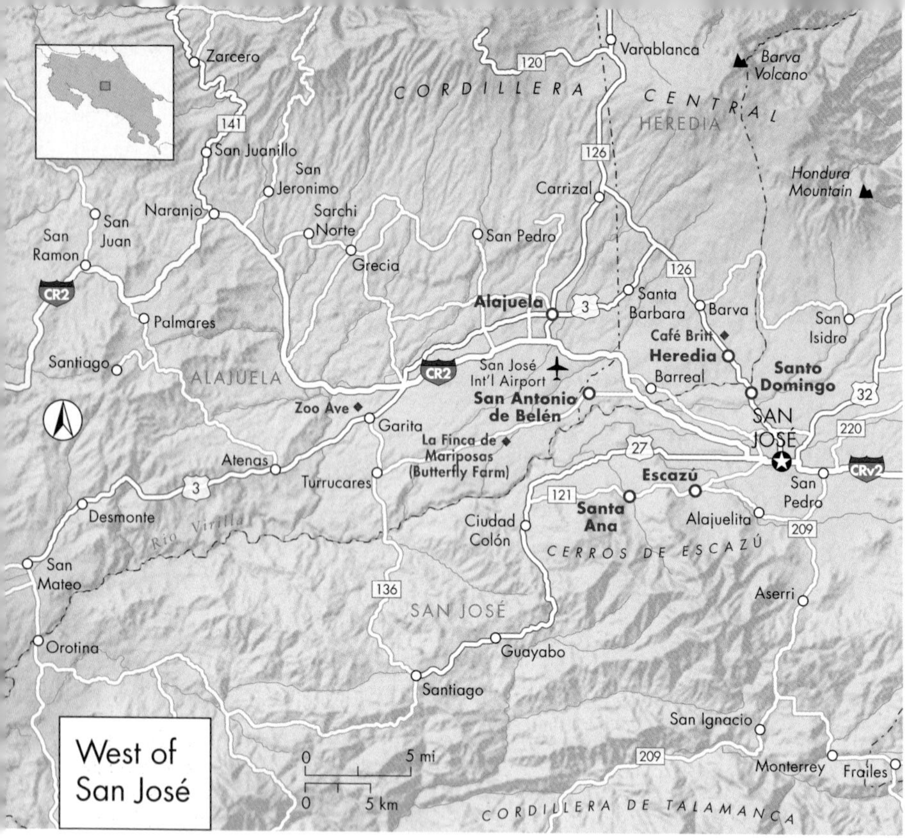

landscape—each year you have to climb higher to find the kind of scene that captured the attention of many a Costa Rican painter in the early 20th century. In their place are plenty of fancy homes and condos, especially in the San Antonio and San Rafael neighborhoods. Escazú's historic church faces a small plaza, surrounded in part by weathered adobe buildings. The town center is several blocks north of the busy road to Santa Ana, which is lined with a growing selection of restaurants, bars, and shops.

GETTING HERE AND AROUND

To drive to Escazú from San José, turn left at the western end of Paseo Colón, which ends at the Parque La Sabana. Take the first right, and get off the highway at the second exit. The off-ramp curves sharply left; follow it about 1 km (½ mi), sticking to the main road, to El Cruce at the bottom of the hill (marked by a large Scotiabank). Continue through the traffic light for San Rafael addresses; turn right for the old road to Santa Ana. The trip takes about 15 minutes. A steady stream of buses for Escazú runs from several stops around Terminal Coca-Cola in San José (✉ *Avdas. 1–3, Cs. 14–16*), with service from 5 AM to 11 PM.

ESSENTIALS

Bank/ATM **Banco Nacional** (✉ *Southwest side of Parque Central* ☎ *2228–0009*). **Banco de Costa Rica ATM** (✉ *North side of church*).

Internet Bagelmen's (✉*San Rafael de Escazú, 500 m southwest of the Trejos Montealegre shopping center* ☎*2228–4460*). **Internet CF** (✉*Northwest corner of Parque Central, upstairs in Plaza Escazú mall* ☎*2289–5706*).

Medical Assistance Farmacia San Miguel (✉*North side of Parque Central* ☎*2228–2339*). **Hospital CIMA** (✉*Next to PriceSmart, just off the highway to Santa Ana* ✥*12 km/7½ mi west of downtown San José* ☎*2208–1000*).

Post Office Correos (✉*100 m north of church*).

Taxis Coopetico (☎*2224–7979*).

HOCUS POCUS

During colonial days, Escazú was dubbed the City of Witches because many native healers lived in the area. Locals say that Escazú is still Costa Rica's most haunted community, home to witches who will tell your fortune or concoct a love potion for a small fee, but you'd be hard-pressed to spot them in the town's busy commercial district. Try a soccer field instead; the city's team is christened Las Brujas ("the witches). You'll see a huge number of witch-on-a-broomstick decals affixed to vehicles here, too.

4

EXPLORING

High in the hills above Escazú is the tiny community of **San Antonio de Escazú,** famous for its annual oxcart festival held the second Sunday of March. The view from here—of nearby San José and distant volcanoes—is impressive by both day and night. If you head higher than San Antonio de Escazú, brace yourself for seemingly vertical roads that wind up into the mountains toward **Pico Blanco,** the highest point in the Escazú Cordillera, which is a half-day hike to ascend. Our preference is **San Miguel,** one peak east. Although you can hike these hills on your own, it is far safer to go with an outfitter. **Aventuras Pico Tours** (☎*2228–2118* 🌐*www.picotours.com*) is based up here. Its Tico owner has scaled some of the world highest summits, and can lead you on a variety of hikes.

WHERE TO EAT

$$ SOUTHERN

Barbecue Los Anonos. For four decades, Costa Ricans have flocked to Los Anonos to enjoy its family-friendly grill fest. The original dining room, a rustic collection of deep booths with wooden benches, has been expanded upon to add a more elegant space decorated with historic photos. The crowd tends toward families on weekend nights, whereas weekdays are busier during lunch, when business executives come for the economical meals. The best bet is the grilled meat, and there is plenty to choose from, including imported U.S. beef and less expensive Tico cuts. Fresh fish, shrimp, and half a dozen salads round out the choices. ✉*400 m west of Los Anonos Bridge* ☎*2228–0180* ▭*AE, D, DC, MC, V* ⊗*Closed Mon.*

$ ITALIAN

Cerros. This San Antonio hills favorite combines smoky thin-crust pizza with the essence of the Central Valley—simple and sincere. Pull up a chair to one of the gingham-covered tables on the semi-enclosed patio, and you have the perfect view of a Costa Rican microcosm. The valley drops down just behind the soccer field and the green-trimmed church across the street, revealing the shimmering panorama of Escazú, Alajuela, and Heredia. The pizza is the main draw, but pastas, meat dishes, and Costa Rican standbys are well represented. ✉*South side of* *soccer field, San Antonio de Escazú* ☎*2228–1831* ▭*No credit cards* ⊙*No lunch weekdays.*

$ SPANISH ✕**El Gaitero.** Generous portions of Spanish tapas and entrées draw diners to this whitewashed adobe house up the hill near San Antonio de Escazú. Wooden-bench tables are distributed along a wraparound porch with views of the Central Valley; inside, settings are arranged in small-to-medium rooms. Antonio and Olga, the passionate Asturian owners, will bring you up to speed with what's best that night and even pull out recipes to share. Presentation isn't the strong suit here: straight-up good food is, as are reasonable prices. Start with a pitcher of sangria and begin sampling; the extensive menu includes dishes such as Spanish omelet. ⊠*Del Cruce de San Antonio and Barrio El Carmen* ✣*100 m east and 50 m south* ☎*2228–1850* ▭*AE, D, DC, MC, V* ⊙*Closed Mon.–Wed.*

$$$ ITALIAN ✕**Restaurante Cerutti.** The diva of the Central Valley's Italian eateries, this little restaurant promises minimalist elegance in a lovely adobe house built in 1817. The extensive menu, focusing on modern Italian cuisine, ranges from roasted scallops with Spanish chorizo to ravioli stuffed with duck and Italian ham. Core dishes are complemented by a variety of selections that change every month or so. No one disputes that the quality of the food is high—with prices to match. ⊠*Southeast corner of El Cruce, San Rafael de Escazú* ☎*2228–9954* ⊕*www.ceruttirestaurante.com* ▭*AE, D, DC, MC, V* ⊙*Closed Tues.*

$$$ INDIAN ✕**Taj Mahal.** This burst of northern Indian flavor is such a rarity in Central America that we can overlook the slightly less-than-factual claim that the restaurant is the isthmus's only such option. Richly swathed in warm fuchsias, red ochres, and golds, the mansion's dining area sprawls through a handful of small, intimate rooms and out to a gazebo in the tree-covered backyard. The price-to-portion ratio is a little high, particularly for North Americans used to good, cheap Indian food, but the sharp tandoori dishes, curries, and *biryanis* (seasoned rice dishes) are a welcome vacation from ubiquitous European and American fare. Vegetarians may swoon at the options. Helpful waiters, in black or maroon traditional Punjabi dress, are frank about recommendations. The restaurant offers free shuttle transport to and from hotels in Escazú, Santa Ana, and San Antonio de Belén. ✣*1 km/½ mi west of Paco mall on old road to Santa Ana* ☎*2228–0980* ▭*AE, D, DC, MC, V* ⊙*Closed Mon.*

WHERE TO STAY

$–$$ **Casa de las Tías.** The gamut of city services is at your doorstep, but you're blissfully apart from them at this tranquil bed-and-breakfast in San Rafael de Escazú. The name means "The Aunts' House," which is appropriate for this yellow house with a front porch and picket fence at the end of a short road. A few old photos of the ladies themselves complete the effect. The rooms and furnishings feel slightly aged, but make up for it in charm, and the large backyard and gardens give the illusion of being far from a major commercial street. **Pros:** tranquility without sacrificing convenience; service that goes the extra mile; excellent breakfast. **Cons:** walls could be a little thicker; slightly dated feel. ⊠*100 m south and 150 m east of El Cruce; turn east just south of*

Costa Rica's oxcarts are folkloric symbols and a common canvas for local artisans.

Restaurante Cerutti ☎ *2289–5517* 🌐 *www.hotels.co.cr/casatias.html* *4 rooms, 1 junior suite* *In-room: no a/c, no TV, Wi-Fi. In-hotel: laundry service, no kids under 12, no-smoking rooms* *AE, D, DC, MC, V* *BP.*

$ **Costa Verde Inn.** When they need to make a city run, many beach-living expats head straight for this quiet B&B on the outskirts of Escazú. Rooms make nice use of local hardwoods and traditional South American art, and the main building serves as a gathering place with a large sitting area, comfortable chairs, and a fireplace. The inn is surrounded by gardens, and at night you can see the lights of San José twinkling to the east, though just three of the rooms take advantage of the view. The inn is at the end of a narrow driveway with an unassuming gate, but you'll see a sign if you've found the right place, so ring the bell. **Pros:** inviting public areas; excellent value. **Cons:** large student groups in summer; can be difficult to find; pool is for plungers, not swimmers. ✉ *From southeast corner of second cemetery (the farthest west), 300 m south* ☎ *2228–4080* 🌐 *www.costaverdeinn.com* *19 rooms, 3 apartments, 3 studios* *In-room: no a/c, kitchen (some), refrigerator. In-hotel: pool* *AE, D, DC, MC, V* *BP.*

$$ **Posada El Quijote.** Perched on a hill in the Bello Horizonte neighborhood, with a great view of the city, this B&B strikes the right balance between a small inn and a private residence. Being here feels like visiting a friend—albeit a friend with great taste. The quiet, homey feel draws low-key, mature travelers. The best view is from the sundeck, just off a spacious living room with a couch, a fireplace, and lots of modern art. The apartments and the two "deluxe" rooms have comparable views. Smaller "standard" rooms overlook the surrounding gardens, and aren't

nearly as nice. The staff is extremely helpful. It's a bit hard to find, so you may want to take a taxi, or call for directions. **Pros:** peaceful, friendly place to spend first or last night; excellent staff. **Cons:** need a car to get around; can be difficult to find. ✉ *Bello Horizonte de Escazú, first street west of Anonos Bridge* ✣ *1 km/½ mi up hill* ☎ *2289–8401* 🌐 *www.quijote.co.cr* *8 rooms, 2 apartments* *In-room: no a/c (some). In-hotel: laundry service, Wi-Fi, some pets allowed* *AE, D, DC, MC, V* *BP.*

PICNIC TIME

Escazú's Saturday-morning farmers' market makes a terrific place to stock up on some fresh fruit and vegetables if you're preparing a do-it-yourself lunch or just want to snack. Vendors start lining the street just north of the church about dawn, and things begin to wind down by late morning.

NIGHTLIFE

Escazú is the Central Valley's hot spot for nightlife—many Josefinos head here for the restaurants, bars, and dance clubs that cater to a young, cell phone–toting crowd. The highest concentration of nightspots is in the shopping center called **Trejos Montealegre** (✉ *On your left as you enter Escazú, off the highway between San José and Ciudad Colón*). One of the more popular watering holes with the under-30 set is **Henry's Beach Cafe** (✉ *500 m west of El Cruce, Plaza San Rafael, 2nd fl.* ☎ *2289–6250*), which features televised sports by day, varied music by night, and an islands decor of beach paintings and surfboards. Costa Ricans refer to this style of bar as an "American bar," which is fairly accurate. A young, sophisticated crowd keeps **Il Panino** (✉ *Centro Comercial Paco* ☎ *2228–3126* 🌐 *www.jazzcafecostarica.com* *$6–$8* *Closed Sun.*) buzzing. It's a great place to start or end an evening. Music fans on the west side of town cheered the 2008 opening of **Jazz Café Escazú** (✉ *Next to Confort Suizo, across the highway from Hospital Cima; first exit after the toll booths* ☎ *2288–4740* 🌐 *www.jazzcafecostarica.com* *$6–$8* *Closed Sun.*). The boxy club hosts an eclectic live-music lineup similar to that of its popular sister venue in San Pedro and has double the capacity. The high-end **Itskatzú** complex, 1 km (½ mi) east of Multiplaza, has a number of restaurants and bars ranging from the low-brow (Hooters) to sophisticated sushi and live Cuban music.

SHOPPING

★ If you get the shopping bug and absolutely must visit a mall while on vacation, Escazú is the place to do it. **Multiplaza,** on the south side of the Autopista Próspero Fernández, approximately 5 km (3 mi) west of San José, is a big, luxurious one. **Biesanz Woodworks** (✉ *Bello Horizonte, 800 m south of Escuela Bello Horizonte* ☎ *2289–4337* 🌐 *www.biesanz.com*) is where local craftsmen ply their trade and expat artist Barry Biesanz creates unique, world-class items from Costa Rican hardwoods, which are turned (a form of woodworking) on-site. It's difficult to find, so take a taxi or call for directions from your hotel.

SANTA ANA

17 km/10 mi southwest of San José.

As metro development, with the accompanying condos and shopping malls, marches westward, it's hard to tell where Escazú ends and the once-tranquil agricultural community of Santa Ana begins. But the town center, with its rugged stone church surrounded by homes and businesses, has changed little in the past decade. The church, which was built between 1870 and 1880, has a Spanish-tile roof, carved wooden doors, and two pre-Columbian stone spheres flanking its entrance. Its rustic interior—bare wooden pillars and beams and black iron lamps—seems appropriate for an area with a tradition of ranching. Because it is warmer and drier than the towns to the east, Santa Ana is one of the few Central Valley towns that doesn't have a good climate for coffee—it is Costa Rica's onion capital, however—and is instead surrounded by pastures and patches of forest; it isn't unusual to see men on horseback here.

GETTING HERE AND AROUND

From San José, turn left at the western end of Paseo Colón, which ends at the Parque La Sabana. Take the first right, and get on the highway. Get off at the sixth exit; bear left at the flashing red lights, winding past roadside ceramics and vegetable stands before hitting the town center, about 2 km (1 mi) from the highway. The trip takes about 25 minutes. Blue buses to Santa Ana leave from San José's Terminal Coca-Cola every eight minutes. To get to places along the Autopista Próspero Fernández or Piedades, take buses marked "Pista" or "Multiplaza." Those marked "Calle Vieja" leave every 15 minutes and pass through Escazú on the old road to Santa Ana. Buses run from 5 AM to 11 PM.

SANTA ANA ESSENTIALS

Bank/ATM Banco de Costa Rica (✉ *100 m west of church* ☎ *2203–4281*). **Banco Popular** (✉ *Southwest corner of church* ☎ *2203–7979*). **Banco Nacional** (✉ *Northwest corner of church* ☎ *2282–2479*).

Internet Internet Café El Sol (✉ *Southwest corner of church, across from Banco Popular* ☎ *2282–8059*).

Medical Assistance Farmacia Sucre (✉ *25 m south of church* ☎ *2282–1296*).

Post Office Correos (✉ *Northwest corner of church*).

WHERE TO EAT & STAY

$$$ ECLECTIC ✕ **Bacchus.** Take a Peruvian chef trained in France and an Italian owner, and you get Bacchus, a welcome addition to the local dining scene. The cuisine is a mix of French and Italian dishes such as duck breast in a port sauce, baked mushroom-and-polenta ragout, and a variety of pizzas. Modern art decorates the simple but elegant interior, and outdoor seating is available. An extensive wine list and reasonable prices make it a great pick for dinner. ✉ *200 m east and 100 m north of church* ☎ *2282–5441* ▭ *AE, D, DC, MC, V* ⊙ *Closed Mon.*

$ MEXICAN ✕ **Tex Mex.** This Gringo favorite serves a fairly standard Mexican menu—tacos, burritos, quesadillas, and so on—plus a few grilled meat items, such as the Argentinean *churrasco* (a thick tenderloin cut), complete

CLOSE UP

Speaking Costa Rican

Spanish in Costa Rica tends to be localized. This is a land where eloquent speech and creative verbal expression are highly valued. For example, here the response to a "thank-you" is the gracious, uniquely Tico "**Cons:** *mucho gusto*" ("With much pleasure") instead of *"De nada"* ("It's nothing"), which is used in much of Latin America. In other cases, informality is preferred: the conventional *Señor* and *Señora*, for example, are eschewed in favor of the more egalitarian *Don* and *Doña*, used before a first name. Even President Oscar Arias is called "Don Oscar." Exercise caution when selecting from the list below, however. Although young Costa Rican men address everyone as *maje* (dude), you'll get a withering look if you, a visitor, follow suit.

adios good-bye; but also used as "hello" in rural areas
agarrar de maje to pull someone's leg
birra beer
brete work
cachos shoes
chunche any thingamajig
clavar el pico to fall asleep
estar de chicha to be angry
estar de goma to have a hangover
harina money
jupa head
macho, macha a person with blond hair
maje buddy, dude, mate
mamá de Tarzán know-it-all
maría a woman's name; also a taxi meter
matar la culebra to waste time
montón a lot
paño towel
pelo de gato cat hair; or fine, misty rain that falls during December
peso colón
pinche a tight-fisted person
ponerse hasta la mecha to get drunk
porfa please
pura vida fantastic, great
rojo red; also a 1,000-colón note
soda an inexpensive local restaurant
torta a big mistake or error
tuanis cool
tucán toucan; also a 5,000-colón note
upe anyone home?
Con mucho gusto used in response to "thank you" instead of "de nada"
Muy bien, gracias a Dios very well, thank goodness
Muy bien, por dicha very well, luckily
Si Dios quiere God willing

with *chimichurri* (diced garlic and parsley in olive oil). There are about two dozen *bocas* (appetizers), which are mostly smaller versions of entrée items. The enchiladas may not be as good as what you find in San Antonio, but the setting is pleasant, with a yard shaded by massive trees. Seating is on a covered brick patio or in an adjacent dining area enclosed by windows, for cool nights. ✉ *50 m northeast of church* ☎ *2282–6342* ▭ *AE, D, DC, MC, V* ⊗ *Closed Mon.*

$$$ ★ **Alta.** The view from this colonial-style hotel perched on a hillside above Santa Ana is impressive, but then, so is the hotel. The sloping stairway entrance lined with tall columns and greenery is reminiscent of a narrow street in southern Spain, an effect reinforced by the barrel-tile roof and ochre-stucco walls; the narrow hallways feel like an old castle. Guest rooms are spacious, with colonial-style furniture and bathrooms with hand-painted tiles; ask for one on the fourth or fifth floor to take advantage of the view. The restaurant, La Luz ($$$), has a hardwood

floor, a beamed ceiling, and plenty of windows for admiring the distant hills and the pool and gardens below. The eclectic and unusual menu includes baked goat cheese salad, macadamia-encrusted fish, and Moroccan chicken. **Pros:** classy service; panoramic views; excellent value for price. **Cons:** lower-floor rooms lose out on the view; little to do within walking distance. *2½ km/1½ mi west of Paco shopping center, on old road between Santa Ana and Escazú, Alto de las Palomas 2282–4160, 888/388–2582 in U.S. www.thealtahotel.com 18 rooms, 5 suites In-room: safe, Internet, Wi-Fi. In-hotel: restaurant, pool, gym, laundry service AE, D, DC, MC, V CP.*

$$ **Hotel Posada Canal Grande.** This small Italian-owned hotel tucked into the hills to the west of Santa Ana is a great value. Each room is different, and most have wicker beds. Second-floor rooms, each with a balcony over the pool, have excellent views, but the first-floor rooms aren't bad either. Two four-poster beds are placed in the shade by the pool, just to lounge on. On a clear day you can see the Gulf of Nicoya to the west. Poolside chatter is in French, Spanish, and German as much as it is in English. **Pros:** great value; international feel. **Cons:** spartan bathrooms; dining options limited. *On the Próspero Fernández highway to Ciudad Colón, 500 m north of Piedades de Santa Ana bus terminal 2282–4089 www.hotelcanalgrande.com 12 rooms In-room: no a/c, safe, refrigerator, Wi-Fi. In-hotel: restaurant, bar, pool, laundry service, Internet terminal AE, D, DC, MC, V CP.*

4

SHOPPING

★ Large glazed pots with ornate decorations that range from traditional patterns to modern motifs are the specialties at **Cerámica Las Palomas** (*Old road to Santa Ana, opposite Alta Hotel 2282–7001*). Flowerpots and lamps are also common works, and the staff will eagerly show you the production process, from raw clay to art.

GOLF

Although it sits inside a residential complex of the same name, **Valle del Sol** (*1,700 m west of HSBC 2282–9222 www.valledelsol.com $94 for 18 holes with cart Mon. 8–6, Tues.–Sun. 6:30–6*) is Costa Rica's preeminent public golf course. Call to reserve tee times at this 7,000-yard, par 72, 18-hole course. Collared shirts and blouses are required; denim shorts and trousers are prohibited.

NORTH OF SAN JOSÉ

As you set out from San José to explore the towns to the north, you first encounter nothing but asphalt, hotels, and malls—not especially scenic. Santo Domingo and San Antonio de Belén blend into the outskirts of San José, and it's only when you get to the heart of these small towns that you feel you've arrived in Central America. Farther north, Alajuela and Heredia are bustling provincial capitals with charismatic central parks. Throughout this area, tucked into the urban scenery and lining volcanic slopes, are fields of that great Costa Rican staple, coffee.

SAN ANTONIO DE BELÉN

17 km/10 mi northwest of San José.

San Antonio de Belén has little to offer visitors but its rural charm and proximity to the international airport. The latter led developers to build several of the San José area's biggest hotels here. The town also lies on the route of entry for Alajuela's Butterfly Farm, and it's a convenient departure point for trips to the western Central Valley, Pacific coast, and northern region. If you stay at the Marriott, you likely won't even see the town, just the busy highway between San José and Alajuela.

GETTING HERE AND AROUND

From San José, turn right at the west end of Paseo Colón onto the Pan-American Highway (Carretera General Cañas). The San Antonio de Belén exit is at an overpass 6 km (4 mi) west of the Heredia exit, by the Real Cariari Mall. Turn left at the first intersection, cross over the highway, and continue 1 km (½ mi) to the forced right turn, driving 1½ km (1 mi) to the center of town. San Antonio is only 10 minutes from the airport.

SAN ANTONIO DE BELÉN ESSENTIALS

Bank/ATM Banco de Costa Rica (✉ *50 m north of rear of church* ☎ *2239–1149*). **BAC San José ATM** (✉ *200 m west of soccer field*).

Internet Belén Web Café (✉ *West end of soccer field* ☎ *2239–4181*).

Medical Assistance Farmacia Sucre (✉ *North side of church* ☎ *2239–3485*).

Post Office Correos (✉ *3 blocks west and 25 m north of church*).

Taxis Asotaxis Belén (☎ *2293–4712*).

WHERE TO STAY

$$$–$$$$ **Doubletree by Hilton Cariari.** This low-rise hotel (formerly the Meliá Cariari, and many still refer to it by that name) was the metro area's original luxury hotel, and it remains popular for its excellent service and out-of-town location. Just off the busy General Cañas Highway, about halfway between San José and the international airport, the Cariari is surrounded by thick vegetation that buffers it from traffic noise. When Doubletree by Hilton took over in 2008, it began an ambitious renovation project, revamping a number of rooms, replacing all beds, and generally sprucing the place up. Spacious, carpeted guest rooms in back overlook the pool area. The relaxed poolside bar, with cane chairs and colorful tablecloths, and nearby casino, are popular spots. Overall, it feels slightly more low-key and less grandiose than the nearby Marriott. **Pros:** resort experience close to both San José and the airport; kid-friendly. **Cons:** tricky car access; close to busy highway. ✉ *Autopista General Cañas, ½ km/¼ mi east of intersection for San Antonio de Belén, Cariari, San Antonio de Belén* ☎ *2239–0022, 800/222–8733 in North America* 🌐 *www.cariarisanjose.doubletree.com* *198 rooms, 24 suites* *In-room: safe, Wi-Fi. In-hotel: 2 restaurants, bars, pool, gym, laundry service, parking (free), no-smoking rooms* 💳 *AE, D, DC, MC, V.*

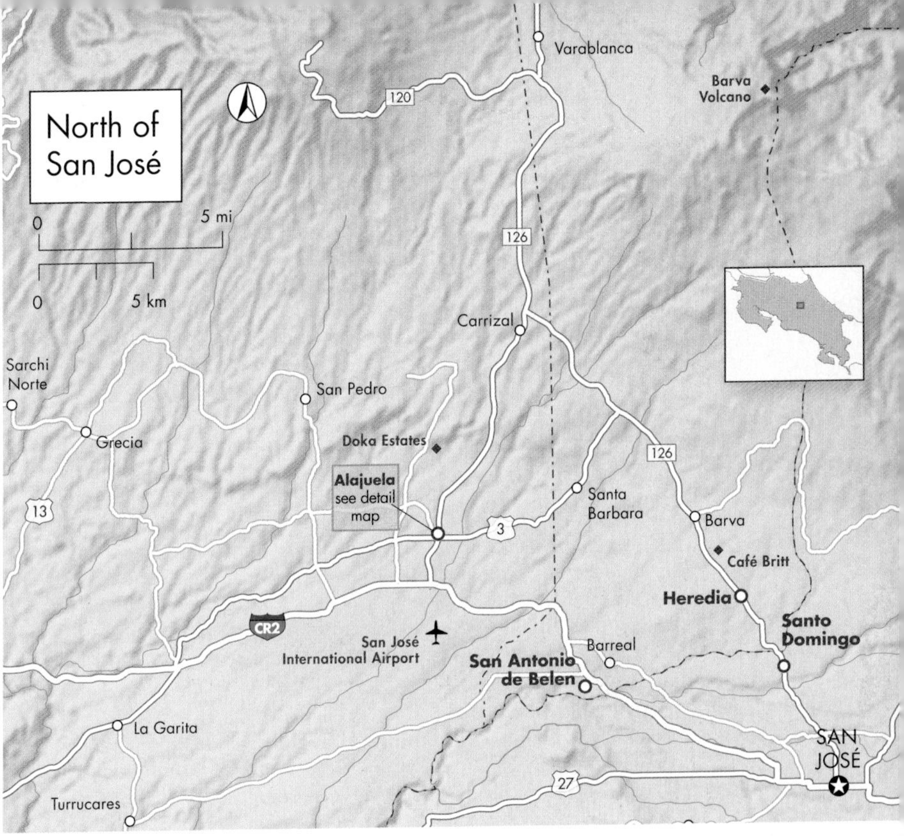

$$–$$$ **El Rodeo.** This quiet hotel bills itself as a "country hotel," though this is more in image than fact—El Rodeo's proximity to the airport and major business parks is the real draw. Spacious rooms, most with polished hardwood floors, high ceilings, and narrow balconies, overlook small gardens and rooms in the adjacent building. An open-air lounge on the second floor has a pool table and wicker furniture. The new Grand Café serves breakfast each morning. The large wooden El Rodeo Steakhouse Restaurant ($$) in front of the hotel is quite popular with Ticos, who pack it on weekends. Decorated with saddles, steer skulls, and other ranching paraphernalia, the restaurant serves an array of grilled meats, from the Argentinean churrascos to T-bones, as well as several fish and shrimp dishes. **Pros:** proximity to airport; newly renovated facilities; spacious rooms. **Cons:** generic feel. ✉ *Road to Santa Ana* ✢ *2 km/1 mi east of Parque Central* ☎ *2293–3909* 🌐 *www.elrodeohotel.com* *26 rooms, 3 suites* *In-room: safe, refrigerator (some), Wi-Fi. In-hotel: restaurant, tennis court, pool, laundry service, Internet terminal* *AE, D, DC, MC, V* *BP.*

$$$$ ★ **Marriott Costa Rica Hotel.** The stately Marriott offers comprehensive luxury close to the airport. Towering over a coffee plantation west of San José, the thick columns, wide arches, and central courtyard are re-creations straight out of the 16th century, and hand-painted tiles and abundant antiques complete the historic appearance. Guest rooms are more contemporary, but they're elegant enough, with hardwood furniture. Some have sliding glass doors that open onto tiny balconies; new rooms feature flat-screen TVs. The place is always abuzz with upscale tourists, business travelers, and participants in the many events that take place at the facilities. **Pros:** excellent service; lavish grounds; close to airport. **Cons:** tendency to nickel-and-dime guests; impersonal feel. ✣ *¾ km/½ mi west of Bridgestone/Firestone, off Autopista General Cañas* ☎ *2298–0000, 800/236–2427 in North America* 🌐 *www.marriott.com* *291 rooms, 9 suites* *In-room: safe, refrigerator, Internet. In-hotel: 4 restaurants, bar, tennis courts, pools, gym, laundry service, Internet terminal, Wi-Fi, parking (free)* ▭ *AE, D, DC, MC, V* *EP.*

ALAJUELA

20 km/13 mi northwest of San José.

Because of its proximity to the international airport (5–10 minutes away) many travelers spend their first or last night in or near Alajuela, but the beauty of the surrounding countryside persuades some to stay longer. Alajuela is Costa Rica's second–most populated city, and a mere 30-minute bus ride from the capital, but it has a decidedly provincial air compared with San José. Architecturally, it differs little from the bulk of Costa Rican towns: it's a grid of low-rise structures painted in dull pastel colors.

GETTING HERE AND AROUND

To reach Alajuela, follow directions to San Antonio de Belén *(above)*. Continue west on the highway past the San Antonio turnoff and turn right at the airport. Buses travel between San José (✉ *Avda. 2, Cs. 12–14, opposite the north side of Parque La Merced*), the airport, and Alajuela, and run every five minutes from 4:40 AM to 10:30 PM The bus stop in Alajuela is 400 meters west, 25 meters north of the central park *(✉ C. 3 and Avda. 1)*. Buses leave San José for Zoo Ave from La Merced church (✉ *C. 14 and Avda. 4*) daily at 8, 9, 10, 11 AM, and noon, returning on the hour from 10 AM to 3 PM.

ALAJUELA ESSENTIALS

Bank/ATM Banco de Costa Rica (✉ *Southwest corner of Parque Central* ☎ *2440–9039*). **Banco Nacional** (✉ *West side of Parque Central* ☎ *2441–0373*).

Hospital Hospital San Rafael (✣ *1 km/½ mi northeast of airport, on main road to Alajuela* ☎ *2436–1001*).

Internet Internet Inter@ctivo (✉ *In front of BAC San José bank, 100 m north of Parque Central* ☎ *2431–1984*).

Medical Assistance Farmacia Chavarría (✉ *Southwest corner of Parque Central* ☎ *2441–1231*). **Farmacia Catedral** (✉ *Northeast corner of Parque Central* ☎ *2441–3555*).

Post Office Correos (✉ *200 m north and 100 m east of Parque Central*).

Taxis Cootaxa (☎ *2443–3030*).

4

EXPLORING

Royal palms and massive mango trees fill the **Parque Central** (✉ *C. Central, Avdas. 1–Central*), which also has a lovely fountain imported from Glasgow and concrete benches where locals gather to chat. Surrounding the plaza is an odd mix of charming old buildings and sterile concrete boxes, including a somewhat incongruous McDonald's.

The large, neoclassical **Alajuela Cathedral** (✉ *C. Central, Avdas. 1–Central* ☎ *2443–2928*) has columns topped by interesting capitals decorated with local agricultural motifs, and a striking red metal dome. The interior is spacious but rather plain, except for the ornate cupola above the altar. It's open daily 5 AM–6 PM.

Alajuela was the birthplace of Juan Santamaría, the national hero who lost his life in a battle against the mercenary army of U.S. adventurer William Walker when the latter invaded Costa Rica in 1856. The **Parque Juan Santamaría** (✉ *C. Central and Avda. 2*) has a statue of the young Santamaría. After a 2005 restoration, Juan should keep his youthful good looks for years to come—which, sadly, is more than can be said for the abandoned-looking, weedy concrete lot he stands on.

Juan Santamaría's heroic deeds are celebrated in the **Juan Santamaría Museum** (Museo Juan Santamaría) housed in the old jail, one block north of Parque Central. It's worth a short look if you have the time; Santamaría's story is an interesting one. ✉ *Avda. 3, Cs. Central–2* ☎ *2441–4775* 🎟 *Free* ⏲ *Tues.–Sun. 10–5:30.*

Spread over the lush grounds of **Zoo Ave** is a collection of large cages holding toucans, hawks, and parrots (the macaws range free), not to mention crocodiles, caimans, a boa constrictor, turtles, monkeys, wild cats, and other interesting critters. The zoo, the best in Costa Rica, runs a breeding project for rare and endangered birds, all of which are destined for eventual release. It has 115 bird species, including such rare ones as the quetzal, fiery-billed aracari, several types of eagles, and even ostriches. An impressive mural at the back of the facility shows Costa Rica's 850 bird species painted to scale. ✉ *La Garita de Alajuela* ✥ *Head west from Alajuela center past cemetery, turn left after stone church in Barrio San José, continue on 2 km/1 mi; or head west of Pan-American Hwy. to Atenas exit, then turn right* ☎ *2433–8989* 🌐 *www.zooave.com* 🎟 *$15* ⏲ *Daily 9–5.*

★ Observe and photograph butterflies up close at **The Butterfly Farm** *(La Finca de Mariposas)*. The farm's several microclimates keep comfortable some 40 species of tropical butterflies. Come when it's sunny if you can—they don't flutter around when it rains. This is the original butterfly farm, but there are other butterfly gardens near Volcán Poás at La Paz Waterfall Gardens and in Monteverde. In 2004 the museum launched an annual mural contest, turning not only its own buildings but surrounding corner stores and houses into canvases for talented Costa Rican artists. You can get here via tours from San José that depart from the capital at 7:20, 10, and 2. ✥ *From San José, turn south (left) at the intersection just past Real Cariari Mall, follow the road to the north side of the church of San Antonio de Belén, take a left at the corner, then follow the butterfly signs* ☎ *2438–0400* 🌐 *www.butterfly*

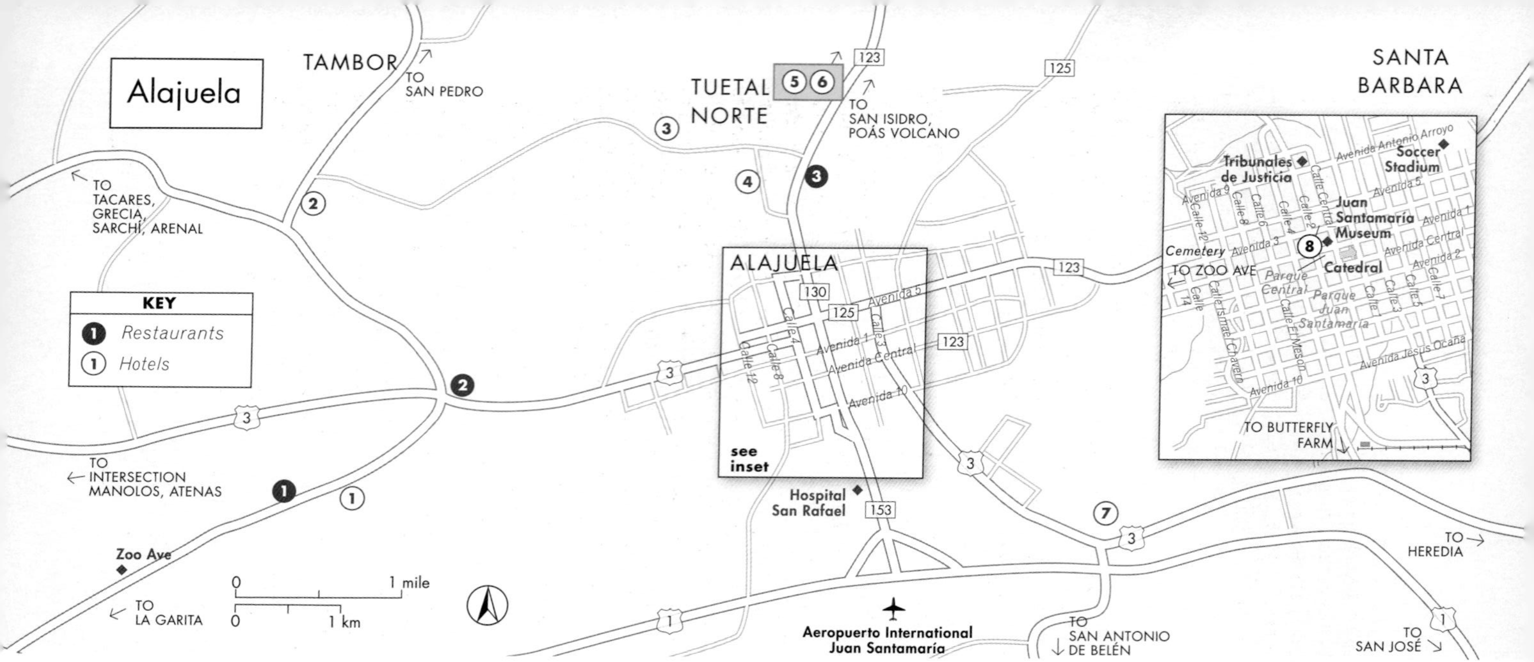

Restaurants ▼

Bar y Restaurante El Mirador **3**
Delicias de Mi Tierra **1**
La Princesa Marina **2**

Hotels ▼

Buena Vista Hotel **5**
Hampton Inn & Suites Airport–San José **7**
Hotel La Rosa de América **1**
Hotel Los Volcanes **8**
Orquideas Inn **2**
Pura Vida Hotel **4**
Siempreverde B&B **6**
Xandari Resort Hotel & Spa **3**

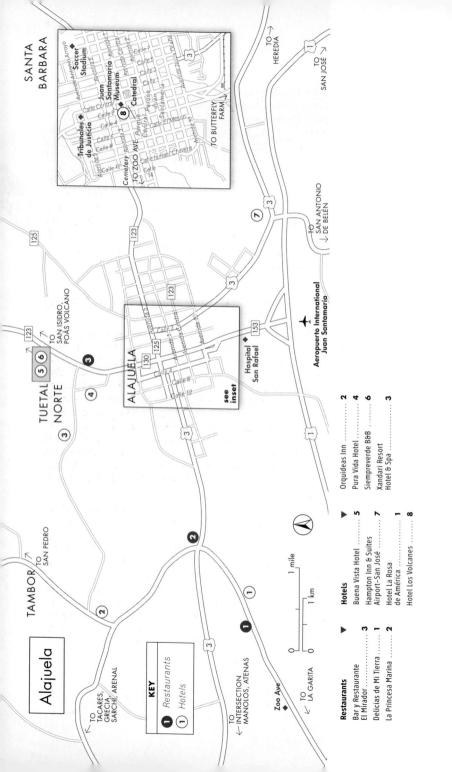

CLOSE UP

A National Hero

When the Costa Ricans drove U.S. invader Walker's army from their country, in 1856, they chased his troops to Rivas, Nicaragua. The army of filibusters took refuge in a wooden fort. Juan Santamaría, a poor, 24-year-old drummer with a militia from Alajuela, volunteered to burn it down to drive them out. Legend says that Santamaría ran toward the fort carrying a torch, and that although he was shot repeatedly, he managed to throw it and to burn the fort down. His bravery wasn't recognized at the time, probably because of his modest origins, but in 1891 a statue depicting a strong and handsome soldier carrying a torch was placed in Alajuela, thus immortalizing Santamaría. For this occasion, Ruben Darío, the great Nicaraguan writer, dedicated a poem to him. The entire account may be apocryphal; some historians doubt there ever *was* such a person. But don't tell that to the average Tico. April 11 is now a national holiday in Costa Rica, called Juan Santamaría Day, which celebrates the Costa Rican victory at the Battle of Rivas.

farm.co.cr *$15, $25 with transportation from San José* *Daily 9–5.*

★ Considering the amount of coffee you'll drive past in the Central Valley, you might want to devote an hour or so of your vacation to learning about the crop's production. **Doka Estate,** a working coffee plantation for more than 70 years, offers a comprehensive tour that takes you through the fields, shows you how the fruit is processed and the beans are dried, and lets you sample the local brew. The best time to take this tour is during the October-to-February picking season. *10 km/6 mi north of Alajuela's Tribunales de Justicia; turn left at San Isidro and continue 6 km/4 mi, follow signs, San Luis de Sabanilla* *2449–5152, 888/946–3652 in North America* *www.dokaestate.com* *$16; transportation from San José, Alajuela, Heredia, Escazú, or San Antonio available* *Tours: daily at 9, 10, 11, 1:30, 2:30, and 3:30; weekends last tour at 2:30.*

EN ROUTE

If you head straight through Alajuela, with the Parque Central on your right, you'll be on the road to Poás Volcano; you should pass the Tribunales de Justicia (the county courthouse) on your right as you leave town. If you turn left upon reaching the Parque Central, and pass the town cemetery on your right, you'll be on the old road to Grecia. About 3 km (2 mi) northwest of town on that road, you'll come upon an old concrete church on the right, which marks your arrival in Barrio San José, a satellite community of Alajuela. A left turn after the church will take you to a lovely rural area called **La Garita** (the Guardhouse), from which the road continues west to Atenas and the Central Pacific beaches. La Garita is a popular weekend destination for Tico families, who head here for the abundant restaurants.

WHERE TO EAT

$$ ECLECTIC **Bar y Restaurante El Mirador.** Perched on a ridge several miles north of town, El Mirador has a sweeping view of the Central Valley that is impressive by day but more beautiful at dusk and night when the

basin is filled with twinkling lights. Get a window table in the dining room, or one on the adjacent porch if it isn't too cool. The menu, which includes *lomito* (tenderloin) and *corvina* (sea bass) served with various sauces, and several shrimp or chicken dishes, plays second fiddle to the view. You could just stop in around sunset for drinks and appetizers. Free transportation from most Alajuela hotels is sometimes available. There are at least two other restaurants nearby with similar names and views—this one is on the main road, close to the Buena Vista Hotel. ✉ *Road to Poás* ✣ *5 km/3 mi north of Tribunales de Justicia* ☎ *2441–9347* ✍ *Reservations essential weekends* ▭ *MC, V.*

¢ COSTA RICAN ✕ **Delicias de Mi Tierra.** A string of típico restaurants lines this road, but the "Delights of My Land" is our favorite. Tasty and traditional Tico favorites are served here: *pozol* (corn-and-pork soup), *casado campesino* (stewed beef with rice, beans, corn, potatoes, and plantains), and *chorreada con natilla* (a corn-bread pancake with sour cream). Long wooden tables and benches are surrounded by cane walls, decorative oxcart wheels, dried gourds, and tropical plants—the kind of decor trying so hard to be traditional that it's anything but. Ordering a few *entraditas* (appetizers) is a good way to sample dishes, as is the *parrillada de campo* (country barbecue), a platter with grilled chicken, beef, pork, rice, beans, fried plantains, and salad, or the larger *fiesta de gallos,* a mixed platter of corn tortillas with various fillings. There are also cheap but hearty breakfasts. Get here early for dinner, as closing time is 8 PM. ✣ *1½ km/1 mi west of the Barrio San José church* ☎ *2433–8536* ▭ *AE, D, DC, MC, V.*

$ SEAFOOD ✕ **La Princesa Marina.** This large open-air eatery (part of a chain) at the intersection of the old Alajuela–Grecia road and the road to La Garita is popular with Ticos, who pack it on weekends to feast on inexpensive seafood. The selection is vast, with 10 types of fish, shrimp, or octopus ceviche, fish fillets served with various sauces, three sizes of shrimp prepared a dozen ways, whole fried fish, lobster tails, and several *mariscadas* (mixed seafood plates). Pastas, rice dishes, beef, and chicken are some other choices, but the seafood is your best bet. The decor is utilitarian—bare tables, ceiling fans, and dividers of potted plants separating the sections—but you avoid that feeling of being in a contrived tourist venue. ✉ *Barrio San José, north of church* ☎ *2433–7117* ▭ *AE, D, DC, MC, V.*

WHERE TO STAY

$$ **Buena Vista Hotel.** Perched high above Alajuela, this hotel's superb staff makes up for the somewhat dated, uninspired decor. It does have the "good view" it is named for, but few of its rooms share in that vista, which is best appreciated from the back lawn. Three balcony rooms on the second floor in back have decent views of the Central Valley, but even better are the views of Poás Volcano from the three rooms above the lobby. Most rooms, however, overlook the lawns or pool area. They are fairly standard—carpeted and sparsely decorated, with small baths and TVs—with none of the pizzazz of similarly priced options. The restaurant behind the lobby serves international dishes and grilled items. **Pros:** excellent service; family friendly. **Cons:** uninspired ambience; mediocre restaurant; farther from the airport than other options.

The Alajuela Cathedral's painted domed cupola was rebuilt after the 1991 earthquake.

6 km/4 mi north of Alajuela's Tribunales de Justicia on road to Poás 2442–8595, 800/506–2304 in U.S. www.hotelbuenavistacr.com 11 rooms, 4 junior suites, 9 deluxe suites, 1 master suite In-room: no a/c, no phone. In-hotel: restaurant, bar, pool, Wi-Fi, no-smoking rooms AE, MC, V CP

$$$ **Hampton Inn & Suites Airport-San José.** A longtime favorite for first-night and last-night stays, this U.S. chain outlet lets you ease into and ease out of Costa Rica in familiar surroundings. Closer to the airport you cannot get: it's just across the highway. **Pros:** airport proximity; U.S. amenities. **Cons:** some noise from planes in the evening; sameness of a chain hotel. *Blvd. del Aeropuerto 2442–3320, 800/426–7866 in North America www.hamptoninncostarica.com 100 rooms In-room: refrigerator (some), Internet. In-hotel: restaurant, pool, gym, Internet terminal, Wi-Fi, no-smoking rooms AE, D, DC, MC, V*

$ **Hotel La Rosa de América.** This small hotel tucked off the road to La Garita is a simple and relaxed place to unwind. The Canadian owners add a welcoming energy and a personalized touch to a place that would otherwise be simply serviceable. There are six buildings, most divided into two units, arranged around the pool and gardens. The white-wall rooms are simple, but it's a quiet place to sleep. Calling ahead for directions is a good idea, but once you're here, you'll have easy access to nearby restaurants and Zoo Ave. All rooms here are nonsmoking. **Pros:** great for families; helpful owners; close to a number of restaurants. **Cons:** lacks flair of other options in this price range; should have car to stay here. *1 km/½ mi east of Zoo Ave 2433–2741 or 2433–2455 www.larosadeamerica.com 12 rooms In-room: no*

The verdant Central Valley is Costa Rica's bread basket.

a/c, no phone, safe. In-hotel: pool, laundry service, Internet, no-smoking rooms ▭*AE, D, DC, MC, V* ¶*BP.*

¢–$ **Hotel Los Volcanes.** Budget travelers looking for airport proximity will find this urban oasis an excellent value. Descendants of the Catalan family that thrived in this heritage house in 1920 still live next door, and historic photos of the mansion in its heyday line the earth-tone walls inside. The spacious rooms have low-slung, wide beds that make the ceilings seem sky-high—but avoid the room next to the washer and dryer. Breakfast is served in a courtyard shaded by a fig tree. Plenty of restaurants are within walking distance, the airport is a 10-minute taxi ride away, and just a few blocks away is the bus stop for La Garita, Poás, and most destinations in central and northwest Costa Rica. **Pros:** airport proximity; good value; historic ambience. **Cons:** some rooms are noisy; no views. ✉*Avda. 3, Cs. 2–Central, or 100 m north, 25 m east of the northwest corner of Parque Central, across from the Juan Santamaría Museum* ☎*2441–0525* ⊕*www.hotellosvolcanes.com* *11 rooms, 7 with bath* *In-room: no a/c (some), safe (some), Internet, Wi-Fi. In-hotel: laundry service, no-smoking rooms* ▭*MC, V* ¶*BP.*

$$ **Orquideas Inn.** A favorite with young couples and families, the friendly Orquideas proves that affordable does not have to equal generic. From a classy Spanish-style main building to a bar dedicated to Marilyn Monroe, this place has style. Deluxe rooms, on a hill with a view of three volcanoes, are spacious, with bamboo furniture, but can smell a bit musty. Smaller rooms have terra-cotta tile floors and Guatemalan fabrics that have seen better days; those on the garden side are quieter, and worth the extra $10. A sumptuous breakfast buffet is served on the bar's patio. The restaurant's ($$) eclectic selection ranges from

straightforward Costa Rican *cuisine* to over-the-top presentations (ceviche served in a half coconut, for one) that have to be seen (and tasted) to be believed. **Pros:** spirited environment; great for first or last night; excellent service. **Cons:** rooms are ready for a face-lift; roadside rooms noisy. *2½ km/1½ mi northwest of the Princesa Marina 2433–9346 www.orquideasinn.com 20 rooms, 6 suites In-room: safe, Wi-Fi. In-hotel: restaurant, bar, pool, laundry service AE, D, DC, MC, V BP.*

$$ ★ **Pura Vida Hotel.** Extremely well-informed, helpful owners and proximity to the airport (15 minutes) make this a good place to begin and end a trip. Thanks to its location on a ridge north of town, several of this hotel's rooms have views of Poás Volcano, and all of them offer tranquility and abundant birdsong. The two rooms in the main house have the best views, but *casitas* (little houses) scattered around the large garden offer more privacy. Bright and cheery bungalows have small terraces with chairs where guests, typically well traveled, lounge. Continental breakfasts and delicious dinners (by reservation) are served on a covered terrace behind the house. Ask about their books-for-schools program. **Pros:** owners active in the local community; stellar breakfast. **Cons:** large dogs may turn off those with less-than-fuzzy feelings for animals; stairs to climb. *Tuetal 2 km/1 mi north of Tribunales de Justicia; veer left at Y 2430–2929 www.puravidahotel.com 2 rooms, 4 bungalows In-room: no a/c, no phone, no TV. In-hotel: restaurant, laundry service, Internet, no-smoking rooms AE, D, DC, MC, V CP.*

$–$$ **Siempreverde B&B.** A night at this isolated B&B in the heart of a coffee plantation might be as close as you'll ever come to being a coffee farmer, or to truly getting away from it all. The attractive wooden house has seven sparsely decorated rooms upstairs, with hardwood floors and small windows; ask for the Cuarto Azul (the Blue Room). There's also a living room, a kitchen, a lounge, and a terrace in back where breakfast is served. Photos of the coffee harvest decorate the walls, and just beyond the yard and manicured gardens that surround the house, neat rows of coffee plants stretch off into the distance. **Pros:** off-the-beaten-path feel; plenty of tranquility. **Cons:** isolated location; tour groups pass by for breakfast most mornings. *12 km/7½ mi northwest of Tribunales de Justicia de Alajuela; turn left at high school 2449–5562 www.siempreverdebandb.com 7 rooms In-room: no a/c, no phone, no TV AE, D, DC, MC, V BP.*

$$$–$$$$ Fodor's Choice ★ **Xandari Resort Hotel & Spa.** The tranquil and colorful Xandari is a strikingly original inn and spa, tailor-made for honeymooners and romantic getaways. Its bold design is the brainchild of a talented couple—he's an architect, she's an artist. Contemporary pueblo-esque villas along a ridge overlooking Alajuela and San José are spacious, with plenty of windows, colorful paintings, large terraces, and secluded lanais (sunbathing patios). It's the kind of place that makes you want to take pictures of your hotel room. Some villas stand alone and some share a building, but nearly all of them have spectacular views. So does the restaurant ($$), which serves tasty, often organic, low-fat food. A 4-km (3-mi) trail through the hotel's forest reserve winds past five waterfalls.

Pros: amazing service; ideal setting for romance; guilt-free gourmet delights. **Cons:** some noise from other rooms; should have car to stay here. *5 km/3 mi north of Tribunales de Justicia; turn left after small bridge, follow signs 2443–2020, 866/363–3212 in U.S. www.xandari.com 22 villas In-room: no a/c, safe, refrigerator, no TV, Wi-Fi. In-hotel: restaurant, bar, pools, spa, laundry service, Internet terminal, no-smoking rooms AE, MC, V CP.*

SANTO DOMINGO

18 km/11 mi northeast of Escazú, 7 km/4½ mi northwest of San José.

Between Heredia and San José, the town of Santo Domingo de Heredia has plenty of traditional architecture and a level of tranquility that belies its proximity to the capital, a mere 15-minute drive away if the traffic gods smile upon you. Established in the early 19th century, Santo Domingo is surrounded by coffee farms and several smaller, even quieter communities. It has two Catholic churches, including one of the country's two basilicas. The Iglesia del Rosario, which faces the town's sparsely planted Parque Central, was built in the 1840s and is open for Mass every morning from 7 to 10. The larger Basílica de Santo Domingo, which stands across from a soccer field in the northeast end of town, is open for evening Mass from 5 to 7, and is a venue for classical music concerts throughout the year, including the July-to-August International Music Festival.

GETTING HERE AND AROUND

For the 30-minute trip from downtown San José, head north on C. Central 4 km (2½ mi) to the central park in Tibás; continue 100 meters (328 feet) and turn left. Follow this road another 2½ km (1¼ mi) to Santo Domingo. From the west end of Paseo Colón, turn right onto the Pan-American Highway (aka the Carretera General Cañas), then right off the highway just before it heads onto an overpass, after the Hotel Irazú (on the right). Keep to this road for about 2 km (1 mi) to the first intersection after it becomes one-way. Turn right at the lights, continue 3 km (2 mi), passing INBioparque, until the road Ts; a left here brings you into town. One of the Heredia bus routes leaves from C. 1, Avdas. 7–9 every three to five minutes and passes through Santo Domingo.

ESSENTIALS

Bank/ATM Banco Nacional (*Across from south side of Iglesia del Rosario 2244–0439*).

Post Office Correos (*Avda. Central, Cs. 2 and 4*).

EXPLORING

Santo Domingo's main attraction is **INBioparque**, which does a good job of explaining the country's various ecosystems. It's a useful, if slightly expensive, primer before you head out to the hinterlands. Wander trails through climate-controlled wetlands and out to tropical dry forest. The forests may not look much different, but your English-speaking guide will explain the subtleties. Along the way, stop at the butterfly farm, snake and insect exhibits, and bromeliad garden. The tour is packed with information—perhaps too much—but if you're visiting Costa Rica for its ecology, it's a worthwhile lesson. Kids love the virtual aerial flyover of Central America introduced by astronaut Franklin Chang. A restaurant serves typical Costa Rican fare, and the gift shop has souvenirs and books on natural history. Reservations are required for tours. ✉ *Road between Santo Domingo and Heredia, 400 m north and 200 m west of Shell gas station* ☎ *2507–8107* 🌐 *www.inbioparque.com* *$23* ⏲ *Tues.–Fri. 8–4 (last admission at 3), weekends 8–5 (last admission at 4). Tours at 9, 11, and 1.*

WHERE TO STAY

$$ **Hotel Bougainvillea.** This hotel is a top choice for business travelers and small-scale conferences, but its extensive grounds, which bump up against coffee farms, are ideal for lazy strolls or families with energetic kids. You might even forget that you're only 20 minutes from San José. The spacious and carpeted but otherwise unremarkable rooms are furnished with local hardwoods. Rooms on the second and third floors have large balconies; get one with a view of the gardens behind the hotel. The 8-acre garden, shaded by large trees, holds an extensive bromeliad collection. Pre-Columbian pottery and paintings by Costa Rican artists decorate the lobby and restaurant ($$), which serves a small but excellent selection of Continental cuisine. An hourly shuttle takes you to the Hotel Villa Tournón in San José. All rooms here are nonsmoking. **Pros:** lush and open spaces; of the urban hotels, one of the better bird-watching sites. **Cons:** slightly institutional smell and feel in the hallways. *2 km/1 mi east of Santo Domingo de Heredia, Santo Tomas* ☎ *2244–1414, 866/880–5441 in North America* 🌐 *www.hb.co.cr* *77 rooms, 4 suites* *In-room: no a/c, Wi-Fi. In-hotel: restaurant, bar, tennis courts, pool, laundry service, Internet terminal, no-smoking rooms* *AE, D, DC, MC, V* *EP.*

HEREDIA

4 km/3 mi north of Santo Domingo, 11 km/6 mi northwest of San José.

Heredia is the capital of the important coffee province of the same name, and contains a few of the country's best-preserved colonial structures. Founded in 1706, the city bears witness to how difficult preservation can be in an earthquake-prone country; most of its colonial structures have been destroyed by the tremors and tropical climate—not to mention modernization. Still, the city and neighboring towns retain a certain historic feel, with old adobe buildings scattered amid the concrete structures. The nearby villages of Barva and Santo Domingo de Heredia have more colonial and adobe buildings, and the roads that wind through the hills above those towns pass through charming scenery and rural enclaves, making them excellent routes for exploration.

GETTING HERE AND AROUND

The narrow routes to Heredia are notoriously clogged at almost all times; avoid them during rush hours if possible. Turn right at the west end of Paseo Colón. Follow Pan-American Highway 2 km (1 mi); take the second exit, just before the highway heads onto an overpass and just after the Hotel Irazú (on the right). To get to the center of Heredia, follow that road for 5½ km (3½ mi), then turn left at the Universidad Nacional; continue north past the university instead of turning to reach the Britt Coffee Tour, Museo de Cultura Popular, Sacramento, Barva, and points beyond. Buses run between San José (300 m east of Hospital San Juan de Dios) and Heredia every 5 to 10 minutes daily (between 5 AM and 10 PM), following the above car route. The steady stream of buses leaving from C. 1, Avdas. 7–9 every three to five minutes passing through Santo Domingo are sometimes a better bet during rush hour, particularly the *directo* buses that start after 3:30 PM; these buses also run from midnight to 3:30 AM on the hour. If you're without a car, a taxi is the best way to get to Café Britt or Barva.

ESSENTIALS

Bank/ATM Banco Popular (⊠ *200 m east of northeast corner of Parque Central* ☎ *2260–9407*). **Banco Nacional** (⊠ *Southwest corner of Parque Central* ☎ *2277–6900*).

Internet Internet Cosmos (⊠ *300 m east of Parque Central* ☎ *2262–4775*).

Pharmacy Farmacia Chavarria (⊠ *Southwest corner of Parque Central* ☎ *2263–4670*).

Post Office Correos (⊠ *Northwest corner of Parque Central*).

EXPLORING

Heredia is centered on tree-studded **Parque Central,** one of the country's loveliest central parks, which is surrounded by a few historic buildings. The park has a cast-iron fountain imported from England in 1879 and a simple kiosk where the municipal band plays Sunday-morning and Thursday-night concerts. ⊠ *C. Central and Avda. Central* .

The impressive **Cathedral of the Immaculate Conception** (Catedral de la Inmaculada Concepción) is a whitewashed stone church built between 1797 and 1804 to replace an adobe temple dating from the early 1700s. Its thick stone walls, small windows, and squat buttresses have kept it intact through two centuries of quakes and tremors. It has a pale interior with marble floors and stained-glass windows, and is flanked by tidy gardens. There are Sunday services at 6 AM, 9 AM, 11 AM, and 6 PM. ⊠ *Eastern end of Parque Central* ☎ *2237–0779* ⊙ *Daily 6–6.*

To the north of the Parque Central stands a strange, decorative tower called the **Little Fort** *(Fortín)*, which was built as a military post in the 1870s by the local oligarch Fadrique Gutiérrez. It never did see action and now serves as a symbol of the province, one of the few military monuments in this army-less country. The tower is closed to the public. The old brick building next to the Fortín is the Town Hall (Palacio Municipal). ⊠ *C. Central and Avda. Central.*

Two blocks south of the Parque Central is Heredia's **Old Market** (Mercado Viejo), which has fewer souvenirs for sale than San José's Mercado Central but is less cramped and safer. On the next block to the southeast is the **New Market** (Mercado Nuevo), which holds dozens of *sodas* (simple restaurants). ⊠ *C. Central and Avda. 6* ⊙ *Mon.–Sat. 7–6.*

At the edge of a middle-class neighborhood between Heredia and Barva is the **Museum of Popular Culture** (Museo de Cultura Popular), which

Continued on page 164

Picking coffee beans from plant

COFFEE, THE GOLDEN BEAN

Tour a working coffee plantation and learn about the product that catapulted Costa Rica onto the world's economic stage, built the country's infrastructure, and created a middle class unlike any other in Central America.

Costa Rica B.C. (before coffee) was a poor, forgotten little colony with scant infrastructure and no real means of making money. Coffee production changed all of that and transformed the country into one of the wealthier and more stable nations in Central America. Coffee remains Costa Rica's bread and butter—the industry employs one-fourth of Costa Rica's population full- or part-time—and coffee plantations are sprinkled throughout the Central Valley and Northern Plains. All cultivate fine Arabica beans (by government decree, the inferior Robusta variety is not grown here). Visit one and learn what makes the country tick.

By Jeffrey Van Fleet

HISTORY IN A CUP

Coffee plantations near Poas Volcano, Central Valley.

The country's first leaders saw this new crop as a tool with which to engineer a better life for their people. After gaining independence, new laws were created to allow average Costa Ricans to become coffee-growing landowners. These farmers formed the foundation of a middle-class majority that has long distinguished the country from the rest of Latin America. Costa Rica's infrastructure, institutional organizations, and means of production quickly blossomed—young entrepreneurs established small import-export houses, growers banded together to promote a better infrastructure, and everyone plowed their profits into improving the country's primitive road system.

SOCIAL TRANSFORMATION

As the coffee business became more profitable, prominent families were sending their children abroad to study, and doctors, lawyers and other skilled professionals in search of jobs began arriving by the

DRINKING THE GOOD STUFF

Here's the kicker for you, dear coffee-loving visitor: It's tough to find a decent cup in Costa Rica. True to the realities of developing-country economics, the good stuff goes for export, leaving a poorer quality bean behind for the local market. Add to that that the typical household here makes coffee with heaps of sugar. Your best bet for a good cup is an upscale hotel or restaurant, which is attuned to foreign tastes and does use export-quality product. The decorative foil bags you see in souvenir shops and supermarkets are also export-quality and make terrific souvenirs.

COFFEE TIMELINE

Native workers harvesting coffee beans in 1800s

1720	Coffee arrives in New World.
1791	Coffee plants introduced to Costa Rica.
1820	First coffee exports go to Panama.
1830	Legislation paves way for coffee profits to finance government projects.
1860	Costa Rican coffee first exported to United States.
1890	Atlantic Railroad opens, allowing for easier port access.

Enjoying a cup of coffee in Montezuma, Nicoya Peninsula

boatload. Returning students and well-educated immigrants brought a new world view that contributed to the formation of Costa Rica's liberal ideology.

MODERN TIMES

Development gobbled up land in the Central Valley by the last half of the 20th century, and coffee production began to spread to other areas of the country. A worldwide slump in coffee prices in the 1990s forced many producers out of the business. Prices have risen since 2002, and the government looks to smooth out any fluctuations with added-value eco-certification standards and innovative marketing.

Today, some 70% of the country's *número uno* agricultural crop comes from small family properties of under 25 acres owned by 250,000 farmers. They seasonally employ over four times that number of people, and kids in rural areas still take class time off to help with the harvest.

CAFÉ CHEAT SHEET

café solo: black

con azúcar: with sugar

con crema: with cream

con leche: with milk

descafeinado: decaffeinated (not easy to find here)

■

grano entero: whole beans

molido: ground

tostado claro or ***tueste claro:*** light roast

tostado oscuro or ***tueste oscuro:*** dark roast

Oxcarts built in the early 1900s to transport coffee.

1897	Coffee barons construct San José's ornate Teatro Nacional.
1992	Costa Rica adopts new environmental laws for coffee industry.
1997	Tourism displaces coffee as Costa Rica's top industry.
Today	Costa Rica turns to eco-certification and fair-trade marketing of coffee.

COSTA RICA'S BEAN COUNTRY

Coffee plantations from Cervantes to Orosi Central Valley

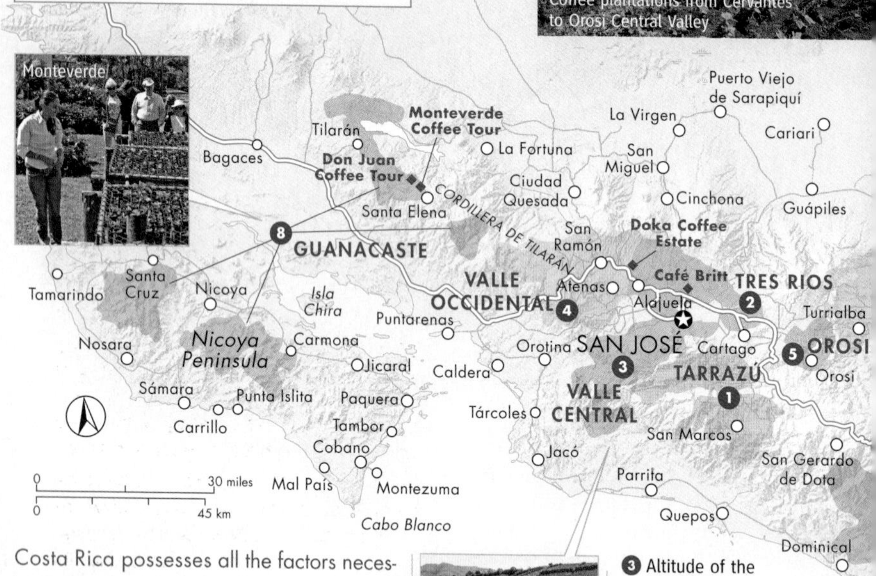

Costa Rica possesses all the factors necessary—moderately high altitude, mineral-rich volcanic soil, adequate rainfall but distinct rainy and dry seasons—to be a major coffee player. Costa Rican growers cultivate only Arabica coffee beans. The industry eliminated the inferior Robusta variety in 1989 and hasn't looked back. The Costa Rican Coffee Institute certifies eight regional coffee varieties.

The coffee-growing cycle begins in April or May, when rains make the dark-green bushes explode in a flurry of white blossoms. By November, the fruit starts to ripen, turning from green to red. The busy harvest begins as farmers race to get picked "cherries" to *beneficios* (processing mills), where beans are removed, washed, machine-dried, and packed in burlap sacks either for export or to be roasted for local consumption.

Coffee plantations, Central Valley

❶ Aficionados wax poetic about the bean that come from **Tarrazú**, the high-altitude Los Santos Region in the Southern Pacific. It has good body, high acidity, and a chocolaty flavor.

❷ Coffee grown in **Tres Ríos**, east of San José, has high acidity, good body, and a nice aroma.

❸ Altitude of the **Central Valley** (around San José, Heredia and Alajuela) affects the size and hardness of the coffee bean and can influence certain components, particularly the acidity. This is an important characteristic of Arabica coffee.

❹ **Valle Occidental,** in the prosperous western Central Valley, gives you hints of apricots and peaches.

Arabica coffee beans

Coffee beans

Coffee bean pickers

Hand picking Coffee beans

Coffee plant

5 Tasters describe **Orosi** coffee, from the southeastern Central Valley, as "floral."

6 The lower altitudes of nearby **Turrialba** give its product a medium body.

7 The high-altitude **Brunca** region, near San Vito in southern Costa Rica, produces coffee with excellent aroma, good body, and moderate acidity.

8 **Guanacaste** is a diverse region that includes Monteverde and the central Nicoya Peninsula. Here they produce a medium-body coffee.

PLANTATIONS WITH TOURS

Wonder where your cup of morning coffee originates? The following purveyors give informative tours of their facilities and acquaint you with the life and times of the country's favorite beverage.

CAFÉ BRITT Barva, Heredia *(see the Central Valley chapter)* Café Britt incorporates a small theater production into its tour, presenting the history of Costa Rican coffee in song and dance. Britt also presents a separate, more academic tour giving you a participatory glimpse into the world of professional coffee tasters.

DOKA COFFEE ESTATE San Luis de Sabanilla, Alajuela *(see the Central Valley)* Doka Coffee Estate offers a comprehensive tour through the entire growing and drying process and lets you sample the local brew. The best time to take this tour is during the October-to-February picking season.

DON JUAN COFFEE TOUR Monteverde *(see the Northern Plains)* A personalized excursion with a small group is the hallmark of this tour to a coffee plantation a few miles outside the town of Santa Elena.

MONTEVERDE COFFEE TOUR Monteverde *(see the Northern Plains)* Monteverde Coffee offers you some hands-on experience. Depending on the time of year, you can help with picking, drying, roasting or packing.

All of the above tours guide you through the plant-to-cup process in English or Spanish, taking you from picking to drying to roasting to packing to brewing.

Reservations are essential and you should plan on spending a half-day for any of these outings. The whole package will set you back about $30 per person.

preserves a farmhouse built in 1885 with an adobe-like technique called *bahareque*. Run by the National University, the museum is furnished with antiques and surrounded by a garden. An adjacent open-air restaurant serves inexpensive Costa Rican lunches on weekends. Just walking around the museum is instructive, but calling ahead to reserve a hands-on cultural tour (such as one on tortilla making) really makes it worth the trip. ✉ *Between Heredia and Barva; from Musmanni bakery in Santa Lucia de Barva, 100 m north ✢ 1 km/½ mi east; follow signs* ☎ *2260–1619* 🌐 *www.ilam.org/cr/museoculturapopular* 🎫 *$2* ⏲ *Weekdays 9–4, Sun. 10–5*; closed Sat.

★ The producer of Costa Rica's most popular export-quality coffee, **Café Britt**, gives a lively tour that highlights Costa Rica's history of coffee cultivation through a theatrical presentation that is admittedly a bit hokey. Your "tour guides" are professional actors, and pretty good ones at that, so if you don't mind the song and dance, it's fun. Take a short walk through the coffee farm and processing plant, and learn how professional coffee tasters distinguish a fine cup of java. One major difference between this tour and that of Doka Estate in Alajuela is that Doka takes you through the mill. Britt, ever the innovator, provides a similar tour add-on by request. A separate "Expert Coffee Lovers Tour" gives a more academic view of the subject and takes you into the world of professional coffee tasters. ✉ *From Heredia, take road to Barva; follow signs* ☎ *2277–1500, 800/462–7488 in North America* 🌐 *www.cafebritt.com* 🎫 *$20 tour only, $27 with transportation, $35 with transportation and lunch* ⏲ *Tours: Dec.–May, daily at 11 and 3; June–Nov., daily at 11.*

WHERE TO EAT

$–$$ ITALIAN ✕ **L'Antica Roma.** The food here more than makes up for the less-than-tasteful red curtains, gold walls, and faded images of the Colosseum. The ample menu offers more than 40 pizza varieties, all baked in a wood-burning oven, and homemade fresh pasta, such as three-mushroom ravioli. Two TVs with sports are suspended indoors; the tables out on the wrought-iron-enclosed patio lend themselves better to conversation. ✉ *C. 7 and Avda. 7, across from the Hotel Valladolid* ☎ *2262–9073* 💳 *AE, D, DC, MC, V.*

WHERE TO STAY

$$$$ Fodor's Choice ★ **Finca Rosa Blanca Country Inn.** There's nothing common about this exclusive B&B overlooking coffee farms; new additions update the Gaudí-esque hideaway's reputation as one of the country's top sumptuous splurges. The main building retains its soaring ceiling and white-stucco arches, set among tropical flowers and shaded by massive fig trees. All rooms—each with its own style—have been spruced up, from the addition of Jacuzzi bathtubs to new 100% bamboo sheets. The spacious two-story suite is out of a fairy tale, with a spiral staircase leading up to a window-lined tower bedroom. The owners work hard to make the hotel as eco-friendly as possible, using composting, solar panels, and other methods. The hotel is one of only four in the country to receive a top rating for sustainable tourism. Prix-fixe gourmet dinners are available at the new El Tigre Vestido restaurant ($$$), and guests can relax in the new bar or full-service spa. All rooms here are

nonsmoking. **Pros:** eco-consciousness; indulgence with style; service par excellence. **Cons:** some units short on closet and drawer space; can be difficult to find. ✉ *800 m north of Café Britt Distribution Center in Santa Barbara de Heredia, Barrio Jesus* ☎ *2269–9392* 🌐 *www.fincarosablanca.com* *11 junior suites, 2 master suites* *In-room: no a/c, safe, kitchen (some), refrigerator (some), no TV, Internet, Wi-Fi. In-hotel: restaurant, bar, pool, spa, laundry service, Internet terminal, no-smoking rooms* *AE, MC, V* *BP.*

$$ **Hotel Valladolid.** This is hands-down the best hotel in downtown Heredia. The tall (for Heredia) and narrow building has just 11 modern rooms, designed for business travelers and visiting professors at the nearby National University, although the typical guests are now just as likely to be vacationers. The tile floors and white walls aren't exactly inspired, but are just fine for a night's sleep. **Pros:** central location; friendly staff. **Cons:** Heredia's charms lie in the outskirts, not in town; a few rooms show their age. ✉ *C. 7 and Avda. 7, 400 m north and 100 m west of the main entrance of La Universidad Nacional* ☎ *2260–2905* 🌐 *www.hotelvalladolid.net* *11 rooms, 1 suite* *In-room: safe, refrigerator, Wi-Fi. In-hotel: bar, laundry service* *AE, D, DC, MC, V* *CP.*

EN ROUTE

At the center of **Barva de Heredia,** a small community about 3 km (2 mi) north of Heredia proper, is the **Parque Central,** surrounded by old adobe shops with Spanish-tile roofs on three sides and a white-stucco church to the east. The stout, handsome church dates from the late 18th century; behind it is a lovely little garden shrine to the Virgin Mary. On a clear day you can see verdant Volcán Barva *(⇨ Chapter 5)* towering to the north, and if you follow the road that runs in front of the church and veer left at the Y, you will wind your way up the slopes of that volcano to Vara Blanca, where you can either drive north to the La Paz Waterfall Gardens or continue straight to Poás Volcano National Park *(⇨ Chapter 5)*. If instead you veer right at the Y and drive up the steep, narrow road, you'll pass through San José de la Montaña and Paso Llano to reach Sacramento, where the road turns into a rough dirt track leading to the Barva sector of Braulio Carrillo National Park *(⇨ Chapter 5)*. If you turn left when you reach Barva's central plaza, you'll head to San Pedro and Santa Barbara, where roads head south to Alajuela and north to Vara Blanca.

CARTAGO AND IRAZÚ VOLCANO

Cartago, due east of San José, was the country's first capital, and thus has scattered historical structures and the remarkable Basílica de Los Angeles. To the north of Cartago towers massive Irazú Volcano, which is covered with farmland and topped by an impressive crater.

CARTAGO

22 km/14 mi southeast of San José.

Cartago is Costa Rica's oldest community, but earthquakes have destroyed most of its structures from the colonial era. Cartago was left behind in 1823, when the seat of government was moved to the emerging economic center of San José. You'll see some attractive old buildings as you move through town, most of them erected after a 1910 earthquake. Most visitors see Cartago on their way to or from the Orosi Valley or Turrialba, and there is little reason (or place) to stay the night. The Orosi Valley, a short drive away, has better choices.

GETTING HERE AND AROUND

For the 25-minute drive from San José, drive east on Avenida 2 through San Pedro and Curridabat to the highway entrance, where you have three road options—take the middle one marked Cartago. Shortly before Cartago, a Y intersection marks the beginning of the route up Irazú, with traffic to Cartago veering right. Buses between San José and Cartago leave every 10 minutes daily (25 m north of the Hotel Balmoral or 300 m south of the Teatro Nacional) from 5 AM to midnight; buses to Paraíso leave weekdays from the same terminal every half hour. Cartago buses to San José pick up 200 meters north of the Parque Central. Buses to Orosi leave Cartago every 15 to 30 minutes from 5:30 AM to 10 PM, 100 meters (328 feet) east, 25 meters (82 feet) south of the southwest corner of Las Ruinas.

CARTAGO ESSENTIALS

Bank/ATM BAC San José (✉ *100 m south of Las Ruinas30101* ☎ *2295–9797*). **Scotiabank ATM** (✉ *Northwest corner of Las Ruinas*).

Hospital Hospital Max Peralta (✉ *200 m south, 150 m east of Las Ruinas* ☎ *2550–1999* 🌐 *www.hmp.sa.cr*).

Pharmacy Farmacia Central (✉ *Just south of Las Ruinas* ☎ *2551–0698*).

Post Office Correos (✉ *Avda. 2, Cs. 15–17*).

Taxis Taxis El Carmen (☎ *2551–0836*).

EXPLORING

Churches in some form or another have stood at the site of the present-day Parque Central since 1575, and have been knocked down by earthquakes and reconstructed many times. Undeterred by complete destruction in 1841, the citizens of Cartago began work on a Romanesque cathedral some years later, but the devastating earthquake of 1910 halted work and put an end to the last attempt at building a structure on the site. **Las Ruinas** (✉ *Avda. 2, Cs. 1–2*), or "the Ruins," of this unfinished house of worship now stand in a pleasant park planted with tall pines and bright impatiens. You won't be able to go inside, but the site is spectacular from outside as well. Among the many legends attributed to the ruins is the gruesome story of the priest of one of the earlier churches at the site, who, after falling in love with his sister-in-law, was murdered by his brother. His ghost, dressed as a priest but headless, still haunts the grounds. Although the park is billed as a Wi-Fi hot spot, we recommend not pulling out your laptop in such a public place—nothing to do with alleged hauntings.

Our Lady of the Angels Basilica (*Basílica de Nuestra Señora de los Angeles;* ✉ *C. 16, Avdas. 2–4, 7 blocks east of central square* ☎ *2551–0465*) is a hodgepodge of architectural styles from Byzantine to Baroque, with

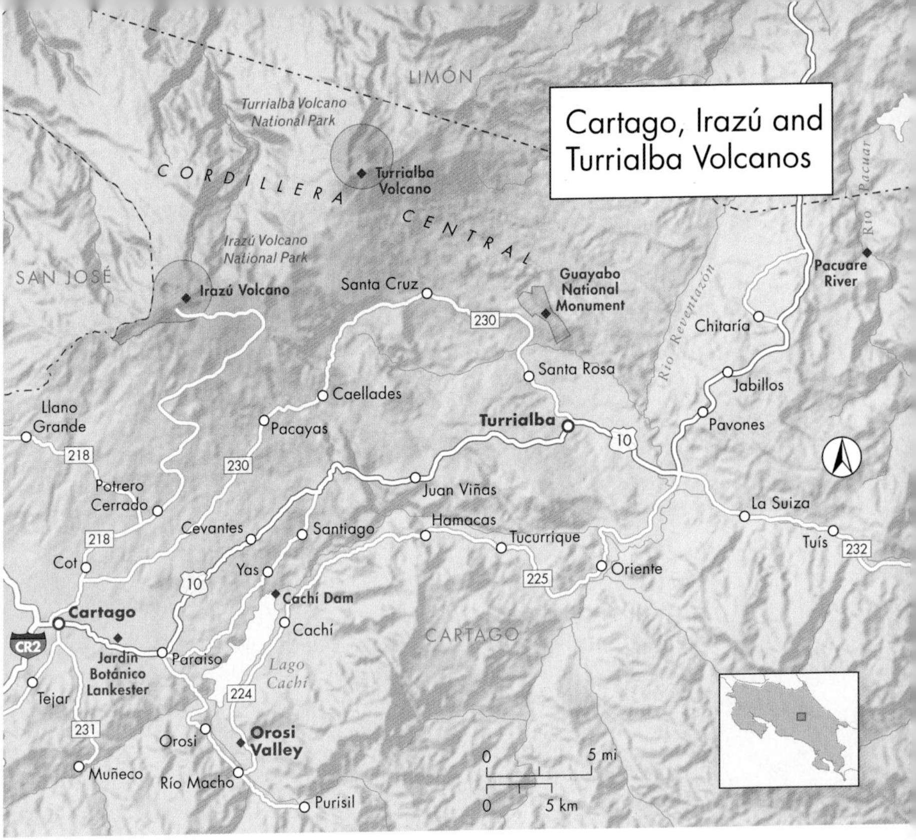

a dash of Gothic. The interior is even more striking, with a colorful tile floor, intricately decorated wood columns, and lots of stained glass. The church is open daily 6 AM to 7 PM. The basilica is also the focus of an annual pilgrimage to celebrate the appearance of La Negrita, or the Black Virgin, Costa Rica's patron saint.

WHERE TO EAT

Although you can find decent pasta and pizza, haute cuisine just doesn't exist here. Instead, Cartago gives you a fine opportunity to eat some *comida típica*. On just about any street downtown you'll find a *soda* (simple café), and the women in the kitchen will serve you the same style of food they cook at home for their own families. There are literally dozens of places of comparable quality. One rule of thumb: the busier the better—the locals know where to eat well.

VOLCÁN IRAZÚ

31 km/19 mi northeast of Cartago, 50 km/31 mi east of San José.

Volcán Irazú is Costa Rica's highest volcano, at 3,422 meters (11,260 feet). Its presence is a mixed blessing: the ash fertilizes the Central Valley soil, but the volcano has caused considerable destruction through the

CLOSE UP

La Negrita

On the night of August 1 and well into the early-morning hours of August 2, the road to Cartago from San José clogs with worshippers, some of whom have traveled from as far away as Nicaragua to celebrate the 1635 appearance of Costa Rica's patron saint, La Negrita (the Black Virgin). The feast day draws an estimated 1 million pilgrims each year, not bad for a country of just 4 million people. At a spring behind the church, people fill bottles with water believed to have curative properties. Miraculous healing powers are attributed to the saint, and devotees have placed thousands of tiny symbolic crutches, ears, eyes, and legs in a room to the left of the altar. Tour buses and school groups, along with shops selling the saint's likeness, make the scene a bit of a circus.

centuries. ☎ *2551–9398, 8200–5025 for ranger station* ✉ *$7* ⊙ *Daily 8–3:30.*

GETTING HERE AND AROUND

Follow directions to Cartago *(⇨ above)*, but shortly before the city a Y intersection marks the beginning of the road up Irazú; traffic to Cartago veers right, then left immediately past the first lights. From downtown Cartago, a 45-minute trip, take the road to Irazú at the northeast corner of the Basilica. Signs from Cartago lead you to the park. Buses head to Volcán Irazú from San José (✉ *Avda. 2, Cs. 1–3*) daily at 8 AM and return at 12:30 PM.

WHERE TO EAT

$ COSTA RICAN ✕ **Restaurant 1910.** Decorated with vintage photos of early-20th-century buildings and landscapes, this restaurant documents the disastrous 1910 earthquake that rocked this area and all but destroyed the colonial capital of Cartago. The menu is predominantly Costa Rican, with such traditional specialties as *trucha* (trout), and rice with chicken. One of the less common dishes is *corvina* (sea bass) fillet with béarnaise sauce. The *típico* buffet is a great introduction to Costa Rican cooking. ✉ *Road to Parque Nacional Volcán Irazú; 300 m north of Cot–Pacayas turnoff* ☎ *2536–6063* ▭ *AE, MC, V* ⊙ *No dinner Sun.*

$ COSTA RICAN Fodor's Choice ★ ✕ **Restaurante Noche Buena.** If you've raced up Irazú to catch the clear early-morning views, a late breakfast or early lunch at this bright roadside stop is a great excuse to linger in the area. Sample stick-to-your-ribs *gallo pinto* (a traditional dish made with rice and beans), *tres leches* (literally "three milks," a light and airy cake), and—not to be missed—the best fried yucca around. The pale wood floors and walls inside have a studied rustic charm, but the ample patio is a fresher option; neither has particularly impressive views. The Costa Rican owner, Federico Gutiérrez, has added a 3-km (2-mi) trail to waterfalls and a high-tech, interactive volcano museum ($4) that shouldn't be missed. Get here early, as the restaurant closes at 3 on weekdays and 4:30 on weekends. ✉ *At Km 24.5, road to Parque Nacional Volcán Irazú* ☎ *2530–8013* 🌐 *www.nochebuena.org* ▭ *AE, D, DC, MC, V* ⊙ *No dinner.*

Cartago's Basilica de Nuestra de is the focus of the annual pilgramage to celebrate the appearance of the Black Virgin.

THE OROSI VALLEY

If you have a day to spend near San José, this route past coffee plantations, small towns, and verdant landscapes, with countless breathtaking views, makes a classic day trip, popular with locals on the weekend but still off the beaten path. The region is one of the few areas in Costa Rica that still has remnants (ruins and churches) of the 17th-century Spanish colonial era. A good road makes a loop around the valley, easy to do if you have your own vehicle, or if you go on a guided tour—it's a staple of most San José tour operators' offerings. Public transportation is trickier here: buses travel clockwise and counterclockwise, but neither route completes the loop.

ESSENTIALS

Bank/ATM Banco Nacional (✉ *300 m south of soccer field, Orosi* ☎ *2533–1390* ✉ *West side of central park, Paraíso* ☎ *2574–7274*).

Internet PC Orosi (✉ *200 m south of church, Orosi*).

Pharmacy Farmacia Sucre (✉ *200 m west of central park, Paraíso* ☎ *2574–7286*). **Farmacia Tabor** (✉ *Southeast corner of soccer field, Orosi* ☎ *2533–3395*).

Post Office Correos (✉ *125 m north of central park, in the Edificio Flor María, Paraíso*).

EXPLORING

At the basílica in the center of Cartago, turn right, and then left onto the busy road to Paraíso and Orosi. After 6 km (4 mi), a blue sign on the right marks the short road to the lush gardens of the **Jardín Botánico**

Bulls dressed in their finest for an oxcart parade in Cartago.

Lankester (*West entrance to Paraíso* *2552–3247* *www.jardinbotanicolankester.org* *$5* *Daily 8:30–4:30*), one of the world's foremost orchid collections, with more than 1,100 native and introduced species of orchids. Bromeliads, heliconias, and aroids also abound, along with 80 species of trees, including rare palms. The best time to come is February through April, when the most orchids are in bloom. The garden's gift shop is one of the few places in Costa Rica to buy orchids that you can take home legally. (They come in small bottles and don't flower for four years, so you'll need some serious patience.)

Head east toward Paraíso and then into the town itself. Hang a right at the central park. Some 2 km (1 mi) beyond is the **Sanchiri Mirador**, one of the valley's best miradores (lookout points). But our favorite vantage point is at a point on the road just beyond Sanchiri where the earth appears to drop away and the valley comes into view as you make the steep descent to the town of Orosi. Here's a case for letting someone else do the driving.

The town of Orosi, in the heart of the valley, has but one major attraction: the squat but beautifully restored 1743 **Iglesia de San José de Orosi** (*Across from soccer field* *2533–3051* *Museum $1* *Church Tues.–Sun. 9–noon and 1–5; museum Tues.–Fri. 1–5, weekends 9–5*), the country's oldest house of worship still in use, and one of the only structures still remaining from the colonial era. It has a low-slung whitewashed facade; the roof is made of cane overlaid with terra-cotta barrel tiles. Inside are an antique wooden altar and ancient paintings of the stations of the cross and the Virgin of Guadalupe, all brought to Costa Rica from Guatemala. A religious-art museum next door has officially posted hours and yet does not always adhere to them.

Continue past the dam into the small hamlet of Ujarrás, then follow the signs to the site of the ruins of Costa Rica's first church, **Iglesia de Ujarrás** (✉*In a small park, 1 km/½mi from Restaurante Típico Ujarrás* ☎*2574–8366* 🎟*Free* ⏲*Daily 6–6*). Built between 1681 and 1693 in honor of the Virgin of Ujarrás, the church, together with the surrounding village, was abandoned in 1833 after a series of earthquakes and floods wreaked havoc here, at the lowest point of the Orosi Valley. An unlikely Spanish victory in 1666 over a superior force of invading British pirates was attributed to a prayer stop here. A final 6-km (4-mi) drive to Paraíso from Ujarrás completes the road that loops the valley.

WORD OF MOUTH

"Orosi Valley is beautiful: [there weren't many] tourists but it was busy with agriculture, with many trucks on the roads. It's nice and cool in the valley, with beautiful evenings, so bring a sweater. We had a glorious morning to view Irazu Volcano; the nearby Turrialba Volcano was sputtering and smoking. We are fascinated by volcanoes, and these ones don't disappoint."
—4explore

South of Orosi, the road becomes a rugged track following the Río Grande de Orosi past coffee plantations, elegant fincas (farmhouses), and seasonal barracks for coffee pickers before it's hemmed in by the steep slopes of thick jungle. At the bottom of the loop road, follow signs for **Tapantí National Park** (✉*14 km/8 mi south of Orosi,* ☎*2551–2970* 🎟*$6* ⏲*Weekdays 8–4, weekends 7–5*). Though it's worth the trip for just an hour or two of exploring, you could easily fill a day in the park. Stretching all the way to the Talamanca Mountains, the reserve encompasses 47 square km (18 square mi) of largely pristine, remote cloud forest, refuge for more than 400 bird species, including the emerald toucanet, violaceous trogon, and most of the country's hummingbirds. The rangers' office and visitor center are on the right just after the park entrance. You can leave your vehicle at a parking area 1½ km (1 mi) up the road. From here loop trails head off into the woods on both sides. One trail passes a picnic area and several swimming holes with (cold) emerald waters. The other trail is along a forested hillside. About 1½ km (1 mi) up from the parking area is an entrance to the La Pava Trail on the right, leading down a steep hill to the riverbank. If you continue ½ km (¼ mi) past the trailhead, you arrive at a 91-meter (300-foot) stair trail leading to a lookout. Get an early start. The park clouds over markedly by afternoon.

WHERE TO EAT

$ ECLECTIC ✕**Gecko's.** This textbook backpacker hangout is affiliated with a Dutch-Canadian-owned Spanish school and hostel in Orosi. The café is bright and open, with groovy music and free-spirited clothes for sale. The creative menu ranges from traditional Costa Rican food to Kroket (deep-fried meat roll on a bun) and shish kebab. Helpful staff run a tourist-information desk inside. ✉*400 m south of church* ☎*2533–3640* 💳*No credit cards.*

Iglesia de San José de Orosi is the county's oldest church that is still in use.

$ COSTA RICAN **La Casona del Cafetal.** The valley's best lunch stop is on a coffee plantation overlooking the Cachí Reservoir. It's firmly on the beaten path, which means frequent visits from tour groups. The spacious brick building has a high barrel-tile roof, with tables indoors and on a tiled portico on the lake side. Casados and other Costa Rican staples accompany inventive dishes such as corvina guarumos (bass stuffed with mushrooms). Expect a wait on weekends, when diners come from miles around for the 18 lunch buffet. After lunch, take a stroll down to the lake or check out the gift shop. *2 km/1 mi south of Cachí Dam* *2577–1414* *AE, D, DC, MC, V* *No dinner.*

WHERE TO STAY

$$ **Hotel Río Perlas Spa & Resort.** Thermal springs fill one of the pools at this hotel squeezed into a small valley. The place has a condo community feeling, with a driveway running the length of the property and the rooms divided among many smaller buildings. Rooms are nice, but not especially luxurious; they have tile floors and wood furniture. Ask for one of the wooden cabins at the back of the property. There is a replica of the Orosi church here, too. *6 km/3 mi south of Paraíso, turn right at bridge, then 2½ km/1½ mi; look for large sign* *2533–3341* *www.rioperlasspaandresort.com.* *In-hotel: restaurant* *AE, D, DC, MC, V.*

$ **Kiri Mountain Lodge.** This small, family-run hotel has easy access to the park and its own 175-acre private reserve close to waterfalls and most of the same wildlife seen at Tapantí. The number of bird species in the lodge's gardens alone is impressive, especially hummingbirds. Rooms are small and simple, with tile floors and tiny bathrooms, but their porches have views of a jungle-laden hillside. The restaurant serves a small selection of Costa Rican food; fresh trout, raised in nearby ponds, is the best option. You can also catch your own trout and have them cook it for you. **Pros:** secluded location; friendly owners. **Cons:** basic rooms; need a car to stay here. ✉*Turnoff 2 km/1 mi before Tapantí park entrance* ☎*2533–2272* 🌐*www.kirilodge.net* *6 rooms* *In-room: no a/c, no phone, no TV. In-hotel: restaurant* *MC, V* *BP.*

$ **Orosi Lodge.** Run by a German couple who have built a warm rapport with the community, the little lodge blends in with Orosi's pretty, old-town architecture: whitewashed walls are trimmed in blue, ceilings are high, and natural wood is used throughout. Some furnishings, such as the clay lamps in the rooms, are done by local artisans. Common areas are colorful, with paintings and sculpture by local artists. Double beds have two twin-size comforters. Second-floor rooms have views of the Orosi Valley and Irazú Volcano. The hip coffee shop brews a great cup of joe, and Latin music usually plays from a 1960s jukebox in the foyer. ✉*350 meters south, 100 meters west of soccer field* ☎*2533–3578* 🌐*www.orosilodge.com* *6 rooms* *In-room: no a/c, no phone, refrigerator, no TV. In-hotel: restaurant* *AE, D, DC, MC, V* *EP.*

SHOPPING

Stop in at the unique artisan shop Casa del Soñador (*House of the Dreamer;* ✉*2 km/1 mi south of the Cachí Dam* ☎*2577–1186 or 2577–1983*), established by local wood sculptor Macedonio Quesada. Though Macedonio died years ago, his sons Miguel and Hermes and a former apprentice are still here, carving interesting, often comical little statues out of coffee roots.

THE TURRIALBA REGION

The agricultural center of Turrialba and the nearby Guayabo ruins lie considerably lower than the Central Valley, so they enjoy a more moderate climate, a transition between the cooler Central Valley and the sweltering Caribbean coast. There are two ways to reach this area from San José, both of which pass spectacular scenery. The more direct route, accessible by heading east through both Cartago and Paraíso, winds through coffee and sugar plantations before descending abruptly into Turrialba. For the second route, turn off the road between Cartago and the summit of Irazú near the town of Cot, heading toward Pacayas. That narrow route twists along the slopes of Irazú and Turrialba volcanoes past some stunning scenery—stately pollarded trees lining the road, riotous patches of tropical flowers, and metal-girder bridges across crashing streams. As you begin the descent to Turrialba town, the temperature rises and sugarcane alternates with fields of neat rows of coffee bushes.

TURRIALBA

58 km/36 mi east of San José.

The relatively well-to-do agricultural center of Turrialba suffered when the main San José–Limón route was diverted through Guápiles in the late 1970s. The demise of the famous Jungle Train that connected these two cities was an additional blow. But today, because of the beautiful scenery and a handful of upscale nature lodges, ecotourism is increasingly the focus of the town's efforts. The damming of the Reventazón River has cut down on the number of tourists, but significant numbers of kayakers and rafters flock here to run the Pacuare. Turrialba has two major factories: Conair, which you'll see on the road to Siquirres, and a Rawlings factory, which makes all the baseballs used in the major leagues. (Rawlings, unfortunately, does not offer tours.) Though pleasant enough and with a youthful vibe from the nearby university and the white-water folk, Turrialba doesn't have much to offer, but the surrounding countryside hides some spectacular scenery and patches of rain forest. Finally, there's Volcán Turrialba, which you can ascend on foot or horseback.

CORRUPTION CRACKDOWN

Long a proponent of do-as-I-say, not-as-I-do anticorruption policies, Costa Rica got tough on bigwigs in 2004. Two former presidents were taken into custody for allegedly accepting bribes in a telecommunications deal. A third—José María Figueres—lives in Switzerland and faces arrest if ever he returns to Costa Rica. The sight of former leaders being led away in handcuffs has shaken many Costa Ricans' faith in their democracy, but others see it as a positive sign that no one is above the law.

GETTING HERE AND AROUND

The road through Cartago continues east through Paraíso, where you turn left at the northeast corner of the central park to pick up the road to Turrialba. Marked by signs, this road leads north to Guayabo National Monument. Buses between San José and Turrialba leave hourly (5:15 AM to 10:30 PM) from Calle 13, Avenida 6, just west of the downtown court buildings. Direct buses depart from the Turrialba terminal (at the entrance to Turrialba) for San José on the hour; on the half hour to Cartago, and every two hours to Siquirres.

ESSENTIALS

Bank/ATM Banco Nacional (✉ *C. 1 at Avda. Central30501* ☎ *2556–1211*). **Banco de Costa Rica** (✉ *Avda. 0, C. 130501* ☎ *2556–0472*).

Hospital Hospital Dr. William Allen (✉ *Avda. 2, 100 m west of C. 4* ☎ *2558–1300*).

Internet Dimensión Internet (✉ *East side of central park* ☎ *2556–1586*).

Pharmacy Farmacia San Buenaventura (✉ *50 m south of west side of central park* ☎ *2556–0379*).

Post Office Correos (✉ *Avda. 6 at C. Central 50 m north of central park*).

Taxis Transgalo (☎ *2556–9393*).

EXPLORING

Although you can't easily drive up to its summit as you can at Poás and Irazú, **Volcán Turrialba** is worth visiting, albeit with some precautions these days. The easiest way to arrange the excursion is to call the **Volcán Turrialba Lodge** (☎*2273–4335*) and request a guide. You can ascend the 6 km (4 mi) from the lodge on foot or horseback in one to two hours (allow up to four hours for the round-trip, plus exploring time), and at 3,340 meters (10,958 feet) with luck you'll see clear down to the Caribbean coast. At this writing visits are limited to a 20-minute max—a protective measure implemented in response to heightened volcanic rumbling. Volcanologists are concerned about the heavy content of sulfur dioxide in fumes emanating from the volcano since 2007, a phenomenon that has taken its toll on plant and animal life here. ⚠**If you suffer from any type of heart or respiratory condition or are pregnant, stay away.**On the road that runs from Pacayas to Turrialba through Santa Cruz there is a signed turnoff at La Pastora, west of Santa Cruz, that leads up the mountain. The drive up is 15 km (9 mi) and starts paved, but the road gets worse the higher you go. In most cases you'll need a 4WD to make the last section before the trailhead, which is in a very small community called La Central de Turrialba. The road veers left toward the Volcán Turrialba Lodge, and a very washed-out road leads right, toward the summit. If you want to take the latter route, you can park on the left just after the school; usually someone is around to charge you a few dollars for the privilege, but as elsewhere in the country, this in no way guarantees your car's safety. We recommend parking at Volcán Turrialba Lodge—they don't charge, they'll point out the way, and you can rest up with some snacks and hot chocolate at the restaurant when you're finished. Get an early start and dress for the weather—it can get chilly up here even during the day. A park employee sometimes hangs out at the top to collect the $1 entrance fee and hand out maps.

OFF THE BEATEN PATH

A good place for bird-watching, the **Tropical Agricultural Research and Higher Education Center** (Centro Agronómico Tropical de Investigación y Enseñanza), better known by its acronym, CATIE, is one of the leading tropical research centers in Latin America. You might catch sight of the yellow-winged northern jacana or the purple gallinule in the lagoon near the main building. The 10-square-km (4-square-mi) property includes landscaped grounds, seed-conservation chambers, greenhouses, orchards, experimental agricultural projects, a large swath of rain forest, labs and offices, and lodging for students and teachers. Behind the administration building lies the lake that once was rapids on the Reventazón River. The CATIE staff is working to improve visitor access; two-hour guided tours (call ahead to reserve) of the impressive botanical garden have been added, and forest trails are planned for the future. Groups of 10 or more now may add on lunch at the new café (Costa Rican and Spanish plates) and/or a fruitful tasting session of bounty from the garden ($4 per person extra). *3 km/2 mi outside Turrialba, on road to Siquirres ☎2558–2000 www.catie.ac.cr $5; $15 with guide; $25 for full facility tour, $10 per person for groups of more than 5 Daily 7–4.*

CLOSE UP

White-Water Thrills

You're struggling to hang on and paddle, you can't hear a thing over the roar, and you were just slammed with a mighty wall of water. Sound like fun? Then you're in the right place. The **Río Pacuare** and the **Río Reventazón** draw rafters and kayakers from all over the world to Turrialba. Right next to Turrialba, the Reventazón has Class II, III, and IV rapids. The Pacuare, farther from Turrialba, has a spectacular 29-km (18-mi) run with a series of Class III and IV rapids. The scenery includes lush canyons where waterfalls plummet into the river and expanses of rain forest.

Nearly every outfitter has day trips, but some also have multiday trips that include jungle hikes. Costa Rica Nature Adventures and Ríos Tropicales even have their own lodges on the river. Age requirements for children vary by outfitter; Costa Rica Expeditions runs a family trip on the gentler Pejibaye River that kids as young as five can enjoy. The typical trip starts with a van ride to the put-in; including a breakfast stop, it usually takes about 2½ hours from hotel to river. After the first half of the run, guides flip one of the rafts over to form a crude lunch table. Then you continue up the river to Siquirres, and pile back in the van for the ride home.

It would be unwise to choose your company based merely on price: those with bargain rates are probably skimping somewhere. Good outfitters require you to wear life vests and helmets, have CPR-certified river guides with near-fluent English skills, and have kayakers accompany the rafts in case of emergencies. A 5:1 guest-to-guide ratio is good, 10:1 is not. Local Turrialba companies have better prices and allow you to book a trip at the last minute. Hotels and travel agencies book trips with larger outfitters, who can pick you up from nearly anywhere in the Central Valley. Prices range from about $75 to $100.

People fall out of the raft all the time, and it is no big deal. The worst-case scenario is getting caught underwater or under the raft, but surprisingly, most fatalities are heart-attack victims, so don't participate if you're high-risk. You should also be able to swim. Almost every long-standing company has had a death—it is an unfortunate reality of the business. Don't hesitate to ask about safety records. The vast majority of trips, however, are pure exhilarating fun.

In 2006 the government decided to keep long-stalled plans to dam the Pacuare on ice for the time being, but reserves the right to revive them in the future. This would be the last nail in the coffin for the rafting industry (the Reventazón was dammed in the 1960s) and would destroy one of nature's real gems. Locals will surely put up a fight, but run it now while you can.

On the slopes of Turrialba Volcano is **Guayabo National Monument,** Costa Rica's most significant archaeological site. It's interesting, but definitely no Machu Picchu. Records mentioning the ruins go back to the mid-1800s, but systematic investigations didn't begin until 1968, when a local landowner out walking her dogs discovered what she thought was a tomb. Archaeologists began excavating the site and unearthed the base wall of a chief's house in what eventually turned out to be the ruins of a large community (around 10,000 inhabitants) covering

"For a fun ride, try rafting the Pacuare River in October or November when the water is high." —photo by Linda137, Fodors.com member

49 acres, 10 of which have been excavated. The city was abandoned in AD 1400, probably because of disease or war. Guided tours (about two hours) in Spanish or English are provided by freelance guides who wait at the entrance. They'll take you through the rain forest to a *mirador* (lookout) from which you can see the layout of the excavated circular buildings. Only the raised foundations survive, since the conical houses themselves were built of wood. As you descend into the ruins, notice the well-engineered surface and covered aqueducts leading to a trough of drinking water that still functions today. Next you'll pass the end of an 8-km (5-mi) paved walkway used to transport the massive building stones; the abstract patterns carved on the stones continue to baffle archaeologists, but some clearly depict jaguars, which were revered as deities. The hillside jungle is captivating, and the trip is further enhanced by bird-watching possibilities: 200 species have been recorded. If you arrive from the east via the Santa Teresita (Lajas) route, you can make it in any car, but via the alternative Santa Cruz route you'll need a 4WD vehicle to get here. ✣ *Drive through the center of Turrialba to a girdered bridge; take road northeast 16 km/10 mi (about 20 minutes' driving); take a left at the well-marked turnoff, continue another 3 km/2 mi to the monument. If you've taken the scenic Irazú foothills route to Turrialba and have a 4WD, the Santa Cruz route—11 km/7 mi (about 35 minutes' driving)—is an option. Turn left on rough road from Santa Cruz; climb 5 km/3 mi, past the Escuela de Guayabo; turn right at the sign for the monument; the road descends 6 km/4 mi to the site.* ☎ *2559–1220* 🎫 *$4* ⏲ *Daily 8–3:30.*

Costa Rica's first church, Iglesia de Ujarrás was abandoned in 1833 after a series of earthquakes and floods wreaked havoc.

OUTDOOR ACTIVITIES

The two best ways to reach the summit of Turrialba Volcano are on foot or on horseback. **Volcán Turrialba Lodge** (☎*2273–4335*) arranges guided horseback and hiking trips.

WHITE-WATER OUTFITTERS

Most outfitters are based in San José, and many offer both rafting and kayaking. Tico's River Adventures, Costa Rica Ríos (multiday packages only), and Rainforest World are in Turrialba. **Costa Rica Expeditions** (☎*2257–0766* 🌐*www.costaricaexpeditions.com*). **Costa Rica Nature Adventures** (☎*2225–3939 or 2224–0505, 800/283–5032 in North America* 🌐*www.costaricanatureadventures.com*). **Costa Rica Ríos** (☎*2556–9617 or 888/434–0776* 🌐*www.costaricarios.com*). **Exploradores Outdoors** (☎*2222–6262 or 646/205–0828 toll-free* 🌐*www.exploradoresoutdoors.com*). **Rainforest World** (☎*2556–0014 or 8357–7250* 🌐*www.rforestw.com*). **Ríos Tropicales** (☎*2233–6455 or 866/722–8273* 🌐*www.riostropicales.com*).

WHERE TO EAT

¢–$ COSTA RICAN **La Garza Bar y Restaurante.** Similar to La Feria in scope but slightly more atmospheric and with a bar, La Garza also runs the gamut from hamburgers to chicken, but has a better seafood selection. (Sorry, vegetarians, "beetsteak" is a misprint.) This is a good place for a late dinner, as it's open until 11. ✉*Northwest corner of park* ☎*2556–1073* 💳*AE, D, DC, MC, V.*

$ COSTA RICAN **Restaurante La Feria.** A permanent exhibition of national art and the Turrialba expertise of owner Don Roberto (if you speak Spanish) make this a worthwhile stop. This family-style restaurant has the usual midscale Costa Rican fare, ranging from fast food to filet mignon. Casados and gallo pinto compete with more familiar chicken and seafood dishes. Even paella is on the menu (with three hours' notice). ✉ *Just west of Hotel Wagelia, at entrance to town* ☎ *2556–0386* ▭ *AE, D, DC, MC, V* ⊙ *No dinner Tues.*

KEEPING COOL

The Central Valley's climate is often a great surprise to first-time visitors—it's not at all the steamy tropics you've imagined. It's usually cool enough at night to go without air-conditioning, so don't be surprised if many hotels don't have it.

WHERE TO STAY

$$–$$$ ★ **Casa Turire.** Set near sugar plantations and overlooking an artificial lake, this timeless hotel is an elegant base for nearby adventure day trips. The building looks like a manor house that has survived mysteriously intact from the turn of the 20th century. In fact, it's the product of more recent imaginations. From the royal palms that line the driveway to the tall columns and tile floors, Casa Turire is an exercise in attention to detail. High-ceiling guest rooms have hardwood floors and furniture, small balconies, and bright bathrooms with tubs. The central courtyard is a civilized spot in which to relax after a day's adventure, and the restaurant serves reasonably priced international cuisine. The master suite is exceptional, built on two floors with a huge wraparound balcony. A model farm on the property gives kids hands-on time with animals. **Pros:** excellent value; beautiful grounds; good base for adventure trips. **Cons:** mediocre restaurant; need a car to stay here. ✣ *8 km/5 mi south on Carretera a la Suiza from Turrialba* ☎ *2531–1111* 🌐 *www.hotelcasaturire.com* *12 rooms, 4 suites* *In-room: no a/c (some), safe, DVD. In-hotel: restaurant, room service, bar, pool, bicycles, laundry service, Internet terminal, Wi-Fi* ▭ *AE, MC, V* 🍽 *BP.*

$$$ **Rancho Naturalista.** Customized guided bird-watching within a 160-acre private nature reserve is the reason to stay here. The ranch is a birder's paradise, and the narrow focus may be too much for those not interested in our feathered friends. More than 400 species of birds and thousands of different kinds of moths and butterflies live on the reserve and nearby sites, and a resident ornithologist helps you see and learn as much as you want. The two-story lodge is upscale modern with rustic touches, as are the separate cabins. Good home cooking is served in the indoor and outdoor dining rooms, both of which have beautiful views of Volcán Irazú and the Turrialba Valley. Guided tours, meals, horseback riding, and your birding guide are all included in the price. **Pros:** birder's paradise; hiking trails for guests; warm atmosphere. **Cons:** rooms can be musty with dated feel; not a great base for adventure day trips; need a car to stay here. ✣ *20 km/12 mi southeast of Turrialba, 1½ km/1 mi south of Tuís, then up a rough road* ☎ *2433–8278 for reservations, 2554–8100 for directions* 🌐 *www.ranchonaturalista.net* *15 rooms, 13 with bath* *In-room: no a/c, no phone, no TV, Internet. In-hotel: restaurant, laundry service, no-smoking rooms* ▭ *No credit cards* 🍽 *FAP.*

$ **Turrialtico.** Dramatically positioned on a hill overlooking the valley east of Turrialba, this hotel has impressive views of the surrounding

4

countryside; it's the best budget option in the area. An open-sided restaurant occupies the ground floor, above which are handsome rooms with hardwood floors. Ask for one on the west side—these have dazzling views of Turrialba and, if there are no clouds, Volcán Irazú. The restaurant serves a small selection of authentic Costa Rican and international dishes. The only problem is that the rustic wooden construction makes the rooms anything but soundproof. **Pros:** rich views at budget prices; good opportunity to mingle with Ticos. **Cons:** thin walls; less service oriented than other options; need a car to stay here. *8 km/5 mi east of Turrialba on road to Siquirres 2538–1111 www.turrialtico.com 14 rooms, 6 cabins In-room: no a/c, no phone, no TV, Wi-Fi (some). In-hotel: restaurant, bar, laundry service AE, D, DC, MC, V BP.*

$$ **Volcán Turrialba Lodge.** On the slope of the volcano, usually accessible only by 4WD vehicle (which the lodge will arrange for a fee), the lodge has simple but comfortable rooms, most with a wood-burning stove. Rates include three meals. You'll eat well: the proprietors serve healthful Costa Rican food. Even more compelling are the tours. Mountain-biking and horseback-riding trips can be arranged, as well as a 10-hour trek from the Volcán Turrialba to Guápiles via Braulio Carrillo National Park. This place is not for everyone—it gets chilly at over 10,000 feet—but it's a unique mountain escape and a great value. A variety of packages, with one, two, or all three meals, is yours for the booking. ■ **TIP→Day-trippers are welcome.** **Pros:** good value; proximity to volcano; friendly staff. **Cons:** gets chilly; options limited on rainy days; need a car to stay here. *20 km/12 mi east of Cot, turn right at Pacayas on road to Volcán Turrialba, 4 km/2½ mi on dirt road 2273–4335 www.volcanturrialbalodge.com 28 rooms In-room: no a/c, no phone, no TV. In-hotel: restaurant, bar, pool AE, MC, V BP, MAP, FAP.*

The Northern Plains

WORD OF MOUTH

"Here is a beautiful view of the Arenal Volcano, the most active volcano in Costa Rica. We stayed at a nearby hotel and had a room with a volcano view, as well as skies so clear we could see the summit."

—photo by Msoberma, Fodors.com member

WELCOME TO NORTHERN PLAINS

TOP REASONS TO GO

★ **Walk in a cloud:** Explore Monteverde's misty world on treetop walkways up to 41 meters (138 feet) off the ground.

★ **Windsurfing:** Lake Arenal is one of the top windsurfing spots on earth; winds can reach 50 to 60 MPH December through April.

★ **Arenal Volcano:** You can hear the rumblings of the world's third–most active volcano for miles around, and, on clear nights, watch crimson rock and gas ooze down its flanks.

★ **Watching wildlife:** Waterbirds, monkeys, turtles, crocodiles, jaguars, and sloths abound in the 25,000-acre Caño Negro National Wildlife Refuge.

★ **Walk down to the waterfall:** The reward for a tough hike down to Cataratas de la Fortuna is a magnificent series of waterfalls.

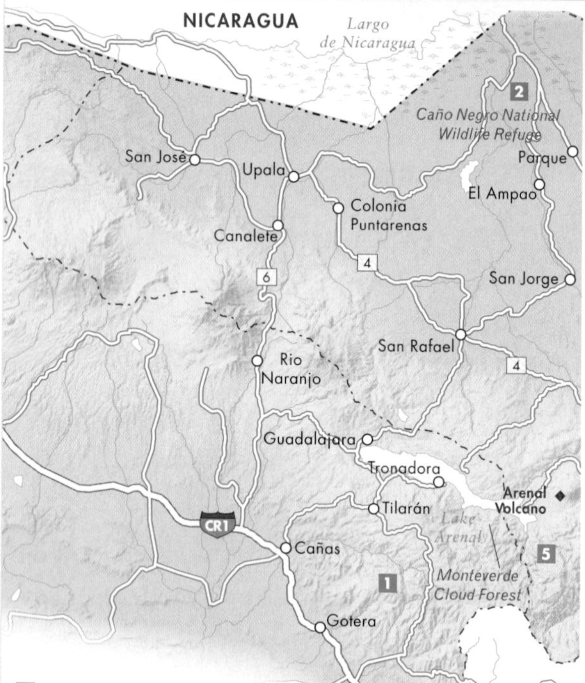

1 Monteverde Cloud Forest Area. Home to the rainiest of cloud forests, the Monteverde Cloud Forest Area is also the canopy-tour capital of Costa Rica. Hanging bridges, treetop tram tours, and zip lines: it's got it all. As if that's not enough, horseback riding, rappelling, and nature hikes are also available.

2 The Far North. Caño Negro National Wildlife Refuge, in the Far North, is great for fishing, birdwatching, and communing with nature.

3 The Sarapiquí Loop. The Sarapiquí Loop circles Braulio Carrillo National Park, rare for its easy-to-access primary rain forest. The loop's highlight is Poás Volcano; its turquoise crater lake and steaming main crater make it the favorite volcano of many visitors.

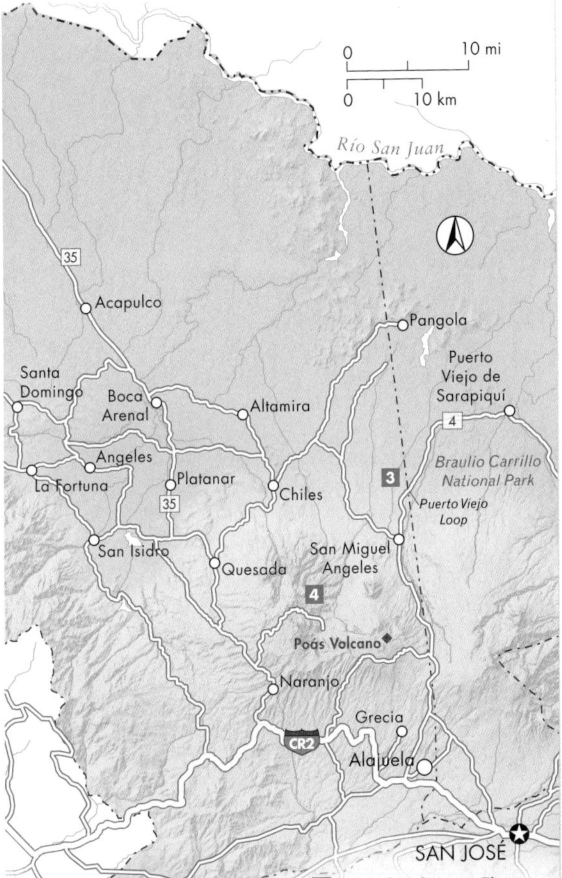

4 Northwest of San José. Northwest of San José are one of the country's best crafts communities, Sarchí, and some luxurious countryside lodges.

5 Arenal Volcano. The Arenal Volcano area is one of the hottest tourist destinations in Costa Rica. La Fortuna is the closest town to the volcano; among many nearby diversions are the Tabacón Hot Springs. Tilarán, west of Lake Arenal, is the place to be if you're a windsurfer.

GETTING ORIENTED

Geographically, the Zona Norte (Northern Zone), as it is known locally, separates neatly into two alluvial plains. The rich, lush terrain runs from the base of the Cordillera Central in the south to the Río San Juan, on the border with Nicaragua in the north. Most visitors begin their visit to Costa Rica in San José, many then heading north to La Fortuna, using it as a base for exploring the volcano, waterfall, and Caño Negro, and participating in activities like sportfishing, windsurfing, and kitesurfing at Lake Arenal, and rafting on the Sarapiquí River.

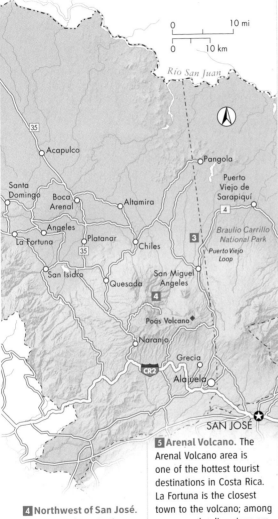

NORTHERN PLAINS PLANNER

The Northern Plains: Plainly Kid-Friendly

Perhaps no region of Costa Rica offers as many activities of interest to the under-18 set. Young children especially will "ooh" (and "eeewwww") at various area animal exhibits devoted to bats (Monteverde, La Virgen de Sarapiquí), frogs (Monteverde, Braulio Carrillo National Park, La Virgen de Sarapiquí, La Paz Waterfall Gardens), butterflies (Monteverde, La Fortuna, La Paz Waterfall Gardens), and snakes (Grecia, Monteverde, La Virgen de Sarapiquí, Braulio Carrillo National Park, La Paz Waterfall Gardens). Guided nature hikes abound; shorter treks can be entertaining and cater to younger ones' shorter attention spans. Most sure-footed and confident teenagers can participate in adult activities. We recommend white-water rafting and canopy tours.

A few operators around here will tell you that kids older than eight can participate in canopy tours. We're skeptical of such claims, even if their brochures show children happily zipping from platform to platform. The gondola-like trams (Braulio Carrillo National Park, Monteverde) are far safer ways to see the rain forest canopy.

Rain Forests Are . . . Rainy

We frequently overhear comments such as "I didn't know it would be so rainy in the rain forest." You heard it here first: that's why they call it the rain forest! During the rainy season it's not unusual for it to rain for several days straight, and even during the dry season, brief showers will come up without notice. Be sure to bring a poncho or rain jacket and waterproof footwear.

The Early Bird Catches the Sun

In the rainy season it's almost a given that you'll get a bit damp on your canopy tour, hike, or horseback ride, and most tour operators provide ponchos. But to avoid a thorough soaking, plan activities for the morning. Rains usually begin around 2 PM, like clockwork, from July through December, although they can be more prolonged in September and October. The clearest time of day is normally before 8 AM.

Safety First

This region is Costa Rica's capital of adventure tourism—it gave birth to the canopy tour—so any risks up here are far more likely to be natural than criminal. Before you set out rafting, zip-lining, rappelling, or bungee jumping, be brutally frank with yourself about your abilities, your physical condition, and your fear levels. (It's almost impossible to turn back on many excursions once you've started.) Even an activity as innocuous as hiking or horseback riding poses a certain amount of risk, and you should never go alone. Nature here is not an amusement park. As Dorothy says in The Wizard of Oz, "Toto, I don't think we're in Kansas anymore."

Remember also that little government oversight over adventure tourism exists here. Pay close attention during any safety briefings and orientation. Don't be afraid to ask questions, and don't be afraid to walk away if something seems off to you.

When to Go

Climate is difficult to pinpoint in this vast region. The Northern Plains links the rainier Caribbean in the east to drier Guanacaste in the west. It's a pretty good rule of thumb to say that precipitation decreases from east to west. Grecia, Sarchí, and Naranjo enjoy a climate similar to Costa Rica's higher-elevation Central Valley, with pleasant springlike days year-round, and well-defined rainy and dry seasons.

Throughout the entire region, the warm and humid rainy season normally takes place June to December. But rains can occur outside the official wet season since the area's low elevation frequently hosts battles between competing weather fronts. Expect highs of 26°C to 32°C (80°F to 90°F) and lows of 15°C to 20°C (60°F to 70°F). Nights are cool and comfortable.

At almost 1,524 meters (5,000 feet), Monteverde has a significantly different climate: it's cool, damp, and breezy much of the time, with average highs around 20°C (70°F) and lows around 13°C (55°F), and high winds in January and February.

Visibility changes daily (and hourly), so your chances of seeing the Arenal and Poás craters are more or less the same year-round, though you may have more luck from February to April, the hottest and driest time of the year.

Early December to April is considered a weather-related high season, although many places in Arenal and Monteverde are beginning to impose high-season rates in July and August to correspond with prime North American and European vacation times.

Dining and Lodging

WHAT IT COSTS IN DOLLARS

	¢	$	$$	$$$	$$$$
Restaurants	under $5	$5–$10	$10–$15	$15–$25	over $25
Hotels	under $50	$50–$75	$75–$150	$150–$250	over $250

Restaurant prices are per person for a main course at dinner. Hotel prices are for two people in a standard double room in high season, excluding service and tax (16.4%).

How Much Time?

Although not centrally located, the Northern Plains can be easily tacked onto stays in other regions of Costa Rica. Fairly decent—decent for Costa Rica, that is—transportation links the region to San José, the Central Valley, and the North Pacific. (Always the exception, Monteverde sits isolated, approached only by rugged roads from all directions.)

If your stay here is limited to two or three days, make La Fortuna your base. Don't miss the volcano, the Tabacón Hot Springs, or Caño Negro Wildlife Refuge.

Most tour operators who have volcano hikes end the day at one of the various thermal springs in the area. "Half-day" tours to Caño Negro actually take most of a day, from around 7:30 AM to 4 PM.

A week in the Northern Plains is more than enough time to experience a great deal of this area—especially if you're longing to get out and get moving. Give yourself four days in La Fortuna/Arenal for rafting trips on area rivers, horseback rides, and kitesurfing or windsurfing on Lake Arenal. Devote the rest of your week to Monteverde Cloud Forest.

Driving yourself between Monteverde and Arenal means negotiating some pretty horrendous roads. Tour operators can arrange for boat or even horse transfers.

CAÑO NEGRO WILDLIFE REFUGE

Think a smaller version of Florida's Everglades and you'll have a good picture of the Refugio Nacional de Vida Silvestre Caño Negro.

This lowland rain-forest reserve in the far northern reaches of Costa Rica near the Nicaraguan border covers 98 square km (38 square mi). It looks remote on the map, but is easily visited on an organized day tour if you're up this way. In 2007 Caño Negro was designated the core of a new UNESCO biosphere called Agua y Paz (Water and Peace), which encompasses more than 2 million acres of wildlife habitat in Costa Rica and Nicaragua.

Caño Negro has suffered severe deforestation over the years, but most of the length of the Río Frío, its principal river, is still lined with trees. The park's vast lake, which floods according to seasonal rains, is an excellent place to watch waterfowl. On land, pumas, tapirs, ocelots, cougars, and the always elusive jaguar make up the mammal life found here—consider yourself fortunate if you spot that last one. Caimans snap everywhere in the knee-deep marshy waters, too.

BEST TIME TO GO

It gets *hot* here, with March and April brutally so, but the January–March dry season is the best time to spot the reserve's migratory bird population. Opportunities abound the rest of the year too, though. No matter what the season, bring sunscreen, water, insect repellant, and a brimmed hat.

FUN FACT

In addition to other bird species, the reserve is the best place to spot the Nicaraguan grackle—the border is just 12 mi away after all. This New World blackbird is only found in Nicaragua and Northern Costa Rica. It's medium-sized, with a long, graduated tail and fairly long bill and legs. Listen for its distinctive whistling, whining call

BOAT TOURS

In the dry season you can ride horses, but a visit here chiefly entails a wildlife-spotting boat tour. You could drive up here on your own—roads to the area are in good shape—but once here, you'd need to arrange for boat transportation. Visiting with a tour company out of La Fortuna—it's a 90-minute ride one way—is the easiest way to see the park.

BIRD-WATCHING

This is the best place in the country to see water birds. Just sit back in your tour boat and survey the passing parade. You're sure to see anhingas spreading their wings to dry; both glossy and white ibis recognizable by their long curved beaks; roseate spoonbills often mistaken for flamingos; and the jabiru, king of the storks. Herons and kingfishers lurk on the banks, ready to spear fish; while jacanas, with their huge feet, forage in the water lettuce, looking as though they are actually walking on water. Above the water, watch for gray-colored snail kites, which true to their name, are hunting for snails.

CAIMAN LAND

Famous for its caimans, Caño Negro still boasts a sizeable population. They're smaller than crocodiles, though—at most 8 feet long—and they are relatively unthreatening since they're too small to eat large mammals (this includes humans). It's a thrill to see them sunning on a bank or to see their spectacled eyes floating just above the water line. Unfortunately, the caimans here are under serious threat from hunters who sneak across the Nicaraguan border and slaughter them by the hundreds for their skins. The proof is sadly on display in the souvenir shops in Nicaragua, where you will see purses and belts made from caiman hides.

TOP REASONS TO GO

BIRD-WATCHING

The reserve is one of Costa Rica's lesser sung bird-watching and wildlife viewing destinations. Caño Negro is growing in popularity, but, for now, a visit here still gives you that "I'm in on a secret the rest of the world doesn't know about" satisfaction.

FISHING

It's not all about wildlife viewing here: Caño Negro is also one of Costa Rica's prime freshwater fishing destinations, with snook and marlin yours for the catching and the bragging rights during the July–March season. (There's barely enough water in the lake the other months of the year, so fishing is prohibited then.) The two lodges inside the reserve can hook you up.

GREAT TOURS

It's easy to get here from the Arenal area, with top-notch operators and their teams of knowledgeable guides organizing day tours from La Fortuna and so-called "evening" tours that actually get you here by the very warm mid-afternoon and depart around dusk. Opt for the morning tours if your schedule permits.

5

VOLCÁN ARENAL

The mile-high Volcán Arenal, Costa Rica's youngest and most active volcano, dominates the region's landscape.

Volcanologists estimate Arenal's age at around 4,000 years and it was dormant for at least 400 years until 1968. It may be local folklore, but residents before then referred to Arenal as simply "the mountain" and apparently, despite its conical shape, did not realize it was a volcano. On July 29, 1968, an earthquake shook the area, and 12 hours later Arenal blew.

Since then, Arenal has been in a constant state of activity—thunderous, rumbling eruptions are sometimes as frequent as one per hour. These earthshaking events remind everyone what it really means to coexist with the world's third most active volcano. Night is the best time to view the action: on a clear evening you can see rocks spewing skyward. Although everyone refers to "lava," "pyroclastic flow," a mix of incandescent rock and gas, is a more apt description of what the volcano churns out. Call it what you will: the spectacle rarely fails to impress.

BEST TIME TO GO

To be honest, viewing Arenal can be hit or miss any time of year. January through April, especially in the early morning, usually means fewer clouds to obscure daytime views. The dry season's clear evenings give the best spectacle of the volcano's flows. Patience is a virtue here.

FUN FACT

Researchers at INBio, the National Biological Institute in Santo Domingo, north of San José have been hard at work around the volcano. They see promise in the lichens growing on Arenal's slopes as a source of new antibiotics.

VOLCANIC TIPS

Two words: "from afar." Under no circumstances should you hike even the volcano's lower slopes on your own. Lava rocks and volcanic gas have killed trekkers who got too close, most recently in 2000. The tour operators we recommend know where the danger lies and take appropriate precautions. Wait until around 2 PM to see if the weather will cooperate, and then book your afternoon volcano hike.

Beyond that, take a liberal interpretation of "exploring" the volcano, and gaze at its majesty from the distance and safety of several area hotels, restaurants, and hot springs that afford postcard views.

HIKING

For intrepid hikers who want to get a little closer to the action, the Las Heliconias trail, which starts at the park reception center, wends through secondary forest and passes by the cooled lava flow from the 1968 eruption. The Los Tucanes trail also leads to the lava fields, but it's more of an uphill hike, beginning near the entrance to the Arenal Observatory Lodge. There's also a hiking trail up to Cerro Chatto, a lopsided, extinct crater, partially filled with water, creating a pretty lake. Since volcano activity and lava flow can change suddenly, check with the park rangers to see which trails are currently safe to hike.

BIRD-WATCHING

If you decide to hike the park's Los Tucanes trail, chances are you'll see at least one of the five species of toucan that have been recorded here: chestnut-billed and keel-billed toucans, the yellow-eared and emerald toucanet, and the collared araçari. You'll never look at a box of Fruit Loops the same after seeing the real thing. Hummingbirds also abound on the volcano's slope. Look for anything tiny and purple.

TOP REASONS TO GO

A PERFECT VOLCANO
Look up "volcano" in the dictionary. You half expect to see a picture of Arenal. Its perfect cone, red-hot flow, plumes of ash, and menacing location close to the tourist town of La Fortuna practically define the term.

SPORTS AND ADVENTURE
No other attraction in Costa Rica has given rise to a list of accompanying entertainment offerings quite so extensive. Come here to pay your respects to Arenal, and you'll find enough other area activities to keep you occupied for days. (You'll also appreciate the backup on those occasions when clouds obscure your view of the volcano.)

ALL BUDGETS WELCOME
We lament that budget and even moderate travelers are being priced out of the market in certain regions of Costa Rica. Not so here. Choose from everything from backpackers' digs to luxury hotels in the area around Arenal. Feel free to stay for days, no matter what your budget.

5

VOLCÁN POÁS

Towering north of Alajuela, the verdant Poás Volcano is covered with a quilt of farms and topped by a dark green shawl of cloud forest.

That pastoral scene disappears once you get to the summit, and you gaze into the steaming, bubbling crater with smoking fumaroles and a gurgling, gray-turquoise sulfurous lake. You'll swear you're peering over the edge of a giant witches' cauldron. That basin, a mile in diameter and nearly 1,000 feet deep, is thought to be the largest active volcanic crater in the world.

Poás is one of Costa Rica's five active volcanoes—it has erupted 40 times since the early 1800s—and is one of those rare places that permit you to see volcanic energy this close with minimal risk to your safety. Authorities closely monitor Poás's activity following several eruptions in March 2006, the first significant increase in activity since 1994. Access is normally open at this writing, but park officials close the route up here on those occasions of any activity they deem "irregular."

BEST TIME TO GO

The peak is frequently shrouded in mist, and you might see little beyond the lip of the crater. Be patient and wait awhile, especially if some wind is blowing—the clouds can disappear quickly. Aim to get here before 10 AM. The earlier in the day you go, the better.

FUN FACT

Forgot your umbrella? (It gets wet up here.) Duck under a *sombrilla de pobre* (poor man's umbrella) plant. These giant leaves can grow to diameters of 4 to 5 feet—plenty big enough to shelter a few hikers caught out in the rain.

VOLCANIC TIPS

A paved road leads all the way from Alajuela to Poás's 8,800-foot summit. The 2009 earthquake wrecked the eastern-approach road from Varablanca, so check before you try that route. No one is allowed to venture into the crater or walk along its edge. ■ **TIP→ Take periodic breaks from viewing: Step back at least every 10 minutes, so that the sulfur fumes don't overcome you. Be sure to bring a sweater or a jacket—it can be surprisingly chilly up here.**

HIKING

From the summit, two trails head into the forest. The second trail, on the right just before the crater, winds through a thick mesh of shrubs and dwarf trees to the eerie but beautiful Botos Lake (**Laguna Botos**), which occupies an extinct crater. It takes 30 minutes to walk here and back, but you'll be huffing and puffing if you're not used to this altitude, almost 9,000 feet above sea level.

BIRD-WATCHING

Although birding can be a little frustrating here because of cloud and mist, more than 330 bird species call Poas home. One of the most comical birds you'll see in Costa Rica is usually spotted foraging in plain sight on the ground: the big-footed finch whose oversized feet give it a clownish walk. Its cousin, the yellow-thighed finch, is easy to recognize by its bright-yellow, er ... thighs. Arrive early and bird around the gate before the park opens, and stop along the road to the visitors center wherever you see a likely birding area. In the underbrush you may find spotted wood-quail or the elusive, buffy-crowned wood-partridge. The trees along the road are a favorite haunt of both black-and-yellow and long-tailed silky flycatchers.

TOP REASONS TO GO

LAVA AND ASH

"Up close and personal with nature" takes on a whole new meaning here. Costa Rica forms part of the Pacific Rim's so-called "Ring of Fire," and a visit to the volcano's summit gives you a close-up view of a region of the earth that is still in formation.

MORE THAN A VOLCANO

The park is not just about its namesake volcano. A few kilometers of hiking trails wind around the summit and let you take in the cloud forest's lichens, ferns, and bromeliads.

A+ FACILITIES

You're on your own in many Costa Rican national parks, which have little by way of facilities. This park is a pleasant exception, with an attractive visitor's center containing exhibits, cafeteria, gift shop, and restrooms.

LOCATION, LOCATION, LOCATION

Poas' proximity to San José, the western Central Valley and many destinations in this chapter makes it an easy half-day trip. Mix and match a volcano visit with several other area attractions.

5

ECO-LODGES IN THE NORTHERN PLAINS

This territory as a whole doesn't garner the attention in eco-circles that other parts of Costa Rica do, but the country has no more diverse region than the Northern Plains.

Cloud forests, rain forests, volcanoes, thermal springs, white-water rivers, waterfalls, coffee and banana plantations, and rolling farmland combine to create the vast landscape that stretches across the northern third of Costa Rica. That translates into a variety of environmentally themed pursuits unmatched anywhere else in the country. The mists of Monteverde define "cloud forest," and the original Quaker settlers stamped their environmental consciousness on the area. La Fortuna and environs have parlayed the presence of the nearby Arenal Volcano into a myriad of activities. The Sarapiquí region is one of the lesser-known (but no less impressive) rain forest regions with a growing selection of small lodges. (And don't forget that this region gave Costa Rica the zip-line canopy tour, one of its best-known and most popular tourist activities.) The tourist industry up here knows what the region has to offer and is keen to preserve what is green. Hotel owners and tour operators are just as eager to show it off to you.

GOOD PRACTICES

Consider public or semi-public transportation for negotiating the Northern Plains. No question: distances are vast, and your own wheels *do* offer you the greatest convenience. It's surprisingly easy, though, to take shuttle transport, base yourself in Arenal or Monteverde, and use occasional taxis to get around once you arrive. Many tour operators in both places are happy to pick you up at your hotel, too.

Also, ask if your hotel recycles. In Monteverde, the answer will usually be "Yes," but it'll be less likely in other places. If enough guests keep requesting it, more lodgings just might hop on the eco-bandwagon.

TOP ECO-LODGES IN THE NORTHERN PLAINS

ARCO IRIS LODGE, MONTEVERDE

The German management here eschews the overused word ecotourism, insisting that many in Costa Rica view the concept as simply e¢otouri$m. But if any lodging were entitled to use the term in its marketing, it would be this one. Comfortable cabins are scattered around the grounds here, and though you're right in the center of town, Arco Iris has managed to create a country feel. (The 135 bird species sighted on the property contribute to that ambience.) That, along with the organic foods, active recycling program, biodegradable materials, and involvement in the community, makes this one of our favorite Costa Rican eco-lodges . . . even if it doesn't call itself that.

LAGUNA DEL LAGARTO LODGE, CIUDAD QUESADA

It doesn't get mentioned in the pantheon of better-known Costa Rican eco-lodges, but this smallish property near the Nicaraguan border offers a variety of nature-themed activities to rival any of the big guys. Accommodation is rustic in this remote locale, but impact on the environment has been minimal. The 1,250-acre rain forest here makes for terrific bird-watching—380 species have been catalogued so far—hiking, and canoeing. Laguna del Lagarto gives back to its community, and has succeeded in bringing employment to a poorer, often forgotten corner of Costa Rica.

LA SELVA, PUERTO VIEJO DE SARAPIQUÍ

You would expect any lodging that functions as a working biological station and where research biologists make up the primary clientele to be eco-friendly. La Selva does not disappoint. The Durham, North Carolina–based Organization for Tropical Studies operates the facility along with two other similar stations in Costa Rica, and offers a fascinating program of nature-themed activities for you, the nonprofessional guest. Keep one caveat in mind, though: scientists take priority in procuring space in the rustic but comfortable cabins.

PLANTING TREES

"Costa Rica" equals "forest" in the minds of most visitors. Truth be told, about half the country has been deforested, much of it occurring in this region. The reasons are mostly understandable: coffee, bananas, and dairy cattle make the Northern Plains the country's breadbasket; for decades, trees have been cleared for farmland.

Enter the *A Que Sembrás un Árbol* program. Loosely translated, that means "May you plant a tree." It forms part of the United Nations' international Planting for the Planet program, whose goal is to plant 3.5 billion trees worldwide each year. Costa Rica's contribution to the agenda, begun in 2008, aims for an annual figure of 7 million trees, around one-third of which are targeted for this region.

Like most environmental initiatives here, the program began at the grassroots level, with area students kicking off the tree planting, soliciting support from area businesses, and petitioning the government to become officially involved in the U.N. project.

THE NORTHERN PLAINS

By Jeffrey Van Fleet

The vast expanse that locals call the Zona Norte (Northern Zone) packs in more variety of activities than any other part of the country. You'll find almost everything in this region that Costa Rica has to offer, except beaches.

Spend any amount of time here and you can partake of—take a deep breath—volcano-viewing, horseback riding, canoeing, kayaking, rafting, rappelling, windsurfing, wildlife-viewing, bird-watching, bungee jumping, shopping, zip-lining, cloud and rain forest hiking, swimming, and hot-springs soaking. Good transportation links to and within the region make it easy to explore.

GETTING HERE

NatureAir and SANSA have daily flights from their respective airports in San José to La Fortuna (FTN). Most travelers to this region fly into San José's Aeropuerto Internacional Juan Santamaría or Liberia's Daniel Oduber Airport. Monteverde and Arenal are equidistant from both. Base your choice of airport on which other areas in Costa Rica you plan to visit in addition to this one.

Buses in this region are typically large, clean, and fairly comfortable, but often crowded Friday through Sunday. Don't expect air-conditioning. Service tends toward the agonizingly slow: even supposedly express buses marked *directo* (direct) often make numerous stops.

Road access to the northwest is by way of the paved two-lane Pan-American Highway (Carretera Interamericana, or CA1), which starts from the west end of Paseo Colón in San José and runs northwest to Peñas Blancas at the Nicaraguan border. Turn north at Naranjo or San Ramón for La Fortuna; at Lagarto for Monteverde; and at Cañas for Tilarán. Calle 3 heading north from downtown San José becomes the Braulio Carrillo Highway and provides the best access to Puerto Viejo de Sarapiquí and environs.

GETTING AROUND

This region manages to mix some of the country's smoothest highways with some of its most horrendous roads. (The road to Monteverde is legendary in the latter regard, but the final destination makes it worth the trip.) Four-wheel-drive vehicles are best on the frequently potholed roads. If you don't want to pay for 4WD, at least rent a car with high clearance. (Many rental agencies insist you take a 4WD vehicle if you mention Monteverde as part of your itinerary.) You'll encounter frequent one-lane bridges; if the triangular CEDA EL PASO faces you, yield to oncoming traffic.

It is possible to rent a car in La Fortuna or Monteverde, but for a far better selection, most visitors pick up their rental vehicles in San José or Liberia.

NORTHWEST OF SAN JOSÉ

The rolling countryside northwest of San José and west of Alajuela holds a mix of coffee, sugarcane, and pasture, with tropical forest filling steep river valleys and ravines. The Pan-American Highway makes a steady descent to the Pacific coast through this region, which is also traversed by older roads that wind their way between simple agricultural towns and past small farms and pastoral scenery. West of San Ramón the valley becomes narrow and precipitous as the topography slopes down to the Pacific lowlands. An even narrower valley snakes northward from San Ramón to the northern lowlands beyond.

GRECIA

26 km/16 mi (45 mins) northwest of Alajuela, 46 km/29 mi (1 hr) northwest of San José.

Founded in 1838, the quiet farming community of Grecia is reputed to be Costa Rica's cleanest town—some enthusiastic civic boosters extend that superlative to all Latin America—but the reason most people stop here is to admire its unusual church.

GETTING HERE AND AROUND

From San José continue west on the highway past the airport—the turnoff is on the right—or head into Alajuela and turn left just before the Alajuela cemetery. Buses leave Calle 20 in San José for Grecia every 30 minutes from 5:30 AM to 10 PM. From Alajuela, buses to Grecia/Ciudad Quesada pick up on the southern edge of town (C. 4 at Avda. 10).

ESSENTIALS

Bank/ATM BAC San José (✉ *100 m north of Central Park*). **Banco Nacional** (✉ *Northwest corner of Central Plaza 20301* ☎ *2494–3600*).

EXPLORING

The brick-red, prefabricated iron **Church of Our Lady of Mercy** (Iglesia de las Mercedes) was one of two buildings in the country made from steel frames imported from Belgium in the 1890s (the other is the metal schoolhouse next to San José's Parque Morazán), when some prominent Costa Ricans decided that metal structures would better withstand the

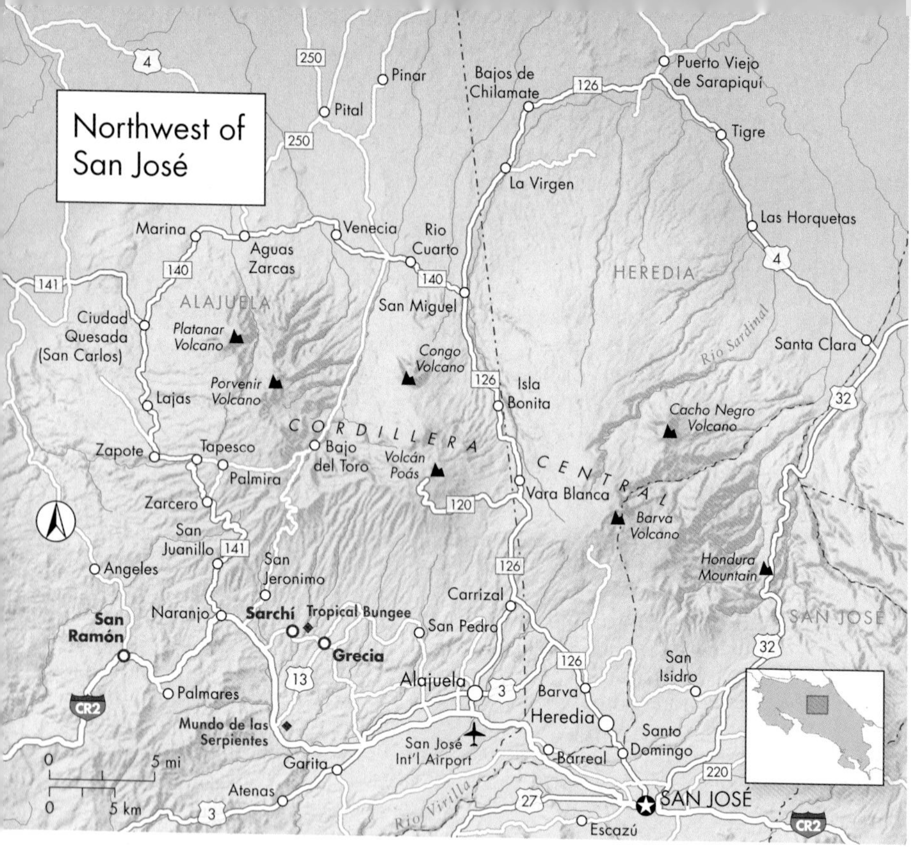

periodic earthquakes that had taken their toll on so much of the country's architecture. The frames were shipped from Antwerp to Limón, then transported by train to Alajuela—from which the walls of the church were carried by oxcarts. Although the park fronting the church is a Wi-Fi hot spot, we advise against pulling out your laptop in such a public setting. ✉ *Avda. 1, Cs. 1–3* ☎ *2494–1616* ⏲ *Daily 8–4.*

On a small farm outside Grecia, the **World of Snakes** (Mundo de las Serpientes) is a good place to see some of the snakes that you are unlikely—and probably don't want—to spot in the wild. Sequestered in the safety of cages here are some 50 varieties of serpents, as well as crocodiles, iguanas, poison dart frogs, and various other cold-blooded creatures. Admission includes a 90-minute tour. ✉ *Poro* ✥ *2 km/1 mi east of Grecia, on road to Alajuela* ☎ *2494–3700* 🌐 *www.theworldofsnakes.com* 🎟 *$11, $6 ages 7–15, free under 7* ⏲ *Daily 8–4.*

OUTDOOR ACTIVITIES

BUNGEE JUMPING

A 79-meter-tall (265-foot-tall) bridge that spans a forested gorge over the Río Colorado is the perfect place to get a rush of adrenaline in a tranquil, tropical setting. Even if you aren't up for the plunge, it's worth stopping to watch a few mad souls do it. **Tropical Bungee** (✉ *Pan-American Hwy.* ✥ *2 km/1 mi west of turnoff for Grecia, down a dirt* *road on the right* ☎*2248–2212 or 8842–0050* 🌐*www.bungee.co.cr* ⏲*Daily 8–11:30 and 1–4*) organizes trips to the bridge. The first jump is $65 and the second is $30. Transportation is free if you jump; $10 if you don't. Reservations are essential. If this is your last hurrah in Costa Rica, a van can take you and your bags straight to the San José airport after your jump.

PAINTED OXCARTS

Coffee has come to symbolize the prosperity of the Central Valley and the nation. Nineteenth-century coffee farmers needed a way to transport this all-important cash crop to the port of Puntarenas on the Pacific coast. Enter the oxcart. Artisans began painting the carts in the early 1900s. Debate continues as to why: the kaleidoscopic designs may have symbolized the points of the compass, or may have echoed the landscape's tropical colors. In any case, the oxcart has become the national symbol. Give way when you see one out on a country road, and marvel at the sight.

WHERE TO STAY

$$–$$$ Fodor'sChoice ★ **Vista del Valle Plantation Inn.** Honeymooners (and many posters to fodors.com) frequent this bed-and-breakfast on an orange and coffee plantation outside Grecia overlooking the canyon of the Río Grande. Cottages are decorated in minimalist style with simple wooden furniture and sliding doors that open onto small porches. Each has its own personality; the Nido, removed from the rest and with the nicest decor, is the most romantic. The hotel's forest reserve has an hour-long trail leading down to a waterfall. Breakfast is served by the pool or in the main house, where you can relax in a spacious living room. The food is quite good, and special dietary requests are accommodated with advance notice. It's a mere 20-minute drive from the airport. **Pros:** attentive staff; secluded cabins; healthful food served. **Cons:** car is necessary for staying here. ✉*On highway 1 km/½ mi west of Rafael Iglesia Bridge; follow signs* 📫*c/o M. Bresnan, SJO–1994, Box 025216, Miami, FL 33102-5216* ☎*2450–0800* 🌐*www.vistadelvalle.com* *10 cottages* *In-room: no a/c, no phone, no TV. In-hotel: restaurant, pool, Internet terminal, Wi-Fi* *AE, MC, V* *BP.*

SARCHÍ

8 km/5 mi west of Grecia, 53 km/33 mi (1½ hrs) northwest of San José.

Tranquil Sarchí rambles over a collection of hills surrounded by coffee plantations. It's Costa Rica's premier center for crafts and carpentry. People drive here from all over central Costa Rica to shop for furniture, and tour buses regularly descend upon the souvenir shops outside town. The area's most famous products are its brightly painted oxcarts—replicas of those traditionally used to transport coffee.

GETTING HERE AND AROUND

To get to Sarchí from San José, take the highway well past the airport to the turnoff for Naranjo; then veer right just as you enter Naranjo. Direct buses to Sarchí depart from Alajuela (C. 8, between Avdas. 1 and 3) every 30 minutes 6 AM–9 PM; the ride takes 90 minutes.

ESSENTIALS

Bank/ATM Banco Nacional (✉ *South side of soccer field* ☎ *2454–3044*).

Post Office Correos (✉ *50 m west of central plaza*).

EXPLORING

Sarchí's **Parque Central** resembles the central park of any other Costa Rican small town—the facade of its church is frequently compared to a wedding cake—but the park's real attraction is the world's largest oxcart, constructed and brightly painted by longtime local factory Taller Eloy Alfaro e Hijos and enshrined in the Guinness Book of World Records. The work logs in at 18 meters (45 feet) and weighs 2 tons. Since no other country is attached to oxcarts quite the way Costa Rica is, we don't look for that record to be broken anytime soon. ✉ *Center of Sarchí.*

Costa Rica's only real oxcart factory left, **Eloy Alfaro and Sons Workshop** *(Taller Eloy Alfaro e Hijos)*, was founded in 1923, and its carpentry methods have changed little since then, although the "e Hijos" portion of the family (the sons) runs the operation these days. The two-story wooden building housing the wood shop is surrounded by trees and flowers—mostly orchids—and all the machinery on the ground floor is powered by a waterwheel at the back of the shop. Carts are painted in the back, and although the factory's main product is a genuine oxcart—which sells for about $2,000—there are also some smaller mementos that can easily be shipped home. ✉ *200 m north of soccer field* ☎ *2454–4131* ⏲ *Weekdays 8–4.*

If you enjoy plants, the **Else Kientzler Botanical Garden** *(Jardìn Botánico Else Kientzler)* is well worth a break from your shopping. The site exhibits some 2,000 plant species, tropical and subtropical, over its sprawling 17 acres. The German owner named the facility, affiliated with an ornamental-plant exporter, after his plant-loving mother. About half of the garden's pathways are wheelchair accessible. ✉ *800 m north of soccer field* ☎ *2454–2070* 🌐 *www.elsegarden.com* 🎟 *$14* ⏲ *Daily 8–4.*

SHOPPING

Sarchí is the best place in Costa Rica to buy miniature oxcarts, the larger of which are designed to serve as patio bars or end tables and can be broken down for easy transport or shipped to your home. Another popular item is a locally produced rocking chair with a leather seat and back.

Fodor's Choice ★ The nicest of the many stores south of town is the **Chaverrí Oxcart Factory** (*Fábrica de Carretas* ✉ *Main road* ✣ *2 km/1 mi south of Sarchí* ☎ *2454–4411*), and you can wander through the workshops in back to see the artisans in action. (Despite the name, much more is for sale here than oxcarts.) Chaverri is a good place to buy wooden crafts; nonwood products are cheaper in San José. Chaverri also runs a restaurant next door, **Las Carretas** (☎ *2454–1633*), which serves a variety of local food all day until 6 PM and has a good lunch buffet.

Taking the plunge. Bunging jumping at the Colorado River Bridge, Grecia.

Sarchí's answer to a shopping mall, the **Plaza de la Artesanía** (✥ *2 km/1 mi south of Sarchí* ☎ *2454–3430*) gathers 34 artisan and souvenir shops under one roof. If you can't find it here, it probably doesn't exist.

SAN RAMÓN

23 km/14 mi west of Sarchí, 59 km/37 mi (1½ hrs) northwest of San José.

Having produced a number of minor bards, San Ramón is known locally as the City of Poets. San Ramón hides its real attractions in the countryside to the north, on the road to La Fortuna, where comfortable lodges offer access to private nature preserves. There's not much to see in San Ramón other than its church.

GETTING HERE AND AROUND

San Ramón is on the Pan-American Highway west of Grecia. To reach the hotel we list north of town, head straight through San Ramón and follow the signs. Buses leave hourly for San Ramón from San José's Terminal de Puntarenas. From Alajuela, buses to San Ramón/Ciudad Quesada pick up on the southern edge of town (✉ *C. 4 at Avda. 10*).

ESSENTIALS

Bank/ATM HSBC (✉ *150 m north of Palí supermarket 20201* ☎ *2445–3602*). **Scotiabank** (✉ *Pan-American Highway, entrance to San Ramón* ☎ *2447–9190*).

Internet Cybercafé San Ramón (✉ *100 m east of Banco Central* ☎ *2447–9007*).

EXPLORING

> **FINDING YOUR WAY**
>
> No sun to help you get your bearings? Just remember that the entrance to most Catholic churches in Costa Rica faces west, so that the congregation can face east toward Rome. Churches in La Fortuna, and the Central Valley's Orosi and Turrialba are notable exceptions.

Aside from its poets, the massive **Church of San Ramón** (Iglesia de San Ramón), built in a mixture of the Romanesque and Gothic styles, is the city's claim to fame. In 1924 an earthquake destroyed the smaller adobe church that once stood here, and the city lost no time in creating a replacement—this great gray concrete structure took a quarter of a century to complete, from 1925 to 1954. To ensure that the second church would be earthquake-proof, workers poured the concrete around a steel frame that was designed and forged in Germany (by Krupp). Step past the formidable facade and you'll discover a bright, elegant interior. ✉ *Across from Parque Central* ☎ *2445–5592* ⏲ *Daily 6–11:30* AM *and 1:30–7* PM.

WHERE TO EAT AND STAY

$ COSTA RICAN ✕ **La Colina.** Here's the only Costa Rican restaurant whose food has been transported into outer space: Retired Costa Rican–American astronaut Franklin Chang, a fan of La Colina's *cajetas especiales,* a sweet orange-coconut dish, took some with him on one of his NASA missions. This roadside diner, with its requisite plastic chairs, has an eclectic menu. Start your meal with a delicious ceviche, moving on to the famous rice and chicken or, for the more adventurous, *lengua en salsa* (tongue in tomato sauce). Meals begin with complimentary chips and pickled vegetables. ✉ *Highway to Puntarenas* ✣ *2 km/1 mi west of San Ramón* ☎ *2445–4956* ▭ *AE, D, DC, MC, V.*

$$$–$$$$ ★ **Villa Blanca.** This charming hotel is on a working dairy and coffee farm constructed and once owned by former Costa Rican president Rodrigo Carazo. The farmhouse contains the reception desk, bar, and restaurant; down the hill are lovely casitas, each a replica of a traditional adobe farmhouse complete with whitewashed walls, tile floors, cane ceilings, and fireplaces. Resident guides lead nature walks through the adjacent cloud-forest reserve, which is excellent bird-watching territory. Horses are available for exploring the rest of the farm. **Pros:** attentive service; many activities; secluded location. **Cons:** far from sights; need car to stay here. ✣ *20 km/12 mi north of San Ramón on road to La Fortuna* 📫 *Apdo. 247–1250, Escazú* ☎ *2461–0300* 🌐 *www.villablancacr.com* *34 casitas* *In-room: no a/c, no phone, refrigerator, no TV, Wi-Fi (some). In-hotel: restaurant, bar, spa, Internet terminal, Wi-Fi* ▭ *AE, D, DC, MC, V* 🍽 *BP.*

EN ROUTE

The small town of **Zarcero,** 15 km (9 mi) north of Sarchí on the road to Ciudad Quesada, looks like it was designed by Dr. Seuss. Evangelisto Blanco, a local landscape artist, modeled cypress topiaries in fanciful animal shapes—motorcycle-riding monkeys, a lightbulb-eyed elephant—that enliven the park in front of the town church. The church interior is covered with elaborate pastel stencil work and detailed religious paintings by the late Misael Solís, a well-known local artist. Sample some cheese if you're in town, too; Zarcero-made cheese is one of Costa Rica's favorites.

THE ARENAL VOLCANO AREA

Whether you come here from San José or Liberia, prepare yourself for some spectacular scenery—and a bumpy ride. As you bounce along on your way to Arenal, you may discover that "paved" means different things in different places, and that potholes are numerous. Any discomfort you experience is more than made up for by the swaths of misty rain forest and dramatic expanses of the Cordillera Central. Schedule at least 3½ hours for the trip.

VOLCANIC BEGINNINGS

Many people who settled the Northern Plains came to the then-isolated region in the 1940s and '50s from other parts of the country to take part in government-sponsored homesteading programs. Thanks to rich volcanic soil, the agricultural region became one of the most productive in Central America. More recently, since the 1968 Arenal eruption (the first eruption in nearly 500 years), Ticos have been drawn by jobs in the ever-expanding tourism industry. In the far northern section of the region, close to the border, a great number of residents are Nicaraguan.

5

CIUDAD QUESADA (SAN CARLOS)

55 km/33 mi (1 hr) northwest of Zarcero.

Highway signs point you to CIUDAD QUESADA, but it's simply "San Carlos" in local parlance. Like so many other places in Costa Rica, the landscape is splendid, but what passes for architecture varies from ordinary to downright hideous. San Carlos is where everyone in the region comes to shop, take in a movie, get medical care, and generally take care of the necessities. There's also an enormous bus terminal (with shopping center and multiplex movie theater) where you can make connections to almost anywhere in the northern half of the country. If you're traveling from San José to points north, your bus will stop here even if it's a so-called express. This lively mountain market town–provincial capital serves a fertile dairy region and is worth a stop for a soak in the soothing thermal waters in the area.

GETTING HERE AND AROUND

Ciudad Quesada lies 55 km (33 mi) off the Pan-American Highway north of Zarcero. Buses from San José leave Terminal Atlántico Norte on the hour, from 5 AM to 7 PM. The trip takes around three hours. The Ciudad Quesada bus terminal is a couple of kilometers from the center of town; taxis wait at the terminal to take you into town. Driving is straightforward in this part of the country, as long as you don't get stuck behind a slow-moving truck transporting sugarcane to the Central Valley. Try to get an early start if you're driving yourself; the road between Zarcero and Ciudad Quesada begins to fog over by early afternoon.

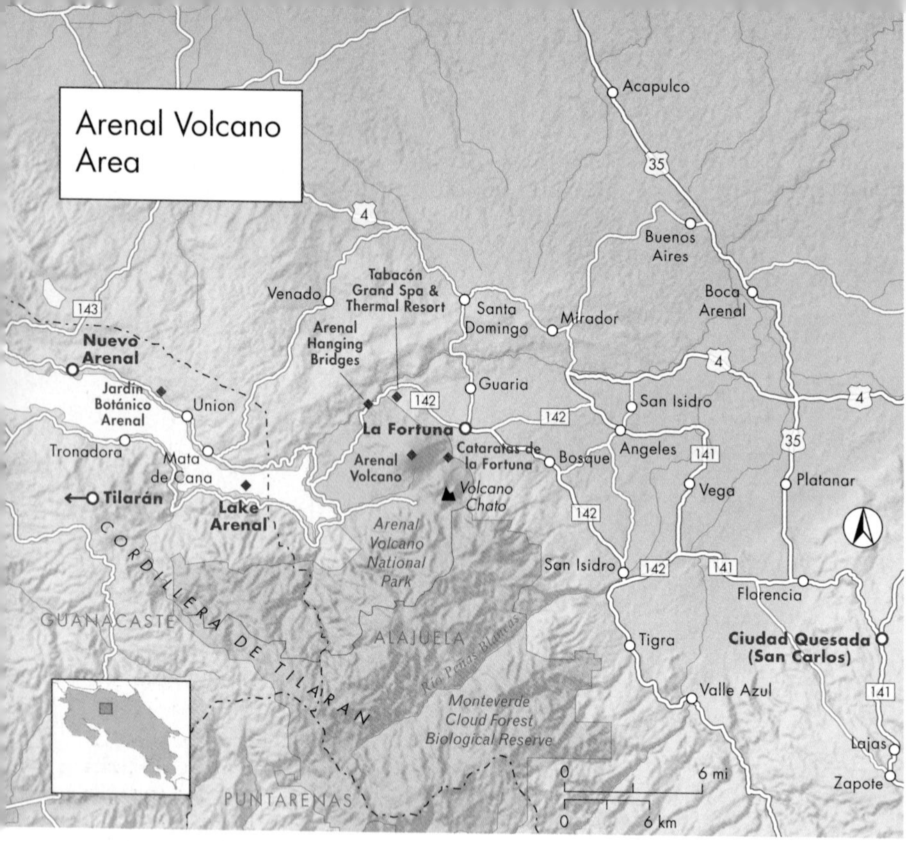

ESSENTIALS

Bank/ATM BAC San José (✉ *100 m north and 125 m west of cathedral*). Banco Nacional (✉ *Across from north side of cathedral* ☎ *2401–2000*). Scotiabank (✉ *Across from Mercado de Artesanías* ☎ *2461–9660*).

Internet Internet Café (✉ *150 m north of park* ☎ *2460–3653*).

Medical Assistance Hospital de San Carlos (✣ *2 km/1 mi north of park* ☎ *2460–1176*).

Post Office Correos (✉ *Across from Escuela Chávez*).

EXPLORING

Termales del Bosque lets you soak those tired muscles, as you watch the birds, for a more reasonable price than most of the other hot springs in the region. ✉ *Hwy. 140* ✣ *7 km/4½ mi east of Ciudad Quesada* ☎ *2460–4740* 🌐 *www.termalesdelbosque.com* *Day pass $12* ⏲ *Daily 8* AM*–10* PM.

WHERE TO STAY

$ ★ **Laguna del Lagarto Lodge.** One of Costa Rica's smaller eco-lodges, this hideaway in a 1,250-acre rain forest near the Nicaraguan border gives shelter to 380 bird species and counting. Rustic cabins come with single beds. Buffet-style meals are served on a patio with river and forest views. Rates include one guided walk on the 10 km (6 mi) of forest trails, a tour of the butterfly garden, and use of canoes. Recommended extras include horseback riding and a boat trip up to the border on the San Carlos River. (Bring your passport, since San Carlos River is officially Nicaraguan territory.) Ask about transfers available (at extra cost) from various points, including San José. The knowledgeable personnel here speak German, in addition to the requisite English and Spanish. **Pros:** small size; attentive service; great excursions. **Cons:** rough road to get here; spartan rooms. *✣7 km/4 mi north of Boca Tapada, 135 km/78 mi northeast of Ciudad Quesada ☎2289–8163 ⊕www.lagarto-lodge-costa-rica.com ⇆20 rooms, 18 with bath ♁In-room: no a/c, no phone, no TV. In-hotel: restaurant, bar, laundry service ▭MC, V ¶◎¶EP.*

CAUTION

The ubiquitous OFFICIAL TOURIST INFORMATION signs around La Fortuna and Monteverde aren't "official" at all, but are merely storefront travel agencies and tour operators hoping to sell you tours.

5

LA FORTUNA

50 km/30 mi (45 mins) northwest of Ciudad Quesada, 75 km/45 mi (90 mins) north of San Ramón, 17 km/11 mi east of Arenal Volcano, 190 km/118 mi (3 hrs by car; 25 mins by plane) northwest of San José.

At the foot of massive Arenal Volcano, the small community of La Fortuna attracts visitors from around the world. Nobody comes to La Fortuna—an ever-expanding mass of hotels, tour operators, souvenir shops, and *sodas* (small, family-run restaurants)—to see the town itself. Instead, thousands of tourists flock here each year to use it as a hub for visiting the natural wonders that surround it. The volcano, as well as waterfalls, vast nature preserves, great rafting rivers, and an astonishing array of birds, are to be found within an hour or less of your hotel. La Fortuna is also the best place to arrange trips to the Caño Negro National Wildlife Refuge *(⇨ below)*.

After the 1968 eruption of Arenal Volcano, La Fortuna was transformed from a tiny, dusty farm town to one of Costa Rica's tourism powerhouses, where visitors converge to see the volcano in action. Volcano-viewing can be hit or miss, though, especially during the rainy season (May–November). One minute Arenal looms menacingly over the village; the next minute clouds shroud its cone. Early morning, especially in the dry season, is always the best time to catch a longer gaze.

NAVIGATING LA FORTUNA

Taxis in and around La Fortuna are relatively cheap, and will take you anywhere; a taxi to the Tabacón resort should run about $8. Get a cab at the stand on the east side of Parque Central.

GETTING HERE AND AROUND

Choose from two routes from San José: for a slightly longer, but better road, leave the Pan-American Highway at Naranjo, continuing north to Zarcero and Ciudad Quesada. Head northwest at Ciudad Quesada to La Fortuna; or for a curvier but shorter route, continue beyond Naranjo on the Pan-American Highway, turning north at San Ramón, arriving at La Fortuna about 90 minutes after the turnoff. Either route passes through a mountainous section that begins to fog over by afternoon. Get as early a start as possible. NatureAir and SANSA fly daily to La Fortuna (FTN); flights land at an airstrip at the hamlet of El Tanque, 7 km (4 mi) east of town. Van transport ($5 one-way) meets each flight to take you into La Fortuna.

Gray Line has daily shuttle bus service between San José, La Fortuna and Arenal ($35), and Monteverde ($35). Interbus also connects San José with La Fortuna, Ciudad Quesada, San Ramón, and Monteverde (all $39) daily, with connections from here to a few of the North Pacific beaches. Public buses depart five times daily from San José's Terminal Atlántico Norte. Travel time is four hours. Although billed as an express route, the bus makes many stops.

Desafío Adventures provides a fast, popular three-hour transfer between Monteverde and La Fortuna via taxi, boat, then another taxi, for $25 each way.

ESSENTIALS

Bank/ATM BAC San José (✉ *75 m north of gas station*). **Banco de Costa Rica** (✉ *Money exchange booth; across from south side of church*). **Banco Nacional** (✉ *Central Plaza* ☎ *2479–9355*).

Bus Contacts Gray Line Tourist Bus (☎ *2220–2126* 🌐 *www.graylinecostarica.com*). **Interbus** (☎ *2283–5573* 🌐 *www.interbusonline.com*).

Internet Expediciones Fortuna (✉ *Across the street from Central Plaza* ☎ *2479–9104*).

Medical Clinic Seguro Social (✉ *300 m east of Parque Central* ☎ *2479–9643*).

Pharmacy FarmaTodo (✉ *50 m north of La Fortuna's gas station* ☎ *2479–8155*).

Post Office Correos (✉ *Across from north side of church*).

Rental Cars Alamo (✉ *100 m west of church, La Fortuna* ☎ *2479–9090* 🌐 *www.alamocostarica.com*). **Mapache** (✉ *800 m west of church, La Fortuna* ☎ *2479–0010* 🌐 www.mapache.com). **Poás** (✉ *25 m south of church, La Fortuna* ☎ *2479–8027* 🌐 www.poasrentacar.com).

Tour Information Desafío Adventures (✉ *Behind church, La Fortuna* ☎ *2479–9464* 🌐 *www.desafiocostarica.com*)

EXPLORING

MAIN ATTRACTIONS

Fodor's Choice ★ Getting to **Fortuna Waterfall** (*Cataratas de la Fortuna*) requires a strenuous walk down ½ km (¼ mi) of precipitous steps, but it's worth the effort. Allow 25 to 50 minutes to reach the falls. Swimming in the pool under the waterfall is usually safe. Wear sturdy shoes or water sandals with traction, and bring snacks and water. You can get to the trailhead from La Fortuna by walking or taking an inexpensive taxi ride. Arranging a tour with an agency in La Fortuna is the easiest option. ✉ *Yellow entrance sign off main road toward volcano* ✣ *7 km/4 mi south of La Fortuna* *$6* *Daily 8–4.*

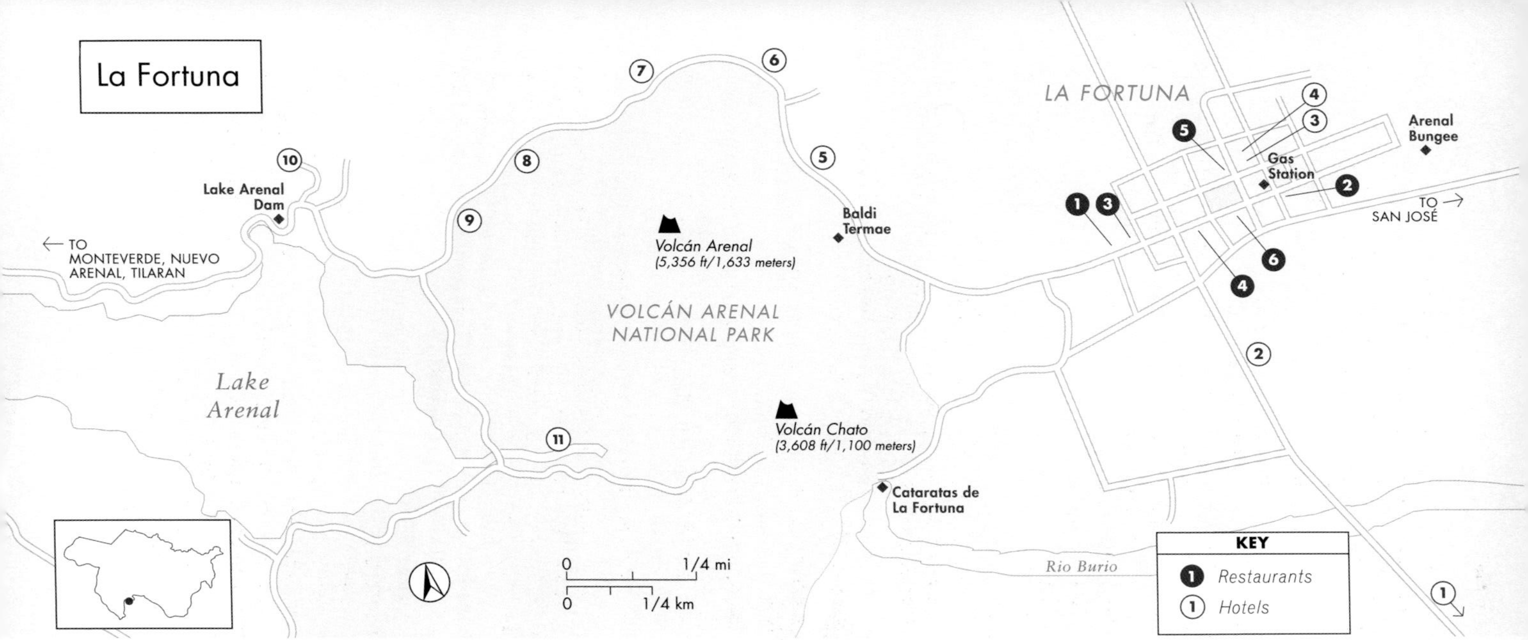

Restaurants ▼

- Don Rufino **2**
- La Choza de Laurel **1**
- Las Brasitas **3**
- Lava Rocks Café **4**
- Rancho La Cascada **5**
- Soda La Parada **6**

Hotels ▼

- Arenal Country Inn **2**
- Arenal Nayara **6**
- Arenal Observatory Lodge **11**
- Cabinas Los Guayabos **8**
- Cabinas Oriuma **3**
- Hotel Bosques de Chachagua **1**
- Hotel San Bosco **4**
- The Lost Iguana Resort ... **10**
- Montaña de Fuego **7**
- La Pradera **5**
- Tabacón Grand Spa & Thermal Resort **9**

5

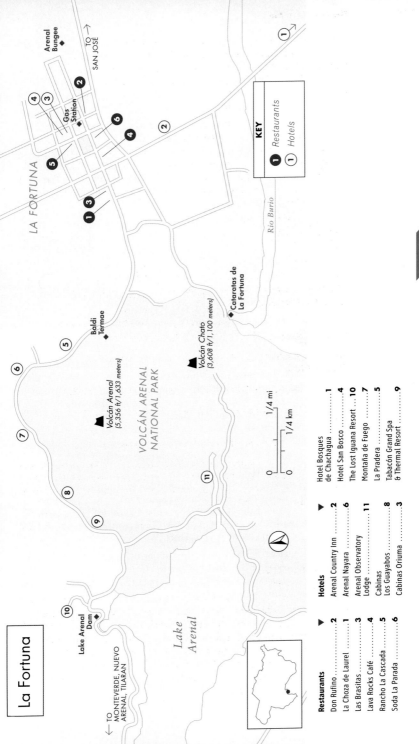

"Our best day in Costa Rica—canyoneering and waterfall rappelling near the active Arenal Volcano." —photo by sportster, Fodors.com member

Arenal Hanging Bridges is actually a series of trails and bridges that form a loop through the primary rain forest of a 250-acre private reserve, with great bird-watching and volcano-viewing. Fixed and hanging bridges allow you to see the forest at different levels. It's open rain or shine, and there are things to do in both climates. Shuttle service from La Fortuna can be arranged. ✉ *Arenal Dam, 4 km/2½ mi west of Tabacón* ☎ *2479–9686 or 2290–0469* 🌐 *www.hangingbridges.com* 🎟 *$34; bird tour $45, shuttle $12* ⏲ *Daily 7–4:30; evening tour at 5:30.*

ALSO WORTH SEEING

The town's squat, pale, concrete **Church of San Juan Bosco,** unremarkable on its own, wins Costa Rica's most-photographed-house-of-worship award. The view of the church from across the central park, with the volcano in the background, makes a great photo of the sacred and the menacing. ✉ *West side of Parque Central.*

OFF THE BEATEN PATH

In 1945 a farmer in the mountain hamlet of Venado fell in a hole, and thus discovered the **Venado Caverns** *(Cavernas de Venado).* The limestone caves contain eight chambers extending about 2½ km (1½ mi). Sunset Tours *(⇨ Outdoor Activities, below)* runs trips. If you're non-claustrophobic, willing to get wet, and don't mind bats—think carefully—this could be the ticket for you. ✉ *45 mins north of La Fortuna and 20 mins southeast of San Rafael* ☎ *2479–9415* 🎟 *$35* ⏲ *Daily 7–8.*

OUTDOOR ACTIVITY

Fodor's Choice ★ **Desafío Adventures** (✉ *Behind church* ☎ *2479–9464* 🌐 *www.desafiocostarica.com*) can take you rafting, horseback riding, hiking, canyoning, and rappelling. **Jacamar Naturalist Tours** (✉ *Across from Parque Central* ☎ *2479–9767* 🌐 *www.arenaltours.com*) launches a variety of tours. **Sunset Tours** (✉ *Across from south side of church* ☎ *2479–9800, 866/417–7352 in North America* 🌐 *www.sunsettourcr.com*) pioneered excursions to the Caño Negro Wildlife Refuge and Venado Caverns and is one of the country's best tour operators.

The **Danaus Ecocenter** (*Ecocentro Danaus*), a small ecotourism project outside of town, exhibits 300 species of tropical plants, abundant animal life—including sloths and caimans—and butterfly and orchid gardens. It's also a great place to see Costa Rica's famed red poison dart frogs up close. A two-hour guided evening tour begins at 6 pm and should be reserved in advance. *4 km/2½ mi east of La Fortuna* ☎ *2479–7019* 🌐 *www.ecocentrodanaus.com* *$6, evening tour $30* *Daily 8–4.*

BUNGEE JUMPING

You don't even need to leave town to plummet from a 39-meter (130-foot tower). **Arenal Bungee** (✉ *500 m east of church* ☎ *2479–7440* 🌐 *www.arenalbungee.com* *Daily 9:30–8:30*), on the east edge of La Fortuna, offers a bungee jump (into a pool if you like) for $50. For another $50, the facility's Rocket Launcher catapults you into the air, with bungeelike recoils to follow. The Big Swing ($50), the third activity here, takes you on a 25-meter-high (85-foot-high), 180-degree arc through the air. You can mix and match activities, too, or do all three for $100. The site is open after dark, but remember that La Fortuna does not face the flow side of Arenal. Twilight is an especially beautiful time to ascend to the top of the tower to catch the sun setting behind the volcano.

CANOPY TOURS

Arenal Rain Forest Reserve, a canopy tour–bridge walk complex near La Fortuna, is operated by the Sky Trek–Sky Walk folks in Monteverde. Alpine-style gondolas transport you to the site, from which you can descend via a zip-line canopy tour or hike through the cloud forest along a series of suspended bridges. ✉ *12 km/7 mi west of La Fortuna, El Castillo* ☎ *2479–9944* 🌐 *www.skytrek.com* *60, $50 tram only, shuttle $8* *Daily 7–4.*

FISHING

Lake Arenal is enormous and stocked with game fish, including tilapia, *guapote* (Central American rainbow bass), and *machaca* (Central American shad). Most tour operators and hotels can set you up with guides. Rates begin at $150. **Jacamar Naturalist Tours** *(⇨ above)* has morning and afternoon sportfishing trips to Lake Arenal and Caño Negro Lagoon.

HORSEBACK RIDING

★ If you're interested in getting up to Monteverde from the Arenal–La Fortuna area without taking the grinding four-hour drive, there's an alternative: **Desafío Adventures** (✉ *Behind church* ☎ *2479–9464* 🌐 *www.desafiocostarica.com*) has a 4½-hour guided horseback trip ($75). The trip involves taxi or van service from La Fortuna to the southern shore

5

of Lake Arenal, and from that trail's end you ride to Monteverde, circumventing poorly maintained trails. A boat ride across Lake Arenal is included. You leave La Fortuna at 7:30 AM and arrive in Monteverde around 2:30 PM. You can also take the trip in reverse. Desafío will provide a driver to transport your rental vehicle, but you must arrange to include that driver in your rental agreement. ■ **TIP→Many other agencies, many of them nothing more than a guy and a horse, lead riding tours between La Fortuna and Monteverde, but along treacherous trails, and some riders have returned with stories of terrified horses barely able to navigate the way. Stick with Desafío.**

ADVENTURE ALTERNATIVE

If you're feeling more community-minded than adventurous, **Desafío Adventures** (✉ *Behind church* ☎ *2479–9464* 🌐 *www.desafiocostarica.com*) has a daylong tour (💵 $75) that takes you to an area animal-rescue center, women's arts-and-crafts cooperative, organic medicinal-plant farm, and recycling center. Lunch is included.

The ride from La Fortuna to the Fortuna Waterfall is appropriate for both novice and experienced riders. **Chaves Horse Tours** (☎ *8354–9159 or 2479–9023*) has guided horseback tours to the waterfall. **Desafío** (*⇨ above*) leads guided horseback tours to the falls.

RAFTING AND KAYAKING

Several La Fortuna operators offer Class III and IV white-water trips on the Río Toro. The narrow river requires the use of special, streamlined boats that seat just four and go very fast. The easier Balsa, Peñas Blancas, Arenal, and San Carlos rivers have Class II and III rapids and are close enough to town that they can be worked into half-day excursions. **Canoa Aventura** (☎ *2479–8200* 🌐 *www.canoa-aventura.com*) can design a canoeing trip with ample wildlife viewing on the Río Peñas Blancas and also has daylong canoe tours of the Caño Blanco Wildlife Refuge. Tours are appropriate for beginners, with a selection of easy floats if you're not feeling too adventurous, and instruction is provided, but the folks here can tailor excursions if you're more experienced.

★ **Desafío Adventures** (✉ *Behind church* ☎ *2479–9464* 🌐 *www.desafiocostarica.com*) pioneered rafting trips in this region, and has day trips on the Río Toro for experienced rafters ($85), half-day rafting and kayaking outings on the nearby Arenal and Balsa rivers ($65) ideal for beginners, as well as a leisurely wildlife-viewing float on the Peñas Blancas ($45). **Ríos Tropicales** (✣ *1 km/½ mi west of La Fortuna* ☎ *2479–0075* 🌐 *www.flowtrips.com*) does the standard trips on the Toro, Peñas Blancas, and Arenal rivers.

RAPPELLING

Rappel down four waterfalls and one rock wall ranging in height from 18 to 45 meters (60 to 150 feet) with **Pure Trek Canyoning** (☎ *461–2110, 866/569–5723 in North America* 🌐 *www.puretrekcostarica.com*). Two guides lead small groups—10 is the maximum size—on a four-hour tour ($90) that departs at 7 AM or noon to a private farm near La Fortuna, with plenty of wildlife-watching opportunities along the way. The excursion includes transportation, all gear, breakfast (for the morning tour), and a light lunch.

CAUTION

What's the newest craze in Monteverde and Arenal? Four-wheel all-terrain vehicles. Seemingly everybody rents them out these days, but we've heard too many reports of rollover accidents and don't recommend them. (They're also very noisy, and we object to them on that principle.)

EN ROUTE

Increased development on the highway between La Fortuna and the Tabacón resort has led to a noticeable increase in traffic. It is hardly the proverbial urban jungle, and it is one of the country's prettiest stretches of road, but you should drive with caution. Cars dart in and out of driveways. Visitors congregate along the side of the road (likely a sloth-spotting). Drivers gaze up at the volcano that looms over the highway. Keep your eyes on the road.

5

WHERE TO EAT

$$–$$$ ECLECTIC

Don Rufino. The town's most elegant-looking restaurant is really quite informal. The L-shaped bar fronting the main street has become a popular expat and tourist hangout and lends a relaxed air to the place. No need to dress up here: this is La Fortuna, after all. The friendly waitstaff might suggest tilapia in bacon-and-tomato sauce or spinach ricotta to the accompaniment of coconut rice. ⊠*Across from gas station* ☎*2479–9997* ▭*AE, D, DC, MC, V.*

$ COSTA RICAN

La Choza de Laurel. Tantalizing rotisserie chicken, and pretty cloves of garlic and bunches of onions dangling from the roof draw in passersby to this old favorite, open-air Costa Rican–style restaurant a short walk from the center of town. The place opens early, perfect for a hearty breakfast on your way to the volcano. ⊠*300 m northwest of church* ☎*2479–7063* ▭*AE, D, DC, MC, V.*

$ COSTA RICAN

Las Brasitas. Chicken turns over wood on a rotisserie in a brick oven at this pleasant restaurant on the road heading out of town toward the volcano. Try the succulent chicken when it ends up in the tasty fajitas or any of the other ample-size Mexican dishes. Service is good, and you have your choice of three open-air dining areas arranged around a garden. Two are secluded and intimate; the third is less so, being closer to the road. ⊠*200 m west of church* ☎*2479–9819* ▭*AE, D, DC, MC, V.*

$$ COSTA RICAN

Lava Rocks Café. A couple of trendy steps above the average *soda* in food and atmosphere (and a bit higher in price), this open-air café has tasty *casados* (plates with rice, beans, fried plantains, and fish, chicken, or meat) and sandwiches, and we love their rich fruit *batidos* (milk shakes). ⊠*Across from south side of church* ☎*2479–8039* ▭*AE, D, DC, MC, V.*

$ COSTA RICAN

Rancho la Cascada. You can't miss its tall, palm-thatch roof in the center of town. The festive upstairs contains a bar, with large TV, neon signs, and flashing lights. Downstairs the spacious dining room—decorated with foreign flags—serves basic, midprice Costa Rican fare. Its location right in the center of town makes it a favorite for tour groups. ⊠*Across from northeast corner of Parque Central* ☎*2479–9145* ▭*AE, D, DC, MC, V.*

¢ COSTA RICAN **Soda La Parada.** Here's a case study in what tourism does to a place: La Fortuna's only 24-hour eatery was once a hole-in-the-wall joint across from the bus stop. It has now expanded greatly and even has sit-down dining. It is still a convenient place to grab a quick and cheap meal, and to stock up on snacks for long bus rides. *Across from Parque Central and regional bus stop 2479–9547 No credit cards.*

RICE & BEANS

"More tico than gallo pinto" is an old saying here, but just how Costa Rican is the country's signature dish? Nicaraguans also claim it as their own, and the rivalry has led to five Guinness Book of World Records bids for the largest batch. Costa Rica captured the first title in 2003, only to have Nicaragua top it a mere 12 days later. Costa Rica recaptured the prize in 2005. After three years of grumbling, in 2008, Nicaragua snatched the title back with a 22,000-dish batch of rice and beans. Costa Rica more than doubled that amount at a March 2009 event with a whopping 50,000 servings. Nicaragua, it's your serve.

WHERE TO STAY

$$ **Arenal Country Inn.** It doesn't quite approximate an English country inn, although it is charming. Each brightly furnished modern room has two queen-size beds and a private patio. The lush grounds have great views of the Arenal Volcano. A big breakfast is served in the restaurant, an open-air converted cattle corral. You can take lunch and dinner there as well. **Pros:** good value; friendly staff. **Cons:** several blocks from center of town; removed from sights. *1 km/½ mi south of church of La Fortuna, south end of town 2479–9670, 2283–0101 in San José www.arenalcountryinn.com 20 rooms In-room: safe, refrigerator. In-hotel: restaurant, bar, pool, laundry service AE, DC, MC, V BP.*

$$$ **Arenal Nayara.** Opened in early 2008 just off the road between La Fortuna and Tabacón, this newest entry into the upscale Arenal sweepstakes has expansive grounds scattered with cabins, all strategically aligned to provide balcony views of the volcano. Each is decorated in bright tropical colors and comes with dark-wood furnishings, four-post canopy beds, plasma TVs, DVD players, whirlpool tubs, and two showers, one indoors and one outdoors. Those are amenities rarely seen up here, and rarely seen in Costa Rica at all, for that matter. All rooms here are no-smoking. **■TIP→Nayara offers frequent Web-only promotions.** **Pros:** luxurious rooms; great volcano views; good restaurant. **Cons:** massive grounds navigable only by golf cart shuttles; can be difficult to find. *5 km/3 mi west of La Fortuna 2479–1600 www.arenalnayara.com 24 rooms In-room: safe, refrigerator, DVD. In-hotel: restaurant, room service, bar, tennis court, pool, spa, laundry service, Wi-Fi, no-smoking rooms AE, D, DC, MC, V EP*

$–$$ **Arenal Observatory Lodge.** You're as close as anyone should be to an active volcano at the end of the winding road leading to the lodge—a mere 1¾ km (1 mi) away. The isolated lodge was founded by Smithsonian researchers in 1987. It's fairly rustic, emphasizing that outdoor activities are what it's all about. Rooms are comfortable and simply furnished (comforters on beds are a cozy touch), and most have stellar

A leisurely stroll across a suspension bridges in Monteverde.

views. Five of the rooms here are wheelchair accessible, as are a couple of miles of the property's trails. After a hike, take a dip in the infinity-edge pool or 12-person hot tub, which face tall pines on one side and the volcano on the other. The dining room, which serves tasty and hearty food, has great views of the volcano and lake. **Pros:** best volcano views; secluded location; numerous activities. **Cons:** rough road to get here; isolated location. ✣ *3 km/2 mi east of dam on Laguna de Arenal; from La Fortuna, drive to Tabacón resort and continue 4 km/2½ mi past resort to turnoff at base of volcano; turn and continue for 9 km/5½ mi* ✉ *Apdo. 13411–1000, San José* ☎ *2479–1070, 2290–7011 in San José* 🌐 *www.arenalobservatorylodge.com* *43 rooms, 38 with bath; 2 suites* *In-room: no a/c, no phone, safe, no TV. In-hotel: restaurant, bar, pool, laundry service* *AE, D, DC, MC, V* *BP.*

$ **Cabinas Los Guayabos.** A great budget alternative to the more expensive lodgings lining the road to the volcano is this group of basic but spotlessly clean cabins managed by a friendly family. The units have all the standard budget-lodging furnishings, but each comes with its own porch facing Arenal—ideal for viewing the evening spectacle. **Pros:** good budget value; friendly owners; great volcano views. **Cons:** rustic rooms; best to have car to stay here. ✣ *9 km/5½ mi west of La Fortuna* ☎ *2479–1444* 🌐 *www.cabinaslosguayabos.com* *8 cabins* *In-room: no phone, refrigerator* *V* *EP.*

¢ **Cabinas Oriuma.** Right in the center of town, Oriuma is a popular choice for budget travelers and tour groups. The modern rooms are sparkling clean. The second-floor balcony is a pleasant spot to relax and read, watch the happenings in the Parque Central across the street, or plan your next adventure. **Pros:** good budget value; close to center of town. **Cons:** some rooms get street noise; boxy design. ✉ *15 m north of Parque Central* ☎ *2479–9111* ✎ *oriuma@ice.co.cr* *25 rooms* *In-room: no a/c (some), no phone, safe* ▭ *MC, V* *EP.*

$$ **Hotel Bosques de Chachagua.** At this working ranch, intersected by a brook, you can see *caballeros* (cowboys) at work, take a horseback ride into the rain forest, and look for toucans from the open-air restaurant, which serves local meat and dairy products. Each cabina (cottage) has a pair of double beds and a deck with a picnic table. Large, reflective windows enclosing each cabina's shower serve a marvelous purpose: birds gather outside your window to watch their own reflections while you bathe and watch them. The lodge is 3 km (2 mi) up a rough track—4WD is a must in rainy season—on the road headed south from La Fortuna to La Tigra. **Pros:** secluded location; many activities. **Cons:** rustic rooms; far from sights. ✣ *12 km/7 mi south of La Fortuna* *Apdo. 476–4005, Ciudad Cariari* ☎ *2468–1010* ⊕ *www.chachaguarainforesthotel.com* *32 cabinas* *In-room: no a/c, no phone, no TV. In-hotel: restaurant, bar, pool* ▭ *AE, D, DC, MC, V* *BP.*

$–$$ **Hotel San Bosco.** Covered in blue-tile mosaics, this two-story hotel is certainly the most attractive and comfortable in the main part of town. Two kitchen-equipped cabinas (which sleep 8 or 14 people) are a good deal for families. The spotlessly clean, white rooms have polished wood furniture and firm beds and are linked by a long veranda lined with benches and potted plants. **Pros:** good value; close to center of town. **Cons:** some rooms get street noise; boxy design. ✉ *220 m north of La Fortuna's gas station* ☎ *2479–9050* ⊕ *www.arenal-volcano.com* *34 rooms* *In-room: no phone, refrigerator (some), Wi-Fi. In-hotel: pool, Internet terminal* ▭ *AE, D, DC, MC, V* *BP.*

$–$$ **La Pradera.** "The Prairie" is a simple roadside hotel with comfortable guest rooms that have high ceilings, spacious bathrooms, and verandas. Two rooms have whirlpool tubs. Beef eaters should try the thatch-roof restaurant next door. The steak with jalapeño sauce is a fine, spicy dish. **Pros:** good value; good restaurant. **Cons:** spartan rooms; lackadaisical staff. ✣ *2 km/1 mi west of La Fortuna* ☎ *2479–9597* ⊕ *www.lapraderadelarenal.com* *28 rooms* *In-room: no phone, refrigerator (some). In-hotel: restaurant, bar, pool* ▭ *MC, V* *BP.*

$$$–$$$$ **The Lost Iguana Resort.** Despite its relative isolation—you're several kilometers beyond Tabacón—the Lost Iguana hums with activity, and is a favorite among fodors.com posters. Buildings here scale a hillside a short drive up a rugged road above the Arenal Dam. Each unit comes with a huge picture window that leads out onto an individual balcony with stupendous volcano views. Rooms are decorated with locally made art and bamboo-frame beds. Suites come with vaulted ceilings, private garden showers, and private whirlpools. A few cottages tuck away on the grounds and make ideal getaways for families. The location makes this a good bet if you have your own vehicle, but taxis can ferry you to and from area attractions, too. **Pros:** secluded location; great volcano views; many activities. **Cons:** removed from sights; rough final stretch of road to get here. ✣ *31 km/19 mi west of La Fortuna on highway toward Nuevo Arenal* ☎ *2479–1555, 2267–6148 in San José* ⊕ *www.*

lostiguanaresort.com ⇨ *42 rooms* ♖ *In-room: safe, refrigerator, Wi-Fi. In-hotel: restaurant, room service, bar, pools, spa, laundry service, no kids under 6 except in houses* ▭ *AE, MC, V* 🍴 *EP.*

$$–$$$ Fodor'sChoice ★ **Montaña de Fuego.** On a manicured grassy roadside knoll, this highly recommended collection of cabins affords utterly spectacular views of Arenal Volcano. (If you don't stay here, Montaña de Fuego's Acuarela Restaurant dishes up tasty Costa Rican cuisine and throws in the same stupendous views.) The spacious, well-made hardwood structures have large porches, and rooms have rustic decor. The friendly management can arrange tours of the area. ■ **TIP→Montaña de Fuego offers periodic Internet-only discounts when you book via its Web site.** **Pros:** great volcano views; many activities for guests only; good restaurant. **Cons:** some cabins face highway noise; sometimes difficult to find space. ⊹ *8 km/5 mi west of La Fortuna* ☎ *2479–1220, 877/383–4612 in North America* ⊕ *www.montanadefuego.com* ⇨ *68 cabinas* ♖ *In-room: safe, refrigerator. In-hotel: restaurant, bars, pools, spa, laundry service, Internet terminal, Wi-Fi* ▭ *AE, DC, MC, V* 🍴 *BP.*

$$$$ ★ **Tabacón Grand Spa & Thermal Resort.** Without question, Tabacón, with its impeccably landscaped gardens and hot-spring rivers at the base of Arenal Volcano, is one of Central America's most famous and compelling resorts, and a 2008 remodeling of all units here cemented that status. The hot springs and small but lovely spa customarily draw visitors inland from the ocean with no regrets. All rooms have tile floors, a terrace or patio, and big bathrooms. Some have volcano views; others overlook the manicured gardens. The suites are some of the country's finest lodgings, with tile floors, plants, beautiful mahogany armoires and beds, and two-person whirlpool baths. The hotel's intimacy is compromised by its scale and its popularity with day-trippers—a reservations system for day passes is limiting the intrusion and improving that situation somewhat—but it has some private areas for overnight guests only, including a dining room and pool. All rooms here are no-smoking, although smoking is permitted in public areas. ■ **TIP→Tabacón offers frequent Internet-only discounts if you book directly through its Web site.** **Pros:** luxurious hot springs; great volcano views; good restaurant. **Cons:** crowded with tour groups; chain-hotel design; music sometimes too loud. ⊹ *13 km/8 mi northwest of La Fortuna on highway toward Nuevo Arenal* ☎ *2460–2020, 2519–1900 in San José, 877/277–8291 in North America* ✉ *Apdo. 181–1007, San José* ⊕ *www.tabacon.com* ⇨ *114 rooms, 11 suites* ♖ *In-room: safe, refrigerator, DVD, Internet. In-hotel: 2 restaurants, room service, bars, pools, gym, spa, Wi-Fi, no-smoking rooms* ▭ *AE, D, DC, MC, V* 🍴 *BP.*

SHOPPING

★ **Toad Hall** (⊠ *Road between Nuevo Arenal and La Fortuna* ☎ *2692–8001*), open daily from 8 to 6, sells everything from indigenous art to maps to recycled paper and used books. The owners can give you the lowdown on every tour and tour operator in the area; they also run a deli-café with light snacks and views of the lake and volcano.

NIGHTLIFE

People in La Fortuna tend to turn in early, though there are a few clubs and discos for night owls. **Volcán Look Disco** (*✣5 km/3 mi west of La Fortuna ☎2479–9616*), which bills itself as the largest Costa Rican disco outside San José, erupts with dancing and music on weekends. Pizzeria **Vagabundo** (*✣3 km/2 mi west of La Fortuna ☎2479–9565*) turns into a lively bar in the evening, with foosball and billiards in the back room.

IN MEMORIAM

Those yellow hearts with halos painted on the pavement mark spots where people have died in car accidents or vehicles have struck and killed pedestrians. An alarming number of them dot streets and roads around the country. Drive (and walk) with utmost caution.

VOLCÁN ARENAL NATIONAL PARK

Shimmering Lake Arenal, all 125 square km (48 square mi) of it, lies between green hills and a rumbling volcano. It's Costa Rica's largest inland body of water. Many visitors are surprised to learn it's a man-made lake, created in 1973 when a giant dam was built. A natural depression was flooded, and a 32-km-long by 14.4-km-wide (20-mi-long by 9-mi-wide) lake was born. The almost constant winds from the Caribbean make this area a windsurfing mecca. Outfitters in La Fortuna, Nuevo Arenal, and Tilarán run fishing, windsurfing, and kite-surfing trips on the lake. Desafío, an operator based in La Fortuna and Monteverde, has a half-day horseback trip between the two towns, with great views of the lake (⇨ *see Exploring in La Fortuna, above*).

NUEVO ARENAL

40 km/25 mi (1 hr) west of La Fortuna.

Much of the original town of Arenal, at one of the lowest points near Lake Arenal, was destroyed by the volcano's 1968 eruption, and the rest was destroyed in 1973, when Lake Arenal flooded the region. The *nuevo* (new) town was created about 30 km (19 mi) away from the site of the old. It doesn't have much to interest tourists, but is about halfway between La Fortuna and Tilarán, making it a good stop for a break, and an even better base with a couple of truly lovely lodgings nearby.

GETTING HERE AND AROUND

The route from La Fortuna to Nuevo Arenal around the north shore of Lake Arenal is in better shape than it has been in years, with only a couple of short atrocious sections to negotiate. Expect smooth sailing west of the Tabacón resort as far as the Arenal Dam, beyond which you should stick to daylight travel only. Watch out for the raccoonlike coatimundis (*pizotes* in Spanish) that scurry along the road. Longtime human feeding has diminished their ability to search for food on their own, and the cookies and potato chips they frequently get make matters worse.

The perfect way to end the day. A nice soak in the hot springs in Arenal Volcano National Park.

Public buses run twice daily from La Fortuna to Nuevo Arenal and beyond to Tilarán.

ESSENTIALS

Bank/ATM Banco Nacional (*West side of church* *2694–4122*).

Internet Tom's Pan (*300 m south of gas station* *2694–4547*).

Post Office Correos (*Next to Guardia Rural*).

WHERE TO STAY

$ Fodor'sChoice ★ **Chalet Nicholas.** John and Cathy Nicholas (and their resident Great Danes) have converted their hillside home into a charming B&B with stunning views of the lake and volcano. The two rosewood rooms downstairs have tile floors. Up a spiral staircase lies the L-shaped, all-wood double loft with three beds and a back porch that overlooks the large garden. All rooms have volcano views. Birds abound: 100 species have been catalogued on the grounds. The entire property is no-smoking. **Pros:** attentive owners; great breakfasts; good value. **Cons:** best for dog lovers; need car to stay here. *3 km/2 mi west of Nuevo Arenal 2694–4041 www.chaletnicholas.com 3 rooms In-room: no a/c, no phone, no TV. In-hotel: restaurant, no-smoking rooms No credit cards BP.*

$$$–$$$$ **La Mansión Inn Arenal.** Halfway between La Fortuna and Nuevo Arenal, the elegant La Mansión Inn sits at the point where the volcano begins to disappear from sight, but the lake views (and the sunsets) remain as spectacular as ever. Individual cottages scatter around the 25-acre grounds on Arenal's north shore. Brightly colored wrought-iron furnishings decorate every split-level unit. As befits such a secluded

place, bird-watching opportunities abound. ■ **TIP→The hotel offers frequent Web-only packages.** **Pros:** luxurious furnishings; stupendous lake views. **Cons:** far from sights; need car to stay here. ✉ *Road between Nuevo Arenal and La Fortuna* ☎ *2692–8018, 877/660–3830 in North America* 🌐 *www.lamansionarenal.com* *18 cottages, 3 suites* *In-room: no a/c (some), no phone, refrigerator, DVD (some), no TV (some). In-hotel: restaurant, bar, pools, spa, laundry service, Wi-Fi* ▭ *AE, D, DC, MC, V* *BP.*

$$ Fodor's Choice ★ **Villa Decary.** There's everything to recommend at this hillside lodging overlooking Lake Arenal, but it all goes back to owners Jeff and Bill and their attentive service. Rooms have large picture windows and private balconies—great places to take in the ample bird-watching opportunities—and bright yellow-and-blue spreads and drapes. Higher up the hill, spacious bungalows afford an even better view. The hotel accepts payment in American Express traveler's checks, too. All rooms here are no-smoking. **Pros:** attentive owners; great breakfasts; good value. **Cons:** need car to stay here. ✥ *2 km/1 mi east of Nuevo Arenal* ☎ *8383–3012* ☎ *2694–4330* 🌐 *www.villadecary.com* *5 rooms, 3 bungalows* *In-room: no a/c, no phone, no TV. In-hotel: restaurant, Wi-Fi, no-smoking rooms* ▭ *MC, V* *BP.*

TILARÁN

Heading west around Laguna de Arenal, you pass a couple of small villages and arrive at the quiet whitewashed town of Tilarán, on the southwest side of the lake. A windmill farm in the hills high above the town attests to its being the windiest place in the country, and it's used as a base by bronzed windsurfers. For those days when you get "skunked" (the wind fails to blow), horseback riding and mountain biking can keep you busy. A lakeside stroll is a pleasant way to while away a few hours.

GETTING HERE AND AROUND

22 km/14 mi (45 mins) southwest of Nuevo Arenal, 62 km/38 mi (1½ hrs) west of La Fortuna.

The road from La Fortuna via Nuevo Arenal is in reasonable shape these days, with a few short potholed stretches. Give yourself sufficient time—say, two hours—for the trip, and make the trip during daylight hours. Public buses travel to and from La Fortuna twice daily, and from a small terminal at Calle 20 and Avenida 3 in San José five times daily.

ESSENTIALS

Bank/ATM Banco Nacional (✉ *Central Plaza* ☎ *2695–5610*). **CooTilarán** (✉ *150 m north of cathedral* ☎ *2695–6155*).

Hospital Clínica Tilarán (✉ *200 m west of Banco Nacional* ☎ *2695–5093*).

Post Office Correos (✉ *115 m west of municipal stadium*).

OUTDOOR ACTIVITIES

WINDSURFING AND KITESURFING

The best selection of wind- and kitesurfing equipment for rent or purchase can be found at **Tilawa Wind Surf** (✉*Hotel Tilawa* ✣*8 km/5 mi north of Tilarán* ☎*2695–5050* 🌐*www.windsurfcostarica.com*). It's the only outfitter here open year-round. Beginner's lessons start at $65.

Rent wind- and kitesurfing equipment at **Tico Wind** (✣*30 km/18 mi west of Nuevo Arenal* ☎*2692–2002* 🌐*www.ticowind.com*) during the December to April season. It offers beginner's lessons starting at $45, or enroll in a multiday course for $200.

WHERE TO STAY

$–$$ **Hotel Tilawa.** This Costa Rican homage to the Palace of Knossos on Crete has neoclassical murals, columns, and plant-draped arches that somehow don't seem dramatically out of place. The large rooms have two queen-size beds with Guatemalan bedspreads and natural wood ceilings; the bathrooms are especially spacious. Sailing tours in a 39-foot catamaran, the windsurfing and kite-surfing school and shop, and the skateboarding park make this a practical place to base yourself if you want an active vacation. Packages include the use of windsurfing gear. The open-air patio restaurant dishes up steaks and seafood. **Pros:** many activities; stupendous lake views. **Cons:** isolated location; lackluster staff. ✣*8 km/5 mi north of Tilarán* ☎*2695–5050* 🌐*www.hotel-tilawa.com* 📫*Apdo. 92–5710, Tilarán* *20 rooms* *In-room: no a/c, no TV. In-hotel: restaurant, bar, pool, spa, water sports, bicycles, laundry service* ▭*MC, V* 🍴*EP.*

MONTEVERDE CLOUD FOREST AREA

Monteverde is a rain forest, but you won't be in the tropics, rather in the cool, gray, misty world of the cloud forest. Almost 900 species of epiphytes, including 450 orchids, are found here; most tree trunks are covered with mosses, bromeliads, ferns, and other plants. Monteverde spans the Continental Divide, extending from about 1,500 meters (4,920 feet) on the Pacific slope and 1,350 meters (4,430 feet) on the Atlantic slope up to the highest peaks of the Tilarán Mountains at around 1,850 meters (6,070 feet).

MONTEVERDE CLOUD FOREST BIOLOGICAL RESERVE

★ *10 km/6 mi (30 mins) south of Santa Elena, 35 km/22 mi (2 hrs) southeast of Tilarán, 167 km/104 mi (5 hrs) northwest of San José.*

Close to several fine hotels, the private Reserva Biológica Bosque Nuboso Monteverde is one of Costa Rica's best-kept reserves, with well-marked trails, lush vegetation, and a cool, damp climate. The collision of moist winds with the Continental Divide here creates a constant mist whose particles provide nutrients for plants growing at the upper layers of the forest. Giant trees are enshrouded in a cascade of orchids, bromeliads, mosses, and ferns, and in those patches where sunlight penetrates, brilliantly colored flowers flourish. The sheer size of everything, especially the leaves of the trees, is striking. No less

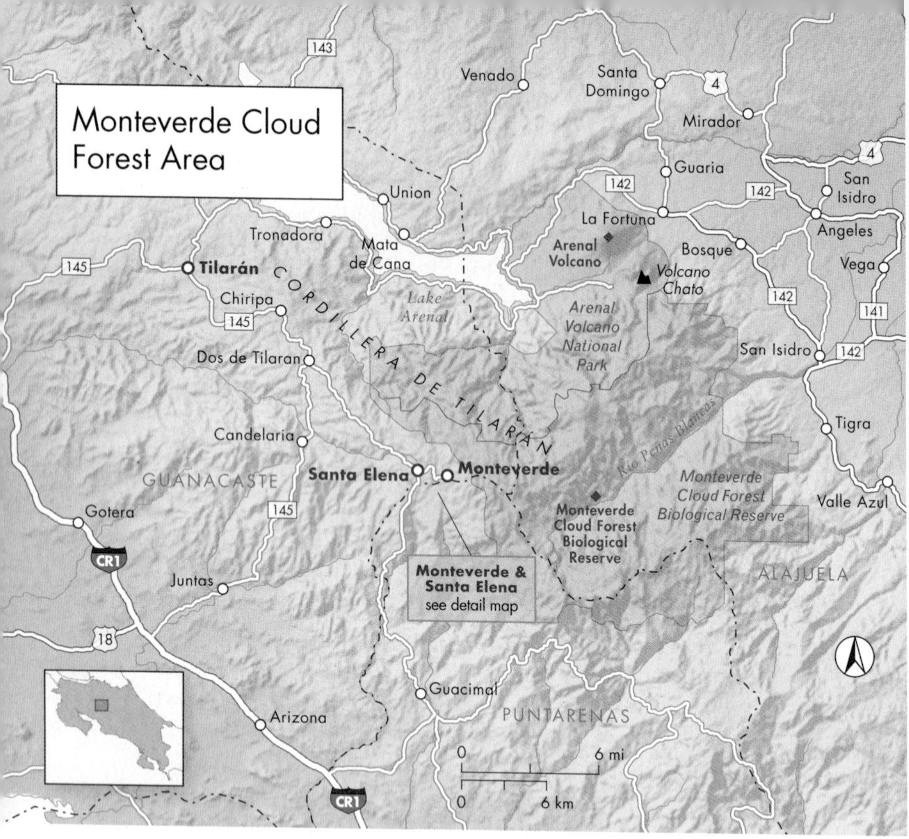

astounding is the variety: 2,500 plant species, 400 species of birds, 500 types of butterflies, and more than 100 different mammals have so far been catalogued at Monteverde. A damp and exotic mixture of shades, smells, and sounds, the cloud forest is also famous for its population of resplendent quetzals, which can be spotted feeding on the *aguacatillo* (similar to avocado) trees; best viewing times are early mornings from January until September, and especially during the mating season of April and May. Other forest-dwelling inhabitants include hummingbirds and multicolor frogs.

For those who don't have a lucky eye, a short-stay aquarium is in the field station; captive amphibians stay here just a week before being released back into the wild. Although the reserve limits visitors to 160 people at a time, Monteverde is one of the country's most popular destinations. We do hear complaints (and agree with them) that the reserve gets too crowded with visitors at times. As they say, the early bird catches the worm, and the early visitor has the best chance at spotting wildlife. Allow a generous slice of time for leisurely hiking to see the forest's flora and fauna; longer hikes are made possible by some strategically placed overnight refuges along the way. At the reserve entrance you can buy self-guide pamphlets and rent rubber boots; a map is provided when you pay the entrance fee. You can navigate the reserve on your own, but a guided tour (7:30 and 11:30 AM and 1 PM) is invaluable for getting the most out of your visit. There's also another option: take advantage of their two-hour guided night tours starting each evening at 7:15 (reservations required), and the reserve provides transport from area hotels for an extra $3. ✉ *10 km/6 mi south of Santa Elena* ☎ *2645–5122* 🌐 *www.cct.or.cr* 🎫 *$17 ($9 for students with International Student Identity Card) plus $17 with guide services; $17 night tour* ⏲ *Daily 7–4.*

CAUTION

The San José–Monteverde public bus route is notorious for theft; watch your bags, and never let your passport and money out of your sight—or off your person.

Never take advice from the street "guides" who meet incoming buses in Monteverde and La Fortuna. They claim to want to help you find accommodations and tours, when in reality they receive kickbacks for sending tourists to less-than-desirable hotels or to unqualified "tour guides."

5

DID YOU KNOW?

Monteverde's Quakers, or more officially, the Society of Friends, no longer constitute the majority here these days, but their imprint on the community remains strong. (Don't expect to see anyone dressed like the man on the Quaker Oats box.) The Friends' meeting house, just south of the Cheese Factory on the road to the reserve, welcomes visitors at meetings of worship, 10:30 AM Sunday and 9 AM Wednesday. Most of the time is spent in quiet reflection.

GETTING HERE AND AROUND

Buses from San José leave twice daily from the Terminal Atlántico Norte (✉ *C. 12 at Avda. 9*), at 6:30 AM and 2:30 PM, stopping in the center of Santa Elena and at various locations on the way up the mountain as far as the Cheese Factory. Buses from Santa Elena leave for San José at 6:30 AM and 2:30 PM daily. Taxis from Santa Elena are $7. Buses from Tilarán to Santa Elena leave once a day, at 12:30 PM. The roads to the area are some of the worst in the country. ■ **TIP→Monteverde's sole gas station, near the entrance to the Hotel Belmar, is closed at this writing because of its alleged failure to meet environmental standards, with tentative plans to reopen sometime in 2009. Fill your tank before you venture up here.**

MONTEVERDE AND SANTA ELENA

Monteverde is 167 km/104 mi (5 hrs) northwest of San José. Santa Elena is 6 km/4 mi (30 mins) north of Monteverde and 35 km/22 mi (2 hrs) southeast of Tilarán.

The area's first residents were a handful of Costa Rican families fleeing the rough-and-ready life of nearby gold-mining fields during the 1940s. They were joined in the early 1950s by Quakers, conscientious objectors from Alabama fleeing conscription into the Korean War. A number of things drew them to Costa Rica: just a few years earlier it had abolished its military, and the Monteverde area offered good grazing. But it was the cloud forest that lay above their dairy farms that soon attracted the attention of ecologists. Educators and artisans followed, giving Monteverde and its "metropolis," the village of Santa Elena, a mystique all their own. In any case, Monteverde looks quite a bit different than it did when the first wave of Quakers arrived. New hotels have sprouted up everywhere, traffic grips the center of town, and a small shopping mall has gone up. A glut of rented all-terrain vehicles contributes to the increasing din that disrupts Monteverde's legendary peace and quiet. Some define this as progress. Others lament the gradual chipping-away at what makes one of Costa Rica's most special areas so, well, special. Locals have taken to posting signs that exclaim "¡PARQUEO, NO! ¡PARQUE SÍ!" ("PARKING LOT, NO! PARK, YES!"). We side with them. You can still get away from it all up here, but you'll have to work harder at it than you used to. In any case, you'll not lack for things to do if seeing nature is a primary reason for your visit.

Note that a casual reference to "Monteverde" generally refers to this entire area, but officially the term applies only to the original Quaker settlement, which is by the dairy-processing plant just down the mountain from the reserve entrance. If you follow road signs exclusively, you'll end up a bit outside the town of Santa Elena.

The only way to see the area's reserves, including the Monteverde Cloud Forest, is to hike them *(⇨Hiking in Outdoor Activities, below)*.

NAVIGATING MONTEVERDE AND SANTA ELENA

There will be times you wish you had your own vehicle, but it's surprisingly easy to get around the Monteverde area without a car. Given the state of the roads, you'll be happy to let someone else do the driving. However, if you do arrive by rental car, the road up the mountain from Santa Elena is paved as far as the gas station near the entrance to the Hotel Belmar. Taxis are plentiful; it's easy to call one from your hotel, and restaurants are happy to summon a cab to take you back to your hotel after dinner. Taxis also congregate in front of the church on the main street in Santa Elena. Many tour companies will pick you up from your hotel and bring you back at the end of the day, either free or for a small fee.

GETTING HERE AND AROUND

Getting here means negotiating some of the country's legendarily rough roads, but don't let that deter you from a visit. Years of promises to pave the way up here have collided with politics and scarce funds, but many residents remain just as happy to keep Monteverde out of the reach of tour buses and day-trippers. ("Do we really want this to be a shore excursion for cruise ships?" some residents ask.) Your own vehicle gives you the greatest flexibility, but a burgeoning number of shuttle-van services connect Monteverde with San José and other tourist destinations throughout the country.

If your bones can take it, a very rough track leads from Tilarán via Cabeceras to Santa Elena, near the Monteverde Cloud Forest Biological Reserve, doing away with the need to cut across to the Pan-American Highway. You need a 4WD vehicle, and you should inquire locally about the current condition of the road. The views of Nicoya Peninsula, Lake Arenal, and Arenal Volcano reward those willing to bump around a bit. Note, too, that you don't really save much time—on a good day it takes about 2½ hours as opposed to the 3 required via Cañas and Río Lagarto on the highway.

Gray Line has daily shuttle bus service between San José, La Fortuna and Arenal ($27), and Monteverde ($38). Interbus also connects San José with La Fortuna, Ciudad Quesada, San Ramón, and Monteverde (all $29) daily, with connections from here to a few of the North Pacific beaches.

Desafío Adventures provides a fast, popular three-hour transfer between Monteverde and La Fortuna. The taxi-boat-taxi service costs $25 one-way.

ESSENTIALS

Bank/ATM Banco Nacional (✉ *50 m north and 50 m west of bus station, Santa Elena* ☎ *2645–5027*).

Bus Information Gray Line Tourist Bus (☎ *2220–2126* 🌐 *www.graylinecostarica.com*). **Interbus** (☎ *2283–5573* 🌐 *www.interbusonline.com*).

Internet Historias Internet Café (✉ *Road to Jardín de Mariposas, 75 m down from Pizzería de Johnny, Cerro Plano* ☎ *2645–6914*).

Medical Clinic Seguro Social (✉ *150 m south of soccer field, Santa Elena* ☎ *2645–5076*).

Pharmacy Farmacia Vitosi (✉ *Across from Super Compro supermarket, Santa Elena* ☎ *2645–5004*).

Post Office Correos (✉ *Center of Santa Elena*).

Rental Cars Hertz (✉ *Cerro Plano, Monteverde* ☎ *2645–6555* 🌐 *www.hertz.com*).

Tourist Information Centro de Visitantes Monteverde (✉ *Across from Super Compro supermarket, Santa Elena* ☎ *2645–6565*). **Desafío Adventures** (✉ *Across from Super Compro supermarket* ☎ *2645–5874* 🌐 *www.monteverdetours.com*).

OUTDOOR ACTIVITIES

ZIP-LINE TOURS

Fodor's Choice ★ **Selvatura**, a cloud forest park outside of Monteverde Reserve, has the only zip-line tour built entirely inside the cloud forest. It has 15 lines and 18 platforms. Mix and match packages to include the complex's hanging bridges, hummingbird and butterfly gardens, and reptile exhibition. *(* *See more on Selvatura, below.**)* ✉ *Office across from church, Santa Elena* ☎ *2645–5929* 🌐 *www. selvatura.com* 🎟 *$40.*

Sky Trek has 11 cables that are longer than those of the Original Canopy Tour—the longest more than 750 meters (2,500 feet). The zip lines here extend between towers above the canopy, rather than between trees, and you'll more likely notice the effects of the wind on this one. ✉ *Office across from Banco Nacional, Santa Elena* ☎ *2645–5238* 🌐 *www.skytrek.com* 🎟 *$44, shuttle $1.*

The **Original Canopy Tour** near Santa Elena was the first zip-line tour in Costa Rica, with 10 platforms in the canopy, and lasting 2½ hours. You arrive at most of the platforms using a cable-and-harness traversing system and climb 12.5 meters (42 feet) inside a strangler fig tree to reach one. ✉ *Cerro Plano* ☎ *2291–4465 in San José for reservations* 🌐 *www.canopytour.com* 🎫 *$45.*

HANGING BRIDGES AND TRAMS

Natural Wonders Tram is an hour-long ride through the rain forest canopy in a two-person carriage on an elevated track. You control the speed of your carriage. Alternatively, a 1½-km (1-mi) walk gives you a ground-level perspective. The site opens for night visits with advance reservations. ✉ *Off main road between Santa Elena and Monteverde, on turnoff to Jardín de Mariposas* ☎ *2645–5960* 🎫 *$15* ⏲ *Daily 8 AM–6 PM.*

★ **Tree Top Walkways**, inside of Selvatura, takes you to heights ranging from 50 meters (150 feet) up to 170 meters (510 feet) on a 3-km (2-mi) walk. These are some of the longest and strongest bridges in the country and run through the same canopy terrain as the zip-line tour. ✉ *Office across from church, Santa Elena* ☎ *2645–5929* 🌐 *www.selvatura.com* 🎫 *$20.*

Sky Walk allows you to walk along five hanging bridges, at heights of up to 41 meters (138 feet), connected from tree to tree. Imposing towers, used as support, mar the landscape somewhat. Reservations are required for guided tours. A tram, similar to that found at the Arenal Rain Forest reserve, is under construction at this writing. ✉ *Across from Banco Nacional, Santa Elena* ☎ *2645–5238* 🌐 *www.skytrek.com* 🎫 *$17* ⏲ *Daily 7–4.*

HORSEBACK RIDING

★ Long-established **Desafío Adventures** (✉ *Across from Super Compro supermarket, Santa Elena* ☎ *2645–5874* 🌐 *www.monteverdetours.com*) leads four-hour horseback tours to the San Luis Waterfall, an area not often taken in by Monteverde visitors, and also has shorter excursions on farms around Santa Elena. For the Monteverde–La Fortuna trip ($65), you travel by car and boat, with a three-hour horseback ride on a flat trail along Lake Arenal. Farms for resting the animals are at each end. It's infinitely more humane for the horses (and you) than the muddy, treacherous mountain trails used by dozens of other individuals who'll offer to take you to Arenal. Tour prices range from $25 to $48.

■ **TIP→** The ride from Monteverde to La Fortuna can be dangerous with outfitters that take inexperienced riders along steep trails. Desafío should be your only choice for getting from Monteverde to La Fortuna on horseback.

Escorted half-day horseback-riding tours ($40) with **Caballeriza El Rodeo** (✉ *West entrance of town of Santa Elena, at tollbooth* ☎ *2645–5764* ✉ *rodeo@racsa.co.cr*) are on a private farm. Excursions are for everyone from beginner to experienced rider. A two-hour sunset tour ($25) begins at 4 PM. Family-operated **El Palomino** (✉ *Just outside Santa Elena* ☎ *2645–5479*) gives escorted afternoon half-day horseback-riding tours on farm areas around Santa Elena. Transportation from your hotel is included.

On a horseback tour with **Gold Tours** (✉ *Monteverde Homestay, 150 m northeast of school, Cerro Plano* ☎ *2645–6914*) you visit a 1920s gold mine. The excursion ($40) includes a demonstration of the panning

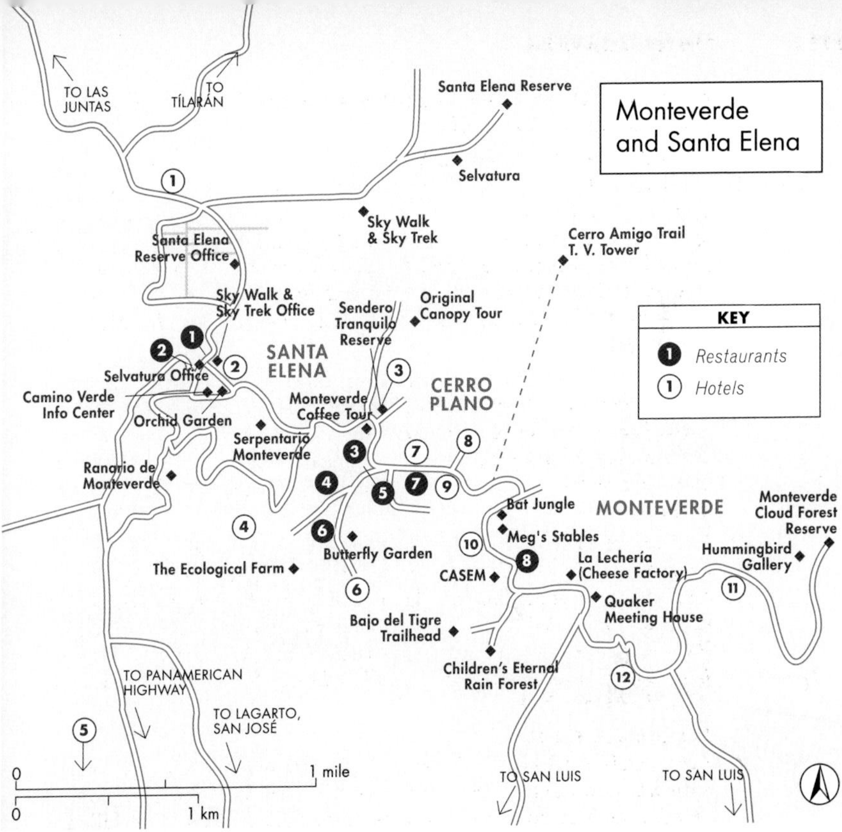

Restaurants ▼

- Cafe Flor de Vida **3**
- Chimera **7**
- De Lucía **4**
- El Márquez **1**
- Moon Shiva **5**
- Sofía **6**
- Stella's Bakery **8**
- Tree House **2**

Hotels ▼

- Arco Iris Lodge **2**
- El Bosque Lodge **10**
- El Establo Mountain Hotel **7**
- Fonda Vela **12**
- Hotel Belmar **8**
- Hotel El Sapo Dorado **3**
- Hotel Montaña Monteverde **9**
- Monteverde Lodge **4**
- Pensión Montverde Inn **6**
- El Sol **5**
- Swiss Hotel Miramontes **1**
- Trapp Family Lodge **11**

methods used during those heady days, and on the trip back a visit to a *trapiche*, a traditional sugarcane mill. Everyone from small children to seasoned experts can participate on these guided horseback-riding trips ($15–$50) with **Meg's Stables** (✉ *Main road, across from CASEM* ☎ *2645–5419*). Reservations are a good idea in high season, and essential if you want an English-speaking guide. A tour to the San Luis waterfalls is geared toward experienced riders.

■ **TIP→Book horseback trips in the morning during rainy season (July–December). Rains usually begin around 2 PM.**

EXPLORING

MAIN ATTRACTIONS

If your time in Monteverde is limited, consider spending it at **Selvatura,** a kind of nature theme park—complete with canopy tour and bridge walks—just outside the Santa Elena Reserve. A 100-bird hummingbird garden, an enormous enclosed 50-species *mariposario* (butterfly garden), a *herpetario* (frog and reptile house), and insect exhibition sit near the visitor center. Transportation from area hotels is included in the price. You can choose from numerous mix-and-match packages, depending on which activities interest you, or take it all in, with lunch and guide included, for $120. Most visitors get by for much less, given that you couldn't take in all there is to do here in one day. ✉ *Office across from church, Santa Elena* ☎ *2645–5929* ⊕ *www.selvatura.com* *Prices vary, depending on package* ⏲ *Daily 8:30–4:30.*

Forty species of butterflies flit about in four enclosed botanical gardens at the **Butterfly Garden** (Jardín de Mariposas). Morning visits are best, since the butterflies are most active early in the day. Your entrance ticket includes an hour-long guided tour. ✉ *Near Pensión Monteverde Inn; take right-hand turnoff 4 km/2½ mi past Santa Elena on road to Monteverde, continue for 2 km/1 mi* ☎ *2645–5512* ⊕ *www.monteverdebutterflygarden.com* *$9, $3 for kids under 12* ⏲ *Daily 9:30–4.*

Only in Monteverde would visitors groove to the nightlife at an exhibition of 20 species of frogs, toads, and other amphibians. Bilingual biologist-guides take you through a 45-minute tour of the terrariums in the **Frog Pond of Monteverde** (Ranario de Monteverde), just outside Santa Elena. For the best show, come around dusk and stay well into the evening, when the critters become more active and much more vocal. (Your ticket entitles you to a second visit the same day.) There's a small frog-and-toad-theme gift shop. ✣ *½ km/¼ mi southeast of Super Compro supermarket, Santa Elena* ☎ *2645–6320* ⊕ *www.ranario.com* *$10, $8 for students, free for kids under 6* ⏲ *Daily 9–8:30.*

Several conservation areas that have sprung up near Monteverde make attractive day trips, particularly if the Monteverde Reserve is too busy. The 765-acre **Santa Elena Reserve** just west of Monteverde is a project of the Santa Elena high school, and has a series of trails of varying lengths and difficulties that can be walked alone or with a guide. The 1.4-km (¾-mi) Youth Challenge Trail takes about 45 minutes to negotiate and contains an observation platform with views as far away as the Arenal Volcano—that is, if the clouds clear. If you're feeling hardy, try the 5-km (3-mi) Caño Negro Trail, clocking in at around four hours. There's a

Continued on page 230

"This is our 5 year old on his first zipline through the rainforest of Manuel Antonio."
—Jill Chapple, Fodors.com member

CANOPY TOURS

Costa Rica invented the concept of the canopy tour, and the idea has spread across the globe. Zip lining through the treetops is a once-in-a-lifetime experience, and exploring the jungle canopy is the best way to see the most eye-catching animals.

A canopy tour is an umbrella term describing excursions that take you to the jungle's ceiling. The experience is distinctly Costa Rican and is one of the country's signature activities for visitors. There are two types of tour: one gives you a chance to see animals (from bridges and platforms), and the other lets you swing through the trees like them (on zip lines). We know of around 80 tours nationwide but recommend only about a third of that number. You'll find tour information in every chapter of this book, even in San José.

By Jeffrey Van Fleet

WHAT EXACTLY IS A CANOPY TOUR?

Canopy cable ride at Monteverde cloud forest

WHAT TO EXPECT

Plan on a half-day for your canopy tour, including transportation to and from your hotel, and a safety briefing for zip line excursions. Most zipline tours begin at fixed times and reservations are always required, or at least advised. Hanging-bridges tours are far more leisurely and can be done at your own pace. The occasional mega-complex, such as Monteverde's Selvatura, offers both types of tours. For most, it's one or the other.

BRIDGES AND TRAMS

These are canopy tours in a literal sense, where you walk along suspension bridges, ride along in a tram, or are hoisted up to a platform to get a closer look at birds, monkeys, and sloths. They're also called hanging-bridges tours, sky walks, or platform tours. If seeing nature at a more leisurely pace is your goal, opt for these, especially the bridge excursions. They're peaceful and unobtrusive. Early mornings are the best time for animal sightings—at 50–250 feet above ground, the views are stupendous—and the weather is usually better.

ZIP LINES

This type of tour is a fast-paced, thrilling experience. You're attached to a zip line with a safety harness, and then you "fly" at about 30 miles per hour from one tree platform to the next. (You may be anywhere from 60–300 feet above the forest floor.) Tree-to-tree zip lines date from the 19th century and have been a bona fide activity for visitors to Costa Rica since the mid-1990s when the first tour opened in Monteverde. When most people say "canopy tour" they're referring this type of excursion. These tours are tremendous fun, but don't plan on seeing the resplendent quetzal as you zip from platform to platform. (Your shouts of exhilaration will probably scare them all away.) An average fitness level—and above-average level of intrepidness—are all you need.

TOP CANOPY TOURS BY REGION

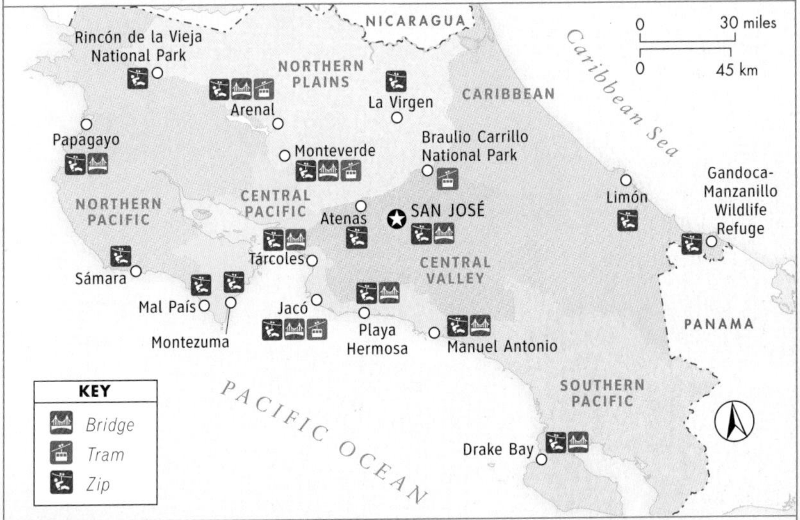

TOUR OPERATOR	LOCATION	TYPE		
Arenal Rain Forest Reserve	Arenal	Zip	Bridge	Tram
Canopy Safari	Manuel Antonio	Zip	Bridge	
Canopy del Pacífico	Malpaís	Zip		
Cocozuma	Montezuma	Zip		
Crazy Monkey Canopy	Gandoco-Manzanillo	Zip		
Hacienda Poco Azul	La Virgen, Sarapiquí	Zip		
Hotel Villa Lapas	Tárcoles	Zip	Bridge	
Natural Wonders Tram	Monteverde			Tram
Original Canopy Tour	Atenas	Zip		
Original Canopy Tour	Drake Bay	Zip	Bridge	
Original Canopy Tour	Veragua, Limón	Zip		
Rain Forest Aerial Tram	Braulio Carrillo National Park			Tram
Rain Forest Aerial Tram	Jacó			Tram
Rincón de la Vieja Canopy	Rincón de la Vieja National Park	Zip		
Selvatura	Monteverde	Zip	Bridge	
Tití Canopy Tour	Manuel Antonio	Zip		
Urban Canopy	San José	Zip	Bridge	
Waterfall Canopy Tour	Jacó	Zip	Bridge	
Wing Nuts Canopy Tour	Sámara	Zip		
Witch's Rock Canopy Tour	Papagayo	Zip	Bridge	

WORD OF MOUTH

Visitors to Arenal should not miss the hanging bridges. Hikers follow a well-marked trail and traverse 16 suspension bridges, each providing a spectacular vista of the surrounding jungle.

tiffnco, Fodors.com member

SAFETY FIRST

(top left) Zip lining Aventuras del Sarapiqui. (bottom right) Brown-Throated Three-Toed Sloth. (right) Sky Tram, Rainforest Canopy Tour, Arenal

PLAYING IT SAFE

Flying through the air, while undeniably cool, is also inherently dangerous. Before you strap into a harness, be certain that the safety standards are first rate. There's virtually no government oversight of the activity in Costa Rica. Here is a list of questions you should ask before you book:

1. How long has the company been in business?

2. Are they insured?

3. Are cables, harnesses, and other equipment manufacturer-certified?

4. Is there a second safety line that connects you to the zip line in case the main pulley gives way?

5. What's the price? Plan on paying $50 to $80—a low price could indicate a second-rate operation.

6. Are participants clipped to the zip line while on the platform? (They should be.)

KEEP IN MIND

- Listen closely to the guides' pre-tour safety briefing and obey their instructions.
- Never argue with the guide when s/he is making a decision to preserve your safety.
- Don't attempt to take photos in flight.
- Gauge your abilities frankly. Remember, once you start, there's no turning back.
- If anything seems "off" or makes you uncomfortable, walk away.

shuttle service to the reserve with fixed departures and returns. Reservations are required, and the cost is $2 each way. ✣*6 km/4 mi north of Santa Elena* ☏*2645–5390* 🌐*www.reservasantaelena.org* *$12, plus $15 with guide services* ⏲*Daily 7–4.*

I LOVE A PARADE

Tread carefully when you see a tiny green parade on the ground before you. It's a troop of leaf-cutter ants carrying compost material to an underground nest.

ALSO WORTH SEEING

Butterflies, frogs, and snakes already have their own Monteverde-area exhibits. The **Bat Jungle** gives its namesake animal equal time with guided tours into the life of one of the planet's most misunderstood mammals. An adjoining museum documents the history of the region, in particular, its early settlement by the Quakers. ✉*Across from Casem Monteverde* ☏*2645–6566* *$10* ⏲*Daily 9:30–8:30*

The 54,000-acre **Children's Eternal Rain Forest** (Bosque Eterno de los Niños) dwarfs the Monteverde and Santa Elena reserves. It began life as a school project in Sweden among children interested in saving a piece of the rain forest, and blossomed into a fund-raising effort among students from 44 countries. The reserve's **Bajo del Tigre trail** makes for a gentle, self-guided 1½-km (1-mi) hike through secondary forest. Along the trail are 27 stations at which to stop and learn about the reserve, many with lessons geared toward kids. A separate guided twilight walk ($15) begins at 5:30 PM and lasts two hours, affording the chance to see the nocturnal side of the cloud forest; reservations are required. Much of the rest of the reserve is not open to the public, but the Monteverde Conservation League offers stays at San Gerardo and Poco Sol, two remote field stations within the forest. The $34 packages include dormitory accommodation and meals. ✉*100 m south of CASEM* ☏*2645–5003* 🌐*www.acmcr.org* *Forest $7; transportation from area hotels $2* ⏲*Daily 8–4:30.*

The **Ecological Farm** (Finca Ecológica) is a private wildlife refuge with four trails on its 75 acres, plus birds, sloths, agoutis, coatimundis, two waterfalls, and a coffee plantation. If you can't make it all the way up to the Monteverde Reserve for the evening hike, there's a top-notch guided, two-hour twilight walk that begins each evening at 5:30. Reservations are required. ✉*Turnoff to Jardín de Mariposas, off main road between Santa Elena and Monteverde* ☏*2645–5869* *$9, twilight walk $15* ⏲*Daily 7–5.*

★ Bite your tongue before requesting Costa Rica's ubiquitous Café Britt up here. Export-quality Café Monteverde is the locally grown product. The **Monteverde Coffee Tour** lets you see the process up close from start to finish, from shade growing on the area's Turín plantation, 7 km (4 mi) north of Santa Elena; transport to the *beneficio,* the processing mill where the beans are washed and dried; and finally to the roaster. Reservations are required, and pickup is from area hotels. ☏*2645–7090* 🌐*www.crstudytours.com* *$25* ⏲*Tours at 8 AM and 1 PM.*

The **Orchid Garden** (Jardín de Orquídeas) showcases more than 400 species of orchids, one of which is the world's smallest. The Monteverde

Orchid Investigation Project manages the gardens. ✉ *150 m south of Banco Nacional* ☎ *2645–5308* *$7* *Daily 8–5.*

The 200-acre **Sendero Tranquilo Reserve** is managed by the Hotel Sapo Dorado and bordered by the Monteverde Cloud Forest Biological Reserve and the Guacimal River. Narrow trails are designed to have as little impact on the forest as possible (only groups of two to six are allowed). A guide leads you through primary and secondary forest and an area that illustrates the effects of deforestation. Because of the emphasis on minimal environmental impact, animals here tend to be more timid than at some other reserves. *3 km/2 mi north of Monteverde Reserve entrance, Cerro Plano* ☎ *2645–5010* *$22* *Tours depart daily at 7:30* AM *and 1* PM*; reservations required.*

At the **Serpentarium of Monteverde** (Serpentario Monteverde), greet 40 species of live Costa Rican reptiles and amphibians with glass safely between you and them. Guided tours in English or Spanish are included in your admission price. ✉ *Just outside Santa Elena on road to Monteverde* ☎ *2645–6002* *www.snaketour.com* *$8* *Daily 9–8.*

5

NEED A BREAK?

Long before tourists flocked up here, dairy farming was the foundation of Monteverde's economy. Quakers still operate what is locally referred to as the Cheese Factory, or La Lechería (*½ km/¼ mi south of CASEM, halfway between Santa Elena and Monteverde Reserve* ☎ *2645–2850, 2645–7090 tours*). The factory store sells local cheeses and ice cream. Stop in for a cone. It's open Monday–Saturday 7:30–5 and Sunday 7:30–4. If you have more time, take a two-hour tour of the operation Monday–Saturday at 9 or 2. Tours are $8 and wind up with a cheese-sampling session. Reserve in advance. If you're not heading up the mountain, these folks also operate a stand across from the Treehouse restaurant on the main street in Santa Elena.

WHERE TO EAT

$ ECLECTIC

Chimera. Karen Nielsen, owner of nearby Sofía, also operates this all-tapas (appetizers) offering, where you can mix and match small plates from the à la carte menu. Prices do add up quickly, but two or three menu items will make a filling meal out of such diverse mini-dishes as sea bass with passion-fruit cream, or coconut shrimp in mango-ginger sauce. Excellent dessert choices include a chocolate mousse or vanilla ice cream with pineapple-ginger-rum syrup, and a terrific selection of tropical-style cocktails and European and South American wines. A scant nine tables dot the place. Arrive before 7 if you want a guaranteed table, although the wait is never too long. ✉ *Cerro Plano60109* ☎ *2645–6081* *AE, D, DC, MC, V.*

$$$ MIDDLE EASTERN

De Lucía. Cordial Chilean owner José Belmar is the walking, talking (in five languages) menu at this elegant restaurant, always on hand to chat with guests. All entrées are served with grilled vegetables and fried plantains, and include sea bass with garlic sauce, and orange chicken. The handsome wooden restaurant with red mahogany tables is given a distinct South American flavor by an array of Andean tapestries and ceramics. An excellent dessert choice is *tres leches* (three milks), a richer-than-rich cake made with condensed, whole, and evaporated milk.

✉ *Turnoff to Jardín de Mariposas, off main road between Santa Elena and Monteverde, Cerro Plano* ☎ *2645–5337* ▭ *AE, MC, V.*

$ SEAFOOD **El Márquez.** Seafood is an unexpected treat up here in the mountains, and it's fresh: the owner gets shipments from Puntarenas several times weekly. The place is nothing fancy—expect plastic tables and chairs, with lots of local flavor—but when area residents want a special restaurant meal, this is where they come. Portions are big, but prices aren't. You could have trouble finishing the generous mixed seafood platter with shrimp, crab, and octopus in a white-wine sauce, or the jumbo shrimp with a sauce of mushrooms and hearts of palm. ✉ *Next to Suárez veterinary clinic, Santa Elena* ☎ *2645–5918* ▭ *MC, V* ⏲ *Closed Sun.*

$ MIDDLE EASTERN **Moon Shiva.** Costa Rica meets the Middle East at this casual place. Falafel, pita, tahini, and baba ghanoush figure prominently on the menu, but fillings for the *gallos* (build-your-own tortilla-wrapped "burritos") include standard Tico black-bean paste as well as hummus. The house sauce of pineapple, curry, and coconut garnishes many a dish. Ice cream with fried bananas in rum and cinnamon is a sweet finale. The place has live music most evenings at 8. ✉ *100 m north of Cerro Plano school, Cerro Plano* ☎ *2645–6270* ▭ *AE, MC, V* ⏲ *No lunch Sun.*

$$ ITALIAN **Pizzería de Johnny.** Everyone makes it to this stylish but informal place with candles and white tablecloths. The Monteverde pizza, with the works, is the most popular dish, and pastas, sandwiches, and a decent wine selection round out the menu. ✉ *Road to Monteverde Reserve, 1½ km/1 mi southeast of Santa Elena* ☎ *2645–5066* ▭ *MC, V.*

$$ ECLECTIC Fodor's Choice ★ **Sofía.** Here's one of the area's most stylish restaurants, but this is still Monteverde, so you can leave your fancy clothes at home. Waiters in crisp black aprons scurry attentively around the three dining rooms with ample window space. We like Sofía for its variety of about a dozen main courses: a mix of chicken, beef, pork, seafood, and vegetarian entrées. Try the chimichanga with corvina and shrimp and a side of coconut rice. There's an extensive wine and cocktail selection, too. ✉ *Turnoff to Jardín de Mariposas, off main road between Santa Elena and Monteverde, Cerro Plano* ☎ *2645–7017* ▭ *AE, D, DC, MC, V.*

$ CAFE **Stella's Bakery.** This local institution is one of the few spots that open at 6 AM. It's a good place to get an early-morning fix before heading to the Monteverde Reserve. Pastries, rolls, muffins, natural juices, and coffee are standard breakfast fare. Take them with you if you're running short of time. Lunch consists of light sandwiches, soups, and pastas. Make it a very early dinner here; the place closes at 6 PM. ✉ *Across from CASEM, Monteverde* ☎ *2645–5560* ▭ *AE, D, DC, MC, V.*

$ ECLECTIC **Tree House.** The name describes the place: this two-story restaurant on Santa Elena's main street is built around a 60-year-old fig tree. Tree branches shelter first-floor tables from the afternoon mist, but not entirely. If that's a problem, grab a table on the covered upper floor. The menu mixes pastas and seafood with Costa Rican cuisine. For a taste of everything, try the *típico* platter. The service here is "leisurely" or "slow," depending on your perspective. Spending at least $6 here gets you 30 minutes of free Internet use at the bank of computers downstairs. ✉ *Across from AyA, Santa Elena* ☎ *2645–5751* ▭ *AE, D, DC, MC, V.*

CLOSE UP

Bird Country

Nearly 850 bird species have been identified in Costa Rica, more than in the United States and Canada combined. Consequently, bird-watchers flock here by the thousands. The big attractions tend to be eye-catching species like the keel-billed toucan, but it is the diversity of shape, size, coloration, and behavior that makes bird-watching in Costa Rica so fascinating.

Tropical superstars: Parrots, parakeets, and macaws; toucans and toucanets; and the elusive but legendary resplendent quetzal are a thrill for those of us who don't see them every day.

In supporting roles: Lesser-known but equally impressive species include motmots, with their distinctive racket tails; oropéndolas, which build remarkable hanging nests; and an amazing array of hawks, kites, and falcons.

Color me red, blue, yellow . . . : Two of the most striking species are the showy scarlet macaw and the quirky purple gallinule; tanagers, euphonias, manakins, cotingas, and trogons are some of the country's loveliest plumed creatures, but none of them matches the iridescence of the hummingbirds *(⇨ below)*.

Singing in the rain: The relatively inconspicuous clay-color robin is Costa Rica's national bird. It may look plain, but its song is melodious, and because the males sing almost constantly toward the end of the dry season—the beginning of their mating season—local legend has it that they call the rains.

The big and the small of it: The scintillant hummingbird is a mere 6¼ cm (2½ inches) tall and weighs just over 2 grams, whereas the jabiru, a long-legged stork, can grow to more than 1.2 meters (4 feet) tall and weigh up to 14 pounds.

Parrots, parakeets, and macaws; toucans and toucanets; and the elusive but legendary resplendent quetzal: Costa Rica hosts 51 members of the hummingbird family, compared with just one species for all of the United States east of the Rocky Mountains. Time spent near a hummingbird feeder will treat you to an unforgettable display of accelerated aerial antics and general pugnacity.

"Snow birds": If you're here between October and April, don't be surprised if you see some feathered friends from home. When northern birds fly south for the winter, they don't all head to Miami. Seasonal visitors like the Kentucky warbler make up about a quarter of the amazing avian panorama in Costa Rica.

Bird-watching can be done everywhere in the country. And don't let the rainy season deter you: seasonal *lagunas* (lagoons) such as Caño Negro and the swamps of Palo Verde National Park, which disappear during the dry months, are excellent places to see birds.

5

WHERE TO STAY

$–$$ ★ **Arco Iris Lodge.** You're almost right in the center of town, but you'd never know it. This tranquil spot has cozy cabins set on 4 acres of birding trails. Cabin decor ranges from rustic to plush, but all lodgings come with porches. Start your day with a delicious breakfast buffet, including homemade bread and granola. You need not be a honeymooner to stay in the sumptuous three-level honeymoon cabin, secluded off on

DID YOU KNOW?

Tree-to-tree zip lines date back to the 19th century, and were introduced to rainforest study in Costa Rica in the 1970s. The first commercial canopy tour opened in Monteverde in the mid-1990s and within a decade, close to 100 canopy tours were operating around the country. Today, they generate $120 million annually and attract a reported 200,000 travelers each year.

a corner of the property, with private patio, whirlpool tub, and DVD player. The laid-back German management can provide good advice about how to spend your time in the area. **Pros:** attentive owner and staff; terrific breakfasts; ecology-minded place. **Cons:** back of bank blocks views; steep walk if on foot. ✉ *50 m south of Banco Nacional, Santa Elena* ☎ *2645–5067* 🌐 *www.arcoirislodge.com* *20 cabins, 1 suite* *In-room: no a/c, no phone, safe (some), DVD (some), no TV (some). In-hotel: laundry service, Internet terminal* ▭ *MC, V* 🍴 *EP.*

THE UBIQUITOUS SODA

In Costa Rica the word *soda* has nothing to do with a carbonated beverage. (That's a *gaseosa* here.) Instead, a soda is a small, often family-run restaurant frequented by locals that you'll find in every town and city. Don't expect anything as fancy as a menu. A board usually lists specials of the day. The lunchtime *casado* (literally, "married")—a "marriage" of chicken, pork, or beef with rice, beans, cabbage salad, and natural fruit drink—sets you back about $2. No one will bring you a bill; just pay the cashier when you're finished.

$ **El Bosque Lodge.** Convenient to the Bajo del Tigre nature trail and Meg's Stables, El Bosque's quiet, simple rooms are grouped around a central camping area. A bridge crosses a stream and leads to the hotel. Brick-oven pizzas are served on the veranda. **Pros:** good budget value; seclusion, especially in rooms away from road. **Cons:** basic rooms; lackluster staff. ✣ *2½ km/1½ mi southeast of Santa Elena on road to Monteverde Reserve, Monteverde* 📫 *Apdo. 5655, Santa Elena* ☎ *2645–5221* 🌐 *www.bosquelodge.net* *27 rooms* *In-room: no a/c, no TV, Internet. In-hotel: restaurant, bar, laundry service, Internet terminal* ▭ *AE, DC, MC, V* 🍴 *EP.*

$$–$$$ **El Establo Mountain Hotel.** "The Stable" began life as just that, a stable near the road, remodeled and apportioned into comfortable rooms with basic furnishings. Over the years, ever-upward expansion has turned this place into a sprawling operation. A newer pink building perches on the hill with large suites with wood-and-stone walls. Some contain lofts; all come with amenities rarely seen up here, such as bathtubs, phones, and enormous windows with views of the Gulf of Nicoya. The two newest buildings, higher on the hill, have rooms with hot tubs, private balconies, and even more commanding views. This is, by far, the area's largest hotel complex—you'll need the minivan shuttle to transport you up and down the hill. In that regard, El Establo is somewhat "un-Monteverde," but its guests undeniably have fun with its many facilities, including a guests-only canopy tour. Oh, and those original stable rooms? They're not in use anymore. **Pros:** luxurious furnishings; many activities. **Cons:** massive grounds; lacks intimacy of other Monteverde lodgings. ✣ *3½ km/2 mi northwest of Monteverde* ☎ *2645–5110, 877/623–3198 in North America* 🌐 *www.hotelelestablo.com* *155 rooms* *In-room: no a/c, safe, refrigerator. In-hotel: 2 restaurants, bars, tennis courts, pool, gym, spa* ▭ *AE, D, DC, MC, V* 🍴 *BP.*

$$ **El Sol.** A charming German family tends to guests at one of those quintessential get-away-from-it-all places just 10 minutes down the mountain from—and a noticeable few degrees warmer than—Santa

Elena. Two fully furnished *ojoche*-wood cabins perch on the mountainside on the 25-acre farm. Every vantage point in the cabins—the living area, the bed, the desk, the shower, and even the toilet—has stupendous views. The property has 3 km (2 mi) of trails, a stone-wall pool, and a Finnish sauna. Meals can be arranged and taken in the main house or brought to your cabin. **Pros:** great views; whimsically decorated cabins. **Cons:** need car to get here; far removed from sights. ✣ *4 km/2½ mi southwest of Santa Elena* ☎ *2645–5838* 🌐 *www.elsolnuestro.com* *2 cabins* *In-room: no a/c, no phone, no TV. In-hotel: restaurant, pool* ▭ *No credit cards* 🍴 *EP.*

$$ **Fonda Vela.** Owned by the Smith brothers, whose family was among
Fodor'sChoice ★ the first American arrivals in the 1950s—their father's paintings grace the lodging's public areas—these steep-roof chalets have large bedrooms with white-stucco walls, wood floors, and huge windows. Some have views of the wooded grounds; others, of the far-off Gulf of Nicoya. The most innovatively designed of Monteverde's hotels is also one of the closest to the reserve entrance. Both restaurants ($$$) prepare local and international recipes with flair, served indoors or on the veranda. The place is a longtime favorite of those who post to fodors.com Latin America discussion board. **Pros:** rustic luxury; secluded location; terrific restaurant. **Cons:** far from town; rough road to get here. ✣ *1½ km/1 mi northwest of Monteverde Reserve entrance, Monteverde* ☎ *2645–5125* 🌐 *www.fondavela.com* *Apdo. 12–5655, Santa Elena, Monteverde* *40 rooms* *In-room: no a/c, refrigerator. In-hotel: 2 restaurants, bar, laundry service, Internet terminal* ▭ *AE, D, DC, MC, V* 🍴 *EP, BP, MAP, FAP.*

$$ **Hotel Belmar.** Built into the hillside, Hotel Belmar resembles two tall Swiss chalets and commands extensive views of the Golfo de Nicoya and the hilly peninsula. The amiable Chilean owners have designed both elegant and rustic rooms, paneled with polished wood; half the rooms have balconies. In the restaurant ($$–$$$) you can count on adventurous and delicious *platos del día* (daily specials) of Costa Rican and international fare. **Pros:** good value; friendly staff. **Cons:** far from town; steep walk if on foot. ✣ *4 km/2½ mi north of Monteverde* ☎ *2645–5201* 🌐 *www.hotelbelmar.net* *Apdo. 17–5655, Monteverde60109* *28 rooms* *In-room: no a/c, no TV, Wi-Fi. In-hotel: restaurant, bar, laundry service, Internet terminal* ▭ *AE, MC, V* 🍴 *EP.*

$$ **Hotel El Sapo Dorado.** After beginning its life as a nightclub, the "Golden Toad" became a popular restaurant and then graduated into a very pleasant hotel. Geovanny Arguedas's family arrived here to farm 10 years before the Quakers did, and he and his wife, Hannah Lowther, have built secluded hillside cabins with polished paneling, tables, fireplaces, and rocking chairs. The restaurant ($$) is well known for its pastas, pizza, vegetarian dishes, and sailfish from Puntarenas. **Pros:** rustic luxury; attentive service. **Cons:** trails between cabins get muddy in rainy season; no screens on some windows, steep walk if on foot. ✣ *6 km/4 mi northwest of Monteverde Reserve entrance, Monteverde* ☎ *2645–5010* 🌐 *www.sapodorado.com* *Apdo. 9–5655, Monteverde60109* *30 rooms* *In-room: no a/c, no phone, refrigerator,*

no TV. In-hotel: restaurant, bar, Internet terminal ⊟*AE, D, DC, MC, V* 🍴*BP.*

$$ **Hotel Montaña Monteverde.** The area's first lodging—it dates from 1979—underwent a 2007 makeover worthy of a reality TV show. Some of the hotel's seclusion has been lost as a result, but the sparkle of the updated furnishings makes up for it. Each room comes with shower and tub, flat-screen TV, brightly colored drapes and spreads, and large windows with super views. On the topic of views, the terrace restaurant also offers superb vistas of the far-off Gulf of Nicoya. **Pros:** luxurious furnishings; new remodeling. **Cons:** a little farther outside Santa Elena than some might want; a few front rooms get noise from road. ✉*Cerro Plano60109* ☎*2645–5338* 🌐*www.monteverdemountainhotel.com* *42 rooms* *In-room: no a/c, safe, refrigerator (some). In-hotel: restaurant, room service, bar, Internet terminal* ⊟*AE, D, DC, MC, V* 🍴*EP.*

$$$ Fodor'sChoice ★ **Monteverde Lodge.** The well-established Costa Rica Expeditions operates this longtime favorite close to Santa Elena. Rooms have vaulted ceilings, bathtubs—an amenity rarely seen here—and great views. A table abuts the angled bay window overlooking the 15 acres of grounds, a perfect place to have a cup of coffee and bird-watch from indoors. The restaurant and bar congregate around an enormous but cozy lobby fireplace. Relax in the whirlpool tub in the enormous solarium, a perfect place to unwind after a day of tromping through the reserves. Or take in the evening slide presentation, showcasing cloud forest life. These folks also offer packages that include meals, guided walks, and round-trip transportation from San José. **Pros:** rustic luxury; attentive service; many activities. **Cons:** ground-floor rooms can be noisy; not centrally located relative to Santa Elena or reserve. ✉*200 m south of Ranario de Monteverde, Santa Elena* *Apdo. 6941–1000, San José* ☎*2645–5057, 2257–0766 in San José* 🌐*www.costaricaexpeditions.com* *27 rooms* *In-room: no a/c, no TV. In-hotel: restaurant, bar, Internet terminal* ⊟*AE, D, DC, MC, V* 🍴*EP, FAP, MAP.*

¢ **Pensión Monteverde Inn.** One of the cheapest inns in the area is quite far from the Monteverde Reserve entrance, on a 28-acre private preserve. The bedrooms are basic, but they have stunning views of the Gulf of Nicoya as well as hardwood floors, firm beds, and powerful, hot showers. Home cooking is served by the chatty David and María Savage and family. **Pros:** good rock-bottom budget value; friendly owners; good views. **Cons:** spartan rooms. ✉*50 m past Butterfly Garden on turnoff road, Cerro Plano* ☎*2645–5156* *13 rooms* *In-room: no a/c, no phone, no TV. In-hotel: restaurant* ⊟*No credit cards* 🍴*BP.*

$ **Swiss Hotel Miramontes.** Switzerland meets the cloud forest at this Swiss-owned and -operated small inn. Each room has a private porch. Guests have access to a private orchid garden with more than 300 varieties. If you're tired of rice and beans, the restaurant serves a variety of Swiss, Austrian, Italian, and French dishes. **Pros:** pleasant, small operation, friendly owners. **Cons:** not many frills; far from sights. ✣*1 km/½ mi south of Santa Elena* ☎*2645–5152* 🌐*www.swisshotelmira*

5

montes.com *8 rooms* *In-room: no a/c. In-hotel: restaurant* *MC, V* *BP.*

$$ **Trapp Family Lodge.** The enormous rooms, with wood paneling and ceilings, have lovely furniture marvelously crafted from—you guessed it—wood. The architectural style is appropriate, as the lodge is surrounded by trees, just a 10-minute walk from the park entrance, making it the closest lodge to the reserve. (This means, though, that the trip into town is longer.) The friendly Chilean owners are always around to provide personalized service. Other than a small hutlike enclosure near the entrance, the entire property is no-smoking. **Pros:** rustic luxury; good value; closest lodging to reserve entrance. **Cons:** far from town; rough road to get here. *Main road from Monteverde Reserve, Monteverde* *Apdo. 70–5655, Monteverde 60109* *2645–5858, 866/255–7476 in North America* *www.trappfamilylodgecr.com* *26 rooms* *In-room: no a/c, no TV (some). In-hotel: restaurant, bar, laundry service, Internet terminal, no-smoking rooms* *AE, D, DC, MC, V* *EP.*

SHOPPING

ARTS AND CRAFTS

Atmosphera (*Turnoff to Jardín de Mariposas, Cerro Plano* *2645–6555*) specializes in locally made primitivist wood carvings. **Bromelia's** (*100 m east of CASEM, Monteverde* *2645–6272*) bills itself as a bookstore, but sells colorful batiks, masks, and jewelry, too. The **Cooperativa de Artesanía de Santa Elena y Monteverde** (*CASEM* *Next to El Bosque Lodge, Monteverde* *2645–5190*), an artisans' cooperative made up of 89 women and 3 men, sells locally made crafts. The prices are higher than at most other places. **Coopesanta Elena** (*Next to CASEM* *2645–5901*) is the distributor for packages of the area's gourmet Café Monteverde coffee and accoutrements. The **Hummingbird Gallery** (*Outside entrance to Monteverde Reserve* *2645–5030*) sells books, gifts, T-shirts, great Costa Rican coffee, prints, and slides by nature specialists Michael and Patricia Fogden, as well as watercolors by nature artist Sarah Dowell.

NIGHTLIFE

"Wild nightlife" takes on its own peculiar meaning here. You can still get up close with nature after the sun has gone down. Several of the reserves have guided evening walks—advance reservations and separate admission are required—and the Ranario, Serpentario, and Bat Jungle keep evening hours. Noted area biologist Richard LaVal presents a slide show called "*Sounds and Scenes of the Cloud Forest*" at the Monteverde Lodge nightly at 6:15 ($5). Advance reservations are required. Beyond that, you'll probably while away the evening in a restaurant or your hotel dining room chatting with fellow travelers. Monteverde is an early-to-bed, early-to-rise kind of place.

CAÑO NEGRO REFUGE AREA

Long a favorite among fishing enthusiasts and bird-watchers, this remote area is off the beaten track and may be difficult to get to if your time in Costa Rica is short. You can cross into Nicaragua, via Los Chiles, but there are almost no roads in this part of southern Nicaragua, making access to the rest of the country nearly impossible. The border crossing at Peñas Blancas, near the north Pacific coast, is far more user-friendly (⇨ *Crossing into Nicaragua at Peñas Blancas, in Chapter 6).*

CAÑO NEGRO NATIONAL WILDLIFE REFUGE

Fodor'sChoice ★ *91 km/57 mi (1½ hrs) northwest of La Fortuna.*

Caño Negro doesn't grab the same amount of attention in wildlife-viewing circles as other destinations in Costa Rica, but the reserve is a splendid place to watch waterfowl and resident exotic animals. ✉ *180 km/108 mi north of La Fortuna* *$7* *Daily 7–4.*

GETTING HERE AND AROUND

The highway from La Fortuna to Los Chiles is one of the best-maintained in the northern lowlands. You can catch public buses in San José at Terminal Atlántico Norte twice a day, a trip of about five hours, with many stops. Public buses also operate between La Fortuna and Los Chiles. If they have room, many tour companies (Sunset Tours included) will allow you to ride along with them on their shuttles, for a cost of around $10. If you're not staying way up here, an organized tour of the reserve is the best way to get to and from it.

OUTDOOR ACTIVITIES

Several La Fortuna–area tour companies have trips to Caño Negro. **Sunset Tours** (☎ *2479–9800, 866/417–7352 in North America* *www.sunsettourscr.com*) pioneered tours to the reserve, and runs top-notch, informative daylong or half-day tours, among the best in the country, to Caño Negro for $80 to $100, with higher rates in effect if you stay at one of the more far-flung Arenal lodgings. Bring your jungle juice: the mosquitoes are voracious. **Jacamar Naturalist Tours** (☎ *2479–9767* *www.arenaltours.com*) is a well-established tour operator with three-hour boat trips ($65) on the Río Frío in the Caño Negro reserve.

DID YOU KNOW?

Now you see it, now you don't: Caño Negro's lake forms during the rainy season when the Río Frío floods its banks. By February, dry conditions begin to shrink the lake, and by April, all that's left are a few spotty lagoons.

WHERE TO STAY

$$ **Caño Negro Natural Lodge.** That such an upscale property exists in this remote place might amaze you, but this Italian-designed, family-operated resort on the east side of the reserve is never pretentious. Rooms have high ceilings, colorful drapes and bedspreads, and huge showers; some rooms have bunk beds. There are two- and three-day packages available for anglers and non-anglers alike. The lodge has a variety of meal options; most guests opt for taking all meals here, since there are few other restaurants in town. Horseback riding can be arranged and miniature golf, croquet, and badminton are a few of the on-site diversions. **Pros:** secluded location; close to reserve. **Cons:** need car to get here. ✉ *Caño Negro village* ☎ *2471–1000, 2265–1204 in San José* *www.canonegrolodge.com* *22 rooms* *In-room: no phone,*

5

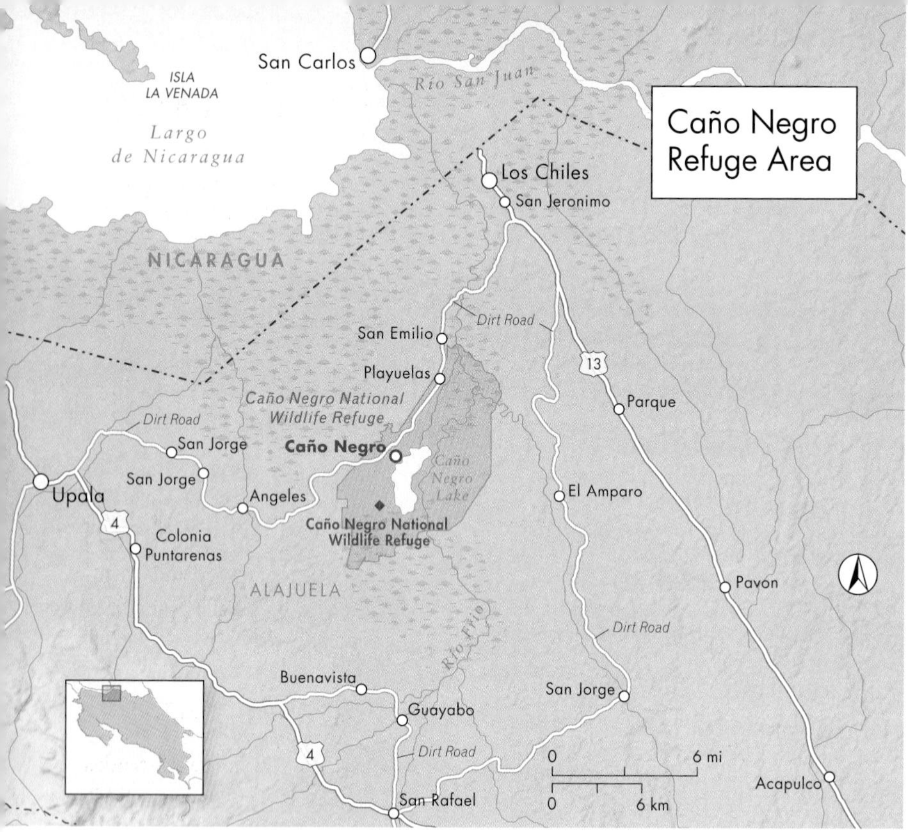

safe, no TV. In-hotel: restaurant, bar, pool, laundry service ▭*AE, MC, V* 🍽*CP.*

$$ **Hotel de Campo.** All are welcome here, though the lodge is best known for its fishing tours, equipment and boat rental, and nearby lake filled with tarpon and bass. Seven white bungalows of high-quality wood each contain two bright, sparkling rooms with terra-cotta tile floors, and are arranged around the wooded property. The produce from the lodge's citrus orchard ends up on your breakfast plate. In addition to credit cards and cash, the lodge accepts American Express traveler's checks. **Pros:** secluded location; close to reserve. **Cons:** need car to get here. ✉*Caño Negro village* ☎*2471–1490* 🌐*www.hoteldecampo.com* *14 rooms* *In-room: no a/c, no phone, no TV. In-hotel: restaurant, bar, pool* ▭*AE, MC, V* 🍽*BP.*

THE SARAPIQUÍ LOOP

The area immediately north of the San José metro area doesn't leap to mind when discussing ecotourism in Costa Rica, but it should. The Sarapiquí River gave its name to this region at the foot of the Cordillera Central mountain range. To the west is the rain forest of Braulio Carrillo National Park, and to the east are Tortuguero National Park and Barra del Colorado National Wildlife Refuge. These splendid national parks share the region with thousands of acres of farmland, including palm, banana, and pineapple plantations, as well as cattle ranching. Cheap land and rich soil brought a wave of Ticos to this area a half century ago. Until the construction of Highway 126 in 1957, which connects the area to San José, this was one of the most isolated parts of Costa Rica, with little or no tourism. Government homesteading projects brought many residents, who cleared massive swaths of the rain forest for cattle grazing and agriculture. Now, ironically, old-growth lowland rain forest, montane cloud forest, and wetlands exist only within the borders of the national parks and several adjoining private reserves. A growing selection of nature lodges have set up shop here, and you can enjoy their offerings 60 to 90 minutes after you leave the capital. (Just try getting to the Osa Peninsula on the Southern Pacific coast in that same time.)

VOLCANO-VIEWING ON AN EMPTY STOMACH

No question: the earlier you get to Poás, the better the views you'll be afforded. If that means skipping breakfast, a number of roadside stands on the way up the volcano sell strawberry jam, *cajeta* (a pale fudge), and rather bland corn crackers called *biscochos* to tide you over until you can have a hearty *típico* breakfast in the park visitor center's cafeteria.

If you don't have much time, **Ecoscape Nature Tours** (☎*2239–8332, 866/887–2764 in North America* 🌐*www.ecoscapetours.com*) has the best daylong Sarapiquí Loop tour, as well as a more leisurely extended itinerary that lasts two days. It also has nighttime jungle tours in the Selva Verde reserve.

VOLCÁN POÁS NATIONAL PARK

Fodor's Choice ★ *37 km/23 mi (45 mins) north of Alajuela, 57 km/35 mi (1 hr) north of San José.*

Arenal may be Costa Rica's most famous volcano, but you can walk right up to the crater here at Poás. That gives it an edge in the "cool volcano visit" department.

GETTING HERE AND AROUND

Taxis from San José are around $80 (and around $40 from Alajuela). From the Pan-American Highway north of Alajuela, follow the signs for Poás. The road is in relatively good condition. One public bus departs daily at 8 AM from San José (✉*Ave. 2, Calle 12–14*), and returns at 2 PM. A slew of tours from San José take in the volcano and combine the morning excursion with an afternoon at the La Paz Waterfall Gardens, or tours of Café Britt near Heredia or the Doka Estate near Alajuela. (⇨*Chapter 4*). ✉*From Alajuela, drive north through town and follow signs* ☎*2482–2424, 192 (national parks hotline) in Costa Rica* 🎟*$10* ⏲*Daily 8:30–3:30.*

EXPLORING

★ Five magnificent waterfalls are the main attractions at **La Paz Waterfall Gardens,** on the eastern edge of Volcán Poás National Park, but they are complemented by the beauty of the surrounding cloud forest, an abundance of hummingbirds and other avian species, and the country's biggest butterfly garden. A concrete trail leads down from the visitor center to the multilevel, screened butterfly observatory and continues to gardens where hummingbird feeders attract swarms of these multicolor creatures. The trail then enters the cloud forest, where it leads to a series of metal stairways that let you descend into a steep gorge to viewing platforms near each of the waterfalls. A free shuttle will transport you from the trail exit back to the main building if you prefer to avoid the hike uphill. Several alternative paths lead from the main trail through the cloud forest and along the river's quieter upper stretch, providing options for hours of exploration—it takes about two hours to hike the entire complex. (Enter by 3 PM to give yourself adequate time.) The visitor center has a gift shop and open-air cafeteria with a great view. The gardens are 20 km (12 mi) northeast of Alajuela, and are a stop on many daylong tours from San José that take in the Poás volcano or area coffee tours. ✣ *6 km/4 mi north of Vara Blanca* ☎ *2482–2720* 🌐 *www.waterfallgardens.com* 🎫 *$35, $47 with lunch, $65 with round-trip transportation from San José* ⏲ *Daily 8–5.*

> **QUAKE ZONE**
>
> In January 2009, a 6.2-magnitude earthquake struck just east of the Poás, killing 23 people. A few listings below (La Paz Waterfall Gardens, Peace Lodge, and Poás Volcano Lodge) suffered damage, but all planned to be up and running again soon.

OUTDOOR ACTIVITIES

HORSEBACK RIDING

Guided horseback tours with **Poás Volcano Lodge** (✣ *6 km/4 mi east of Chubascos restaurant, on road to Vara Blanca* ☎ *2482–2194*) are available in the cloud forest of Finca Legua, a private reserve 5 km (3 mi) north of the lodge. Daily tours ($65), which include lunch, run from 9 AM to 2 PM. Make reservations.

WHERE TO EAT AND STAY

$ COSTA RICAN Fodor's Choice ★ ✕ **Chubascos.** Amid tall pines and colorful flowers on the upper slopes of Poás Volcano, this popular restaurant has a small menu of traditional Tico dishes and delicious daily specials. Choose from the full selection of casados and platters of *gallos* (homemade tortillas with meat, cheese, or potato fillings). The *refrescos* (fresh fruit drinks) are top-drawer, especially the ones made from locally grown *fresas* (strawberries) and *moras* (blackberries) blended with milk. ✣ *1 km/½ mi north of Laguna de Fraijanes* ☎ *2482–2280* 💳 *AE, D, DC, MC, V* ⏲ *Closed Tues.*

$ COSTA RICAN ✕ **Jaulares.** Named after the *jaul*, a tree common in the nearby cloud forest, this spacious restaurant specializes in grilled meat, though there are also several fish dishes and *chicharrones* (deep-fried meaty pork rinds). All the cooking is done with wood, which adds to the rustic ambience of terra-cotta floors, bare wooden beams, and sylvan surroundings. The house specialty, *lomito Jaulares* (Jaulares tenderloin), is a strip of grilled

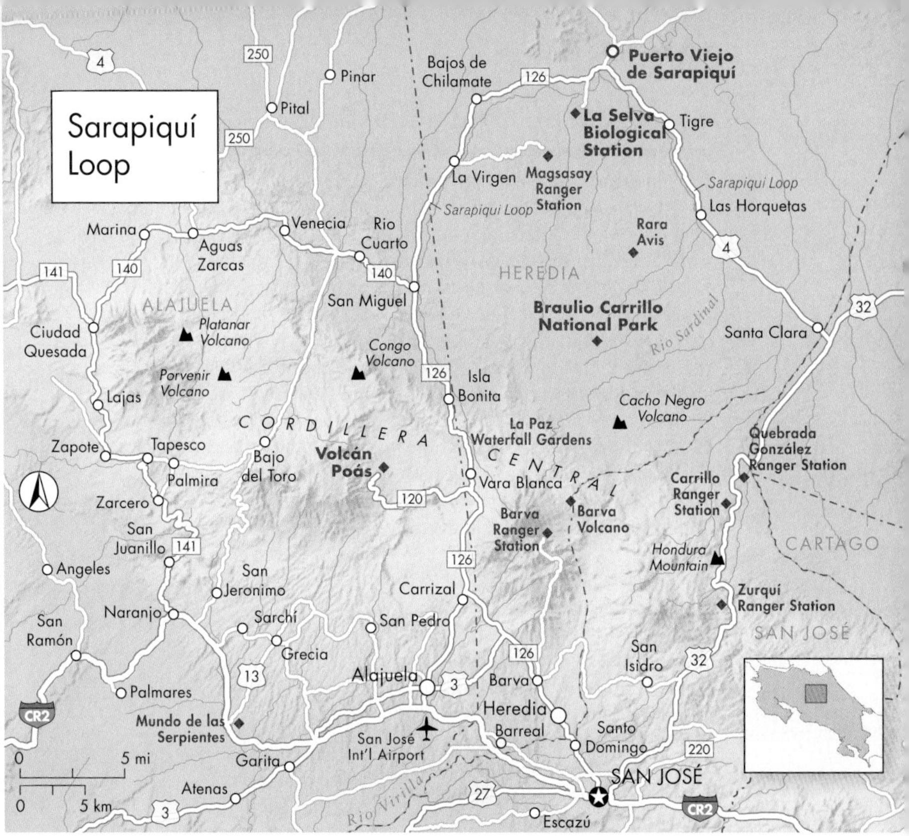

meat served with *gallo pinto* (rice and beans) and a mild *salsa criollo* (creole sauce). Though primarily a lunch spot, Jaulares stays open until midnight on weekends for concerts—Latin music on Friday night and rock on Saturday night. Four basic cabinas in back are an inexpensive overnight option, though you'll need to reserve them early for concert nights. ✣*2 km/1 mi north of Laguna de Fraijanes* ☎*2482–2155* ▭*AE, D, DC, MC, V.*

$$$$ ★ **Peace Lodge.** These rooms overlooking the misty forest of La Paz Waterfall Gardens seem like something out of the *Lord of the Rings,* with their curved, clay-stucco walls, hardwood floors (note that all but the top floors can be noisy because of creaky stairs), stone fireplaces (gas), and four-poster beds made of varnished logs, complete with mosquito-net canopy. They are proper abodes for elfin kings, especially the spacious, grottolike bathrooms with two showers, a whirlpool tub, tropical gardens, and private waterfall. Most hotels settle for a room with a bath. Peace Lodge gives you a bath with a room. And as if that weren't enough, you can soak in your second whirlpool tub on a porch with a cloud-forest view. Being able to explore the waterfall gardens before they open is another perk; room rates include admission. The cuisine here is a couple of notches below the accommodations. The entire place is an old favorite of posters to the fodors.com discussion boards. **Pros:** many activities included in rates; whimsical furnishings;

CLOSE UP

Certificate of Sustainable Tourism

One trip to Costa Rica and you'll swear everything here is eco-lodges, ecotourism, eco-this, eco-that. But *sustainability*, the buzzword in Costa Rican tourism these days, also has to do with conserving cultural, as well as natural, resources. The Certification for Sustainable Tourism (CST) program, administered jointly by the Costa Rican Tourism Institute, National Chamber of Tourism, Ministry of the Environment, and University of Costa Rica, recognizes businesses that adhere to those ideals. Those that submit to a rigorous assessment are evaluated on their employment of local people, respect for local culture, contribution to the economic and social well-being of the community, and preservation of natural resources. Businesses that rely heavily on foreign investment and whose earnings are mostly repatriated outside Costa Rica don't make the cut (but probably don't submit to an evaluation in the first place).

Instead of stars, 84 hotels have earned one to five leaves for their efforts. At this writing, Finca Rosa Blanca, north of Heredia in the Central Valley; Lapa Ríos, at Cabo Matapalo on the South Pacific; Sí Como No, at Manuel Antonio on the Central Pacific; and Hotel Villa Blanca, near San Ramón in the Northern Plains, are the only four lodgings to hold five leaves. The resorts and hotels that are recognized are not all small "mom-and-pop" places: the Four Seasons on the Papagayo Peninsula and Arenal's Tabacón have been recognized as well. Nor are they only places in the middle of the rain forest: San José's large but unobtrusive Clarion Hotel Amón Plaza is among several city lodgings proudly displaying awards.

Although other countries have their own rating systems for eco-friendly lodgings, many of these suffer from corrupt policies that allow ratings to be bought. The CST is one of the best and most thorough awards programs in the world. In fact, the World Tourism Organization has adopted it as its model, and countries from Mexico to Malawi now employ similar standards. You'll find a list of Costa Rica's CST holders at the program's Spanish-English-French Web site, 🌐 *www.turismo-sostenible.co.cr.*

rates include admission to Waterfall Gardens. **Cons:** popular with tour groups; sometimes difficult to find space. ✣ *6 km/4 mi north of Vara Blanca* ☎ *482–2720, 225–0643 in San José, 954/727–3997 in North America* 🌐 *www.waterfallgardens.com* *17 rooms, 1 villa* *In-room: no a/c, no phone, refrigerator. In-hotel: restaurant* ▭ *AE, DC, MC, V* 🍽 *EP.*

$–$$ **Poás Volcano Lodge.** The rustic architecture of this former dairy farmhouse, with rough stone walls and pitched beam roof, fits perfectly into the rolling pastures and forests that surround it. The interior mixes Persian rugs with textiles from Latin America, and Guaitil Indian pottery with North American pieces. The oversize sunken fireplace may be the lodge's most alluring feature. All rooms are different, so if possible, look at a few before you decide: one has an exquisite stone bathtub. The less expensive rooms, though not as opulent, have a more dependable supply of hot water. A small dairy farm and garden supply the kitchen with ingredients for the hearty breakfasts. **Pros:** cozy rooms; close to volcano. **Cons:** rustic rooms. ✈6 *km/4 mi east of Chubascos restaurant, on road to Vara Blanca* ✉*Apdo. 5723–1000, San José* ☎*2482–2194* 🌐*www.poasvolcanolodge.com* *11 rooms, 9 with bath* *In-room: no a/c, no phone, no TV. In-hotel: restaurant, laundry service, Internet terminal* *AE, D, DC, MC, V* *BP.*

SHOPPING

The **Neotrópica Foundation** sells nature-theme T-shirts, cards, and posters in the national park's visitor center and devotes a portion of the profits to conservation projects.

> **WORD OF MOUTH**
>
> "It's a very good idea to hit Poas early—We got there early enough to enjoy five minutes of clear visibility of the crater! We had no choice but to go during the weekend, and it was crowded. It's worth the trip up for Botos Lagoon and the bird trail, which is sublime if you can grab some time alone on it and wait for the birds to emerge." —RAC

5

BRAULIO CARRILLO NATIONAL PARK

30 km/19 mi (45 mins) north of San José.

In a country where deforestation is still rife, hiking through Parque Nacional Braulio Carrillo is a rare opportunity to witness dense, primary tropical cloud forest. The park owes its foundation to the public outcry provoked by the construction of the highway of the same name through this region in the late 1970s—the government bowed to pressure from environmentalists, and somewhat ironically, the park is the most accessible one from the capital thanks to the highway. Covering 443 square km (171 square mi), Braulio Carrillo's extremely diverse terrain ranges from 55 meters (108 feet) to about 2,896 meters (9,500 feet) above sea level and extends from the central volcanic range down the Caribbean slope to La Selva research station near Puerto Viejo de Sarapiquí. The park protects a series of ecosystems ranging from the cloud forests on the upper slopes to the tropical wet forest of the Magsasay sector; it is home to 6,000 tree species, 500 bird species, and 135 mammal species.

For all its immense size and proximity to the capital, visitor facilities in the park are limited. Your exposure will most likely take place when you pass through on the way to the Caribbean, or when you stay at any of the lodgings that fringe Braulio Carrillo. Penetrating the park's depths is a project only for the truly intrepid:

The **Zurquí ranger station** is to the right of the highway, ½ km (¼ mi) before the Zurquí Tunnel. Here a short trail loops through the cloud forest. Hikes are steep; wear hiking boots to protect yourself from mud, slippage, and snakes. The main trail through primary forest, 1½ km (1 mi) long, culminates in a *mirador* (lookout point), but alas, the highway mars the view. Monkeys, tapirs, jaguars, kinkajous, sloths, raccoons, margays, and porcupines all live in this forest, and resident birds include the resplendent quetzal and the eagle. Orchids, bromeliads, heliconias, fungi, and mushrooms live closer to the floor. Another trail leads into the forest to the right, beginning about 17 km (11 mi) after the tunnel, where it follows the Quebrada González, a stream with a cascade and swimming hole. There are no campsites in this part of the park. The **Carrillo ranger station,** 22 km (14 mi) northeast along the highway from Zurquí, marks the beginning of trails that are less steep. Farther north on this highway, near the park entrance/exit toward Guápiles, is the **Quebrada González** ranger station. To the east of Heredia, a road climbs **Barva Volcano** *(⇨ below)* from San Rafael. ☎*2290–8202 Sistemas de Areas de Conservación, 192 (national parks hotline)* *$10* *Daily 7–4.*

The 2,896-meter (9,500-foot) summit of **Barva Volcano** is the highest point in Braulio Carrillo National Park. Dormant for 300 years now, Barva is massive: its lower slopes are almost completely planted with coffee fields and hold more than a dozen small towns, nearly all of which are named after saints. On the upper slopes are pastures lined with exotic pines and the occasional native oak or cedar, giving way to the botanical diversity of the cloud forest near the top. The air is usually cool near the summit, which combines with the pines and pastures to evoke the European or North American countryside.

Barva's misty, luxuriant summit is the only part of Braulio Carrillo where camping is allowed, and it's a good place to see the rare resplendent quetzal early in the morning. Because it's somewhat hard to reach, Barva receives a mere fraction of the crowds that flock to the summits of Poás and Irazú. A two- to four-hour hike in from the Barva ranger station takes you to the main crater, which is about 162 meters (540 feet) in diameter. Its almost vertical sides are covered in sombrillas de pobre, a plant that thrives in the highlands, and oak trees laden with epiphytes (nonparasitic plants that grow on other plants). The crater is filled with an otherworldly black lake. Farther down the track into the forest lies a smaller crater lake. **■TIP→Bring rain gear, boots, and a warm shirt. Stay on the trail when hiking anywhere in Braulio Carrillo; even experienced hikers who know the area have lost their way up here, and the rugged terrain makes wandering through the woods very dangerous. In addition, muggings of hikers have been reported in the park. (This is the closest national park to San José and its attendant urban problems.) Go with a ranger if possible.**

For access to the volcano, start from Sacramento, north of Heredia. North of Barva de Heredia the road grows narrow and steep. At Sacramento the paved road turns to dirt, growing worse as it nears the Barva ranger station. We recommend a 4WD vehicle, especially during the rainy season. From the ranger station you can take a 4WD vehicle over the extremely rocky road to the park entrance (dry season only), or hike up on foot. The walk through the cloud forest to the crater's two lakes takes two to four hours, but your efforts should be rewarded by great views (as long as you start before 8 AM, to avoid the mist). ✉*Access via the park's Barva ranger station* ☎*2283–5906, 192 (national parks hotline) in Costa Rica* *$10 (in addition to $6 Braulio Carrillo Park entrance)* *Tues.–Sun. 7–4.*

San Rafael de Heredia, 2 km (1 mi) northeast of Heredia, is a quiet, mildly affluent coffee town with a large church notable for its stained-glass

Paz Waterfall Gardens attracts 24 different species of hummingbirds and has a huge butterfly garden.

windows and bright interior. The road north from the church winds its way up Barva Volcano to the Hotel La Condesa, ending atop the Monte de la Cruz lookout point.

GETTING HERE AND AROUND

From San José, travel northeast on Calle 3, which becomes the Guápiles Highway (Hwy. 32), toward Limón. This highway winds through the park, entering at the main ranger station, Zurquí, and exiting at the Quebrada González ranger station. The Barva station is on the west side of the park, north of Zurquí, and is the easiest to access. From Heredia, drive north to Sacramento on Highway 114. The station is 4 km (2½ mi) northeast of Sacramento on a trail that's accessible on foot or by 4WD (except during heavy rains).

Any bus going to Guapiles, Siquirres, and Puerto Viejo de Sarapiquí can drop you off at the Zurquí ranger station. Buses ($2) depart from San José Monday through Saturday from the Atlántico Norte bus station (for Guápiles) or the Gran Terminal del Caribe (for Siquirres or Puerto Viejo de Sarapiquí) several times daily. A cab from San José costs $40 to $50. A number of tour companies offer one-day tours from San José.

OUTDOOR ACTIVITIES

HIKING

The upper slopes of **Barva Volcano** have excellent hiking conditions: cool air, vistas, and plentiful birds. The crater lakes topping the volcano can be reached only on foot, and if you haven't got a 4WD vehicle, you'll also have to trek from Sacramento up to the entrance of Braulio Carrillo National Park. The trails are frequently muddy; ask about their condition at the ranger station. The **Sendero Botello** trail, on the east side of the park (entrance near the Quebrada González ranger station off the Guápiles Highway), is a better choice for casual hikers.

> **A WAY OF LIFE**
>
> *Pura vida* means, literally, "pure life," and is used by Costa Ricans to express agreement, greeting, leave-taking, and basically anything positive. If someone asks, "¿Pura vida?" (basically, "How's it going?" or "Everything okay?"), the response could also be "¡Pura vida!" ("Excellent!") It might also be used to wish someone luck or to say, "Have fun!" Once you arrive, you realize that pura vida is also a philosophy of life, and undoubtedly one reason why 2 million visitors (and counting) come here each year.

WHERE TO STAY

$$–$$$ **Hotel & Villas La Condesa Monte de la Cruz.** The stone fireplace surrounded by armchairs and a small bar in the La Condesa lobby is one of the many facets of the hotel that suggest a lodge you'd expect to find in a more northern latitude. In the central courtyard, topped by a giant skylight, is one of the hotel's two restaurants. A tropical garden is similarly enclosed in the pool area. Guest rooms are carpeted and tastefully furnished, and each has a picture window. Suites have bedroom lofts, sitting areas, and the hotel's best views. **Pros:** rustic luxury; easily reached from San José. **Cons:** isolated; not much within walking distance. ⊠*Next to Castillo Country Club* ✣*10 km/6 mi north of San Rafael de Heredia* ☎*2267–6000* 🌐*www.hotellacondesa.com* *70 rooms, 36 suites* *In-room: no a/c, safe, kitchen (some), refrigerator, Wi-Fi. In-hotel: 2 restaurants, bar, pool, laundry service, Internet terminal* ▭*AE, D, DC, MC, V* *BP.*

$ **Las Ardillas.** Surrounded by old pines on a country road, these unpretentious log cabins are inviting retreats for those looking to lock themselves up in front of a fireplace and tune out the world. The small on-site spa is a good reason to venture from the comfortable, romantic rooms. The restaurant specializes in meats roasted over a wood fire and has a nice selection of Spanish wines. All rooms have modest wood furniture and queen-size beds. **Pros:** secluded location; good restaurant. **Cons:** rustic rooms; chilly here at night. ⊠*Main road, Guacalillo de San José de la Montaña* *Apdo. 44–309, Barva* ☎*2260–2172* *19 cabins* *In-room: no a/c, no phone, kitchen, no TV (some). In-hotel: restaurant, bar, spa* ▭*MC, V* *BP.*

PUERTO VIEJO DE SARAPIQUÍ

6½ km/4 mi north of La Selva.

In the 19th century, Puerto Viejo de Sarapiquí was a thriving river port and the only link with the coastal lands straight east. Fortunes nosedived with the construction of a full-fledged port in the town of Moín near Limón, and today Puerto Viejo has a slightly run-down air. The activities of the Nicaraguan Contras made this a danger zone in the 1980s, but now that the political situation has improved, boats once again ply the old route up the Sarapiquí River to the San Juan River on the Nicaraguan frontier, from where you can travel downstream to Barra del Colorado or Tortuguero. A few tour companies have Sarapiquí

River tours with up to Class III rapids in the section between Chilamate and La Virgen, with plenty of wildlife to see. If you prefer to leave the driving to them, many of the lodges operate boat tours on the tamer sections of the river.

CAUTION

Don't confuse Puerto Viejo de Sarapiquí with Puerto Viejo de Talamanca on the south Caribbean coast (⇨ *Puerto Viejo de Talamanca, in Chapter 9*). Locals refer to both as simply "Puerto Viejo." Buses for both towns depart from San José's Gran Terminal del Caribe with nothing more than a PUERTO VIEJO sign in the station to designate either. Point to the map and ask for clarification before boarding.

GETTING HERE AND AROUND

The Braulio Carrillo Highway runs from Calle 3 in San José and passes the Zurquí and Quebrada González sectors of Braulio Carrillo National Park. It branches at Santa Clara, north of the park, with the paved Highway 4 continuing north to Puerto Viejo de Sarapiquí. Alternatively, an older winding road connects San José with Puerto Viejo de Sarapiquí, passing through Heredia and Vara Blanca. The former route is easier, with less traffic; the latter route is more scenic but heavily trafficked. (If you are at all prone to motion sickness, take the newer road.) The roads are mostly paved, with the usual rained-out dirt and rock sections; road quality depends on the time of year, the length of time since the last visit by a road crew, and/or the amount of rain dumped by the latest tropical storm. Heavy rains sometimes cause landslides that block the highway near the Zurquí Tunnel inside the park, in which case you have to go via Vara Blanca. Check conditions before you set out. Get an early start; fog begins to settle in on both routes by midafternoon. **■ TIP→There are gas stations on the Braulio Carrillo Highway at the turnoff to Puerto Viejo de Sarapiquí, as well as just outside of town. Fill the tank when you get the chance.**

Buses travel several times daily via both routes and leave from San José's Gran Terminal del Caribe.

ESSENTIALS

Bank/ATM Banco Nacional (✉ *Across from post office41001* ☎ *2766–6012*).

Internet Internet Sarapiquí (✉ *Next to Joyería Mary* ☎ *2766–6223*).

Medical Clinic Red Cross (✉ *West end of town* ☎ *2766–6901*).

Post Office Correos (✉ *50 m north of soccer field*).

EXPLORING

Bats are not blind, contrary to popular belief, and most have no interest in sucking your blood. These are just a couple of things you learn on the **Bat Tour** at the nonprofit **Tirimbina Rainforest Center.** Also in the "did you know?" category, touching frogs will not give you warts. You'll learn that on Tirimbina's evening Frog Tour. An informative three-hour guided tour during the day is a terrific value. The center encompasses 750 acres of primary forest and 8 km (5 mi) of trails, some of them traversing hanging bridges at canopy level. Reservations are required for all tours. ✉ *La Virgen de Sarapiquí* ✣ *17 km/11 mi southwest of Puerto Viejo* ☎ *2761–1579* 🌐 *www.tirimbina.org* 🎫 *$15, $22 guided*

Insanely steep hills and heavy rainfall make this country a mecca for white-water sports.

tour, $19 bat tour, $22 frog tour, $24 bird-watching tour ⏲ *Daily 7–5. Bat tour daily 7:30* PM*; frog tour daily 7:30* PM*; guided tours daily 8* AM *and 2* PM.

★ Costa Rica's indigenous peoples don't get the visibility of those in Guatemala or Mexico, probably because they number only 40,000 out of a population of 4 million. The **Dr. María Eugenia Bozzoli Museum of Indigenous Cultures** (Museo de Culturas Indígenas Doctora María Eugenia Bozzoli), part of the Centro Neotrópico Sarapiquís, provides a well-rounded all-under-one-roof introduction to the subject. Nearly 400 artifacts of the Boruca, Bribri, Cabécar, Guaymí, and Maleku peoples are displayed, including masks, musical instruments, and shamanic healing sticks. Start by watching a 17-minute video introduction, *Man and Nature in Pre-Columbian Costa Rica.* A botanical garden next door cultivates medicinal plants still used by many traditional groups. In 1999 researchers discovered an archaeological site on the grounds that contains pre-Columbian tombs and petroglyphs dating from the 15th century. The site is still under study. ✉ *La Virgen de Sarapiquí* ✣ *17 km/11 mi southwest of Puerto Viejo* ☎ *2761–1418* 🌐 *www.sarapiquis.org* 🎟 *$12 (includes guide)* ⏲ *Daily 9–5.*

The newest of Costa Rica's serpentaria is the aptly named **Snake Garden,** with some 50 species of reptiles on display, including all the poisonous snakes (and most of the nonpoisonous ones) found here in Costa Rica, as well as pythons, anacondas, and rattlesnakes from elsewhere in North and South America. You can handle a few specimens (the non-venomous varieties, at least) upon request and under supervision. ✉ *La*

Virgen de Sarapiquí, 400 m south of Centro Neotrópico Sarapiquís ☎2761–1059 $6, $5 children under 6 ⏲Daily 9–5.

A working dairy farm and horse ranch, the **Hacienda Pozo Azul** runs guided tours of the ecologically sound 360-cattle dairy operation. It also has many adventure tours *(⇨ Outdoor Activities, below). ✉La Virgen de Sarapiquí ✣17 km/11 mi southwest of Puerto Viejo ☎2761–1360, 877/810–6903 in North America ⊕www.pozoazul.com $10 ⏲By reservation.*

Heliconias abound at the aptly named **Heliconia Island** in the Sarapiquí River. Some 70 species of the flowering plant, a relative of the banana, are among the collections that populate 5 acres of botanical gardens here. Expect to see ample bird and butterfly life, too. *✉La Chaves ✣8 km/5 mi south of Puerto Viejo de Sarapiquí ☎8397–3948 ⊕www.heliconiaisland.com $12, $17 with guide ⏲Daily 9–5.*

OUTDOOR ACTIVITIES

Hacienda Pozo Azul (*✉La Virgen de Sarapiquí ✣17 km/11 mi southwest of Puerto Viejo 41002 ☎2761–1360, 877/810–6903 in North America ⊕www.haciendapozoazul.com*) is a dairy farm and ranch with biking, horseback riding, rafting, canopy tours, float tours, and rappelling excursions that allow you to combine several activities in a day. **Hotel Gavilán Río Sarapiquí** (*☎2766–6743 ⊕www.gavilanlodge.com*) runs wildlife- and bird-watching tours from its site near Puerto Viejo de Sarapiquí up to the San Juan River. Passports are required for the trip, since the San Juan lies entirely within Nicaragua.

CANOPY TOUR

The canopy tour ($45) at **Hacienda Pozo Azul** *(⇨ above)* has 12 zip lines, ranging in height from 18 to 27 meters (60 to 90 feet).

HORSEBACK RIDING

Dairy farm **Hacienda Pozo Azul** *(⇨ above)* is also a horse ranch and has riding excursions for all experience levels through the region around La Virgen. A two-hour tour is $35; a half day is $45. Check out the multiday tours, too, if you're an experienced rider.

MOUNTAIN BIKING

Aventuras de Sarapiquí (*☎2766–6768 ⊕www.sarapiqui.com*) has made-to-order half-day and multiday biking trips for casual and serious riders. **Costa Rica Biking Adventure** (*☎2235–4982 in San José ⊕www.bikingincostarica.com*) runs one-day mountain-biking tours of the area. **Hacienda Pozo Azul** *(⇨ above)* has half-day, full-day, and two-day rough-and-tumble back-roads bike tours ($45–$75).

RAFTING

The Virgen del Socorro area is one of the most popular "put-in points" for white-water rafters, and offers both Class II and III rapids. Trips leaving from the Chilamate put-in are more tranquil, with mostly Class I rapids. The put-in point depends on the weather and season.

Several operators lead tours on the Sarapiquí River. Old standby **Costa Rica Expeditions** (*☎2222–0333 ⊕www.costaricaexpeditions.com*) offers full-day trips on the Sarapiquí from San José. La Fortuna–based **Desafío** (*☎2479–9464 ⊕www.desafiocostarica.com*) brings you in from the west to the Sarapiquí River, but the distance is no longer than making the trip from San José. **Ríos Tropicales** (☎*2233–6455* 🌐*www.riostropicales.com*) takes in the Sarapiquí on day excursions from San José.

RAPPELLING

Hacienda Pozo Azul (⇨*above*) guides you on a 27-meter (90-foot) river canyon descent ($28).

WHERE TO STAY

$$ **Centro Neotrópico Sarapiquís.** Overlooking the Sarapiquí River, the CNS is an environmental educational center, museum, garden, and hotel all rolled into one. Three indigenous-inspired circular *palenque* (indigenous huts) buildings with palm-thatch roofs house the ample-size rooms. All come with a tile floor, pre-Columbian-style decor, wrought-iron fixtures, and a private terrace. There's an extra cost to visit the center's numerous attractions. **Pros:** good value; many activities; whimsical furnishings. **Cons:** no a/c; sometimes difficult to find space. ✉*La Virgen de Sarapiquí* ✉*17 km/11 mi southwest of Puerto Viejo* ☎*2761–1004, 866/581–0782 in North America* 🌐*www.sarapiquis.org* *47 rooms* *In-room: no a/c, no phone (some), no TV. In-hotel: restaurant, bar, laundry service, Internet terminal* *AE, D, DC, MC, V* *EP.*

$$ **Hotel Gavilán Río Sarapiquí.** Beautiful gardens run down to the river, and colorful tanagers and three types of toucan feast in the citrus trees. The two-story lodge has comfortable rooms with white walls, terra-cotta floors, and decorative crafts. The food, Costa Rican *comida típica* (typical fare), has earned its good reputation. Prime activities are horseback jungle treks, boat trips up the Sarapiquí River, and bird-watching—more than 100 species have been spotted here. **Pros:** lovely gardens; many activities. **Cons:** rustic rooms; need car to stay here. ✉*700 m north of Comando Atlántico (naval command) 41001* *Apdo. 445–2010, San José* ☎*2766–6743, 2234–9507 in San José* 🌐*www.gavilanlodge.com* *17 rooms* *In-room: no a/c, no phone, no TV. In-hotel: restaurant* *AE, D, DC, MC, V* *EP.*

¢ **Posada Andrea Cristina.** The Martinez family owns and operates this friendly and comfortable B&B. High-ceiling rooms have private bathrooms and hot water. Two A-frame bungalows share a (cold-water-only) bathroom. All bungalows and rooms have private gardens with hammocks. **Pros:** good value; secluded location; attentive owners. **Cons:** rustic rooms; need car to stay here. *½ km/¼ mi west of town, La Guaria* ☎*2766–6265* 🌐*www.andreacristina.com* *6 cabins, 4 with bath* *In-room: no a/c* *No credit cards* *BP.*

$$ ★ **Selva Verde Lodge.** Built on stilts over the Sarapiquí River, this expansive complex stands on the edge of a 2-square-km (1-square-mi) private reserve of tropical rain forest and caters primarily to natural-history tours. The buildings have wide verandas strung with hammocks, and the rooms come with polished wood paneling and mosquito blinds. Activities include guided walks, boat trips, canoeing, rafting, and mountain biking. Room prices include a bird-watching tour. Reserve a few weeks ahead, especially in high season; the place is very popular with tour groups. **Pros:** ecology-minded staff; many activities. **Cons:** popular with tour groups; sometimes difficult to find space. *7 km/4 mi west of Puerto Viejo de Sarapiquí* *Apdo. 55, Chilamate* ☎*2766–6800,*

800/451–7111 in North America www.selvaverde.com 40 rooms, 5 bungalows In-room: no a/c (some), no phone, safe, refrigerator (some), no TV. In-hotel: restaurant, bar, pool, laundry service AE, MC, V BP, FAP.

LA SELVA BIOLOGICAL STATION

6 km/4 mi south of Puerto Viejo de Sarapiquí, 79 km/49 mi (2–4 hrs) northeast of San José.

At the confluence of the Puerto Viejo and Sarapiquí rivers, La Selva packs about 420 bird species, 460 tree species, and 500 butterfly species into just 15 square km (6 square mi). Spottings might include the spider monkey, poison dart frog, agouti, collared peccary, and dozens of other rare creatures. **■ TIP→If you want to see wildlife without having to rough it too much, skip Rara Avis and come here.** Extensive, well-marked trails and swing bridges, many of which are wheelchair accessible, connect habitats as varied as tropical wet forest, swamps, creeks, rivers, secondary regenerating forest, and pasture. The site is a project of the Organization for Tropical Studies, a research consortium of 65 U.S., Australian, Latin American, and African universities, and is one of three biological stations OTS operates in Costa Rica. To see the place, take an informative three-hour morning or afternoon nature walk with one of La Selva's bilingual guides, who are some of the country's best. Walks start every day at 8 AM and 1:30 PM. You can add a noontime lunch to your walk for $12; schedule it in advance. For a completely different view of the forest, set off on a guided two-hour walk at 5:45 AM, or the night tour at 7 PM. If you get a group of at least five together, you can enroll in the daylong Bird-Watching 101 course or one of the nature-photo workshops, which can be arranged anytime—either is $40 per person. Or get a group of at least six together and tag along with one of the resident research scientists for a half day. Young children won't feel left out either, with a very basic nature-identification course geared to them. Even with all the offerings, La Selva can custom-design excursions to suit your own special interests, too. Advance reservations are required for the dawn and night walks as well as for any of the courses. *6 km/4 mi south of Puerto Viejo de Sarapiquí 41001 OTS, Apdo. 676–2050, San Pedro 2766–6565, 2524–0607 in San José, 919/684–5774 in North America www.ots.ac.cr Nature walk $34, morning and afternoon walks $40, dawn or night walk $40 Walks daily at 8 AM and 1:30 PM.*

GETTING HERE AND AROUND

To get here, drive south from Puerto Viejo, and look for signs on the west side of the road. For those without wheels, La Selva is a $4 taxi ride from Puerto Viejo de Sarapiquí.

WHERE TO STAY

$$$ **La Selva.** Other lodges provide more comfort for the money, but none can match La Selva's tropical nature experience. The dorm-style rooms have large bunk beds, tile floors, and lots of screened windows. Newer family-style cabins can sleep up to four people and offer a greater level of comfort and privacy. The restaurant, something like a school

cafeteria, serves decent food but has a very limited schedule (reserve ahead). It's a good idea to pay the full-board fee, which includes a guided nature walk and three meals a day with your room rate, since there's nowhere else to eat. Priority is given to researchers—this is a working field station—so advance reservations are essential. **Pros:** many activities, ecology-minded staff. **Cons:** rustic room; no a/c; sometimes difficult to procure overnight space. *6 km/4 mi south of Puerto Viejo de Sarapiquí OTS, Apdo. 676–2050, San Pedro 2766–6565, 2524–0607 in San José www.ots.ac.cr 60 bunk beds share 12 baths, 18 cabins In-room: no a/c, no phone, no TV. In-hotel: restaurant, laundry facilities AE, MC, V FAP.*

OFF THE BEATEN PATH

South of Puerto Viejo de Sarapiquí, the tiny hamlet of Las Horquetas is a jumping-off point for two lodges, at different ends of the comfort scale:

$$–$$$ **Rara Avis.** Toucans, sloths, great green macaws, howler and spider monkeys, vested anteaters, and tapirs may be on hand to greet you when you arrive at Rara Avis, one of Costa Rica's most popular private reserves, one open only to overnight guests. There are three lodging options here. The Waterfall Lodge, near a 59-meter (197-foot) waterfall, has hardwood-paneled rooms with chairs, firm beds, balconies, and hammocks. Despite the prices, accommodation is rustic, with minimal amenities and no electricity. More basic, Las Casitas are three two-room cabins with shared bath and cold water. On the high end, ideal for a rustic honeymoon, is the River Edge Cabin, a 10-minute walk through the forest (it's dark at night, but you're given a flashlight), with private bath and balcony and solar panel–generated electricity. Rates include guides and transport from Las Horquetas. It's time-consuming to get here—your journey from Las Horquetas is on a tractor-pulled cart—so the recommended stay is two nights. **Pros:** many activities. **Cons:** rough trip to get here; expensive for amenities provided. *Las Horquetas 2764–1111 www.rara-avis.com 16 rooms, 10 with bath In-room: no a/c, no phone, no TV. In-hotel: restaurant MC, V AI.*

$$ **Sueño Azul Resort.** This nature lodge and wellness retreat is the most luxurious property in the area, and a favorite for honeymooners and those attracted by the wide variety of yoga and other "wellness" disciplines. Spacious rooms have high ceilings, two double beds, large bathrooms, and a private porch overlooking either one of the rivers or a small lake. One large junior suite has its own outdoor whirlpool tub. Meals are served in an open-air dining room with a view. A wide range of tours and activities is offered, including rain forest hikes, horseback riding, mountain biking, and fly-fishing, as well as trips to major attractions. The spa and yoga facility are impressive for an area in which these amenities are unheard of. **Pros:** lovely furnishings. **Cons:** no a/c. *Just west of Horquetas, off Hwy. 4 2764–1000, 2253–2020 in San José www.suenoazulresort.com 65 rooms In-room: no a/c, safe. In-hotel: restaurant, bar, pool, spa, laundry service AE, D, DC, MC, V EP.*

6

North Pacific

WORD OF MOUTH

"Playa Hermosa is a good location for a base. Do try to take a day trip to the Rincón de la Vieja for the mega-combo tour (includes a full day of activities, such as ziplines, mud baths, horseback riding, and waterslides down the mountain). A day trip to Tamarindo can be fun, too."

—shillmac

WELCOME TO NORTH PACIFIC

TOP REASONS TO GO

★ **Beaches:** White sand; black sand; palm-fringed strands; beaches for swimming, partying, surfing, and sunbathing—you can't beat Guanacaste's beaches for sheer variety.

★ **Endangered nature:** Guanacaste's varied national parks protect some of Central America's last remaining patches of tropical dry forest, an unusual ecosystem where you might spot magpie jays or howler monkeys in the branches of a gumbo-limbo tree.

★ **Surfing:** The waves are usually excellent at more than a dozen North Pacific beaches, including Playa Avellanas, Playa Grande, and Playa Negra.

★ **Big wind:** From December to May, the trade winds whip across northern Guanacaste with a velocity and consistency that makes the Bahía Salinas a world-class sailboarding and kitesurfing destination.

★ **Scuba diving:** Forget the pretty tropical fish. Sharks, rays, sea turtles, and moray eels are the large-scale attractions for divers on the Guanacaste coast.

1 Far Northern Guanacaste. Dry, hot Far Northern Guanacaste is traditionally ranching country, but it does include the impressive wildernesses of Santa Rosa and Rincón de la Vieja national parks, the latter of which holds one of Costa Rica's five active volcanoes. Farther to the north is Bahía Salinas, second only to Lake Arenal for wind- and kitesurfing.

2 Tempisque River Basin. National parks Palo Verde and Barra Honda are the main attractions in the Tempisque River Basin. The former is a prime bird-watching park; the latter has caves and tropical forest ripe for exploration.

3 Nicoya Coast. The number and variety of beaches along the Nicoya Coast make it a top tourist destination. Each beach has its specialty, be it surfing, fishing, diving, or just plain relaxing. Hotels and restaurants are in generous supply.

GETTING ORIENTED

Guanacaste Province—a vast swath of land in northwestern Costa Rica—is bordered by the Pacific Ocean to the west and the looming Cordillera de Guanacaste volcanic mountain range to the east. To the south is the Nicoya Peninsula, with almost continuous beaches along more than 100 km (62 mi) of Pacific coastline, as the crow flies. Many roads are unpaved, especially those to the national parks and less developed beaches, so the best way to get around is in a 4WD vehicle. Take a plane, bus, or shuttle van to Liberia and pick up your rental car there.

NORTH PACIFIC PLANNER

Weather or Not

The North Pacific region of Costa Rica is known for reliably beautiful weather, awesome beaches for surfing and sportfishing, and plenty of wildlife-watching opportunities. Guanacaste is the driest region of the country, with only 165 centimeters (65 inches) of average annual rainfall; it's also the hottest region, with average temperatures around 30°C to 35°C (86°F to 95°F). Mid-November through mid-January—the shoulder season—is the best time to visit, when the landscape is green, the evening air is cool, and hotels and restaurants are prepped and excited for the tourist influx. The beaches and trails can get packed during the drier months, especially mid-December to February, when school is out in Costa Rica. February through April are the driest months: skies are clear, but the heat is intense and the landscape is brown and parched. Fishing and scuba diving are at their best during this period. May through October are the rainy months, which bring lower prices, fewer crowds, and a lush green landscape—though most afternoons also see major downpours.

Getting Around the Region

Most roads here alternate between being extremely muddy and treacherous during the rainy season, and being extremely dusty and treacherous during the dry season. That said, it can be a real adventure exploring the coastline if you have a 4WD or a hired driver with a good, sturdy car. The major artery in this region is the Pan-American Highway (CA 1), which heads northwest from San José to Liberia, then due north to the Nicaraguan border. It's poorly maintained, with many potholes and hills. Trucks and buses often create heavy traffic. To skip the hours of driving, consider flying into Liberia, whose airport provides easy access to the region. Local hotels and tour companies can help you arrange for ground transportation in many cases. In Guanacaste, it's usually safe to take pirata (pirate, or unofficial) taxis, but always negotiate the price before getting into the cab.

What to Do

ACTIVITY	WHERE TO DO IT
Fishing	Playa Flamingo, Tamarindo, Puerto Carrillo, Playas del Coco
Diving	Playa Hermosa, Playa Flamingo, Playa Potrero, Playas del Coco, Ocotal
Surfing	Tamarindo, Playa Langosta, Playa Grande, Playa Avellanas, Playa Negra, Santa Rosa National Park, Playa Guiones
Volcanoes	Rincón de la Vieja National Park
Turtle-watching	Playa Grande, Playa Ostional
Wildlife-watching	Palo Verde National Park, Rincón de la Vieja National Park, Santa Rosa National Park, Barra Honda National Park

Getting the Most Out of the North Pacific

Visiting this region for 10 days to 2 weeks will introduce you to its wonders and leave you with a real taste of the North Pacific. Schedule plenty of beach time for lounging, sunbathing, surfing, diving, and snorkeling. Logistically, you also need to take into consideration slow travel over bumpy roads. A beach with lots of restaurants and nightlife can keep you entertained for a week or more, whereas a more solitary beach might merit only a couple of days. Also plan to visit some protected areas to enjoy canopy tours, wildlife-viewing, and hiking. Outdoorsy types should consider spending a few days around Rincón de la Vieja National Park for its amazing hiking, bird-watching, and horseback riding. Other parks to consider are Palo Verde National Park, Santa Rosa National Park, and Barra Honda National Park. Most North Pacific beaches are just a few hours drive from the Arenal Volcano area (⇨Chapter 3), so the region can be combined with the Northern Plains. Macaw Air flies directly from Tamarindo or Liberia to Puerto Jiménez, where you can spend a few days in a jungle lodge off the grid in the Osa Peninsula, a contrast to developed Nicoya beaches.

Recommended Tour Operators

Swiss Travel Service (☎ *2282–4898* 🌐 *www.swisstravelcr.com*) specializes in Guanacaste. Despite the name, it's operated by Costa Ricans with lots of local experience. Custom-design a guided private or small-group tour.

The excellent **Horizontes Nature Tours** (☎ *2222–2022* 🌐 *www.horizontes.com*) has independent, private tours with your own guide/driver and small-group tours.

Dining and Lodging

WHAT IT COSTS IN DOLLARS

	¢	$	$$	$$$	$$$$
Restaurants	under $5	$5–$10	$10–$15	$15–$25	over $25
Hotels	under $50	$50–$75	$75–$150	$150–$250	over $250

Restaurant prices are per person for a main course at dinner. Hotel prices are for two people in a standard double room in high season, excluding service and tax (16.4%).

Where to Stay?

A wide range of lodging options awaits you in the North Pacific, so choose wisely. If your goal is to take leisurely swims and lounge quietly on the beach with a cocktail in hand, then avoid the beaches that are renowned for surfing waves. Super-expensive resorts like the Four Seasons are generally well balanced with budget hotels that charge less than $50 per night. As in all of Costa Rica, the places we recommend most highly are the small owner-operated hotels and bed-and-breakfasts that blend in with unspoiled nature and offer one-on-one attention from the staff and owners. Most hotels will be able to connect you with local tour operators and knowledgeable staff members who can help show you the best aspects of each destination, whether it's a local park with howler monkeys, a great family-run restaurant on the beach, or a thrilling canopy tour.

Word of Mouth

"There is a nice hike [in Rincón de la Vieja] that goes by the hot mud pots and other interesting things. You'll have to cross some streams. You can access the trail from the main park entrance. The hike to the top [of the crater] is pretty strenuous. We weren't allowed up the time we tried because of high winds."

—Suzie2

PALO VERDE NATIONAL PARK

One of the best wildlife- and bird-watching parks in the country, Palo Verde extends over 198 square km (76 square mi) of dry deciduous forest, bordered on the west by the wide Tempisque River.

With fairly flat terrain and less dense forest than a rain forest, wildlife is often easier to spot here. Frequent sightings include monkeys, coatis, peccaries, lizards, and snakes. (Keep an eye out for the harlequin snake. It's nonpoisonous but mimics the deadly coral snake coloring.)

The park contains seasonal wetlands at the end of the rainy season that provide a temporary home for thousands of migratory and resident aquatic birds, including herons, wood storks, jabirus, and flamingo-like roseate spoonbills. Crocodiles ply the slow waters of the Tempisque River year-round, and storks nest on islands at the mouth of the river where it empties into the Gulf of Nicoya. Trails are well marked, but the weather here can be very hot and windy. Mosquitoes, especially in the marshy areas, are rampant.

BEST TIME TO GO

The best time of year to go is at the beginning of the dry season, especially in January and February, when the seasonal wetlands are shrinking and birds and wildlife are concentrated around smaller ponds. Set off early in the morning or after 3 in the afternoon, when the sun is lower and the heat is less intense.

FUN FACT

The park is named after the lacy, light-green Palo Verde bush, also known as the Jerusalem thorn. Even when it loses its leaflets, this tree can still photosynthesize through its trunk, so it can withstand the droughts common to this area.

PARK STRATEGIES

Unlike many of the other national parks, you can drive 7 km (5 mi) of fairly rough road from the park entrance to the Organization for Tropical Studies (OTS) research station, where most of the trailheads begin. From that point, the best way to see the park is on foot. Plan to spend a couple of nights in the dormitory-style park lodge so that you can get an early-morning start. You'll want to start early because this is a very, very hot area. Hike open areas in the cooler mornings and then choose shaded forest trails for hikes later in the day. Make sure you have a good sun hat, too.

BIRD-WATCHING

The greatest number of creatures you're likely to see here are birds, close to 300 recorded species. Many of them are aquatic birds drawn to the park's vast marshes and seasonal wetlands. The most sought-after aquatic bird is the jabiru stork, a huge white bird with a red neck and long black bill. You'll most likely see it soaring overhead—it's hard to miss. Other birds endemic to the northwest, which you may find in the park's dry-forest habitat, are streaked-back orioles, banded wrens, and black-headed trogons.

There's a raised platform near the OTS station with a panoramic view over a bird-filled marsh. Be prepared to climb a narrow metal ladder.

RIVER CRUISE

A river does run through the park, so a delightful and less strenuous wildlife-viewing option is to cruise down the Tempisque River on a chartered boat with a guide who'll do the spotting for you. Without a boat, you are limited to observing the marshy areas and riverbanks from a long distance. Be sure the boat you choose has a bilingual naturalist on board who knows the English names of birds and animals.

TOP REASONS TO GO

BIRDS, BIRDS, BIRDS

Even if you're not used to looking at birds, you'll be impressed by the waves of migratory water birds that use this park as a way station on their migratory routes. Think of the 2001 documentary *Winged Migration,* and you'll have an idea of the numbers of birds that flock here.

LOTS OF WILD ANIMALS

Hiking the forest trails is hot work, especially in the dry season. But the wildlife-viewing here makes it worthwhile. Watch for monkeys, peccaries, large lizards, and coatis. Take plenty of water with you wherever you walk, and use repellent or wear long sleeves and pants.

OUTDOOR ADVENTURES

The Organization for Tropical Studies has a number of activites that are good for just about any type of group. Choose from guided nature walks, mountain biking, boat tours, and even an occasional nighttime tour. Accomodations can be a little rugged here, but that's half the fun.

RINCÓN DE LA VIEJA NATIONAL PARK

Rincón de la Vieja National Park is Costa Rica's mini-Yellowstone, with volcanic hot springs and bubbling mud pools, refreshing waterfalls, and cool forest trails. Often shrouded in clouds, the volcano dominates the landscape northwest of Liberia, rising above the sunbaked plains.

It has two windswept peaks, Santa María, 1,916 meters (6,323 feet) high on the east slope, and Rincón de la Vieja at 1,895 meters (6,254 feet) on the west. The latter slope has an active crater that hardy hikers can climb up to, and easily accessible fumaroles on its lower slope that constantly let off steam. The park protects more than 177 square km (54 square mi) of the volcano's forested slopes. The wildlife list includes more than 250 species of birds, plus mammals such as white-tailed deer, coyotes, howler and capuchin monkeys, armadillos, and the occasional harlequin snake (not poisonous). The Las Pailas entrance has the most accessible trails, including an easy loop trail that wends past all the interesting volcanic features.

BEST TIME TO GO

Good times to visit are January through May, during the dry season. May to November—the green season—is when the fumaroles and boiling mud pots are most active, but the crater is often covered in clouds so it's not the best time to hike to the top. Trails can get crowded during school break (mid-December through February). Get here early if you plan a long hike or a climb to the crater, since the park entrance closes at 3 PM.

FUN FACT

Volcán Rincón de la Vieja, which literally means "the corner of the old lady," refers to the legend of a wise woman/healer who once lived on its slopes.

HIKING

The only way to explore the park trails is on foot, along well marked paths that range from easy loops to longer, more demanding climbs. The ranger station at the Las Pailas entrance provides maps of the park trails and washrooms before you set off. The easiest hike is the Las Pailas loop, which starts just past the ranger station; it takes about two hours to hike. If you want to venture farther afield, follow the signs for the La Cangreja trail. After passing through dense, cool forest, you'll emerge through an avenue of giant agave plants into an open, windy, meadow. Your reward is the cool waterfall and swimming hole at the end of the trail. There are also warm springs in the rocks surrounding the pool, so you can alternate between warm and cool water in this natural spa.

BIRD-WATCHING

Wherever you walk in this park, you are bound to hear the three-note song of the long-tailed manakin. It sounds something like "Toledo," and that's what the locals call this bird. Along with their lavish, long tail feathers, the males are famous for their cooperative courting dance: two pals leap back and forth over each other, but only the senior male gets any girl who falls for this act. The hard-to-spot rock wren lives closer to the top of the volcano. Birding is excellent most of the year here except for January when the weather is dry but often too windy to distinguish between a fluttering leaf or a flittering bird.

ON HORSEBACK

Saddle up to explore the lower slopes of the volcano, just outside the park borders. Local ranches and lodges organize day-long trail rides to waterfalls and sulfur springs. Your nose will tell you when you are approaching the springs—it's not the picnic lunch gone bad, it's the distinctive rotten-egg smell of sulfur.

TOP REASONS TO GO

GEOLOGICAL WONDERS

The 3-km (2-mi) Las Pailas loop trail showcases the park's famous geothermal features. Along the trail you'll see fumaroles with steam hissing out of ground vents, a *volcancito* (baby volcano), and boiling mud fields named after pots (*pailas*) used for boiling down sugar cane.

CLIMBING TO THE CRATER

The hike to the crater summit is the most demanding, but also the most dramatic. The trail climbs 8 km (5 mi) through shaded forest, then up a sunbaked, treeless slope to the windswept crater, where temperatures plummet. Be sure to check wind and weather conditions at the ranger station before attempting this hike.

BIRDING

The park's forest, alive with the haunting songs of the long-tailed manakin and the loud whinnies of the ivory-billed woodcreeper, is prime bird-watching territory. For intrepid birders, the winding trail leading to the crater is home to the rock wren, which can only be found on these slopes.

6

SANTA ROSA NATIONAL PARK

Renowned for its wildlife, Santa Rosa National Park protects the largest swath of extant lowland dry forest in Central America, about 91,000 acres. *Dry* is the operative word here, with less than 162 centimeters (64 inches) of rainfall a year.

If you station yourself near watering holes in the dry season—January to April—you may spot deer, coyotes, coatis, and armadillos. The park also has the world's only fully protected nesting beach for olive ridley sea turtles. Treetop inhabitants include spider, capuchin, and howler monkeys, as well as hundreds of bird species. The deciduous forest here includes giant kapok, Guanacaste, and mahogany trees, as well as calabash, acacia, and gumbo-limbo trees with their distinctive peeling bark. The park is also of historical significance to Costa Rica because it was here, in 1856, that an army of Costa Rican volunteers decisively defeated an invading force of mercenaries led by an American adventurer named William Walker.

BEST TIME TO GO

Dry season is the best time to visit if you want to see wildlife. The vegetation is sparse, making for easy observation. It's also the best time to drive to the park's beaches. Be aware: it can get very hot and very dry, so take plenty of water if you plan on hiking. In the rainy season, trails can become mud baths.

FUN FACT

Moving from sparse, sunlit secondary forest into the park's shady primary forest areas, you can experience an instant temperature drop of as much as 5°C (9°F). It's a little like walking into a fridge, so wear layers.

GETTING AROUND

Only the first 12 km (7 mi) of the park's roads are accessible by vehicles. The rest of the park's 20 km (12 mi) of trails are for hiking only. It's easy to drive to the La Casona headquarters along a paved road and pick up a loop hiking trail, but beyond that point you need a four-wheel-drive vehicle. During the rainy season, the roads beyond La Casona are impassable even to four-wheel-drive vehicles. Get an early start for any hikes to take advantage of cooler temperatures.

HISTORY

Costa Rica doesn't have many historical sites—relics of its colonial past have mostly been destroyed by earthquakes and volcanic eruptions. So La Casona, the symbolic birthplace of Costa Rica's nationhood, is a particularly revered site. Most Costa Ricans come to Santa Rosa on a historical pilgrimage. Imagine the nation's horror when the place was burned to the ground in a fire purposely set in 2001 by disgruntled poachers, who had been fined by park rangers. The government, school children, and private businesses came to the rescue, raising the money to restore the historic hacienda and replace the exhibits of antique farm tools and historical photos.

TURTLES

Thousands of olive ridley sea turtles emerge from the sea every year, from July to December, to dig nests and deposit eggs on the park's protected beaches at Playa Nancite and Playa Naranjo. Green sea turtles and the huge leatherbacks also clamber ashore, but in much smaller numbers. If you're a hardy outdoors type, you can hike the 12 km (8 mi) to Playa Naranjo and pitch your tent near the beach. Unlike most other turtle-nesting beaches with organized tours, this is a natural spectacle you'll get to witness far from any crowds.

TOP REASONS TO GO

EXPLORE THE FOREST

The short (about a half a mile) La Casona nature-trail loop, which starts from the park headquarters, is a great way to get a sampling of dry tropical forest and to spot wildlife. Look for signs leading to the *Indio Desnudo* (Naked Indian) path, named after the local word for gumbo-limbo trees.

WILDLIFE WATCHING

Wildlife is easy to spot here thanks to the low-density foliage of this tropical dry forest. Scan the treetops and keep an eye out for spider, white-faced capuchin, and howler monkeys. If you're lucky you might even spot an ocelot.

SERIOUS SURFING

Off Playa Naranjo lies the famous Witch's Rock, a towering rock formation famous for its surfing breaks. If you're interested in checking it out but don't feel like walking for miles, take a boat from Playa del Coco, Playa Hermosa, or Playa Tamarindo.

6

ECO-LODGES IN THE NORTH PACIFIC

On the mainland, sweeping plains bordered by volcanoes hold remnants of Central America's tropical dry forest. On the Pacific-edged Nicoya Peninsula, conservationists try to protect turtle-nesting beaches from the encroachments of ever-grander resort hotels and vacation houses.

These tropical dry forest change from relatively lush landscapes during the rainy season to desertlike panoramas in the dry months. The national parks of Santa Rosa, Rincón de la Vieja, Palo Verde, and Barra Honda all protect vestiges of dry forest, as do the private reserves of Hacienda Guachipelín and Rincón de la Vieja Mountain Lodge, where guests can explore on horseback. Visitors can experience the region's wetlands and waterways by riverboat tours and raft. The Nicoya Peninsula is also the site of Las Baulas National Marine Park, where massive leatherback sea turtles lay their eggs on Playa Grande from October to March; and Ostional National Wildlife Refuge, where thousands of olive ridley turtles clamber ashore on moonlit nights from July to January.

GOOD PRACTICES

After a decade of uncontrolled development in the North Pacific province of Guanacaste, Guanacastecation became a pejorative watchword in Costa Rica for unsustainable development.

Playas Junquillal, Negra, Nosara, and Punta Islita are some of the notable exceptions to overdevelopment, managing to maintain a balance between nature and commercial development. Eco-minded tourists who are planning a beach vacation may want to visit these less-developed areas and reward lodge owners who have worked hard to keep their pieces of paradise as sustainable as possible.

TOP ECO-LODGES IN THE NORTH PACIFIC

HARMONY HOTEL

Steps from Playa Guiones in Nosara, this former surfer hotel has been transformed into a low-key, luxury resort with a sustainable mind-set. From permaculture-inspired landscaping with native plants and the use of biodegradable cleaning products and toiletries, to solar-heated hot water and conscientious recycling and waste-management policies, the hotel owners cover all the sustainable stops. Hotel employees, most of them local hires, also volunteer in the town schools, mentoring and teaching English classes and computer literacy.

LAGARTA LODGE

Perched high on a hill, Lagarta Lodge has a wonderful view of distant Ostional National Wildlife Refuge bordering the Pacific. With only six guest rooms, the hotel minimizes its environmental impact by keeping an sharp eye on its consumption of water and energy, as well as on waste management and recycling. Its eco-friendly hospitality practices have garnered it two leaves in the national Green Leaf sustainability program. By far the most salient eco-aspect of the lodge, though, is its 90-acre private Nosara Biological Reserve, with trails crisscrossing a huge mangrove forest bordering the Nosara River and snaking through primary forest on the steep slopes leading from the lodge down to the river.

BORINQUEN MOUNTAIN RESORT & SPA

This luxury resort of stylish villas on the western slope of Rincón de la Vieja doesn't fit the typical eco-lodge profile. But the hotel's eco-conscious policies have won it three leaves in the Green Leaf sustainability program. As well as putting sustainable practices to work, staff members teach the local community about the importance of recycling, waste separation, and organic gardening. The hotel uses earth-friendly, biodegradable products; conserves energy consumption and water use; and helps support community schools with proceeds from recycling refunds.

NESTING LEATHERBACK TURTLES

You simply cannot believe how big a leatherback turtle is. Weighing in at 550 kilos (more than 1,200 pounds), females come ashore under cover of night to lay clutches of up to 100 golf ball–size eggs in nests they dig out of the sand with their flippers. It's equally hard to believe the lengths people will go to in the hopes of catching this incredible sight. Your best chance is at Playa Grande in Las Baulas National Marine Park. As night falls, groups of visitors, each shepherded by a local guide, hunker down at the park entrance, waiting for the summons to sprint down the beach to take their turn, standing silently and witnessing the monumental egg laying. A decade ago, it was almost a sure thing to find at least one laying turtle on the beach during the nesting season. But today, some groups will come away disappointed, a sad reminder of how in the past 25 years, shore development and commercial fishing have reduced sea turtle populations by 99%.

NORTH PACIFIC

Updated by David Dudenhoefer and Heidi Leigh Johansen

Beautiful weather and a windswept coastline bring surfers to the North Pacific area of Costa Rica, an abundance of marine life and stellar diving spots lure underwater aficionados, and a sturdy flow of tourism paired with a laid-back attitude make this an all-around top spot to experience Costa Rica's charms.

GETTING HERE AND AROUND

Aeropuerto Internacional Daniel Oduber Quirós (LIR) in Liberia is an international gateway to the coast. Tamarindo, Playa Nosara, Playa Sámara, Playa Carrillo, and Punta Islita also have airstrips. Flying in from San José to these airports is the best way to get here if you are already in the country. If your primary destination lies in Guanacaste or Nicoya, make sure you or your travel agent investigates the possibility of flying directly into Liberia instead of San José, which saves some serious hours on the road.

SANSA and Nature Air have scheduled flights between San José and destinations on the Nicoya Peninsula. Macaw Air flies small planes between Liberia and Tamarindo, as well as between destinations on the Nicoya Peninsula and to other destinations, including Quepos and Puerto Jiménez.

The northwest is accessed via the paved two-lane Pan-American Highway (CA 1), which begins at the top of Paseo Colón in San José. Take the bridge across the Tempisque river to get to the Pacific beaches south of Liberia. Paved roads run down the spine of the Nicoya Peninsula all the way to Playa Naranjo, with many unpaved and potholed stretches. Once you get off the main highway, dust, mud, potholes, and other factors come into play, depending on which beach you visit. The roads to Playa Flamingo, Playa Conchal, Playa Brasilito, Tamarindo, Playa Grande, Playa Sámara, Playas del Coco, Hermosa, and Ocotal are paved all the way; every other destination requires some dirt-road maneuvering.

You can ride in a comfortable, air-conditioned minibus with Gray Line Tourist Bus, connecting San José, Liberia, Playa Flamingo, Playa Conchal, Playa Potrero, Playa Brasilito, Playa Hermosa, Playas del Coco, Ocotal, Tamarindo, Rincón de la Vieja, and Playa Langosta. Fares range from $27 to $45, depending on destination. The Gray Line Tourist Bus from San José to Liberia and Tamarindo begins picking up passengers from hotels daily around 8 AM. The return bus leaves the Tamarindo and Flamingo areas around 8:30 AM and 3:30 PM. Interbus has door-to-door minivan shuttle service from San José to all the major beach destinations (Papagayo, Canas, Flamingo, Tamarindo, Cocos, Ocotal, Nicoya, and Sámara), for $35 to $43 per person. Reserve at least one day in advance.

ESSENTIALS

Bus Contacts Gray Line Tourist Bus (☎ *2232–3681 or 2220–2126* 🌐 *www.graylinecostarica.com*). **Interbus** (☎ *2283–5573* 🌐 *www.interbusonline.com*).

FAR NORTHERN GUANACASTE

The mountains, plains, and coastline north of Liberia up to the border of Nicaragua make up Far Northern Guanacaste. Liberia, the capital of Guanacaste province, is the closest town to Costa Rica's second-largest airport. You'll most likely pass through it on your way to the beaches southwest of the city or to the nearby national parks of Guanacaste, Santa Rosa, or Rincón de la Vieja. This last park is home to Volcán Rincón de la Vieja, an active volcano that last erupted in 1991.

Northwest of Rincón de la Vieja, on the coast, Parque Nacional Santa Rosa (Santa Rosa National Park) is a former cattle ranch where Costa Ricans defeated the invading mercenary army of American William Walker in 1856. Together with adjacent Guanacaste National Park, Santa Rosa protects the country's largest remnant of tropical dry forest, as well as an important nesting beach for olive ridley sea turtles, which lay their eggs in the sand between July and November. Closer still to the Nicaraguan border is the town of La Cruz, overlooking the lovely Golfo de Santa Elena, and the remote beaches and windswept hotels of Bahía Salinas.

RINCÓN DE LA VIEJA NATIONAL PARK

★ *25 km (15 mi) northeast of Liberia.*

Parque Nacional Rincón de la Vieja is Costa Rica's mini-Yellowstone, with volcanic hot springs and boiling, bubbling mud ponds. The park protects more than 140 square km (54 square mi) of the volcano's upper slopes, which are covered with forest. Often enveloped in clouds, the volcano dominates the scenery to the east of the Pan-American Highway. It has two peaks: Santa María (1,916 meters [6,323 feet]) and the barren Rincón de la Vieja (1,895 meters [6,254 feet]). The latter has an active crater and fumaroles on its lower slope that constantly let off steam, making an eruption unlikely anytime soon. The wildlife here is diverse: more than 250 species of birds, including long-tailed manakins and blue-crowned motmots; plus mammals such as white-tailed deer, coyotes, howler and capuchin monkeys, and armadillos. There are two main entrances: Santa María and Las Pailas; the latter is the most common place to enter the park because it has the most accessible trails and there are several hotels along the road leading up to it. ■ **TIP→If you**

6

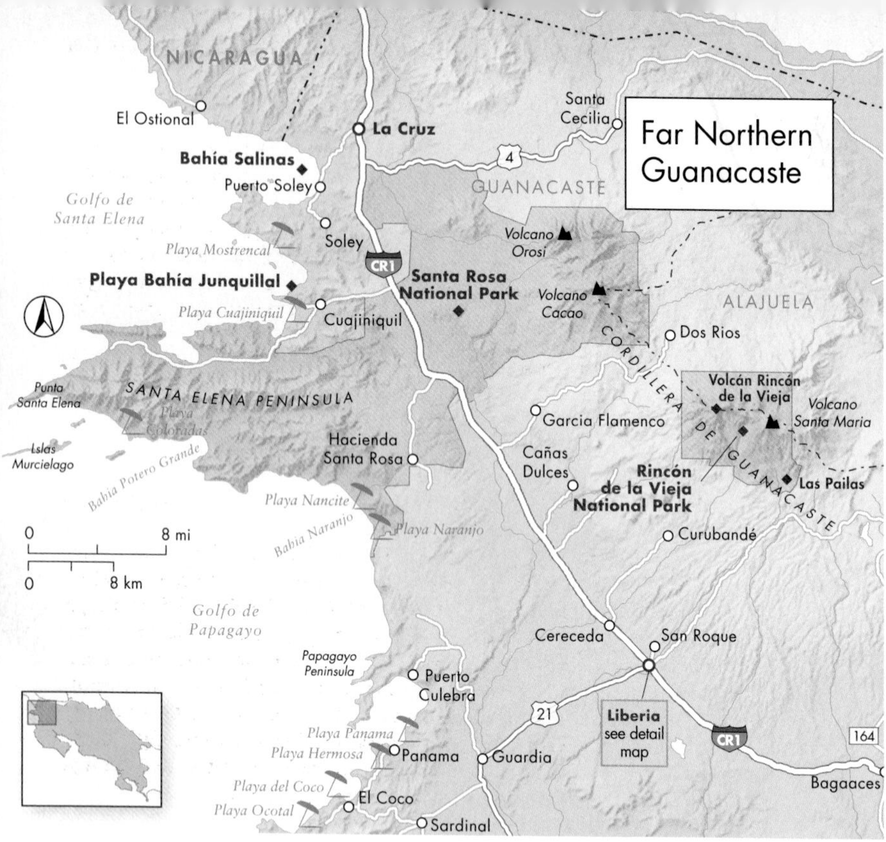

want to explore the slopes of the volcano, go with a guide—the abundant hot springs and geysers have given unsuspecting visitors some very nasty burns. In addition, the upper slopes often receive fierce and potentially dangerous winds—before ascending, check at either ranger station for conditions. The park does not have guides; we recommend the guides at Hacienda Guachipelín and Rincón de la Vieja Volcano Mountain Lodge *(⇨ below)*. You must sign in and pay at the ranger station. Many of the attractions people visit in Rincón de la Vieja are accessible without actually entering the park, since the ranches that border it also hold significant forest and geothermal sites. ☎ *2666–5051* ✉ *$10* ⏲ *Daily 7–5, last entry at 3* PM.

DID YOU KNOW?

The name Rincón de la Vieja translates as "the old woman's corner" and may come from a variety of local legends—it is said, for example, that a witch once lived at the top of the mountain and could send columns of smoke and steam into the air at will.

GETTING HERE AND AROUND

There are two park entrances on the volcano's southern slope: the less traveled one at Hacienda Santa María on the road leading northeast from Liberia (one hour); and the one at Las Pailas, past Curubandé off the Pan-American Highway. To get to the Las Pailas entrance from

CLOSE UP

More Texan than Tropical

Guanacaste, Costa Rica's "Wild West," looks different from the rest of Costa Rica. It was originally covered in dry tropical forests, but beginning in early colonial times, and then picking up speed in the 1950s (when cattle ranching became big business), the dry forest was cleared to create vast cattle ranges. Harder-to-access forests covering the volcanic slopes survived. The resulting flat, sunbaked landscape makes the inland parts of the province look a little like the American Southwest. Cowboy culture still takes center stage during seasonal fiestas and a few rodeos. But these days more and more *sabaneros* (cowboys) are trading in their horses for pickup trucks.

Liberia, take the first entrance road 5 km (3 mi) northwest of Liberia off the Pan-American Highway. The turnoff is easy to miss—follow signs for Hacienda Guachipelín or the town of Curubandé. It's a rough 23-km (14-mi) dirt road, and you have to pay a small toll. The Santa María entrance is 25 km (15 mi) northeast of Liberia along the Colonia Blanca route, which follows the course of the Río Liberia. The turnoff from the Pan-American Highway to the hotels on the western slope of the volcano is 12 km (7 mi) northwest of Liberia, turning right at the road signed for Cañas Dulces. A 4WD vehicle is recommended, though not essential, for all these slow and bone-rattling rides.

OUTDOOR ACTIVITIES

Borinquen Mountain Resort & Spa (*12 km/7½ mi northwest of Liberia on the Pan-American Hwy., then 23 km/14 mi north on the dirt road that passes Cañas Dulces* ☎*2690–1900* *www.borinquenhotel.com*) offers a day package ($90) that begins with a horseback ride and a 90-minute canopy tour, followed by lunch and free time in the hotel's hot springs and natural steam bath. **Buena Vista Lodge & Adventure Center** (*Western slope of volcano* *10 km/6 mi north of Cañas Dulces* ☎*2690–1414* *www.buenavistalodgecr.com*), west of the park, lies on a large ranch contiguous with the park where visitors enjoy horseback riding, waterfall hikes, a canopy tour, hanging bridges, a 480-meter (1,600-foot) (long, not steep) waterslide through the forest, and hot springs. Tours are $20 to $40 per person; a combo ticket is $85, including lunch. **Hacienda Guachipelín Adventure Tours** (*Road to Rincón de la Vieja National Park* ☎*2666–8075 or 2442–2818* *www.guachipelin.com*) has horseback riding, river tubing, hot springs and mud baths, and guided waterfall and volcano hikes. The popular canyon tour includes rock climbing, rappelling, zip lines, suspension bridges, and a Tarzan swing. A one-day, all-you-can-do adventure pass is $80, including lunch. Playa Hermosa–based Mainor Lara Bustos of **Tours Your Way** (☎*8820–1829* *www.tours-your-way.com*) guides tours to Rincón de la Vieja or Palo Verde for $80, including transportation, entrance fees, lunch, and snacks.

CANOPY TOURS

The zip-line canopy tour ($40) with **Buena Vista Lodge & Adventure Center** *(⇨above)* has cables that are up to 27 meters (90 feet) off the ground and up to 135 meters (450 feet) long. **Rincón de la Vieja Canopy** (*✉Rincón de la Vieja Volcano Mountain Lodge ☎2200–0238 🌐www.rincondelaviejalodge.net*) runs four-hour horseback and canopy tours ($45), which include a 16-platform zip line, a ride to the Los Azufrales sulfur springs, or a forest hike to a waterfall with a box lunch.

HIKING

Nearly all the lodges and outfitters in the area offer guided hikes through the park to the fumaroles, hot springs, waterfalls, summit, or the edge of the active crater.

If you're doing a self-guided hike, stop for trail maps and hiking information at the park stations at both entrance gates. The 8-km (5-mi) **trail to the summit** heads up into the forest from the Las Pailas park entrance, then emerges onto a windy, exposed shale slope that's slippery and hard going, and has poor visibility owing to clouds and mist. It's a trip for serious hikers, best done in dry season with preparation for cold weather at the top. A less strenuous option is the fascinating 3-km (2-mi) **loop through the park,** which takes about two hours to complete, starting at the Las Pailas entrance. Along the well-marked trail you'll see fumaroles exuding steam, a *volcáncito* (little volcano), and Las Pailas, the boiling mud fields named after pots used for boiling down sugarcane. If you tread softly in the nearby forest, you may spot animals such as howler, capuchin, and spider monkeys, as well as raccoonlike coatis looking for handouts. ■ **TIP→** Remember the cardinal rule of wildlife encounters: don't feed the animals. Another popular hike out of Las Pailas is a four-hour, 10-km (6-mi) **La Cangreja Waterfall loop,** passing through beautiful primary forests and windswept savannas. The *catarata* (waterfall) has a cool swimming hole below; the surrounding rocks have pockets of hot springs.

HORSEBACK RIDING

Borinquen Mountain Resort & Spa *(⇨above)* offers horseback tours ($80) on a 494-acre ranch that holds patches of forest and ridges with views of nearby Rincón de la Vieja that can be combined with a hike to waterfalls, or a canopy tour. The tour combos include lunch and use of hot springs, and range in price from $70 to $90.

Buena Vista Mountain Lodge & Adventure Center *(⇨above)* has horseback trips to hot springs ($40) and to Borinquen Waterfall ($45). If not everyone in your party is a horse lover, tractor transport ($35) is available to the hot springs as well. **Rincón de la Vieja Volcano Mountain Lodge** (*⇨above*) has guides for hiking or horseback riding near the park. **Hacienda Guachipélin** *(⇨above)* is a working ranch with more than 100 horses and miles of trails to three waterfalls, tropical dry forest, and hot springs. Fees range from $35 for an hour to $200 for a 10-hour tour.

WHERE TO STAY

$$$–$$$$ **Borinquen Mountain Resort & Spa.** The spacious villas on this 12,000-acre ranch overlook lawns shaded by tropical trees on the volcano's windy west slope. They are the nicest accommodations in the

DID YOU KNOW?

In the geothermal areas around Rincón de la Vieja, you'll find mudpots (pools of bubbling mud), fumerals (holes that emit steam and gases) and hot springs.

area, with sloping wooden ceilings, large porches, and plenty of amenities, but they are by far the most expensive as well. Elegant deluxe bungalows have king-size canopy beds, whereas the junior suites have amazing views. Though 90 minutes from the park entrance, the ranch holds most of the same natural attractions, including three waterfalls and patches of forest that hold monkeys, parrots, deer, and other wildlife. The spa has volcanic mud baths, hot springs, and a wooden sauna heated by steam from a fumarole, all included in room rates. Activities include hiking, horseback riding, ATV trips, a canopy tour, and a trip to the park in a Land Rover followed by a hike. The rooms are separated from the restaurant and spa by steep climbs, but the staff can transport you in a golf cart. **Pros:** attractive, well-equipped bungalows; peaceful environment; lots of outdoor activities. **Cons:** far from park entrance; overpriced; restaurant a notch below accommodations. ✣*13 km/8 mi northwest of Liberia on Pan-American Hwy., then 29 km/18 mi north on the dirt road toward Cañas Dulces* ☎*2690–1900* 🌐*www.borinquenhotel.com* *22 villas, 17 bungalows* *In-room: refrigerator. In-hotel: restaurant, bar, pool, spa, laundry service, Internet terminal* *AE, DC, MC, V* *BP.*

$ ★ **Hacienda Guachipelín.** Day-trippers come here, perhaps one of the best values in the Rincón area, for hair-raising adventure tours *(⇨ Outdoor Activities, above)*, but this 3,706-acre working ranch is also famous for its horses—more than 100 of them—and its nature trails leading to several waterfalls, hot springs, and mud baths. Rugged ranch hands swaggering around give the place a real cowboy flavor. Rooms are large and pleasantly furnished, with windows front and back to let in cool mountain air. The newer rooms, numbers 32 and up, are more colorful and larger, though a bit of a walk from the restaurant. Avoid rooms 24 to 31, right beside the corral, unless you enjoy the aroma of horses; try to get one between 32 and 39, which have volcano views from the front terrace. Hearty buffet meals are served in the open-air restaurant, which has valley views. Dairy and beef products come fresh from the hacienda's own herd; vegetarians may have trouble finding meat-free dishes. Large groups often stay here, but you can always find a quiet trail on the vast, partially forested property. The hotel's spa offers an array of treatments, from mud wraps to massages. **Pros:** near park entrance; lots of activities; good value. **Cons:** caters to lots of large groups and day visitors; no a/c in rooms. ✣*17 km/10 mi northeast of the Pan-American Hwy., on road to Las Pailas park entrance* ☎*2666–8075 or 2442–1828* 🌐*www.guachipelin.com* *52 rooms* *In-room: no a/c, no phone, safe, no TV. In-hotel: restaurant, bar, pool, spa, laundry service, Internet terminal* *AE, DC, MC, V* *BP.*

$ **Rincón de la Vieja Mountain Lodge.** This is the closest you can stay to the Las Pailas park entrance, which makes it a good spot for hikers and nature lovers who aren't terribly demanding. Hiking and horse trails lead to a hot sulfuric pool, and farther through the forest, to a blue lake and waterfall, and the volcano's crater deep in the park. The sunny log cabins (room numbers 39 and up), with colorful tiled bathrooms and porches with hammocks, are the best choices. Avoid the rows of connected older rooms (1 to 28), which are dark and gloomy.

The dining room is claustrophobic, with mediocre food served buffet-style, but the alfresco bar is lively in the evening, usually filled with small groups of international ecotourist types. The grounds are shaded by giant malinche trees, and there is a tiny dipping pool. **Pros:** close to park; lots of tour options; reasonably priced. **Cons:** rustic rooms; mediocre food. ✣*21 km/12 mi northeast of Pan-American Hwy.; 5 km/3 mi north of Hacienda Guachipelín; 2 km/1 mi south of Las Pailas park entrance* ☎*2200–0238* 🌐*www.rincondelaviejalodge.net* *38 rooms* *In-room: no a/c, no phone, no TV. In-hotel: restaurant, bar* *AE, MC, V* *BP.*

SANTA ROSA NATIONAL PARK

35 km/22 mi northwest of Liberia.

Renowned for its wildlife, which is easy to spot in the dry season, thanks to sparser foliage, Santa Rosa protects the largest swath of tropical dry forest in Central America. Camping expeditions serving bird-watchers, naturalists, and backpackers often venture deep into the interior, but it's possible to experience a good bit of its impressive flora and fauna on a full-day or half-day visit. Treetop inhabitants include spider, capuchin, and howler monkeys, as well as hundreds of bird species. If you station yourself next to water holes during the dry season, you may also spot deer, coyotes, coatis, or armadillos. Typical dry-forest vegetation includes kapok, Guanacaste, mahogany, calabash, acacia thorn, and gumbo-limbo trees.

Santa Rosa's wealth of flora and fauna is due in part to its remoteness, since much of it is still inaccessible to the common tourist. To get anywhere in the park, you must have a vehicle—preferably 4WD. The park headquarters, a historic ranch house and museum called La Casona, and a nearby camping area are 8 km (5 mi) from the Pan-American Highway via a paved road. Within this dense, shady forest, temperatures drop by as much as 5°C (9°F).

In rainy season the park's rough road to the beach cannot be accessed by even 4WD vehicles, but several short trails head into the forest from its first, flat stretch, and day hikers can easily explore the first stretch of the steep part on foot. Park off the road just before it descends into the forest. From the park headquarters it's 13 km (8 mi) to **Playa Naranjo,** where famed Witch's Rock surf break is located (surfers often get there by boat). **Playa Nancite**—the site of one of the world's only completely protected olive ridley turtle *arribada,* or mass nesting (accessible primarily to biologists and students; permit required)—is an additional 5 km (3 mi) by footpath north of Playa Naranjo. ✉*Km 269, Pan-American Hwy.* ✣*35 km/22 mi north of Liberia* ☎*2666–5051* *$10* ⏲*Daily 8–4:30.*

GETTING HERE AND AROUND

The turnoff for Santa Rosa National Park from the Pan-American Highway is well marked, about 30 minutes out from Liberia. From Liberia you can hop on a bus heading north to La Cruz and get off at the park entrance, but you'll have to hitchhike or hike 8 km (5 mi) in the hot sun to La Casona from here.

OUTDOOR ACTIVITIES

HIKING

The short (about half a mile) **La Casona nature-trail loop** from the park headquarters is worth taking to get a brief sampling of the woods. Look for the INDIO DESNUDO, or "Naked Indian," path, named after the local word for gumbo-limbo trees. ■ **TIP→Carry plenty of water and insect repellent.**

Several other short trails lead off the road **to the beaches** before it becomes impassable to vehicles. The hike to Playa Naranjo (13 km [8 mi] west of La Casona) and Playa Nancite (5 km [3 mi] north of Naranjo) requires good physical condition and lots of water. You can get a map of the trails at the park entrance.

> **WALKER'S LAST STAND**
>
> Santa Rosa Park was the site of the 1856 triumph over American invader William Walker in the famous Battle of Santa Rosa—one of the few historic military sites in this army-less country. The rambling colonial-style ranch house called **La Casona** was the last stand of a ragged force of ill-equipped Costa Ricans who routed the superior mercenary army of the notorious Walker. Disgruntled poachers burned La Casona to the ground in 2001, but it has since been rebuilt.

SURFING

★ **Witch's Rock** towers offshore over a near-perfect beach break off Playa Naranjo in Santa Rosa National Park. If you are interested in surfing Witch's Rock, take a boat tour from Playas del Coco, Playa Hermosa, or Playa Tamarindo, to the south.

WHERE TO STAY

There are basic, dormitory-style lodgings and a camping area near the park's administrative center and at a biological station at Playa Naranjo. You can also camp within Santa Rosa National Park at the very basic and remote campsites at the beaches of Naranjo and Murcielego. Call the park headquarters (☎ *2666–5051 or 2666–0630*) for information. Most people visit the park on day trips from Liberia, or nearby Cuajiniquil.

PLAYA BAHÍA JUNQUILLAL

26 km/16 mi northwest of Santa Rosa National Park entrance.

This 2½-km (1½-mi), tree-fringed, Blue Flag beach is as close as you can get to white-sand beach in this part of Guanacaste. The warm, calm water makes it one of the best swimming beaches on the Gulfo de Santa Elena. Not to be confused with the Playa Junquillal on the western coast of the Nicoya Peninsula farther south, this beach is part of the Guanacaste National Wildlife Refuge to the north of Santa Rosa. Stay for the day or camp out in the well-kept, shaded camping area with cold-water showers, grills, and picnic tables. You can snorkel if you've got your own gear. ✥ *18 km/11 mi west of Pan-American Hwy. Cuajiniquil turnoff.*

GETTING HERE AND AROUND

From the Pan-American Highway, take the road signed for Cuajiniquil, 43 km (26 mi) northwest of Liberia and 8 km (5 mi) north of Santa Rosa National Park. Follow the paved road 14 km (8 mi) to the beach turnoff, along a dirt road for another 4 km (2½ mi). From the Bahía Salinas area, take the scenic dirt road (4WD recommended); then follow the road near Puerto Soley (signed for Cuajiniquil) 7 km (4 mi) to the beach entrance. It's about 30 minutes from the Pan-American turnoff and one hour from Bahía Salinas.

WHERE TO STAY

$ **Santa Elena Lodge.** This simple family-run lodge on the outskirts of Cuajiniquil provides the closest accommodations to both Playa Bahía Junquillal and Santa Rosa National Park, making it a good option for nature lovers and anyone who wants to stray from the vacationing crowds. The owner, Manuel Alán, is a former fisherman who switched to tourism a few years ago, converting his family home into a B&B. The rooms have varnished hardwood walls and ceilings, plenty of windows, and small bathrooms—rooms 5 and 6 are the nicest, since they overlook the garden. Breakfast is served in back, whereas lunch and dinner are available at the adjacent seafood restaurant. Manuel rents bikes, kayaks, and snorkeling equipment, and offers an array of tours that include horseback riding, a hike through the Murcielago sector of Santa Rosa National Park, a boat tour of a mangrove estuary, and whale-watching from August to February. **Pros:** friendly; near beach and park; lots of outdoor options. **Cons:** little English spoken; basic accommodations; close to road. ✉ *Cuajiniquil* ✢ *10 km/6 mi west of Pan-American Hwy., 8 km/5 mi east of Junquillal* ☎ *2679–1038* 🌐 *www.santaelenalodge.com* *9 rooms* *In-room: no phone, no TV. In-hotel: restaurant, water sports, bicycles, laundry service, Internet terminal* ▭ *AE, DC, MC, V* 🍽 *EP.*

6

LA CRUZ

40 km/25 mi northwest of Liberia.

North of Santa Rosa National Park on the west side of the highway is the turnoff to La Cruz, a scruffy, bustling little town. For travelers, it's noteworthy only for the stunning views of Bahía Salinas from its bluff and its proximity to the nearby windswept beaches on the south shore of Bahía Salinas, in the hamlet of Jobo, and in the Golfo de Santa Elena. The Nicaraguan border lies just north of La Cruz at Peñas Blancas. ■ **TIP→All travelers are stopped at two checkpoints south of La Cruz for passport and cursory vehicle inspection. Police vigilance is heightened in the region.**

GETTING HERE AND AROUND

La Cruz is a straight-shot, one hour's trip north of Liberia on the Pan-American Highway. Buses leave Liberia for La Cruz, or you can flag down a bus that says LA CRUZ on its windshield anywhere along the highway north of Liberia.

CLOSE UP

Guanacaste National Park

The 325-square-km (125-square-mi) Parque Nacional Guanacaste, bordering the east side of the Pan-American Highway 30 km (18 mi) north of Liberia, was created in 1989 to preserve rain forests around Cacao Volcano (1,633 meters [5,443 feet]) and Orosi Volcano (1,464 meters [4,879 feet]), which are seasonally inhabited by migrant wildlife from Santa Rosa. The park isn't quite ready for tourism yet. There are very few facilities and no well-marked trails; if you want to hike, it's best to hire a professional guide. In rainy season, roads are impassable; a 4WD vehicle is required year-round. The park is a mosaic of interdependent protected areas, parks, and refuges; the goal is to eventually create a single Guanacaste megapark to accommodate the migratory patterns of animals, from jaguars to tapirs. Much of the park's territory is cattle pasture, which, it is hoped, will regenerate into forest. Today the park has more than 300 different birds and more than 5,000 species of butterflies.

To really explore the park, you must stay in the heart of it, at one of three biological stations. They are mostly reserved for students and researchers, but you can request accommodations from the **park headquarters** (☎ *2666–5051*).

ESSENTIALS

Bank Banco Nacional (✉ *Pan-American Hwy. across from Ursa gas station* ☎ *2679–9389*). **Banco Popular** (✉ *1 block east of Central Park* ☎ *2679–9352*).

Hospital Hospital Area de Salud La Cruz (✉ *Main highway at entrance to town* ☎ *2679–9311*).

Pharmacy Farmacia La Cruz (✉ *1 block north of Central Park* ☎ *2679–8048* 🕓 *Weekdays 8–8, weekends 9–4*).

Internet Internet Café (✉ *Beside Banco Popular*).

Post Office Correo (✉ *Behind police station on west side of Central Park*).

CROSSING INTO NICARAGUA AT PEÑAS BLANCAS

Costa Rica and Nicaragua share a busy border crossing at Peñas Blancas, 18 km (11 mi) north of La Cruz along a paved highway. ■ **TIP→Rental vehicles may not leave Costa Rica.** Tica Bus and Transnica bus companies *(⇨ Bus Travel in Travel Smart Costa Rica)* travel direct between San José and Managua via this route. You can also take a Tralapa bus to the border from other points in Costa Rica. You'll make your crossing, then catch a Nicaraguan bus or taxi to Rivas, 35 km (22 mi) farther, which is the regional hub for buses departing to other parts of Nicaragua. The fee to cross the border is $7 (paid on the Nicaraguan side), plus a $2 surcharge if you cross from noon to 2 PM or on weekends. Nicaraguan shuttle taxis transport people between the border posts. Returning to Costa Rica is basically the same process in reverse; you are charged a $1 municipal tax and $2 exit tax to leave Nicaragua by land. The crossing is open daily 6 AM–8 PM; get there with time to spare or you *will* be stranded. Banks on both sides of the border change their own currency and U.S. dollars. Colones are not accepted or exchanged in Nicaragua; likewise for córdobas in Costa Rica. Overland border crossing procedures can be confusing if you don't speak Spanish.

THIEVES ON THE BEACHES

The North Pacific's idyllic landscapes and friendly people belie an ever-present threat of theft. Though a tiny minority, Costa Rica's thieves manage to ruin a lot of vacations by absconding with backpacks, cameras, wallets, and passports, the last of which necessitates a trip to San José. Keep your valuables in your hotel safe and don't ever leave anything in an unattended car, even while checking into your hotel. Hotel parking lots are popular spots for local kleptomaniacs, as are beaches.

BAHÍA SALINAS

15 km/9 mi west of La Cruz.

The large windswept bay at the very top of Costa Rica's Pacific coast is the second-windiest area in the country, after Lake Arenal, making it ideal for windsurfing and kitesurfing. Strong breezes blow from November to May, when only experienced surfers are out on the water and the water grows steadily cooler. The south (bay) side has the strongest winds, and choppy, colder water from January to May.

6

In July and August the wind is more appropriate for beginners, whereas any time of year you can enjoy the area's diving and beaches. On the sheltered Golfo de Santa Elena, to the west, are two beaches that rank among the most beautiful in all of Costa Rica: Playa Rajada and Playa Jobo, a far cry from the overdeveloped beaches of Guanacaste's gold coast farther to the south.

GETTING HERE AND AROUND

From a high point in La Cruz, the road to Salinas descends both in altitude and condition. It's only 15 km (9 mi) southwest to Hotel Ecoplaya, but the road can be jilted and broken, so may take up to 45 minutes or an hour. Signs direct you to Puerto Soley and El Jobo, an end-of-the-road hamlet, about 2 km (1 mi) past the turnoff for Ecoplaya. Playa Copal is about 13 km (8 mi) along the same road from La Cruz.

EXPLORING

Playa Copal (✣ *About 2 km/1 mi east of the branch road that leads to Ecoplaya*) is a narrow, dark-beige beach that wouldn't be worth visiting except for the fact that it is one of the main venues for kitesurfing. There are villas and rooms for rent. A couple of kilometers to the east, Playa Papaturro also has kitesurfing and simple accommodations.

Gorgeous, horseshoe-shaped **Playa Rajada** (✣ *5 km/3 mi west of Ecoplaya Beach Resort or 3 km/2 mi north of the town of El Jobo*) is a wide sweep of almost-white, fine-grain sand. Shallow, warm waters make it perfect for swimming, and an interesting rock formation at the north end invites snorkelers. It's also a favorite beach for watching sunsets.

★ **Playa Jobo** (✣ *3 km/2 mi walk or drive, west from Ecoplaya Beach Resort*) is a gem with fine sand and calm water. It's fringed with acacia trees that have sharp thorns, so keep your distance. There's a shady parking area about 150 meters (500 feet) off the beach where you have to leave your car.

DID YOU KNOW?

Holy Week, or Semana Santa, runs from Palm Sunday through Easter Sunday and is a huge celebration in this very Catholic country. On Good Friday you'll see religious processions on all over the country.

CLOSE UP

Semana Santa

Don't underestimate how completely Costa Rica shuts down for Holy Week, the week preceding Easter. Cities become ghost towns—San José turns beguilingly peaceful—save for religious processions. Many businesses close the entire week; little opens on Thursday or Friday. Tourists, local and international, flock to the beaches. Make reservations months in advance if you plan to be here during that week, and expect greatly inflated room rates. Know that Holy Thursday and Good Friday are, by law, dry days. Bars and liquor stores must close, and no one, including restaurants or your hotel dining room, is permitted to sell alcohol.

6

OUTDOOR ACTIVITIES

Inshore fishing is quite good in the bay during windy months, when snapper, roosterfish, wahoo, and other fighters abound. Scuba divers also encounter plenty of big fish from December to May, though visibility can be poor then. From May to December the snorkeling is good around the rocky points and Isla Bolaños. **Ecoplaya Beach Resort** (✉ *La Coyotera Beach* ✣ *15 km/10 mi west of La Cruz on a rough dirt road* ☎ *2676–1042* 🌐 *www.ecoplaya.com*) organizes local adventure tours that include kayaking to Isla Bolaños (a tiny island that is a refuge for such seabirds as the brown pelican), inshore fishing, horseback riding, hiking, and scuba diving, as well as farther-afield adventure tours to Santa Rosa National Park, Hacienda Guachipelín, and the historic city of Granada, in nearby Nicaragua.

KITESURFING AND WINDSURFING

The **Kite Surfing School** (☎ *8826–5221* 🌐 *www.bluedreamhotel.com*) on Playa Papaturro (9 km [5½ mi] west of La Cruz, turn left at sign for Papaturro) is run by Nicola, a multilingual instructor with lots of experience; eight hours of beginner's kitesurfing lessons cost $240, including equipment. The school has 10 inexpensive rooms on a ridge with ocean views and a restaurant, called Blue Dream Hotel. **Cometa Copal Kite Surfing Centre and School** (☎ *2676–1192*), on Playa Copal (10 km [6 mi] west of La Cruz), is run by an American who provides kitesurfing lessons and rents equipment.

WHERE TO STAY

$$ **Ecoplaya Beach Resort.** Set between La Coyotera Beach and a mangrove estuary, this small resort has a sprawling collection of villas and two-story concrete buildings (with several types of spacious rooms) that dot ample grounds. Be warned—it's in a high-wind zone. Even with glass buffers and windbreak trees and shrubs, the large swimming pool usually has waves. The 1-km-long (½-mi-long) beach has coarse brown sand flecked with broken shells, and the water is extremely shallow and murky during the windy months. Jobo, Copal, and Rajada beaches are just a short drive away. The hotel organizes activities and tours that

include fishing, diving, horseback riding, and full-day tours to the province's national parks, or historic towns in nearby Nicaragua. Since the resort is also a time-share, it's often packed with Costa Rican families and is full during the holidays. The restaurant, set beneath a massive thatch roof, serves good food, though the service is inconsistent. **Pros:** friendly; quiet; lots of activities. **Cons:** timeworn; service inconsistent; pool gets packed during holidays. ✉ *La Coyotera Beach* ✣ *15 km/10 mi west of La Cruz on a rough dirt road* ☎ *2676–1010, 2228–7146 in San José* 🌐 *www.ecoplaya.com* *16 villas, 20 rooms* *In-room: safe, kitchen (some). In-hotel: restaurant, bar, pool, beachfront, diving, water sports, laundry service* 💳 *AE, MC, V* 🍽 *FAP.*

¢ **Pura Vida Residence.** An affordable base for exploring the area, this Italian-built and -managed hilltop residence overlooks Playa Copal, the premier beach for windsurfing and kitesurfing. Studio rooms are in a white concrete building on a ridge overlooking a small pool. Fully equipped villas are perfect for groups. High ceilings, lots of cool stone and tile, and huge windows to catch the winds off the bay help you keep your cool despite the lack of air-conditioning in the rooms and some of the villas. The small restaurant above those rooms serves the best food in the area ($), such as fresh pastas, baked whole fish, risottos, stuffed calamari, and a selection of pizzas. It's a great lunch option, since the view from its rustic wooden tables is impressive. **Pros:** good value; near surfing beach. **Cons:** isolated; weather-worn. ✉ *Playa Copal* ✣ *13 km/8 mi west of La Cruz* ☎ *8389–6794* 🌐 *www.progettopuravida.com* *7 rooms, 5 villas* *In-room: no a/c (some), no phone, kitchen (some), no TV. In-hotel: restaurant, pool* 💳 *No credit cards* 🍽 *EP.*

LIBERIA

214 km/133 mi (4–5 hrs) northwest of San José.

Once a dusty cattle-market town, Liberia is now galloping toward modernization. Though you can spot the occasional *sabanero* (cowboy) on horseback, the capital of Guanacaste province is well on its way to becoming one big shopping mall, complete with fast-food restaurants and a multiplex theater. The whitewashed adobe houses for which Liberia was nicknamed the "White City" are the only traces of its colonial past. Today Liberia is essentially a good place to have a meal and make a bank stop, though it can serve as a base for day trips to Santa Rosa and Rincón de la Vieja national parks. The drive from San José takes between four and five hours, so it makes sense to fly directly into Liberia if you're going only to the North Pacific. It's easy to rent a car near the airport.

NAVIGATING LIBERIA

The *avenidas* (avenues) officially run east–west, whereas the *calles* (streets) run north–south. Liberia is not too big to walk easily, but there are always taxis lined up around the central park.

GETTING HERE AND AROUND

From San José, follow the Pan-American Highway west past the Puntarenas exit, then north past Cañas to Liberia. The road is paved but is poorly maintained in places. It's a heavily traveled truck and bus route, and there are miles and miles where it is impossible to pass, but

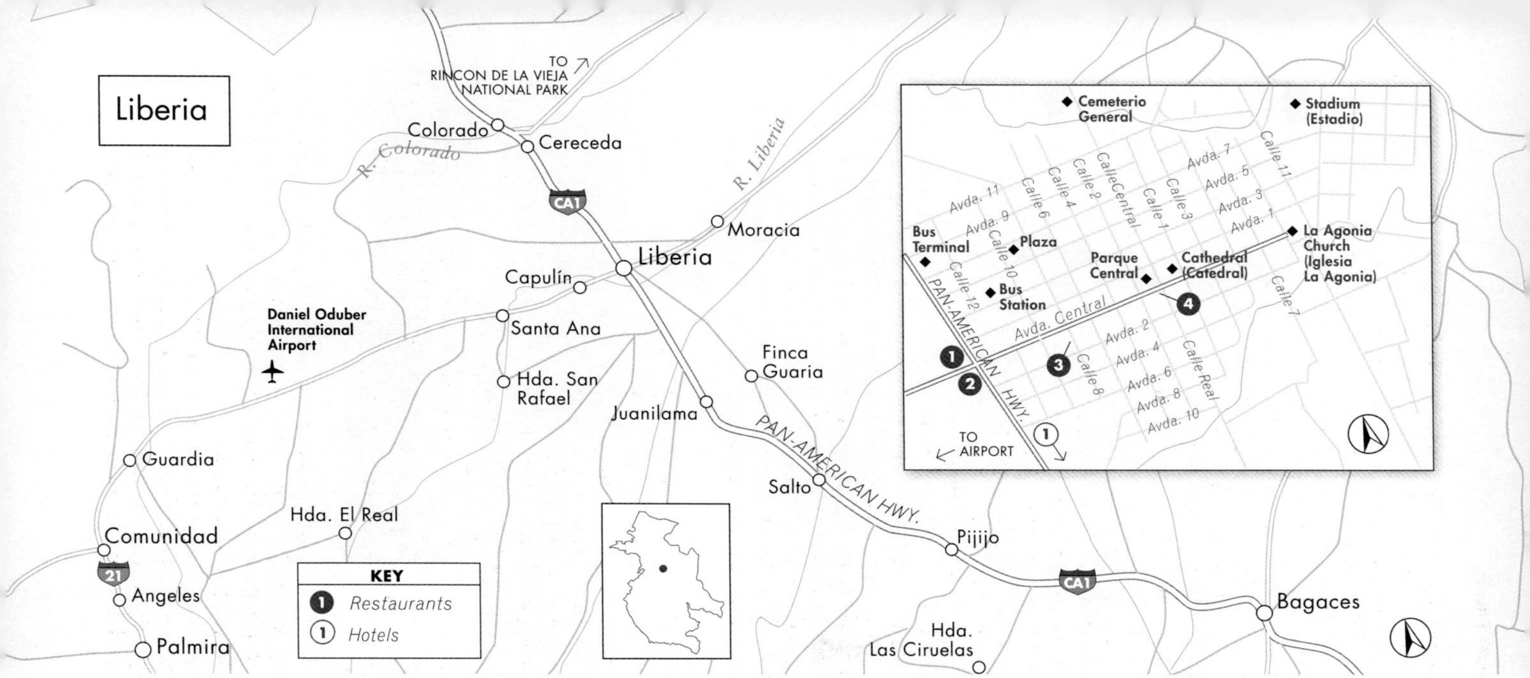

Restaurants ▼

Burger King/ATM **1**

El Café Liberia **3**

La Toscana **2**

Restaurante y Marisquería Paso Real **4**

Hotels ▼

Best Western Hotel Las Espueleas **1**

many drivers try, making this a dangerous road. Hourly direct buses leave San José for Liberia each day, and there are half a dozen daily flights, so it might be worth busing or flying to Liberia and renting a car from here.

ESSENTIALS

Bank/ATM Banco de Costa Rica (*⊠ C. Central at Avda. 1; diagonally across from Central Park ☎ 2666–9002*). **Bancredito** (*⊠ Avda. Central, 2 blocks north of highway*).

Hospital Liberia Hospital (*⊠ North end of town ☎ 2399–0399*).

Pharmacy Farmacia Lux (*⊠ C. 4 and Avda. Central ☎ 2666–0061 ⊙ Weekdays 8–10, Sat. 8–4*).

Internet Ciber Enl@ce (*⊠ C. 4 and Avda. Central ⊙ Daily 8 AM–10 PM*).

Post Office Correo (*⊠ 300 m west of highway, 200 m north of Avda. Central*).

Rental Cars Alamo (*✣ 2 km/1 mi northeast of Liberia airport, Liberia ☎ 2668–1111, 800/462–5266 in U.S.* **Budget** (*✣ 1 km/½ mi southwest of Liberia airport, Liberia ☎ 2668–1118*). **Economy** (*✣ 3½ km/2 mi southwest of Liberia airport, Liberia ☎ 2666–2816 or 2666–7560*). **Hola Rentacar** (*✣ 2 km/1 mi southwest of Liberia airport, Liberia ☎ 2667–4040*). **Payless Car Rental** (*✣ 5 km/3 mi southwest of Liberia airport, Liberia ☎ 2667–0511*).

EN ROUTE

Yes, that is a life-size dinosaur standing beside the highway 20 minutes north of Puntarenas. It is one of 26 lifelike models of extinct and endangered animals arranged along a 1½-km (1-mi) forest trail at Parque MegaFauna Monteverde (*⊠ Pan-American Hwy. ☎ 2645–5029*). Along with the spectacular models outdoors, the $4 entrance fee includes an impressive insect museum. The park is open daily 8 AM to 4:30 PM.

WHERE TO EAT

¢ CAFE — ✕ **El Café Liberia.** The smell of roasting coffee is the best advertisement for this sophisticated café in the center of Liberia. New owners have kept some of the former French-Canadian owner's excellent dishes, including refreshing soups—the mint pea is a winner—savory quiches, and hot sandwiches. Save room for homemade desserts like ice cream in exotic fruit flavors. The casual bar is a cool place to relax, sip a glass of wine, and browse through the paperbacks in the book exchange. *⊠ C. 8, 75 m south of Banco Nacional ☎ 2665–1660 ▭ No credit cards ⊙ Closed Sun.*

$ ITALIAN — ✕ **La Toscana.** Billing itself as "spaghetteria, pizzeria, grigliata, and cafe," this restaurant uses real Italian ingredients. Properly aged Parmigiano cheese and prosciutto from Parma give authenticity to the 40 types of wood-oven pizzas. Tender tuna carpaccio and ensalada caprese are tasty starters. Risottos are the chef's specialty; a nutty, brown, three-mushroom version is cooked perfectly *al dente* and flavored with truffle oil—rare in these parts. *⊠ Centro Comercial Santa Rosa, across from Burger King, on road to airport ☎ 2665–0653 ▭ AE, DC, MC, V.*

$–$$ SEAFOOD — ✕ **Restaurante y Marisquería Paso Real.** A Liberia institution, this second-floor restaurant's terrace overlooks Liberia's Parque Central, which makes for great people-watching. Fresh, tangy ceviches or seafood-laden *sopas de mariscos* (seafood soup) are great light lunches. Save the *filet*

CLOSE UP

Making a Difference

National park or reserve entrance fees help support the preservation of Costa Rica's wildlife and places. You can also make your visit beneficial to the people living nearby by hiring local guides, horses, or boats; eating in local restaurants; and buying things (excluding wild-animal products) in local shops. You can go a few steps further by making donations to local conservation groups or to such international organizations as Conservation International, the Rainforest Alliance, and the Worldwide Fund for Nature, all of which support important conservation efforts in Costa Rica. It's also helpful to explore private preserves off the beaten path and to stay at lodges that contribute to environmental efforts and to nearby communities. By planning your visit with an eye toward grassroots conservation efforts, you join the global effort to save Costa Rica's tropical ecosystems and help ensure that the treasures you traveled so far to see remain intact for future generations.

gratinado al brandy con camarones (fish fillet topped with grilled shrimp and smothered in a brandy cream sauce) for when you're really hungry. Service is efficient and pleasant. It's open daily 11 AM to 10 PM. ✉ *Avda. Central, south side of main square* ☎ *2666–3455* ▭ *AE, MC, V.*

6

WHERE TO STAY

$$ **Best Western Las Espuelas.** From the gigantic Guanacaste tree that shades its parking lot to the local paintings and indigenous stone statues that decorate its lobby, this motel just south of town has more character than one might expect. Rooms are a little institutional, but the grounds are verdant and the rectangular pool is quite large. Two suites, by the pool, have private whirlpool tubs. Rooms facing the highway can be a little noisy; numbers 17 and up are quieter. The restaurant, which resembles a coffee shop, serves complimentary buffet breakfasts, but you're best off heading into town for dinner. The hotel's casino is popular with locals. **Pros:** reasonable rates; big pool. **Cons:** highway noise; mediocre rooms; insects sometimes a problem. ✉ *Pan-American Hwy.* ✣ *2 km/1 mi south of Liberia* ☎ *2666–0144* 🌐 *www.bestwestern.co.cr* *44 rooms, 2 suites* *In-room: safe. In-hotel: restaurant, bar, pool, laundry service, Wi-Fi* ▭ *AE, D, MC, V* *BP.*

THE NICOYA COAST

Strung along the coast of the Nicoya Peninsula are sparkling sand beaches lined with laid-back fishing communities, and hotels and resorts in every price category. As recently as the 1970s, fishing and cattle ranching were the area's mainstays. Development is barreling ahead full speed, though, bringing with it sophisticated restaurants, hotels, and shops, along with congestion, construction chaos, water pollution, and higher prices. Roads are only starting to catch up, so you'll find the interesting anomaly of a trendy restaurant or upscale hotel plunked at the end of a tortuous dirt road. The key to enjoying Nicoya is to slow down. You'll soon be as mellow as the locals.

PAPAGAYO PENINSULA

The Papagayo Peninsula, a crooked finger of land cradling the west side of Bahía Culebra (Snake Bay), is the site of a government-sponsored development program modeled after Cancún. Five large hotels are already situated around Papagayo Bay, and many others are slated to be built here. Although the hotels are modeled on their Caribbean counterparts, the beaches are distinctly Costa Rican, with brown sand and aquamarine water that grows cool from January to April. Isolation is the name of the game, which means that getting out of man-made "paradise" to explore anything off-property often entails a pricey tour.

High season here coincides with dry season. There's guaranteed sun January to April, but there's also intense heat, and the landscape becomes brown and brittle. In the rainy season (August to December), the landscape is greener and more lush. Sparkling water and spectacular sunsets are beautiful year-round.

GETTING HERE AND AROUND

All hotels here have airport pickup. To get to the Four Seasons from the Liberia airport (the hotel refuses to put up directional signs in order to "protect its privacy"), drive 10 km (6 mi) south of Guardia, over the Río Tempisque Bridge, then take the turn on the right signed for Papagayo Allegro Resort. Follow this road about 20 km (12 mi) to its end at the entrance to the resort.

OUTDOOR ACTIVITIES

CANOPY TOUR

Taking advantage of one of the few remaining patches of dry tropical forest on the Papagayo Peninsula, **Witch's Rock Canopy Tour** (☎ *8371–3685* ✉ *witchsrockcanopytour@hotmail.com*) gives you your money's worth: 23 platforms, with a thrilling 450-meter (1,485-foot) cable zip between two of them; four hanging bridges; a waterfall in rainy season; and hiking trails. The 1½-hour tour is $70 per person.

WHERE TO STAY

$$$$ **Four Seasons Resort Costa Rica.** By far one of the most luxurious hotels in Costa Rica, the Four Seasons is extremely secluded (it's nearly 30 minutes from the main road). Service, provided by a cream-of-the-crop, bilingual staff, is faultless. The decor is tasteful and arty. Huge rooms have king-size beds, marble baths, and screened-in living-room terraces. The breezy 18-hole Arnold Palmer signature golf course has breathtaking views—and prices ($185 per round). The state-of-the-art spa is impressive but a little sterile. Dishes created at the dinner-only Di Mare restaurant are worth their wildly expensive price tags, but the rest of the hotel's food has been disappointing. **Pros:** impeccable service; lovely beach. **Cons:** isolated; expensive. ✣ *25 km/15 mi west of Guardia; follow signs to Papagayo Allegro Resort and continue to end of road* ☎ *2696–0000* 🌐 *www.fourseasons.com/costarica* *123 rooms, 36 suites, 21 villas* *In-room: safe, refrigerator, Wi-Fi. In-hotel: 4 restaurants, room service, bars, golf course, pools, gym, spa, beachfront, water sports, children's programs (ages 4–12), laundry facilities, Internet terminal, no-smoking rooms* ▭ *AE, DC, MC, V* *EP.*

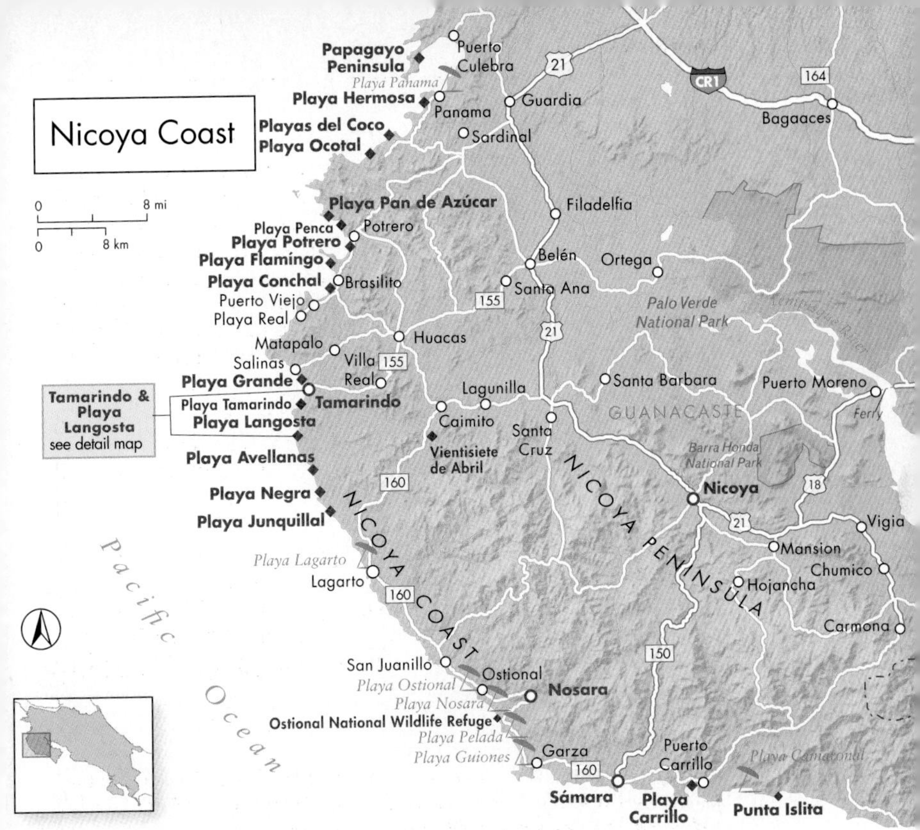

PLAYA HERMOSA

27 km/17 mi southwest of Liberia airport.

Beautiful Playa Hermosa is one of the last laid-back beach towns on this part of the coast. It's the kind of place where the beach is still the town's main thoroughfare, filled with joggers, people walking their dogs, and families out for a stroll. Not to be confused with the mainland surfers' beach of the same name south of Jacó, this Playa Hermosa is experiencing heavy development pressures, with new crops of sunny villas and high-rise condos filling up with American and Canadian expatriates. Luckily, though, the full length of the beach has long been occupied by small hotels, restaurants, and homes, so the newer hotel behemoths and other developments are forced to set up shop off the beach or on other beaches in the area.

Hermosa's mile-long crescent of dark gray volcanic sand attracts heat, so the best time to be out on the beach is early morning or late afternoon, in time for the spectacular sunsets. The beach fronts a line of trees, so there's a welcome respite from the heat of the sun. The crystal-clear water—it's a Blue Flag beach—is usually calm, with no strong currents and with comfortable temperatures of 74°F to 80°F (23°C to 27°C). Sea views are as picturesque as they get, with bobbing fishing boats, jagged profiles of coastline, rocky outcroppings, and at night the twinkling lights of the Four Seasons Resort across the bay. At the beach's north end, low tide creates wide, rock-lined tidal pools.

GETTING HERE AND AROUND

From the Comunidad turnoff of Highway 21, heading from Liberia, Playa Hermosa is about 15 km (9 mi) northwest. The paved road forks after the small town of Sardinal, the right fork heading into Hermosa and the left leading to Playas del Coco. Local directions usually refer to the first and second entrance roads to the beach, the first entrance being the southern one. There is no through beachfront road, so you have to approach the beach from either of these two roads. Transportes La Pampa buses leave from Liberia for Playa Hermosa daily at 5:30, 7:30, and 11:30 AM and 1, 3:30, 5:30, and 7:30 PM. A taxi to Playas del Coco costs about $12 and takes about an hour.

ESSENTIALS

Playa Hermosa has few resources. Get what you need in Liberia or Playas del Coco, just to the south.

Internet Villa Acacia (✉ *Second entrance to Playa Hermosa; south on beach road* ☎ *2672–1000*).

OUTDOOR ACTIVITIES

Aqua Sport (✉ *Beach road; heading south, take second entrance to Playa Hermosa and follow signs* ☎ *2672–0050* 🌐 *www.costa-rica-beach-hotel.com*) organizes fishing, surfing, and snorkeling trips and rents every kind of boat and board. **Charlie's Adventure** (✉ *Hotel Condovac, north end of beach* ☎ *2672–1041 or 2672–0275* 🌐 *www.papagayotours.typepad.com*) organizes ATV tours ($75), horseback riding ($45), and sunset sails ($50), as well as boat tours of Hermosa Bay ($75, including drinks). **Velas de Papagayo** (✉ *Hotel Playa Hermosa Bosque del Mar* ☎ *2223–2598 or 2223–8010* 🌐 *www.velasdepapagayo.com*) runs morning and sunset cruises of Papagayo Bay that include snorkeling, drinks, and snacks ($100). **Hotel El Velero** (✉ *100 m north of Aqua Sport* ☎ *2672–1017* 🌐 *www.costaricahotel.net*) will take you out for a five-hour sunset cruise on a 38-foot sailing yacht ($50 per person). Daytime tours include snorkeling, cave exploring, canopy touring, and diving.

DIVING AND SNORKELING

Average temperatures of 75°F to 80°F (23°C to 27°C), 20 to 60 feet (32 to 95m) of visibility, and frequent sightings of sea turtles, sharks, manta rays, moray eels, and very big fish make Hermosa a great place to dive. There is little coral in the area, but rock reefs attract large schools of fish, and countless critters lurk in their caves and crannies.

Charlie's Adventure (⇨ *above*) organizes snorkeling and diving trips. **Diving Safaris** (✉ *Second entrance road to Playa Hermosa, almost at beach on right side* ☎ *2672–1259* 🌐 *www.costaricadiving.net*) has a range of scuba activities, from beginner training to open-water PADI certification courses. Multitank dives are organized at more than 20 sites. Guides and trainers are very good, and their safety standards have the DAN (Divers Alert Network) seal of approval. This dive shop has also earned the coveted five-star, gold-palm status from PADI. Prices range from

$75 for two-tank morning dives to $425 and up for the PADI open-water certification course.

FISHING

The fishing at Playa Hermosa is mostly close to the shores, and yields edible fish like *dorado* (mahimahi), amberjack, rooster fish, snapper, and yellowfin tuna. Local restaurants are happy to cook your catch for you. You can rent a boat with **Aqua Sport** *(⇨ above)*. **Charlie's Adventure** *(⇨ above)* runs fishing trips. **Papagayo Gulf Sport Fishing** *(☎ 2670–1564 ⊕ www.papagayofishing.typepad.com)* also runs various fishing tours in the area.

WHERE TO EAT

A few of Playa Hermosa's best restaurants are at hotels *(⇨ Where to Stay, below)*.

$ ECLECTIC ★ ✕ **Ginger.** This tapas restaurant, in a modernistic glass-and-steel tree house cantilevered on the side of a hill, is a big hit. The chef has created an Asian-fusion menu with a few Mediterranean dishes. It includes such intriguing appetizer-size offerings as chicken satay with a macadamia-nut rub, mahimahi with a ginger mango sauce, and a taco basket filled with seared pepper-crusted tuna and pickled ginger slaw. Portions are small, but layers of condiments and garnishes make them surprisingly satisfying. The fun thing to do is order several dishes and share. *✉ Main highway, south of Hotel Condovac ☎ 2672–0041 Reservations essential ▭ MC, V ⊗ Closed Mon.*

WHERE TO STAY

$$$ ★ **Casa Conde del Mar.** Spread over verdant grounds just behind relatively pristine Playa Panama—a mile north of Playa Hermosa—this is the place to head for privacy and relaxation. Rooms are in one-story buildings with a traditional Costa Rican decor: Spanish tile roof; red-tile floors; high, sloping ceilings; and covered front terraces offering a glimpse of the sea through the forest that lines the nearby beach. Standard rooms are spacious and equipped with amenities you might expect from any big luxury hotel, whereas the suites are bigger, and more elegant, with a Jacuzzi in the bathroom and pullout couch in the living room. There's a large pool with a waterfall and swim-up bar, and an elegant, airy restaurant ($$) that serves pizza, pastas, and other Italian fare as well as local seafood and beef. The people at the tour desk offer an array of tours, and placid, tree-lined Playa Panama is mere steps away. **Pros:** spacious rooms; immaculate grounds; quiet. **Cons:** not much nightlife; remote. *✉ Playa Panama ✣ 2 km/1 mi north of Playa Hermosa ☎ 2226–0808 or 2672–1001 ⊕ www.grupocasaconde.com 120 rooms, 6 junior suites In-room: safe, Wi-Fi. In-hotel: restaurant, room service, bars, pool, beachfront, laundry service, Internet terminal ▭ AE, DC, MC, V EP.*

$$ **Hotel El Velero.** This laid-back hotel is right on the beach, and though nothing fancy, it's an excellent option if you're watching your expenses. The open-air bar and restaurant, hemmed by exuberant greenery and a small pool, is often hopping with local expats and visitors exchanging fishing, boating, and real-estate stories. The Canadian general manager is an ebullient host, full of local lore and advice. Attractive rooms have

tropical decor with terra-cotta tiles, bamboo furniture, and large windows. Those on the second floor are nicer, with high, sloping wooden ceilings. Only two rooms have ocean views, but you're likely to spend plenty of your time in one of the many chairs and hammocks overlooking the beach, some of which are a shell's toss from the surf at high tide. The hotel runs daily snorkeling and sunset cruises on its own handsome 38-foot sailboat. In the restaurant, jumbo shrimp and always-fresh mahimahi are fixtures. Come on Wednesday or Saturday for beach barbecues. In high season, there's live music on Saturday night. Drinks are two-for-one every day during happy hour, 4 to 6 PM. **Pros:** on the beach; competitive rates; friendly; informal. **Cons:** tiny pool; most rooms have lousy views; can be noisy. ✉*Second entrance to Playa Hermosa, on beach road* ☎*2672–0036* 📠*2672–0016* 🌐*www.costaricahotel.net* *22 rooms* *In-room: safe. In-hotel: restaurant, bar, pool, water sports, laundry service* 💳*AE, MC, V* *EP.*

$$ **Hotel La Finisterra.** From its perch 250 meters (825 feet) up the ridge that defines the southern end of Playa Hermosa, this hotel enjoys a commanding view of the beach and bay. The restaurant ($$), which overlooks the pool and sea, is popular with local expats, who come for the Peruvian-style ceviche, octopus sautéed in a tomato sauce, macadamia-encrusted sea bass, and Mediterranean chicken. The rooms, above the restaurant, are simple but comfortable, with two doubles or one king-size bed, picture windows, and nature paintings by local artists. Rooms on the north side of the building have the best view, though the vista from the common balcony and pool area below are even more impressive. **Pros:** good food; friendly staff; great view. **Cons:** steep road up from beach; small pool. ✉*First entrance to Playa Hermosa, left before Hotel Playa Hermosa, 250 m/825 feet up hill* ☎*2672–0227* 🌐*www.lafinisterra.com* *10 rooms* *In-room: no phone, no TV, Wi-Fi. In-hotel: restaurant, pool, Wi-Fi* 💳*AE, MC, V* *EP.*

$$ ★ **Hotel Playa Hermosa Bosque del Mar.** Century-old trees shade this low-lying hotel on the southern end of Playa Hermosa. The most popular activity here is lounging in hammocks strung around the garden, but floating in the blue-tile pool surrounded by lush landscaping is a close second. Flashes of sunlit ocean, just a few barefoot steps away, periodically penetrate the cool greenery, and now and then an iguana, bird, or monkey rustles the foliage above. Rooms complement the surrounding nature, with trees growing through porches, stained-wood furniture, earth tones, and ceramic bathrooms. Beachfront rooms are the nicest, since you can open the screened windows at night and catch the breeze and the sound of the ocean. The restaurant serves truly fresh fish and beef tenderloin raised on the owner's own ranch. **Pros:** recently remodeled; great food. **Cons:** spotty service; few bathroom amenities. ✉*End of first entrance to Playa Hermosa* ☎*2672–0046* 🌐*www.hotelplayahermosa.com* *20 rooms, 12 deluxe suites* *In-room: safe, refrigerator. In-hotel: restaurant, bar, beachfront, water sports, Wi-Fi* 💳*AE, DC, MC, V* *EP.*

$$ **Villa del Sueño.** Although the handsome garden restaurant ($$$) is the main attraction at this elegant hotel, the spacious rooms are quite nice, too, though it's about a block from the beach. Rooms have up-to-

date bathrooms, comfortable mattresses, and tropical color schemes. The smaller "standard" rooms around the pool are a good deal, and they open onto small terraces with chairs. Larger "superiors" above the restaurant sleep more people, but aren't as nice. If you need more room, spring for a one- or two-bedroom suite in the development across the street, which have kitchenettes, large balconies, or terraces, and are steps away from a larger pool. The restaurant has formal food and polished service, but a casual atmosphere. Filet mignon with a brandy-and-peppercorn sauce, perfectly cooked mahimahi in shrimp sauce, and garlicky butterfly shrimp are among the options. **Pros:** excellent restaurant; good value. **Cons:** not on the beach; can be noisy. ✉ *First entrance to Playa Hermosa, 350 m west of main highway* ☎ *2672–0026* 🌐 *www.villadelsueno.com* *14 rooms, 16 junior suites, 12 suites* *In-room: safe, kitchen (some), refrigerator (some), no TV (some). In-hotel: restaurant, room service, bar, pools, laundry service, Internet terminal, Wi-Fi, no-smoking rooms* *AE, MC, V* *EP.*

NIGHTLIFE

Hotel El Velero (✉ *Second entrance to Playa Hermosa, then 100 m north of Aqua Sport on beach road*) hosts beach barbecues with live music on Wednesday and Saturday nights in high season. The crowd is 30-ish and up. In high season there's live music on Tuesday, Friday, and Sunday nights at **Villa del Sueño** (✉ *First entrance to Playa Hermosa, 350 m west of main highway*).

SHOPPING

You can shop for a beach picnic at **Aqua Sport** (✉ *Second entrance to Playa Hermosa; follow signs heading south on beach road*) mini-market and liquor store and buy souvenirs in the gift shop. The gift shop at **Villa del Sueño** (✉ *First entrance to Playa Hermosa, 350 m west of main highway*) has original oil paintings, exotic crafts from around the world, locally made mother-of-pearl jewelry, and unique ivory bracelets made of local Brahma cow bones. **Kaltak Art and Craft Market** (✉ *South of airport on road to Santa Cruz*) has five rooms of high-quality crafts and gifts, including organic-cotton blouses and dresses and traditional leather-and-wood rocking chairs, which they will ship for you.

6

PLAYAS DEL COCO

25 km/16 mi southwest of Liberia airport.

Messy, noisy, colorful, and interesting, Playas del Coco is first and foremost a fishing port, with a port captain's office, a fish market, and an ice factory for keeping the catch of the day fresh—not for cooling margaritas, although many are enjoyed here. The town (called "El Coco" by locals) is not particularly scenic. The dark-sand beach is mostly a workplace, and it hasn't yet met the Blue Flag standards of cleanliness. The main street becomes a sea of mud when it rains and a dust bowl when it doesn't. So why do visitors flock here? Although fresh seafood, myriad souvenir shops, and plenty of bars draw some tourism, the primary reasons to come to Playas del Coco are the diving, fishing, and surfing at remote breaks such as Ollie's Point and Witch's Rock. Because El Coco is mere minutes from Playa Hermosa, however, you

Continued on page 297

Choosing a Beach

From pulverized volcanic rock and steady waves to soft white sand and idyllic settings, all of the beaches along Nicoya's coast have their own distinct merits. Playa Brasilito has restaurants so close to the ocean the surf spray salts your food; Playas Hermosa and Sámara are family-friendly spots with swimmable waters; and Playas Langosta and Pelada are made for contemplative walks.

NORTHERN NICOYA PENINSULA

Playa Tamarindo

❶ Popular all-inclusive resorts line the beaches of the **Papagayo Peninsula**.

❷ **Playa Hermosa** is one of the few Costa Rican beaches with calm, crystal-clear waters.

❸ Surfing, diving, and fishing are the name of the game at **Playas del Coco** and its scruffy beach town.

❹ **Playa Ocotal** is a quiet beach with great views and good snorkeling.

❺ **Playa Pan de Azúcar** is difficult to access, but practically deserted once you get there.

❻ **Playa Potrero** is the jumping-off point for diving trips to the Catalina Islands.

❼ Busy white-sand **Playa Flamingo** is ideal for swimming and sunning.

❽ Shells sprinkle the sand at chilled-out **Playa Conchal**, near a small fishing village.

❾ Lively **Tamarindo** is a hyped up surfing and water-sports beach with wild nightlife.

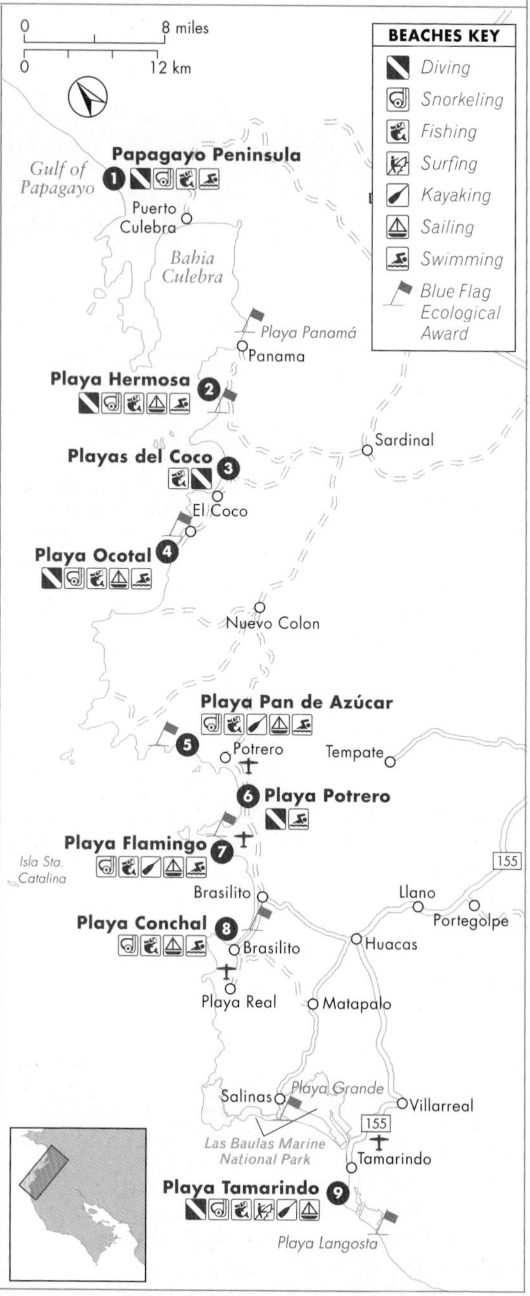

CENTRAL NICOYA PENINSULA

(top) Playa Avellanas (bottom) Sunset at Sámara

❶ Black-sand **Playa Langosta** is great for walks up its estuary and watching dramatic sunsets.

❷ **Playa Avellanas** is a no frills backwater surf spot.

❸ **Playa Negra** has some of Costa Rica's best surfing waves.

❹ Peaceful and pretty **Playa Junquillal** is all about relaxation.

❺ Hemmed in by rocks, **Playa Pelada** is a calm beach staked out by territorial Tico surfers.

❻ Long, clean **Playa Guiones** has a coral reef and is backed by dense jungle.

❼ **Sámara's** gentle waters make it perfect for kayaking and swimming.

❽ Perhaps the most beautiful beach in the country, **Playa Carrillo** fronts an idyllic half-moon bay.

❾ Rocky **Punta Islita** has interesting tidal pools to explore.

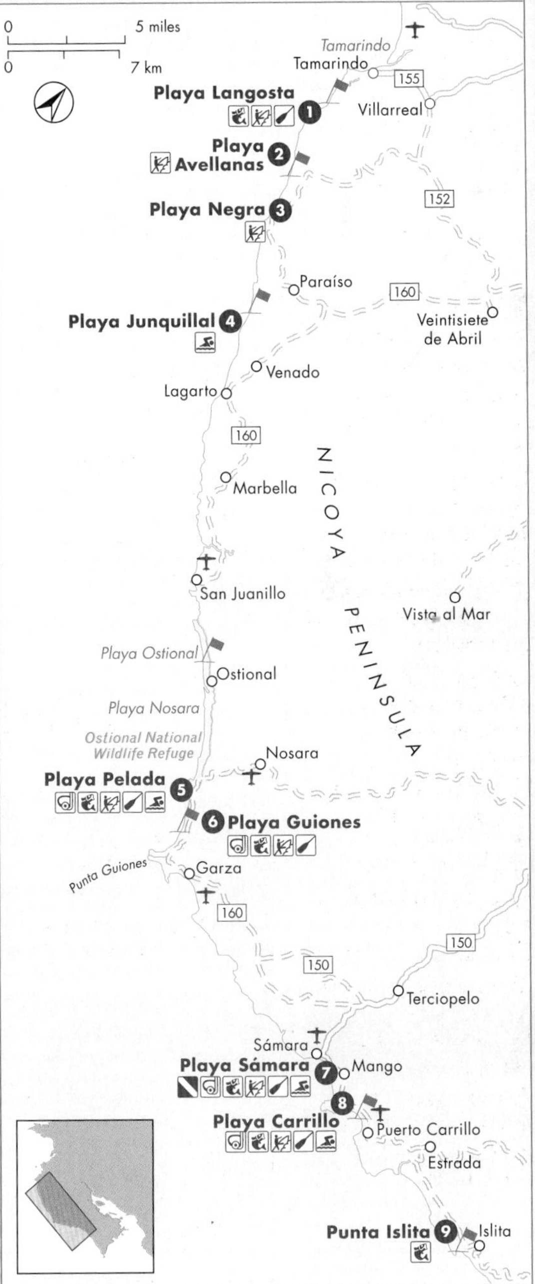

SOUTHERN NICOYA PENINSULA

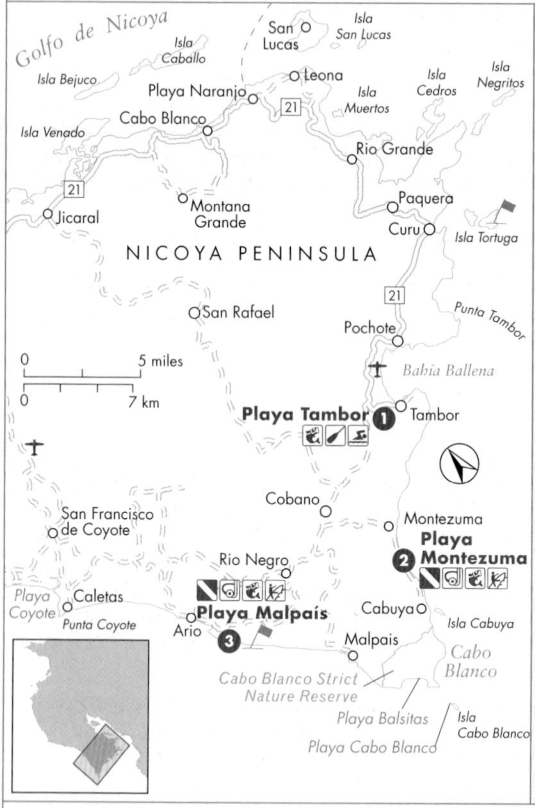

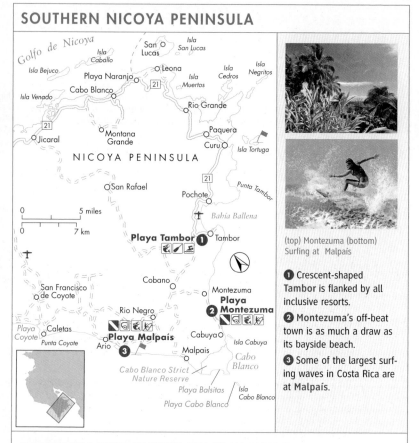

(top) Montezuma (bottom) Surfing at Malpaís

❶ Crescent-shaped **Tambor** is flanked by all inclusive resorts.

❷ **Montezuma's** off-beat town is as much a draw as its bayside beach.

❸ Some of the largest surfing waves in Costa Rica are at **Malpaís**.

MAKING THE BEST OF YOUR BEACH VACATION

Horseback riding at Tamarindo Beach

■ Tamarindo, Nosara, and Sámara are good for beginning surfers. Playas Grande, Avellanas, and Negra are best left to those with experience; other surfing waters are somewhere in between.

■ Tamarindo, Nosara, Sámara, and Tambor are beaches with air service to San José.

■ The beach road connecting most Nicoya Peninsula beaches is hard to stomach any time of year, and virtually impassable during the August through December rains. Take easier inland routes instead.

■ Riptides are seriously dangerous and hardly any Costa Rican beaches have lifeguards; get information from your hotel about where to swim.

can just as easily enjoy those sports while staying at that more pleasant beach. If you like to party, and want some local color, Coco's slightly down-at-the-heels ambience can be appealing.

GETTING HERE AND AROUND

The easy drive from the Liberia airport to Playas del Coco takes about 30 minutes. The paved highway turns into a grand, divided boulevard as you enter town and then dissolves into the dusty main street that leads directly to the beach. If you don't have a car, the best way to get here from Playa Hermosa is in a taxi, for about $12 each way.

ESSENTIALS

Bank/ATM Banco Nacional (✉ *Main street, at entrance to town*).

Hospital Public Health Clinic (✉ *Next to Hotel Coco Verde* ☎ *2670–0987*).

Pharmacy Farmacia Cocos (✉ *100 m east of Banco Nacional* ☎ *2670–1186* ⏲ *Mon.–Sat. 8:30–8, Sun. 10–6* ☞ *Resident doctor*).

Post Office Correo (✉ *Beachfront, beside police station*).

OUTDOOR ACTIVITIES

DIVING AND SNORKELING

Half a dozen dive shops populate this small town. The standard price for a two-tank dive is $70; Catalina Island dives are $95. This coast doesn't have the coral reefs or the clear visibility of the Caribbean coast, but it does have a lot of plankton (hence the lower visibility) that feeds legions of fish, some of them really, really big. Manta rays and sharks (white-tipped, nurse, and bull varieties) are among the stars of the undersea show. It takes about 20 to 45 minutes to reach most dive sites.

Most of the dive shops have instruction, including **Summer Salt Dive Center** (✉ *Main street* ☎ *2670–0308* 🌐 *www.summer-salt.com*). **Deep Blue Diving Adventures** (✉ *Main street, in Hotel Coco Verde parking lot* ☎ *2670–1004* 🌐 *www.deepblue-diving.com*) is a reliable option. **Rich Coast Diving** (✉ *Main street, across from A&A office* ☎ *2670–0176* 🌐 *www.richcoastdiving.com*) has enthusiastic guides and instructors and limits tours to 5 divers per instructor and 15 divers per boat.

FISHING

Fishing charter boats go out 24 to 64 km (15 to 40 mi) seeking yellowfin tuna, mahimahi, grouper, and red snapper close-in, and sailfish, marlin, and roosterfish offshore (beyond 64 km [40 mi]). Boats, moored here and in nearby Ocotal, can pick you up from a beach near your hotel. **TranquilaMar** (✉ *Behind Louisiana Bar & Grill, off main street* ☎ *2670–0833* 🌐 *www.tranquilamar.com*) has four 28-foot Cummins diesel-power boats moored in nearby Ocotal. They can pick you up at any local beach. Just bring sunscreen and your hat, says the owner. Trips are $450 for a half day and $650 for a full day. **Blue Marlin Service** (✉ *Main street* ☎ *2670–0707 or 8348–6510* 🌐 *www.sportfishingbluemarlin.com*) goes out in either a 25-foot boat for close-in fishing ($325 half day) or in a luxury 52-footer for a full day offshore ($2,200).

GOLF

The brand-new **Papagayo Golf & Country Club** (*2 km/1 mi south of Sardinal on road to San Blas* *2697–0169 or 2697–1313* *www.papagayo-golf.com*) is an 18-hole, par-72 course. It's also affordable; you can play the whole course for $80, including golf cart and a cooler with ice, or play 9 holes for $50. There's a restaurant and bar, and a tournament every Sunday morning.

SURFING

★ Legendary **Witch's Rock and Ollie's Point** surfing spots are a one-hour boat ride away from Playas del Coco off the coast of Santa Rosa National Park. You can surf as long as you pay the $6 park entrance fee.

You can sign up for a surfing trip with any beach-town tour operator, but local authorities allow excursions to Witch's Rock and Ollie's Point to originate only from the main dock at Playas del Coco, in boats owned by local boat owners, in order to curb overcrowding and undue environmental stress.

WHERE TO EAT AND STAY

$$–$$$ SOUTHERN **Luz de Papagayo.** This second-story restaurant is cool and breezy, but the Cajun cuisine is hot, with the most authentic jambalaya in town and a spicy gumbo loaded with shrimp, crab, and sausage. The fish is fresh, and it's served any way you like it, with a choice of 10 intriguing sauces, including macadamia pesto or orange-chipotle sauce. *Main street, across from Hotel Coco Verde Casino* *2670–0400* *AE, MC, V.*

$$–$$$ SEAFOOD **Restaurante Papagayo Seafood.** The food here is straightforward, reliably fresh, and flavorful. Start with fish ceviche, or seafood soup generously packed with shrimp, squid, fish, and crab. Then sink your teeth into the catch of the day (including lobster, most notably), prepared any one of a dozen ways, or Papagayo seafood au gratin, which is a mix of sautéed seafood in a tarragon cream sauce. Meat lovers can order from the menu of the contiguous Papagayo Steakhouse, which has local and USDA beef, as well as a kids' menu. Seating is available downstairs, between the stuffed fish and potted plants, or on the cooler, quieter second floor. *Main street, across from Hotel Coco Verde* *2670–0298* *AE, DC, MC, V.*

$$ **La Puerta del Sol.** Facing a formal garden with sculpted shrubs and a lovely pool just two blocks from the beach, this tranquil enclosure of stylish suites has modern, airy Mediterranean-style guest rooms shot through with hot, tropical colors. Each room has high ceilings, plenty of windows, and gleaming white, tiled bathrooms. King-size beds roost atop adobe platforms, whereas single beds nearby double as sofas by day. Pasha, the resident Newfoundland dog, can usually be found lolling around the reception area, and there are various pet cats prowling in the garden. The restaurant, El Sol y La Luna (*above*), is excellent. **Pros:** intimate; comfortable. **Cons:** a walk to the beach; small. *180 m to right (north) off main road to town* *2670–0195* *lapuertadelsolcostarica@hotmail.com* *9 rooms* *In-room: safe, refrigerator. In-hotel: restaurant, pool, gym, laundry service, Wi-Fi* *MC, V* *BP.*

THE ECOLOGICAL BLUE FLAG

The tourist industry here estimates that three-quarters of visitors to Costa Rica make a beach excursion. With that in mind, the national water utility, Acueductos y Alcantarillados, in conjunction with the Instituto Costarricense de Turismo, began evaluating and ranking water and environmental quality in coastal communities in 1996. Those that achieved at least a 90 percent score were awarded a Bandera Azul Ecológica (ecological blue flag) to fly as a symbol of excellence. The program, modeled on one begun in Spain in 1986, awards flags as prizes for communities, rather than to individual hotels. Participants are required to form a Blue Flag committee, a move that brings together diverse sectors of an area's population, many of which otherwise fiercely compete for tourist dollars. The program has prompted communities to put resources into improving environmental quality of life for themselves and for their guests.

Only 10 beaches earned a flag that first year, a fact that Costa Rica sheepishly decided not to publicize, not wanting to call attention to the high number of communities that didn't make the cut. When 19 succeeded the following year, the results went public. Blue Flag locales receive year-round inspections of water quality—both ocean and drinking water—trash cleanup, waste management, security, signage, and environmental education. (Winners dare not rest on their laurels: a few know the shame of having their flags yanked.) In 2002, the competition was opened to inland communities; 2006 saw schools recognized; eco-friendly businesses were added in 2008, including the Rain Forest Aerial Tram; and rivers became eligible for inclusion in 2009.

Blue flags fly proudly in the following locations covered in this book:

CENTRAL VALLEY

Carrizal (Alajuela).

NORTHERN PLAINS

La Fortuna, Las Horquetas, San Rafael de Heredia, Vara Blanca.

NORTH PACIFIC

Bahía Junquillal, Nosara (Playa Guiones), Ostional, Playa Avellanas, Playa Carrillo, Playa Conchal, Playa Flamingo, Playa Grande, Playa Hermosa, Playa Junquillal, Playa Langosta, Playa Pan de Azúcar, Playa Panamá, Punta Islita.

CENTRAL PACIFIC

Barú, Isla Tortuga, Malpaís, Manuel Antonio (Playa Manuel Antonio, Playa Espadilla Sur, Puerto Escondido, Playa Gemelas), Puntarenas, Punta Leona (Playa Blanca, Playa Limoncito, Playa Mantas).

SOUTH PACIFIC

Ballena National Marine Park (Playa La Colonia, Playa Piñuela, Playa Ballena, Punta Uvita), San Gerardo de Rivas, San Marcos de Tarrazú.

CARIBBEAN

Cahuita (Puerto Vargas, Playa Blanca, Playa Negra), EARTH, Gandoca-Manzanillo Wildlife Refuge, Puerto Viejo de Talamanca (Playa Chiquita, Playa Cocles, Punta Uva), Rain Forest Aerial Tram.

NIGHTLIFE

Most local expats prefer **Coconutz** (✉*Main road, across from Hotel Coco Verde*), which is usually packed around happy hour (4 *to* 6), when they often have live music. They also have pool tables, lots of big TVs for games, and bar food. At the **Lizard Lounge** (✉*Main road, west of Hotel Coco Verde*) there's dancing every night on a big thatch-roof dance floor. The reggae, techno, and rap beats appeal to a very young crowd. **Zouk Santana** (✉*Main road, west of Hotel Coco Verde*) is a split-level lounge with a funky ambience that combines bars, couches, and small dance floors for moving to the eclectic mix of music.

SHOPPING

If you can't find it at **Galería & Souvenirs Susy** (✉*Main street, next to Coco Verde Hotel*), chances are they don't make it in Costa Rica. Along with a huge selection of interesting notebooks and albums made of botanical materials, the place also sells locally made shell belts.

PLAYA OCOTAL

3 km/2 mi north of Playas del Coco.

One of the most dramatic beaches in the country, this serene crescent is ringed by rocky cliffs. The sparkling, clean turquoise water contrasts with the black sand. It's only ½ km (mi) long, but the vistas are endless, with offshore islands and the jagged profile of the Santa Elena Peninsula 34 km (21 mi) away. Right at the entrance to the Gulf of Papagayo, it's a good place for sportfishing enthusiasts to hole up between excursions. There's good diving at Las Corridas, just 1 km (½ mi) away, and excellent snorkeling in nearby coves and islands, as well as right off the beach around the rocks at the east end of the beach.

GETTING HERE AND AROUND

The drive is 10 minutes from Playas del Coco on a paved road to the gated entrance of Playa Ocotal. The road winds through a heavily populated Tico residential area, so be on the lookout, especially at night, for bicyclists without lights, children, dogs, cows, and horses on the road. There are no buses from Playas del Coco to Ocotal, but it's about $7 by taxi.

OUTDOOR ACTIVITIES

DIVING AND SNORKELING

The rocky outcrop at the north end of the beach near Los Almendros is good for close-to-shore snorkeling. The dive shop at the **Ocotal Beach Resort** (✉*3 km/2 mi south of Playas del Coco* ☎*2670–0321* 🌐*www.ocotaldiving.com*) is the only PADI Instruction Development Center in Costa Rica, offering the highest-level diving courses. The shop has excellent equipment, safety standards, and instruction. A regular dive costs $75; equipment rental is $25. The shop also rents snorkeling equipment for $10 per day.

FISHING

Ocotal Beach Resort *(⇨above)* has a sportfishing operation with three 32-foot Morgan hulls powered by twin 260-horsepower Cummins engines ($499 half day; $800 full day for up to four fishers). Marlins are catch-and-release, but you can keep—and eat—the mahimahi, yellowfin tuna, grouper, and amberjack you catch.

HIKING

Take an exhilarating and engrossing morning walk ($20) in the hills of Ocotal with retired vet and very active naturalist **Will Abrams** (☎*2670–0553*). The energetic, knowledgeable Kentucky native entertains and educates with stories about the secret lives of trees, plants, and animals spotted along the way.

WHERE TO EAT AND STAY

$$$ COSTA RICAN **Picante.** It's hot and it's tropical, and, as the name warns (*picante* means "spicy"), everything here makes your taste buds tingle. The menu spices up (literally) local fish and tropical fruits in dishes like fresh-tuna *salade niçoise* and grilled mahimahi with a picante mango sauce. (There's also a milder kids' menu.) The large terrace restaurant is poolside, facing the gorgeous beach backed by a cookie-cutter condominium development at Bahía Pez Vela. The cheap dinette furniture is out of sync with the innovative food, but you'll forgive the furniture faux pas when you taste the tart margarita pie or mango cobbler. Their Sunday brunch (10–2) is quite popular. ✉*At the beach, Bahía Pez Vela* ✢*1½ km/1 mi south of Ocotal* ☎*2670–0901* ▭*MC, V.*

$$ ★ **Hotel Villa Casa Blanca.** For romance, you can't beat this Victorian-style, all-suites B&B in a hillside building buried in a bower of tropical plantings. Four-poster beds, plush furniture, and Victorian detailing set the mood. The honeymoon suites have deep soaking tubs built for two. The pool is small but pretty. There's no room service, but the obliging staff can arrange for local restaurants to deliver dinners *á deux*, to be enjoyed by candlelight at the pool or on the terrace. Waffles, pancakes, muffins, and savory dishes provide fuel in the morning. Breakfast entertainment is provided by various pet parrots who are vociferous as well as notorious moochers. Judging by the guest comments, people love them. **Pros:** romantic; fabulous breakfasts. **Cons:** small rooms; sometimes dingy. ✉*Inside gated entrance to El Ocotal Beach Resort* *Apdo. 176–5019, Playas del Coco* ☎*2670–0448* *www.hotelvillacasablanca.com* *12 suites* *In-room: no phone, safe, no TV. In-hotel: pool, laundry service, Internet terminal, Wi-Fi, no-smoking rooms* ▭*AE, MC, V* *BP.*

$$$ **Ocotal Beach Resort.** This resort has the best sea views hereabouts and is one of the best dive and sportfishing resorts in the country. All rooms have ocean views, but those with the nicest views are on the hilltop, even though they may be a bit cramped with furniture. Down the hill to the beach, comfortable triangular bungalows each have two separate suites that share a semiprivate pool. Swimming pools dot the property; be prepared, though, for a steep hike to the biggest one down at the beach, or call for a golf cart to take you there. The best feature of the restaurant, which specializes in Mediterranean and Asian flavors, is the 270-degree view from the terrace. **Pros:** lots of excursions; great infrastructure; lovely view. **Cons:** resort-y; spotty service. ✢*3 km/2 mi south of Playas del Coco, down newly paved road* ☎*2670–0321* *www.ocotalresort.com* *42 rooms, 5 suites, 12 bungalow suites* *In-room: safe.*

DID YOU KNOW?

Magnificent beaches and a dramatically sculpted shoreline are the Nicoya Penisula's trademarks. Here you'll find no shortage of wildlife watching opportunities. Be sure to check out the tide pools that form on the rocky headlands at each end of Playa Ocotal.

In-hotel: 2 restaurants, room service, bars, tennis court, pools, spa, diving, laundry service, Internet terminal, Wi-Fi ▭*AE, MC, V* 🍽*BP.*

NIGHTLIFE

Enjoy a quiet margarita with an ocean view at **Father Rooster Sports Bar & Grill** (✉*Next door to El Ocotal Beach Resort* ✣*3 km/2 mi south of Playas del Coco*) on the beach. The action heats up later in the evening with big-screen TV, music, pool, beach volleyball, and Tex-Mex bar food. During peak holiday weeks, crowds of partiers descend on the bar to dance by torchlight.

PLAYA PAN DE AZÚCAR

8 km/5 mi north of Flamingo Beach.

Playa Pan de Azúcar (literally "Sugar Bread Beach," though most people call it simply Sugar Beach) has a quality that can be hard to come by in this area: privacy. With only one built-up property, the entire stretch of soft, light-colored sand feels practically deserted. The north end of the beach has some good snorkeling when the sea is calm—usually around low tide—and the swimming out from the middle of the beach is relatively safe. But if the swell is big, children and weak swimmers shouldn't go in past their waist. Playa Penca, a short walk south along the beach, can be a good swimming beach as well. A large part of the attraction here is the forest that hems the beach, where you may see howler monkeys, black iguanas, magpie jays, trogons, and dozens of other bird species.

6

GETTING HERE AND AROUND

Getting to this beach is an adventure in itself. It's still a very bumpy road 20 minutes from Flamingo Beach. If you have a 4WD vehicle and an excellent sense of direction, you can attempt to drive (dry season only) the 16-km (11-mi) Monkey Trail, which cuts through the mountains from Coco to Flamingo. But even some Ticos get lost on this route, so keep asking for directions along the way. There are no buses to Playa Pan de Azúcar; a taxi from Playa Flamingo costs about $15.

OUTDOOR ACTIVITIES

Most of the operators who work out of Flamingo (⇨*below*) can pick up guests at the Hotel Sugar Beach for skin diving, sportfishing, sailing, horseback riding, and other excursions. The Hotel Sugar Beach (⇨*below*) offers outrigger tours to a secluded beach 40 minutes to the north, which has a large reef and calm water for snorkeling.

WHERE TO STAY

$$–$$$ 🏨 **Hotel Sugar Beach.** The theme of this secluded hotel with a shimmering pool and thin, curving beach is harmony with nature. Its owners have gone to great lengths to protect the surrounding environment, as the abundant wildlife on its 25 acres of protected forest attests. Spacious one- and two-bedroom suites, with high ceilings and private terraces with idyllic sea views, are great for couples and families (kids under 12 stay free). If you like serenity and want to spend a little less on lodging, opt for a standard room in one of the duplexes scattered through the forest. Each room is decorated in earth tones, with elegant wicker

Fodor's Choice ★

furniture, a wooden door with a hand-carved local bird or animal, and a veranda with a garden or ocean view (the best ocean views are from rooms 21 and 22). The open-air rotunda restaurant serves good seafood dishes ($$$), and there's a kids' menu. The hotel's recycling, energy and water conservation, and community service programs are exemplary. **Pros:** friendly; natural setting; practically private beach. **Cons:** waves and rocks can make ocean dangerous for kids. *⊕8 km/5 mi north of Playa Flamingo ☎2654–4242 ⊕www.sugar-beach.com 22 rooms, 6 suites, 2 houses In-room: safe, kitchen (some), refrigerator. In-hotel: restaurant, room service, bar, pool, water sports, laundry service, Internet terminal, Wi-Fi ▭AE, D, MC, V BP.*

PLAYA POTRERO

4 km/2½ mi north of Flamingo.

The small town of Potrero is a classic Tico community, with a church, school, and supermarket arranged around a soccer field. But Potrero Beach stretches for 4 km (2½ mi) all the way south from the village to the skyline of Flamingo. Development is picking up speed, with large houses and condominium developments springing up on any hill with a view. There's a large Italian contingent here, adding some style and flavor to area hotels. The brown-sand beach is safe for swimming, but Potrero is neither the prettiest, nor cleanest, of this region's beaches. The best area for swimming is midway between Flamingo and Potrero town, near the hotel Bahía del Sol. The best beach view and best breeze are from a bar stool at Bar Las Brisas. About 10 km (6 mi) offshore lie the Catalina Islands, a barrier-island mecca for divers and snorkelers, which dive boats based in Flamingo can reach in 10 minutes.

GETTING HERE AND AROUND

Just before crossing the bridge at the entrance to Flamingo, take the right fork signed for Playa Potrero. The road, which is alternately muddy or dusty, is rough and follows the shoreline. Local buses run from Flamingo to Potrero, but it's so close that you're better off taking a taxi.

OUTDOOR ACTIVITIES

DIVING

Marked as Santa Catarina on some maps, the **Catalina Islands,** as they are known locally, are a major destination for dive operations based all along the coast. These barrier islands are remarkable for their diversity, and appeal to different levels of divers. On one side, the islands have 20- to 30-foot drops, great for beginners. The other side has deeper drops of 18 to 24 meters (60 to 80 feet), better suited to more experienced divers. The top dive sites around the Catalina Islands are **The Point** and **The Wall.** From January to May, when the water is colder, you are almost guaranteed manta-ray sightings at these spots. Cow-nosed and devil rays are also spotted here in large schools, as well as bull and white-tipped sharks, several types of eels, and an array of reef fish. Dive operators from Playa Hermosa south to Tamarindo offer trips to these islands. Reserve through your hotel.

Costa Rica Diving (*⊕1 km/½ mi south of Flamingo on the main highway ☎2654–4148 ⊕www.costarica-diving.com*) has been specializing in

Catalina Islands dives for more than 16 years, with two-tank, two-location trips limited to five divers costing $75. The German owners also offer courses and are noted for their precision and high safety standards.

WHERE TO EAT

¢–$ MEXICAN **Bar Las Brisas.** The perfect beach bar, Las Brisas is a shack with a view of the entire sweep of Playa Potrero. The kitchen serves up fairly basic bar fare and some fresh seafood such as rice with shrimp, and a grilled mahimahi sandwich. The fish tacos are outstanding—breaded strips of fish smothered in lettuce, tomato, and refried beans and encased in both a crisp taco and a soft tortilla shell. Wednesday is ladies' night, when the joint really jumps. The place is decorated with old surfboards, rusty U.S. license plates, and wall murals. ✉ *100 m west of soccer field, across from supermarket* ☎ *2654–4047* ▭ *V.*

$ ECLECTIC **El Castillo Gourmet Eatery.** You won't find a better peanut-butter cookie in the country. This bakery/restaurant is also famous for its gooey cinnamon buns and pizza, which you can pick up to eat on the beach or back at your hotel. A mix of Latin and American food—from breakfast eggs Benedict through sandwiches and salads, Tex-Mex standards, shrimp skewers, and fish-and-chips—is served at casual terrace tables shaded by an ancient fig tree. The only drawback is the location on a busy corner, since the traffic tends to kick up a lot of dust. There's live music on Thursday night, and karaoke on Friday night. ✉ *Across from Club Bahía Potrero* ☎ *2654–4271* ▭ *MC, V.*

$ ITALIAN **Ristorante Marco Polo.** They came, they saw, they built a whole Tuscan-style village and imported a chef from Italy to cater to a demanding Italian clientele. Marco Polo, the main restaurant at the Villagio Flor de Pacífico mega-development of red-roof villas east of Potrero, serves properly *al dente* pasta with homemade sauces and a dozen different wood-oven pizzas. They also serve more substantial dishes such as grilled tuna, chicken cordon bleu, and tenderloin with a béarnaise sauce. There's even a pool in back that you can use while you wait for lunch. ✣ *1 km/½ mi east of Potrero* ☎ *2654–5504* ▭ *AE, MC, V.*

WHERE TO STAY

$$–$$$ ★ **Bahía del Sol.** It has the premier location on the beach, with rooms surrounding lush gardens shaded by tropical trees. But this luxury hotel doesn't rest on its well-situated laurels. The service matches the unbeatable surroundings. At the restaurant ($$$), next to the gorgeous palm-fringed pool, smartly uniformed waiters serve jumbo shrimp, lobster, fresh fish, and various meat dishes prepared in an eclectic mix of ways, from blackened tuna to Moroccan lamb. Seating is under a massive thatch roof or at several tables on the lawn overlooking the beach. Rooms are spacious and elegant, with Costa Rican wicker and wood furniture, patterned ceramic-tile floors, and paintings by Costa Rican artists. They open onto a portico with chairs, hammocks, and views of the garden; deluxe rooms also have a back patio with a Jacuzzi hemmed by greenery. Spacious one- and two-bedroom suites also have kitchens and living rooms. **Pros:** on the beach; lovely grounds; excellent restaurant; friendly. **Cons:** noise from nearby bars; room could use updating. ✉ *South end of Potrero Beach, across from El Castillo*

☎2654–4671 🌐www.potrerobay.com ⇆28 rooms, 11 suites ♘In-room: safe, refrigerator, Wi-Fi. In-hotel: restaurant, room service, bar, pool, beachfront, bicycles, laundry service, Internet terminal, Wi-Fi ▭AE, MC, V ⊙BP.

$ **Bahía Esmeralda Hotel & Restaurant.** Although it's not on the beach, this Italian-run hotel has style at an affordable price. It's a great place for families or groups. Ochre-color villas are spread out around pretty pool gardens and lawn. Large glass doors bring in lots of light, and the fans hung from high wooden ceilings keep things cool. The well-equipped apartments sleep four, six, or eight people, and have handsome fabrics and bathrooms tiled in cool green. An alfresco restaurant serves breakfast and light Italian dishes. The friendly owner-manager is always on the premises. It's a five-minute walk through the village to the beach. **Pros:** friendly service; economical. **Cons:** not on the beach. *✉1 block east of Potrero village ☎2654–4480 🌐www.hotelbahiaesmeralda.com ⇆4 rooms, 8 apartments, 4 suites ♘In-room: no phone, kitchen (some). In-hotel: restaurant, pool, laundry service, Wi-Fi ▭AE, MC, V ⊙EP apartments, BP rooms.*

PLAYA FLAMINGO

80 km/50 mi southwest of Liberia.

Flamingo was the first of the northern Nicoya beaches to experience the wonders of overdevelopment, a fact immortalized in the concrete towers that straggle up the hill above Flamingo Bay. The place is still abuzz with real-estate activity, and any ledge of land with a view is a building site. The beach, hidden away to the southwest of the town, is one of the loveliest strands in Costa Rica, with light-beige sand sloping into a relatively calm sea and buttonwood trees separating it from the road. This beach is great for swimming, with a fine-sand bottom and no strong currents, though there are a few submerged rocks in front of the Flamingo Beach Resort, so you should swim a bit farther south. There's sometimes a bit of surf, so if the waves are big, keep your eye on little paddlers. There is little shade along the beach's kilometer-long stretch, and no services, though there are restaurants in the beach resort and the adjacent town. To find the beach, go straight as you enter town, instead of going up the hill, and turn left after the Flamingo Beach Resort.

Flamingo is perhaps most famous for its large sportfishing fleet, temporarily moored out in the bay while the government grants a new concession to update and operate the marina here. Lured by boatloads of single-for-the-week fishermen, working girls abound here, adding a faint salacious whiff to the nightspots.

GETTING HERE AND AROUND

To get to Playa Flamingo from Liberia, drive 45 km (28 mi) south to Belén and then 35 km (22 mi) west on a good, paved road. The trip takes about three hours. If you're coming from the Playas del Coco and Ocotal area, you can take a 16-km (10-mi) shortcut, called the Monkey Trail, starting near Sardinal and emerging at Potrero. It's then 4 km (2½ mi) south to Flamingo. Attempt this only in dry season and in a 4WD. You can also take a bus from Liberia (⇨ *Bus Travel in Travel Smart Costa Rica*).

ESSENTIALS

Bank/ATM Banco de Costa Rica (✉ *Right from main street, halfway up hill, in Condominio Marina Real* ☎ *2654–4984*).

Pharmacy Santa Fe Medical Center & Pharmacy (✉ *Halfway up hill*).

Internet Shark Point at Costa Rica Diving (✣ *1 km/½ mi south of town* ☎ *2654–4148* ⏲ *Daily 10–6*).

OUTDOOR ACTIVITIES

Flamingo offers the quickest access to the **Catalina Islands**, visible from its beach, where big schools of fish, manta rays, and other sea creatures gather. Coastal reefs to the north are visited on day trips that combine snorkeling with time on undeveloped beaches. **Aquacenter Diving** (✉ *Below Flamingo Marina Resort* ☎ *2654–4072 or 2654–4141* 🌐 *www.aquacenterdiving.com*) runs two-tank dives at the Catalina Islands ($75) and snorkeling trips ($49), as well as offering a range of PADI certification courses.

BOATING

Lazy Lizard Catamaran Sailing Adventures (☎ *2654–5900* 🌐 *www.lazylizardsailing.com*) offers a morning or afternoon snorkeling and sunbathing tour on a 38-foot catamaran. The four-hour tours start at 9:30 AM and 1:30 PM and cost $75, with snorkeling equipment, kayaks, drinks, and food included. If you're up for a more energetic sea expedition, paddle with **Guanacaste Outriggers** (☎ *8383–3013* 🌐 *www.guanacaste outriggers.com*) to remote beaches for snorkeling, swimming, and beachcombing ($57, including fruit buffet). Canoes seat seven, plus two guides.

Sail off for an afternoon of snorkeling, snacking, and sunset drinks on **Samonique III** (☎ *2654–5280 or 2654–7870* 🌐 *www.costarica-sailing.com*), a *trés jolie* 52-foot French ketch ($75). The ship sails daily at 2 and returns at 6:30 PM.

FISHING

Although the marina is still closed down while officials consider bids to rebuild it, there are plenty of sportfishing boats bobbing in Flamingo Bay. In December the wind picks up and many of the smaller, 31-foot-and-under boats head to calmer water farther south. But the wind brings cold water and abundant baitfish, which attract marlin (blue, black, and striped), Pacific sailfish, yellowfin tuna, wahoo, mahimahi, grouper, and red snapper. January to April is consequently prime catch-and-release season for billfish. One of the established fishing operations that sticks around all year is **Billfish Safaris** (✉ *Lower level, Mariner Inn, at entrance to town* ☎ *2654–5244* 🌐 *www.billfishsafaris.com*). Its 42-foot boat with twin 350-horsepower diesel engines can go anywhere in any kind of sea. Trips on a smaller 35-foot boat are also available. Half-day trips are $1,030–$1,425 for up to seven anglers; full-day trips run $1,265–$2,000. You can also go out night fishing for snapper and grouper ($120 per person).

WHERE TO EAT

$$$ FRENCH ★ **Mar y Sol.** Come early to catch the sunset from the second-floor tapas lounge here, then linger over a fine French-accented dinner at this elegant, torchlighted terrace restaurant perched on a hillside. The chef/owners Alain and Jean Luc Taulere represent the fifth and sixth generations of a family of French restaurateurs, so of course there's bouillabaisse on the menu, along with escargots and Chateaubriand for two, sliced tableside. More interesting, though, are their fusions of French traditions with tropical flavors in dishes such as grilled mahimahi with a mango salsa and buerre blanc sauce, or seared tuna with an Asian reduction, wakame, and wasabi mashed potatoes. The succulent rack of lamb is served with a rosemary Bordelaise sauce, and the crispy duck, with a Cognac guava sauce. A Sunday brunch menu, served from 10:30 AM to 2:30 PM, has omelets, quiches, and scallops au gratin. There's an extensive wine cellar to match the sophisticated menu, and they serve two dozen wines by the glass. Service is smoothly professional. *150 m uphill (west) from the Banco de Costa Rica* *2654–4151* *AE, MC, V* *Closed Sun.* and *Oct.*

$ SEAFOOD **Marie's Restaurant.** A Flamingo institution, serving beachgoers and locals for more than two decades, this popular restaurant serves an array of sandwiches and salads, as well as reliably fresh seafood in large portions at reasonable prices. Settle in at one of the wooden tables beneath the ceiling fans and massive thatched roof for a traditional Costa Rican ceviche, avocado stuffed with shrimp, or heart of palm and pejivalle (palm fruit). The main fare includes whole-fried red snapper, shrimp and fish shish kebabs, and a delicious *plato de mariscos* (shrimp, lobster, and fish served with garlic butter, potatoes, and salad). Save room for Marie's signature banana-chocolate bread pudding. At breakfast, try unusual papaya pancakes, French toast made with cream cheese and jam, or Marie's special omelet with cheese, onion, sweet pepper, bacon, and ham. *Main road, near north end of beach* *2654–4136* *AE, MC, V.*

WHERE TO STAY

$$ **Flamingo Beach Resort.** This three-story concrete hotel has a great location overlooking beautiful Flamingo Beach, and though few of its rooms have ocean views, they are all mere steps away from the sand and surf. A family-friendly inn, it has the comfortable, if slightly anonymous, look of an international hotel. You can't beat its beach-accessible location, though, or the huge, centerpiece swimming pool with 25-meter lap lanes along one side. The kids' pool has a sunburn-preventive thatch roof, and is close enough to the swim-up bar that you could save a toddler without spilling your piña colada. There's a dive shop on-site as well as water-sports equipment, and there are several pool tables and children's activities. Rooms are standard size, with high ceilings and private balconies or terraces. Get a pool view, preferably on the second or third floor; those with higher numbers have ocean views. The restaurants are not exciting, so don't take the all-inclusive option. There are good restaurants within walking distance or a quick shuttle trip away. **Pros:** beachfront; big pool; good value. **Cons:** inconsistent service; mediocre food. *Hotel entrance on left past Marie's Restaurant* *2654–4444,*

The reclusive zebra moray eel likes to hide it's entire body in in rock or corral holes.

2283–8063 in San José 🌐*www.resortflamingobeach.com* ⇆*88 rooms, 8 suites* 👍*In-room: safe, kitchen (some), refrigerator, Wi-Fi. In-hotel: restaurant, room service, bars, tennis court, pools, gym, beachfront, diving, children's programs (ages 2–12), laundry service, Wi-Fi* ▭*AE, MC, V* 🍴*EP, AI.*

$$–$$$ **Flamingo Marina Resort.** Though a short walk from Flamingo beach, this collection of hillside villas has lots to do. There are four pools, tennis courts, a beach, a dive shop, and a tour desk. The fashionably decorated rooms, color-washed in a mango hue, have terra-cotta lamps, hand-carved wooden furniture, and shell-shaped sinks. The luxurious condos have modern kitchens and spacious sitting areas with leather couches. Nearly all rooms and condos have large verandas with views of the sea and Playa Potrero. **Pros:** spacious rooms; sea views; ample grounds. **Cons:** not on main beach; no nightlife. ✉*Hill above Flamingo Bay* 📫*Apdo. 321–1002, San José* ☎*2654–4141* 🌐*www.flamingomarina.com* ⇆*22 rooms, 6 suites, 80 condos* 👍*In-room: safe, kitchen (some), Wi-Fi. In-hotel: restaurant, room service, bar, pools, beachfront, diving, laundry service, Internet terminal* ▭*AE, DC, MC, V* 🍴*EP.*

$ **Hotel Guanacaste Lodge.** On the outskirts of Flamingo, a short drive from the beach, this Tico-run lodge offers basic accommodations for a fraction of what the town's big hotels charge. Ten simple, duplex bungalows have high-beamed ceilings, wood furniture, walk-in closets, and spacious bathrooms. Each room has a picture window looking out onto a garden that holds the pool, a thatched shelter, and a cascading fountain. **Pros:** very private; friendly. **Cons:** no in-room phones; simple. ✉*200 m south of the Potrero-Flamingo crossroads* ☎*2654–4494* *www.guanacastelodge.com* *10 rooms* *In-room: no phone. In-hotel: pool* *V* *BP.*

NIGHTLIFE

The **Mariner Inn Bar** (*Bottom of hill, entering Flamingo*) is often boisterous and thick with testosterone, as fishermen trade fish tales. If you're interested in fishing of a different sort, or just like to watch, restaurant/disco/casino **Amberes** (*Halfway up hill in Flamingo*) is the late-night meeting place.

THE GUANACASTE TREE

Massive and wide spreading, with tiny leaflets and dark brown, ear-like seedpods, the Guanacaste tree is common through this region, and is Costa Rica's national tree.

PLAYA CONCHAL

8 km/5 mi south of Flamingo.

Lovely, secluded Playa Conchal is named for the bits of broken shells that cover its base of fine white sand (the Spanish word for shell is concha). It's an idyllic strand of sugary sand sloping steeply into aquamarine water and lined with an array of trees. The point that defines Conchal's northern end is hemmed by a lava-rock reef that is a popular snorkeling area—locals rent equipment on the beach—whereas the beach's southern extreme is often deserted. Although the sprawling Paradisus Playa Conchal resort covers the hinterland behind the beach, you don't need to stay at that all-inclusive resort to enjoy Conchal, since it's a short walk, or drive, south to Brasilito.

GETTING HERE AND AROUND

The drive south from Flamingo is 10 minutes on a paved highway. Both town and beach are just 1 km (½ mi) north of the entrance to Paradisus Playa Conchal. To reach Playa Conchal, turn left at the end of the town square and follow the dirt road across a stretch of beach and over a steep hill; the beach stretch is impassable at high tide. Buses run from Flamingo to Conchal three times daily, at 7:30 and 11:30 AM and 2:30 PM. A taxi from Flamingo is about $6.

ESSENTIALS

The closest bank and ATM are in Flamingo.

Hospital Costa de Emergencias (*Crossroads at Huacas* *2653–6440*).

Pharmacy Farmacia El Cruce (*Crossroads at Huacas* *2653–8787* *Daily 8 AM–10 PM*).

Internet Internet Café (*Near Supermarket López, 200 m south of school* *Daily 9–8*).

EXPLORING

A small, scruffy fishing village just 1 km (½ mi) north of Conchal, **Brasilito** has ramshackle houses huddled around its main square, which doubles as the soccer field. It's cluttered, noisy, and totally Tico, a lively contrast to the controlled sophistication of the Playa Conchal resort and residential development. Fishing boats moor just off a wide beach, about 3 km (2 mi) long, with golden sand flecked with pebbles and a few rocks. The surf is a little stronger here than at Flamingo Beach, but the shallow, sandy bottom keeps it swimmable. The sea is cleaner off nearby Playa Conchal, which is also a more attractive beach. A few casual *marisquerias* (seafood eateries) and a couple of notable restaurants line Brasilito's beach.

OUTDOOR ACTIVITIES

GOLF

One of the best golf courses in the country, the Paradisus Playa Conchal megaresort's **Reserva Conchal Golf Club** (✉*Paradisus Playa Conchal, entrance, less than 1 km/½ mi south of Brasilito* ☎*2654–4123*) is an 18-hole, par-71 course designed by Robert Trent Jones Jr. The course is reserved for hotel guests only, who can try out their swing on 18 holes for $160, cart included.

WHERE TO EAT AND STAY

$$ SEAFOOD **El Camarón Dorado.** Much of the appeal of this open-air bar-restaurant whose name translates as "The Golden Shrimp" is its shaded location on Brasilito's beautiful beach. Some tables are practically on the beach, with the surf lapping just yards away, making it the perfect spot for sunset drinks. The white-plastic tables and chairs are not up to the standards of the food, which is mostly locally caught fish and seafood served in bountiful portions. The house specialties include mahimahi prepared various ways, arroz a la marinera (rice with seafood), grilled lobster, and either jumbo, or the smaller pinky shrimp al ajillo (sautéed with garlic). If you have a reservation, a van can pick you up from Flamingo or Tamarindo hotels. ✉*200 m north of Brasilito Plaza* ☎*2654–4028* ▭*AE, DC, MC, V.*

$–$$ ITALIAN **Il Forno.** For a break from seafood, try lunch or dinner at this romantic Italian garden restaurant. There are 17 versions of thin-crust pizzas, plus fine homemade pastas and risotto. Vegetarians have lots of choices (if you can get past the thought that veal is on the menu), including an eggplant lasagna and interesting salads. They also serve some tasty seafood and meat dishes. At dinner, fairy lights and candles glimmer all through the garden, and some private tables are set apart under thatched roofs. Spanish and Italian wines are available by the glass or bottle. ✉*Main road, 200 m east of the bridge in Brasilito* ☎*2654–4125* ▭*No credit cards* ⊙*Closed Mon. and Oct.*

¢ **Hotel Brasilito.** Backpackers and travelers who don't need amenities will love this vintage, two-story, wooden hotel's seafront location, if not its no-frills rooms. Those rooms are a bit devoid of decor, though they do have hot water and either air-conditioning or a fan. Be prepared for some noise: kids playing, dogs barking, and motors revving. Ask for one of the two larger rooms above the restaurant; they share a veranda with unobstructed sea views. You can't beat the price for seaside rooms. Outback Jack's ($$), the Australian restaurant that occupies the open-air lobby, is a colorful, lively spot that specializes in grilled meat and seafood. **Pros:** inexpensive; across the street from beach; good restaurant. **Cons:** very basic rooms; can be noisy. ✉*Between soccer field and beach, Brasilito* ☎*2654–4237* ⊕*www.brasilito.com* *18 rooms* *In-room: no a/c (some), no phone, no TV. In-hotel: restaurant, beachfront, laundry service, Wi-Fi* ▭*MC, V* *EP.*

6

$$$$ **Paradisus Playa Conchal Beach & Golf Resort.** So vast that guests ride around in trucks covered with striped awnings and the staff gets around on bicycles, this all-inclusive resort, the top of the line of the Spanish Melía hotel chain, is luxurious, if lacking a bit in personality. The grounds encompass almost 4 square km (1½ square mi) that include a distant, picture-perfect beach. But in the labyrinthine guest village, the ocean disappears and the only views are of gardens and other buildings exactly like yours. The split-level Spanish Colonial–style villas have huge marble bathrooms and elegant sitting rooms. More than 100 "Royal Service" rooms are closer to the beach and have a private concierge. There's a kids' club and the largest—and perhaps warmest—pool in Central America. Grownups can amuse themselves sailing, snorkeling, kayaking, gambling at the casino, playing the gorgeous 18-hole golf course, or rejuvenating at the spa. If you're into the beach, try to get booked into a building between 1 and 5, or 33 and 40. More expansive Royal Service rooms are far from the beach. **Pros:** lovely rooms; beach access; abundant activities. **Cons:** expensive; massive; most rooms far from beach. ✉ *Entrance less than 1 km/½ mi south of Brasilito* ☎ *2654–4123* 🌐 *www.paradisus-playa-conchal.com* *292 villas, 122 Royal Service villas* *In-room: safe, refrigerator, Wi-Fi. In-hotel: 7 restaurants, room service, bars, golf course, tennis courts, pools, gym, spa, beachfront, water sports, bicycles, children's programs (ages 3–12), laundry service, Internet terminal, Wi-Fi* *AE, DC, MC, V* *AI.*

NIGHTLIFE

Live music, both acoustic guitar and rowdier dance bands, keeps **The Happy Snapper** (✉ *On main street across from beach in Brasilito*) hopping from Wednesday to Saturday nights. Owner Mike Osborne often mans the bar and spikes the drinks with his own brand of wry humor.

EN ROUTE

Gas stations are few and far between in these hinterlands. If you're heading down to Tamarindo from the Flamingo/Conchal area, fill up first. Your best bet is the 24-hour Oasis Exxon, 3 km (2 mi) east of Huacas.

TAMARINDO

82 km/51 mi southwest of Liberia.

Once a funky beach town full of spacey surfers and local fishermen, Tamarindo has become a pricey, hyped-up hive of commercial development and real-estate speculation, with the still-unpaved roads kicking up dust and mud alternately, depending on the season. On the plus side, there's a dizzying variety of shops, bars, and hotels, and probably the best selection of restaurants of any beach town. Strip malls and high-rise condominiums have obscured views of the still-magnificent beach, and some low-life elements are making security an issue. But once you're on the beach, almost all the negatives disappear (just keep your eyes on your belongings). Wide and flat, the sand is packed hard enough for easy walking and jogging. How good it is for swimming and surfing, however, is questionable, since the town has twice lost its

Blue Flag clean-beach status (because of overdevelopment and the total absence of water treatment). The water quality is especially poor during the rainy months, when you'll want to do your swimming and surfing at nearby Playa Langosta, or Playa Grande. **■TIP→ Strong currents at the north end of the beach get a lot of swimmers into trouble, especially when they try to cross the estuary without a surfboard.**

Surfing is the main attraction here, and there's a young crowd that parties hard after a day riding the waves. Tamarindo serves as a popular base for surfing at the nearby Playas Grande, Langosta, Avellanas, and Negra. There are plenty of outdoor options in addition to surfing, though, among them diving, sportfishing, wildlife-watching, and canopy tours. You can play 18 rounds at the nearby Hacienda Pinilla golf course, or simply stroll the beach and sunbathe.

GETTING HERE AND AROUND

Both Nature Air and SANSA fly to Tamarindo from San José. Macaw Air flies between Liberia and Tamarindo and to other Nicoya Peninsula towns. By car from Liberia, travel south on the highway to the turnoff for Belén, then head west and turn left at the Huacas crossroads to Tamarindo. Stretches of the paved road from Belén are in deplorable states of disrepair. There are no direct bus connections between Playa Grande or Playa Avellanas and Tamarindo. A taxi is the way to go from nearby towns if you don't have wheels. The **Tamarindo Shuttle** (☎ *2653–1326*) ferries passengers between the various beaches in a comfortable van.

6

ESSENTIALS

Bank/ATM Banco Nacional (✉ *Across from Tamarindo El Diria Hotel*).

Internet Internet Café (✉ *Road to Hotel Pasatiempo, next to ABC Realty*).

Medical Assistance Farmacia Tamarindo (✉ *Main road into town* ☎ *2653–1239*). **Emergencias 2000** (✥ *4 km/2½ mi east of Tamarindo at Villa Real crossroad* ☎ *8380–4125 or 2653–0611* 🌐 *www.emergencias2000.com*).

Rental Cars Alamo (✉ *Hotel Diría, main road, Tamarindo* ☎ *2653–0727*). **Budget** (✉ *Hotel Zullymar, main road, Tamarindo* ☎ *2653–0756*). **Economy** (✉ *Main road entering Tamarindo, next to Restaurant Coconut, Tamarindo* ☎ *2653–0752*). **Hola Rentacar** (✉ *Hacienda Pinilla, Tamarindo* ☎ *2653–2000*).

Taxis Olman Taxi (☎ *2653–1143 or 8356–6364 [cell]*); the SANSA shuttle van from the airport into town (☎ *2653–0244*) charges $4 per person.

OUTDOOR ACTIVITIES

BOATING

Rocky Isla El Capitán, just offshore, is a close-in kayaking destination, full of sand-dollar shells. Exploring the tidal estuaries north and south of town is best done in a kayak at high tide, when you can travel farther up the temporary rivers. Arrange kayaking trips through your hotel. **Iguana Surf** (✉ *Road to Playa Langosta* ☎📠 *2653–0148* 🌐 *www.iguanasurf.net*) has an office with information on guided kayaking tours of the San Francisco Estuary and a full roster of local tours, including snorkeling. Sail off into the sunset aboard a 50-foot traditional schooner with cruise company **Mandingo Sailing** (☎ *2653–2323* 🌐 *www.*

tamarindosailing.com). Soft drinks, beer and wine, and bocas (snacks) are included on the three-hour cruise. The boat leaves at 3 PM from in front of El Pescador restaurant on the beach ($80 per person).

FISHING

A number of fishing charters in Tamarindo cater to saltwater anglers. The most experienced among them is **Tamarindo Sportfishing** (☎ *2653–0090* 🌐 *www.tamarindosportfishing.com*), run by Randy Wilson, who has led the way in developing catch-and-release techniques that are easy on the fish. Wilson has roamed these waters since the 1970s, and he knows where the big ones lurk. His 38-foot *Talking Fish* is equipped with a marlin chair and a cabin with a shower, and costs $1,500 for a full day, $850 for a half. A fishing trip for up to four anglers on one of two 28-foot boats costs $825 to $975 for a full day; $550 to $675 for a half.

GOLFING

Mike Young, who has designed some of the best golf courses in the southern United States, designed the par-72 championship course at **Hacienda Pinilla** (*10 km/6 mi south of Tamarindo via Villa Real* ☎ *2680–7062 or 2680–3000* 🌐 *www.haciendapinilla.com*). It has ocean views and breezes, and plenty of birds populate the surrounding trees. Guests pay $225 for 18 holes in high season.

SURFING

Iguana Surf 2 (✉ *At beach near Frutas Tropicales* ☎ *2653–0148* 🌐 *www.iguanasurf.net*) rents surfboards and Boogie boards and offers lessons (for ages 3 to 88). **Maresias Surf Shop** (✉ *Next to Banco Nacional* 🌐 *www.maresiasurfcostarica.com* ☎ *2653–0224*) has equipment, lessons, and lots of local knowledge. Check out **Robert August Surf Shop** (✉ *Tamarindo Vista Villas* ☎ *2653–0221* 🌐 *www.robertaugust.com*) for boards to buy or rent, surfing gear, swimsuits, and sunblock. The shop operates a kids' surfing school as well as offering adult lessons. **High Tide Surf Shop** (✉ *Road to Langosta, about 200 m west of Hotel Pasatiempo* ☎ *2653–0108*) has high-end surfing equipment and clothing and a large selection of beachwear in a second-story shop.

WILDLIFE TOURS

ACOTAM (☎ *2653–1687*), a local conservation association, conducts turtle-viewing tours with local guides for $35. The group picks you up at your hotel and briefs you at their headquarters on the estuary that separates Tamarindo and Playa Grande. An open boat then takes you across the estuary, where you wait at the park station until a turtle has been spotted. The turtle-nesting season runs from mid-October to February. They also offer mangrove tours year-round. They don't speak much English.

WHERE TO EAT

$$ ECLECTIC ★ **Dragonfly Bar & Grill.** A low-key, natural ambience with tree-trunk columns, sculptural hanging lamps, and a cool soundtrack make this immensely popular, friendly restaurant a great place to spend an evening. The chef offers a limited but enticing menu of innovative dishes that combine the flavors of Asia and Latin America, with a few Mediterranean accents. Settle in and tingle your taste buds with spicy shrimp

Tamarindo and Playa Langosta

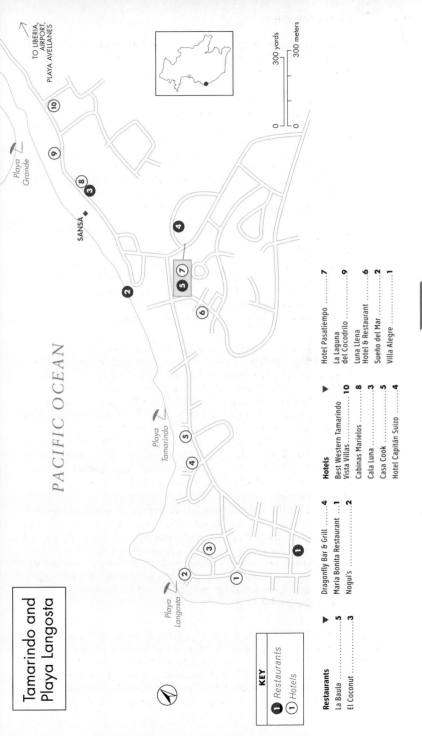

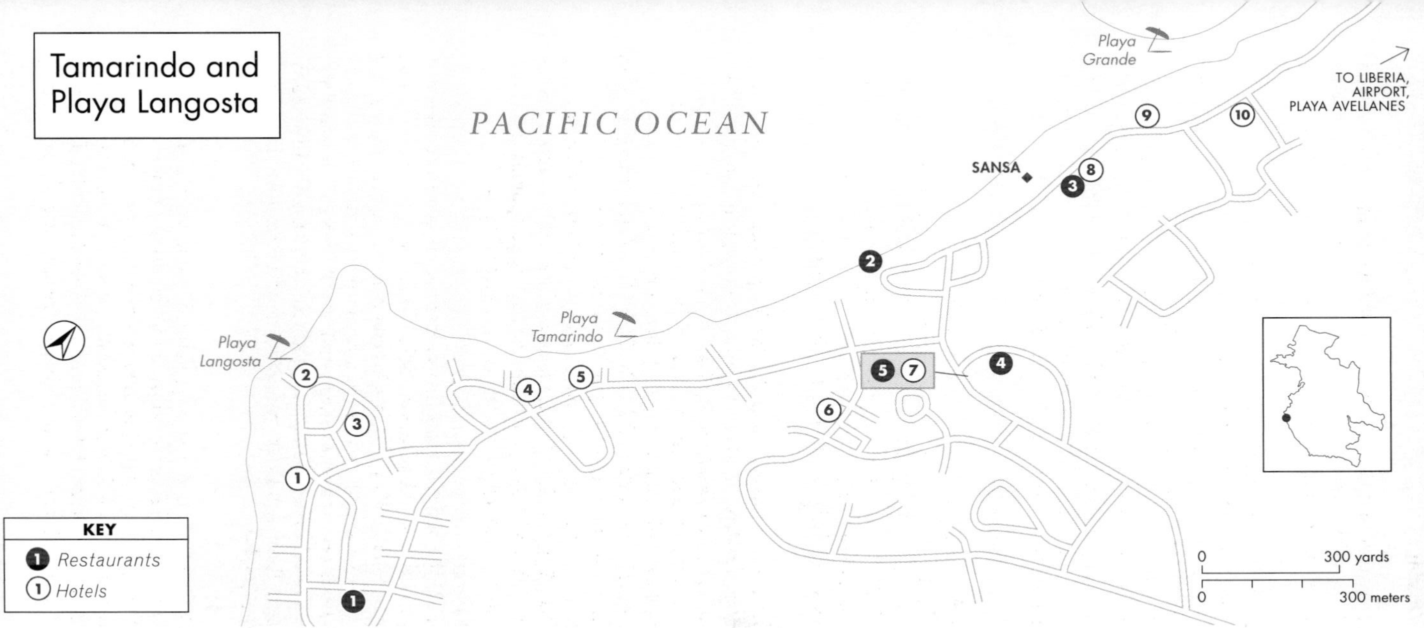

Restaurants ▼

La Baula 5
El Coconut 3
Dragonfly Bar & Grill 4
María Bonita Restaurant ...1
Nogui's 2

Hotels ▼

Best Western Tamarindo Vista Villas 10
Cabinas Marielos 8
Cala Luna 3
Casa Cook 5
Hotel Capitán Suizo 4
Hotel Pasatiempo 7
La Laguna del Cocodrilo 9
Luna Llena Hotel & Restaurant 6
Sueño del Mar 2
Villa Alegre 1

rolls, or a roasted beet, Gorgonzola, and walnut salad. Then sink your incisors into a pork chop over roasted garlic potato puree, or a Thai-style crispy fish cake with curried sweet corn. There are various vegetarian options, and the daily fish specials are always a good bet. ✉ *100 m east of Hotel Pasatiempo* ☎ *2653–1506* 🌐 *www.dragonflybarandgrill.com* ✍ *Reservations recommended* ▭ *AE, DC, MC, V* ⏱ *Closed Sun. and Sept. No lunch.*

$$$$ SEAFOOD ✕ **El Coconut.** The red, black, and dark-wood interior of this high-gloss, dinner-only restaurant with giant stone sculptures and a coconut tree growing through the roof feels like a lacquered Japanese *bento* box. Seafood is the main event, with the catch of the day—usually mahimahi—served half a dozen ways, but they also serve a good tenderloin, with a choice of sauces, and the classic surf and turf. The innovative jumbo shrimp or lobster in a pineapple, raisin, and ginger sauce are delicious, and the list of sauces for the fish includes the traditional Norwegian sandelfjords smor (a cream sauce with lime)—the owner is from Norway. Service is smooth and more formal than at most beach restaurants, and they have a good wine list, but the food and drink are much more expensive here than at the competition. ✉ *Main street, 150 m south of Tamarindo Vista Villas* ☎ *2653–0086* ▭ *AE, MC, V* ⏱ *Closed Mon. during low season. No lunch.*

$ PIZZA ✕ **La Baula.** Popular with the locals, this alfresco pizzeria on a quiet side street has plenty of cars parked outside most nights. Families are especially fond of La Baula—the Costa Rican name for the "leatherback turtle"—because of its reasonable prices and adjacent playground. Everyone enjoys the consistently delicious thin-crust pizzas, though if you don't like pizza, stay away. It's about the only thing on the menu, which consists of two dozen pies and a mixed salad. They also offer a tasty little tiramisu. ✉ *100 m north of Hotel Pasatiempo* ☎ *2653–1450* ▭ *AE, MC, V* ⏱ *No lunch.*

$$ SEAFOOD ✕ **Nogui's.** Pleasing a loyal legion of local fans since 1974, Nogui's offers a hearty Costa Rican menu and an ocean view. It is one of Tamarindo's best options for lunch, with a good selection of sandwiches and huge salads. It's also a good spot for dinner, when they offer a full seafood menu and various meat dishes. The recipes and presentation are nothing fancy, but the seafood is fresh and the price is right. Instead of the ubiquitous rice and beans on the side, Nogui's has a puree of *tiquisque,* a potatolike tuber. The homemade pies are legendary, notably the coconut cream. They also serve a signature margarita made with tamarind fruit. On weekends the restaurant on Nogui's second floor, called the Sunset Lounge, offers a small selection of innovative tapas, with a strong Asian influence, and a hipper ambience. ✉ *South side of Tamarindo Circle, on beach* ☎ *2653–0029* ▭ *AE, MC, V* ⏱ *Closed Wed. and 2 wks in Oct.*

WHERE TO STAY

$$ **Best Western Tamarindo Vista Villas.** If you're into surfing, this is where you want to be. Even though it's across the street from the beach, it's quite close to Tamarindo's beach break, and a quick paddle to the river-mouth break and Playa Grande. Around the pool and bar the talk is all about waves. There's a surf school and a surf shop, and surfing legends

Robert August and Wing Nuts, of *Endless Summer* movie fame, are frequent guests. The large villas with kitchens have a bedroom with a double bed and two futon couches; they are slowly being redecorated. Avoid rooms 101 to 107, which face the pool's supporting wall. Poolside rooms can be noisy when the pool is filled with frolicking kids. The hotel has a helpful tour desk. **Pros:** near beach break; villas view ocean. **Cons:** not on the beach; spotty service. ✉ *Main road entering Tamarindo, on left* ☎ *2653–0114, 800/536–3241 in U.S.* 🌐 *www.tamarindovistavillas.com* *12 rooms, 17 villas* *In-room: safe, kitchen (some). In-hotel: restaurant, room service, bar, pool, water sports, laundry service, Wi-Fi* 💳 *AE, MC, V* *CP.*

¢ **Cabinas Marielos.** Rooms at this well-situated, locally owned hotel are among the best of the budget category in Tamarindo. Two wings, decorated with floral motifs in the style of the artisans of Sarchí, are well back from the busy main road, on grounds with colorful gardens, coconut palms, and other trees. The beach and surf break are a short walk away. Rooms are quite basic, with cold-water showers and either a fan or air-conditioning. Guests sometimes share meals in the well-equipped common kitchen. The atmosphere is surprisingly serene, and the friendly staff can arrange turtle-watching, horseback riding, and other tours. **Pros:** cheap; near beach; relatively quiet. **Cons:** basic rooms; no hot showers. ✉ *Across main dirt road from beach, on left after Best Western* ☎ *2653–0141* 🌐 *www.cabinasmarieloscr.com* *24 rooms* *In-room: no a/c (some), no phone, safe, refrigerator (some), no TV. In-hotel: no-smoking rooms* 💳 *AE, MC, V* *EP.*

$$$ ★ **Casa Cook.** With just a few rooms on the quiet, southern end of the beach, this friendly, family-run place is one of Tamarindo's most secluded lodging options. Two cabinas on the beach have sleeping areas separated by 5-foot-high walls from living rooms with futon couches and kitchenettes. Narrow front terraces have ocean views through a high iron fence—security first—with hammocks hung between the trees on the other side of the gate. Behind those bungalows is a small tile pool hemmed by gardens, and the casita, which occupies the ground floor of the building that holds the owners' apartment. Though less private than the cabinas, the casita is slightly larger, with two futon couches, a kitchen, and glass doors that open onto the pool area. There are several restaurants and a supermarket within walking distance. **Pros:** small; secluded, beachfront; friendly. **Cons:** often full; extremely tiny. ✉ *Road to Playa Langosta, 100 m before Hotel Capitán Suizo* ☎ *2653–0125* 🌐 *www.casacook.net* *2 cabinas, 1 casita, 1 apartment* *In-room: no phone, safe, kitchen. In-hotel: pool, beachfront, water sports, laundry service, Wi-Fi, no kids under 12, no-smoking rooms* 💳 *AE, MC, V* *EP.*

$$$–$$$$ Fodor's Choice ★ **Hotel Capitán Suizo.** For folks who like nature, intimacy, and a beautiful beach setting, this is the best choice in town. Nestled in the forest on the relatively quiet southern end of Tamarindo's beach, elegant balconied rooms and airy bungalows surround a lovely pool shaded by large trees and greenery. Second-floor rooms have high, angled ceilings and lots of screens, which keeps them relatively cool despite their lack of air-conditioning. Lower rooms are smaller and darker, but have air-

A group of local musicians rocking out in Tamarindo.

conditioning, and terraces with views of the forested grounds, which are home to iguanas, raccoons, howler monkeys, and an array of birds. All rooms are decorated with fascinating vintage sepia photos depicting early-20th-century Costa Rican life. The two-level bungalows have king-size four-poster beds, futon couches, sensuous bathrooms with sunken whirlpool tubs, and outdoor garden showers—only two have an ocean view. The four-bedroom apartment has a kitchen and whirlpool tub. A beautifully decorated terrace restaurant overlooking the pool and beach serves contemporary cuisine and hosts lively beach barbecues on Friday night. Service is friendly and polished. **Pros:** beachfront; secluded; friendly; lovely gardens and pool. **Cons:** sand fleas and mosquitoes can be a problem; pricey. ✉ *Right side of road toward Playa Langosta* 📫 *Apdo. 22–5159, Villa Real, Guanacaste* ☎ *2653–0075 or 2653–0353* 🌐 *www.hotelcapitansuizo.com* *22 rooms, 7 bungalows, 1 apartment* *In-room: no a/c (some), safe, refrigerator, no TV. In-hotel: restaurant, room service, bar, pool, beachfront, water sports, bicycles, laundry service, Internet terminal, Wi-Fi* 💳 *AE, MC, V* 🍽 *BP.*

$$ **Hotel Pasatiempo.** Come for Sunday football, open mike on Tuesday night, or great eggs Benedict any morning. One way or another, you are bound to pass some time at this friendly, laid-back place. This is one of the last relatively tranquil hotels in the sea of Tamarindo construction. Duplex bungalow rooms are scattered around lushly landscaped grounds and the pool, next to which towers the restaurant's thatch roof. Each unit, named after a Guanacaste beach, has a small patio with a hammock or swinging chair and a hand-painted beach mural; newer deluxe rooms are nicer and more secluded. Suites are good for young families, since they have one bedroom and small daybeds in the living room. The Oasis Restaurant ($$) serves a mix of above-average bar food and pizza, along with more sophisticated fare, such as macadamia-encrusted mahimahi with a mango sauce, or chicken in a Stroganoff sauce. **Pros:** lush grounds; relatively quiet. **Cons:** several blocks from beach; noisy Sunday to Tuesday. ✉ *Off dirt road to Playa Langosta, 180 m from beach behind Tamarindo Circle* ☎ *2653–0096* 🌐 *www.hotelpasatiempo.com* *23 rooms, 2 suites* *In-room: no phone, safe. In-hotel: restaurant, bar, pool, laundry service, Internet terminal, Wi-Fi* *AE, MC, V* *BP.*

$–$$ **La Laguna del Cocodrilo.** This hotel's name, which translates as "The Crocodile's Lagoon," refers to a pond between the hotel and the beach that is frequented by one of those giant lizards. A short trail leads from past that pond to the north end of Playa Tamarindo and the estuary. Standard rooms here should be avoided, since they are too close to Tamarindo's main road and are dark, but the ocean views and junior suites are a good deal, especially since they're practically on the beach. The only problem is their proximity to the restaurant and bar, which stays open till 11 PM, so this isn't the place for early-to-bed types. No matter where you stay, though, you should dine at the hotel's restaurant ($$$), where tables are scattered amid tropical greenery and coconut palms decorated with light spirals. The young American chef produces some tasty seafood inventions such as red snapper stuffed with a Cognac mousse, potato-wrapped sea bass, and a decent bouillabaisse. The French bakery in front serves good breakfasts, light lunches, and sweets. **Pros:** almost beachfront; good restaurant. **Cons:** standard rooms dark; can be noisy. ✉ *Main street, on right entering town* ☎ *2653–0255* 🌐 *www.lalagunadelcocodrilo.com* *10 rooms, 2 suites, 1 studio* *In-room: no phone, safe, refrigerator. In-hotel: restaurant, bar* *MC, V* *EP.*

6

$$$$ **Los Altos de Eros Luxury Inn & Spa.** This intimate adults-only inn is the place to be for honeymooning couples with enough money left over after the wedding to pamper themselves. Rooms, with queen or king beds, are elegant and comfortable, opening out onto a large pool with expansive views as far as the ocean. But the main draw here is the spa, built into the side of a mountain and staffed by a team of professional therapists, offering such sybaritic pleasures as volcanic mud wraps, honey-cucumber-lime facials, papaya body polishes, and relaxing massages. Day packages are available for nonguests. Gourmet breakfast and lunch are included, as is dinner two nights a week. Other evenings, you can take a free shuttle into nearby Tamarindo to experience the local dining scene. Early-morning yoga classes and hikes around the 70-acre property keep you active. **Pros:** secluded; small; romantic. **Cons:** scheduled mealtimes; pricey. ✉ *Cañafistula, 14 km/8½ mi southeast of Tamarindo* ☎ *850–4203, 786/866–7039 in U.S.* 🌐 *www.losaltosdeeros.com* *4 rooms, 1 suite* *In-room: safe, refrigerator. In-hotel: restaurant, bar, pool, gym, spa, Wi-Fi* *MC, V* *Closed Oct.* *MAP.*

$$ **Luna Llena Hotel & Residence.** This place looks a little like a Fellini film set of a fantasy tropical village. Bright-yellow conical thatch-roof huts on different levels circle a small pool and tropical gardens. Interiors

are colorful and whimsical, with unusual fabrics, furniture, and walls painted by co-owner Simona Daniela, who, along with husband Pino Trimarchi, adds Italian panache to the place. They also serve good Italian food in the tiny restaurant on the grounds. Four bright double rooms on the second floor have queen-size beds, high ceilings, spacious bathrooms, and colorful, creative decors. Bungalows with their own kitchens are great for families. The ground floor holds a kitchenette, bathroom, and a queen bed, whereas a steep, curving stair leads to a wooden loft with two single beds. The hotel is a 10-minute walk from the beach, in a relatively quiet area. **Pros:** secluded; lush grounds. **Cons:** several blocks away from beach; small pool. ✉ *From road to Playa Langosta, first left (uphill); 1 block past Iguana Surf* ☎ *2653–0082* 🌐 *www.hotellunallena.com* *5 rooms, 7 bungalows* *In-room: safe, kitchen (some). In-hotel: restaurant, room service, pool, laundry service, Internet terminal, Wi-Fi* *AE, MC, V* *CP.*

NIGHTLIFE

Tamarindo is one of the few places outside of San José where the nightlife really jumps. In fact, it has the dubious distinction of being featured on Entertainment Television's explicit *Wild On* series, which spotlights the rowdiest party scenes around the world.

Although party-hearty hot spots come and go with the tides, Tamarindo does have some perennial, low-key options. For a pleasantly sedate Friday evening, try barbecue on the beach at the **Hotel Capitán Suizo** (✉ *Right side of road toward Playa Langosta; veer left before circle*), starting at 6:30 with a cocktail, then on to a lavish barbecue buffet and live folk music and dancing ($29, reserve in advance). During the week, **Hotel Pasatiempo** (✉ *Off dirt road to Playa Langosta*) has wildly popular Tuesday open-mike sessions. Friday nights at **Crazy Monkey Bar** (✉ *Tamarindo Vista Villas, main road entering Tamarindo*) is ladies' night. The live music attracts a crowd of locals who really know how to move. **Restobar La Caracola** (✉ *Tamarindo Circle, beside Nogui's* ☎ *2653–0583*) often has live music and dancing on weekends. There are tango, salsa, and merengue dance lessons for novices.

SHOPPING

Most stores in the strip malls lining the main road sell the same souvenirs. It's hard to leave town without at least one sarong in your suitcase. At **Calypso** (✉ *Main Street at Tamarindo El Diria Hotel* ☎ *2653–1436*), Parisian Anne Loriot has raised the bar on beach fashion with fabulous Indonesian- and Mexican-style coverups and elegant, cool dresses, all available in real women's sizes.

★ You'll also find original clothing and jewelry at **Azul Profundo** (✉ *Main street, Plaza Tamarindo* ☎ *2653–0395*), designed by a talented young Argentine woman. All her jewelry is made with real and semiprecious stones. For a good selection of swimsuits and a wide range of kiddie beachwear, check out **Tienda Bambora** (✉ *On beach, south side of Tamarindo Circle* ☎ *2653–0865*).

PLAYA LANGOSTA

2 km/1 mi south of Tamarindo.

Playa Langosta is actually two beaches divided by the San Francisco Estuary, the mouth of which is a knee-high wade at low tide, and a deep river with dangerous currents around high tide. To the north is residential Langosta, where every foot of beachfront has been built up, but the contractors' hammers are now ringing out in every building space inland as well. It is sort of a bedroom community of Tamarindo, just five minutes away by car. To the south of the estuary is pristine Langosta, a protected annex of Las Baulas National Marine Park, where leatherback turtles nest at night and beachcombers roam by day. Luckily, most of the development on the northern half is tucked behind the buttonwood trees, so you can enjoy an unsullied dramatic beachscape, with surf crashing against rocky outcroppings. The beach here is rather narrow, since the coast is lined with rocks, and the light-gray sand is rather coarse. There's a wider, less rocky stretch in front of the Barceló Resort, where you can walk across the San Francisco Estuary at low tide to stroll and swim on the beach's southern half. If you walk a ways up that shallow tidal river at low tide, you may see snowy egrets, baby blue herons, tail-bobbing spotted sandpipers, and, if your eyes are sharp, tiny white-lored gnatcachers, endemic to these parts.

GETTING HERE AND AROUND

The dirt road from Tamarindo is alternately dusty or muddy, but reliably rough. Or you can walk along the beach, at low tide, all the way from Tamarindo Beach. Most car-free visitors get picked up from Tamarindo by their hotels. Or you can take a taxi.

OUTDOOR ACTIVITIES

Tour operators in Tamarindo, just a few miles north, offer activities in the Playa Langosta area.

WHERE TO EAT

$$ CARIBBEAN ★ ✕ **Maria Bonita Restaurant.** This popular Latin-Caribbean restaurant is owned by a couple with years of hotel and restaurant experience in Cuba and throughout the Caribbean. Cheerful Adela serves (and makes delicious desserts) while Tom slaves away in the kitchen, turning out mouthwatering, perfectly spiced dishes such as smoked pork chops smothered in a tart tamarind sauce, coconut chicken casserole, and daily seafood specials. The wine list focuses on South American and Spanish vintages. There are just six tables in the pretty patio garden and four tables inside the intimate dining room—and they fill up fast. ✉ *Beside the Playa Langosta supermarket* ☎ *2653–0933* ✍ *Reservations essential* 💳 *MC, V* ⏲ *Closed Sun. and Oct. No lunch.*

WHERE TO STAY

$$$ **Cala Luna.** This gorgeous collection of bungalows sequestered in a private jungle can be alternately as lifeless as a tomb and raucously noisy, with parties around the extravagantly landscaped pool. Standard rooms in ochre-color bungalows—reached via a labyrinth of high hibiscus hedges—have king-size beds, high wooden ceilings, softly lighted alcoves, and oversize bathrooms with sunken, tiled tubs. The secluded

villas, with hidden driveways and private pools, have two or three bedrooms and kitchens. The beach is a short walk away, across a road and through the forest, but it's narrow and lined by rocks here. The glorious pool is bordered by the pretty, Provençal-style Cala Moresca restaurant ($$$), where the cuisine is Mediterranean with Asian touches. On the other end of the pool is an excellent sushi bar, making this a good place to dine if you stay at one of the B&Bs nearby. **Pros:** excellent grounds; lovely villas. **Cons:** lots of nearby construction; a/c only in the bedrooms. ✉ *100 m south of Hotel Capitán Suizo, veer right.* ☎ *2653–0214* 🌐 *www.calaluna.com* *20 rooms, 26 villas* *In-room: safe. In-hotel: restaurant, bar, pool, laundry service, Internet terminal, Wi-Fi* *AE, MC, V* *CP.*

$$$–$$$$ Fodor's Choice ★ **Sueño del Mar.** The name of this place means "Dream of the Sea," and the front gate opens into a dreamy world of intimate gardens, patios, frescoes, hand-painted tiles, and a jungle of Latin American *objets d'art.* This nearly flawless B&B occupies an adobe-style house with spacious double rooms, two larger casitas with kitchens and loft bedrooms, and a second-floor suite. The downstairs rooms are a little dark, but are full of interesting, often amusing folk art, and have Balinese showers that open to the sky. All rooms but the suite have queen-size beds, and the casitas have couches that convert into two single beds. If privacy is paramount, opt for the breezy honeymoon suite, a sensuous sultan's lair with rich, red fabrics, rugs, and hanging glass lamps and an ocean view. A lavish breakfast is served on the patio next to a tiny garden pool. Or you can take your morning coffee on the beach, with chairs and hammocks amid the trees and driftwood—it's also the perfect spot for sunsets. At low tide a large snorkeling pool forms in the rocks that surround the beach, but the swimming area is a 10-minute walk to the south. **Pros:** intimate; well appointed. **Cons:** small pool; awful roads nearby. ✉ *130 m south of Capitán Suizo, veer right for 45 m, then right again for about 90 m to entrance gate, across from back of Cala Luna Hotel* *Sueño del Mar, detras de Cala Luna Hotel, Playa Langosta-Guanacaste* ☎ *2653–0284* 🌐 *www.sueno-del-mar.com* *3 rooms, 1 suite, 2 casitas* *In-room: no phone, kitchen (some), no TV, Wi-Fi. In-hotel: restaurant, pool, beachfront, water sports, laundry service, Internet terminal, no-smoking rooms* *MC, V* *BP.*

$$$ ★ **Villa Alegre.** A visit here is like coming to stay with friends who just happen to have a really terrific house on the beach. Owned by congenial and helpful Californians Barry and Suzye Lawson, this homey but sophisticated Spanish-style B&B overlooks a small forest reserve and a somewhat rocky section of Langosta Beach, which is visible only from the terrace and pool. Rooms, villas, and casitas are furnished with souvenirs from the Lawsons' international travels, including Japan, Russia, and Guatemala. The Mexican honeymoon suite has a Frida Kahlo–esque canopy bed and a huge outdoor bathroom/patio. Spacious villas have kitchens, living rooms with several futons, and terraces overlooking the forest. Lavish breakfasts are served family-style at 8:30 on a terrace overlooking the small pool—they're a chance to meet other guests and to ask the Lawsons for travel advice or other help, which they happily provide. The hotel often plans and hosts weddings;

ceremonies take place at a huge boulder on the beach dubbed Marriage Rock. **Pros:** lovely grounds; friendly. **Cons:** dark rooms; pricey. ✉*Playa Langosta, 300 m south of Hotel Capitán Suizo* ☎*2653–0270* 🌐*www.villaalegrecostarica.com* *4 rooms, 2 villas, 1 casita* *In-room: no phone, no TV, Wi-Fi. In-hotel: pool, beachfront, laundry service, Internet terminal, no-smoking rooms* *AE, MC, V* *BP.*

PLAYA GRANDE

21 km/13 mi north of Tamarindo.

Down the (long, paved) road from Tamarindo, but only five minutes by boat across a tidal estuary, lies beautiful Playa Grande. The beach has thus far escaped the overdevelopment of nearby Tamarindo, and is consequently lined with thick vegetation instead of hotels and strip malls. It is one of the world's most important nesting beaches for the giant leatherback sea turtle, and is consequently protected within a national park, though admission is free unless you go on a turtle tour during the nesting season (October 20 *to* February 15). The beach's protected status is in part because a surfer who arrived here more than 30 years ago was so upset by the widespread turtle-egg poaching that he adopted a conservationist's agenda. Louis Wilson, owner of Las Tortugas Hotel, spearheaded a campaign to protect the nesting *baulas* (leatherback turtles) that eventually resulted in the creation of Las Baulas Marine National Park. The long Blue Flag beach is also a paradise for surfers and sunbathers by day, and the forest that lines it holds howler monkeys and an array of birds, whereas the mangrove estuary on the north end of the beach has crocodiles. The only problem with Playa Grande is the abundance of mosquitoes during the rainy months, especially near the estuary, so bring plenty of repellent.

6

Playa Grande isn't immune to development, though; developers have sold hundreds of lots, and there are at least 100 finished houses. The good thing is that the homes are well back from the beach, thanks to a legislated buffer zone and a decree that no lights can be visible from the beach, to avoid disturbing the turtles. A few hotels and restaurants make this a pleasant, tranquil alternative to Tamarindo. And if you want to go shopping, Tamarindo is only a boat ride away. **■TIP→Recent trip reports suggest that crime in the Playa Grande area has increased of late. Take reasonable precautions, choose a hotel with room safes, bring very few valuables, and stay alert.**

GETTING HERE AND AROUND

The road from Tamarindo is paved for the duration of the 30-minute drive. Palm Beach Estates, where most hotels are, is about 3 km (2 mi) south of the main Playa Grande entrance on a dirt road. Alternatively, you can take a small boat across the Tamarindo Estuary for about $2 per person and walk 30 minutes along the beach to the surf break; boats travel between the guide kiosk at the north end of Tamarindo and either Villa Baulas or Hotel Bula Bula in Playa Grande.

EXPLORING

Both **Las Baulas Marine National Park** *(Parque Nacional Marino Las Baulas)*, which protects the long Playa Grande, and the **Tamarindo Wildlife Refuge,** a mangrove estuary with some excellent bird-watching, have been under some developmental pressure of late.

TURTLE-WATCHING

Playa Grande hosts the world's largest visitation of nesting giant leatherback turtles. From October 20 to February 15, during the peak nesting season, the beach is strictly off-limits from 6 PM to 6 AM. You can visit only as part of a guided tour, waiting your turn at the park entrance, beside Hotel Las Tortugas, until spotters find a nesting turtle. At their signal, you'll walk down the beach as silently as you can, where in the darkness you'll witness the remarkable sight of a 500-pound creature digging a hole in the sand large enough to deposit up to 100 golf ball–size eggs. About 60 days later, the sight of hundreds of hatchlings scrambling toward open water in the early morning is equally impressive. Turtle-watching takes place around high tide, which can be shortly after sunset, or in the early morning. From December to mid-February, try to reserve your tour a week ahead of time, or stop by the ranger station early the morning of the day you want to do the tour, since they allow only 40 people on the beach per night, half of which can register that day. Plan on spending one to four hours at the ranger station waiting for a turtle to come up, during which you can watch a video on the turtles in English (the guides speak mostly Spanish). ✉ *Playa Grande, 100 m east of main beach entrance* ☎ *2653–0470* 🎟 *$20, includes guided tour* ⏲ *Oct. 20–Feb. 15 by reservation made between 8 AM and 5 PM.*

OUTDOOR ACTIVITIES

■ **TIP→ Unless you are a strong swimmer attached to a surfboard, don't go in any deeper than your waist here.** There is calmer water for snorkeling about a 20-minute walk north of Las Tortugas, at a black-sand beach called Playa Carbón.

All the hotels can arrange boat tours of the estuary, where you may see crocodiles, monkeys, herons, kingfishers, and an array of other birdlife; go either early in the morning or late in the afternoon, and bring insect repellent. **Hotel Las Tortugas** (✉ *Las Baulas Marine National Park* ☎ *2653–0423* 🌐 *www.lastortugashotel.com*) has a full menu of nature tours, including guided nature walks, and canoeing on the estuary; they also rent snorkeling equipment and explain how to get to Playa Carbón, the nearest skin-diving spot ($25 to $55).

SURFING

Playa Grande is renowned for having one of the most consistent surf breaks in the country. Only experienced surfers should attempt riding this beach break, which often features big barrels and offshore winds. The waves are best at high tide, especially around a full moon. **Hotel Las Tortugas** *(⇨ above)* rents boards for $20 a day. **Hotel Bula Bula** (✉ *Palm Beach Estates* ✣ *2 km/1 mi east of Playa Grande* ☎ *2653–0975* 🌐 *www.hotelbulabula.com*) rents both long and short boards for $25 a day.

Continued on page 330

BIRD-WATCHING

by Dorothy McKinnon

Even if you've never seen yourself as a bird-watcher, Costa Rica will get you hooked. Waking you before dawn, calling to you throughout the day, and serenading you through tropical nights, birds are impossible to ignore here.

Luckily, Costa Rica has a wealth of world-class ornithologists and local bird guides that can answer all your questions. Even licensed naturalist guides have some birding expertise, so virtually every tour you take in the country will include some bird-watching.

The sheer variety and abundance of birds here makes bird-watching a daily pastime—with less than 0.03% of the planet's surface, Costa Rica counts some 875 bird species, more than the United States and Canada combined. You don't have to stray far from your hotel or even need binoculars to spot, for instance, a kaleidoscopic-colored Keel-billed Toucan, the one of Fruit Loops cereal fame. But armed with a pair of binoculars and a birding guide, the sky is literally the limit for the numbers of birds you can see.

Part of the thrill of walking along a jungle trail is the element of surprise: What is waiting around the path's next curve? Catching sight of a brilliantly colored bird is exciting, but being able to identify it after a couple of encounters is even more thrilling. For kids, spotting birds makes a great game. With their sharp, young eyes, they're usually very good at it—plus it's wildly educational.

About 10% of Costa Rica's birds are endemic, so this is a mecca for bird-watchers intent on compiling an impressive life list.

DID YOU KNOW?

There are more than 400 bird species in Monteverde Cloud Forest Preserve. In 1997, a group of local bird watchers started out early and managed to identify 368 of them in one day!

BEST BIRDING DESTINATIONS

The most sought-after bird is the aptly named Resplendent Quetzal, sporting brilliant blue, green, and red plumage and long tail feathers. The best places to spot it are the new **Los Quetzales National Park** in the Cerro de la Muerte highlands, the **San Gerardo de Dota valley,** and the **Monteverde Cloud Forest Reserve.**

Another bird high on many bird-watchers' lists, is the Scarlet Macaw, the largest of the parrot family here. You'll see pairs performing aerial ballets and munching in beach almond trees in **Corcovado National Park,** along the **Osa Peninsula's coastline,** and around **Carara National Park** in the Central Pacific region.

The **Tempisque River delta's** salty waters, at the north end of the Gulf of Nicoya, are famous for its wealth of water birds, notably Wood Storks, Glossy Ibis, and Roseate Spoonbills. A little farther north, in **Palo Verde and Cano Negro National Parks,** look for the rarest and largest of wading birds, the Jabiru.

The network of jungle-edged natural canals in **Tortuguero National Park,** in the northern Caribbean, is home to a host of herons, including the spectacular Rufescent Tiger-Heron and the multi-hued Agami Heron.

More than 50 species of hummingbirds hover around every part of the country. Look for them around feeders at lodges in the **Cerro de la Muerte area, Monteverde,** and the **Turrialba region.**

WHEN TO GO: The best time to bird is November to May, when local species are joined by winter migrants. Breeding season, which varies by species throughout the year, is the easiest time to spot birds, as males put on displays for females, followed by frequent flights to gather nesting material and then food for the chicks. Also keep your eye on fruit-bearing trees that attract hungry birds.

BIRD-WATCHING 101

Quetzal in Valley of the Quetzals; Krasinsky, Fodors.com member

Binoculars are the most important piece of equipment. They don't have to be a very expensive pair, but they should have good light-gathering lenses and be waterproof. A magnification of 7 to 8 is ideal; any higher and your range of vision becomes very limited.

A good guidebook is essential. The standard "bible" has been a comprehensive tome written by Dr. Alexander Skutch, but beginners (and experienced birders) will probably find the new field guide, written by Richard Garrigues and illustrated by Robert Dean, much more useful—and lighter to carry. It has range maps for every bird and lists the most obvious field marks to help you identify each species. Gift shops and hotels also sell plastic-laminated, one-page guides for local birds that can get you started.

The most important advice for new birders is to find the bird with your naked eye and then bring your binoculars to your eyes, without losing your focus on the bird. Look for beak shape; characteristic rings around the eye; bars, stripes, spots, and mottling on plumage; and, of course, colors on feathers, eyes, beaks, legs, and feet.

10 EASY-TO-IDENTIFY BIRDS FOR BEGINNERS

❶ Blue-Crowned Motmot
Unmistakable with those long tail feathers that look like tennis racquets, this gorgeous turquoise and green bird perches low in trees often close to a stream. They're usually silent but their call is easy to identify: a repeated, low "whoop."

❷ Keel-Billed Toucan
Half a dozen of these rainbow-colored, huge-billed birds often travel together, hunting for berries and fruits. Look for them in Cecropia trees, and listen for the loud, rapid beat of their wings.

❸ Great Kiskadee
You can tell the kiskadee from the similar looking flycatchers by its *pecho amarillo* (yellow breast), black-and-white-striped head, reddish tinted wings, and its call—it really does say *Kiss-kah-deeee*!

❹ Orange-fronted Parakeet
Found in forest canopy on the Pacific side of the country, these highly social and noisy little birds feed in flocks of up to 100. The adults are mainly green, and have shorter tails than their crimson-fronted cousins. The head is distinctive, with a blue crown, and orange forehead. Sadly, the population has been decreasing for a number of years thanks to the pet trade.

❺ Rufous-tailed Hummingbird
Stake out hibiscus hedges or any flowering shrub for the country's most common hummingbird. An iridescent green color, with a long red beak and reddish-brown tail, it makes a loud "tse, tse" chipping sound as it goes about its business.

❻ Scarlet Macaw

Look for this huge scarlet, yellow, and blue parrot in the beach almond trees that edge South Pacific beaches. They usually travel in pairs and you'll probably hear their raucous squawks before you see them.

❼ Blue-Gray Tanager

Abundant everywhere—cities, towns, gardens, and countryside—this bluish-gray bird, always seen in pairs, loves fruit. You'll often find them at feeding platforms and in fruiting fig trees.

❽ Black Vulture

Almost every large black bird you see circling high in the sky will be a vulture; these have white-tipped wings. You'll also see them hopping along the roadside feasting on roadkill.

❾ Roadside Hawk

This raptor sits quietly on low perches in trees alongside fields and roads, waiting to pounce on lizards, large insects, and small mammals. It has a gray head, a yellow beak and legs, and a brown and white striped chest.

❿ Cherrie's Tanager (aka Passini's Tanager)

The unmistakable scarlet-rumped, velvety-black male travels with a harem of olive-and orange-colored females, making a lot of scratchy noises as they hunt insects in dense shrubbery.

WHERE TO EAT

$$$ CONTINENTAL ✕ **Hotel Cantarana.** Chef Manfred Margraf brings to the table 30 years of cooking experience in Switzerland, Germany, and the Caribbean. The menu changes depending on availability of local ingredients—think lots of seafood—and on the chef's inspired whims, but is always classically Continental, with elegant presentation. ✉ *Palm Beach Estates* ✥ *2 km/1 mi east of park headquarters* ☎ *2653–0486* 🌐 *www.hotelcantarana.com* ▭ *MC, V*

$$$ ECLECTIC ★ ✕ **Rip Jack Inn.** Located a block from the beach, this place usually has an ocean breeze to complement the ceiling fans, which are best enjoyed from the hammock in the corner. They have rooms for rent downstairs, but most people who head here come to eat, or party at the long bar, which occupies about a third of the restaurant. The food is quite good, and the menu ranges from sesame-crusted tuna with rice and tempura vegetables to grilled tenderloin with mashed potatoes. The lunch menu has a good selection of salads and sandwiches. Save room for a mud pie, or cheesecake with strawberries. ✉ *100 m south of park headquarters* ☎ *2653–0480* 🌐 *www.ripjackinn.com* ▭ *AE, DC, MC, V* ⊙ *Closed Wed.*

WHERE TO STAY

$$ **Hotel Bula Bula.** At the eastern edge of the estuary near Palm Beach Estates, Bula Bula has its own dock and boat for ferrying guests and restaurant patrons the short distance to and from Tamarindo. The hotel forms a 45-degree angle to the curvy pool bordered by a garden. (Be careful of the cactus!) Rooms have king-size beds and high ceilings, and open onto a portico with wicker rocking chairs, with walls painted in brilliant colors and hung with Central American art. They don't offer a lot of privacy, but the friendly American owners provide complimentary sarongs, fluffy pool towels, coffeemakers, DVD players, and other amenities. They can arrange a two-hour boat tour of the estuary, or rentals of nearby houses. The menu at the alfresco Great Waltini's Restaurant & Bar ($$–$$$) reads like that of a U.S.-style eatery: seafood enchiladas, peel-and-eat shrimp, pork chop, filet mignon, and New York strip steak. They have good fresh seafood specials. Save room for the homemade tres leches dessert. **Pros:** friendly; good food; lots of amenities. **Cons:** rooms small for price; 10-minute walk from beach; far from surf break. ✉ *Palm Beach Estates* ✥ *3 km/2 mi east of Playa Grande* ☎ *2653–0975, 877/658–2880 in U.S.* 🌐 *www.hotelbulabula.com* *10 rooms* *In-room: no phone, refrigerator. In-hotel: restaurant, bar, pool, laundry service, Wi-Fi* ▭ *AE, MC, V* *BP.*

¢–$ **Hotel El Manglar.** If you like cooking for yourself, consider the apartments at this French-run hotel. Painted in tropical colors, they also have a Provençal touch, with French doors and lace curtains. Sitting rooms, kitchens, and terraces give you lots of room to relax, and there is even a grill on the terrace. The cheaper upstairs guest rooms are much more basic, with minimalist decor and loft bedrooms with fans instead of air-conditioners. The hotel has a pretty garden and a pool inlaid with bright mosaic tile. It's a short walk from the beach. **Pros:** quiet; near beach. **Cons:** foam mattresses; no restaurant; far from surf break. ✉ *Palm Beach Estates* ✥ *2 km/1 mi south of Playa Grande, south of Hotel*

La Cantarana ☎☎2653–0952 🌐www.hotel-manglar.com ⇨5 rooms, 4 apartments ♨In-room: no a/c (some), no phone, safe, kitchen (some), no TV (some). In-hotel: pool ▭MC, V 🍽EP.

¢–$$ ★ **Hotel Las Tortugas.** With a prime location on the beach, steps away from Playa Grande's famous surf break, this place is perfect for surfers, nature lovers, and sun worshippers. The name, which means "The Turtles," is no accident; this hotel was designed with turtles in mind. Owner/conservationist Louis Wilson made sure, for instance, that room and restaurant lights don't shine on the beach, because light disorients the turtles. Rooms are spacious, with good beds, stone floors, and colorful tile bathrooms. Most have either a terrace or a balcony. Las Tortugas accommodates all budgets, with rooms ranging from spacious suites to dorm-style rooms in an annex that Louis built for student groups and volunteers. They also offer an array of apartments up the hill, some with kitchenettes, that rent by the night, week, or month. All of this adds up to the best value in Playa Grande, and one of the best deals on the Pacific coast. The main surf break is just to the south of the hotel, and turtle tours start at the nearby ranger station. Rip currents are a danger on the beach here, which is why many guests prefer the pool shaped like a leatherback turtle (the turtle's head is the kiddie pool). Lush gardens slung with hammocks round out the grounds' appeal. The restaurant ($$$) serves a good selection of fresh seafood and grilled meat dishes. **Pros:** on the beach; friendly owners; good value. **Cons:** busy spot; spotty service at times. ✉*Entrance to Las Baulas Marine National Park ✥33 km/20 mi north of Tamarindo ☎2653–0423 🌐www.lastortugashotel.com ⇨11 rooms, 3 dorms, 17 apartments ♨In-room: no phone, safe (some), kitchen (some), refrigerator (some), no TV. In-hotel: restaurant, bar, pool, beachfront, water sports, laundry service, Internet terminal, Wi-Fi ▭MC, V 🍽EP.*

PLAYA AVELLANAS

17 km/11 mi south of Tamarindo.

Traditionally a far cry from Tamarindo's boom of real-estate development, this relatively undeveloped beach's main claim to fame is surfing. As you bump along the rough beach road, most of the cars you pass have surfboards on top. Nevertheless, Avellanas (pronounced ah-vey-*ya*-nas) is a lovely spot for anyone who likes the sea and sand, though you shouldn't go in deeper than your waist when the waves are big, because of rip currents. Tamarindo escapees have been slowly encroaching on Avellanas for years, building private houses and a smattering of small hotels, but the inauguration of a massive Marriott here in 2008 marked the beginning of major development. The beach itself is a beautiful, 1-km (½-mi) stretch of pale-gold sand with rocky outcroppings at its southern end, a small river mouth, and a mangrove swamp behind its northern half. It is also home to a very big pig named Lola, who likes to cool off in the surf. Unfortunately, security is an issue here, as at most Costa Rican beaches; posted signs warn visitors not to leave anything of value in parked cars or unattended on the beach.

Costa Rica's shores are visited by the green turtle, the olive ridley, the hawksbill, the loggerhead, and the leatherback turtle.

GETTING HERE AND AROUND

You have to drive 30 minutes inland from Tamarindo to Villa Real, where you turn right for the 13-km (8-mi) trip down a bumpy road to reach Playa Avellanas. There are rivers to cross in rainy season, when you may want to drive via Paraíso and Playa Negra. If you're without a car, take the **Tamarindo Shuttle** (☎*2653–1326*) van, $10 to $20 one-way for one to four people.

OUTDOOR ACTIVITIES

SURFING

Locals claim there are eight breaks here when the swell is big, which means Avellanas doesn't suffer the kind of overcrowding the breaks at Playas Negra and Langosta often do. Tamarindo-based surf schools can arrange day trips here. You can rent boards and find kindred surfing spirits at **Cabinas Las Olas** (✉*Main road, on right* ☎*2652–9315*), $2 an hour or $25 a day.

WHERE TO EAT AND STAY

$–$$ VEGETARIAN ★ ✕**Lola's.** In deference to Lola, the owners' free-roaming pet pig, the menu at this hip beach café is heavily vegetarian. It has exactly the kind of ambience one comes to Costa Rica for, with tables scattered along the beach amid palms and Indian almond trees, hammocks swinging in the wind, palm fronds rustling, and surfers riding the glistening waves in front. Seating, or more precisely, lolling, is all on the sand at low hardwood tables and reclining chairs, or on colorful cushions on rattan mats. Along with the fresh-fruit smoothies and ultrathin vegetarian pizzas, the menu includes organic chicken and "responsible fish" (fish caught in nets that don't also trap turtles). Seared ahi tuna with sun-dried tomato and olive tapenade served on ciabatta bread is a winner, as are the ceviche, fish-and-chips, and assorted salads. You can arrange in advance for private beach dinners by candlelight (the pig isn't invited). ✉ *At main entrance to Playa Avellanas* ☎ *2652–9097* ▭ *No credit cards* ⊗ *Closed Mon. No dinner.*

$ **Cabinas Las Olas.** Frequented mainly by surfers, this place is a good option for anyone seeking beach access and relative solitude. The hotel's spacious glass-and-stone bungalows are scattered across a leafy property behind Playa Avellanas, which guests reach via an elevated boardwalk through a protected mangrove estuary. Each cabina has a queen and a single bed, high wooden ceiling, and covered terrace with a hammock. There's no air-conditioning, but high ceilings, a shady location, and good cross ventilation keep the rooms cool at night. Monkeys, iguanas, and other critters lurk in and around the extensive, forested grounds. The restaurant, under the shade of a giant Guanacaste tree, serves a good selection of Costa Rican and continental cuisine at reasonable prices ($$) for breakfast, lunch, and dinner. **Pros:** near beach; in forest; secluded. **Cons:** mosquitoes a problem in rainy season; simple rooms. ✣ *1 km/½ mi before Avellanas, on right* ☎ *2652–9315* ⊕ *www.cabinaslasolas.co.cr* *10 rooms* *In-room: no a/c, no phone, safe, no TV. In-hotel: restaurant, water sports, laundry service, Wi-Fi* ▭ *AE, MC, V* ⊗ *Closed 15 days in Oct.* *EP.*

6

PLAYA NEGRA

3 km/2 mi south of Playa Avellanas.

Surfer culture is apparent here in the wave of beach-shack surfer camps along the beach road. But there's also a big residential development here called Rancho Playa Negra, with more upscale development on the drawing boards. Contrary to the name, the beach is not black, but rather beige with dark streaks. It's not a great swimming beach, because it tends to have big waves and is lined with rocks, though there is one short stretch of clear sand to the south of the hotel, and at low tide a large tidal pool forms in front of the hotel. The spindly buttonwood trees that edge the beach provide sparse shade.

GETTING HERE AND AROUND

From Playa Avellanas, continue south 10 minutes on the rough beach road to Playa Negra. If it's rainy season and the road is too rough, you can approach along a slightly more civilized route from Santa Cruz. Drive 27 km (16½ mi) west, via Veintisiete de Abril, to Paraíso, then follow signs for Playa Negra for 4 km (2½ mi). Taxis are the easiest way to get around if you don't have a car.

OUTDOOR ACTIVITIES

SURFING

Surfing cognoscenti dig the waves here, which are almost all rights, with beautifully shaped barrels. It's a spectacular, but treacherous, rock-reef break for experienced surfers only. There's also a small beach break to the south of the rocks where neophytes can cut their teeth. Both breaks can be ridden from mid- to high tide. The point break is right in front of the **Hotel Playa Negra** (✣ *4 km/2½ mi northwest of Paraíso* *on dirt road, then follow signs carefully at forks in road* ☎*2652–9134 or 2652–9298* 🌐*www.playanegra.com*), which can arrange surfing classes ($25 per hour), and rents boards ($20 per day).

> **A SURF CLASSIC**
>
> Americans—surfer Americans, at least—got their first look at Playa Negra in 1994's *The Endless Summer II*, a film by legendary surf documentarian Bruce Brown.

WHERE TO STAY

$$ ★ **Hotel Playa Negra.** Brilliantly colored thatch-roof cabinas are sprinkled across sunny lawns strewn with tropical plantings at this gorgeous oceanfront place. Each hut has curvaceous tile bathrooms plus built-in sofas that can double as extra beds. There's no air-conditioning, but conical thatch roofs keep the cabinas cool. Ocean tidal pools, swimming holes, and rock reefs provide plenty of opportunities for lazy afternoon exploration. This is paradise for surfers, with a good swell running right in front of the hotel. The round restaurant serves typical food with a few continental dishes under a giant thatch roof, but the ocean view is more of an attraction than the food. There's also an air-conditioned Internet café in the beach boutique, which arranges kayaking and horseback tours. **Pros:** in front of reef break; friendly. **Cons:** not a great swimming beach; concrete-floor rooms. ✣*4 km/2½ mi northwest of Paraíso on dirt road (watch signs for Playa Negra), then follow signs carefully at forks in road* ☎*2652–9134* 📠*2652–9035* 🌐*www.playanegra.com* *10 cabinas* *In-room: no a/c, no phone, safe, no TV. In-hotel: restaurant, bar, pool, beachfront, water sports, laundry service* 💳*AE, DC, MC, V* ⏲*Restaurant closed Sept. 15–Nov. 1* *EP.*

PLAYA JUNQUILLAL

4 km/2½ mi south of Paraíso, 34 km/22 mi southwest of Santa Cruz.

Seekers of tranquility need look no farther than Junquillal (pronounced hoon-key-*yall*). A short drive to the south of Playa Negra, this wide swath of light brown sand stretches over 3 km (2 mi), with coconut palms lining much of it and hardly a building in sight. Two species of sea turtle nest here, and a group of young people collect and protect their eggs, releasing the baby turtles after sunset. Although it qualifies as a Blue Flag beach, the surf here is a little strong, so watch children carefully. There's a kids' playground right at the beach, and a funky little restaurant with concrete tables amid the palms. It's also a perfect beach for taking long, romantic strolls. Surfers head here to ride the beach break near Junquillal's northern end, since it rarely gets crowded. A surprisingly cosmopolitan mélange of expats has settled in this area, as the selection of goods in the small supermarket in town confirms, but Junquillal is still barely on the tourist map. Its handful of hotels consequently offer some of the best deals on the North Pacific coast.

GETTING HERE AND AROUND

In rainy season, the 4-km-long (2½-mi-long) beach road from Playa Negra to Playa Junquillal is sometimes not passable. The alternative is driving down from Santa Cruz one hour on a road that's paved part of the way. The Castillos bus company runs a bus to Junquillal from the central market in Santa Cruz four times a day (at 5 and 10:30 AM, and 2:30 and 5:30 PM); the trip takes about an hour. A taxi from Santa Cruz costs about $25; from Tamarindo, $35.

ESSENTIALS

The closest town for most services is Santa Cruz, 34 km (22 mi) northeast.

Hospital Clínica (✉ *Veintisiete de Abril* ✣ *16 km/10 mi northeast of Playa Junquillal*).

Internet Supermercado Junquillal (✉ *Near beach entrance*).

DID YOU KNOW?

Guanacaste was a political monkey-in-the-middle for centuries, bouncing between Spain, Nicaragua, and independence. In 1858 Guanacastecans finally voted to annex themselves to Costa Rica, an event celebrated every July 25 with a national holiday.

OUTDOOR ACTIVITIES

HORSEBACK RIDING

At German-run **Paradise Riding** (☎ *2658–8162* 🌐 *www.paradiseriding.com*) the 16 horses are in tip-top shape, as is the impressive tack room, with top-quality saddles lined up in a neat row. There are two-hour trail rides (about $50), or you can set off for a whole day of riding. The maximum number of riders they can handle is 10. You'll saddle up at the friendly owner's house, across from the entrance to Guacamaya Lodge.

6

WHERE TO EAT

$$$ ITALIAN ★ ✕ **La Puesta del Sol.** Italian food aficionado Alessandro Zangari and his wife, Silvana, have created what he modestly calls "a little restaurant in my home." But regulars drive all the way from Tamarindo to sit at one of his five tables and enjoy the dinner-only, haute-Italian menu. It's one of the priciest restaurants on the coast, but Alessandro spares no expense or effort to secure the best ingredients, buying only locally caught seafood and importing his own truffles from Italy. The pasta is made from scratch, and the sauces are prepared to order. The fettucine *boscaiolo* contains a woodsy trio of cremini, porcini, and Portobello mushrooms and the ravioli *al tartufo* (with truffle) is simply sublime. Another favorite is fresh fish *livornesca* (in a caper, olive, and tomato sauce). The softly lighted patio restaurant, tinted in tangerine and deep blue, overlooks a lush garden within earshot of the surf. ✉ *Just north of main entrance to Playa Junquillal* ☎ *2658–8442* ✍ *Reservations essential* ▭ *No credit cards* ⊗ *Closed end of Easter week to mid-Nov. No lunch.*

$ COSTA RICAN ✕ **Restaurante Playa Junquillal.** This funky, open-air restaurant with concrete tables amid the coconut palms is a classic Costa Rican beach bar. It regularly fills up in the evening, when local expats gather to watch the sunset. The lunch options include a small selection of appetizers, a fish sandwich, and the typical Costa Rican casado (fish fillet, or barbecued steak with rice and beans). At dinner, you can also get a fish fillet, or shrimp sautéed with garlic, barbecued chicken, or beef, and a few vegetarian options. It's basically just a good spot for a drink and snack on the beach. ✉ *Main entrance to Playa Junquillal* ☎ *2658–8432* ▭ *MC, V.*

WHERE TO STAY

$–$$ ☺ Fodor's Choice ★ **Guacamaya Lodge.** Spread across a breezy hill with expansive views of the surrounding forest and the sea above the treetops, the Guacamaya is a real find. Spacious cabinas surround a generous-size pool, lawn, and tropical plants. The large restaurant ($–$$) shaded by a conical thatch roof serves excellent Continental cuisine, including such Swiss specialties as *Rösti* (hash browns with bacon and cheese) and *Zürcher Geschnetzeltes* (beef medallions and mushrooms in a creamy sauce), various pastas, fresh seafood dishes, and a good salad selection. Meals come with deliciously dense homemade bread. The spacious duplex bungalows with plenty of windows and small terraces are a real deal. Screened windows let in the cooling evening breezes, so you probably won't need the quiet air-conditioners in each room. Well-equipped studios in a two-story building have kitchenettes, big bathrooms, and covered porches; those on the second floor are more spacious and have better views. The modern house, with a full kitchen and a large covered veranda, is perfect for rental by families. There's also a kids' pool, a playground, and a resident little girl happy to have playmates. The place fills up fast, so book early. **Pros:** good value; clean; friendly. **Cons:** 1,000 feet from the beach. ✉ *275 m east of Playa Junquillal* *Apdo. 6, Santa Cruz* ☎ *2658–8431* ⊕ *www.guacamayalodge.com* *6 cabinas, 4 studios, 1 villa* *In-room: no phone, kitchen (some), no TV. In-hotel: restaurant, bar, tennis court, pool, laundry service, Internet terminal, Wi-Fi* ▭ *AE, MC, V* ⊗ *Closed Sept. and Oct.* *EP.*

¢ **Hotel TaTanka.** This attractive Italian-run hotel has tasty food and very comfortable rates. Ten big rooms are lined up under a tile-roof veranda facing a kidney-shaped pool. They have Mayan-style wall paintings, arty bamboo closets, and large tiled bathrooms. Wood-oven pizzas and homemade pastas—the *spaghetti a la carbonara* is *delicioso*—are served in a huge alfresco restaurant with elegant furniture. The beach is a three-minute walk away. **Pros:** inexpensive; near beach. **Cons:** rooms a bit dark; musty. ✉ *Main Junquillal road, just south of Guacamaya Lodge* ☎ *2658–8426* ⊕ *www.hoteltatanka.com* *10 rooms* *In-room: no phone, no TV. In-hotel: restaurant, pool, laundry service, Internet terminal* ▭ *MC, V* ⊗ *Closed Sept. and Oct.; restaurant closed Mon.* *BP.*

$$ **The Hotel Villa Serena.** Serenely spread across verdant grounds a short walk from the beach, this hotel is certainly aptly named. The rooms are slightly old, but bright and spacious, with high wooden ceilings, big bathrooms, and soothing pastels and local art on the walls. They open onto narrow terraces with wooden chairs, most of which overlook the gardens; only rooms 1 and 2 have ocean views. A large, rectangular pool is surrounded by coconut palms, and across the street is a small shelter at the edge of the beach, perfect for watching the sunset. The second-floor bar and restaurant ($$$) also have a nice ocean view. The menu ranges from fish-and-chips to filet mignon, with daily seafood specials. Coffee is delivered to rooms in the morning, and free snorkeling gear and kayaks are available to guests. **Pros:** closest rooms to

beach; quiet. **Cons:** only TV is at the bar; bugs. ✉*Main Junquillal road, south of main beach access* ☎*2658–8430* 🌐*www.land-ho.com/villa* *12 rooms* *In-room: no phone, no TV. In-hotel: restaurant, bars, pool, gym, spa, water sports, laundry service, Wi-Fi* 💳*AE, DC, MC, V* *EP.*

NOSARA

28 km/17 mi southwest of Nicoya.

One of the last beach communities for people who want to get away from it all, Nosara's attractions are the wild stretches of side-by-side beaches called Pelada and Guiones, with surfing waves and miles of sand on which to stroll, and the tropical dry forest that covers much of the hinterland. The town itself is inland and not very interesting, but the surrounding flora and fauna keep nature lovers entertained. Regulations here limit development to low-rise buildings 600 feet from the beach, where they are, thankfully, screened by trees. Americans and Europeans, with a large Swiss contingent, are building at a fairly rapid pace, but there appears to be an aesthetic sense here that is totally lacking in Tamarindo and Sámara.

For years, most travelers headed here for the surf, but the Nosara Yoga Institute, which offers instructor training, and daily classes for all levels, is increasingly a draw for health-conscious visitors. Bird-watchers and other nature enthusiasts can explore the tropical dry forest on hiking trails, on horseback, or by boating up the tree-lined Nosara River. The access roads to Nosara are abysmal, and the labyrinth of woodsy roads around the beaches and hard-to-read signs make it easy to get lost, which is why most hotels here provide local maps for their guests.

GETTING HERE AND AROUND

From Nicoya, drive south, almost to Sámara, but take the very first road signed for Nosara, 1 km (½ mi) south of the big gas station before Sámara. This high road is rough for about 8 km (5 mi), but there are bridges over all the river crossings. When you join up with the beach road near Garza, you still have a very bumpy 10 km (6 mi) to go. The roads into Nosara are in really bad shape, so a 4WD vehicle is definitely recommended. Budget about one hour for the trip. You can also fly directly to Nosara on daily scheduled SANSA and Nature Air flights, or take an air-conditioned shuttle van from San José. Several major rent-a-car companies have offices in Nosara.

ESSENTIALS

Bank/ATM Banco Popular (✉*In strip mall next to Café de Paris on road to Playa Guiones* ☎*2682–0267*).

Hospital Centro Médico Nosara (✉*In front of strip mall next to Café de Paris, on road to Playa Guiones* ☎*2682–1212*).

Pharmacy Farmacia Nosara (✉*In front of strip mall next to Café de Paris, on road to Playa Guiones* ☎*2682–1148* ⏲*Mon.–Sat. 8–noon and 1:30–5*).

Internet Café de Paris (✉*At entrance to Playa Guiones* ☎*2682–0087*).

Post Office Correo (✉*Next to soccer field*).

Rental Cars Alamo (✉ *Café de Paris shopping center, main road, Nosara* ☎ *2682–0052*).

Taxis Independent drivers provide taxi service. **Abel's Taxi** (☎ *8812–8470*) is reliable.

> **CAUTION**
>
> To approach Nosara along the coast from Junquillal to the north, you have to ford many rivers, including the Río Ostional, which is sometimes impassable during the wet season. This beach road requires 4WD. If you have a compact car, or it has been raining a lot, you are better off driving via Nicoya on the paved road.

EXPLORING

With some of the most consistent surf on the Pacific coast, **Playa Guiones** attracts a lot of surfboard-toting visitors. But the breezy beach, with vegetation rising up from the high-tide mark for its length, is also a haven for shell seekers, sun lovers, and anyone who wants to connect with nature. The only building in sight is the bizarre Hotel Nosara, which was originally the only choice for lodging in town, but which is now a rambling private residence complete with observation tower. Otherwise, this glorious beach has 7 km (4 mi) of hard-packed sand, great for jogging and riding bikes. Because there's a 9-foot tide, the beach is expansive at low tide but rather narrow at high tide, when waves usually create strong currents that can make the sea deadly for nonsurfers. Most hotels post tide charts. Guiones is at the south end of the Nosara agglomeration, with three public accesses. The easiest one to find is about 300 meters (1,000 feet) past the Hotel Harmony, heading straight at the intersection.

North along the shore, Playa Guiones segues seamlessly into crescent-shape **Playa Pelada**, where the water is a little calmer. There are tide pools to explore and a blowhole that sends water shooting up when the surf is big. Lots of trees provide shade. This is the locals' favorite vantage point for watching sunsets. Olga's Bar, a ramshackle Tico beach bar, is a great place for a cool beer; or sip a sunset cocktail at the funky La Luna Bar & Grill, next door.

Ostional National Wildlife Refuge *(Refugio Nacional de Fauna Silvestre Ostional)* protects one of Costa Rica's major nesting beaches for olive ridley turtles. Locals have formed an association to run the reserve on a cooperative basis, and during the first 36 hours of the *arribadas* (mass nesting) they are allowed to harvest the eggs, on the premise that eggs laid during this time would likely be destroyed by subsequent waves of mother turtles. Though turtles nest here year-round, the largest arribadas, with thousands of turtles nesting over the courses of several nights, occur from July to December, though smaller arribadas take place between January and May. They usually take place around high tide, the week of a new moon. People in Nosara usually know when an arribada has begun. The mandatory guided tours of the nesting and hatching areas cost $10 per person. Stop at the kiosk at the entrance to the beach to arrange a tour. ✣ *7 km/4½ mi north of Nosara* ☎ *2682–0428 or 2682–0400* 🎫 *$10 for tour.*

Beginning surfers love Samara's almost placid water and it's undeveloped palm-fringed beach.

★ **Nosara Biological Reserve** (Reserva Biológica Nosara) is a treasure. The 90-acre private reserve includes trails through a huge mangrove wetland and old-growth forest along the Nosara River. A concrete walkway passes over an eerily beautiful mangrove swamp, with fantastical stilt roots and snap-crackling sound effects from respiring mollusks. More than 250 bird species have been spotted here, and there's an observation platform for watching birds. There are always crabs, lizards, snakes, and other creatures rustling in the grass and howler monkeys and iguanas in the trees. Pick up a self-guided trail map from the Hotel Lagarta Lodge when you pay your admission fee, or better yet, hire the resident nature guide; call ahead if you want to hire a guide. The best times to do the hike, which takes about two hours, are early in the morning or late in the afternoon, which means you can follow your trek with breakfast, or sunset cocktails at the Hotel Lagarta Lodge. ✉ *Trailhead 168 steps down from Hotel Lagarta Lodge, top of hill at the north end of Nosara* ☎ *2682–0035* 🎫 *$6, free for kids under 15, $12 with guide (reserve 1 day in advance).*

MASSAGE AND YOGA

The Nosara Yoga Institute (✉ *Southeast end of town, on main road to Sámara* ☎ *2682–0071, 866/439–4704 in U.S.* 🌐 *www.nosarayoga.com*) focuses on teacher certification, but also offers several daily yoga classes to the public ($10), weeklong workshops, and retreats. Relaxing massages in a jungle setting ($55 per hour) are available by appointment at **Tica Massage** (✉ *Across from the Hotel Harmony [formerly the Hotel Villa Taype]* ☎ *2682–0096*), plus spa services such as facials and salt glows.

OUTDOOR ACTIVITIES

Iguana Expeditions (✉ *Gilded Iguana, Playa Guiones* ☎ *2682–4089* 🌐 *www.iguanaexpeditions.com*) organizes kayaking on the Nosara River, a hike to a waterfall, horseback riding, fishing, surfing, and nature tours. The **Harbor Reef Surf Resort** (✉ *Follow signs from Café de Paris turnoff, Playa Guiones* ☎ *2682–0059 or 2682–1000* 🌐 *www.harborreef.com*) has an excellent tour desk that can arrange fishing, surfing, nature tours, and a day trip to the Tempisque River that combines a boat and canopy tour.

HELP ON THE ROAD

The more remote the area, the more likely that someone will stop to help you change a tire or tow you out of a river. Usually, Good Samaritans won't accept any payment and are more trustworthy than those who offer to "help" in the States. Near Ostional, there's a farmer named Valentin who regularly pulls cars out of the flooded river with his tractor. So he is known as Valentin *con chapulin* (with a tractor).

BIRD-WATCHING

On river trips with **Nosara Boat Tours** (✉ *Boat moored at bottom of hill leading to Hotel Lagarta Lodge, follow signs to the boca [mouth] of Nosara River* ☎ *2822–1806 or 2682–0610* 🌐 *www.nosaraboattours.com*), you glide up the Nosara and Montaña rivers in a flat-bottom catamaran with an almost noiseless electric motor. Wading herons, egrets, roseate spoonbills, ospreys, and kingfishers are common sights. The German-born naturalist guide also knows where river otters play and crocodiles hunker down in mud caves along the riverbank. Trips are $30 per person ($15 for kids under 14).

HORSEBACK RIDING

German equestrienne Beate Klossek and husband Hans-Werner take small groups of up to six people on 3½-hour horseback nature tours through the jungle and along the beach ($60 to $90 per person, according to group size) with **Boca Nosara Tours** (✉ *150 m below Hotel Lagarta Lodge, at mouth of Nosara River* ☎ *2682–0280* 🌐 *www.bocanosaratours.com*). Horses are well mannered and well treated. There are smaller saddles for kids over eight.

SURFING

If you ever wanted to learn to surf, Nosara is the place. Guiones is the perfect beginners' beach, with no rocks to worry about. Local surf instructors say that the waves here are so consistent that there's no week throughout the year when you won't be able to surf. In March and April, the Costa Rican National Surf Circuit comes here for surf trials. Especially recommended for beginners, **Safari Surf School** (✉ *Road to Playa Guiones; ask for directions at Casa Tucán* ☎ *2682–0573* 🌐 *www.safarisurfschool.com*) is run by two surfing brothers from Hawaii, one of whom lives here year-round. A one-hour private lesson costs $40, equipment included. The school is closed in October. **Corky Carroll's Surf School** (✉ *Near Casa Romántica, on the Playa Guiones road* ☎ *2682–0385* 🌐 *www.surfschool.net*) has its own hotel for surfing students. **Coconut Harry's Surf Shop** (✉ *Main road, across from Café de Paris* ☎ *2682–0574* 🌐 *www.coconutharrys.com*) has boards ($15 to

$20 per day), gear, and lessons ($45 per hour, board included). **Nosara Surf Shop** (✉ *Café de Paris, road to Playa Guiones* ☎ *2682–0186* 🌐 *www.nosarasurfshop.com*) rents boards by the day ($15 to $20) and has lots of gear, too.

> **CAUTION**
>
> Many restaurants do not include the legally required 13% tax and 10% service in their menu prices, but tack them onto the bill at the end. It might be indicated somewhere on the menu that tax and tip are not included, but that's not always the case. If you're not sure, ask.

WHERE TO EAT

$$ ECLECTIC **Café de Paris.** The French-Swiss owners have turned this corner restaurant into a chic, alfresco eatery. Fresh-baked pastries and desserts are a major draw. Sweet and savory croissants are excellent, as is the divine chocolate tart. In addition to the tried-and-true wood-oven pizzas, nachos, and hearty sandwiches, they have such Continental treats as fish and vegetables baked in papillote, jumbo shrimp flambé, and lamb stew with mushrooms. ✉ *Main road at Playa Guiones entrance* ☎ *2682–0087* ▭ *AE, MC, V.*

$$ ITALIAN ★ **Giardino Tropicale.** Famous for its crispy-crust, wood-oven pizzas loaded with toppings as well as the bowls of homemade chili-pepper sauce that grace every table, this thatch-roof multilevel restaurant casts a wide net to include daily fresh seafood and fish specials. Sit on one of the upper decks by day, and you'll dine amid the treetops. Service is always fast and very friendly. ✉ *Giardino Tropical Hotel, main street, past entrance to Playa Guiones* ☎ *2682–0258* ▭ *AE, MC, V* ⏲ *No lunch.*

$$ AMERICAN **Marlin Bill's.** Sink your teeth into classic rib-eye steak, pork chops, and lobster in American-size portions at this open-air restaurant with a distant ocean view. Lighter choices include eggplant parmigiana and delicious "dorado fingers"—battered fish fillet strips served with tartar sauce. The decor is decidedly fishy, with a mounted marlin, fish murals, and a photo wall of happy fishers and their prize catches. Fishing and real estate talk over beer and chicken wings keeps the U-shaped bar abuzz. ✉ *Hilltop above main road, near Coconut Harry's Surf Shop* ☎ *2682–0458* ▭ *MC, V* ⏲ *Closed Sun.*

WHERE TO STAY

$–$$ ★ **Casa Romántica Hotel.** The name ("Romantic House") says it all: the Spanish Colonial–style house has a balustraded veranda upstairs and a graceful arcade below. The young Swiss owners renovated the original rooms and built new rooms in separate wings. All are bright, with big bathrooms and shared terraces with views of the glorious gardens. There's a kidney-shaped pool next to a thatch shelter with hammocks, and a short path through the surrounding forest leads to the beach. The small patio restaurant where the complimentary buffet breakfast is served becomes a truly romantic, candlelighted restaurant ($–$$) at night, when the menu includes such Continental favorites as chicken cordon bleu, beef Stroganoff, a creamy shrimp curry, and daily fish and seafood specials. **Pros:** near beach; good restaurant; good value. **Cons:** rooms not spectacular; can be noisy. ✉ *100 m west of Giardino Tropical, on left,* ☎📠 *2682–0272* 🌐 *www.casa-romantica.net* *10 rooms*

6

In-room: no a/c (some), no phone, safe, refrigerator, no TV. In-hotel: restaurant, pool, beachfront, laundry service, Wi-Fi ☰MC, V ǀ◎ǀBP.

$–$$ **Giardino Tropicale Hotel.** In the lush gardens downhill from the popular restaurant (⇨*above*), shaded by large trees, are comfortable cabinas and a sparkling 40-foot swimming pool—the only good lap pool in town. The handsome suites have everything you need to make breakfast: electric kettles, coffeemakers, refrigerators, and sinks. Two spacious apartments also have full kitchens. The four smaller cabinas have solar-heated hot water, ceiling fans, coffeemakers, and refrigerators; use of air-conditioning costs extra. Inexpensive, hearty breakfasts are served by the pool, and the restaurant is one of the best in town. **Pros:** good value; environmentally friendly; helpful owners. **Cons:** road noise; extra charge for a/c; short walk to beach. ✉*Main street, past entrance to Playa Guiones* ☎*2682–4000* 🌐*www.giardinotropicale.com* *4 cabinas, 4 suites, 2 apartments* *In-room: no phone, refrigerator, kitchen (some), no TV (some). In-hotel: restaurant, pool, Wi-Fi* ☰*AE, DC, MC, V* ǀ◎ǀ*EP.*

$ **The Gilded Iguana.** This lively hotel/bar/restaurant has been a Nosara fixture for more than 15 years. Televised sports, live music, and lots of friendly regulars make the open-air bar a popular place. The on-site tour desk can arrange almost any outing you can imagine. Six large, air-conditioned rooms are lined up behind a small, kidney-shaped pool with a refreshing waterfall. For traditionalists, the original rooms have more character, in a shaded wooden building with louvered, screened windows letting in fresh breezes in lieu of air-conditioning. **Pros:** economical; laid-back. **Cons:** spotty service; needs updating. ✉*Playa Guiones, Nosara* ☎*2682–0259* 🌐*www.gildediguana.com* *10 rooms, 2 suites* *In-room: no a/c (some), no phone, refrigerator, no TV. In-hotel: restaurant, bar, pool, laundry service* ☰*MC, V* ǀ◎ǀ*EP.*

$$ **Harbor Reef Surf Resort.** Lose yourself in the junglelike garden grounds centered around two small pools, one presided over by a concrete crocodile, the other by a tiny waterfall. Your wake-up call is the bellowing of a resident howler monkey, and you can bird-watch at breakfast. Rooms and suites cater to surfers of every age, with plenty of space for boards and gear inside, but the decor is rudimentary. "Surf city" rooms have two queen beds in slightly separate alcoves, whereas larger suites are great for families, with two bedrooms, two baths, a loft with twin beds, and a kitchen. The surf break at Playa Guiones is a 300-meter (1,000-foot) walk away. The open-air restaurant ($–$$) serves an American menu, with fresh fish, steak, chicken, pastas, and some Tex-Mex dishes. A large souvenir shop and a beachwear shop are on the grounds. Owner Randy Bombard has a wealth of information about the area. **Pros:** attractive grounds; near beach; good restaurant. **Cons:** bland rooms; pricey. ✉*Follow signs from Café de Paris turnoff* ☎*2682–0059 or 2682–1000* 🌐*www.harborreef.com* *13 rooms, 9 suites, 18 houses* *In-room: no phone, kitchen (some), refrigerator. In-hotel: restaurant, bar, pools, laundry service, Internet terminal, Wi-Fi* ☰*AE, DC, MC, V* ǀ◎ǀ*EP.*

$$$ ★ **The Harmony Hotel.** Surf's up . . . upscale, that is. This formerly frayed surfer's haunt has been reborn as an ultracool hipster's retreat. The

American owners are surfers, but of an age where comfort and quiet are more appealing than partying. The rooms surround a huge garden that holds a gorgeous, chlorine-free pool and sundeck—an oasis of tranquility. Every room, villa, and bungalow has soft sage-and-cream-color walls, a king-size bed dressed in white linen, and natural and polished wood trim and furniture. Enclosed back decks with hammocks expand what are otherwise standard-size rooms. The slightly larger duplex bungalows in back offer a little more privacy for an extra $60. The retro '60s lounge bar with basket chairs and adjacent restaurant add to the sophisticated ambience, but chic is not cheap—this place is markedly more expensive than its neighbors. For the health-conscious traveler there's a "healing center" complete with spa, yoga classes, and juice bar. The best surf breaks are just 180 meters (600 feet) away, down a shaded path. **Pros:** near beach; chic; nice details. **Cons:** pricey; not overly kid-friendly. ✉ *From Café de Paris, take road almost all the way to Playa Guiones, on right* ☎ *2682–4114* 🌐 *www.harmonynosara.com* *10 rooms, 15 bungalows* *In-room: safe, refrigerator, no TV, Wi-Fi. In-hotel: restaurant, bar, pool, spa, beachfront, laundry service, no-smoking rooms* *AE, DC, MC, V* *BP.*

6

$ ★ **Hotel Lagarta Lodge.** A birders' and nature lovers' Valhalla, this magnificent property on a promontory has amazing views of the forest, river, and coast north of Nosara. The private Nosara Biological Reserve is directly below the lodge. A 10-minute walk down a steep path takes you through a monkey-filled forest to beautiful Playa Guiones and surfing waves. The bright, spacious rooms are simple but comfortable, with balconies and terraces perfect for admiring the sweeping vista. Swiss managers Regina and Amadeo Amacker oversee the eagle's-nest lobby-restaurant ($–$$, reservations essential), which features a Swiss-inspired menu that is strong on fresh fish and seafood, such as skewered prawns with bacon, and poached fish with a lemon sauce. There is also a cocktails-and-canapés Sunset Bar that you must visit even if you stay elsewhere. The breakfast buffet is delicious, with fresh breads and homemade jams. Both the garden and reserve are maintained without any chemical fertilizers, insecticides, herbicides, or the use of electric machinery. **Pros:** amazing views and grounds; close to nature. **Cons:** not on the beach; plain rooms. ✉ *Top of hill at north end of Nosara* ☎ *2682–0035* 🌐 *www.lagarta.com* *6 rooms* *In-room: no a/c, no phone, no TV. In-hotel: restaurant, bar, pool, Internet terminal* *MC, V* *EP.*

$$ ★ **Luna Azul.** Sequestered in the hills above Playa Ostional, several miles north of Nosara, Luna Azul is a tranquil, tasteful spot full of clever design and healthful attributes—supplied by the zoologist and homeopathist Swiss owners. Abundant birds and wildlife, thanks to the surrounding private nature reserve, make this an excellent spot for nature lovers; it is also the most convenient lodge for seeing turtles nesting. Rooms are spacious, and the bathrooms are elegant, with hot-water showers open to nature. Three separate rooms have very private decks, cooled by overhead fans; four others have their own gardens. Acupuncture and homeopathic treatments and massages are available. The chic seafood restaurant overlooking the small tile pool and treetops draws

Soft music and cocktails on the beach at the La Vela Latina in Samara.

customers from Nosara, with perfectly prepared seafood, fresh fish, tenderloin, and organic chicken. The only drawback to this picture-perfect place is that it's hard to get to when the Lagarto River swells in rainy season, but you can always reach it via Veintisiete de Abril, near Tamarindo. **Pros:** isolated in a picturesque environment; good restaurant. **Cons:** off the beaten path. ✣*1 km (½ mi) north of Ostional, 5 km (3 mi) north of Nosara* ☎*2821–0075* ⊕*www.hotellunaazul.com* *3 bungalows, 4 rooms* *In-room: no phone, safe, refrigerator, no TV. In-hotel: restaurant, bar, pool, laundry service* ▭*AE, DC, MC, V* ⊙*Closed Oct.* *BP.*

NIGHTLIFE

There's always plenty of surfing talk at **Kaya Sol** (✉*Playa Guiones* ☎*2682–0080*) a friendly, laid-back bar near the beach with a pool table, tree-trunk tables, and a light, inexpensive menu. **The Gilded Iguana** (✉*Playa Guiones* ☎*2682–0259*) has live acoustic music on Tuesday night that draws a big crowd.

Sunset is the main event in the evening, and people gather to watch it at **Olga's Bar** (✉*Playa Pelada* ☎*No phone*), a ramshackle beach shack. Saturday night, the popular **Tropicana** (✉*Downtown Nosara, beside the soccer field* ☎*No phone*) is where the action is.

SHOPPING

Arte Guay (✉*Commercial center, just past Café de Paris on road to Playa Guiones* ☎*2682–0757*) has local crafts and beachwear. Along with surfing wear and gear, **Coconut Harry's Surf Shop** (✉*Main road, across from Café de Paris*) has an interesting selection of jewelry and bottled hot sauces made by Harry himself. (The Iguana Atomic Hot

Sauce will rip your tongue out!) At the **Chenoa Boutique** (✉ *Commercial center, just past Café de Paris on road to Playa Guiones*) has an interesting selection of jewelry, handbags, and beachwear.

SÁMARA

36 km/23 mi southwest of Nicoya, 26 km/16 mi south of Nosara.

The drive to Sámara from Nicoya may be one of the most scenic in Costa Rica, passing rolling hills and green vistas before descending to a wide, south-facing bay hemmed by palm-shaded sand. Long a favorite summer-home spot with well-off Costa Ricans, Sámara's combination of safe swimming water and relative proximity to San José make it a popular destination for working-class Ticos as well. The town of Sámara has an abundance of budget accommodations, which makes it a good destination for travelers with limited budgets. It can be a lively place on weekends, with bars on the beaches and handicraft vendors on the main drag, but it isn't the cleanest of beaches (no Blue Flag), and those seeking solitude should head to the beach's western or eastern ends. Though it lacks the rip currents that make many Costa Rican beaches dangerous, Sámara has pollution problems, and thus is not the best beach for swimming from September to December, when daily rains flush plenty of things you wouldn't want to swim with into the sea.

Sámara's wide sweep of light-gray sand is framed by two forest-covered hills jutting out on either side. It's the perfect hangout beach, with plenty of natural shade, bars, and restaurants to take refuge in from the sun. There is, however, a sandy roadway running through the coconut palms and Indian almond trees that line the beach, so be sure to look both ways when you move between the surf and margaritaville. The waves break out on a reef that lines the entrance of the cove, several hundred yards offshore, which keeps the water calm enough for safe swimming but leaves enough surf to have fun in. The reef holds plenty of marine attractions for diving and snorkeling excursions. Isla Chora, at the south end of the bay, provides a sheltered area that is especially popular for kayakers and snorkelers—it even has a tiny beach at lower tides.

GETTING HERE AND AROUND

The road from Nicoya is paved all the way for the scenic one-hour drive to Sámara. ■ **TIP→ Potholes are spreading, so keep your eyes on the road instead of the beautiful views.** A rough beach road from Nosara is passable in dry season (it's more direct, but takes just as long); do not attempt this road when it rains. To get from Nosara to Sámara via the paved road, drive south, 5 km (3 mi) past Garza. At the "T" in the road, ignore the road toward Sámara (the beach road) and take the road to the left, toward Nicoya. This will take you uphill to merge with the main Nicoya–Sámara highway. Sámara-bound buses leave Nicoya from a stop 300 meters east of the central park. They depart hourly from 5 AM to 3 PM and then at 4:30, 6:30, 8, and 9:45 PM.

ESSENTIALS

Bank/ATM Banco Nacional (✉ *50 m west of church, 100 m west of main road* ☎ *2656–0089*).

6

Hospital **Transportes Médicos** (☏ *8304–2121*).

Pharmacy **Farmacia Sámara** (✉ *North end of soccer field* ☏ *2656–0123*).

Internet **Se@net** (✉ *Across from soccer field* ☏ *2656–0302* ⏲ *Daily 8–8*).

Post Office **Correo** (✉ *Beside church, across from soccer field*).

Rental Cars **Alamo** (✉ *Calle Principal, Sámara* ☏ *2656–0958*). **Budget** (✉ *100 m east of Hotel Giada, Sámara* ☏ *2436–2000*).

OUTDOOR ACTIVITIES

Sámara is known more for gentle water sports such as snorkeling and kayaking than for surfing, although there are a couple of surf schools in town. There are also two high-flying adventures here: zip-line tours and ultralight flights and flying lessons. ATV tours, tearing along dirt roads, are popular with travelers who are particularly fond of dust, or mud, according to the season. For information on area activities, visit the town's official Web site at 🌐 *www.samarabeach.com*.

Tío Tigre Tours (✉ *50 m east of school and 100 m north* ☏ *2656–0098*) has a full line of guided outdoor activities, including kayaking ($25), snorkeling ($30), horseback riding ($30), and dolphin- and whale-watching tours ($35). **Sámara Travel Center** (✉ *Main street, across from Century 21* ☏ *2656–0922*) offers an array of local tours and bus and plane tickets to other parts of the country, and rents bikes and motorcycles.

CANOPY TOURS

Wing Nuts Canopy Tour (✉ *In the hills above Sámara* ☏ *2656–0153*) has a three-hour, 12-platform zip-line tour through a patch of tropical forest just south of town, with ocean views from some of the platforms ($55).

DIVING AND SNORKELING

The reef offshore is the best place to snorkel. Kayakers also paddle out to Isla Chora to snorkel on the leeward side of the island. The lone dive shop here, French-run **Pura Vida Dive** (✉ *Sámara, 600 m west of church* ☏ *2656–0643* 🌐 *www.puravidadive.com*), takes a maximum of five divers ($90 each) about 8 km (5 mi) out to explore rock formations off Playa Buena Vista and Playa Carrillo. Turtles, white-tipped sharks, and lots of big fish are the star sightings. The company also rents scuba equipment and arranges snorkeling trips.

KAYAKING

Plastic sit-on-top kayaks can be rented at Villas Playa Sámara (⇨ *below*), which is quite close to Isla Chora and the reef. **C&C Surf Shop** (✉ *On beach across from Casa del Mar* ☏ *2656–0628*) runs kayak snorkeling tours to Isla Chora and the nearby reef ($30). **Tío Tigre** (⇨ *above*) offers various kayaking tours.

SURFING

The surf is relatively gentle at Sámara, so it's a good place for beginners. The challenging waves for more experienced surfers are farther south, at Playa Camaronal, which has both left and right breaks. **C&C Surf Shop** (⇨ *above*) has a beachfront surf school ($40 per lesson), and rents boards ($4 per hour).

ULTRALIGHT FLIGHTS

Flying Crocodile Lodge (✉ *Playa Buena Vista* ⊕ *6 km/4 mi northwest of Sámara* ☎ *2656–8048* 🌐 *www.flying-crocodile.com*) gives ultralight flights and flying lessons ($75 for 20-minute tour).

WHERE TO EAT

$$$ STEAK ★ **El Lagarto.** With varnished wooden tables scattered across the sand amid ficus and Indian almond trees, close enough to the sea to hear the surf above the mix of Latin music on the stereo, El Lagarto has Sámara's best ambience by far. But its big draw is the food—fresh local seafood and high-quality meat grilled to perfection on a massive, open-air barbecue. The name means "The Crocodile," but you won't find croc steaks on the menu. You can, however, sink your teeth into juicy tenderloin, lamb chops, mahimahi, prawns, tuna, veal ribs, mussels, chicken breast stuffed with mushrooms and cheese, portobello mushrooms, or a whole-grilled lobster. You won't find any barbecue sauce on the meat here; everything is simply brushed with extra-virgin olive oil seasoned with a bit of garlic, salt, and pepper to complement the flavor of the wood. Dinners include grilled vegetables and potatoes; a salad is à la carte. They have a kids' menu, an ample wine list, and an extensive cocktail selection, not to mention banana splits. ✉ *200 m west and 200 m south of Banco Nacional* ☎ *2656–0750* 💳 *AE, DC, MC, V* ⊗ *No lunch. Closed Oct.*

6

$ ITALIAN ★ **El Manglar.** Hidden on a rutted side street, this informal Italian eatery beneath a large thatch roof doesn't look like much, but there are usually plenty of cars parked in front, since it's a favorite of local expatriates. The owner, Letizia Vendittelli, is invariably in the kitchen, preparing fresh pasta, fish, and meat dishes to order, or sliding another one of her super-thin, crispy pizzas out of the oven. She makes the best pizza in town, with two dozen varieties to choose from. The ricotta-and-spinach ravioli with porcini mushrooms and zucchini have made many a mouth water, as have the homemade gnocchi—but ask for the mahimahi ravioli, which isn't on the menu but is often available, and have Letizia smother them in her creamy shrimp sauce. She makes nearly everything fresh, which means you have to wait a little longer here than at the competition, but she is happy to modify recipes to suite your taste. ✉ *200 m west and 150 m south of Banco Nacional* ☎ *2656–0096* 💳 *MC, V* ⊗ *No lunch. Closed 2 wks in May and 2 wks in Sept.*

$ ITALIAN **Pizza & Pasta a Go-Go.** An ample selection of high-quality Italian food, including 25 fabulous pizzas, 26 pastas, generous salads, and a lengthy Italian wine list, is just one reason to drop in at this sidewalk trattoria. Unlike the checkered tablecloths you'd find elsewhere, here you have glass tabletops showcasing shells, or plain wooden tables by the pool. Save room for a tiramisu that transcends the tropics and delivers your taste buds to Italy. ✉ *Hotel Giada lobby, main strip, 150 m north of beach* ☎ *2656–0132* 💳 *AE, MC, V.*

WHERE TO STAY

¢–$ **Hotel Casa del Mar.** Less than a block from the beach, this pleasant, well-tended hotel is one of Sámara's best values. The bright, tidy rooms have dark-wood furniture, white walls, and ceramic floors. Eleven of the rooms have a/c and private bath, and some have queen-size beds.

Six of the rooms lack air-conditioning and share baths, but they share a common balcony with an ocean view, and sea breezes help to cool them. The hotel has a giant cold-water whirlpool in a small garden and a big cage holding a parrot named Lolita. **Pros:** helpful staff; easy on the wallet. **Cons:** not right on the beach; no swimming pool. ✉*Main strip, 45 m east of school* ☎*2656–0264* 📠*2656–0129* 🌐*www.casadelmarsamara.com* *17 rooms, 11 with bath* *In-room: no a/c (some), no phone, refrigerator (some), no TV (some). In-hotel: no-smoking rooms* *AE, MC, V* *BP.*

$ **Hotel Giada.** Giada means "jade" in Italian, and this small hotel in the heart of town has been decorated with the artistic Italian owners' precious, polished creations. Watermelon, terra-cotta, and yellow washes give the walls an antique Mediterranean look, and the terraces of the back rooms overlook a curvaceous blue pool surrounded by tropical greenery. The rooms have whimsical bamboo furniture and sea creatures on the hand-painted bathroom tiles. Pizza & Pasta a Go-Go *(⇨above)*, the hotel's restaurant, is an excellent Italian restaurant. The hotel's drawback is noise from the restaurant and the street, which is why roadside rooms should be avoided; ask for a room overlooking the pool. **Pros:** affordable; friendly. **Cons:** not right on the beach; small rooms. ✉*Main strip, 250 m from beach* ☎*2656–0132* 🌐*www.hotelgiada.net* *24 rooms* *In-room: safe, refrigerator (some). In-hotel: restaurant, pool* *AE, DC, MC, V* *BP.*

$$–$$$ **Hotel Las Brisas del Pacífico.** One of the few beachfront hotels in Sámara, Las Brisas has been here for nearly two decades, and much of the place shows its age. The standard rooms, in two rows of white, Spanish-style bungalows hugging the bottom of a steep hill, can be hot and stuffy. "Sky rooms," in the two-story building at the top of the hill, are more expensive, but much nicer, with ocean-view balconies and a nearby pool, as well as a separate parking lot, so that you don't have to climb up and down the steep hill. Newer "on-top" rooms above the office are closer to the beach and have balconies, but most view the restaurant's roof. You'll want to eat everything but breakfast in town. The receptionist can arrange diving trips and other outings. **Pros:** great location; two nice pools. **Cons:** rooms and grounds somewhat neglected; service inconsistent. ✉*South of town* ☎*2656–0250* 🌐*www.brisas.net* *34 rooms* *In-room: no a/c (some), no phone, safe. In-hotel: restaurant, bar, pools, beachfront, laundry service, Wi-Fi* *AE, D, MC, V* *BP.*

$$ ★ **Villas Kalimba.** You may never want to leave this tranquil oasis hidden behind scrolled white-and-orange walls. The architecture is Mexican, but the style is all Italian. Ochre-washed villas with hammocks and dining tables on their front porches circle an exuberant garden and pool with a cool waterfall. Rooms have state-of-the-art kitchens, and you can dine alfresco at a long wooden table on your own tiled terrazza. All the comforts of a luxury home—king-size bed, cable TV, a personal portable phone—are here, just across the street from the beach. Barbecues and pasta dinners for guests are offered several times a week beneath a Spanish-tile roof by the pool. **Pros:** spacious villas; lovely garden; quiet. **Cons:** not on beach; uninspired dining. ✉*200 m east of the Sámara*

Idyllic Playa Carrillo is perfect for swimming, snorkeling, or just sunning.

Police Station, along beach road ☎2656–0929 🌐www.villaskalimba.com ⇆6 villas, 2 casas ☝In-room: kitchen. In-hotel: pool, laundry service ▭MC, V ⊚EP.

$$$ **Villas Playa Sámara.** Families come back to this property year after year for good reason: there's lots to do, the villas are spacious and practical, and the setting is fabulous. It is spread along the picture-perfect southern end of the beach, where the ocean is cleaner than it is near town, and shallow and safe enough for swimming. The spacious, Spanish-style one-, two-, and three-bedroom villas of white stucco are sprinkled across the property's gardens and wide lawns. They have kitchens and dining areas with daybeds that are perfect for kids (under 12 stay free), and shaded terraces with either a hammock or chairs, but they are quite timeworn and lack such basics as a phone and a TV. Most have ocean views through the palms, but the duplex villas 2A/B and 11A/B are especially close to the beach, and thus cost an extra $20; 17 A/B is a close second. The restaurant food is not terrific; it's best to cook for yourself or dine in town. **Pros:** great location; spacious villas; ample grounds. **Cons:** villas timeworn; cleaning inconsistent. *✉Off main road ✣2 km/1¼ mi south of town ☎☎2656–0372, 2256–8228 in San José 🌐www.villasplayasamara.com ⇆59 villas ☝In-room: no phone, kitchen, no TV (some). In-hotel: restaurant, bar, pool, beachfront, water sports, bicycles, laundry service, Internet terminal, Wi-Fi ▭AE, MC, V ⊚EP.*

NIGHTLIFE

The liveliest, noisiest beach bar is **Las Olas** (✉ *On beach, 200 m west and 200 m south of Banco Nacional* ☎ *2656–1100*). Three pool tables, bright lights, and a pulsing Latin soundtrack attract a mix of locals and young backpackers. **Tutifruti** (✉ *50 m west of police station*), on the beach, is the local dance club. It opens only on Friday and Saturday, when it gets packed with young Costa Ricans. **Shake Joe's** (✉ *On beach, center of town*) is the place for music, drinks, and an international menu.

★ **La Vela Latina** (✉ *Across from Villas Kalimba, on beach*) is the cool place for grown-up soft music and cocktails on the beach.

SHOPPING

Souvenir stands set up along the main street and at the entrance to the beach. Most shops here have pretty much the same beachwear and souvenirs for sale. **Tienda Licia** (✉ *Main street*) has a wall hung with pretty glass fish and butterfly ornaments made by a San José artist. Arts-and-crafts gallery **Dragonfly Galería** (✉ *Across the street from Licia*) sells local paintings and carvings, and shell, feather, and bead jewelry. It also paints temporary henna tattoos.

PLAYA CARRILLO

Fodor's Choice ★ *7 km/4 mi southeast of Sámara.*

With its long, reef-protected beach backed by an elegant line of swaying palms and sheltering cliffs, Playa Carrillo (interchangeably called Puerto Carrillo) is a candidate for the most picturesque beach in Costa Rica. Unmarred by a single building, it's ideal for swimming, snorkeling, walking, and lounging—just remember not to sit under a loaded coconut palm. There are some concrete tables and benches, but they get snapped up quickly. This is a popular beach with locals, and it gets quite busy on weekends. The main landmark here is the Hotel Guanamar, high above the beach. Unfortunately the former private fishing club and previously grand hotel has been bought and sold so often that its charm has faded. But its bar still has the best view.

GETTING HERE AND AROUND

You can fly into Playa Carrillo on SANSA or Nature Air and land at the airstrip, or head south 15 minutes on the smooth, paved road from Sámara. If you're not staying at a hotel in Carrillo, you'll have to park your car either in a sunbaked concrete lot halfway along the beach or on the grassy median at the south end of the beach. You can also leave the driving to Interbus (⇨ *North Pacific Essentials, at end of chapter*) and get here in an air-conditioned van.

ESSENTIALS

Sámara is the closest town for banks and other services.

EXPLORING

Most nature lovers are no fans of zoos, but **La Selva Zoo & Bromeliad Garden,** a small zoo with mostly rescued small animals, is a great chance to see them up close in chest-high corrals under the shade of trees. The zoo's focus is on hard-to-see nocturnal animals, so the best time to visit is at sunset when the roly-poly armadillos and big-eyed kinkajous are starting to stir. There are also skunks, spotted pacas, raccoons, and scarier species like bats, boas, poison dart frogs, caimans, and crocodiles. A bromeliad and orchid collection is artistically arranged around the zoo. If you come early in the day, your ticket is also good for a return evening visit. ✉ *Road behind Hotel Esperanza* ☎ *8305–1610* 🎫 *$8* ⏲ *Daily 10–9.*

OUTDOOR ACTIVITIES

FISHING

From January to April, the boats moored off the beach take anglers on fishing expeditions. Experienced local skipper Rob Gordon lives right in Puerto Carrillo and runs fishing trips on the five-passenger *Kitty Kat* (☎ *2656–0170 or 8359–9039* 🌐 *www.sportfishcarrillo.com*), a 28-foot aluminum boat with twin diesels ($950 full day, $500–$650 half day). He offers catch-and-release marlin and sail fishing as well as good-eating dorado, yellowfin tuna, and wahoo. There are also dolphins and occasional whales to watch if the fishing is slow.

6

PUNTA ISLITA

8 km/5 mi south of Playa Carrillo in dry season, 50 km/31 mi south of Carrillo by alternative route in rainy season.

Punta Islita is named for a tiny tuft of land that becomes an island at high tide, but the name is synonymous in Costa Rica with Hotel Punta Islita, one of the country's most luxurious and gorgeous resorts. The curved beach is rather rocky but good for walking, especially at low tide when tidal pools form in the volcanic rock. Another interesting stroll is through the small village, which has become a work in progress, thanks to a community art project led by renowned Costa Rican artists who use town buildings as their canvas. Everything—from outdoor activities to food—revolves around, and is available through, the resort.

GETTING HERE AND AROUND

During the dry season, it's a quick trip south of Playa Carrillo in a 4WD vehicle, but in the rainy season, it's often impossible to cross the Río Ora, so you have to make a much longer detour along rough dirt roads with spectacular mountain views. Most guests consequently fly into the hotel's private airstrip.

WHERE TO STAY

$$$$ Fodor'sChoice ★ **Hotel Punta Islita.** Overlooking the ocean from a forested ridge, this secluded hotel is luxury incarnate. Hidden around the hillside are villas, casitas, suites, and spacious rooms, each with a private porch and a hammock. Beds have rough-hewn wooden bedposts, and bathrooms are tiled, with deep tubs. Casitas have their own private plunge pools or outdoor whirlpools and private gardens, one of the main attractions for the many honeymooners. A massive thatched dome covers the restaurant and opens onto an infinity-edge pool with a swim-up bar. If you overdo it with the activities here—including golfing, mountain biking, and zip-line tours—stop by the spa for massage treatments using local herbs. **Pros:** gorgeous views; lots of activities. **Cons:** isolated; mediocre

beach. ✣ *8 km/5 mi south of Playa Carrillo* ✉ *Apdo. 242–1225, Plaza Mayor, San José* ☎ *2661–4044, 2231–6122 in San José* 🌐 *www.hotelpuntaislita.com* ⇨ *14 rooms, 8 suites, 8 casitas, 17 villas* ♘ *In-room: DVD (some). In-hotel: 2 restaurants, bars, golf course, tennis courts, pools, gym, spa, beachfront, laundry service, Wi-Fi, no-smoking rooms* ▭ *AE, DC, MC, V* 🍴 *BP.*

THE TEMPISQUE RIVER BASIN

The parks in and around the Río Tempisque are prime places to hike, explore caves, and spot birds and other wildlife. The town of Nicoya is the commercial and political hub of the northern Nicoya Peninsula. By road, Nicoya provides the best access to Sámara, Nosara, and points south and north and is linked by a smooth, well-paved road to the artisan community of Guaitil and the northern Nicoya beach towns.

The Friendship Bridge, built with donated funds from Taiwan and more commonly referred to as the Río Tempisque Bridge, crosses the Río Tempisque just north of where passengers used to weather long waits for a ferry. To get to the bridge, head north from San José on the Pan-American Highway, turn left about 48 km (30 mi) north of the Puntarenas turnoff, and drive 27 km (17 mi) west.

PALO VERDE NATIONAL PARK

52 km/32 mi south of Liberia.

One of the best wildlife- and bird-watching parks in Costa Rica, Palo Verde is bordered on the west by the Río Tempisque. Extending over 198 square km (76 square mi), the park protects a significant amount of deciduous dry forest. The terrain is fairly flat—the maximum elevation in the park is 268 meters (879 feet)—and the forest is less dense than a rain forest, which makes it easier to spot the fauna. The park holds seasonal wetlands that provide a temporary home for thousands of migratory birds toward the end of the rainy season, whereas crocodiles ply the Tempisque's waters year-round. From September through March you can see dozens of species of migratory and resident aquatic birds, including herons, wood storks, jabirus, and elegant, flamingo-like roseate spoonbills. **■ TIP→ A raised platform near the ranger station, about 8 km (5 mi) past the park entrance, gives you a vantage point over a marsh filled with ducks and jacanas. But be prepared to climb a narrow metal ladder.** Lodging in rustic dormitory facilities ($10) and meals ($5 breakfast; $7 for lunch or dinner) can be arranged through the park headquarters. ✣ *29 km/18 mi southwest of Bagaces* ☎ *2200–0125* 🎟 *$10* ⏲ *Daily 8–dusk; entrance gates open 8–noon and 1–4.*

GETTING HERE AND AROUND

To get to Palo Verde from Liberia, drive south along the Pan-American Highway to Bagaces, then turn right at the small, easy-to-miss sign for Palo Verde, along a rough dirt road for 28 km (17 mi). Count on an hour to drive the distance from the main highway to the park entrance; it's a very bumpy road. You'll have to pay the $10 park entrance fee to get to the Organization for Tropical Studies station. The OTS station

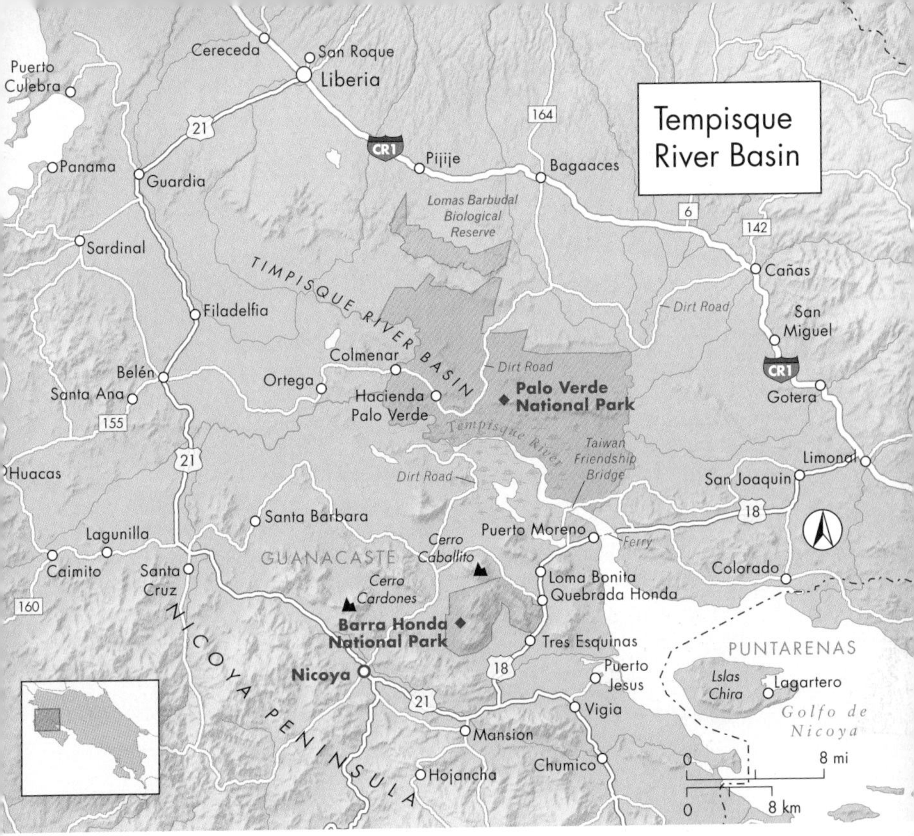

is about 7 km (5 mi) beyond the park entrance; the park headquarters is just another kilometer farther. The gatekeeper takes lunch from noon to 1 PM. The drive should take a total of about three hours.

EXPLORING

Just 3 km (2 mi) north of the Palo Verde road at Bagaces, take the dirt road signed for **Llanos de Cortés** to get to this hidden waterfall less than 2 km (1 mi) off the highway. About half a kilometer along the dirt road you'll see on your right a large rock with CATARATAS scrawled on it. Follow this bumpy road about 1.3 km (.8 mi) to its end and then clamber down a steep path to the pool at the bottom of a spectacular, wide, 50-foot waterfall. This is a great place for a picnic. ■ **TIP→Don't leave anything of value in your car.**

Sad but sobering, one of the few places left in the country where you are guaranteed to see large wild cats, including a jaguar, is **Las Pumas Rescue Shelter** (Centro de Rescate Las Pumas) (*4½ km/3 mi north of Cañas on main highway* ☎*2669–6044* *www.laspumas.org*). The small enclosures also hold jaguarundis, pumas, margays, ocelots, and oncillas. Some small animals and birds are rehabilitated and released into the wild. The larger cats are probably here for life, as it's dangerous for them to be released. The refuge relies on contributions. It's open daily 8 to 4.

OUTDOOR ACTIVITIES

The **Organization for Tropical Studies** (☎*2524–0607* 🌐*www.ots.ac.cr*), a nonprofit, scientific consortium, offers overnight packages with a guided walk, meals, and lodging in rustic, bunk-bedded double rooms with private bath ($65 per person). Their biological research station overlooks the Palo Verde wetlands, and they also offer a boat tour plus longer hikes as affordable add-ons to the package.

BIRD-WATCHING

The best bird-watching in Palo Verde is on the wetlands in front of the Organization for Tropical Studies' (OTS) biological station. The OTS has expert guides who can help you see and identify the varied birds in the area, but if you have good binoculars and a bird book, you can identify plenty of species on your own. A boat excursion to Isla Pájaros south of the Río Tempisque is interesting for birders. Toward the end of rainy season this 6-acre island near Puerto Moreno is an exciting place to see hundreds of nesting wood storks, cormorants, and anhingas. You can get close enough to see chicks being fed in nests. ■ **TIP→** **The best time to go is very early in the morning, to avoid heat and to guarantee the most bird sightings.** **Aventuras Arenal** (☎*2479–9133* 🌐*www.arenal adventures.com*) guides have good eyes and usually know the English names for birds. The company specializes in ecological tours. Tours depart from docks along the Río Tempisque, including the dock at Palo Verde. **CATA Tours** (☎*2674–0180, 2296–2133 in San José*) runs $45 wildlife- and bird-watching boating adventures down the Río Bebedero into Palo Verde. Arrange hotel pickup from Nicoya beaches and Papagayo Peninsula when you book.

Safaris Corobici(☎*2669–6191* 🌐*www.nicoya.com*) is a small company that specializes in the Class I and II floats down the Río Corobicí ($35 to $60; children under 14 half price) that start from (and end at) the Restaurante Rincón Corobicí, on the Pan-American Highway 5 km (3 mi) north of Cañas.

WILDLIFE WATCHING

On a calm adventure trip with **Safaris Corobicí** (✉*Main highway to Liberia at Km 193, south of Corobicí* ☎*2669–6091* 🌐*www.nicoya.com*), guides do the rowing on large inflatable rafts while you look at the flora and fauna. Two- or three-hour float trips ($35 to $60) cover wildlife-rich territory not far from Palo Verde. Trips require two or more passengers, and they start from the Restaurante Rincón Corobicí, on the Pan-American Highway 5 km (3 mi) north of Cañas. **Ríos Tropicales** (☎*2233–6455* 🌐*www.riostropicales.com*) lets you paddle down the easy Class I and II rafting route on the Río Corobicí. Those two- to three-hour trips ($50 excluding ground transportation) are great for bird- and monkey-watching and are safe enough for kids ages seven and older.

WHERE TO STAY NEAR PALO VERDE

$ **La Ensenada Lodge.** This is the most comfortable base for bird-watching and nature appreciation near the Río Tempisque. Part of a national wildlife refuge, the property is also a 1,000-acre cattle ranch and salt

Rafting on the Corobici River, North Guanacaste.

producer. The salt flats and nearby shallow waters attract wading birds (and crocodiles that snack on them). The Isla Pájaros Biological Reserve, the country's largest breeding ground for black-crowned night herons, is a short boat ride away. The wood cabins are comfortable, with verandas and big screened windows that let the light and breeze in, but because most of them are duplexes, they don't afford a lot of privacy, so see if you can get a freestanding one. The rancho restaurant serves buffet-style Italian and Costa Rican meals, including beef raised on the ranch. **Pros:** wildlife; interesting setting. **Cons:** very simple rooms. ✥*13 km/8 mi southwest of Pan-American Hwy. along a dirt road, 40 km/25 mi north of the Puntarenas turnoff* ☎*2289–6655* 🌐*www.laensenada.net* ⇆*26 cabin rooms* 👍*In-room: no a/c, no phone, no TV. In-hotel: restaurant, bar, pool, laundry service* ▭*No credit cards* 🍽*EP.*

EN ROUTE

The approach to the town of Santa Cruz from the east is like a giant pit stop, with one car-parts shop after another. One of the few reasons to visit is to eat at **Coope-Tortillas** (✉*Drive through business district, 200 m past church turn right and look for peaked-roof metal structure, Santa Cruz* ☎*2680–0688*), where you can watch hand-rolled corn tortillas being cooked the old-fashioned way over an open fire. Friendly women in blue uniforms, members of a local women's cooperative, heap your plate with your choice of traditional *Guanacasteco* foods and bring it to one of the picnic tables in a high-ceiling, corrugated-metal building. Try the delicious *arroz de maiz,* a corn stew. The restaurant is open 4 AM to 5 PM. Tortillas sometimes run out before 4 PM.

BARRA HONDA NATIONAL PARK

100 km/62 mi south of Liberia, 13 km/8 mi west of Río Tempisque Bridge.

Once thought to be a volcano, 390-meter (1,184-foot) **Barra Honda Peak** actually contains an intricate network of caves, a result of erosion after the ridge emerged from the sea. Some caves on the almost 23-square-km (14-square-mi) park remain unexplored, and they're home to abundant animal life, including bats, birds, blindfish, salamanders, and snails.

THE FIRST GUANACASTECOS

The Chorotega tribe first settled the Guanacaste area and grew corn and fished. Chief Nicoya was the Chorotegan leader who greeted the conquistadors in 1523 and bequeathed his name to the town and peninsula.

GETTING HERE AND AROUND

From the Río Tempisque Bridge, drive west along a paved highway. Then follow a dirt road (signed off the highway) for 10 km (6 mi) to the park entrance. There are buses that come here from the town of Nicoya, but they don't leave until 12:30 and 4 PM, a little late to start a hike. You can also take a taxi from Nicoya to the park entrance or go with one of many tour companies in beach towns on the Nicoya Peninsula.

EXPLORING

Every day from 7 AM to 1 PM local guides take groups rappelling 18 meters (58 feet) down into **Terciopelo Cave,** which shelters unusual formations shaped (they say) like fried eggs, popcorn, and shark's teeth. You must wear a harness with a rope attached for safety. The tour costs $26, including equipment rental, guide, and entrance fee. Kids under 12 are not allowed into this cave, but they can visit the kid-size La Cuevita cavern ($6), which also has interesting stalagmites. Both cave visits include interpretive nature hikes.

If you suffer a fear of heights, or claustrophobia, the cave tour is not for you, but Barra Honda still has plenty to offer, thanks to its extensive forests and abundant wildlife. You can climb the 3-km (2-mi) Los Laureles trail (the same trail that leads to the Terciopelo cave) to Barra Honda's summit, where you'll have sweeping views over the surrounding countryside and islet-filled Gulf of Nicoya. Wildlife you may spot on Barra Honda's trails includes howler monkeys, white-faced monkeys, skunks, coatis, deer, parakeets, hawks, dozens of other bird species, and iguanas. Local guides charge $6 for hiking tours. An off-site **park office** (✉*Across from colonial church, Nicoya* ☎*2686–6760*) provides information and maps of the park. It's open weekdays 7–4. It's a good idea to hire a local guide from the **Asociación de Guias Ecologistas.** The park has camping facilities. Make reservations for weekend lodging in the park. *13 km/8 mi west of Río Tempisque Bridge* ☎*2659–1551* *$10* *Daily 7:30–4.*

NICOYA

27 km/15 mi west of the Río Tempisque Bridge.

Once a quaint provincial town, Guanacaste's colonial capital is now bustling because of tourism and real-estate booms along the nearby coast. With all the commercial bustle, Nicoya is rapidly losing what small-town charm it once had. But there are still a few historical remnants around the central park. A noticeable Chinese population, descendants of 19th-century railroad workers, has given Nicoya numerous Chinese restaurants. The town has Internet cafés and ATMs that take international cards.

GETTING HERE AND AROUND

The town of Nicoya is 40 minutes west of the Río Tempisque Bridge on a paved road. If you're running out of gas, oil, or tire pressure, the Servicentro Nicoyano on the north side of Nicoya, on the main road, is open 24 hours.

ESSENTIALS

Bank/ATM **Banco de Costa Rica** (✉ *West side of central park* ☎ *2685–5110*). **Coopmani ATH** (✉ *Main street, beside Fuji Film store*).

Hospital **Hospital de L'Anexion** (✉ *Main road into town from highway* ☎ *2685–8400*).

Pharmacy **Farmacia Clinica Medica Nicoyana** (✉ *Main street, near Restaurante Nicoya* ⏲ *Weekdays 8–7:30, Sat. 8–6*).

Internet **CiberClub** (✉ *Across from Hotel Yenny, 1 block south of central park* ☎ *2686–7143* ⏲ *Mon.–Sat. 8:30 AM–9 PM*).

Post Office **Correo** (✉ *Southwest corner of park*).

Taxis **Taxi Service** (☎ *2686–2466*).

EXPLORING

Nicoya's only colonial landmark is the whitewashed, mission-style **Church of San Blas.** Originally built in 1644, the church was reconstructed after the original was leveled by an 1831 earthquake. The spare interior is made grand by seven pairs of soaring carved-wood columns. Inside are folk-art wood carvings of the Stations of the Cross arrayed around the stark white walls, a small collection of 18th-century bronze mission bells, and some antique wooden saints. Arched doorways frame verdant views of park greenery and distant mountains. ✉ *North side of central park* ☎ *No phone* *By donation* ⏲ *Erratic hours.*

OUTDOOR ACTIVITIES

Hiking in Barra Honda is the main outdoor adventure here. If that's too strenuous for you, **Tempisque Eco Adventuras** (*4 km/2½ mi southwest of Río Tempisque Bridge* ☎ *2687–1212* *ecoaventuras@racsa.co.cr*) can show you flora and fauna similar to Barra Honda's on a seven-cable canopy tour ($35). For a fun day, you can combine the canopy tour with a Palo Verde boat tour. Lunch is in a charming open-air restaurant accompanied by traditional marimba music.

6

WHERE TO EAT AND STAY

$ CHINESE ✕ **Restaurante Nicoya.** There are many Chinese restaurants from which to choose in Nicoya. This one is the most elegant, with hanging lanterns, a colorful collection of international flags, and an enormous menu with 85 Asian dishes, such as stir-fried beef with vegetables. The fresh sea bass sautéed with fresh pineapple, chayote, and red peppers is excellent. ✉*Main road, 70 m south of Coopmani Bldg.* ▭*AE, DC, MC, V* ⊙*Closed daily 3–5.*

¢ COSTA RICAN ✕ **Soda Colonial.** One of the town's last vestiges of local color is this vintage all-day restaurant with white-adobe walls. Facing the shady central park, it's a great place to watch small-town life go by. Sit at a wooden bench in the wainscotted interior and sip a tamarindo refresco or order hearty portions of typical Tico food, heavy on the beans and rice. ✉*Southeast corner of central park* ▭*No credit cards.*

$ **Hotel de Lujo Río Tempisque.** There aren't many reasons to stay overnight in Nicoya, but if you get stuck here, this "luxury" lodge is the best option. The rooms here, with high wooden ceilings and big picture windows, are comfortable by any standards. Huge white-tile bathrooms have mirrored closets and showers big enough for two. The best thing about the place, though, is its tranquil location north of town, and its ample gardens and small pool. **Pros:** quiet; convenient. **Cons:** simple; not memorable. ✉*Highway north to Santa Cruz, outside Nicoya* ☎*2686–6650* *30 rooms* *In-room: no phone, refrigerator. In-hotel: restaurant, pool* ▭*AE, MC, V* *EP.*

¢ **Hotel Mundiplaza.** This hotel is the town's most modern. On the second floor above a medical clinic, it doesn't have much personality. But if you need a bed for the night, it has fresh rooms with all the modern conveniences. There's also a small restaurant and Internet café in the same building. ✉*Main road into Nicoya, near hospital* ☎*2685–3535* *25 rooms* *In-room: no phone. In-hotel: laundry service* ▭*AE, DC, MC, V* *EP.*

Central Pacific

WORD OF MOUTH

"At the end of a hike through Manuel Antonio, we finally reached a beach where a troop of White-faced Capuchins had gathered. They entranced everyone as they ran along low hanging branches, tantalizing close."

—photo by Gwendolyn Morris, Fodors.com member

WELCOME TO CENTRAL PACIFIC

TOP REASONS TO GO

★ **Nature and wildlife:** Explore seaside flora and fauna at Manuel Antonio National Park, Curú National Wildlife Refuge, and Cabo Blanco Absolute Nature Reserve.

★ **Fishing:** Deep-sea fishing at Quepos, Tambor, Jacó, or Herradura is a chance to hook a sailfish, marlin, wahoo, or yellowfin tuna.

★ **Sunsets:** Whether you view it from the beach in Malpaís or while sipping hilltop cocktails in Manuel Antonio, this region has some of the country's best venues for watching the sunset.

★ **Surfing:** This is Costa Rica's surf central. Jacó, Malpaís, and Playa Hermosa swarm with surfers, from beginners to pros.

★ **Adventure sports:** Snorkel among colorful fish, get muddy on ATV mountain rides, and zip through treetops near Jacó, Manuel Antonio, or Montezuma.

1 Southern Nicoya Tip. On the Southern Nicoya Tip, across the gulf from the "mainland," towns are more tranquil and more spread out. Beaches and surfing dominate.

GETTING ORIENTED

Most of the Central Pacific is mountainous, and beach towns are backed by forested peaks. Humid evergreen forests, oil-palm plantations, and cattle pastures blanket the land. The coastal highway connects all towns from Tárcoles to the southern Pacific. The hub town of Jacó makes a good base for visiting surrounding beaches and wildlife areas. Farther south are Quepos and its neighbor, Manuel Antonio, followed by smaller towns barely touched by tourism. Across the Gulf of Nicoya, the more tranquil southern tip of the Nicoya Peninsula is also surrounded by impressive mountains, but with dry tropical forests that change radically from the rainy to the dry season.

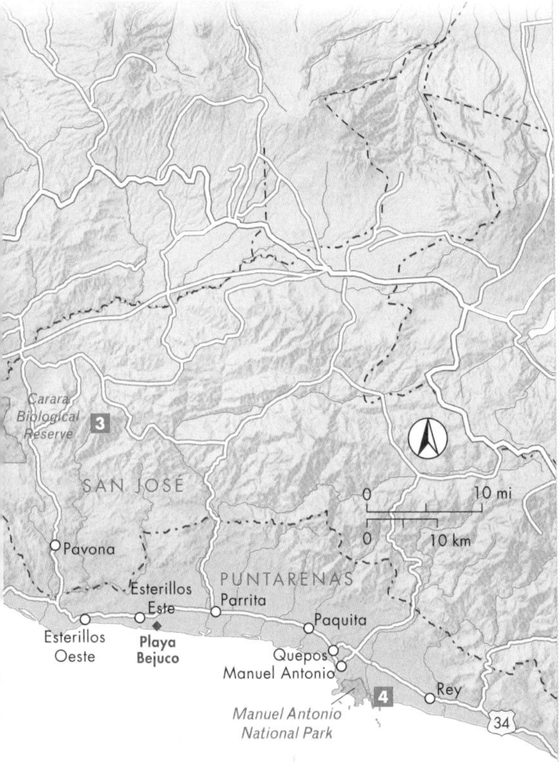

2 Inland. Humid evergreen forests, coffee fields, and cattle pastures blanket the Inland portions of the Central Pacific.

3 Carara National Park. Carara National Park is home to a very impressive collection of plants and animals.

4 Coast. From Tárcoles, the highway along the Coast connects lively tourist hubs Jacó, Quepos, and Manuel Antonio, and on down to the South Pacific. This is the place to surf, do a multitude of active tours, laze on the beach, and explore Manuel Antonio National Park.

CENTRAL PACIFIC PLANNER

Beating the Crowds

The dry season here is the high season: visitors (lots of them) arrive December through May, pushing hotel prices up and crowding the beaches. During Holy Week and the last week of the December, rooms are even harder to come by. A great time to visit the area is during July and August, which see warm, sunny days with the occasional light shower. If you are in the area in high season and want to visit one of the parks, get an early start and arrive by 7 AM.

Choosing a Place to Stay

The Central Pacific has a good mix of high-quality hotels, nature lodges, and *cabinas* (low-cost Tico-run hotels, often laid out like motels), including some of the country's priciest lodgings. As a rule, prices drop 20% to 30% during the rainy season. Reserve as far in advance as possible during the busy dry season. Near Manuel Antonio National Park, Manuel Antonio is the more activity-rich, attractive, and expensive place to stay (though we've culled the best budget options).

Do It Your Own Way

This popular area is also easily reachable. If you're not pressed for time, and you'd like to experience more than just resorts, beaches, and, depending on when you go, crowds, then rent a car or travel by bus, shuttle, or private driver instead of flying from San José. Your rewards will be plenty: beautiful landscapes, typical rural towns, and easy-going Ticos. Distances from San José are not overwhelming, and the ferry ride across the Gulf of Nicoya has great views of the mountainous coast and its islands. Buses are timely and economical, but if you prefer an air-conditioned ride, shuttles leave from San José and can drop you off at your hotel's doorstep. Most travelers heading to the southern tip of the Nicoya Peninsula arrive by car via the ferry from Puntarenas to Paquera. You can also fly into Tambor's airstrip and taxi to your beach from here.

What to Do

ACTIVITY	WHERE TO DO IT
Fishing	Quepos, Manuel Antonio, Playa Herradura, Tambor, Jacó
Snorkeling	Isla Tortuga, Manuel Antonio, Montezuma
Surfing	Jacó, Playa Hermosa, Malpaís
Wildlife-viewing	Manuel Antonio National Park, Rio Tárcoles, Cabo Blanco Absolute Nature Reserve, Curú National Wildlife Refuge, Carara National Park
Yoga	Montezuma, Malpaís, Jacó, Manuel Antonio
Zip-line tours	Malpaís, Montezuma, Jacó, Playa Herradura, Playa Hermosa, Manuel Antonio, Quepos

Recommended Tour Operators

Costa Rica 4u (CRT ☎2508–5000 🌐www.costarica4u.com) has a variety of Central Pacific tours, plus car rentals, private drivers, shuttle vans, and a 4WD off-the-beaten-path "adventure" transfer between San José and Manuel Antonio.

Cruise West (☎888/851–8133 🌐www.cruisewest.com) runs four 11- to 15-day cruises that visit coastal reserves in Panama and Costa Rica.

King Tours (☎8819–1920, 2643–2441, or 800/213–7091 🌐www.kingtours.com) arranges trips to the top Central Pacific attractions, including Manuel Antonio National Park and Carara National Park.

Ríos Tropicales (☎2233–6455 or 866/722–8273 🌐www.riostropicales.com), a high-quality adventure tour company, runs a four-day, three-night sea-kayaking trip ($600) based at Curú National Wildlife Refuge and meanders among the islands of the Gulf of Nicoya. White-water rafting trips on rivers near Manuel Antonio cost $70 to $99.

Dining and Lodging

WHAT IT COSTS IN DOLLARS

	¢	$	$$	$$$	$$$$
Restaurants	under $5	$5–$10	$10–$15	$15–$25	over $25
Hotels	under $50	$50–75	$75–$150	$150–$250	over $250

Restaurant prices are per person for a main course at dinner. Hotel prices are for two people in a standard double room in high season, excluding service and tax (16.4%).

Planning the Days and Nights

Nightlifers of all ages, Ticos as well as travelers, flock to Jacó to party until sunrise, making it the country's liveliest beach town. Jacó draws everyone from partying college kids to groups of men seeking to savor the local beer. Be aware that Jacó also attracts a fair number of ladies of the night.

South of Quepos along the coastal highway lie tranquil beaches, where time seems to stand still, a real contrast with the busy Manuel Antonio area. Dominical makes a great surf spot after Jacó, whereas Punta Uvita has a vast beach and more wildlife than people. From the southern tip of Nicoya, head up the west coast to hop along the endless stretch of beaches. Or ferry back to the mainland to explore Monteverde's cloud forest.

Timing

A week gives you enough time to visit several beaches on the central coast or get a good grasp of the tip of Nicoya.

Word of Mouth

"Finca Rosa Blanca [Country Inn] is out in the country a ways, but it is not to be missed, and you definitely should include a gourmet dinner in their restaurant. Enjoy Costa Rica. It is a beautiful destination."

—MarciaM

7

CARARA NATIONAL PARK

One of the last remnants of an ecological transition zone between Costa Rica's drier northwest and more humid southwest, Carara National Park holds a tremendous collection of plants and animals.

Squeezed into its 47 square km (18 square mi) is a mixed habitat of evergreen and deciduous forest, river, lagoon, and marshland. Much of the park's terrain is blanketed with dramatic primary forest, massive trees laden with vines and epiphytes. This is a birder's and plant-lover's haven. The sparse undergrowth makes terrestrial wildlife and ground birds easier to see, but of course nothing is guaranteed. Your chances of seeing wildlife increase dramatically the earlier you get here. The most famous denizens—apart from the crocodiles in the adjoining Río Tarcoles—are the park's colorful and noisy scarlet macaws, which always travel in pairs. An oxbow lake (a U-shaped body of water that was once part of a river) adds an extra wildlife dimension, attracting turtles and waterfowl—and the crocodiles that dine on them. Bring lots of drinking water; this park can get very hot and humid.

BEST TIME TO GO

Dry season, January to April, is the best time to visit. The trails get very muddy during the rainy season and may even close in the wettest months. This small park can feel crowded at the trailheads, so arrive early and walk far. Bird-watchers can call the day before to arrange early admission.

FUN FACT

The crowning glory of Carara is the successful conservation program that has doubled its scarlet macaw population. You can't miss these long-tailed, noisy parrots—look for streaks of brilliant blue and red in the sky.

HIKING

The best and really only way to explore this park is on foot. Rubber boots or waterproof shoes are essential in the rainy season, and still a good idea, even in the drier months. Trails are well marked and maintained but the ground is often muddy—this is rainforest, after all. The shortest—and most popular—loop trail can be done in only 15 minutes. But if you venture farther afield, you'll quickly be on your own, except for the wildlife you're bound to encounter. The longer trail that connects with the Quebrada Bonita loop takes one to three hours to hike. There is also a short wheelchair-accessible route that starts at the main entrance. It goes deep enough into the forest to give visitors a sense of its drama and diversity.

BIRD-WATCHING

With more than 350 species recorded here, Carara is on every bird-watcher's must-visit list. It's an especially good place to see elusive ground birds, such as antpittas (a small ground dwelling bird that eats ants), early in the morning and late in the afternoon. Around the lake and in the marshy areas, you may also spot roseate spoonbills, northern jacanas, and stately boat-billed herons. The park's most famous fliers are the Scarlet Macaws. Once almost absent from the area, a decades-long conservation program has revitalized the local population.

WILDLIFE

Carara is famous for an amazing variety of wildlife, given its relatively small area. Keep alert (and quiet) while walking and you'll have a good chance of spotting big and small lizards, coatimundis (a member of the raccoon family), and sloths. You're almost guaranteed to see white-faced monkeys and, with luck, howler and spider monkeys, too. You may even surprise a nine-banded armadillo snuffling along the ground, or a northern tamandua (anteater) patrolling low branches.

TOP REASONS TO GO

WILDLIFE
For most visitors, wildlife is the park's main attraction. You can count on seeing monkeys and lots of lizards as you walk the trails. Although they are a little harder to spot, look for anteaters, sloths, and armadillos.

BIRDS
With a varied habitat that attracts both forest and water birds, Carara is a treasure trove for birders. Even if you're not a birder, you'll get a thrill hearing the raucous crowing of beautiful Scarlet Macaws as they soar over the forest canopy.

THE JUNGLE
The forest here is simply magnificent. Even if you don't spot a single bird or animal, you will experience the true meaning of jungle. Carara has one of the most diverse collections of trees in the country. Breathe deeply, be alert to the symphony of forest sounds, and bask in a totally natural world.

MANUEL ANTONIO NATIONAL PARK

At only 7 square km (3 square mi), Manuel Antonio National Park—Costa Rica's smallest park—has an impressive collection of natural attractions: wildlife, rain forest, white-sand beaches, and rocky coves with abundant marine life.

The forest is dominated by massive gumbo-limbo trees, recognizable by their peeling bark. It's home to both two- and three-toed sloths, green and black iguanas, agoutis (similar to the guinea pig, but with longer legs), three species of monkeys, and more than 350 species of birds.

Trails are short, well maintained—and heavily traveled. Make no mistake about it: this is no undiscovered wilderness. In fact, Manuel Antonio is Costa Rica's second-most-visited attraction. There are 5 km (3 mi) of coastline, and it's one of the few parks where you can combine nature walks with swimming off idyllic beaches. There's absolutely no commercial beach development, so the beaches are picture-perfect pristine. The park entrance is across a shallow river mouth, so be prepared to get your feet wet or shuttle across in a rowboat (for less than $1).

BEST TIME TO GO

Visit any day but Monday, when the park is closed, and any month but September or October, when it's very wet. Come early, ideally between 7 and 8 AM, because park rangers allow only 600 to 800 people at a time inside.

FUN FACT

The park's territory is too small to support all of its monkeys, so forested corridors and suspended bridges have been built to allow the monkeys to come and go.

HIKING

Don your hiking shoes and set off on the main trail from the ranger station. You'll immediately find yourself in rain forest and then emerge onto sparkling Playa Espadilla Sur. Another trail leads to Playa Manuel Antonio, which has a good coral reef for snorkeling. These two beaches lie on either side of a *tombolo*, a sandy strip that connects the mainland to rocky Punta Catedral, which used to be an island. Farther east, where fewer visitors venture, Playa Escondido is rocky and secluded. Trails from the entrance to Punta Catedral and Playa Escondido are in good shape. Trails farther east are progressively rougher going. Sturdy walking sandals are good enough for most of the trails, but light hiking boots or closed shoes will help you avoid nasty encounters with biting ants.

WILDLIFE

Manuel Antonio is famous for its monkeys, especially the noisy white-faced monkeys that pester tourists at the beach. A troop of rarer squirrel monkeys also live here, one of the few places in the country where you can still find them. These tiny monkeys—*mono titi* in Spanish—are an endangered species. Catching sight of them is a real wildlife coup. The smallest of Costa Rica's four monkey species, these little guys have squirrel-like bushy tails but they only use them for balance—they can't swing from them.

Watch, too, for less active creatures, such as the more-or-less stationery sloth, especially along the park's Sloth Trail. They sleep much of the day, curled up high in the trees. Look for clumps of green and brown and watch carefully to see if they move.

You'll see many more animals and birds with a guide than without one. You can hire an official guide at the park entrance. If you're interested in seeing birds, be sure to hire a guide carrying a scope, so you can get close-up views of far-away birds.

TOP REASONS TO GO

BEACHES

Gorgeous beaches without any commercial clutter or noise are one of the best reasons to visit Manuel Antonio. Bring your own snorkeling gear, snacks, and drinks since there's nowhere to buy them. There are very basic toilet facilities and cold-water, open-air showers.

HIKING

Hiking is one of the main attractions. The farther east you go, the rougher and less traveled the trails become, and the greater your chances increase of seeing wildlife.

PELICANS

Just off Playa Espadilla, you can swim out to some rocks and tread water while pelicans dive for fish, oblivious to visitors who bob quietly in the water.

VIEWS

For a fabulous coastal view, take the steep path that leads up to Punta Catedral's rocky hill, draped with thick jungle. You'll pass a lookout point from which you can gaze out at the Pacific and the park's islets.

ECO-LODGES IN THE CENTRAL PACIFIC

The Central Pacific is more renowned for its hedonistic Pacific beaches and resort nightlife than for wildlife or ecotourism. But there are some small pockets of original forest and habitat, and a couple of greener lodging choices.

An ecological transition zone between the dry forests of the North Pacific and the rain forests of the South Pacific, the Central Pacific is home to animals and plants of both regions. It is one of the easiest places to get a good look at the American crocodile, many of which gather near the bridge over the Tarcoles River. It's also easy to spot scarlet macaws in and around nearby Carara National Park, which protects the largest expanse of forest left in the region. Nearby Rainmaker Reserve is another good place to experience wildlife. At Manuel Antonio Park farther down the Pacific coast, you can see wildlife and enjoy an ocean swim at the same time. Over on the Nicoya Peninsula, the smaller Curú National Wildlife Reserve and Cabo Blanco Absolute Nature Reserve (its name says it all) are farther off the beaten path but worth a visit if wild is what you seek.

GOOD PRACTICES

No matter how many warning signs are posted, visitors still feel compelled to feed the animals. At Manuel Antonio National Park, the white-faced monkeys have become a nuisance down at the beach, begging for food and even stealing backpacks and ripping food packages open. They are very cute, but they can also be quite mean and deliver nasty bites to the hands that feed them.

It's not only animal behavior, but also animal health that has been compromised. The white-faced monkeys in Manuel Antonio show elevated levels of cholesterol from all the fried chips they have been fed over decades!

TOP ECO-LODGES IN THE CENTRAL PACIFIC

HOTEL SÍ COMO NO

From its meticulous recycling policy and energetic reduction of waste and energy consumption to its innovative conservation programs, Sí Como No has led the way in sustainable tourism. Perched on a hillside in the center of developed Manual Antonio, this luxury hotel is not a classic "eco-lodge." But owner Jim Damalas has worked hard to minimize the hotel's environmental impact. Guests may notice another more ephemeral but no less important policy here: good-natured hospitality. By creating a harmonious workplace, the hotel has retained well-trained, happy staff, who in turn do their best to make guests happy, too.

The hotel's most notable contribution to local ecotourism is the nearby Butterfly Garden and a 30-acre wildlife refuge. Sí Como No also promotes local culture in Quepos and its surrounding farm villages. The hotel is a member of the Green Hotels of Costa Rica and has attained the country's highest sustainability award: Five Green Leaves.

ARENAS DEL MAR BEACH AND NATURE RESORT

One of the newest hotels in the Central Pacific, this luxury hotel has an impressive eco pedigree. It is the brainchild of Teri and Glenn Jampol, owners of Finca Rosa Blanca in the Central Valley, one of the first lodges in the country to achieve five-leaf sustainability status. Their goal here was to create a five-star luxury resort that is also a five-leaf sustainable hotel. The first most obvious eco-aspect guests encounter is the reception center in a forest clearing, where you leave your car behind and ride an electric golf cart to the main open-air lobby.

You may also not be able to see your room for the trees. For 20 years, the Jampols reforested and allowed these formerly farmed slopes to regenerate before they began building, often wrapping terraces around established trees. The result is a totally natural landscape, home to lots of wildlife.

FROM OUR WRITER

Conserving natural habitat is not only a good idea, ecologically speaking, but also makes for potentially unpredictable and memorable wildlife sightings. On a visit to Arenas del Mar Beach and Nature Resort, in Manuel Antonio, I was relaxing by one of the hotel's two swimming pools, watching white-faced monkeys scrambling among branches over the nearby restaurant roof, throwing down half-eaten fruits and the occasional partially vivisected grasshopper (headless but still squirming).

Suddenly, my peripheral vision caught sight of a coatimundi emerging from the forest at the far side of the pool. He dove into the pool, dog-paddled diagonally across, climbed out, and made a beeline into the forest. It was a surprise to me to learn that coatis could even swim. This one was obviously so at home here that he thought nothing of using the hotel pool as a cool shortcut.

—Dorothy MacKinnon

7

Updated by David Dudenhoefer & Heidi Leigh Johansen

The Central Pacific region of Costa Rica is a long swath of gorgeous land, from sublime coastline dotted with national parks to inland stretches of ranches, coffee plantations, small villages, and forested mountains. There's a reason this is a popular place to visit: the region has a lot of "Pura Vida" to offer.

GETTING HERE AND AROUND

The 30-minute flight between San José and Quepos can save you the three-hour drive or bus trip, which involves a serpentine mountain road. Flights from San José to Tambor take 20 minutes—a fraction of the time it takes to drive to Puntarenas and ferry over, and from here it's a reasonable taxi trip to Montezuma and Malpaís.

From San José the best way to get to the southern tip of Nicoya is to take the Pan-American Highway (CA1) west to Puntarenas (two hours), and board a car ferry bound for Paquera (one hour). Take the road to Cóbano, which passes Tambor. Turn left in Cóbano to reach Montezuma (40 minutes), or drive straight to reach Malpaís and Santa Teresa (one hour). The quickest way to the Central Pacific coast from San José is to take the Pan-American Highway (CA1) west to the exit for Atenas (the sign will say Atenas/Orotina/Jacó), where you turn left (south). Once you leave the highway, the road is one lane in each direction for the rest of the route. Between Atenas and Orotina it is steep and full of curves. If you don't have experience in mountain driving, you're better off taking a bus, shuttle van, or flight to the coast. The coastal highway, or Costanera, heads south from Orotina to Tárcoles, Jacó, Hermosa, Bejuco, and Quepos. It is well marked and paved. An asphalt road winds its way over the hill between Quepos and Manuel Antonio National Park. It takes about 2½ hours to drive to Jacó and 3 to Quepos.

Buses are very inexpensive and easy to use. From San José to Puntarenas you'll pay about $4, and from San José to Quepos or Manuel Antonio you'll pay about $7.

A comfortable, air-conditioned alternative to regular bus service to Montezuma, Tambor, Puntarenas, Punta Leona, Playa Herradura, Jacó, Manuel Antonio, and some destinations in between is the hotel-to-hotel shuttle service offered by Gray Line, which serves Jacó and Manuel Antonio. Prices from San José are $27 to Jacó and $35 to Manuel Antonio, and there are departures every morning and afternoon. You can request that vans to Jacó drop you off at Carara National Park. Vans to Manuel Antonio can drop you off at Playa Hermosa's hotels. There is also once-daily service connecting Jacó and Manuel Antonio to the major North Pacific beaches, Monteverde, and Arenal; rates range from $35 to $45.

ESSENTIALS

Bus Contacts Gray Line (☎ *2220–2126 or 2643–3231* 🌐 *www.graylinecostarica.com*).

THE SOUTHERN NICOYA TIP

Reached by a one-hour ferry ride from Puntarenas, the southern tip of the Nicoya Peninsula is one of Costa Rica's less-developed regions, where some of the country's most gorgeous beaches, rain forests, waterfalls, and tidal pools lie at the end of some of its worst roads. Within the region are quiet, well-preserved parks where you can explore pristine forests or travel by boat or sea kayak to idyllic islands for bird-watching or snorkeling. Other outdoor options include horseback riding, gliding through the treetops on a canopy tour, or surfing on some of the country's most consistent waves. In the laid-back beach towns of Montezuma, Santa Teresa, and Malpaís, an international cast of surfers, nature lovers, and expatriate massage therapists live out their dreams in paradise.

PUNTARENAS

110 km/68 mi west of San José.

A docking point for international cruise ships and the launching pad for ferries heading southeast to the coast of the Nicoya Peninsula, Puntarenas could easily be relegated to what you see from your car as you roll through town. Unless you're waiting to catch the ferry, there's really no reason to stay in Puntarenas. Parts of its urban beach look almost like a Dumpster. How this stretch of shoreline got a Blue Flag for cleanliness is a mystery. Nonetheless, it's a city with a past as an affluent port town and principal vacation spot for San José's wealthy, who arrived by train in the last century. Once the port was moved and roads opened to other beaches, Puntarenas's economy crashed. Recent attempts by politicians and hotel owners to create tourism-boosting diversions have been unsuccessful thus far. But if you have some downtime here, head for the Paseo de los Turistas, a beachfront promenade lined with concrete benches. From this narrow spit of sand—*punta de arenas* literally means "point of sand"—which protrudes into the Gulf of Nicoya, you get impressive sunsets and vistas of the Nicoya Peninsula. On days when cruise ships arrive, local artisans sell their wares at a market near the dock.

GETTING HERE AND AROUND

The drive from San José to Puntarenas takes about two hours. From downtown San José, take the Pan-American Highway (CA1) west toward the airport, then continue west on CA1 for another 90 minutes to the turnoff for Puntarenas. From here it's another 15 minutes to the ferry dock. Buses run every hour between San José and Puntarenas. If you travel to Puntarenas by bus, take a taxi to the ferry dock.

Ferries shuttle passengers between Puntarenas and Paquera on the Nicoya Peninsula, where they are met by buses bound for Cóbano, Montezuma, and Santa Teresa. The passenger and car ferries run by **Naviera Tambor** (☎*2661–2084*) depart both Puntarenas and Paquera at 5, 7:30, and 10 AM, and 12:30, 3, 5:30, and 10 PM. The trip takes about 60 minutes.

Asociación de Desarrollo Integral Paquera (☎*2641–0118*) runs a small passenger-only ferry that departs from behind Puntarenas Mercado daily at 11:30 AM and 4 PM, with return trips at 7:30 AM and 2 PM. The trip takes 90 minutes.

ESSENTIALS

Bank/ATM Banco de Costa Rica (*BCR* ✉*100 m north of municipal market*). **Banco Nacional** (✉*200 m west of municipal market* ☎*2661–0233*). **Mutual Alajuela ATH** (✉*Across from Ferretería Tung Sing, near municipal market*).

Hospital Hospital Monseñor Sanabria (*8 km/5 mi east of Puntarenas* ☎*2663–0033*).

Pharmacy Farmacia Andrea (✉*75 m east of Victoria Park* ☎*2661–2866*).

Internet Millennium Cyber Café (✉*Paseo de Los Turistas, east of Hotel Tioga* ☎*2661–4759*).

Post Office Correos (✉*Avda. 3, near Parque Victoria*).

Tourist Information La Camara de Turismo (✉*Plaza de las Artesanías, in front of Muelle de Cruceros* ☎*2661–2980* *Weekdays 8–12:30 and 1:30–5:30; weekends when cruise ships are in port*). **La Oficina de Información Turistica** (✉*Near car ferry terminal* ☎*2661–9011* *Daily 8–5*).

WHERE TO EAT AND STAY

$–$$ ECLECTIC ✕ **Gugas.** Simple but elegant, Gugas receives high praise from locals for its fine dining alfresco. "Chicken of the Sea" (fish stuffed with shrimp and spices), pasta dishes, vegetarian options, seafood, and meat plates are all on the menu of this German-owned restaurant. ✉*100 m north of the cruise-ship port or 100 m from the bus terminal, across from the fishing pier* ☎*2661–4231* ▭*AE, DC, MC, V.*

$–$$ COSTA RICAN ✕ **Restaurante La Yunta.** In a 1928 wooden building that originally served as a vacation home for San José's upper class, this old-fashioned steak house is presided over by mounted ox heads (*yunta* means "a yoked pair of oxen"). Seating is on a large veranda with a view of the ocean and of passersby strolling down the Paseo de los Turistas. The specialty is *churrasco* (tenderloin), but the diverse menu includes seafood dishes like lobster and sea bass cooked 10 different ways. The liquor list is impressively long. ✉*West end of Paseo de los Turistas, east of Hotel Tioga* ☎*2661–3216* ▭*AE, DC, MC, V.*

$$ **Hotel Las Brisas.** Close to the ferry docks, this white, three-story motel-style building wraps around its pool, where the views of the sun setting over the Nicoya Peninsula are terrific. Superior rooms have balconies with views of the ocean, and a few of them also have Jacuzzis. Standard rooms on the third floor cost a little bit more, but they are worth it for the ocean view. Pictures of Greece taken by the owner hang in the hallways and a few rooms. The restaurant menu ($$–$$$) reflects the owners' nationalities with Greek-influenced seafood and meat and some Mexican dishes. **Pros:** ocean views; decent restaurant. **Cons:** expensive, considering location; plain rooms. ✉ *West end of Paseo de los Turistas* ☎ *2661–4040* 🌐 *www.lasbrisashotelcr.com* *19 rooms* *In-room: safe some), Wi-Fi some). In-hotel: restaurant, room service, bar, pool, gym, laundry service, Wi-Fi* 💳 *AE, DC, MC, V* *BP.*

$–$$ **Hotel Tioga.** Across the street from a tree-filled park and the cleanest part of the city's beach, Hotel Tioga opened in 1959 and is run by the original owner's son. Face-lifts over the years have modernized it a bit, but it's still rather timeworn. Glimpses of the past hang in hallways of the first to third floors with black-and-white photographs of Puntarenas in the early 1900s. Your best bets are the 11 "executive" guest rooms upstairs, with balconies overlooking the gulf, pleasantly decorated with colorful, tropical prints and heavy varnished dark-wood furniture. Rooms around the courtyard, which holds a small pool, can

CLOSE UP

A Darker Side of Tourism

Despite Costa Rica's relative affluence in Central America—in large part because of its thriving tourism industry—the fact remains that 10% of the country's population still lives in poverty. And although burgeoning tourism has benefited portions of the population, it has manifested itself in less fortunate ways in more impoverished sectors of society by giving rise to a sex-for-sale trade that some experts say rivals that in Thailand.

The case is bleak for impoverished Costa Ricans, but is worst for women and young girls. Forty percent of girls do not attend school, and 41% of births in Costa Rica are to unwed mothers. Prostitution is legal for those over 18 in Costa Rica, but pimping is not, and prostitution of minors certainly is not. There are no statistics on the number of minors involved in prostitution, but it's clear from the many Web sites promoting travel to Costa Rica as a sex-tourism paradise with plenty of young girls available that the problem is ongoing. In 1996 the National Institute for Children (PANI) targeted Limón, San José, and Puntarenas as the places where poor children are most susceptible to entering into prostitution.

In 2004 the U.S. Human Trafficking Report listed Costa Rica as one of the world's worst offenders in the trafficking of women and children into prostitution. To their credit, the administrations of Presidents Abel Pacheco and Oscar Arias have taken steps to combat the problem of the underage sex trade, a refreshing change from their predecessor, Miguel Angel Rodríguez, who famously denied in an interview on the ABC News program *20/20* in 2001 that such a problem existed. Steps taken thus far have included crackdowns on brothels, closer surveillance, harsher penalties for offenders, and a Web site that lists photos of missing children.

be noisy. The second-floor restaurant is open to cool breezes off the gulf. **Pros:** good value; across street from beach. **Cons:** timeworn; a bit cramped; busy on weekends. ✉ *Paseo de los Turistas, 8 blocks west of dock* ☎ *2661–0271* 🌐 *www.hoteltioga.com* *52 rooms* *In-room: safe. In-hotel: restaurant, bar, pool, laundry service, Wi-Fi* ▭ *AE, DC, MC, V* 🍽 *BP.*

EN ROUTE

If you take the ferry from Puntarenas to the southern tip of the Nicoya Peninsula, you'll arrive at a ferry dock 5 km (3 mi) north of the small community of **Paquera.** The only reason to stop here is to pick up supplies or fill up your tank on the way to the beach.

CURÚ NATIONAL WILDLIFE REFUGE

7 km/4½ mi south of Paquera, 1½ to 2 hrs southwest of Puntarenas by ferry.

Established by former farmer and logger-turned-conservationist Frederico Schutt in 1933, Refugio Nacional de Vida Silvestre Curú was named after the indigenous word for the pochote trees that flourish here. Trails lead through the forest and mangrove swamps where you see hordes of phantom crabs on the beach, howler and white-faced capuchin monkeys in the trees, and plenty of hummingbirds, kingfishers, woodpeckers, trogons, and manakins (including the coveted long-tailed manakin). The refuge is working to reintroduce spider monkeys and scarlet macaws into the wild. Some very basic accommodations, originally designed for students and researchers, are available by the beach ($8 per person); call ahead to arrange for lodging, guides, horseback riding, and early-morning bird-watching walks. ✉ *7 km/4½ mi south of Paquera on road to Cóbano, left side of road* ☎ *2641–0100* 🌐 *www.curuwildliferefuge.com* 🎫 *$8* 🕑 *Daily 7–3.*

HABLA INGLES?

Although some Central Pacific areas like Jacó and Manuel Antonio are very touristy, don't assume everyone speaks English. Taxi and bus drivers often won't understand your directions in English. To make traveling smoother, write down the name of the place you're headed to or ask someone at your hotel's reception desk to write out directions in Spanish, which you can pass on with a smile to your driver.

DID YOU KNOW?

The land that is now Curú National Wildlife Refuge was once owned by the Pacific Lumber Company, which logged the area's rosewood, cedar, and mahogany trees. Thanks to its protected status, the area is now home to more than 230 species of birds, 78 species of mammals, and 500 species of plants.

GETTING HERE AND AROUND

From the town of Paquera it's a short drive to Curú National Wildlife Refuge. You can also take a bus bound for Cóbano, asking the driver to drop you off at the refugio.

OUTDOOR ACTIVITIES

Curu Tourism (✉ *Main road, across from Esso station* ☎ *2641–0004* 🌐 *www.curutourism.com*) gives horseback tours of the refuge ($16) and also has a ride to sparkling-white Quesera Beach ($16). The company also offers inexpensive kayaking trips ($26) and tours to Isla Tortuga ($23).

EN ROUTE

Paquera is the closest city to Tambor, but if you're headed to Montezuma or Malpaís, you'll pass through **Cóbano,** 12 km (7½ mi) southwest of Tambor. The town has a supermarket, gas station, and Banco Nacional with the area's only ATM.

PLAYA TAMBOR AREA

27 km/17 mi south of Paquera.

Known for massive, all-inclusive hotels and housing developments, Playa Tambor runs along the large half-moon Bahía Ballena, whose waters are more placid than those of other beaches on Nicoya's southern tip. Playa Tambor is one of the country's least attractive beaches, although there are two small but lovely ones to the south. The tiny fishing village hasn't developed as much as Montezuma or Malpaís, which makes it a better destination for those who want to get away from the crowds. It can serve as a convenient base for fishing excur-

Isla Tortuga, just off the coast near Curú National Wildlife Refuge.

sions, horseback-riding trips, and day trips to Curú National Wildlife Refuge and Isla Tortuga.

GETTING HERE AND AROUND

You can fly directly to Tambor from San José on SANSA and Nature Air. Taxis meet every flight and can take you to a nearby hotel ($10 to $15), to Montezuma ($30), or to Malpaís ($40).

ESSENTIALS

Internet Compu-Office del Pacífico (✉ *In small strip mall on left after Costa Coral Hotel, coming from Paquera* ☎ *2683–0582* ⏲ *9–7*).

OUTDOOR ACTIVITIES

Unlike other beach towns, Tambor doesn't have tour operators on every corner or rental shops of any kind—not even for a basic bike. The receptionist at your hotel can set up tours of the area's diverse natural attractions.

FISHING In the open sea off the Gulf of Nicoya, sailfish, marlin, tuna, and wahoo are in abundance from November to March. Local fishermen in small boats are your best guides to finding fish in the gulf, including snapper, sea bass, and jacks, almost year-round. Prices for inshore fishing range from $250 for half-day trips to $500 for full-day excursions. Tambor's best deep-sea fishing boat is the 29-foot *Phoenix*, owned by **End of the Line Sportfishing** (✉ *Road from Paquera, just before Playa Tambor's entrance* ☎ *2683–0453* ✉ *endofthelinefishing@yahoo.com*). Captain Robert Ranck offers full-day excursions ($750) or half-day trips that last around five hours ($450). The boat carries six people. Lunch, drinks, and fishing gear are included.

HIKING An easy and quick excursion from Tambor is the 1-km (½-mi) hike south of town to the secluded beach of Palo de Jesús. From the town's dock, follow the road south until it becomes a shady trail that winds its way over rocks and sand around Punta Piedra Amarilla. The trees along the way resound with squawks of parakeets and the throaty utterings of male howler monkeys.

HORSEBACK RIDING Both the Hotel Tambor Tropical and the Tango Mar have their own stables and offer a selection of horseback tours that can take you down trails through the rain forest or down to the beach to see an array of wildlife. Set off early in the morning or late in the afternoon, when it is cooler and you are more likely to see birds and animals. Tours range from $30 to $60, depending on the duration.

WHERE TO EAT

$ SEAFOOD ✕ **Bahía Ballena Yacht Club.** Get fishing tips—as well as the catch of the day grilled or served with butter and garlic—at this dockside fishermen's haunt. The menu is small, but has shrimp and lobster prepared several ways, a few salads, and other light fare. The square central bar is cooled by several ceiling fans, making a cold beer that much more appealing in the heat of the afternoon. The pool table provides entertainment for tourists and locals alike. ✉ *First left after main entrance to Playa Tambor* ☎ *2683–0213* ▭ *MC, V.*

$–$$ SWISS ✕ **Beach Combers.** Between the row of private residences built along Playa Tambor is this restaurant that serves a dozen different pasta dishes, cheese fondue, and chicken *cordon bleu,* among other international plates. Surrounded by thick foliage, tables are arranged on an open-air terrace area beneath a white stucco building. The restaurant is a couple of minutes from town on foot along the beach. ✉ *In Tambor, across from the ocean on the main street.* ☎ *2683–0152* ▭ *MC, V.*

$ ITALIAN ★ ✕ **Trattoria Mediterránea.** This colorful restaurant in an old wooden house is often packed with local epicureans who come to savor the homemade pastas, thin-crust pizzas, and fresh seafood. The young Italian owners, Maurizio and Sandra, welcome guests with complimentary bruschetta made with fresh-baked bread, and everything is made to order, so the food can take awhile to arrive. They offer a selection of about a dozen pizzas and authentic dishes such as linguine *con gamberi* (with shrimp), *scaloppini con esparagi* (chicken medallions with asparagus) and *pescado de la trattoria* (baked fish with olive oil, lemon, garlic, and spices). ✉ *On left after main entrance to Playa Tambor* ☎ *2683–0400* ✍ *Reservations essential* ▭ *MC, V* ⊙ *Closed Mon. (and Tues. in low season) and end of Sept. to end of Oct. No lunch.*

WHERE TO STAY

$ **Costa Coral del Pacifico.** On the road from Paquera, a few meters from Tambor's entrance, stands this festive blue-and-orange hotel with spacious and tastefully decorated Mexican-theme rooms. Those with terraces face the pool and hot-tub area, and all have well-kept kitchenettes. The top floor holds a restaurant and bar, with karaoke on Thursday night. The beach lies about 300 meters (1,000 feet) away. This place makes for a good overnight stop on your way to or from Paquera. **Pros:** wonderful staff; clean. **Cons:** very out of the way; little English spoken. ✉ *Road to Cóbano, 200 m from Tambor's cemetery, left-hand side* ☎ *2683–0105 or 2683–0280* *10 rooms* *In-room: kitchen. In-hotel: restaurant, bar, pool, laundry service* ▭ *MC, V* *BP.*

$$$ **Tambor Tropical.** Though a stone's throw from the beach, this small hotel isn't a great place for beach lovers, because it isn't a great beach. But it is a convenient base for anyone interested in sportfishing or horseback riding, or for those who simply seek an intimate setting in which to loll by the pool. The attractive, spacious suites have floors, ceilings, walls, and even toilet seats made of varnished tropical hardwoods. The large windows running across the front give them a great view of the sea and surrounding gardens—second-floor rooms have the best. Platform beds provide sunrise views. The sea breeze and ceiling fans cool the rooms better than air-conditioning, and the lack of televisions inspires rest and relaxation. Meals are served by a lovely, blue-tile pool or in the thatch dining room during the rainy months; on Monday they have a popular barbecue. **Pros:** lovely rooms; tranquil. **Cons:** not on nice beach; no a/c in rooms. ✉ *Main street of Tambor, turn left at beach* ☎ *2683–0011, 866/890–2537 in U.S.* *www.tambortropical.com* *12 suites* *In-room: no a/c, no phone, kitchen, no TV, Wi-Fi. In-hotel: restaurant, room service, bar, pool, beachfront, laundry service, no kids under 16* ▭ *AE, MC, V* *CP.*

$$$ Fodor's Choice ★ **Tango Mar Resort.** This idyllic resort south of Tambor was featured on the TV series *Temptation Island*. The 150-acre grounds include a small 9-hole golf course, exuberant gardens, tropical forests, and stunning Playa Quitzales, a beach lined with coconut palms and lush foliage. There is a large rock reef just offshore, and an impressive waterfall on the beach a short hike away. Colorful villas with two to five bedrooms and ample porches overlook the beach. Smaller suites are housed in raised octagonal wooden bungalows with whirlpool tubs and ocean views. The standard rooms are in a three-story concrete building that is a stone's throw from the surf. Two restaurants serve Costa Rican and Continental cuisine. On-site activities include snorkeling, horseback riding, hiking through a private nature reserve, and golf (greens fee $20). They also offer a dozen tours to nearby attractions, as well as sportfishing excursions. **Pros:** gorgeous setting; friendly; quiet; lots of activity options. **Cons:** not the place for partyers; hard to get to. ✥ *3 km/2 mi south of Tambor* *Apdo. 1–1260, Escaz* ☎ *2683–0001* *www.tangomar.com* *18 rooms, 17 suites, 4 villas* *In-room: safe, kitchen some), refrigerator. In-hotel: 2 restaurants, bars, golf course, tennis courts, pools, spa, beachfront, water sports, bicycles, laundry service, Internet terminal, Wi-Fi* ▭ *AE, DC, MC, V* *BP.*

ISLA TORTUGA

90 mins by boat from Puntarenas.

Soft white sand and casually leaning palms fringe this island of tropical dry forest off the southern coast of the Nicoya Peninsula. Sounds heavenly? It would be if there weren't quite so many people. Tours from Jacó, Herradura, San José, Puntarenas, and Montezuma take boatfuls of visitors to drink from coconuts and snorkel around a large rock. You'll see a good number of colorful fish, though in the company of many tourists. But it does make for an easy day trip out to sea. On the boat ride from Playa Tambor or Montezuma you might spot passing dolphins. A 40-minute hiking trail wanders past monkey ladders, strangler figs, bromeliads, orchids, and the fruit-bearing *guanabana* (soursop) and *marañón* (cashew) trees up to a lookout point with amazing vistas. Though state owned, the island is leased and inhabited by a Costa Rican family. Day trips here cost $17 to $99, depending on the duration and departure point.

GETTING HERE AND AROUND

Every tour operator in Playa Tambor and Montezuma *(⇨ below)* offers trips to Isla Tortuga, one of the area's biggest attractions, or you can kayak from the nearby Curú National Wildlife Refuge. Admission to the island is $7 (included in tour prices).

OUTDOOR ACTIVITIES

KAYAKING **Curu Tourism** (✉ *Main road, across from Esso station* ☎ *2641–0004* 🌐 *www.curutourism.com*) arranges year-round kayak excursions to Isla Tortuga for $23, including entrance fee to the island. Snorkeling equipment is available for an additional fee. **Calypso Cruises Island Tours** (☎ *2256–2727* 🌐 *www.calypsocruises.com*) takes you to Isla Tortuga from San José, Jacó, Manuel Antonio, or anywhere in between with bus and boat transportation included ($119, kids under six $65).

MONTEZUMA

7 km/4½ mi southeast of Cóbano, 45 km/28 mi south of Paquera, 18 km/11 mi south of Tambor.

Beautifully positioned on a sandy bay, Montezuma is hemmed in by a precipitous wooded shoreline that has prevented the overdevelopment that has affected so many other beach towns. Its small, funky town center is a pastel cluster of New Age health-food cafés, trendy beachwear shops, jaunty tour kiosks, noisy open-air bars, and older *sodas* (casual eateries). Most hotels are clustered in or around the town's center, but the best ones are on the coast to the north and south, where the loudest revelers are the howler monkeys in the nearby forest. The beaches north of town, especially Playa Grande, are lovely.

Montezuma has been on the international vagabond circuit for years, attracting backpackers and alternative-lifestyle types. At night, the center of town often fills up with tattooed travelers and artisans who drink in the street and entertain each other and passersby. When college students are on break, the place can be a zoo.

North and south of the town center, however, are always quiet, and the attractions here include swaths of tropical dry forest, waterfalls, and beautiful virgin beaches that stretch across one national park and two nature preserves. One especially good walk (about 2½ hours) or horseback ride leads to a small waterfall called El Chorro that pours into the sea, where there is a small tidal pool at lower tides.

Jumping through one of the two waterfalls in Montezuma.

GETTING HERE AND AROUND

Most people get here via the ferry from Puntarenas to Paquera, which is an hour's drive from Montezuma. The quickest way to get here, however, is to fly to nearby Tambor *(Air Travel Travel Smart Costa Rica)* ⇨ *in*. One of the taxis waiting at the airstrip will take you to Montezuma for $35, about a 1½-hour drive. There are also one-hour water taxis ($35) that travel every morning between Herradura, near Jacó, and Montezuma, departing from Montezuma at 6:30 and 9:30 AM, and Herradura at 7:45 and 10:45 AM.

ESSENTIALS

ATM Banco Nacional (✉ *Main road, C⊠bano* ☎ *2642–0210*).

Internet Surf the Banana Internet Café (✉ *Main road, next to El Sano Banano* ☎ *2642–0944*).

Post Office Librería Topsy (✉ *Next door to school*).

OUTDOOR ACTIVITIES

In Montezuma it seems that every other storefront is occupied by a tour operator. The town's oldest and most experienced tour company, **Cocozuma Traveller** (✉ *Main road, next to El Sano Banano* ☎ *2642–0911* 🌐 *www.cocozumacr.com*), offers horseback riding to a beachfront waterfall ($40), a full-day snorkeling trip to Isla Tortuga with lunch ($50), various sportfishing options ($170–$750), scuba diving ($120–$200), and a canopy tour ($40).

★ Hiking is one of the best ways to explore Montezuma's natural treasures, including beaches, lush coastline, jungles, and waterfalls. There are plenty of options around town or in nearby parks and reserves. Just over a bridge, 10 minutes south of town, a slippery path patrolled by howler monkeys leads upstream to two waterfalls and a fun swimming hole. If you value your life, don't jump or dive from the waterfalls. Guides from any tour operator in town can escort you, but save your money. This one you can do on your own. To reach the beachfront waterfall called **El Chorro,** head left from the main beach access and hike about two hours to the north of town along the sand and through the woods behind the rocky points. The trip takes you across seven adjacent beaches, on one of which there is a small store where you can buy soft drinks. Bring water and good sunblock. El Chorro can also be reached on a horseback tour with a local tour operator.

WHERE TO EAT

$–$$ ECLECTIC ✕ **Cocolores.** Follow the line of multicolor lanterns to this open-air eatery. The simple wooden tables are on a patio bordered with gardens or, during the drier months, on the beach. The Italian and Argentine owners serve an eclectic menu ranging from shrimp curry to seafood pasta to tenderloin with porcini mushrooms. They also have a good selection of pizzas. ✉ *Behind Hotel Pargo Feliz* ☎ *2642–0348* ▭ *AE, DC, MC, V* ⊙ *Closed Mon. and Oct. No lunch June–Dec.*

$$ ECLECTIC ✕ **El Sano Banano Restaurant.** Freshly caught seafood, organic chicken, sushi, Thai dishes, and a half-dozen pasta dishes are included on the menu at Montezuma's first natural-food restaurant. Named after the dried bananas sold by the owners, the eatery serves mostly vegetarian fare, including some excellent salads. On the terrace, which is a popular people-watching spot, you can enjoy a delicious Mocha Chiller, made with frozen yogurt, or a wide variety of coffee drinks. A battalion of ceiling fans keeps the air moving in the spacious, adobe-style dining room. A free movie is shown nightly at 7:30 in the dining room, which is a popular diversion, but don't expect a romantic dinner during this time. Rooms to rent on the second floor are a comfortable option if the other hotels are full. ✉ *Main road* ☎ *2642–0944* ▭ *AE, MC, V.*

$$$ ITALIAN Fodor's Choice ★ ✕ **Playa de los Artistas.** This open-air restaurant with driftwood tables scattered along the beach specializes in modern Mediterranean-style seafood, meat dishes, and pizza. Flickering lanterns combine with crashing surf to create a romantic and relaxed dinner experience. Portions are plentiful and dramatically presented on huge platters. The eclectic menu changes daily, and on weekends they fire up a barbecue. An outdoor, coffee-wood oven gives a tropical aroma to pizza, fish, and pork. Meals are accompanied with freshly baked, savory focaccia. ✉ *275 m south of town, near Los Mangos Hotel, C bano* ☎ *2642–0920* ▭ *No credit cards* ⊙ *Closed Sun., mid-May–mid-June, and mid-Sept.–mid-Nov.*

$$–$$$ ECLECTIC ★ ✕ **Ylang-Ylang Restaurant.** One of Montezuma's best restaurants, Ylang-Ylang is nestled between the beach and the jungle. The lunch menu—a selection of sushi, salads, and sandwiches—makes it well worth the 10-minute walk down the beach. The inventive dinner menu ranges from a Thai-style teriyaki tuna steak and stir-fries to penne in a seafood sauce. There are also various vegan and raw live dishes. Whatever you choose, you'll want to save room for one of the scrumptious desserts, such as the tiramisu espresso crepe. At night, they provide free transportation from the Sano Banano, in town. ✉ *On beach, ½ km/¼*

7

mi north of town, at Ylang-Ylang Beach Resort ☎*2642–0636* ▭*AE, DC, MC, V.*

WHERE TO STAY

¢–$$ **Hotel Amor de Mar.** About ½ km (¼ mi) south of town, this ruggedly handsome hotel sits across from the entrance to Montezuma's famous waterfall. A grassy lawn stretches to the rocky seashore, where you can cool off in a natural tidal pool at low tide or lounge about in one of the palm-shaded hammocks. The place has a peaceful and intimate atmosphere in which to savor the homemade breakfasts served each morning. Wood-panel rooms are rustic but comfortable; second-floor rooms have more windows. Two rooms share a bathroom and are considerably cheaper. The two-story oceanfront houses next door have four bedrooms, making them great for larger groups. **Pros:** beautiful property; friendly. **Cons:** most of the rooms are small; can be a little worn. ✉*300 m south of town, past bridge* ☎*2642–0262* ⊕*www.amordemar.com* *11 rooms, 9 with bath; 2 houses* *In-room: no a/c (some), no phone, no TV. In-hotel: restaurant* ▭*MC, V* *EP.*

$$ **Hotel El Jardín.** Spread across a hill several blocks from the beach, this hotel has rooms with ocean, pool, and garden views. True to its name, the rooms are scattered around a lush garden populated with bright red ginger flowers and faux stone indigenous sculptures. Teak paneling and furniture, stained-glass pictorial panels, and terraces with hammocks give this hotel style as well as comfort. If you don't mind the climb, ask for an upper room and you'll get a better view. There's no formal breakfast, but fresh fruit and coffee are laid out in the reception area each morning. **Pros:** central location; good value. **Cons:** noise from bars in town; pricey. ✉*West end of main road* ☎*2642–0074* ⊕*www.hoteleljardin.com* *15 rooms, 2 villas* *In-room: no phone, refrigerator, no TV. In-hotel: pools* ▭*AE, DC, MC, V* *EP.*

¢–$$ ★ **Hotel Los Mangos.** Within sight and sound of the sea, these affordable octagonal wood bungalows are spread across a shady mango grove. Hammocks and rocking chairs furnish the wraparound decks on each. Less attractive, though cheaper, are the rooms in a two-story, orange-and-blue building by the road. Here you'll find verandas and rocking chairs facing the sea. Four of the second-floor rooms share baths, for half the price. The secluded, scenic pool with a waterfall overlooks the ocean. Memorable yoga classes are given in an open-air pavilion. **Pros:** great pool; lots of wildlife. **Cons:** noisy; needs updating. ✉*Near entrance to waterfall trail, ½ km/¼ mi south of town* ☎*2642–0076* ⊕*www.hotellosmangos.com* *10 rooms, 6 with bath; 9 bungalows* *In-room: no a/c, no phone, refrigerator (some), no TV. In-hotel: pool* ▭*AE, DC, MC, V* *EP.*

$$ **Nature Lodge Finca los Caballos.** A dirt road leads to this cozy equestrian paradise high on a hill, just a short ride from Montezuma center. Horses graze on the 14-acre estate when they aren't taking guests to nearby waterfalls, mountains, or beaches. The open-air restaurant and pool terrace have bird's-eye views of the ocean and the surrounding valley. The small, simple rooms have pastel walls decorated with stencils of lizards and frogs; all have hammocks in front. Only four have forest views, so ask for one of these when you reserve. Massages and other spa services

Enjoying a snack at Playa De Los Artistas restaurant in Montezuma.

are available to guests. **Pros:** clean rooms; relaxing ambience. **Cons:** not a great location; no screens on the windows. *⊕3 km/2 mi north of Montezuma on main road ☎📠2642–0124 🌐www.naturelodge.net ⇆12 rooms ♂In-room: no a/c, no phone, safe, refrigerator, no TV. In-hotel: restaurant, bar, pool, laundry service, no-smoking rooms ▭AE, MC, V ⊙Closed Oct. ¦◎¦BP*

$$–$$$ Fodor'sChoice ★ **Ylang-Ylang Beach Resort.** Secluded and quiet, this tropical resort with a holistic slant is a 10-minute beach walk from town. Nestled between the sea and a lush forest, the geodesic-dome bungalows are snug but charming, with outdoor showers and terraces. Some have sea views and cozy loft sleeping areas. Facing the beach, a three-story building has two-story suites with balconies and simple but colorful standard rooms below. Rustic "jungalows"—large tents with beds and decks—offer a back-to-nature experience, but they share bathrooms. The grounds are covered with trees that hold iguanas, howler monkeys, tricolor squirrels, and an array of birds. Adding to the romance is a jungle-fringed pool with a waterfall. Yoga classes and spa services are offered, and a restaurant with tables under the stars serves some of the tastiest fusion dishes in Montezuma. **Pros:** gorgeous, natural setting; great restaurant; friendly. **Cons:** jungalows offer limited privacy; some rooms are small. *⊠700 m north of school in Montezuma 📫El Sano Banano, Montezuma ☎2642–0636 🌐www.elbanano.com ⇆3 rooms, 3 suites, 8 beachfront bungalows, 6 tents ♂In-room: no a/c (some), no phone, safe, refrigerator (some), no TV. In-hotel: restaurant, bar, pool, beachfront, water sports, laundry service, Internet terminal, Wi-Fi ▭AE, MC, V ¦◎¦MAP.*

NIGHTLIFE

Though options are extremely limited, Montezuma's nightlife scene is growing. Locals and foreigners mix at pool tables or late-night clubs, a refreshing change from larger beach towns where the clientele tends to be more segregated. Street-side artisans selling their creations often animate the area with drumming and dancing that draws passersby to stop and shake their hips, too.

Chico's Bar (✉ *Next to Hotel Moctezuma*) blasts music from its dark, uninviting entrance, but farther back is a brighter, spacious deck with pool tables and dancing. Directly behind is an open-air beach bar with a more laid-back atmosphere. The bar at **Restaurante Moctezuma** (✉ *Under Hotel Moctezuma* ☎ *2643–0657*) serves the cheapest beers in town. At night, tables in the sand are lighted by candles and moonlight.

SHOPPING

Beachwear, banana paper, wooden crafts, and indigenous pottery are some of what you find in colorful shops in the town's center. During the dry season, traveling artisans from around the world unfold their street-side tables just before the sun begins to set; candles light up the handmade leather-and-seed jewelry, dream catchers, and knit tops. For some intellectual stimulation at the beach, head to **Librería Topsy** (✉ *Next door to school* ☎ *2642–0576*), where you can buy, exchange, or rent a book—one whole room is devoted to a lending library. Some foreign newspapers are available.

CABO BLANCO ABSOLUTE NATURE PRESERVE

10 km/6 mi southwest of Montezuma, about 11 km/7 mi south of Malpaís.

Conquistadores named this area Cabo Blanco on account of its white earth and cliffs, but it was a more benevolent pair of foreigners—Nicolas Wessberg and his wife, Karen, arriving here from Sweden in the 1950s—who made it a preserve (Reserva Natural Absoluta Cabo Blanco, in Spanish). Appalled by the first clear-cut in the Cabo Blanco area in 1960, the pioneering couple launched an international appeal to save the forest. In time their efforts led not only to the creation of the 12-square-km (4½-square-mi) reserve but also to the founding of Costa Rica's national park service, the National Conservation Areas System (SINAC). Wessberg was murdered on the Osa Peninsula in 1975 while researching the area's potential as a national park. A reserve just outside Montezuma was named in his honor. A reserve has also been created to honor his wife, who dedicated her life to conservation after her husband's death.

Informative natural-history captions dot the trails in the moist evergreen forest of Cabo Blanco. Look for the sapodilla trees, which produce a white latex used to make gum; you can often see V-shaped scars where the trees have been cut to allow the latex to run into containers placed at the base. Wessberg catalogued a full array of animals here: porcupine, hog-nosed skunk, spotted skunk, gray fox, anteater, cougar, and jaguar. Resident birds include brown pelicans, white-throated magpies, toucans, cattle egrets, green herons, parrots, and blue-crowned motmots.

A fairly strenuous 4-km (2½-mi) hike, which takes about two hours in each direction, follows a trail from the reserve entrance to **Playa Cabo Blanco.** The beach is magnificent, with hundreds of pelicans flying in formation and paddling in the calm waters offshore—you can wade right in and join them. Off the tip of the cape is the 7,511-square-foot **Isla Cabo Blanco,** with pelicans, frigate birds, brown boobies, and an abandoned lighthouse. As a strict reserve, Cabo Blanco has restrooms and a visitor center but no other tourist facilities. Rangers and volunteers act as guides. ✉ *10 km/6 mi southwest of Montezuma via Cabuya* ☎ *2642–0093* 🎫 *$8* ⏲ *Wed.–Sun. 8–4.*

GETTING HERE AND AROUND

Roads to the reserve are usually passable only in the dry season, unless you have a 4WD. From Montezuma or Malpaís, take the road to Cabuya. Taxis can take you to or from Montezuma, but buses toward the park also leave from Montezuma daily at 8 and 9:50 AM and 2 PM, returning at 9 AM, and 1 and 4 PM.

MALPAÍS AND SANTA TERESA

12 km/7½ mi southwest of Cóbano, 52 km/33 mi south of Paquera.

This remote fishing area was once frequented only by die-hard surfers in search of some of the country's largest waves and by naturalists en route to the nearby Cabo Blanco Absolute Nature Preserve. The town and its miles of beach are accessible only down a steep and bumpy dirt road. But now hotels, restaurants, and shopping centers are springing up at an alarming rate, especially toward the Santa Teresa side. Still, the abundant forest, lovely beaches, and consistent surf make this a great place to spend some time.

Coming from Montezuma, the road hits an intersection, known locally as El Cruce, marked by hotel signs and a strip mall on the right. To the left is the rutted route to tranquil Malpaís, and to the right is the road to Santa Teresa, with plenty of hotels, restaurants, and shops. Playa Carmen, straight ahead, is the area's best place for surfing, though swimmers will want to be careful of rip currents there. Malpaís and Santa Teresa are so close that locals disagree on where one begins and the other ends. You could travel up the road parallel to the ocean that connects them and not realize you've moved from one town to the other.

GETTING HERE AND AROUND

From Paquera it's a 90-minute drive to Malpaís via Cóbano. After Cóbano, the road quickly deteriorates. It can become quite muddy in the rainy season, so you'll want a 4WD vehicle. There are no direct buses between Paquera and Malpaís; to get here you have to change buses in Cóbano. Taxis waiting at Tambor's airstrip will take up to four people to Malpaís for $40. The trip between Jacó and Malpaís takes about two hours, thanks to the daily boat service from Montezuma. **Tropical Tours** (✉ *North of El Cruce* ☎ *2640–1900*) can set you up with a shuttle to San José ($35), or a taxi and boat from Malpaís and to Jacó ($55).

7

ESSENTIALS

ATM Banco Nacional (✉ *Centro Comercial Playa Carmen* ☎ *2640–0598*).

Internet Tropical Tours (✉ *50 m north of El Cruce* ☎ *2640–1900*) has two Internet cafés in Santa Teresa.

Pharmacy Farmacia Amiga (✉ *Centro Comercial Playa Carmen* ☎ *2640–0463*).

WORD OF MOUTH

"I highly recommend the Malpais area. You can take a 30 minute flight to Tambor and then drive 30 minutes and you're there! There is a nice mix of Ticos and foreigners. It's not like many places that have been overly Americanized yet. It has natural beauty and amazing beaches. There is plenty to do there, too: You can fish, surf, canopy tour, hike, snorkel, and ATV ride through the jungle to go to Montezuma waterfalls. Also check out the nice local restaurants and bars at night." —siempretrvls

OUTDOOR ACTIVITIES

CANOPY TOUR **Canopy del Pacífico** (✉ *In front of fishermen's village* ☎ *2640–0360 or 8817–1679*) is the only canopy tour in the area ($35 for a two-hour, nine-platform tour). You can walk, glide, or rappel through 64 acres of forest. **Tropical Tours** (✉ *North of El Cruce* ☎ *2640–1900*) can set you up with a canopy tour, horseback-riding jaunt, or day trip to Isla Tortuga.

SURFING From November to May, the Malpaís area has some of Costa Rica's most consistent surf, as well as clear skies and winds that create idyllic conditions. **Playa Carmen** is the area's most consistent surf spot for all levels, and has dozens of beach breaks scattered along its shores. The sea grows rough and dirty during the May to December rainy season, with frequent swells that make it impossible to get out. **Playa Santa Teresa** is a better option when the waves at Playa Carmen are too gnarly. In Malpaís, at **Mar Azul**, more advanced surfers can try the break over a rock platform. **Corduroy to the Horizon** (✉ *20 m east of Playa Carmen* ☎ *2640–0173*), Malpaís's original surf shop, rents surfboards ($10 per day); arranges lessons ($30 per hour); and sells wax, boards, and beachwear.

WHERE TO EAT

$$$ SEAFOOD ★ ✕ **Nectar.** Resort Florblanca's alfresco restaurant by the pool has some tables that provide calming sea views through the tropical foliage. Fresh seafood is the specialty here, with inventive daily specials that focus on the day's catch. Asian and Mediterranean influences shine through in dishes ranging from spicy prawn fettuccine, to succulent pork ribs, to seared tuna with sweet Thai rice and braised bok choy. There's always a pizza of the day and a small sushi menu. ✉ *Resort Florblanca* ✣ *2 km/1 mi north of soccer field* ☎ *2640–0232* ✍ *Reservations essential* ▭ *AE, DC, MC, V.*

$ SEAFOOD ✕ **Piedra Mar.** With all the new restaurants popping up along the beach road, the favorite standby is still this old shack down on the beach. Tables and plastic chairs are set up under a corrugated tin roof, and the only decor is the rocky seascape, 10 feet away. Your shrimp or lobster (just $15) comes flavored with garlic and—on windy days—the sea spray crashing against the rocks. Sunset is popular with locals, so come early. Or come for breakfast at 7 and watch the early-morning sun lighting up the ocean. ✉ *275 m south of Blue Jay Lodge* ☎ *2640–0069* ▭ *No credit cards* ⊙ *Closed Sun.*

$ PIZZA ✕ **Pizzeria Playa Carmen.** This restaurant's location, under the trees on the area's most popular beach, makes it the perfect choice for lunch. It's extremely casual, so you don't even have to put on a shirt. Oven-baked pizza is the house specialty, and these thin-crust pies are big enough for two people, especially if you start with one of the oversize salads. The kitchen also serves shrimp scampi, various pastas, and other dishes. ✉ *Playa Carmen, east of El Cruce* ☎ *2640–0110* ▭ *No credit cards* ⊙ *Closed Tues. and Sept.–Nov.*

$$$ SEAFOOD ★ ✕ **Soma.** This small, tranquil restaurant within the Milarepa hotel serves delicious and creative Asian-inspired plates based on fresh local ingredients. The menu changes each night, but usually has fresh tuna, mahimahi, or other seafood, plus a chicken or beef dish. Any of the dishes can be prepared without meat, so vegetarians can choose from a wide selection. Tables are arranged under an open-air poolside deck a short walk from the beach. ✉ *Milarepa* ⊕ *2 km/1 mi north of soccer field* ☎ *2640–0023 or 2640–0663* ✍ *Reservations essential* ▭ *MC, V* ⊙ *Closed Oct.*

WHERE TO STAY

$ **Blue Jay Eco-Lodge.** Perched along a forested mountainside, these wooden bungalows feel like tree houses; you'll hear howler monkeys and an array of birdsong from your bed. Steep trails lead to the rustic aeries built on stilts, with screens for walls on three sides, comfortable beds, and balconies hung with hammocks. Once you drag your luggage up the hill, you will be rewarded with great views from the upper rooms. Blankets buffer you against the sometimes cool, breezy nights. Blue Jay's three lower cabins are larger, but lack the arboreal charm of the rest. Breakfast is in the open-air restaurant, next to an attractive, blue-tile pool. Head to the nearby beach, or climb the mountain trail behind the cabins, to look for birds. **Pros:** natural setting; good value. **Cons:** not well maintained; steep terrain. ✉ *From El Cruce, 800 m south toward Malpa s* ☎ *2640–0089 or 2640–0340* 📠 *2640–0141* 🌐 *www.bluejaylodgecostarica.com* *10 cabins* *In-room: no a/c, no phone, safe, no TV. In-hotel: pool, laundry service, no-smoking rooms* ▭ *AE, D, MC, V* *BP.*

$$$$ Fodor'sChoice ★ **Florblanca.** Named for the white flowers of the frangipani trees growing between the restaurant and the beach, this collection of luxurious villas is scattered through the forest mere steps from the surf. It's a tasteful, friendly resort dedicated to relaxation and rejuvenation. The wonderfully decorated and spacious villas have an Asian feel, especially in the outdoor Balinese-inspired bathrooms with rain showers and sunken tubs. Airy living rooms open onto porches with large hammocks. Most villas have one air-conditioned bedroom with a king-size bed; two-bedroom villas have a second room with twin beds. Only three villas have sea views through the trees, so request one of these when you book. Free yoga classes are given in a studio that faces the ocean, and the massage therapist at the beachfront spa will happily work out your kinks. The only TV is in a comfortable lounge. **Pros:** gorgeous villas and grounds; friendly; great yoga classes. **Cons:** very expensive; on

Santa Teresa beach, southern tip of the Nicoya Peninsula.

rocky stretch of beach; insects sometimes a problem. *2 km/1 mi north of soccer field* *Apdo. 131–5361, Cóbano* *2640–0232* *www.florblanca.com* *10 villas* *In-room: safe, refrigerator, no TV, Wi-Fi. In-hotel: restaurant, room service, bar, pools, gym, spa, beachfront, water sports, bicycles, laundry service, Internet terminal, Wi-Fi, no kids under 14* *AE, DC, MC, V* *EP.*

$$ **Luz de Vida.** This laid-back, beachfront lodge owned by a group of Israeli surfers is a good value. Simple bungalows, spread around forested grounds, have sloping wooden ceilings, lofts, a couch, or extra beds downstairs (kids under 10 stay free). Smaller standard rooms in two-story concrete buildings close to the road are not nearly as good a deal. The pool has a waterfall and is surrounded by trees, gardens, and thatch parasols. The open-air restaurant, nearby, has an ocean view and serves everything from falafel to filet mignon. Good waves break right in front of the hotel, so when the staff offers to arrange surfboard rentals and lessons, be sure to take them up on it. **Pros:** beachfront; nice grounds; friendly. **Cons:** service inconsistent; standard rooms too close to road. *From El Cruce, 800 m south toward Malpa s* *2640–0568 or 2640–0320* *www.luzdevida-resort.com* *6 bungalows, 8 rooms* *In-room: safe, refrigerator, no TV. In-hotel: restaurant, bar, pool, beachfront, water sports, laundry service, Wi-Fi* *MC, V* *EP.*

$$$ ★ **Milarepa.** Named after a Tibetan Buddhist saint who gained enlightenment in just one lifetime, Milarepa is a perfect place for peaceful renewal, whether romantic or spiritual. The four bamboo bungalows are spaced apart to ensure privacy and are furnished in ascetic but exquisite taste, with carved Indonesian wooden beds draped with mosquito netting, and bamboo armoires. Bathrooms are open to the sky,

with alcoves for Buddhist deities. Each bungalow has a veranda looking out onto the beach, shaded by a grove of palms and lined with volcanic rocks. Beachfront bungalows cost a bit more than those with ocean views set farther back. A large pool lies next to Soma (⇨*above*, the hotel's excellent restaurant [$$$]). **Pros:** secluded; small; beachfront; great restaurant. **Cons:** loosely managed; insects can be a problem; on rocky section of beach. *2 km/1 mi north of school, beside Resort Florblanca 2640–0023 www.milarepahotel.com 4 cottages In-room: no a/c, no phone, safe, no TV. In-hotel: restaurant, bar, pool, beachfront, water sports, laundry service, Wi-Fi, no-smoking rooms MC, V BP.*

¢ ★ **Ritmo Tropical.** Tranquil, comfortable, and nicely priced, this small hotel a short walk from the beach is the best deal in Malpaís. Red-tile-roof bungalows here are simple yet tasteful, with high wooden ceilings, large bathrooms, lots of windows, and front terraces. Some cabins, arranged in a semicircle around the large pool and gardens, have views of the sea and the jungle. A couple of rooms in back are even cheaper than the others. The reasonably priced Italian restaurant ($) in front of the property serves two dozen types of pizza, fresh fish with a selection of sauces, and tasty pasta dishes such as farfalle with fish and shrimp curry sauce. **Pros:** very clean rooms; economical. **Cons:** variety in room type; a walk to town. *100 m south of El Cruce on road toward Malpa s 2640–0174 7 bungalows, 2 rooms In-room: no a/c, no phone, safe, no TV. In-hotel: restaurant, bar, pool, laundry service MC, V EP.*

7

INLAND

Beaches may be this region's biggest draw, but the countryside holds some splendid scenery, from the steep coffee farms around Atenas to the tropical forests of the lowlands. In the wilderness of Carara National Park and surroundings, you might encounter white-faced capuchin monkeys in the trees or crocodiles lounging on a riverbank. The region is extremely biologically diverse, making it an excellent destination for bird-watchers and other wildlife enthusiasts.

ATENAS

42 km/26 mi west of San José.

Known for its excellent climate, Atenas is a pleasant, friendly town surrounded by a hilly countryside of coffee and cane fields, cattle ranches, and patches of forest. The small city is off the tourist circuit, which means that here, unlike other highly popular destinations, you'll walk alongside more locals than foreigners and get a more authentic idea of the country. Gazing at the tree-covered peaks and exploring the coffee farms are the main activities in this traditional town. Atenas's center has a concrete church, some well-kept wooden and adobe houses, and a park dominated by royal palms.

GETTING HERE

Atenas lies about one hour west on the route between San José and beaches such as Herradura, Jacó, and Manuel Antonio. Take the Pan-American Highway past the airport and turn right at the overpass with the signs for beach resorts and Zoo Ave. Turn left from the exit and stay on the main road. Buses to Atenas leave frequently from the Coca-Cola terminal in San José and arrive near the center of town.

ESSENTIALS

Bank/ATM **Banco de Costa Rica** (⊠ *200 m west of Catholic church* ☎ *2446–6034*). **Banco Nacional** (⊠ *Northern corner of central park* ☎ *2446–5157*).

Hospital **Clínica Pública** (⊠ *150 m south of the fire station* ☎ *2446–5522*).

Pharmacy **Farmacia Don Juan** (⊠ *West corner of Catholic church* ☎ *2446–5055*).

Internet **C@fé K-puchinos** (⊠ *Northwest corner of Parque Central* ☎ *2289–0082*).

Post Office **Correos** (⊠ *50 m southeast of northeast corner of market*).

WHERE TO EAT AND STAY

$ LATIN AMERICAN ✕ **Mirador del Cafétal.** An obligatory stop even if it's just for a cup of coffee, this open-air restaurant next to the road between Atenas and Jacó is a great spot to enjoy the view of steep hillsides covered with coffee trees. The best view is from the long countertops with stools that line the edge of the building, but the wooden tables and chairs might be more comfortable. The food is a mix of Costa Rican and Mexican cuisine, including burritos, chicken with rice, and *sopa azteca* (a tomato-base soup). The restaurant's own brand of coffee is sold by the pound. ⊠ *Road to Jac* ✣ *6 km/3 mi west of Atenas* ☎ *2446–7361* ▭ *AE, MC, V.*

$$ **El Cafétal Inn.** This charming bed-and-breakfast feels and looks more like a home than a hotel, since they go out of their way to help with your travel plans. On a hilltop coffee farm, the two-story concrete lodge has comfortable accommodations with fabulous vistas. Most rooms have balconies, and those on the corners of the second floor have curved windows offering panoramic views. They also have a bungalow near the pool, and two small houses for rent nearby. Breakfast, which includes homegrown coffee roasted on the premises, is served on the back garden patio. The fact that it lies just 25 minutes from the airport makes this a tranquil place to begin or end a Costa Rica trip. **Pros:** superb food; lovely grounds. **Cons:** not all rooms have views. ✣ *8 km/5 mi north of Atenas; heading west from San José on highway to Puntarenas, turn left (south) just before bridge 5 km/3 mi west of Grecia, Santa Eulalia de Atenas* ☎ *2446–5785* 🌐 *www.cafetal.com* *14 rooms, 1 bungalow, 2 houses* *In-room: no a/c, no phone, no TV. In-hotel: restaurant, bar, pool, laundry service, no-smoking rooms* ▭ *AE, MC, V* *BP.*

CARARA NATIONAL PARK

43 km/25 mi southwest of Atenas, 85 km/51 mi southwest of San José.

On the east side of the road between Puntarenas and Playa Jacó, Parque Nacional Carara protects one of the last remnants of an ecological transition zone between Costa Rica's drier northwest and the more humid southwest. It consequently holds a tremendous collection of plants and animals. Much of the 47-square-km (18-square-mi) park is covered with primary forest on steep slopes, where the massive trees are laden with vines and epiphytes. The sparse undergrowth makes wildlife easier to see here than in many other parks, but nothing is guaranteed. If you're lucky, you may glimpse armadillos, basilisk lizards, coatis, and any of several monkey species, as well as birds such as blue-crowned motmots, chestnut-mandibled toucans, and trogons.

The first trail on the left shortly after the bridge that spans the Río Tárcoles (a good place to spot crocodiles) leads to a horseshoe-shaped *laguna meandrica* (oxbow lake). The small lagoon covered with water hyacinths is home to turtles, crocodiles, and waterfowl such as the northern jacana, roseate spoonbill, and boat-billed heron. It is a two- to four-hour hike from the trailhead to the lagoon and back, depending on how much bird-watching you do. ■ **TIP→Cars parked at the trailhead have been broken into. If you don't see a ranger on duty at the *sendero laguna meandrica* trailhead, avoid leaving anything of value in your vehicle. You may be able to leave your belongings at the main ranger station (several miles south of the trailhead), where you can also buy drinks and souvenirs and use the restroom. Otherwise, visit the park as a day trip from a nearby hotel.**

Two trails lead into the forest from the parking lot. The shortest one can be done in 15 minutes, whereas the longer one that connects with the Quebrada Bonita loop takes one to three hours to hike. The latter can be quite muddy during the rainy months, when you may want rubber boots. Carara's proximity to San José and Jacó means that tour buses arrive regularly in high season, scaring some animals deeper into the forest. Come very early or late in the day to avoid crowds. Bird-watchers can call the day before to arrange admission before the park opens. Camping is not permitted.

Local travel agencies and tour operators arrange transport to and guides through the park (⇨ *Park Tours, below*). The park itself has guides, but you must arrange in advance. ✉ *East of Costanera just south of bridge over Rio Tárcoles* ☎ *8383–9953* 🎫 *$10* ⏲ *Daily 7–4.*

GETTING HERE

From Atenas, pass through Orotina and follow the signs to Jacó and Quepos. The reserve is on the left after you cross Río Tárcoles. From San José, hop on a bus to Jacó, Quepos, or Manuel Antonio and ask to be dropped off near the park entrance, about a two-hour drive.

PARK TOURS

Johnny Marin at **Jaguar RIders** (☎ *2643–0180 or 8393–6626*), in Jacó, has been guiding people through the forests of Carara for years. **Costa Rica Expeditions** (☎ *2222–0333* 🌐 *www.costaricaexpeditions.com*), the country's original ecotour operator, offers day trips to Carara from San José, and includes the park in several of its multiday trips. **Horizontes** (☎ *2222–2022* 🌐 *www.horizontes.com*), the country's premier nature-tour operator, can arrange visits to Carara as a day trip from San José or as part of a longer tour.

THE COAST

> **BASE CAMP**
>
> Visitors to Costa Rica prefer using Atenas as their first- and last-night base camp instead of San José, because Atenas is smaller, friendlier, and more tranquil. The international airport is geographically closer to Atenas, but the hilly roads make the ride slightly longer than on San José's express highway.

Along a short stretch of Costa Rica's Pacific coast from Tárcoles to Manuel Antonio are patches of undeveloped jungle, the popular Manuel Antonio National Park, and some of the country's most accessible beaches. The proximity of these strands to San José leads Costa Ricans and foreigners alike to pop down for quick beach vacations. Surfers have good reason to head for the consistent waves of Playas Jacó and Hermosa, and anglers and golfers should consider Playa Herradura for its golf courses and ocean access. You might find Herradura and Jacó overrated and overdeveloped. Manuel Antonio could be accused of the latter, but nobody can deny its spectacular natural beauty.

TÁRCOLES

90 km/54 mi southwest of San José.

Crocodile boat tours on the Río Tárcoles are this small town's claim to fame. In fact, you don't actually have to drive to Tárcoles to do the tour, because operators can pick you up in Herradura or Jacó. The muddy river has gained a reputation as the country's dirtiest, thanks to San José's inadequate sewage system, but it amazingly remains an impressive refuge for wildlife. A huge diversity of birds results from a combination of transitional forest and the river, which houses crocodiles, herons, storks, spoonbills, and other waterbirds. This is also one of the only areas in the country where you can see scarlet macaws, which you may spot on a boat tour or while hiking in a private reserve nearby.

GETTING HERE

By car, head through Atenas to Orotina and follow the signs to Herradura, Jacó, and Quepos. After crossing the bridge over the Rio Tárcoles, look for the entrance to the town of Tárcoles on the right. On the left is the dirt road that leads to the Hotel Villa Lapas and the waterfall reserve. Any bus traveling to Jacó can drop you off at the entrance to Tárcoles. Let the driver know in advance.

OUTDOOR ACTIVITIES

On the two-hour riverboat tours through the mangrove forest and Tarcoles River you might see massive crocodiles, Jesus lizards, iguanas, and some of roughly 50 colorful bird species, including the roseate spoonbill and boat-billed heron. Tours reach the river's mouth, providing nice sea views, especially at sunset. ■ **TIP→ Around noon is the best time to spot crocs sunbathing; bird enthusiasts prefer afternoon rides to catch scarlet macaws. During the rainy season (May to November), the river may grow too rough for boats in the afternoon.**

Two brothers run **Crocodile Man Tour** (✉ *Main road into Tárcoles* ☎ *2637–0771 or 8822–9042* 🌐 *www.crocodilemantour.com*). The small scars

on their hands are the result of the tour's most original (and optional) attraction: feeding fish to the crocs. The boats are small enough to slide up alongside the mangroves for a closer look. Transportation is provided from nearby beaches, but not from San José.

CANOPY TOUR **Hotel Villa Lapas** (✉ *Off Costanera, after bridge over Rio Tárcoles* ☎ *2637–0232* 🌐 *www.villalapas.com*) manages a suspension-bridge nature walk and a zip-line tour. **Sky Way** consists of five suspension bridges spread out over a 2½-km (1½-mi) old-growth-forest nature trail. You can do the trail with a guide ($20). A shuttle picks you up at the Hotel Villa Lapas. **Villa Lapas Canopy** has zip lines through primary forest ($30).

WHERE TO EAT AND STAY

¢–$ COSTA RICAN ✕ **Soda los Mangos.** Next to Soda las Veraneras, this place is similar, with casados and fresh fried fish or fish fillets in garlic sauce. Most tables are outdoors except for one beneath the television indoors. ✉ *Near entrance to Tárcoles* ☎ *2637–0672* ▭ *No credit cards.*

$$ ECLECTIC ✕ **Steve n' Lisa's.** A convenient location, an ocean view, and good food make this roadside restaurant overlooking Playa La Pita, just south of the entrance to Tárcoles, a popular pit stop for those traveling between San José and the Central Pacific beaches. Sit on the covered porch or at one of the concrete tables on the adjacent patio, and enjoy the view

CLOSE UP

Diving the Deep at Coco Island

Rated one of the top diving destinations in the world, Isla del Coco is uninhabited and remote, and its waters are teeming with marine life. It's no place for beginners, but serious divers enjoy 30-meter (100-foot) visibility and the underwater equivalent of a big-game park: scalloped hammerheads, white-tipped reef sharks, Galápagos sharks, bottlenose dolphins, billfish, and manta rays mix with huge schools of brilliantly colored fish.

Encompassing about 22½ square km (14 square mi), Isla del Coco is the largest uninhabited island on earth. Its isolation has led to the evolution of dozens of endemic plant and animal species. The rocky topography is draped in rain forest and cloud forest and includes more than 200 waterfalls. Because of Isla del Coco's distance from shore (484 km [300 mi]) and its craggy topography, few visitors to Costa Rica—and even fewer Costa Ricans—have set foot on the island.

Costa Rica annexed Coco in 1869, and it became a national park in 1978. Today only extremely high-priced specialty-cruise ships, park rangers and volunteers, and scientists visit the place Jacques Cousteau called "the most beautiful island in the world." The dry season (November to May) brings calmer seas and is the best time to see silky sharks. During the rainy season large schools of hammerheads can be seen, but the ocean is rougher.

Two companies offer regular 10-day dive cruises to Isla del Coco that include three days of travel time on the open ocean and cost roughly $3,735 to $4,395, depending on the boat and dates. The *Okeanos Aggressor* (☎ *2289–2261, 800/348–2628 in U.S.* 🌐 *www.aggressor.com*) offers 8- and 10-day dive safaris to Coco Island year-round. *Undersea Hunter* (☎ *2228–6613, 800/203–2120 in U.S.* 🌐 *www.undersea hunter.com*) runs 10-day dive trips to the island year-round.

of the Gulf of Nicoya through the palm fronds. The menu includes breakfast options and a wide selection of lunch and dinner entrées that ranges from tacos and hot dogs to a pricey surf and turf. ✉ *On the Costanera* ✢ *1 km/½ mi south of Tárcoles turnoff, on right* ☎ *2637–0594* 💳 *AE, DC, MC, V.*

$$ 🏨 **Hotel Villa Lapas.** Within a tranquil rain-forest preserve, far from other hotels (and the beach), Villa Lapas is a great escape for nature lovers, but also has on-site entertainment to keep you busy, such as a large-screen television, a pool table, and foosball. You can cross a suspension bridge to reach a small replica of a Costa Rican colonial village with a restaurant, cantina, church, and gift shops. Follow the river flowing through the protected forest for a pleasant hike. There is a canopy tour on the property *(see Canopy Tour, above)*. The austere rooms are nothing special, but they have terra-cotta floors, hardwood ceilings, and large baths. An all-inclusive meal plan is available, but you're better off eating your lunch and dinner elsewhere. **Pros:** surrounded by forest; lots of activities; birds; kid-friendly. **Cons:** rooms sometimes musty; air conditioners old; mediocre buffets. ✉ *Off Costanera* ✢ *3 km/2 mi after bridge over Rio Tárcoles, turn left on dirt road, up 600 m* ☎ *2637–0232* 🌐 *www.villalapas.com* *55 rooms* *In-room: safe,*

no TV (some). In-hotel: 2 restaurants, bars, pool, laundry service, Wi-Fi ▭*AE, DC, MC, V* 🍽*BP.*

EN ROUTE

Even if you choose to bypass Tárcoles and its crocodile tours, you can still get a peek at the huge reptiles as they lounge on the riverbanks: on the Costanera, pull over just after crossing the Río Tárcoles bridge and walk back onto it. Bring binoculars if you have them. ■ **TIP→Be sure to lock your car—vehicles have been broken into here.**

BETWEEN TÁRCOLES AND PLAYA HERRADURA

Past Tárcoles, the first sizable beach town of the Central Pacific coast is Playa Herradura. In between, you'll pass two exclusive hotels, hidden from view at the end of long winding roads.

About a kilometer (½ mi) south after the entrance to Tárcoles, the Costanera passes a small beach called **Playa La Pita,** which provides your first glimpse of the Pacific if you're coming down from San José or the Central Valley. The beach is rocky, and its proximity to the Rio Tárcoles makes the water murky and unfit for swimming, but it's a nice spot to stop and admire the ocean. From here the road heads inland again, and you'll come across the entrance to Punta Leona, a vast hotel and residential complex. The road then winds its way up a steep hill, atop which is the entrance to the luxury hotel Villa Caletas. On the other side of that ridge is the bay and beach of Herradura.

WHERE TO EAT AND STAY

$$$–$$$$ ✕ **El Mirador Restaurant.** White tablecloths, glass walls, and yellow-and-blue-checked curtains contribute to the sophisticated but not overly stuffy atmosphere of this restaurant at Villa Caletas. Expensive prix-fixe meals include your choice of appetizer, main dish, and dessert. Appetizers range from the traditional escargots to a shrimp and lobster bisque. The entrées include beef tenderloin with a red wine and espresso sauce, jumbo shrimp sautéed with coconut and vanilla, and a combination of a veal chop and roast duck. A covered terrace below the restaurant is popular for sunset viewing over a cocktail, and the tapas menu is much less expensive than the main restaurant. ✉*Villa Caletas hotel, off coastal highway* ✣*3 km/1½ mi south of Punta Leona* ☎*2637–0505* ▭*AE, DC, MC, V.*

$$–$$$ **Hotel Punta Leona.** This 740-acre private reserve and resort community is an odd and overwhelming mix of nature, residential development, and vacation spot. Punta Leona's attractions include three beaches, a tropical forest, a butterfly farm, and guided bird-watching hikes. Punta Leona (Lion's Point) made headlines as the setting of the Ridley Scott film *1492: Conquest of Paradise* and more recently for blocking public access to its beaches, which is illegal in Costa Rica. The little "city" contains everything from restaurants and pools to a grocery store and church, plus plenty of amusements, including a zip-line tour, tennis court, and mini–golf course. Frequent shuttles travel between the rooms, restaurants, and beaches. Hotel guests, home owners, and time-share members contribute to crowded beaches on weekends, especially in the dry season, when this place can be a bit of a zoo. **Pros:** ample beachfront; lots of variety in activities. **Cons:** far from town;

DID YOU KNOW?

For experienced scuba divers only, Coco Island is the underwater equivalent of a big-game park and according to the late Jacques Cousteau, it's "the most beautiful island in the world." We agree.

dingy rooms; spotty service. *✈15 km/9 mi south of Tárcoles on west side of road to Jacó ☎2231–3131 or 2630–1000 🌐www.hotelpuntaleona.com ⇨108 rooms, 13 suites, 27 apartments ♿In-room: safe, refrigerator. In-hotel: 3 restaurants, room service, bars, tennis court, pools, beachfront, water sports, laundry service, Wi-Fi ▭AE, DC, MC, V ¶BP.*

$$$–$$$$ ★ **Villa Caletas.** Perched 365 meters (1,200 feet) above the sea on a promontory south of Punta Leona, this collection of elegant rooms sequestered in the jungle has jaw-dropping views of the surrounding foliage and sea below. Spectacular sunset views should be enjoyed from the bar, even if you stay elsewhere. Freestanding suites and villas are gorgeous, but rooms in the main building are far inferior; if a villa isn't within your budget, do try to get a deluxe room. Victorian, French colonial, and Hellenistic motifs are combined throughout, with Ionic columns, varied artwork, cookie-cutter trims, and cane chairs. The regular pool is rather small and chilly, but the new Zephyr Palace complex has amazing views and an impressive infinity pool. The closest beach, Playa Caletas, is attractive, but small and rocky. Though a great place for romance or relaxation, this hotel has little to offer kids or active travelers. **Pros:** gorgeous views, forest, and sunsets; good food. **Cons:** abundant insects; little to do; lots of stairs; inconsistent service. *✉Off coastal highway ✈3 km/1½ mi south of Punta Leona, on right 📪Apdo. 12358–1000, San Jos ☎2637–0505 or 2630–3000 🌐www.villacaletas.com ⇨10 rooms, 14 villas, 7 junior suites, 13 suites ♿In-room: safe. In-hotel: 2 restaurants, bars, pool, gym, spa, laundry service, no-smoking rooms ▭AE, DC, MC, V ¶EP.*

PLAYA HERRADURA

20 km/12 mi south of Tárcoles.

If sportfishing and golf are your priorities, this is a good option. If you're looking for nature, seclusion, a beautiful beach, or a bargain, keep driving. Rocky Playa Herradura, a poor representative of Costa Rica's breathtaking beaches, gets its name from the Spanish word for "horseshoe," referring to the shape of the deep bay in which it lies. Its tranquil waters make it considerably safer for swimming than most central and southern Pacific beaches, and that, coupled with its proximity to San José, has turned it into a popular weekend getaway for Josefinos, who compete for shade beneath the sparse palms and Indian almond trees that line the beach. On the north end of the beach is the Los Sueños development, which includes a large marina, shopping center, hundreds of condos, a golf course, and a massive Marriott hotel.

GETTING HERE

By car, head 20 minutes straight down the Central Pacific highway. The town's entrance is on the right-hand side, where a long paved road leads to the beach. Follow the signs to the Marriott.

OUTDOOR ACTIVITIES

Few activities are available directly in Playa Herradura, but that doesn't mean you have to settle for less. Most of the area's diverse outfitters can pick you up at your hotel for activities near Jacó and Playa Hermosa.

Your hotel's reception desk is often a good source of information.

King Tours (✉*Main road into Playa Herradura, in front of Los Sueños* ☎*2643–2441, 8819–1920, or 800/213–7091* 🌐*www.kingtours.com*) arranges trips to renowned attractions like Manuel Antonio National Park and Carara National Park, as well as crocodile boat tours, deep-sea and coastal fishing trips, horseback rides, and canopy tours. The company can also book tours to destinations elsewhere in the country, such as Poás and Arenal volcanoes, Monteverde Cloud Forest, and Isla Tortuga. **Costa Rica Dreams** (✉*Los Sueños Marina* ☎*2637–8942, 732/901–8625 Ext. 2 in U.S.* 🌐*www.costaricadreams.com*) is one of the area's oldest and most reputable sportfishing outfitters.

THE HAUNTED CART

If you're out late one night and hear a slow scraping of wheels against the road, it just might be the *carreta sin bueyes* (cart without oxen) of ghostly legend. Its owner reputedly stole building materials from a church, and was condemned to perpetually traverse the country's highways and byways in the cart he used to transport his stolen goods. (The oxen were blameless for their role and escaped the curse.)

WHERE TO EAT AND STAY

$–$$$ SEAFOOD ✕**Restaurante El Pelícano.** It may not look like much at first glance, but this open-air restaurant across the street from the beach serves some dishes you'd be hard-pressed to find in other casual beach-town places. The decor is limited to green-tile floors, thin wooden columns, lime tablecloths, and soft candlelight. Starters include fish croquettes in a lemon sauce, green pepper stuffed with shrimp and mushrooms, or clams *au gratin*. Grilled tuna in a mango sauce, sea bass in a heart-of-palm sauce, lobster, and tenderloin are a few of the main dishes. ✉*Turn left at end of main road into Playa Herradura* ☎*2637–8910* ▭*AE, DC, MC, V.*

$$$$ **Los Sueños Marriott Ocean and Golf Resort.** This mammoth multimillion-dollar resort in a palatial colonial-style building has a gorgeous view of Herradura Bay. It combines modern amenities with traditional Central American decorative motifs, such as barrel-tile roofing and hand-painted tiles. Rooms here, though attractive and some of the country's most expensive, are nothing special compared with those at smaller hotels in the same price range. They have marble baths, wooden furniture, and tiny balconies. Be sure to get a room with an ocean view, or you'll be contemplating condos. An enormous pool with islands and swim-up bars, a Ted Robinson golf course called La Iguana, a modern marina, and various diversions are designed to keep you on-site and entertained. **Pros:** impeccable grounds; great service; memorable. **Cons:** so-so service; beach can be dirty. ✉*800 m west of road to Jacó from San José, follow signs at entrance of road to Playa Herradura* ☎*2630–9000, 800/228–9290 in U.S.* 🌐*www.marriott.com* *191 rooms, 10 suites* *In-room: safe, refrigerator, Internet. In-hotel: 5 restaurants, room service, bars, golf course, tennis courts, pool, gym, spa, beachfront, children's programs (ages 5–15), laundry service, Internet terminal, Wi-Fi, no-smoking rooms* ▭*AE, DC, MC, V* *EP.*

7

JACÓ

2 km/1 mi south of Playa Herradura, 114 km/70 mi southwest of San José.

Its proximity to San José has made Jacó the most developed beach town in Costa Rica. Nature lovers and solitude seekers should skip this place, which is known mostly for its nightlife, surf scene, and prostitution. More than 50 hotels and cabinas back its long, gray-sand beach, and the mix of restaurants, shops, and bars lining Avenida Pastor Diaz (the town's main drag) give it a cluttered appearance devoid of any greenery. Any real Costa Rican–ness evaporated years ago; U.S. chain hotels and restaurants have invaded, and you can pretty much find anything you need, from law offices and dental clinics to DVD-rental shops and appliance stores. It does have a bit of everything in terms of tours and outdoor activities, and makes a convenient hub for exploring neighboring beaches and attractions.

GETTING HERE AND AROUND

The drive from San José takes about three hours; take the Pan-American Highway past the airport to the exit for Atenas, then follow the signs to Orotina, Jacó, and Quepos. The exit, on the right after Herradura, is well marked. Buses leave from San José's Coca-Cola station five times daily. **Pacific Travel & Tours** (☎ *2643–2520* 🌐 *www.pacifictravelcr.com*) brings passengers across the Gulf of Nicoya to Montezuma.

ESSENTIALS

Bank/ATM BAC San José (✉ *Il Galeone mall*). **Banco Nacional** (✉ *Avda. Pastor Diaz* ☎ *2643–3621*).

Hospital Ambulance (☎ *2643–1690*). **Clínica Pública** (✉ *In front of Plaza de Deportes* ☎ *2643–1767*).

Pharmacy Farmacia Jacó (✉ *Diagonally across from Mas X Menos supermarket* ☎ *2643–3205*).

Internet Centro de Computación (✉ *Avda. Pastor Diaz, center of town*).

Post Office Correos (✉ *Avda. Pastor Diaz*).

Rental Cars Budget (✉ *Avda. Pastor Diaz* ☎ *2643–2665* 🌐 *www.budget.com*). **Economy** (✉ *Avda. Pastor Diaz* ☎ *2643–1098* 🌐 *www.economyrentacar.com*). **Alamo** (✉ *Avda. Pastor Diaz* ☎ *2643–1752* 🌐 *www.alamo.com*). **Payless** (✉ *Avda. Pastor Diaz* ☎ *2643–3224* 🌐 *www.paylesscarrental.com*).

Taxis Taxi services (☎ *2643–2020, 2643–2121, or 2643–3030*).

Tourist Information Pacific Travel & Tours (✉ *Centro Comercial La Casona [La Casona shopping center]* ☎ *2643–2520* 🌐 *www.pacifictravelcr.com*).

EXPLORING

Long, palm-lined **Playa Jacó**, west of town, is a pleasant enough spot in the morning, but can burn the soles of your feet on a sunny afternoon. Though the gray sand and beachside construction make it less attractive than most other Costa Rican beaches, it's a good place to soak up the sun or enjoy a sunset. Playa Jacó is popular with surfers for the consistency of its waves, but when the surf is up, swimmers should

Hotels ▼

Aparthotel Flamboyant **7**

Aparthotel Girasol **11**

Club del Mar .. **12**

Docelunas **13**

Hotel Canciones del Mar **1**

Hotel Tangerí **4**

Las Orquideas **10**

Mar de Luz **3**

Tropical Garden Hotel **8**

Nightlife ▼

Jungle **2**

Nacho Daddy's ... **9**

Restaurante El Colonial **6**

Tabacón **5**

Shopping ▼

Cocobolo **1**

El Cofre **3**

Guacamole **2**

beware of dangerous rip currents. During the rainy months the ocean here is not very clean.

OUTDOOR ACTIVITIES

You don't have to physically step into any tour office, because everyone from a reception desk attendant to a boutique salesperson can book you a local adventure. Almost every tour can pick you up at your hotel's doorstep. ■ **TIP→Keep in mind that part of your price tag includes the salesperson's commission, so if you hear higher or lower prices from two different people, it's likely a reflection of a shift in the commission. You can try negotiating a better deal directly from the outfitter.**

Jaguar Riders (☎ *2643–0180 or 8393–6626*) specializes in ATV tours of the mountains east of town and trips to Carara National Park, but can arrange all kinds of personalized excursions. **Fantasy Tours** (✉ *Best Western Jacó Beach Resort* ☎ *2643–2231 or 2220–2126* 🌐 *www.graylinecostarica.com*) deals primarily with large groups, arranging day trips from Jacó to Arenal and Poás volcanoes, Manuel Antonio National Park, Sarchí, Isla Tortuga, and raft trips on the Savegre River. **Pacific Travel & Tours** (✉ *Centro comercial La Casona [La Casona shopping center]* ☎ *2643–2520* 🌐 *www.pacifictravelcr.com*) sells an array of tours in and around Jacó.

ATV TOURS Because ATV tours are fairly new here, the vehicles are in good condition. But they're not exactly the most eco-friendly way to see the area's rain forest and wildlife. Some operators will ask you to put up a credit card voucher of roughly $500. **ATV Tours** (☎ *2778–8172 or 8812–1789*) runs two- or three-hour tours ($65–$85) through rain forests, rivers, and waterfalls that lie about 15 minutes south of Jacó. **Ricaventura** (✉ *In the center of Playa Jacó, behind Subway* ☎ *2818–6973 or 2643–3395* 🌐 *www.ricaventura.com*) is considered by locals to be the best ATV tour with the longest routes. Ricaventura offers various options: a two-hour sunset tour ($69), a four-hour Carara Park and nearby river tour ($89), a six-hour Pacayal Waterfall trip ($110), and full-day trips ($150).

CANOPY TOURS In the hills across the highway from Jacó Beach, **Chiclets Canopy Tour** (☎ *2643–3271*) takes you sliding through one of the area's more pristine forests along cables strung between 14 treetop platforms between 60 and 130 feet above the ground. The price is $60 per person. **Waterfalls Canopy Tour** (☎ *2643–3322* 🌐 *www.waterfallscanopy.com*), in a private reserve 4 km (2½ mi) from Jacó, is a zip-line tour with a view of rain forest and waterfalls. You can combine the tour, which costs $58 per person, with nature walks and a visit to a butterfly and frog garden, or do it at night.

A modified ski lift offers easy access to the rain-forest canopy, with six-seat gondolas that float through the treetops at the **Rain Forest Aerial Tram** (☎ *2257–5961* 🌐 *www.rainforestram.com*). This tram lies within a 222-acre private reserve 3 km (2 mi) west of Jacó. The company offers guided tours that explain a bit of the local ecology ($55), as well as early-morning bird-watching tours (six-person minimum; $110 per person). There is also a small serpentarium and medicinal plant garden.

HANG GLIDING A truly unique experience, hang gliding gives you the chance to see not just Jacó, but a huge expanse of Pacific coastline. With **Hang Glide Costa**

Rica (☎ *8353–5514*) you can take a tandem hang-gliding flight or fly in a three-seat, open cockpit ultralight plane. You are picked up in Jacó and taken to the airstrip 6 km (4 mi) south of Playa Hermosa. Prices start at around $70 per person.

HORSEBACK RIDING **Discovery Horseback Tours** (☎ *8830–7550*) is owned by a British couple who run *2½-hour* trail rides on healthy horses. You'll spend some time in the rain forest and also stop at a small waterfall where you can take a dip ($60). **Horse Tours Jacó at Hacienda Agujas** (☎ *2637–0808 or 8838–7940*) are serene enough for all ages and skill levels. Late-afternoon tours are on a cattle ranch about 25 minutes north of Jacó, where the trail winds through a rain forest and down a beach. The ride ends with a colorful sunset bang ($65).

RIPTIDES

Riptides (or rip currents), common in Jacó and Manuel Antonio's Playa Espadilla, are dangerous and have led to many deaths in the area. If you get caught in one, don't panic and don't try to swim against it. Let the current take you out just past the breakers, where its power dissipates, then swim parallel to shore. Once the current is behind you, swim back to the beach. The best policy is not to go in deeper than your waist when the waves loom large.

KAYAKING AND CANOEING **Kayak Jacó Costa Rica Outriggers** (☎ *2643–1233* 🌐 *www.kayakjaco.com*) takes you to waters calmer than those at Jacó Beach. Instead, you'll visit Playa Agujas for sea-kayaking tours and Hawaiian-style outrigger canoe trips ($60). The half-day tours include snorkeling (conditions permitting) at secluded beaches.

SURFING Jacó has several beach breaks, all of which are best around high tide. Surfboard-toting tourists abound in Jacó, but you don't need to be an expert to enjoy the waves—the swell is often small enough for beginners, especially around low tide. Abundant surf shops rent boards and give lessons. Prices range from $25 to $45 an hour and usually include a board and transportation. If you plan to spend more than a week surfing, it might be cheaper to buy a used board and sell it before you leave *(⇨ Shopping, below)*. If you don't have much experience, don't go out when the waves are really big—Jacó sometimes gets very powerful swells, which result in dangerous rip currents. During the rainy season, waves are more consistent than in the dry months, when Jacó sometimes lacks surf.

SWIMMING The big waves and dangerous rip currents that make surfing so popular here can make swimming dangerous. Lifeguards are on duty only at specific spots, and only sporadically. If the ocean is rough, stay on the beach—dozens of swimmers have drowned here over the years.

When the ocean is calm, especially around low tide, you can swim just about anywhere along Jacó Beach. The sea is always calmer near the beach's northern and southern ends, but the ocean bottom is littered with rocks there, as it is in front of the small rivers that flow into the sea near the middle of this beach.

WHERE TO STAY

$–$$ ★ **Apartotel Flamboyant.** Though nothing special, this small beachfront hotel is a good deal, especially if you take advantage of the cooking facilities. Half the rooms have small kitchenettes; the others have air-conditioning instead. Larger apartments can fit five to six people. Terraces with chairs overlook a garden and pool area, where there's a grill for your use. Second-floor rooms have balconies with sea views. It's all just a few steps from the surf, and a block east of Jacó's busy main strip. **Pros:** beachfront; good value; quiet; centrally located. **Cons:** very simple rooms; looks a little worn. ✉ *100 m west of Centro Comercial Il Galeone* ☎ *2643–3146* 🌐 *www.apartotelflamboyant.com* *20 rooms, 3 apartments* *In-room: no a/c (some), safe, kitchen (some), Wi-Fi (some). In-hotel: pool, beachfront, laundry service, Wi-Fi* *AE, DC, MC, V* *EP.*

$$ **Apartotel Girasol.** A great option for families, or small groups of friends looking for comfort and quiet, Girasol is a quiet beachfront hotel with a neighborly feel. The cozy apartments face the small pool and grill area and include a bedroom with a queen and single bed, a living and dining room with another bed, a complete kitchen, and a terrace with chairs. A winding pathway crosses the well-maintained front lawn with an impressive ficus tree in the middle, and leads to a small gate that opens directly onto the beach, where you should take at least one evening to enjoy a spectacular sunset. **Pros:** beachfront; quiet grounds; big apartments. **Cons:** far from town center; often full. ✉ *100 m west of Motoshop, end of C. Republica Dominicana* ☎ *2643–1591* 🌐 *www.girasol.com* *16 apartments* *In-room: safe, kitchen, Wi-Fi. In-hotel: pool, beachfront, laundry service* *MC, V* *EP.*

$$–$$$ Fodor's Choice ★ **Club del Mar.** Secluded at the beach's southern end, far from Jacó's crowds, Club del Mar is the area's priciest, and nicest, lodging option. In the main building, above the restaurant, bar, and reception, standard green-and-cream-hue rooms have private teak balconies with screen doors that keep the sea breeze circulating. Comfortable condos, clustered in two-story buildings amid massive trees and verdant lawns, are considerably nicer. One- and two-bedroom apartments have abundant windows, modern kitchens, and pleasant furnishings; two-bedroom condos are a bargain for two couples. The nicest condos are those nearest the sea (nos. 13 to 16). Las Sandalias restaurant ($$–$$$) serves some of the area's finest food (⇨ *above*). **Pros:** beachfront; tranquil; friendly; lush grounds; tasteful decor. **Cons:** some highway noise reaches back to condos; some insects. ✉ *Costanera, 275 m south of gas station* *Apdo. 107–4023, Jac* ☎ *2643–3194, 866/978–5669 in U.S.* 🌐 *www.clubdelmarcostarica.com* *8 rooms, 22 condos, 2 suites* *In-room: safe, kitchen (some). In-hotel: restaurant, room service, bar, pool, beachfront, water sports, laundry facilities, Wi-Fi* *AE, DC, MC, V* *EP.*

$$–$$$ **Docelunas.** Most of Jacó's hotels and visitors huddle around the beach, but "Twelve Moons" sits a couple of miles from the sea and sand. With a mountainous green backdrop, this hotel spreads out across 5 acres of lawns shaded by tropical trees and luxuriant gardens. Spacious teak furniture–filled rooms have large bathrooms with showers,

bathtubs, and double sinks. Yoga classes are given daily in a hilltop, hardwood-floor room with windows for walls. The full-service spa uses the hotel's own homemade beauty products, and the open-air restaurant ($$–$$$) serves creative seafood, meat, vegetarian, and vegan dishes. ✉ *On coastal highway from San Jos , pass the first entrances to Jac ; take dirt road on left with signs for Docelunas* ☎ *2643–2211* 🌐 *www.docelunas.com* *20 rooms* *In-room: safe, refrigerator, Wi-Fi. In-hotel: restaurant, room service, bar, pool, spa, laundry service, no-smoking rooms* ▭ *AE, DC, MC, V* *BP.*

$$ **Hotel Canciones del Mar.** The poetically named "Songs of the Sea" is a tranquil, intimate, and charming hotel with rooms that are among the closest to the ocean of any hotel in the area. Tastefully and individually decorated, the one- and two-bedroom suites are in a two-story cream-color building, with well-equipped kitchens. Five ocean-view rooms cost a bit more, but the rest have porches overlooking the lush gardens and blue-tile pool. Breakfast and drinks can be enjoyed under a thatch roof next to the beach or in the shade of palms on the beach itself, whereas the rooftop tapas bar is a great spot to watch the sunset. A communal tree house–like space behind the pool makes a pleasant reading or relaxing spot. **Pros:** close to ocean; rooms have kitchens. **Cons:** too close to Jacó; rooms feel worn. ✉ *End of C. Bri Bri* *Apdo. 86–4023, Jac* ☎ *2643–3273* 🌐 *www.cancionesdelmar.com* *12 suites* *In-room: safe, kitchen, refrigerator, Wi-Fi. In-hotel: restaurant, bar, pool, beachfront, laundry service* ▭ *AE, MC, V* *BP.*

Fodor's Choice ★

$$–$$ **Hotel Tangerí.** One of Jacó's older hotels, the Tangerí has an excellent beachfront location and ample grounds shaded by coconut palms. The accommodations range from spacious rooms by the sea to villas big enough for a large family. The bright but bland standard rooms in a two-story concrete building by the beach are a good deal for couples. Beachfront rooms have balconies or terraces with lovely ocean views through the palms. Ocean-view rooms are over the lawn, and some have a rather distant glimpse of the sea. The villas, complete with kitchens and one to three bedrooms, are set back from the beach; avoid nos. 5, 6, and 8, which are too close to the road. This is a popular spot with Costa Rican families, thanks to its convenient beach access, several pools, a playground, Ping-Pong, and pool table, which means it can be quite busy during the holidays. There's a snack bar by the pool and a steak house ($$$) near the entrance. **Pros:** beachfront; spacious rooms; centrally located. **Cons:** rooms a bit timeworn; musty. ✉ *Avda. Pastor Diaz, north of river* ☎ *2643–3001 or 2258–4012* 🌐 *www.hoteltangeri.com* *14 rooms, 10 villas* *In-room: kitchen (some), refrigerator. In-hotel: restaurant, bar, pools, gym, beachfront, laundry service, Wi-Fi* ▭ *AE, MC, V* *EP.*

¢–$ **Las Orquideas.** Just far enough from the beach and main tourist beat to be a bargain, but close enough to be convenient, this pleasant little hotel provides cleanliness and comfort at reasonable rates. Colorful, narrow rooms have tile floors, two beds, and the basic amenities; air-conditioning costs $10 extra. Small front terraces overlook the gardens and small pool, where the predominantly surfer guests tend to congregate. **Pros:** good location; clean. **Cons:** no frills; no beachfront. ✉ *East*

7

"I caught this beautiful heron just outside our beachfront hotel at Jacó." —photo by Leethal33, Fodors.com member

of Frutastica supermarket ☎*2643–4056* *10 rooms* *In-room: no phone, safe, refrigerator, Internet. In-hotel: pool, laundry service* *AE, MC, V* *EP.*

$$ **Mar de Luz.** It may be a few blocks from the beach, and it doesn't look like much from the street, but Mar de Luz is a surprisingly pleasant place full of flowering plants and shady, bird-attracting trees. The Dutch owner is dedicated to cleanliness and providing lots of amenities, such as poolside grills, a kids' game room, plentiful common areas—like the large open-air reading lounge—and inexpensive tours. Rooms vary in decor: the bright, pastel-hue rooms have two queen-size beds and kitchenettes; top-floor rooms have a small living room with checkered sofas and a double bed; the cozy split-level rooms with kitchenettes and stone walls are reminiscent of European B&Bs. **Pros:** attentive owner; plenty to do. **Cons:** rooms a bit dark; service can be spotty. ✉*East of Avda. Pastor Diaz, behind Jungle bar* ☎*2643–3000 or 877/623–3198* *www.mardeluz.com* *27 rooms, 2 suites* *In-room: safe, kitchen (some), refrigerator, Wi-Fi (some). In-hotel: pool, laundry service, Internet terminal, no-smoking rooms* *AE, DC, MC, V* *BP.*

$ **Tropical Garden Hotel.** As its name suggests, this hotel's special charm comes from the impressive lush gardens that fill almost every inch of its property, making it one of the most verdant places in Jacó. Meters from the beach and from the main strip, rooms lack style but have very basic kitchenettes and front porches for iguana- and bird-spotting. It's one of Jacó's original hotels (formerly known as Villas Miramar), and the rooms show their age, but it's competitively priced. **Pros:** pleasant grounds; economical. **Cons:** timeworn; simple. ✉*50 m west of Il Galeone mall, toward the beach* ☎*2643–3003* *www.tropicalgardenhotel.com*

12 studios, 1 suite In-room: no a/c (some), no phone, safe, kitchen. In-hotel: pool AE, MC, V EP.

NIGHTLIFE AND THE ARTS

Whereas other beach towns may have a bar or two, Jacó has an avenue full of them, with enough variety for many different tastes. After-dinner spots range from restaurants perfect for a quiet drink to loud bars with pool tables to dance clubs or casinos.

BARS For a laid-back cocktail, people-watching, and a tropical feel, head to **Restaurante El Colonial** (*Avda. Pastor Diaz, across from Il Galeone mall 2643–3326*) on the main drag, which has a large circular bar in the center and lots of wicker chairs and tables in the front. Sometimes it has live music. A mix of bar and disco, **Nacho Daddy's** (*Avda. Pastor Diaz, 1st fl of Il Galeone mall 2643–2270*) is Jacó's after-hours nightspot, open from 10 PM to 4 AM. The restaurant **Tabacón** (*Avda. Pastor Diaz, north of Il Galeone mall 2643–3097*) is a nice place for a cocktail, after-dinner drinks, or a late-night meal. It has a big bar in back, pool tables, and live music on weekends. **Jungle** (*Avda. Pastor Diaz, across from Hotel Tangerí, above Subway*) has a large, second-floor bar, has wide-screen TVs, several pool tables, dartboards, a large bar, and a dance floor in back.

CASINOS **Jazz Casino and Sportsbook** (*Hotel Amapola, 130 m east of the Municipalidad government building, southern end of town 2643–2316*), Jacó's first casino, has rummy, slot machines, and craps. There's also a roomy bar area.

SHOPPING

Souvenir shops with mostly the same mass-produced merchandise are crowded one after the other along the main street in the center of town. Most of the goods, like wooden crafts and seed jewelry, are run-of-the-mill souvenir fare, but a few shops have more unusual items. The two neighboring shops at **Cocobolo** (*Avda. Pastor Diaz, next to Banana Café 2643–3486*) are jam-packed with merchandise hanging from the ceiling, walls, and shelves. It's much of what you find in other stores, but with more international and tasteful items and a richer variety. **El Cofre** (*Avda. Pastor Diaz, across from Banco Nacional 2643–1912*) claims to sell only handmade goods and specializes in mostly wooden furniture, including heavy Guatemalan pieces and Indonesian teak; it also sells masks, drums, Moroccan lamps, and even carved doors. Curious religious statues of saints and angels from Central America are big sellers. **Guacamole** (*Centro Comercial Costa Brava, south of Il Galeone mall 2643–1120*) sells beautiful and comfortable batik clothing produced locally, along with Brazilian bathing suits, Costa Rican leather sandals and purses, and different styles of jewelry.

SURFBOARDS AND GEAR **Carton** (*Calle Madrigal 2643–3762*) sells new and used boards and has a selection of surf wear, sunglasses, and accessories. **Jass** (*Centro Comercial Ureña 2643–3549*) has a good variety of surf gear at decent prices. It sells new and used boards. **TIP→Most shops that sell boards also buy used boards.**

PLAYA HERMOSA

5 km/3 mi south of Jacó, 113 km/70 mi southwest of San José.

On the other side of the rocky ridge that forms the southern edge of Jacó Beach is Playa Hermosa, a swath of gray sand and driftwood stretching southeast as far as the eye can see. Despite its name—Spanish for "Lovely Beach"—Playa Hermosa is hardly spectacular. The southern half of the wide beach lacks palm trees or other shade-providing greenery; its sand is scorchingly hot in the afternoon; and frequent rip currents make it unsafe to swim when there are waves. But board-riders find beauty in its consistent surf breaks. The beach's northern end is popular because it often has waves when other spots are flat, and the ocean is cleaner than at Jacó. There is also plenty of forest covering the hills, and scarlet macaws sometimes gather in the Indian almond trees near the end of beach. For nonsurfers, outdoor options include horseback and canopy tours in the nearby, forested hills or ultralight and hang-gliding flights over the coast. But all of these can be done from other beaches. As for the town itself, there's really not much, which is part of the attraction for travelers who want to escape Jaco's crowds and concrete towers. Most of the restaurants, bars, and hotels have cropped up one after the other on a thin stretch separating the highway and the beach. From June to December, olive ridley turtles nest on the beach at night, especially when there's not much moonlight.

GETTING HERE

If you have a car, take the coastal highway 5 km (3 mi) past Jacó. You'll see the cluster of businesses on the right. If you don't, take a taxi from Jacó or a local bus toward Quepos.

ESSENTIALS

Internet Goola Café and Internet (✉ *Costanera, north of soccer field* ☎ *2643–3696*).

OUTDOOR ACTIVITIES

You can arrange activities throughout the Central Pacific from Playa Hermosa. Most tour operators and outfitters include transportation in their prices. *For more options than we list here, see Outdoor Activities in Jacó, above, or consult your hotel's reception.* Raul Fernandez of **Playa Hermosa Turtle Tours** (☎ *8817–0385*) takes small groups to look for nesting sea turtles on Playa Hermosa between July and December ($35), as part of a project to collect the eggs and raise them in a hatchery. Tour times vary depending on the tide; he can provide transportation from hotels in Jacó.

CANOPY TOUR **Chiclets Canopy Tour** (✉ *West of Costanera* ✣ *½ km/¼ mi north of Hermosa* ☎ *2643–3271* 🌐 *www.jacowave.com*) runs four guided tours daily that take you through the rain-forest canopy ($60). Cables strung between platforms perched high in a dozen trees have views of tropical foliage, wildlife, and the nearby coast.

HORSEBACK RIDING **Discovery Horseback** (☎ *8838–7550* 🌐 *www.discoveryhorsetours.com*) runs various tours through the nearby mountains to a waterfall and along the beach. Their most popular tour is a 2½-hour ride through the rain forest ($60). You can also arrange riding lessons.

SURFING Most people who bed down at Playa Hermosa are here for the same reason—the waves that break just a shell's toss away. There are a half-dozen breaks scattered along the beach's northern end, and the surf is always best around high tide. Because it is a beach break, though, the waves here often close out, especially when the surf is big. If you don't have much experience, don't go out when the waves are really big—Hermosa sometimes gets very powerful swells, which result in dangerous rip currents. If you're a beginner, don't go out at all. Surf instructors in Hermosa take their students to Jacó, an easier place to learn the sport.

Reggae-theme **Restaurante Jammin'** (✉ *Next to Cabinas Las Arenas* ☎ *2643–1853*) offers surf lessons ($45) and buys, rents, and sells boards as they're available. Andrea Díaz, a professional surfer with **Waves Costa Rica** (✉ *Next to the Backyard* ☎ *2643–7025 or 8829–4610* 🌐 *www.wavescr.com*), takes surf students to calmer Playa Jacó for two-hour lessons ($55 per person for group sessions; $100 for a private surf package). She also offers surf-camp packages, which include room and board and yoga.

WHERE TO EAT AND STAY

$–$$ ECLECTIC ✕ **The Backyard.** Playa Hermosa's original nightlife spot, the North American–style Backyard has two seating areas, each with its own bar. Television sets on the wraparound bar in the front room show sports matches and surf videos. A wooden deck in back overlooking the beach is great for lunch and sunset, mostly because of the pleasant sea breezes and view. The usual bar food—Tex-Mex standards and burgers—is complemented by fresh seafood, including ceviche, grilled tuna, lobster, and jumbo shrimp. It's popular especially on Friday and Saturday, when there's live music. ✉ *Costanera, southern end of town next to the Backyard hotel, below)* ☎ *2643–7011* 💳 *AE, DC, MC, V.*

$–$$ SEAFOOD ✕ **Jungle Surf Café.** This simple, open-air eatery decorated with a colorful rain-forest mural serves some of Hermosa's best food. Seating is on a patio and wooden deck hemmed by tropical trees, with views of the road and soccer field. Breakfasts are hearty—try the banana pancakes—and the eclectic lunch selection ranges from shish kebabs to fish sandwiches. The dinner menu changes nightly, but usually includes big portions of fresh tuna or mahimahi. ✉ *Costanera, north of soccer field* ☎ *2643–1495* 💳 *No credit cards* 🍷 *BYOB* ⊗ *Closed Wed.*

$$$ 🏨 **The Backyard.** Surfers—not the budget backpacking kind—are the main clientele at this small, cream-color hotel on the beach. Rooms have high ceilings, clay-tile floors, and sliding-glass doors that open onto semiprivate balconies and terraces, most of which have good views of Playa Hermosa. Second-floor rooms have better views, as do the two spacious corner suites with separate bedrooms and large balconies—they're a good deal for small groups. There's a nice little pool surrounded by tropical foliage in back. **Pros:** steps from the surf; nice views from second floor; friendly. **Cons:** expensive; bar next door noisy on weekends. ✉ *Costanera, southern end of town* ☎📠 *2643–7011* 🌐 *www.backyardhotel.com* ⇆ *6 rooms, 2 suites* ♿ *In-room: safe, refrigerator, Wi-Fi. In-hotel: restaurant, bar, pool, laundry service* 💳 *AE, DC, MC, V* 🍽 *CP.*

7

Continued on page 415

SURFING COSTA RICA

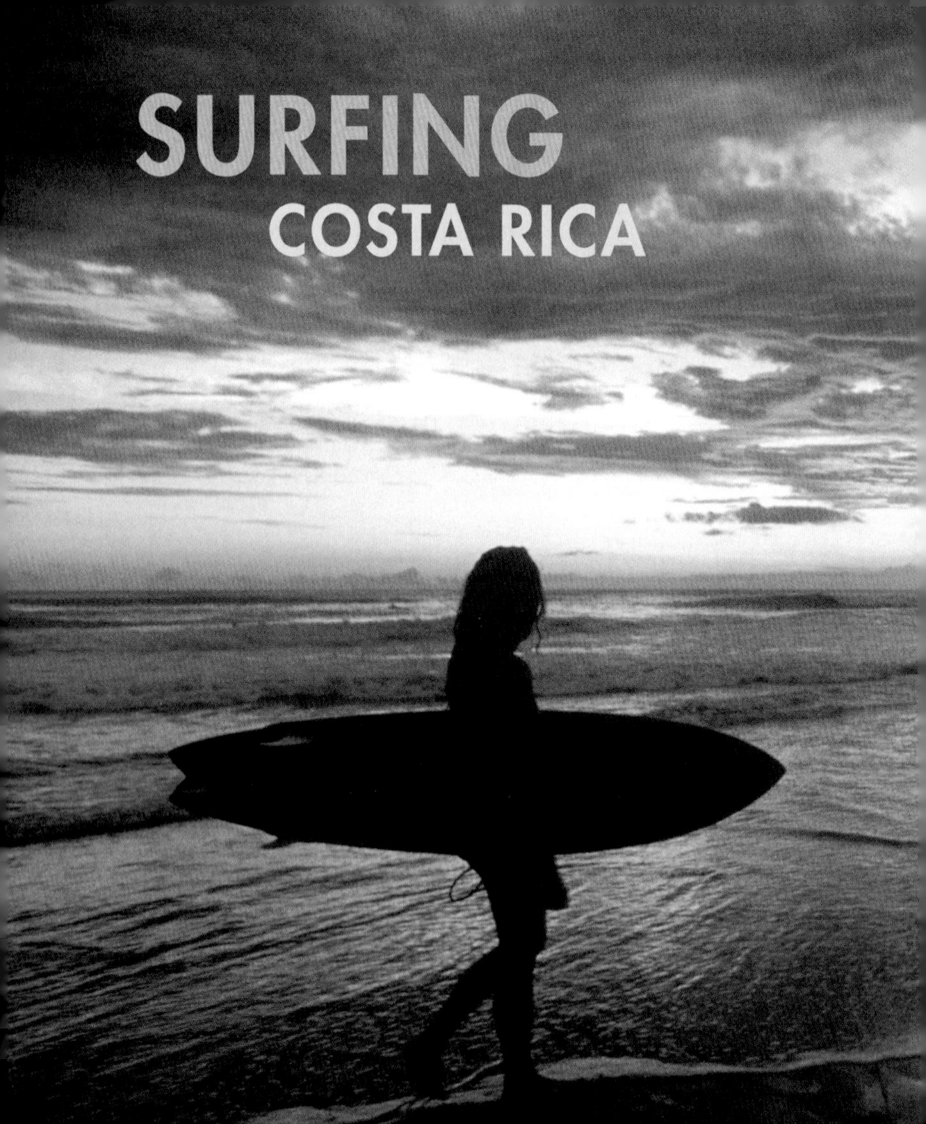

Costa Rica's big surfing community, consistent waves, and not-too-crowded beaches make surfing accessible to anyone who is curious enough to give it a whirl; surf schools, board rentals, and beachside lessons are plentiful. At the most popular beaches, surf tourism is a regular part of the scene. Many instructors are able to bridge generational divides, giving lessons tailored for anyone from tots to retirees. First timers would be wise to start at a beginner beach and take some lessons

by Leland Baxter-Neal

Costa Ricans are known for their laid-back attitude, and this usually translates into a welcoming vibe in the water. Of course, as the waves get more intense, and the surfers more serious, the unspoken rules get stricter, so beginners are advised to stay close to the shore. A good instructor should help keep you out of the way anywhere you go, and if you're on your own, just steer clear of the hot shots until you know the local protocol.

COSTA RICA'S SURF FINDER

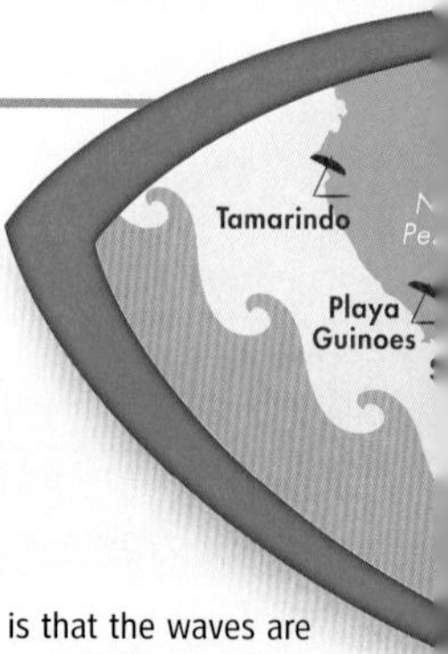

THE PACIFIC COAST

For those new to surfing, destinations on the Pacific coast are more welcoming in a number of ways. There are more beaches, hotels, bars, and surf schools than in the Caribbean, and the waves are friendlier. Access to the Northern and Central Pacific coast is also made easy by (sometimes) paved and well-marked roads. As you head southward down the coast, the route becomes untamed. The remoteness of the Osa Peninsula has guarded a couple of world-class breaks surrounded by some of the country's most untouched jungle.

WHEN TO GO: waves are most consistent from December through April. As you move southward down the coast, the breaks are best from May to November.

THE CARIBBEAN

Costa Rica's truncated Caribbean has comparatively few beaches and they draw only the most dedicated surf seekers. The laid-back culture of that coast seems a perfect match for the surfer vibe. Among the Caribbean waves is perhaps Costa Rica's most famous: Puerto Viejo's Salsa Brava.

WHEN TO GO: Best conditions January through April.

TYPES OF BREAKS

BEACH BREAK: The best type for beginners. Waves break over sandbars and the seafloor. Jacó, Hermosa, and Sámara are all beach breaks.

POINT BREAK: Created as waves hit a point jutting into the ocean. With the right conditions, this can create very consistent waves. Pavones is a point break.

REEF BREAK: Waves break as they hit reef. It can create great (but dangerous) surf. There's a good chance of getting smashed and scraped over extremely sharp coral or rocks. Salsa Brava, in Puerto Viejo, is a reef break.

general

PACIFIC

1 Tamarindo: Very popular with all levels of surfers. Beach breaks are great to learn on; nice waves are formed at a rock outcropping called Pico Pequeño and at the river mouth at the beach's north end. Neighboring Playa Grande is a big, fast beach break for advanced riders.

2 Playa Guiones: If not the best surf in the vicinity of Nosara, it's the best for beginners and longboarders, second only to Sámara. Lots of long, fun beach breaks.

3 Sámara: Protected, mellow beach breaks where the greatest danger is that the waves are too small. Great for beginners and close to lots of breaks for more advanced surfers.

4 Mal País: A variety of beach breaks plus a point break that's good when waves get big. Good for beginners and advanced surfers.

5 Jacó: Unless the surf gets too big, the consistent beach breaks produce forgiving waves that are good to begin and advance on. The south end is best for beginners. Avoid water pollution problems and the occasional crocodile by staying clear of river mouths.

Tamarindo

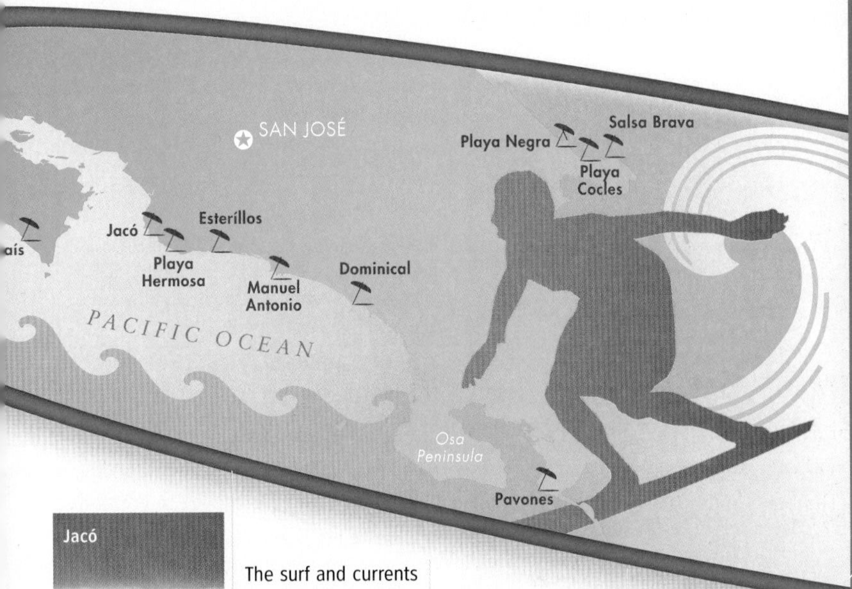

6 Playa Hermosa: A steep beach break just south of Jacó with some of the country's best waves and surfers. Waves can get big, mean, and thunderously heavy; beginners should enjoy the show from the shore. Rip currents make swimming much too dangerous.

7 Esterillos: Divided into three beaches, going north to south: Oeste, Centro, and Este. A beautiful stretch of coast, uncrowded to the point of desolation. The surf and currents can be tough for beginners, and Este and Centro have waves much like Hermosa. Oeste has a variety of beach breaks with softer, friendlier waves.

8 Manuel Antonio: Just outside the national park you'll find a variety of beach breaks. Playitas, at the park's north end, is perhaps the most consistent.

9 Dominical: At the foot of beautiful, forested coastal mountains. A long set of beach breaks that are fun and great for all levels. When waves do get big, beginners should head south to Dominicalito. Rip currents make Dominical too dangerous for swimming.

10 Pavones: Legendary, remote, and surrounded by rain forest, Pavones is said to be the world's longest, or second-longest, left-breaking wave, with a perfect ride lasting nearly three minutes. But with fickle conditions and a tough drive to get here, it's best for the very experienced and dedicated.

CARIBBEAN

11 Playa Negra: A largely undiscovered but quality beach break for all skill levels.

12 Salsa Brava: When the conditions are right, this is arguably Costa Rica's best and most powerful wave; it's placed right over a shallow coral reef. For advanced surfers only.

13 Playa Cocles: Plenty of beach breaks to pick from, good for all levels. But beware the currents or you'll drift out to sea.

SURF SCHOOL TIPS

Surf lesson

Surfing is for the young and the young of heart. At many of Costa Rica's top surf beaches, a wide range of ages and skill sets can be found bobbing together in the water. With the right board and some good instructions, just about anybody can stand up and have some fun in the waves. We strongly recommend taking a lesson or two, but be sure to take them from an actual surf school (there's one on just about every beach) rather than the eager kid who approaches you with a board. Trained instructors will be much better at adapting their lesson plans to different skill levels, ages, and body types.

If you're a first timer, there are a few things you need to know before getting in the water.

- **Pick your beach carefully:** Sámara is a good choice, as is Jacó or Tamarindo. You want beach breaks and small, gentle waves. Make sure to ask about rip tides.
- **Expect introductory lessons to cover the basics:** how to lie on the board, paddle out, duck the incoming waves, and how to pop up onto your surf stance. If you're a natural, you'll be able to hop up and stay standing in the white wash of the wave after it breaks.
- **Have realistic expectations:** even if you have experience in other board sports, like snowboarding or skateboarding, don't expect to be surfing on the face of the wave or tucking into barrels on your first day.
- **Choose the right gear:** if you're a beginner, start on a longboard. Be sure to wear a T-shirt or a wet suit to help protect your chest and stomach from getting scraped.

SURF SLANG (or how not to sound like a dork).

Barrel: The area created when a wave breaks onto itself in a curl, creating a surfable tube that's the surfer's nirvana. Also called the green room.

Drop in: To stand up and drop down the face of a wave. Also used when one surfer cuts another off : "Hey, don't drop in on that guy!"

Duck dive: A maneuver where the surfer first pushes his or her board underwater and then dives with it, ducking under waves that have already broken or are about to break. It's difficult with a longboard *(see Turtle roll).*

Goofy foot: Having a right-foot-forward stance on the surfboard. The opposite is known as natural.

Close out: When a wave or a section of a wave breaks all at once, rather than breaking steadily in one direction. A frustrating situation for surfers, giving them nowhere to go as the wave comes crashing down.

Ding: A hole, dent, crack, or other damage to a board.

Funboard: A little longer than a shortboard with a broad, round nose and tail. Good for beginners looking for something more maneuverable than a longboard.

Outside: The area farther out from where waves are most regularly breaking. Surfers line up here to catch waves.

Shortboard: Usually 6 to 7 feet long with a pointed nose. A tough board to learn on.

Stick: A surfboard.

Turtle roll: A maneuver where the surfer rolls over on the surfboard, going underwater and holding the board upside down. Used by longboarders and beginners to keep from being swept back toward shore by breaking waves.

¢–$$ **Cabinas Vista Hermosa.** Playa Hermosa's original hotel, Cabinas Vista Hermosa sits at the edge of a pleasant grove of coconut palms and almond trees. It can be a bit hard to find. The hotel was renovated in 2007, and the new rooms in a two-story concrete building are simple but comfortable. Pay the extra $20 for an ocean-view room, with sliding doors that open onto a common terrace, since the ones in back overlook the road and parking lot. A separate building on the beach has rustic backpacker rooms that share a bathroom for half the price. The rooms and restaurant overlook two pools, a grill for guest use, and tables on the beach. Common areas have hammocks and diversions like foosball and Ping-Pong. **Pros:** economical; lots of activities. **Cons:** very simple; hard to find. *Costanera, 150 m south of soccer field 2643–7022 or 2643–7040 www.vistahermosa.20m.com 10 rooms In-room: refrigerator. In-hotel: restaurant, pools, laundry service No credit cards BP.*

PLAYA BEJUCO

27 km/16 mi south of Playa Hermosa, 32 km/19 mi south of Jacó.

Surfers wanting to escape the crowds at Jacó and Playa Hermosa, or anyone simply seeking to stray from the beaten path, need only drive 20 minutes south to this relatively deserted palm-lined beach. One could stroll for an hour along the light-gray swath of sand and hardly encounter a soul. Several vacation homes and two small hotels sit behind the first part of the beach, and behind them is a large mangrove forest where you might see macaws or white-faced monkeys. The surf is as big and consistent as at Playa Hermosa, but with a fraction of the surfers. It's a Blue Flag beach, but like Hermosa, it can develop dangerous rip currents, so swimmers should go in no deeper than their waist when the waves are big. Aside from surfing and beachcombing, there is little to do here, which makes it a good place for people wanting to do nothing at all. The mosquitoes can be quite fearsome during the rainy months.

GETTING HERE

If you have a car, take the coastal highway 27 km (16 mi) south past Playa Hermosa to the turnoff for Playa Bejuco, which is 1 km (½ mi) west of the highway. If you don't, take a taxi from Jacó, or local bus toward Quepos.

OUTDOOR ACTIVITIES

SURFING There are various high-tide beach breaks scattered along Playa Bejuco. Waves tend to close out here when the swell is big, but then you can try the mouth of the estuary, 1 km (½ mi) south of the hotels. Bejuco is a do-it-yourself beach, with neither surf schools nor board rental nearby, and because the waves break so close to shore, it's not a good spot for beginners.

WHERE TO STAY

$$ **Delfin Beach Front Resort.** Every room in this two-story hotel has an ocean view, and the surf breaks right in front of it. Tastefully decorated rooms are standard size, with one king or two queen beds, and a small

bathroom. They all have either a large balcony or a terrace; those on the ground floor tend to have better views of the sea, past the skinny coconut palms. The bright, airy restaurant ($$) also overlooks the beach, but the menu is very limited, with tilapia instead of ocean fish, oddly enough. There's a small pool in back, near which hang a few hammocks. **Pros:** beachfront; clean rooms. **Cons:** limited selection at restaurant; so-so management. ✉ *On beach, Playa Bejuco* ☎ *2778–8054* 🌐 *www.delfinbeachfront.com* 12 *rooms* *In-room: no phone, safe. In-hotel: restaurant, bar, pool, beachfront, laundry service* *AE, DC, MC, V* *CP.*

$$ **Hotel Playa Bejuco Hotel.** Playa Bejuco's less expensive accommodations are 50 meters (165 feet) away from the beach, so the views are of pool and gardens rather than surf and sand. The rooms are spacious and well equipped, and the hotel is nicely designed with ochre walls, lots of foliage, and a large, blue-tile pool. They cater to families by putting several beds in some rooms, such as the second-floor rooms with one king and a loft with two twin beds. The restaurant ($$–$$$) has an extensive menu that includes sea bass served with various sauces, pastas, pork loin, filet mignon, and jumbo shrimp. **Pros:** big pool; decent restaurant. **Cons:** lacks ocean view. ✉ *Road to Playa Bejuco, on left* ☎ *2778–8181* 🌐 *www.hotelplayabejuco.com* *20 rooms* *In-room: no phone, safe, refrigerator. In-hotel: restaurant, bar, pool, laundry service, Wi-Fi, no-smoking rooms* *AE, DC, MC, V* *BP.*

QUEPOS

23 km/14 mi south of Parrita, 174 km/108 mi southwest of San José.

This hot and dusty town serves as a gateway to Manuel Antonio. It also serves as the area's hub for banks, supermarkets, and other services. Because nearby Manuel Antonio is so much more attractive, there is no reason to stay here, but many people stop for dinner, for a night on the town, or to go sportfishing. Quepos's name stems from the indigenous tribe that inhabited the area until the Spanish conquest wiped them out. For centuries the town of Quepos barely existed, until the 1930s, when the United Fruit Company built a banana port and populated the area with workers from other parts of Central America. The town thrived for nearly two decades, until Panama Disease decimated the banana plantations in the late 1940s. The fruit company then switched to less lucrative African oil palms, and the area declined. Only since the 1980s have tourism revenues lifted the town out of its slump, a renaissance owed to the beauty of the nearby beaches and nature reserves. Forests around Quepos were destroyed nearly a century ago, but the massive Talamanca Mountain Range, some 10 km (6 mi) to the east, holds one of the largest expanses of wilderness in Central America.

GETTING HERE

It's just over a three-hour drive from San José to Quepos; follow the directions for Jacó and continue south another 40 minutes. Buses from San José's Coca-Cola bus station drop you off in downtown Quepos. SANSA and Nature Air run multiple flights per day between San José and Quepos, as well as direct flights between Quepos and other tourist destinations.

WORD OF MOUTH

"Quepos has become more commercial, but the national park is still unspoiled. Outside the park, they have been strict in enforcing the protected maritime zone, which keeps the hotels off the beach. There is a long public beach outside the park—it's very scenic, and has many restaurants and bars."
—Pat_Hewitt

ESSENTIALS

Bank/ATM **BAC San José** (✉ *Avda. Central*). **Banco Nacional** (✉ *50 m west and 100 m north of bus station* ☎ *2777-0113*).

Hospital Ambulance (☎ *2777-0118*). **Quepos hospital** (✣ *4 km/2½ mi on road to Dominical* ☎ *2777-0020*).

Pharmacy **Farmacia Fischel** (✉ *Near bus station, in front of municipal market* ☎ *2777-0816*).

Post Office **Correos** (✉ *C. Central*).

Rental Cars **Alamo** (✉ *Downtown, 50 m south of Korean school* ☎ *2777-3344, 800/462-5266 in U.S.* 🌐 *www.alamo.com*). **Payless** (✉ *Main road between Quepos and Manuel Antonio* ☎ *2777-0115* 🌐 *www.paylesscarrental.com*).

Taxis **Taxi services** (☎ *2777-0425, 2777-1693, or 2777-1068*).

Travel Agency **Lynch Travel** (✉ *Downtown, behind bus station* ☎ *2777-1170* 🌐 *www.lynchtravel.com*).

7

EXPLORING

Spread over Fila Chota, a lower ridge of the Talamanca Range 22 km (13 mi) northeast of Quepos, **Rainmaker** is a private nature reserve that protects more than 1,500 acres of lush and precipitous forest. The lower part of the reserve can be visited on guided tours from Manuel Antonio, or as a stop on your way to or from Quepos. Tours begin at 7:30. There are two tours available: a walk up the valley of the Río Seco, which includes a dip in a pool at the foot of a waterfall; or a hike into the hills above the waterfall and over a series of suspension bridges strung between giant tropical trees. The park also offers an early-morning bird-watching tour and a night hike. The best value is a half-day package ($70) that includes transport from Manuel Antonio or Quepos, a guided tour, a river swim, and breakfast and lunch. The reserve is home to many of Costa Rica's endangered species, and you may spot birds here that you won't find in Manuel Antonio. It isn't as good a place to see animals as the national park, but Rainmaker's forest is different from the park's—lusher and more precipitous—and the view from its bridges is impressive. It's best to visit Rainmaker in the morning, since—true to its name—it often pours in the afternoon. ✣ *22 km/13 mi northeast of Quepos* ☎ *2777-3565, 504/349-9849 in U.S.* 🌐 *www.rainmakercostarica.org* 🎟 *$75–$100 for guided tours* ⏲ *Mon.–Sat. 7:30–4.*

OUTDOOR ACTIVITIES

There's a tour operator or travel agency on every block in Quepos that can sell you any of about a dozen tours, but some outfitters give discounts if you book directly through them. The dry season is the best time to explore the area's rain forests. If you're here during the rains, do tours first thing in the morning.

CANOPY TOUR There are many zip-line tours in the area that take you flying through the treetops, but **Canopy Safari** (✉*Downtown, next to the Poder Judicial* ☎*2777–0100* 🌐*www.canopysafari.com*) has earned a reputation for long and fast-paced rides. The company's privately owned forest is about a 45-minute car ride from Quepos, and the tour ($65) includes gliding down nine zip lines and a swim in a river pool.

FISHING Quepos is one of the best points of departure for deep-sea fishing in southwestern Costa Rica. The best months for hooking a marlin are from October to February and in May and June, whereas sailfish are abundant from November to May, and are caught year-round. From May to October you're more likely to catch yellowfin tuna, rooster fish, mahimahi, and snapper. **Bluefin Tours** (✉*Downtown, across from the soccer field* ☎*2777–2222 or 2777–1676* 🌐*www.bluefinsportfishing.com*) has catch-and-release sportfishing, conventional fishing, and fly-fishing on a fleet of 25-, 28-, and 31-foot boats. Half-day charters run $545– to $775, whereas a full day costs $645 to $995. **Costa Mar Dream Catcher** (✉*Entrance to Quepos, next to Café Milagro* ☎*2777–4700 or 2777–0593* 🌐*www.costamarsportfishing.com*) has the largest fleet of boats in Quepos, with 11 boats ranging from 25 to 36 feet, and consequently has a wide range of rates. Half- and full-day charters run $500–$1,100. Half-, three-quarter-, and full-day catch-and-release fly and conventional trips ($600–$900 for a full day) with **Luna Tours Sport Fishing** (✉*Downtown, next to Casino Kamuk* ☎*2777–0725, 888/567–5488 in U.S.* 🌐*www.lunatours.net*) are available on 27-, 32-, and 33-foot boats.

KAYAKING AND RAFTING **Iguana Tours** (✉*Downtown Quepos, across from soccer field* ☎*2777–2052* 🌐*www.iguanatours.com*) specializes in exploring the area's natural beauty through white-water rafting on the Naranjo and Savegre rivers and kayak adventures at sea or in a mangrove estuary. They also offer bird-watching, horseback riding, and canopy tours.

MOUNTAIN BIKING The area's green mountains are great for biking, but in the dry season it's hot—very, very hot. The rainy season is slightly cooler, but be prepared to get muddy. **Estrella Tour** (✉*Downtown, across the street from Restaurante El Pueblo* ☎*2777–1286 or 8843–6612* 🌐*www.puertoquepos.com/ecotourism/mountain-biking.html*) has an array of bike tours for intermediate and expert riders ranging from a couple of hours to a full day ($40 to $95). They also offer two- and three-day trips ($140 to $310) that include meals and lodging in mountain cabins.

WHERE TO EAT

$$ SEAFOOD ★ ✕**El Gran Escape.** A favorite with sportfishermen ("You hook 'em, we cook 'em"), the Great Escape is the town's best place for seafood. The menu is dominated by seafood entrées, from shrimp scampi to fresh tuna with mushrooms to bouillabaisse and paella. You can also get hearty

Restaurants ▼

- Agua Azul **10**
- Anaconda Restaurant **11**
- Barba Roja **7**
- Café Milagro **8**
- El Gran Escape ... **1**
- Hotel Vela Bar Restaurant **12**
- Kapi Kapi **6**
- Marlin Restaurant **13**
- El Patio **2**
- Resturante Mar Luna **4**
- Ronny's Place **3**
- Salsipuedes **5**
- Sunspot Bar & Grill **9**

Hotels ▼

- Arenas del Mar **1**
- Cabinas Espadilla **12**
- Cabinas Piscis **9**
- Costa Verde **7**
- Hotel Inn on the Park **14**
- Hotel Manuel Antonio **11**
- Hotel Playa Espadilla **15**
- Hotel Sí Como No **6**
- Hotel Vela Bar **16**
- Hotel Verde Mar **10**
- Makanda by the Sea **2**
- El Mango Moon .. **3**
- La Mariposa **4**
- La Posada **13**
- Villas de la Selva **8**
- Villas Nicolás ... **5**

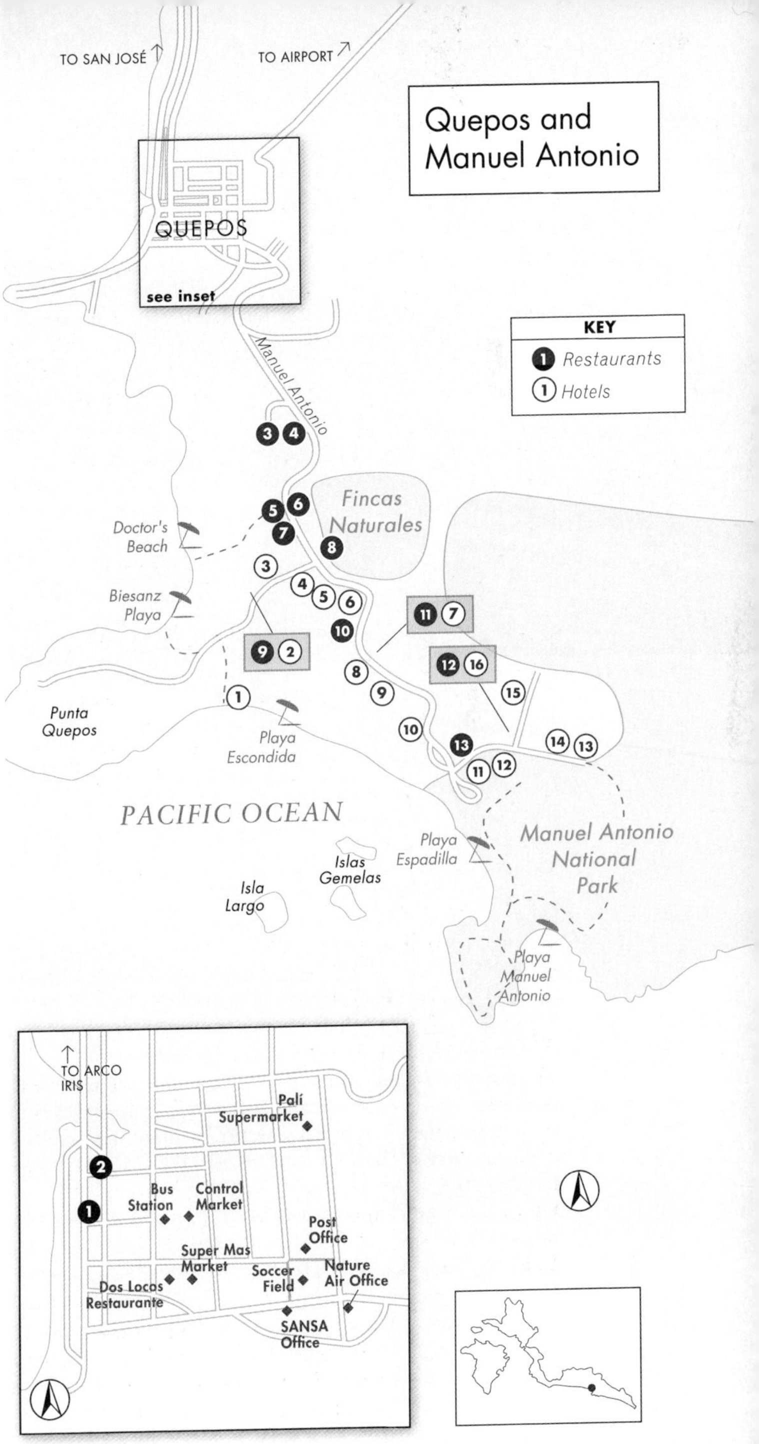

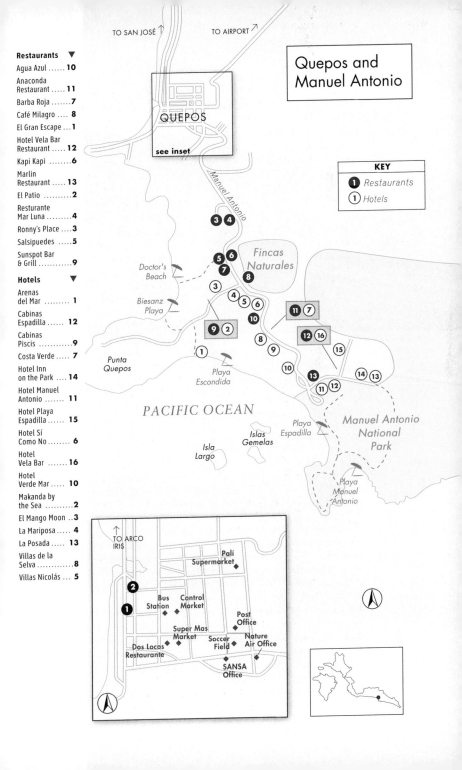

"I was in complete awe as my fantastic local Quepos guide led me along a delightful path up in the hills outside of Quepos." —photo by Colleen George, Fodors.com member

burgers, or a handful of Mexican dishes, and there's a kids' menu. You won't find any billfish, like marlin or swordfish, on the menu, owing to their conservation policy, but the back wall is covered with pictures of them (and their proud reelers). Weathered fishing caps hang from the bar's ceiling. ✉ *150 m north of Hotel Kamuk* ☎ *2777–0395* 🌐 *www.elgranescape.net* 💳 *AE, DC, MC, V* ⏲ *Closed Tues.*

$$–$$$
LATIN AMERICAN
★

✕ **El Patio.** It would be easy to miss this small restaurant squeezed between a couple of shops south of the bridge into town, but don't. The nouveau Latin American cuisine includes some delectable innovations on traditional Central American and Caribbean flavors. Start with some chicken tamales, ceviche, or a mango and chayote (green squash) salad, then sink your teeth into a slice of pork loin in a creole mojo (spicy tomato sauce), shrimp in a rum coconut sauce, or mahimahi cooked in a banana leaf with a smoked tomato mojo and a squash puree. The lunch menu has a good selection of salads, sandwiches, and wraps. The nicest tables are in back, around a lush garden and fountain. ✉ *250 m north of Hotel Kamuk* ☎ *2777–4982* 💳 *AE, DC, MC, V* ⏲ *Closed Sun.*

NIGHTLIFE

Large, air-conditioned **El Arco Iris** (✉ *Over last bridge into Quepos* ☎ *2777–0449*) is the only dance club in the area. Locals and tourists of all ages pack in after midnight, after warming up in other bars. A DJ spins a mix of salsa, merengue, reggae, and pop. Older American expats often congregate at Tex-Mex **Dos Locos Restaurante** (✉ *Avda. Central at C. Central, near bus station* ☎ *2777–1526*) day and night to people-watch or, on Wednesday and Friday nights, to listen to live music.

MANUEL ANTONIO

3 km/2 mi south of Quepos, 179 km/111 mi southwest of San José.

You need merely reach the top of the forested ridge on which many of Manuel Antonio's hotels are perched to understand why it is one of Costa Rica's most popular destinations. That sweeping view of beaches, jungle, and shimmering Pacific dotted with rocky islets confirms its reputation. And unlike the tropical forests in other parts of the country, Manuel Antonio's humid tropical forest remains green year-round. The town itself is spread out across a hilly and curving 5-km (3-mi) road that originates in Quepos and dead-ends at the entrance to Manuel Antonio National Park. Along this main road, near the top of the hill or on its southern slope, are the area's most luxurious hotels and fine-dining restaurants, surrounded by rain forest with amazing views of the beaches and offshore islands. The only problem with staying in one of those hotels is that you'll need to drive or take public transportation to and from the main beach and national park, about 10 minutes away. More hotel and restaurant options are available at the bottom of the hill, within walking distance of the beach, but they lack the sweeping view.

Manuel Antonio is a very gay-friendly town. Many hotels and bars cater to gay travelers, and all of them offer a warm welcome to anyone walking in the door. The area doesn't especially cater to budget travelers, but there are a few cheap places near the end of the road, and various mid-range lodging options.

GETTING HERE

Manuel Antonio is a 15-minute drive over the hill from Quepos and 25 minutes from the Quepos airport. Between SANSA and NatureAir, there are 10 flights per day linking San José and Quepos, as well as direct flights between Quepos and other tourist destinations. Buses depart from San José's Coca-Cola bus station for Manuel Antonio three times a day, at 6 AM, noon, and 6 PM, traveling the opposite direction at 6 AM, noon, and 5 PM; they pick up and drop off passengers in front of hotels on the main Quepos–Manuel Antonio road. Gray Line offers door-to-door service to and from San José, Jacó, Monteverde, Arenal, and major North Pacific beaches. The trip from San José takes about 3½ hours by car or bus. A local public bus makes the 20-minute trip from Quepos to Manuel Antonio every half hour from 7 to 7, then hourly until 10 PM.

ESSENTIALS

Bank/ATM Banco Proamerica (✉ *Main road, next to Economy Rent a Car*).

Pharmacy Farmacia Manuel Antonio (✉ *Main road, across from Marlin Restaurant* ☎ *2777–5370*). **Farmacia La Económica** (✉ *Main road, across from soccer field* ☎ *2777–2130*).

Internet Cantina Internet (✉ *Main road, across from Costa Verde* ☎ *2777–0548*). **Sí Como No Internet** (✉ *Main road, inside Regalame Art Gallery* ☎ *2777–0777*).

Taxis Taxi services (☎ *2777–0425, 2777–0734, or 2777–1693*).

Rental Cars Economy (✉ *Next to Banca Proamerica* ☎ *2777–5353* 🌐 *www.economyrentacar.com*).

EXPLORING

Fodor's Choice ★ **Parque Nacional Manuel Antonio (Manuel Antonion National Park)** proves that good things come in small packages. Costa Rica's smallest park packs in an impressive collection of natural attractions: lots of wildlife, rain forest, white-sand beaches, and rocky coves with abundant marine life. Trails are short, well maintained, and easy to walk. The forest is dominated by massive ficus and gumbo-limbo trees, and is home to two- and three-toed sloths, green and black iguanas, agoutis, four species of monkeys, and more than 350 species of birds.

Despite being Costa Rica's smallest national park, this is its second most visited, after Poás Volcano. Why? Maybe because it is one of two places in Costa Rica to see adorable squirrel monkeys. It's also one of the best places in Costa Rica to see white-faced capuchin monkeys and three-toed sloths. Make no mistake about it: Manuel Antonio is no undiscovered wilderness. It's one of Costa Rica's most-visited attractions, so if you're looking for an undisturbed natural oasis, this is not it. But what Manuel Antonio does have is great diversity of wildlife, all easily spotted from the well-marked trails. And because animals are so used to humans, this is one of the best places to see them up close.

From the ranger station a trail leads through the rain forest behind Playa Espadilla Sur, the park's longest beach. It's also the least crowded because the water can be rough. The coral reefs and submerged volcanic rocks of white-sand Playa Manuel Antonio make for good snorkeling. The 1-km-long (½-mile-long) beach, tucked into a deep cove, is safe for swimming. At low tide you can see the remains of a Quepos Indian turtle trap on the right—the Quepos stuck poles in the semicircular rock formation, which trapped turtles as the tide receded. Olive ridley and green turtles come ashore on this beach May through November. Espadilla and Manuel Antonio beaches lie on opposite sides of a tombolo, or a sandy strip that connects the mainland to Punta Catedral (Cathedral Point), which used to be an island. The steep path that leads up Punta Catedral's rocky hill draped with thick jungle passes a lookout point from which you can gaze over the Pacific at the park's islands.

Farther east, Playa Escondido (Hidden Beach) is rocky and secluded, but it's also more difficult to access. Before you head out to Escondido, find out when the tides come in so you're not stranded. It's quiet and secluded. Kayaking trips might take you down to Punta Serrucho near the southern border of the park, whose jagged peaks explain its name. (Serrucho means "saw.")

WORD OF MOUTH

"We've been to Manuel Antonio during the first week of July, and it was very hot with afternoon rain each day. The rain didn't stop us from doing anything; we kind of expected it, so just did our tours early in the day. You don't really need a car in MA. Everything is easy to walk to and cabs are inexpensive; the guides will usually pick you up for tours." —volcanogirl

A few tips: Hire a guide—you'll walk away with a better understanding of the flora and fauna and see things you probably would have missed otherwise. Get here as early as possible—between 7 and 8 AM is ideal. Rangers permit only 600 to 800 people inside at a time, and during peak season visitors line up to enter. Early morning is also the best time to see animals. And beware of manzanillo trees (indicated by warning signs)—their leaves, bark, and applelike fruit secrete a gooey substance that irritates the skin. ✉*Manuel Antonio* ☎*2777–5185* *$10* ⏲*Tues.–Sun. 7–4*).

DID YOU KNOW?

More than 100 species of mammals and nearly 200 species of birds call Manuel Antonio home. Superstars include the squirrel monkey, white-nosed coati, snakes, bats, iguanas, dolphins, woodpeckers, motmots, mantled howler monkeys, and sloths.

As the road approaches the national park, it skirts the lovely, forest-lined beach of **Playa Espadilla,** which stretches for more than 2 km (1 mi) north from the rocky crag that marks the park's border to the base of the ridge that holds most of the hotels. One of the most popular beaches in Costa Rica, Playa Espadilla fills up with sunbathers, surfers, volleyball players, strand strollers, and sand-castle architects on dry-season weekends and holidays, but for most of the year it is surprisingly quiet. Even on the busiest days it is long enough to provide an escape from the crowd, which tends to gather around the restaurants and lounge chairs near its southern end. Though it is often safe for swimming, beware of rough seas, which create deadly rip currents.Near the northern end of Playa Espadilla is a rocky ridge that separates the main beach from a short, secluded beach called **Playitas,** which has a decent surf break and is the area's nude beach.

Fincas Naturales, a former teak plantation, has been reforested to allow native trees to spring back among the not-so-native ones. A footpath winds through part of the 30-acre tropical forest, and naturalist guides do a good job of explaining the local ecology and identifying birds. The reserve is home to three kinds of monkeys, as well as iguanas, motmots, toucans, tanagers, and seed-chomping rodents called agoutis. Guided walks are given throughout the day: the first starts at 6:30 AM for bird-watching, then at 9 AM and 1 PM, plus a nighttime jungle trek that departs at 5:30 PM. The quickest and least expensive tour is an hourly walk through displays on butterflies, reptiles, and amphibians. Unfortunately, you can't explore the reserve at your own pace. ✉*Entrance across street from Sí Como No Hotel* ☎*2777–0850* 🌐*www.butterflygardens.co.cr* *$15–$45, kids under 12 $10–$35, depending on tour* ⏲*Daily 7 AM–6 PM.*

OUTDOOR ACTIVITIES

Manuel Antonio's list of outdoor activities is almost endless. Tours generally range from $40 to $90 per person and can be booked through your hotel's reception desk or directly through the outfitter. During the rainy season, some outdoor options might lose their appeal, but clouds usually let loose in the afternoon, so take advantage of sunny mornings.

CANOPY TOURS ★ **Tití Canopy Tours** (☎*2777–3130*) has a relatively slow-paced zip-line tour ($55) through a forest reserve that is contiguous with the national park. Guides go above and beyond to make you feel comfortable and safe, and will help you spot animals.

TOUR OPERATORS A small company run by friendly young locals with a good grasp of the area's activities, **Espadilla Tours** (☎*2777–5334*) can arrange any kind of activity in the Manuel Antonio area, from surf lessons to sunset sails. The Internet café next to the Marlin Restaurant has information.

IN THE THICK OF IT

There's more rain forest on private land than in Manuel Antonio National Park, which means it's not unusual to see many of the animals the park is famous for from the balcony of your hotel room or from your breakfast table. It also means that local landowners play an important role in conserving the area's flora and fauna.

HIKING Highly visited Manuel Antonio National Park is the obvious place to go, but in private reserves like Fincas Naturales *(⇨above)* and Rainmaker *(⇨Quepos, above)* you can also gain a rich appreciation of the local forests' greenery and wildlife. ■**TIP→Bring binoculars!**

HORSEBACK RIDING **Brisas del Nara** (☎*2779–1235* 🌐*www.horsebacktour.com*) takes riders of all ages and levels through the protected Cerro Nara mountain zone, 32 km (20 mi) from Manuel Antonio, and ends with a swim in a natural pool at the foot of a 350-foot waterfall. Full-day tours ($65) include three hours on horseback, with breakfast and lunch included; the ride on the half-day tour ($50) lasts two hours, and there's no lunch. **Finca Valmy Tours** (☎*2779–1118* 🌐*www.valmytours.com*) is known for its attentive service and healthy horses. Its six-hour horseback tours take you through the forested mountains above Villa Nueva, east of Manuel Antonio ($65). Lunch and swimming in a pool below a small waterfall on their property are included.

Beach riding is the specialty of **Rancho Savegre** (☎*2779–4430 or 8834–8687* 🌐*www.costaricahorsevacation.com*). Trips set out from a cattle ranch about 15 minutes south of Manuel Antonio and include a stop at a waterfall for swimming or trail walking. Of the two half-day tours, only the morning tour includes a meal.

KAYAKING **Iguana Tours** (☎*2777–2052* 🌐*www.iguanatours.com*) runs sea-kayaking trips ($65) to the islands of Manuel Antonio National Park—which require some experience when the seas are high—and a mellower paddle through the mangrove estuary of Isla Damas, where you might see monkeys, crocodiles, and various birds.

SNORKELING AND DIVING The islands that dot the sea in front of Manuel Antonio are surrounded by volcanic rock reefs with small coral formations and attract schools of snapper, jacks, barracudas, rays, sea turtles, moray eels, and other marine life. **Manuel Antonio Divers** (☎*2777–7878* 🌐*www.manuelantoniodivers.com*) offers half-day tours ($85) at half a dozen spots offshore where an array of fish and other marine life congregate around volcanic rocks. Full-day trips to Caño Island ($235), a 90-minute boat trip away, as well as snorkeling excursions ($135) to the Islas Gemelas, complement the complete selection of PADI certification courses they provide. **Oceans Unlimited** (☎2777–3171 🌐*www.oceansunlimitedcr.com*) offers various offshore sites, an all-day diving excursion to Caño Island ($149–$220), PADI certification courses, and snorkeling. Several tour operators in town can put you on an organized snorkel excursion to the calm waters of Biesanz Beach.

SWIMMING When the surf is up, riptides are a dangerous problem on Playa Espadilla, Manuel Antonio's main beach, which runs parallel to the road to the park's entrance. For a less turbulent swim and smaller crowds, head to **Playa Biesanz** (✉*Near Hotel Parador*), which lies within a sheltered cove and also has good snorkeling. Manuel Antonio's safest swimming area is sheltered **Playa Manuel Antonio**, the second beach in the national park. Its white sand makes it attractive for lounging around, and it's also a good place for snorkeling. ■**TIP→Never leave your valuables unattended while you're swimming.**

ULTRALIGHT FLYING **Sky Riders** (*2777–4101* 🌐*www.costaricaskyriders.com*) has open-cockpit, slow-flying ultralights that glide between sea level and 304 meters (1,000 feet). One tour is a one-passenger, 24-minute ride over Manuel Antonio and several surrounding beaches ($95). The other is a two-person 35-minute flight over Damas Island's canals and mangroves ($125).

WHITE-WATER RAFTING The three white-water rivers in this area have limited seasons. The rains from August to October raise the rivers to their perfect peak. **Río Savegre**, which flows past patches of rain forest, has two navigable stretches: the lower section (Class II to III), which is a mellow trip perfect for neophytes, and the more rambunctious upper section (Class III to IV). It is usually navigable from June to March. **Río Naranjo** (Class III to IV) has a short but exciting run that requires some experience and can be done only from June to December. **Río Parrita** (Class II to III) is a relatively mellow white-water route, and in the dry season it can be navigated only in two-person, inflatable duckies.

Manuel Antonio's original rafting outfitter, **Adventure Manuel Antonio** (☎*2777–1084* 🌐*www.adventuremanuelantonio.com*), leads trips down the Savegre and Naranjo on half-day and full-day tours ($69–$98). Naranjo River tours can be combined with kayaking in the nearby estuary. **Ríos Tropicales/h2O Adventures** (☎*2777–4092* 🌐*www.h2ocr.com*), the biggest rafting outfitter in the country, runs kayaking excursions and rafting trips on the Savegre and Naranjo ($70 to $98).

WHERE TO EAT

$$–$$$ SEAFOOD ★ ✕**Agua Azul.** This simple second-floor restaurant with a small kitchen in one corner offers a breathtaking view by day and a deliciously inventive selection of seafood at night. The lunch menu is strong on salads and sandwiches, but the dinner options include some of the best entrées in town. In addition to nightly fish and pasta specials, they offer such inventive delicacies as seared tuna over a tequila-and-lime cucumber salad, calamari sautéed with capers and olives, and coconut-crusted mahimahi. ✉*Main road, above the Villas del Parque office* ☎*2777–5280* 💳*V* ⊗*Closed Wed. and Oct.*

$$ ECLECTIC ✕**Anaconda Restaurant.** Named for the humongous snake whose skin is mounted on the wall behind the bar, this open-air restaurant is hidden

in the rain forest. You won't see any anacondas (they are found in South America), but you may spot iguanas, squirrel monkeys, or various species of birds from one of the restaurant's oversize chairs. You are sure to enjoy the view of the coast. The eclectic menu ranges from Japanese-style tuna to Tuscan mahimahi. They also serve excellent pastas and salads. The restaurant is a short drive from the beach, making it an excellent option for a quiet lunch. ✉ *Costa Verde Hotel* ☎ *2777–1973* ▭ *AE, DC, MC, V.*

$ CAFÉ ✕ **Café Milagro.** The only place in town that serves its own fresh-roasted coffee, Café Milagro is a colorful, cozy choice for breakfast food any time of the day, or to satisfy a chocolate-chip-cookie craving. The North American menu includes bagels, breakfast burritos, baked goods like brownies and muffins, an inventive selection of sandwiches, and a fruit plate with granola. Tables on the front porch overlook the road, but there's also seating in the back garden. ✉ *Main road to park, across from La Mariposa* ☎ *2777–0794* ▭ *AE, DC, MC, V* ⏲ *No dinner.*

$$ ECLECTIC ✕ **Hotel Vela Bar Restaurant.** This small, open-air restaurant retains an intimate atmosphere behind a hedge of tropical foliage and beneath a conical thatch roof. They serve a variety of dishes in generous proportions, including mahimahi with an array of sauces, shrimp with ginger, and pork chops in pineapple sauce. There are vegetarian options as well. Service can be slow when it gets busy. ✉ *Up road from Marlin Restaurant* ☎ *2777–0413* ▭ *AE, DC, MC, V.*

$$$ ECLECTIC ★ ✕ **Kapi Kapi.** This elegant restaurant at the edge of the forest offers Manuel Antonio's best ambience for dinner, with low lighting, ochre walls, dark hardwoods, and potted palms. The name is a greeting in the indigenous Maleku language, but the menu is the cosmopolitan invention of a Californian chef. It includes such un–Costa Rican starters as a lemongrass, chicken, and coconut soup, and "seafood cigars"—a mix of fresh tuna, shrimp, and mahimahi deep-fried in an egg-roll wrapper and served on a cabbage salad. The main courses include such Asian-inspired dishes as prawns with a tamarindo-coconut-rum glaze and macadamia-encrusted mahimahi with a plum chili sauce. Only in dessert does the chef reveal his nationality, with the chocolate s'more cake. ✉ *East side of main road, across from Pacifico Colonial condos* ☎ *2777–5049* ✍ *Reservations essential* ▭ *MC, V* ⏲ *No lunch.*

$–$$ COSTA RICAN ✕ **Marlin Restaurant.** The outdoor tables of this two-story concrete restaurant are pretty much always full, owing to its location on Manuel Antonio's busiest corner, across the street from the beach. It's a convenient place to grab breakfast after an early-morning hike through the park—be it banana pancakes or a *t pico,* with eggs and *gallo pinto* (black beans and rice). The lunch and dinner menu ranges from the ubiquitous *arroz con pollo* (rice with chicken) to tenderloin with french fries, and jumbo shrimp in garlic and lemon butter. The fresh mahimahi and tuna are always a good bet. Breakfast is also available. ✉ *Main road, south of the hill, on corner across from bus stop and beach* ☎ *2777–1134* ▭ *AE, DC, MC, V.*

$$$ SEAFOOD ✕ **Restaurante Mar Luna.** Easy to overlook, this simple blue wooden restaurant propped on the hillside is often packed. The decor is limited to illuminated plastic fish, ceramic mobiles, potted palms, and colorful

Espadilla Beach, not far from Quepos, is one of the few beaches in Costa Rica with life guards.

tablecloths, but the restaurant has a pleasant view of treetops and the sea below. The fresh seafood, caught each morning by one of the cooks, is what draws the crowd. You might start with sashimi or seafood soup, and move on to one of the popular entrées: grilled tuna with peppers and onions, lobster in a brandy sauce, the humongous mariscada—a sautéed seafood platter for two—or one of the surf-and-turf options. They have live Latin music Thursday to Saturday, and a small bamboo bar in front. ✉ *East side of road, 100 m north of Manuel Antonio Elementary School* ☎ *2777–5107* ▭ *AE, MC, V* ⏲ *No lunch.*

$–$$ COSTA RICAN ✕ **Ronny's Place.** A spectacular sunset view and friendly, attentive service are this simple, open-air restaurant's best qualities. The small menu includes such typical Tico dishes as *sopa negra* (black-bean soup), ceviche, shrimp and fish on a skewer, and filet mignon wrapped with bacon and topped with a mushroom sauce. Ronny's is somewhat secluded down a long dirt road that crosses a green valley on a narrow ridge in front of the sea. ✣ *1 km/½ mi west of main road, down dirt road across from Amigos del Río* ☎ *2777–5120* ▭ *AE, DC, MC, V.*

$ ECLECTIC ✕ **Salsipuedes.** This colorful, friendly tapas bar nestled behind a rock formation at the edge of the forest has one of the best sunset views in town, making it a great cocktail and appetizer option. The tapas are fun to share, three to five per couple, depending on how hungry you are. They range from sashimi and grilled tuna or mahimahi to fajitas. Such Costa Rican favorites as frijolitos blancos (white beans stewed with chicken) and chicharrones con yuca (fried pork and cassava root) are also available. They offer half a dozen full dinners, including larger cuts of fish, and some rice and pasta dishes, plus they're willing to turn any of the tapas dishes into a full meal. ✉ *Main road, across from Banco Proamerica* ☎ *2777–5091* ▭ *MC, V* ⊙ *Closed Tues. No lunch.*

$–$$$ ECLECTIC ★ ✕ **Sunspot Bar and Grill.** The open-air, poolside restaurant of the exclusive Makanda by the Sea hotel has tables beneath purple cloth tents overlooking the sea and surrounding jungle. Its kitchen, cleverly hidden beneath the bar, serves up such succulent treats as jumbo shrimp in a ginger sauce and grilled beef tenderloin with a choice of sauces. The menu also includes poultry, lamb, and pasta dishes, along with nightly specials. At lunch they offer great pizzas, salads, and sandwiches. You'll want to put on insect repellent at night. ✉ *Makanda by the Sea hotel* ✣ *1 km/½ mi west of La Mariposa* ☎ *2777–0442* ✍ *Reservations essential* ▭ *AE, DC, MC, V.*

WHERE TO STAY

$$$$ Fodor'sChoice ★ **Arenas del Mar Beach and Nature Resort.** What you don't see is what you get at this new eco-luxury hotel: no cars, no crowds, no clutter. You can hardly see the hotel's seven sage-and-beige modern buildings camouflaged on reforested hillsides sloping down to two pristine, almost deserted beaches. Rooms here are chic and elegant but still "green," decorated with gorgeous natural fabrics, king-size beds, and flamboyant local art. Bathrooms are spacious, with round, glass-brick shower stalls. Huge private terraces, some with ocean view and mosaic-tiled hot tubs, have comfortable outdoor sitting areas. Two pools, two beaches to choose from, and a spa all spell luxury. Even the eco element here is an added luxury, with 12 acres of beach and forest alive with birds, butterflies, and wildlife. The main restaurant is practically in the trees, and the menu is innovative and ambitious. There's also a more casual daytime restaurant at the lower pool nearest the beach. **Pros:** best of both worlds: luxury and eco-consciousness; best beach access in Manuel Antonio; wonderful bird-watching and wildlife viewing. **Cons:** very steep paths and stairs, although electric carts constantly transport guests. ✉ *Far west end of Playa Espadilla, down the El Parador road, in Manuel Antonio* ☎ *2777–2777* 🌐 *www.arenasdelmar.com* ⇆ *38 rooms* ♨ *In-room: safe, kitchen, Wi-Fi . In-hotel: 2 restaurants, bar, 2 pools, spa, beachfront, laundry service, Internet terminal, Wi-Fi, parking (free)* ▭ *AE, MC, V* 🍽 *BP*

$$ **Cabinas Espadilla.** Owned by the same family that runs the nearby Hotel Playa Espadilla, these quiet cabinas close to the beach are more affordable but have fewer amenities. Rooms open onto porches overlooking tropical gardens and a wide lawn, shaded by hammock-strung palm trees, and a large pool. The rooms with kitchenettes cost $10 more, but are a bit cramped. Guests have access to the hotel's restaurant, tennis court, and forest trail. **Pros:** good value; short walk from beach; nice grounds. **Cons:** mediocre rooms; not very friendly. ✉ *On road beside Marlin Restaurant* ☎ *2777–0903* 🌐 *www.cabinasespadilla.com* ⇆ *16 cabinas* ♨ *In-room: no phone, safe, kitchen (some), refrigerator, no TV. In-hotel: pool, laundry service* ▭ *AE, MC, V* 🍽 *EP.*

¢ **Cabinas Piscis.** A short walk through the woods from the beach, this tranquil hotel shaded by tall trees is one of the area's best options for budget travelers. Most rooms are in a concrete building with a wide porch; they are simple but spacious, with small bathrooms and lots of windows. The tiny, lower-price rooms that share a separate, cold-water bathhouse are marketed to backpackers. Also available are a separate cabin with a refrigerator, and an open-room, fully equipped *casita* for four. A small restaurant serves breakfast and light lunches. Bathrooms do not have hot water. **Pros:** forested property on the beach; inexpensive. **Cons:** spartan rooms; soft beds. ✉ *Road to park, past Hotel Karahe* ☎ *2777–5320* *15 rooms, 10 with bath; 1 casita; 1 cabin* *In-room: no a/c, no phone, no TV* *MC, V* *EP.*

$$–$$$ ★ **Costa Verde.** You're likely to see monkeys, iguanas, and all kinds of birds on the forest trails surrounding this extensive hotel's buildings, which are scattered on both sides of the main road. Adult-only studios are spacious, with large balconies and screened walls that let the breeze through. Those in the other buildings are smaller but are air-conditioned. Splurge for a "Studio-Plus," which all have ocean views. Three fully equipped bungalows are also available for groups of up to six. The cheaper "efficiencies" are a mixed lot—only those in Building D, in the jungle overlooking the sea, are recommended; Buildings B and C aren't. The hotel's Anaconda Restaurant *(⇨ above)* is excellent. The dinner-only La Cantina ($$), across the street, serves good grilled meats and seafood, and has live music. **Pros:** great ocean views; wildlife; restaurants; studios and Building D efficiencies a good value. **Cons:** most efficiencies suffer road noise; no beach access; service inconsistent. ✉ *Road to park, south side of hill, on left* ☎ *2777–0584, 2777–0187, or 866/854–7958* *www.costaverde.com* *10 efficiencies, 15 studios, 3 bungalows* *In-room: no a/c (some), no phone (some), kitchen. In-hotel: 2 restaurants, bars, pools, laundry service, Internet terminal* *AE, MC, V* *EP.*

$$$ **El Mango Moon.** This B&B's intimate atmosphere and hospitable staff make you feel like you're staying with a friend rather than at a hotel. The comfy, open living-room area extends to a balcony lined with a wooden counter and stools with views to the mango-shaped pool below and a tranquil cove framed by the rain forest. The cream-color rooms vary in size and amenities; more expensive rooms have semiprivate balconies. Rooms on the top floor can connect for families. Monkey-attracting mango trees surround the building, and a steep 20-minute trail leads to a secluded beach. **Pros:** nice view; tranquil area; friendly. **Cons:** far from main beaches; not much privacy; some rooms dark; relatively expensive. ✉ *Between La Mariposa and Makanda* ☎ *2777–5323* *www.mangomoon.net* *9 rooms, 2 suites* *In-room: no phone, safe. In-hotel: restaurant, bar, pool, no kids under 12, no-smoking rooms* *AE, MC, V* *BP.*

¢–$$ ★ **Hotel Manuel Antonio.** One of Manuel Antonio's original hotels, this economical place is close to the national park entrance and across the street from the beach. The rooms, in two-story concrete buildings, have tile floors, simple pastel drapes and bedspreads, and large balconies or terraces, many of which have ocean views. Unfortunately, the ocean view is often obstructed by souvenir vendors' stalls and cars lining the road. The rooms are comfortable but not fancy, equipped with air-conditioning and cable TV, and just steps away from the beach and park. Backpackers can stay in one of the rustic wooden rooms above

The pacific coast is backed by mangrove, rain, transitional, and tropical-dry forests.

the restaurant, which lack air-conditioning and TV, but are a third of the price. **Pros:** near beach, park; a real bargain. **Cons:** busy area on weekends; service inconsistent. ✉ *End of road to park* ☎ *2777–1237 or 2777–1351* *hotelmanuelantonio@racsa.co.cr* *28 rooms* *In-room: safe. In-hotel: restaurant, room service, bar, laundry service, no-smoking rooms* *AE, MC, V* *EP.*

$$–$$$ **Hotel Playa Espadilla.** A short walk from the beach, this friendly hotel spreads across grounds bordered on two sides by the tall trees of Manuel Antonio National Park, and it has a trail through an area of the park that few people visit. The simple but spacious mint-green rooms with big windows are housed in two-story buildings surrounded by green lawns; for a bit more money, some rooms have good-size kitchens with modern appliances. A small blue-tile pool and patio have a pleasant adjacent bar area with a billiard table. Directly behind are a large, open-air restaurant and a tennis court, but there are better places to dine in the area. **Pros:** surrounded by forest; close to beach. **Cons:** service inconsistent; very small pool. ✉ *150 m up side road from Marlin Restaurant, first left* ☎ *2777–0903* *www.hotelespadilla.com* *16 rooms* *In-room: safe, kitchen (some), Wi-Fi. In-hotel: restaurant, room service, bar, tennis court, pool, laundry service, Wi-Fi, no-smoking rooms* *AE, DC, MC, V* *BP.*

$$$–$$$$ **Hotel Sí Como No.** This luxury resort goes to great lengths to be eco-friendly, and has earned a level-five Certificate of Sustainable Tourism, the highest level possible. It's also quite family-friendly, with a separate kids' pool, complete with waterslide, and an in-house cinema. Rooms of varying sizes (and prices) are in two-story buildings scattered through the rain forest, decorated in earth tones to complement the surrounding

nature. Spring for a spacious deluxe room for a sea view, which you can enjoy from your private balcony. Smaller "superior" rooms, in the ground floors, have less impressive views, whereas standard rooms view the forest. There is live music nightly at the Claro Que Sí restaurant (dinner only; $$$), which specializes in Caribbean-style seafood, and the Rico Tico ($$) grill, which serves lighter fare. A free shuttle makes scheduled trips to the beach, about 3 km (2 mi) away. **Pros:** friendly; nice views; environmentally sustainable; good restaurants. **Cons:** 3 km (2 mi) from beach; standards overpriced; several suites too close to road. ✉ *Road to park, just after Villas Nicolás, right-hand side* ☎ *2777–0777* 🌐 *www.sicomono.com* *38 rooms, 20 suites* *In-room: safe, kitchen (some), refrigerator, no TV. In-hotel: 2 restaurants, bars, pools, spa, laundry service, Wi-Fi* ▭ *AE, MC, V* *BP.*

¢–$ ★ **Hotel Vela Bar.** Abutting the jungle not far from Playa Espadilla, this low-key, eclectic hotel has small but attractive rooms and very competitive rates. Though a bit cramped, each room has its own rustic charm, with white stucco walls, simple wooden furniture, and terracotta tile or wood floors. Room 7 is particularly nice, thanks to large windows and a bathtub. Shared front terraces with rocking chairs and hammocks overlook lush gardens. Two bungalows with private patios, air-conditioning, and TV sleep four. The restaurant, under a conical thatch roof in front, serves an eclectic mix of seafood and meat dishes with an array of sauces. **Pros:** very affordable; laid-back. **Cons:** basic rooms; spotty service. ✉ *Up road from Marlin Restaurant, on left* ☎ *2777–0413* 🌐 *www.velabar.com* *8 rooms, 2 bungalows, 1 apartment* *In-room: no a/c (some), no phone, safe, kitchen (some), refrigerator (some), no TV (some). In-hotel: restaurant, bar, Internet terminal* ▭ *AE, DC, MC, V* *EP.*

$$ **Hotel Verde Mar.** This whimsical little hotel and its helpful staff are in the rain forest, with direct access to the beach and minutes away from the park. The rooms in a long two-story concrete building are on the small side, with one queen bed, but have colorfully artistic interiors, kitchenettes, and large windows with views of the ubiquitous tropical foliage. Suites are a bit bigger than standard rooms and have two queen beds and a walk-in closet. There's a small pool, from which a wooden catwalk leads through the woods to the beach. **Pros:** good value; mere steps from beach; in forest; friendly. **Cons:** rooms smallish; very basic. *½ km/¼ mi north of park* ☎ *2777–1805 or 2777–2122* 🌐 *www.verdemar.com* *22 rooms* *In-room: no phone, safe, kitchen (some), no TV. In-hotel: pool, Internet, no-smoking rooms* ▭ *AE, DC, MC, V* *EP.*

$$ **Inn on the Park.** This family-friendly inn has a quiet location near the beach and national park. The papaya-color building has three floors with two rooms each. Half are master suites with separate bedrooms, kitchens, and pullout couches, which can be a deal for small families (kids under 12 stay free). Upper rooms share balconies with verdant views. A small pool area with a wooden deck has a grill and tables where complimentary Continental breakfast is served. The rain forest rises up just behind it. **Pros:** good for families; lovely locale. **Cons:** no frills; rooms can be dingy. ✉ *200 m up side road from Marlin*

Restaurant ☎ *2777–5115* 🌐 *www.innontheparkhotel.com* ↩ *6 rooms* ⚐ *In-room: safe, kitchen (some). In-hotel: pool, laundry service, Internet, no-smoking rooms* 🍽 *CP.*

$$$–$$$$ Fodor'sChoice ★ **La Mariposa.** The best view in town—a sweeping panorama of verdant hills, the aquamarine ocean, and offshore islands—is Mariposa's claim to fame. A confusing array of accommodations ranges from standard rooms overlooking the rain forest to bright suites with ocean-view balconies, to a penthouse. All are spacious and are in a series of buildings between the jungle and gardens ablaze with colorful flowers. The four-story main building holds the lobby and restaurant, above which are three floors of ocean-view rooms reached by external spiraling stairways, which aren't for people who have trouble with stairs or suffer from vertigo. They are big, though rather plain, and have semiprivate balconies with amazing views; book a bright corner room on an upper floor (No. 31, 35, 36, or 40). Older ocean-view rooms on the hillside have low ceilings, Spanish decor, and big balconies overlooking the coast and park. Newer standard ocean views, down the hill, have lesser vistas, but TV sets. Larger premier rooms offer more privacy and great views, and have daybeds for kids (under 10 stay free), though the modern, new units suffer design flaws. The sundeck and wraparound pool are lovely. Transportation is provided to and from the beach, several times a day. **Pros:** gorgeous views; decent restaurant; central location. **Cons:** 4 km (2½ mi) from beach, ocean-view balconies separated by cane barriers. ✉ *West of main road, right after Barba Roja* 📮 *Apdo. 4, Quepos* ☎ *2777–0355, 800/572–6440 in U.S.* 🌐 *www.hotelmariposa.com* ↩ *60 rooms* ⚐ *In-room: safe, kitchen (some), no TV, Internet. In-hotel: restaurant, room service, bars, pools, laundry service, Wi-Fi* 💳 *AE, DC, MC, V* 🍽 *BP.*

$$ Fodor'sChoice ★ **La Posada Private Jungle Bungalows.** Nestled on the edge of the national park, this cluster of bungalows is also just a short walk from the beach. Each bungalow has its own name—Fisherman's Wharf, Birds of Paradise, Jungle—and is decorated accordingly. The palm-thatch terraces face the small pool and lush greenery of the rain forest, which is regularly animated by troops of squirrel monkeys and other animals. As the charming North American owner, Michael, says, it's as close as you'll get to sleeping in the park. The main building holds three spacious apartments and a fully equipped casita (small house) on the second floor with two bedrooms, two baths, and a futon. Complimentary breakfast and cheap pizza are served in a small restaurant ($) in front. **Pros:** good value; near beach and park; wildlife; friendly. **Cons:** a bit isolated; small pool. ✉ *250 m up side road from Marlin Restaurant* 📮 *Apdo. 155–6350, Quepos* ☎📠 *2777–1446* 🌐 *www.laposadajungle.com* ↩ *4 bungalows, 2 apartments, 1 casita* ⚐ *In-room: no phone, safe, refrigerator. In-hotel: pool, laundry service, no-smoking rooms* 💳 *MC, V* 🍽 *BP.*

$$$$ Fodor'sChoice ★ **Makanda by the Sea.** Hypnotic views of the jungle-framed Pacific Ocean make this secluded rain-forest retreat perfect for honeymooners. The bright, spacious, white-and-cream villas are among the country's most tasteful (and expensive). They have a comfortable seating area and king-size bed facing the sliding glass doors that lead to large balconies

with ocean views and hammocks. The modern kitchens won't be necessary for breakfast, which is delivered to your room. Windows behind the bed maximize natural light, and the small Japanese-style garden out back adds to the subtle, well-designed touches. The smaller studios are darker, and have less impressive views, but they have access to the lovely, colorful pool and the Sunspot Bar and Grill (⇨ *above*), one of the best restaurants in town. Adventurous hikers can make the 20-minute trek through the jungle to a tiny, private beach. **Pros:** secluded; tranquil; surrounded by nature; ocean views. **Cons:** far from beach; studios need updating. *1 km/½ mi west of La Mariposa Apdo. 29, Quepos 2777–0442, 888/625–2632 in North America www.makanda.com 6 villas, 5 studios In-room: safe, kitchen, Internet. In-hotel: restaurant, room service, pool, beachfront, laundry service, Internet terminal, no kids under 16 AE, DC, MC, V BP.*

$$ **Villas de la Selva.** Hidden from the main road behind a mural of monkeys, this unique hillside hotel has comfortable accommodations and great views of the ocean. Straight down the long stairway, and perched on a cliff facing the ocean, are three airy rooms, each with its own color scheme, kitchenette, and ample terrace. There's also a casita that fits several people. Up the side of the hill, two much smaller rooms with balconies have nice views, but tiny bathrooms. A 300-meter (990-foot) trail leads to the beach. **Pros:** nice views; beach access; good value. **Cons:** unfriendly owner; not much privacy. *Road to park, past Costa Verde and La Arboleda hotels 2777–1137 www.villasdelaselva.com 6 rooms, 1 casita In-room: no a/c (some), no phone, safe (some), kitchen (some), refrigerator. In-hotel: pool, laundry service MC, V EP.*

$$–$$$ Fodor'sChoice ★ **Villas Nicolás.** On a hillside about 3 km (2 mi) from the beach, terraced Mediterranean-style privately owned (and rented) villas have impressive views. Villas on the upper levels have ocean views, and those on the lower level overlook the jungle, where you may spot monkeys, iguanas, and an array of birds. (Avoid units 1 and 2, which overlook the hotel next door.) Each room is decorated differently, but the predominant motif is tropical. Most have balconies, some of which are large enough to hold a table, chairs, and hammock. Narrow walkways wind through this tranquil property's lush grounds to the villas and blue-tile pool. During the high season a tiny restaurant by the pool offers breakfasts and light meals. **Pros:** great location; most rooms have great views. **Cons:** some units need updating; inconsistent service. *Road to park, across from Hotel Byblos Apdo. 236, Quepos 2777–0481 www.villasnicolas.com 12 villas In-room: safe, kitchen (some), refrigerator, no TV. In-hotel: pool, laundry service, no-smoking rooms AE, DC, MC, V EP.*

NIGHTLIFE

BARS The **Billfish Bar** (*Main road, across from Barba Roja 2777–0411*), with large-screen TVs and pool tables, fills up on game nights.

★ **Salsipuedes** (*Main road, north of Barba Roja 2777–5019*), a colorful tapas bar hidden behind tropical foliage, is a great sunset venue. It's one of the few places you can enjoy a quiet drink.

7

DANCE CLUB **Barba Roja** (✉ *Main road, across from Hotel Divisamar* ☎ *2777–0331*) has a popular sunset happy hour. The bar becomes a dance club late on Saturday night. **Tutu** (✉ *Above Gato Negro, Casitas Eclipse* ☎ *No phone*) is Manuel Antonio's late-night gay bar. It's an elegant place, with light reflected off a deep blue pool. **The Lounge** (✉ *Main road, above La Hacienda Restaurant* ☎ *2777–5143*) is a popular late-night spot, with reggae playing Monday and Wednesday and a mix of Latin rhythms other nights.

SHOPPING

There's no shortage of shopping in this town. The beach near the entrance to the park is lined with a sea of vendors who sell T-shirts, hats, and colorful beach wraps. More authentic handicrafts are sold at night by artisans positioned along the sidewalk in central Manuel Antonio.

La Buena Nota (✉ *Main road, past Hotel Karahe* ☎ *2777–1002*) has an extensive selection of beachwear, souvenirs, sunscreen, hats, postcards, and English-language books and magazines. **Regalame** (✉ *Next to Sí Como No Hotel* ☎ *2777–0777*) is primarily an art gallery, with paintings, drawings, pottery, and jewelry by dozens of artists.

South Pacific

WORD OF MOUTH

"This was taken at sunset on Dominical Beach. The tide goes way out and the sand stays wet. We found this to be one of the most picturesque beaches in Costa Rica."

—photo by Chad Clark, Fodors.com

WELCOME TO SOUTH PACIFIC

TOP REASONS TO GO

★ **Enormous Corcovado National Park:** The last refuge of such endangered species as jaguars and tapirs.

★ **Mountain hikes:** Hikes that range from easy daytime treks from luxurious lodges to Costa Rica's toughest: 3,810-meter (12,500-foot) Cerro Chirripó.

★ **Kayaking:** Head to the Golfo Dulce or along the Sierpe or Colorado rivers' jungly channels.

★ **Bird-watching:** Yields such beauties as scarlet macaws and the resplendent quetzal.

★ **Wild places to stay:** Relax in the top eco-lodges, thatch-roof beach bungalows, and cozy mountain cabins.

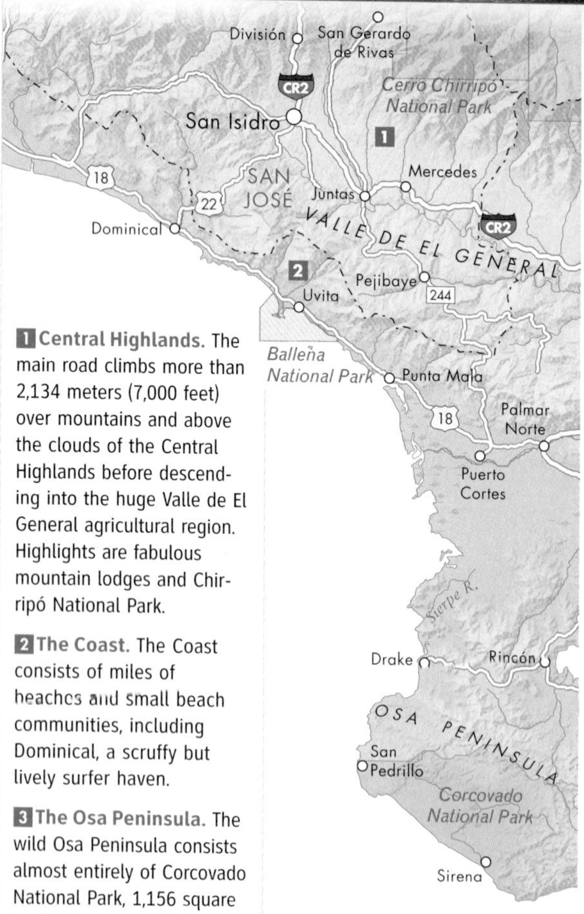

1 Central Highlands. The main road climbs more than 2,134 meters (7,000 feet) over mountains and above the clouds of the Central Highlands before descending into the huge Valle de El General agricultural region. Highlights are fabulous mountain lodges and Chirripó National Park.

2 The Coast. The Coast consists of miles of beaches and small beach communities, including Dominical, a scruffy but lively surfer haven.

3 The Osa Peninsula. The wild Osa Peninsula consists almost entirely of Corcovado National Park, 1,156 square km (445 square mi) of primary and secondary rain forest straight out of a David Attenborough nature documentary.

4 Golfo Dulce. The eastern Golfo Dulce draws anglers to Golfito, slow-paced beach bums to Zancudo, and serious surfers to Pavones.

GETTING ORIENTED

The most remote part of Costa Rica, the South Pacific encompasses the southern half of Puntarenas Province and La Amistad International Biosphere. The region descends from mountainous forests just an hour south of San José to the humid Golfo Dulce and the richly forested Osa Peninsula, 8 to 10 hours from the capital by car.

SOUTH PACIFIC PLANNER

Climate and Weather

The climate swings wildly in the south, from frigid mountain air to steamy coastal humidity. In the mountains it's normally around 24°C (75°F) during the day and 10°C (50°F) at night, though nighttime temperatures on the upper slopes of Cerro de la Muerte can be close to freezing. Temperatures in coastal areas are usually 24°C–32°C (76°F–90°F), but it's the humidity that does you in. If you're traveling from San José through the mountains on your way to points south, be sure to pack a warm sweater or jacket.

The dry season, from January through April, has the most reliably dry weather. But the shoulder seasons can be delightful, especially in early December when the landscape is lush and green and crowds of tourists have yet to arrive. The May-to-December rainy season is the worst in the Osa Peninsula, where rains usually last through January. Roads sometimes flood and lodges might close in the rainiest months (October and November). Elsewhere during the rainy season, mornings tend to be brilliant and sunny, with rain starting in midafternoon.

Choosing a Place to Stay

Expect reasonable comfort in unbelievably wild settings. Most accommodation is in small hotels, cabins, and lodges run by hands-on owners, many of them foreigners who fell in love with the place on a visit and stayed. Generally speaking, the farther south and more remote the lodge, the more expensive it is. Bad roads (causing supply problems) and lack of electricity and communications make hotelkeeping costly, especially in the Osa Peninsula and Golfo Dulce. When you look at the per-person prices, take into account that most of these places include meals, transport, guides, and unique locations.

The country's premier eco-lodges are almost all in the Southern Zone, ranging from simple tents to sophisticated lodges. But keep in mind that if you yearn to be close to nature, you have to be prepared for encounters of the natural kind in your shower or bedroom. Keep a flashlight handy for nighttime trips to the bathroom and always wear sandals.

A World Apart

Visitors go south to heed the call of the wild. On land, hiking, bird-watching, horseback riding, and wildlife-viewing are the main activities, along with some thrilling tree-climbing, zip-line, and waterfall-rappelling opportunities. On the water, there's surfing, snorkeling, diving, fishing, sea-kayaking, and whale- and dolphin-watching, as well as swimming and beachcombing. There's even a sky option, flying in a two-seater ultralight plane.

What makes many of these activities special in the Southern Zone is that, given the wildness of the locations, the focus is more on nature than on entertainment. No matter what you're doing, you'll come across interesting flora and fauna and natural phenomena. Another key to what sets the Southern Zone apart is the large number of trained naturalist guides. Most eco-lodges have resident guides who know not only where to find the birds and wildlife, but also how to interpret the hidden workings of the natural world around you.

Getting Here and Around

You need at least a week to truly experience any part of the Osa Peninsula. Even if you fly, transfers to lodges are slow, so plan two days for travel alone. Choose one home base and take day trips. In three weeks, though, you can experience the entire Southern Zone: mountains, beaches, and the Osa Peninsula.

For points between San José and San Vito, driving is a viable option, as long as you give yourself lots of time. Direct buses to San Isidro, Golfito, and Puerto Jiménez are cheap and reliable and are reasonably comfortable. The best and fastest way to get to the far south, though, is to fly directly to Golfito, Puerto Jiménez, Drake, Palmar Sur, or Carate. Many lodges arrange flights, taxi, and boat transfers all the way from San José as part of a package. If you want your own car to go exploring, you can rent 4WD vehicles in Puerto Jiménez and Golfito.

If you are driving south, keep in mind that Cerro de la Muerte is often covered with fog in the afternoon, so plan to cross the mountains in the morning. Don't try to cover too much ground on a set schedule. It is simply impossible to underestimate how long it takes to drive the roads or make transportation connections in this part of the country, especially during rainy season when flooding and landslides can close roads and bad weather can delay flights. But remember, getting there is part of the adventure.

Dining and Lodging

WHAT IT COSTS IN DOLLARS

	¢	$	$$	$$$	$$$$
Restaurants	under $5	$5–$10	$10–$15	$15–$25	over $25
Hotels	under $50	$50–$75	$75–$150	$150–$250	over $250

Restaurant prices are per person for a main course at dinner. Hotel prices are for two people in a standard double room in high season, excluding service and tax (16.4%).

Kids Gone Wild

The Southern Zone is like Outward Bound for families, where kids and parents can face challenges—such as no TV or video games!—and have adventures together. Plunge the family into real-life adventures with added natural-history educational value. You might inspire a future herpetologist or marine biologist amongst your progeny.

Go horseback riding to waterfalls and swimming holes. Steal into the night with infrared flashlights to scout out frogs and other fascinating, nocturnal creepy-crawlies. Enjoy kayaking in a calm gulf where dolphins play. Rappel down a waterfall, climb inside a hollow tree, or zip-line through the trees.

The remoter areas of the South are ideal for kids ages 7 and up. Babies and all their paraphernalia are hard to handle here, and toddlers are tough to keep off the ground where biting insects and snakes live.

Tour Operators

Horizontes Nature Tours (☎2222–2022 🌐www.horizontes.com) is an expert ecotourist company that arranges custom tours with naturalist guides and ornithologists.

Costa Rica Expeditions (☎2257–0766 🌐www.costaricaexpeditions.com) is the original ecotourist outfit in Costa Rica, specializing in countrywide nature tours with local naturalist guides.

CHIRRIPÓ NATIONAL PARK

Chirripó National Park is all about hiking. The ascent to Mount Chirripó, the highest mountain in Costa Rica, is the most popular and challenging hike in the country. It's also the most exclusive, limited to 40 hikers per day.

From the trailhead to the peak, you gain more than 2,438 meters (8,000 feet) of elevation, climbing through shaded highland forest, then out into the wide-open, windswept wilds of the páramo, scrubby moorland similar to the high Andes. It's a 48-km (30-mi) round-trip, and you need at least three days to climb to the hostel base, explore the summits, and descend. The modern but chilly stone hostel is the only available accommodation, with small rooms of four bunks each, shared cold-water bathrooms, and a cooking area. You need to bring your own sleeping bag, pillow, and provisions. A new generator and some solar panels provide some electricity, but the hostel is still bare-bones rustic. Trails from the hostel lead to the top of Chirripó—the highest point in Costa Rica—and the nearby peak of Terbi, as well as half a dozen other peaks and glacier lakes. ■ **TIP→Pack plenty of warm clothes.**

BEST TIME TO GO

Between sometimes freezing temperatures and more than 381 centimeters (150 inches) of rain a year, timing is of the essence here. The best months are in the dry season, January to May. The park is often closed from September through mid-December, when the trails are too wet and slippery for safety.

FUN FACT

A climb up Chirripó is a rite of passage for many young Costa Ricans, who celebrate their graduation from high school or college with a group expedition.

HIKING

There's no getting around it: the only way to explore this park is on foot. And the only way is up. It's a tough climb to Mount Chirripó's base camp—6 to 10 hours from the official park entrance, depending on your physical condition—so most hikers head out of San Gerardo de Rivas at the first light of day. You can hire porters to lug your gear up and down for you, so at least you can travel relatively light.

People who live in Costa Rica train seriously for this hike, so be sure you are in good enough shape to make the climb. Smart hikers also factor in a couple of days in the San Gerardo de Rivas area to acclimatize to the high altitude before setting out. The hike down is no picnic, either: your knees and ankles will be stretched to their limits. But it's an adventure every step of the way—and the bragging rights are worth it.

MOUNTAIN HIGHS

The base-camp hostel at Los Crestones is at 11,152 feet above sea level, so you still have some hiking ahead of you if you want to summit the surrounding peaks. Take your pick: Chirripó at 12,532 feet; Ventisqueros at 12,467 feet; Cerro Terbi at 12,336; and, for the fainter of heart, Mt. Uran at a measly 11,811 feet. Mountain hikers who collect "peaks" can add all four mountain tops to their list.

BIRD-WATCHING

Although your eyes will mostly be on the scenery, there are some highland species of birds that thrive in this chilly mountain air. Watch for the Volcano Junco, a sparrow-like bird with a pink beak and a yellow eye ring. Only two hummingbirds venture up this high—the fiery-throated, which lives up to its name; and the Volcano hummingbird, which is the country's smallest bird. If you see a raptor soaring above, chances are it's a red-tailed hawk.

TOP REASONS TO GO

DID IT!
The sheer sense of accomplishing this tough hike is the number one reason hikers take on this challenge. You don't have to be a mountain climber but you do need to be in very good shape.

TOP OF THE WORLD
The exhilaration of sitting on top of the world, with only sky, mountain peaks, and heath as far as the eye can see, motivates most visitors to withstand the physical challenges and the spartan conditions in the hostel.

UNIQUE ENVIRONMENT
A climb up Chirripó gives visitors a unique chance to experience extreme changes in habitat, from pastureland through rainforest and oak forest to bleak, scrubby páramo (a high elevation ecosystem). As the habitat changes, so does the endemic wildlife, which thins out near the top, along with the air.

OCEAN VIEWS
On rare, perfectly clear days, the top of Chirripó is one of the few places in the country where you can see both the Pacific and Atlantic oceans.

8

CORCOVADO NATIONAL PARK

For those who crave untamed wilderness, Corcovado National Park is the experience of a lifetime. Covering one-third of the Osa Peninsula, the park is blanketed primarily by virgin rain forest and holds Central America's largest remaining tract of lowland Pacific rain forest.

The remoteness of Corcovado and the difficult access to its interior make it one of the most pristine parks in the country—barely disturbed by human presence—where massive, vine-tangled primary-forest trees tower over the trails, and birds and wildlife abound. Your chances of spotting endangered species are better here than anywhere else in the country, although it still takes a combination of determination and luck. The rarest and most sought-after sightings are the jaguar and Baird's tapir. Corcovado also has the largest population of scarlet macaws in the country. Bordering the park are some of Costa Rica's most luxurious jungle lodges and retreats, all of which are contributing to the effort to save Corcovado's wildlife, which has been under heavy pressure in recent years from poachers.

BEST TIME TO GO

Dry season, January to April, is the best time to visit, but it's also the most popular. With so little accommodation available, it's crucial to reserve well in advance. June through August will be wetter, but may also be a little cooler. The trails are virtually impassable from September to December.

FUN FACT

Warning signs to stay on the trails should be heeded: in 2007, the Minister of Tourism got lost and wandered around in a daze for three days after following a baby tapir off the trail and being attacked by its mother.

GETTING HERE AND AROUND

The easiest way to visit the park is on a day trip by boat, organized by a lodge or tour company in Drake Bay, Puerto Jiménez, or Sierpe. The well-heeled can fly in on an expensive charter plane to the Sirena air field. But no matter how you get there, the only way to explore is on foot. There are no roads, only hiking trails. If you have a backpack, strong legs, and a reservation for a tent site or a ranger station bunk, you can enter the park on foot at three staffed ranger stations and spend up to five days, deep in the wilds.

HIKING

There are three main hiking routes to Corcovado. When you're planning your itinerary, keep in mind that the hike between any two ranger stations takes at least a day. The hike from San Pedrillo to Sirena is the longest, at 25 km (15 mi), mostly along the beach, then 7 km (4 mi) through a majestic forest. The hike from La Leona to Sirena is about 16 km (10 mi) and requires crossing a wide river mouth and a stretch of beach best crossed at low tide. Some people plan this hike before dawn to avoid the blistering sun. The 17.4-km (10.8-mi) trail from Los Patos to Sirena is the coolest trail, through forest all the way.

BIRD-WATCHING AND WILDLIFE

The holy grail of wildlife spotting here is a jaguar or a Baird's tapir. You may be one of the lucky few to see one of these rare, elusive animals. In the meantime, you can content yourself with coatis, peccaries, and agoutis on the ground and, in the trees, some endemic species of birds you will only see in this part of the country: Baird's trogon, riverside wren, and black-cheeked ant-tanager, to name a few.

TOP REASONS TO GO

FLORA AND FAUNA
The sheer diversity of flora and fauna and the chance to see wildlife completely in the wild are the main draws here. The number of catalogued species, to date, includes 500 trees (49 of them in peril of extinction), 150 orchids, 370 birds, 140 mammals (17 on the endangered list), 123 butterflies, 116 amphibians, and more than 6,000 insects.

OFF THE BEATEN TRACK
Day visitors get to taste the thrill of being completely off the beaten track, in an untamed natural world. But for campers and guests at the park's main lodge, La Sirena, the chance to spend days roaming miles of trails without hearing a single man-made sound is a rare treat.

TEST YOUR LIMITS
The physical challenges of hiking in high humidity and living very basically, along with the psychological challenge of being completely out of touch with "the real world," appeal to the kind of people who like to test their limits. It's not quite "Survivor," but you do need to be prepared..

8

PARQUE NACIONAL MARINO BALLENA

Great snorkeling, whale-watching, and beachcombing draw visitors and locals to Parque Nacional Marino Ballena (Whale Marine National Park), which protects four relatively tranquil beaches stretching for about 10 km (6 mi), as well as a mangrove estuary, a recovering coral reef, and a vast swath of ocean.

Playa Uvita, fronting the small town of Bahía Ballena, is the longest and most visited beach, and the embarkation point for snorkeling, fishing, and whale-watching tours. Restaurants line the nearby main street of the town. Playa Colonia has a safe swimming beach with a view of rocky islands. Playa Ballena, south of Playa Colonia, is a lovely strand backed by lush vegetation. Finally, tiny Playa Piñuela is the prettiest of the park beaches, in a deep cove that serves as the local port. Along with the tropical fish you'll see while snorkeling, you may be lucky enough to see humpback whales and dolphins. Above the water there are frigate birds and brown boobies, a tropical seabird, nesting on the park's rocky islands.

BEST TIME TO GO

December to April is the best time for guaranteed sunny beach weather, as well as for sightings of humpback whales with their young. The whales also roam these waters in late July through late October. Bottlenose dolphins abound in March and April. Avoid weekends in December to February, and Easter week, if you want the beach to yourself.

FUN FACT

Playa Uvita features a *tombolo,* a long swath of sand connecting a former island to the coast. At low tide, the exposed brown sandbar resembles a whale's tail, in keeping with the bay's name: Bahía Ballena (Whale Bay).

BEACH COMBING

The park's beaches are ideal to explore on foot, especially the Blue Flag–designated Playa Uvita, which has the longest and widest stretch of beach. Visitors and locals flock here in the late afternoon to catch spectacular sunsets. Don't forget your camera! At low tide, you can walk out onto the Whale's Tail sandbar. During the day, you'll see moving shells everywhere—hermit crabs of every size are constantly scuttling around. Although it all looks idyllic—and it mostly is—don't leave valuables unattended on the beach.

IN, ON, AND OVER THE WATER

Swimming here is relatively safe, but check with the park ranger or your hotel about the best swimming spots. Or just watch where the locals are frolicking in the water. Get a little further out in the water on a fishing charter and try your hand at reeling in mahimahi, tuna, and mackerel. Whale- and dolphin-watching excursion are also a fun option—bottle-nose dolphins are most often spotted, but humpback whales, especially mothers with babes, are the stars of the show. If you want to be the captain of your boat, sea kayaks are a popular way to explore the park's mangroves and river estuaries. Playa Ventanas, just south of the park's official border, has tidal rock caves you can kayak through. You can also paddle out to close-in islets and look for brown boobies, the tropical seabird kind that nest here. For the ultimate bird's eye view, take an ultra-light flight over the park.

CAMPING

If you brought a tent, pitch it here. Camping on the beach is allowed at Playas Ballena, Colonia, and Piñuela. You can't beat the price, as camping is included in the park admission. Costa Ricans are avid—and often noisy—campers, so try to avoid busy weekends and Semana Santa (Easter Week).

TOP REASONS TO GO

ALONE TIME

If solitude is what you're after, the park's beaches are relatively uncrowded, except on weekends and school holidays when locals come to relax. Neither Playa Colonia nor Playa Piñuela see a lot of traffic, so you can have them virtually to yourself almost anytime.

BEACHES

Miles of wide, sandy beach backed by palm trees and distant green mountain ridges make this one of the most scenic and accessible coastlines in the country. Playa Uvita and Playa Ballena, with their warm, swimmable waters and soft sand, attract the most beachgoers.

WHALES AND DOLPHINS

Catching sight of a humpback whale with her youngster swimming alongside is a thrill you won't forget. And watching dolphins cavorting around your excursion boat is the best entertainment on water.

WATER BOUND

Water activities include fishing, snorkeling, and sea-kayaking. There are snorkeling and dive trips out to Caño Island, about 45 minutes by boat.

8

ECO-LODGES IN THE SOUTH PACIFIC

The South Pacific Zone is Costa Rica's last frontier, with a wealth of protected biodiversity. It's also the cradle of the country's ecotourism, including some of the world's best eco-lodges.

Costa Rica's wildest corner has vast expanses of wilderness ranging from the majestic cloud forests and high-altitude páramo of the Talamanca highlands to the steamy, lowland rain forest of Corcovado National Park. Quetzals and other high-elevation birds abound in the oak forests of the San Gerardo de Dota valley, and scarlet macaws congregate in beach almond trees lining the shores of the Osa Peninsula. The Southern Zone has some of the country's most impressive, though least accessible, national parks—towering Chirripó and mountain-studded La Amistad; and Corcovado, where peccaries, tapirs, and, more rarely, jaguars still roam. Stunning marine wonders can be found in the Golfo Dulce, the dive and snorkeling spots around Caño Island Biological Reserve, and Ballena Marine National Park, famous for seasonal whale migrations. The lodges around Drake Bay, together with the off-the-grid lodges of Carate and Cabo Matapalo, provide unequaled immersion in tropical nature.

GOOD PRACTICES

The signage you'll often see in natural areas sums up ecotourism's principal tenets: Leave nothing but footprints; take away nothing but memories.

A few more tips:

Walk softly on forest trails and keep as quiet as you can. You'll spot more wildlife and maintain the natural atmosphere of the forest for other visitors, too.

Stay on marked trails and never approach animals; use your zoom lens to capture close-ups.

Ecotourism is also about getting to know the locals and their culture. Visit a local farm, an artisan's co-op, or a village school.

TOP ECO-LODGES IN THE SOUTH PACIFIC

LAPA RÍOS

Lapa Ríos is the premier eco-lodge in Costa Rica. Along with providing top-notch, sustainable hospitality, the lodge's mission is to protect the 1,000 acres of forest in its private preserve edging Corcovado National Park. Its main weapon is education, through local school programs and community involvement. The lodge owners spearheaded the building of the local school and provide direct employment to more than 45 area families. Lapa Ríos was the first area lodge to offer a free sustainability tour, highlighting innovative eco-friendly practices, including feeding organic waste to pigs to produce methane fuel. As a guest, you'll be thankful for the absence of motor noise—gardeners work exclusively with manual tools.

CASA CORCOVADO

This jungle lodge, bordering Corcovado National Park, gets top eco marks for its energy-saving solar and micro-hydroelectric systems, and its recycling and waste-management leadership in the area. The lodge financed the building of a recycling center in Sierpe, and all the area's glass and aluminum is now recycled. Guests receive refillable bottle to use throughout their stay. Owner Steve Lill is co-founder and president of the Corcovado Foundation, a major supporter of local initiatives to preserve wildlife on the Osa Peninsula.

PLAYA NICUESA RAINFOREST LODGE

From its initial construction to its daily operations, this Golfo Dulce lodge, accessible only by boat, has been committed to sustainability. The main lodge and guest cabins were built with fallen wood and recycled materials. Solar power, an organic septic system, composting, and a chemical-free garden also attest to the owners' eco credentials. The kitchen uses local produce and cooks up fish caught in the gulf. Lodge owners Donna and Michael Butler match guests' donations to the Osa Campaign, a cooperative conservation program.

AFTER DARK

The first night in a remote Southern Zone eco-lodge can be unnerving. You may have looked forward to falling asleep to the sounds of nature, but you may not be prepared for the onslaught of night noises: the chirping of geckos as they hunt for insects in the thatch roof, the thwack of flying insects colliding against window screens, the swish of bats swooping, and the spine-tingling calls of owls and nightjars. Add in the chorus of croaking frogs and you may have trouble falling asleep. Once you realize that you are safe under your mosquito net, you can start to enjoy the nocturnal symphony. And after the first day of waking up at dawn to the roars of howler monkeys and the chatter of songbirds, you'll be more than ready to crash the next night shortly after dinner. Most guests are asleep by 8 PM and rise at 5 AM, the best time to spot birds and wildlife as they start their day, too. For nighttime visits to the bathroom, be sure to keep a flashlight handy and something to put on your feet if you want to avoid creepy-crawlies.

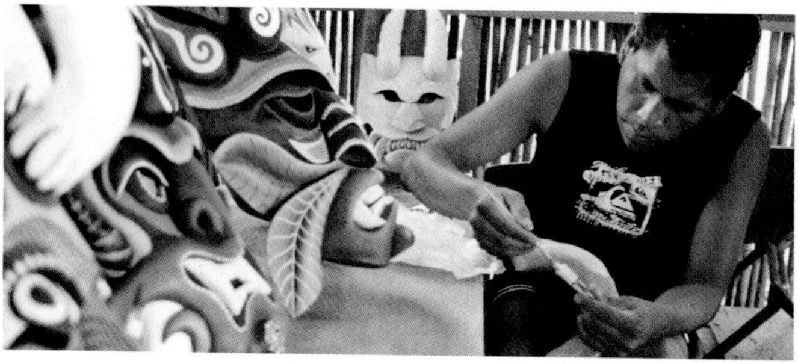

By Dorothy MacKinnon

The South Pacific encompasses everything south of San José, down to the border with Panama, and all the territory west of the Talamanca mountains, sloping down to the Pacific coast. World-class mountain hikes and bird-watching abound in the highlands, just south of the capital.

The beaches attract surfers, fishers, whale-watchers, and beachcombers. But the jewels in the South Pacific crown are the idyllic Golfo Dulce and the wild Osa Peninsula, brimming with wildlife and natural adventures.

GETTING HERE AND AROUND

SANSA and Nature Air have direct flights to Drake Bay, Palmar Sur, and Puerto Jiménez. SANSA has the most flights to Golfito and the only flights to Coto 47 (for San Vito). *For more information about air travel to the South Pacific from San José, see Air Travel in Travel Smart Costa Rica.*

Alfa Romeo Aero Taxi, at the Puerto Jiménez airport (really more of an airstrip), flies small charter planes to Carate, Tiskita, and Corcovado National Park's airstrip at La Sirena. The one-way price is $385 for up to five people.

Owing to the dismal state of the roads and hazardous driving conditions—flooded rivers and potholes—we don't recommend driving to the South Pacific, especially in rainy season. If you decide to drive, make sure your vehicle has 4WD and a spare tire. Give yourself lots of daylight time to get to where you are going. You can also fly to Golfito or the Osa Peninsula and rent a 4WD vehicle locally.

Bus fares from San José range from about $3 to $10, depending on distance and number of stops. The best way to get around the region's roads is by bus—let someone else do the driving. Bus fares are cheap, and you'll meet the locals. But the going is generally slow, buses often leave very early in the morning, and schedules change frequently, so check the day before you want to travel.

Based in Dominical, Easy Ride has two daily shuttle-van services in each direction between San José and the Dominical/Uvita/Ojochal area for $30 to $45 per person. For an extra $5 they will take you to the San José airport.

ESSENTIALS

Bus Contacts Easy Ride (☎ *2253–4444* 🌐 *www.easyridecr.com*).

THE CENTRAL HIGHLANDS

Less than an hour south of San José the Pan-American Highway climbs up into the scenic Central Highlands of Cerro de la Muerte, famous for spectacular mountain vistas, high-altitude coffee farms, cloud-forest eco-lodges, and challenging mountain hikes.

ZONA DE LOS SANTOS

Santa María de Dota is 65 km/40 mi south of San José. The Route of the Saints is 24 km/15 mi long.

Empalme, at Km 51 of the Pan-American Highway, marks the turnoff for Santa María de Dota, the first of the blessed coffee-growing towns named after saints that dot this mountainous area known as the Zona de Los Santos (Zone of the Saints).

The scenic road that winds through the high-altitude valley from ★ Empalme to San Pablo de León is appropriately called **La Ruta de Los Santos** *(Route of the Saints).* It's well paved to facilitate shipping the coffee produced in the region, which is central to Costa Rica's economy. On the 30-minute (24-km [15-mi]) drive from Empalme to San Pablo de León Cortés, you see misty valleys ringed by precipitous mountain slopes terraced with lush, green coffee plants. The route also captures the essence of a traditional Tico way of life built around coffee growing. Stately churches anchor bustling towns full of prosperous, neat houses with pretty gardens and 1970s Toyota Land Cruisers in a rainbow of colors parked in front.

GETTING HERE From San José, drive an hour and a half southeast on the paved Pan-American Highway, heading toward Cartago, then follow the signs south for San Isidro de El General. The two-lane road climbs steeply and there are almost no safe places to pass heavy trucks and slow vehicles. Make an early start, because the road is often enveloped in mist and rain in the afternoon. At Km 51 turn right at Empalme to reach Santa María de Dota, 14 km (8½ mi) along a wide, curving, paved road.

WHERE TO EAT AND STAY

¢ CAFE ✕ **Café de Los Santos.** This pretty café, within sight of the majestic, domed San Marcos church, showcases the area's high-altitude *arabica* Tarrazú coffee, the "celestial drink" for which this zone is famous. There are more than 30 specialty coffee drinks, plus homemade sweet and savory pastries, and light lunches. It's open weekdays 9 to 6:30, weekends 2 to 5:30. ✉ *100 m east of church* ✥ *6 km/4 mi west of Santa María de Dota, San Marcos de Tarrazú* ☎ *2546–7881* ▭ *No credit cards.*

$–$$ 🏨 **El Toucanet Lodge.** For serenity and mountain greenery, you can't beat this family-run lodge with plenty of pastoral scenery on view from the glassed-in dining room. Each of the six large rooms in three wooden

8

cabins above the main lodge has its own private veranda and tile bathroom with skylight. Two new junior suites have fireplaces, whirlpool baths, and king-size beds. Owners Gary and Edna Roberts are known for hearty breakfasts, baked trout dinners, and creative vegetarian dishes. Gary leads a free quetzal hunt every day at 7 AM along the road, bordering Los Quetzales National Park. He also arranges horseback rides, mountain hikes, and tours of neighboring coffee *fincas* (farms). With at least six hours' notice, he can fire up the natural-stone hot tub for an end-of-day soak under the stars. **Pros:** fresh mountain air; tranquility; low-key; affordable. **Cons:** simple furnishings; limited menu. *7 km/4½ mi east of Santa María de Dota along steep, winding paved road, Copey; or from Km 58 of the Pan-American Hwy., turn right at sign for Copey and follow dirt road 8 km/5 mi 2541–3131 2541–3045 www.eltoucanet.com 6 rooms, 2 junior suites In-room: no a/c, no phone, no TV. In-hotel: restaurant AE, MC, V Closed Sept. BP.*

> **THE FINAL FRONTIER**
>
> The Southern Zone was the very last part of Costa Rica to be settled. The first road, from San José to San Isidro, wasn't begun until the 1950s.

SHOPPING

The best place to buy local coffee is where the farmers themselves bring their raw coffee beans to be roasted and packed into jute bags, the **Coopedota Santa Maria** (*Main road, just after the bridge as you enter Santa María de Dota 2541–2828*). You can buy export-quality coffee at their new coffee shop for about $10 per kilo (2.2 pounds). Choose between *en grano* (whole bean) or *molido* (ground), and between light or dark roast. The shop is open 8 to 6, daily in high season. You can also reserve a tour ($13) of the coffee co-op by calling ahead.

SAN GERARDO DE DOTA

89 km/55 mi southeast of San José, 52 km/32 mi south of Santa María de Dota.

Cloud forests, invigorating, cool mountain air, well-kept hiking trails, and excellent bird-watching make San Gerardo de Dota one of Costa Rica's premier nature destinations. The tiny hamlet is in the narrow Savegre River valley, 9 km (5½ mi) down a twisting, partially asphalted track that descends abruptly to the west from the Pan-American Highway. The peaceful surroundings look more like the Rocky Mountains than Central America, but hike down the waterfall trail and the vegetation quickly turns tropical again. Beyond hiking and bird-watching, activities include horseback riding and trout fly-fishing.

GETTING HERE

The drive from San José takes about three hours, and from Santa María de Dota about one hour. At Km 80 on the Pan-American Highway, turn down the dirt road signed SAN GERARDO DE DOTA. It's a harrowing, twisting road for most of the 9 km (5½ mi), with signs warning drivers to gear down and go slow. Some newly paved sections help to ease the

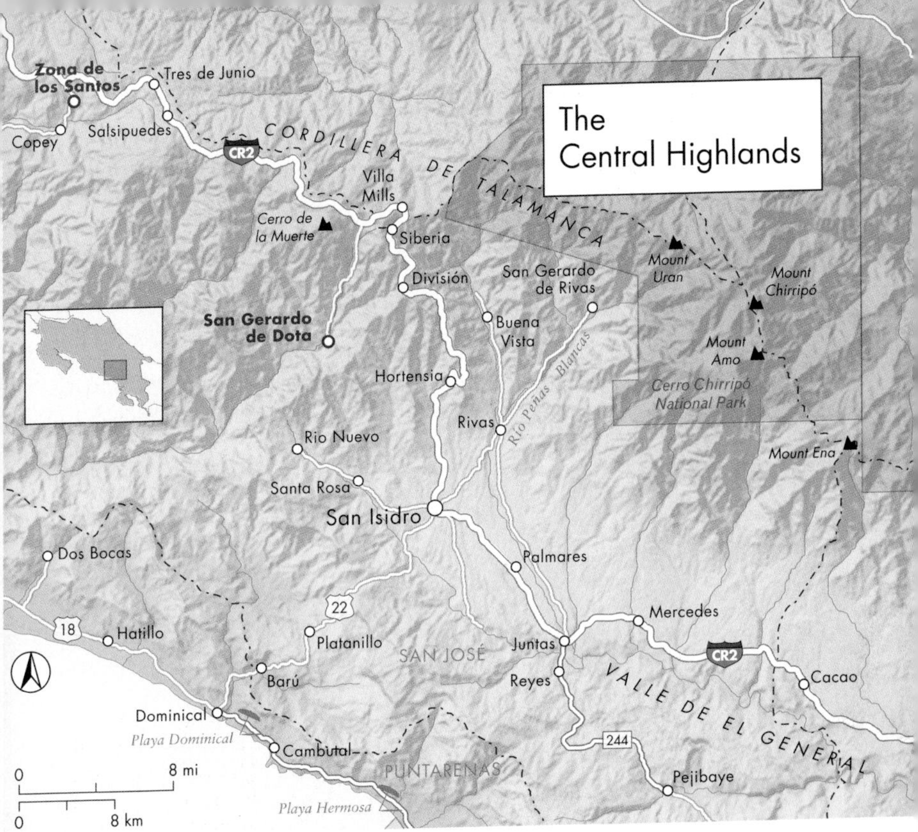

worst curves. Tourist vans often stop along the road when the guides spot birds; grab your binoculars and join them!

OUTDOOR ACTIVITIES

BIRD-WATCHING ★ This area is a must for bird-watchers, who flock here with small package tours *(⇨ Tours in Travel Smart Costa Rica)*. Individual birders can choose from a roster of expert local guides; check with your hotel for recommendations. **Savegre Hotel de Montaña** (☎ *2740–1028* 🌐 *www.savegre.co.cr*) has the best bird guides in the area ($70 for a half day) and organizes hiking tours in the surrounding mountains.

Although you can see many birds from your cabin porch, most bird-watching requires hiking, some of it along steep paths made extra challenging by the high altitude (from 7,000 to 10,000 feet above sea level). Come fit and armed with binoculars and layers of warm clothing. The early mornings are brisk up here, but you'll warm up quickly with the sun and the exertion of walking.

HIKING Some of the best hiking in the country is in this valley. Expert birder Marino Chacón of Savegre Hotel *(⇨ below)* leads a daylong natural-history hike (about $150 for up to nine people, including transportation and a packed lunch) that starts with a drive up to the *páramo* (high-altitude, shrubby ecosystem) of **Cerro de la Muerte.** The trail begins at the cluster of communication towers, near Km 89, and descends through the forest into the valley. Miles of prime bird-watching/hiking trails wind through the forest reserve belonging to the Chacóns. ■**TIP→Night temperatures on the slopes of Cerro de la Muerte can approach freezing—it's called the Mountain of Death for the very simple reason that long-ago travelers attempting to cross it on foot often froze to death during the night. Pack accordingly.**

The most challenging trail in the area is the one that begins at the ★ Hotel Savegre and follows the **Río Savegre** down to a spectacular waterfall. To get to the trailhead, follow the main road past Savegre Hotel to a fork, where you veer left, cross a bridge, and head over the hill to a pasture that narrows to a footpath. Although it is only 2 km (1¼ mi) each way, the hike is steep and slippery, especially near the bottom, and takes about three hours.

THE RESPLENDENT QUETZAL

The damp, epiphyte-laden oak-tree forest around San Gerardo de Dota is renowned for resplendent quetzals, considered by many to be the most beautiful bird in the Western world. Male quetzals in full breeding plumage are more spectacular than females, with metallic green feathers, crimson stomachs, helmetlike crests, and extravagantly long tail feathers. Ask guides or hotel staff about common quetzal hangouts; early morning during the March-to-May nesting season is the best time to spot them.

WHERE TO STAY

$ **Albergue de Montaña Paraíso del Quetzal.** Nestled in a cloud forest just minutes off the main highway, this rustic lodge is, indeed, a paradise for resplendent quetzals and for the visitors who want to see this most beautiful and sought-after bird in Costa Rica. Even if you don't catch sight of a quetzal, the vistas of cloud-enshrouded mountains and valleys will keep you busy, as will the hiking and birding trails through ancient oak forests dripping with moss and epiphytes. Each cozy cabin, set in splendid isolation, has a double bed plus a bunk bed, and lots of blankets. Nighttime temperatures drop into the 40s (around 4°C to 7°C at this altitude (about 2,377 meters [7,800 feet] above sea level), and you'll be happy for the tiny, tiled bathrooms with steaming-hot showers. The main lodge has a wood-burning stove and a deck abuzz with brilliant hummingbirds. Meals are simple *comida tipica* (typical food), cooked on a woodstove. All the family pitches in, cooking, serving, and guiding. This is the first hotel in this world-renowned birding area to receive the country's coveted Blue Flag for eco-friendliness. Per-person rates include dinner and breakfast, and guided hiking and birding tours. **Pros:** scenic views; pristine cloud forest; amazing bird-watching and hikes. **Cons:** very simple lodging and food; steep paths to some cabins; very cold nights. ✉ *Km 70, Pan-American Hwy., Cerro de la Muerte* ☎ *2200–0241 or 8390–6894* 🌐 *www.paraisodelquetzal.com* *8 cabins* *In-room: no a/c, no phone, no TV. In-hotel: restaurant* *MC, V* *EP.*

$ **Cabañas y Senderos Las Cataratas.** One of the best deals—and meals—in the valley is at this rustic restaurant and cabins run by a Tico family, who all join in (kids, too) to help serve meals. Three simple, wooden cabins, one with a wood-burning fireplace, have red-velvet decor

A male white-throated mountain-gem hummingbird in a defense posture. Rio Savegre, San Gerardo de Dota.

reminiscent of a bordello, but they are cheap and comfortable. There are some short, steep forest trails to explore. At the restaurant ($) you can dine on fresh trout—pulled directly out of the adjoining pond when you place your order—with salad, vegetables, dessert, and juice for less than $10. If you haven't got the time or the courage to face the steep road all the way down to San Gerardo, this is a good compromise, only 3 km (2 mi) in from the highway. It's a good idea to call ahead on a weekday, and Bernardo, the owner, will be ready for you. **Pros:** cheap; excellent fresh trout; authentic Tico culture. **Cons:** rustic, simple; call ahead on a week day to make sure someone is there. *✢3 km/2 mi down steep road to San Gerardo de Dota ☎8393–9278 or 2740–1064 🌐www.cataratas.guiapz.com ⇆3 cabins ♁In-room: no a/c, no phone, no TV. In-hotel: restaurant ▭MC, V 🍴EP.*

8

$$ **Dantica Lodge and Gallery.** High style at high altitude, this avant-garde lodge clinging to the side of a mountain has unbeatable valley views. Spacious white-stucco casitas with two bedrooms and baths are perfect for families. New casitas in a forest clearing provide the ultimate in seclusion and close-to-nature experiences, including the honeymoon hideaway with sunken whirlpool tub big enough for two, a private garden, and forest trail. All the casitas have living rooms with huge picture windows, private terraces, kitchenettes, and electric heaters, along with fluffy, warm duvets. Some have the added luxury of sunken whirlpool tubs and fireplaces. Mixing modern European style with Colombian antiques, the young Dutch/Colombian owners have an unerring eye for style, reflected in their stunning, glassed-in gallery of Latin American *artesanía* (arts and crafts); even if you don't stay here, check out the gallery. Enjoy a hearty breakfast or light lunch served on exquisite china in a glass-walled house with a heart-stopping view. **Pros:** stylish, comfortable casitas; gorgeous natural setting; 5 km (3 mi) of trails. **Cons:** no dinner served, so bring your own food, go off-property, or order dinner from a nearby restaurant; steep access to forest casitas along narrow trails. ✉ *Road to San Gerardo de Dota* ✣ *4 km/2 mi west of Pan-American Hwy.* ☎ *2740–1067* 🌐 *www.dantica.com* ⇨ *7 casitas, 1 suite, 1 house* ♧ *In-room: kitchen, refrigerator. In-hotel: restaurant, no-smoking rooms* ▭ *AE, MC, V* 🍽 *BP.*

$$ Fodor's Choice ★ **Savegre Hotel de Montaña.** Famous for its miles of bird-watching trails and expert guides, this once-rustic lodge has been upgraded to luxury, including new cabins with handsome wood furniture, fireplaces, and deep bathtubs—unthinkable luxuries back in the 1950s when Don Efrain Chacón first bushwhacked his way through these mountains. Still run by Efrain's children and grandchildren, the main lodge has a big fireplace, a cozy bar, and a veranda buzzing with hummingbirds. Breakfast and lunch can be served on a sunny terrace also abuzz with hummingbirds. Homegrown trout is the restaurant's specialty. You can avoid the twisting drive here by taking a bus to Km 80 on the Pan-American Highway and arranging to get a lift to the hotel ($12). **Pros:** great trails; amazing birdlife; excellent guides. **Cons:** buffet-style meals when hotel has lots of groups; older cabins are very simple and lack privacy; be prepared for very cold nights. *Turn right at sign to San Gerardo de Dota on Pan-American Hwy., about 80 km/50 mi southeast of San José, and travel 9 km/5½ mi down very steep gravel road* 📫 *Apdo. 482, Cartago* ☎ *2740–1028* 🌐 *www.savegre.co.cr* ⇨ *25 cabinas, 20 cabin-suites* ♧ *In-room: no a/c, no TV. In-hotel: restaurant, bar, Internet terminal* ▭ *AE, MC, V* 🍽 *BP.*

$$ **Trogón Lodge.** Overlooking the same cloud forest and boulder-strewn river as Savegre Hotel de Montaña, Trogón Lodge is more a relaxing hideaway than a hiking-heavy destination. The green wooden cabins encircle a fantasy garden bursting with color and a riot of roses, calla lilies, and geraniums. Each cabin has two separate rooms with big windows, queen-size beds, and white-tile baths with hot showers and rain-forest showerheads. Gas heaters and extra blankets guard against chilly mountain nights. The only drawback is shared verandas. A honeymoon cabin perched in solitary splendor has a king-size bed and a whirlpool tub with a panoramic view. Meals are served in a restaurant with tree-trunk tables, adjoined by a new bar and dining terrace with a river view. Quetzal-watching, horseback riding, waterfall hikes, and an 11-platform canopy tour are some of the diversions, or you can relax with a massage at the new spa. **Pros:** pretty, lush garden; pleasant, convivial public area. **Cons:** steep, short trails that end at road; little privacy except in honeymoon suite. ✣ *Turn right at sign to San Gerardo de Dota on Pan-American Hwy., about 80 km/50 mi southeast of San José, and follow signs; lodge is 7½ km/4½ mi down a dirt road* 📫 *Apdo. 10980–1000, San José* ☎ *2740–1051, 2293–8181 in San José* 🌐 *www.grupomawamba.com* ⇨ *22 rooms, 1 suite* ♧ *In-room: no a/c, no phone, no TV. In-hotel: restaurant, bar, bicycles* ▭ *AE, MC, V* 🍽 *EP.*

VALLE DE EL GENERAL REGION

The Valle de El General (The General's Valley) is bounded to the north and west by the central highlands of the massive Cordillera de Talamanca and to the south by La Amistad International Park, above San Vito. The valley is named for the Río de El General, one of the many rivers that rise in the Talamancas and run down through the valley, making it ideal for farming. This area includes vast expanses of highland wilderness on the upper slopes of the Cordillera de Talamanca and the high-altitude *páramo* (shrubby ecosystem) of Chirripó National Park, as well as prosperous agricultural communities amid vast, sunbaked fields of pineapple and sugarcane.

SAN ISIDRO DE EL GENERAL

54 km/34 mi south of San Gerardo de Dota.

Although San Isidro de El General has no major attractions, the bustling market town is a good place to have lunch, get cash at one of the many ATMs (most accept only Visa/Plus cards), or fill your tank—the main highway into town is lined with service stations, some operating 24 hours. Advice to map readers: There are other San Isidros in Costa Rica, but this is the only San Isidro e El General. Just to confuse matters more, this town also goes by the name Peréz Zeledon.

GETTING HERE AND AROUND

The Pan-American Highway takes you straight into San Isidro. It's 129 km (80 mi) south of San José and about 1½ hours' drive south of the San Gerardo de Dota highway exit. Truck traffic can be heavy. Buses to Dominical leave San Isidro from the Quepos bus terminal, 100 meters south and 200 meters east of the cathedral, near the main highway. Buses to San Gerardo de Rivas, the starting point of the trail into Chirripó National Park, depart from San Isidro at 5 AM from the central park and at 2 PM from a stop at the central market.

ESSENTIALS

Bank/ATM Banco de Costa Rica (✉ *1 block south of southwest corner of park* ☎ *2771-3287*). **ATH Coopealianza** (✉ *South side of central park, beside Hotel Chirripó* ☞ *ATM only*).

Hospital Hospital Escalante Pradilla (✉ *North end of town* ☎ *2771-3122*).

Pharmacy Farmacia Santa Marta (✉ *Across from cultural center* ☎ *2771-4506*).

Internet Internet El Balcón (✉ *150 m east of Central Market, near Banco de Costa Rica* ☎ *2771-6300*).

Post Office Correo (✉ *200 m south of City Hall, south side of park*).

Visitor Information Ciprotur (✉ *Behind the MUSOC bus station, where San José buses arrive* ☎ *2771-6096*). **Selva Mar** (✉ *45 m south of central park* ☎ *2771-4582* 🌐 *www.exploringcostarica.com*).

8

EXPLORING

The **National Parks Service** (✉*Across from Cámara de Cañeros* ☎*2771–3155*) has an office in town where you can get information on Chirripó National Park.

In a lush valley 7 km (4½ mi) northeast of San Isidro, the community-managed **Las Quebradas Biological Center** is a *centro biológico* (nature reserve) that protects 1,853 acres of dense forest in which elegant tree ferns grow in the shadows of massive trees, and colorful tanagers and euphonias flit about the foliage. A 3-km (2-mi) trail winds uphill through the forest and along the Río Quebradas, which supplies water to San Isidro and surrounding communities. There's also an easily accessible sensory garden, with plants to smell and taste. *At bottom of mountain as you approach San Isidro, take sharp left off Pan-American Hwy. at sign for Las Quebradas, go 7 km/4½ mi northeast; center is 2 km/1 mi north of town, along unpaved road* ☎*2771–4131* *$2* *Tues.–Sun. 8–3.*

Los Cusingos Neotropical Bird Sanctuary was the home of the late Dr. Alexander Skutch, Central America's preeminent ornithologist/naturalist and a co-author of *A Guide to the Birds of Costa Rica,* the birders' bible. His 190-acre estate, an island of forest amid a sea of new farms and housing developments, is now run by the nonprofit Tropical Science Center, which has improved the trails and restored the simple house where Dr. Skutch lived—without electricity—from 1941 until his death in 2004, just a week shy of his 100th birthday. Bird species you might see include fiery-billed araçaris—colorful, small members of the toucan family—and mixed tanager flocks. *12 km/7½ mi southeast of San Isidro, Quizarrá* ☎*2200–5472* *www.cct.or.cr* *$10* *Daily 7–4, preferably by reservation.*

OUTDOOR ACTIVITIES

Selva Mar (✉*Half a block south of the cathedral* ☎*2771–4582*) is the most experienced Southern Zone tour operator.

BIRD-WATCHING **Sunny Travel/Tropical Feathers** (☎*2771–9686 or 2772–3275* *www.costaricabirdingtours.com*), run by expert birder Noel Urena, has multiday bird-watching packages and arranges customized tours in the San Isidro and Dominical area.

HIKING The major tourist draw is climbing Mount Chirripó (the highest peak is 3,820 meters or about 12,530 feet high) in Chirripó National Park. **Costa Rica Trekking Adventures** (☎*2771–4582* *www.chirripo.com*), run by Selva Mar, can arrange everything you need to climb the mountain, including transportation, guide, porters to carry your gear, meals, snacks, and beverages. But you still have to make the tough climb yourself, about eight hours uphill to the park lodge, and five hours to come down. The two-night, three-day packages are $440 per person, with at least two people. It's much cheaper to do it on your own, but you have to make all the advance arrangements yourself.

WHERE TO EAT AND STAY

¢–$ COSTA RICAN **El Trapiche de Nayo.** This rustic open-air restaurant with a panoramic valley view serves the kind of food Ticos eat at *turnos* (village fund-raising festivals), including hard-to-find *sopa de mondongo* (tripe soup).

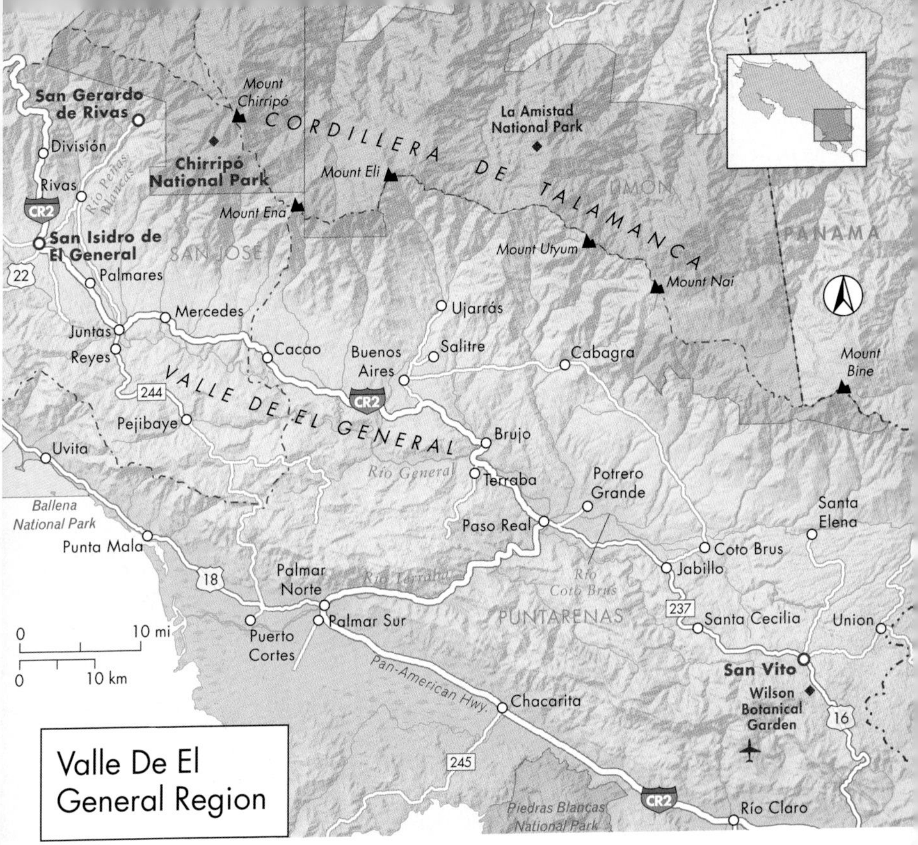

Valle De El General Region

Easier to stomach are the *gallos* (do-it-yourself filled tortillas), which you can stuff with hearts of palm, other root vegetables, and wood-fire-cooked chicken. On Saturdays, raw sugarcane is pressed in an antique mill and boiled in huge iron cauldrons to make smooth *sobado,* a molasses-flavor fudge. Service is leisurely, to say the least, and the restrooms—with seatless toilets—leave much to be desired. ✉ *Pan-American Hwy.* ⊕ *6 km/4 mi north of San Isidro* ☎ *2771–7267* ▭ *AE, MC, V.*

$ MEXICAN ✕ **Taquería Mexico Lindo.** Locals, expats, and tourists crowd into this casual cantina, famous for its authentic Mexican food cooked and served by an extended Mexican family. It's cheap and cheerful, with hearty servings of burritos (including veggie options), enchiladas, chiles rellenos, tuna-stuffed avocados, and daily specials served on terra-cotta dishes under a flutter of festive paper cutouts on the ceiling. Unusually for a Mexican place, the desserts are standouts and all homemade. ✉ *Shopping arcade beside Hotel Chirripó, outside of Central Park in downtown San Isidro* ☎ *2771–8222* ▭ *AE, MC, V* ⊙ *Closed Sun.*

$ **Hotel Los Crestones.** Flowering hedges give this pleasant, two-story, motel-style building between the sometimes noisy local stadium and a sedate funeral home a homey feel. Affordable rooms are large and comfortable, with tile floors, pretty floral linens, and some bathtubs. The quietest rooms are numbers 18 to 21. There's a small pool in a pleasant garden at the back where you can cool off. **Pros:** affordable, pleasant rooms; secure, covered parking for car. **Cons:** avoid rooms at the front, which can be noisy; a few rooms lack a/c. ✉*Southwest side of stadium, on road to Dominical* ☎*2770–1200* 🌐*www.hotelloscrestones.com* *27 rooms* *In-room: no a/c (some), Wi-Fi. In-hotel: restaurant, pool* ▭*AE, MC, V* *EP.*

> **HITTING THE TRAILS**
>
> The hiking in the south is simply spectacular, so don't leave home without your boots. The most challenging hike in the country is Chirripó Mountain, a 6- to 10-hour haul up to the national-park hostel, a base camp for exploring surrounding peaks. Dramatic but less challenging hikes include the well-maintained, wide trails in the cool high-altitude forests of the Savegre Valley; the narrow Coastal Path south of Drake; and forest trails to waterfalls and swimming holes in the Golfo Dulce, Osa Peninsula, and around Dominical.

¢ **Hotel Zima.** Close to the main bus station and especially popular with backpackers heading up to Chirripó, this hotel's pleasant rooms are in bungalows arranged in a nicely landscaped row, reminiscent of a 1950s motel, complete with swimming pool. There are also rooms in a two-story building with porches. Some rooms have queen-size beds and air-conditioning; others have double or single beds and ceiling fans. Have breakfast at the small terrace restaurant or cross the highway and forage among the inexpensive eateries. **Pros:** handy to bus station and restaurants in town. **Cons:** not a scenic location, just off main highway; smallish rooms. ✉*Half a block east of main highway into San Isidro, across from MUSOC bus terminal* ☎*2770–1114* *2770–9888* *14 bungalows, 13 rooms* *In-room: no a/c (some), no phone. In-hotel: restaurant, pool, laundry service, Internet terminal* ▭*AE, MC, V* *EP.*

SAN GERARDO DE RIVAS

20 km/12½ mi northeast of San Isidro.

Chirripó National Park is the main reason to venture to San Gerardo de Rivas, but if you aren't up for this physically challenging adventure it's still a great place to spend a day or two. Spread over steep terrain at the end of the narrow valley of the boulder-strewn Río Chirripó, San Gerardo de Rivas has a cool climate, good bird-watching, spectacular views reminiscent of Nepal, and an outdoor menu that includes waterfall hikes.

GETTING HERE

More than half the one-hour drive from San Isidro is on a very rocky, very hilly, dirt road; 4WD is strongly recommended. There is a bus from San Isidro and it is a slow, dusty ride up the mountain.

EXPLORING

The **Hot Springs** (Aguas Termales), on a farm above the road to Herradura, are a favorite tourist stop. To get here, you must cross a river on a rickety bridge, then manage a steep climb on foot or by 4WD vehicle to a combination of natural rock and concrete pools in a forested area. It's nothing fancy and can be crowded with locals on weekends, so

CLOSE UP

A Mosaic of Forests

Though the rain forest is the most famous region in Costa Rica, there are other types of forests here equally rich in life and well worth exploring. The **tropical dry forests** of the northwestern lowlands are similar to rain forests during the rainy season, but once the weather turns dry, most trees lose their leaves, and some burst simultaneously into full flower, notably the yellow-blossom buttercup tree and the pink tabebuia. Cacti, coyotes, and diamondback rattlesnakes can be found, in addition to typical rain-forest flora and fauna.

The **cloud forests** on the upper reaches of many Costa Rican mountains and volcanoes are so deeply lush that it can be hard to find the bark on a tree for all the growth on its trunk and branches. Vines, orchids, ferns, aroids, and bromeliads are everywhere. More light reaching the ground means plenty of undergrowth, too. Cloud forests are home to a multitude of animals, ranging from delicate glass frogs, whose undersides are so transparent that you can see many of their internal organs, to the legendary resplendent quetzal. The foliage and mist can make it hard to see wildlife.

Along both coasts are extensive **mangrove forests,** extremely productive ecosystems that play an important role as estuaries. Mangroves attract animals that feed on marine life, especially fish-eating birds such as cormorants, herons, pelicans, and ospreys. The forests that line Costa Rica's northeastern coast are dominated by the water-resistant *jolillo* palm or *palma real.* Mangroves are home to many of the same animals found in the rain forest—monkeys, parrots, iguanas—as well as river dwellers such as turtles and crocodiles.

8

aim for a weekday soak. ✉ *Above road to Herradura* ✣ *About 1½ km/1 mi past the ranger station, north of town* ☎ *2742–5210* 🎫 *$3* ⏲ *Daily 7–5:30.*

Cloudbridge Private Nature Reserve, a private nature reserve staffed by volunteers, has an easy trail to a waterfall, plus almost 20 km (12 mi) of river and ridge trails bordering Chirripó National Park. It's a pleasant alternative for hikers who aren't up to the challenge of Chirripó. ✣ *2 km/1 mi northeast of San Gerardo de Rivas* 🌐 *www.cloudbridge.org* 🎫 *By donation* ⏲ *Daily sunrise–sunset.*

OUTDOOR ACTIVITIES

HIKING **Ruta Urán.** Really fit hikers can undertake a five-day guided hike up a new alternative route to Chirripó led by experienced local guides. The hike eventually arrives at the Chirripo National Park hostel, and then descends by the usual national park route. The price of $550 for two hikers includes lodging, meals, and guide and park fees. ✣ *Comité de Turismo y Guias de Herradura, in National Park Office in San Gerardo de Rivas* ☎ 2742–5073 🌐 *www.chirriporural.org*

Selva Mar *(⇨ San Isidro, above)* also runs tours around San Gerardo de Rivas.

WHERE TO STAY

¢ **Albergue de Montaña El Pelícano.** On a precipitous ridge south of town, this wooden lodge is named for a chunk of wood that resembles a pelican—one of dozens of idiosyncratic wooden sculptures carved out of tree roots by owner Rafael Elizondo. Above the restaurant, which has a gorgeous view of the valley below San Gerardo, are economical small rooms with shared bath. More comfortable options are the two private wooden cabins with kitchenettes near the pool. The owners can help arrange everything for a climb up Chirripó. The climb to the hotel itself is quite steep and 4WD is advisable. **Pros:** proximity to Chirripó and a free ride to the trailhead; very cheap. **Cons:** shared bath; very tiny rooms, but most visitors are only here to sleep before setting off early to climb Chirripó. ✉*260 m south of national park office* ☎*2742–5050* 🌐*www.hotelpelicano.net* *10 rooms with shared bath, 2 cabins* *In-room: no a/c, no phone, no TV. In-hotel: restaurant, tennis court, pool, Internet terminal* ▭*MC, V* *EP.*

$–$$ **Río Chirripó Retreat.** A popular place for yoga retreats, this lodge has clear mountain air, a rushing river, and a huge conical-roof adobe temple hung with a monastery bell and Tibetan prayer flags. You'll feel as though you have arrived in the Himalayas. The bougainvillea-bedecked bed-and-breakfast is a great place for bird-watching, clambering along the river rocks strewn with Druidic-looking stone seats and altars, or acclimatizing before climbing Chirripó. Or you can relax in the hot tub or the swimming pool overlooking the tumultuous river. Two-story wood cabins are cantilevered over a steep ravine, with twig-railing porches. The comfortable rooms have large bathrooms and walls stenciled with mysterious symbols. A new yoga platform with a view also doubles as a palatial guest room. **Pros:** dramatic scenic location; extravagant breakfasts with copious fresh fruits; meal package available. **Cons:** reserve well in advance to avoid group retreats; smallish rooms with two single beds each; shared balconies. ✉*Down a steep drive, just past cemetery* ☎*2742–5109* 🌐*www.riochirripo.com* *8 rooms, 2 cabins, 1 suite* *In-room: no a/c, no phone, no TV. In-hotel: restaurant, pool, 1 suite with kitchen, Wi-Fi* ▭*No credit cards* *BP.*

CHIRRIPÓ NATIONAL PARK

The park entrance is a 4-km/2-mi hike uphill from San Gerardo de Rivas.

The main attraction of this national park is Mount Chirripó, the highest mountain in Costa Rica and a mecca for both hikers and serious peak summiters. If you want to take up the challenge, be sure to make arrangements well in advance. The number of hikers in the park each day is limited to 40. Thirty reservations are booked months ahead and usually snapped up by locals and tour companies, leaving only 10 spaces for hikers who show up at the park. Without reservations, you can try your luck and check in at the San Gerardo ranger station, which grants entrance on a first-come, first-served basis. Maximum stay is three days, two nights.

DID YOU KNOW?

Although it takes the fittest hikers at least four hours to get to the base camp of Chirripó, hundreds of competitors from around the world converge on tiny San Gerardo de Rivas every February to run a 34-km (22-mi) race up and down Chirripó. A local family of hardy brothers shares the record time: three hours and 15 minutes!

GETTING HERE

You are required to report to the **San Gerardo de Rivas National Parks Service** (✉ *Main street* ☎ *2742–5083 reservations* ✉ *reservacioneschirripo@gmail.com*) before you start, either the day before, or the morning of your climb. The office is open 6:30–4, park admission is $15 per day, and they have trail maps. Don't try to sneak in: a park ranger will stop you at a checkpoint on the trail and ask to see your reservation voucher. You can reserve lodgings over the phone or e-mail; ask for a copy of the wonderfully informative visitor's guide to be sent to you via e-mail.

OUTDOOR ACTIVITIES

Hikes and other activities in the park are arranged by **Selva Mar** *(⇨ San Isidro, above)* and by the **Guides and Porters Association of San Gerardo** (☎ *2742–5073* 🌐 *www.chirriporural.org*), who provide guides, porters, and provisions for Chirripó hikes, as well as an alternative hike up the Ruta Urán.

SAN VITO

110 km/68 mi southeast of San Isidro, 61 km/38 mi northeast of Golfito.

Except for the tropical greenery, the rolling hills around the bustling hilltop town of San Vito could be mistaken for a Tuscan landscape. The town actually owes its 1952 founding to 200 Italian families who converted forest into coffee, fruit, and cattle farms. The Italian flavor lingers in outdoor cafés serving ice cream and pastries and an abundance of shoe stores. A statue dedicated to the *pioneros* stands proudly in the middle of town. San Vito is also the center of the Coto Brus coffee region. Many coffee pickers are from the Guaymí tribe, who live in a large reserve nearby and also over the border in Panama. They're easy to recognize by the women's colorfully embroidered cotton dresses.

GETTING HERE AND AROUND

If you are driving south from San Isidro, your best route is along the wide, smooth Pan-American Highway via Buenos Aires to Paso Real, about 70 km (43 mi). Then take the scenic high road to San Vito, 40 km (25 mi) farther along. This road has recently been paved, and it's the most direct and the prettiest route. Another route, which many buses take, is via Ciudad Neily, about 35 km (22 mi) northeast of Golfito, and then 24 km (15 mi) of winding steep road up to San Vito, at almost 1,000 meters (3,280 feet) above sea level. At this writing, the road is potholed and in *mal estato* (bad shape). There are direct buses from San José four times a day, and buses from San Isidro seven times a day. You can also fly to Coto 47 and take a taxi to San Vito.

A ginger flower at the Wilson Botanic Gardens in San Vito.

ESSENTIALS

Most of the banks in town have cash machines that accept foreign cards.

Bank/ATM Banco Nacional (✉ *Across from central park* ☎ *2773–3601*). **ATH Coopealianza** (✉ *Center of town, north of hospital*).

Hospital Hospital San Vito (✉ *South end of town on road to Wilson Botanical Garden* ☎ *2773–3103*).

Pharmacy Farmacia Coto Brus (✉ *Center of town across from La Flor pastry shop* ☎ *2773–3076*).

Internet Cybershop (✉ *1 block west of main street at north end of town* ☎ *2773–3521*).

Post Office Correo (✉ *Far north end of town, beside police station*).

Taxis Taxi service (✉ *Taxi stand beside park at center of town* ☎ *2773–3939*).

EXPLORING

Fodor'sChoice ★ The compelling tourist draw here is the world-renowned **Wilson Botanical Garden,** a must-see for gardeners and bird-watchers and enchanting even for those who are neither. Paths through the extensive grounds are lined with exotic plants and shaded by avenues of palm trees and 50-foot-high bamboo stalks. In 1961 U.S. landscapers Robert and Catherine Wilson bought 30 acres of coffee plantation and started planting tropical species, including palms, orchids, bromeliads, and heliconias. Today the property extends over 635 acres, and the gardens hold around 2,000 native and more than 3,000 exotic species. The palm collection—more than 700 species—is the second largest in the world.

Fantastically shaped and colored bromeliads, which usually live in the tops of trees, have been brought down to the ground in impressive mass plantings, providing one of many photo opportunities. The property was transferred to the Organization for Tropical Studies in 1973, and in 1983 it became part of Amistad Biosphere Reserve. Under the name **Las Cruces Biological Station,** Wilson functions as a research and educational center, so there is a constant supply of expert botanists and biologists to take visitors on natural-history tours in the garden and the adjoining forest trails. If you spend a night at the garden lodge, you have the garden all to yourself in the late afternoon and early morning, when wildlife is most active. ✣ *6 km/4 mi south of San Vito on road to Ciudad Neily* ✉ *Apdo. 73–8257, San Vito* ☎ *2773–4004* 🌐 *www.esintro.co.cr* 🎟 *$12* ⏲ *Daily 8–5.*

OUTDOOR ACTIVITIES

BIRD-WATCHING In addition to its plants, **Wilson Botanical Garden** *(⇨ Exploring, above)* is renowned for its birds. There are about 250 species of birds in the garden alone, including half of the country's hummingbird species, and 410 species total in the immediate area. Competing with the birds for your attention are more than 800 butterflies. Naturalist guides lead visitors on birding and natural-history tours through the garden ($18 per person). The Río Java trail, open only to overnight guests of Wilson, is also a great place to see birds.

WILDLIFE-WATCHING If you are an overnight guest at **Wilson Botanical Garden** *(⇨ Exploring, above)*, you can walk the Río Java trail, through a forest thick with wildlife, particularly monkeys.

WHERE TO EAT AND STAY

$ ITALIAN ★ ✕ **Pizzería Liliana.** Follow the locals' lead and treat yourself to authentic pizza at the classiest restaurant in town or dig into the macaroni *sanviteña*-style: with white sauce, ham, and mushrooms. The classics are here as well, and they're all homemade—lasagna, cannelloni, and ravioli. The authentically Italian vinaigrette salad dressing is a welcome change from more acidic Tico dressings. In true Italian fashion, the friendly, family-run restaurant can be noisy, but it's a happy buzz. For a more romantic dinner, ask for a table on the pretty garden terrace. ✉ *150 m west of central square* ☎ *2773–3080* ▭ *MC, V.*

$$$ 🏨 **Hacienda La Amistad Lodge & Rainforest Preserve.** Here's a rare opportunity to explore La Amistad Park, which borders this 25,000-acre family estate, most of which is primary forest studded with rivers and spectacular waterfalls. The alpine-style lodge offers comfortable quarters, great home-cooked food, and excellent cappuccino and espresso, made from the estate's own organic coffee beans. New junior suites are a little more luxurious, with queen beds. Daylong guided hikes or horseback rides traverse the property's 57 km (35 mi) of trails, excellent for bird watching. The really adventurous can take the Feel Green hiking tour, hiking to four camps over the course of five days. The staff, including a cook, carries all your gear and food in the truck and meets you at each camp. The cabins are as rustic as it gets; the shared baths have only (very) cold water. But the wildlife and walks are beyond exhilarating, and the food cooked in a wood-fire stove is simple but delicious. Bring

along a really good sleeping bag for the cold mountain nights. You can also visit the camps on day tours. **Pros:** unequaled hiking trails; scenic waterfalls. **Cons:** rough access road; bring your own sleeping bag/pillow for camps. *✢32 km/20 mi east of San Vito along a rough, rocky road ☎2200–5037, 2289–7667 in San José 🌐www.haciendalaamistad.com ⇨8 rooms, 4 junior suites in lodge, 6 cabins at each camp ♂In-room: no a/c, no phone, no TV. In-hotel: restaurant, bar, laundry service, Internet terminal ▭AE, MC, V ♀|FAP.*

¢ **Hotel El Ceibo.** The best deal in town, El Ceibo is tucked in a quiet cul-de-sac behind the main street, an Italian-style oasis with graceful arcades and decorative balustrades overlooking potted palms. Rooms are compact but tidy, bright, and comfortable. Rooms 1 to 10 and 21 to 32 have small balconies opening onto a wooded ravine alive with birds. The restaurant, illuminated by a skylight, serves home-style Italian and Tico food at reasonable prices. **Pros:** central location; good price; relative quiet. **Cons:** some rooms are quite small; furnishings are nothing special. *✉140 m east of San Vito's central park, behind Municipalidad ☎2773–3025 🖷2773–5025 ⇨40 rooms ♂In-room: no a/c, no phone. In-hotel: restaurant, bar ▭MC, V ♀|EP.*

$–$$ Fodor's Choice ★ **Wilson Botanical Garden.** A highlight of any Costa Rican visit, this magical botanical garden has comfortable rooms in two modern buildings built of glass, steel, and wood that blend into a forested hillside. The smaller rooms have two single beds, and larger ones have three singles. Private balconies cantilevered over a ravine make bird-watching a snap even from your room. Each room is named after the exotic plant growing at the doorway. Room rates include three excellent home-style meals, a guided tour of the grounds, and 24-hour access to the garden. Staying overnight is the only way to see the garden at dusk and dawn or to walk the Sendero Río Java, a trail that follows a stream through a forest teeming with birds and monkeys. The staff here is cheerful and professional, and the youthful enthusiasm of visiting research students is contagious. **Pros:** unparalleled setting with 24-hour access to garden and nature trails; excellent birding and wildlife-viewing. **Cons:** rooms are becoming a little shabby; meals are served family-style, strictly on time. *✢6 km/4 mi south of San Vito on road to Ciudad Neily ✉OTS, Apdo. 676–2050, San Pedro ☎2524–0628 San José office, 2773–4004 lodge 🌐www.esintro.co.cr ⇨12 rooms ♂In-room: no a/c, no TV. In-hotel: restaurant, Internet terminal ▭AE, MC, V ♀|FAP.*

SHOPPING

In an old farmhouse on the east side of the road between San Vito and the botanical garden, **Finca Cántaros** (*✉Road to Ciudad Neily ✢3 km/2 mi south of San Vito ☎2773–3760*) sells crafts by indigenous artisans from near and far, including Guaitil ceramic figures and *molas* (colorful appliqué work) made by Kuna women from the San Blas Islands in Panama. You can also find a great selection of colorful, high-glaze ceramics from San José artists. Profits help support the adjacent children's library. **■TIP➜** Along with shopping, you can walk bird-filled nature trails around a lake behind the shop.

EN ROUTE

The 33-km (21-mi) road from **San Vito to Ciudad Neily** is twisting and spectacular, with views over the Coto Colorado plain to the Golfo

Dulce and Osa Peninsula beyond. Watch out for killer potholes, though. The road from **San Vito to Paso Real** is equally scenic, traveling along a high ridge with sweeping valley views on either side. As you descend, the wide valley of the El General River opens up before you, planted with miles of spiky pineapples and tall sugarcane. The road has been repaved, and once again even drivers can enjoy the scenery without falling into potholes.

MAKING OUT

Kissing in public, among heterosexual couples at least, is rarely frowned upon, with parks a favorite venue. But a growing number of locally patronized restaurants have posted signs: ESCENAS AMOROSAS PROHIBIDA, literally "Amorous scenes prohibited."

THE COAST

On the other side of a mountain ridge, just a scenic hour-long drive west of San Isidro, you reach the southern Pacific coast with its miles of beaches for sunning, surfing, kayaking, and snorkeling. Ballena National Marine Park alone encompasses almost 10 km (6 mi) of protected beaches. Scattered along the coast are small communities with increasing numbers of international residents and interesting restaurants and lodging options.

DOMINICAL

34 km/21 mi southwest of San Isidro, 40 km/25 mi south of Quepos.

8

Sleepy fishing village–turned–scruffy surfer town, Dominical is changing again as luxury villas pop up all over the hillsides above the beaches, bringing new wealth that is boosting the local economy. It's still a major surfing destination, attracting surfers of all ages, with a lively restaurant and nightlife scene. Bars and restaurants come and go with the waves of itinerant foreigners, so don't hesitate to try something new. Dominical's real magic lies beyond the town, in the surrounding terrestrial and marine wonders: the rain forest grows right up to the beach in some places, and the ocean offers world-class surfing.

GETTING HERE AND AROUND

The road west over the mountains and down to Dominical is scenic at its best and fog-shrouded and potholed at its worst. It has recently been repaved, but there are lots of curves, and potholes pop up unexpectedly, so take your time and enjoy the scenery along the hour-long drive from San Isidro. From Quepos, the road south is the only section of the Costanera still not paved, and it's a bumpy, dusty ride past palm-oil plantations. Buses from San Isidro leave four times a day, two times daily from Quepos. If you want to avoid driving altogether, Easy Ride (⇨ *Shuttle Van in Travel Smart Costa Rica*) has air-conditioned minibuses with room for six to eight passengers that make two trips to and from San José daily ($35).

ESSENTIALS

Bank/ATM Banco de Costa Rica (✉ *Plaza Pacífica* ☎ *2787–0381*).

CLOSE UP

La Amistad National Park

By far the largest park in Costa Rica, at more than 1,980 square km (765 square mi), La Amistad is a mere portion of the vast La Amistad Biosphere Reserve that stretches into western Panama. Altitudes range from 1,000 meters (3,280 feet) to 3,500 meters (11,480 feet). There are miles of rugged, densely forested trails and plenty of wildlife (two-thirds of the country's vertebrate species live here), but because access is extremely difficult, it's not worth visiting the park unless you plan to spend several days, making this a trip only for experienced hikers. Unless you're comfortable being lost in the wilderness, hire a local guide for $20 a day from ASOPROLA, the local guide association (☎2743–1184), which also organizes strenuous three-day guided trips, with two overnights at a mountain refuge ($143 per person with all meals). ASOPROLA also operates El Albergue La Amistad, at the Altamira park entrance, with both private and dormitory rooms with hot-water showers ($12), as well as an organic restaurant run by a local women's cooperative. The alternative is rustic campsites (bring your own tent) for $5 per person at the Potrero Grande park entrance. Reserve space about a week in advance. To get to the park entrance (4WD essential), drive 31 km (20 mi) west from San Vito along the road to Paso Real. Turn right at the park sign at Guacimo, near two small roadside restaurants. Then drive about 20 km (13 mi) uphill on a rough road. The last couple of kilometers are on foot. ☎*2200–5355* *$10 per day* *Daily 8–4.*

Hospital Clínica González Arellano (*Next to pharmacy* ☎*2787–0129*).

Pharmacy Farmacia Dominical (*Pueblo del Río Center at entrance to town* ☎*2787–0454*).

Internet Dominical Internet Cafe (*Above San Clemente Bar, main street* ☎*2787–0191*). **Super Diuwak** (*Next to Hotel Diuwak on road to beach* ☎*2787–0143*).

Post Office San Clemente Bar (*Main street, at bus stop, a mail drop-off only*).

Rental Cars Alamo (*Hotel Villas Río Mar, Dominical* ☎*2787–0052* *www.alamocostarica.com*).

Visitor Information Southern Expeditions (*On Main Street across from San Clemente Bar* ☎*2787–0100*).

EXPLORING

★ The **Hacienda Barú** nature reserve is a leader in both ecotourism and conservation, with a turtle protection project and nature education program in the local school. The bird-watching is spectacular, with excellent guides. You can stay at the cabins and poolside rooms or just come for the day to walk the forest and mangrove trails, zip through the canopy on cables, climb a tree, or stake out birds on an observation platform. *3 km/2 mi north of bridge into Dominical* ☎*2787–0003* *www.haciendabaru.com* *$6, tours $20–$60* *Daily 7 AM–dusk.*

Five years in the making, **Parque Reptilandia** is an impressive reptile exhibit with more than 300 specimens of snakes, lizards, frogs, turtles, and other creatures in terrariums and large enclosures. You can see Central America's only Komodo dragon, Gila monsters, and a 150-pound, African spur-thighed tortoise that likes to be petted. Kids love the maternity ward showcasing newborn snakes. More mature snakes live under a retractable roof that lets in sun and rain. Although snakes are generally more active in sunlight, this is still a great rainy-day-at-the-beach alternative activity. Guided night tours ($20) can also be arranged to watch nocturnal animals at work. If you're not squeamish, feeding day is Friday. *11 km/7 mi east of Dominical on road to San Isidro* *2787–8007* *www.crreptiles.com* *$10* *Daily 9–4:30.*

The **Nauyaca Waterfalls** (Cataratas de Nauyaca), a massive double cascade tumbling down 45 meters (150 feet) and 20 meters (65 feet), are one of the most spectacular sights in Costa Rica. The waterfalls—also known as Barú River Falls—are on private property, so the only way to reach them is to take a hiking or horseback tour (⇨ *Outdoor Activities, below*).

Playa Dominical is long and flat, rarely crowded, and good for beachcombing among all the flotsam and jetsam that the surf washes up onto the brown sand. Swimmers should beware of fatally dangerous rip

"Nauyaca waterfall is 3-tiered waterfall. Well worth the visit." —photo by Richard Bueno, Fodors.com member

currents. In high season, flags mark off a relatively safe area for swimming, under the watchful gaze of a professional lifeguard.

Playa Dominicalito, just 1 km (½ mi) south of Playa Dominical, is usually calmer and more suited to Boogie boarding.

A considerably smaller waterfall than Nauyaca Waterfalls, **Pozo Azul** is in the jungle about 5 km (3 mi) south of town. Off the main highway, head up the road toward Bella Vista lodge and take the first road to the right, past the new school and through a stream; follow the road straight uphill for about 300 meters (1,000 feet) to where the road widens. You can park here and climb down the steep trail to the river on the right, where there is a lovely swimming hole and waterfall, often populated by local kids when school is out. There sometimes is a guard on duty in the parking lot (tip him about 350 colones per hour), but be sure not to leave anything of value in your parked car.

OUTDOOR ACTIVITIES

Southern Expeditions (✉ *On main street, across from San Clemente Bar & Grill* ☎ *2787–0100* 🌐 *southernexpeditionscr.com*), a major tour operator in the area, can arrange kayaking, white-water rafting, scuba diving, fishing, and nature tours in and around Ballena Marine National Park, Caños Island, and all the way down to Corcovado National Park.

Much of the lush forest that covers the steep hillsides above the beaches is protected within private nature reserves. Several of these reserves, such as Hacienda Barú and La Merced (⇨ *Ballena Marine National Park below*), are financing a biological corridor and preservation of the rain forest.

FISHING Angling options range from expensive sportfishing charters to a trip in a small boat to catch red snapper and snook for supper. The five most common fish species here, in the order in which you are likely to catch them, are sailfish, dorado, yellowfin tuna, wahoo, and marlin. **Mark Hendry** (☎*2787–8224*) runs trips 28 nautical miles out to the Furuno Bank, which he claims is the most reliable area for finding the big ones, including sailfish and marlin. Trips ($650) are in a 21-foot Mako boat and include food, drinks, and gear. **Nick Fortney** (☎*2786–5273* ⊕*www.costaricahooksetters.net*), a U.S. Coast Guard–licensed captain, comes down from Alaska every year to spend November to April in Dominical, offering inshore and offshore fishing trips on his custom 25-foot El Hooksetter. A half day for up to four fishers is $375; full day, with lunch included, is $650.

PACK YOUR BOARD

The surfing is great in Dominical, thanks to the runoff from the Barú River mouth, which constantly changes the ocean bottom and creates well-shaped waves big enough to keep intermediate and advanced surfers challenged. The best surfing is near the river mouth, and the best time is two hours before or after high tide, to avoid the notorious riptides.

HORSEBACK RIDING **Don Lulo** (☎*2787–8137 or 2787–8013*) operates tours to Nauyaca Waterfalls that depart Monday to Saturday at 8 AM from the road to San Isidro, 10 km (6 mi) northeast of Dominical. The tour is $50 and includes breakfast and lunch at Don Lulo's family homestead near the falls. You can swim in the cool pool beneath the falls, so bring a bathing suit. There is a river to cross, but otherwise the ride is easy; horses proceed at a walk. Be sure to reserve a day in advance.

Friendly, well-trained horses at **Bella Vista Lodge** (*5 km/3 mi southeast of Dominical* ☎*2787–8069*) also take riders to the Nauyaca, via a scenic valley route, with lunch and a ride in an aerial tram included for $45. For the same price you can go for a gallop on the beach in the morning or afternoon, depending on tides. These tours include lunch. The three- to four-hour tours start at the lodge, then head down the steep Escaleras road 2 km (1 mi), passing Pozo Azul. Riders staying in hotels on the beach can also pick up the ride right on the beach.

SURFING **Green Iguana Surf Camp** (☎*2787–0157* ⊕*www.greeniguanasurfcamp.com*) gives two-hour individual lessons for $50 or $40 per person for small groups of two or more. They also have weeklong packages that include lodging, board rental, lessons, and transport to whichever nearby beach has the best waves each day (from $585). These longer packages include transportation to and from San José.

WHERE TO EAT

$–$$$ THAI ✕**Coconut Spice.** If you like rice with spice, you've come to the right place. This sophisticated restaurant has authentic Southeast Asian flavor in both food and furnishings. Try the hot-and-sour tom yan goong soup, tart with lemongrass and lime and heated up with chilies. The jumbo shrimp vary in price and can get quite expensive, but they're worth it: buttery, sweet, and cooked in spicy coconut sauce. There are also satays, curries, and other Indian standards. The restaurant recently moved to a larger location by the river, so bring along repellent. It's daily from 1 PM. ✉ *Pueblo del Río at entrance to Dominical* ☎ *2787–0073* ▭ *MC, V*

$$ ITALIAN ✕ **ConFusione.** The location—on a dead-end road at the southern end of the beach—may confound you on your first visit, but there's nothing confusing about the sophisticated Italian menu. Along with the usual dishes, the menu has some interesting tropical twists: fish sauces blending coconut with Cognac, and pineapple with cream. The most popular dish here is the lomito, local beef tenderloin expertly aged and cooked. Appetizers are big enough to share, and pizzas are popular among the more budget-conscious surfers. The terrace dining room, though, is all grown up, glowing with gold light and warm earth tones. The wine list is varied and interesting, with a good selection of Italian wines at modest prices. BYOR—Bring Your Own Repellent. ✉ *Domilocos Hotel, south end of Dominical Beach* ☎ *2787–0244* ▭ *MC, V* ⊙ *No lunch.*

$$–$$$ SEAFOOD ✕ **La Parcela.** Picture a dream location: a high headland jutting out into the sea with vistas up and down the coast. Throw in a breeze-swept terrace, polished service, and some fine seaside cuisine. This restaurant has had its ups and downs, often relying on its unmatched location, but the current management has got it right: a wide-ranging menu of pastas, salads, and seafood. Generous servings of perfectly cooked fish are topped with some interesting sauces, including a standout roasted red pepper sauce with almonds. Desserts here are rich—mud pie and a delectable chocolate cake—and substantial enough to share. If you're just passing through Dominical, this is a good place for a cold beer or a *naturale,* a tall glass of freshly whipped fruit juice. Sunsets here are spectacular. There is some controversy about this restaurant's eco-sensitive location, so call ahead to make sure it's still up and running. ✣ *4 km/2½ mi south of Dominical* ☎ *2787–0016* ▭ *AE, DC, MC, V.*

¢–$ COSTARICAN ✕ **Restaurant Su Raza.** Among the handful of sodas (casual eateries) in town serving typical Costa Rican food, this one is notable for its whole fish. Hearty portions of seafood are served on a wooden veranda that's a great bird-watching spot. Bring your binoculars, especially if you come just before sunset or for breakfast. Stick to the *desayuno típico* for breakfast, with traditional rice and beans and eggs. The omelets are great, but they come with limp frozen french fries, the bane of Tico restaurants. ✉ *Across from San Clemente Grill, main road* ☎ *2787–0105* ▭ *No credit cards.*

$ TEX MEX ✕ **San Clemente Mexican-American Bar & Grill.** Signs you're in the local surfer hangout: dozens of broken surfboards affixed to the ceiling, photos of the sport's early years adorning the walls, and a big sound system and dance floor. Fresh seafood, sandwiches, and Tex-Mex standards like burritos and nachos make up the menu. The bargain "starving surfer's breakfast"—two eggs with *gallo pinto* (black beans and rice) or pancakes, plus coffee—is always popular. Owner Mike McGinnis is famous for making a blistering hot sauce and for being a super source of information about the area. ✉ *Middle of main road* ☎ *2787–0055* ▭ *AE, MC, V.*

$ MEXICAN ✕ **Tortilla Flats.** Another perennially popular surfer hangout, this casual place has the advantage of being right across from the beach. Fresh-baked baguette sandwiches are stuffed with interesting combinations; the grilled chicken, avocado, tomato, and mozzarella California sandwich is the most popular. Light eaters can buy half a sandwich. Fresh-fish specials and typical Mexican fare round out the casual menu. The margaritas are excellent, and ladies are served free shots on Thursday night. ✉ *On beach, Dominical* ☎ *2787–0033* ▭ *AE, MC, V.*

WHERE TO STAY

Lodgings in the lowlands of Dominical and the area a little to the north tend to be hot and muggy and not as comfortable as the more luxurious, private, and breezy places up in the hills above Dominicalito, to the south.

$–$$ **Coconut Grove Oceanfront Cottages.** Right on the beach, this well-maintained cluster of cabins and beach houses is ideal for couples or families who want to fend for themselves. The two bamboo-furnished beach houses sleep two to six and have full kitchens; the smaller cabins have kitchenettes and room for three. At night you can turn off the a/c, open the screened windows, and fall asleep to the sound of the sea. The largest cottage, No. 5, is also closest to the beach. There's a pretty pool, and yoga classes take place twice a week. The American owners have dogs, including two large but lazy Great Danes. **Pros:** best location in town: right on beach; close to cool ocean breezes; communal barbecue; friendly owner/hosts. **Cons:** furnishings are simple, not fancy; guests must love dogs. ✉ *Turn off main highway at Km 147* ✣ *3 km/2 mi south of Dominical* ☎ *2787–0130* 🌐 *www.coconutgrovecr.com* *3 cabins, 2 beach houses* *In-room: kitchen (some). In-hotel: pool, beachfront* ▭ *No credit cards* *EP.*

$$$ **Cuna del Angel Hotel and Spa.** Hosts of decorative angels abound at this made-in-heaven fantasyland for grown-ups. The over-the-top decor may not suit everyone, but this is a perfect spot for those who like to indulge themselves. The original 16 rooms are luxurious, chock-full of delightful touches, including luxurious linens and towels, stained-glass windows, and spectacular lamps. Nine new Jungle Rooms are smaller and darker, but cheaper and very comfortable, with pickled-wood walls, antiqued armoires, and balconies facing forest or garden. The spa is small and intimate, with a sensual Turkish bath, a selection of soothing massages, and a full-service hair salon. Once you feel rejuvenated, a lush garden, a terrace restaurant, and a pretty pool with an ocean view draw you outdoors. Dinner in the terrace restaurant is pleasant, with a sophisticated menu, and if your timing is right, there's entertainment by top national musicians at the hotel's once-a-month dinner concerts. **Pros:** endlessly amusing decor to keep you talking, admiring, and laughing; friendly service in hotel and spa, which is small and intimate. **Cons:** room balconies and terraces are quite close together, so not a lot of privacy; rooms that face the pool can be noisy if children are playing; steep steps to new Jungle Rooms. ✉ *Puertocito* ✣ *9 km/5 m south of Dominical* ☎ *2787–8012* *2787–8015 Ext. 304* 🌐 *www.cunadelangel.com* *25 rooms* *In-room: Wi-Fi. In-hotel: restaurant, bar, pool, spa, no-smoking rooms* *BP.*

$ **Hacienda Barú National Wildlife Refuge and Ecolodge.** Base yourself in this model eco-lodge to explore vast tracts of surrounding forest,

8

mangroves, and a Blue Flag beach with nesting turtles. The six original cabins have sitting rooms with wood furniture, kitchenettes, screened-in porches, and lush flower borders. Each cabin sleeps three or four people. Six handsome new guest rooms built with plantation teak have high ceilings, tiled showers, and small porches, looking onto a brand new swimming pool. A new solar system provides plenty of hot water for showers. Linger for an hour or two atop a lofty bird observation platform in the hotel's rain-forest canopy, zip along the canopy tour, climb a 114-foot-high tree with ropes, or stay overnight at a shelter in the heart of the forest. Excellent local guides interpret the miles of trails, or you can follow the self-guided trail with the help of a handbook. There's a great gift shop here with lots of local crafts and nature books. **Pros:** prime wildlife viewing; excellent guides; trails and outdoor activities; spacious cabins with kitchens; comfortable new guest rooms; perfect for groups. **Cons:** cabins are not fancy and have small, basic bathrooms. *3 km/2 mi north of bridge into Dominical* *Apdo. 215–8000, Pérez Zeledón 11901* *2787–0003* *www.haciendabaru.com* *6 cabinas, 6 guest rooms* *In-room: no a/c, no phone, some kitchens, no TV. In-hotel: restaurant, beachfront* *AE, MC, V* *BP.*

$–$$ ★ **Necochea Inn.** The forest setting feels primeval, but the decor at this handsome mountain retreat is a sophisticated mix of plush, contemporary furniture and wood, stone, and animal-print fabric. Downstairs living and dining rooms face a wall of sliding glass doors looking onto a stone-deck pool in the jungle and a slice of ocean for a view. Two streams run through the forested property, supplying a natural, burbling soundtrack. A curved stone stairway leads up to two luxurious, large rooms that share a spacious bath. The huge upstairs suite and a slightly smaller regular room have private porches, decadent bathrooms with deep tubs, antique armoires, and gleaming hardwood floors. A new creek-side suite has its own TV, a/c, and a romantic whirlpool tub on a private terrace. Host Yvonne de Necochea is full of energy and makes every guest feel at home. **Pros:** luxurious accommodation with a personal touch, including Yvonne's mural-size wildlife paintings; excellent breakfasts; and, if you ask, a rollicking night of karaoke. **Cons:** up a steep road that can be muddy; need your own car to get down hill to restaurants and beaches. *South of Km 147, turn 2 km/1 mi up, past the Pozo Azul, Dominicalito* *2787–8072 or 8395–2984* *www.thenecocheainn.com* *3 rooms with shared bath, 2 suites, 1 room with private bath* *In-room: a/c (in 1 room), no phone, TV (1 room). In-hotel: restaurant, pool* *MC, V* *BP.*

¢–$ ★ **Pacific Edge.** Unbeatable views and affordable prices set these stylishly rustic cabins apart. The forest grows right up to the edge of the property, high on a mountain ridge south of town. Private, spacious wood cabinas—one sleeps six; others sleep four—have kitchenettes, tiled bathrooms, hammocks strung on wide porches, and comfortable orthopedic mattresses covered with colorful Guatemalan bedspreads. Host Susie Atkinson serves great breakfasts in the lodge's bamboo-roof, pagoda-style dining room. Dinner—Thai-style shrimp, perhaps—is cooked on request. Two lookout towers at each end of the tiny pool catch the spectacular sunsets and passing whale pods. The road up to

LIVING OFF THE GRID

Many hotels in remoter areas of the South Pacific generate their own electricity, so don't count on air-conditioning, using a hair dryer, calling home, checking your e-mail, or paying with a credit card (unless it's arranged in advance). Some lodges do have radio contact with the outside world and satellite phone systems you can use in emergencies, but bad weather can often block the satellite signal. On the positive side, you really can get away from it all in the Southern Zone. Pack as though you are a castaway from modern civilization. Be sure to bring the following:

- Flashlight with extra batteries, or better still, one of the new kinetic flashlights that need no batteries
- Insect repellent (lots of it)
- Sunscreen (ditto)
- After-sun lotion
- All toiletries and medications you could conceivably need in small travel containers
- Sturdy, breathable hiking shoes and lots of socks (your feet will get wet)
- Waterproof walking sandals
- Binoculars
- Sun hat
- Refillable water bottle
- Portable, battery-operated reading light
- Zip-lock baggies of all sizes to keep cameras, snacks, etc., dry and bug-free

8

this lofty perch requires a 4WD vehicle, but a hotel shuttle can pick you up in town with advance notice. Be prepared for a barky welcome; Susie and her husband, George, love big (but gentle) dogs. The reception desk closes at 6 PM. **Pros:** fabulous views; bargain prices; serene setting; can make your own breakfast and simple snacks. **Cons:** very steep road that requires 4WD to get back and forth to town restaurants and beaches; must love dogs. ✉*Drive 4 km/2½ mi south of Dominical to Km 148, then turn up a rough road 1.2 km/1 mi* ☎📠*2787–8010* 🌐*www.pacificedge.info* *4 cabinas* *In-room: no a/c, no phone, refrigerator, no TV. In-hotel: restaurant, bar, pool* *AE, MC, V* *EP.*

$ **Roca Verde.** This small, friendly hotel has the best beach access in the area. Rooms are sunny and stylish, with swirling flower murals, luxurious bathrooms, and cane-balustraded verandas looking onto a garden and a small pool. There's no TV reception in the rooms, but if you're lucky, you'll be here on a night when the local little theater group is performing in the hotel's open-air lobby. The fish-sculpture-festooned lobby is a gathering place for locals and also a gallery displaying work by local artists. The hotel arranges surfing lessons and fishing trips. Late-night dances on Saturdays, sometimes with live music, draw *bailarinas* (dancers) from surrounding towns. **Pros:** right on the beach; friendly bar; reasonably priced. **Cons:** can be very noisy Saturday night if you're not a party lover; restaurant is just average. ✉*1 km/½ mi south of Dominical* ☎*2787–0036* 🌐*www.hotelrocaverde.com* *10 rooms* *In-room: no phone, no TV. In-hotel: restaurant, pool, beachfront, laundry service* *AE, MC, V* *EP.*

$$–$$$ ★ **Villas Río Mar.** Upriver from the beach on exquisitely landscaped grounds, this hotel is awash in clouds of terrestrial orchids and aflame with bright bougainvillea and hibiscus. Rooms are in adobe-style cabinas with thatched roofs and cane ceilings, and have clean white-tile bathrooms. The newer junior suites have king-size beds, cable TV, and air-conditioning—a must, since the cabinas bake in the sun. Four suites also have whirlpool tubs. Every room has a private porch screened with mosquito netting and furnished with bamboo chairs and hammocks. Plants and elegant table settings fill the huge thatch-roof restaurant with pool views. The breakfast buffet ($6.50 for nonguests) is a good deal here, as are theme-night buffets. A luxurious, large pool has a swim-up bar and handsome teak pool furniture. **Pros:** huge pool; lovely grounds; good restaurant. **Cons:** about half the rooms have no a/c, and it can get hot here; there are small beaches along the river, but it's a 15-minute walk along an alternately dusty/muddy road to town and the ocean beach. *1 km/½ mi west of Dominical; turn right off highway into town and then right again under bridge and follow bumpy river road ☎2787–0052 www.villasriomar.com 40 rooms, 12 junior suites In-room: no a/c (some), refrigerator, no TV (some). In-hotel: restaurant, bar, tennis court, pool, spa, Wi-Fi AE, MC, V BP.*

NIGHTLIFE

During the high season, Dominical hops at night, and when the surfers have fled to find bigger waves, there are enough locals around to keep some fun events afloat. At Friday night's **Movies in the Jungle** (✉*Marina Vista 3, high up on the Escaleras road at Cinema Escaleras in a private house with no sign; call for directions* ☎*2787–8065*), after a potluck dinner at 5, the movies start at 6, in dry season from December to April. Movie buff Harley "Toby" Toberman presents self-proclaimed weird shorts from his huge collection plus a full-length feature on a huge screen, with state-of-the-art equipment. Admission is $6, which goes into a projector-bulb fund. Saturday night the dance action is at the **Roca Verde** (*1 km/½ mi south of Dominical* ☎*2787–0036*), with a mixed crowd that doesn't usually get warmed up until 11 PM. Friday night there's live music and dancing at **San Clemente Bar** (✉*On main road* ☎*2787–0055*). At **Maracatu World Music Bar** (✉*Main street, across from San Clemente* ☎*2787–0091*) the crowd is young and edgy, with an open mike on Tuesday, and salsa music on Wednesday, which is also ladies' night. An older crowd gathers at **Río Lindo Resort** (✉*At entrance to town* ☎*2787–0028*) on Sunday from 4 to 9 PM for an alfresco fiesta by the pool, including barbecue, horseshoes, and calypso and bluesy music. Bring your swimsuit. There's live music and dancing in the hotel's Rum Bar on occasion.

SHOPPING

Banana Bay Gallery & Gifts (✉*Plaza Pacífica shopping center, highway just above Dominical* ☎*2787–0106* *Closed Sun.*) is not only air-conditioned, but also stocked with an always-intriguing and always-amusing mix of arts and crafts and unusual items, along with indigenous crafts such as tropical masks and lots of insect-theme toys for kids of all ages.

BALLENA MARINE NATIONAL PARK

20 km/12 mi southeast of Dominical.

Parque Nacional Marino Ballena (Whale Marine National Park) boasts four separate beaches, stretching for about 10 km (6 mi), and encompasses a mangrove estuary, a recovering coral reef, and more than 12,350 acres of ocean, home to tropical fish, dolphins, and humpback whales who use it as a nursery. *Park begins at Playa Uvita, about 20 km/20 mi south of Dominical ☎2743–8236 $6 Daily 6–6.*

GETTING HERE AND AROUND

The park area includes the communities of Uvita, Bahía Ballena, and Ojochal, all easily accessible off the Costanera, a wide, paved highway. As soon as you get off the highway, however, the roads are bumpy and dusty. Alternatively, take a taxi or bus from Dominical. Buses leave Dominical at 10:30 AM and 5:30 PM daily, and there are longer-haul buses that pass along the Costanera and can drop you off in Uvita. Each of the park's four sectors has a small ranger station where you pay your admission.

ESSENTIALS

Uvita Information Center (☎8843–7142 or 2743–8889 www.uvita.info).

EXPLORING

Playa Ventanas, just 1½ km (1 mi) south of Ballena Marine Park, is a beautiful beach that's popular for sea-kayaking, with some interesting tidal caves. The mountains that rise up behind these beaches hold rain forests, waterfalls, and wildlife. There is guarded, private parking here for 350 colones (about 75¢) an hour (except on Wednesday, when you park at your own risk).

At **La Merced National Wildlife Refuge**, owned by Selva Mar, you can ride the range or beach on horseback, explore the forest on a nature hike, or go bird-watching with an excellent guide. Tours include transportation from your hotel and a guide; the full-day tour includes lunch. For $6 you can explore the 10 kilometers (6 mi) of trails on your own with a trail map. *Reception center at Km 159 on the Costanera, north of Uvita ☎8861–5147 www.rancholamerced.com $35 half-day tour, $60 full-day tour By reservation only.*

You'll find excellent bird-watching and hiking a little farther up the hill in the **Oro Verde Private Nature Reserve**, which offers daily two-hour birding tours at 6 AM and 2 PM ($35), as well as guided hikes through their primary forest reserve ($20 to $35) and a three-hour morning or afternoon horseback tour to a waterfall ($35). You can also have a hot lunch with a local family for an extra $5 per person. *3 km/2 mi uphill from Rancho La Merced, north of Uvita ☎2743–8072 By reservation only.*

OUTDOOR ACTIVITIES

Outfitters in Dominical *(⇨above)* run tours to the park and surrounding beaches. **La Merced National Wildlife Refuge** *(⇨above)* has birding, forest hikes, and horseback riding. For local bookings and information, contact the Uvita Information Center *(⇨above)*.

8

CLOSE UP

Wildlife-Watching Tips

If you're accustomed to nature programs on TV, with visions of wildebeest and zebra swarming across African savanna, your first visit to a tropical forest can be a bewildering experience. If these forests are so diverse, where are all the animals? Web sites, brochures, and books are plastered with lovely descriptions and close-up images of wildlife that give travelers high hopes. Reality is much different but no less fascinating. Below are some tips to make your experience more enjoyable.

■ Don't expect to see rarely sighted animals. It might happen; it might not. Cats (especially jaguars), harpy eagles, and tapirs are a few rare sightings.

■ Monkeys can be the easiest animals to spot, but although they are as reliable as the tides in some locations, in others they are rare indeed.

■ Remember that nearly all animals spend most of their time avoiding detection.

■ Be quiet! Nothing is more unsettling to a wary animal than 20 *Homo sapiens* conversing as they hike. It's best to treat the forest like a house of worship—quiet reverence is in order.

■ Listen closely. Many visitors are surprised when a flock of parrots overhead is pointed out to them, despite the incredible volume of noise they produce. That low-pitched growl you hear is a howler monkey call, which is obvious if nearby, but easily missed over the din of conversation. Try stopping for a moment and closing your eyes.

■ Slowly observe different levels of the forest. An enormous caterpillar or an exquisitely camouflaged moth may be only a few inches from your face, and the silhouettes in the tree 100 meters (330 feet) away may be howler monkeys. Scan trunks and branches where a sleeping sloth or anteater might curl up. A quick glance farther down the trail may reveal an agouti or peccary crossing your path.

■ In any open area such as a clearing or river, use your binoculars and scan in the distance; scarlet macaws and toucans may be cruising above the treetops.

■ Cultivate some level of interest in the less charismatic denizens of the forest—the plants, insects, and spiders. On a good day in the forest you may see a resplendent quetzal or spider monkey, but should they fail to appear, focus on an intricate spiderweb, a column of marching army ants, mammal footprints in the mud, or colorful seeds and flowers fallen from high in the canopy.

DIVING AND SNORKELING **Mystic Dive Center** (☎2786–5217 🌐*www.mysticdivecenter.com*) specializes in dive and snorkel trips to Caño Island, about 50 km (31 mi), or an hour and 15 minutes, from Playa Ventanas ($95 full-day snorkeling; $145 full-day diving, including equipment, lunch, park fees, and guide). **Crocodive** has complete PADI-certified diving and snorkeling courses, including introductory dive courses in a pool ($60) or at Caño Island ($159). A four-hour dive or snorkeling trip around Ballena Marine Park is $57 per snorkeler or $95 per diver (with two tanks). They also have night dives and trips to Caño Island ($85 to $135). ✉*At entrance to Ojochal, Playa Tortuga* ☎2786–5417 🌐*www.crocodive.com*.

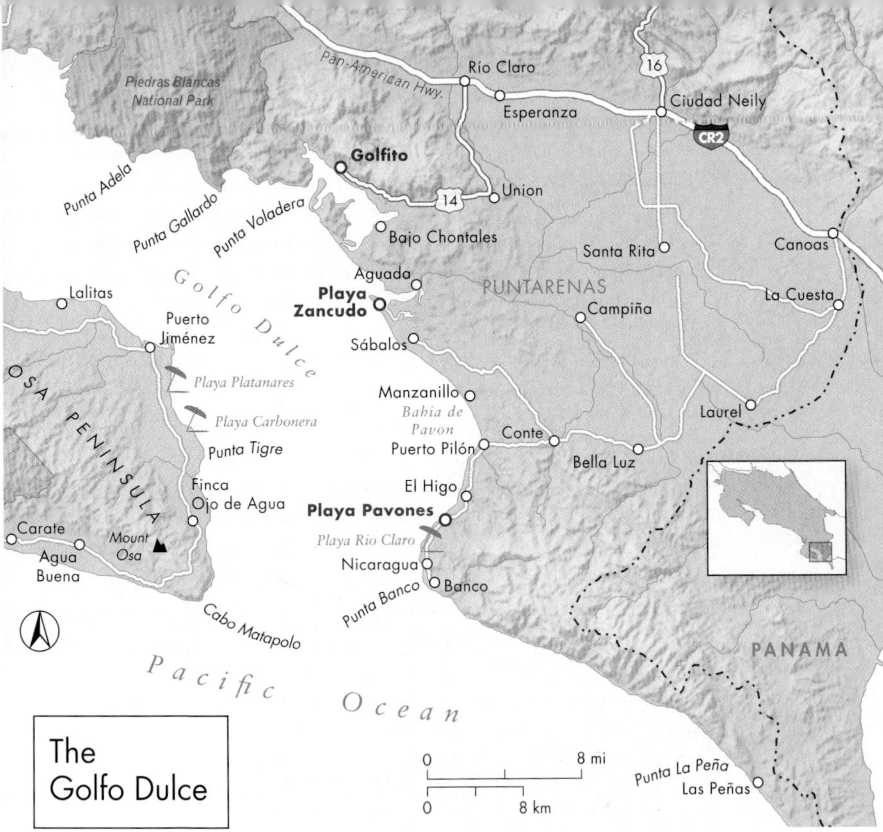

The Golfo Dulce

by boat. Early morning is the best time, when the water in the gulf is at its calmest. Most lodges include the boat transport in their rates.

GETTING HERE

From San José the trip is a long and often grueling eight-hour drive along paved roads crossing over often-foggy mountains. Your best bet, especially if you are visiting one of the lodges on the gulf, is to fly to Golfito, which takes only about an hour. Direct buses from San José leave twice daily.

ESSENTIALS

Bank/ATM ATH Coopealianza (✉ *Across from hospital, north end of town*). **Banco Nacional** (✉ *South of hospital* ☎ *2775–1101*).

Hospital Regional Hospital (✉ *American Zone, near Deposito* ☎ *2775–1001*).

Pharmacy Farmacia Golfito (✉ *Main street, across from city park* ☎ *2775–2442*).

Internet Wi-Fi is now widely available if you have your own laptop. Locals use computers at **Daisy's Ropa Americana** (✉ *Across from hospital* ☎ *2775–2187*).

Post Office Correo (✉ *Across from soccer field; climb flight of stairs off the main road, south of central park*).

Taxis Taxi service (☎ *2775–2020*).

Visitor Information Land Sea Services (✉ *Next to Banana Bay Marina on left as you enter town* ☎ *2775–1614*); they also sell SANSA tickets. **Visitor Information Center** (✉ *At municipal dock* ☎ *2775–1820* ⏲ *Mon.–Sat. 8–noon*).

EXPLORING

The northwestern end of town is the so-called **American Zone,** full of wooden houses on stilts, where the expatriate managers of United Fruit lived amid flowering trees imported from all over the world. Some of these vintage houses, built of durable Honduran hardwoods, are now being spruced up.

Golfito doesn't have a beach of its own, but **Playa Cacao** is a mere five-minute boat ride across the bay from town. Hire a boat at the city dock or from a mooring opposite the larger cruise-ship dock, north of Golfito's center. Playa Cacao has two casual restaurants and one collection of basic cabinas, but it makes a cooler, quieter option when the heat and noise in Golfito get unbearable.

Piedras Blancas National Park has some great birding. The park is verdant forest, home to many species of endemic plants and animals. It's also an important wildlife corridor because it connects to Corcovado National Park. Follow the main road northwest through the old American Zone, past the airstrip and a housing project: the place where a dirt road heads into the rain forest is ground zero for bird-watchers. ✉ *Adjacent to Golfito National Wildlife Refuge* ☎ *No phone* *Free* ⏲ *Daily dawn–dusk.*

A Garden of Eden with mass plantings of ornamental palms, bromeliads, heliconias, cycads, orchids, flowering gingers, and spice trees, **Casa** ★ **Orquideas** has been tended with care for more than 25 years by American owners Ron and Trudy MacAllister. The 2½-hour tour, available Sunday and Thursday at 8:30 AM, includes touching, tasting, and smelling, plus spotting toucans and hummingbirds. Trudy is also a font of information on local lore and medicinal plants. Guided tours, given for a minimum of three people, are $8 per person. Self-guided visits cost $5. The garden is accessible only by boat; a water taxi from Golfito to the garden (about $60 to $75 round-trip for up to four people) is a tour in itself. ✉ *North of Golfito on the Golfo Dulce* ☎ *8829–1247* *$5–$8* ⏲ *Tours Thurs. and Sun. at 8:30* AM ⏲ Closed Fri.

OUTDOOR ACTIVITIES

FISHING The open ocean holds plenty of sailfish, marlin, and rooster fish during the dry months, as well as mahimahi, tuna, and wahoo during the rainy season; there's excellent bottom fishing any time of year. Captains are in constant radio contact with one another and tend to share fish finds.

Banana Bay Marina (☎ *2775–0838 or 2775–1111* 🌐 *www.bananabaymarina.com*) has a fleet of five boats skippered by world-record-holding captains. A day's fishing for up to four averages $1,000. **C-Tales** (✉ *Las Gaviotas Hotel* ☎ *2775–0062* 🌐 *www.c-tales.com*) operates fishing boats with English-speaking captains and mates. **Land Sea** (✉ *Waterfront next to Banana Bay Marina* ☎ *2775–1614* 🌐 *www.marinaservices-yachtdelivery.com*) can hook you up with independent captains in the area.

WHERE TO EAT

$–$$ AMERICAN ✕ **Banana Bay.** For consistently good American-style food, you can't beat this breezy marina restaurant with a view of expensive yachts and fishing boats. Locals complain that the prices are high, but portions are hefty, and include generous salads, excellent chicken fajitas wrapped in homemade tortillas, and a delicious grilled dorado fish sandwich with a mountain of fries—a deal at $7.50. While you're waiting for your order, take advantage of the free Wi-Fi. It's open for breakfast, too. ✉ *Golfito main street, south of town dock* ☎ *2775–0838* ▭ *MC, V.*

$ COSTA RICAN ✕ **Restaurante Mar y Luna.** Strings of buoys, nets, and fishing rods give a nautical air to this casual, affordable terrace restaurant jutting out into Golfito Harbor. Twinkling fairy lights frame a pleasant harbor view. The seafood-heavy lineup includes shrimp and grilled whole fish. Chicken fillets smothered in a mushroom sauce and vegetarian dishes round out the menu. The quality varies, depending on who's in the kitchen, but during a recent visit the kitchen was in top form. ✉ *South end of Golfito main street, just north of Hotel Las Gaviotas* ☎ *2775–0192* ▭ *MC, V* ⊗ *Closed Mon.*

WHERE TO STAY

The atmosphere of the in-town hotels differs dramatically from that of the lodges in the delightfully remote east coast of the Golfo Dulce. The latter is a world of jungle and blue water, birds and fish, and desert-island beaches, with lodges accessible only by boat from either Golfito or Puerto Jiménez.

$$ **Esquinas Rainforest Lodge.** This well-managed eco-lodge is a model conservation project run by Austrians who have tried to instill a sense of Teutonic order. (More than 80% of the guests here are from Germany and Austria.) But the tidy gravel paths winding past wooden cabins in manicured gardens are constantly being encroached upon by wild forest, with the garden looking wilder every year. A spring-fed pool is delightful, and fragrant white ginger and ylang-ylang encircle a pond that is home to contented, well-fed caimans. Another nearby pond has a new lookout for bird-watchers. Local guides lead visitors along thrilling trails that head to the waterfalls and primary forest of Piedras Blancas National Park. Rooms have tile floors, good reading lamps, and airy bathrooms with plenty of hot water. The dining room, romantically candlelit at night, serves excellent food. For families or foursomes, there is a new, fully equipped Jungle Villa with forest views (minimum stay four nights). **Pros:** excellent trails and wildlife-viewing opportunities in unique natural setting; hearty meals. **Cons:** no a/c and it can get hot here; some trails are challenging and you need to be steady on your feet; lodge is geared to nature lovers who aren't looking for luxury. ✉ *Near La Gamba* ✣ *5 km/3 mi west of Villa Briceño turnoff* ☎ *2741–8001, 2775–0140 in Golfito* 🌐 *www.esquinaslodge.com* *14 rooms in 7 bungalows* *In-room: no a/c, no phone, no TV. In-hotel: restaurant, bar, pool* ▭ *AE, MC, V* *FAP.*

¢–$ **Hotel Las Gaviotas.** Just south of town on the water's edge, this hotel has wonderful views over the inner gulf. Rooms have terra-cotta floors, teak furniture, and a veranda with chairs overlooking the well-tended tropical gardens and the shimmering gulf beyond. A pleasant open-air

"Taken in the road to Puerto Jimenez. It was such a beautiful view of Gulfo Dulce." —photo by jamie722, Fodors.com member

restaurant with fresh-tasting food looks onto the large pool, whose terrace is barely divided from the sea. The restaurant has an extensive wine and cocktail list, and the weekend barbecue buffets ($18) are the best deal in town. The hotel offers sportfishing trips from its own dock and has a good gift shop. **Pros:** great location and large pool; safe parking. **Cons:** fairly utilitarian furniture and spare decor; bathrooms are a little dreary. *3 km/2 mi south of Golfito town center* *Apdo. 12–8201, Golfito* *2775–0062* *www.resortlasgaviotas.com* *18 rooms, 3 cabinas* *In-room: safe. In-hotel: restaurant, bar, pool* *AE, MC, V* *EP.*

¢ COSTA RICAN **Hotel Samoa del Sur.** Nautical kitsch at its best, this dockside hotel has a ship-shaped restaurant ($–$$$), complete with a billowy sail and a mermaid figurehead. This is definitely fisherman territory, with a pool table, loud music, and big TVs. Unexpectedly, the breakfast omelets may be the best in Costa Rica. The seaside theme carries through to spacious rooms, from shell-pattern bedspreads to shell-shaped hand soap. Rooms have two double beds, remote-control air-conditioning, and tile bathrooms with hot water (a rarity in these parts). The mattresses are a little soft, and you are at the mercy of adjoining neighbors and the thumping music from the bar, but things usually quiet down by 11 PM. The eccentric French owner designed a swimming pool in the shape of butterfly wings, plus a kids' pool and play area. Guests who want to get out on the water can paddle complimentary kayaks. **Pros:** affordable and fun; lively restaurant. **Cons:** can be lots of rambunctious kids in pool; noisy bar in evenings; guard dogs at night may scare off some guests. *Main street, 1 block north of town dock* *2775–0233* *www.samoadelsur.com* *14 rooms* *In-room: no phone, Wi-Fi (some). In-hotel: restaurant, bar, pool, bicycles, laundry service, Wi-Fi in restaurant* *AE, MC, V* *EP.*

$$$ Fodor's Choice ★ **Playa Nicuesa Rainforest Lodge.** Hands down, this is the best lodge on the gulf, with an emphasis on adventure on both land and sea. Out the front door of the lodge are beach, bay, and mangroves, with kayaks, snorkeling, fishing, sailing, and swimming; out the back door is a forested mountain with hiking trails, a waterfall, and plenty of wildlife and a resident naturalist to interpret the trails. For more contemplative types, there is a new yoga deck and a resident yoga instructor in high season. The two-story main lodge is a palatial tree house, crafted from 15 kinds of wood. Luxurious, hexagonal wooden cabins with open-air showers are scattered around a lush garden that ensures privacy. A stucco guesthouse with four large, comfortable rooms is shaded by mango trees. Solar power ensures a steady supply of electricity, and there's always lots of hot water. Imaginative meals are served in the second-story dining room–cum–lounge with an unbeatable tropical-garden view. The owners are active ex–New Yorkers devoted to running an eco-friendly operation and delivering top-level service. **Pros:** everything you need to have an active vacation; excellent food and service; idyllic setting; friendly, intelligent owners who interact with guests. **Cons:** no a/c; cabins are fairly open to nature, so there will be some insects outside the mosquito netting at night. *Golfo Dulce, north of Golfito; accessible only by boat from Golfito or Puerto Jiménez* *Apdo. 56, Golfito* *8824–6571, 2256–0085 in San José, 866/504–8116 in U.S.* *www.nicuesalodge.com* *5 cabins, 4 rooms* *In-room: no a/c, no phone, no TV. In-hotel: restaurant, bar, beachfront, water sports, no kids under 6* *MC, V* *Closed Oct.–Nov. 15* *AI.*

8

SHOPPING

Ticos are drawn to Golfito's duty-free bargains on such imported items as TV sets, stereos, tires, wine, and liquor. To shop at the **Depósito Libre** you have to spend the night in Golfito, because you have to register in the afternoon with your passport to shop the next morning. Shopping is sheer madness in December. It's closed on Monday. **Tierra Mar** (*Waterfront next to Banana Bay Marina*) has an excellent selection of painted wood masks. It also has one-of-a-kind local crafts, such as woven straw hats, cotton purses, and painted gourds, and local paintings. In a class all its own, the **Mercado Artesania** (*Hotel Samoa Sur, main street, 1 block north of town dock*) is filled with every imaginable—and unimaginable—souvenir. Large paintings by local artists, huge painted fans from Thailand, hammocks, beach clothes, and life-size snake carvings are just a few of the offerings here. Even if you don't buy a thing, it's fun to look. Ask the hotel manager to unlock the door and visit the Shell Museum, the hotel owner's personal, lifelong collection of shells.

NIGHTLIFE

The bar at **Banana Bay Marina** (*Main street, south of town dock*) is usually full of English-speaking fishermen in the evening. Every night, **Bar Los Comales** (*Near the large dry dock at north end of town*) has dancing and karaoke until 2 AM. It's in a rougher section of town, so go with a group and leave in a taxi.

The bar at **Samoa del Sur** (✉ *1 block north of town dock*) has a mix of Ticos and foreigners, mostly of the male persuasion, who gather for the loud music until 11 PM.

TO FLUSH OR NOT TO FLUSH?

Costa Rican toilets *do* flush, but in most of Costa Rica, septic systems weren't designed to accommodate toilet tissue (the pipes are too narrow). If you don't want to be the *gringo* who clogs up the works, watch for signs asking you not to put anything in the toilet. A wastebasket (*basurero*) is almost always provided to hold used tissue. Even upscale resorts and other places with modern septic systems have the basket, since the habit has been ingrained in locals.

PLAYA ZANCUDO

51 km/32 mi south of Golfito.

For laid-back beaching involving hammocks strung between palms and nothing more demanding than watching the sun set, you can't beat breezy Playa Zancudo, with its miles of wide, flat beach and views of the Osa Peninsula. It isn't picture-perfect: the 10 km (6 mi) of dark brown sand is often strewn with flotsam and jetsam. But there's a constant breeze and a thick cushion of palm and almond trees between the beach and the dirt road running parallel. The standout feature is the magnificent view across the gulf to the tip of the Osa Peninsula. The beach runs almost due north–south, so you have center-stage seats for sunsets, too. Away from the beach breezes, be prepared for biting *zancudos* (no-see-ums).

There's a flurry of new construction here, with Canadians and Americans building substantial beachfront homes. Most hotels and restaurants are within sight of the beach. Life here is laid-back and very casual, centering on walking the beach, fishing, kayaking, swimming, and hanging out at the local bars and restaurants. Zancudo has a good surf break at the south end of the beach, but it's nothing compared with Playa Pavones a little to the south. Swimming is good two hours before or after high tide, especially at the calmer north end of the beach, and if you get tired of playing in the surf and sand, you can arrange a boat trip to the nearby mangrove estuary to see birds and crocodiles. Zancudo is also home to one of the area's best sportfishing operations, headquartered at the Zancudo Lodge.

GETTING HERE AND AROUND

The road from Golfito is paved for the first 11 km (7 mi), but after the turnoff at El Rodeo the trip entails almost two hours of bone shaking and a short ride on—but sometimes a long wait for—a cable river ferry (600 colones, about $1.10). You are much better off without a car here. You can hire a boat at the municipal dock in Golfito for the 25-minute ride ($30 for two) or take a $5 *collectivo* (communal) boat that leaves Zancudo Monday to Friday in high season at 7 AM, Saturday at 8 AM; the return boat leaves Golfito's Hotel Samoa del Sur at noon. (In low season, the shuttle runs Monday, Wednesday, and Friday only.) **Cabinas Los Cocos** (✉ *Beach road* ☎ *2776–0012*) has water-taxi service to Golfito ($20 per person; minimum $60) and service to Puerto Jiménez ($20 per person; minimum $60).

Getting around Playa Zancudo doesn't take much, since there's really only one long, dusty road parallel to the beach. You can rent a bike at Cabinas Sol y Mar or Tres Amigos Supermercado, both on the main road in Zancudo, for about $10 per day.

ESSENTIALS

Internet Oceano Internet Café (✉ *In Oceano Cabinas, 50 m south of Supermercado Bellavista* ☎ *2776–0921*).

OUTDOOR ACTIVITIES

FISHING If you've got your own gear, you can do some good shore fishing from the beach or the mouth of the mangrove estuary, or hire a local boat to take you out into the gulf. The main edible catches are yellowfin tuna, snapper, and snook; catch-and-release fish include marlin, rooster fish, and swordfish.

The Zancudo Lodge (✉ *North end of town on main road* ☎ *2776–0008* 🌐 *www.thezancudolodge.com*) runs the biggest charter operation in the area, with 15 boats ranging in length from 25 feet to 36 feet. A day's fishing includes gear, food, and drinks (about $750 for two fishers), and you can arrange to be picked up in Golfito or Puerto Jiménez. Captain John Olson at **Sportfishing Unlimited** (☎ *2776–0036*) offers 28-foot center-console boats with both fly and conventional tackle. The rate is $650 per day for two fishers, which includes lunch, drinks, and gear. Born and raised in Golfito, **Captain Ronny** (☎ *2776–0201* ✉ *golfitocr@yahoo.com*) has worked at all the area fishing lodges. The daily rate is an all-inclusive $800 for a maximum of four fishers.

KAYAKING The kayaking is great at the beach and along the nearby Río Colorado, lined with mangroves. **Cabinas Los Cocos** (✉ *Beach road* ☎ *2776–0012*) has a popular tour ($50) that takes you for a 1½-hour motorboat ride up the river, then a 2-hour kayak tour along a jungly mangrove channel. The company also rents user-friendly sit-on-top kayaks with backrests for $5 per hour.

8

WHERE TO EAT

$–$$ ITALIAN ✕ **Macondo.** There's absolutely nothing fancy about this tiny restaurant, but it serves the best homemade pasta in the Southern Zone. Chef Daniel Borello comes from the Piemonte region in northern Italy, and his pasta is light, almost tissue-paper thin, and perfectly sauced. There's no written menu, just a recitation of pasta shapes available with your choice of sauce. There's also meat or spinach-and-cheese ravioli and, sometimes, lasagna, as well as jumbo shrimp and beef tenderloin. But stick to the pasta—it's a sure bet. The only disappointment is that none of the wine choices is worthy of the food. End your meal with an authentic espresso or cappuccino. Lunch is also offered in high season, from December to May. ✉ *Across from Ferreteria, on beach road, center of town* ☎ *2776–0157* ▭ *No credit cards* ⊙ *Closed Sept.–Nov.*

$–$$ ECLECTIC ✕ **Oceano Bar & Restaurant.** This popular beachfront restaurant has a wide-ranging menu that gets raves from the locals. Choose from seafood, steaks, and creative salads, such as watermelon with feta bathed in a balsamic-mint dressing. The young Canadian owners make what is probably the country's only *poutine* (a Quebecois comfort food with french fries, gravy, and chunks of cheese). Fish sandwiches are also popular, along with enormous hamburgers. There's an alfresco tapas bar and a lounge where you can sip martinis. Bring your laptop and surf on their Wi-Fi connection. ✉ *Beach road, 50 m south of Supermercado Bellavista60704* ☎ *2776–0921* ▭ *MC, V* ⊙ *Closed Oct.*

$–$$ ECLECTIC ★ ✕ **Restaurant Sol y Mar.** On a breezy porch with a palm-fringed beach view, this restaurant has the most cosmopolitan food in Zancudo, with an eclectic menu of spicy *quesadillas* and super-stuffed burritos, savory chicken *cordon bleu,* and fresh fish with elegant French sauces. There's a touch of Thai here, too; one of the most popular dishes is mahimahi in a coconut-curry sauce. Desserts are decadent and delicious, including a standout carrot cake. As at a lot of restaurants catering to tourists, prices do not include tax and service, so be sure to factor in an extra 23% to the bill. ✉ *Hotel Sol y Mar, main road* ☎ *2776–0014* ▭ *No credit cards.*

WHERE TO STAY

$ **Cabinas Los Cocos.** This cluster of castaway-island, self-catering cabins is designed for people who want to kick back and enjoy the beach. Artist Susan England and her husband, Andrew Robertson, are Zancudo fixtures and can organize any activity, including river safaris, kayaking tours, and visits to nature preserves. Two idyllic tropical cabins have thatch roofs and hammocks. The others are renovated 40-year-old banana-company houses moved here from Palmar Norte. These charming pastel wooden cottages give you the rare chance to share a little bit of Costa Rican history. Book early, because so many guests return the same time every year. **Pros:** like having your own beach house on a practically deserted, idyllic beach, with everything you need to live well; friendly, funny hosts who help you get the most out of your stay. **Cons:** no a/c, but there are ceiling fans and ocean breezes. ✉ *Beach road, about 200 m north of Sol y Mar* ☎ *2776–0012* 🌐 *www.loscocos.com* *4 cabins* *In-room: no a/c, no phone, kitchen, no TV. In-hotel: beachfront, laundry service* ▭ *No credit cards* *EP.*

¢ **Cabinas Sol y Mar.** As its name implies, Cabinas Sol y Mar has sun and sea, plus a beach fringed by coconut palms. Wooden cabinas painted leaf green have porches and high ceilings looking onto the gulf with spectacular views of the Osa Peninsula. Each breezy, roomy cabina sleeps four. Two of the sunny bathrooms feature pebble-lined showers. There's also an economy cabin for two, with its own fridge; and a three-story rental house. The alfresco restaurant *(⇨ above)* consistently serves the best food in town. The popular U-shaped bar is an easy place to meet new friends, including Laurie and Rick, the friendly Canadian-American owners. A well-stocked gift shop sells colorful sarongs and clothing from Thailand. **Pros:** beach location; affordable price; lively restaurant and bar. **Cons:** no a/c; simple cabins. ✉ *Main road, south of Cabinas Los Cocos, Playa Zancudo* ☎ *2776–0014* 🌐 *www.zancudo.com* *5 cabinas, 1 house* *In-room: no a/c, no phone, no TV. In-hotel: restaurant, bar, beachfront, Wi-Fi* ▭ *MC, V* *EP.*

$$–$$$ **The Zancudo Lodge.** Most people who stay here are anglers on all-inclusive sportfishing packages, taking advantage of the lodge's 15 fishing boats. But new owners are making the comfortable beachfront hotel a good choice even if you've never caught anything but a cold. Kayaks

and surfboards are available for guests to enjoy the gulf without dropping a fishing line. The verdant grounds surround an inviting pool and an open-air restaurant that serves both buffet and table-service meals. The rate includes all meals and drinks, including alcohol. Women are more than welcome here, but remember this place is usually full of rowdy fishermen—which can be a good or bad thing, depending on your tastes. The sea foam–green two-story hotel, enlivened with colorful murals, has huge rooms with hardwood floors, firm queen beds, and ocean views. Eight new rooms and a luxury suite are in the works. **Pros:** fishers' delight with excellent boats and captains; most luxurious hotel in Zancudo, with a/c, a rarity in these parts. **Cons:** if you don't like a testosterone-charged fisherman atmosphere, this is not the place for you; evenings can get a little rowdy. ✉*Main road, north end of town, 200 m past police post, Playa Zancudo* *Apdo. 41, Golfito* ☎*2776–0008, 800/854–8791 in U.S.* *www.thezancudolodge.com* *20 rooms, 1 suite* *In-room: refrigerator. In-hotel: restaurant, bar, pool, beachfront, Wi-Fi* *AE, MC, V* *FAP.*

PLAYA PAVONES

53 km/33 mi south of Golfito.

One of the most scenic beaches to drive past is remote Playa Pavones, on the southern edge of the mouth of Golfo Dulce. Through a fringe of palms you catch glimpses of brilliant blue water, white surf crashing against black rocks, and the soft silhouette of the Osa Peninsula across the gulf. The area attracts serious surfer purists, but also has pristine black-sand beaches and virgin rain forest. The coast is very rocky, so it's important to ask locals which beach to try. One of the best places to swim is in the Río Claro, under the bridge or at the river mouth (dry season only). The town of Pavones itself is an unprepossessing collection of *pensiones* and *sodas* (casual eateries) clustered around a soccer field.

8

GETTING HERE

There's no avoiding the bumpy road from Golfito to Conte, where the road forks north to Zancudo and south to Pavones. But the dirt road to Pavones is usually well graded. A public bus leaves from Golfito very early in the morning, and the drive takes about 2½ hours. A taxi from the airstrip in Golfito costs $90.

OUTDOOR ACTIVITIES

SURFING Pavones is famous for one of the longest waves in the world, thanks to the mouth of the Río Claro, which creates ideal sandbanks and well-shaped waves. The ocean bottom is cobblestone where the surfing waves break. The most consistent waves are from April to September, and that's when the surfing crowd heads down here from the Central Pacific coast beaches. But even at the crest of its surfing season Pavones is tranquility central compared with the surfing hot spots farther north.

Most surfers here are serious about their sport and bring their own boards. You can buy used surfboards and other surfing gear or sign up for a lesson ($35 plus $20 board rental) at **Sea Kings Surf Shop** (✉*In town, by soccer field* ☎*2776–2015* *www.surfpavones.com*). **Cabinas**

La Ponderosa (⇨ *Where to Stay and Eat, below*) rents surfboards ($30) as well as bicycles ($20). **Río Claro Sports & Adventures** (☎ *2776–2416*) offers surf lessons ($50), including board rental; they also rent surfboards and snorkeling gear for $15 per half day, and bicycles for $5 per hour.

> **CAUTION**
>
> In the unlikely event that you are bitten by a snake, stay calm, move slowly, and try to remember what the snake looked like, to tell the clinic staff. Allow antivenom to be administered only by a trained person, in case of side effects. Five hours is the window before any tissue loss. To avoid snakebites, stay on trails and wear long, loose pants; in some areas high rubber boots are recommended.

WHERE TO EAT

$ VEGETARIAN **Café de la Suerte.** Fortunately for food lovers, the "Good Luck Café" serves truly astonishing vegetarian food from 7:30 to 5 that even a carnivore could love, along with intriguing exotic juice combinations and thick fruit smoothies. The homemade yogurt is a revelation: light, almost fluffy, and full of flavor. The Israeli owners serve it over a cornucopia of exotic fruits, sprinkled with their own granola, and mix it into refreshing fruit-flavor *lassis* (a yogurt-base drink from India). Healthful sandwiches are heavy on excellent hummus, and hot daily specials might include curried hearts of palm. Don't leave without buying a fudgy brownie or a brown-sugar oatmeal square for the road. Bring your laptop and use their Wi-Fi—the $1 an hour is donated to the local school. ✉ *Next to soccer field* ☎ *2776–2388* 🌐 *www.cafedelasuerte.com* 💳 *No credit cards* ⏲ *No dinner. Closed Sun.*

WHERE TO STAY

$–$$ **Cabinas La Ponderosa.** The world-famous Playa Pavones surfing break is just a 10-minute walk from this surfer-owned hotel, the only beach resort in the area. It's a cut above the usual surfer place, though, with a recent remodeling and a new swimming pool. Rooms have crisp white linens, new orthopedic mattresses, freshly tiled bathrooms, and a/c or screened windows to let in the sea breezes. Two of the three spacious suites have screened-in porches overlooking the lush garden and pool. A two-bedroom villa with fridge and a two-story house with full kitchen are available as weekly rentals. If you're not into surfing, there are nature trails winding through 14 acres of garden and forest, plus a yoga deck and massages. Everything is within walking distance, including a swimmable beach and restaurants, so you don't need a car. **Pros:** a surfer's haven, with gear for rent and lots of local knowledge, courtesy of surfing owners and other guests; affordable; close to beach and town. **Cons:** tends to attract a younger crowd; mosquitoes love the garden when there's no breeze. ✉ *On beach* ☎ *2776–2076, 954/771–9166 in U.S.* 🌐 *www.cabinaslaponderosa.com* *2 rooms, 3 suites, 2 houses* *In-room: no a/c (some), phone, refrigerator (some), DVD. In-hotel: restaurant, beachfront, bicycles* 💳 *No credit cards* *EP.*

$$ **Casa Siempre Domingo.** High on a breezy hill, this spacious B&B has the town's best view of the Golfo Dulce. Two of the four enormous rooms have 20-foot ceilings and double beds set high to catch the view out the large windows. The other two have pretty garden views. A new

infinity swimming pool gives you yet another opportunity to enjoy the view poolside. The owners have a young son and welcome visiting playmates. Substantial breakfasts, prepared by owner Heidi, a food professional in her former life, are served at a large communal table in a screened-in great room, and there's a communal fridge for storing food and drinks. The steep driveway up to this lofty perch can be a little daunting. You'll need 4WD or else you can build up a set of steely muscles climbing up on foot. **Pros:** the view, the view, the view; spacious, well-appointed rooms; great breakfasts; kids welcome. **Cons:** a very steep drive uphill; a thigh-cramping walk up and down to the beach. ✣ *2 km/1 mi south of town; follow signs after Río Claro Bridge* ☎ *8820–4709* 🌐 *www.casa-domingo.com* *4 rooms* *In-room: no phone, no TV. In-hotel: pool* *No credit cards* *BP.*

$$ **Tiskita Jungle Lodge.** This last outpost lodge is one of the premier
Fodor's Choice ★ attractions in the Southern Zone for nature lovers. Peter Aspinall, a passionate farmer and conservationist, and his wife, Lisbeth, homesteaded here in 1977, and today the property includes a vast fruit orchard, with more than 100 varieties of trees that attract monkeys, coatis, birds, and other wildlife. Surrounding the orchard are 800 acres of primary and secondary forest, a habitat for the more than 275 species of birds and a 90-strong troop of squirrel monkeys. Peter leads tours of the orchard, and a naturalist guide leads bird-watching and nature tours. Comfortable screened wooden cabins on stilts have rustic furniture and tiled bathrooms, some of them open-air. Trails invite you to explore the jungle and a cascading waterfall with freshwater pools. Very simple buffet meals are served in an open-air dining room. Throughout the day you can help yourself to freshly squeezed tropical juices in the fridge, and the cookie jar is always full. Cabins are spread out, with lots of steps to climb. Recently rebuilt No. 6 has the most privacy, with a huge porch looking onto a beautiful ocean view. The beach, with swimmable waters, is a steep 15-minute downhill walk. Most guests arrive by small plane at the hotel's private airstrip. **Pros:** unrivaled wildlife-viewing and birding; splendid natural isolation; excellent guides and opportunity to get to know the friendly, knowledgeable owners. **Cons:** some steep walks to cabins in forest; no a/c; expect some insect visitors in rustic cabins; not a lot of privacy in joined double and triple cabins, which share verandas; food is simple and there's not a whole lot of it. ✣ *6 km/4 mi south of Playa Pavones* *Apdo. 13411–1000, San José* ☎ *2296–8125* 🌐 *www.tiskita.com* *17 rooms arranged in 4 single cabins, 3 doubles, and 1 triple* *In-room: no a/c, no phone, no TV. In-hotel: restaurant, bar, pool, beachfront, bicycles* *No credit cards* *Closed Sept. 15–Oct. 31* *AI.*

NIGHTLIFE

The town's main watering hole is **Cantina Esquina del Mar** (⊠ *Beachfront, center of town*). It's nothing fancy, but it's lively.

8

THE OSA PENINSULA

If you came to Costa Rica seeking wilderness and adventure, this is it. You'll find the country's most breathtaking scenery and most abundant wildlife on the Osa Peninsula, a third of which is protected by Corcovado National Park. You can hike into the park on any of three routes or fly in on a charter plane. Corcovado also works for day trips from nearby luxury nature lodges, most of which lie within private preserves that are home for much of the same wildlife you might see in the park. And complementing the peninsula's lush forests and pristine beaches is the surrounding sea, with great fishing and some surfing.

There are two sides to the Osa: the gentler Golfo Dulce side, much of it accessible by car, albeit along rocky roads; and the much wilder and dramatic Pacific side, which is accessible only by boat, by charter plane, or by hiking a sublimely beautiful coastal trail.

PUERTO JIMÉNEZ

130 km/86 mi west of Golfito, 364 km/226 mi from San José.

You might not guess it from the rickety bicycles and ancient pickup trucks parked on the main street, but Puerto Jiménez is the largest town on the Osa Peninsula. This one-iguana town has a certain frontier charm, though. New restaurants, hotels, and "green" newcomers lend an interesting, funky edge. It's also the last civilized outpost on the peninsula. Heading south, you fall off the grid. That means no public electricity or telephones. So make your phone calls, send your e-mails, get cash, and stock up on supplies here. Be prepared for the humidity and mosquitoes—Puerto Jiménez has plenty of both. If you need a refreshing dip, head south of the airport to Playa Platanares, where there is a long stretch of beach with swimmable, warm water.

The main reason to come to Puerto Jiménez is to spend a night before or after visiting Corcovado National Park, since the town has the best access to the park's two main trailheads and an airport with flights from San José. It's also the base for the *collectivo* (public transport via pickup truck) to Carate.

GETTING HERE AND AROUND

Most visitors fly to the newly upgraded Puerto Jiménez airfield from San José, since the drive is grueling and long. Driving from Golfito is not recommended either—although the road from Chacarita to Rincón has recently been paved, the road from Rincón to Jiménez is dust-filled rough going all the way (although it may be paved soon). A better option from Golfito is the motorboat launch. A rickety old passenger launch ($1.50 each way) leaves Golfito at 11:30 AM every day and takes 1½ hours. Faster motorboat launches ($4) make the trip in 45 minutes, leaving Golfito seven times a day starting at 5:10 AM. The fast launches heading to Golfito leave Puerto Jiménez at 6 AM, noon, and 4 PM. You can also hire private taxi boats at the city dock. Prices are $50 to $65 between Golfito and Puerto Jiménez. Water taxis can also take you to beachfront lodges.

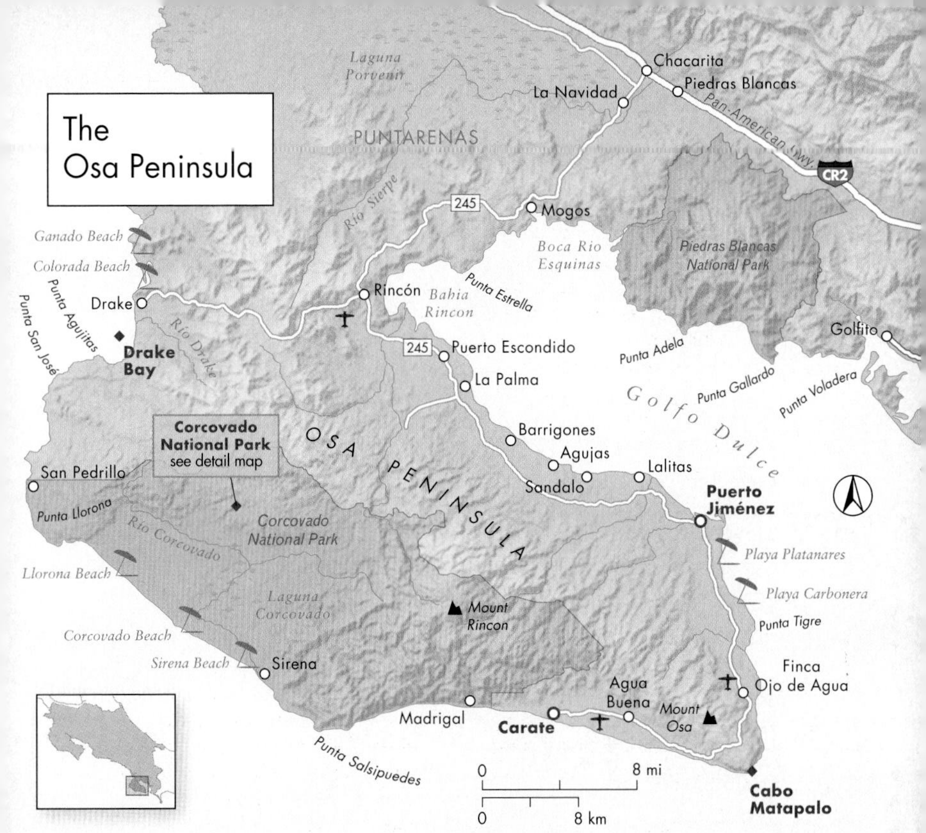

A *collectivo* ($8) leaves Puerto Jiménez twice daily for Cabo Matapalo and Carate. It's the cheapest way to travel, but the trip is along a very bumpy road—not recommended in rainy season (May–December). The collectivo leaves from a stop 200 meters west of the Super 96 at 6 AM and 1:30 PM.

Once you get to the main street in town, you can get around on foot or by bicycle. You can rent a bike for $10 a day ($15 for mountain bikes) at **Tom's Bike Rentals** (✉ *100 m east of Cabinas Marcellina* ☎ *2735–5414*). If you don't have a car and are staying outside of town, you are at the mercy of taxis to get anywhere. Water taxis, hired at the city dock, can take you to waterfront lodges, nearby beaches, or Golfito.

ESSENTIALS

Bank/ATM Banco Nacional (✉ *500 m south of Super 96, directly across from church* ☎ *2735–5020*).

Hospital Public Clinic and First Aid Station (✉ *25 m west of post office* ☎ *2735–5063*).

Pharmacy Farmacia Hidalgo (✉ *Main street, across from Carolina Restaurant* ☎ *2735–5564* ⏲ *Mon.–Sat. 8–8*).

Internet CaféNet El Sol (✉ *Main street, next to Juanita's* ☎ *2735–5719*). **Café Internet Osa Corcovado** (✉ *1 block east of Tom's Bikes* ☎ *2735–5230* ⏲ *Closed*

Continued on page 500

Scuba Diving and Snorkeling

by Gillian Gillers

For snorkelers and scuba divers, Costa Rica is synonymous with swarms of fish and stretches of coral that hug the country's 910 miles of coastline. Submerge yourself in crystalline waters and enter another world, with bull sharks, brain coral, and toothy green eels. The variety and abundance of marine life are awe-inspiring.

WHEN AND WHERE TO GO

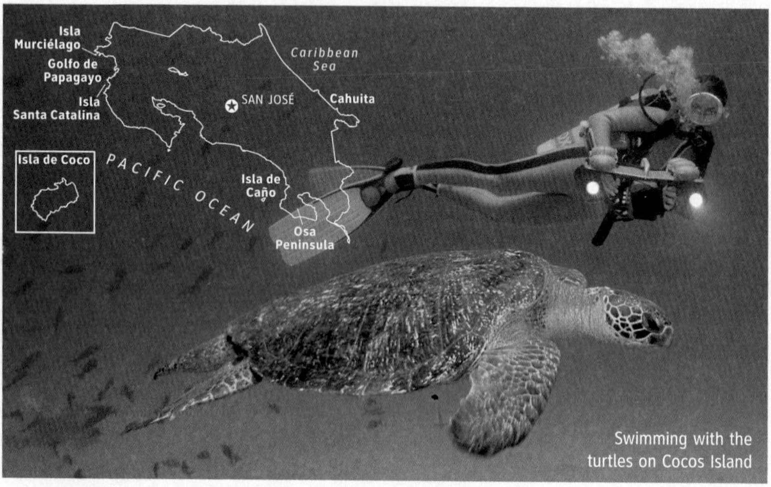

Swimming with the turtles on Cocos Island

The Pacific tends to be clearer than the Caribbean, and the fish are bigger and more abundant. Northern waters are generally best May through July, after winds die down and the water turns bluer and warmer. The southern Osa Peninsula is popular during the dry season, from January to April.

The Caribbean, known for its diverse coral and small fish, is good for beginners because it has less surge. The best months are September and October, when the ocean is as calm and flat as a swimming pool. April and May also offer decent conditions, but steer clear during the rest of the year, when rain and strong waves cloud the water.

CAHUIT Mounds of coral and a barrier reef (dubbed Long Shoal) run from Cahuita to Punta Mona, along 25 kilometers of Caribbean coastline. Arches, tunnels and canyons in the reef form a playground for small fish, crabs, and lobsters. Even though sediment and waste water have damaged much of the coral, the healthy sections are dense, colorful, and delightfully shaped. Gentle pools right off the beach allow for some of the country's best snorkeling.

ISLA DEL COCO (Cocos Island) Some 295 nautical miles and a 36-hour sail from Puntarenas, Cocos Island is one of the world's premier sites for advanced divers. Visibility is good all year, and hammerhead and white-tipped reef sharks are the main attractions.

ISLA DEL CAÑO (Caño Island) With clear water, big schools of fish, and healthy coral, this biological reserve is the second-best dive spot after Cocos. Stronger currents make Caño better suited for advanced divers, but novice snorkelers can frolic in the Garden, a shallow area to the north.

ISLA SANTA CATALINA (Santa Catalina Island) Known for sightings of golden cownose rays and giant mantas, these big rocks near Playa Flamingo have spots for beginner and advanced divers. Snorkelers should head to shallower waters near the beach.

GOLFO DE PAPAGAYO (Papagayo Gulf) This northern gulf has Costa Rica's highest concentration of snorkel and dive shops. Calm, protected waters make it the best place for beginner divers on the Pacific.

ISLA MURCIÉLAGO (Bat Island) Located inside Santa Rosa National Park, this cluster of rocks is good for advanced divers and famous for its fearsome bull sharks.

DIVING SCHOOLS

The beach towns on both coasts are riddled with diving schools and equipment rentals shops. If you're a first-timer and plan to go diving just once, taking a basic half-day class isn't difficult, and it will allow you to dive up to 40 feet with an instructor. A three- or four-day certification course gets you a lifetime license and allows you to dive up to 130 feet and without a guide. Outfitters can point snorkelers towards pristine spots. We list only the most reputable schools under the Outdoor Activity section throughout every chapter; look for the ones that are PADI (Professional Association of Diving Instructors) trained or give PADI certifications.

IN CASE OF AN EMERGENCY

DAN (Divers Alert Network) is an organization that provides emergency medical advice and assistance for underwater diving injuries. Doctors, emergency medical technicians, and nurses are available 24 hours a day to answer questions. If you would like to discuss a potential diving-related health problem, contact the non-emergency DAN switchboard (☎800/446–2671) or check out their website (🌐www.diversalertnetwork.org). Their emergency telephone line is 919/684–8111 or 919/684–9111 for international calls.

SNORKELING TIPS

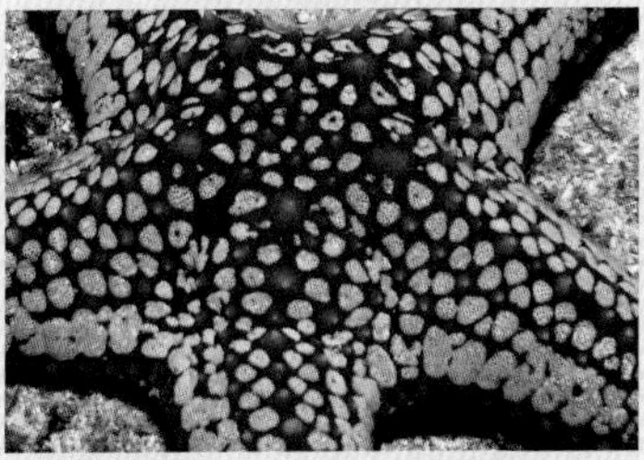

Sea Star in Catalina Islands

- Never turn your back on the ocean, especially if the waves are big.
- Ask about rip tides before you go in.
- Enter and exit from a sandy beach area.
- Avoid snorkeling at dusk and never go in the water after dark.
- Wear lots of sunscreen, especially on your back and butt cheeks.
- Don't snorkel too close to the reef. You could get scratched if a wave pushes you.
- Be mindful of boats.

DIVING TIPS

- Make sure your instructor is certified by a known diving agency, such as PADI.
- Stick to the instructor's guidelines on depth and timing.
- Never hold your breath.
- Never dive or snorkel (or swim or surf) alone. Also, never touch the coral or the fish—this is for your own good and the good of the marine life.
- Don't drink alcohol before diving.
- Never dive while taking medicine unless your doctor tells you it's safe.
- Diving can be dangerous if you have certain medical problems. Ask your doctor how diving may affect your health.
- If you don't feel good or if you are in pain after diving, go to the nearest emergency room immediately.
- Don't fly for 12 hours after a no-decompression dive, even in a pressurized airplane.

CREATURES OF THE SEA

Underwater exploration is as close to visiting another world as you can come. Here you'll encounter some of the most bizarre creatures on this planet.

Pillar Coral

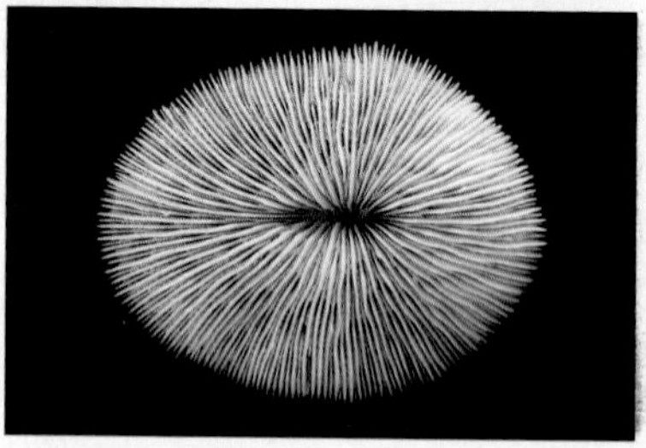

Calcareous skeleton of the coral

CORAL

Coral tends to cluster in colonies of identical individuals. The most diverse coral (at least 31 types) in Costa Rica can be found on the Caribbean coast, near Puerto Viejo. Like other plant-looking sea animals, many types of coral reproduce by spawning.

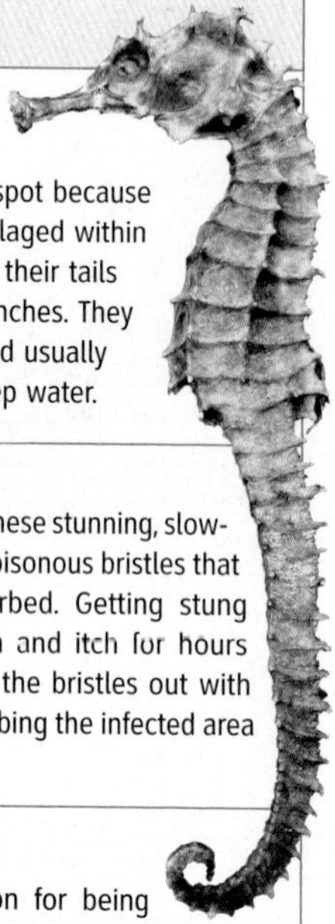

SEAHORSE

These magical little creatures are hard to spot because they are often camouflaged within black coral trees, with their tails curled around the branches. They are bottom feeders and usually found in 10 meter deep water.

FIREWORM

Look but don't touch! These stunning, slow-moving worms have poisonous bristles that flare out when disturbed. Getting stung is no fun; it will burn and itch for hours afterwards. Try taking the bristles out with adhesive tape and dabbing the infected area with alcohol.

GREEN EEL

Eels have a reputation for being vicious and ill-tempered, but they're really shy and secretive. Eels will only attack humans in self-defense. Though they may accidentally bite the hand that feeds them, it's just because they can't see or hear very well.

SPONGES

Common in the Caribbean, these strange animals don't have nervous, digestive, or circulatory systems. Instead, they rely on a constant water flow for food and oxygen, and to remove wastes. To reproduce, some sponges release both sperm and eggs into the water and hope the two collide.

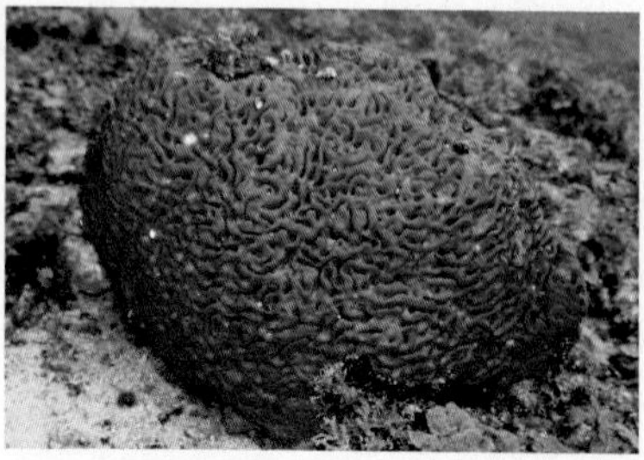

Orange sponge

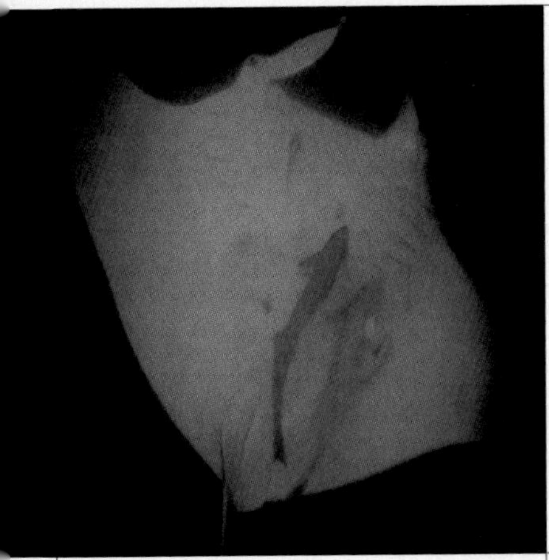

BOTTLENOSE DOLPHIN

Everybody loves dolphins. In some parts of the world they work with local fishermen, driving schools of fish into the nets and then eating the fish that escape. They've also been known to help injured divers to the surface.

GIANT MANTA RAY

Commonly spotted near Isla Santa Catalina, mantas often hang out at reef-side "cleaning stations" where small fish (like wrasses and angelfish) congregate. These cleaner fish feed in the manta's gills and over its skin, simultaneously scrubbing it free of parasites and dead skin.

BARRACUDA

Barracudas are not aggressive towards humans, but are vicious predators. Their diet consists of all sorts of fish. Large barracudas, when gorged, will even try to herd a school of fish into shallow water so that they can guard over them and eat them off when they're hungry again.

HAMMERHEAD SHARK

These sharks are distinctive not only for their strangely shaped, mallet-like head but also because they're one of the few creatures in the animal kingdom (besides humans and pigs) that can tan. If they spend too much time in shallow waters, they'll become noticeably darker. In 2007, scientists also discovered that hammerheads can reproduce asexually through a rare process called parthenogenesis: female hammerheads can actually develop an embryo without ever having been fertilized.

PARROTFISH

Parrotfish are named for their external set of tightly packed teeth that look just like a parrots beak. These strange looking teeth are used to rasp the algae off of coral and rock, thus feeding themselves and keeping the coral clean and healthy.

Sun.) has a more reliable high-speed connection, plus laptop data ports and, best of all, really strong air-conditioning.

The **National Parks Service Headquarters** (✉ *Next to airport* ☎ *2735–5036*) has information about hiking trails in Corcovado National Park. The office is open weekdays 8 to 4.

Post Office Correo (✉ *West side of soccer field*).

Rental Cars Solid Car Rental (✉ *150 m north of airport, Puerto Jiménez* ☎ *2735–5777* 🌐 *www.solidcarrental.com*).

Visitor Information Osa Tropical (✉ *Across from Banco Nacional on main street* ☎ *2735–5062* ✉ *osatropical@ice.co.cr*).

WORD OF MOUTH

"I love the Osa Peninsula in July. The local bus from San Jose will take 9 hours or more—this is why most people fly. Once in Puerto Jiménez, there are several budget hotels in or near town. If you want to head down to the park, you can take the collectivo [communal truck] in the morning and then take it back to Puerto Jiménez in the afternoon: Very inexpensive but also uncomfortable. Think Indiana Jones. I didn't mind the back of a pickup at all but some people really hate it. In Puerto Jiménez, head to the Pearl of the Osa restaurant/bar and check out the beach there—it's one of the prettiest in the area." —Suzie2

OUTDOOR ACTIVITIES

Escondido Trex (✉ *Restaurante Carolina, 200 m south of soccer field* ☎ *2735–5210* 🌐 *www.escondidotrex.com*) arranges kayaking, charter-fishing, and small-boat outings for watching wildlife, and land-based outings, including a half-day hike around Matapalo ($50). Isabel Esquivel at **Osa Tropical** (✉ *Main road, across from Banco Nacional* ☎ *2735–5062*) runs the best general tour operation on the peninsula. Whatever travel question you ask the locals, they will usually say, "Ask Isabel." Along with arranging flights, ground transport, hotel bookings, tours, and car rentals, Osa Tropical is the radio communications center for many of the off-the-grid Osa lodges and tour operators.

BIRD-WATCHING The birding around the Osa Peninsula is world renowned, with more than 400 species. Endemic species include Baird's trogon, yellow-billed cotinga, whistling wren, black-cheeked ant tanager, and the glorious turquoise cotinga. There have even been sightings of the very rare harpy eagle in the last couple of years. One of the best spots on the peninsula to find a yellow-billed cotinga or a white-crested coquette is the bridge over the river at **Rincón** (✣ *40 km/25 mi north of Puerto Jiménez*), if you get there before 7 AM.

★ The best English-speaking birding guides are Liz Jones and Abraham Gallo, who run **Bosque del Río Tigre Lodge** (✉ *Dos Brazos del Tigre* ✣ *12 km/7½ mi northwest of Puerto Jiménez* 🌐 *www.osaadventures.com*). They lead birding trips all around the peninsula, including visits to Corcovado National Park.

FISHING Along with Golfito across the water, Puerto Jiménez is a major fishing destination, with plenty of billfish and tuna, snapper and snook, almost all year, with the exception of June and July, when things slow down. The best offshore fishing is between December and April.

Beach views at Drake Bay on the Osa Peninsula.

Osa Yacht Club (☎*2735–5920* 🌐*www.costaricasportsman.com*) in Puerto Jiménez is one of the most highly recommended fishing operations on the Osa Peninsula. Captain Mark Corn has 13 years of experience fishing these waters. A full-day of fishing for up to six fishers, on state-of-the-art Wellcraft and Blackin sportfishing boats, includes lunch and drinks ($1,400); half-day fishing is $850. Check out their Web site for multiday fishing packages that include lodging.

8

Taboga Aquatic Tours (☎*2735–5265 or 8379–0705*), a more modest local fishing outfit, offers half-day inshore fishing for up to four for $400; a whole day offshore costs $500.

HIKING If you have 4WD, it's just a 30-minute ride west to the village of Dos Brazos and the **Tigre Sector** of Corcovado Park. Few hikers come to this pristine part of the park because it's difficult to access, which means you'll likely have it to yourself. You can take a taxi to Dos Brazos and hike from here, or use rustic but comfortable Bosque del Río Tigre Lodge as a base.

★ **Osa Aventura** (☎*2735–5758* 🌐*www.osaaventura.com*) specializes in multiday Corcovado hiking adventures led by Mike Boston, an ebullient tropical biologist who sounds like Sean Connery and looks like Crocodile Dundee. Hikers stay in way-off-the-beaten-track rustic lodges en route, and camp or stay in basic cabins in Corcovado. Mike also employs three young bilingual biologists to lead hikes and conduct scientific research projects, in which visitors can sometimes participate.

HORSEBACK RIDING The most popular horse trails in the area are at remote **Río Nuevo Lodge** (✉*Office next to La Carolina Restaurant, main street* ☎*2735–5411* 🌐*www.rionuevolodge.com*), about 12 bumpy km (7½ mi) west of town. Rides along the river and up onto scenic forested ridges last from three to seven hours and include transportation there and back and a home-cooked hot meal for $50 per person.

KAYAKING Puerto Jiménez is a good base for sea-kayaking trips on the calm Golfo Dulce and for exploring the nearby mangrove rivers and estuaries. Alberto Robleto, an enterprising local, has amassed an impressive fleet of kayaks with excellent safety equipment at **Aventuras Tropicales Golfo Dulce** (*South of airport on road to Playa Platanares* *2735–5195* *www.aventurastropicales.com*). Tours include snorkeling, dolphin-watching, and bird-watching. The most popular is the three-hour mangrove tour ($30). A three- to five-day kayaking tour ($90 per day, four-person minimum) teaches survival skills in the tropical forest. Outrigger canoe trips ($60 for six hours) are also offered. A six-hour bike tour takes you through a local village, over hills, and across rivers ($50). All tours longer than three hours include a picnic lunch. **Escondido Trex** *(above)* has kayak fishing trips, mangrove tours, and popular sunset dolphin tours (all tours $40).

Finca Köbö Chocolate Tour (*18 km/11 mi west of Puerto Jiménez, near La Palma* *8398–7604* *www.fincakobo.com* *$28, kids age 6–8, half price* *Tours 9 AM and 2 PM*) takes you right to the source to see how cacao grows and becomes chocolate at this organic cacao plantation. The two-hour tour includes a naturalist-guided walk around the roughly 50-acre property, which includes gardens, orchards, and both primary and secondary forest. The highlight of the tour is the tasting—dipping an array of tropical fruits grown on-site into a pot of homemade chocolate fondue.

WHERE TO EAT

¢–$ CAFÉ **Café la Onda.** The latest place for locals and visitors to meet and greet is this new-wave, college-style café, complete with easy chairs, magazines, a book exchange, and the added allure of air-conditioning. The casual fare runs from bagels—try their popular bagelwich, with ham, bacon, tomato, and jalapeño peppers—to stuffed sandwiches on homemade white or whole wheat rolls, and salads. There are homemade cookies and cakes to accompany the excellent coffee, espresso, and refreshing fruit smoothies and shakes. You can also order box lunches here to take on hikes. *100 m north, then 100 m west of the Banco Nacional on main street* *2735–5312* *Weekdays 7:30–4:30; until 3 PM on Sat. Closed Sun.*

¢–$$ SEAFOOD **Corcovado Marisquería, Restaurante y Bar.** If you're hungry for a bargain and enjoy a little local atmosphere, join the fishermen, local families, and young backpackers at this tiny restaurant that has spilled over into a large waterfront garden. Customers happily sit at a jumble of plastic and wood tables sheltered by makeshift tents and palm trees, ordering from a vast menu that offers more than 40 *bocas* (small bites) and *platos fuertes* (main courses) that run the gamut from seafood rice to whole lobster. You can make a meal of one or two bocas—say, clams in garlic butter and a cup of tangy ceviche or a shrimp omelet with salad—and walk away for less than $5. Wash it down with local or imported beer and sit as long as you like, looking out on the Golfo Dulce. It's open

CLOSE UP

Where Have All the Forests Gone?

The world gives high marks to Costa Rica for its environmental awareness, but accolades don't always match reality. In the last half century more than two-thirds of Costa Rica's original forests have been destroyed. Forests have traditionally been considered unproductive land, and their destruction was for a long time synonymous with development. In the 1970s and 1980s, international and domestic development policies fueled the destruction of large tracts of wilderness. Fortunately, in the 1970s alarmed Costa Rican conservationists began creating what is now the best national park system in Central America. The government has since made progress in curbing deforestation outside the national parks, too.

As you travel through Costa Rica, you see that its predominant landscapes are not cloud and rain forests but the coffee and banana plantations and cattle ranches that have replaced them. Deforestation not only spells disaster for endangered animals like the jaguar and the harpy eagle, but can also have grave consequences for human beings. Forests absorb rain and release water slowly, playing an important role in regulating the flow of rivers—which is why severely deforested regions often suffer twin plagues of floods during the rainy season and drought during the dry months. Tree covers also prevent topsoil erosion, thus keeping the land fertile and productive; in many parts of the country erosion has left once-productive farmland almost worthless.

---

from 10 AM to 11 PM daily. ✉ *25 m south of city dock, on the waterfront* ☎ *2735–5659 or 8898–2656* ▭ *MC, V.*

$–$$ ITALIAN **✕ Il Giardino.** Northern Italian cooking, in the form of tasty homemade pastas and excellent salads, is alive and well in Puerto Jiménez at this popular garden restaurant. Sadly, wood-oven pizzas are not the restaurant's forte, and service can be painfully slow. The owner is also a master carpenter, so the curvy blond-wood bar and hand-carved detailing in the casual restaurant are handsome indeed. Choose a table in the back garden if you're in the mood for a leisurely, romantic dinner. It's open from 5 to 10 PM. ✉ *25 m south of La Carolina, then 25 m west, downtown Puerto Jiménez* ☎ *2735–5129* ▭ *No credit cards.*

¢–$ COSTA RICAN **✕ Restaurante Carolina.** This simple alfresco restaurant in the heart of Puerto Jiménez on the main drag is the central meeting place for every foreigner in town, ergo a good place to pick up information. The place also serves decent *comida típica* (typical food) and reliably fresh seafood. Don't count on using a credit card, though, as phone lines are dodgy. ✉ *Main road, center of town* ☎ *2735–5185* ▭ *MC, V.*

WHERE TO STAY

Playa Platanares is only about 6 km (4 mi) outside of Puerto Jiménez, but lodgings there have a very different feeling from those in town, since they are on a lovely and quiet beach. Bosque del Río Tigre is also outside of town, but inland, in a forested area beside a river.

$$$ **Bosque del Río Tigre Lodge.** You can't get any closer to nature than this off-the-grid lodge, famous for its birding trails, wedged between the forest and the banks of the Río Tigre. Four second-story rooms have chest-

"Sweetie, a spider monkey, quickly found refuge from the rain underneath Alex's rain poncho!" —photo by hipvirgochick, Fodors.com member

high walls, and then are open to nature to the roof with no screens, just mosquito nets over the beds. You're at eye level with the trees and, despite the almost-alfresco rooms, you'll sleep comfortably with linens and pillows that always feel fresh. Electricity is solar-generated and limited, but on-demand gas heaters provide plenty of hot water in the garden showers. The gourmet food rivals that of the best luxury-lodge kitchens. Guests gather around a communal table at dinner with owners Liz Jones and Abraham Gallo, the best bird guides in the area. More than 360 species have been spotted on the property, including 250 species from the lodge porch. Abraham, a lifelong local, can show you hidden mountain trails into Corcovado National Park, less than a mile away. Miners still pan for gold in the nearby river, which has a great swimming hole. **Pros:** a birder's paradise; great hiking trails; fabulous food. **Cons:** shared bathroom (except in one separate cabin) and outdoor showers; limited electricity; must love the outdoors. ✉ *Dos Brazos del Tigre* ✢ *12 km/7 mi west of Puerto Jiménez* ☎ *888/875–9543 in U.S.* 🌐 *www.bosquedelriotigre.com* *4 rooms with shared bath, 1 cabin with private bath* *In-room: no a/c, no phone, no TV. In-hotel: restaurant* ▭ *MC, V* ⏲ *Closed Sept. and Oct.* *FAP.*

¢–$ **Cabinas Jiménez.** Overlooking the harbor, these creatively renovated rooms and bungalows set in a lush garden have the best water views in town. You can enjoy the sound of the surf from your own terrace or the new hammock hut, or jump right into the gulf when it laps up against the hotel garden at high tide. Colorful wall murals, fresh tiled bathrooms, and air-conditioning make this affordable place a cut above the others in town. Coffeemakers and small fridges are another nice touch.

The owner is a keen fisherman and offers fishing trips and dolphin tours on his own boat. **Pros:** watery views; a/c; bungalows have pleasant, private terrace with hammock; helpful, knowledgeable manager Chris. **Cons:** rooms are on the small side; no food service. ✉ *200 m west of town dock* ☎ *2735–5090* 🌐 *www.cabinasjimenez.com* *7 rooms, 3 bungalows* *In-room: no phone, safe, refrigerator, no TV (some). In-hotel: beachfront, water sports* *AE, D, MC, V* *EP.*

¢ **Cabinas Marcelina.** Two elderly Italian sisters run the best bargain hotel in town. Fresh, spotlessly clean rooms look out onto the pleasant garden and have homey, old-fashioned touches like lace shower curtains. All have private bathrooms and hot water, and half are air-conditioned. If you're traveling solo or need a break from your traveling companion, two single rooms with fans are $22 each. The lavish Continental breakfast, served in the garden, is an additional $6. **Pros:** affordable; some rooms have a/c; pleasant garden oasis in middle of town. **Cons:** rooms are quite small; fan-only rooms are very cheap but can be hot and sticky. ✉ *Main street, north side of Catholic church* ☎ *2735–5007* *cabmarce@hotmail.com* *8 rooms* *In-room: no a/c (some), no phone, no TV* *No credit cards* *EP.*

$ **Danta Corcovado Lodge.** This artistically rustic lodge within walking distance of the western edge of Corcovado National Park is reminiscent of an Adirondacks camp, with creatively designed twig chairs and headboards, twisted-branch windows, and furniture made of leftover tree stumps. Kids of all ages will like the cabin-in-the-woods atmosphere. An ideal place to start a hike into Corcovado, the 100% locally run lodge offers accommodations to suit all budgets, from bunk-bed rooms with shared bath to spacious forest cabins, to a wheelchair-accessible master suite with a spacious, semi-alfresco bathroom, paved with smooth river stones. Breakfast is included and traditional Costa Rican meals are served in an alfresco restaurant, joined to the lodge by a covered breezeway. The Los Patos entrance to the park is 8 km (5 mi) away; if you'd rather not walk, the lodge offers a horseback tour to the park entrance, with lunch by a waterfall. You can enjoy much of the same national park wildlife by walking the trails of this 86-acre, reforested property. **Pros:** proximity to Corcovado National Park; comfortable rusticity; affordable. **Cons:** no a/c; close encounters of the insect kind in cabins. ✉ *Guadalupe* ✣ *3 km/2 mi northwest of La Palma* ☎ *2735–1111* 🌐 *www.dantacorcovado.net* *3 rooms, 1 suite, 4 cabins sleeping 3–8 people* *In-room: no a/c, some shared bath. In-hotel: restaurant* *MC, V* *BP.*

$$–$$$$ Fodor's Choice ★ **Iguana Lodge.** If a long stretch of deserted beach is your idea of heaven, this luxury lodge with breezy, screened-in, two-story cabins set among mature trees is for you. The gentle Golfo Dulce waters are perfect for swimming, sea-kayaking, and Boogie boarding. Cabins are furnished elegantly in bamboo, with thoughtful touches like Egyptian cotton sheets and a raft of candles for romantic evenings. The upper-level cabins have the nicest views and catch the best breezes. Pebble-lined showers have plenty of solar-heated hot water and excellent water pressure. Eight new rooms in the former Pearl of the Osa Hotel, adjoining Iguana Lodge, have been upgraded, with marble bathrooms and

8

upscale detailing. Extravagant buffet-style dinners, with exotic foods reflecting the owners' worldwide travels, are served in a thatch-roof dining room with a huge table that can accommodate up to 32 diners. The lavish breakfasts are worth getting up for. You can opt for lunch or dinner in the Pearl of the Osa restaurant, on the beach. A yoga platform and a Japanese soaking tub add a contemplative touch. Birds are plentiful in the Playa Preciosa Platanares Mixed Refuge, which borders the lodge. **Pros:** top-of-the-line accommodation and food in tranquil tropical setting; complimentary kayaks; interesting turtle conservation program. **Cons:** no a/c, so can be hot; new club rooms are small and can be noisy; leave your hair dryer at home and be prepared to get friendly with an insect or two. ✉*Playa Platanares* ✣*5 km/3 mi south of Puerto Jiménez airport* ☎*8848–0752* 📠*2735–5436* 🌐*www.iguanalodge.com* *4 duplex cabins with 2 rooms each, 8 rooms in hotel, 1 house* *In-room: no a/c, no phone, no TV. In-hotel: restaurant, beachfront, water sports* ▭*MC, V* MAP

WORD OF MOUTH

"We stayed at the Iguana Lodge for two nights before going to Bosque del Cabo. Really enjoyed the stay there: food was great, place was well laid out, a bit more secluded than the Black Turtle and I think a little more upscale. It was nice being on the beach for a couple of days. If you do stay at the Iguana Lodge, just make sure you ask for a cabina upstairs, it's where we would have preferred to have been."

—owlwoman

NIGHTLIFE

The sidewalks are usually rolled up by 9 PM in Puerto Jiménez, but there are a few evening options. **Bar La Taberna** (✉*1 block east of El Tigre Mini Mercado, downtown* ☎*2735–9533* ⏲*5 PM–2 AM*). Every night of the week, this surprisingly sophisticated hangout is where the action is. Locals and visitors mingle around the curvy, polished wood bar, knocking back exotic cocktails or local beers; snacking on bocas at the tree-trunk tables; or playing darts or foosball on the adjoining terrace. The music is eclectic and always tuanis (cool). With live salsa music, **Pearl of the Osa** (✉*Next door to Iguana Lodge on Playa Platanares*) attracts a big crowd Friday night. The crowd is a mix of ages, and the music is loud and a lot of fun.

SHOPPING

★ Jewelry maker Karen Herrera (✉*Beside airport*) has collected the finest arts and crafts in the area and displayed them in an impressive shop. **Jagua Arts & Crafts** has some rare items, including colorful cotton dresses and woven Panama hats made by the Guaymí people. Other interesting items are exquisitely detailed bird carvings made by a family in Rincón; stained-glass mosaic boxes, mirrors, and trivets made by a San José artist; local paintings; and serious art ceramics. There's also a selection of natural-history field guides and books.

CORCOVADO NATIONAL PARK

Fodor'sChoice ★ Corcovado National Park is the last and largest outpost of virgin lowland rain forest in Central America and teeming with wildlife. Visitors who tread softly along the park's trails may glimpse howler, spider, and squirrel monkeys, peccaries (wild pigs), poison-arrow frogs, scarlet macaws, and, very rarely, jaguars and tapirs.

Most first-time visitors to Corcovado come on a daylong boat tour or hike. But to get to the most pristine, wildlife-rich areas, you need to walk, and that means a minimum of three days: one day to walk in, one day to walk out, and one day inside.

GETTING HERE AND AROUND

The easiest way to visit remote Corcovado is on a day trip via boat from a Drake Bay lodge or on foot from Carate. The 20-minute boat trip from Drake Bay gets you to the San Pedrillo entrance in the dry season (January–April). The boat trip from Drake to Sirena takes 45 minutes to 1 hour. From Carate airfield, where the collective taxi from Puerto Jiménez stops, it's about a 45-minute walk along the beach to the La Leona park entrance.

For getting to Corcovado from elsewhere, the most expensive option—but also the easiest way to get right to the heart of the park—is flying in on a small charter plane ($275) to the tiny La Sirena airstrip in the park. **Alfa Romeo Aero Taxi** (*E Puerto Jiménez airport* ☎ *735–5178*).

Less expensive is hiring a taxi in Puerto Jiménez ($45) to the Los Patos trailhead, or at least to the first crossing of the Río Rincón (from which you hike a few miles upriver to the trailhead). The cheapest, and least convenient, option is to take a morning bus for less than $1 from Puerto Jiménez at 8 AM to La Palma and then hike or take a taxi to the Los Patos entrance.

ESSENTIALS

Hours of Operation Ranger stations are officially open from 8 AM to 4 PM daily, but you can walk in almost anytime as long as you pay in advance.

Contacts National Parks Service in Puerto Jiménez (☎ 2735–5580 🌐 *www.pncorcovado.com* *$10* per day ⏲ *Daily 8–4*).

OUTDOOR ACTIVITIES

If your reason for coming to the Osa is Corcovado, choose a lodge that has resident naturalist guides. On the Drake Bay and gulf sides of the park, all the lodges arrange guided trips into Corcovado, most with their own guides, but some with freelance guides. Tour operators in Puerto Jiménez and Drake Bay also run guided trips in the park.

HIKING There are three main hiking routes to Corcovado. One begins near La Palma, at the Los Patos entrance. There are also two beach trails to the park: one begins in Drake Bay and follows the coast down to the San Pedrillo entrance to the park; the other is an easy 45-minute beach walk from Carate to the La Leona entrance.

Hiking is always tough in the tropical heat, but the forest route (Los Patos) is cooler than the two beach hikes (La Leona and San Pedrillo). San Pedrillo is accessible only at low tide, and although it is possible to hike La Leona at high tide, it's more difficult since you have to walk on a slope rather than the flat part of the beach. The hike between any two stations takes all day or more, and the longest hike is San Pedrillo to Sirena; it's 21 km (13 mi) along the beach, then 7 km (4 mi) on the forest trail. ■ **TIP→ This trail is passable only in the dry season, as the rivers get too high to cross in the rainy months and the river mouths are home to snakes, bull sharks, and crocodiles!**

> **WARNING**
>
> Swimming on the beach near Sirena is not advised because of rip currents and bull sharks. Also steer clear of the brackish Río Sirena, home to crocs, bull sharks, and snakes. The only advisable swimming area is the Río Claro.

The hike from La Leona to Sirena is about 16 km (10 mi) and requires crossing one big river mouth and a stretch of beach that can be crossed only at low tide. It takes planning ahead, and some guides do it at night, by the light of the moon and stars, to avoid the blistering heat along the beach.

The 17.4-km (10.8-mi) trail from Los Patos to Sirena is lovely and forested. But to get to the Los Patos station you first walk 8 km (5 mi) along the verdant Río Rincón valley. The Sirena ranger station has great trails around it that can easily fill a couple of days.

Osa Aventura (⇨ *see Outdoor Activities in Puerto Jiménez, above*) specializes in wildlife tours.

WHERE TO EAT

Basic meals can be arranged at Sirena if you reserve in advance with the National Parks Service office in Puerto Jiménez. It's always a good idea to ask about what meals are available for sale when you make your reservation.

WHERE TO STAY

Camping or sleeping in the ranger's stations are your only lodging options inside the park, and both take planning and preparation. You must reserve in advance, during peak visitor times, at least 30 days ahead. Bunks at the Sirena ranger station (which is in a lamentable state of disrepair) are limited to 20 people a day, as are meals, which are very basic. Bring your own sheets, a pillow, and a good mosquito net. Campers planning to camp at La Leona, San Pedrillo, or La Sirena need to bring their own tents, gear, and food (although meals are sometimes available at La Leona). At the time of this writing, the Los Patos camping area had been closed but should be opened shortly.

There is a maximum stay of four nights and five days. To make reservations you must fill out a request, via e-mail or in person at the park office in Puerto Jiménez, then make a deposit in the park's Banco Nacional account, then e-mail, fax, or present the receipt in person to the park office. Lodging is $8 per night, not including meals; camping costs $4 per person per night. Check theWeb site for online reservations and information on lodging and camping availability

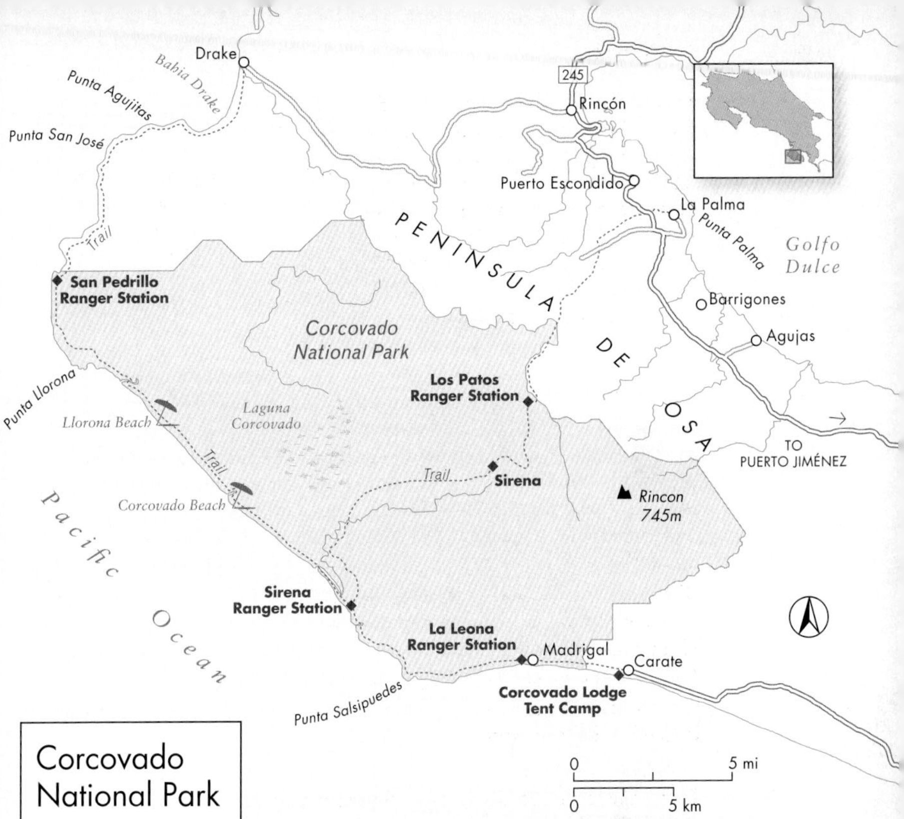

Corcovado National Park

DID YOU KNOW?

Corcovado has 13 ecosystems within its boundaries, ranging from mangroves and swamps to lowland rain forest. The park also has more forest giants—trees that stand 50 to 80 meters (165 to 264 feet) high—than anywhere in Central America.

CABO MATAPALO

21 km/14 mi south of Puerto Jiménez.

The southern tip of the Osa Peninsula, where virgin rain forest meets the sea at a rocky point, retains the kind of natural beauty that people travel halfway across the world to experience. From its ridges you can look out on the blue Golfo Dulce and the Pacific Ocean, sometimes spotting whales in the distance. The forest is tall and dense, with the highest and most diverse tree species in the country, usually draped with thick lianas. The name Matapalo refers to the strangler fig, which germinates in the branches of other trees and extends its roots downward, eventually smothering the supporting tree by blocking the sunlight. Flocks of brilliant scarlet macaws and troops of monkeys are the other draws here.

GETTING HERE AND AROUND

If you drive one hour south from Puerto Jiménez, be prepared for a bumpy ride and a lot of river crossings. In rainy season cars are sometimes washed out along rivers to the ocean. Most hotels arrange transportation in 4WD taxis or their own trucks. The cheapest—and the roughest—way to travel is by *collectivo,* an open-air communal truck ($8), that leaves Puerto Jiménez twice a day (at 6 AM and 1:30 PM). Buses do not serve Cabo Matapalo.

OUTDOOR ACTIVITIES

Outfitters in Puerto Jiménez run tours in this area. Each of the lodges listed has resident guides who can take guests on nature hikes. For extreme forest sports, **Everyday Adventures** (☎*8353–8619* ⊕*www.psychotours.com*) takes you on not-so-everyday adventures: rappelling down waterfalls ($85), climbing up a 43-meter (140-foot) strangler fig tree ($55), ocean kayaking (with an optional 9-meter [30-foot] dive, $55), and rain-forest hiking ($35). Or you can go all out with a combination rappelling/climbing tour for $120.

SURFING On the eastern side of Cabo Matapalo, waves break over a platform that creates a perfect right, drawing surfers from far and wide, especially beginners. Local surf expert **Richard Gardela** (☎*2735–5857 or 8866–4657*) will take you to where the best waves are on any given day, at Matapalo, or in Pavones directly across the gulf, for $200 to $400, including transportation, lunch, and drinks for one to three surfers. A two-hour introductory lesson costs $80, including transportation and equipment.

WHERE TO STAY

$$$$ Fodor'sChoice ★ **Bosque del Cabo.** Atop a cliff at the tip of Cabo Matapalo, this lodge has unparalleled views of the Golfo Dulce merging with the endless blue of the Pacific. The property, with hundreds of acres of animal-rich primary forest, also has the most beautiful landscaping on the peninsula. Deluxe thatch-roof cabins have king-size beds, with private, outdoor garden showers with hot water. Private decks are perfect for sunning by day and stargazing at night. A suspension bridge through the forest links the main lodge with three more rustic cabins set in a tropical garden that is great for bird-watching. Excellent meals are served in a rancho restaurant overlooking a garden alive with hummingbirds by day and serenaded by a chorus of frogs at night. Solar- and hydro-powered generators provide enough light to read by, and with the ocean breezes, you won't miss air-conditioning. Resident guides are on hand to lead you along forest trails—on foot or along a canopy zip line—and down to the beach with its natural warm tidal whirlpools and river waterfalls. The owners work hard to make their lodge as environmentally responsible as possible. **Pros:** luxurious, artistic bungalows; fabulous trails and guides; congenial atmosphere among guests at cocktail hour and dinner. **Cons:** steep trail to beach and back; very small pool; limited electricity supply. *+22 km/14 mi south of Puerto Jiménez on road to Carate* *Box 02-5635, Miami, FL 33102* ☎*2735–5206* ⊕*www.bosquedelcabo.com* *10 ocean-view cabins; 2 garden cabins; 3 houses, 1 with pool* *In-room: no a/c, no phone, kitchen (some), no TV. In-hotel: restaurant, bar, pool, beachfront* *MC, V* *FAP.*

"This is the view from the deck of the Tucan cabina at Bosque del Cabo." —photo by Monica Richards, Fodors.com member

$$$$ ★ **El Remanso.** You'll find tranquility and elegant simplicity at this almost spiritual retreat in a forest brimming with birds and wildlife, 122 meters (400 feet) above a beach studded with tide pools. Luxurious two-person cabinas have screened windows, large verandas, and showers behind curving Gaudí-like walls. A new deluxe cabin, on the path to the beach, has stunning ocean views and lots of privacy. There's also a large family cabin and a very private, deluxe two-story cabin, perfect for honeymoons. Four spacious rooms and two suites in a new two-story building have king-size beds, bathtubs, and verandas overlooking a swimming pool. Meals using local produce are served on a newly expanded deck restaurant. Waterfall rappelling, zip-line access to a canopy platform, and biologist-guided nature walks are the highlights, apart from soaking in the serenity. This is the most relaxed lodge in the area. **Pros:** gorgeous natural setting; privacy in cabins; jungle views; access to beach. **Cons:** no a/c; no hair dryers; food is often good but not spectacular. ✉ *South of entrance to Bosque del Cabo on road to Carate* ☎ *2735–5569* *www.elremanso.com* *4 rooms, 2 suites, 5 cabinas* *In-room: no a/c, no phone, no TV. In-hotel: restaurant, bar, beachfront, Internet terminal* *MC, V* *FAP.*

$$$$ Fodor'sChoice ★ **Lapa Ríos.** The most spectacular eco-resort in Costa Rica, Lapa Ríos has won numerous awards for its mix of conservation and comfort at the edge of civilization. After catching your breath when you see the view from the high, breezy jungle ridge rife with wildlife, your next sharp intake may be when you see the bill. But in this case the price is not inflated. Spacious, airy cabins built of gleaming hardwoods have four-poster queen beds, stylish bathrooms, and showers with one

8

screened wall open to nature. Private teak-decked garden terraces allow you to view passing monkeys and toucans from a lounge chair. There's an infinity pool, a spa, and a yoga deck. Inspired meals, served under a soaring thatch roof, include lots of seafood, exotic local fruits and vegetables, and mouthwatering desserts. You can eat whenever—and as much as—you want. Resident naturalist guides lead tours through pristine wilderness and to nearby beaches on foot or on horseback. Along with the high cost of transporting and providing all these luxuries in a remote location, it's the exceptional service that justifies the high price tag, which includes transfers from Puerto Jiménez in new 4WD vehicles. Don't miss their free sustainability tour called Twigs, Pigs, and Garbage, which highlights the resort's ingenious eco-friendly infrastructure, including pigs' contribution to energy fuels. ■ **TIP→If you don't like to climb stairs, request a cabin close to the main lodge.** **Pros:** excellent, professional service; Tico-flavor atmosphere with local employees; delicious typical and international dishes. **Cons:** steep price, but this is a once-in-a-lifetime experience; some steps to climb to farther cabins; steep trail to beach, but there is a shuttle service. *✣20 km/12 mi south of Puerto Jiménez ✉Apdo. 100–8203, Puerto Jiménez ☎2735–5130 📠2735–5179 🌐www.laparios.com 🛏16 cabinas ☝In-room: no a/c, no phone, no TV. In-hotel: restaurant, bar, pool, spa, beachfront, laundry service 💳AE, MC, V 🍽AI.*

CARATE

60 km/37 mi west of Puerto Jiménez.

Carate is literally the end of the road. The black volcanic-sand beach stretches for more than 3 km (2 mi), with surf that's perfect for Boogie boarding and body surfing but not for serious board surfing or safe swimming. The main entertainment at the beach is watching the noisy but magnificent scarlet macaws feasting on almonds in the beach almond trees that edge the shore. Carate has no phone service; a couple of lodges have satellite phones and iffy Wi-Fi and cell-phone connections.

GETTING HERE AND AROUND

The road from Matapalo to Carate covers 40 suspension-testing km (25 mi); at this writing, the road is graded and relatively smooth, but that can all change with one drenching wet season. You're better off taking the *collectivo* from Puerto Jiménez *(⇨To and From Puerto Jiménez, above)*. Or give yourself a break and fly via charter plane to Carate's small airstrip, arranged through your lodge. From here it's just 3 km (2 mi), roughly a 40-minute walk along the beach to the La Leona ranger station entrance to Corcovado National Park. In rainy season (May to December) it is sometimes impossible to cross the raging Río Carate that separates the landing strip from the beach path to the park, and you may end up stranded on either side. Parking at the store in Carate is $5 per day.

OUTDOOR ACTIVITIES

Activities here revolve around Corcovado National Park and its environs. Hiking, horseback riding, canopy tours, and other adventures must be organized through your hotel.

WHERE TO STAY

$$$ ★ **Lookout Inn.** The only hotel on Carate's beach, this barefoot inn—shoes come off at the bottom step—is set on a precipitous hillside (steep stairs are plentiful here, including a 500-step "Stairway to Heaven" up to a lofty lookout). Luxurious rooms in the lodge have huge ceramic bathrooms. Two screened-in wooden cabins are perfect for those craving privacy, and one new cabin, the Monkey House, is great for families, with a queen bed and two singles in a loft. It's also under the monkeys' favorite treetop freeway. Cheaper tentlike "tiki" cabinas sit on 10-foot platforms and share a bathhouse. This place is full of quirky artistic touches, including a swinging bed in another new cabin, the Swing Inn Spa. But the quirkiest element is owner Terry Conroy, an energetic host who makes sure everyone joins in on activities. His serene Tica wife, Katya, balances her husband and makes a mean margarita. Inventive meals with lots of fresh fish and Asian flavors are served on two breezy terraces with spectacular views of the coastline. Dozens of scarlet macaws frequent the garden, and monkeys come to feast on bananas. There's also a spring-fed plunge pool with a hammock rancho, a yoga deck, a new spa, a shaded pavilion on the beach, and a bird-watching trail through primary forest. The hotel organizes beach and trail rides on horseback. **Pros:** proximity to beach and access on foot to Corcovado Park; excellent food; party atmosphere; guaranteed scarlet macaw sightings (or your money back!). **Cons:** very steep drive/stair climb up to lodge and down to beach; very limited communication with outside world; cabins have more privacy than main lodge rooms. ⊠ *300 m east of Carate landing strip* ☎ *2735–5431, 815/955–1520 in U.S.* 🌐 *www.lookout-inn.com* *3 rooms, 4 cabins, 2 tiki cabins with shared bath* *In-room: no a/c, no phone, no TV. In-hotel: restaurant, bars, pool, spa, beachfront, laundry service, some pets allowed* ▭ *MC, V* 🍽 *AI.*

$–$$ ★ **Luna Lodge.** Luna Lodge's ultimate charm lies in its remoteness and tranquility. On a mountaintop overlooking the ocean and the rain forest, it's a true retreat, with a huge hardwood pavilion for practicing yoga or contemplating magnificent sunsets. Just below the yoga platform there's an elegant massage hut with ethereal views. Round bungalows in the garden, spaced apart for privacy, have thatch roofs, garden showers, and decks for bird-watching or relaxing in wood-and-leather rocking chairs. Three deluxe rooms near the main lodge have private baths and share a spacious deck. For real adventure, bed down in one of the lodge's comfortable new platform tents, set on a hilltop with ocean view and private bathrooms. Guided hikes to nearby waterfalls and swimming holes are precipitous and thrilling, and lounging around the beautiful new pebble-deck pool is pure nirvana. Healthful meals have an imaginative vegetarian flair, tempered with servings of fish and chicken spiced with herbs from a hilltop organic garden. Host Lana Wedmore is a model of amiable helpfulness. **Pros:** scenic setting for peace, yoga, and therapeutic massage; comfortable lodging and healthful food; excellent birding. **Cons:** extremely steep road up to lodge; beach is quite a hike back down (and up!); no a/c and limited electricity; open cabins mean there may be some encounters of the small wildlife kind. ✥ *2 km/1 mi up a steep, partially paved road from Carate* *Box 025216–5216,*

8

One of Punta Marenco Lodge's boat excursions.

Miami, FL 33102 ☎8380–5036 or 8358–5848, 888/409–8448 in U.S. 🌐www.lunalodge.com ⇨8 bungalows, 3 rooms, 5 tents ♿In-room: no a/c, no phone, no TV. In-hotel: restaurant, bar, pool, spa ▭MC, V 🍴FAP.

DRAKE BAY

18 km/11 mi north of Corcovado, 40 km/25 mi southwest of Palmar Sur, 310 km/193 mi south of San José.

This is castaway country, a real tropical adventure, with plenty of hiking and some rough but thrilling boat rides. The rugged coast that stretches south from the mouth of the Río Sierpe to Corcovado probably doesn't look much different from what it did in Sir Francis Drake's day (1540–96), when, as legend has it, the British explorer anchored here. Small, picture-perfect beaches with surf crashing against dark volcanic rocks are backed by steaming, thick jungle. Nature lodges scattered along the coast are hemmed in by the rain forest, which is home to troops of monkeys, sloths, scarlet macaws, and hundreds of other bird species.

GETTING HERE AND AROUND

The fastest way to get to Drake Bay is to fly directly to the airstrip. You can also fly to Palmar Sur and take a taxi to Sierpe and then a boat to Drake Bay. From the airport, it's a 25-minute taxi ride to Sierpe; small, open boats leave at low tide, usually 11 to 11:30 AM for the one-hour trip to Drake. Captains will often stop along the way to view wildlife in the river mangroves. Many lodges arrange boat transportation from Drake Bay or Sierpe. From Rincón you can drive to Drake on a 20-km

(12-mi) graded dirt road. Buses leave Puerto Jiménez for La Palma every two hours from 6 AM to 8 PM, connecting in La Palma with buses to Drake Bay at 10:30 AM and 4 PM. Buses leave Drake at 4 AM and 1 PM for La Palma, to connect with buses to either Puerto Jiménez or San José. The drive from San José to Drake is scenic, but an exhausting seven hours long.

Exceptionally fit backpackers can hike to the northern entrance of Corcovado along an 18-km (11-mi) coastal path that follows the shoreline, cutting through shady forest when the coast gets too rocky. But it is impossible to walk during rainy season (September to December), when rivers flood and tides are too high.

ESSENTIALS

Drake just got electricity in 2004, so there are still very few services.

Internet Internet Cafe (✉ *Corcovado Expeditions, Drake village* ☎ *8818–9962* ⏲ *Daily 10–8*).

Visitor Information Corcovado Expeditions (✉ *Drake* ☎ *8818–9962* 🌐 *www.corcovadoexpeditions.net*).

The cheapest accommodations in the area can be found in the town of **Drake,** which is spread out along the bay. A trio of upscale nature lodges—Drake Bay Wilderness Resort, Aguila de Osa Inn, and La Paloma Lodge—are also clumped near the Río Agujitas on the bay's southern end. They all offer comprehensive packages, including trips to Corcovado and Caño Island. Lodges farther south, such as Punta Marenco Lodge and Casa Corcovado, run excursions from even wilder settings. During the dry season you can reach the town of Drake via a graded dirt road from Rincón.

8

OUTDOOR ACTIVITIES

Jinetes de Osa (✉ *Drake village, west side of bay* ☎ *8826–9757* 🌐 *www.jinetesdeosa.com*) has diving ($95 plus $20 for gear) and snorkeling ($70) and dolphin-watching tours ($100), as well as a canopy tour ($65) with some interesting bridge, ladder, and rope transitions between platforms.

WHERE TO STAY

$$$$ **Aguila de Osa Inn.** A sportfisher's dream lodge, Aguila de Osa has spacious rooms with hardwood interiors, oversize bamboo beds, and luxurious tile-and-glass-brick bathrooms. Stained-glass lamps with tropical themes and hand-carved doors add artistic flair. Be prepared for a steep climb up stone stairs to your room with a view of Drake Bay. Morning coffee arrives outside your room before 6 AM. Dinner here is a real event, with huge platters of perfectly cooked fish—sometimes guests' own catches—and meats, served family-style. The lodge has two 31-foot, high-tech sportfishing boats, as well as dive trips and excursions into Corcovado Park. Two-night packages include transfers from Drake Bay or Palmar Sur airports. **Pros:** great for fishing enthusiasts; elegant lodge and rooms; convivial, communal dining with wine included. **Cons:** no ocean views or breezes, and heat and humidity can be stifling; steep climb to some rooms, on sometimes slippery stone stairs; some rooms have little privacy, notably No. 10. ✉ *South end of Drake*

CLOSE UP

Snorkelers' Paradise

Most of uninhabited 2½-square-km (1-square-mi) **Caño Island Biological Reserve** is covered in evergreen forest that includes fig, locust, and rubber trees. Coastal Indians used it as a burial ground, and the numerous bits and pieces unearthed here have prompted archaeologists to speculate about pre-Columbian long-distance maritime trade. Occasionally, mysterious stones that have been carved into perfect spheres of varying sizes are discovered. The uninhabited island's main attraction now is the ocean around it, superb for scuba diving and snorkeling.

The snorkeling is best around the rocky points flanking the island's main beach; if you're a certified diver, you'll probably want to explore Bajo del Diablo and Paraíso, where you're guaranteed to encounter thousands of good-size fish, including white-tip, nurse, and trigger sharks.

The only way to get to the island, 19 km (12 mi) due west of the Osa Peninsula, is by boat arranged by your lodge or a tour company. Lodges and the Jinetes de Osa tour company in Drake Bay run day trips here, as do tour companies in Dominical, Uvita, and Sierpe.

at mouth of Río Agujitas ✉ *Interlink 898 Box 025635, Miami, FL 33102* ☎ *2296–2190 in San José* 🖷 *2232–7722* 🌐 *www.aguiladeosa.com* *11 rooms, 2 suites* *In-room: no a/c, no phone, refrigerator (some), no TV. In-hotel: restaurant, bar, water sports, laundry service, Internet terminal, Wi-Fi* ▭ *AE, MC, V* 🍴 *FAP.*

$$$–$$$$ ★ **Casa Corcovado Jungle Lodge.** This hilltop jungle lodge has it all: a prime location on the edge of Corcovado National Park, luxury accommodations, and first-class service. Spanish colonial–style bungalows are spread out, each with its own garden for maximum privacy. The bungalows have elegant furniture, four-poster beds, and huge tile bathrooms, some with open-air garden showers. Laundry service is extra, but each room has clotheslines for drying your sure-to-be-damp clothes. Two swimming pools and self-guided nature trails on the property keep you busy outdoors, and the games room has books and board games to occupy evenings and rainy afternoons. The hilltop sunset margarita bar has excellent views of the sun setting behind Caño Island. The vast restaurant, studded with art deco stained glass, serves excellent breakfasts and packs hearty picnic lunches. At this writing, dinners are less successful, but new chefs are revising the menu. The minimum stay is two nights, but the best deal is a three-night package that includes transportation from San José, all meals, and a trip to Caño Island and Corcovado National Park. **Pros:** unrivaled location adjoining national park and close to Caño Island; excellent tours, service, and facilities. **Cons:** an adventure to get here: be prepared for a hair-raising, wet landing; steep climb to lodge from beach, but there is a tractor-pulled cart to transport guests and luggage; no a/c; limited electricity. ✉ *Northern border of Corcovado* ✉ *Apdo. 1482–1250, Escazú* ☎ *2256–3181* 🌐 *www.casacorcovado.com* *14 rooms* *In-room: no a/c, no phone, no TV. In-hotel: restaurant, bars, pools, beachfront, water sports* ▭ *AE, MC, V* ⏲ *Closed mid-Sept.–mid-Nov.* 🍴 *AI.*

$-$$ **Drake Bay Wilderness Resort.** On a grassy point between Río Aguji-tas and the ocean, this breezy resort has the best views of Drake Bay. It's also kid-friendly, with a pool, open ground for romping, and tidal pools to explore. Keep an eye out for precocious squirrel monkeys. The wooden cabins are camp-style, three rooms to a building. But with hot water, tile bathrooms, and carved animal bedposts supporting firm queen-size beds, this is very comfortable camping. There's no air-conditioning, but ocean breezes make for cool evenings. There are also five less expensive, tentlike cabanas on platforms with shared baths, right at the water's edge. Kayaks are at your disposal for exploring the river. Most guests come to see the rain forest, but you can also opt for mangrove, scuba diving, sportfishing, and dolphin- and whale-watching tours. **Pros:** great location; family-friendly and affordable; good food; free laundry service. **Cons:** not a lot of privacy; no a/c; noisy generator provides limited electricity. ✉ *On peninsula at mouth of Río Agujitas, on southern end of bay* *Apdo. 1370010–1000, San José* ☎ *8337–8004, 561/371–3437 in U.S.* *2770–8012* *www.drakebay.com* *20 rooms* *In-room: no a/c, no phone, no TV. In-hotel: restaurant, bar, pool, laundry facilities, Internet terminal, Wi-Fi* *AE, MC, V* *FAP.*

$$-$$$ **Jinetes de Osa.** The most comfortable and reasonably priced place to stay right in the village of Drake, this small bay-side hotel with a casual open-air restaurant has simple rooms, all with tile floors and hot-water showers. Rooms open out onto a pleasant terrace with a view of the town and the bay. Guests get to leave their artistic signatures on painted driftwood mobiles that decorate the restaurant. The on-site diving operation is well run, so the lodge is often filled with groups of divers. **Pros:** convenient location; affordable; adventuresome, active clientele. **Cons:** standard rooms are smallish, so opt for the larger deluxe room if you can; no a/c. ✉ *Drake village, west side of bay* ☎ *8826–9757* *2231–5801 in San José* *www.costaricadiving.com* *9 rooms* *In-room: no a/c, no phone, no TV. In-hotel: restaurant, beachfront* *MC, V* *FAP.*

$$$$ ★ **La Paloma Lodge.** Sweeping ocean views and lots of tropical-foliage privacy make this villa lodge the area's most romantic. Planted in a jungle garden on a ridge jutting into Drake Bay, elegant, spacious wooden villas have bedroom lofts, spiffy bathrooms, and large porches with summery green wicker furniture. Numbers 1 and 3 have the best sea views. Four standard rooms lined up in a shared building are anything but standard: they're spacious and luxurious with jungle and garden views. Room D has a wraparound deck overlooking an expanse of jungle that will delight bird-watchers. A small pool overlooks forest and ocean, or you can head down the hill to Playa Cocolito, the hotel's gem of a beach at the edge of the coastal path to Corcovado. The hotel runs a diving school and offers river kayaking. The flower-filled restaurant serves tropical fare, and there's always afternoon tea and baked treats when you can mingle with the other guests. Manager Nichole Dupont maintains a high standard of service. There's a three-night minimum stay; packages are the best bet, as they include transportation from San José, all meals, and some tours. **Pros:** idyllic setting with ocean

8

views and easy access to Coastal Footpath; great service; interesting guests from all over the world. **Cons:** expensive; no a/c; open cabins mean you will have to contend with some insect visitors. ✉ *Drake Bay, 300 m past Drake Bay Wilderness Resort* 📭 *Apdo. 97–4005, Heredia* ☎ *2293–7502* 🌐 *www.lapalomalodge.com* 🛏 *4 rooms, 7 cabinas* 👍 *In-room: no a/c, no phone, no TV. In-hotel: restaurant, bar, pool, beachfront, diving, water sports, Wi-Fi in restaurant* 💳 *MC, V* ⏲ *Closed mid-Sept.–Oct.* 🍽 *FAP.*

WORD OF MOUTH

"We enjoyed our stay very much at La Paloma Lodge in Drake Bay. They make everything so easy. The food was good. Our guide to Corcovado was fantastic—we learned so much from him! We saw as many animals on their property as we saw in the park. We did the Cano Island snorkeling trip. We knew the snorkeling would not be comparable to some of the Caribbean islands but we did see quite a few fish and sharks."

—wego

$$ 🏨 **Punta Marenco Lodge.** This rustic lodge has the best location on the Pacific side of the Osa, and it's the best deal on the coast. After a bumpy period when the lodge was leased out, the owners have returned to upgrade and run it themselves. South Seas island–style cabins with thatch roofs perch on the spine of a ridge overlooking the sea. Private porches are perfect for siestas, sunsets, and stargazing. Four new, spacious cabins have garden and sea views, ideal for bird-watchers; No. 4 has a huge bed with a frog headboard. Toucans and scarlet macaws visit every morning, and paths lead to the scenic coastal trail and deep into the Río Claro National Wildlife Refuge. A resident guide is on hand for nature walks, and the lodge can arrange oceangoing tours, including diving and dolphin-watching excursions. The rancho restaurant has a family feel, with communal tables and typical Tico food. There is electricity for only a few hours in the evening, and no hot water. Insects frequent the thatch roofs, but so do tiny lizards that eat them up. You can hike here from Drake or take a boat from Drake or Sierpe (included in packages). **Pros:** castaway-island remoteness; trails are as good as those in Corcovado National Park; very reasonable price. **Cons:** very rustic; steep climb uphill to lodge after thrilling wet landing on beach; simple food; very limited electricity and contact with outside world. ✉ *Beachfront, directly east of Caño Island and north of Casa Corcovado* 📭 *Apdo. 2133–1100, Tibas* ☎ *2292–2775 for reservations* 🌐 *www.corcovadozone.com* 🛏 *14 cabinas* 👍 *In-room: no a/c, no phone, no TV. In-hotel: restaurant, beachfront* 💳 *MC, V* 🍽 *FAP.*

NIGHTLIFE

When you're on the Osa Peninsula, the wildest nightlife is outdoors. ★ Join entomologist Tracie Stice, also known as the Bug Lady, on the **Night Tour** (☎ *8812–6673 or 8867–6143* 🌐 *www.thenighttour.com*) of insects, bats, reptiles, and anything else moving around at night. Tracie is a wealth of bug lore, with riveting stories from around the world. Headlamps and infrared flashlights help you see in the dark. Tours are $35 per person.

Caribbean

WORD OF MOUTH

"Probably the best decision of our trip was to visit the Caribbean side. The people, beaches, and food were exceptional. We went snorkeling and hikes in the Cahuita National Park—both incredible experiences. While snorkeling, we saw a nurse shark, manta ray, sea urchins, coral reef, parrot fish, and needle fish."

–skiobx

WELCOME TO CARIBBEAN

TOP REASONS TO GO

★ **Turtles:** People from around the world flock to the northern Caribbean for the annual nesting of four species.

★ **Food and flavors:** Leave gallo pinto behind in favor of mouthwatering *rondón* (meat or fish stew), or *caribeño* (Caribbean) rice and beans, stewed in coconut milk.

★ **Dolphin-watching:** Bottlenose, tucuxi, and Atlantic-spotted dolphins ply the southern Caribbean coast.

★ **Music:** Mix reggae and calypso with your salsa. Rhythms waft in from the far-off Caribbean Islands; and home-grown musicians are making names for themselves, too.

★ **Sportfishing:** World-class tarpon and snook attract serious anglers to the shores off Barra del Colorado and Tortuguero national parks.

1 Northern Lowlands. The Northern Lowlands have little to offer tourists in their own right, but are close to Braulio Carrillo Park and rafting-trip put-in points.

2 Northern Caribbean Coast. The Northern Caribbean Coast encompasses the coastal jungles and canals of Tortuguero National Park and Barra del Colorado Wildlife Refuge. Boat and air travel are the only ways to reach this roadless region.

3 Southern Caribbean Coast. The Southern Caribbean Coast stretches south from port-of-call Limón to Panama. Towns along the coast have an Afro-Caribbean vibe—some are more backpacker-ish than others. Beaches are fringed with forest and waters are rough. Surfers make the trip for Salsa Brava.

GETTING ORIENTED

Costa Rica's Caribbean coast is sometimes called its Atlantic coast, so as not to confuse tourists looking for the white sand and clear-blue waters of the Caribbean Islands. This Caribbean is very different, with sands in shades of brown and black, waters that are rough and murky (ideal for surfing), dense jungle, heavy and frequent rain, and a less sophisticated, laid-back approach to tourism. It is beautiful and fascinating in its own way, but it's definitely not St. Barths.

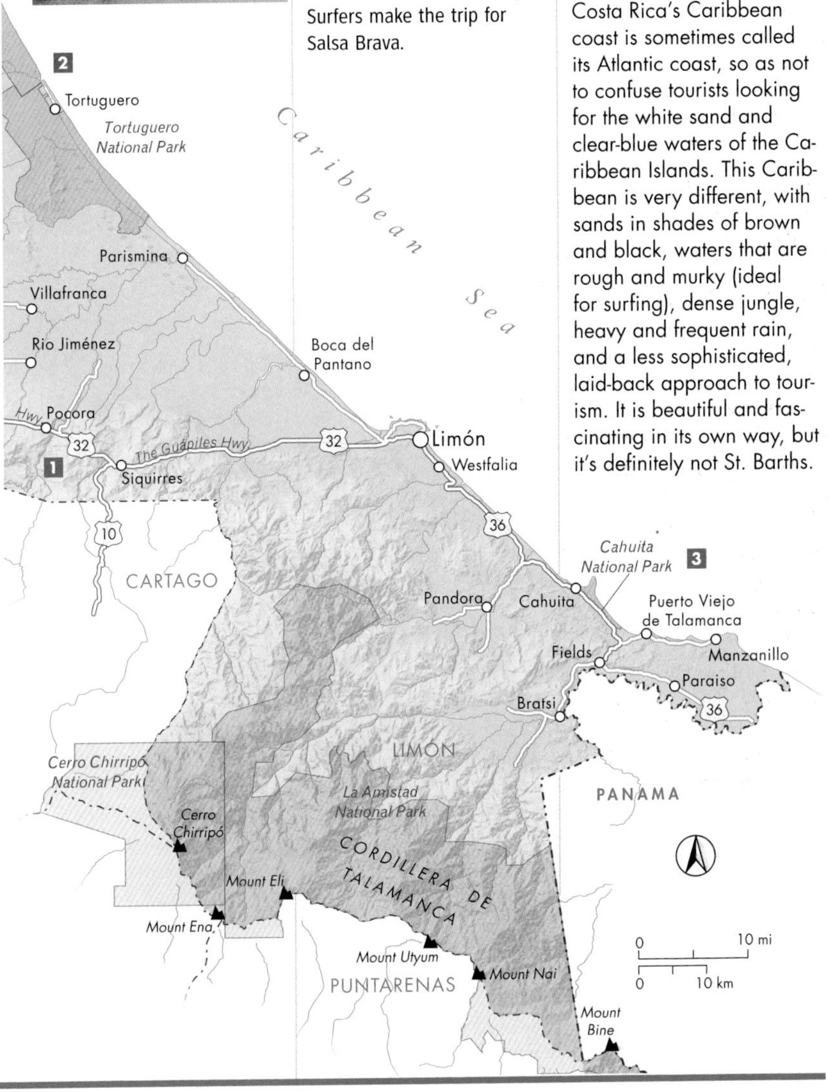

CARIBBEAN PLANNER

When to Go

Climate is the Caribbean's bugaboo and will forever prevent it from becoming the same high-powered tourist destination that the North Pacific is. (Frankly, we consider that to be a blessing.) The Caribbean lacks a true dry season, though February to April and September to October could be called drier seasons, with many sunny days and intermittent showers. The heaviest rains (and periodic road closures) come in December and January, high season elsewhere. During the rainiest months prices are lower and visitors fewer.

Temperatures remain constant year-round, with daily highs of 29°C to 31°C (84°F to 88°F) and lows of 21°C to 23°C (69°F to 73°F). Yet, despite weather patterns that differ from the rest of Costa Rica, places here charge high-season rates from December to April, and again in July and August. (Tortuguero sets its own high and low seasons, with higher prices the norm during prime turtle-watching months of July through September.) Not to fear though: prices skew a bit lower in the Caribbean than elsewhere in the country.

Getting There

Old-timers still remember the days when the only access to this region was the railroad that once connected San José with Limón. From there, boats would take them up and down the coast. Today, this historically isolated area is one of the country's most accessible. The southern coast is a three- to four-hour drive from San José, over mostly decent roads (by Costa Rican standards), and public transportation is frequent and reliable. Gas stations are plentiful between Guápiles and Limón, but their numbers dwindle to one between Limón and Puerto Viejo de Talamanca. The northern Caribbean coast is another story: the total absence of roads means you have to arrive by plane or boat. Most travelers go with a tour booked through one of the large lodges.

If your driving here, remember that fog often covers the mountains in Braulio Carrillo National Park, north of San José, by early afternoon. Cross this area in the morning if you can. Always exercise utmost caution on the portion of highway that twists and turns through the park. Check road conditions before you set out; occasional closures through Braulio Carrillo necessitate leaving San José from the southeast, passing through Cartago, Paraíso, and Turrialba, then rejoining the Caribbean highway at Siquirres.

The Complete Package

One of Costa Rica's most remote regions is also one of its prime tourist destinations. No roads lead to Tortuguero on the northeast coast, so plane or boat are your only options. If you don't want to bother with logistics, consider booking a package tour with one of the lodges we list. It will include all transport from San José, overnights, meals, and guided tours. Prices look high at first, but considering all you get, they are quite reasonable. Other types of tours regional tours are also available: **Horizontes** (☎2222–2022 🌐www.horizontes.com) tours include naturalist guides and transport by 4WD vehicle. **Talamanca Adventures** (☎2224–3570 🌐www.talamanca-adventures.com) leads off-the-beaten-path tours on everything from Caribbean cooking to rain forest conservation.

What to Do

ACTIVITY	WHERE TO DO IT
Biking	Cahuita, Puerto Viejo de Talamanca
Bird-watching	EARTH, Tortuguero, Gandoca-Manzanillo Wildlife Refuge
Butterfly-viewing	Cahuita, Puerto Viejo de Talamanca, Limón
Diving	Gandoca-Manzanillo Wildlife Refuge
Dolphin-watching	Gandoca-Manzanillo Wildlife Refuge
Fishing	Barra del Colorado, San Juan River, Tortuguero
Kayaking	Gandoca-Manzanillo Wildlife Refuge, Tortuguero
Snorkeling	Cahuita National Park, Gandoca-Manzanillo Wildlife Refuge
Surfing	Cahuita, Puerto Viejo de Talamanca, Limón
Turtle-watching	Gandoca-Manzanillo Wildlife Refuge, Tortuguero
White-water rafting	Siquirres
Wildlife-viewing	Tortuguero, Barra del Colorado, Gandoca-Manzanillo Wildlife Refuge, Guápiles
Zip-lining	Gandoca-Manzanillo Wildlife Refuge, Limón

Dining and Lodging

WHAT IT COSTS IN DOLLARS

	¢	$	$$	$$$	$$$$
Restaurants	under $5	$5–$10	$10–$15	$15–$25	over $25
Hotels	under $50	$50–$75	$75–$150	$150–$250	over $250

Restaurant prices are per person for a main course at dinner. Hotel prices are for two people in a standard double room in high season, excluding service and tax (16.4%).

How Much Time?

Attractions near Guápiles and Siquirres lend themselves to long day trips from San José. Tour operators also have whirlwind daylong Tortuguero trips from San José. We recommend you avoid these—the area really deserves two or, ideally, three days. Choose a single Caribbean destination and stay put if you have just a few days. (Cahuita and Puerto Viejo de Talamanca are ideal for that purpose.) If you have a week, you can tackle the north and south coasts.

Choosing a Place to Stay

The high-rise, glitzy resorts of the Pacific coast are nowhere to be found in the Caribbean. The norm here is small, independent lodgings, usually family owned and operated. Fewer visitors in this region mean plenty of decent lodging at affordable prices most of the year. But tourism *is* growing, so it's risky to show up without reservations. Surprisingly few places here have air-conditioning, but sea breezes and ceiling fans usually provide sufficient ventilation. Smaller places frequently don't take credit cards; those that do may give discounts if you pay with cash.

PARQUE NACIONAL TORTUGUERO

BEST TIME TO GO

The July–October nesting season for the green turtle is Tortuguero's most popular time to visit. It rains here (a lot!) year-round, so expect to get wet no matter when you go. February through April and September and October are a tad drier.

At various times of the year, four species of sea turtles—green, hawksbill, loggerhead, and giant leatherback—lumber up the 35 km (22 mi) of beach to deposit their eggs for safekeeping.

In 1975 the Costa Rican government established Parque Nacional Tortuguero to protect the sea turtle population, which had been decimated after centuries of being aggressively hunted for its eggs and carapaces. This is the best place in Costa Rica to observe these magnificent creatures' nesting and hatching rituals. Still, despite preservation efforts, less than 1% of the hatchlings will make it to adulthood.

Turtles may be the name of the game here, but keep your eyes peeled for nonturtle species, too: tapirs, jaguars, anteaters, ocelots, howler monkeys, white-faced capuchin monkeys, three-toed sloths, collared and white-lipped peccaries, coatis, and blue morpho butterflies also populate the park. The palm-lined beaches of the park stretch off as far as the eye can see. You can wander the beach independently when the turtles aren't nesting, but riptides make swimming dangerous, and shark rumors persist.

FUN FACT

One of nature's mysteries is how turtles find their way back to the same beach years later. It's thought that the sand leaves a biological imprint on the turtle hatchlings during their scurry to the sea, which directs females to return here years later to nest.

BEST WAY TO EXPLORE

TOURS

Most visitors opt for a fully escorted tour with one of the big lodges, because you're looked after from the moment you're picked up at your San José hotel until you're dropped off a day or two or seven later. All include a couple of standard tours of the park in their package prices. It's entirely possible to stay at a smaller in-town place and make à la carte arrangements yourself. No matter which way you go, your park tour will be on foot or by boat. Remember: no four-wheeled vehicles up here.

BOAT RIDES

It's not quite "The African Queen," but a boat ride along the narrow vine-draped canals here is pretty close. Once you're off the main canal, the specially designed, narrow tour boats glide relatively quietly—using mandated electric motors—and very slowly, which makes for better wildlife spotting and less waves that erode the lagoon banks. Another alternative is to rent a kayak and go at your own speed along the canals.

BIRD-WATCHING AND WILDLIFE

This is a birder's dream destination. Some of the rarer species you'll find here include the snowy cotinga, palm warbler, and yellow-tailed oriole. Water birds and herons abound. On a recent foray, members of the Birding Club of Costa Rica were treated to a close-up view of a wide-eyed rufescent tiger-heron chick sitting in his nest, squawking impatiently for food. You'll also see iguanas, caimans, and sloths. Bird watching and wildlife spotting sometimes collide: while watching two beautiful agami herons feeding on a muddy bank, birders were shaken up by the sudden splash of a crocodile attacking the herons. Happily, the herons were quicker off the mark than the birders were!

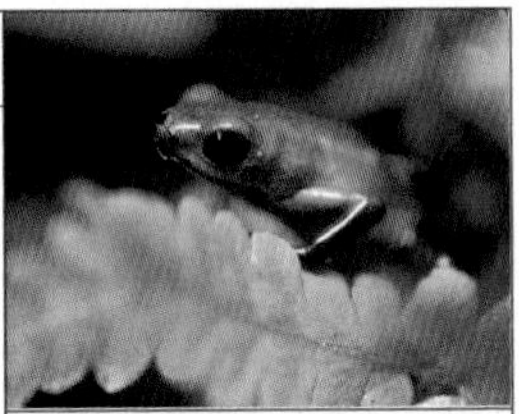

TOP REASONS TO GO

TURTLES

Tortuguero takes its name from the Spanish word for turtle (*tortuga*) and here you'll get the chance to observe the nesting and hatching of four species of sea turtle, and to ponder one of nature's amazing rituals.

PLANE OR BOAT ONLY

Whoever coined the old adage "Getting there is half the fun" might have had Tortuguero in mind. Plane and boat are the only ways to get to this no-road sector of Costa Rica. If you have the time, the fully escorted boat trips to and from the jungle give you a real Indiana Jones experience.

LUXURY IN THE JUNGLE

Don't let tales of Tortuguero's isolation dissuade you from making a trip. No question: the place is remote. But the lodges up here package everything (overnight lodging, meals, tours, and, best of all, guided round-trip transport) into one price in true "leave the driving to them" fashion. You won't lift a finger.

CAHUITA NATIONAL PARK

In a land known for its dark-sand beaches, the coral-based white sand of Cahuita National Park (Parque Nacional Cahuita) is a real standout.

The only Costa Rican park jointly administered by the National Parks Service and a community, it starts at the southern edge of the village of Cahuita and runs pristine mile after pristine mile to the southward. Whereas most of the country's protected areas tender only land-based activities, this park entices you offshore as well.

Roughly parallel to the coastline, a 7-km (4-mi) trail passes through the forest to Cahuita Point. A hike of a few hours along the trail—always easiest in the dry season—lets you spot howler and white-faced capuchin monkeys, coatimundis, armadillos, and raccoons. The coastline is encircled by a 2½-square-km (1-square-mi) coral reef, protection of which was the reason for the park's creation. You'll find superb snorkeling off Cahuita Point, but sadly, the coral reef is slowly being killed by sediment, intensified by deforestation and the erosive effects of the 1991 earthquake that hit the coast.

BEST TIME TO GO

As is the case on this coast, you can expect rain here no matter what the time of year. February through April and September and October are drier months, and offer the best visibility for snorkeling. (Those are the least desirable months if you're here to surf.)

FUN FACT

When Costa Rica began charging admission to national parks, residents successfully requested an exemption, fearing that such charges would harm the local economy. Your admission fee to this park is voluntary.

BEST WAY TO EXPLORE

CYCLING
Cycling makes a pleasant way to see the park in the dry season. Seemingly everybody in Cahuita and Puerto Viejo de Talamanca rents bicycles. (The southern entrance to the park is close enough to Puerto Viejo that it could be your starting point, too.) The park trail gets pretty muddy at times, and you run into logs, river estuaries, and other obstacles.

HIKING
A serious 7-km (4-mi) hiking trail runs from the park entrance at Kelly Creek all the way to Puerto Vargas. Take a bus or catch a ride to Puerto Vargas and hike back around the point in the course of a day. Remember to bring plenty of water, food, and sunscreen.

SNORKELING
Tour operators in Cahuita will bring you to a selection of prime snorkeling spots offshore. If you want to swim out on your own, the best snorkeling spot is off Punta Vargas at the south end of the park. Along with the chance to see some of the 500 or so species of tropical fish that live here, you'll see some amazing coral formations, including impressive elk horn, majestic blue stag horn, and eerie yellowbrain corals. When the water is clear and warm, the snorkeling is great. But that warm water also appeals to jelly fish—if you start to feel a tingling sensation on your arms or legs, make a beeline for the shore. Each little sting doesn't hurt much, but accumulated stings can result in a major allergic reaction in some people.

BEACHING IT
The waves here are fabulous for body surfing along the section of beach at the Puerto Vargas entrance. This wide swath of shoreline is also great for strolling, jogging, or just basking in the Caribbean sun—be careful of rip tides along this stretch of coast. The safest swimming is in front of the camping area.

TOP REASONS TO GO

SNORKELING
Costa Rica's largest living coral reef just offshore means the snorkeling is phenomenal here. Watch for blue parrot fish and angelfish as they weave their way among equally colorful species of coral, sponges, and seaweeds. Visit during the Caribbean coast's two mini–dry seasons for the best visibility.

EASY ACCESS
With one of its two entrances sitting in "downtown" Cahuita, access to the park is a snap. But ease of access does not mean the place is overrun with visitors. Fortunately, this is no Manuel Antonio.

LOTS OF LODGING
Closeness to Cahuita and Puerto Viejo de Talamanca and their spectrum of lodging options means you'll have no trouble finding a place to stay that fits your budget. You can even camp in the park if you're up to roughing it.

ECO-LODGES IN THE CARIBBEAN

Year-round rainfall begets year-round greenery on the Caribbean coast. You can count on lushness here when the rest of Costa Rica's landscape turns dusty during its dry season.

Not only does Costa Rica's Caribbean region host a different culture than the rest of the country, but its landscape is entirely different, too. Things are verdant all year, and that gives the eastern portion of the country a more tropical feel than the rest of Costa Rica. Development has been slow to come to the coast—anyone over the age of 20 well remembers the days of few roads, no phones, and no television. For you, that means far fewer visitors than along north and central Pacific coasts and a far more authentic experience since the environment is better preserved and the local culture respected. *Small* is the watchword for tourism around here—always has been and always will be. Developers do float occasional trial balloons about international mega-tourism projects in this region, but they get shot down quickly by the folks here who do not want their Caribbean coast to turn into the Pacific coast, thank you very much.

GOOD PRACTICES

Stay at locally owned lodgings. That's easy in the Caribbean, since the international chains are nowhere to be found here. Smaller lodgings that support the local economy are the universal norm. A stay here means that you are supporting those communities, too.

Consider taking public or semi-public transportation when visiting the Caribbean. Cahuita and Puerto Viejo de Talamanca are have good bus and shuttle service; your own two feet, bicycles, and taxis make it easy to get around once you arrive. Of course, a Tortuguero visit means you leave the transportation to someone else. There's no other choice.

TOP ECO-LODGES IN THE CARIBBEAN

CASA MARBELLA, TORTUGUERO

Most visitors to Tortuguero opt for a stay at one of the big all-inclusive lodges lining the canals outside the village. Yet our favorite in-town lodging provides a far more intimate Tortuguero experience with one-on-one nature tours, rather than big groups, for just a fraction of the cost. Canadian owner and naturalist Daryl Loth is a knowledgeable and well-respected figure in the area. Though onetime outsiders, the folks at Casa Marbella have become arguably the town's biggest boosters, working closely with people here to develop sustainable, nonintrusive tourism that will benefit the entire community. We like and appreciate this "transplanted foreigner" model.

ALMONDS & CORALS TENT LODGE CAMP, GANDOCA-MANZANILLO WILDLIFE REFUGE

At first blush, the concept does sound a bit cheesy: you camp in a tent, but that tent sits on a platform and you have a thatch roof above your tent—guaranteed to stay snug and dry. Almonds & Corals scatters its "campsites" unobtrusively throughout its forest property along the coast and connects them with each other and to its restaurant, reception, and the beach by softly lighted paths. That and the myriad of environmentally themed activities conducted by local guides really does give that "get away from it all" experience with a bit of rustic luxury.

RAIN FOREST AERIAL TRAM, BRAULIO CARRILLO NATIONAL PARK

Yes. Despite the name, there is accommodation here. The park is one of the Caribbean region's premier attractions, and staying here lets you enjoy the place after the day-trippers have left. The unobtrusive cabins are so inconspicuously tucked away that few people even know they exist. In an effort to minimize impact, cabins are not available for stays unless at least two can be rented at a time. Food is locally grown, and electricity shuts off after 9 PM. Of course, the rates include the full complement of the site's eco-theme activities.

BIOGEM

In 2009, the nonprofit Natural Resources Defense Council (NRDC) named the entire country one of its BioGems, a designation the New York–based environmental crusader usually reserves for a single site or species. In doing so, NRDC recognizes the country's wealth of biodiversity and its fragile status. The organization has pledged to work with the Costa Rican government in areas of reforestation and development of renewable energy technology. (With approximately 99% of Costa Rica's energy coming from hydroelectric and wind power, the country already does an impressive job in that latter regard.)

Caribbean residents know NRDC well. The organization worked closely with people in the region at the grassroots level to block attempts to turn the southern Caribbean coast over to offshore oil exploration. Such drilling would have damaged the coast's fragile mangroves, sand beaches, and coral reefs. After many years, the oil companies' proposals have, thankfully, been put to rest for good.

By Jeffrey Van Fleet

Everything about Costa Rica's Caribbean coast seems different: different culture, different history, different climate, and different activities. It is rainier here than in other parts of Costa Rica, so the region will never draw the typical fun-in-the-sun crowd that frequents the drier Pacific coast.

Never fear though: you'll find a year-round forested lushness and just as many activities at a more reasonable price. This region was long ago discovered by European adventure seekers but is much less known in North American circles.

GETTING HERE AND AROUND

You can fly daily from San José to the airstrip in Tortuguero (TTQ) or three times weekly to Barra del Colorado (BCL) via SANSA. Nature Air flies daily to Tortuguero. Nature Air also flies three times weekly to the small airport in Bocas del Toro, Panama (BOC).

Autotransportes MEPE, which has a lock on bus service to the south Caribbean coast, has a reputation for being lackadaisical, but is really quite dependable. Drivers and ticket sellers are accustomed to dealing with foreigners; even if their English is limited, they'll figure out what you want. Bus fares to this region are reasonable. From San José, expect to pay $2 to Guápiles, $4 to Limón, $7 to Cahuita, $8 to Puerto Viejo de Talamanca, and $10 to Sixaola and the Panamanian border.

If you prefer a more private form of travel, consider taking a shuttle. Gray Line Tourist Bus has daily service that departs from many San José hotels for Cahuita and Puerto Viejo de Talamanca. Tickets are $35 and must be reserved at least a day in advance. Comfortable air-conditioned Interbus vans depart from San José hotels daily for Guápiles, Siquirres, Cahuita, and Puerto Viejo de Talamanca. Reserve tickets ($35) a day in advance.

ESSENTIALS

Bus Contacts Gray Line Tourist Bus (☎ *2220–2126* 🌐 *www.graylinecostarica.com*). **Interbus** (☎ *2283–5573* 🌐 *www.interbusonline.com*).

THE NORTHERN LOWLANDS

That proverbial fork in the road presents you with a choice just beyond the immense Braulio Carrillo National Park north of San José. The highway branches at Santa Clara, having completed its descent onto the Caribbean plain. A left turn takes you north to Puerto Viejo de Sarapiquí and the forest-clad hills of the eastern slope of the Cordillera Central (⇨ *Chapter 3*). If you stay on the well-maintained main Guápiles Highway, you head southeast toward Limón and the Caribbean coast. The highway passes through sultry agricultural lowlands, home to large banana and cacao plantations, but bypasses the region's three main communities: burgeoning Guápiles and the smaller towns of Guácimo and Siquirres. You may not see any reason to stop when driving through the region—the Caribbean coast beckons, after all—but a couple of lesser-known sights might be an incentive to take a break.

GUÁPILES

60 km/38 mi northeast of San José.

Guápiles, one of the country's fastest-growing cities, is the hub of northeastern Costa Rica, and with all the facilities in town, residents of the region barely need to trek to San José anymore. The smaller town of Guácimo lies 12 km (7 mi) east on the Guápiles Highway.

GETTING HERE AND AROUND

Guápiles lies just north of Braulio Carrillo National Park and straddles the highway to the Caribbean. It's an easy one-hour drive from San José just 60 km (38 mi) to the southwest, or Limón 84 km (50 mi) to the east. Empresarios Guapileños buses connect San José's Gran Terminal del Caribe with Guápiles every hour from early morning until late evening, and provide service seven times daily to Guácimo.

9

ESSENTIALS

Bank/ATM BAC San José (✉ *Across from AyA* ☎ *2710–7434*). **Banco Nacional** (✉ *400 m east of Palí supermarket* ☎ *2713–2000*).

Hospital Hospital de Guápiles (✉ *90 m south of fire station* ☎ *2710–6801*).

Pharmacy Farmacia San Martín (✉ *Across from Palí* ☎ *2710–1115*). **Farmacia Santa Marta** (✉ *Across from Banco Nacional* ☎ *2710–6253*).

Post Office Correos (✉ *North of MUCAP*).

EXPLORING

Curious about how those tropical houseplants you have at home started out? Ornamental plant farm **Costa Flores** conducts 1½-hour English-language tours—advance reservations are required—through its gardens and facilities. (Riotously colored heliconias are a specialty here.) The tour ends at the packinghouse, where you see how plants are prepared for export. You get to create your own floral bouquet to take with you as a souvenir. ✣ *3½km/2 mi north of Guácimo on road to Río Jiménez* ☎ *2716–7645* 🎫 *$18* ⏲ *Daily 6–4.*

The nonprofit university called **EARTH** (Escuela de Agricultura de la Región Tropical Húmeda, or Agricultural School of the Humid Tropical

CLOSE UP

Rain Forest Aerial Tram

Just 15 km (9 mi) beyond the northeastern boundary of Braulio Carrillo, a 1,200-acre reserve houses a privately owned and operated engineering marvel: a series of gondolas strung together in a modified ski-lift pulley system. (To lessen the impact on the jungle, the support pylons were lowered into place by helicopter.) The tram gives you a way of seeing the rain forest canopy and its spectacular array of epiphyte plant life and birds from just above, a feat you could otherwise accomplish only by climbing the trees yourself. Though purists complain that it treats the rain forest like an amusement park, it's an entertaining way to learn the value and beauty of rain forest ecology.

The 21 gondolas hold five people each, plus a bilingual biologist-guide equipped with a walkie-talkie to request brief stops for gaping or snapping pictures. The ride covers 2½ km (1½ mi) in 80 minutes. The price includes a biologist-guided walk through the area for ground-level orientation before or after the tram ride. Several add-ons are possible, too, with frog, snake, and butterfly exhibits, a medicinal-plant garden, and a zip-line canopy tour on-site, as well as a half-day birding tour. You can arrange a personal pickup in San José for a fee; alternatively, there are public buses (on the Guápiles line) every half hour from the Gran Terminal del Caribe in San José. Drivers know the tram as the *teleférico.* Many San José tour operators make a daylong tour combining the tram with another half-day option; combos with the Britt Coffee Tour or INBioparque in Santo Domingo, both near Heredia, are especially popular. Ten rustic (no a/c or TV) but cozy cabinas (cottages) are available on-site for $94 per person. The facility operates the lodging only if at least two cabins are being rented at the same time. (Reservations are required.) Electricity shuts off after 9 PM. Cabin rates include meals, tram tours, and guided walks. A café is open to all for breakfast, lunch, and dinner. If you're traveling the Central Pacific coast, you'll find similar installations near the town of Jacó (⇨ *Chapter 7*) 3 km (2 mi) north of Supermercado Maxi Bodega, although without the accommodation, and a restaurant open for breakfast and lunch only. The admission price at the Pacific facility includes the tram ride, nature walk, snake exhibit, heliconia and medicinal plant gardens, and transport from Jacó-area hotels, as opposed to the à la carte pricing used at the Braulio Carrillo tram. The company also operates trams in the Caribbean-island nations of Jamaica, Dominica, and St. Lucia, all outside the scope of this book.

Reservations: ✉Teleférico del Bosque Lluvioso, Avda. 7 at C. 7, San José ☎2257–5961, 866/759–8726 in North America 🌐www.rainforestrams.com 🎫$55, $27.50 for children under 12; $100, $72.50 for children under 12, includes round-trip transportation to the site from San José hotels 🕘Tours: Mon. 9–4, Tues.–Sun. 6:30–4. Call for reservations 6 AM–9:30 PM 💳AE, D, DC, MC, V.

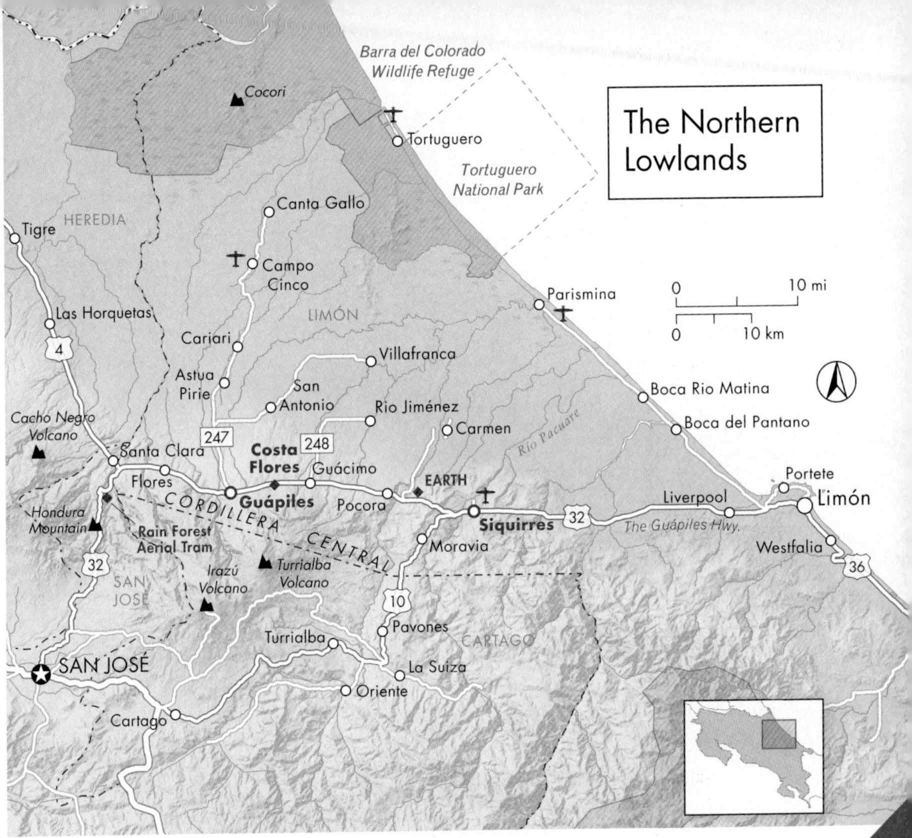

Region) researches the production of less pesticide–dependent bananas and other forms of sustainable tropical agriculture, as well as medicinal plants. The university graduates some 100 students from Latin America and Africa each year. EARTH's elegant stationery, calendars, and other paper products are made from banana stems, tobacco leaves, and coffee leaves and grounds, and are sold at the on-site Oropéndola store and in many tourist shops around the country. The property encompasses a banana plantation and a forest reserve with nature trails. Half-day tours are $15; full-day, $25; and lunch is $12 for day visitors. Though priority is given to researchers and conference groups, you're welcome to stay in the school's 50-person lodging facility, with private bathrooms, hot water, and ceiling fans, for $65 a night, which includes the use of a swimming pool and exercise equipment. The site is a bird-watchers' favorite; some 250 species have been spotted here. Reservations are required. ✉ *Pocora de Guácimo* ✣ *15 km/9 mi east of Guápiles on Guápiles Hwy.* 📫 *Apdo. 4442–1000, San José* ☎ *2713–0000* 🌐 *www.earth.ac.cr.*

Rainforest trams are a great way to experience the Braulio Carrillo National Park.

SIQUIRRES

28 km/17 mi east of Guápiles.

Its name is a corruption of the words *Si quieres* (if you want), fittingly impassive for this lackluster town. It anchors a fertile banana- and pineapple-growing region, and marks the transition point between the agricultural lowlands and the tropical, palm-laden coast. Siquirres has the unfortunate historical distinction of having once been the westernmost point to which Afro-Caribbean people could migrate. Costa Rica implemented the law in the late 1880s—when large numbers of Afro-Caribbeans immigrated (mainly from Jamaica) to construct the Atlantic Railroad—but abolished it in the 1949 constitution.

GETTING HERE

Siquirres lies just off the main highway and is easily accessible from the east, west, or south (if you're arriving from Turrialba). Autotransportes Caribeños buses connect San José's Gran Terminal del Caribe with Siquirres several times daily.

ESSENTIALS

Bank/ATM Banco Nacional (*✉ 50 m south of Acón gas station ☎ 2768–8128*).

Medical Clinic Centro de Salud de Siquirres (*✉ East side of soccer field ☎ 2768–6138*).

Pharmacy Farmacia Santa Lucía (*✉ 50 m west of fire station ☎ 2768–9304*).

Post Office Correos (*✉ Next to Guardia Rural*).

EXPLORING

Pineapples don't get the same attention in world circles as Costa Rican coffee and bananas, but the **Agri Tours Pineapple Tour** (⊠*On highway* ✣*7 km/4 mi east of Siquirres* ☎*2282–1316 in San José* 🌐*www.agritourscr.com*), affiliated with Del Monte Foods, can acquaint you with the life and times of this lesser-known crop, from cultivation to drying and packing at a farm just east of town. The two-hour tour is $17, samples included. Call to make a reservation.

OUTDOOR ACTIVITIES

RAFTING ★ Siquirres's proximity to the put-in sites of several classic rafting excursions makes it an ideal place to begin a trip. Old standby **Ríos Tropicales** (⊠*On the highway in Siquirres* ☎*2233–6455, 866/722–8273 in North America* 🌐*www.riostropicales.com*) has tours on a Class III to IV section of the Pacuare River between Siquirres and San Martín, as well as the equally difficult section between Tres Equis and Siquirres. Not quite so wild, but still with Class III rapids, is the nearby Florida section of the Reventazón. Day excursions normally begin in San José, but if you're out in this part of the country, you can kick off your excursion here at the company's operations center in Siquirres.

THE NORTHERN CARIBBEAN COAST

Some compare these dense layers of green set off by brilliantly colored flowers—a vision doubled by the jungle's reflection in mirror-smooth canals—to the Amazon. That might be stretching it, but there's still an Indiana Jones mystique to the journey up here, especially when you get off the main canals and into the narrower lagoons. The region remains one of those Costa Rican anomalies: roadless and remote, it's nevertheless one of the country's most-visited places. The tourism seasons here are defined not by the rains or lack thereof (it's wet most of the year) but by the months of prime turtle hatching in Tortuguero, or by what's biting in sportfishing paradise Barra del Colorado.

In 1970 a system of canals running parallel to the shoreline was constructed to provide safer access to the region than the dangerous journey up the seacoast. You can continue up the canals, natural and man-made, that begin in Moín, near Limón, and run all the way to Tortuguero and beyond to the less-visited Barra del Colorado Wildlife Refuge. Or you can embark at various points north of Guápiles and Siquirres, as do public transportation and most of the package tours. (The lodges' minivans bring you from San José to the put-in point, where you continue your journey by boat.)

TORTUGUERO

North of the national park of the same name, the hamlet of Tortuguero is a pleasant little place with 600 inhabitants, two churches, three bars, a handful of souvenir shops, and a growing selection of inexpensive lodgings. (And one more plus: there are no motor vehicles here, a refreshing change from the traffic woes that plague the rest of Costa Rica.) You can also take a stroll on the 32-km (20-mi) beach,

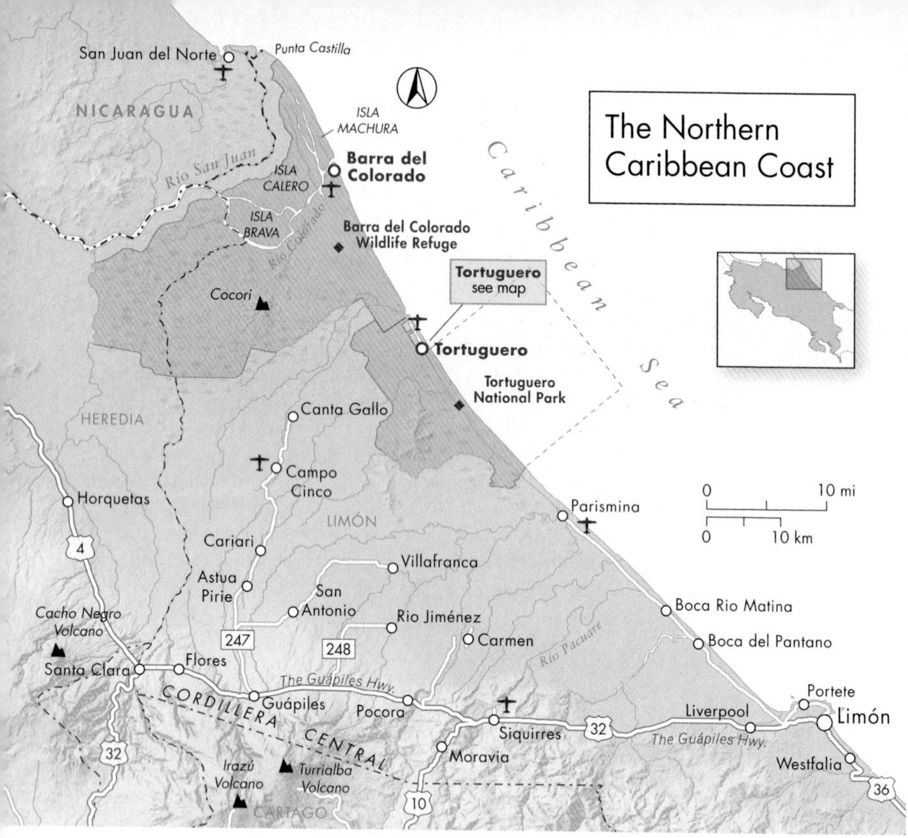

but swimming is not recommended because of strong riptides and large numbers of bull sharks and barracuda.

The stretch of beach between the Colorado and Matina rivers was first mentioned as a nesting ground for sea turtles in a 1592 Dutch chronicle. Nearly a century earlier, Christopher Columbus compared traversing the north Caribbean coast and its swimming turtles to navigating through rocks. Because the area is so isolated—there's no road here to this day—the turtles nested undisturbed for centuries. By the mid-1900s, however, the harvesting of eggs and poaching of turtles had reached such a level that these creatures faced extinction. In 1963 an executive decree regulated the hunting of turtles and the gathering of eggs, and in 1970 the government established Tortuguero National Park; modern Tortuguero bases its economy on tourism.

GETTING HERE AND AROUND

It's easier than you'd think to get to remote Tortuguero. Flying is the quickest (and most expensive) option. SANSA and Nature Air provide early-morning flights to and from San José. SANSA agent **Victor Barrantes** (☎*2709–8055 or 8838–6330*) meets both planes—they arrive and depart within 15 minutes of each other—and offers boat-taxi service to and from town for $3. Call and confirm with him the day before if you need a ride. If you're staying at one of the lodges, its boat will meet you at the airstrip.

The big lodges all have packages that include transportation to and from San José along with lodging, meals, and tours. Guide-staffed minivans pick you up at your San José hotel and drive you to the put-in site, usually somewhere north of Siquirres, where you board a covered boat for the final leg on the canals to Tortuguero. The trip up entails sightseeing and animal-viewing. The trip back to San José stops only for a lunch break. This is the classic "leave the driving to them" way to get to Tortuguero.

NICARAGUA CANAL?

During the 1840s California gold rush, the Río San Juan became an important crossroads allowing miners and gold to move between New York and San Francisco some 70 years before the Panama Canal opened. Cornelius Vanderbilt financed the dredging of the waterway to allow ships to pass up the river to Lake Nicaragua. From here a rail line connected to the Pacific Ocean. As the Panama Canal ages, there is again talk of resurrecting this "wet-dry" canal. So far, plans remain on the drawing board.

A boat from the port of Moín, near Limón, is the traditional budget method of getting to Tortuguero if you are already on the Caribbean coast. Arrive at the docks by 9 AM and you should be able to find someone to take you there. The going price is $30 per person one way, $50 round-trip, and travel time is about three hours. **Alexis Soto and Sebastián Torres** (☎*900/296–2626 beeper*) partner to provide a reliable boat service between Moín and Tortuguero for about $50 round-trip. Arrange in advance. If you arrive in Moín in your own vehicle, JAPDEVA, Costa Rica's Atlantic port authority, operates a secure, guarded parking facility for your car while you are in Tortuguero.

It's entirely possible to make the trip independently from San José, a good option if you are staying in the village rather than at a lodge. A direct bus departs from San José's Gran Terminal del Caribe to Cariari, north of Guápiles, at 9 AM. At Cariari, disembark and walk five blocks to the local terminal, where you can board a noon bus for the small crossroads of La Pavona. From here, boats leave at 1:30 PM to take you to Tortuguero, arriving around 3 PM. The Cariari–La Pavona–Tortuguero bus-boat service is provided by **COOPETRACA** (☎*2767–7137*) or **Viajes Clic-Clic** (☎*2709–8155, 8844–0463, or 8308–2006*) for $10 one way. La Pavona has secure parking facilities. **■ TIP→Avoid Rubén Bananero, a company that provides bus-boat transport from Cariari via an inconvenient route through the Geest banana plantation.** They begin to hustle you the minute you get off the bus in Cariari, insisting the La Pavona route does not exist. They also require that you buy a round-trip ticket, limiting your return options, and do everything they can to steer you toward hotels that pay them a commission. Others will also try to take you to their own dedicated "information dock" in the village, steering you toward their own guides. If you've made advance reservations for guides or hotels, stand your ground and say "*No, gracias.*"

Water taxis provide transport from multiple points in the village to the lodges. Expect to pay about $2 to $3 per trip.

ESSENTIALS

Internet La Casona (*North side of soccer field 2709–8092*).

Visitor Information Kiosk (*Town center Information on the town's history, the park, turtles, and other wildlife; unstaffed booth with free brochures*). **Tortuguero Information Center** (*Across from Catholic church 2709–8011 or 8833–0827 tortugueroinfo@yahoo.com*).

EXPLORING

Fodor's Choice ★ **Tortuguero National Park.** The name Tortuguero means "turtle region," and what better place to see sea turtles and observe the age-old cycle of these magnificent animals nesting, hatching and scurrying to the ocean? *2710–2929 or 2710–2939 $10 Daily 6–6.*

DID YOU KNOW? **Some people still believe turtle eggs to be an aphrodisiacal delicacy, and some bars (illegally) serve them as snacks. It's a big part of the human contribution to turtles' disappearance.**

The **Caribbean Conservation Corporation** (*CCC*) runs a visitor center and a museum with excellent animal photos, a video narrating local and natural history, and detailed discussions of the latest ecological goings-on and what you can do to help. There's a souvenir shop next door. For the committed ecotourist, the **John H. Phipps Biological Field Station,** affiliated with the CCC, has camping areas and dorm-style quarters with a communal kitchen. If you want to get involved in the life of the turtles, helping researchers to track turtle migration (current research, using satellite technology, has tracked turtles as far as the Florida Keys), or helping to catalog the population of neotropical migrant birds, arrange a stay in advance through the center. *From beach, walk north along path and watch for sign Apdo. 246–2050, San Pedro 2709–8091, 800/678–7853 in North America www.cccturtle.org $1 Mon.–Sat. 8–4, Sun. 9–5.*

OUTDOOR ACTIVITIES

Tortuguero is one of those "everybody's a guide" places. Quality varies, but most guides are quite knowledgeable. If you stay at one of the lodges, guided tours are *usually* included in your package price (check when you book). If you hire a private guide, $5 per person per hour is the going rate, with most excursions lasting three hours.

TOUR GUIDES AND OPERATORS Call or stop by the visitor center at the **Caribbean Conservation Corporation** (*2709–8091, 2297–5510 in San José www.cccturtle.org*) to get a recommendation for good local guides.

★ **Daryl Loth** (*8833–0827 or 2709–8011 safari@racsa.co.cr*) has a wealth of information about the area and conducts boat excursions on the canals and responsible turtle-watching tours in season with advance notice. **Victor Barrantes** (*2709–8055 or 8838–6330 tortuguero_info@racsa.co.cr*) is the local SANSA agent who conducts hiking tours to Cerro Tortuguero and around the area when he's not meeting the early-morning flights.

Hotels ▼

Casa Marbella	8
Evergreen Lodge	6
Laguna Lodge	2
Manatus Hotel	4
Mawamba Lodge	5
Pachira Lodge	7
Somoa Lodge	3
Tortuga Lodge	1

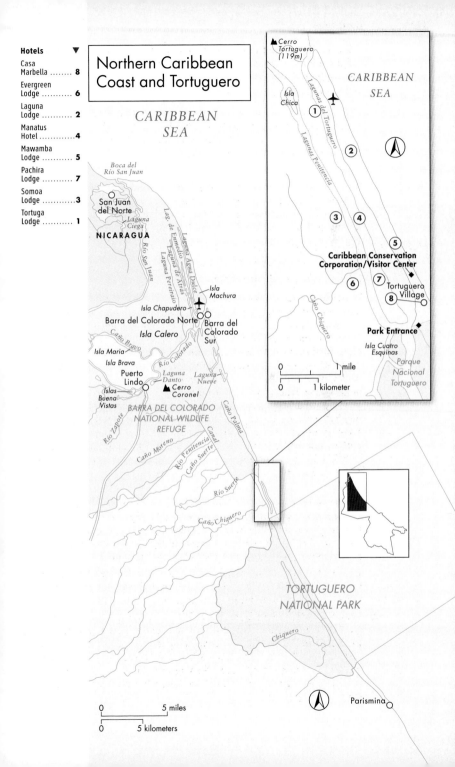

Northern Caribbean Coast and Tortuguero

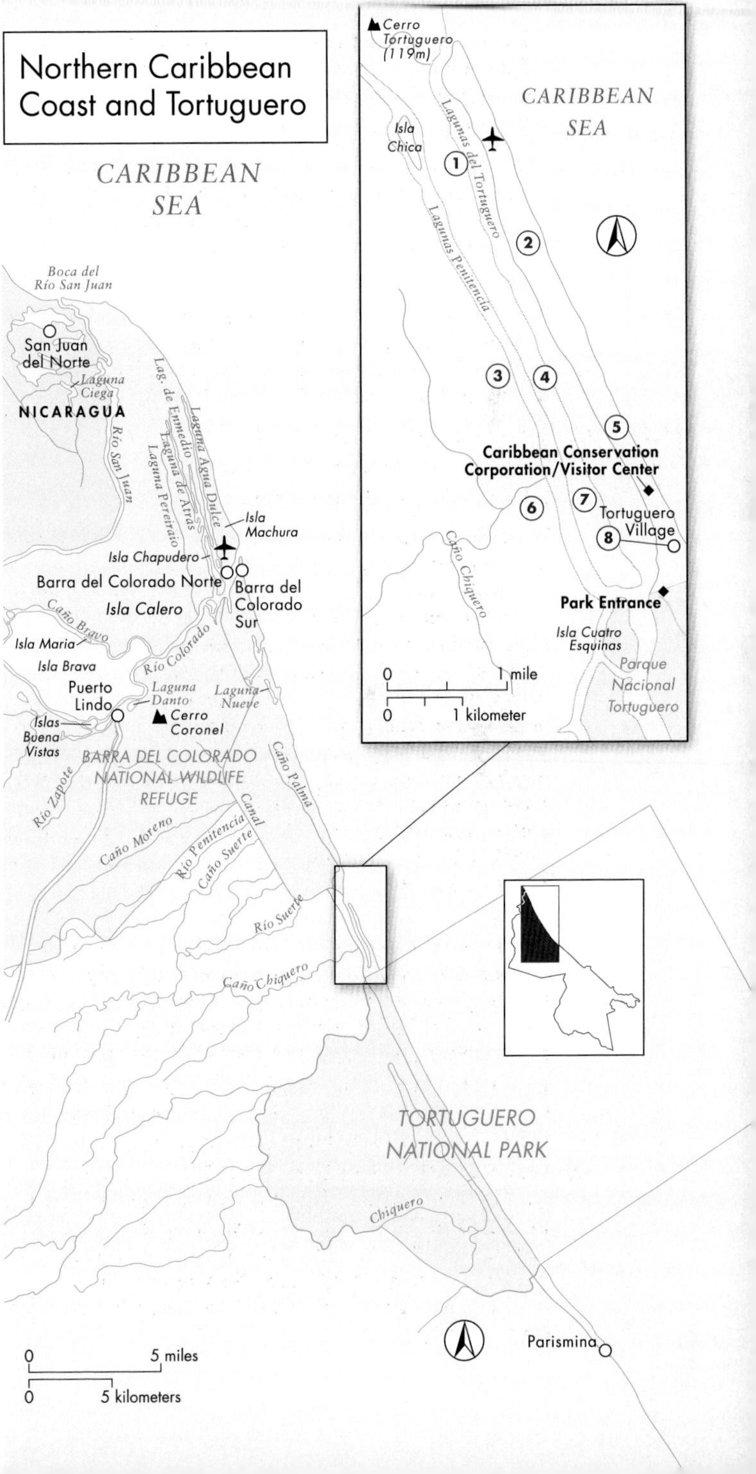

FISHING You have your choice of mackerel, tarpon, snook, and snapper if you fish in the ocean; snook and calba if you fish in the canals. If you opt for the latter, the National Parks Service levies a $30 license fee (you are fishing in the confines of Tortuguero National Park), good for one month. Operators add the fee to your price.

CAUTION

Wear mosquito repellent in low-lying coastal areas, where a few cases of dengue have been reported.

Longtime area fishing expert **Eddie Brown** (☎*2710–8016*) is based out of Tortuga Lodge and has daylong fishing packages for $500. **Elvin Gutiérrez** (☎*2709–8115* 🌐*www.tortuguerosportsfishing.com*), known as "Primo" to everyone in town, takes two passengers out for two hours or more, at $75 per hour, or for a full nine-hour day ($500). Prices include boat, motor, guide, and refreshments.

TURTLE-WATCHING If you want to watch the *deshove* (egg laying), contact your hotel or the parks office to hire a certified local guide, required on turtle-watching excursions. Note that you won't be allowed to use a camera—flash or nonflash—on the beach, and only your guide is permitted to use a flashlight (and that must be covered with red plastic), because lights can deter the turtles from nesting. ■**TIP**➔A few unscrupulous locals will offer to take you on a turtle-watching tour outside the allowed February-through-November season, disturbing sensitive nesting sites in the process. If it's not the season, don't go on a turtle excursion. As the signs around town admonish: DON'T BECOME ANOTHER PREDATOR.

WHERE TO EAT

The big lodges here offer one- or two-night excursion packages. (Given the choreography it takes to get up here, opt for a more leisurely two-night stay if you can.) Rates are expensive, but prices include everything from guides, tours, meals, and snacks to minivan and boat transport, and in some cases air transport to and from San José. If you stop and calculate what you get, the price may not be as bad as it first seems, and the tours are undeniably great fun. Usually *not* included in package prices? Alcoholic beverages, soda, bottled water, and the $10 entrance to Tortuguero National Park. Ask to be sure. Few of the lodges have phones, although all have radio contact with the outside world. All reservations must be made with their offices in San José. Be sure to travel light; you get a baggage allowance of 25 pounds, usually strictly enforced. There's just no space in the boats for you to bring more.

$ ITALIAN ✕**Budda Café.** Hip was never a word that went hand in hand with Tortuguero, but this place has changed the rules. Pizza, crepes, pastas, and fresh fish are on the menu at this small, canal-side café in the center of town. Lattice wood over the windows, a thatched roof, and of course, a Buddha statue make up the furnishings. Jazzy cha-cha or a Dean Martin ballad might be playing in the background. ✉*Next to police station, Tortuguero village* ☎*2709–8084* ▭*No credit cards* ⏲*Closed Wed.*

$ COSTA RICAN ✕**Miss Junie.** Longtime Tortuguero doyenne Miss Junie has supposedly retired as the village's best-known cook, a tradition she learned at her mother's knee more than a half century ago, but still can be seen in the

DID YOU KNOW?

Manatees also live in Tortuguero's canals, but they're slow moving and often hit by motorboats. Manatees are herbivores at eat up to 150 pounds of plants a day. They're also notorious for having gas, so keep your eyes peeled for bubbles in the water and drive slowly.

kitchen of the open-air restaurant adjoining her home. (Fidel Castro and Che Guevara were among the early diners here.) Selection is limited, and reservations are required, but you can usually count on a chicken, beef, or fish platter with rice and beans simmered in coconut milk. Your meal includes a beverage and dessert. ✉ *150 m north of Para so Tropical, Tortuguero village* ☎ *2709–8102* ✍ *Reservations essential* ▭ *No credit cards.*

PACKAGE DEALS

Be sure to ask lodges about two-day/one-night packages. They often offer discounted rates for two people.

¢ CAFE ✕ **The Vine Bakery.** Pastas, pizzas, and sandwiches are on the menu, but this small bakery and coffee shop is also a great place to stop for breads made with banana, carrot, and *natilla* (cream), for example. ✉ *25 m north of Catholic church, Tortuguero village* ☎ *2709–8132* ▭ *No credit cards* ⏲ *No dinner.*

WHERE TO STAY

¢–$ Fodor'sChoice ★ **Casa Marbella.** This bed-and-breakfast, the best of the in-town lodgings, is a real find. Canadian owner and naturalist Daryl Loth is a respected authority on all things Tortuguero, and one of the community's biggest boosters. If he's unable to take you out in his boat himself, he'll find someone who can. Immaculate rooms have tile floors and varnished-wood finishing with vaulted ceilings and skylights in the bathrooms. Ample breakfasts are served on the covered back patio facing the lodging's own private canal dock. The terrace is also a relaxing place for a coffee break on a rainy afternoon. There's a small kitchenette for your use. **Pros:** knowledgeable owner; immaculate rooms. **Cons:** some street noise; no access to lodge-package amenities of big lodges. ✉ *Across from Catholic church, Tortuguero village* ☎ *2709–8011* 🌐 *casamarbella.tripod.com* *8 rooms* *In-room: no a/c, no phone, no TV* ▭ *No credit cards* *BP.*

$$$$ Fodor'sChoice ★ **Evergreen Lodge.** Owned by the Pachira Lodge people, the Evergreen offers an entirely different (and intimate) concept in Tortuguero lodging: whereas other lodges have cabins arranged around a clearing, at Evergreen they penetrate deep into the forest. A network of walking trails extends to Canal Chiquerito, the third waterway inland. Cabins are made from deep-red almond wood or gypsum wood. All have one double and one single, as well as venetian blinds for privacy. Honeymooners make up a substantial portion of the clientele here. Watch for the whimsical ANT CROSSING signs as you walk around the grounds. **Pros:** seclusion from other lodges; lush wooded setting. **Cons:** rustic rooms; farther from town than other lodges. ✥ *2 km/1 mi from Tortuguero village on Canal Penitencia* *Apdo. 1818–1002, San José* ☎ *2257–7742, 800/644–7438 in North America* 🌐 *www.evergreentortuguero.com* *36 cabins* *In-room: no a/c, no phone, no TV. In-hotel: restaurant, bar* ▭ *AE, D, DC, MC, V* *AI.*

$$$$ **Laguna Lodge.** Laguna is the largest of the Tortuguero lodges, and it hums with activity. Jam-packed package tours begin in San José and embark from boats at Caño Blanco, north of Siquirres. A mix of concrete and wood buildings spread out over 12 acres of grounds on a thin

sliver of land between the ocean and the first canal inland. Rooms have wood paneling and floors, and tiled bathrooms. The property includes a butterfly garden and a small network of trails through secondary forest. Meals are served buffet-style at the open-air restaurant that extends out over the canal. The snazzy combo reception–gift shop–meeting room building seems to have sprung straight from the mind of Gaudí. **Pros:** many activities; unique architecture. **Cons:** large numbers of guests; not for those who crave anonymity. ☎*2709–8082, 2272–4943 in San José* 🌐*www.lagunatortuguero.com* *80 rooms* *In-room: no a/c, no phone, no TV. In-hotel: 2 restaurants, bars, pool, laundry service, Internet terminal* ▭*AE, D, DC, MC, V* *AI.*

$$$$ **Manatus Hotel.** Take one longtime budget lodging, give it a makeover worthy of a television reality show, reincarnate it as Tortuguero's luxurious hotel, and you've got yourself Manatus Hotel. Amenities such as air-conditioning, massage, and television are simply not found up here, but Manatus has them. Bright rooms with large windows each have two four-post queen-size beds with flowered quilted spreads, all under vaulted ceilings. Packages include round-trip van and boat transportation from San José, as well as all meals in the snazzy riverside restaurant. **Pros:** intimate surroundings; numerous creature comforts. **Cons:** fills up quickly in high season; degree of luxury may feel out of place in Tortuguero. *Across river, about 1 km/½mi north of Tortuguero* ☎*2709–8197, 2239–4854 in San José* 🌐*www.manatuscostarica.com* *12 rooms* *In-room: no phone, refrigerator. In-hotel: restaurant, room service, bar, pool, gym, laundry service* ▭*AE, D, DC, MC, V* *AI.*

$$$$ ★ **Mawamba Lodge.** Nestled between the river and the ocean, Mawamba is the perfect place to kick back and relax. It is also the only jungle lodge within walking distance (about 10 minutes) of town. Packages include transport from San José; when you arrive at the river town of Matina, you're whisked into a launch for a 2½-hour ride to a 15-acre site with comfortable (hot water!) rustic cabinas with bright colors and garden views. Meals are taken in the spacious dining room, and are included in the price, along with transfers and guided tours of the jungle and canals; trips to turtle-heavy beaches cost $10 extra. Packages begin at $263 per person. **Pros:** many activities; walking distance to village. **Cons:** rustic rooms; not for those who crave anonymity. *½km/¼mi north of Tortuguero on ocean side of canal* *Apdo. 10980–1000, San José* ☎*2293–8181 in San José* 🌐*www.grupomawamba.com* *58 cabinas* *In-room: no a/c, no phone, no TV. In-hotel: restaurant, bar, pool, beachfront, laundry service, Internet terminal* ▭*AE, D, DC, MC, V* *AI.*

$$$$ Fodor's Choice ★ **Pachira Lodge.** This is the prettiest of Tortuguero's lodges, but not the costliest. Each almond-wood cabina in the lush, well-manicured gardens contains four guest rooms with high ceilings, king-size beds, and bamboo furniture. The stunning pool is shaped like a giant sea turtle: the head is a whirlpool tub, the left paw is a wading pool, and the right paw is equipped for swimmers with disabilities. There is no cross-river transportation into town. Package deals include transport from San José, a jungle tour, and all meals; rates begin at $209 per person. Pachira

9

"Cruising down the canal in Tortuguero Park, we discovered this emerald basilisk, a magnificient looking creature." —photo by Liz Stuart, Fodors.com member

is known for being the most competitive marketer of the lodges here, and the place is often full. **Pros:** many activities; good value. **Cons:** large numbers of guests; can be difficult to find space; not for those who crave anonymity. ✉ *Across river from Mawamba Lodge* 📫 *Apdo. 1818–1002, San José* ☎ *2223–1682 in San José, 800/644–7438 in North America* 🌐 *www.pachiralodge.com* ⇨ *88 rooms* 👍 *In-room: no a/c, no phone, no TV. In-hotel: restaurant, bar, pool, laundry service* 💳 *AE, MC, V* 🍽 *AI.*

$$$$ **Samoa Lodge.** A location on the inland side of the second canal in from the ocean gives this place plenty of room to spread out, and indeed, a network of hiking trails on the lodge's grounds is one of the attractions here. Buildings are scattered around manicured gardens and contain rooms with vaulted ceilings, all with either one double and one single bed or three single beds. **Pros:** seclusion from other lodges; ample grounds; network of hiking trails. **Cons:** rustic rooms; farther from town than other lodges. ✣ *2 km/1 mi from Tortuguero village on Canal Penitencia* 📫 *Apdo. 10736–1000, San José* ☎ *2258–6244 in San José* 🌐 *www.samoalodge.com* 👍 *In-room: no a/c, no phone, no TV. In-hotel: restaurant, bar, pool, no-smoking rooms* 💳 *AE, D, DC, MC, V* 🍽 *AI.*

$$$$ ★ **Tortuga Lodge.** Lush lawns, orchids, and tropical trees surround this thatched riverside lodge owned by Costa Rica Expeditions and renowned for its nature packages and top-notch, personalized service. Tortuga sets itself apart with its smaller size, and markets itself to a higher-budget clientele than do its major competitors here (Laguna, Mawamba, and Pachira). Tortuga's packages all include its own charter

flights to Tortuguero rather than the land/boat combos from San José used by the other lodges. Guest rooms are comfortable, with much-appreciated mosquito blinds. The penthouse suite, with two king-size beds and an extra smaller bed, has ample room for a family. The chefs do an excellent job preparing hearty food, which is served family-style rather than in a buffet line as at other lodges. Tortuguero National Park is 20 minutes south by boat. **Pros:** many activities; seclusion from other lodges. **Cons:** rustic rooms; farther from park than most lodges here. ✉*Across the river from airstrip* ✣*2 km/1 mi from Tortuguero* ☎*2710–8016, 2257–0766 in San José* 🌐*www.costaricaexpeditions.com* *26 rooms* *In-room: no a/c, no phone, no TV. In-hotel: restaurant, bar, pool, laundry service* ▭*AE, MC, V* 🍴*FAP.*

BARRA DEL COLORADO

Up the coast from Tortuguero is the ramshackle hamlet of Barra del Colorado, a popular sportfishing hub characterized by plain stilted wooden houses, dirt paths, and a complete absence of motorized land vehicles (though some locals have added motors to their hand-hewn canoes).

EXPLORING

Bordered to the north by the Río San Juan and the frontier with Nicaragua is the vast, 905-square-km (350-square-mi) **Barra del Colorado Wildlife Refuge***(Refugio Nacional de Vida Silvestre Barra del Colorado)*, Costa Rica's largest reserve, and really the only local attraction for non-anglers. Most people arrange trips here through their lodge. Transportation once you get here is almost exclusively waterborne, as there are virtually no paths in this swampy terrain. The list of species that you're likely to see from your boat is almost the same as that for Tortuguero; the main difference here is the feeling of being farther off the beaten track. You can realistically get as far as the 640,000-acre **Río Indio-Maíz Biological Reserve** when crossing the border here. The reserve is a continuation of the Barra del Colorado Wildlife Refuge, but in Nicaraguan territory. ✣*30 km/18 mi north of Tortuguero* ☎*No phone* *Free* ⏲*24 hrs.*

9

TO AND FROM BARRA DEL COLORADO

25 km/16 mi northwest of Tortuguero.

SANSA and Nature Air have very early morning flights from San José. You're likely staying at a fishing lodge if you come this far, and a representative will meet your flight and escort you to your lodge and back.

THE SOUTHERN CARIBBEAN COAST

The landscape along the Guápiles Highway changes from farmland to tropics as you approach the port city of Limón. Place names change, too. You'll see signs to towns called Bristol, Stratford, and Liverpool, reflecting the region's British Caribbean heritage. European backpackers discovered tourist towns par excellence Cahuita and Puerto Viejo de Talamanca; now visitors of all nationalities and budgets flock there.

LIMÓN

100 km/62 mi southeast of Guápiles, 160 km/100 mi north and east of San José.

The colorful Afro-Caribbean flavor of one of Costa Rica's most important ports (population 90,000) is the first sign of life for seafaring visitors to Costa Rica's east coast. Christopher Columbus was the first tourist here: he dropped anchor on his final voyage to the New World in 1502. Limón (sometimes called "Puerto Limón") is a lively, if shabby, town with a 24-hour street life. The wooden houses are brightly painted, but the grid-plan streets look rather worn, partly because of the damage caused by a 1991 earthquake. Street crime, including pickpocketing and nighttime mugging, is not uncommon here. Long charged with neglecting the city, the national government has now turned attention to Limón. New businesses are coming in, a positive sign of urban renewal, and the town has beefed up security with a more visible police presence.

Limón receives thousands of visitors every year, owing in large part to its newest incarnation as a port of call. Carnival, Celebrity, Holland America, Princess, and Royal Caribbean cruise ships all dock here on certain of their Panama Canal or Western Caribbean itineraries. The downtown Terminal de Cruceros hums with activity between October and May, with one or two boats each day December through March, but many fewer outside those peak months. This is the place to find telephones, Internet cafés, manicurists (they do quite a brisk business), a tourist-information booth, and tour-operator stands, too. Downtown shopkeepers have all learned how to convert their colón prices to dollars, and post the day's exchange rate. St. Thomas or Puerto Vallarta it is not—perhaps someday, residents hope—but Limón has a tourist vibe these days that the city has never before experienced. The terminal contains souvenir stands staffed by low-key vendors who invite you to look, but don't pester you if your answer is "*No, gracias.*"

NAVIGATING LIMÓN

Avenidas (avenues) run east and west, and *calles* (streets) north and south, but Limón's street-numbering system differs from that of other Costa Rican cities. "Number one" of each avenida and calle begins at the water and numbers increase sequentially as you move inland, unlike the evens-on-one-side, odds-on-the-other scheme used in San José. But the scarcity of street signs means everyone uses landmarks anyway. Official red taxis ply the streets, or wait at designated taxi stands near Parque Vargas, the Mercado Municipal, and the cruise-ship terminal.

GETTING HERE AND AROUND

If you're coming to the Caribbean coast, you'll pass through Limón. The Guápiles Highway that began in San José ends here at the ocean, but bypasses the heart of downtown by a couple of blocks. Budget about 3½ hours for the trip. Just after the sign to SIXAOLA and the coastal highway south to Cahuita and Puerto Viejo de Talamanca is the city center. The main bus terminal lies at Avenida 2 and Calle 8, across from the soccer stadium, and serves routes from San José, Guápiles, and Siquirres, with buses arriving several times daily from each. Opt for the *directo* (express) service from San José rather than the *corriente* buses, which

Continued on page 551

It was so awesome to see this huge dorado (mahi-mahi) my husband boated with help from a great first mate. – janenicole, Fodors.com member

SPORTFISHING

by Elizabeth Goodwin

Adventurous anglers flock to Costa Rica to test their will—and patience—against an assortment of feisty fresh- and saltwater fish. Just remember: catch-and-release is sometimes expected, so the pleasure's all in the pursuit.

With so many options the hardest decision is where to go. Inshore fishing in the country's rivers and lakes yields roosterfish, snapper, barracuda, jacks, and snook. Fly-fishing afficiondas love the extra-large tarpon and snook because of their sheer size and fight. The country's coasts swarm with a multitude of bigger game, including the majestic billfish that Hemingway made famous—the marlin and the sailfish.

There are a multitude of top-notch fishing outfitters up and down both coasts and around rivers and lakes, so planning a fishing trip is easy. We list our favorites throughout the book under Outdoor Activities. Charter boats range from 22 feet to 60 feet in length. With a good captain, a boat in the 22- to 26-foot range for up to three anglers can cost from $500 to $750 a day. A 28- to 32-foot boat fits four and costs from $800 to $1,200 per day. A boat for six people costs $1,400 to $1,800 and measures between 36 and 47 feet. A 60-foot boat for up to ten anglers costs about $3,000 a day. A good charter boat company employs experienced captains and offers good equipment, bait, and food and beverages.

CHOOSING A DESTINATION

Costa Rica teems with a constant supply of *pescado* (fish), some of which might seem unique to North Americans. Below are some local catches and where you'll find them.

A local fisherman in Puerto Viejo.
xelas, fodors.com member.

Barra del Colorado *(See Chapter 9)* is a popular sportfishing hub and a great departure point for freshwater fishing on the Caribbean side of the country. Fly fishers looking for the ultimate challenge head to **San Juan River** for its legendary tarpon. The **Colorado River** lures anglers with jack, tuna, snook, tarpon, and dorado. Transportation and tours can be arranged by the hotels listed in **Puerto Viejo de Sarapiquí** and **Las Horquetas** *(See Chapter 4)*.

Lake Arenal and **Caño Negro Lagoon** are also great freshwater spots to snag extra-large tarpon, snook, and the ugly-but-fascinating guapote bass. Start your fishing journey in nearby **La Fortuna** *(See Chapter 5)*.

On the Pacific side, **Tamarindo** is the main departure point for anglers looking to find big game, including tuna, roosterfish, and marlin. Boats also leave

from **Playas del Coco, Ocotal, Tambor,** and **Flamingo Beach**, which are best fished May through August. All are close to the well-stocked northern Papagayo Gulf. If you're hunting sailfish and marlin between December and April, head to the Central Pacific coast around **Los Sueños** and **Quepos**, where up to 10 sailfish are caught per boat *(See Chapters 6 and 7)*. The southern Pacific towns, like **Puerto Jimenez, Golfito,** and **Zancudo,** are less developed than the other Pacific regions and are famous for their excellent inshore fishing for snapper and roosterfish, though offshore big game is also good in the area, especially November through January *(See Chapter 8)*.

FISHING LICENSE

Costa Rica requires that all anglers have a valid Costa Rica fishing license. You can usually pick one up at the dock entrance on the morning of your first day of fishing for $24.00. It's good for one year from the date of purchase. Keep in mind that, many charters do not fold this into their costs because license enforcement is lax and it is occasionally difficult to track down people who sell fishing licenses. You may want to ask about this before you head out.

(top) Osa Peninsula, (bottom left) *Plat de jour* is Wahoo, (bottom right) School of Tarpon

THE FISH YOU'LL FIND

By law billfish are catch-and-release only.

GASPAR (alligator gar), found in Barra del Colorado River and Lake Arenal, looks like a holdover from prehistoric times and has a long narrow snout full of sharp teeth; they make great sport on light tackle. Gar meat is firm and sweet (some say shrimplike), but the eggs are toxic to humans.

Snook

MARLIN AND SAILFISH migrate northward through the year, beginning about November, when they are plentiful in the Golfito region. From December into April they spread north to Quepos, which has some of the country's best deep-sea fishing, and are present in large numbers along the Nicoya Peninsula at Carrillo and Sámara from February to April, and near Tamarindo and Flamingo from May to September. Pacific sailfish average more than 45 kilos (100 pounds), and are usually fought on a 15-pound line or less. Costa Rican laws require that all sails be released and bans sportsfishers from bringing them on board for photo ops.

Sailfish

GUAPOTE (rainbow bass) make their home in Lake Arenal. It's a hard-hitting catch: 5- to 6-pounders are common. Taxonomically, guapote are not related to bass, but are caught similarly, by casting or flipping plugs or spinner bait. Streams near the Cerro de la Muerte, off the Pan-American Highway leading south from San José, are stocked with guapote. The fish tend to be small, but the scenery makes a day here worthwhile.

TARPON AND SNOOK fishing are big on the Caribbean coast, centered at the mouth of the Barra del Colorado River. The acrobatic tarpon, which averages about 38 kilos (85 pounds) here, is able to swim freely between salt water and freshwater and is considered by many to be the most exciting catch on earth. Tarpon sometimes strike like a rocket, hurtling 5 meters (16 feet) into the air, flipping, and twisting left and right. Anglers say the success rate of experts is to land about 1 out of every 10 tarpon hooked. In the Colorado, schools of up to 100 tarpon following and feeding on schools of titi (small, sardinelike fish) travel for more than 160 km (100 mi) to Lake Nicaragua. The long-standing International Game Fishing Association all-tackle record was taken in this area.

WHEN TO GO

In Costa Rica, you're guaranteed a few good catches no matter what the season, as demonstrated by the cadre of sportsmen who circle the coasts year-round chasing that perfect catch. If your heart is set on an area or a type of fish, do your research ahead of time and plan accordingly.

CLOSE UP

The Nicas

Immigration issues generate intense debate in the United States and Western Europe. Who would guess that it has become a contentious matter here in Costa Rica, too? Over the past four decades, war, poverty, dictatorship, revolution, earthquakes, and hurricanes have beset Nicaragua, Costa Rica's northern neighbor. Each new calamity has brought a wave of refugees fleeing south. Approximations vary—no one can know for sure—but high-end estimates guess that 20% of Costa Rica's population today is Nicaraguan. Speaking with a faster, more clipped accent than Costa Ricans, they do not fade into the scenery.

The refrain among Ticos is a familiar one: "They're taking our jobs!" Yet, truth be told, Nicaraguans are performing the low-end labor that Costa Ricans just won't do anymore: your hotel chambermaid may likely be Nicaraguan; the glitzy resort where you're staying was probably built with the sweat of many Nicaraguan construction workers; and the beans that went into that delicious morning cup of Costa Rican java were likely harvested by Nicaraguan coffee pickers.

make many stops along the route. Buses to Cahuita and Puerto Viejo de Talamanca and all points on the south coast arrive and depart from a stop across from Radio Casino on Avenida 4 between calles 3 and 4.

ESSENTIALS

Bank/ATM **BAC San José** (*Avda. 3, Cs. 2–3* *2798–0155*). **Banco Nacional** (*Avda. 2, Cs. 3–4* *2758–0094*). **Scotiabank** (*Avda. 3 and C. 2* *2798–0009*).

Hospital **Hospital Dr. Tony Facio** (*Highway to Portete* *2758–2222*).

Internet **Café Internet** (*Gran Terminal del Caribe, Avda. 2 and C. 8, across from the soccer stadium* *2798–0128*). **Internet Cinco Estrellas** (*50 m north of Terminal de Cruceros* *2758–5752*).

Pharmacy **Farmacia Buenos Aires** (*25 m east of Mercado Municipal* *2798–4732*). **Farmacia Limonense** (*1st fl., Radio Casino* *2758–0654*).

Post Office **Correos** (*Avda. 2 and C. 4*). **DHL** (*Across from Terminal de Cruceros* *2758–1256*). **UPS** (*West side of Parque Vargas* *2798–3637*).

Visitor Information **JAPDEVA** (*Atlantic Port Authority* *Terminal de Cruceros* *Accessible to cruise-ship passengers only*).

EXPLORING

The aquamarine wooden port building faces the cruise terminal, and just to the east lies the city's palm-lined central park, **Parque Vargas.** From the promenade facing the ocean you can see the raised dead coral left stranded by the 1991 earthquake. Nine or so Hoffman's two-toed sloths live in the trees of Parque Vargas; ask a passerby to point them out, as spotting them requires a trained eye.

A couple of blocks west of the north side of Parque Vargas is the lively enclosed **Municipal Market** (*Mercado Municipal* *Pedestrian mall, Avda. 2,*

9

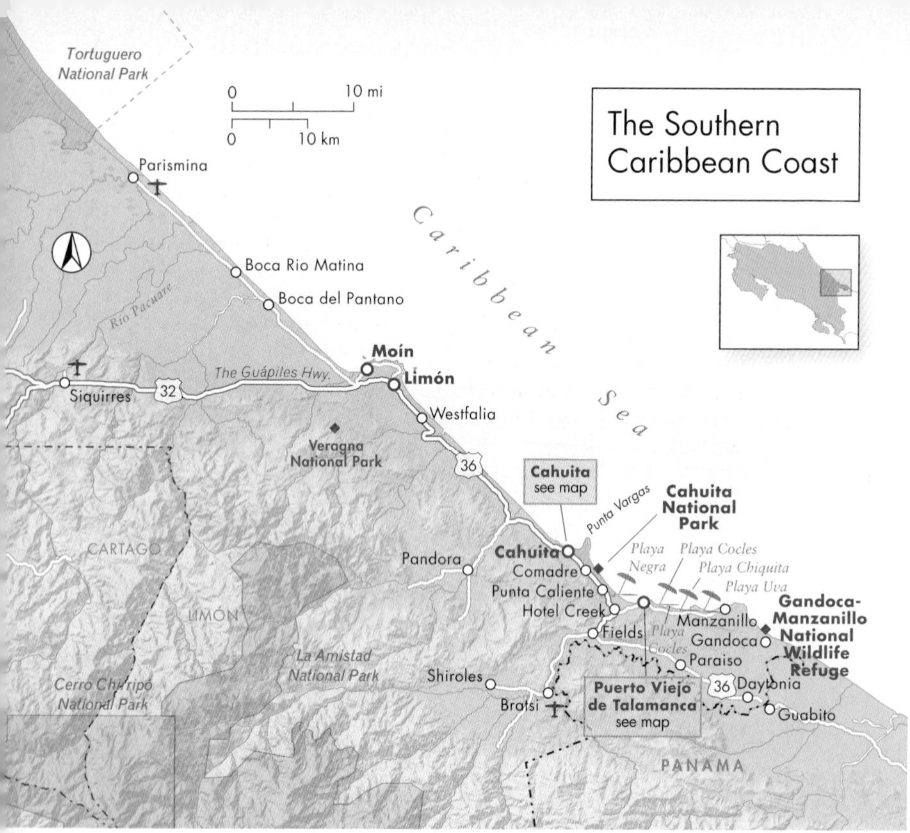

Cs. 3–4), where you can buy fruit for the road ahead and experience the sights, sounds, and smells of a Central American market.

On the left side of the highway as you enter Limón is a large **cemetery.** Notice the COLONIA CHINA ("Chinese colony") and corresponding sign in Chinese on the hill in the cemetery: Chinese workers made up a large part of the 1880s railroad-construction team that worked here. Thousands died of malaria and yellow fever.

OUTDOOR ACTIVITIES

Limón's growing crop of tour operators serves cruise-ship passengers almost exclusively. **Laura Tropical Tours** (✉ *Terminal de Cruceros* ☎ *2758–1240*) has excursions to banana plantations, Tortuguero, and Cahuita National Park. **Mambo Tours** (✉ *Terminal de Cruceros* ☎ *2798–1542*) can take you on three- to eight-hour excursions around the region, and even on an all-day trip to the Rain Forest Aerial Tram or San José.

The region's newest attraction, **Veragua Rainforest Adventure Park**, is a 4,000-acre nature theme park, about 30 minutes west of Limón. It's popular with cruise-ship passengers in port for the day, but if you're in the area, it's well worth a stop. Veragua's great strength is its small army of enthusiastic, super-informed guides who take you through a network of nature trails and exhibits of hummingbirds, snakes, frogs, and butterflies and other insects. A gondola ride overlooks the complex and transports you through the rain forest canopy. A branch of Monteverde's **Original Canopy Tour** is here, too, and offers you the chance to zip from platform to platform—10 in all—through the rain forest canopy. The $45 tour lasts 1½ hours and can be done separately from the other attractions. The canopy tour is included in the all-inclusive daylong, walk-in tour, but not the half-day tour or the tour from San José. (*Veragua de Liverpool ✣15 km/9 mi west of Limón ☎2296–5056 in San José 🌐www.veraguarainforest.com 🎫Half-day tour 65, children under 12, 45; full-day tour 99, children under 12, 70; full-day tour with transportation from San José, $139, children under 12, $99 ⏲Tues.–Sun. 8–4*)

CANOPY TOURS

SHIP AHOY!

If you arrive in Limón on a cruise ship, a day in the Caribbean is yours for the taking. The Tortuguero canals, the beaches at Puerto Viejo de Talamanca, the sloth rescue center at Aviarios del Caribe near Cahuita, or the Veragua Rainforest Adventure Park, just a few miles away, are four popular excursions. A few hardy souls venture as far away as the Rain Forest Aerial Tram or San José. A legion of taxi drivers waits at the terminal exit if you have not arranged an organized shore excursion through your cruise company.

WHERE TO EAT AND STAY

$ SEAFOOD ✕**Brisas del Caribe.** Here's a case study in what happens when cruise ships come to town. This old downtown standby, once as charmingly off-kilter as the crooked umbrellas on its front tables, got rid of its video poker machines (and the locals who always hoped to get lucky playing them), tiled the floors, and remodeled. The food is still good—seafood and surprisingly decent hamburgers, a real rarity in Costa Rica, are the fare here—but a bit of the local color has faded. Passenger or not, you can partake of the lunch buffet on cruise days. ✉*North side of Parque Vargas* ☎*2758–0138* ▭*AE, D, DC, MC, V.*

$ 🏨**Hotel Maribú Caribe.** Perched on a cliff overlooking the Caribbean Sea between Limón and Portete, these white conical thatch huts have great views, but you're a long way from the ocean itself. The lovely grounds have green lawns, shrubs, palm trees, and a large, kidney-shaped pool. The poolside bar discourages exertion. The hotel is immensely popular on weekends, but during the week you'll likely have the place to yourself. **Pros:** good moderate value; secluded location. **Cons:** no access to beach; far from center of town. ✣*4 km/2½ mi north on road to Portete* 📫*Apdo. 623–7300* ☎*2795–2543* ✉*maribucaribe@hotmail.com* *50 rooms* *In-room: Wi-Fi. In-hotel: restaurant, bar, laundry service* ▭*AE, D, DC, MC, V* 🍽*EP.*

¢ 🏨**Hotel Park.** The prices at this pastel-and-pink business-class hotel in central Limón can't be beat. All rooms have modern furnishings and private balconies, so opt for one fronting the ocean. The air-conditioned dining room is a pleasant respite from the heat of the port city. **Pros:** good budget value; great ocean views. **Cons:** small rooms; air-conditioning too icy at times. ✉*Avda. 3, Cs. 2–3* ☎*2798–0555* ✉*parkhotellimon@ice.co.cr* *32 rooms* *In-hotel: restaurant* ▭*AE, DC, MC, V* 🍽*EP.*

9

A carnival in Limón.

SHOPPING

The cruise-ship terminal contains an orderly maze of souvenir stands. Vendors are friendly; there's no pressure to buy. Many shops populate the restored port building across the street as well. Spelling is not its forte, but the **Caribean Banana** (✉ *50 m north Terminal de Cruceros, west side of Parque Vargas*) stands out from the other shops in the cruise-terminal area with a terrific selection of wood carvings.

MOÍN

5 km/3 mi north of Limón.

The docks at Moín are a logical next stop after visiting neighboring Limón, especially if you want to take a boat north to explore the Caribbean coast.

GETTING HERE

Moín is a quick taxi ride from the center of Limón.

You'll probably be able to negotiate a waterway and national-park tour with a local guide, and if you call in advance, you can arrange a tour with the man considered the best guide on the Caribbean coast:

★ **Modesto Watson** (☎ *2226–0986* 🌐 *www.tortuguerocanals.com*), a local Miskito Indian guide. He's legendary for his bird- and animal-spotting skills as well as his howler monkey imitations. The family's *Riverboat Francesca* can take you up the canals for two-day–one-night excursions to Tortuguero for $165 to $220 per person, depending on the lodge used.

CAHUITA

44 km/26 mi southeast of Limón.

Dusty Cahuita, its main dirt street flanked by wooden-slat cabins, is a backpackers' vacation town—a hippie hangout with a dash of Afro-Caribbean spice tossed in. And after years of negative crime-related publicity, Cahuita has beefed up security—this is one of the few places in the country where you will be conscious of a visible and reassuring, though not oppressive, police presence—and has made a well-deserved comeback on the tourist circuit. Tucked in among the backpackers' digs are a few surprisingly nice get-away-from-it-all lodgings, and restaurants with some tasty cuisine at decent prices. No question that nearby Puerto Viejo de Talamanca has overtaken Cahuita and become the hottest spot on the southern Caribbean coast. But as Puerto Viejo grows exponentially, Cahuita's appeal is that it remains small and manageable. It's well worth a look.

NAVIGATING CAHUITA

Cahuita's tiny center is quite walkable, if dusty in the dry season and muddy in the wet season. It's about a 30-minute walk to the end of the Playa Negra road to Hotel La Diosa. Take a taxi to or from Playa Negra after dark. Cahuita has no officially licensed red taxis; transportation is provided informally by private individuals. To be on the safe side, have your hotel or restaurant call a driver for you.

Bicycles are a popular means of utilitarian transport in Cahuita. Seemingly everyone rents basic touring bikes for $5 to $10 per day, but quality varies widely. **Cabinas Brigitte** (⊠*Playa Negra road* ⊠*1½ km/1 mi from town* ☎*2755–0053*) rents good bikes for $6 per day. **Cahuita Tours** *(**⇨below**)* also has bike rentals.

GETTING HERE AND AROUND

Autotransportes MEPE buses travel from San José five times a day, and approximately hourly throughout the day from Limón and Puerto Viejo de Talamanca. Car travel is straightforward: watch for signs in Limón and head 45 minutes south on the coastal highway. Road conditions wax and wane with the severity of the previous year's rains and with the speed at which highway crews patch the potholes. Cahuita has three entrances from the highway: the first takes you to the far north end of the Playa Negra road, near the Magellan Inn; the second, to the middle section of Playa Negra, near the Atlántida; and the third, to the tiny downtown.

The proximity of the Panamanian border means added police vigilance on the coastal highway. No matter what your mode of transport, expect a passport inspection and cursory vehicle search at a police checkpoint just north of Cahuita. If you're on public transportation, you'll disembark from the bus while it is searched.

ESSENTIALS

Bank/ATM Banco de Costa Rica (⊠*Entrance to town* ☎*2755–0401* ▭*Visa only*).

Internet Cabinas Palmer Internet (⊠*50 m east of Coco's* ☎*2755–0435*).

CLOSE UP

The Old Atlantic Railroad

Christopher Columbus became the Caribbean's (and the country's) first tourist when he landed at Uvita Island near Limón during his fourth voyage to the New World in 1502. But the region was already home to thriving, if small, communities of Kekoldi, Bribrí, and Cabécar indigenous peoples. If Costa Rica was an isolated backwater, its Caribbean coastal region remained even more remote from colonial times through most of the 19th century.

New York industrialist Minor Keith changed all that in 1871 with his plan to launch the British-funded Atlantic Railroad, a mode of transportation that would permit easier export of coffee and bananas to Europe. Such a project required a massive labor force, and thousands of West Indians, Asians, and Italians were brought to Costa Rica to construct the 522-km (335-mi) railroad from Limón to San José. Thousands are reputed to have died of yellow fever, malaria, and snakebite during construction of the project. Those who survived were paid relatively well, however, and by the 1930s many Afro-Caribbean residents owned their own small plots of land. When the price of cacao rose in the 1950s, they emerged as comfortable landowners. Not that they had much choice about going elsewhere: until the Civil War of 1948, black Costa Ricans were forbidden from crossing into the Central Valley lest they upset the country's racial balance, and they were thus prevented from moving when United Fruit abandoned many of its blight-ridden northern Caribbean plantations in the 1930s for green-field sites on the Pacific plain.

Costly upkeep of rail service, construction of the Braulio Carrillo Highway to the coast, declining banana production, and an earthquake that rocked the region in 1991 all sounded the death knell for the railroad. The earthquake was also a wake-up call for many here. The long lag time for aid to reach stricken areas symbolized the central government's historic neglect of the region. Development has been slow to reach this part of the country. (Telephones and electricity are still newfangled inventions in some smaller communities here.) As elsewhere in the country, communities now look to tourism to put colones in the coffers. San José has resurrected commuter-rail service, and a few folks here hold out faint hopes that Caribbean train service will start up once again, but that's likely a long way off.

EXPLORING

A full-fledged nature center a few miles northwest of Cahuita and well worth a stop,

Fodor's Choice ★ **Aviaries of the Caribbean** (Aviarios del Caribe) has dense gardens that have attracted more than 300 bird species. Proceeds go to good-hearted owners Judy and Luis Arroyo's sloth-rescue center on the premises. Buttercup, the very first of their charges, holds court in the nature-focused gift shop. *9 km/5 mi northwest of Cahuita, follow signs on Río Estrella delta* ☎ *2750–0775* *www.slothrescue.org* *$25 for tours* *Daily 6–2:30.*

At most butterfly gardens around Costa Rica you get wet during the rainy season. (The mesh enclosures don't offer much protection from the moisture.) But that's not the case at the **Cahuita Butterfly Garden,** where a wood roof covers the perimeter of the 1,100-square-meter (11,800-square-foot) facility. The friendly owners conduct tours in English, French, and Spanish. There's a souvenir shop and small café that serves refreshments, as well as a lounge area outfitted with whimsical wooden chairs. (The owner is a sculptor.) ✉ *Coastal highway, 200 m before main entrance to Cahuita* ☎ *2755–0361* 🎫 *$8* ⏲ *Sun.–Fri. 8:30–3:30, Sat. 8:30–noon.*

RECYCLE!

Unfortunately it's difficult to recycle in most places in Costa Rica, but Cahuita and Puerto Viejo de Talamanca have made it a breeze. Deposit your aluminum cans and glass and plastic beverage bottles in the *Recicaribe* barrels you'll see in either community.

The chocolate trade contributed substantially to this region's economy in the 19th century, and you can get a figurative and literal taste of that fact at **Cacao Trails,** an outdoor museum devoted to the cultivation of cacao and its transformation into chocolate. There is also a museum documenting indigenous history on-site, with an emphasis on shaman-style healing. Finish off with a visit to the thatch-roof restaurant and a hearty Caribbean lunch. ✉ *Coastal highway* ✣ *5 km/3 mi south of main entrance to Cahuit* ☎ *2756–8186* 🌐 *www.cacaotrails.com* 🎫 *$15, $25 with guided tour* ⏲ *Daily 8–4.*

OUTDOOR ACTIVITIES

Cahuita is small enough that its tour operators don't focus simply on the town and nearby national park, but instead line up excursions around the region, even as far away as the Tortuguero canals to the north and Bocas del Toro, Panama, to the south. **Cahuita Tours** (✉ *Main street, 180 m north of Coco's* ☎ *2755–0000 or 2755–0101* 🌐 *www.cahuitatours.com*) is the town's largest and most established tour operator. They can set you up with any of a variety of adventures, including river rafting, kayaking, and visiting indigenous reserves (for a glimpse into traditional life). They can also reconfirm flights and make lodging reservations. We recommend them over their competitors.

9

WHERE TO EAT

$–$$ ECLECTIC Fodor's Choice ★ ✕ **Cha Cha Chá.** Québécois owner Bertrand Fleury's sign triumphantly announces CUISINE OF THE WORLD at the entrance to his restaurant on Cahuita's main street. (He counts French, Italian, Brazilian, and Canadian heritage in his family tree.) Thai shrimp salad and Tex-Mex fajitas are two of the typically eclectic dishes. The menu is small, but what's done is done impeccably well. A delectable specialty is *langosta cha cha chá* (lobster in a white-wine garlic sauce with fresh basil). Paintings by local and Cuban artists hang on the walls of the candlelit semi-outdoor dining area, separated from the street by miniature palm trees. The place is (deservedly) popular and has a scant 32 places. Make it a stop; it's one of the country's top restaurants. ✉ *Main street, 200 m north of Coco's* ☎ *2755–0476* ✍ *Reservations essential* 💳 *MC, V* ⏲ *Closed Mon. No lunch.*

$ CARIBBEAN ✕ **Miss Edith.** Miss Edith is revered for her flavorful Caribbean cooking, vegetarian meals, and herbal teas for whatever ails you. Back in

Restaurants ▼
Cha Cha Chá 2
Miss Edith 1

Hotels ▼
Alby Lodge 8
Atlántida Lodge 1
Bungalows Aché 7
Bungalows Malú 4
El Encanto Bed & Breakfast 5
Hotel La Diosa ...3
Kelly Creek Hotel & Restaurante ...6
Magellan Inn 2

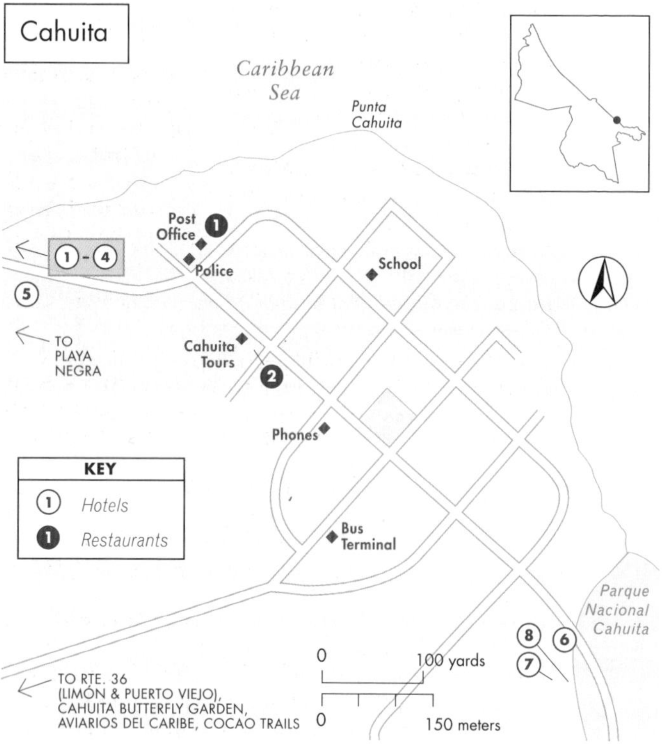

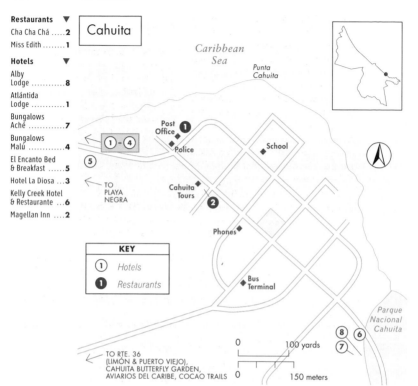

the old days, she served on her own front porch; she's since moved to more ample surroundings on an easy-to-miss side street at the north end of town. A bit of the mystique disappeared with the move, but her made-to-order dishes—*rondón* (stew of vegetables and beef or fish) and spicy jerk chicken—are good no matter where they are served. You can get breakfast here (except on Sunday). ✉*East of police station* ☎*2755–0248* ▭*No credit cards.*

WHERE TO STAY

$ **Alby Lodge.** You're right in town, but you'd never know it at this friendly lodging. Cabins with hardwood floors are propped up on stilts and have hot-water baths, log tables, mosquito nets, and a hammock on the front porch. Make use of the shared kitchen facilities and outdoor barbecue. The forested grounds and high thatch roof keep the temperature pleasantly bearable in otherwise balmy Cahuita. It's next to the park, so the howler monkeys are your morning alarm clock. **Pros:** central location; friendly staff. **Cons:** sometimes a bit noisy; spartan rooms. ✉*180 m west of national park entrance* ☎*2755–0031* 🌐*www.albylodge.com* *4 cabins* *In-room: no a/c, no phone, no TV, Wi-Fi* ▭*No credit cards* *EP.*

$ **Atlántida Lodge.** Attractively landscaped grounds, the beach across the road, and a large pool are Atlántida's main assets. You're welcomed to your room by a lovely assortment of fresh and dried flowers; the rooms themselves are a little on the rustic side, but have tile floors and pretty terraces. Two rooms have hot tubs. All the coffee and bananas you can drink and eat are yours as well. **Pros:** good value; decent pool. **Cons:** some dark rooms; lackluster staff. ✉ *Next to soccer field at Playa Negra* ☎ *2755–0115* ✍ *atlantis@racsa.co.cr* *32 rooms, 2 suites* *In-room: no a/c, no phone, no TV. In-hotel: restaurant, bar, pool, gym, laundry service* ▭ *AE, D, DC, MC, V* *EP.*

CAUTION

That man on the street who asks you, "Do you want a smoke?" isn't offering you a Marlboro. A simple "*No, gracias*" is all you need. The problem is no worse here than anywhere else in Costa Rica, but drugs get more publicity in the Caribbean.

¢–$ **Bungalows Aché.** Like Alby Lodge next door, Aché scatters wooden bungalows—three octagonal structures in this case—around wooded grounds that make the close-by town center seem far away. The buildings come with a rocking chair and porch hammock. The largest bungalow sleeps four. The Swiss owner accepts euros, dollars, and colones. **Pros:** central location; friendly staff. **Cons:** small rooms; spartan rooms. ✉ *180 m west of national park entrance* *Apdo. 740–7300, Limón* ☎ *2755–0119* 🌐 *www.bungalowsache.com* *3 bungalows* *In-room: no a/c, no phone, refrigerator, no TV* ▭ *No credit cards* *EP.*

$ **Bungalows Malú.** This is one of the rare places with air-conditioning on the coast, but it doesn't need it: the octagonal stone-and-wood bungalows spread out on the grounds here get plenty of cool breezes from the beach across the road. Each unit has shuttered screened windows, hardwood floors, and a private porch with a hammock. **Pros:** good value; air-conditioning. **Cons:** far from sights; bungalows are dark inside. ✉ *Playa Negra road* ✉ *2 km/1 mi north of Cahuita* ☎ *2755–0114* ✍ *bungalowmalu@gmail.com* *6 bungalows* *In-room: no phone, refrigerator, no TV. In-hotel: restaurant, bar, pool, Internet terminal* ▭ *MC, V* *BP.*

9

$–$$ **El Encanto Bed & Breakfast Inn.** Zen Buddhist owners have cultivated
Fodor'sChoice ★ a serene and beautiful environment here, ideal for physical and spiritual relaxation. Lodgings are in a garden with an extensive bromeliad collection and Buddha figures. Choose between comfortable rooms or bungalows, all decorated with art from around the globe; some rooms have a double vaulted ceiling with strategically placed screens that keep the place wonderfully ventilated. Amenities include queen-size beds, hot water, and secure parking. Breakfast comes complete with homemade breads and cakes. The beach is across the street, and massage and yoga classes are available on weekends. **Pros:** friendly owners; good value; central location. **Cons:** not for young travelers looking for a scene. ✉ *200 m west of police station on Playa Negra road* *Apdo. 7–7302, Cahuita* ☎ *2755–0113* 🌐 *www.elencantobedandbreakfast.com* *3 rooms, 3 bungalows, 1 apartment* *In-room: no a/c, no phone, kitchen (some), no TV (some). In-hotel: pool* ▭ *AE, MC, V* *BP.*

$$ **Hotel La Diosa.** The owners' interest in Eastern religions is evidenced in the hotel's name (La Diosa means "goddess") and by the sign depicting

a Hindu goddess. They have also opted for little touches such as the rounding of corners and cachá-wood rails to "enhance feminine energy." The place hosts occasional yoga workshops, too, but that's as New Age as it gets. Brightly painted stone or wood cabins—a few have air-conditioning, a rarity here—are scattered around the grounds. All have bright furnishings and art posters hang on the walls, and one room even comes with a whirlpool tub. A bridge leads from the pool to the beach. **Pros:** seclusion; air-conditioning available. **Cons:** far from sights; small rooms. ⊕ *2 km/1 mi north of town at end of Playa Negra road* ☎ *2755–0055, 877/623–3198 in North America* 🌐 *www.hotelladiosa.net* *13 cabins* *In-room: no a/c (some), no phone, no TV. In-hotel: restaurant, bar, pool, Wi-Fi* ▭ *AE, D, DC, MC, V* *BP.*

A TOWN THAT WON'T LET YOU DOWN

Cahuita's first tourist of note was Costa Rican president Alfredo González, whose boat shipwrecked on this stretch of coast in 1915. The president was so grateful for the aid settlers gave him that he purchased a tract of land here and donated it to them to construct a town.

$ **Kelly Creek Hotel & Restaurante.** Owners from Madrid have created a wonderful budget option in a handsome wooden hotel on the creek bank across a short pedestrian bridge from the park entrance. Each of the four hardwood-finished guest rooms is big enough to sleep a small army and has two double beds. Owner Andrés de Alcalá barbecues meat and fresh fish on an open-air grill and also cooks paella and other Spanish specialties. Stop by the restaurant ($–$$) for dinner, even if you're not staying here, but order the paella by 2 PM. Caimans come to the creek bank in search of snacks, and the monkeys and parrots who live in the national park are just yards away, as is the lively center of Cahuita. You'll get a small discount if you pay in cash. **Pros:** good value; terrific Spanish restaurant; friendly owners. **Cons:** dark rooms; occasional, but rare, street noise. ✉ *Next to park entrance* ☎ *2755–0007* 🌐 *www.hotelkellycreek.com* *4 rooms* *In-room: no a/c, no phone, no TV. In-hotel: restaurant* ▭ *AE, MC, V* *EP.*

$$ ★ **Magellan Inn.** Arguably Cahuita's most elegant lodging, this group of bungalows is graced with tile-floor terraces facing a pool and gardens growing on an ancient coral reef. Carpeted rooms have original paintings and custom-made wooden furniture. Feast on intensely flavored French and creole seafood specialties at the Casa Creole ($–$$), open for dinner each evening on the hotel's patio; don't miss the house pâté or the homemade ice cream. The open-air bar rocks to great blues and jazz recordings in the evening and mellows with classical music at breakfast. **Pros:** seclusion; good value; scrumptious dinners. **Cons:** far from sights; staff can be too businesslike. ⊕ *2 km/1 mi north of town at end of Playa Negra road* *Apdo. 1132–7300, Limón* ☎ *2755–0035* 🌐 *www.magellaninn.com* *6 rooms* *In-room: no a/c (some), no phone, no TV, Wi-Fi. In-hotel: restaurant, bar, pool, laundry service* ▭ *AE, D, DC, MC, V* *CP.*

Wildlife watching in Cahuita National Park.

NIGHTLIFE

Aside from a local bar or two, Cahuita's nightlife centers on restaurants, all pleasant places to linger over dinner for the evening. Lively reggae, soca, and samba blast weekend evenings from the turquoise **Coco's Bar** (✉ *Main road* ☎ *No phone*). The assemblage of dogs dozing on its veranda illustrates the rhythm of local life.

CAHUITA NATIONAL PARK

Just south of Cahuita.

Parque Nacional Cahuita begins at the southern edge of the town of the same name. Its rain forest extends right to the edge of its curving, utterly undeveloped 3-km (2-mi) white-sand beach. ☎ *2755–0461 Cahuita entrance, 2755–0302 Puerto Vargas entrance* *By donation at Cahuita entrance, $10 at Puerto Vargas entrance* ⏲ *Daily 6–5 Cahuita entrance, daily 7–4 Puerto Vargas entrance.*

GETTING HERE AND AROUND

Choose from two park entrances: one is at the southern end of the village of Cahuita; the other is at Puerto Vargas, just off the main road, 5 km (3 mi) south of town. If you don't have a car, you can get here easily via bike or taxi.

OUTDOOR ADVENTURES

Operators in Cahuita or Puerto Viejo de Talamanca can hook you up with excursions to and in the park, or you can go on your own, especially if you use the entrance at the south edge of the village.

SNORKELING Cahuita's reefs are just one of several high-quality snorkeling spots in the region. Rent snorkeling gear in Cahuita or Puerto Viejo de Talamanca or through your hotel; most hotels also organize trips. It's wise to work with a guide, as the number of good snorkeling spots is limited and they're not always easily accessible. Cahuita established a community lifeguard team in 2002, unusual in Costa Rica. ■ **TIP→As elsewhere up and down the Caribbean coast, the undertow poses risks for even experienced swimmers. Use extreme caution and never swim alone.**

PUERTO VIEJO DE TALAMANCA

16 km/10 mi south of Cahuita.

This muddy, colorful little town is one of the hottest spots on the international budget-travel circuit, and swarms with surfers, New Age hippies, beaded and spangled punks, would-be Rastafarians of all colors and descriptions, and wheelers and dealers—both pleasant and otherwise. Time was when most kids came here with only one thing on their mind: surfing. Today many seem to be looking for a party, with or without the surf.

But if alternative lifestyles aren't your bag, there are plenty of more "grown-up" offerings on the road heading southeast and northwest out of town. At last count, some 50 nationalities were represented in this tiny community, and most are united in concern for the environment and orderly development of tourism. (Few want to see the place become just another Costa Rican resort community.) Some locals bemoan the loss of their town's innocence, as drugs and other evils have surfaced, but only in small doses: this is still a fun town to visit, with a great variety of hotels, cabinas, and restaurants in every price range. Unlike some other parts of Costa Rica, no one has been priced out of the market here.

Locals use "Puerto Viejo" to refer to the village. They drop the "de Talamanca" part; we use the complete name to avoid confusion with the other Puerto Viejo: Puerto Viejo de Sarapiquí in the Northern Plains. You have access to the beach right in town, and the Salsa Brava, famed in surfers' circles for its pounding waves, is here off the coast, too. The best strands of Caribbean sand are outside the village: Playa Cocles, Playa Chiquita (technically a series of beaches), and Punta Uva, all dark-sand beaches, line the road heading southeast from town. Playa Negra—not the Playa Negra near Cahuita—is the black-sand beach northwest of town. Punta Uva, with fewer hotels and the farthest from the village, sees fewer crowds and more tranquility. Playa Negra shares that distinction, too—for now—but developers have eyed the beach as the next area for expansion.

NAVIGATING PUERTO VIEJO DE TALAMANCA You can manage the town center quite easily on foot, though it is dusty in the dry season and muddy when it rains. (The main street is, thankfully, paved.) Everyone gets around by bike here, and seemingly everyone has one for rent. Quality varies widely. Expect to pay $10 per day for a good bike. **Cabinas Grant** (✉ *100 m south of bus stop* ☎ *2750–0292*) has the best selection of quality bikes in town. Priority is given to guests at **Casa Verde Lodge** (✉ *200 m south and 200 m east* *of bus stop* ☎*2750–0015*), but they usually have extra bikes you can rent for a half or full day even if you don't stay here. There are a couple of official red licensed cabs, but most taxi service here is informal, with private individuals providing rides. To be on the safe side, have your hotel or restaurant call one for you.

GETTING HERE AND AROUND

The turnoff to Puerto Viejo de Talamanca is 10 km (6 mi) down the coastal highway south of Cahuita. (The highway itself continues south to Bribrí and Sixaola at the Panamanian border.) The village lies another 5 km (3 mi) beyond the turnoff. The paved road passes through town and continues to Playas Cocles and Chiquita and Punta Uva before the pavement peters out at the entrance to the village of Manzanillo. "Badly potholed" describes the condition of the road from the highway into town, and as far as Playa Cocles. The newer paved sections beyond Cocles haven't disintegrated . . . yet. Autotransportes MEPE buses travel from San José five times a day, and approximately hourly throughout the day from Limón and Cahuita. All buses from San José go into Puerto Viejo de Talamanca; most, though not all, Limón-originating buses do as well, but a couple drop you off on the highway. Check if you board in Limón.

A scant four buses per day ply the 15-km (9-mi) paved road between Puerto Viejo and Manzanillo, so unless your schedule meshes exactly with theirs, you're better off biking or taking a taxi to and from the far-flung beaches along the way. Taxis charge $7 to Playas Cocles and Chiquita (as well as north to Playa Negra), $8 to Punta Uva, and $12 to Manzanillo.

ESSENTIALS

Bank/ATM Banco de Costa Rica (✉*50 m south of bridge at entrance to town* ☎*2750–0707* ☞*Visa only*).

Internet ATEC (✉*Across from Restaurant Tamara* ☎*2750–0398*). **Café Internet Río Negro** (✉*Playa Cocles* ✣*4 km/2½ mi southeast of town* ☎*2750–0801*). **El Tesoro** (✉*Playa Cocles* ☎*2750–0128*).

Pharmacy Farmacia Amiga (✉*Next to Banco de Costa Rica* ☎*2750–0698*).

Post Office Correos (✉*50 m west of ATEC*).

Visitor Information ATEC (✉*Across from Restaurant Tamara* ☎*2750–0191* 🌐*www.ateccr.org*).

EXPLORING

At the **Finca la Isla Botanical Garden** you can explore a working tropical fruit, spice, and ornamental plant farm. Sloths abound, and you might see a few poison dart frogs. A $10 guided tour includes admission and a glass of the farm's homemade fruit juice. You get the fruit juice if you wander around on your own, too—a $1 self-guided-tour book is available in English, Spanish, French, or German. Watch the demonstration showing how cacao beans are turned into chocolate, and sample some of the product at the end of the tour. ✣*½ km/¼ mi west of town at Playa Negra* ☎*2750–0046* 🌐*www.greencoast.com/garden.htm* 🎟*5, guided tour 10* ⏲*Fri.–Mon. 10–4.*

9

Restaurants ▼

Amimodo 8
Bread & Chocolate 2
Café Viejo 3
Chile Rojo 6
Gatta Ci Cova .. 10
El Loco Natural 1
La Pecora Nera 9
Salsa Brava 7
Soda Miss Sam 5
Tex Mex 4

Hotels ▼

Agapi 6
Azania Bungalows 9
Cariblue Hotel............ 8
Casa Camarona 11
Casa Verde Lodge 1
Coco Loco Lodge 2
La Costa de Papito 10
Escape Caribeño 5
Hotel La Perla Negra 3
Pachamama .. 14
El Pizote Lodge 4
Shawandha Lodge 13
Totem 7
Yaré Bungalows ... 12

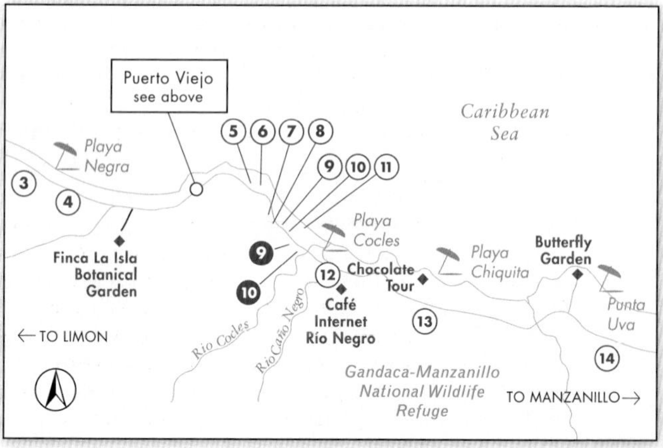

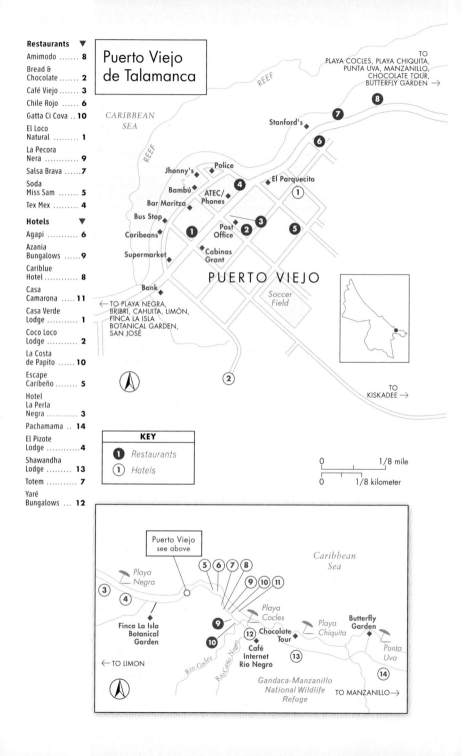

Cacao once ruled the Talamanca region, but few plantations are left these days. One friendly Swiss couple continues the tradition and shows you the workings of their chocolate plantation on their **Chocorart** chocolate tour. Follow the little-known life cycle of this crop from cultivation to processing. There's sampling at the tour's conclusion. Call or e-mail to reserve a tour (you need a minimum of four people) and to be picked up from the Playa Chiquita School. Since these folks are Swiss, they can tailor the commentary in German, French, or Italian, in addition to English or Spanish. *6 km/4 mi southeast of town at Playa Chiquita 2750–0075 chocorart@racsa.co.cr 15 per person By appointment.*

Unlike most such establishments in Costa Rica, which are for show only, the working **Butterfly Garden** cultivates 60 to 80 species of butterflies, three of which are unique to the area, for shipment to similar facilities around the world. The knowledgeable staff provides guided tours with bilingual commentary. *7 km/4½ mi southeast of town at Punta Uva 2750–0086 5, free for kids under 6 Daily 8–4.*

OUTDOOR ACTIVITIES

As in Cahuita, tour operators and outfitters here can set up tours and activities anywhere on the south Caribbean coast.

Tours with **ATEC** (*Talamancan Association of Ecotourism and Conservation) Across from Restaurant Tamara 2750–0191 www.ateccr.org*) have an environmental or cultural bent, such as Afro-Caribbean or indigenous-culture walks—tours to the nearby Kekoldi indigenous reserve are especially popular—rain forest hikes, coral-reef snorkeling trips, fishing trips, bird-watching tours, night walks, and adventure treks. Local organizations and wildlife refuges receive 15% to 20% of ATEC's proceeds. Well-established operator **Terra Aventuras** (*100 m south of bus stop 2750–0750 www.terraventuras.com*) can lead you around Puerto Viejo de Talamanca and Cahuita, or take you on excursions to Tortuguero, the Gandoca-Manzanillo Wildlife Refuge, and Bocas del Toro in Panama. It also rents good-quality surfboards, bicycles, Boogie boards, and snorkeling gear.

RAFTING ★ Rafting excursions lie about two hours away, but one San José–based outfitter has an office here. **Exploradores Outdoors** (*Across from ATEC 2750–2020, 2222–6262 in San José www.exploradoresoutdoors.com*) is highly regarded and has day excursions on the Pacuare and Reventazón rivers, with a pickup point here or in San José, and the option to start in one place and be dropped off at the other. The outfitter also offers sea-kayaking excursions off the coast of the Gandoca-Manzanillo Wildlife Refuge.

SURFING Surfing is the name of the game in Puerto Viejo, for everyone from newbies to Kelly Slaters. The best conditions are late December through March, but there's action all year. Longtime surfers compare the south Caribbean to Hawaii, but without the "who-do-you-think-you-are?" attitude. There are a number of breaks here, most famously **Salsa Brava**, which translates to "wild sauce." It breaks fairly far offshore and requires maneuvering past some tricky currents and a shallow reef. Hollow and primarily right-breaking, Salsa Brava is one gnarly wave

9

CLOSE UP

Reefs at Risk

One of the most complex organisms in the marine world, a coral reef is an extraordinary and extraordinarily delicate habitat. Coral reefs are the result of the symbiotic relationship between single-cell organisms called zooxanthellae and coral polyps. The zooxanthellae grow inside the cells of the polyps, producing oxygen and nutrients that are released into the coral tissues. Corals secrete calcium carbonate (limestone) that, over time, forms the vast coral reef "superstructure." Zooxanthellae require exposure to sunlight to thrive. The healthiest coral reefs are in clear, clean, tropical seawater at a temperature of 20°C to 25°C (70°F to 80°F). Healthy coral reefs are biologically rich gardens occupied by a diverse selection of life forms, from microscopic unicellular algae and phytoplankton to a wide range of fish.

Unfortunately, coral reefs in Costa Rica are in danger. Dirt and sediment from banana plantations and logging areas, as well as runoff from pesticide use, are killing them. The dirty runoff literally clogs the pores of the zooxanthellae and smothers them. In the Golfo Dulce, 98% of one of the oldest reefs in Costa Rica has been destroyed by this sedimentation. The once-enormous reefs of Cahuita are almost entirely gone.

Human visitors, including careless snorkelers, have also damaged reefs. Just touching a reef damages it. When exploring a coral reef, look but don't touch, and snorkel only on its outer side, preferably in calm weather. Can the reefs be saved? With commitment and time, yes. Coral is resilient, and will grow back—if the Costa Rican government makes it a priority.

when it gets big. If it gets *too* big, or not big enough, check out the breaks at Punta Uva, Punta Cocles, or Playa Chiquita. Boogie boarders and bodysurfers can also dig the beach-break waves at various points along this tantalizingly beautiful coast.

If you're, say, over 30, but have always wanted to try surfing, consider the friendly, three-hour $35 surf school at **Aventuras Bravas** (✉ *Across from Stanford's* ☎ *8849–7600*). You start out with a small wave near the bus stop, and get a money-back guarantee that you'll be standing by the end of the lesson. You can also rent equipment here.

WHERE TO EAT

$$ ITALIAN ★ ✕ **Amimodo.** The name translates to "my way," and the exuberant Italian owners really do it their way, combining the cuisine of their native northern Italy with Caribbean flavors. Your antipasto might be classic bruschetta or *jamón de tiburón* (shark ham with avocado dressing), and your ravioli might be stuffed with tropical shrimp, pineapple, and curry, with avocado sauce on the side. The tropical veranda with gingerbread trim spills over onto the beach with abundant greenery, and the restaurant is a popular gathering place for Puerto Viejo's Italian community. ✉ *200 m east of Stanford's* ☎ *2750–0257* ▭ *MC, V* ⊗ *Closed Tues. or Thurs., varies*

¢ COSTA RICAN ★ ✕ **Bread & Chocolate.** The take-away line for brownies forms at the gate before this place opens at 6:30 AM, but stick around and fortify yourself with a hearty breakfast of cinnamon-oatmeal pancakes,

French toast, or creamy scrambled eggs, washed down with a cup of French-press coffee. Lunch brings jerk chicken, roasted red peppers, and chocolate truffles. Everything is homemade, right down to the mayonnaise. Make your dinner early; the place closes at 6 PM. This is one of several bakery-slash-breakfast-and-lunch cafés open in town; the friendly owner gives this place the edge. ✉ *50 m south of post office* ☎ *2750–0723* ▭ *No credit cards* ⏲ *Closed Mon. and Tues. No dinner Sun.*

CAUTION

The conditions that make the Caribbean so popular among surfers spell danger for swimmers. Drownings occur each year. Strong riptides can pull you out to sea, even in waist-deep water, before you realize what's happening. Never swim alone in these parts—good advice anywhere.

$ ITALIAN **Café Viejo.** This has fast become the hot place to see and be seen on Puerto Viejo's main drag. The owners, four brothers who learned to cook at the knee of their Italian grandmother back in Rimini, have concocted a menu, several pages long, of pizzas and handmade pastas. Recorded reggae and mambo music bops in the background. ✉ *Across from ATEC* ☎ *2750–0817* ▭ *MC, V* ⏲ *Closed Tues. No lunch.*

$ THAI **Chile Rojo.** There's not a thing about the name or furnishings to reflect its Thai and Middle-Eastern offerings, but business is brisk here, so brisk that the restaurant moved into spacious new digs in early 2009. Choose from Thai grilled tuna, falafel, hummus, and samosas. Sushi is available on Saturday. In deference to the town's European tourist trade, the restaurant accepts euros as payment, too. ✉ *Across from Stanford's* ☎ *2750–0319* ▭ *No credit cards* ⏲ *Closed Mon.*

$ ECLECTIC Fodor's Choice ★ **El Loco Natural.** El Loco Natural epitomizes Puerto Viejo: lively, organic, all the rage, but confident enough not to seek trendiness. Popularity meant a move to much larger quarters in late 2008, and seating is much more spacious than it used to be. Ordering is by sauces: Thai peanut, Indonesian-Caribbean curry, Mexican chipotle, Jamaican jerk-style, or Malaysian-guayaba curry. Then select vegetables, chicken, shrimp, or fish (marlin or tuna). You'll be better able to converse with your fellow diners if you sit at the tables inside. Live music gets going late on Thursday and Sunday evenings. ✉ *100 m south of bus stop* ☎ *2750–0530* ▭ *No credit cards* ⏲ *No lunch.*

$ ITALIAN **Gatta Ci Cova.** Chef-owner Ilario Giannoni strolls the 100 meters over from his La Pecora Nera restaurant to watch over his new baby these days. The restaurant, whose name comes from an Italian expression meaning "things kept secret," provides a less formal, less expensive alternative to the original, but still has all the flair and all the fun. Lunch offerings focus on the $10 plato del día, a bargain with appetizer, salad, a rotating selection of pastas, dessert, and a glass of wine. ✣ *3 km/2 mi southeast of town at Playa Cocles* ☎ *2750–0730* ▭ *AE, D, DC, MC, V* ⏲ *Closed Mon.*

$$$ Fodor's Choice ★ **La Pecora Nera.** Though the name means "black sheep" in Italian, there's nothing shameful about this thatch-roof roadside restaurant. There's always a lot more to choose from than you'll see on the sparse-looking menu. Wait for owner/chef Ilario Giannoni to come out of the

9

kitchen and triumphantly announce—with flair worthy of an Italian opera—which additional light Tuscan entrées, appetizers, and desserts they've concocted that day. Be prepared for a long, leisurely dining experience with attentive service. It's worth the wait; this is one of the country's top Italian restaurants. *✢3 km/2 mi southeast of town at Playa Cocles ☎2750–0490 ▭AE, D, DC, MC, V ⏲Closed Mon. No lunch.*

$ SEAFOOD ✕ **Salsa Brava.** The restaurant overlooking the Salsa Brava break—with sublime surf vistas—has taken the name of this famed surfing spot. Opt for casual counter service or grab a seat at one of the colorful roadside tables. Lunch and dinner center on grilled fish and meat, with red snapper prepared in olive oil, garlic, and cayenne pepper a specialty. *✉100 m east of Stanford's ☎2750–0241 ▭AE, D, DC, MC, V ⏲Closed Mon.*

¢ CARIBBEAN ✕ **Soda Miss Sam.** Longtime restaurateur Miss Sam still dishes up hearty Caribbean cuisine at this small restaurant, a Puerto Viejo institution—she prefers not to divulge how many years she's been doing so—and the front porch is still full of diners. Rice and beans are usually going, or you can get a *casado* (plate with rice, beans, and fried plantains) with chicken, beef, pork, or fish and freshly squeezed fruit juices as accompaniment. It's open for breakfast, too. *✉300 m south, 200 m east of bus stop ☎2750–0108 ▭No credit cards ⏲Closed Tues.*

$ MEXICAN ✕ **Tex Mex.** Puerto Viejo's newest eatery begins the day with hearty Gringo- or Tico-style breakfasts. (Expect *gallo pinto* [rice and beans] or an ample fruit plate if you opt for the latter.) Lunch and dinner give way to standard nachos, burritos, tacos, and enchiladas. Tex Mex screens free DVD movies, yours for the price of a drink, each evening except Thursday. *✉ 50 m east of ATEC ☎2750–0525 ▭No credit cards ⏲Closed Thurs.*

WHERE TO STAY

$–$$ **Agapi.** Agapi means "love" in Greek, and Costa Rican–Greek owners Cecilia and Tasso lovingly watch over their guests with some of the most attentive service around. Seven furnished apartments overlook the beach and come complete with fully equipped kitchen, hot-water bath, hammock, mosquito nets over the beds, and private balcony. An additional six rooms have two full-size beds each, and all have an ocean view. A common area in the back contains a beachside barbecue. **Pros:** kitchens; central location. **Cons:** not for travelers who want anonymity; first-floor rooms are dark. *✢1 km/½ mi southeast of Stanford's ☎2750–0446 ⊕www.agapisite.com 5 rooms, 12 apartments In-room: no a/c (some), no phone, kitchen (some), refrigerator, no TV (some). In-hotel: laundry service, Wi-Fi ▭AE, D, DC, MC, V EP.*

$$ **Azania Bungalows.** Eight thatch-roof, A-frame bungalows spread around Azania's ample gardens, and sleep four. The first floor contains a queen-size bed, and a ladder leads to the second floor with a pair of single beds. Much-appreciated mosquito netting covers all of them. You'll luxuriate in the semi-open shower in the blue-tile bathrooms. Meals are served in the hotel's Argentine restaurant next to the free-form pool. **Pros:** good value; good Argentine restaurant. **Cons:** difficult to make reservations; bungalows are dark inside. *✢1½ km/1 mi southeast of*

town at Playa Cocles ☎2750–0540 ⊕www.azania-costarica.com ⇨8 bungalows ♁In-room: no a/c, no phone, refrigerator, no TV. In-hotel: restaurant, bar, pool, laundry service, Internet terminal, Wi-Fi ▭AE, D, DC, MC, V ¶○¦BP.

$$ Fodor'sChoice ★ **Cariblue Hotel.** The youthful Italian owners who came here to surf years ago stayed on and built a lodging that combines refinement with that hip Puerto Viejo vibe in exactly the right proportions. Cariblue's finely crafted all-wooden bungalows are spaciously arrayed on the edge of the jungle, across the road from the splendid white-sand beaches of Punta Cocles. Cabinas are linked to the main ranch-style building by paths that meander across a gently sloping lawn shaded by enormous trees. Expansive verandas and beautiful tile mosaics in the bathrooms add an air of refinement; hammocks add an air of relaxation. Breakfasts are huge. Italian cuisine dominates for lunch, and dinner is served at the lively Soleluna restaurant ($–$$) on-site. **Pros:** friendly owners; good restaurant. **Cons:** need car to stay here; a few reports of lackluster staff. *✢2 km/1 mi southeast of town at Playa Cocles ✆Apdo. 51–7304, Puerto Viejo de Talamanca ☎2750–0035 ⊕www.cariblue.com ⇨21 bungalows ♁In-room: no a/c (some), no phone, safe, no TV (some). In-hotel: restaurant, bars, pool, laundry service, Wi-Fi ▭AE, D, DC, MC, V ¶○¦BP.*

$ **Casa Camarona.** Though half the rooms have air-conditioning at this secluded lodging, you hardly need it. The abundant shade and sea breezes keep the rooms delightfully cool. All the spacious, wooden, rustic rooms front the ocean—the second-story rooms have the best view—and have two double beds. Meals are served at the seaside Caribbean restaurant. **Pros:** good value; air-conditioning. **Cons:** need a car to stay here; some dark rooms. *✢3 km/2 mi south of town at Playa Cocles ✆Apdo. 2070–1002, San Jos ☎2750–0151 or 283–6711 in San José ⊕www.casacamarona.co.cr ⇨17 rooms ♁In-room: no a/c (some), no phone, no TV. In-hotel: restaurant, bar, laundry service, no-smoking rooms ▭AE, DC, MC, V ¶○¦CP.*

¢–$ Fodor'sChoice ★ **Casa Verde Lodge.** If you've graduated from your backpacker days and are a bit more flush with cash but still want to be near the action, this old standby on a quiet street a couple of blocks from the center of town is ideal. The comfortable cabinas are decorated with an interesting variety of touches such as shell mobiles, watercolor frescoes, and indigenous tapestries. Overall, rooms at this Swiss-run lodging have a neat-as-a-pin quality. Exotic birds flutter constantly through the lush plantings that screen the cabinas from the street. The place is immensely popular, since the price is low and it's clean and well run; reserve well in advance. You'll receive a small discount if you pay in cash. **Pros:** good value; immaculate. **Cons:** difficult to find space; businesslike staff. *✉200 m south and 200 m east of bus stop ✆Apdo. 37–7304, Puerto Viejo de Talamanca ☎2750–0015 ⊕www.cabinascasaverde.com ⇨17 rooms, 9 with bath; 2 apartments ♁In-room: no phone, refrigerator (some), no TV. In-hotel: restaurant, pool, bicycles, laundry service ▭AE, MC, V ¶○¦EP.*

$ **Coco Loco Lodge.** The cool, forested grounds here lie close to the center of town but seem far away. The Austrian owners lavish you with lots of personal attention. The bungalows on stilts are simply furnished

9

but contain hot-water baths, mosquito nets over the beds (you'll need them), and hammocks on the porch. There are also two fully furnished houses available for short- or long-term rental. Great coffee is included in the room rate; a huge buffet breakfast is extra. You'll receive a discount if you pay with cash. **Pros:** good budget value; central location. **Cons:** rustic rooms; dark road at night. ✉ *180 m south of bridge at entrance to town* P *2750–0281* 🌐 *www.cocolocolodge.com* *8 cabins, 2 houses* *In-room: no a/c, no phone, kitchen (some), refrigerator (some). In-hotel: Internet terminal, Wi-Fi* ▭ *MC, V* *EP.*

$ **El Pizote Lodge.** El Pizote observes local architectural mores while offering more than most in the way of amenities. All standard rooms have polished wood paneling, reading lamps, mirrors, and firm beds. Each of the two-room bungalows sleeps six. The restaurant serves breakfast, dinner, and drinks all day. Guanábana and papaya grow on the grounds, and hiking trails lead off into the jungle. Tranquil Playa Negra is just across the road. **Pros:** good value; air-conditioning available. **Cons:** small rooms; far from sights. ✉ *300 m before entrance to town at Playa Negra* *Apdo. 1371–1000, San José* ☎ *2750–0088* 🌐 *www.pizotelodge.com* *8 rooms, 12 bungalows* *In-room: no a/c (some), no phone, TV. In-hotel: restaurant, bar, pool, laundry service* ▭ *MC, V* *EP.*

$–$$ **Escape Caribeño.** Wonderfully friendly Italian owners Gloria and Mauro Marchiori are what make this place: they treat you like family. A dozen immaculate hardwood bungalows line a pleasant garden amply populated with hummingbirds, just outside of town. All cabins have hammocks, mosquito nets, double beds, and even a bunk bed or two for larger groups. Across the road lie two stucco cabins in a wooded spot on the beach. Breakfast is served in a thatch-roof dining area in the center of the garden. You'll receive a small discount if you pay with cash. **Pros:** central location; gregarious owners. **Cons:** some small rooms; some spartan rooms. ✉ *400 m southeast of Stanford's* P *2750–0103* 🌐 *www.escapecaribeno.com* *14 cabins* *In-room: no phone, safe, refrigerator, Wi-Fi* ▭ *AE, D, DC, MC, V* *EP.*

$$ **Hotel La Perla Negra.** Fine design is evident in the construction of this handsome, two-story dark-wood structure across a tiny dirt road near the end of Playa Negra. All rooms have balconies, half with ocean views, half with jungle views. The three-meal restaurant features grilled meats and fish. Between the building and the beach is a spacious, inviting pool. Though the hotel does not accept credit cards, you can make your payment through PayPal. **Pros:** secluded; quality construction of buildings. **Cons:** far from sights; situated on lesser-known Playa Negra. ✉ *Playa Negra* ✣ *1 km/½ mi north of Puerto Viejo* ☎ *2750–0111* 🌐 *www.perlanegra-beachresort.com* *24 rooms, 7 houses* *In-room: no a/c (some), no phone, no TV. In-hotel: restaurant, bar, tennis court, pool, laundry service, Wi-Fi* ▭ *AE, D, DC, MC, V* *CP.*

$–$$ **La Costa de Papito.** Papito's raised cabins are deep in the property's wooded grounds and furnished with whimsical bright tropical-blue and zebra-stripe prints. Breakfast, with an extra cost of $6, is served at the table and chairs on your porch, which has a hammock or swing chair. You'll get a 15% discount if you pay in cash. **Pros:** good value; friendly

Calm waters over the reef just off of Punta Uva Beach near Puerto Viejo de Talamanca.

owner. **Cons:** need car to stay here; some noise from bar area. *2 km/1 mi southeast of town at Playa Cocles* P2750–0080 *www.lacostadepapito.com* *13 cabins* *In-room: no phone, no TV. In-hotel: restaurant, spa, bicycles, Internet terminal* *AE, D, DC, MC, V* *EP.*

$ **Pachamama.** So cool and shady is this place set within the confines of the Gandoca-Manzanillo Wildlife Refuge that the owners took out the ceiling fans. No one ever needed them. Though still within sight of the Puerto Viejo–Manzanillo road, Pachamama delivers a get-away-from-it-all nature experience at a fraction of the cost of other Costa Rican eco-lodges. Cozy wood cabins are simply furnished with two beds and mosquito netting and have colorful spreads and drapes. A house can be rented by the week or month. Personal touches such as breakfast (included in the rates of the bungalows, but not the kitchen-equipped house) brought to the porch of your cabin are standard. The bungalows are joined by a kitchen and are ideal for renting by a group or family. **Pros:** seclusion; friendly owners. **Cons:** far from sights; need car to stay here. *9 km/5½ mi southeast of town at Punta Uva* P2759–9196 *www.pachamamacaribe.com* *2 bungalows, 3 houses* *In-room: no a/c, no phone, kitchen (some), no TV. In-hotel: bicycles, laundry service* *MC, V* *EP, BP.*

$$ ★ **Shawandha Lodge.** The service is personalized and friendly at Shawandha, whose spacious, beautifully designed bungalows are well back from the road at Playa Chiquita. The thatch-roof bungalows have elegant hardwoods, four-poster beds, and verandas with hammocks. Each bathroom has a unique and beautiful tile mosaic. The hearty breakfast starts off with an impressive fruit plate. A white-sand beach lies 180 meters (600 feet) away, across the road. Even if you don't stay

here, stop by and enjoy a distinctive French-Caribbean dinner in the open-air restaurant. **Pros:** elegant bungalows; sumptuous restaurant. **Cons:** far from sights. *6 km/4 mi southeast of town at Playa Chiquita* *2750–0018* *www.shawandhalodge.com* *13 bungalows* *In-room: no a/c, no phone, safe, no TV. In-hotel: restaurant, bar, laundry service* *AE, MC, V* *BP.*

A BAD RAP

The Caribbean has a reputation among Costa Ricans for being crime-ridden, mainly because of a few high-profile cases here years ago, the nearness of the Panamanian border, and the fact that this is an impoverished region compared with other parts of the country. In actuality, the problem is no better or worse here than elsewhere. Just take the standard precautions you would when you travel anywhere and stick to well-traveled tourist paths.

$$ **Totem.** Each of the tropical-blue units here contains a living room and bedroom with bamboo furnishings, a queen bed, and bunks. We like the two rooms on the upper balcony with stupendous ocean views and overlooking the gurgling, fountain-fed pool. The restaurant serves superb pizza. **Pros:** good value; terrific restaurant. **Cons:** need car to stay here; some reports of lackluster staff. *1½ km/1 mi southeast of town at Playa Cocles* *2750–0758* *www.totemsite.com* *12 rooms, 6 suites* *In-room: no a/c (some), refrigerator. In-hotel: restaurant, bar, pool, Internet terminal, Wi-Fi* *AE, D, DC, MC, V* *BP.*

¢–$ **Yaré Bungalows.** The sound of the jungle is overpowering, especially at night, as you relax in your brightly pastel-painted Yaré cabina. All rooms have hot water and verandas with hammocks. The restaurant is open for breakfast, lunch, and dinner. **Pros:** good value, whimsical bungalows. **Cons:** sound travels far; far from sights. *3½ km/2 mi southeast of town at Playa Cocles* *Apdo. 117–1007, San José* *2750–0106, 888/250–6472 in North America* *www.bungalowsyare.com* *22 rooms* *In-room: no phone, safe (some), kitchen (some), refrigerator (some), no TV. In-hotel: restaurant, bar, laundry service* *AE, D, DC, MC, V* *BP.*

NEED A BREAK?

At first glance, this small café could use a spelling lesson, but since Caribeans deals in coffee, the play on words is apt. Treat yourself to a latté, mocha, or coconut cappuccino, all made from organic, fair-trade coffee from the Turrialba region in the far-eastern Central Valley, and roasted here. The place is open daily except Tuesday. ***50 m west of bus stop*** ***8836–8930.***

NIGHTLIFE

The distinction between dining spot and nightspot blurs as the evening progresses, as many restaurants become pleasant places to linger over dinner. Bars each have their special nights for live music. The town's main drag between El Loco Natural and Salsa Brava is packed with pedestrians, bicycles, and a few cars most evenings, the block between Café Viejo and El Parquecito getting the most action. Wander around; something is bound to entice you in. **TIP→When out after dark, ask a staff member at the restaurant, bar, or club to call you a taxi at the end of the night.**

BARS **Bar Maritza** (✉ *50 m east of bus stop*) is frequented by locals, and has live music on Sunday night. Grab a beer, and chow down on pizza or sandwiches at **El Dorado** (✉ *Across from ATEC*), a much quieter alternative to the noisier bars. **Tex Mex** (✉ *50 m east of ATEC*) serves drinks and two big-screen movies every evening except Thursday.

DANCE CLUBS Ticos come from miles around for the Friday and Monday reggae nights at **Bambú** (✉ *Next to Jhonny's*), but the place is closed most other evenings. **Jhonny's Place** (✉ *230 m east of bus stop*) has nights variously devoted to reggae, jazz, R&B, and hip-hop. **Stanford's** (✉ *100 m from the town center on the road to Manzanillo*) is the place to merengue or salsa the weekend nights away. Partake of light meals on the new second-floor patio dining room if dancing isn't your thing.

LIVE MUSIC Caribbean restaurant **El Parquecito** (✉ *50 m east of ATEC*) pulls live-music duty Tuesday, Friday, and Saturday evenings. You're bound to hear "No Woman No Cry" and all the other reggae anthems. Organic-food restaurant **El Loco Natural** (✉ *150 m west of ATEC* ☎ *2750–0263*) has live music Thursday and Sunday evenings.

SHOPPING

Vendors set up stands at night on the beach road near El Parquecito, jewelry being the prime fare. But the town counts a few honest-to-goodness souvenir stores, too.

Buy your semi-official Puerto Viejo T-shirt at **Color Caribe** (✉ *100 m south of bus stop*), and check out the huge selection of Rastafarian clothing, plus hammocks, wood carvings, and whimsical mobiles.

★ Puerto Viejo's best shop, **Luluberlu** (✉ *200 m south and 50 m east of bus stop*), sells a wonderful selection of local indigenous carvings—balsa and *chonta* wood are especially popular—and jewelry, paintings, and ceramics by 30 artists from the region.

GANDOCA-MANZANILLO NATIONAL WILDLIFE REFUGE

15 km/9 mi southeast of Puerto Viejo.

The Refugio Nacional de Vida Silvestre Gandoca-Manzanillo stretches along the southeastern coast beginning southeast of Puerto Viejo de Talamanca to the town of Manzanillo and on to the Panamanian border. Its limits are not clearly defined. Because of weak laws governing the conservation of refuges and the rising value of coastal land in this area, Gandoca-Manzanillo is less pristine than Cahuita National Park and continues to be developed. However, the refuge still has plenty of rain forest, *orey* (a dark tropical wood) and jolillo swamps, 10 km (6 mi) of beach where four species of turtles lay their eggs, and almost 3 square km (1 square mi) of *cativo* (a tropical hardwood) forest and coral reef. The Gandoca estuary is a nursery for tarpon and a wallowing spot for crocodiles and caimans.

GETTING HERE

The road from Puerto Viejo de Talamanca ends at the entrance to the village of Manzanillo. Just three buses each day—morning, midday, and late afternoon—connect the two. All taxi drivers in Puerto Viejo charge $10 for the trip here.

"We found Playa Manzanillo while visiting the Caribbean side of Costa Rica. A beautiful beach and very laid back atmosphere." —photo by dgray, Fodors.com member

EXPLORING

The easiest way to explore the refuge is to hike along the coast south of Manzanillo. You can hike back out the way you came in or arrange (in Puerto Viejo de Talamanca) to have a boat pick you up at Punta Mono (Monkey Point), a three- to four-hour walk from Manzanillo, where you find secluded beaches hidden by tall cliffs of fossilized coral. The mangroves of Gandoca, with abundant caimans, iguanas, and waterfowl, lie six to eight hours away. Park administrators can tell you more and recommend a local guide; inquire when you enter Manzanillo village and the locals will point you toward them. ✉ *15 km/9 mi southeast of Puerto Viejo de Talamanca* ☎ *2750–0398 for ATEC* ⏲ *Daily 7–4.*

The nearby village of **Manzanillo** maintains that "end of the world" feel. Tourism is still in its infancy this far down the coast, though with the road paved all the way here, the town is now a popular destination among people in Limón for weekend day trips. The rest of the week, you'll likely have the place to yourself.

OUTDOOR ACTIVITIES

A guide can help you get the most out of this relatively unexplored corner of the country. The **Association of Indigenous Naturalist Guides of Manzanillo** (✉ *Main road* ☎ *2759–9064 or 8843–9122* ✉ *guiasmant@yahoo.com.mx*) is a consortium of high-quality, knowledgeable local guides who know the area well and lead a variety of half- and full-day tours. (The U.S. Agency for International Development planted the seed money to get the project going.) They can take you for a hike in the reserve or out to Monkey Point, with a return trip by boat. They also have horseback riding; bird-, dolphin-, and turtle-watching; and traditional fishing excursions.

DIVING AND SNORKELING

The friendly staff at **Aquamor Talamanca Adventures** (✉ *Main road* ☎ *2759–0612* 🌐 *www.greencoast.com/aquamor.htm*) specializes in land- and ocean-focused tours of the Gandoca-Manzanillo Wildlife Refuge, and can tend to all your water-sporting needs in these parts, with guided kayaking, snorkeling, and scuba-diving tours, as well as equipment rental. They also offer the complete sequence of PADI-certified diving courses. Companies in Puerto Viejo de Talamanca (⇨ *above*) can arrange boat trips to dive spots and beaches in the refuge as well.

DOLPHIN-WATCHING

The **Talamanca Dolphin Foundation** (✉ *Main road, Manzanillo* ☎ *2759–9188* 🌐 *www.dolphinlink.org*) has 2½-hour dolphin observation tours—excellent opportunities to see bottlenose, *tucuxi* (gray), and Atlantic spotted dolphins swimming this section of the coast.

WHERE TO EAT AND STAY

$ SEAFOOD

✕ **Restaurant Maxi's.** Cooled by sea breezes and shaded by tall, stately palms, this two-story, brightly painted wooden building offers weary travelers cold beer, potent cocktails, and great seafood at unbeatable prices after a day's hike in the refuge. Locals and expatriates alike—and even chefs from Puerto Viejo's fancier restaurants—come here for their lobster fix, and the fresh fish is wonderful, too. At one time, perhaps before tourism became big in this area, Costa Ricans made Maxi's into an entire day trip. Now that the road is paved all the way to Manzanillo, the weekend crowds are getting ever larger. Locals tend to congregate in the rowdy but pleasant downstairs bar, where reggae beats into the wee hours. ✉ *Main road, Manzanillo* ☎ *2759–9073* ▭ *No credit cards.*

$$$$

Almonds & Corals Tent Lodge Camp. Buried in a dark, densely atmospheric beachfront jungle within the Gandoca-Manzanillo Wildlife Refuge, Almonds & Corals takes tent camping to a new level. The "campsites" are freestanding platforms raised on stilts and linked by boardwalks lighted by kerosene lamps. Each safari-style tent is protected by a peaked roof and enclosed in mosquito netting, and has beds, electric lamps, hammocks, and hot water. A fine three-meal restaurant is tucked into the greenery halfway down to the property's exquisite, secluded beach. Rustic camping this is not, but the locale does provide that close-to-nature experience. Your wake-up call is provided by howler monkeys and chatty parrots. These folks also offer multiday packages that include round-trip transportation from San José. **Pros:** rustic comfort; lots of activities. **Cons:** far from sights; need car to stay here. ✉ *Near end of road to Manzanillo* *Apdo. 681–2300, San José* ☎ *2759–9056, 2272–2024 in San José* 🌐 *www.almondsandcorals.com* *24 tent-cabins* *In-room: no a/c, no phone (some), refrigerator (some), no TV. In-hotel: restaurant, bar, laundry service, Internet terminal* ▭ *AE, D, DC, MC, V* *MAP.*

¢

Cabinas Something Different. On a quiet street, these shiny, spic-and-span motel-style cabinas are the nicest option in the village of Manzanillo. Each bright tile-floor unit comes with a TV—quite a rarity in these parts—a table, and a small porch. Several sleep up to four people. **Pros:** good budget value; television. **Cons:** small rooms; spartan rooms. ✉ *180 m south of Aquamor, Manzanillo* ☎ *2759–9014* *18 cabinas* *In-room: no a/c (some), no phone, refrigerator* ▭ *No credit cards* *EP.*

9

CROSSING INTO PANAMA VIA SIXAOLA

Costa Rica's sleepy border post at Sixaola fronts Guabito, Panama's equally quiet border crossing, 44 km (26 mi) south of the turnoff to Puerto Viejo de Talamanca. Both are merely collections of banana-plantation stilt houses and a few stores and bars; neither has any lodging or dining options, but this is a much more low-key crossing into Panama than the busy border post at Paso Canoas on the Pan-American Highway near the Pacific coast. If you've come this far, you're likely headed to **Bocas del Toro,** the real attraction in the northwestern part of Panama. This archipelago of 68 islands continues the Afro-Caribbean and indigenous themes seen on Costa Rica's Atlantic coast, and offers diving, snorkeling, swimming, and wildlife-viewing. The larger islands are home to a growing selection of hotels and restaurants, everything from funky to fabulous. "Bocas" has acquired a cult following among long-term foreign visitors to Costa Rica, who find it a convenient place to travel when their permitted three-month status as a tourist has expired, since a quick 72-hour jaunt out of the country gets you another three months in Costa Rica.

ANOTHER GOOD BOOK

If you're headed to Panama, we'd be remiss in not recommending that you pick up a copy of *Fodor's Panama* for far more detail about Bocas del Toro and the rest of the country than we can provide here.

■ **TIP→Whatever your destination in Panama, come armed with dollars.** Panama uses U.S. currency, but refers to the dollar as the *balboa.* (It does mint its own coins, all the same size as their U.S. counterparts.) No one anywhere will accept or exchange your Costa Rican colones.

Costa Rican rental vehicles may not leave the country, so crossing into Panama as a tourist is an option only via public transportation. The public bus route from San José to Cahuita and Puerto Viejo de Talamanca terminates here at the border approximately six hours after leaving the capital. Taxis in Puerto Viejo de Talamanca charge about $50 for the jaunt to the border, a much quicker and reasonable option if you can split the fare among a group. Disembark and head for the Costa Rican immigration office (☎ *2754–2044*) down a flight of stairs from the west end of a former railroad bridge. Officials place an exit stamp in your passport, after which you walk across the bridge and present your passport to Panamanian immigration. U.S., U.K., and Canadian visitors must also purchase a $5 tourist card for entry into the country; Australian and New Zealand citizens need only their passports.

The **Consulate of Panama** (☎ *2280–1570*) in San José can provide more information. The border crossings are open 7 AM–5 PM (8 AM–6 PM Panamanian time) daily. Set your watch one hour ahead when you enter Panama.

Taxis wait on the Panamanian side to transport you to the small city of Changuinola, the first community of any size inside the country, from which there are bus and air connections for travel farther into Panama. Taxis can also take you to Almirante, where you'll find boat launches to Bocas del Toro.

UNDERSTANDING COSTA RICA

COSTA RICA AT A GLANCE

FAST FACTS

Capital: San José

Type of government: Democratic republic

Independence: September 15, 1821 (from Spain)

Population: 4,248,508

Population density: 82 persons per square km (204 persons per square mi)

Literacy: 95%

Language: Spanish (official); English spoken by most in the tourism industry

Ethnic groups: White (including mestizo) 94%, black 3%, Amerindian 1%, Asian 1%, other 1%

Religion: Roman Catholic 76%, Evangelical Protestant 15%, other 6%, none 3%

GEOGRAPHY & ENVIRONMENT

Land area: 51,100 square km (19,730 square mi); slightly smaller than the U.S. state of West Virginia

Coastline: 1,290 km (802 mi)

Terrain: Rugged central range with 112 volcanic craters that separates the eastern and western coastal plains

Natural resources: Hydroelectric power, forest products, fisheries products

Natural hazards: Droughts, flash floods, thunderstorms, earthquakes, hurricanes, active volcanoes, landslides

Flora: 9,000 species, including 1,200 orchid species and 800 fern species; tidal mangrove swamps, tropical rain forest, subalpine forest

Fauna: 36,518 species, including 34,000 species of insects and 2,000 species of butterflies

Environmental issues: Deforestation, rapid industrialization and urbanization, air and water pollution, soil degradation, plastic waste, fisheries protection

ECONOMY

Currency: Colón, (*pl.*) colones

GDP: $37.97 billion

Per capita income: $4,670

Unemployment: 6.6%

Major industries: Tourism, microprocessors, food processing, textiles and clothing, construction materials, fertilizer, plastic products

Agricultural products: Bananas, coffee, pineapples, sugarcane, corn, rice, beans, potatoes, beef

Exports: $6.2 billion

Major export products: Bananas, coffee, pineapples, electronic components, fertilizers, sugar, textiles, electricity

Export partners: (in order of volume) U.S., Hong Kong, Holland, Guatemala, Canada, Malaysia, Nicaragua, Germany

Imports: $7.84 billion

Major import products: Chemicals, consumer goods, electronic components, machinery, petroleum products, vehicles

Import partners: U.S. (41%), Japan (5.6%), Venezuela (4.8), Mexico (4.8%), Ireland (4.2%), China (4.2%), Brazil (4.2%)

DID YOU KNOW?

- Tourism earns more foreign exchange than bananas and coffee combined.
- Costa Rica did away with its military in 1949.
- Five percent of the world's identified plant and animal species are found in this country.
- Costa Rica is the home of five active volcanoes—including Volcán Arenal, the second-largest active volcano in the world.

A BRIEF HISTORY

First Encounters

In mid-September 1502, on his fourth and last voyage to the New World, Christopher Columbus was sailing along the Caribbean coast of Central America when his ships were caught in a violent tropical storm. He found sanctuary in a bay protected by a small island; ashore, he encountered native people wearing heavy gold disks who spoke of great amounts of gold in the area. Sailing farther south, Columbus encountered more natives wearing gold. He was convinced that he had discovered a land of great wealth.

The Spanish Colonial Era

The first few attempts by the Spanish to conquer Costa Rica, beginning in 1506, were unsuccessful owing to sickness and starvation among the Spanish troops, hearty resistance by the indigenous population, and rivalries between various expeditions. By 1560, almost 60 years after its discovery, no permanent Spanish settlement existed in Costa Rica, and early settlers were largely left to their own devices. But that all changed in 1563, when explorer Juan Vásquez de Coronado—a "good Coronado" as Ticos are fond of saying, to distinguish him from other pillaging conquistadors named Coronado—founded the colonial capital of Cartago.

Costa Rica remained the smallest and poorest of Spain's Central American colonies, producing little wealth for the empire. Unlike other mineral-rich colonies around it, Costa Rica was largely ignored. The population stayed at fewer than 20,000 for centuries, and was mainly confined to small, isolated farms in the highland Central Valley and the Pacific lowlands. By the end of the 18th century, however, Costa Rica began to emerge from isolation. Some trade with neighboring Spanish colonies was carried out and the population began to expand across the Central Valley.

When Napoléon defeated and removed King Charles IV in 1808 and installed his brother Joseph on the Spanish throne, Costa Rica pledged support to the old regime, even sending troops to Nicaragua in 1811 to help suppress a rebellion against Spain. By 1821, though, sentiment favoring independence from Spain was prevalent throughout Central America, and a declaration of independence for all of Central America was issued by Guatemala on September 15 of that year. Costa Rica then became part of the Mexican empire until 1826, when it became part of the United Provinces of Central America. Costa Rica declared its independence as a sovereign nation in 1838.

The only major threat to that sovereignty took place in 1856, when the mercenary army of U.S. adventurer William Walker invaded the country from Nicaragua, which it had conquered the year before. Walker's plan to turn the Central American nations into slave states was cut short by Costa Rican president Juan Rafael Mora, who raised a volunteer army and repelled the invaders, pursuing them into Nicaragua and joining troops from various Central American nations to defeat the mercenaries. This conflict produced national hero Juan Santamaría, a young drummer boy from a poor family *(⇨CloseUp "A National Hero" in Chapter 4)*.

Foundations of Democracy

For most of the 19th century the country was ruled by a succession of wealthy families. Coffee was introduced to the country in the 1820s and bananas in the 1870s, and these crops became the country's major sources of foreign exchange. The government spent profits from the coffee trade on improving roads and ports, and other civic projects that included San José's Teatro Nacional.

In 1889 the first free popular election was held, characterized by full freedom of the press, frank debates by rival candidates, an honest tabulation of the vote, and the first peaceful transition of power from a ruling group to the opposition. This provided the foundation of political stability that Costa Rica enjoys to this day.

Booming exports were cut short by the arrival of World War I, followed by the Great Depression and World War II. Poverty soared and a social revolution threatened in the late 1930s, as the popular Communist Party threatened strikes and violence. Costa Rica's version of the New Deal came in 1940, when conservative president Rafael Angel Calderón Guardia allied with the Catholic Church and implemented many of the Communist Party's demands, leading to a system of socialized medicine, minimum-wage laws, low-cost housing, and worker-protection laws.

The success of Calderón's social reforms was tainted by accusations of corruption, which resulted in a civil uprising in 1948, led by the still-revered José "Don Pepe" Figueres Ferrer, who had been exiled by Calderón as the political leader of the opposition. After a few months of armed conflict, a compromise was reached—Figueres would respect Calderón's social guarantees and preside over an interim government for 18 months. In 1949 Figueres abolished Costa Rica's military and created a national police force, nationalized the banking system and public utilities, and implemented health and education reforms. He stepped down after 18 months, only to be reelected twice in free elections.

The Modern Era

During the 1950s and 1960s, insurance, telecommunications, the railroad system (now defunct), ports, and other industries were nationalized. The state-led economic model, although increasingly inefficient, led to a rising standard of living until the early 1970s, when an economic crisis introduced Costa Ricans to hyperinflation. By the mid-1980s Costa Rica had begun pulling out of its economic slump, in part thanks to efforts to diversify the economy. By the mid-1990s, tourism had surpassed bananas as the country's largest earner of foreign exchange, and high-tech companies such as Intel and Motorola opened plants and service centers in Costa Rica, providing well-paid jobs for educated professionals.

Recent years have seen the continued growth of the tourism industry, and the establishment of a thriving but controversial Internet-based gambling industry tied to U.S. sporting events. The economy continues to bedevil Costa Rica: inflation hovers around 10% annually and the country's currency continues to be devalued on a regular basis. Attempts to privatize state-owned industries have been unsuccessful, and the process of negotiating a Central American free-trade agreement with the United States (and its mandated opening of state enterprises to competition) continues to generate heated debate.

Today the challenge facing Costa Rica is how to conserve its natural resources while still permitting modern development. The government has been unable or unwilling to control illegal logging, an industry that threatens to destroy the country's old-growth forests. Urban sprawl in the Central Valley and the development of megaresorts along the Pacific coast threaten forests, wildlife, and the slow pace of life that makes Costa Rica so enjoyable for visitors. Although tourism provides a much-needed injection of foreign exchange into the economy, the government has not fully decided which direction it should take. The buzzwords now are "ecotourism" and "sustainable development," and it is hoped that Costa Rica will find it possible to continue down these roads.

WILDLIFE AND PLANT GLOSSARY

Here is a rundown of some of the most common and attention-grabbing mammals, birds, reptiles, amphibians, plants, and even a few insects that you might encounter. We give the common Costa Rican names, so you can understand the local lingo, followed by the latest scientific terms.

Fauna

Agouti (*guatusa*; *Dasyprocta punctata*): A 20-inch, tail-less rodent with small ears and a large muzzle, the agouti is reddish brown on the Pacific side, more of a tawny orange on the Caribbean slope. It sits on its haunches to eat large seeds and fruit and resembles a large rabbit without the long ears.

Anteater (*oso hormiguero*): Three species of anteater inhabit Costa Rica—the very rare giant (*Myrmecophaga tridactyla*), the nocturnal silky (*Cyclopes didactylus*), and the Collared, or Vested (*Tamandua mexicana*). Only the last is commonly seen, and too often as roadkill. This medium-size anteater, 30 inches long with an 18-inch tail, laps up ants and termites with its long, sticky tongue and has long, sharp claws for ripping into insect nests.

Armadillo (*cusuco*; *Dasypus novemcinctus*): The nine-banded armadillo is widespread in Costa Rica and also found in the southern United States. This nocturnal and solitary edentate roots in soil with a long muzzle for a varied diet of insects, small animals, and plant material.

Baird's Tapir (*danta*; *Tapirus bairdii*): The largest land mammal in Costa Rica (to 6½ feet), Baird's tapir is something like a small rhinoceros without armor. Adapted to a wide range of habitats, it's nocturnal, seldom seen, but said to defecate and sometimes sleep in water. Tapirs are herbivorous and use their prehensile snouts to harvest vegetation. The best opportunities for viewing wild tapirs are in Corcovado National Park.

Bat (*murciélogo*): With more than 100 species, Costa Rica's bats can be found eating fruit, insects, fish, small vertebrates, nectar, and even blood, in the case of the infamous vampire bat (*vampiro, Desmodus rotundus*), which far prefers cattle blood to that of any tourist. As a group, bats are extremely important ecologically, and are essential to seed dispersal, pollination, and controlling insect populations.

Butterfly (*mariposa*): Estimates of the number of butterfly species in Costa Rica vary, but all range in the thousands. The growing number of butterfly gardens popping up around the country is testament to their popularity among visitors. Three Costa Rican Morpho species—spectacular, large butterflies—have a brilliant-blue upper wing surface, giving them their local nickname of *pedazos de ciel* (pieces of sky). The blue morpho (*Morpho peleides*), arguably the most distinctive, is common in moister areas and has an intense ultraviolet upper surface. Adults feed on fermenting fruit; they never visit flowers.

Caiman (*caiman*): The spectacled caiman (*Caiman crocodilus*) is a small crocodilian (to 7 feet) inhabiting fresh water, subsisting mainly on fish. Most active at night (it has bright-red eye shine), it basks by day. It is distinguished from the American crocodile by a sloping brow and smooth back scales.

Coati (*pizote*; *Nasua narica*): This is a long-nose relative of the raccoon, its long tail often held straight up. Lone males or groups of females with young are active during the day, on the ground, or in trees. Omnivorous coatis feed on fruit, invertebrates, and small vertebrates. Unfortunately, many have learned to beg from tourists, especially in Monteverde and on the roads around Arenal.

Cougar (*puma*; *Felis concolor*): Mountain lions are the largest unspotted cats (to 8 feet, including the tail) in Costa Rica. Widespread but rare, they live in essentially all-wild habitats and feed on vertebrates ranging from snakes to deer.

Crocodile (*lagarto*; *Crocodylus acutus*): The American crocodile, up to 16 feet in length, is found in most major river systems, particularly the Tempisque and Tárcoles estuaries. It seldom attacks humans, preferring fish and birds. It's distinguished from the caiman by size, a flat head, narrow snout, and spiky scales.

Ctenosaur (*garrobo*; *Ctenosaura similis*): Also known as the black, or spiny-tailed, iguana, this is a large (up to 18 inches long with an 18-inch tail) tan lizard with four dark bands on its body and a tail ringed with sharp, curved spines, reminiscent of a dinosaur. Terrestrial and arboreal, it sleeps in burrows or tree hollows. It lives along the coast in the dry northwest and in wetter areas farther south. The fastest known reptile (clocked on land), the ctenosaur has been recorded moving at 21.7 mi per hour.

Dolphin (*delfín*): Several species, including bottlenose dolphins (*Tursiops truncatus*), frolic in Costa Rican waters. Often seen off Pacific shores are spotted dolphins (*Stenella attenuata*), which are small (up to 6 feet), with pale spots on the posterior half of the body; they commonly travel in groups of 20 or more and play around vessels and in bow wakes. Tucuxi dolphins (*Sotalia fluviatilis*) have also been spotted in small groups off the southern Caribbean coast, frequently with bottlenose dolphins.

Frog and Toad (*rana,* frog; *sapo,* toad): Some 120 species of frog exist in Costa Rica; many are nocturnal. The most colorful daytime amphibians are the tiny strawberry poison dart frog (*Dendrobates pumilio*) and green-and-black poison dart frog. The bright coloration of these two species, either red with blue or green hind legs or charcoal black with fluorescent green markings, warns potential predators of their toxicity. The red-eyed leaf frog (*Agalychnis callidryas*) is among the showiest of nocturnal species. The large, brown marine toad (*Bufo marinus*), also called cane toad or giant toad, comes out at night.

Howler Monkey (*mono congo*; *Alouatta palliata*): These dark, chunky-bodied monkeys (to 22 inches long with a 24-inch tail) with black faces travel in troops of up to 20. Lethargic mammals, they eat leaves, fruits, and flowers. The males' deep, resounding howls sound like lions roaring, but actually serve as communication among and between troops.

Hummingbird (*Trochilidae*): Weighing just a fraction of an ounce, hummingbirds are nonetheless some of the most notable residents of tropical forests. At least 50 varieties can be found in Costa Rica, visiting typically red, tubular flowers in their seemingly endless search for energy-rich nectar. Because of their assortment of iridescent colors and bizarre bills and tail shapes, watching them can be a spectator sport. Best bets are hummingbird feeders and anywhere with great numbers of flowers.

Iguana (*iguana*): Mostly arboreal but good at swimming, the iguana is Costa Rica's largest lizard: males can grow to 10 feet, including tail. Only young green iguanas (*Iguana iguana*) are bright green; adults are much duller, females dark grayish, and males olive (with orangish heads in breeding season). All have round cheek scales and smooth tails.

Jaguar (*tigre*; *Panthera onca*): The largest New World feline (to 6 feet, with a 2-foot tail), this top-of-the-line predator is exceedingly rare but lives in a wide variety of habitats, from dry forest to cloud forest. It's most common in the vast Amistad Biosphere Reserve, but it is almost never seen in the wild.

Jesus Christ Lizard (*gallego*): Flaps of skin on long toes enable this spectacular lizard to run across water. Costa Rica has three species of this lizard, which is more properly called the basilisk: lineated (*Basiliscus basiliscus*) on the Pacific side is brown with pale lateral stripes; in the Caribbean, emerald (*Basiliscus plumifrons*) is marked with turquoise and black on a green body; and striped (*Basiliscus vittatus*), also on the Caribbean side, resembling the lineated basilisk. Adult males grow to 3 feet (mostly tail), with crests on the head, back, and base of the tail.

Leaf-Cutter Ant (*zompopas*; *Atta spp.*): Found in all lowland habitats, these are the most commonly noticed neotropical ants, and one of the country's most fascinating animal phenomena. Columns of ants carrying bits of leaves twice their size sometimes extend for several hundred yards from an underground nest to plants being harvested. The ants don't eat the leaves; their food is a fungus they cultivate on the leaves.

Macaw (*lapas*): Costa Rica's two species are the scarlet macaw (*Ara macao*), on the Pacific side (Osa Peninsula and Carara Biological Reserve), and the severely threatened great green macaw (*Ara ambigua*), on the Caribbean side. These are huge, raucous parrots with long tails; their immense bills are used to rip fruit apart to reach the seeds. They nest in hollow trees and are victimized by pet-trade poachers and deforestation.

Magnificent Frigatebird (*tijereta del mar*; *Fregata magnificens*): A large, black soaring bird with slender wings and forked tail, this is one of the most effortless and agile flyers in the avian world. More common on the Pacific coast, it doesn't dive or swim but swoops to pluck its food, often from the mouths of other birds.

Manatee (*manatí; Trichechus manatus*): Although endangered throughout its range, the West Indian manatee can be spotted in Tortuguero, meandering along in shallow water, browsing on submerged vegetation. The moniker "sea cow" is apt, as they spend nearly all their time resting or feeding. Their large, somewhat amorphous bodies won't win any beauty contests, but they do appear quite graceful.

Margay (*caucel*; *Felis wiedii*): Fairly small, this spotted nocturnal cat (22 inches long, with an 18-inch tail) is similar to the ocelot but has a longer tail and is far more arboreal: mobile ankle joints allow it to climb down trunks head first. It eats small vertebrates.

Motmot (*pájaro bobo*): These handsome, turquoise-and-rufous birds of the understory have racket-shaped tails. Nesting in burrows, they sit patiently while scanning for large insect prey or small vertebrates. Costa Rica has six species.

Northern Jacana (*gallito de agua*; *Jacana spinosa*): These birds are sometimes called "lily trotters" because their long toes allow them to walk on floating vegetation. Feeding on aquatic organisms and plants, they're found in almost any body of water. They expose yellow wing feathers in flight. Sex roles are reversed; "liberated" females are larger and compete for mates (often more than one), whereas the males tend to the nest and care for the young.

Ocelot (*manigordo*; *Felis pardalis*): Mostly terrestrial, this medium-size spotted cat (33 inches long, with a 16-inch tail) is active night and day, and feeds on rodents and other vertebrates. Forepaws are rather large in relation to the body, hence the local name, *manigordo,* which means "fat hand."

Opossum (*zorro pelón*; *Didelphis marsupialis*): Like the kangaroo, the common opossum belongs to that rare breed of mammals known as marsupials, distinguished by their brief gestation period and completion of development and nourishment following birth in the mother's pouch. The Costa Rican incarnation does not "play possum," and will bite if cornered rather than pretend to be dead.

Oropendola (*oropéndola*; *Psarocolius* spp.): These crow-size birds in the oriole family have a bright-yellow tail and nest in colonies, in pendulous nests (up to 6 feet long) built by females in isolated trees. The Montezuma species has an orange beak and blue cheeks, the chestnut-headed has a yellow beak. Males make an unmistakable, loud, gurgling liquid call. The bird is far more numerous on the Caribbean side.

Parakeet and Parrot (*pericos*, parakeets; *loros*, parrots): There are 15 species in Costa Rica (plus two macaws), all clad in green, most with a splash of a primary color or two on the head or wings. They travel in boisterous flocks, prey on immature seeds, and nest in cavities.

Peccary: Piglike animals with thin legs and thick necks, peccaries travel in small groups (larger where the population is still numerous); root in soil for fruit, seeds, and small creatures; and have a strong musk odor. You'll usually smell them before you see them. Costa Rica has two species: the collared peccary (*saíno, Tayassu tajacu*) and the white-lipped peccary (*chancho de monte, Tayassu pecari*). The latter is now nearly extinct.

Pelican (*pelícano*): Large size, a big bill, and a throat pouch make the brown pelican (*Pelecanus occidentalis*) unmistakable in coastal areas (it's far more abundant on the Pacific side). Pelicans often fly in V formations and dive for fish.

Quetzal One of the world's most exquisite birds, the resplendent quetzal (*Pharomachrus mocinno*) was revered by the Maya. Glittering green plumage and the male's long tail coverts draw thousands of people to highland cloud forests for sightings from February to April.

Roseate Spoonbill (*garza rosada*; *Ajaja ajaja*): Pink plumage and a spatulate bill set this wader apart from all other wetland birds; it feeds by swishing its bill back and forth in water while using its feet to stir up bottom-dwelling creatures. Spoonbills are most common around Palo Verde and Caño Negro.

Sloth (*perezoso*): Costa Rica is home to the brown-throated, three-toed sloth (*Bradypus variegatus*) and Hoffmann's two-toed sloth (*Choloepus hoffmanni*). Both grow to 2 feet, but two-toed (check forelegs) sloths often look bigger because of longer fur and are the only species in the highlands. Sloths are herbivorous, accustomed to a low-energy diet, and well camouflaged.

Snake (*culebra*): Costa Rica's serpents can be found in trees, above and below ground, and even in the sea on the Pacific coast. Most of the more than 125 species are harmless, but are best appreciated from a distance. Notable members of this group include Costa Rica's largest snake, the boa constrictor (*Boa constrictor*), reaching up to 15 feet, and the fer-de-lance (*terciopelo, Bothrops asper*), which is a much smaller (up to 6 feet) but far more dangerous viper.

Spider Monkey (*mono colorado, mono araña*): Lanky and long-tailed, the black-handed spider monkey (*Ateles geoffroyi*) is the largest monkey in Costa Rica (to 24 inches, with a 32-inch tail). Moving in groups of two to four, they eat ripe fruit, leaves, and flowers. Incredible aerialists, they can swing effortlessly through branches using long arms and legs and prehensile tails. They are quite aggressive and will challenge onlookers and often throw down branches. Caribbean and southern Pacific populations are dark reddish brown; northwesterners are blond.

Squirrel Monkey (*mono tití*): The smallest of four Costa Rican monkeys (11 inches, with a 15-inch tail), the red-backed squirrel monkey (*Saimiri oerstedii*) has a distinctive facial pattern (black cap and muzzle, white mask) and gold-orange coloration on its back. It is the only Costa Rican monkey without a prehensile tail. The species travels in noisy, active groups of 20 or more, feeding on fruit and insects. Numbers of this endangered species have been estimated between 2,000 and 4,000 individuals. Most squirrel monkeys in Costa Rica are found in Manuel Antonio National Park, in parts of the Osa Peninsula, and around the Golfo Dulce.

Three-Wattled Bellbird (*pájaro campana*; *Procnias tricarunculata*): Although endangered, the bellbird can be readily identified in cloud forests (around Monteverde, for example), where it breeds by its extraordinary call, a bold and aggressive "bonk," unlike any other creature in the forest. If you spot a male calling, look for the three pendulous wattles at the base of its beak.

Toucan (*tucán, tucancillo*): The keel-billed toucan (*Ramphastos sulfuratus*) with the rainbow-colored beak is familiar to anyone who's seen a box of Froot Loops cereal. Chestnut-mandibled toucans (*Ramphastos swainsonii*) are the largest (18 inches and 22 inches); as the name implies, their lower beaks are brown. The smaller, stouter emerald toucanet (*Aulacorhynchus prasinus*) and yellow-eared toucanet (*Selenidera spectabilis*) are aptly named. Aracaris (*Pteroglossus Spp.*) are similar to toucans, but colored orange-and-yellow with the trademark toucan bill.

Turtles (*tortuga*): Observing the nesting rituals of the five species of marine turtles here is one of those truly memorable Costa Rican experiences. Each species has its own nesting season and locale. The olive ridley (*lora*; *Lepidochelys olivacea*) is the smallest of the sea turtles (average carapace, or hardback shell, is 21–29 inches) and the least shy. Thousands engage in nighttime group nesting rituals on the North Pacific's Ostional. At the other extreme, but only slightly farther north on Playa Grande, nests the leatherback (*baula*; *Dermochelys coriacea*) with its five-foot-long shell. On the north Caribbean coast, Tortuguero hosts four of them: the leatherback, the hawksbill (*carey*; *Eretmochelys imbricata*), the loggerhead (*caguama*; *Caretta caretta*), and the green (*tortuga verde*; *Chelonia mydas*), with its long nesting season (June–October) that draws the most visitors and researchers.

Whales (*ballena*): Humpback whales (*Megaptera novaeanglia*) appear off the Pacific coast between November and February; they migrate from California and as far as Hawaii. You can also spot Sey whales, Bryde's whales, and farther out to sea, blue whales and sperm whales. On the Caribbean side, there are smaller (12 to 14 feet) Koiga whales.

White-Faced Capuchin Monkey (*mono cara blanca*; *Cebus capuchinus*): Medium-size and omnivorous, this monkey (to 18 inches, with a 20-inch tail) has black fur and a pink face surrounded by a whitish bib. Extremely active foragers, they move singly or in groups of up to 20, examining the environment closely and even coming to the ground. It's the most commonly seen monkey in Costa Rica. It's also the most often fed by visitors, to the point where some monkey populations now have elevated cholesterol levels.

White-Tailed Deer (*venado*; *Odocoileus virginianus*): Bambi would feel at home in Costa Rica, although his counterparts here are slightly smaller. As befits the name, these animals possess the distinctive white underside to their tail (and to their bellies). They are seen in drier parts of the country, especially in the northwest province of Guanacaste.

White-Throated Magpie-jay (*urraca*; *Calocitta formosa*): This southern relative of the blue jay, with a long tail and distinctive topknot (crest of forward-curved feathers), is found in the dry northwest. Bold and inquisitive, with amazingly varied vocalizations, these birds travel in noisy groups of four or more.

Flora

Ant-acacia (*acacia; Acacia* spp.): If you'll be in the tropical dry forest of Guanacaste, learn to avoid this plant. As if its sharp thorns weren't enough, acacias exhibit an intense symbiosis with various ant species (*Pseudomyrmex* spp.) that will attack anything—herbivores, other plants, and unaware human visitors that come in contact with the tree. The ants and the acacias have an intriguing relationship, though, so do look, but don't touch.

Bromeliad (*piña silvestre*): Members of the family Bromeliaceae are *epiphytes,* living on the trunk and branches of trees. They are not parasitic, however, and so have adapted to acquire all the necessary water and nutrients from what falls into the central "tank" formed by the leaf structure. Amphibians and insects also use the water held in bromeliads to reproduce, forming small aquatic communities perched atop tree branches. In especially wet areas, small bromeliads can even be found on power lines. Their spectacular, colorful efflorescences make popular—and expensive—houseplants in northern climes.

Heliconia (*helicónia; Heliconia* spp.): It's hard to miss these stunning plants, many of which have huge inflorescences of red, orange, and yellow, sometimes shaped like lobster claws, and leaves very much the size and shape of a banana plant. With luck, you'll catch a visiting hummingbird with a beak specially designed to delve into a heliconia flower—truly a visual treat.

Mangroves (*manglares*): Taken together, this handful of salt-tolerant trees with tangled, above-ground roots make up their own distinct ecosystem. Buttressing the land against the sea, they serve as nurseries for countless species of fish, crabs, and other marine animals and provide roosting habitat for marine birds. Mangroves are found on the coast in protected areas such as bays and estuaries.

Naked Indian Tree (*indio desnudo; Bursera simaruba*): This tree can be found in forests throughout Costa Rica, often forming living fences, and is instantly identifiable by its orange bark that continually sloughs off, giving rise to another common name, the sunburnt tourist tree. One theory suggests that the shedding of its bark aids in removing parasites from the tree's exterior.

Orchid (*orquídea*): The huge Orchidaceae family has more than 1,200 representatives in Costa Rica alone, with nearly 90% percent living as epiphytes on other plants. The great diversity of the group includes not only examples of great beauty but exquisite adaptations between flowers and their insect pollinators. With a combination of rewards (nectar) and trickery (visual and chemical cues), orchids exhibit myriad ways of enticing insects to cooperate.

Strangler Fig (*Matapalo*; *Ficus spp.*): Starting as seedlings high in the canopy, these aggressive plants grow both up toward the light, and down to the soil, slowly taking over the host tree. Eventually they encircle and appear to "strangle" the host, actually killing it by hogging all the available sunlight, leaving a ring of fig trunk around an empty interior. Figs with ripe fruit are excellent places for wildlife spotting, as they attract monkeys, birds, and an assortment of other creatures.

MENU GUIDE

Rice and beans are the heart of Costa Rica's *comida típica* (typical food). It's possible to order everything from sushi to crepes in and around San José, but most Ticos have a simple diet built around rice, beans, and the myriad fruits and vegetables that flourish here. Costa Rican food isn't spicy, and many dishes are seasoned with the same five ingredients—onion, salt, garlic, cilantro, and red bell pepper.

SPANISH	ENGLISH

GENERAL DINING

Almuerzo	Lunch
Bocas	Appetizers or snacks (literally "mouthfuls") served with drinks in the tradition of Spanish tapas.
Casado	Heaping plate of rice, beans, fried plantains, cabbage salad, tomatoes, macarrones (noodles), and fish, chicken, or meat—or any variation thereof; casado and plato del día are often used interchangeably.
Cena	Dinner
Desayuno	Breakfast
Plato del día	Plate of the day
Soda	An inexpensive café; casados are always found at sodas.

ESPECIALIDADES (SPECIALTIES)

Arreglados	Sandwiches or meat and vegetable puff pastry.
Arroz con mariscos	Fried rice with fish, shrimp, octopus, and clams, or whatever's fresh that day.
Arroz con pollo	Chicken with rice
Camarones	Shrimp
Ceviche	Chilled, raw seafood marinated in lime juice, served with chopped onion and garlic
Chilaquiles	Meat-stuffed tortillas
Chorreados	Corn pancakes, served with natilla (sour cream)
Corvina	Sea bass
Empanadas	Savory or sweet pastry turnover filled with fruit or meat and vegetables.
Empanaditas	Small empanadas

SPANISH	ENGLISH
Gallo pinto	Rice sautéed with black beans (literally, "spotted rooster"), often served for breakfast.
Langosta	Lobster
Langostino	Prawns
Olla de carne	Soup of beef, chayote squash, corn, yuca (a tuber), and potatoes.
Palmitos	Hearts of palm, served in salads or as a side dish.
Pejibaye	A nutty, orange-colored palm fruit eaten in salads, soups, and as a snack.
Pescado ahumado	Smoked marlin
Picadillo	Chayote squash, potatoes, carrots, or other vegetables chopped into small cubes and combined with onions, garlic, and ground beef.
Pozol	Corn soup
Salsa caribeño	A combination of tomatoes, onions, and spices that accompanies most fish dishes on the Caribbean coast.

POSTRES (DESSERTS) & DULCES (SWEETS)

Cajeta de coco	Fudge made with coconut and orange peel
Cajeta	Molasses-flavored fudge
Dulce de leche	Thick syrup of boiled milk and sugar
Flan	Caramel-topped egg custard
Mazamorra	Cornstarch pudding
Pan de maiz	Sweet corn bread
Torta chilena	Flaky, multilayered cake with dulce de leche filling.
Tres leches cake	"Three milks" cake, made with condensed and evaporated milk and cream.

FRUTAS (FRUITS)

Aguacate	Avocado
Anon	Sugar apple; sweet white flesh; resembles an artichoke with a thick rind
Banano	Banana
Bilimbi	Looks like a miniature cucumber crossed with a star fruit; ground into a savory relish.

SPANISH	ENGLISH
Fresa	Strawberry
Cas	A smaller guava
Granadilla	Passion fruit
Guanábana	Soursop; large, spiky yellow fruit with white flesh and a musky taste.
Guayaba	Guava
Mamon chino	Rambutan; red spiky ball protecting a white fruit similar to a lychee.
Mango	Many varieties, from sour green to succulently sweet Oro (golden); March is the height of mango season.
Manzana de agua	Water apple, shaped like a pear; juicy but not very sweet.
Marañon	Cashew fruit; used in juices
Melon	Cantaloupe
Mora	Blackberry
Palmito	Heart of palm
Piña	Pineapple
Papaya	One of the most popular and ubiquitous fruits.
Pipa	Green coconut; sold at roadside stands with ends chopped off and straws stuck inside.
Sandia	Watermelon
Carambola	Star fruit

BEBIDAS (BEVERAGES)

Agua dulce	Hot water sweetened with raw sugarcane.
Batido	Fruit shake made with milk (con leche) or water (con agua).
Café con leche	Coffee with hot milk
Café negro	Black coffee
Fresco natural	Fresh-squeezed juice
Guaro	Harsh, clear spirit distilled from fermented sugarcane.
Horchata	Cinnamon-flavored rice drink.
Refrescos	Tropical fruit smoothie with ice and sugar.

VOCABULARY

	ENGLISH	SPANISH	PRONUNCIATION
BASICS			
	Yes/no	Sí/no	see/no
	OK	De acuerdo	de a-**kwer**-doe
	Please	Por favor	pore fah-**vore**
	May I?	¿Me permite?	may pair-**mee**-tay
	Thank you (very much)	(Muchas) gracias	(**moo**-chas) **grah**-see-as
	You're welcome	Con mucho gusto	con **moo**-cho **goose**-toe
	Excuse me	Con permiso	con pair-**mee**-so
	Pardon me	¿Perdón?	pair-**dohn**
	Could you tell me?	¿Podría decirme?	po-dree-ah deh-**seer**-meh
	I'm sorry	Disculpe	Dee-**skool**-peh
	Good morning!	¡Buenos días!	**bway**-nohs **dee**-ahs
	Good afternoon!	¡Buenas tardes!	**bway**-nahs **tar**-dess
	Good evening!	¡Buenas noches!	**bway**-nahs **no**-chess
	Goodbye!	¡Adiós!/¡Hasta luego!	ah-dee-**ohss/ah**-stah-lwe-go
	Mr./Mrs.	Señor/Señora	sen-**yor**/sen-**yohr**-ah
	Miss	Señorita	sen-yo-**ree**-tah
	Pleased to meet you	Mucho gusto	**moo**-cho **goose**-toe
	How are you?	¿Cómo está usted?	**ko**-mo es-**tah** oo-**sted**
	Very well, thank you.	Muy bien, gracias.	**moo**-ee bee-**en**, **grah**-see-as
	And you?	¿Y usted?	ee oos-**ted**
DAYS OF THE WEEK			
	Sunday	domingo	doe-**meen**-goh
	Monday	lunes	**loo**-ness
	Tuesday	martes	**mahr**-tess
	Wednesday	miércoles	me-**air**-koh-less
	Thursday	jueves	hoo-**ev**-ess

ENGLISH	SPANISH	PRONUNCIATION
Friday	viernes	vee-**air**-ness
Saturday	sábado	**sah**-bah-doh

MONTHS

ENGLISH	SPANISH	PRONUNCIATION
January	enero	eh-**neh**-roh
February	febrero	feh-**breh**-roh
March	marzo	**mahr**-soh
April	abril	ah-**breel**
May	mayo	**my**-oh
June	junio	**hoo**-nee-oh
July	julio	**hoo**-lee-yoh
August	agosto	ah-**ghost**-toh
September	septiembre	sep-tee-**em**-breh
October	octubre	oak-**too**-breh
November	noviembre	no-vee-**em**-breh
December	diciembre	dee-see-**em**-breh

USEFUL PHRASES

ENGLISH	SPANISH	PRONUNCIATION
Do you speak English?	¿Habla usted inglés?	**ah**-blah oos-**ted** in-**glehs**
I don't speak Spanish	No hablo español	no **ah**-bloh es-pahn-**yol**
I don't understand (you)	No entiendo	no en-tee-**en**-doh
I understand (you)	Entiendo	en-tee-**en**-doh
I don't know	No sé	no seh
I am American/ British	Soy americano (americana) / inglés(a)	soy ah-meh-ree- **kah**-no (ah-meh-ree- **kah**-nah) / in-**glehs (ah)**
What's your name?	¿Cómo se llama usted?	koh-mo seh **yah**-mah **oos**-ted
My name is..	Me llamo..	may **yah**-moh
What time is it?	¿Qué hora es?	keh **o**-rah es
It is one, two, three ... o'clock.	Es la una ... Son las dos, tres	es la **oo**-nah/sohn lahs dohs, tress

ENGLISH	SPANISH	PRONUNCIATION
How?	¿Cómo?	**koh**-mo
When?	¿Cuándo?	**kwahn**-doh
This/Next week	Esta semana / la semana que entra	**es**-teh seh-**mah**- nah / lah seh-**mah**- nah keh **en**-trah
This/Next month	Este mes/el próximo mes	**es**-teh mehs/el **proke**-see-mo mehs
This/Next year	Este año/el año que viene	**es**-teh **ahn**-yo/el **ahn**-yo keh vee-**yen**-ay
Yesterday/today/ tomorrow	Ayer/hoy/mañana	ah-**yehr**/oy/mahn- **yah**-nah
This morning/ afternoon	Esta mañana/ tarde	**es**-tah mahn-**yah**- nah/ **tar**-deh
Tonight	Esta noche	**es**-tah **no**-cheh
What?	¿Qué?	keh
What is it?	¿Qué es esto?	keh es **es**-toh
Why?	¿Por qué?	pore **keh**
Who?	¿Quién?	kee-**yen**
Where is...?	¿Dónde está...?	**dohn**-deh es-**tah**
the bus stop?	la parada del autobus?	la pah-**rah**-dah del oh-toh-**boos**
the post office?	la oficina de correos?	la oh-fee-**see**-nah deh koh-**reh**-os
the museum?	el museo?	el moo-**seh**-oh
the hospital?	el hospital?	el ohss-pee-**tal**
the bathroom?	el baño?	el **bahn**-yoh
Here/there	Aquí/allá	ah-**key**/ah-**yah**
Open/closed	Abierto/cerrado	ah-bee-**er**-toh/ ser-**ah**-doh
Left/right	Izquierda/derecha	iss-key-**er**-dah/ dare-**eh**-chah
Straight ahead	Derecho	dare-**eh**-choh
Is it near/far?	¿Está cerca/lejos?	es-**tah** **sehr**-kah/ **leh**-hoss
I'd like...	Quisiera...	kee-see-ehr-ah

ENGLISH	SPANISH	PRONUNCIATION
a room	un cuarto/una habitación	oon **kwahr**-toh/ **oo**-nah ah-bee- tah-see-**on**
the key	la llave	lah **yah**-veh
a newspaper	un periódico	oon pehr-ee-**oh**- dee-koh
a stamp	la estampilla	lah es-stahm-**pee**-yah
I'd like to buy...	Quisiera comprar...	kee-see-**ehr**-ah kohm-**prahr**
a dictionary	un diccionario	oon deek-see-oh- **nah**-ree-oh
soap	jabón	hah-**bohn**
suntan lotion	loción bronceadora	loh-see-**ohn** brohn- seh-ah-**do**-rah
a map	un mapa	oon **mah-**pah
a magazine	una revista	**oon**-ah reh-**veess**-tah
a postcard	una tarjeta postal	**oon**-ah tar-**het**-ah post-**ahl**
How much is it?	¿Cuánto cuesta?	**kwahn**-toh **kwes**-tah
Telephone	Teléfono	tel-**ef**-oh-no
Help!	¡Auxilio!	owk-**see**-lee-oh
	¡Ayuda!	ah-**yoo**-dah
	¡Socorro!	soh-**kohr**-roh
Fire!	¡Incendio!	en-**sen**-dee-oo
Caution!/Look out!	¡Cuidado!	kwee-**dah**-doh

SALUD (HEALTH)

I am ill	Estoy enfermo(a)	es-**toy** en-**fehr**- moh(mah)
Please call a doctor	Por favor llame a un médico	pohr fah-**vor ya**-meh ah oon **med**-ee-koh
acetaminophen	acetaminofen	a-say-ta-**mee**-no-fen
ambulance	ambulancia	ahm-boo-**lahn**-see-a
antibiotic	antibiótico	ahn-tee-bee-**oh**-tee-co
aspirin	aspirina	ah-spi-**ree**-na
capsule	cápsula	**cahp**-soo-la

ENGLISH	SPANISH	PRONUNCIATION
clinic	clínica	**clee**-nee-ca
cold	resfriado	rays-free-**ah**-do
cough	tos	toess
diarrhea	diarrea	dee-ah-**ray**-a
fever	fiebre	fee-**ay**-bray
flu	Gripe	**gree**-pay
headache	dolor de cabeza	doh-**lor** day cah- **bay**-sa
hospital	hospital	oh-spee-**tahl**
medication	medicamento	meh-dee-cah-**men**-to
pain	dolor	doh-**lor**
pharmacy	farmacia	fahr-**mah**-see-a
physician	médico	**meh**-dee-co
prescription	receta	ray-**say**-ta
stomach ache	dolor de estómago	doh-**lor** day eh-**sto**-mah-go

Travel Smart Costa Rica

WORD OF MOUTH

"We've never used Interbus, but it's a great alternative for those who wish not to rent a car and drive. I can honestly say that, as a frequent solo traveler (and at 55, an older gal!), I find the public bus system lots of fun! Yes, [it helps that] I pack lightly, hang on to my bag, and speak intermediate Spanish. [Regardless], I've never had a negative experience—except for riding a couple of hours while standing in the aisle! If you can pack lightly and can speak enough Spanish to purchase your ticket, it's a great way to get around for next to nothing!"

—shillmac

www.fodors.com/forums

GETTING HERE & AROUND

AIR TRAVEL

If you are visiting several regions of the country, flying into San José's Aeropuerto Internacional Juan Santamaría, in the center of the country, is the best option. Flying into Liberia's Daniel Oduber Quirós International Airport makes sense if you are planning to spend your vacation in Guanacaste. Bus travel time between the Liberia airport and most of the resorts is less than two hours.

Most travelers fly into the larger San José airport, the transportation hub to nearly every point in the country. Rarely does an international flight get into San José early enough to make a domestic connection, particularly in the rainy season, as the weather is typically unsuitable for flying in the afternoon. So you'll likely end up spending your first night in or near the city, and leave for your domestic destination the next morning out of the SANSA terminal next to the international airport or via Nature Air out of tiny Tobias Bolaños Airport.

Heavy rains in the afternoon and evening during the May-to-November rainy season sometimes cause flights coming into San José to be rerouted to Panama City, where you may be forced to spend the night. October tends to be the worst month for reroutes. **TIP→In the rainy season, always book a flight with the earliest arrival time available.**

Once you're in Costa Rica, some airlines recommend that you call the San José office about three days before your return flight to reconfirm; others, such as TACA, explicitly say it's not necessary. It's always a good idea to call the local office the day before you are scheduled to return home to make sure your flight time hasn't changed.

The tiny, domestic passenger planes in Costa Rica require that you pack light. A luggage weight limit of 12 kilograms (27 pounds) is imposed by SANSA; Nature Air allows 13.6 kilograms (30 pounds). On some flights extra luggage is allowed, but is charged about $0.55 to $1 per pound. Heavy packers can leave their surplus for free in a locked area at Nature Air's terminal. SANSA does not store extra baggage.

If you arrive in Costa Rica and your baggage doesn't, the first thing you should do is go to the baggage claims counter and file an official report with your specific contact information. Then call your airline to find out if they can track it and how long you have to wait—generally bags are located within two days. Continue on your trip as you can; bags can be sent to you just about anywhere in the country. Don't expect too much from local officials; try to get updates from the airline directly.

If your bag has been searched and contents are missing or damaged, file a claim with the TSA Consumer Response Center as soon as possible. If your bags arrive damaged or fail to arrive at all, file a written report with the airline before leaving the airport.

When you fly out of Costa Rica, you'll have to pay a $26 airport departure tax in colones or with a Visa credit card. You can pay the tax upon arrival or departure at the Bancrédito counter in the airport, or at any Bancrédito or Banco de Costa Rica branch in Costa Rica during your trip. Lines can be long, so don't leave it until the last minute. The Hotel Presidente in the capital allows you to pay for the tax on your hotel bill and gives you the receipt for the airport. If you're staying at an upscale hotel, ask—the program is catching on fast.

Airline Security Issues Transportation Security Administration (🌐 *www.tsa.gov*) has answers for almost every question that might come up.

AIRPORTS

Costa Rica has two international airports. Aeropuerto Internacional Juan Santamaría (SJO) is the country's main airport. It's about 17 km (10 mi), or 30 minutes by car, northwest of downtown San José, just outside the city of Alajuela. The SANSA terminal for domestic flights is here. The country's other international airport is Daniel Oduber Quirós International Airport (LIR), a small airport near Liberia, in the North Pacific, the hub for domestic charter airline Macaw Air. Six commercial airlines fly to Liberia: United Airlines, from Chicago (December to April); Northwest, from Minneapolis; American Airlines, from Dallas and Miami; Delta, from Atlanta and Los Angeles; Continental, from Houston and Newark; and US Airways from Charlotte, North Carolina; regularly scheduled charter flights from the United States are few. The tiny Tobias Bolaños airport, in the San José suburb of Pavas (west of the city), serves domestic airline Nature Air, domestic charter companies, and a handful of private planes.

Other places where planes land in Costa Rica aren't exactly airports. They're more like a carport with a landing strip, at which an airline representative arrives just minutes before a plane is due to land or take off.

Prepare yourself for long waits at immigration and customs, and for check-in and security checkpoints, especially at Juan Santamaría, where you need to get to the airport three hours before your flight. This is slowly improving—eight new gates were finished in December 2007—but infrastructure improvements and other issues still face a bumpy road. Most North American flights arrive at this airport in the evening and depart early in the morning, which are the busiest times.

Liberia is a tiny airport, so check-in times are usually shorter. However, infrastructure hasn't quite caught up to the exponential increase in flights, so we recommend that you arrive at least two hours before international departures.

Juan Santamaría is a full-service airport with many arrivals and departures each day, so if you miss your flight or have some other unexpected mishap, you're better off here. Fares are usually lower to San José than to Liberia.

Airport Information Aeropuerto Internacional Daniel Oduber Quirós (*LIR* ✣ *13 km/8 mi west of Liberia* ☎ *506/2668–1010 in Costa Rica*). **Aeropuerto Internacional Juan Santamaría** (*SJO* ✣ *17 km/10 mi northwest of downtown San José, just outside Alajuela* ☎ *506/2437–2400, 506/2437–2626 in Costa Rica for departure and arrival info*). **Aeropuerto Internacional Tobías Bolaños** (✣ *6 km/4 mi west of San José, Pavas* ☎ *506/2232–2820 in Costa Rica*).

GROUND TRANSPORTATION

At Aeropuerto Internacional Juan Santamaría, you exit the terminal into a fume-filled parking area flanked by hordes of taxis and tour vans. If you're with a tour, you need only look for a representative of your tour company with a sign that bears your name. If you need a taxi, first buy a voucher at a counter just to the left of the arrivals exit, then present it to the driver of one of the orange Taxis Unidos cabs (no other taxis are allowed in the arrivals area). Rates are standardized to the various parts of town; most areas of San José are $18 to $20. Avoid the shuttle companies' *collectivos*, or minivans—they're almost the same price as a taxi (for two or fewer people), but the van is often crammed with other passengers, and you'll have to make stops at their hotels, making your transfer another journey in itself.

FLIGHTS

From the United States: Miami has the highest number of direct flights, but nonstop flights are also available from New York, Houston, Dallas, Atlanta, Phoenix, Charlotte, Fort Lauderdale, and Los Angeles. Continental, American, Delta, US Airways, and United are the major U.S. carriers with nonstop service to Costa Rica. Martinair has nonstop flights from Orlando and Miami. From New York, flights to San José are 5½ hours nonstop or 7 to 8 hours via Miami. From Los Angeles, flights are about 5½ hours nonstop or 8½ hours via Houston; from Houston, 3½ hours nonstop; from Miami, 3 hours; from Charlotte, 4 hours; and from Chicago, 7 hours, through Houston or Charlotte. In general, nonstop flights aren't that much more expensive. Median ticket prices from hubs such as New York, Los Angeles, and Seattle hover between $400 and $600, although the range can vary widely up or down.

Spirit Air, the first of the low-cost U.S. carriers to fly to Costa Rica, offers nonstop service to San José from Fort Lauderdale. Frontier Airlines followed suit in late 2007, with direct flights from Denver for the first part of the year (January to mid-August). Other than obvious considerations such as price and scheduling, a regional airline like Mexicana and TACA (a Central American airline) is a good choice if you're visiting more than one Central American country; major U.S. airlines don't serve routes such as Costa Rica–Honduras.

From elsewhere in Central America: international flights to Costa Rica tend to be cheaper than those to Nicaragua or Panama, so if you're doing two or three countries, it makes sense, budget-wise, to start in Costa Rica. Copa, TACA, and Lacsa fly between Panama City and San José and between Managua, Nicaragua, and San José. Nature Air flies between Bocas del Toro, Panama, and San José. At this writing, Nature Air flights into Limón were still on offer, but the fate of the route was uncertain because of infrastructure problems. Given Costa Rica's often difficult driving conditions, distances that appear short on a map can represent hours of driving on dirt roads pocked with craters; buses can be a slow and uncomfortable way to travel. Domestic flights are a desirable and practical option. And because 4WD rental rates can be steep, flying is often cheaper than driving. Most major destinations are served by daily domestic flights.

The informality of domestic air service—"airports" other than Liberia and San José usually consist of only an airstrip with no central building at which to buy tickets—means you might want to purchase your domestic airplane tickets in advance (by phone or online), although you can buy them at the San José or Liberia airports or at travel agencies once you're in the country. In theory, you can purchase tickets up to two hours before the flight departs. This is a potentially viable option in the May-through-November low season, but we recommend grabbing a seat as soon as you know your itinerary.

There are two major domestic commercial airlines: SANSA and Nature Air. Most Nature Air and SANSA flights leave from the San José area *(⇨ Airports)*. Commercial planes are small—holding between 6 and 19 passengers. Charter company Macaw Air flies its five-passenger Cessna 206 out of Liberia, allowing you to bypass San José altogether. Domestic flights originating in San José are generally nonstop, with the exception of some flights to the far south, where you might stop in Drake Bay first, then continue on to Puerto Jiménez, for example. SANSA and Nature Air both have a few nonstop inter-destinational flights, such as Tamarindo–Liberia, and a number of flights with quick connections or stops. You can buy SANSA and Nature Air tickets online, over the phone, and at most travel agencies in Costa Rica. Reserve Macaw Air tickets by e-mail or by phone.

Charter flights within Costa Rica are not as expensive as one might think, and can be an especially good deal if you are traveling in a group. If a group this size charters a small plane, the price per person will be only slightly more than taking a regularly scheduled domestic flight, and you can set your own departure time. The country has dozens of airstrips that are accessible only by charter planes. Charter planes are most often booked through

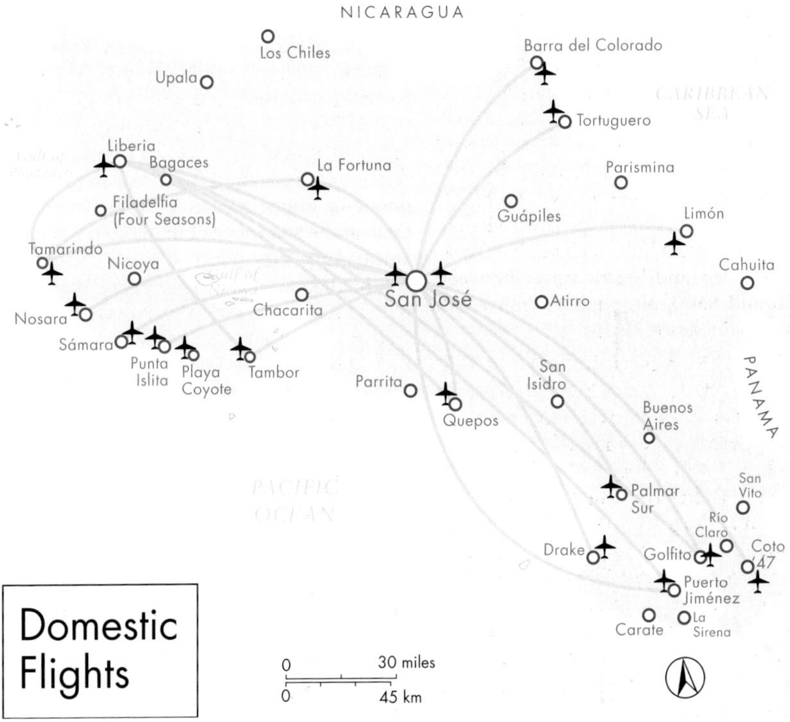

Domestic Flights

tour operators, travel agents, or remote lodges. Most charter planes are smaller than domestic commercial planes.

■ **TIP→Don't book a domestic flight for the day you arrive in or leave Costa Rica**; connections will be extremely tight, if possible at all, and you'll be at the mercy of temperamental weather and delays.

Airline Contacts American Airlines (☎ *800/433-7300, 506/2257-1266 in Costa Rica* ⊕ *www.aa.com*). **Continental Airlines** (☎ *800/231-0856 for international reservations, 0800/2044-0005 in Costa Rica* ⊕ *www.continental.com*). **Delta Airlines** (☎ *800/241-4141 for international reservations, 0800/2056-2002 in Costa Rica* ⊕ *www.delta.com*). **United Airlines** (☎ *800/538-2929 for international reservations, 0800/2052-1243 in Costa Rica* ⊕ *www.united.com*). **US Airways** (☎ *800/622-1015 for international reservations, 0800/2011-0793 in Costa Rica* ⊕ *www.usairways.com*).

Domestic and Charter Airlines Aerobell Air Charter (☎ *506/2290-0000 in Costa Rica* ⊕ *www.aerobell.com*). **Copa** (☎ *800/359-2672 in U.S. and Canada, 506/2223-2672 in Costa Rica* ⊕ *www.copaair.com*). **Macaw Air** (☎ *506/8364-1223 in Costa Rica* ⊕ *www.macawair.com*). **Nature Air** (☎ *800/235-9272 in North America, 506/2299-6000 in Costa Rica* ⊕ *www.natureair.com*). **SANSA** (☎ *506/2290-4100 or 2221-9414 in Costa Rica* ⊕ *www.flysansa.com*). **TACA** (☎ *800/400-8222 in U.S., 506/2299-8222 in Costa Rica* ⊕ *www.grupotaca.com*).

BUS TRAVEL

Tica Bus has daily runs between Costa Rica and Panama or Nicaragua; Transnica has daily service between Costa Rica and Granada and Managua. We recommend choosing Tica Bus if at all possible, but Transnica is acceptable in a pinch. Both companies have comfortable, air-conditioned coaches with videos and onboard toilets, and help with border procedures.

All Costa Rican towns are connected by regular bus service. Bus service in Costa Rica is reliable, comprehensive, and inexpensive. Buses between major cities are modern and air-conditioned, but once you get into the rural areas, you may get a converted school bus without air-conditioning. The kind of bus you get is the luck of the draw (no upgrades here). Bus travel in Costa Rica is formal, meaning no pigs or chickens inside and no people or luggage on the roof. On longer routes, buses stop midway at modest restaurants. Near the ends of their runs many nonexpress buses turn into large taxis, dropping passengers off one by one at their destinations; to save time, take a *directo* (express) bus. Be prepared for bus-company employees and bus drivers to speak Spanish only.

The main inconvenience of long-distance buses, aside from being much slower than flying, is that you usually have to return to San José to travel between outlying regions. For example, a bus from San José to the Osa Peninsula is nine hours or more, whereas the flight is one hour. Shorter distances reduce the difference—the bus to Quepos is 3½ hours and the flight 30 minutes—and in those cases the huge price difference might be worth the extra hours of travel. There is no main bus station in San José; buses leave from a variety of departure points, depending on the region they serve.

■ TIP→Don't put your belongings in the overhead bin unless you have to, and if you do, keep your eye on them. If anyone—even someone who looks like a bus employee—offers to put your luggage on the bus or in the luggage compartment underneath for you, politely decline. If you must put your luggage underneath the bus, get off quickly when you arrive to retrieve it.

Most bus companies don't have printed bus schedules to give out, although departure times may be printed on a sign at the bus company's office and ticket window. Bus-line phones are usually busy or go unanswered. The schedules and prices we list are accurate at this writing, but change frequently. **■ TIP→For the most-reliable schedule information, go to the bus station a day before your departure.** The ICT tourist office (⇨ *Visitor Information below*) hands out bus schedules and provides a PDF version on its Web site, but this should be used as only a rough guide, as it is updated infrequently. Hotel employees can usually give you the information you need.

Buses usually depart and arrive on time; they may even leave a few minutes before the scheduled departure time if full.

Tickets are sold at bus stations and on the buses themselves; reservations aren't accepted, and you must pay in person with cash. If you pay on the bus, be sure to have loose change and small bills handy; avoid paying with a 10,000 colón bill. Buses to popular beach and mountain destinations often sell out on weekends and the days before and after a holiday. It's also difficult to get tickets back to San José on Sunday afternoon. Some companies won't sell you a round-trip ticket from the departure point; especially during the peak season, make sure the first thing you do upon arrival in your destination is to buy a return ticket. Sometimes tickets include seat numbers, which are usually printed on the tops of the chairs. Smoking is not permitted on buses.

Two private bus companies, Gray Line Tours Fantasy Bus and Interbus, travel to the most popular tourist destinations in modern, air-conditioned vans. Interbus vans usually seat seven people, and coaches can also be reserved for large groups; Gray Line vans seat 14 to 28 people. Be sure to double-check information that is listed on the Web site—published prices may not be accurate and routes are not always running. This service costs about $25 to $50 one way, but can take hours off your trip. Gray Line has a Fantasy Bus Pass (around $115, depending on route) good for unlimited travel for one week on a specific route of your choice; reservations need to be made 24 hours in advance. Interbus offers three- to seven-trip Flexipasses; prices range from $117 to $262 and the passes are good for one month. Hotel-to-hotel service is offered as long as your lodging is on the route; if you're heading off the beaten track, it's a hotel-to-nearest-hotel service.

Bus Information Tica Bus (✉ *200 m north and 100 m west of Torre Mercedes, Paseo Colón, San José* ☎ *2223–8680 or 2221–0006* 🌐 *www.ticabus.com*). **Transnica** (✉ *C. 22, Avdas. 3–5, San José* ☎ *2223–4123 or 2223–4242* 🌐 *www.transnica.com*).

Shuttle-Van Services Costa Rica Shuttle (☎ *2289–9509* 🌐 *www.costaricashuttle.com*). **Gray Line Tourist Bus** (☎ *2291–2222 or 2220–2126* 🌐 *www.graylinecostarica.com*). **Interbus** (☎ *2479–9796 or 2283–5573* 🌐 *www.interbusonline.com*).

CAR TRAVEL

Hiring a car with a driver makes the most sense for sightseeing in and around San José. You can also usually hire a taxi driver to ferry you around; most will stick to the meter, which at this writing will tick at a rate of about $5 per hour for the time the driver is waiting for you. At $75 to $120 per day plus the driver's food, hiring a driver for areas outside the San José area costs almost the same as renting a 4WD, but is more expensive for multiday trips, when you'll also have to pay for the driver's room. Some drivers are also knowledgeable guides; others just drive. Unless they're driving large passenger vans for established companies, it's doubtful that drivers have any special training or licensing. Hotels can usually direct you to trusted drivers; you can also find recommendations on fodors.com. Alternatively, Alamo (*⇨ below*) provides professional car-and-driver services for minimum three-day rentals (available May to November only). You pay $75 on top of the rental fee, plus the driver's food and lodging. Costa Rica Shuttle (⇨By Bus) provides drivers on similar terms for $130 per day.

Most rental companies have an office close to Aeropuerto Internacional Juan Santamaría where you can drop off your car (even if you picked up the car at another San José branch) and provide transport to get you to your flight. Leave yourself a half hour for the return time and shuttle.

GASOLINE

There is no self-service gas in Costa Rica; 24-hour stations are generally available only in San José or on the Pan-American Highway. Most other stations are open from about 7 to 7, some until midnight. It is not customary to tip attendants.

Gas prices are fixed by the government, and gas stations around the country are legally bound to stick to the determined prices. Try to fill your tank in cities—gas is more expensive (and more likely to be dirty) at informal fill-up places in rural areas, where gas stations can be few and far between. Major credit cards are widely accepted. Ask the attendant if you want a *factura* (receipt). Regular unleaded gasoline is called *regular* and high-octane unleaded is called *super*. Gas is sold by the liter.

PARKING

On-street parking is scarce in downtown San José; where you find it, you'll also find *guachimanes* (informal, usually self-appointed guards). They freely admit they don't get paid enough to actually get involved if someone tries something with your car, but it's best to give them a couple of hundred colones per hour anyway. In centers such as San José, Alajuela, and Heredia, you'll find several signs with a large E in a red circle, and the words con boleto (with a ticket). These tickets can be bought for ½ hour (190 colones), 1 hour (375 colones) or 2 hours (750 colones) at the respective municipal hall. *It's a 3,700-colón fine (about $7) if you're caught in one of these spaces without a ticket.*

Safer and ubiquitous are the public lots (*parqueos*), which average flat rates of approximately $1.25 per hour. Most are open late, especially near hopping night-spots or theaters, but check beforehand. Never leave anything inside the car. It is illegal to park in the zones marked by yellow curb paint, or in front of garage doors or driveways, usually marked with signs reading *No Estacionar* (No Parking). Downtown parking laws are strictly enforced; the fine for illegal parking is 5,000 colones (about $10). However, the city center's narrow throughways are often bottlenecked by "waiting" cars and taxis—double-parked with someone in the car. Despite the cacophonic honking, this is largely tolerated. Outside of the main hubs of the Central Valley, parking rules are far more lax, and *guachimanes*, private walled, and guarded hotel or restaurant parking are the rule, with few public lots.

RENTAL CARS

When you reserve a car, ask about cancellation penalties, taxes, drop-off charges (if you're planning to pick up the car in one city and leave it in another), and surcharges (for being under or over a certain age, for additional drivers, or for driving across state or country borders or beyond a specific distance from your point of rental). All these things can add substantially to your costs. Request such extras as car seats and GPS devices when you book.

Rates are sometimes—but not always—better if you book in advance or reserve through a rental agency's Web site. There are other reasons to book ahead, though: for popular destinations, during busy times of the year, or to ensure that you get certain types of cars (vans, SUVs, exotic sports cars).

■ **TIP→If you're planning to go to only one or two major areas, taking a shuttle van or a domestic flight is usually a better and cheaper option than driving.** Renting is a good choice if you're destination hopping, staying at a hotel that's a trek to town, or going well off the beaten path. Car trips to northern Guanacaste from San José can take an entire day, so flying is probably better if you don't have long to spend in the country. Flying is definitely better than driving for visiting the South Pacific.

A standard vehicle is fine for most destinations, but a *doble-tracción* (4WD) is often essential to reach the remoter parts of the country, especially during the rainy season. Even in the dry season, you must have a 4WD vehicle to reach Monteverde and some destinations in Guanacaste. The big 4WD vehicles, such as a Suzuki Grand Vitara, can cost roughly twice as much as an economy car, but compact 4WDs, such as the Daihatsu Terios, are more reasonable, and should be booked well in advance. Most cars in Costa Rica have manual transmissions. ■ **TIP→Specify when making the reservation if you want an automatic transmission; it usually costs about $5 more per day, but some companies, such as Alamo and Hertz, don't charge extra.** Larger, more expensive automatic Montero and Sorento models are also available.

If you plan to rent any kind of vehicle between December 15 and January 3, or during Holy Week (the week leading up to Easter)—when most Costa Ricans are on vacation—reserve several months ahead of time.

Costa Rica has around 30 car-rental firms. Most local firms are affiliated with international car-rental chains and offer the same guarantees and services as their branches abroad; local company Tricolor gets high marks from travelers on our Fodor's Forum. At least a dozen rental offices line San José's Paseo Colón; most large hotels and Aeropuerto Internacional Juan Santamaría have representatives. Renting in or near San José is by far the easiest way to go. It's getting easier to rent outside of San José, particularly on the Pacific coast. Several rental companies have set up branches in Liberia, Quepos, Jacó, Tamarindo, and La Fortuna. In most other places across the country it's either impossible or very difficult and expensive to rent a car.

Car seats are compulsory for children under four years old, and can be rented for about $5 per day; reserve in advance. Rental cars may not be driven across borders to Nicaragua and Panama. For a $50 fee, National and Alamo will let you drop off a Costa Rican rental car at the Nicaragua border and provide you with a Nicaraguan rental on the other side. Seat-belt use is compulsory in the front seat. Fuel-efficiency measures restrict certain cars from San José's city center during rush hours once a week, according to the final license-plate number (e.g., plates that end in 9 are restricted on Friday). This also applies to rental cars; if you are stopped, do not pay a bribe. To rent a car, you need a driver's license, a valid passport, and a credit card. The minimum renter age varies; agencies such as Economy, Budget, and Alamo rent to anyone over 21; Avis sets the limit at 23, Hertz at 25. Though it's rare, some agencies have a maximum age limit.

High-season rates in San José begin at $45 a day and $300 a week for an economy car with air-conditioning, manual transmission, unlimited mileage, plus obligatory insurance; but rates fluctuate considerably according to demand, season, and company. Rates for a 4WD vehicle during high season are $70 to $90 a day and $450 to $550 per week. Often companies will also require a $1,000 deposit, payable by credit card.

Cars picked up at or returned to Aeropuerto Internacional Juan Santamaría incur a 12% surcharge. Arrangements can be made to pick up cars directly at the Liberia airport, but a range of firms have offices nearby and transport you from the airport free of charge—and with no surcharge for an airport pickup. Check cars thoroughly for damage before you sign the rental contract. Even tough-looking 4WD vehicles should be coddled. **■TIP→The charges levied by rental companies for damage—no matter how minor—are outrageous even by U.S. or European standards.** It's very wise to opt for full-coverage insurance. One-way service surcharges are $50 to $150, depending on the drop-off point; National allows travelers free car drop-off at any of its offices with a minimum three-day rental. To avoid a hefty refueling fee, fill the tank just before you turn in the car. It's almost never a deal to buy the tank of gas that's in the car when you rent it; the understanding is that you'll return it empty, but some fuel usually remains. Additional drivers are about $5 to $10 per day if there is any charge at all. Almost all agencies, with the exception of Budget Rent-a-Car, have cell-phone rental; prices range between $2 and $6 per day, with national per-minute costs between 50¢ and $2.

International driving permits (IDPs), which are used only in conjunction with a valid driver's license and translate your license into 10 languages, are not necessary in Costa Rica. Your own driver's license is good for the length of your initial tourist visa. You must carry your passport, or a copy of it with the entry stamp, to prove when you entered the country.

Major Agencies Alamo (☎ *506/2242–7733 in Costa Rica* 🌐 *www.alamocostarica.com*). **Avis** (☎ *506/2293–2222 in Costa Rica* 🌐 *www.avis.co.cr*). **Budget** (☎ *506/2436–2000 in Costa Rica* 🌐 *www.budget.co.cr*). **Dollar** (☎ *877/767–8651 or 866/746–7765 in North America, 506/2443–2950 in Costa Rica* 🌐 *www.dollarcostarica.com*). **Hertz** (☎ *888/437–8927 in North America, 506/2221–1818 in Costa Rica* 🌐 *www.costaricarentacar.net*). **National Car Rental** (☎ *877/862–8227 in North America, 506/2242–7878 in Costa Rica* 🌐 *www.natcar.com*).

Local Agencies Economy (☎ *877/326–7368 in North America, 506/2299–2000 in Costa Rica* 🌐 *www.economyrentacar.com*). **Tricolor** (☎ *800/949–0234 in North America, 506/2440–3333 in Costa Rica* 🌐 *www.tricolorcarrental.com*).

ROAD CONDITIONS

Many travelers shy away from renting a car in Costa Rica, if only for fear of the road conditions. Indeed, this is not an ideal place to drive: in San José traffic is bad and car theft is rampant (look for guarded parking lots or hotels with lots); in rural areas roads are often unpaved or potholed—and tires aren't usually covered by the basic insurance. And Ticos are reckless drivers—with one of the highest accident rates in the world. But though driving can be a challenge, it's a great way to explore certain regions, especially Guanacaste, the Northern Plains, and the Caribbean coast (apart from Tortuguero and Barra del Colorado). Keep in mind that mountains and poor road conditions make most trips longer than you'd normally expect.

San José is terribly congested during weekday morning and afternoon rush hours (7 to 9 AM and 4 to 6 PM). Avoid returning to the city on Sunday evening, when traffic to San José from the Pacific coast beaches backs up for hours. The winding Pan-American Highway south of the capital is notorious for long snakes of traffic stuck behind slow-moving trucks. Look out for potholes, even in the smoothest sections of the best roads. Also watch for unmarked speed bumps where you'd least expect them, particularly on rural main thoroughfares. During the rainy season roads are in much worse shape. Check with your destination before setting out; roads, especially in Limón Province, are prone to washouts and landslides.

San José has many one-way streets and traffic circles. Streets in the capital are narrow. Pedestrians are supposed to have the right-of-way but do not in reality, so be alert when walking. The local driving style is erratic and aggressive but not fast, because road conditions don't permit too much speed. Frequent fender benders tie up traffic. Keep your windows rolled up in the center of the city, because thieves may reach into your car at stoplights and snatch your purse, jewelry, and so on.

Signage is notoriously bad, but improving. Watch carefully for *No Hay Paso* (Do Not Enter) signs; one-way streets are common, and it's not unusual for a street to transform from a two-way to a one-way. Streetlights are often out of service and key signs missing or knocked down because of accidents.

Outside of San José you'll run into long stretches of unpaved road. Frequent hazards in the countryside are potholes, landslides during the rainy season, and cattle on the roads. Drunk drivers are a hazard throughout the country on weekend nights. Driving at night is not recommended anyway, since roads are poorly lighted and many don't have painted center lines or shoulder lines.

ROADSIDE EMERGENCIES

Costa Rica has no highway emergency service organization. In Costa Rica 911 is the nationwide number for accidents. Traffic police are scattered around the country, but Costa Ricans are very good about stopping for people with car trouble. Whatever happens, don't move the car after an accident, even if a monstrous traffic jam ensues. Call 911 first if the accident is serious (nearly everyone has a cell phone here and it's almost a given that someone will offer to help). Also be sure to call the emergency number your car-rental agency has given you. For fender benders, contact the Traffic Police, who will try to locate a person to assist you in English—but don't count on it. If you don't speak Spanish, you may want to contact the rental agency before trying the police. If your own car is stolen, call the Judicial Investigative Police (OIJ, pronounced oh-ee-hota), which will find an English-speaking representative to assist you.

Emergency Services Ambulance and Police (☎ *911*).

RULES OF THE ROAD

Driving is on the right side of the road in Costa Rica. The highway speed limit is usually 90 KPH (54 MPH), which drops to 60 KPH (36 MPH) in residential areas. In towns limits range from 30 to 50 kph (18 to 31 MPH). Speed limits are enforced in all regions of the country. Seat belts are required, and an awareness campaign has increased enforcement. *Alto* means "stop" and *ceda* means "yield." Right turns on red are permitted except where signs indicate otherwise, but in San José this is usually not possible because of one-way streets and pedestrian crossings.

Local drunk driving laws are strict. You'll get nailed with a 10,000-colón fine if you're caught driving in a "pre-drunk" state (blood alcohol levels of 0.049% to 0.099%). If your level is higher than that, you'll pay 20,000 colones, the car will be confiscated, and your license will be taken away. Policemen who stop drivers for speeding and drunk driving are often looking for payment on the spot—essentially a bribe. Whether you're guilty or not, you'll get a ticket if you don't give in. Asking for a ticket instead of paying the bribe discourages corruption and does not compromise your safety. You can generally pay the ticket at your car-rental company, which will remit it on your behalf.

Car seats are required for children ages four and under, but car-seat laws are not rigorously enforced. Children over 12 are allowed in the front seat. Drivers are prohibited from using handheld cell phones, but this is almost never enforced, and distracted chatters are the norm.

CRUISE SHIP TRAVEL

The quality of shore excursions at Costa Rica's Pacific ports (Caldera, Quepos, Golfito) and Limón, on the Caribbean, has skyrocketed in past years, as operators scramble to serve the influx of cruisers who stop in, usually on their way to or from the Panama Canal. Most large cruises stop in the country only once, although some make stops on both coasts. Small-scale ships, including Windstar Cruises (capacity for 145), Seabourn (60 guests), and highly recommended, conservation-minded Lindblad (62 guests) offer Costa Rica–focused cruises along the Pacific coast.

Cruise Lines Lindblad (☎ *800/397–3348 in North America* 🌐 *www.expeditions.com*). **Seabourn Cruise Line** (☎ *800/929–9391* 🌐 *www.seabourn.com*). **Windstar Cruises** (☎ *206/292–9606 or 800/258–7245* 🌐 *www.windstarcruises.com*).

TAXI TRAVEL

Taxis are cheap and your best bet for getting around San José. Just about every driver is friendly and eager to use a few English words to tell you about a cousin or sister in New Jersey; however, cabbies truly conversant in English are scarce. Most are knowledgeable, but given the haphazard address system, may cheerfully engage passersby or other taxi drivers to find your destination. Tipping is not expected, but a good idea when you've had some extra help.

Cabs are red, usually with a yellow light on top. To hail one, extend your hand and wave it at about hip height. If it's available, the driver will often flick his headlights before pulling over. Cabs can be scarce when it's raining or during rush hour. The city is dotted with *paradas de taxi*, taxi lineups where you stand the best chance of grabbing one. Your hotel can usually call you a reputable taxi or private car service, and when you're out to dinner or on the town, the restaurant or disco can just as easily call you a cab—it's much easier than trying to hail one on the street in the wee hours, and safer, too.

TIP→Taxi drivers are infamous for "not having change." If it's just a few hundred colones, you may as well round up. If it's a lot, ask them to drive to a store or gas station where you can make change. They'll often miraculously come up with the difference, or wait patiently while you get it. To avoid this situation, never use a 10,000-colón bill in a taxi, and avoid paying with 5,000-colón bills unless you've run up almost that much in fares.

Technically this system applies throughout the country, but rural and unofficial cabs often use their odometers to creatively calculate fares. Manuel Antonio drivers are notorious for overcharging. It's illegal, but taxis charge up to double for hotel pickups or fares that take them out of the province (such as San José to Alajuela or vice versa). Ask the manager at your hotel about the going rate for the destination to which you're heading. Drivers have a fairly standard list of off-the-meter illegal fares.

In the capital there's usually no reason to take the risk with an unofficial taxi (*pirata*), but they are often the only option outside main hubs. See the regional chapters for recommended drivers, or check with your hotel or restaurant for reliable service.

It's always a good idea to make a note of the cab number (painted in a yellow triangle on the door), and sit in the backseat for safety.

TRAIN TRAVEL

An earthquake in 1991 wreaked havoc on the country's century-old rail links, and service was completely suspended in 1995. Revived interest in commuter trains as a solution to the city's traffic snarls has been hit-and-miss.

More popular is the Tico Train, a tourist day trip that leaves from the Pacific station in southern San José to the Pacific port of Caldera. Trains leave Saturday and Sunday at 7 AM, returning by 8:30 PM ($39 per passenger over four years old). Fueled as much by nostalgia as hydrocarbons, the scenic trip (four hours each way) follows a historic route; passengers are serenaded by a strolling guitar player, given traditional snacks, and free to wander about on a five-hour beach stop.

Information **Tico Train Tour to Caldera** (☎ *506/2233–3300 in Costa Rica* 🌐 *www.ticotraintour.com*).

ESSENTIALS

ACCOMMODATIONS

Low-end alternatives are often referred to as *cabinas* whether they offer concrete-block motels or freestanding cottages. Most have private rooms, cold-water concrete showers, fans instead of air-conditioning, and limited—if any—secure parking or storage, and may share bathrooms. Owners tend to be Costa Rican. Often without Web sites, e-mail, or links to major agencies, these hotels tend to follow a first-come, first-served booking policy. They may have room during peak seasons when mid- or upper-end options are booked solid.

Midrange options include boutique hotels, tasteful bungalows, bed-and-breakfasts, and downtown casino hotels. Those in the hotter beach areas may not have hot-water showers. Many have pools, Internet access, and meal options. They tend to be foreign-owned and, with the exception of the casinos, have personalized service. Because they're generally small, you may have to book one or two months ahead, and up to six months in the high season. Booking through an association or agency can significantly reduce the time you spend scanning the Internet, but you can often get a better deal and negotiate longer-stay or low-season discounts. The Costa Rican Hotel Association has online search and booking capabilities. ICT provides hotel lists searchable by star category. Costa Rica Travel Review lists and rates properties and provides a number of links.

High-end accommodations can be found almost everywhere. They range from luxury tents to exquisite hotels and villa rentals, and are often more secluded. You'll find all the amenities you expect at such areas, with one notable exception: the roads and routes to even five-star villas can be atrocious. This category is sometimes booked up to a year in advance for Christmas, and during this season you may be able to book only through agents or central reservations offices. Resorts are generally one of two kinds: luxurious privileged gateways to the best of the country (such as Punta Islita) or generic budget all-inclusives (such as the Barceló) that probably run counter to what you're coming to Costa Rica for. Several chain hotels have franchises in Costa Rica, leaning toward the generic and all-inclusive. The upside is that they are rarely booked solid, so you can always fall back on one in a worst-case scenario, and they often have member discounts.

Nature lodges and hotels in the South Pacific (where restaurants aren't an option) may be less expensive than they initially appear, as the price of a room usually includes three hearty meals a day, and sometimes guided hikes. These, and other remote accommodations, may not have daily Internet access even though they have a Web site: be patient if you're attempting to book directly. Since many of the hotels are remote and have an eco-friendly approach (even to luxury), air-conditioning, in-room telephones, and TVs are exceptions to the rule. Consider how isolated you want to be; some rural and eco-lodges are miles from neighbors and other services and have few rainy-day diversions.

The ICT's voluntary "green leaf" rating system evaluates establishments in terms of sustainable-tourism criteria; a detailed description of the program and a search function to find lodging by sustainability level can be found at 🌐*www.turismo-sostenible.co.cr*.

The lodgings we list are Costa Rica's cream of the crop in each price category. We always list the facilities that are available, but we don't specify whether they cost extra; when pricing accommodations, always ask what's included and what costs extra. Properties are assigned price categories based on the range from the least-expensive standard double room at high season (excluding holidays) to the most expensive. Keep in mind that hotel prices we list exclude 16.4% service and tax.

For Costa Rica's popular beach and mountain resorts, be sure to reserve well in advance for the dry season (mid-December–April everywhere except the Caribbean coast, which has a short September–October "dry" season). During the rainy season (May–mid-November except on the Caribbean coast, where it's almost always rainy) most hotels drop their rates considerably, which sometimes sends them into a lower price category than the one we indicate.

TIP→If you're having trouble finding a hotel that isn't completely booked, consider contacting a tour operator who can arrange your entire trip. Because they reserve blocks of rooms far in advance, you might have better luck.

Most hotels and other lodgings require you to give your credit-card details before they will confirm your reservation. If you don't feel comfortable e-mailing this information, ask if you can fax it (some places even prefer faxes). However you book, get confirmation in writing and have a copy of it handy when you check in.

Be sure you understand the hotel's cancellation policy. Some places allow you to cancel without any kind of penalty—even if you prepaid to secure a discounted rate—if you cancel at least 24 hours in advance. Others require you to cancel a week in advance or penalize you the cost of one night. Small inns and B&Bs are most likely to require you to cancel far in advance. Most hotels allow children under a certain age to stay in their parents' room at no extra charge, but others charge for them as extra adults; find out the cutoff age for discounts.

Hotels operate on the European Plan (EP, no meals) unless we specify that they use the Breakfast Plan (BP, with full breakfast), Continental Plan (CP, Continental breakfast), Full American Plan (FAP, all meals), or Modified American Plan (MAP, breakfast and dinner), or are all-inclusive (AI, all meals and most activities).

Lodging Resources Costa Rica Travel Review (*www.costaricatravelreview.com*). **Costa Rican Hotel Association** (*506/2248–0990 in Costa Rica* *www.costaricanhotels.com*). **Instituto Costarricense de Turismo** (*ICT* *866/267–8274 in North America, 506/2299–5800 in Costa Rica* *www.visitcostarica.com*).

APARTMENT AND HOUSE RENTALS

Rental houses are now common all over Costa Rica, and are particularly popular in the Pacific coast destinations of Manuel Antonio, Tamarindo, Ocotal, and Jacó. Furnished rentals accommodate a crowd or a family, often for less and at a higher comfort level. Generally properties are owned by individual owners or consortiums, most of them based in the United States with house managers in Costa Rica. Resort communities with villa-style lodgings are also growing. Nosara Home Page lists apartments and villas on the Nicoya Peninsula; Villas International has an extensive list of properties in Quepos and Tamarindo. For the southern Nicoya Peninsula check Costa Rica Beach Rentals. The House of Rentals, a Century 21 affiliate, arranges houses and condos in the Flamingo and Potrero areas.

Contacts Century 21 (*506/2654–4004 in Costa Rica, 877/661–2060 from U.S.* *www.century21costarica.net*). **Costa Rica Beach Rentals** (*506/2640–0065* *www.costarica-beachrentals.com*). **Nosara Beach Rentals** (*506/2682–0153* *www.nosarabeachrentals.com*).

Villas & Apartments Abroad (*212/213–6435 in U.S., 800/433–3020* *www.vaanyc.com*). **Villas Caribe** (*800/645–7498* *www.villascaribe.com*).

Villas International (*415/499–9490 in U.S., 800/221–2260* *www.villasintl.com*).

BED-AND-BREAKFASTS

A number of quintessential B&Bs—small and homey—are clustered in the Central Valley, generally offering hearty breakfasts and friendly inside information for $50 to $70 per night. You'll also find them scattered through the rest of the country, mixed in with other self-titled B-andBs that range from small cabins in the mountains to luxurious boutique hotel–style digs in northern Guanacaste.

Reservation Services Bed & Breakfast.com (☎ *512/322–2710 or 800/462–2632* ⊕ *www.bedandbreakfast.com*) also sends out an online newsletter. **Bed & Breakfast Inns Online** (☎ *615/868–1946 or 800/215–7365* ⊕ *www.bbonline.com*). **Pamela Lanier's Bed and Breakfasts, Inns and Guesthouses International** (⊕ *www.lanierbb.com/Costa_Rica*).

HOME EXCHANGES

With a direct home exchange you stay in someone else's home while they stay in yours. Some outfits also deal with vacation homes, so you're not actually staying in someone's full-time residence, just their vacant weekend place.

A handful of home exchanges are available; this involves an initial small registration fee, and you'll have to plan ahead. It's an excellent way to immerse yourself in the true Costa Rica, particularly if you've been here before and aren't relying so heavily on the tourism support that hotels can offer. Drawbacks include restricted options and dates. Many companies list home exchanges, but we've found HomeLink International, which lists a handful of jazzy houses in Costa Rica, and Intervac to be the most reliable.

Exchange Clubs Home Exchange (☎ *800/877–8723* ⊕ *www.homeexchange.com*); $59.95 for a one-year online listing. **HomeLink International** (☎ *800/638–3841* ⊕ *www.homelink.org*); $80 yearly for Web-only membership; $125 includes Web access and two catalogs. **Intervac U.S.** (☎ *800/756–4663* ⊕ *www.intervacus.com*); $95 for Web-only membership; $195 includes Web access and a catalog.

WORD OF MOUTH

Did the resort look as good in real life as it did in the photos? Did you sleep like a baby, or were the walls paper thin? Did you get your money's worth? Rate hotels and write your own reviews in Travel Ratings or start a discussion about your favorite places in Travel Talk on www.fodors.com. Your comments might even appear in our books. Yes, you, too, can be a correspondent!

HOSTELS

Hostels offer bare-bones lodging at low, low prices—often in shared dorm rooms with shared baths—to people of all ages, though the primary market is young travelers, especially students. Most hostels serve breakfast; dinner and/or shared cooking facilities may also be available. In some hostels you aren't allowed to be in your room during the day, and there may be a curfew at night. Nevertheless, hostels provide a sense of community, with public rooms where travelers often gather to share stories. Many hostels are affiliated with Hostelling International (HI), an umbrella group of hostel associations with some 4,500 member properties in more than 70 countries. Other hostels are completely independent and may be nothing more than a really cheap hotel.

Costa Rica has a sprinkling of youth hostels and hotels affiliated with Hostelling International; most are tantamount to inexpensive hotels, appropriate for families. Youth-oriented Hostal Toruma in San José, part of the Costarrican [sic] Hostel Network, is an exception, as is Hostel Playa Tamarindo; the former offers private rooms as well as dorms, and the latter has surf racks. Tranquilo Backpackers, Gaudy's Backpackers, and Hostel Costa Linda also lean toward boisterous, younger guests.

ADDRESSES

In Costa Rica addresses are usually given in terms of how many meters the place is from a landmark. Street names and building numbers are not commonly used. Churches, stores, even large trees that no longer exist—almost anything can be a landmark, as long as everyone knows where it is, or where it used to be. A typical address in San José is *100 metros este y 100 metros sur del Más X Menos* (100 meters east and 100 meters south from the Más X Menos supermarket). **TIP→In towns and cities in Costa Rica, each block is assumed to be 100 meters, although some blocks may be much longer and some may be shorter. So if someone tells you to head down the road 500 meters, they mean five blocks.** Ticos, as Costa Ricans call themselves, are generally happy to help lost visitors, and they spend a lot of time describing where things are. But be warned—even if they don't know where something is, Ticos will often give uncertain or even wrong information rather than seem unhelpful; triangulated direction-asking is a must. Ask at least two, if not three, people in quick succession to avoid getting hopelessly lost. Key direction terms are *lugar* (place), *calle* (street), *avenida* (avenue), *puente* (bridge), *piso* (floor), *edificio* (building), *cruce* (intersection), *semáforo* (traffic light), *rotonda* (traffic circle), and *cuadra* (block).

COMMUNICATIONS

INTERNET

Downtown San José is full of Internet cafés with high-speed connections; prices are usually less than $1 per hour. As you move away from the capital, prices rise to $2 to $4 per hour and connections become slower and more unreliable. Wildly expensive satellite Internet is available at some remote, exclusive hotels. Cafés are generally good places to make international Internet calls, but expect echoes and a mediocre connection. Most major hotels have free wireless access or use of a guest Internet computer. Eateries such as Denny's, Bagelmen's, and a number of upscale cafés are also Wi-Fi friendly. Dial-up access is spotty and frustrating, but if you're desperate and have both a computer and access to a telephone line, you can buy one of RACSA's prepaid Internet cards in three amounts: 1,800 colones (5 hours), 3,550 colones (10 hours), and 5,300 colones (15 hours). Cards are sold at Kodak stores, Perimercado supermarkets, and some branches of the Banco Nacional. The cards come with the access numbers, and a help line with English-speaking operators.

Contacts Cybercafes (🌐 *www.cybercafes.com*) lists more than 4,000 Internet cafés worldwide.

PHONES

The good news is that you can now make a direct-dial telephone call from virtually any point on earth. The bad news? You can't always do so cheaply. Calling from a hotel is almost always the most expensive option; hotels usually add huge surcharges to all calls, particularly international ones. In some countries you can phone from call centers or even the post office. Calling cards usually keep costs to a minimum, but only if you purchase them locally. And then there are mobile phones (⇨ *below*), which are sometimes more prevalent—particularly in the developing world—than landlines; as expensive as mobile phone calls can be, they are still usually a much cheaper option than calling from your hotel.

CALLING WITHIN COSTA RICA

In 2008, all phone numbers in Costa Rica were assigned an extra number. A 2 was tacked on to the front of all landline numbers and an 8 was added to the front of all mobile phone numbers. In-country 800 numbers were not affected by the change.

The Costa Rican phone system is very good by the standards of other developing countries. However, phone numbers do change often. Some phones have a card reader on the right-hand side, but the readers are hit-and-miss. There are no area codes in Costa Rica, so you only need dial a seven-digit number, without the 506 country code. Fewer and farther between are the gray coin-operated phones; posted on each are the coins accepted (it varies from phone to phone).

CALLING OUTSIDE COSTA RICA

The country code for the United States is 1.

Internet telephony is by far the cheapest way to call home; it is a viable option in the Central Valley and major tourist hubs. For other regions or for more privacy, a pay phone using an international phone card *(⇨ Calling Cards, below)* is the next step up; you can also call from a pay phone using your own long-distance calling card. Dialing directly from a hotel room is very expensive, as is recruiting an international operator to connect you. ■ **TIP→**Watch out for pay phones marked CALL USA/CANADA WITH A CREDIT CARD. They are *wildly* expensive.

To call overseas directly, dial 00, then the country code (dial 1 for the U.S. and Canada), the area code, and the number. You can make international calls from almost any phone with an international calling card purchased in Costa Rica. First dial 199, then the PIN on the back of your card (revealed after scratching off a protective coating), then dial the phone number as you would a direct long-distance call.

When requesting a calling card from your phone provider, ask specifically about calls from Costa Rica. Most 800-number cards don't work in Costa Rica. Callingcards.com is a great resource for prepaid international calling cards. At this writing, it lists at least two calling-card companies with rates of 29¢ and 56¢ per minute for calls from Costa Rica to the United States.

You may find the local access number blocked in many hotel rooms. First ask the hotel operator to connect you. If the hotel operator balks, ask for an international operator, or dial the international operator yourself. For service in English, you'll have more luck dialing the international operator (☎ 175 or 116). One way to improve your odds of getting connected to your long-distance carrier is to sign up with more than one company: a hotel may block Sprint, for example, but not MCI. If all else fails, call from a pay phone.

AT&T, MCI, and Sprint access codes make calling long distance relatively convenient but can be very expensive.

To make a person-to-person direct-dial call from any phone, dial 09 (instead of 00 for a regular call), the country code for the country you're calling, and then the number. The operator will ask for the name of the person you're contacting, and billing at direct-dial rates begins only once that person comes to the phone.

Direct-dial calls to the United States and Canada are 27¢ per minute.

Phone Resources **Callingcards.com** (🌐 *www.callingcards.com*). **International information** (☎ *124*). **International operator** (☎ *175 or 116*).

CALLING CARDS

Most public phones require phone cards (for local or international calls), but phone cards can also be used from any non-rotary telephone in Costa Rica, including residential phones, cell phones, and hotel phones. It's rare to be charged a per-minute rate for the mere use of the phone in a hotel.

Phone cards are sold in an array of shops, including Más X Menos supermarkets, post offices, offices of the Costa Rican Electricity Institute (ICE), and at any business displaying the gold-and-blue TARJETAS TELEFÓNICAS sign. International cards tend to be easier to find in downtown San José and in tourism areas.

Tarjetas para llamadas nacionales (domestic calling cards) are available in denominations of 500 colones and 1,000 colones. Phone-card rates are standard throughout the country, about 1¢ per minute, half that at night; a 500-colón card provides about 125 minutes of daytime landline calls. This decreases sharply if calling a cell phone; rates vary. *Tarjetas para llamadas internacionales* (international calling cards) are sold in $10, $20, 3,000-colón, and 10,000-colón amounts (denominations are inexplicably split between dollars and colones). It's harder to find the 10,000-colón cards; your best bet is to try a Fischel pharmacy or an ICE office. In busy spots, roaming card-hawkers abound; feel free to take advantage of the convenience—they're legit.

Some public phones accept *tarjetas chip* ("chip" cards), which record what you spend. **■TIP→**Avoid buying chip cards: they malfunction, you can use them only at the few-and-far-between chip phones, and they are sold in small denominations that are not sufficient for international calls.

MOBILE PHONES

If you have an unblocked phone (some countries use different frequencies than what's used in the United States) and your service provider uses the world-standard GSM network (as do T-Mobile, Cingular, and Verizon), you can probably use your phone abroad. **■TIP→**If you travel internationally frequently, save one of your old mobile phones or buy a cheap one on the Internet; ask your cell phone company to unlock it for you, and take it with you as a travel phone, buying a new SIM card with pay-as-you-go service in each destination.

If your cell phone company has service to Costa Rica, you theoretically can use it here, but expect reception to be impossibly bad in many areas of this mountainous country. Costa Rica works on a 1,800 MHz system—a tri- or quad-band cell phone is your best bet. Note that roaming fees can be steep.

Most car-rental agencies have good deals on cell phones, often better than the companies that specialize in cell-phone rental. If you're not renting a car, a number of companies will rent TDMA or GSM phones; remember, coverage can be spotty. Although service is evening out, TDMA phones have tended to work best in the Central Valley and Guanacaste; GSM is better for remote areas such as Dominical, Sámara, and Tortuguero. Specify your destination when renting. Rates range from $5 to $15 per day, plus varying rates for local or international coverage and minimum usage charges. Local calls average 70¢ per minute, international $1.25 to $1.50. You'll need your ID, a credit card, and a deposit, which varies per phone and service but averages $300 to $400; some rent only to those over 21. The deposit drops significantly with companies that can hook you up with a rented local chip for your own phone.

Friendly and professional, Cell Service Costa Rica will get you hooked up and provides door-to-door service; it doesn't rent SIM cards. Cellular Telephone Rentals Costa Rica has higher daily rates but free local calls, and will set you up with a card for your phone. Most rental companies in Costa Rica do not charge for text messages.

Contacts Cell Service Costa Rica (☎ *506/2296–5553 in Costa Rica* 🌐 *www.cellservicecr.com*). **Cellular Telephone Rentals Costa Rica** (☎ *800/769–7137 in U.S., 506/2290–7534 or 506/8845–4427 in Costa Rica* 🌐 *www.cellulartelephonerentals.com*).

CUSTOMS AND DUTIES

You're always allowed to bring goods of a certain value back home without having to pay any duty or import tax. But there's a limit on the amount of tobacco and liquor you can bring back duty free, and some countries have separate limits for perfumes; for exact figures, check with your customs department. The values of so-called duty-free goods are included in these amounts. When you shop abroad, save all your receipts, as customs inspectors may ask to see them as well as the items you purchased. If the total value of your goods is more than the duty-free limit, you'll have to pay a tax (most often a flat percentage) on the value of everything beyond that limit.

When shopping in Costa Rica, keep receipts for all purchases. Be ready to show customs (*aduanas*) officials what you've bought. Pack purchases together in an easily accessible place. The Patrimony Protection Department recommends obtaining a letter (free) from its office in the National Museum attesting that high-quality replicas of pre-Columbian artifacts are in fact copies, to avoid customs hassles. In practice, few people request such a letter, and problems with such souvenirs are infrequent. The only orchids you can take home are packaged in a tube and come with an export permit.

If you think a duty is incorrect, appeal the assessment. If you object to the way your clearance was handled, note the inspector's badge number. In either case, first ask to see a supervisor. If the problem isn't resolved, write to the appropriate authorities, beginning with the port director at your point of entry.

It usually takes about 10 to 30 minutes to clear customs when arriving in Costa Rica.

Visitors entering Costa Rica may bring in 500 grams of tobacco, 5 liters of wine or spirits, 2 kilograms of sweets and chocolates, and the equivalent of $500 worth of merchandise. One camera and one video camera, six rolls of film, binoculars, and electrical items for personal use only are also allowed. Make sure you have personalized prescriptions for any medication you are taking. Customs officials at San José's international airport rarely examine tourists' luggage, but if you enter by land, they'll probably look through your bags. Officers at the airport generally speak English and are usually your best (only, really) option for resolving any problem. You can try calling the Customs office, but if you get through and get results, let us know!

Pets (cats or dogs) with updated health and vaccination certificates are welcome in Costa Rica; no prior authorization is required if bringing a dog or cat that has up-to-date health and vaccination cards. The Servicio Nacional de Salud Animal can provide more info.

Information in Costa Rica Customs (☎ *506/2441–6069 in Costa Rica* 🌐 *www.hacienda.go.cr*). **Patrimony Protection Office** (☎ *506/2291–3517 in Costa Rica*). **Servicio Nacional de Salud Animal** (☎ *506/2260–8300 in Costa Rica* 🌐 *www.senasa.go.cr*).

U.S. Information U.S. Customs and Border Protection (🌐 *www.cbp.gov*).

EATING OUT

The cilantro-and-onion-flavored pot of rice and beans known as *gallo pinto* is synonymous with all things Tico, as evidenced by the expression "As Tico as *gallo pinto*." Nonetheless, Nicaraguans fiercely beg to differ, claiming the dish as their own and spurring a back-and-forth competition for the world's largest batch of the dish.

Mounds of this hearty breakfast can be found at the quintessential Costa Rican informal eatery—the *soda*. For lunch the dish is called *casados:* the beans and rice are served separately, accompanied by meat, coleslaw, and fried plantains. Increasingly common as you move away from San José are the thatched conical roofs of the round, open *rancho* restaurants that serve a combination of traditional staples with simple international fare. Kitchens cooking up sophisticated cuisine from Thailand, India, Italy, Lebanon, and more dot the capital and popular tourist centers. Vegetarians sticking to lower-budget establishments won't go hungry, but may develop a love-hate relationship with rice, beans, and fried cheese. A simple *sin carne* (no meat) request is often interpreted as "no beef," and you may get a plate of pork, chicken, or fish, so don't be afraid to sound high-maintenance. Specify *solo vegetales* (only vegetables), and for good

LOCAL DO'S AND TABOOS

CUSTOMS OF THE COUNTRY

Ticos tend to use formal Spanish, preferring, for example, *con mucho gusto* (with much pleasure) instead of *de nada* for "you're welcome." Family is very important in Costa Rica. It is considered polite to ask about your marital status and family.

Ticos can be disarmingly direct; don't be surprised (or offended) if locals pick up on a physical trait and give you a nickname: *Chino* for anyone with the slightest slant to the eye, or *Gordita* if you have even an extra ounce around your hips. It's meant affectionately. In almost every other situation, a circumspect approach is advised; North American straightforwardness often comes across as abrupt here. Preceding requests with a bit of small talk (even if it's a hotel employee) goes a long way. Also, be very aware of body language and other cues—Costa Ricans don't like to say no, and will often avoid answering a question or simply say *gracias* when they really mean no.

A large number of Costa Rican men make a habit of ogling or making gratuitous comments when young women pass on the street. Women should take care not to dress in skimpy clothing.

The expression "Tico time" was coined for a reason. Transportation, theaters, government, and major businesses tend to stick to official schedules. Anything else is flexible, and best handled by building in a little buffer time and sliding into the tropical groove.

GREETINGS

Costa Ricans are extremely polite, quick to shake hands (light squeezes are the norm) and place a kiss on the right cheek (meaning you need to bear left when going in for the peck). The formal pronoun *usted* (you) is used almost exclusively; the slangier *vos* is thrown about in informal settings and among close or young friends and relatives.

SIGHTSEEING

As you would anywhere, dress and behave respectfully when visiting churches. In churches men and women should not wear shorts, sleeveless shirts, or sandals; women should wear pants or skirts below the knee. Bathing suits, short shorts, and other skimpy attire are inappropriate city wear, but tend to be the uniform in beach towns; even here, however, cover up for all but the most informal restaurants. Locals tend to dress somewhat formally, with women favoring clothes that show off their curves.

Beggars are not a major problem, but if you're in San José, you'll come across a few. It's always better to give to an established organization, but the safety net for Costa Ricans with disabilities is riddled with holes, so even a couple of hundred colones will be appreciated. Simply keep walking past the addicts—they will almost always just move on to the next person. A couple of savvy panhandlers speak excellent English and will try to draw you into conversation with a sob story about a lost passport. Keep walking.

Banks and other offices allow pregnant women and the elderly to move immediately to the front of the line, and this respect is carried over to other establishments and crowded buses. If you're in a crowd and need to step in front of them, murmur, *"Con permiso"* ("Excuse me").

OUT ON THE TOWN

To catch a waiter's attention, wave discreetly or say, *"Disculpe, señor"* (or *señora* for women); best to leave the finger-snapping to the locals. For the bill, ask for *"La cuenta, por favor."* Pockets of no-smoking sections are growing, especially in the swankier restaurants, but smoking is still tolerated in many public spaces. It's prohibited in government buildings, cinemas, theaters, other public entertainment venues, and public transport. Excessive displays of affection draw frowns, clearly lost on the gaggles of lip-locked couples. Locals tend to dress up to go out, whatever the activity: a snazzy (but not too dressy) outfit will serve you well in San José. If invited to someone's home, bring a gift such as flowers or a bottle of wine or some trinket from your home country. If offered food at someone's home, it's polite to accept it and eat it (even if you aren't hungry).

LANGUAGE

One of the best ways to avoid being an Ugly American is to learn a little of the local language. You need not strive for fluency; even just mastering a few basic words and terms is bound to make chatting with the locals more rewarding.

Spanish is the official language, although many tour guides and locals in heavily touristed areas speak English. You'll have a better time if you learn some basic Spanish before you go and if you bring a phrase book with you. At the very least, learn the rudiments of polite conversation—niceties such as *por favor* (please) and *gracias* (thank you) will be warmly appreciated. *For more words and phrases, see the Spanish glossary in the "Understanding Costa Rica" chapter.* In the Caribbean province of Limón a creole English called Mekatelyu is widely spoken by older generations. English is understood by most everyone in these parts.

An open-ended *"Dónde está . . ."* ("Where is . . .") may result in a wall of rapid-fire Spanish. Better to avoid language as much as possible when asking for directions. You're going to have to stop often anyway, so it can be helpful to make the journey in segments: in the city, say the name of the place you want to go, and point [adding a questioning *izquierda* (left), *derecha* (right), or *directo* (straight)]; do this frequently, and you'll get there. On longer journeys, keep a good map handy, and use the same strategy, asking for a nearby town on your journey rather than the final destination—you're more likely to get accurate directions.

And of course, you can't go wrong with an amiable *Pura vida,* which serves as "hello," "goodbye," "thanks," "cool," "how's it going," and all things amiable.

A phrase book and language-tape set can help get you started. *Fodor's Spanish for Travelers* (available at bookstores everywhere) is excellent.

measure, *nada de cerdo, pollo o pescado* (no pork, chicken, or fish). More cosmopolitan restaurants are more conscious of vegetarians—upscale Asian restaurants often offer a vegetarian section on the menu. In a pinch, the vegetarian fast-food chain Vishnu is always good for a quick meal. If your kids balk at the choices on the menu, ask for plain grilled chicken, fish, or beef: "*Pollo/pescado/carne sencillo para niños*" ("Grilled chicken/fish/meat for children"). Most restaurants are willing to accommodate with options and portion size.

Natural juices, called *frescos*, come with teeth-shattering amounts of sugar. If you're watching your child's intake, request one with only a little sugar (*con poco azúcar*); chances are it will be sweet enough, but you can always top it off if need be. Water is generally safe to drink (especially around San José), but quality can vary; to be safe, drink bottled water.

MEALS AND MEALTIMES

In San José and surrounding cities, *sodas* are usually open daily 7 AM to 7 or 9 PM, though some close on Sunday. Other restaurants are usually open 11 AM to 9 PM. In rural areas restaurants are usually closed on Sunday, except around resorts. In resort areas some restaurants may be open late. Most all-night restaurants are in downtown San José casinos. However, Nuestra Tierra and Manolos are both good 24-hour options, and for late-night cravings the doors at Denny's at the Best Western Irazú just north of San José are always open. Normal dining hours in Costa Rica are noon to 3 and 6 to 9. *Desayuno* (breakfast) is served at most sodas and hotels. The traditional breakfast is *gallo pinto*, eggs, plantains, and fried cheese; hotel breakfasts vary widely and generally offer fruit and lighter international options in addition to the local stick-to-your-ribs plate. *Almuerzo* (lunch) is *casado* time, and *cena* (supper) runs the gamut of just about anything you choose.

Except for those in hotels, many restaurants close between Christmas and New Year's Day and during Holy Week (Palm Sunday to Easter Sunday). Call before heading out. Those that do stay open may not sell alcohol between Holy Thursday and Easter Sunday. Even if you keep your base in San José, consider venturing to the Central Valley towns for a meal or two.

Unless otherwise noted, the restaurants listed in this guide are open daily for lunch and dinner.

Credit cards are not accepted at most restaurants in rural areas. Always ask before you order to find out if your credit card will be accepted. Visa and MasterCard are the most commonly accepted cards; American Express and Diners Club are less widely accepted. The Discover card is increasingly accepted. **■TIP→**Remember that 23% is added to all menu prices: 13% for tax and 10% for service. Because a gratuity (propina) is included, there's no need to tip, but if your service is good, it's nice to add a little money to the obligatory 10%.

RESERVATIONS AND DRESS

Costa Ricans generally dress more formally than North Americans. For dinner, long pants and closed-toe shoes are standard for men except for beach locations, and women tend to wear dressy clothes that show off their figures, with high heels. Shorts, flip-flops, and tank tops are not acceptable, except at inexpensive restaurants in beach towns.

WINES, BEER, AND SPIRITS

The ubiquitous sodas generally don't have liquor licenses, but getting a drink in any other eatery isn't usually a problem. Don't let Easter Thursday and Friday or a local election catch you off guard—the country's dry laws are strictly in effect. Bars close, and coolers and alcohol shelves in restaurants and stores are sealed off with plastic and police tape. In general, restaurant prices for imported alcohol—which includes just about everything except beer, rum, and *guaro*, the local sugarcane firewater—may be more than what you'd like to pay.

House wines are typically a low-end Chilean choice (this simply isn't wine-drinking country), so unless you see a familiar wine on the list, you might want to take a pass. Our advice? Go tropical! The country's abundant tropical fruit juices mix refreshingly well with rum, and to a lesser extent, *guaro*. You may also want to make a trip to the local supermarket to pick up something for an aperitif in your room—the selection will often be larger, and the prices much lower.

Costa Rica's brewery—run by Florida Ice & Farms—has a virtual monopoly on beer production, but produces some respectable lagers that pair well with beach lounging. Emblematic Imperial (known by the red, black, and yellow eagle logo that adorns bar signs and tourist T-shirts) is the favorite. The slightly more bitter Pilsen is a close runner-up, followed by the gold, dark, and light variations of Bavaria. Rock Ice is a relatively new product marketed to the younger crowd, with a higher alcohol content. The brewery also produces Heineken, and distributes imported brands such as Mexico's Corona. Those with exotic tastes (and deep pockets) can also find beers from as far away as Italy.

ELECTRICITY

North American appliances are compatible with Costa Rica's electrical system (110 volts) and outlets (parallel two-prong). Australian and European appliances require a two-prong adapter and a 220-volt to 110-volt transformer. Never use an outlet that specifically warns against using higher-voltage appliances without a transformer. Dual-voltage appliances (i.e., they operate equally well on 110 and 220 volts) such as most laptops, phone chargers, and hair dryers need only a two-prong adapter, but you should bring a surge protector for your computer.

WORD OF MOUTH

Was the service stellar or not up to snuff? Did the food give you shivers of delight or leave you cold? Did the prices and portions make you happy or sad? Rate restaurants and write your own reviews in Travel Ratings or start a discussion about your favorite places in Travel Talk on www.fodors.com. Your comments might even appear in our books. Yes, you, too, can be a correspondent!

Consider making a small investment in a universal adapter, which has several types of plugs in one lightweight, compact unit. Always check labels and manufacturer instructions to be sure. Don't use 110-volt outlets marked FOR SHAVERS ONLY for high-wattage appliances such as hair dryers.

Contacts Steve Kropla's Help for World Travelers (🌐 *www.kropla.com*) has information on electrical and telephone plugs around the world. **Walkabout Travel Gear** (🌐 *www.walkabouttravelgear.com*) has a good coverage of electricity under "adapters."

EMERGENCIES

Dial 911 for an ambulance, the fire department, or the police. Costa Ricans are usually quick to respond to emergencies. In a hotel or restaurant, the staff will usually offer immediate assistance, and in a public area passersby can be counted on to stop and help.

For emergencies ranging from health problems to lost passports, contact your embassy.

U.S. Embassy United States Embassy (*Embajada de los Estados Unidos* ✉ *C. 120 and Avda. 0, Pavas, San José* ☎ *506/2519–2000, 506/2519–2280 in Costa Rica for after-hours emergencies* 🌐 *www.usembassy.or.cr*).

General Emergency Contacts Ambulance (Cruz Roja), Fire, Police (☎ *911*). **Traffic Police** (☎ *2222–9330*).

HEALTH

Most travelers to Costa Rica do not get any vaccinations or take any special medications. However, according to the U.S. Centers for Disease Control, travel to Costa Rica poses some risk of malaria, hepatitis A and B, dengue fever, typhoid fever, and rabies. The CDC recommends getting vaccines for hepatitis A and B and typhoid fever, especially if you are going to be in remote areas or plan to stay for more than six weeks.

Check with the CDC for detailed health advisories and recommended vaccinations. In areas with malaria and dengue, both of which are carried by mosquitoes, bring mosquito nets, wear clothing that covers your whole body, and apply repellent containing DEET in living and sleeping areas. There are some pockets of malaria near the Nicaraguan border on the Caribbean coast. You probably won't need to take malaria pills before your trip unless you are staying for a prolonged period in the north, camping on northern coasts, or crossing the border into Nicaragua or Panama. You should discuss the option with your doctor. Children traveling to Central America should have current inoculations against measles, mumps, rubella, and polio.

SPECIFIC ISSUES IN COSTA RICA

Malaria is not a problem in Costa Rica except in some remote northern Caribbean areas near the Nicaraguan border. Poisonous snakes, scorpions, and other pests pose a small (often overrated) threat. The CDC marks Costa Rica as an area infested by the *Aedes aegypti* (dengue-carrier) mosquito, but not as an epidemic region. A few thousand cases in locals are recorded each year; the numbers had been dropping, but dramatic spikes in 2005 and 2007 have spurred major eradication efforts. Cases of fatal hemorrhagic dengue are rare. The highest-risk area is the Caribbean, and the rainy season is peak dengue season elsewhere. You're unlikely to be felled by this disease, but you can't take its prevention too seriously: *repelente* (insect repellent spray) and *espirales* (mosquito coils) are sold in supermarkets and small country stores. U.S. insect repellent brands with DEET are sold in pharmacies and supermarkets. Mosquito nets are available in some remote lodges; you can buy them in camping stores in San José. **TIP→**Mild insect repellents, like the ones in some skin softeners, are no match for the intense mosquito activity in the hot, humid regions of the Caribbean, Osa Peninsula, and Southern Pacific. Repellants made with DEET or picaridin are the most effective. Perfume, aftershave, and other lotions and potions can actually attract mosquitoes.

It's unlikely that you will contract malaria or dengue, but if you start suffering from high fever, the shakes, or joint pain, make sure you ask to be tested for these diseases when you go to the local clinic. Your embassy can provide you with a list of recommended doctors and dentists.

Government facilities—the so-called Caja hospitals (short for Caja Costarricense de Seguro Social, or Costa Rican Social Security System)—and clinics are of acceptable quality, but notoriously overburdened, a common complaint in socialized-medicine systems anywhere. Private hospitals are more accustomed to serving foreigners. They include Hospital CIMA, Clínica Bíblica, and Clínica Católica, which all have 24-hour pharmacies. Outside of San José most major towns have pharmacies that are open until at least 8 or 9 PM, but usually the nearest hospital emergency room is the only after-hours option. The long-established and ubiquitous Fischel pharmacies are great places for your prescription needs, and usually staff a doctor who can help with minor ailments. Antibiotics and psychotropic medications (for sleep, anxiety, or pain) require prescriptions in Costa Rica. Little else does. But plan ahead and bring an adequate supply with you from home; matches may not be exact.

For specific clinic, hospital, and pharmacy listings, see Chapters 3 through 9.

Most food and water is sanitary in Costa Rica. In rural areas you run a mild risk of encountering drinking water, fresh fruit, and vegetables contaminated by fecal matter, which in most cases causes a bit of *turista* (traveler's diarrhea) but can cause leptospirosis (which can be treated by antibiotics if detected early). You can stay on the safe side by avoiding uncooked food, unpasteurized milk (including milk products), and ice—ask for drinks *sin hielo* (without ice)—and by drinking bottled water. Mild cases of turista may respond to Imodium (known generically as loperamide) or Pepto-Bismol (not as strong), both of which can be purchased over the counter. Drink plenty of purified water or tea; chamomile (*manzanilla* in Spanish) is a good folk remedy. In severe cases, rehydrate yourself with a salt-sugar solution (½ teaspoon salt and 4 tablespoons sugar per quart of water).

Ceviche, raw fish cured in lemon juice—a favorite appetizer, especially at seaside resorts—is generally safe to eat. **■ TIP→ Buy organic foods whenever possible; chemicals, many of which have been banned elsewhere, are sprayed freely here without regulation.**

Heatstroke and dehydration are real dangers, especially for hikers, so drink lots of water. Take at least 1 liter per person for every hour you plan to be on the trail. Sunburn is the most common traveler's health problem. Use sunscreen with SPF 30 or higher. Most pharmacies and supermarkets carry sunscreen in a wide range of SPFs, though it is relatively pricey.

The greatest danger to your person actually lies off Costa Rica's popular beaches—riptides are common wherever there are waves, and tourists run into serious difficulties in them every year. If you see waves, ask the locals where it's safe to swim; and if you're uncertain, don't go in deeper than your waist. If you get caught in a rip current, swim parallel to the beach until you're free of it, and then swim back to shore. **■ TIP→ Avoid swimming where a town's main river opens up to the sea. Septic tanks aren't common.** Do not fly within 24 hours of scuba diving.

OVER-THE-COUNTER REMEDIES

Farmacia is Spanish for "pharmacy," and the names for common drugs *aspirina,* Tylenol, and *ibuprofen* are basically the same as they are in English. Pepto-Bismol is widely available. Many drugs for which you need a prescription back home are sold over the counter in Costa Rica. Pharmacies throughout the country are generally open from 8 to 8, though it's best to consult with your hotel's staff to be sure. Some pharmacies in San José affiliated with clinics stay open 24 hours.

HOURS OF OPERATION

Like the rest of the world, Costa Rica's business hours have been expanding. Megamalls are usually open seven days a week, opening around 10 AM and closing around 9 PM; tourism-based businesses and museums also usually keep a Monday-to-Sunday schedule but open an hour earlier. Many smaller or rural museums are open Monday to Friday. National parks often close one day for maintenance; for example, Manuel Antonio is closed Monday. Restaurants in the city often close on Sunday, and sometimes Monday. Eateries in beach towns and other tourism-oriented areas are more likely to open seven days a week. Bars and nightclubs are generally open until 1 or 2 AM, at which time night owls flock to places like the El Pueblo center in San José to keep partying until 4 AM. Last calls vary from place to place, but it's not hard to find bartenders happy to sell you a drink for the road at closing time.

Some government offices and smaller businesses close for lunch, but *jornada continua* (without the lunch break) is becoming more common, and most commercial establishments follow an 8 AM to 5 PM schedule.

Three public holidays (April 11, July 25, and October 12) are bumped to the following Monday when they fall on a weekend or midweek. Government offices and commercial establishments observe all the holidays. The only days the country truly shuts down are Easter Thursday and Friday; some buses still run, but no alcohol can be purchased, and most restaurants and all stores are closed.

HOLIDAYS

January 1: First day of the year

April 11: Juan Santamaría Day, a national hero

Easter Week: Thursday and Good Friday, religious activities

May 1: International Labor Day

July 25: Anniversary of the Annexation of Guanacaste Province

August 2: Day of the Virgin of Los Angeles (patron saint of Costa Rica)

August 15: Mother's Day

September 15: Independence Day

October 12: Culture Day (*Día de la Cultura*, or *Día de la Raza*)

December 25: Christmas Day

MAIL

The Spanish word for post office is *correo*. Mail from the United States can take up to two to three weeks to arrive in Costa Rica (occasionally it never arrives at all). Within the country, mail service is even less reliable. Outgoing mail is marginally quicker, with delivery to North America in 5 to 10 days, especially when sent from San José. It's worth registering mail; prices are only slightly higher. All overseas cards and letters will automatically be sent airmail. Mail theft is a chronic problem, so do not mail checks, cash, or anything else of value.

Minimum postage for postcards and letters from Costa Rica to the United States and Canada costs the equivalent of U.S. 32¢.

You can have mail sent poste restante (*lista de correos*) to any Costa Rican post office (specify Correo Central to make sure it goes to the main downtown office). In written addresses, *apartado*, abbreviated *apdo.*, indicates a post office box.

Post offices are generally open weekdays 7:30 to 5:30, and on Saturday 8 to noon. Stamps can be purchased at post offices and some hotels and souvenir shops. These vendors will also accept the mail you wish to send; don't bother looking for a mailbox, as only a handful (usually in rural areas with no post office) have been authorized. Always check with your hotel, which may sell stamps and post your letters for you.

SHIPPING PACKAGES

Shipping parcels through the post office is not for those in a hurry, because packages to the United States and Canada can take weeks. Also, packages may be pilfered. However, post-office shipping is the cheapest way to go, with rates at $6 to $13 per kilogram.

Some stores offer shipping, but it is usually quite expensive. If you can, carry your packages home with you.

UPS has offices in San José, Tamarindo, Jacó, Manuel Antonio, Sarchí, Nuevo Arenal, La Fortuna, and Limón. DHL has drop-offs in San José (Rohrmoser, Paseo Colón), Curridabat, Escazú, Heredia, Liberia, Limón, Ciudad Quesada, Jacó, Quepos, and San Isidro. Both have central information numbers with English-speaking staff to direct you to the nearest office. FedEx has offices in San José; it offers package pickup service in San José and other centers, such as Limón; call for availability. Prices are about 10 times what you'd pay at the post office, but packages arrive in a matter of days. ("Overnight" is usually a misnomer—shipments to most North American cities take two days.)

Express Services Main Offices DHL (✉ *600 m northwest of the Real Cariari Mall, La Aurora, Heredia* ☎ *506/2209–6000 in Costa Rica* ☞ *Call for other locations*). **Federal Express** (✉ *Zona Franca Metropolitana, Ciudad Barreal de Heredia, Local 1B, Heredia* ✉ *Centro de Servicio Mundial, Paseo Colón, 100 m east of León Cortés statue, San José*

☎800/463–3339 in North America). **United Parcel Service** (UPS ✉50 m east of Pizza Hut, Pavas, San José ☎506/2290–2828 in Costa Rica ☞Call for other locations).

MONEY

In general, Costa Rica is cheaper than North America or Europe, but travelers looking for dirt-cheap developing-nation deals may find it's more expensive than they bargained for—and prices are rising as more foreigners visit and relocate here.

Food in modest restaurants and public transportation are inexpensive. A one-mile taxi ride costs about $1. Here are some sample prices to give you an idea of the cost of living in Costa Rica: the local currency is the colón (plural: colones).

Prices throughout this guide are given for adults. Substantially reduced fees are almost always available for children, students, and senior citizens.

ATMS AND BANKS

Lines at San José banks would try the patience of a saint; instead, get your spending money at a *cajero automático* (automatic teller machine). If you do use the bank, remember that Monday, Friday, and the first and last days of the month are the busiest days.

Although they are springing up at a healthy rate, don't count on using an ATM outside of San José. Though not exhaustive, the A Todas Horas (ATH) company Web site lists locations of its ATH cash machines, and notes which ones offer colones (usually in increments of 1,000 colones), dollars (in increments of $20), or both; choose your region or city in the box on the homepage called *Busqueda de Cajeros*.

All ATMs are 24-hour; you'll find them in major grocery stores, some hotels, gas stations, and even a few McDonald's, in addition to banks. ATH, Red Total, and Scotiabank machines supposedly accept both Cirrus (a partner with MasterCard) and Plus (a partner with Visa) cards, but often don't. If you'll be spending time away from major tourist centers, particularly in the Caribbean, get most or all of the cash you need in San José and carry a few U.S. dollars in case you run out of colones. It's helpful to have both a Visa and a MasterCard—even in San José—as many machines accept only one or the other. Both companies have sites with fairly comprehensive lists of accessible ATMs around the world (⇨ *below*).

ATMs are sometimes out of order and sometimes run out of cash on weekends. **■TIP→PIN codes with more than four digits are not recognized at some Costa Rican ATMs, such as those at Banco Nacional or Banco de Costa Rica.** If you have a five-digit PIN, change it with your bank before you travel, or use only cash machines marked ATH.

The Credomatic office, housed in the Banco de San José central offices on C. Central between Avdas. 3 and 5, is the local representative for most major credit cards; get cash advances here, or at any bank (Banco Nacional and Banco San José are good for both MasterCard and Visa; Banex, Banco Popular, and Banco Cuscatlan always accept Visa).

State banks have branches with slightly staggered hours; core times are weekdays 9 to 4, and some are open Saturday morning. Several branches of Banco Nacional are open until 6, or occasionally 7. Private banks—Scotiabank, Banco Banex, and Banco de San José—tend to keep longer hours and are usually the best places to change U.S. dollars and traveler's checks; rates may be marginally better in state banks, but the long waits usually cancel out any benefit. The Banco de San José in Aeropuerto Internacional Juan Santamaría is open every day 5 AM to 10 PM.

■TIP→Whenever possible use ATMs only during bank business hours. ATMs here have been known to "eat" cards, and are frequently out of cash. When the bank is open, you can go in to retrieve your card or get cash from a teller. As a safety precaution, look for a machine in a bank with a guard nearby.

Resources A Todas Horas (*ATH* *www.ath.fi.cr*). **MasterCard** (*www.mastercard.com/atmlocator/index.jsp*). **Visa** (*www.visalatam.com/e_index.jsp*).

CREDIT CARDS

Throughout this guide, the following abbreviations are used: **AE,** American Express; **D,** Discover; **DC,** Diners Club; **MC,** MasterCard; and **V,** Visa.

It's a good idea to inform your credit-card company before you travel, especially if you're going abroad and don't travel internationally very often. Record all your credit-card numbers—as well as the phone numbers to call if your cards are lost or stolen—in a safe place. Both MasterCard and Visa have general numbers you can call (collect if you're abroad) if your card is lost, but you're better off calling the number of your issuing bank, since MasterCard and Visa usually just transfer you to your bank; your bank's number is generally printed on your card.

All major credit cards are accepted at most major hotels and restaurants in this book; establishments affiliated with Credomatic now also accept the Discover card. As the phone system improves and expands, many budget hotels, restaurants, and other properties have begun to accept plastic; but plenty of properties still require payment in cash. Don't count on using your credit card outside of San José. **■ TIP→Carry enough cash to patronize the many businesses without credit-card capability.** Note that some hotels, restaurants, tour companies, and other businesses add a surcharge (around 5%) to the bill if you pay with a credit card, or give you a 5% to 10% discount if you pay in cash. It's always a good idea to pay for large purchases with a major credit card if possible, so you can cancel payment or get reimbursed if there's a problem.

CURRENCY AND EXCHANGE

At this writing, the colón is 518 to the U.S. dollar and 691 to the euro. Coins come in denominations of 5, 10, 20, 25, 50, 100, and 500 colones and a range of styles, as new coins mingle with the older ones. For example, a 10-colón coin can be small, heavy, and bronze; large, heavy, and silver-color (currently being phased out); or small and extremely light (feels almost like plasticky play money)—and all are legal tender. Be careful not to mix up the very similar 100- and 500-colón coins. Bills are more standardized, and come in denominations of 1,000, 2,000, 5,000, and 10,000 colones. Avoid using the two larger denomination bills in taxis or small stores. U.S. dollars are widely accepted.

Costa Rican colones are sold abroad at terrible rates, so you should wait until you arrive in Costa Rica to get local currency. U.S. dollars are still the easiest to exchange, but euros can be exchanged for colones at just about any Banco Nacional branch and San José and Escazú branches of other banks, such as BAC San José. Private banks—Scotiabank, Banco Banex, and Banco de San José—are the best places to change U.S. dollars and traveler's checks. There is a branch of the Banco de San José in the airport (open daily 5 AM to 10 PM) where you can exchange money when you arrive—it's a much better deal than the Global Exchange counter. Taxi and van drivers who pick up at the airport accept U.S. dollars.

Outdoor money changers are rarely seen on the street, but avoid them if they approach; you will most certainly get a bad deal.

■ TIP→Even if a currency-exchange booth has a sign promising no commission, rest assured that there's some kind of huge, hidden fee. (Oh . . . that's right. The sign didn't say no *fee*.) And as for rates, you're almost always better off getting foreign currency at an ATM or exchanging money at a bank.

PACKING

Travel light, and make sure you can carry your luggage without assistance. Even if you're planning to stay only in luxury resorts, odds are that at least once you'll have to haul your stuff a distance from bus stops, the shuttle drop-off, or the airport. Another incentive to pack light: domestic airlines have tight weight restrictions (at this writing 11.3 to 13 kilograms [25 to 30 pounds]) and not all buses have luggage compartments. Frameless backpacks and duffel bags can be squeezed into tight spaces and are less conspicuous than fancier luggage.

Bring comfortable, hand-washable clothing. T-shirts and shorts are acceptable near the beach and in tourist areas; long-sleeve shirts and pants protect your skin from ferocious sun and, in some regions, mosquitoes. Leave your jeans behind—they take forever to dry. Pack a waterproof, lightweight jacket and a light sweater for cool nights, early mornings, and trips up volcanoes; you'll need even warmer clothes for trips to Chirripó National Park or Cerro de la Muerte and overnight stays in San Gerardo de Dota or on the slopes of Poás Volcano. Bring at least one good (and wrinkle-free) outfit for going out at night.

Women might have a tough time finding tampons, so bring your own. For almost all toiletries, including contact lens supplies, a pharmacy is your best bet. Don't forget sunblock, and expect to sweat it off and reapply regularly in the high humidity. Definitely bring sufficient batteries, since they're expensive here.

Snorkelers staying at budget hotels should consider bringing their own equipment; otherwise, you can rent gear at most beach resorts.

You have to get down and dirty—well, more like wet and muddy—to see many of the country's natural wonders. This following packing list is not comprehensive; it's a guide to some of the things you might not think to bring. For your main piece of luggage, a sturdy internal-frame backpack is great, but a duffel bag works, too. You can get by with a rolling suitcase, but then bring a smaller backpack as well.

PASSPORTS

U.S. citizens need only a passport to enter Costa Rica for stays of up to 90 days. Make sure it's up to date—you'll be refused entry if the passport is due to expire in less than one month. To be on the safe side, make sure it is valid for at least six months. The only way to extend your stay is to spend 72 hours in Nicaragua or Panama—but don't expect to do that undetected more than a couple of times. New customs forms ask how many visits you've made to Costa Rica in the past year.

Because of high rates of passport theft, travelers in Costa Rica are not required to carry their original documents with them at all times, although you must have easy access to them. Photocopies of the data page and your entry stamp are sufficient. Although there have been reports from around the world about security problems with in-room safes, if your hotel doesn't have a safe in reception, locking a passport in a hotel-room safe is better than leaving it an unlocked hiding place or carrying it with you.

TIP→ For easy retrieval in the event of a lost or stolen passport, before you leave home scan your passport into a portable storage device (like an iPod) that you're carrying with you or e-mail the scanned image to yourself.

If your passport is lost or stolen, first call the police—having the police report can make replacement easier—and then call your embassy (⇨ *Emergencies, below*). You'll get a temporary Emergency Travel Document that will need to be replaced once you return home. Fees vary according to how fast you need the passport; in some cases the fee covers your permanent replacement as well. The new document will not have your entry stamps;

PACKING LIST FOR COSTA RICA

- Quick-drying synthetic-fiber shirts and socks
- Hiking boots or shoes that can get muddy and wet
- Waterproof sport sandals (especially in the Osa Peninsula, where most transportation is by boat, and often there are no docks)
- Knee-high socks for the rubber boots that are supplied at many lodges
- A pair of lightweight pants (fire ants, mosquitoes, and other pests make covering yourself a necessity on deep-forest hikes)
- Pants for horseback riding (if that's on your itinerary)
- Waterproof, lightweight jacket, windbreaker, or poncho
- Day pack for hikes
- Sweater for cool nights and early mornings
- Swimsuit
- Insect repellent (with DEET, for forested areas and especially on the northern Caribbean coast, where there are pockets of malaria)
- Flashlight or headlamp with spare batteries (for occasional power outages or inadequately lighted walkways at lodges)
- Sunscreen with a minimum of SPF 30 (waterproof sunscreens are best; even if you're not swimming, you might be swimming in perspiration)
- Large, portable water bottle
- Hat and/or bandannas (not only do they provide shade, but they prevent perspiration from dripping down your face)
- Binoculars (with carrying strap)
- Camera (waterproof, or with a waterproof case or dry bag, sold in outdoor-equipment stores)
- Film (film in Costa Rica can be expired and is expensive)
- Imodium and Pepto-Bismol (tablet form is best)
- Swiss Army knife (and remember to pack it in your checked luggage, never your carry-on—even on domestic flights in Costa Rica)
- Ziplock bags (they always come in handy)
- Travel alarm clock or watch with an alarm (don't count on wake-up calls)
- Nonelectric shaving utensils
- Toilet paper (rarely provided in public bathrooms)

ask if your embassy takes care of this, or whether it's your responsibility to get the necessary immigration authorization.

GENERAL REQUIREMENTS FOR COSTA RICA	
Passport	Must be valid for 1 month after date of arrival
Visa	Required for Americans (free upon entry)
Vaccinations	None required
Driving	International driver's license not required; CDW is optional on car rentals
Departure Tax	US$26

RESTROOMS

Toilet paper is not discarded into the toilet in Costa Rica, but rather in a trash bin beside it. Septic systems are delicate and the paper will clog the toilet. At some public restrooms you might have to pay 50¢ or so for a few sheets of toilet paper. At others, there may not be any toilet paper at all. It's always a good idea to have some tissues at the ready. Gas stations generally have facilities, but you may decide not to be a slave to your bladder once you get a look at them. On long trips, watch for parked buses; generally this indicates some sort of better-kept public facilities.

Find a Loo The Bathroom Diaries (*www.thebathroomdiaries.com*) is flush with unsanitized info on restrooms the world over—each one located, reviewed, and rated.

SAFETY

Violent crime is not a serious problem in Costa Rica, but thieves can easily prey on tourists, so be alert. The government has been shamed into creating a Tourism Police unit, whose 250+ officers can be seen on bikes or motorcycles patrolling areas in Guanacaste, San José, and the Arenal area. Crimes against property are rife in San José. In rural areas theft is on the rise.

For many English-speaking tourists, standing out like a sore thumb can't be avoided. But there are some precautions you can take:

- Don't bring anything you can't stand to lose.
- Don't wear expensive jewelry or watches.
- In cities, don't carry expensive cameras or lots of cash.
- Carry backpacks on your front; thieves can slit your backpack and run away with its contents before you notice.
- Don't wear a waist pack, because thieves can cut the strap.
- Distribute your cash and any valuables (including credit cards and passport) between a deep front pocket, an inside jacket or vest pocket, and a hidden money belt. (If you use a money belt, carry some cash in your purse or wallet so you don't have to reach for the hidden pouch in public.)
- Keep your hand on your wallet if you are in a crowd or on a crowded bus.
- Don't let your purse just dangle from your shoulder; always hold on to it with your hand for added security.
- Keep car windows rolled up and car doors locked at all times in cities.
- Park in designated parking lots, or if that's not possible, accept the offer of the guachimán (a term adopted from English, pronounced "watchie man")—men or boys who watch your car while you're gone. Give them the equivalent of a dollar per hour when you return.
- Never leave valuables visible in a car, even in an attended parking lot.
- Padlock your luggage.
- Talk with locals or your hotel staff about crime in the area. Never walk in a narrow space between a building and a car parked on the street close to it, a prime hiding spot for thieves. Never leave a drink unattended in a club or bar: scams involving date-rape drugs have been reported in the past few years, targeting both men and women.

- Never leave your belongings unattended anywhere, including at the beach or in a tent.
- If your hotel room has a safe, use it, even if there's an extra charge. If your room doesn't have one, ask the manager to put your valuables in the hotel safe and ask him or her to sign a list of what you are storing there.
- If you are involved in an altercation with a mugger, immediately surrender your possessions and walk away quickly.

Scams are common in San José, where a drug addict may tell tales of having recently been robbed, then ask you for donations; a distraction artist might squirt you with something, or spill something on you, then try to clean you off while his partner steals your backpack; and pickpockets and bag slashers work buses and crowds. To top it all off, car theft is rampant. Beware of anyone who seems overly friendly, aggressively helpful, or disrespectful of your personal space. Be particularly vigilant around the Coca-Cola bus terminal, one of the rougher areas but a central tourism hub.

Don't believe taxi drivers when they say the hotel is closed, unless you've personally gotten out and checked it yourself. Many want to take you somewhere else to earn a commission. If a taxi driver says he does not have change and the amount is substantial, ask him to drive to a store or gas station where you can get change. This might be enough to prompt him to suddenly "find" the difference to give you. Avoid paying with large bills to prevent this.

A number of tourists have been hit with the slashed-tire scam: someone punctures the tires of your rental car (often right at the airport, when you arrive) and then comes to your "aid" when you pull off to the side of the road and robs you blind. Forget about the rims: always drive to the nearest open gas station or service center if you get a flat.

Lone women travelers will get a fair amount of attention from men; to avoid hassles, avoid wearing short shorts or skirts. On the bus, try to take a seat next to a woman. Women should not walk alone in San José at night or venture into dangerous areas of the city at all. Ask at your hotel which neighborhoods to avoid. Ignore unwanted comments. If you are being harassed on a bus, at a restaurant, or in some other public place, tell the manager. In taxis, sit in the backseat. If you want to fend off an earnest but decent admirer in a bar, you can politely say, "*Por favor, necesito un tiempo a solas*" (I'd like some time on my own, please). Stronger is "*Por favor, no me moleste*" (Please, stop bothering me), and for real pests the simple "*Váyase!*" (Go away!) is usually effective.

TAXES

The airport departure tax for tourists is $26, payable in cash or with Visa. All Costa Rican businesses charge a 13% sales tax. Hotels charge a 16.4% fee covering service and tax. Restaurants add 13% tax and 10% service fee to meals. Tourists are not refunded for taxes paid in Costa Rica.

TIME

Costa Rica does not observe daylight saving time, so from November to April it's six hours behind GMT, the equivalent of Central Time in the United States (one hour behind New York). The rest of the year, it is seven hours behind GMT, the equivalent of Mountain Time in the United States (two hours behind New York).

Time Zones Timeanddate.com (*www.timeanddate.com/worldclock*).

TIPPING

TIPPING	
Bellhop	$1–$5 per bag, depending on the level of the hotel
Hotel Concierge	$5 or more, if he or she performs a service for you
Hotel Doorman	$1–$2 if he helps you get a cab
Hotel Maid	$1–$3 a day (either daily or at the end of your stay, in cash)
Hotel Room-Service Waiter	$1–$2 per delivery, even if a service charge has been added
Tour Guide	$10 per day
Waiter	10%–15%, with 15% being the norm at high-end restaurants; nothing additional if a service charge is added to the bill
Restroom Attendants	In more expensive restaurants expect some small change or $1.
Coat-check personnel	Tip coat-check personnel at least $1–$2 per item checked unless there is a fee, then nothing.

Costa Rica doesn't have a tipping culture, but positive reinforcement goes a long way to fostering a culture of good service, which is hit-and-miss. Tip only for good service. Taxi drivers aren't tipped, but it's common courtesy to leave an extra 200–300 colones if they've helped you navigate a complicated set of directions. **TIP→Do not use U.S. coins to tip, because there is no way for locals to exchange them.**

Chambermaids get 1,000 to 1,500 colones per day; for great service try to leave up to 10% of your room bill. Concierges are usually not tipped. Room-service waiters should be tipped about 500 colones, as should bellhops (more in the most expensive hotels).

Restaurant bills include a 13% tax and 10% service charge—sometimes these amounts are included in prices on the menu, and sometimes they aren't. If the menu doesn't indicate whether service is included, ask. An additional gratuity is not expected, especially in cheap restaurants, but people often leave something extra when service is good. Leave a tip of about 200 colones per drink for bartenders, too.

At some point on a trip, most visitors to Costa Rica are in the care of a naturalist guide, who can show them the sloths and special hiking trails they'd never find on their own. Give $10 (or 5,000 colones) per day per person to guides if they've transported and guided you individually or in small groups, and about 10% of the rental to a hired driver of a small car. Give less to guides or drivers on bigger tours. For tour guides, it's okay to pay with U.S. dollars.

TOURS

BIKING

Costa Rica is mountainous and rough around the edges. It's a rare bird that attempts a road-biking tour here. But the payoff for the ungroomed, tire-munching terrain is uncrowded, wildly beautiful off-road routes. Most bike-tour operators want to make sure you're in moderately good shape and do some biking at home. Others, such as Coast to Coast Adventures, have easier one- and two-day jaunts. Lava Tours offers great expert- and intermediate-level riding, as well as "gravity-assisted" (cruising down the paved road from Poás Volcano, for example) trips. Bike Arenal has biking packages in the Arenal area for all skill levels, with short and long ride options for each day. Operators generally provide top-notch equipment, including bikes and helmets, but welcome serious bikers who bring their own ride. Leave the hybrids at home—this is mountain-biking territory. Operators usually meet you at the airport and take care of all logistics. All companies can design custom tours for extreme cyclists if requested.

Topographical maps (not biking maps per se) are generally provided as part of the tour, and include unpaved roads that are useful. If you're striking out on your own, these maps can usually be found at San José's Lehmann bookstore for about $3. Some basic Spanish is highly recommended if you're going to do it yourself.

■ **TIP→Check with individual airlines about bike-packing requirements and blackouts.** Cardboard bike boxes can be found at bike shops for about $15; more secure options start at $40. International travelers often can substitute a bike for a piece of checked luggage at no charge (if the box conforms to regular baggage dimensions), but U.S. and Canadian airlines will sometimes charge a $100 to $200 handling fee each way.

■ **TIP→Most airlines accommodate bikes as luggage, provided they're dismantled and boxed.**

Contacts Bike Arenal (☎ *506/2479–7150, 866/465–4114 in North America* 🌐 *www.bikearenal.com*). **Coast to Coast Adventures** (☎ *506/2280–8054 in Costa Rica* 🌐 *www.ctocadventures.com*). **Jungle Man Adventures** (☎ *506/2225–8186* 🌐 *www.adventurerace.com*). **Lava Tours** (☎ *506/2281–2458, 888/862–2424 in North America* 🌐 *www.lava-tours.com*).

BIRD-WATCHING

You will almost definitely get more out of your time in Costa Rica by taking a tour rather than trying to find birds on your own. Bring your own binoculars but don't worry about a spotting scope; if you go with a tour company that specializes in birding tours, your guide will have one. Expect to see about 300 species during a weeklong tour. Many U.S. travel companies that offer bird-watching tours subcontract with the Costa Rican tour operators listed below. By arranging your tour directly with the Costa Rican companies, you avoid the middleman and save money. Selva Mar, a tour agency specializing in the Southern Zone, runs comprehensive tours through Birding Escapes Costa Rica.

Contacts Birding Escapes Costa Rica (☎ *506/2771–4582 in Costa Rica* 🌐 *www.birdwatchingcostarica.com*). **Costa Rica Expeditions** (☎ *506/2257–0766 in Costa Rica* 🌐 *www.costaricaexpeditions.com*). **Horizontes** (☎ *506/2222–2022 in Costa Rica* 🌐 *www.horizontes.com*).

DIVING

Costa Rica's Cocos Island—one of the best dive spots in the world—can be visited only on a 10-day scuba safari with *Aggressor* or *Undersea Hunter*. But Guanacaste, the South Pacific, and to a lesser extent, the Caribbean, offer some respectable underwater adventures. Bill Beard's Costa Rica in the Gulf of Papagayo, Guanacaste, is a diving-tour pioneer and has countrywide options. Diving Safaris, in Playa Hermosa, has trips to dive sites in Guanacaste. In the South Pacific, Costa Rica Adventure Divers in Drake Bay arranges five-night trips. In this same area, Caño Island is a good alternative if you can't afford the money or time for Cocos Island, particularly in the rainy season, when dive sites closer to shore are clouded by river runoff.

Contacts Aggressor (☎ *800/348–2628 in North America* 🌐 *www.aggressor.com*). **Bill Beard's Costa Rica** (☎ *877/853–0538 in U.S.* 🌐 *www.billbeardcostarica.com*). **Costa Rica Adventure Divers** (☎ *506/2231–5806, 866/553–7073 in the U.S.* 🌐 *www.costaricadiving.com*). **Diving Safaris** (☎ *506/2672–1260 or 506/2672–1259 in Costa Rica* 🌐 *www.costaricadiving.net*). *Undersea Hunter* (☎ *506/2228–6613, 800/203–2120 in North America* 🌐 *www.underseahunter.com*).

FISHING

If fishing is your primary objective in Costa Rica, you are better off booking a package. During peak season you may not even be able to find a hotel room in the hot fishing spots, let alone one of the top boats and skippers. If you're less of a planner, some Fodor's readers say they've had good luck hanging out at "fish bars" in popular areas and asking around for recommendations. The major fish populations move along the Pacific coast through the year, and tarpon and snook fishing on the Caribbean is subject to the vagaries of seasonal wind and weather, but viable year-round. San José–based Costa Rica Outdoors has been in business since 1995, arranging fishing packages; it is one of the best bets for full service and honest advice about where to go, and works with the widest range of operators around the country. More than 100 outfits have high-quality, regionally based services. Anglers in the know recommend Kingfisher Sportfishing in Playa Carrillo, Guanacaste; Blue Fin Sportfishing and J.P. Sportfishing Tours in Quepos; The Zancudo Lodge near Golfito; and Río Colorado Lodge on the northern Caribbean coast.

Contacts Blue Fin Sport Fishing (☎ *506/2777–1676 in Costa Rica* 🌐 *www.bluefinsportfishing.com*). **Costa Rica Outdoors** (☎ *506/2231–0306, 800/308–3394 in U.S.* 🌐 *www.costaricaoutdoors.com*). **J.P. Sportfishing Tours** (☎ *506/2777–1613, 866/620–4188 in U.S.* 🌐 *www.jpsportfishing.com*). **Kingfisher Deep Sea Fishing** (☎ *506/2656–0091 in Costa Rica* 🌐 *www.costaricabillfishing.com*). **Río Colorado Lodge** (☎ *506/2232–4063, 800/243–9777 in North America* 🌐 *www.riocoloradolodge.com*). **The Zancudo Lodge** (☎ *506/2776–0008, 800/854–8791 in U.S.* 🌐 *www.thezancudolodge.com*).

GOLF

Putting on a green against a dramatic Pacific backdrop isn't the first image that springs to mind for Costa Rican vacations, but the increase in luxury resorts and upscale tourism has created a respectable, albeit small, golfing circuit in the Central Valley and along the Pacific coast. Most packages maximize links time with side excursions to explore the country's natural riches. Costa Rica Golf Adventures Ltd. organizes multiday tours at four- and five-star lodgings. Costa Rican–run Golfing Costa Rica sets up packages around the country, largely in its own or affiliated accommodations.

Contacts Costa Rica Golf Adventures (☎ *506/2239–5176, 877/258–2688 in U.S.* 🌐 *www.golfcr.com*).

HIKING

Most nature-tour companies include hiking as part of their itineraries, but these hikes may be short and not strenuous enough for serious hikers. Let the tour operator know what you expect from a hike. Ask a lot of questions about hike lengths and difficulty levels before booking the tour or you may be disappointed with the amount of time you get to spend on the trails. The following companies cater to both moderate and serious hikers.

Contacts Gap Adventures (☎ *800/708–7761 in North America* 🌐 *www.gapadventures.com*). **Serendipity Adventures** (☎ *877/507–1358 in North America, 506/2558–1000 in Costa Rica* 🌐 *www.serendipityadventures.com*). **The Walking Connection** (☎ *800/295–9255 in North America* 🌐 *www.walkingconnection.com*).

SURFING

Most Costa Rican travel agencies and tour companies have packages that ferry both veteran and would-be cowboys (and cowgirls) of the ocean to and between the country's famed bi-coastal breaks. Local experts at Alacran Surf (which works with Surf Costa Rica) really know their stuff, and offer standard or custom packages. Del Mar Surf Camp on the Pacific specializes in women-only surf lessons and packages. Learn how to surf, camp on the beach, and delve into personal development on the Costa Rican Rainforest Outward Bound School's weeklong adult surf journeys.

Contacts Costa Rican Rainforest Outward Bound School (☎ *800/676–2018 in North America, 506/2278–6058 in Costa Rica* 🌐 *www.crrobs.org*). **Del Mar Surf Camp** (☎ *506/2643–3197 in Costa Rica* 🌐 *www.costaricasurfingchicas.com*). **Alacran Surf** (☎ *506/2280–7328 in Costa Rica, 888/751–0135 or 619/955–7171 in North America* 🌐 *www.surf-costarica.com*).

SPANISH-LANGUAGE PROGRAMS

Thousands of people travel to Costa Rica every year to study Spanish. Dozens of schools in and around San José offer professional instruction and homestays, and there are several smaller schools outside the capital. Conversa has schools off Paseo Colón, and in Santa Ana, west of the capital, offering hourly classes as well as a "Super Intense" program (5½ hours per day). On the east side of town, ILISA provides cultural immersion in San Pedro. Mesoamérica is a low-cost language school that is part of a nonprofit organization devoted to peace and social justice. La Escuela D'Amore is in beautiful Manuel Antonio. Language programs at the Institute for Central American Development Studies include optional academic seminars in English about Central America's political, social, and economic conditions.

Contacts Conversa (☎ *506/2221–7649, 888/669–1664 in North America* 🌐 *www.conversa.net*). **ILISA** (☎ *506/2280–0700, 800/464–7248 in U.S.* 🌐 *www.ilisa.com*). **Institute for Central American Development Studies** (*ICADS* ☎ *506/2225–0508 in Costa Rica* 🌐 *www.icads.org*). **La Escuela D'Amore** (☎ *506/2777–1143, 800/261–3203 in North America* 🌐 *www.edcostarica.com*). **Mesoamérica** (☎ *506/2253–3195 in Costa Rica* 🌐 *www.mesoamericaonline.net*).

VOLUNTEER PROGRAMS

In recent years more and more Costa Ricans have realized the need to preserve their country's precious biodiversity. Both Ticos and far-flung environmentalists have founded volunteer and educational concerns to this end.

Volunteer opportunities span a range of diverse interests. You can tag sea turtles as part of a research project, build trails in a national park, or volunteer at an orphanage. Many of the organizations require at least rudimentary Spanish. Most of the programs for volunteers who don't speak Spanish charge a daily fee for room and board. The Caribbean Conservation Corporation (CCC) is devoted to the preservation of sea turtles. Earthwatch Institute leads science-based trips studying monkeys, turtles, or the rain forest. The Talamancan Association of Ecotourism and Conservation (ATEC), as well as designing short group and individual outings centered on Costa Rican wildlife and indigenous culture, keeps an updated list of up to 30 local organizations that welcome volunteers. Beach cleanups, recycling, and some wildlife projects don't require proficiency in Spanish. The Costa Rican Humanitarian Foundation has volunteer opportunities with indigenous communities, women, community-based clinics, and education centers. They also organize homestays.

The Institute for Central American Development Studies (ICADS) is a nonprofit social justice institute that runs a language school and arranges internships and field study (college credit is available); some programs are available only to college students. ICADS can also place students with local social service organizations, environmental groups, and other organizations, depending on interests. The Costa Rica Rainforest Outward Bound School offers two adult programs that combine self-exploration with a truly rural learning experience.

Contacts Costa Rica Rainforest Outward Bound School (☎ *506/2278–6058, 800/676–2018 in U.S.* 🌐 *www.crrobs.org*). **Costa Rican Humanitarian Foundation** (☎ *506/2390–4192 or 506/2282–6358 in Costa Rica* 🌐 *www.crhf.org*). **Institute for Central American Development Studies** (*ICADS* ☎ *506/2225–0508 in Costa Rica* 🌐 *www.icads.org*).

FODORS.COM CONNECTION

Before your trip, be sure to check out what other travelers are saying in Talk on www.fodors.com.

Caribbean Conservation Corporation (☎ *506/2297–5510 in Costa Rica, 800/678–7853 or 352/373–6441 in U.S.* *www.cccturtle.org*). **Earthwatch Institute** (☎ *978/461–0081 or 800/776–0188 in North America* *www.earthwatch.org*). **Talamancan Association of Ecotourism and Conservation (ATEC)** (☎ *506/2750–0398 in Costa Rica* *www.greencoast.com/atec.htm*).

VISITOR INFORMATION

The official tourism board, the Instituto Costarricense de Turismo (ICT), has free maps, bus schedules, and brochures. These folks could do better with the information they provide, but their Web site is comprehensive. Arrive armed with specific questions and know that they will not recommend hotels. At this writing, the Juan Santamaría airport desk had reopened. Visitor information is provided by the Costa Rica Tourist Board in Canada and in the United States.

Contacts Instituto Costarricense de Turismo (*ICT* ☎ *506/2299–5800, 866/267–8274 in North America* *www.visitcostarica.com* ✉ *Aueropuerto Internacional Juan Santamaría* ☎ *506/2437–2400* ⏲ *Closed Wed. and Sun.* ✉ *Plaza de la Cultura, C. 5, Avdas. Central–2* ☎ *506/2222–1090*).

ONLINE TRAVEL TOOLS

Info Costa Rica has a Web site with good cultural info, and chat rooms. For real estate, travel information, and traditional recipes, **Costa Rica.com** is a good bet. Horizontes is a tour operator that offers nature vacations but also has extensive information on Costa Rica and sustainable tourism on its Web site. The **U.S. Embassy's comprehensive site** has health information, travel warnings, lists of doctors and dentists, and much more. **The REAL Costa Rica** slips in a bit of attitude with its information, and is a bit lax on updating, but scores high marks for overall accuracy. Scope out detailed maps, driving distances, and pictorial guides to the locations of hotels and businesses in some communities at **CostaRicaMap.com.** The **Association of Residents of Costa Rica** online forums are some of the region's most active and informed, with topics ranging from business and pleasure trips to the real-estate market. For current events, check out the English-language newspaper **the Tico Times.**

Contacts All About Costa Rica Association of Residents of Costa Rica online forums (*www.arcr.net*). **The REAL Costa Rica** (*www.therealcostarica.com*). **InfoCostaRica** (*www.infocostarica.com*). **Costa Rica.com** (*www.costarica.com*). **Horizontes** (*www.horizontes.com*). **U.S. Embassy's Costa Rica** (*www.usembassy.or.cr*). **The Tico Times** (*www.ticotimes.net*).

INDEX

Photo Credits: 1, kallielukasik, Fodors.com member. 2, Monica Richards, Fodors.com member. 5, carsinio, Fodors.com member. **Chapter 1: Experience Costa Rica:** 8-9, Robert Harding Travel/photolibrary.com. 10, Jaimi DeFeo, Fodors.com member. 11 (left), Plumboy, Fodors.com member. 11 (right), Vogelmutter, Fodors.com member. 14 (left), Gwendolyn Morris, Fodors.com member. 14 (top center), Susana Mingote. 14 (top right), raquel_z , Fodors.com member. 14 (bottom right), Highwind1, Fodors.com member. 15 (top left), Christie Bernick, Fodors.com member. 15 (bottom left), Pablo Arroyo and Margaret Kalacska. 15 (top center), Juan Amighetti/Costa Rica Tourist Board (ICT). 15 (right), Pablo Arroyo and Margaret Kalacska. 16, Danmike, Fodors.com member. 17 (left), Hotel Sí Como No. 17 (right), Thornton Cohen. 18, Arenas Del Mar Beach & Nature Resort. 19 (left), Edgar Moneste/Costa Rica Tourist Board (ICT). 19 (right), Café Britt Costa Rica, S.A. 20, Soccerchump, Fodors.com member. 21 (left), Casa Corcovado. 21 (right), steph270, Fodors.com member. 22, Michael G Smith/Shutterstock. 23, Daniel P. Kraft, Fodors.com member. 28, colibri, Fodors.com member. **Chapter 2: Biodiversity:** 29, Justin Hubbell, Fodors.com member. 30, Jaimi DeFeo, Fodors.com member. 31, Costa Rica Tourist Board (ICT). 34-35, urosr/Shutterstock. 36 (top), blickwinkel/Alamy. 36 (2nd from top), Philipp Weigell/wikipedia.org. 36 (3rd from top), O. Baudys/wikipedia.org. 36 (bottom), Dennis Frates/Alamy. 37 (top), Ben Lunsford/wikipedia.org. 37 (2nd from top), wikipedia.org. 37 (3rd from top), Stefan

Laube/wikipedia.org. 37 (bottom), EML/Shutterstock. 38, Pietro Scozzari/Tips Italia/photolibrary.com. 39 (top), Martin Shields/Alamy. 39 (bottom), danmike, Fodors.com member. 40-41, Sylvain Grandadam/age fotostock. 42 (top), Jason Kremkau. 42 (2nd from top), Peter Arnold, Inc./Alamy. 42 (3rd from top), Túrelio/wikipedia.org. 42 (bottom), wikipedia.org. 43 (top), Danita Delimont/Alamy. 43 (2nd from top), wikipedia.org. 43 (3rd from top), Danita Delimont/Alamy. 43 (bottom), Ken Thornsley/NASA/wikipedia.org. 44, Nik Wheeler/Alamy. 45 (top), piper35w, Fodors.com member. 45 (bottom), Marco13, Fodors.com member. 46-47, Alvaro Leiva/age fotostock. 48 (top), John Seiler/iStockphoto. 48 (2nd from top), Peter Arnold, Inc./Alamy. 48 (3rd from top), Orchi/wikipedia.org. 48 (bottom), Peter Arnold, Inc./Alamy. 49 (top), Papilio/Alamy. 49 (2nd from top), Erlaubnis des Autors/wikipedia.org. 49 (3rd from top), wikipedia.org. 49 (bottom), Danita Delimont/Alamy. 50, Ronald Reyes. 51 (top), maddytem, Fodors.com member. 51 (bottom), Martin Rugner/age fotostock. 52-53, Alvaro Leiva/age fotostock. 54 (top), Avancari/wikipedia.org. 54 (2nd from top), plumboy, Fodors.com member. 54 (3rd from top), Louise Wolff/wikipedia.org. 54 (bottom), Cody Hinchliff/wikipedia.org. 55 (top), David Jensen (Storkk)/wikipedia.org. 55 (2nd from top), matt knoth/wikipedia.org. 55 (3rd from top), Jerry Oldenettel/wikipedia.org. 55 (bottom), Andrew Hewitt/Alamy. 56, Costa Rica Tourist Board (ICT). 57 (top), reedjoella, Fodors.com member. 57 (bottom), frans lemmens/Alamy. 58-59, Andoni Canela/age fotostock. 60 (top), William Tait/Alamy. 60 (2nd from top), Wibowo Djatmiko/wikipedia.org. 60 (3rd from top), Arco Images GmbH/Alamy. 60 (bottom), Florida Images/Alamy. 61 (top), WaterFrame/Alamy. 61 (2nd from top), Steven G. Johnson/wikipedia.org. 61 (3rd from top), Mike Baird/wikipedia.org. 61 (bottom), Mehmet Karatay/wikipedia.org. 62, Thornton Cohen. 63 (top), Liz Stuart, Fodors.com member. 63 (bottom), StupFD, Fodors.com member. 64-65, Alvaro Leiva/age fotostock. 66 (top), wikipedia.org. 66 (2nd from top), Daniel J. Cox/Alamy. 66 (3rd from top), Wilfredo Rodríguez/wikipedia.org. 66 (bottom), Andrewtappert/wikipedia.org. 67 (top), Thierry Caro/wikipedia.org. 67 (2nd from top), Jim Lebster/wikipedia.org. 67 (3rd from top), Patrick Verdier/wikipedia.org. 67 (bottom), Dori (http://dori.merr.info)/wikipedia.org. 68, Juan Amighetti/Costa Rica Tourist Board (ICT). 69 (top), TorontoJeff, Fodors.com member. 69 (bottom), Justin Hubbell, Fodors.com member. **Chapter 3: San José:** 71, R1/Alamy. 72, Lindy Drew. 73 (top), R1/Alamy. 73 (bottom), Costa Rica Tourist Board (ICT). 77, Pietro Scozzari/age fotostock. 78, Choice Hotels International, Inc. 79 (top), Hotel Rincón de San José. 79 (bottom), Hotel Presidente. 80, Ronald Reyes. 91, R1/Alamy. 96, José Fuste Raga/age fotostock. 107, Neil McAllister/Alamy. 111, Liz Stuart, Fodors.com member. 118-119, Lindy Drew. 118 (bottom), Andre Nantel/iStockphoto. 120 (top and center), Lindy Drew. 120 (bottom), David L Amsler/iStockphoto. 121-23 (all), Lindy Drew. **Chapter 4: The Central Valley:** 127, jvcostarica, Fodors.com member. 128, Pablo Arroyo and Margaret Kalacska. 129 (top and bottom), Costa Rica Tourist Board (ICT). 132, mrsviv07, Fodors.com member. 133 (top), Alvaro Leiva/age fotostock. 133 (bottom), R1/Alamy. 134, Xandari Resorts. 135 (top and bottom), Dawn Pando. 136, Brian Allen, Fodors.com member. 141, Lindy Drew. 153, travelib costa rica/Alamy. 154, Gay Bumgarner/Alamy. 159 (top), Index Stock Imagery/photolibrary.com. 159 (bottom) and 160 (top), Jordi Camí/age fotostock. 160 (center), steve bly/Alamy. 160 (bottom), North Wind Picture Archives/Alamy. 161 (top), Yadid Levy/age fotostock. 161 (bottom), steve bly/Alamy. 162 (top left), Kenneth Hong/Flickr. 162 (top right), Angela Hampton Picture Library/Alamy. 162 (center), JORDI CAMI/Alamy. 162 (bottom),), Jordi Camí/age fotostock. 163 (top left), ©Marvin Dembinsky Photo Associates/Alamy. 163 (top center), Index Stock Imagery/photolibrary.com. 163 (top right), J1/Alamy. 163 (bottom), Arco Images GmbH/Alamy. 169, Ronald Reyes. 170, Lindy Drew. 172, Neil McAllister/Alamy. 177, Linda137, Fodors.com member. 178, Costa Rica Tourist Board (ICT). **Chapter 5: The Northern Plains:** 181, Msoberma, Fodors.com member. 182, Leethal33, Fodors.com member. 183 (top), Pablo Arroyo. 183 (bottom), Costa Rica Tourist Board (ICT). 186, robrick, Fodors.com member. 187 (top), imagebroker/Alamy. 187 (bottom), JORDI CAMI/Alamy. 188, owlwoman, Fodors.com member. 189 (top), vogelmutter, Fodors.com member. 189 (bottom), racegirl, Fodors.com member. 190, Jason Kremkau. 191 (top), Ginita215, Fodors.com member. 191 (bottom), Fernando Ramírez/age fotostock. 192, Chris Fredriksson/Alamy. 193 (top), Laguna del Lagarto Lodge. 193 (bottom), Danita Delimont/Alamy. 194, Lindy Drew. 199, JuanAmighetti/Costa Rica Tourist Board (ICT). 206, sportster, Fodors.com member. 211, Jan Csernoch/Alamy. 215, Sylvain Grandadam/age fotostock. 225, Jill Chapple, Fodors.com member. 226, Y.Levy/Alamy. 228, Tiffnco, Fodors.com member. 229 (top left), Kevin Schafer/Alamy. 229 (bottom left), Justine Evans/Alamy. 229 (right), Kevin Schafer/Alamy. 234, Pattie Steib/Shutterstock. 247, Lindy Drew. 250, Errol Barrantes/Costa Rica Tourist Board (ICT). **Chapter 6: North Pacific:** 255 and 256, Thornton Cohen. 257 (top), Mark Gabrenya/Shutterstock. 257 (bottom), Gpkbrand, Fodors.com member. 260, Danita Delimont/Alamy. 261 (top), Zach Holmes/Alamy. 261 (bottom), Catherine Scott/iStockphoto. 262, imagebroker/Alamy. 263 (top), Sylvia Cordaiy Photo Library Ltd/Alamy. 263 (bottom), R1/Alamy. 264, Thornton Cohen/Alamy. 265 (top), Mark Gabrenya/Shutterstock. 265 (bottom), Kevin Schafer/Alamy. 266, Tim Calver. 267 (top), The Harmony Hotel, Nosara. 267 (bottom), Borinquen Mountain Resort & Spa. 268, PDSF, Fodors.com member. 273, Luis Alberto Aldonza/age fotostock. 280, R1/Alamy. 292-93, John Coletti/age fotostock. 294, Antonio Jorge Nunes/Shutterstock. 295 (top), Mboja, Fodors.com member. 295 (bottom), Chinamom, Fodors.com member. 296 (left), Juan Amighetti/Costa Rica Tourist Board (ICT). 296 (top right), Sam Chadwick/Shutterstock. 296 (bottom right), imagebroker/Alamy. 302, Eyal Nahmias/Alamy. 309, Guillen Photography/UW/Costa Rica/Alamy. 318, Yadid Levy/Alamy. 325, Peter Arnold, Inc./Alamy. 326, Inger Hogstrom/age fotostock. 327, Krasinsky, Fodors.com member. 328 (left), Stephen Turner/wikipedia.org. 328 (top center), Jaimi DeFeo, Fodors.com member. 328 (bottom center), wikipedia.org. 328 (top right), Snowmanradio/wikipedia.org. 328 (bottom right), www.birdphotos.com/wikipedia.org. 329 (top left), JUNIORS BILDARCHIV/age fotostock. 329 (bottom left and top right), wikipedia.org. 329 (bottom center), Dario Sanches/wikipedia.org. 329 (bottom right), Jerry Oldenettel/wikipedia.org. 332, Jason Bazzano/age fotostock. 339 and 344, ImageSync Ltd/Alamy. 349, Jon Arnold Images Ltd/Alamy. 355, Costa Rica Tourist Board (ICT). **Chapter 7: Central Pacific:** 359, Gwendolyn Morris, Fodors.com member. 360 (top), TorontoJeff, Fodors.com member. 360 (bottom), Plumboy, Fodors.com member. 361, Ruthalan, Fodors.com member. 363, TorontoJeff, Fodors.com member. 364, ARCO/F Scholz/age fotostock. 365 (top), jwb5555, Fodors.com member. 365 (bottom), Stephen Saks Photography/Alamy. 366, volcanogirl, Fodors.com member. 367 (top), LynneL, Fodors.com member. 367 (bottom), Highwind1, Fodors.com member. 368, Hotel Sí Como No. 369 (top), Arenas Del Mar Beach & Nature Resort. 369 (bottom), Freank Duffy. 370, esp05, Fodors.com member. 376, Hemis /Alamy. 380, R1/Alamy. 383 and 388, Yadid Levy/Alamy. 396-97, Reinhard Dirscherl/photolibrary.com. 406, Leethal33, Fodors.com member. 410-411, Chris Cheadle/age fotostock. 412 (top), Timur Kulgarin/Shutterstock. 412 (bottom), Thornton Cohen. 413 (left), Sandra Salvadó/age fotostock. 413 (right), LOOK Die Bildagentur der Fotografen GmbH/Alamy. 414, Pablo Arroyo. 420, Colleen George, Fodors.com member. 427, Costa Rica Tourist Board (ICT). 430, Sylvain Grandadam/age fotostock. **Chapter 8: South Pacific:** 435, Chad Clark, Fodors.com member. 436 (top), Cutestcookie, Fodors.com member. 436 (bottom), Carsinio, Fodors.com member. 437 (top), Volcanogirl, Fodors.com member. 437 (bottom), buckscofamily, Fodors.com member. 440, RobertoRamos/Costa Rica Tourist Board (ICT). 441 (top), Justin Hubbell, Fodors.com member. 441 (bottom), Danita Delimont/Alamy. 442, Highwind1, Fodors.com member. 443 (top), Timur Kulgarin/Shutterstock. 443 (bottom), drs, Fodors.com member. 444, R1/Alamy. 445 (top), Jason Kremkau. 445 (bottom), David South/Alamy. 446, Casa Corcovado. 447 (top), Playa Nicuesa Rainforest Lodge. 447 (bottom), Elle Schuster. 448, Ronald Reyes. 453, Danita Delimont/Alamy. 462, Pep Roig/Alamy. 468, Richard Bueno, Fodors.com member. 477, Justin Hubbell, Fodors.com member. 484, jamie722, Fodors.com member. 494-95, Dirscherl Reinhard/age fotostock. 496, Dirscherl Reinhard/age fotostock. 497, Guillen Photography/UW/Costa Rica/Alamy. 498 (top left), Florida Keys National Marine Sanctuary/wikipedia.org. 498 (bottom left), Photo Collection of Dr. James P. McVey, NOAA Sea Grant Program. 498 (top right), Jon Zander/wikipedia.org. 498 (bottom right), NURC/UNCW and NOAA/FGBNMS. 499 (top left), Mila Zinkova/wikipedia.org. 499 (bottom left), suneko/wikipedia.org. 499 (top right), M. Herko/OAR/National Undersea Research Program. 499 (center right), Laban712/wikipedia.org. 499 (bottom right), Adona9/wikipedia.org. 501, LOETSCHER CHLAUS/Alamy. 504, hipvirgochick, Fodors.com member. 511, Monica Richards, Fodors.com member. 514, ticopix/Alamy. **Chapter 9: Caribbean:** 519, John Cancalosi/age fotostock. 520 (top), Costa Rica Tourist Board (ICT). 520 (bottom), Stjerne, Fodors.com member. 521, Costa Rica Tourist Board (ICT). 524, Wendler/age fotostock. 525 (top), Andoni Canela/age fotostock. 525 (bottom), Stjerne, Fodors.com member. 526, Costa Rica Tourist Board (ICT). 527 (top), jhubson1, Fodors.com member. 527 (bottom), Costa Rica Tourist Board (ICT). 528, Almonds & Corals Tent Lodge Camp. 529 (top), Hotel Casa Marbella. 529 (bottom), Almonds & Corals Tent Lodge Camp. 530, JuanAmighetti/Costa Rica Tourist Board (ICT). 534, Danita Delimont/Alamy. 541, Jordi Camí/age fotostock. 544, Liz Stuart, Fodors.com member. 547 (top), janenicole, Fodors.com member. 548, xelas, Fodors.com member. 549 (top), David Kleyn/Alamy. 549 (bottom left), Nordicphotos/Alamy. 549 (bottom right), Andrew Hyslop/iStockphoto. 550 (top), CuboImages srl/Alamy. 554, Sylvain Grandadam/age fotostock. 561, Rodrigo Montenegro/Costa Rica Tourist Board (ICT). 571, Ronald Reyes. 574, dgray, Fodors.com member.

ABOUT OUR WRITERS

Journalist **Leland Baxter-Neal** has been based in Costa Rica for the better part of five years. He's worked as a reporter for The Beach Times and The Tico Times, and freelanced for *The Miami Herald*, *People Magazine*, and *International Living*. He writes about environmental issues, coastal development, tourism, and politics. Leland combats his nostalgia for his home state of Oregon by surfing, immersing himself in nature and dancing a mean salsa.

Freelance writer **David Dudenhoefer** has spent the better part of the past two decades in Costa Rica. He first arrived in 1986 as an exchange student at the Universidad de Costa Rica, where he concentrated on tropical biology and surfing. In the ensuing years, he wrote for dozens of newspapers and magazines and contributed to seven other Fodor's guides. David is currently based in Lima, Peru, from where he covers much of Latin America and works for organizations that promote sustainable development and conservation.

Dorothy MacKinnon arrived in Costa Rica in 1999, promptly fell in love with the country, and took up a post in San José to contribute stories to *The Tico Times* on ecotourism—and to write the Bird Watching feature and the South Pacific chapter of this guide. Along the way, she has learned passable Spanish and become a passionate birder and enthusiastic nature-lover. In her past life, she was a reporter and copy editor for *The Financial Post* in Canada and *The Washington Post*.

Suzanna Starcevic came to Costa Rica in 2000 on a whim, and is mildly surprised (and somewhat pleased) to find herself still there. A journalist by trade, she has worked her way across Canada as a writer and editor, and spent three years as Weekend Editor at *The Tico Times*. She currently works as a translator and freelance writer.

Mark Sullivan has written or edited dozens of travel guides, including *Fodor's Central America*, *Fodor's South America*, and *Fodor's Pocket Aruba*. His cultural reporting has also appeared in many magazines, including *Billboard*, *InStyle*, and *Interview*. When not on the road, he splits his time between a shoebox apartment in New York City and a rambling Victorian in the Catskills. Mark wrote Experience Costa Rica for the guide this year

San José–based freelance writer and pharmacist **Jeffrey Van Fleet** has spent the last one-and-one-half decades enjoying Cos Rica's long rainy seasons and Wisconsi cold winters. (Most people would try to it the other way around.) He saw his fi resplendent quetzal, that bird-watche Holy Grail, while researching this guide. Jeff is a regular contributor to Costa Rica's English-language newspaper, *The Tico Times*, and has written for Fodor's guides to Guatemala, Chile, Argentina, Peru, and Central and South America.

Special thanks to the following writers for their contributions to this edition:

Gillian Gillers wrote the Scuba Diving and Snorkeling feature; Liz Goodwin contributed the Sport Fishing article; and Holly Sonneland lent her expertise to the Last Minute Souvenirs piece.

Ancient Rome

Using Evidence

Pamela Bradley

Edward Arnold
A division of Hodder & Stoughton
MELBOURNE LONDON NEW YORK AUCKLAND

Edward Arnold (Australia) Pty Ltd
(The Educational Academic and Medical Publishing
division of Hodder & Stoughton)
A division of Hodder & Stoughton
80 Waverley Road
Caulfield East Victoria 3145

First published by
Edward Arnold (Australia) Pty Ltd in 1990

National Library of Australia
Cataloguing-in-publication data

Bradley, Pamela.
Ancient Rome: using evidence.

Bibliography.
Includes index.
ISBN 0 7131 8328 4.

1. Rome — History — Sources. 2. Rome — History.
I. Title.

937.6

Text and cover design by R. T. J. Klinkhamer
Illustrations by Alan Smith
Typeset in Goudy Old Style by SRM Production
Printed by Macarthur Press Pty Ltd

Front cover: This onyx cameo with a relief of the Roman imperial eagle was carved around AD 40 — its setting much later. (Kunsthistorisches Museum, Vienna)

Contents

List of illustrations

List of maps

PART

1

Introduction to Roman history

The evidence

1

Literature and epigraphy

Records before third century few and unreliable

THERE IS A LARGE BODY of written evidence that can be used by a student of Roman history, although records for the period before the third century BC are 'few and scanty and those that did exist in the public and private archives almost all perished in the burning of Rome'[1] which followed the invasion of the Gauls in 390 BC. Later writers reconstructed these years, often falsely and sometimes deliberately, to serve the interests of the important Roman families who wished their family traditions to be seen in a favourable light. Most later historians writing about the early years of Rome's history used their imagination freely.

Great variety of written evidence from third century

The extensive written evidence from the third century includes official government documents inscribed on stone and bronze; day-to-day business records on papyrus; the lengthy works of annalists and historians such as Livy, Polybius and Tacitus; the biographies of Plutarch; the personal histories of the aristocratic families; the speeches and letters of Cicero; the accounts of the civil wars by Appian; Caesar's account of his Gallic wars, and even the graffiti scrawled on the walls and buildings of cities such as Pompeii.

Roman epigraphy is the study of texts inscribed on materials such as bronze and stone. The oldest surviving inscription was thought to be the signature on a gold brooch of a craftsman of the late seventh century, but this is now generally regarded as a forgery. The earliest on stone is a regulation of the late sixth century that relates to religion and was found in the Roman Forum.

A portion of the consular *fasti*

A fragment of the Roman calendar

Numerous official documents

Official documents include treaties, laws (*leges*), plebiscites (*plebiscita*), senatorial decrees (*senatus consulta*), edicts (*edicta*), communications of Roman magistrates and governors, year lists of the consuls (*fasti consulares*) and the yearly calendar compiled by the chief priest (*pontifex maximus*). In his job of drawing up the calendar each year and noting the religious festivals, the chief priest added important events that would occur during the year and a list of the magistrates; these were later collected and published in the eighty volumes of the *Annales Maximi* by Mucius Scavola (pontifex maximus) in 130 BC. The *fasti* (lists of consuls) were used to date all public and private business. Both these sources provided a chronological outline for historians.

Calendars and fasti

The thousands of inscriptions—both in Greek and in Latin—that have been found, some of which give evidence of the life of the common people, help to complement the work of the historians, whose views were predominantly upper-class.

Evidence from coins

Pictorial representations and writing on coins and gems provide details of many aspects of Roman life such as types of buildings, monuments, religious practices, wars and triumphs, domestic politics and administration in the provinces.

The calendar

Before the time of Julius Caesar, inaccurate intercalations had caused the Roman calendar to be about three months ahead of the solar calendar. Caesar adjusted this, and then introduced a year of 365¼ days.

The purpose of the calendar was to tell Romans when to come to the city to attend the assemblies, when a religious celebration or an important festival was to be held, which days were market days and which were the dates of court actions.

The days were classified with the letters N, NP, EN, F or C.

- N signified *dies nefastus*—a day on which no business could be carried out.
- NP indicated one of the great public festivals of the state. The word represented by the added 'P' is uncertain, the most likely one being *publicus*. There were 49 NP days in the calendar.
- EN marked a *dies endotercisus*—a 'cut day'—on which a religious festival was to be held in the morning and in the evening. On such a day the people's assemblies could not meet and some aspects of public business could not be concluded.
- F was a business day— a *dies fastus*.
- C was a day—*dies comitialis*—on which the *comitia* (assembly) could meet.

Each day was prefixed with a letter of the alphabet from A to H. They were known as the 'nundinal' (of the ninth day) letters, and their purpose was to identify every ninth day—these being, originally, the Roman market-days (later equivalent to a *dies fastus*).

The following extracts are from the early Roman calendar that has been reconstructed from fragments found at Antium, just south of Rome.[2]

April		*August*	
A	**Kalends** of April	A	**Kalends** of April
	Business in court		To Hope To the two Victories
B	Business in court	B	Business in court
C	Business in Assembly	C	Business in Assembly
D	Business in Assembly	D	Business in Assembly
E	**Nones** No business	E	**Nones** No business
	To Fortune and the State		Public Holiday To Safety
F	No business	F	Business in Court
G	No business	G	Business in Assembly
H	No business	H	Business in Assembly
A	No business	A	Business in Court
B	No business	B	Business in Assembly
C	No business To Mighty Idaean	C	Business in Assembly
	Mother of the Gods	D	Business in Assembly
D	No business	E	**Ides** No business
E	**Ides** No business		Public Holiday To Diana,
	Public Holiday		Vortumnus Fortune Horse-rider,
	To Jupiter Conqueror,		Hercules Conqueror, Castor,
	Jupiter Liberty		Pollux, Goddesses of Song
F	No business		

April		*August*	
G	Festival: Sacrifice of Cows in calf No business Public Holiday	F	Business in Court
H	No business	G	Business in Assembly
B	No business	H	Business in Assembly
C	Festival: of Ceres No business Public Holiday To Ceres, Liber and Libera	A	Festival: of God of our Harbour No business Public Holiday
D	No business	B	Business in Assembly
E	Festival: of Pales No business Public Holiday	C	Festival: of Vintage Business in court in the morning To Venus
F	No business	D	Business in Assembly
G	Festival: of Vintage Business in court	E	Festival: of God of Sowing No business
A	Festival: of God of Mildew No business Public Holiday	F	Midsplit
B	Business in Assembly	G	Festival: of Vulcan No business Public Holiday To Vulcan, Hera, Quirinus, Maia above the Meeting-Place
C	Business in Assembly	H	Business in Assembly
D	Business in Assembly	A	Festival: of Goddesses of Good Sowing No business Public Holiday
E	Business in Assembly	B	Business in Assembly
		C	Festival: of Volturnus No business Public Holiday
		D	Business in Assembly
		E	Business in Assembly

Dedications

Dedications to notable Romans, often in the form of epitaphs (words inscribed on a tomb), are very revealing. They usually include details of a person's career and achievements, and some complimentary remarks.

The following inscriptions are dedications—found on their tombs on the Appian Way, just outside Rome—to two members of the Scipio family. The first is the epitaph of Lucius Cornelius Scipio Barbatus (Scipio Longbeard), who was consul in 298 and censor in 290. This verse was inscribed on the front of his tomb some time after the year 200.

> Lucius Cornelius Scipio Longbeard, Gnaeus' begotten son, a valiant gentleman and wise, whose fine form matched his bravery very well was aedile consul and censor among you; he took Taurasia and Cisuana, in fact Samnium; he overcame all the Lucanian land and brought hostages therefrom.[3]

On the same tomb is inscribed '[P]aulla Cornelia, daughter of Gnaeus, wife of Hispallus'. This was obviously a later burial, in the same tomb, of Scipio Longbeard's sister.

The second epitaph was of the son of Scipio Longbeard. Painted on the lid of the tomb in vermilion (a brilliant red colour) were the words 'Lucius

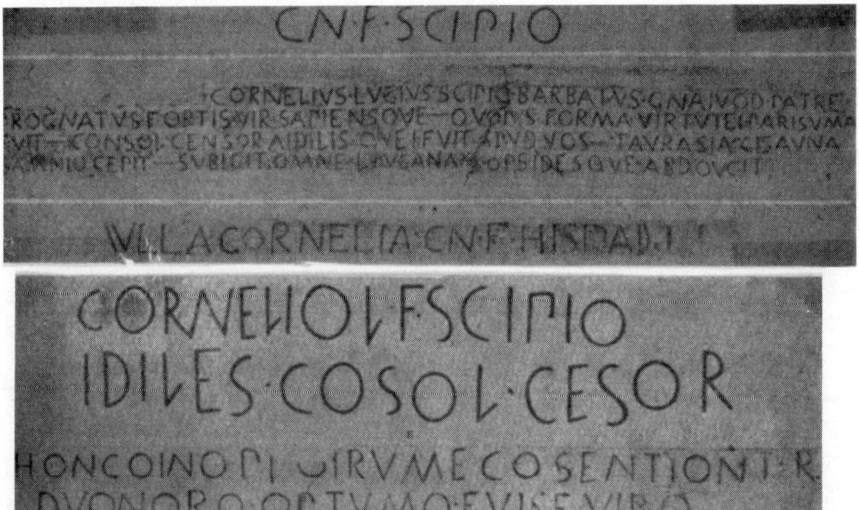

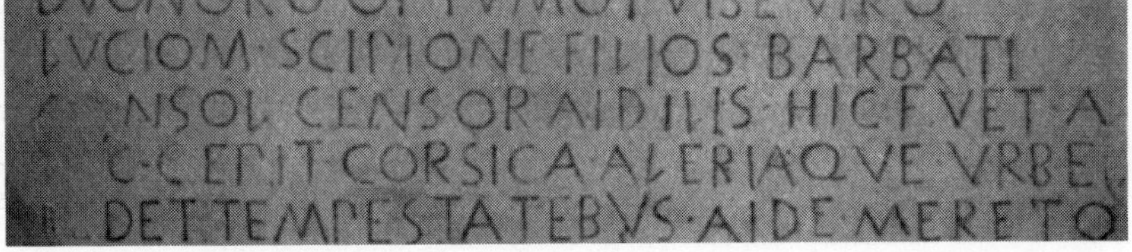

Cornelius Scipio, son of Lucius, aedile, consul, censor'. Carved on a stone tablet at a later date, and found in his grave, was the following:

> This man Lucius Scipio, as most agree, was the very best of all good men at Rome. A son of Long-beard, he was aedile, consul and censor among you; it was he who captured Corsica, Aleria [capital of Corsica] too a city. To the Goddess of Weather he gave a temple in return for benefits received.[4]

Signs of daily life

Some of the most interesting inscriptions are not those that record important government decisions or outline the achievements of outstanding Romans, but rather the numerous and varied examples referring to everyday life.

Graffiti

Painted on the walls of the city of Pompeii were many examples of what would be referred to today as graffiti. Thousands of these abbreviated messages have been found, some of which are extremely vulgar.

The following are a few of the comments written prior to the elections of AD 80.

Graffito from the walls of the gladiators' barracks in Pompeii

Graffito from the wall of the House of Menander in Pompeii giving the address of a woman of easy virtue: 'Ask for Novella Primigenia in the Vicolo Venereio at Nuceria, near Porta Romana'

Numerius Barcha, a fine man: I appeal to you to elect him a member of the Board of Two. So may Venus of Pompeii, holy hallowed Goddess, be kind to you.

Numerius Veius Barcha, may you rot!

Quintius. Let anyone who votes against him take a seat by [on] an ass.[5]

Lost property

As well, there are what would be the equivalent of modern-day lost-and-found columns in a newspaper. A message offering a reward for the recovery of a stolen pot was painted on a wall in Pompeii.

Lost from this shop—a bronze water-pot. 65 sesterces REWARD to anyone who brings back the same. If he produces the thief, from whom we may rescue our property, 84 sesterces.[6]

An inscribed Roman milestone: these were erected every 5000 Roman feet and recorded distances as well as the names of the people responsible for the construction of the road

Official notices

Boundary-stones, marking private and public property, provide another insight into ordinary Roman life. The following inscription on a private boundary stone corresponds to the 'trespassers will be prosecuted' signs today frequently seen on fences.

The lower road is private property of Titus Umbrenius, son of Gaius. Pedestrian traffic, by request only. No person to drive cattle or cart.[7]

The equivalent of an anti-litter notice (no dumping of rubbish) was found on a boundary-stone on the Esquiline hill in Rome. It was inscribed somewhere about the year 79 under the supervision of a praetor called Lucius Sentius.

In God's name: Let none be minded to make a burning-ground [for cremation of the dead] or cast dung or carcass within the limits of the boundary-stones on the side nearer the city.

Also painted on the stone were the words 'Carry away dung far off, lest you come to grief'.[8]

Situations wanted

Skilled tradesmen sometimes advertised for work. A Sicilian stonemason from Panormus thought it best to advertise in both Greek and Latin. His grammar was fairly weak:

Greek—Here slabs for holy temples are modelled and engraved with letters by public labours through us.

Latin—Here inscriptions for holy temples are arranged by public labours through we.[9]

Exercise

Referring to the inscriptions described above (calendar, epitaphs, graffiti, boundary-stones and advertisements) compile a table under the following headings.

Type of document	*Author/s*	*To whom it is addressed*	*Purpose*

Archaeology

The material remains left by the Romans are extensive and not limited to the Italian peninsula. They are found throughout the Mediterranean basin and in areas as far afield as Britain and Iraq.

Extensive material remains

They range from the spectacular—such as amphitheatres, triumphal arches, public baths, catacombs, temples, roads, aqueducts, walls and houses—to vivid wall paintings, statues, busts of notable individuals, household utensils, jewellery, weapons and armour. The ancient cities of Pompeii, Herculaneum and Ostia, to name just a few, reveal clearly what life in the Roman world was like.

The Arch of Titus, built to commemorate the sack of Jerusalem by Titus in AD 70

The aqueduct of Segovia, which was erected during the Augustan period

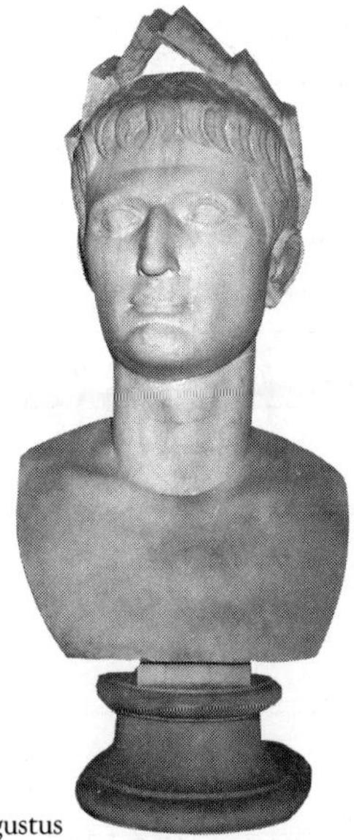

Marble bust of Augustus

The Temple of Fortuna Virilis in the Forum Boarium (cattle market) in Rome

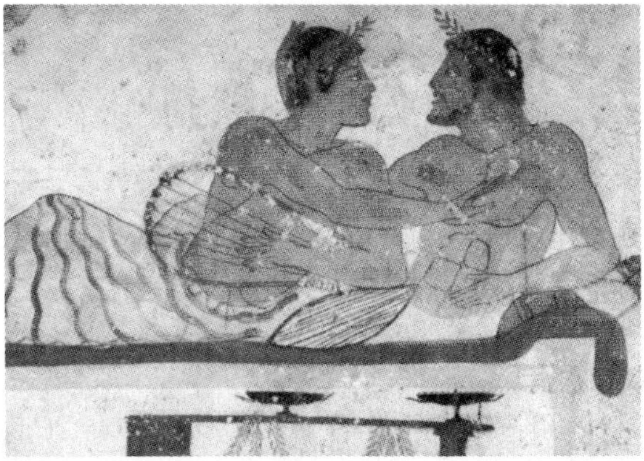

Wall paintings from Paestum in southern Italy

2 The geography of Italy and its influence on the development of Rome

Physical characteristics

The plain of Latium and the site of Rome

Physical influences on development of Rome

THE GROWTH OF ROME—from a small agricultural village on the Tiber River, struggling to maintain itself against its neighbours, to a world power dominating the whole Mediterranean basin—cannot be explained by any one factor. However, the physical characteristics of Italy, Rome's location on the fertile plain of Latium midway along the western side of the peninsula and Italy's central position within the Mediterranean all contributed to Rome's success.

Physical characteristics

Location

Central position in Mediterranean

Opposite: Italy's central position in the Mediterranean basin

Italy had an ideal location in the Mediterranean basin: its position gave access to the lands of the west (Gaul and Spain) and south (North Africa), and later to the Hellenic east. When Rome became an imperial power, this position made it easier to maintain control, while the Mediterranean Sea, *Mare Nostrum* (Our Sea), linked the provinces within the empire.

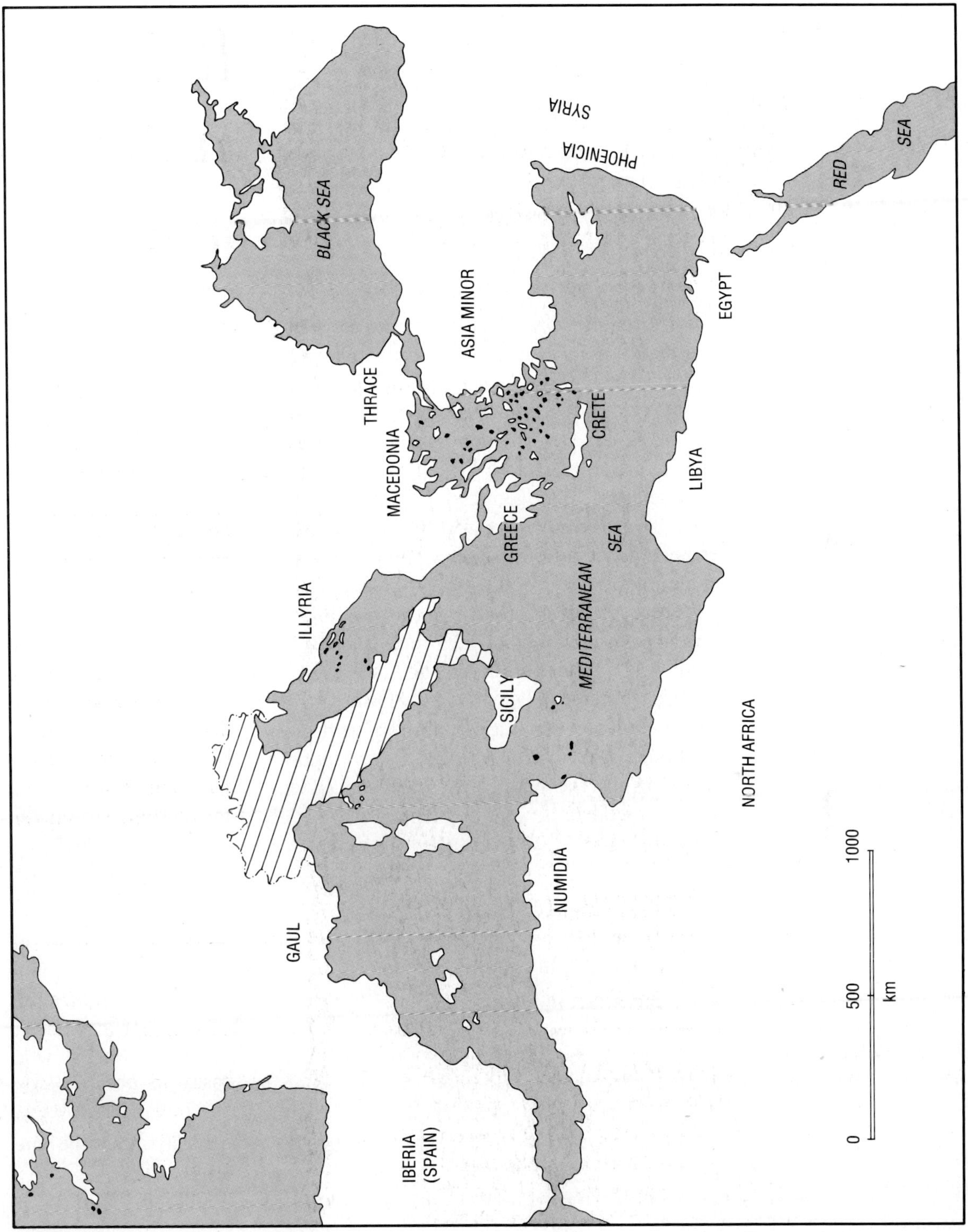
BLACK SEA
SYRIA
PHOENICIA
RED SEA
ASIA MINOR
EGYPT
THRACE
CRETE
MACEDONIA
LIBYA
GREECE
SEA
MEDITERRANEAN
ILLYRIA
SICILY
NORTH AFRICA
NUMIDIA
GAUL
IBERIA (SPAIN)
0
500
1000
km

Landform

Mountains, uplands and volcanoes

Italy is bordered on the north by the very impressive Alps, while the Apennine Ranges run like a backbone from north to south through the entire length of the peninsula. Unlike the tangle of mountains and isolated valleys in Greece, the mountains of Italy have not had such an effect on the political and economic developments of the inhabitants.

Alps no real barrier to invasion

The Alps, despite their height, did not shut out invaders or prevent movement into the peninsula. Several passes provided relatively easy passage for the early migrations into Italy in about 2000 BC and enabled the Gauls to make their successful invasion, reaching and sacking Rome about 390 BC. The easy route into Italy from Gaul and Spain along the west coast made the crossing of the Alpine barrier unnecessary.

Apennines no barrier to unity

The Apennines, ranging in height from about 1400 to 3000 metres, ran closer to the coast and were steeper in the east than in the west, where they fell in a more gentle slope. Although they were not high enough to be a barrier to unity as were the mountains in Greece, they did provide strongholds for the hardy Samnite people—an Italic group who settled in the mountains of central Italy—in their conflicts with Rome.

Volcanic influences on soils and drainage

Along the west coast of the peninsula a series of volcanoes had produced a covering of lava and volcanic ash that had weathered into fertile soils. Volcanic deposits had, however, disrupted the natural drainage system, producing lagoons and marshes which became breeding grounds for mosquitoes: malaria was always a real problem for the people of Italy. Although most of the volcanoes were extinct, three remained active—Vesuvius on the mainland, Stromboli on the island of that name, and Etna in Sicily; the city of Pompeii was totally destroyed by Vesuvius in AD 79.

Plains

Fertile plains in west

The largest and most fertile plains in the peninsula (except for those of the River Po in the north) lay along the western side—Etruria, Latium and Campania. In the east, where the steep slopes of the Apennines ran close to the coast, the land was generally not as fertile, except in Apulia.

Major settlements in west

The plains of the west supported dense populations of farmers, who formed the reliable backbone of the Roman army; therefore, since the centres of population were in the west, it was natural that Rome's first expansion beyond Italy (the Punic Wars against Carthage) should be into the western Mediterranean.

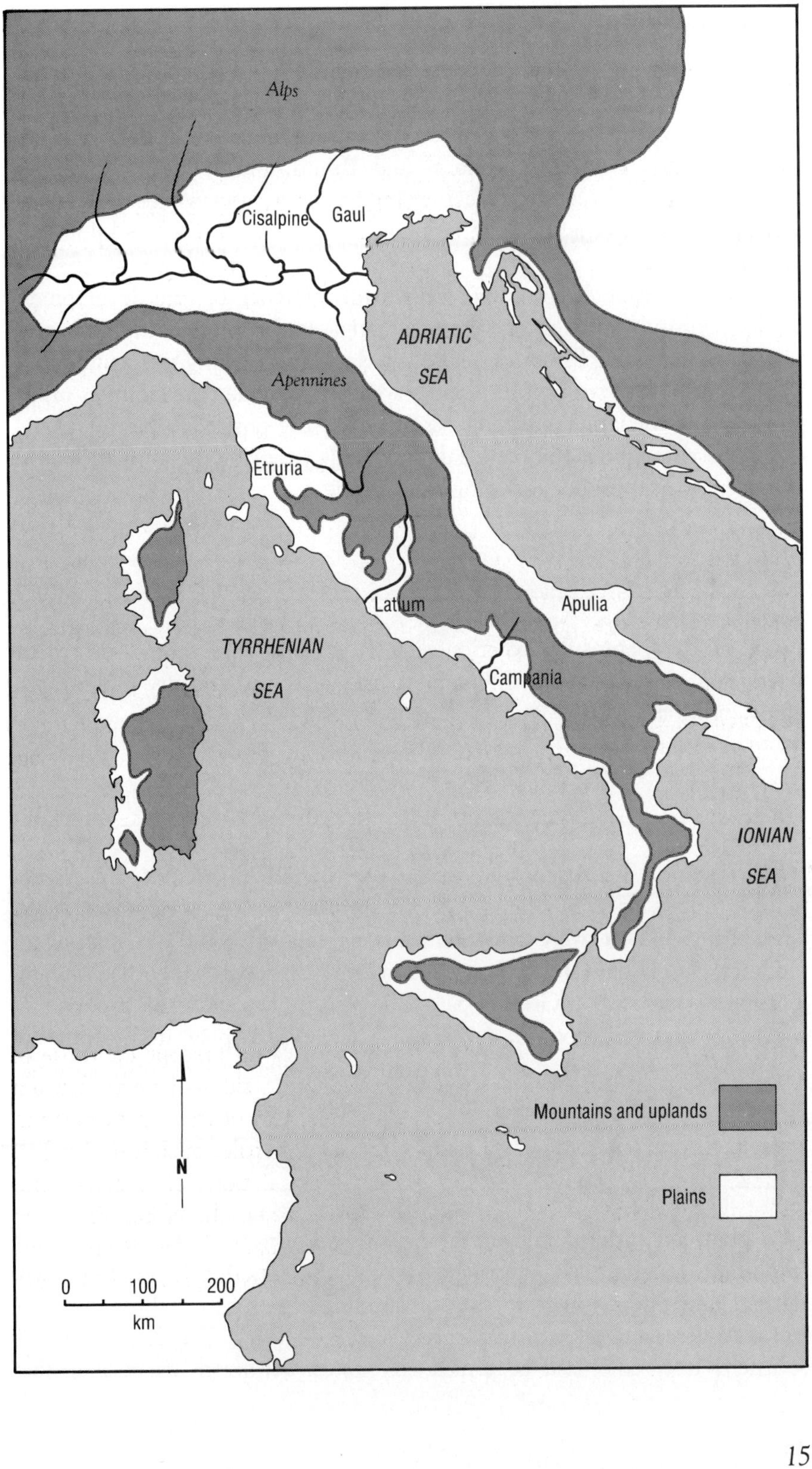

The landform of Italy

Ports and rivers

Very few good harbours

Unlike conditions in Greece where the highly indented coastline brought most Greeks into close contact with the sea, the Italian coastline, although long, had very few good harbours; the best were in the south and east—Naples, Puteoli, Tarentum and Brundisium. However, ships of ancient times did not need deep-water harbours, and where a river was navigable, as was the Tiber, a city could be established a few kilometres upstream from the sea.

Rivers generally unnavigable

Generally, though rivers had very little influence on the development of the peninsula since most were not navigable, being torrential in winter and dry in summer. Estuaries were often dangerous, owing to accumulation of silt and lack of strong tides, and so did not provide port facilities unless they were artificially regulated—as at Ostia, the port of Rome.

Travel throughout the peninsula was made easier by the construction of a fine network of roads radiating from Rome.

Climate

Most of the peninsula experienced—as it still does today—a typical Mediterranean climate with summers bright, sunny and dry and winters rainy, mild and short.

Resources

The slopes of the Apennines were well-wooded in ancient times, providing timber for shipbuilding and other purposes such as to provide roofs and beams. There were also plentiful supplies of stone and marble for building, and clays for pottery. However, although Italy had greater

Lack of mineral resources

natural resources than Greece, particularly in timber and grain products, it was comparatively poor in minerals. There was copper in Etruria, but Rome had to obtain iron from the island of Elba and silver from Sardinia.

The plain of Latium and the site of Rome

Physical advantages of plain of Latium

The plain of Latium, midway along the western side of Italy, had an important geographical advantage. It was the junction of several great natural and direct routes to the surrounding regions with those running north to Etruria and south to Magna Graecia—'Great Greece', an area of southern Italy colonised by Greek city-states. Although there were few

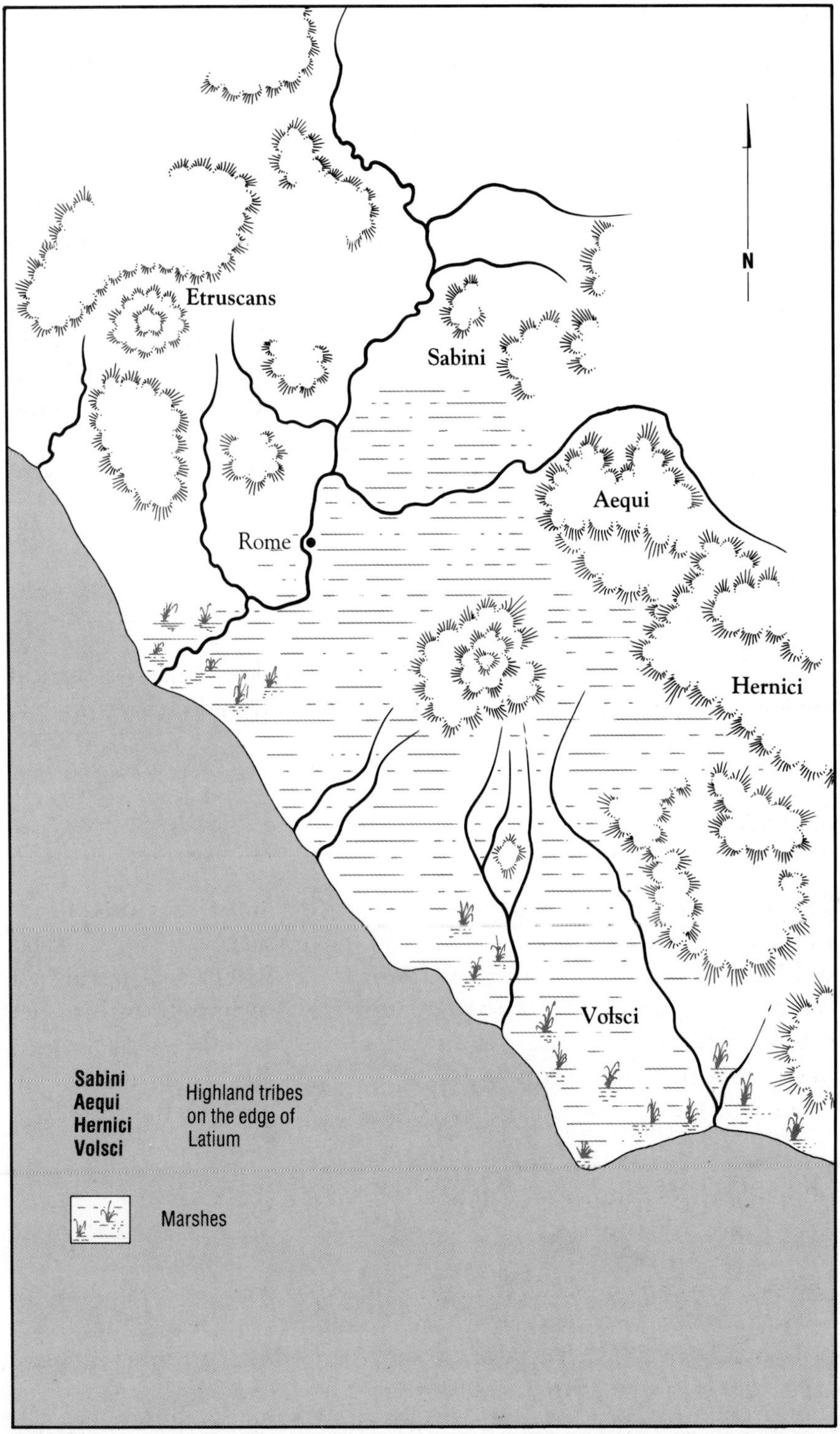

The plain of Latium

Opposite: Early migrations to Italy, Sicily and North Africa

bays and harbours the Tiber River, which formed the northern frontier of Latium, gave swift access to the coast and to the centre of the peninsula.

The fertile valleys of Latium could support a dense population and later, when marshy areas were drained, the area for settlement was greatly expanded. The peoples of the neighbouring uplands, envious of Latium's fertility, continually raided the area until the fourth century.

Rome grew at a site on the River Tiber where volcanic outflows had produced a group of tightly knit hills. These hills were easily defended by the early communities of shepherds and farmers, and reached to the Tiber where an island in the river—the only one—allowed it to be easily bridged (crossed). The city of Rome thus from the start had geographical assets which played a part in its development:

- fertile farming land
- easily defended hills
- access to the sea
- a position where the river could be bridged
- a central position as a road junction

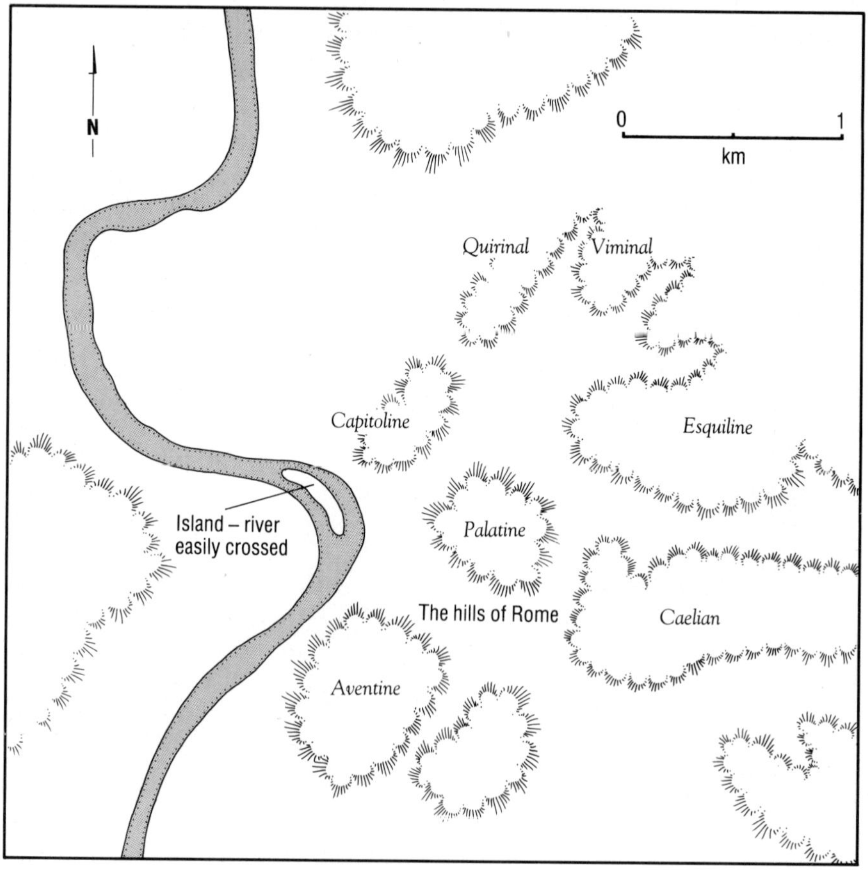

The site of Rome

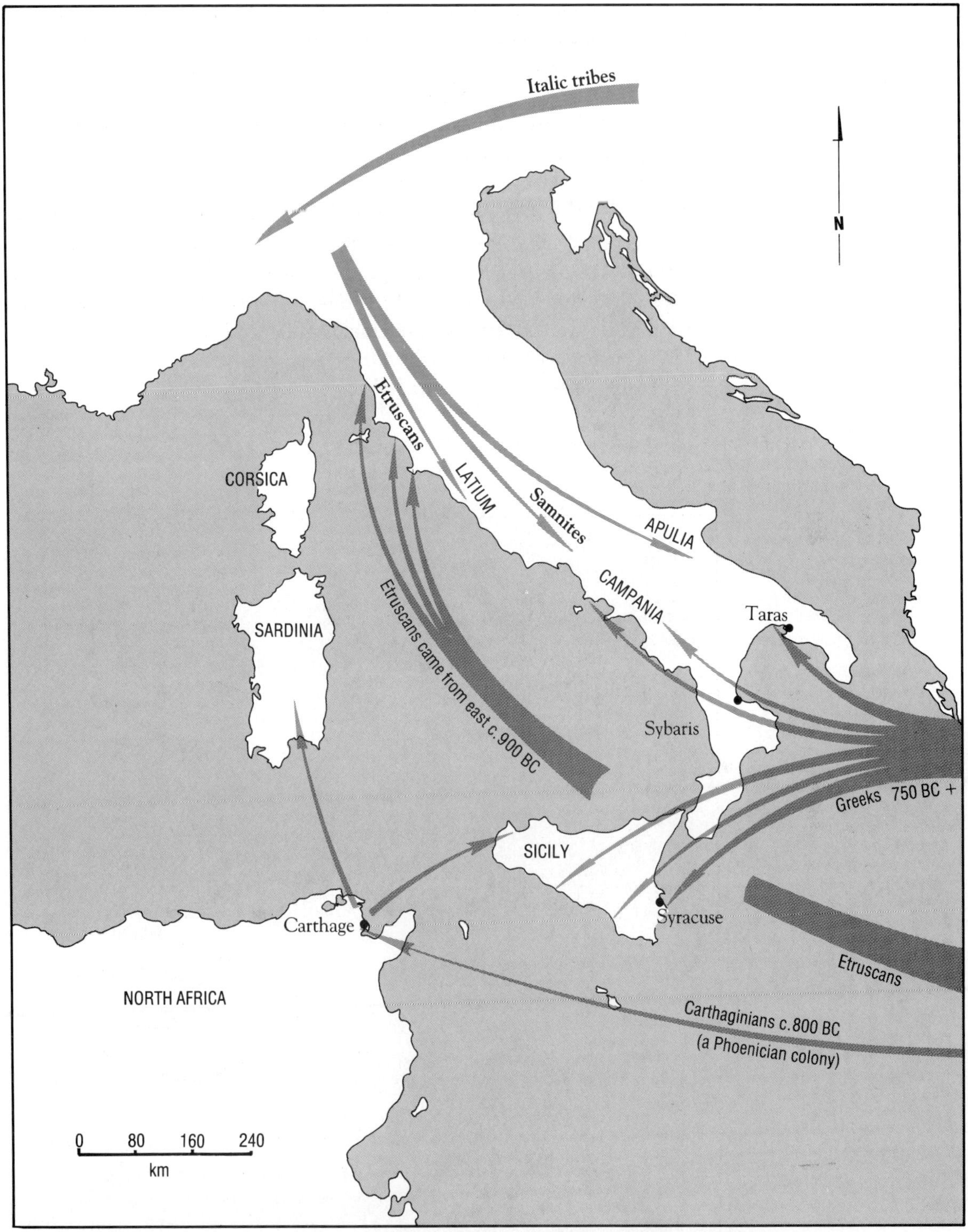
Italic tribes
N
Etruscans
CORSICA
LATIUM
Samnites
APULIA
SARDINIA
Etruscans came from east c. 900 BC
CAMPANIA
Taras
Sybaris
Greeks 750 BC +
SICILY
Syracuse
Carthage
Etruscans
NORTH AFRICA
Carthaginians c. 800 BC
(a Phoenician colony)
0 80 160 240
km

Origin of the Latins

Italic tribes entered the peninsula about 1500–1000 BC in a number of waves, and were Indo-European people similar to the early Greeks. One group of these *Italici* were the Latins, a small tribe who settled on the coastal plain of Latium in agricultural villages. The development soon far surpassed that of the other Italic tribes living in the more mountainous areas of the peninsula.

However, while Rome was still just one of the small, agricultural Latin villages, other civilisations—superior to the Latins—were flourishing in the peninsula. The Etruscans—a people whose origin is even now uncertain—occupied the area north of Latium (Etruria), while the Greeks had established colonies in southern Italy and in Sicily (Magna Graecia). Both cultures were to have considerable influence on Rome.

The Carthaginians in North Africa and Sicily were also to have a considerable effect on events in Italy.

The foundation and early development of Rome 3

The legends

The Etruscan Influence

The Greeks in southern Italy

THE TRADITIONAL ACCOUNT of the origins of Rome centres on two legends.

According to one, refugees from the Trojan War led by Aeneas made their way to Italy and settled in Latium. Aeneas' son, Ascanius, founded the Latin city of Alba Longa and Romulus, one of his descendants, founded Rome.

Legendary founders of Rome

The second legend maintains that the twin grandsons of the legitimate ruler of Alba Longa were cast into the Tiber River by a usurper to the throne but that the twins, Romulus and Remus, were miraculously saved and suckled by a she-wolf. When they grew up, they restored the throne

A bronze statue representing the she-wolf supposed to have suckled Romulus and Remus — the twins are a later addition

to their grandfather and decided to found a city of their own. Romulus founded a settlement on the Palatine Hill in 753, and later killed his brother Remus during a quarrel.

Traditional account of regal period

According to this tradition, Rome was ruled by seven kings — Romulus, Numa Pompilius, Tullus Hostilius, Ancus Marcus, Lucius Tarquinius Priscus, Servius Tullius and Lucius Tarquinius Superbus (Tarquin). The last three kings were Etruscan and were responsible for splendid public works, but during the reign of Tarquin the people revolted and the king was deposed and sentenced to exile. The monarch was replaced by two annually elected magistrates, called consuls, whose authority was the same as the king's had been.

A large part of the traditional account can be discredited, but some aspects of it have been verified by archaeologists.

Material finds on Palatine Hill

Archaeological finds have revealed that there was a settlement in the vicinity of Rome as early as the Bronze Age (before 1000 BC), but remains on the Palatine Hill indicate that this was the site of the original nucleus of the city. The first settlement (in about the eighth century) was nothing more than a shepherds' village, but other settlements were made on the outer hills and the growth of the city resulted from an amalgamation of these hill villages, some of which were settled by the Sabines, an Italic but non-Latin people. By the seventh century the city of Rome included the Palatine, Caelian, Esquiline, Viminal and Quirinal hills.

Hut-shaped urns from which archaeologists, using them as examples of dwellings, have reconstructed the early settlements on the Palatine Hill

Etruscan conquest of Rome in the sixth century

In about the middle of the sixth century Etruscans took over the villages at the Tiber crossing and made them into a true urban community with a paved and drained forum (marketplace) and a temple on the Capitoline Hill. The lands of the farmers in the surrounding area were extended by construction of drainage and irrigation channels.

Monarchy in Rome

Rome was first ruled by kings similar to the type found in Greece. The king was the chief among the leading group of men, who acted as his advisers and chose his successor. The identities, dates and exploits of the kings are obscure, but it was during the regal period that the Romans increased their territory by conquering and absorbing villages. Expansion towards the mouth of the Tiber occurred early and the important centre of Alba Longa was captured and destroyed.

Early expansion of Rome

Last Etruscan king ousted; republic established

The traditional view that the last king of Rome was overthrown by a revolt of the people because of his despotic behaviour seems to be corroborated by the fact that the title *rex* (king) was held in great abhorrence in Rome as late as the first century BC. It is believed that the kings were ousted in about 509, but that the complete break with the Etruscans occurred some time later.

The Etruscans and their influence on Rome

Origin

Possible origin in Asia Minor

The Etruscans settled in the area northwest of Rome that is today called Tuscany. Although their origin is still a mystery, it is generally believed that they migrated by sea from the east, probably from northern Asia Minor in about 900 BC but possibly even as early as 1200–1180.

Lifestyle

Many material remains

Although the large number of Etruscan inscriptions found (about 15 000) can be read since the language uses Greek letters, they cannot generally be understood. Most of what we know of the Etruscans comes from examining the remains of their towns and the objects and wall paintings in their many and varied tombs.

Love of life reflected in tomb wall paintings

The paintings in the magnificent family tombs cut out of rock reveal a people who enjoyed feasting, dancing, music, and watching and taking part in all forms of amusements, such as athletic contests. The nobility enjoyed a luxurious lifestyle and the women, who enjoyed high status,

Painting of the head of an Etruscan woman from the wall of a tomb in Tarquinia

Wall paintings from the Tomb of the Leopards at Tarquinia, revealing the Etruscans' love of music and feasting

dressed elaborately and were adorned with finely made jewellery. The rich furniture, gold ornaments, bronze mirrors, embossed work in bronze and silver, cups, chests, candelabra and statuettes found in their burial chambers testify to the Etruscans' skill in metalwork and their love of luxury.

Religion

Extensive and elaborate burial sites

The importance of life after death for the Etruscans is seen in the large and elaborate *necropoleis* (cities of the dead) surrounding each town and in the size and variety as well as the decoration of the rock-cut tombs. The Etruscan necropolis was a well-kept garden with trees, flowers and fountains. The tombs were usually cut to a depth of three or four metres into the volcanic tufa; on top of some of them were altars, and many had *tumuli* (bell-shaped mounds). They were usually family vaults similar in design to their houses and with elaborately carved—as well as painted—walls.

The dead person was buried with his or her possessions. Before the fifth century the body was laid on a stone couch with a stone pillow, but after that date the Etruscans were buried in elaborately carved and painted sarcophagi, usually with a reclining figure of the dead person on top. Judging by the way they represented gods and demons on the walls of their

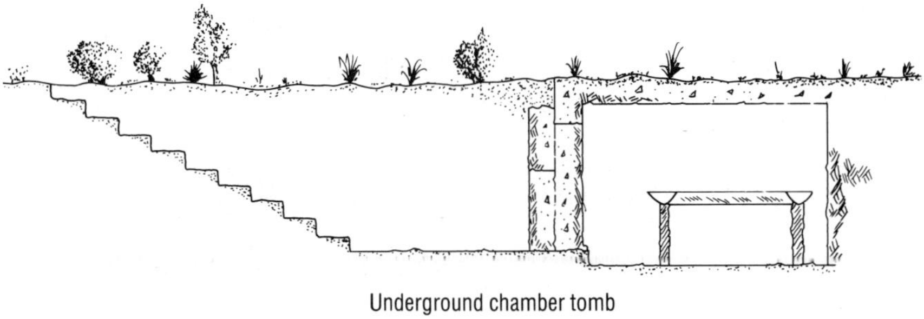

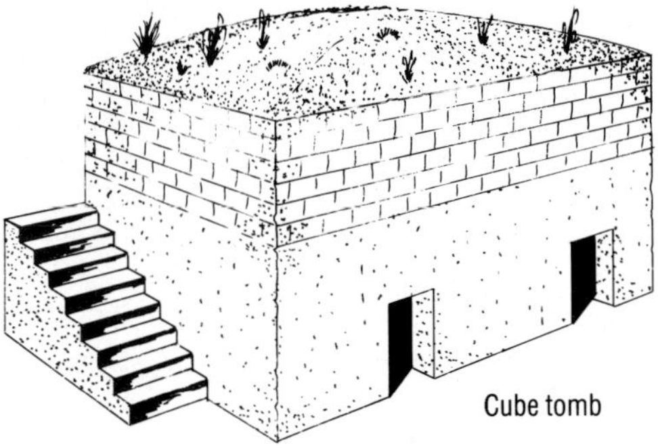

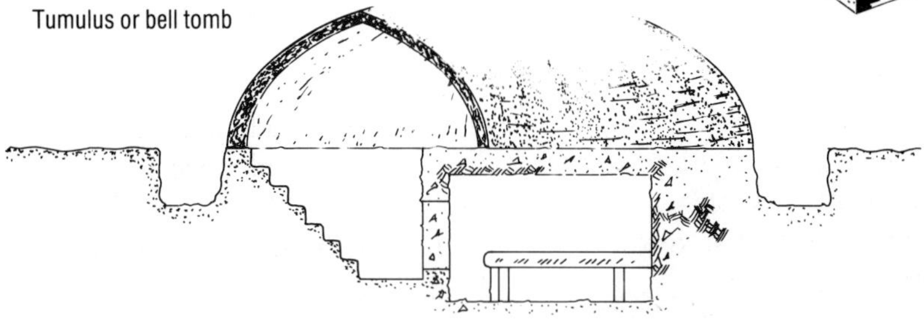

Three types of Etruscan tombs

The Painted Lion Tomb at Cerveteri

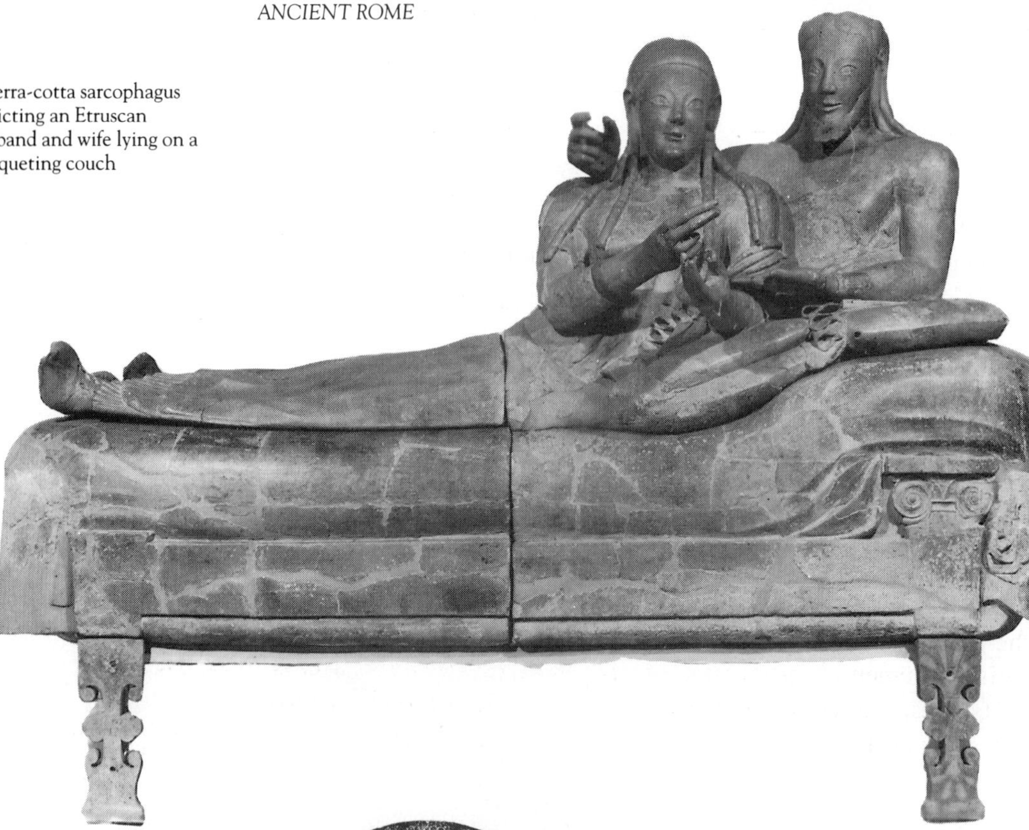

A terra-cotta sarcophagus depicting an Etruscan husband and wife lying on a banqueting couch

An Etruscan engraved mirror (4th century BC) showing the diviner, Chalcas, examining the entrails of a sacrificial animal according to the practice of haruspicy

Bronze model of a liver (3rd century BC) found near Piacenza

tombs, as their power declined they seem to have developed a rather gloomy view of life after death in contrast to joyous scenes earlier depicted.

Divination an important aspect of religion

A triad of gods was worshipped (Tini, Uni and Menrva) and an elaborate ritual of divination was practised in which the priests inspected the organs of sacrificial animals (*haruspicy*). Etruscan religion was probably inseparable from the administration of the state—as was religion in Rome—and used as a means of dominating the people.

Achievements

The Etruscans were a seafaring, commercial and agricultural people with an advanced culture and a high standard of technical expertise, particularly in metalwork; it may have been the mineral resources of Etruria and the adjacent island of Elba which attracted them to the area.

Towns

Unlike the Greek colonies, Etruscan towns and cities were not restricted to the coastline. In fact they often settled on fortified plateaus far from the coast, but with access to the sea; for example, the important settlement of Caere (Cerveteri) was built on a tufa plateau 5 kilometres from the sea but had access to three major ports.

Planned towns

These towns were carefully planned, laid out in a chequerboard pattern with broad, paved streets intersecting at right angles. A ploughed furrow around the town signified the spiritual boundary, or *pomerium*. Stone walls (often with monumental gateways), underground drains and cisterns, aqueducts, bridges, tunnels and temples all were evidence of the Etruscans' great engineering skills, and in all these buildings they made extensive use of the arch, which they introduced into Italy.

Extensive use of arch in buildings

The Cloaca Maxima (Great Drain), built by the Etruscans to drain the Forum, reveals their mastery in the construction of the arch and the vault

Tombs in similar style to homes

Although they built their houses from perishable materials, so that none survive, it is relatively easy to form a clear picture of what they were like by studying the interior design of their tombs, which as has been mentioned was very similar to that of their houses. The Etruscan house was the ancestor of the Roman house, containing an *atrium* (open court) off which were two rooms, probably for slaves, with a door at the opposite end leading to the *triclinium* (banqueting hall); three doors off the triclinium led to the sleeping quarters.

Good road builders

The Etruscans created a considerable road network between their cities which the Romans used and improved. Many of these are still in use today.

Political organisation

Etruscan towns were not united in any strong league but were joined in a loose federation, probably for religious purposes.

Governed as a political elite

The native people whom the Etruscans conquered were not entirely assimilated; they served as conscripts in the lower ranks of the armies and were used as serfs to cultivate the land. The Etruscans ruled as an upper class with exclusive rights to positions of authority, to membership of the state's religion and to knowledge of the law.

Agricultural and industrial development

Great agricultural knowledge

In the field of agriculture forests were cleared, marshes drained, land reclaimed, irrigation systems developed, rivers dammed and vines and olive trees planted.

An example of their great industrial development was the city of Fufluna (Populonia). It had iron furnaces, forges, foundries, a busy port with merchant vessels for exporting the great iron-ore barges, and a naval arsenal. Along the docks there would be enormous piles of crude iron, and finished products ready for export. During World War 1 the Italians mined the slag heaps (waste products from furnaces) for the metals they still contained.

Important smaller industries manufactured gold, silver, ivory, bronze and alabaster products.

Pottery influenced by Greeks

Pottery production was inspired by the contemporary Greek ceramics, but the Etruscans lacked the precision and accuracy of the Greeks and preferred a touch of fantasy in their decoration.

Trade

Widespread trade

The Etruscans traded with Carthage, with the Greeks of southern Italy and Sicily and with the Phoenicians. Their products have been found in France, Germany and Britain, and as far afield as Scandinavia. They exchanged iron, copper and metalwork for gold, silver and tin from Carthage and for vases and art products from the Greeks in the east and the west.

Caere, the leading city in maritime trade in southern Etruria, had its own fleet, with which it was able to protect its trading sphere of influence. It forced the Greeks out of Corsica in spite of the strong cultural ties between Etruscans and Greeks.

A fine example of Etruscan metalwork — a bronze chimera (5th century BC)

Expansion and decline

In the seventh century the Etruscans crossed the Tiber River and conquered a large part of Latium, pushing on to the fertile plains of Campania where they founded new towns at strategic points. The most important in Campania were Capua, Nola and Pompeii.

Influence spread from Po valley to Campania

In the following century they expanded north into the Po valley as far as the Alps and continued their policy of founding towns, some of which are today important centres in modern Italy: Milan, Bologna, Parma and Ravenna. Their southward conquests brought them into direct contact with the Greeks, whose colonies also controlled large parts of the north shore of the Mediterranean. This encouraged the Etruscans to form an alliance with the Carthaginians.

By the end of the sixth century they were the most powerful political group in Italy, but their dominance was short-lived. Between 509 and 507 the Romans and Latins shook off Etruscan rule, and in 474 the Etruscans were severely defeated by the Greeks. When the Samnites of central Italy seized Capua in 424 and the Gauls overran the cities of the Po valley, Etruscan power was broken and their control was restricted to Etruria proper.

Their failure stemmed from the lack of unity and co-operation between cities, which made it impossible to maintain control over hostile subjects. However, although their power declined in the sixth century, their culture continued to influence Italy.

Culture influenced Rome

Influences on Rome

Physical appearance of Rome

The Etruscans transformed Rome from a loose group of agricultural villages into a powerful city (*urbs*). The name Roma (Ruma) was Etruscan and the growth of the city followed the Etruscan pattern even to the extent of the religious boundary-line (pomerium). There were many surviving examples of Etruscan domination in the state religion and in the symbols of political authority. The Roman deities of Jupiter, Juno and

Roman religion

Minerva were associated with the Etruscan triad of gods and the temple on the Capitoline Hill was built by the Etruscans. Divination (the act of finding out whether the gods approved of an action or not by studying the organs of animals and the flights of birds) was also introduced by the Etruscans. Throughout the period of the Roman republic no public event or action could take place without the chief magistrates taking the auspices.

An inscribed stone funerary stele showing an Etruscan carrying a double-headed axe — this later became one of the symbols of authority of a Roman consul

Other Etruscan symbols of authority that continued to be used by the Romans included the *fasces* (bundles of rods within which was tied an axe). These were carried by the twelve *lictors* who were the attendants of the two consuls (the chief magistrates), and indicated the consuls' supreme authority or *imperium* (their right to flog or execute). The colour purple, which had been used for the robe of the king, was later perpetuated in the robe of a Roman general celebrating a triumph and in the stripe that bordered the toga of a high magistrate.

Various forms of Roman entertainment, such as gladiatorial contests and chariot races, also originated with the Etruscans, but their chief legacy to Rome was in practical matters such as planned towns, paved streets, buildings in hewn stone, sewers, drainage channels, bridges and aqueducts, all of which utilised the arch and the vault. Roman military camps were always set up on the plan used for Etruscan towns. However, although Rome was under this Etruscan influence for a time, it always remained a Latin city.

The influence of the Greeks of southern Italy

Greeks in the western Mediterranean

From the eighth century the Greeks had colonised the coasts of Sicily (except in the west), southern Italy from the Bay of Tarentum to the Bay of Naples, and along the southern coasts of Gaul. The Etruscans and Carthaginians prevented them from moving further west or north.

Etruscans influenced by Greeks

The Greek colonies reached the peak of their prosperity in the sixth and fifth centuries; they first influenced Rome indirectly through the Etruscans, who traded extensively with them as is evidenced by the amount of Greek pottery in Etruscan tombs and the themes from Greek myths and legends used as subjects of Etruscan and Roman works of art. The Etruscans passed on Greek architecture, the art of writing, religious cults and social practices.

Stronger Greek influence

When the Romans conquered Magna Graeca, in the third century, Greek influence in the areas of literature, science, philosophy, education, and political and legal institutions became stronger. Two Greek centres which had a considerable influence on Rome in the regal period and during the early and middle republic were Cyme (Cumae) and Posidonia (Paestum).

Cumae and the sibyl

Control of Campania by Cumae in sixth century

Cumae was founded on the northern Campanian plain by Greeks from Chalcis before 750, and in turn it established other settlements including that at Neapolis (Naples). During the seventh and sixth centuries Cumae controlled much of the Campanian coastline, which included the settlement of Baiae (for a long time the largest thermal centre in the Roman empire) and the port city of Puteoli.

The oracle of the sibyl

In the late fifth century Cumae began to play an important part in the early religion of the Romans because it was the site of the oracle of the sibyl (priestess) and it became the practice for Romans to consult the oracle.

The sibyl was supposed to reside in a grotto or cave, and the following illustration shows the site today almost exactly as it was described by the Roman writer, Virgil. The cave was entered through a *dromos* 137 metres long and 5 metres high. There were three identical tunnels hewn out of the stone on one side.

The grotto of the Sibyl

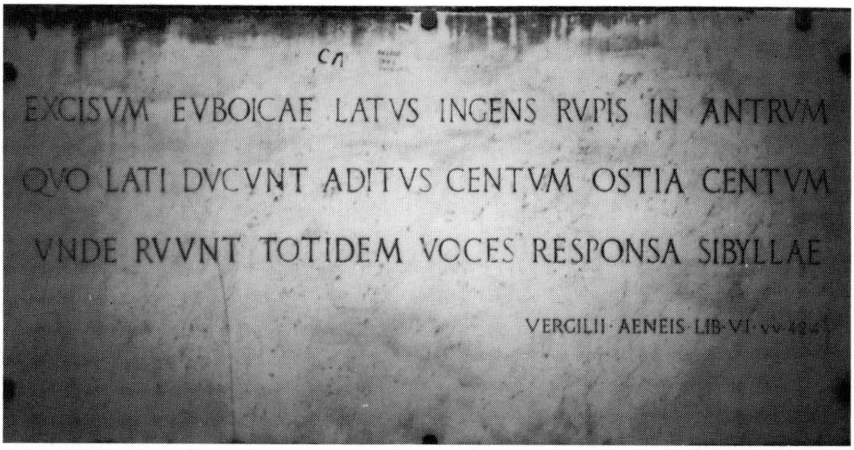
EXCISVM EVBOICAE LATVS INGENS RVPIS IN ANTRVM
QVO LATI DVCVNT ADITVS CENTVM OSTIA CENTVM
VNDE RVVNT TOTIDEM VOCES RESPONSA SIBYLLAE
VERGILII · AENEIS · LIB · VI

A description of the grotto in Latin by Virgil reads: 'The huge side of the Euboean rock is cut into a grotto to which a hundred broad entrances lead, a hundred doors, whence as many voices rush, the replies of the Sibyl'

Sibyl's prophecies in the Books of Fate

The prophecies of the sibyl, which were written in Greek, were collected by the Romans and kept permanently in the form of the Sibylline Books, or Books of Fate. They were entrusted to one of the colleges of Roman priests (a board of ten men whose job it was to perform sacred rights), who consulted these sacred books in times of crisis. It usually happened that whenever the prophecies were interpreted they instructed the Romans to introduce a new Greek god or Greek ritual into the framework of traditional Roman religion, and in this way Roman religion was transformed over the centuries, eventually becoming receptive to the cults of the east.

Introduction of new Greek gods

Posidonia/Paestum

Posidonia—naval ally of Rome

Posidonia, like other Greek commercial and artistic centres in southern Italy, had a profound cultural effect on the early Romans and also contributed to their early naval protection.

Colony of Sybaris

About the middle of the seventh century the Greek city of Sybaris, on the eastern coast of the toe of Italy, wanted to establish a trading station on the western side of the peninsula. Its aim was to take advantage not only of the overland trade from the Ionian to the Tyrrhenian Sea, but to share in the riches of the trade with Latium and Etruria further north. The settlement was given the name of Posidonia and its foundation can be dated from an entirely Greek necropolis found there.

Ideal geographic location

The town prospered and grew as a result of its ideal geographic position (fertile soil, and the safe anchorage for ships in the river Sele), the decline of Etruscan influence in the area in the sixth century and the destruction of Sybaris in 510, which opened the way for Posidonia to become the leading commercial centre in the area. Also, refugees fleeing from Sybaris settled in Posidonia, bringing with them their wealth and spirit of initiative. It is believed that the underground sanctuary at Posidonia is the *heroon* dedicated by the refugees to Is, the mythical founder of Sybaris.

A leading commercial centre

Posidonia was at its greatest between 560 and 440 when the three temples were built—the temple to Ceres (550), the so-called Basilica (500) and the Temple of Poseidon or Neptune (450).

The great temples of Posidonia

At the height of its power Posidonia had close to 20 000 inhabitants and the beautifully preserved Temple of Neptune, the terracotta statues and the tomb frescoes are evidence of the wealth and splendour of the city.

Somewhere about 410 Posidonia came under the control of the Lucanians (from the southwest of Italy), who changed its name to Paistom. It remained under their domination until 273, but the city retained its Greek appearance and culture—coinage was still Greek, and a Greek school of potters and painters flourished. The tombs were rich in paintings and objects indicating that Paistom did not decline during this period. The Italic people as well as the Romans—like the Etruscans before them—imitated the style of Greek vases in both form and decoration.

Italian control of Posidonia

The Temple of Neptune at Paestum

Roman colony at Posidonia

In the year 273 the Romans established a colony at Posidonia, changing its name yet again—to Paestum, the name by which it is known today. The relationship between Rome and Paestum was always very close. The inhabitants of the colony were naval allies (*socii navales*) of Rome, and never failed to supply the Romans with ships and sailors in time of need; they remained loyal to Rome in all circumstances. It was the loyalty of Paestum and others like it during the Hannibalic War that enabled Rome to overcome the Carthaginians in the third century.

Decline due to Via Appia

The Romans added further buildings to the city, such as the forum, the gymnasium and the amphitheatre, but unintentionally contributed to its gradual decline when they built the Via Appia, a road linking Rome with the Adriatic, by-passing Paestum and cutting it off from the valuable eastern trade.

The Via Appia, originally constructed to link Rome and Capua, was later extended to the main port of Brundisium

Roman society in the early republic

4

Social structure

Political organisation

Religion

Military forces

Social structure

An understanding of the way in which early republican society was organised and functioned is necessary in order to appreciate the political, social, economic and military developments that occurred in Rome and Italy during the middle and late republican periods. The following charts and text—and those in the subsequent sections—illustrate the importance of the social relationships between Roman citizens, the varying degrees of political responsibility held by them, the importance of religion in their private and public lives and their military obligations.

Social organisation of the Roman people

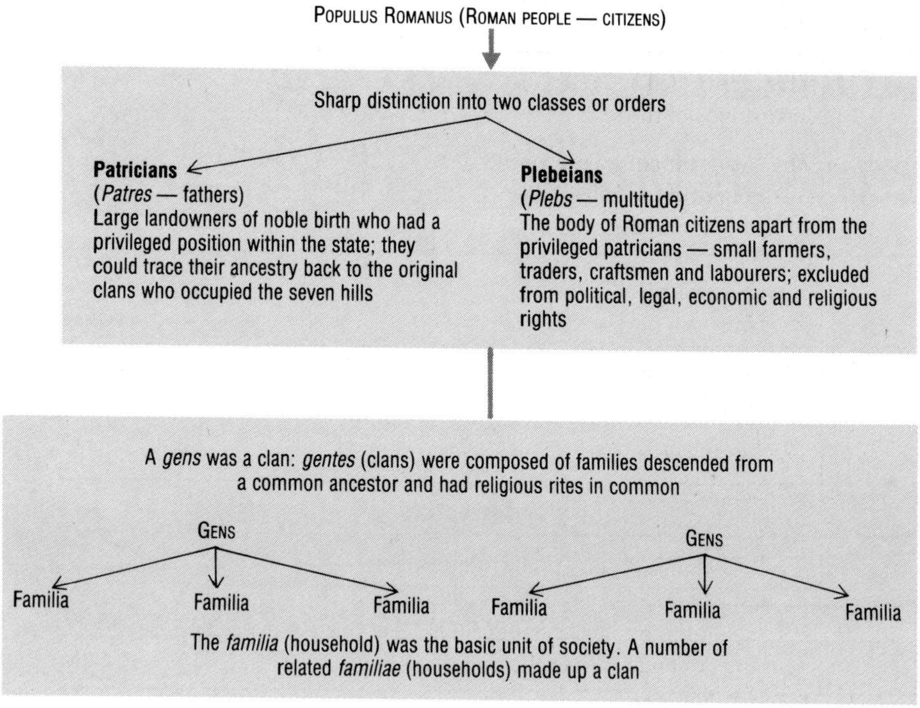
POPULUS ROMANUS (ROMAN PEOPLE — CITIZENS)
Sharp distinction into two classes or orders
Patricians
(*Patres* — fathers)
Large landowners of noble birth who had a privileged position within the state; they could trace their ancestry back to the original clans who occupied the seven hills
Plebeians
(*Plebs* — multitude)
The body of Roman citizens apart from the privileged patricians — small farmers, traders, craftsmen and labourers; excluded from political, legal, economic and religious rights
A *gens* was a clan: *gentes* (clans) were composed of families descended from a common ancestor and had religious rites in common
GENS
Familia
Familia
Familia
GENS
Familia
Familia
Familia
The *familia* (household) was the basic unit of society. A number of related *familiae* (households) made up a clan

The relative positions of the patricians and the plebeians within the state		
Status	*Patricians*	*Plebeians*
Political	They controlled the state by their monopoly of all positions of authority — consuls and senators. Patrician magistrates controlled the assembly.	They were exposed to the authority of the consuls, who had control over the lives of the citizens and against whose decisions there was no appeal. They did not have the right to hold public office; they were excluded from the senate, which was an aristocratic body. In the assembly, those not clients (tenants or dependants) of patricians were outvoted by the patricians and those who were clients.

Status	*Patricians*	*Plebeians*
Religious	They controlled the religious institutions of the state. The two great colleges of priests — the Pontiffs and the Augurs — were in the hands of the patricians. Religion played a very important part in political decisions.	They were excluded from any part in the administration of the state religion and important priesthoods.
Legal	All civil and criminal law was in their hands. The legal code was not written down and only the patricians could interpret and administer it. They did this to suit themselves.	They had neither knowledge of the laws nor access to the administration of the legal system. They had no right of appeal against a harsh decision of the patricians.
Social	A special form of marriage was performed, conducted by the pontifex maximus and the flamen Dialis (priest of Jupiter). They were forbidden to intermarry with plebeians.	They had their own form of marriage. They could not legally intermarry with patricians, but if they did, the children of the union were automatically classed as plebeian.
Economic	They were large landowners. They could afford to lease large tracts of public land (*ager publicus*). They did not engage in industry or trade, but left that to plebeians and foreigners, e.g. Greeks.	Clients were granted land in return for economic and political support. Many plebeians endured poverty owing to occasional absences from their land on military service. The law of debt (unwritten) was extremely harsh. They had to pay a *tributum* (military tax) during time of war. They received no share in the distribution of public lands and were excluded from use of the grazing land. Many plebeians did make a great deal of money through trade, and were often wealthier than the exclusive patricians. It was these wealthy plebeians who resented their lack of political rights.

Status	*Patricians*	*Plebeians*
Military	They dominated the army — entrance was based on property qualifications, since a soldier had to provide his own equipment. They could afford to keep their properties running when away at war.	They served in the army but had to leave their lands unattended meanwhile. Membership of the Roman army was the greatest strength the plebeians had. They were able to put pressure on the patricians to introduce reform during military crises. Some rich plebeians had a sort of equality with the patricians by being able to provide themselves with cavalry equipment.
The grievances of the plebeians and their attempts to gain equality with the patricians persisted in the internal history of Rome for over 200 years of the early republic (see chapter 6).		

The Roman family

The Roman family and its dependants

The basic unit of Roman society was the household (*familia*), in which the oldest male (*paterfamilias*) held absolute authority.

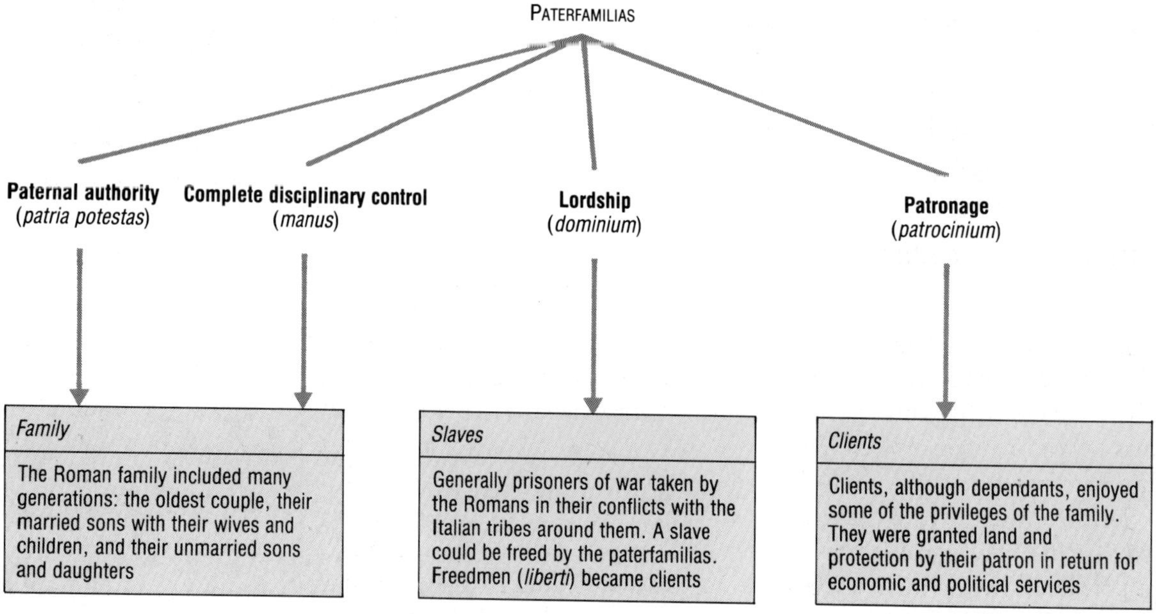
PATERFAMILIAS
Paternal authority (patria potestas)
Complete disciplinary control (manus)
Lordship (dominium)
Patronage (patrocinium)
Family
The Roman family included many generations: the oldest couple, their married sons with their wives and children, and their unmarried sons and daughters
Slaves
Generally prisoners of war taken by the Romans in their conflicts with the Italian tribes around them. A slave could be freed by the paterfamilias. Freedmen (liberti) became clients
Clients
Clients, although dependants, enjoyed some of the privileges of the family. They were granted land and protection by their patron in return for economic and political services

Qualities learned within the family

Authority of paterfamilias

Although the paterfamilias theoretically had the power of life and death over those in the household, he was restrained from abusing his authority by custom and public opinion. To decide a point at issue it was customary for the father to call a meeting of all the close relatives and submit the case to them.

Values taught within the home

Under the authority of the paterfamilias, young people in the household grew up learning the following:
- obedience and respect for their elders;
- the performance of all one's obligations to the family and the gods (*pietas*);
- *mos maiorum* (ancestral custom), which involved the belief that what their ancestors had done before them was important.

Other virtues emphasised were courage, persistence and faithfulness.

Attitudes towards family carried over into public life

Obligations to the state

Respect for the authority of the older members of a household was reflected in attitudes towards elder statesmen. Those Romans who had served the state well and had acquired prestige (*dignitas*) and reputation (*auctoritas*) because of their superiority very rarely had their leadership questioned. The correct performance of one's obligations to the family and the household gods extended to include obligations to the state.

The teaching of obedience, discipline and the importance of ancestral custom meant that Romans did not usually question the established way of doing things (conservatism). They believed in freedom (*libertas*), but this did not include the freedom to disobey the laws or to change those things which had been built up by custom and precedent. Moreover, as a result of their long years of conflict with the peoples around Latium, the Romans developed a seriousness (*gravitas*) about life.

A Roman holding busts of two of his ancestors

Patron–client relationship

In early Rome, the heads of patrician families agreed to protect a number of poorer citizens in return for assistance in their public and private lives. This became a hereditary relationship, and was recognised in the early laws of the republic. In the Twelve Tables (a code of laws) it was stated: 'If a patron defrauds his client he shall be solemnly forfeited [outlawed]'.[1]

Hereditary relationship

Importance in politics

This patron–client relationship was one of the most important and long-lasting features of Roman society, and was of considerable influence in politics. The institution was extended to include freed slaves and later in the republican period, when Rome acquired overseas territory, officials and generals became the patrons of very large groups of foreign people.

Patron–client relationship

PATRON

Duties (*officia*)

To follow patron to war

To vote for patron in elections and support his view in the assembly

To give respectful attention to patron

To support the patron in certain economic matters, such as helping to provide a dowry for the patron's daughter

Benefits (*beneficia*)

Received land to farm

Received legal help and protection in the courts

Received food rations (occasionally payment in cash)

CLIENTS
Tenants who worked on or farmed the estates of the patricians

Patron and client could not give evidence against one another

Roman names

Significance of Roman names

Upper-class Romans had three names.

1 *Praenomen* (personal name), of which there were about thirty. The following are some examples, with their abbreviations:

Aulus	A.	Publius	P.	Gaius	C.
Quintus	Q.	Gnaeus	Cn.	Sextus	S.
Decimus	D.	Lucius	L.	Manius	M'
Titus	T.	Marcus	M.	Tiberius	Ti.

2 *Nomen* (clan name), of which there are thought to have been about a thousand. Some examples of these clan (*gens*) names are Cornelius (Cornelian clan), Claudius (Claudian clan), Julius (Julian clan), Aemilius (Aemilian clan) and Licinius (Licinian clan).

3 *Cognomen* (family name), which indicated the particular branch of the clan to which a man belonged. Within the Cornelian clan (Cornelii) there were families with names such as Scipio, Sulla, Gallus, Lentulus, Balbus, Celsus, Cinna, Dolabella and so on. Sometimes a cognomen

was an obvious reference to a particular physical or mental peculiarity, such as Naso (*nasus* – nose), Capito (*caput* – head) and Caesar (curly-haired).

Special names

An additional cognomen (sometimes referred to as an agnomen) was added to a man's name to perpetuate a great military victory or outstanding exploit in a particular country. Such examples are Africanus, Macedonicus and Creticus. A few prominent Romans had such words as Magnus (great) and Felix (fortunate) added to their names.

Adoptive names

Adoptions also gave rise to an additional cognomen. The adopted person assumed the names of the adopter but retained the name of his original clan as a cognomen; when the son of L. Aemilius Paullus was adopted by P. Cornelius Scipio, he became P. Cornelius Scipio Aemilianus. C. Octavius was adopted by his great-uncle, Julius Caesar. He later assumed the name Augustus.

Praenomen	*Nomen*	*Cognomen*	*Cognomen (agnomen)*
Publius	Cornelius	Scipio	Africanus
Gaius	Julius	Caesar	
Lucius	Cornelius	Sulla	Felix
Publius	Cornelius	Scipio	Aemilianus (adoption)
Gaius	Julius	Caesar	Octavianus (adoption)

Number of names

If a Roman had only two names, this indicated that he did not belong to any of the established clans—for example, Gaius Marius. This did not prevent such a man from reaching a high position within the state, but he did need to have a noble patron who would promote him.

Indications of ancestry

Informally, a Roman man was addressed by a single name—usually his family name, such as Scipio, Caesar or Cicero. On formal occasions his full name was used, and for official records it was usual to insert the names of a man's father and grandfather before his cognomen. This was shown in the following way:

P. Cornelius P.f. P.n. Scipio Aemilianus

M. Tullius M.f. M.n. Cicero

L. Cornelius L.f. P.n. Sulla Felix

P.f. meant *Publii filius* (son of Publius), M.n. meant *Marci nepos* (grandson of Marcus); therefore Sulla was the son of Lucius and the grandson of Publius.

Women's names

A woman usually bore only the name of her clan in the feminine form, such as Julia, Tullia, Cornelia, Sempronia, Livia, Scribonia, Antonia and Aemilia. Sometimes there were two daughters in the family with the same name, and in order to distinguish between them they were referred to as, for example, Antonia major and Antonia minor.

Political organisation

When the last of Rome's kings was overthrown in about 509 (see chapter 3), the form of republican government that replaced the monarchy comprised

- The consuls — two patrician magistrates
- The senate — council of nobles
- The *comitia curiata* — people's assembly

The consuls

The positions of the consuls is summarised below.

Powers	Limitations
Imperium • *Auspicium* • *Right of veto*	*Collegiality* • *Annuality*
The consuls retained the full imperium of the king (supreme executive authority — military, civil and judicial, implying particularly the power to command an army). The symbol of this imperium was the fasces (a double-headed axe enclosed in a bundle of rods) carried by attendants called lictors. The fasces symbolised the consuls' power to flog. They also wore the toga *praetexta*, bordered with a purple band. A part of the imperium was the right of *auspicium* (the right to take the auspices in order to see if the gods approved of an important public act). Each consul had the right of veto (to suspend or prevent the actions of the other).	The dual or collegiate nature of the consulship (shared powers) allowed each one to be a check on the other. The restriction of the length of office to one year meant that a consul could not become too powerful.

As Rome expanded, there was a need for more magistrates to help the consuls administer the state, and by the end of the fourth century the Roman magistracy had developed the form it was to keep until the end of the republic (the structure of republican government is discussed in chapter 6). The consuls eventually lost some of their original functions to other magistrates.

Increase in number of magistrates

The senate

Major features of the senate were these:

- Originally there were 100 members (later 300), recruited from patrician clans only.
- Seats were held for life unless members were found guilty of serious misconduct.
- It served as an advisory body to consuls.
- It had the power to veto resolutions of assembly if the latter acted against the senate's advice.

Although it was an advisory body only, from the third century it gained in influence and power, becoming in effect the virtual government of Rome in the second and first centuries (see chapters 6 and 13).

The assembly of the people

This assembly—the curiate assembly (comitia curiata)—originated in the time of the kings. Rome was divided into 'parishes' (*curiae*) and the people voted according to the curia in which they lived.

The assembly elected the consuls; it then voted for or against any proposals the consuls put before it, but could not raise or discuss any issues. Later, as Rome expanded and developed, a number of other assemblies came into existence (see chapter 6).

Development of assemblies

Religion

Religio in Latin means 'something which binds'. For the Romans, religion was a force that bound man to the gods and involved the correct performance of ritual. The ritual of worship involved sacrifice and prayer, and the two were always combined. Only when the proper procedures on both state and household level were observed would the gods answer their prayers. If there was any mistake—however minute—in the performance of the ritual, the whole process would have to be started again.

Meaning of religion for the Romans

Roman religion was cold, formal and lacked emotional involvement, but it did give the Romans a tolerance towards the beliefs and practices of other people, including those whom they conquered.

Religion at state level

The Roman pantheon (gods)

The state cult centred on a triad of gods, Jupiter (protector of the state), Juno (protector of women) and Minerva (patroness of craftsmen), but the guardians of the fields and flocks worshipped in the household also were worshipped publicly. The later influence of Greek literature and legend resulted in the Roman gods becoming identified with their Greek counterparts: for instance, Jupiter with Zeus, Juno with Hera and Minerva with Athena.

Religion as part of administration

The state religion represented a special branch of the administration and the priests, who were nominated (from their own group) for life, were usually active politicians such as magistrates or senators. Religion was subordinated to the interests of the state, and played a very important part in political decisions.

Priestly colleges

There were a number of colleges (groups) of priests and priestesses who looked after specific areas of the state religion, the most important being the Pontiffs, the Augurs, the Fetiales, the Flamens and the Vestal Virgins. The head of all state priests was the pontifex maximus who, unlike the other priests, was elected for life by the people.

Divination, the act of finding out by various means whether the gods did or did not approve of a proposed action, was an important aspect of the state religion: before any important civil or military action was taken by the state, a magistrate with imperium had to receive assurance that the gods approved. The magistrates took the auspices, which originally meant

A sacrificial procession involving a bull, a sheep and a pig: sacrifices were made prior to all important events, such as the departure of an army or a fleet or the construction of a temple

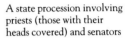

A state procession involving priests (those with their heads covered) and senators

An augur holding his ceremonial wand (*lituus*), with one of the sacred chickens at his feet

observing natural phenomena such as the flights of birds and flashes of lightning (augury). It also involved the study of the size, shape, colour and other markings of the vital organs of animals (haruspicy), unusual events such as earthquakes and eclipses (portents) and unusual births (prodigies). These were all regarded as omens from the gods, and it was the college of Augurs who interpreted them.

A priest (*haruspex*) examining the entrails of a sacrificial animal

Chief colleges of priests			
	Number	*Selection*	*Function*
Pontiffs	Originally 9, later 16	Nominated (co-opted) for life	Advised chief magistrates Were guardians of the 'Divine Law' Established the earliest criminal code Arranged the calendar — fixed dates of religious festivals, special events; announced on which days there was to be no business
Augurs	Originally 3, later 16	Nominated for life	Supervised and interpreted auspices
Fetiales	20	Nominated for life	Intepreted laws governing international relations In charge of rituals for declaring war and concluding treaties Protected foreign ambassadors and supervised extradition
Flamens	15	Nominated — 3 major *flamines* (those of Jupiter, Mars and Quirinus)	Were specialised priests of individual gods, to whom they sacrificed
Vestal Virgins	4–6	Chosen from children, aged 10–16, of freeborn citizens	Cared for the sacred fire of Vesta, goddess of the hearth; were responsible for seeing that the flame did not go out

Religion at the household level

The Roman household worshipped the protectors of its home and its livelihood, chief of which are shown below.

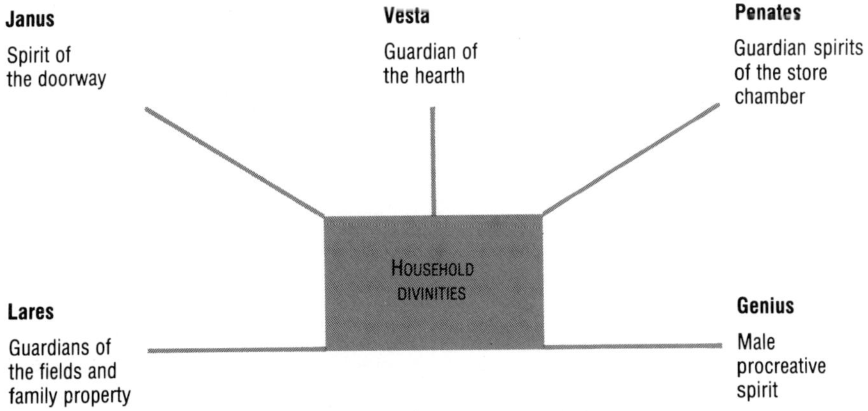

A Roman republican coin bearing the double-headed profile of Janus — the Temple of Janus had its doors open when Rome was at war and closed when peace was restored

Bronze statuette of a Lar: images of these Lares were found in household shrines

Exercise: The Vestal Virgins

Read the two extracts below and answer the questions that follow.

They were required to remain undefiled by marriage for the space of thirty years, devoting themselves to offering sacrifices and performing the other rites ordained by law. During the first ten years their duty was to learn their functions, in the second ten to perform them, and during the remaining ten to teach others . . . And severe penalties have been established for their misdeeds. It is the pontiffs who by law both inquire into and punish these offences; those Vestals who are guilty of lesser misdemeanors they scourge with rods, but those who have suffered defilement they deliver up to the most shameful and the most miserable death. For while they are yet alive they are carried upon a bier with all the formality of a funeral, their friends and relations attending them with lamentations, and after being brought as far as the Colline Gate, they are placed in an underground cell prepared within the walls, clad in their funeral attire.

If a Vestal allowed 'the extinction of the fire, which the Romans dread above all misfortunes' as it indicated to them 'the destruction of the city', she was stripped naked and flogged by the chief priest in the dark.[2]

The Vestals were expected to wear long, old-fashioned wool mantles, and in 420 a Vestal Virgin called Postumia found herself in serious trouble for looking too chic.

Postumia, a Vestal Virgin, was tried for incest, a crime of which she was not guilty but suspicion had been raised by the fact that she was always got up prettily, and she had a wit which was a little too loose for a Virgin. After an adjournment she was found 'not guilty'. Delivering judgment on behalf of the Board of Priests, the Chief Priest told her to stop making jokes, and in her dress and appearance, to aim at looking holy rather than smart.[3]

1. Who was in charge of the Vestals?
2. For how long was a Vestal required to remain unmarried?
3. Describe the punishment inflicted for failure to remain celibate.
4. What was the chief duty of a Vestal?
5. What punishment did she receive for failing to carry out her duty properly?

A fragment showing Vestal Virgins at a banquet

Military organisation

Regal army

The very early Roman army under the kings was traditionally composed of 3000 infantry and 300 cavalry, all of whom were drawn from the patrician class. However, during the early republican period Rome's continual wars with her neighbours made it necessary to increase the size of the army, and this meant that a new recruiting system had to be devised.

Basis of recruitment in the republic

A board of censors called on all men—patricians and plebeians alike—to give details of their property, and once an assessment (*censi*) was made the people were enrolled into five property classes. Before the third century the class in which a man was placed depended on the amount of land and cattle he owned, but this was later replaced with an assessment based on a unit of coinage called an *as*.

Provision of own weapons

Since Roman soldiers were expected to provide their own arms and equipment, the wealthiest citizens were enrolled in the cavalry and first class, while the poorly armed citizens were in the fifth class. Those whose only property was their offspring were called the *proletarii* (*proles* – offspring).

Division within the class

Each class was divided into a number of units or companies called centuries (*centuriae*), theoretically of one hundred men each, and each century was further divided into juniors (aged from seventeen to forty-five) and seniors (over forty-five). The juniors were on active service, while the seniors were used for garrison duty.

Arrangement according to wealth

The centuriate assembly

In the new military arrangement of classes decided according to wealth, citizens would be summoned to muster in the Campus Martius—the field of Mars (god of war)—outside the city. Here they would gather in their centuries, and this military (centuriate) assembly soon became a political organisation, in which the citizens voted on important issues concerned with war and peace. Decisions were made by block voting—that is, each century had one vote, and the wealthiest classes voted first.

In the original *phalanx* formation the better armed, richer classes made up the six ranks of the heavy infantry, but this lacked flexibility; it depended on weight and push rather than on manoeuvrability.

Introduction of pay

At the time of the siege of the Etruscan city of Veii (the beginning of the fourth century) pay was introduced to allow the farmer soldiers to stay at war for longer periods. This meant that each man could now provide himself with arms, and consequently the arrangement of the troops no longer depended on wealth, but rather on skill, experience and age.

Further military changes

When the Romans came into conflict with Italic peoples further afield such as the Samnite tribes in the mountains of central Italy, further changes occurred in the manner of fighting and the arrangement of the troops. The new tactical unit became the *maniple*. The legion (which comprised approximately 4000 men) was divided into three lines of ten maniples, and each maniple was further divided into two centuries.

The three lines of the legion

The light-armed soldiers, *velites*, attacked first, then withdrew between the maniples of the lines. These were followed by the *hastati*, who first hurled their *pila* (a *pilum* was a 2-metre javelin) and then fought hand-to-hand with swords. If they were defeated, the next line (the *principes*) advanced. The *triarii* were the reserves, and generally were not required to fight.

The organisation of a Roman legion

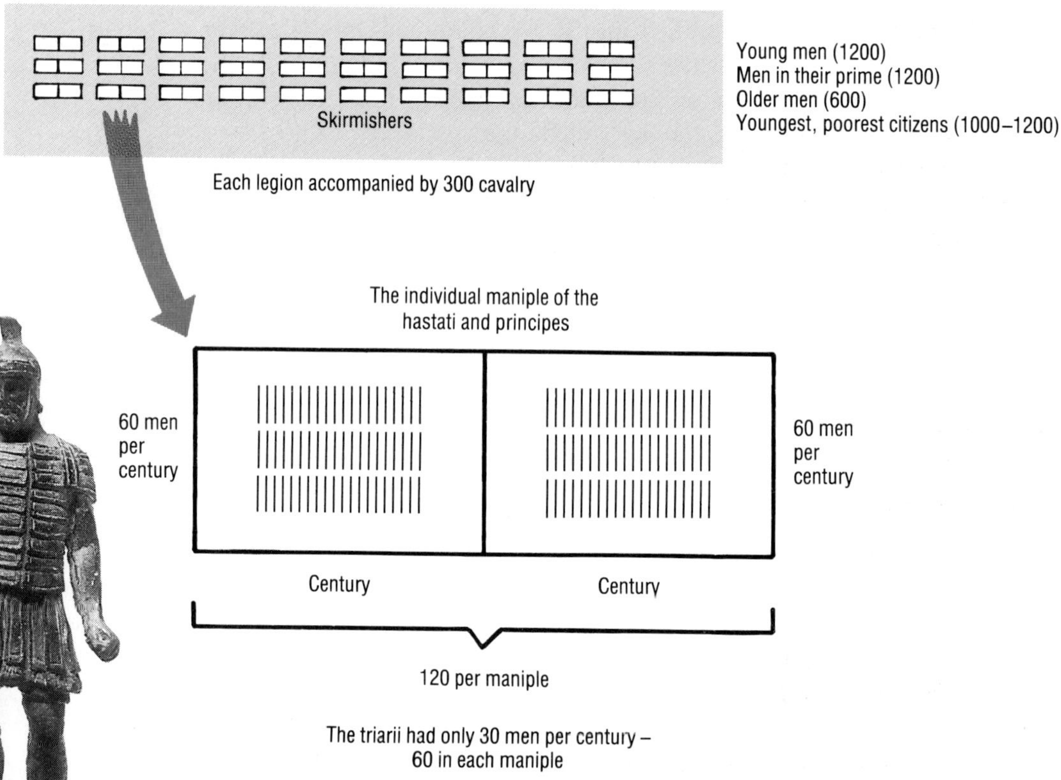

Bronze statuette of a Roman legionary

In the early years of the republic the usual number of troops recruited in time of war was approximately 8000, or two legions. As Rome extended her control over Italy, the army was divided into *legionaries* (Roman citizens in the legions) and *socii* (allies); the latter provided both infantry and cavalry (10 000 and 1800 respectively), and fought on the wings of the legions.

Leadership

The legionaries and the socii were commanded by the two consuls, who combined political and military leadership for their year of office. They exercised imperium (supreme authority) in the field, including the power of life or death over all soldiers, and were assisted by military tribunes.

This organisation of the army remained unchanged until the reforms of Marius, about 104–103 BC.

The Romans had virtually no navy until the First Punic War, in the middle of the third century. Until that time they relied predominantly on the ships of their Greek allies in the south of Italy.

Greek allies provided naval forces

Essay topics

1 Who were the Etruscans? What part did they play in early Roman history? Which aspects of Roman life were permanently influenced by them?

2 Outline the main social, political and religious features of early Roman society.

Further reading

Ancient sources

Livy. *The Early History of Rome*, Books 1–5.

Modern sources

Bloch, R. *The Etruscans*.
_____ . *The Origins of Rome*.
Kagen, D. *Problems in Ancient History*, vol. 2: *The Roman World*.
Lewis, N. & Reinhold, M. *Roman Civilisation—Sourcebook 1: The Republic*.
Ogilvie, R. M. *The Romans and Their Gods*.
Scullard, H. H. *A History of the Roman World, 753–146 BC*.

PART

2

The Roman conquest of Italy and constitutional development

Conquest and organisation 5

The conquest in four phases

Rome and her allies

The Italian conquests

First phase, 509–390

FOR THE ROMANS, the fifth century was marked by intermittent, defensive wars against hostile neighbours—the Sabines, the Aequians (Aequi) and the Volscians (Volsci). In 493, however, the Romans signed a treaty with a league of eight Latin towns (the Latin League), and this gave them a certain amount of protection against their aggressive neighbours.

Roman alliance with Latin towns

> . . . Let them neither make war upon one another themselves nor call in foreign enemies, nor grant safe passage to those who shall make war upon either, but let them assist one another with all their might when warred upon and let each have an equal share of the spoils and booty taken in their common wars.[1]

Rome's most serious enemy during this period was the powerful Etruscan city of Veii, which had been making raids into Roman territory. Veii was placed under siege; it was eventually destroyed (this is generally believed to have been in 396) and the land was annexed by Rome. Soon after this, all southern Etruria was brought under Roman control.

Destruction of Veii

The significance of this period

Effects of Roman expansion

- The treaty signed with the Latin League lasted approximately 150 years and provided Rome with allies to help her fight later battles.
- Rome's territory was almost doubled.

The Roman conquest of Italy

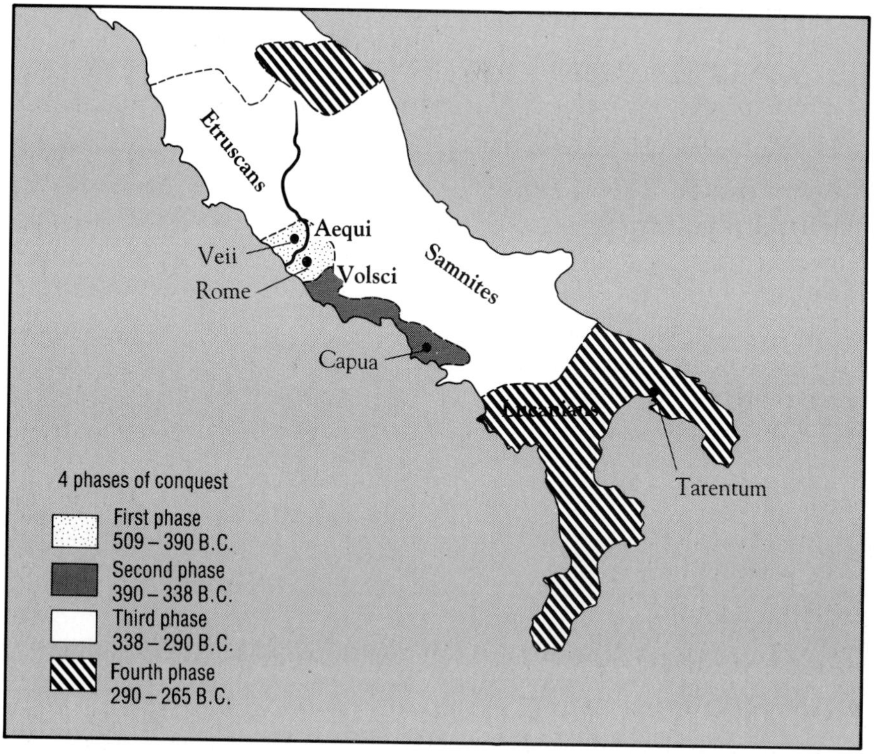

- As the plebeians became more aware of their importance in the army, they were able to threaten to refuse to fight in order to gain some concessions from the patricians. They carried out this threat in 449 when they 'seceded' from the state.
- It was during the siege of Veii that pay was introduced for soldiers, since they were required to be absent from home for long periods.

Second phase, 390–338

In 390 Rome suffered a disaster when the Gauls invaded central Italy, burned and looted the city, and occupied it for seven months.

Destruction of Rome by Gauls

> When they first arrived in Italy, the Celts [Gauls] not only took possession of this northern region [Po Valley], but subjugated many of the neighbouring peoples and terrified them by their audacity. Not long afterwards they defeated the Romans and their allies in a pitched battle, pursued their routed opponents and three days later, occupied the whole of Rome with the exception of the Capitol. But at that moment an invasion of their own territory by the Veneti diverted their attention, and so they made a treaty with the Romans, handed back the city and returned home.[2]

> Thereupon the Senate met and instructed the tribunes of the soldiers to arrange the terms. Then, at a conference between Quintus Sulpicius, the tribune, and the Gallic chieftain Brennus, the affair was settled and a thousand pounds of gold was agreed on as the price of a people that was destined presently to rule the world.[3]

Roman power in central Italy collapsed for a time and the Etruscans, Hernici, Aequi and Volsci took advantage of this weakened position. However, owing to the patriotism of the people and to firm leadership, Rome was rebuilt and its power over its neighbours was re-established.

Roman recovery

In 343 the Romans successfully helped the city of Capua, in Campania, which was being threatened by warlike Samnites from the mountains of central Italy. They were thus able to exert control over Campania. However, the Romans' growing power made the cities of the Latin League fear for their independence; they fought an unsuccessful war with Rome, and in 338 Rome dissolved the League and isolated the cities from one another by signing separate treaties with each one. However, the Latins were given a share in many of the benefits and responsibilities of the Roman people.

Expansion southwards

Separate treaties with Latins

The significance of this period

- After the Gallic invasions, Rome was rebuilt and fortified with a wall 4 metres thick, 8 metres high and 10 kilometres long. Remains of this so-called Servian Wall can still be seen.
- The plebeians, who suffered great economic distress as a result of the invasion by the Gauls, made insistent demands for constitutional reform.
- Rome now controlled approximately 7500 square kilometres and one million people.
- By creating a confederacy in which the Latins were bound to Rome by ties of common interest, and by offering full Roman citizenship in time, Rome assured itself of Latin loyalty in the future.

Beginning of Roman Confederacy

Third phase, 338–290

This period was marked by a long and bitter series of wars against the Samnites, and subsequently by a coalition of Samnites, Etruscans, Umbrians and Gauls, between 327–304 and 298–290.

Long, hard wars with Samnites

The Samnites were well-organised for mountain fighting, and were able to inflict a humiliating defeat on the Romans in 321. Rome spent the next few years strengthening its position by surrounding the Samnites with fortress colonies as bases for attack and reorganising the army for greater flexibility in mountain areas.

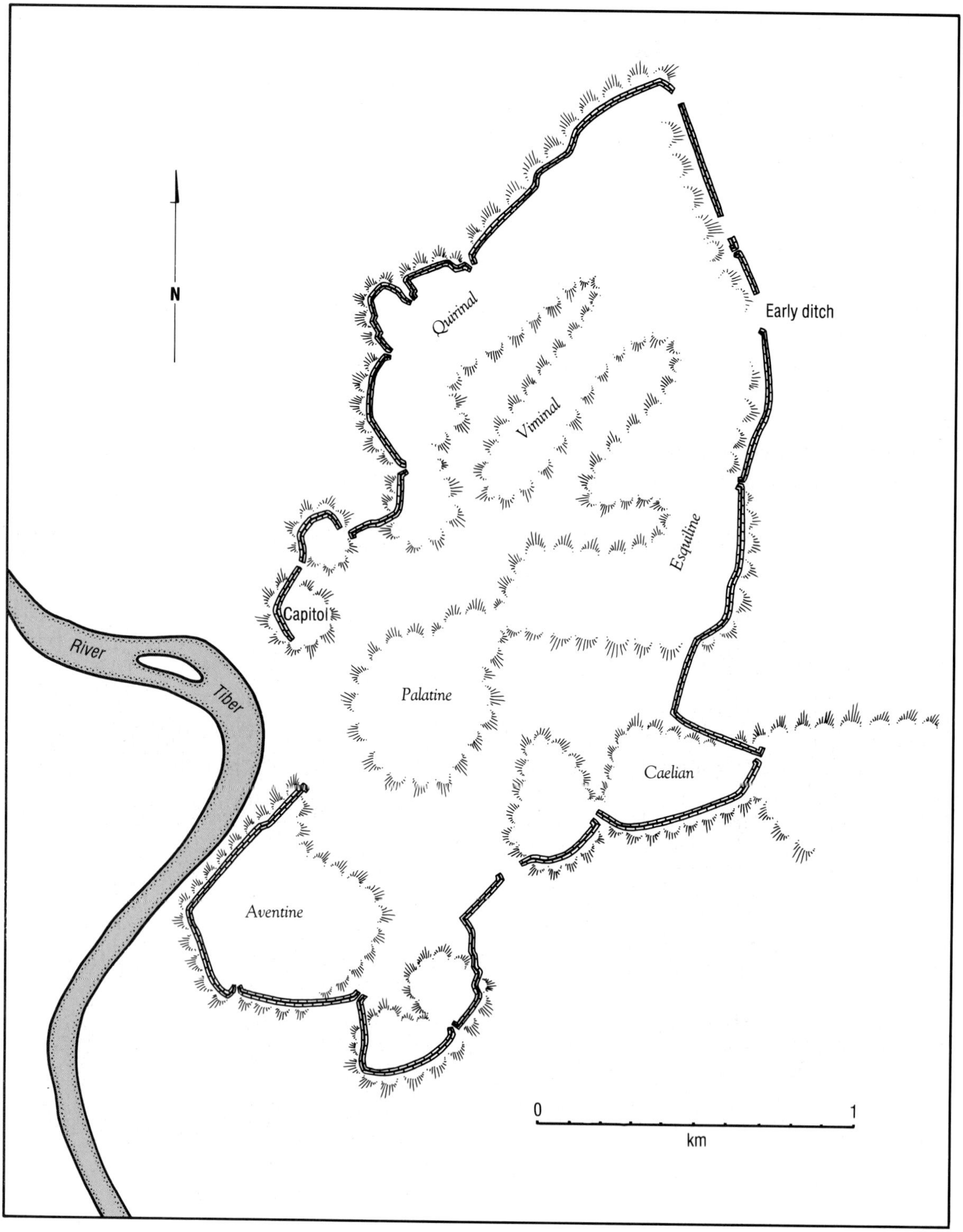
N
Quirinal
Viminal
Esquiline
Early ditch
Capitol
River
Tiber
Palatine
Caelian
Aventine
0
1
km

When the Etruscans entered the conflict on the side of the Samnites, Rome was forced to divide its forces. The cities of northern Etruria were reduced in two quick campaigns, and by 304 the Samnite capital had been taken. The Samnites, however, continued their struggle until 290; the long wars for mastery of central Italy at last came to an end when they accepted the status of Roman allies.

Opposite: The 'Servian' Wall, constructed after the destruction of Rome by the Gauls in 390 — portions of it can still be seen in Rome

The significance of this period

- During this phase of conflict and expansion, the Romans proved their unity, tenacity and adaptability.
- As a result of fighting in the mountains against the Samnites, the Romans further reorganised their army. The rigid phalanx was replaced with maniples — more flexible tactical units. Improvements in equipment were also made.

Changes in methods of fighting

- As Rome's sphere of influence widened, Roman and Latin colonies were planted at strategic points and were later linked by a network of roads which helped Rome keep control in the newly acquired areas.

Colonies planted at strategic points

Bronze figurine of a Samnite warrior, possibly the only true representation of one in existence

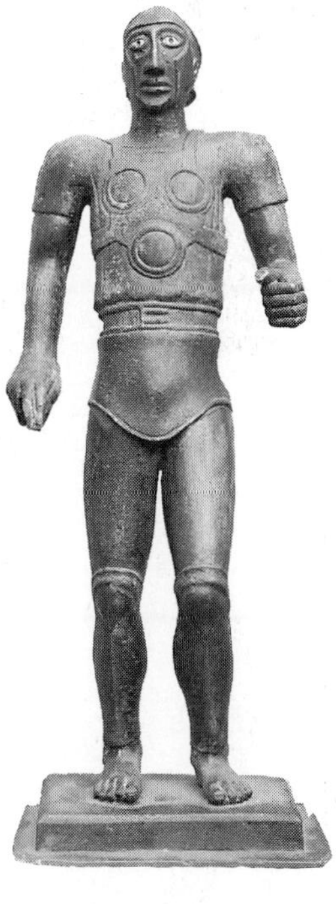

A Samnite warrior from a wall painting at Paestum

- More land, confiscated from conquered people, became available for Roman citizens and this helped to ease the problem of overpopulation and social discontent in Rome among the poorer masses.

Contribution of allies to Roman army

- Rome's military resources were increased. The treaties signed with conquered cities and tribes included provisions for placing allied troops at the disposal of Rome when necessary.

Fourth phase, 290–265

In 284 Rome defeated another coalition of Etruscans and Gauls. This left only the Greek cities of the south outside its sphere of influence.

Trouble with Greeks in south

The cities of Magna Graecia had suffered for some time from repeated attacks by the southern Italian tribes, and in the past the powerful Greek city of Taras (Tarentum) had taken on the role of protector of those cities. However, in 285 the smaller Greek cities, led by Thurii, asked for Rome's protection rather than that of Tarentum. When Rome stepped into that role Tarentum attacked some Roman ships, and also Thurii. When the Romans demanded reparations Tarentum, fearing for its independence, asked for help from Pyrrhus, King of Epirus, who was a skilled and ambitious military leader. He answered the appeal from Tarentum and arrived in Italy with an army of 20 000 skilled professional infantry, a cavalry of 3000 and about twenty elephants.

Greeks helped by Pyrrhus

Pyrrhus and his Greek allies were the greatest threat yet faced by Rome, and in the first two battles of the campaign—Heraclea in 280 and Asculum in 279—the Romans were soundly defeated.

> After a long struggle the Roman line began to give way at the point where Pyrrhus himself was pressing his opponents hardest, but the factor which did most to enable the Greeks to prevail was the weight and fury of the elephants' charge. Against this even the Romans' courage was of little avail: they felt as they might have done before the rush of a tidal wave or the shock of an earthquake, and it was better to give way than to stand their ground to no purpose, and suffer a terrible fate without gaining the least advantage...
>
> The two armies disengaged and the story goes that when one of Pyrrhus' friends congratulated him on his victory, he replied, 'One more victory like that over the Romans will destroy us completely!' He had lost a great part of the force he had brought with him, with a few exceptions almost all his friends and commanders had been killed, and there were no reinforcements which he could summon from home.[4]

Despite their losses the Romans did not make peace with Pyrrhus, but signed a mutually defensive treaty with Carthage (see chapter 7).

Bust of Pyrrhus, King of Epirus, found at Herculaneum

A coin from Tarentum showing Taras riding a dolphin and beneath it an elephant commemorating Pyrrhus

Pyrrhus eventually defeated

Pyrrhus crossed over to Sicily in answer to a call for help from the Sicilians, and during his absence his Greek and Italian allies deserted him. When he returned in 275 he was defeated at Beneventum, and his career in Italy was finished.

Tarentum surrendered in 272, and by 270 all Magna Graecia was under Roman control. Five years later Roman dominance extended from the Po valley in the north to the tip of the peninsula in the south.

The significance of this period

Roman control of whole peninsula

- Rome had brought the whole peninsula (approximately 79 000 square kilometres) into an Italian federation under its leadership. More colonies were established at strategic points.
- This was the first time elephants had been used in Italian warfare.
- The defeat of Pyrrhus made a strong impression on the Hellenistic world, and for the first time Rome was recognised as a world power.
- The treaty with Carthage marked the first intervention of Carthage in Italian affairs.

Reasons for Rome's successful conquest of Italy

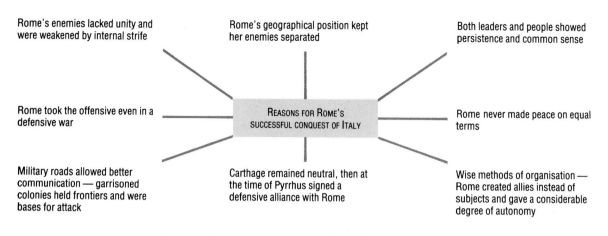

- Rome's enemies lacked unity and were weakened by internal strife
- Rome's geographical position kept her enemies separated
- Both leaders and people showed persistence and common sense
- Rome took the offensive even in a defensive war
- Rome never made peace on equal terms
- Military roads allowed better communication — garrisoned colonies held frontiers and were bases for attack
- Carthage remained neutral, then at the time of Pyrrhus signed a defensive alliance with Rome
- Wise methods of organisation — Rome created allies instead of subjects and gave a considerable degree of autonomy

Rome's organisation of Italy

Rome's expansion within the peninsula was not the result of a deliberate and consisent policy of aggression, but at the same time not all the wars fought by the Romans in the fifth and fourth centuries were — as was claimed by later Romans — purely defensive. Some of the conquered areas were annexed and the land and people incorporated into the Roman state (*ager Romanus*), while the rest were bound to Rome by separate treaties which varied in specific details.

The Roman confederation: citizens and allies

By the middle of the third century Rome was the leader of a great military confederation made up of Roman citizens, Latin allies and Italian allies, but it would take another two centuries of struggle, suffering, rebellions and gradual Romanisation before the military confederation was transformed into a united nation.

Roman citizenship	
Public rights	*Private rights*
To vote in the Roman assembly To hold office as a magistrate To pay taxes To serve in the Roman legions To be subject to Roman magistrates	*connubium* — recognising the validity of a marriage, the bequests in a will and the right to hold inherited property *commercium* — giving the right to buy land and to get a fair price for what was sold *provocatio* — providing the right of appeal to an assembly against the act of a magistrate

The Roman confederation			
		Socii (allies)	
	The Roman state (ager Romanus)	*Latin allies (nomen Latinum)*	*Italian allies (socii Italici)*
Constituents	The city of Rome Annexed territory in Latium, S. Etruria and Campania, and through Sabine territory to the Adriatic Roman colonies (27), small garrisons of Roman citizens at strategic posts on coast — not liable for military duty	A few original Latin towns not absorbed by Rome New Latin colonies — 21 large towns of 2500–6000 households, given land for farming but primarily military in function, on non-Roman territory	150 communities (Greeks, Etruscans and Italians), each bound to Rome by a special treaty (*foedus*) defining its particular relations with Rome.
Rights and duties	Two classes of citizens: • Full citizens (*optimo iure*) with political and private rights — usually lived in or near Rome to enable them to attend the assemblies • Citizens without political rights (*sine suffragio*) — without a vote but with private rights. Communities of these citizens called *municipia* — autonomous in local affairs Both groups subject to taxation and military service in the legions	Private rights of *commercium* and *connubium* (see previous table) Full rights of local self-government Right to move to Rome and become a Roman citizen if a son of military age remained in the colony Service not in Roman legions but in separate divisions of infantry and cavalry under own commanders. All allied troops under overall control of Roman generals	Full rights of local self-government No taxes due to Rome — not placed under regular Roman magistrates Foreign policy controlled by Rome Liable for a military quota — service not in Roman army but in separate divisions under own commanders. All allied troops under the overall control of Roman generals

6 The plebeian struggle for equality and the government of Rome

ROME'S expansion in Italy was inseparable from the internal developments in patrician–plebeian relations that occurred during the same period.

Effects of wars on Rome's internal development

- More magistrates were needed to administer the growing state, and the newly created magistracies were monopolised by the patricians.
- More men and money were required to meet the constant threats from hostile neighbours, and this growing burden of military service and taxation fell heavily on the plebeians.
- Long absences from home, bad seasons, the monopolising of increasing amounts of public land by the patricians and the prevalence of debt among the small farmer-soldiers added to the discontent of the plebeians.

Recognition of power by plebeians

The plebeians, conscious of their importance in the army, used each military crisis to demand concessions from the patricians; they refused to fight the state's battles unless their demands were answered. The discipline, co-operation and organisation acquired during the long years of fighting helped them to claim their rights more effectively.

There was a growing number of plebeians who were equal to the patricians in ability and wealth and who had distinguished themselves in battle; these men were able to act as spokesmen, but nevertheless the struggle for political, social, religious and legal equality was long and bitter since the patricians, with their wealth and experience, contested every demand. When they felt the patrician monopoly of a particular position was threatened, they lessened its importance by transferring some of its functions to a new, exclusively patrician magistracy.

Bitter struggle for equality

MAJOR LANDMARKS IN THE PLEBEIAN STRUGGLE FOR EQUALITY

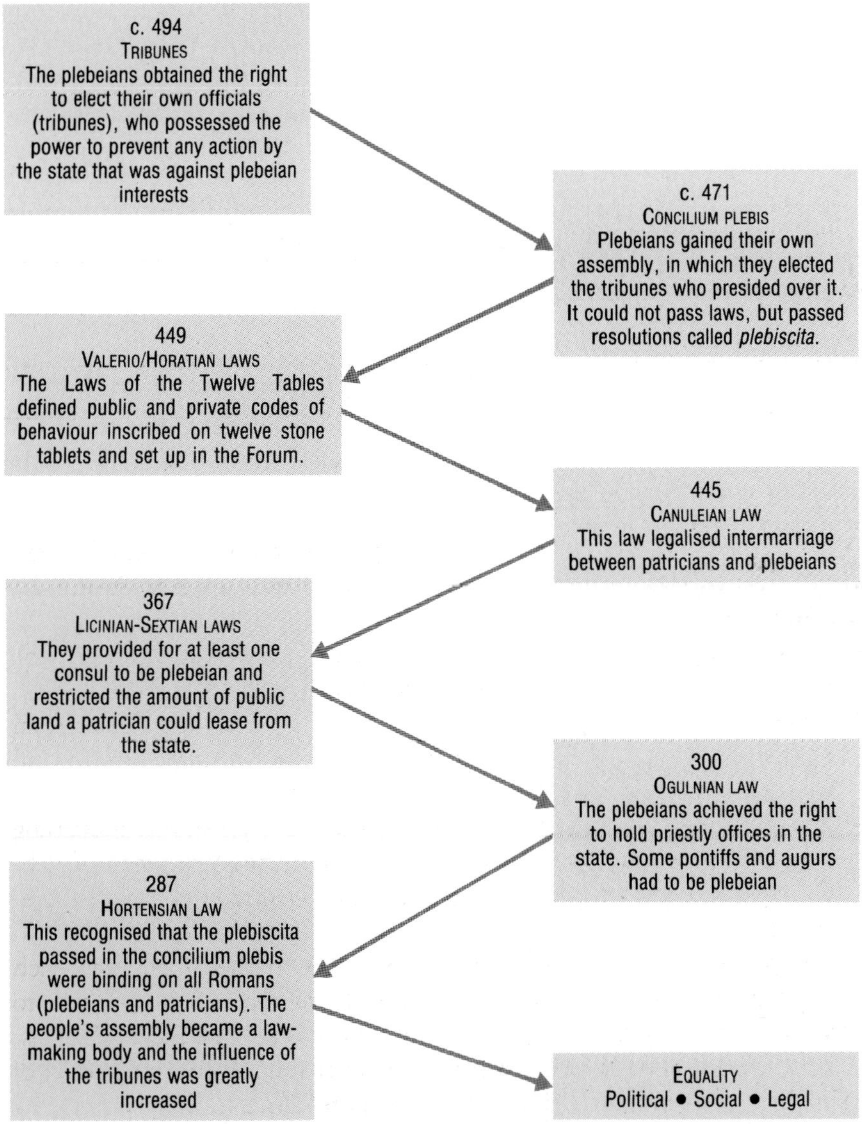

c. 494
TRIBUNES
The plebeians obtained the right to elect their own officials (tribunes), who possessed the power to prevent any action by the state that was against plebeian interests
c. 471
CONCILIUM PLEBIS
Plebeians gained their own assembly, in which they elected the tribunes who presided over it. It could not pass laws, but passed resolutions called *plebiscita*.
449
VALERIO/HORATIAN LAWS
The Laws of the Twelve Tables defined public and private codes of behaviour inscribed on twelve stone tablets and set up in the Forum.
445
CANULEIAN LAW
This law legalised intermarriage between patricians and plebeians
367
LICINIAN-SEXTIAN LAWS
They provided for at least one consul to be plebeian and restricted the amount of public land a patrician could lease from the state.
300
OGULNIAN LAW
The plebeians achieved the right to hold priestly offices in the state. Some pontiffs and augurs had to be plebeian
287
HORTENSIAN LAW
This recognised that the plebiscita passed in the concilium plebis were binding on all Romans (plebeians and patricians). The people's assembly became a law-making body and the influence of the tribunes was greatly increased
EQUALITY
Political • Social • Legal

By the year 287 the political differences between plebeians and patricians had disappeared and intermarriage between the two orders had broken down the old social barriers. The only reminders of the former prestige of the patricians were a few nonpolitical religious positions that they continued to hold and a special patrician magistracy.

However, the lex Hortensia did not mean a victory for democracy over aristocracy. Although the law had recognised that the people in their assembly were the supreme law-making body, in practice the senate had a stronger hold on government in the third and second centuries than ever before. (This will be dealt with in detail in chapter 13). The main difference now was that the old patrician aristocracy, which previously controlled the senate, was gradually replaced with a plebeio-patrician timocracy. Members of the old patrician families, whose numbers were declining, intermarried and associated in office with the new wealthy plebeian families, creating a new ruling nobility that was as exclusive as the old.

Republican government in the third and second centuries

No written constitution

The Romans did not have a written constitution, but rather one which had evolved in the course of the struggle between the patricians and plebeians. The timeline on p. 78 traces this development, showing when magistrates, other than consuls, were introduced to help administer the growing state. By 264 the republican government had virtually acquired the form it was to retain, although it did undergo further changes in the second and first centuries.

SPQR

These letters stand for *Senatus Populusque Romanus*—the Senate and the People of Rome. The Roman government followed the usual pattern of other ancient constitutions—the administrative structure included a council (senate), magistrates and people's assemblies.

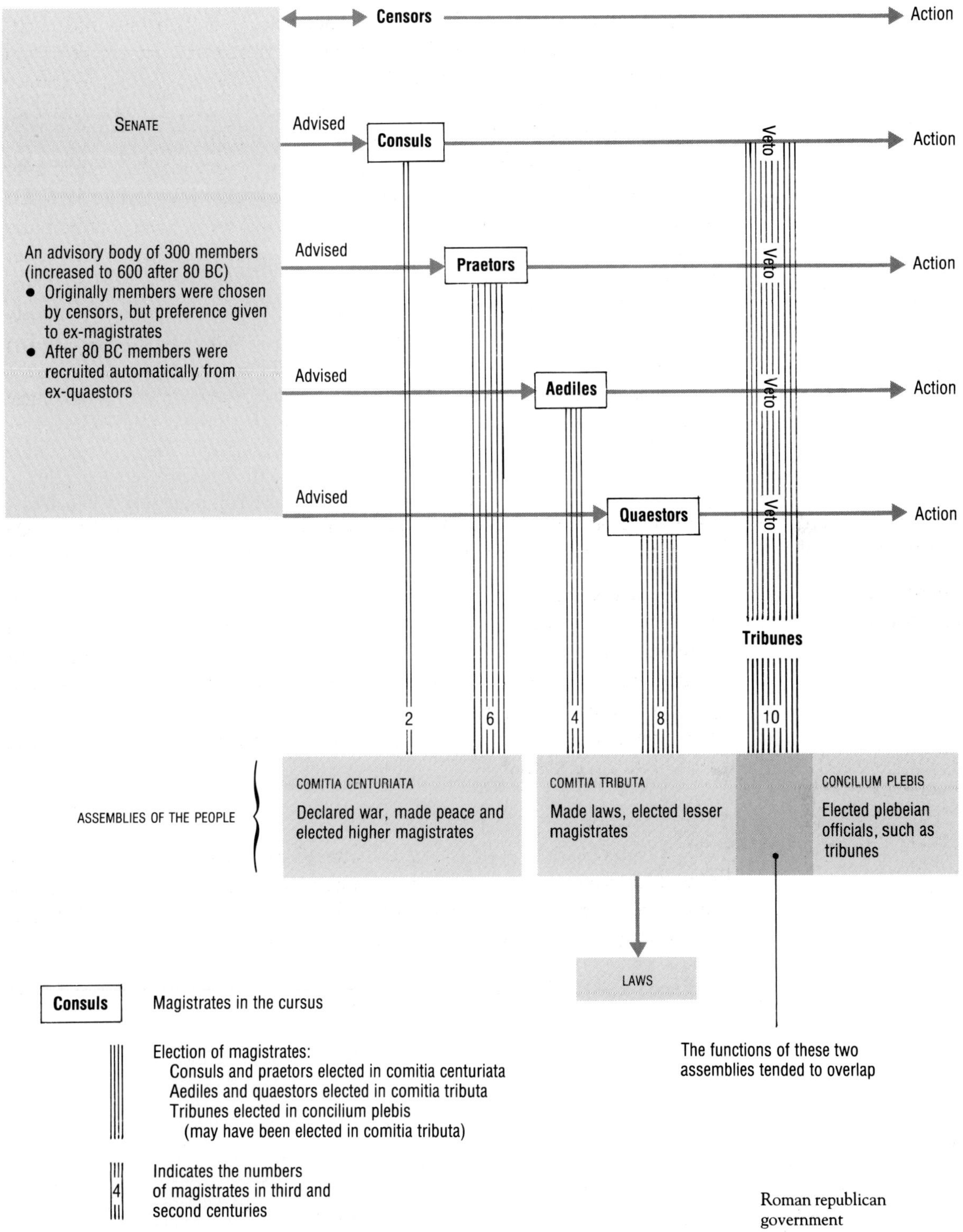

Roman republican government

The senate

In theory the senate was a purely advisory body, but in practice it became the real governing body in Rome. Its power increased during the wars with Carthage, and its supremacy in the state was consolidated during the second century (see chapter 13). Senatorial power was based not on law but purely on custom, precedent and the prestige of its individual members.

The following extract from Polybius VI:13 describes the Roman constitution at its prime.

> Let us now consider the Senate. This body has control of the treasury and regulates the flow of all revenue and expenditure; the quaestors require a decree of the Senate to enable them to authorise expenditure on any given project, with the exception only of payments made to the consuls. The senate also controls what is by far the largest and most important item of expenditure —that is, the programme which is laid down by the censors every five years to provide for the repair and construction of public buildings—and it makes a grant to the censors for this purpose. Similarly any crimes committed in Italy which require a public investigation such as treason, conspiracy, poisoning and assassination, also come under the jurisdiction of the Senate... It is also responsible for dispatching embassies or commissions to countries outside Italy, either to settle differences, or to offer advice, to impose demands, to receive submissions, or to declare war; in the same way whenever any delegations arrive in Rome, it decides how they should be received and what answer should be given to them.

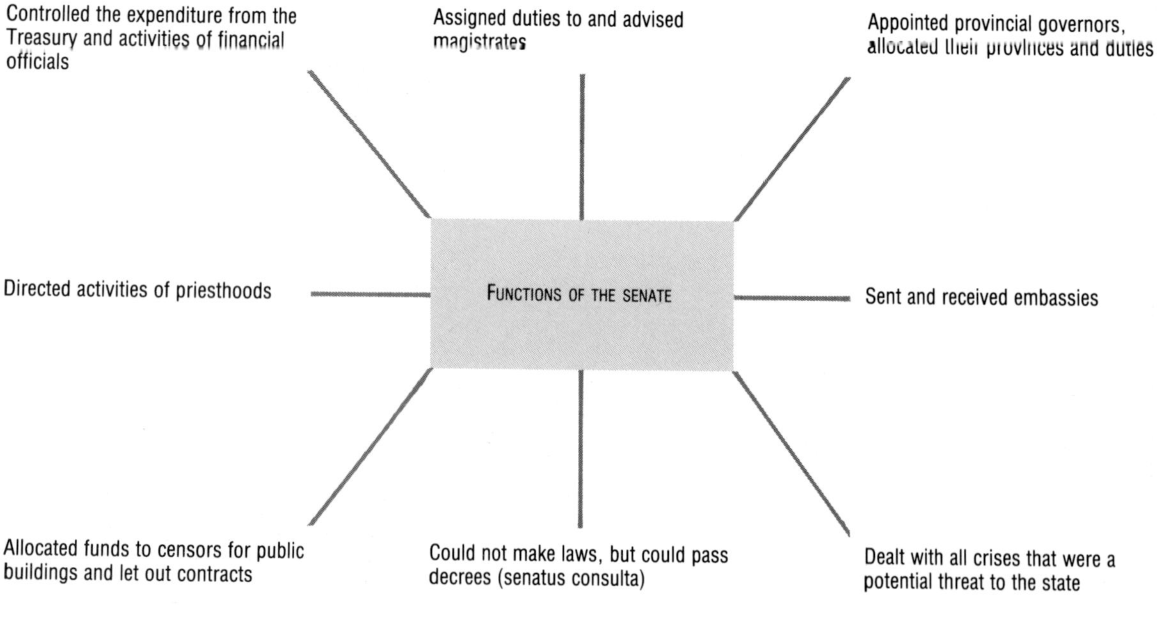
Controlled the expenditure from the Treasury and activities of financial officials
Assigned duties to and advised magistrates
Appointed provincial governors, allocated their provinces and duties
Directed activities of priesthoods
FUNCTIONS OF THE SENATE
Sent and received embassies
Allocated funds to censors for public buildings and let out contracts
Could not make laws, but could pass decrees (senatus consulta)
Dealt with all crises that were a potential threat to the state

The magistrates and the cursus honorum

A magistrate was an elected government official, occupying a position of power and prestige, both of which increased with the rank of his office. However, before a young man started on a political career he was expected to have spent at least ten years in some military position.

'Ladder' of offices

The regular magistrates, in ascending order, were
- quaestors
- aediles (not imperative, but usual)
- praetors
- consuls

These positions comprised what was referred to as the *cursus honorum* (ladder of offices), and any aspiring young politician was expected to proceed up the political ladder in this way. This cursus was formalised in the lex Villia Annalis, passed in 180. Certain essential requirements were laid down including minimum ages for the various offices, a two-year interval between the holding of consecutive offices and a ten-year interval between the holding of the same office. This law made sure that those who reached high office had the necessary qualifications in both military and political affairs.

Lex Villia Annalis

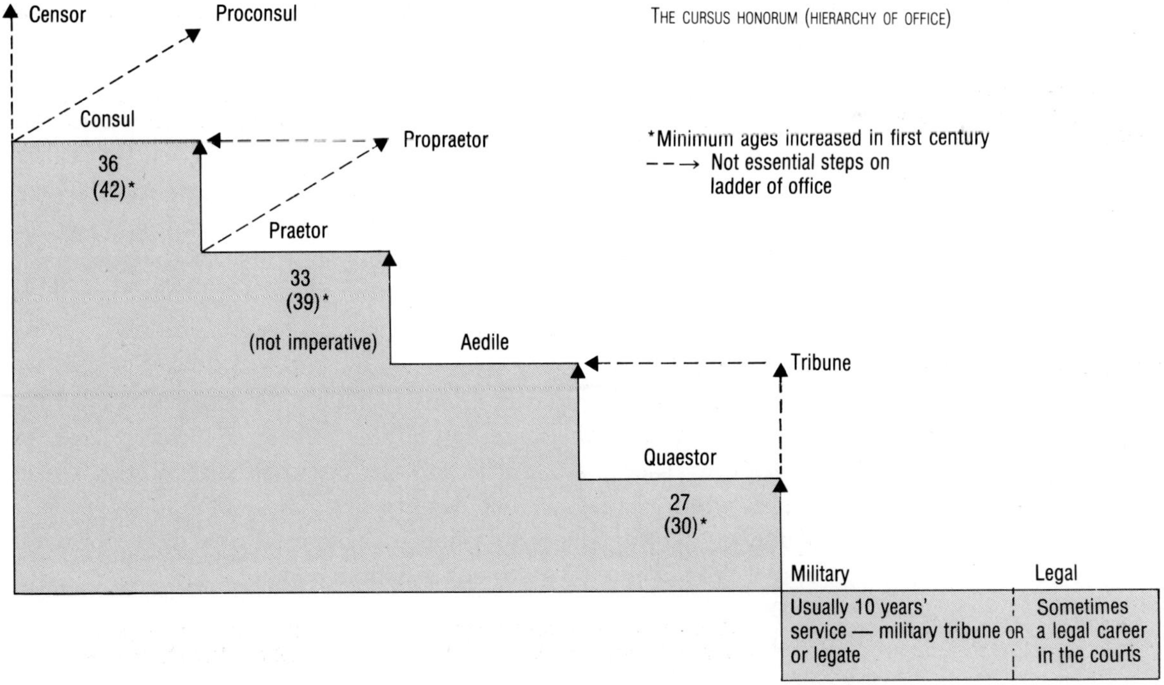

THE CURSUS HONORUM (HIERARCHY OF OFFICE)

Politics the only career for a young Roman noble

Since members of the senatorial class were prevented by the Claudian law of 218 from engaging in commercial activities, the only worthwhile career open to them was politics. Although great personal ability was an asset, it did not automatically ensure career opportunities in Rome; far more important was a distinguished family background and important connections with other leading families. Sometimes, however, a man without the right family background might reach the position of consul if he had shown military brilliance or had built up a high profile through a successful legal career, but in both cases he would still need the patronage of one of the leading senatorial families or factions. Such a man was referred to as a *novus homo* (new man) and was usually not accepted socially within the senatorial clique.

'New men'

To advance to the highest positions in the state the young ambitious man had to develop a successful high profile.

As a junior officer in the army he would hope to attract the notice of his superiors, who might later support him in his bid for election to a quaestorship. If he then reached the position of aedile, he would have plenty of opportunity for self-advertisement and vote-catching since he would be responsible for the city's food supply and the staging of public games. It was of course very expensive to provide lavish games and festivals, but the more memorable they were the more likely it was that he would gain the support of the people when presenting himself for a praetorship.

Private expense incurred in holding aedileship

To seek election to any position cost an enormous amount of money, and even many well-to-do senators often found that the family estate did not provide enough to cover the expenses entailed in the election campaign and especially when holding the position of aedile. Often, to pursue their political careers they were obliged to borrow from the wealthy commercial class (the equestrian class) in return for some political favour.

Senatorial class often borrowed from equites

As Rome expanded and aquired overseas territories, a consul at the end of his term of office looked forward to being appointed to the governship of a province. This gave him the opportunity to reimburse himself for some of his previous costs as it was possible, by various means, to make money in the provinces.

Money-making opportunities in provinces

There were of course other positions which a politically ambitious man could and did hold in his career, but although these are often referred to as magistracies they were either not an essential part of the cursus honorum or not regarded as 'true' magistracies. These were

Important official positions not included in the cursus

- tribune of the people — this came to be one of the most powerful, because of its ability to obstruct legislation;
- censor;
- dictator and master of the horse (*magister equitum*).

A Roman magistrate was permitted to hold other offices at the same time, such as one of the priesthoods.

Forms of power held by magistrates

Imperium This was supreme authority, involving command in war and the interpretation and execution of law, including the infliction of the death penalty. The magistrates with imperium were accompanied by attendants (lictors) who carried the symbol of the imperium—the fasces (bundles of rods). Consuls were attended by twelve lictors each, praetors by six lictors each and the dictator by twenty-four lictors.

Potestas This was the general term for the power of a magistrate to enforce the law by the authority of his office; the power was restricted to the carrying out of certain defined actions. All magistrates had potestas.

A curule magistrate—the curule aedile, praetor, consul or censor—had the right to sit on a special chair of office, called the *sella curulis*, and to wear the *toga praetexta*, the toga with a purple band.

Position and function of magistrates

		Number	*Length of office*	*Authority*	*Elected by*	*Functions*
In the cursus honorum	Consuls	Two	1 year	Imperium	Comitia centuriata	Commanded the army Conducted the chief elections Presided over meeting of the senate Implemented senate decisions
In the cursus honorum	Praetors[1]	Six	1 year	Imperium	Comitia centuriata	Praetor urbanus (city praetor): • Was supreme civil judge of Rome • sometimes commanded an army • could summon comitia centuriata • could introduce legislation Praetor peregrinus (alien praetor): • dealt with lawsuits involving foreigners

		Number	*Length of office*	*Authority*	*Elected by*	*Functions*
In the cursus honorum						• issued annual 'edicts' that were an important source of Roman law
In the cursus honorum	Aediles (curule and plebeian)	Four	1 year	Potestas	Comitia tributa Concilium plebis[2]	Maintained the streets of Rome Regulated traffic Were in charge of public buildings Took care of the city's water supply Controlled the markets and supervised weights and measures Arranged the public festivals and games
In the cursus honorum	Quaestors[1]	Eight	1 year	Protestas	Comitia tributa	Financial and administrativ officials: • maintained public records • superintended the treasury • acted as paymasters when accompanying generals on campaigns • supervised the sale of war booty • were financial assistants to governors
Not in the cursus honorum	Tribunes	Ten	1 year	Potestas	Concilium plebis Comitia tributa[2]	Defended the lives and property of the plebieans[3] Had the right of veto (*intercessio*) against elections of magistrates, laws and decrees of the senate and actions of magistrates

		Number	*Length of office*	*Authority*	*Elected by*	*Function*
Not in the cursus honorum						Could each veto the actions of any of his nine colleagues Summoned the concilium plebis (plebeian assembly) and gained resolutions (plebiscita) from it
	Censors	Two	18 months (elected every 5 years)	Potestas	Comitia centuriata	Took the census (list of citizens) Had right to take judicial proceedings against any citizen suppressing information regarding his property Controlled public morals (could expel senators for lax morality) Prepared the list of members of the senate Supervised the leasing of public lands and buildings and letting of government contracts
	Dictator	One	6 months, in a crisis	Imperium of 2 consuls	*Appointed* by consul on proposal of senate	Superseded all other magistrates in a millitary or serious domestic emergency
	Master of the horse	One	As above	Imperium	*Appointed* by dictator	Was the dictator's lieutenant

[1] Their numbers were gradually increased as the empire grew.
[2] The comitia tributa and the concilium plebis came to be indistinguishable, and it is not certain if those plebeian magistrates (plebeian aedile and tribune) were elected from one or the other. However, the elections for both these positions were held under the supervision of a tribune.
[3] Their homes had to be open to give asylum; they had sacrosanctity, by which they were secure against personal danger.

The following extract is from Plutarch's *Cato the Elder*, and describes the functions of the censors.

The Roman censor

This office [censorship] was regarded as the crowning honour of Roman civic life, and in a sense the culminating achievement of a political career. Its

> powers were very extensive and they included the right to inquire into the lives and manners of the citizens . . . The Romans believed that a man's true character was more clearly revealed in his private life than in his public or political career, and they therefore chose two officials, one from among the so-called patricians and the other a plebeian, whose duty it was to watch, regulate and punish any tendency to indulge in licentious or voluptuous habits and to depart from the traditional and established way of living . . . they had the authority to degrade a Roman knight or to expel a senator who led a vicious or disorderly life. They also carried out and maintained a general census of property, kept a register of all citizens according to their social and political classification, and exercised various other important powers.[1]

Promagistrates

The word 'prorogation' meant 'the extension of the imperium of a consul and praetor' and was first introduced in 326 when it became necessary to extend the yearly period of command of a consul so that he could complete a military campaign. Sometimes a campaign could be jeopardised if a consul's term had expired and he was replaced by the consul for the following year. During a period of continuous war (such as the Hannibalic War, 218–201) it was quite common for commands to be prorogued for long periods.

Increasing use of prorogation

As the number of provinces in the empire increased, prorogation became an important part of the administrative system. At the end of a term of office, a consul was always prorogued as a proconsul and given a provincial command. Sometimes praetors were also prorogued as propraetors, and sent off to the provinces.

Few Romans who were elected to public office reached the highest positions, because there were few places available and the competition was fierce. Also, not all those who achieved a consulship followed the strict procedure of the cursus. There were many irregular careers and this trend increased, particularly in the first century. (Refer to the careers of Marius and Pompey, chapters 15 and 16.)

Exercise: Magistrates for the year 198

The following extract is taken from T. R. S. Broughton's *Magistrates of the Roman Republic*, a two-volume work revealing something of the political career pattern of selected Romans.[2] It is obvious that there is a great deal of information missing.

Use this extract and the information on the preceding pages to answer the questions that follow.

Consuls

SEX. AELIUS Q. f. P. n. PAETUS CATUS (105)
T. QUINCTIUS T. f. L. n. FLAMININUS Pat.

Liv. 32.7.12, and 8.1; *Fast. Cap.*, Degrassi 48f., 121, 452f.; Chr. 354; *Fast. Hyd.*; *Chr. Pasc.*; Cassiod.; Zon. 9.16; on Paetus, Liv. 32.27.5; *Dig.* 1.2.2.38; and on Flamininus, Cic. *Phil.* 5.48; Polyb. 18.46.5; Oros. 4.20.1; and inscriptions, most of them to be dated after his consulships, *ILS* 8766—*SIG*³ 592; *SIG*³ 593; 591, line 65; 674, line 51; and offerings at Delos, *I. de Délos*, 439a, 77; 442b, 85f.; 1429a, 21f.; 1441a, 105f.; 1446,15. Flamininus was assigned Macedonia (Liv. 32.8.4), successfully carried the war into Greece, and attempted to win the Achaean league to the Roman side (Liv. 32.9–15, and 17.4–24; Diod. 28.11; Frontin. *Str.* 2.13.8; Plut. *Flam.* 3–5; App. *Mac.* 5–7; Pausan. 7.8.2–3; Flor. 1.7.11; Auct. *Vir. Ill.* 51.1). His successess led to a parley with Philip at Nicaea, a truce, and the despatch of embassies to Rome (Polyb. 18.1–10; Liv. 32.32–36; Plut. *Flam.* 5–7; App. *Mac.* 8; Iustin. 30.3.8–10; Zon. 9.16). On Flamininus, see Lübker, no. 11.

Praetors

Election: Liv. 32.7.13 Provinces and armies 32.8.5–8

M. CLAUDIUS MARCELLUS (222) Cos. 196 Sicily
Liv. 32.27.3.

L. CORNELIUS MERULA Pat. (270) Cos. 193 Pr. Urbanus
Suppressed a conspiracy of slaves and Carthaginian hostages (Liv. 32.26.4–18).

C. HELVIUS (1) Gaul
Liv. 32.9.5, and 26.2–3.

M. PORCIUS CATO Cos. 195 Sardinia
Instituted a strict regime, expelling the moneylenders and reducing his own expenses (Liv. 32.27.2–4; Nep. *Cato* 1.4. Plut. *Cat. Mai.* 6.1–3; Auct. *Vir. Ill.* 47.1). See D.–G., no. 15, Lübker, no. 4.

Aediles, Curule

Q. MINUCIUS THERMUS (65) Cos. 193, Pr. 196
TI. SEMPRONIUS LONGUS (67) Cos. 194, Pr. 196
Liv. 32.27.8.

Aediles of the Plebs

C. SEMPRONIUS TUDITANUS (90) Pr. 197
M. HELVIUS (4) Pr. 197
Liv. 32.27.7.

Tribunes of the Plebs

M. FULVIUS (56)
M'. CURIUS (4)
They opposed for a time the candidacy of Flamininus for the consulship because he had held no curule office (Liv. 32.7.8–11; Plut. *Flam.* 2.1–2).

Promagistrates

CN. CORNELIUS BLASIO Pat. (74) Pr. 194
Continued as Proconsul in Hither Spain; see 197.

L. CORNELIUS LENTULUS Pat. (188) Cos. 199
His command in Gaul was prorogued until the coming of the Consul with a new army (Liv. 32.8.3, and 26.2).

L. Stertinius (5)
Continued as Proconsul in Farther Spain; see 197.

P. Villius Tappulus (3) Cos. 199, Pr. 203
His successor, the Consul Flamininus, arrived early in the year (Liv. 32.6.4, and 9.6–8; Plut. *Flam.* 3.1–4).

Tribunes of the Soldiers

Ap. Claudius (Nero?) Pat. (245) Pr. 195
Attended Flamininus during his conference with Philip at Nicaea (Liv. 32.35.7; Polyb. 18.8.6).

Legates, Envoys

1. L. Calpurnius (13)
Sent by L. Flamininus at the Consul's suggestion to the assembly of the Achaean League (Liv. 32.19.11, cf. 5).

2. Ap. Claudius Nero Pat. (245) Pr. 195
Q. Fabius (Buteo?) Pat. (31, 57) Pr. 196
Q. Fulvius Flaccus (26, 60) Cos. 180, Pr. 187
Sent to the Senate by Flamininus along with the envoys of Philip, the real allies of Rome (Polyb. 18.10.8; Liv. 32.36.10)

Abbreviations of public offices: cos. – consul
pr. – praetor pat. patrician

1 Identify the patrician families represented among the magistrates of 198.
2 What was the name of the plebeian consul's father? (refer to p. 41 of this text).
3 Which of the praetors became consul soonest?
4 How many of the praetors for 198 are not known?
5 Which was the city praetor and which one served overseas?
6 Are all the aediles for 198 known? Give a reason for your answer.
7 What is noticeable about the later careers of the curule aediles in contrast to the aediles of the plebs? What explanation might be offered for this?
8 From the evidence, which men became consuls together five years later in 193?
9 How many of the tribunes of the plebs are not known for 198?
10 What kinds of duties did the promagistrates have?
11 What position on the cursus honorum is not represented in this extract?

Coin showing a Roman voter dropping a tally into an urn

The popular assemblies

Of the four popular assemblies that functioned in Rome, three were referred to as *comitiae* which meant 'meetings of the whole citizen body'—that is, both plebeians and patricians: the comitia centuriata, in which the people voted in their military centuries; the comitia tributa, in which they voted in their tribes and the comitia curiata, in which they voted in their curiae. The fourth assembly was the concilium plebis, which was meeting of the plebeians only.

The four popular assemblies	
Assembly	*Conditions and functions*
Comitia curiata	Met only for formal purposes • conferred imperium on consuls and praetors
Comitia centuriata	Could be summoned only by a magistrate with imperium and met outside the city on the Campus Martius (Field of Mars) because it was originally a military assembly • elected magistrates with imperium • decided between peace and war • acted as a court of appeal in criminal cases
Comitia tributa	Could be summoned by consuls, praetors or tribunes • elected lesser magistrates • voted on bills put before it by the presiding magistrate — a law-making body • acted as a court of appeal in cases not involving capital punishment
Concilium plebis	Admitted only plebeians to membership • issued resolutions (plebiscita) binding on all citizens after 287 • may have elected tribunes and plebeian aediles

Revision exercise

1 Define the following terms:
- imperium
- potestas
- fasces
- lictors
- cursus honorum
- prorogation
- veto

2 List the magistrates who had (a) imperium and (b) potestas.

3 What were the essential steps in a young Roman's rise to power in politics?

4 Link the following list of magistrates with the appropriate functions.

(a) aedile
(b) praetor urbanus
(c) quaestor
(d) consul
(e) censor
(f) dictator
(g) magister equitum
(h) tribune

(i) to lead the Romans during a military crisis
(ii) to supervise the letting of state contracts
(iii) to assist the dictator

(iv) to look after the interests of the plebeians
(v) to command the army and preside over the senate
(vi) to superintend the treasury
(vii) to arrange public festivals and games and to look after the city of Rome
(viii) to preside over major trials in Rome

5 Which official positions were not of one year's duration?
6 Which assembly elected the magistrates with imperium?
7 Which assembly was the chief law-making body?
8 How was the senate recruited
(a) in the third and second centuries and
(b) in the first century?
9 Why was the censor's position regarded as the high point of a politician's career?
10 What was meant by the term *novus homo?*

Timeline: Expansion and organisation

	Conquest of Italy	*Date*	*Struggle between the orders — constitutional developments*
First phase	Rome against the Latins	499	
		c.494	Appointment of two plebeian magistrates (tribunes)
	Treaty with Latins	493	
	War with Veii		
	Intermittent wars with Aequi and Volsci for next fifty years		
		471	Plebeians obtain own assembly (*concilium plebis*) with right of electing own officers and passing own resolutions (*plebiscita*)
		460	Number of tribunes increased to ten
		451	Laws published — the Twelve Tables
		449	Secession of the plebeians
		447	Quaestors appointed
		445	Lex Canuleia — intermarriage recognised
		443	Six military tribunes replaced consuls Censorship established
	Decisive battle against Aequi	431	
		421	Quaestors increased to four
		409	First plebeian quaestor

	Conquest of Italy	Date	*Struggle between the orders — constitutional developments*
First phase		400	First plebeian military tribune
	Destruction of Veii	396	
	Sack of Rome by Gauls	390	
Second phase	Rome rebuilt	370	
		367	Licinian-Sextian laws
		366	first plebeian consul; first praetor appointed
		356	First plebeian dictator
		351	First plebeian censor
	First Samnite War	343	
	War with Latin League	338	
		337	First plebeian praetor
Third phase		330	Lex Ogulnia — admission of plebeians to colleges of augurs and pontiffs
	Second Samnite War	327	
	Rome's humiliation by Samnites	321	
	Third Samnite War	304	
	Rome facing coalition of Gauls, Etruscans, Umbrians and Samnites	298 290	
Fourth phase		287	Lex Hortensia — resolutions of *concilium plebis* made binding on all people
	Rome's defeat by Pyrrhus	280	
	Defeat of Pyrrhus	275	
	Surrender of Tarentum	270	
	All Italian peninsula under Roman control		

Essay topics

1 What grievances did the plebeians have in the early republican period? Outline the steps by which they gradually gained equality with the patricians.

2 Explain the Romans' success in conquering the peoples of Italy between the fifth and third centuries. How did they organise them into a strong Roman confederacy?

Further reading

Ancient sources

Livy. *Rome and Italy*.

Modern sources

Kagan, D. *Problems in Ancient History*, vol 2: The Roman World.
Lewis, N. & Reinhold, M. *Roman Civilisation — Sourcebook 1: The Republic*.
Scullard, H. H. A *History of the Roman World, 753–146* BC.

PART

3

Rome's expansion in the Mediterranean, 264–146: Carthage, Macedonia, Greece and Asia

By 270 Rome had conquered Italy and organised it into a confederation of Roman citizens and Latin and Italian allies (refer to the map on p. 84)

In the western Mediterranean Carthage was the dominant power, controlling a large part of North Africa, Sicily, Sardinia and Corsica and part of southern Spain. To the east, there were three Hellenistic kingdoms, divisions of the former empire of Alexander the Great: Egypt under the Ptolemies, Syria ruled by the Seleucids and Macedon under the Antigonids. There were also a number of minor powers, such as the eastern kingdom of Pergamum, and two Greek leagues, the Achaean and Aetolian.

Background to the wars with Carthage

7

The historians

The Carthaginian empire

Treaties between Rome and Carthage

Polybius says that the Romans, 'once having made themselves masters of Italy, applied themselves to the conquest of countries further afield'.[1] However, some modern scholars believe that Rome's contact with the Mediterranean powers came about partly by design but more by accident. The fact that the most populated parts of Italy were along the western side made it inevitable that Rome's first contact in the Mediterranean would be with Carthage, since the latter controlled most of Sicily and also Sardinia and Corsica, islands close to the Italian peninsula.

Inevitability of Rome's expansion westward

Since the Carthaginians came originally from Phoenicia and the Latin word for Phoenician was *Poenicus* or *Punicus*, from the Greek word *Phoinix*, the wars between Rome and Carthage are referred to as the Punic Wars. This exhausting conflict was, according to Caven, a 'contest in three rounds'[2] in which the Romans fought first for control of Sicily, then for the leadership of the western Mediterranean and finally to determine the survival or extinction of Carthage. The second of these three wars marked a turning point for Rome, in both her domestic and her foreign policy. It also involved her in hostilities with Macedon and alliance with the Greeks.

Three wars with Carthage — Punic Wars

As Rome became more and more involved in the politics of the east, it became the natural protector of the smaller states against the aggression of the Hellenistic empires. These great monarchies in the east, weakened by internal economic and social problems, were no match for the Romans.

Roman contact with Hellenistic east after 200 BC

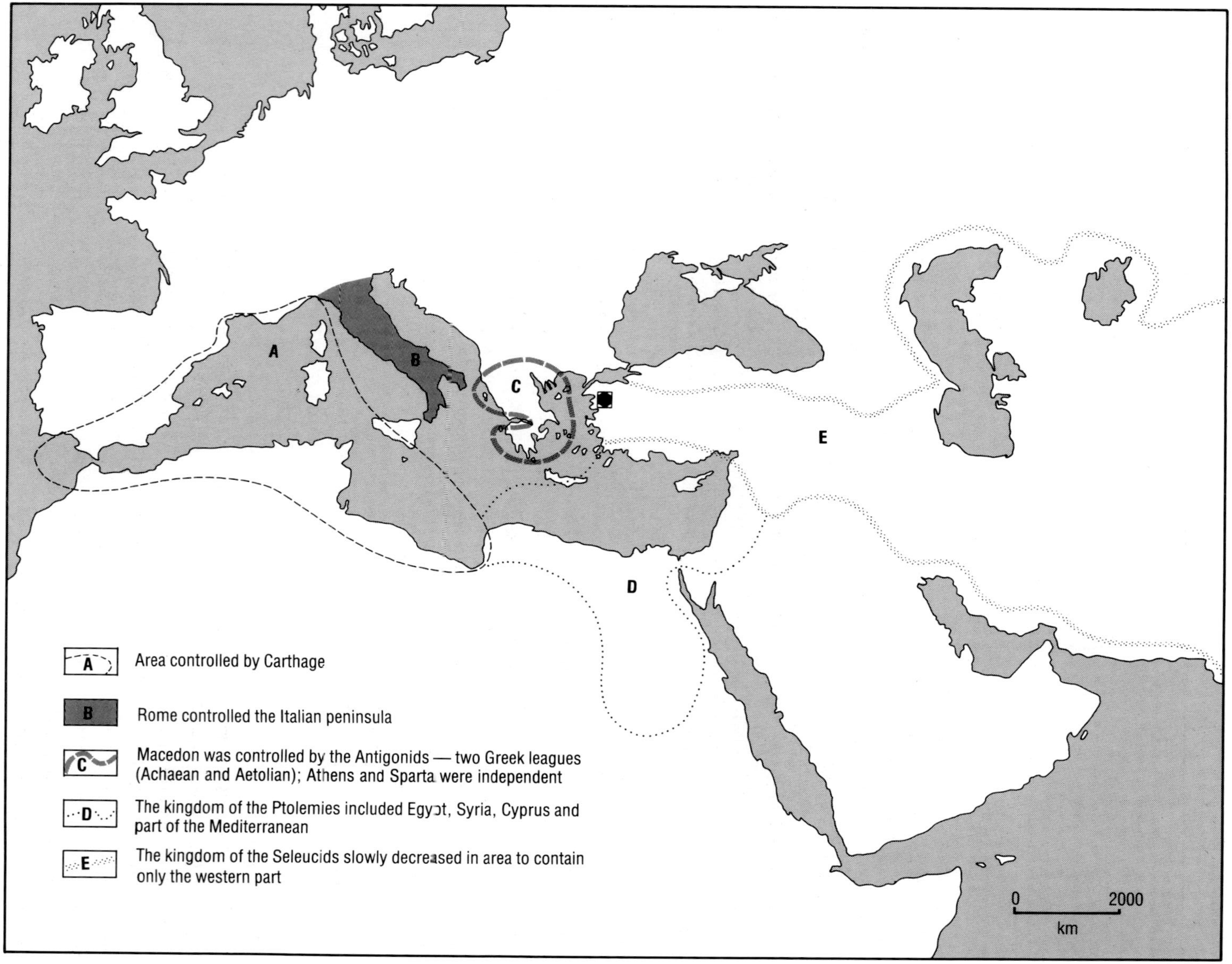
A
B
C
D
E
A
Area controlled by Carthage
B
Rome controlled the Italian peninsula
C
Macedon was controlled by the Antigonids — two Greek leagues (Achaean and Aetolian); Athens and Sparta were independent
D
The kingdom of the Ptolemies included Egypt, Syria, Cyprus and part of the Mediterranean
E
The kingdom of the Seleucids slowly decreased in area to contain only the western part
0
2000
km

Sources for the period

Written evidence

Polybius (c.200–118)

Polybius a Greek citizen

Polybius was a Greek, born in the Achaean city of Megalopolis. As the well-educated son of an Achaean statesman, he became politically active in the affairs of his city and of the Achaean League at a critical time in the affairs of the Greek states.

The Romans, who had been involved in Greek affairs since 200, were sensitive to Greek attitudes towards them and after 168 they carried out a political purge of those suspected of disloyalty to Rome. Polybius was among 1000 prominent Achaeans carried off to Rome for possible trial and detention; he remained in Rome for the next sixteen years, becoming a close friend and adviser of Scipio Aemilianus through whom he met many members of leading Roman families and also foreign envoys.

Taken to Rome as a hostage

Close association with Scipio

Well-travelled

Polybius was well-travelled, having visited many of the places he wrote about. In 151 he accompanied Scipio Aemilianus to Spain, he met Masinissa, the great Numidian chieftain of the Second Punic War, and he crossed the Alps, following the route taken by Hannibal years before. He was also an eyewitness to the destruction of Carthage in 146, and later made a journey to Alexandria, in Egypt.

Acted as mediator

When he returned to Greece, he acted as mediator between the Greek states and Rome. As an ally of Rome, he did his country a great service by 'quenching Rome's anger against Greece'[3] and by helping the Greeks accept the reality of their new relationship with Rome. Since he was articulate, much-travelled, politically experienced and on intimate terms with many prominent Romans, he regarded himself as qualified to record history. Polybius believed that a historian should be a man of action, whose most important duty was to make first-hand enquiries.

Qualified to be historian

His work

Theme: Rome's rise to power in Mediterranean

Polybius' *Histories*, written in forty books of which only five survive intact, covered the years 264–146. He traced the dissolution of the Hellenistic world and the domination of the Mediterranean by the Romans. He began his account of Rome's rise to power with the First Punic War, although he saw this as simply a prelude to the second, the war with Hannibal, and it was with the latter that his main narrative began.

His aim in writing was to show

- 'by what means and under what system of government the Romans succeeded in less than fifty-three years in bringing under their rule

Opposite: The Mediterranean world in the Hellenistic Age, 270 BC

almost the whole inhabited world, an achievement which is without parallel in human history';[4]

- how the Greeks, who were having some problems in adjusting to the Roman domination of their states, should cope with disasters. He hoped that his readers would profit from the experience of others rather than by learning painfully from their own mistakes.

His method and sources

Often an eye witness to events

Polybius believed that personal investigation was of prime importance in writing history, and in many cases he could say that he was himself an eyewitness and therefore had personal knowledge of the course of events. Where this was not the case he was able, because of his association with many influential Romans and Greeks, to interview those who had witnessed the events of which he wrote.

Access to official Roman documents

Also, because of his privileged position in Rome he was able to consult official Roman documents and inscriptions now lost to us, such as the treaties between Rome and Carthage and Scipio Africanus' letter to Philip V of Macedonia, giving his reasons for attacking Cartagena.

For the early period, however, he had to make use of some written sources, his two chief ones being Philinus of Agrigentum, a pro-Carthaginian who lived during the First Punic War, and Quintus Fabius Pictor, the earliest Roman historian, who lived through the Hannibalic War and aimed at justifying Roman policy to the Greeks. According to Polybius, both 'failed to report the truth as they should have done' and 'if history is deprived of truth we are left with nothing but an idle unprofitable tale'.[5]

Critical of many earlier writers

His faults

Honest, but with minor faults

Generally Polybius displayed a high standard of honesty, but he does have his faults.

- He reveals some bias in his treatment of Scipio Aemilianus.
- There is some confusion in his chronology.
- He is inconsistent in his attitude to religion.
- In his account of the Roman constitution he represents it as a 'balanced' constitution rather than an aristocratic one.
- He makes concessions to patriotism. 'I would admit that authors should show partiality towards their own country, but they should not make statements about it which are false.'[6]

Livy (Titus Livius, c.59 BC–AD 17)

Livy was born in Patauium (Padua) in northern Italy somewhere between 64 and 59, and sometime after 31 he moved to Rome. He developed a long and close relationship with the Emperor Augustus, under whose patronage he wrote. As a man of purely literary interests, he had no experience of war or politics and no knowledge of the places about which he wrote. Unlike Polybius, he was an armchair historian, whose chief value to the student lies in his ability to visualise people and scenes.

Little practical experience — an armchair historian

His work

He probably began his history, *Ab Urbe Condita* (From the Foundation of the City), around the year 31, and used an annalistic (year-by-year) approach. The work covered the period from 753 to 9 BC and was a massive undertaking, comprising 142 books of which only thirty-five survive. The years 753–293 and 219–167 are fully covered but the books of the intervening period are lost; Livy is therefore no use as a source for the First Punic War (264–241).

Year-by-year approach

His aim in writing was 'to put on record the story of the greatest nation in the world'[7] and to guide men to adopt correct ways of behaving, by showing them the achievements of the great republican heroes.

Highlighted virtues of great Romans

His method and sources

Livy had to base his work on the written accounts of others; he relied a great deal on Polybius and on two earlier annalists, Valerius Antias and Claudius Quadrigarius, but many sources available to him have since been lost. He tended to follow one source closely for a time and then switch to another, rewriting what was said but adding vivid details from his own imagination.

Followed Polybius closely

He followed the usual practice of presenting speeches, some of which were his own inventions while others were updated versions of his sources.

His weaknesses

Livy's mistakes were due to

Many weaknesses

- the nature of his sources — some were dishonest, while others bent the facts to increase the fame of the Roman people or to enhance the honour and reputation of particular families;
- his lack of opportunity to verify his sources when there were conflicting accounts;
- his imaginative use of the sources;
- his intense patriotism, which led to an unsympathetic attitude towards the Carthaginians in the Second Punic War.

Failed to verify sources

Chronology He sometimes reports the same event twice, and confuses dates based on the four-year Olympiad of Polybius with those based on the Roman consular year.

Confusion with dates

Geography and topography He did not travel, so made many serious geographical mistakes in his accounts of the campaigns in Spain and

Little geographical knowledge

Africa; his account of Hannibal's crossing of the Alps is full of geographical inconsistencies.

Military ignorance

Ignorance of military matters He was ignorant of battle tactics, weapons and military life.

Naivety regarding power politics

Lack of political experience He idealised the part played by the senate and its leaders at the expense of the reputation of popular commanders. Ignorance of power politics made him unaware of the part played by family alliances in dominating particular factions and in controlling elections.

His strengths

What can be learned from Livy? He is a valuable authority on

- the role of individuals in political and military events;
- descriptions of meetings of the senate and assemblies in Rome;
- senatorial administration and the appointments of magistrates;
- military and population figures, Italian colonies, state income, taxation, names of allies, emergency measures such as loans and patriotic sacrifices, war plunder and indemnities.

Plutarch (c.AD 46–120)

Plutarch was born in Chaeronea in Greece; he spent most of his life there although he travelled widely, knew Athens well, and spent some time teaching and lecturing in Rome.

Biographies of famous Romans

Plutarch's *Lives* provide the reader with details of the careers of many great men and an understanding of the life and customs of the ancient world. Those which throw light on this period are *Fabius Maximus*, *Marcellus* and *Cato the Elder*.

Appian (c.AD 95–165)

Appian was a Greek from Alexandria who after gaining Roman citizenship moved to Rome, where he practised law. He wrote the history of Rome in twenty-four books of which only eleven have survived complete. Appian used an ethnographic approach to his history (the characteristics and customs of racial groups).

Appian's chief interest was war

The most relevant parts for this period are books VII and VIII, which cover the Punic Wars. Since Appian was predominantly interested in wars, his material on the conditions and institutions of the republic is unreliable.

Archaeological, numismatic and epigraphic evidence

Great variety of material remains

There is abundant archaeological evidence for this period, such as remains of towns (Corinth and Carthage), sites of important battles (Lake Trasimene), weapons, reliefs depicting soldiers and ships of the period, and bronze or marble busts of outstanding personalities (Scipio Africanus, Claudius Marcellus).

Coins minted in Sicily, Carthage, Spain and Italy provide valuable evidence concerning some of the people (Hamilcar Barca, Hannibal, Masinissa) and events of this vital period of Rome's history.

Inscriptions on monuments, sarcophagi and coins, to name just a few, also complement the written sources.

Exercise

1 Which of the ancient writers mentioned would be the best to consult for information on the First Punic War? Explain why this is so.

2 Whose history of the Second Punic War is likely to be the more reliable? Give reasons for your answer.

3 To which ancient source would you refer for details of the family background, education and personality of leading individuals?

Carthage

Origin of the Carthaginians and their expansion in the western Mediterranean

A Phoenician colony in Africa

The city of Carthage, on the coast of North Africa, was one of a number of settlements in the western Mediterranean founded by the Phoenicians from Tyre some time in the ninth century BC. Originally the Phoenicians were not interested in making permanent settlements but set up entrepots (trading stations), where they exchanged and stored goods and maintained ships.

The site of Carthage

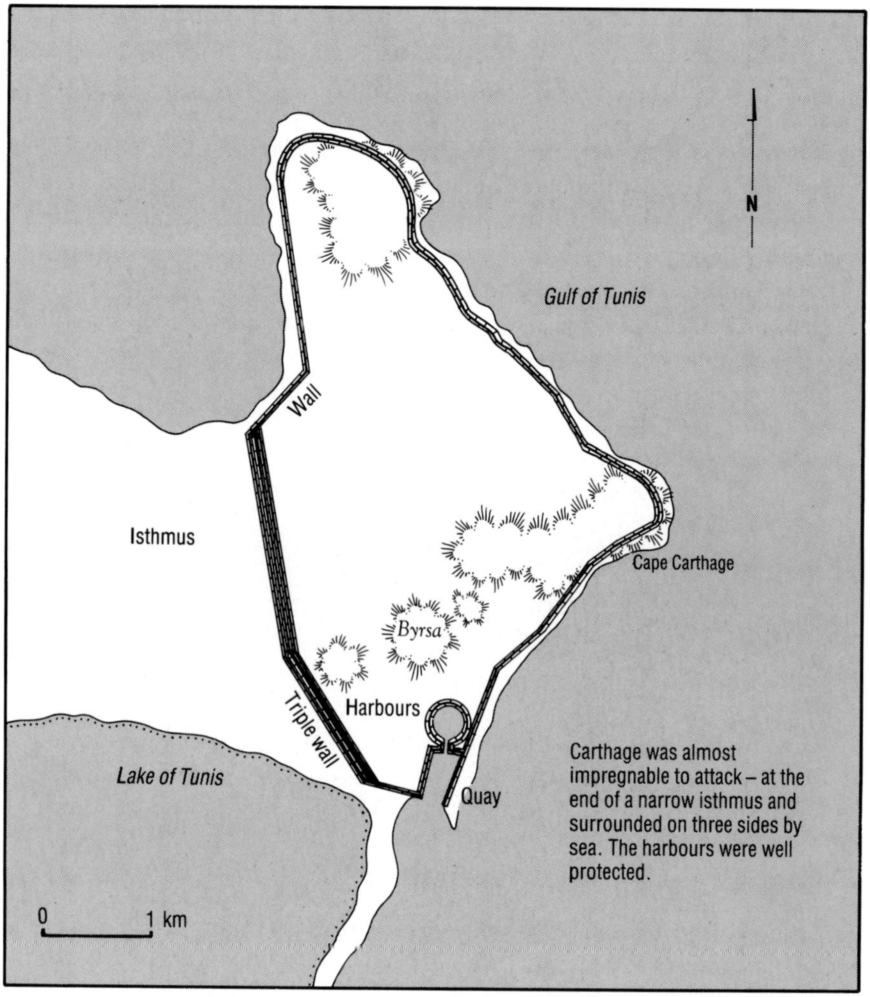

Ideal location and site

Carthage was established on the seaward side of a peninsula that provided both a sheltered harbour and protection from attack by land. There was room for expansion, and the Carthaginians developed the rich hinterland which was guarded by a frontier called the 'Phoenician Trenches'. The city's position, midway along the Mediterranean coast, was ideal for trade with both east and west.

Leader of Phoenician settlements in the west

When the great monarchies of the east conquered Phoenicia, its 'colonies' in the western Mediterranean (including Carthage) were left to their own devices, and with the appearance of the Greek colonists in the area in the eighth century, the Phoenician settlements saw that the best way to survive and maintain a monopoly of trade was to unite under the strongest city, Carthage.

Developed an empire

In the sixth century the Carthaginians embarked on a deliberate policy of expansion by which they conquered the Libyan hinterland (adding close to 25 000 square kilometres to their territory), extended their control in southern Spain and secured a foothold in Sardinia.

For three centuries (the sixth to the third) the Carthaginians had been involved in a series of conflicts with the Greeks of Sicily for control of the island. In 278 the Sicilian Greeks asked a Greek adventurer called Pyrrhus who was campaigning in southern Italy to help them against Carthage; Pyrrhus, however, failed to complete the task, and by 276 Carthage had extended her control in Sicily as far as the borders of Syracuse.

A stele inscribed with Punic symbols, found in Sicily

The Carthaginians were cautious people who avoided war where possible, preferring to solve their problems by peaceful means; however, they were prepared to defend their territory and to protect their trading interests if necessary.

Government

There were essentially four facets in the structure of Carthaginian government, although effective power was in the hands of a group of wealthy nobles who were successful merchants and landowners.

Nobles			*Citizens*
Two annually elected magistrates (*suffetes*)	Grand council of 300; inner committee of 30	Court of 104 judges	Assembly of citizens elected magistrates and councillors

Commerical interests determined Carthage's actions

The ruling oligarchs could hold more than one office (this was known as pluralism) and expected to make a profit out of office tenure; factions often ruled in their own interests, preventing a unified approach when dealing with an enemy. However, although the landlords and merchants, relieved of personal war service, became a ruling elite living in luxury, promoting their interests and exploiting their subjects, they did manage to hold together an empire for six hundred years.

Economic and military resources

The resources of the Carthaginian state can be summarised in the following way.

Revenue

- Carthage controlled a large and prosperous commercial empire.
- Trade included metals (such as tin and gold) from England, Africa and Spain—the last an inexhaustible source of wealth.
- Customs dues were imposed within the empire.
- Direct tribute was paid by subjects.
- Produce came from the great agricultural plantations of North Africa, cultivated by slaves.

Navy

- Carthage relied on a large fleet — manned by its own citizens, skilled in all areas of seamanship — to protect its commercial fleet and its spheres of influence.
- Only part of the navy was in operation at any one time; the remainder was in dry dock with the crews on call. This created problems during emergencies.
- The navy had never really been tested in battle.

Army

- Unlike the navy, the army was recruited from subject states and from mercenaries (soldiers who fought only for the money and were always a potential danger) as there were too few Carthaginian citizens to serve as soldiers.

Relief of a Phoenician ship

- Generals and officers were always Carthaginians who made a profession of war.
- Unsuccessful generals were often put to death (crucified); on the other hand, commanders who were too successful were regarded with suspicion.
- For their cavalry, extensive use was made of the outstanding horsemen from Numidia.
- Elephants were introduced as the 'tanks' of the army about 270.

Early contact with Rome

Diplomatic relations had existed between Rome and Carthage from the sixth century. Polybius had access to two early treaties which were inscribed on bronze tablets in the treasury of the aediles beside the Temple of Jupiter Capitolinus, and the text of which give evidence of (a) Carthage's determination to maintain her commercial monopoly in the western Mediterranean and (b) Rome's lack of interest in overseas trade.

Early treaties favoured Carthage

The earliest, dated in the first year of the republic (509–508), was a mutual recognition of interests. Carthage insisted on the proper regulation of trade and the exclusion of all foreign shipping from the coast of North Africa and the far west of the Mediterranean. Rome, on the other hand, was interested in the recognition of her rights in Latium.

A second treaty, signed in 348, was designed to take account of changed conditions. According to Polybius, the treaty 'runs more or less as follows':

> There shall be friendship on the following conditions between the Romans and their allies, and the Carthaginians, Tyrians, people of Utica and their respective allies. The Romans shall not make raids, or trade or found a city on the farther side of the Fair Promontory, Mastia or Tarsium [perhaps in Spain].
>
> If the Carthaginians capture any city in Latium which is not subject to Rome, they shall keep the goods and the men, but deliver up the city.
>
> If any Carthaginians take prisoner any of a people with whom the Romans have a treaty of peace in writing, but who are not subject to Rome, they shall not bring them into Roman harbours, but if one be brought in and a Roman claims him, he shall be set free. The Romans shall not do likewise.
>
> If a Roman obtains water and provisions from any place under Carthaginian rule, he shall not use these supplies to do harm to any member of a people with whom the Carthaginians enjoy peace and friendship. Neither shall a Carthaginian act in this way. If either party does so, the injured person shall not take private vengeance, and if he does so, his wrongdoing shall be a public offence.

> No Roman shall trade or found a city in Sardinia or in Africa, or remain in a Sardinian or African port longer than he needs to obtain provisions or to repair his ship. If he is driven there by a storm, he shall depart within five days.
>
> In the Carthaginian province of Sicily and at Carthage he may transact business and sell whatever is permitted to a citizen. A Carthaginian in Rome may do likewise.[8]

It is possible that the two republics may have formed a closer political agreement in about 306, when Rome was expanding to the south. In 279, when Pyrrhus was active in southern Italy, an emergency alliance was arranged between the two powers to ensure that neither would assist Pyrrhus against the other.

	The relative strengths and weaknesses of Carthage and Rome at the beginning of the First Punic War	
	Carthage	*Rome*
Strengths	Dominant power in western Mediterranean Large revenue from commercial empire, e.g. trade, tribute Large navy manned by citizens — experienced in seamanship Professional generals — Carthaginian citizens City of Carthage virtually impregnable — control of coastal strongholds in Sicily	Dominant power in Italy Unlimited source of manpower from citizens and allies Favourable policy towards allies secured their loyalty Citizen army patriotic — years of experience during wars in Italy Reasonably stable government
Weaknesses	Reliance on mercenary troops — could be unreliable Members of the empire were subjects, not allies — expected to pay tribute Ruling oligarchy made up of factions with vested interests	No real navy — reliance on Greek allies to provide ships for patrolling coastline Roman commanders were the consuls, elected for one year only

8 The First Punic War, 264–241

The importance of the First Punic War

POLYBIUS began his account of Rome's rise to power with the First Punic War because 'it was the first occasion on which the Romans crossed the sea with an army'[1] and because

> it would be difficult to find any contest which was longer in its duration, more intensively prepared for on both sides or more unremittingly pursued once begun, or one which involved more battles or more decisive changes of Fortune.[2]

Cordial relations before 264

It appears that prior to 264 relations between Rome and Carthage were reasonably cordial and there is no evidence that Rome was planning any expansion beyond Italy. However, it is likely that at some time her interests in southern Italy would have clashed with those of Carthage in Sicily, and some historians maintain that owing to the racial and cultural differences between the two nations, they would have come into conflict sooner or later.

In 264 there seemed no reason to expect war to break out between the two powers. Why then was there a drift into hostilities?

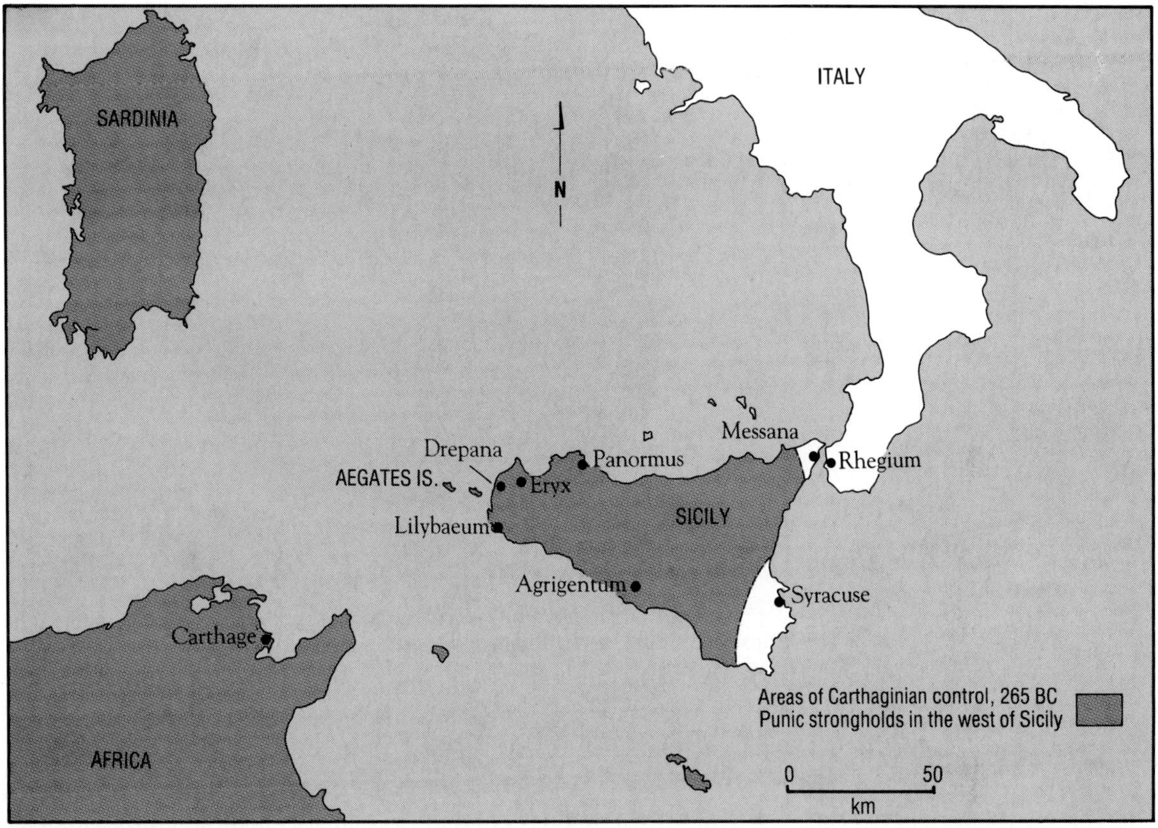

Sicily, at the time of the First Punic War, 264–241 BC

The cause

The conflict between the two powers began as a minor incident involving the town of Messana (formerly called Zancle) on the northeast tip of Sicily and the powerful city of Syracuse in the southeast of the island. The rest of the island was under Carthaginian influence.

Conflict centred on Sicily

The Mamertine Incident

The town of Messana, situated across the straits from the town of Rhegium in Italy, was strategically important. It had a good harbour and was in a position to control traffic passing through the straits.

Strategic location of Messana

About 288 a group of unemployed Campanian mercenaries, who had some years earlier served in the army of Agathocles, King of Syracuse, seized Messana. They were hard, ruthless men, who worshipped Mamers

Mamertines seized Messana

Bronze coin of an armed Mamertine warrior

(Mars) god of war, and adopted the name 'Mamertines' (sons of Mars). They plundered the surrounding districts, causing trouble for both the Syracusans and Carthaginians.

Hiero of Syracuse hoped to recover Messana

Across the straits a garrison of Campanians mutinied and seized the town of Rhegium in about 282, following the Mamertine example. This probably gave the Mamertines a feeling of security, but by 272, however, they faced a serious threat from Syracuse. Hiero, the commander-in-chief, was anxious to establish himself as the ruler of Syracuse and so carried out a campaign to recover Messana, which had once been part of the kingdom of Syracuse. Hiero defeated the Mamertines convincingly, and it appeared that Messana would be captured. However, although Syracuse and Carthage were on reasonably good terms at this stage, the Carthaginians did not want to see Messana fall into Syracusan hands. The commander of a Punic naval force patrolling the straits persuaded the Mamertines to allow a Carthaginian garrison into the town, and Hiero temporarily withdrew.

Carthage garrisoned Messana

Mamertines appealed for an alliance with Rome

The Mamertines, free for the moment, had time to consider what to do next. Perhaps because they were concerned that the Carthaginians might occupy Messana permanently, it was decided to seek an alliance with Rome which seemed 'to offer better long-term security than Carthage'.[3]

Rome's reaction to the Mamertines' appeal

Senate reluctant to form an alliance

The Roman senate hesitated to commit Rome to such an alliance for some of the following reasons:

- The Mamertines were undesirable allies.

Arguments against an alliance with Mamertines

- It would be inconsistent to help the Mamertines when they had just put to death a number of Campanians involved in similar activities at Rhegium, across the straits.
- An alliance with the Mamertines might involve Rome in a wider conflict with the Carthaginians, with whom their relationship was cordial at this stage.
- A war in Sicily might help popular leaders to rise to prominence, and the senate would want to avoid increasing the power of the people.

On the other hand:

- it was the usual Roman practice to protect weaker communities who asked for help;
- many Romans may have feared that if they did not ally themselves with Messana the Carthaginians might use the trouble there as an excuse to annex Messana themselves.

Some concern over possible Carthaginian motives

Since Carthage always sought trading monopolies, Rome's new Greek allies might find their Sicilian trade curtailed and Rome could not afford to neglect their interests. Polybius believed that the Carthaginians would prove to be

> the most vexacious and dangerous of neighbours, since they would encircle Italy on all sides and threaten every part of the country and this was a prospect which the Romans dreaded.[4]

Matter referred to people's assembly

Unable to reach a decision, the senate referred the question to the people in the assembly, who voted to accept the Mamertines into their alliance.

The Roman people way have agreed to the alliance for the following reasons:

- Many plebeians, since the passing of the lex Hortensia in 287, were seeking military glory to help them in a political career. They may have hoped that the alliance would lead to a wider conflict from which they could benefit.
- Some may have believed, as did Polybius, that Carthage was interested in extending its sphere of influence into southern Italy and so they needed to gain a secure outpost (Messana) for the safety of Italy—defensive imperialism. However, there is no evidence that Carthage was interested in such expansion at this stage.
- They may have wanted simply to keep Syracuse in check and did not realise that 'they were involving themselves in a situation out of which a major war might develop nor realise that they were going to come into collision with Carthage'.[5]

Romans crossed to Messana

In 264 the consul Appius Claudius Caudex, with a small force, was sent to Messana to announce the Roman acceptance of the Mamertines into their alliance. When the Mamertines learned of this they asked the Carthaginian garrison commander to leave the city, and the Punic

Carthaginians retired temporarily

general, having no legal right to be there, evacuated the citadel. (On account of his cautious behaviour and lack of initiative this Carthaginian commander was later crucified.)

Carthage and Syracuse joined forces

The acceptance of the Mamertines into the Roman alliance had the effect of forcing the Syracusans and Carthaginians to co-operate in order to prevent Messana falling into the hands of the Romans and threatening their interests in Sicily.

Declaration of war

Carthaginians and Hiero surrounded Messana

Before the main Roman force arrived in Messana, Hiero and the Carthaginians decided that the time 'had come for the barbarians who had occupied Messana to be driven out of Sicily once and for all'.[6] The Carthaginians took up a position north of Messana while Hiero camped to the south. A Carthaginian fleet anchored offshore.

This forced the Roman legions to make the crossing of the straits at night, and at some point the Roman consul sent a message to Hiero and the Carthaginian general to raise the siege of Messana, which was under Roman protection. As this request was refused, war was declared. Thus, it seems that a purely local incident and a misunderstanding of motives led to the outbreak of war.

Roman ultimatum refused

Bust of Hiero of Syracuse

The Romans acted quickly, attacking first Hiero's camp and then that of the Carthaginians. Hiero retreated to Syracuse while Hanno, the Carthaginian general, withdrew to garrison the cities under their control.

As far as Rome and Carthage were concerned, the war could have ended at this point. The Romans had shown that they were prepared to protect the Mamertines, and Carthage had no reason to destroy them. However, Rome had to force Syracuse to recognise her alliance with the Mamertines, and in 264–263 the Roman army beseiged the great city.

Romans besieged Syracuse

Peace treaty between Hiero and the Romans

Hiero, believing that he would gain little support from the Carthaginians, asked for peace with Rome. The Romans granted him a treaty of friendship and alliance by which he retained his control of Syracuse; he became a loyal ally of Rome and remained so until his death.

Subsequently certain of Carthage's subject cities in eastern Sicily defected to Rome, and the Romans now took on a new role — as defenders of the Sicilian Greeks against the 'barbarians'.

The First Punic War was the classic example of an incident that got out of hand.

Agrigentum and its significance

Carthage mustered forces at Agrigentum

The Carthaginians were not prepared to see the revolts of their subjects extended, and began recruiting mercenaries in Liguria, Gaul and Spain. A huge force of approximately 50 000 men was sent to the Carthaginian base at Agrigentum.

Roman siege of Agrigentum

The Romans seized the initiative, broke off their other engagements and concentrated all their forces about 1½ kilometres from Agrigentum, confining the Carthaginians within its walls. After a siege of approximately five months, Agrigentum was taken by the Romans, although their losses were considerable. The city was systematically sacked and the inhabitants sold into slavery, an act of barbarity that disgusted many of the Sicilian coastal towns which in consequence went over to Carthage. It would have been far better for the future of Rome in Sicily had the Romans shown some leniency.

Carthaginians determined to continue the war

The fall of Agrigentum did not destroy Carthage: it had a huge army billeted in the west of the island, its fleet patrolled the coastline, and raids against the Italian coast were initiated from Sardinia. Carthage did not intend to see its remaining possessions whittled away by the Romans, who showed no signs of leaving Sicily but stayed at Messana throughout the winter.

Polybius describes how Rome's objectives in Sicily were now greatly extended.

Roman war objectives changed

> When the news of the events of Agrigentum was received in Rome, the Senate was beside itself with rejoicing. In this exultant mood their aspirations soared far above their original designs, and they were no longer content with having rescued the Mamertines nor with what they had gained in the fighting. They now cherished the hope that they could drive the Carthaginians out of Sicily altogether, and that once this goal was attained their own power would be greatly increased; accordingly they made this their prime objective and gave their whole attention to plans designed to bring it about.[7]

The Romans realised that they could never achieve this while the Carthaginians controlled the sea, and when they saw

Romans realised importance of sea power

> that while the Italian coasts were repeatedly raided and devastated, those of Africa suffered no damage, they were filled with a desire to take to the sea and meet the Carthaginians there.[8]

The importance of sea power

Roman decision to build a fleet

The Romans had shown little interest in the sea, since they were predominantly an agricultural people. They had established a small coast-guard force in 311, but still tended to rely on ships provided by their allies in southern Italy. Their limited naval forces were totally inadequate for challenging Carthage, and it was 'because they saw that the war was dragging on that they first applied themselves to building ships'.[9]

Although Carthage did not ever spend any more on its navy than was necessary for efficiency, it had 100 ships in commission, most of which were quinquiremes ('fivers'). Rome could possibly have built a fleet as large as the Carthaginians' but would have found it virtually impossible to equal the proficiency of their rowers, the skill of their tactics and their experience in navigation. Yet—according to Polybius—the Roman decision to take to the sea illustrated 'the extraordinary spirit and audacity of the Romans'.[10]

Rome's great determination

They used a captured Carthaginian quinquireme as the model for most ships of their fleet, which they built from scratch in sixty days—a remarkable achievement. Approximately 33 000 rowers were recruited from Rome's allies and, according to Polybius, trained on benches on land before spending a short time in rowing practice at sea. To counteract their lack of skill in manoeuvring and ramming, they devised a method of converting sea battles into land battles. A moveable boarding bridge, with an iron spike attached beneath its outer end, rotated on a mast and was dropped on the deck of an enemy ship when it came within reach. The spike held the enemy fast alongside while the Roman soldiers boarded; this device was known as the *corvus* ('crow' or 'raven'), because of its iron

Methods used to train rowers

A working model of a corvus

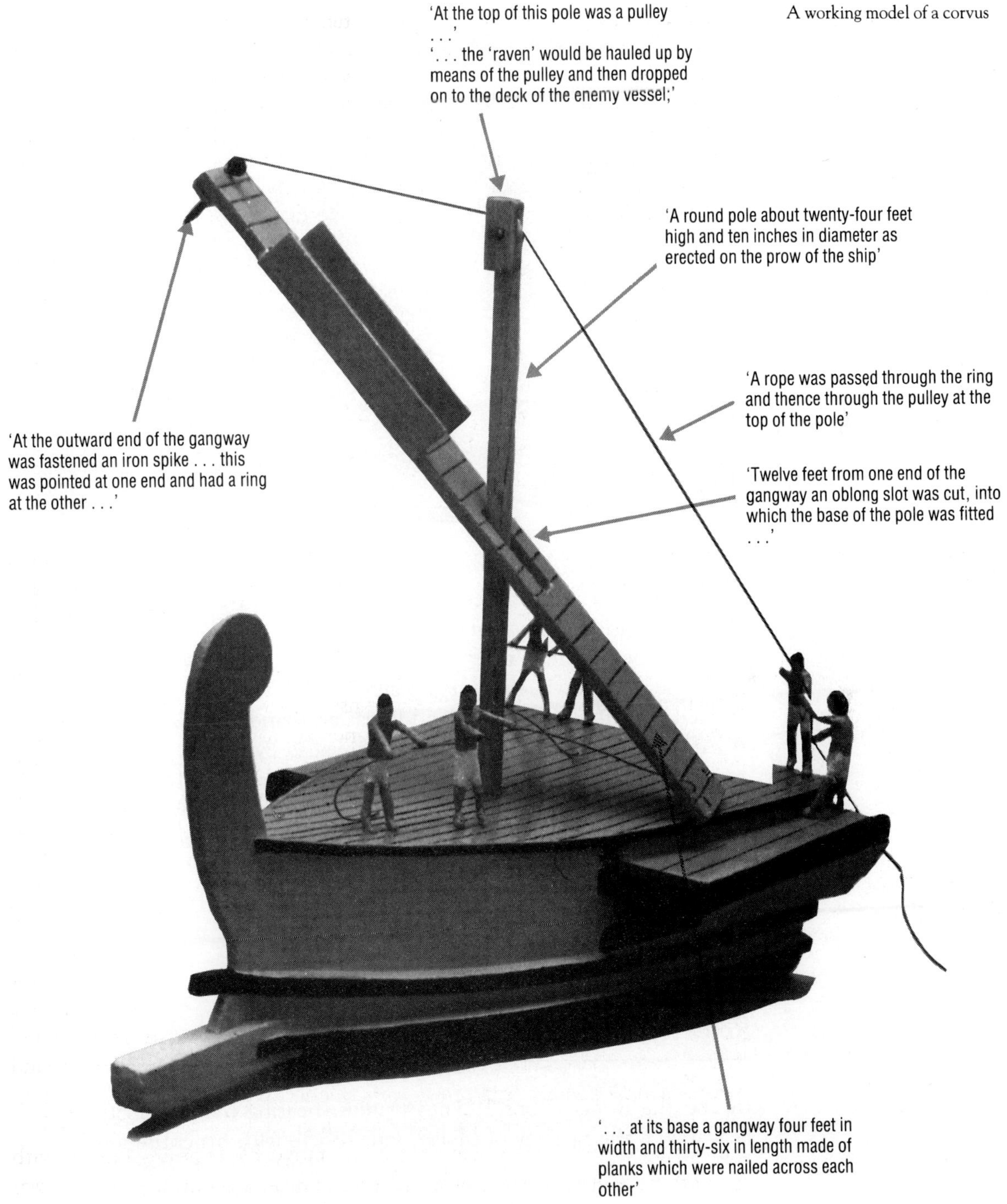
'At the top of this pole was a pulley . . .'
'. . . the 'raven' would be hauled up by means of the pulley and then dropped on to the deck of the enemy vessel;'
'A round pole about twenty-four feet high and ten inches in diameter as erected on the prow of the ship'
'A rope was passed through the ring and thence through the pulley at the top of the pole'
'At the outward end of the gangway was fastened an iron spike . . . this was pointed at one end and had a ring at the other . . .'
'Twelve feet from one end of the gangway an oblong slot was cut, into which the base of the pole was fitted . . .'
'. . . at its base a gangway four feet in width and thirty-six in length made of planks which were nailed across each other'

A relief from the Temple of Praeneste, showing a Roman warship with fully armed crew

Difficulties to be faced by Rome

'beak'. However, on many occasions during this war the Romans were to discover that building a fleet was one thing, but that making competent sailors out of farmers was another.

Naval power would decide the war

It became apparent early in hostilities that whichever side had naval supremacy would win the war, because

- Sicily was the focal point, and it was an island;
- Africa and Carthage could only be invaded by sea;
- the coastline of Italy could be raided by sea from Sicily and Sardinia;
- the Carthaginian strongholds along the southern and western coastlines could be effectively blockaded, being supplied with provisions and fresh recruits only by sea;
- the opposing armies in Sicily were relatively evenly matched.

The map summary on page 113 illustrates the naval reverses and successes experienced by both sides.

Rome's first naval victory — Mylae, 260

In 260 the Roman consul Gaius Duilius, hearing that the Carthaginian fleet was in the vicinity of Mylae, sailed there with his entire force.

> No sooner had the Carthaginians sighted him than they eagerly put to sea with their fleet of one hundred and thirty sail; their spirits were high, for at this stage they felt nothing but contempt for the inexperience of the Romans. They steered straight for the enemy and thought they could risk an attack without

keeping any formation, as though they were seizing a prize which was already theirs for the taking.[11]

As they neared the enemy and saw the 'ravens' [corvi] hoisted aloft in the bows of several ships, the Carthaginians did not know what to make of these devices, which were completely strange to them. However, as they still felt an utter contempt for their opponents, the leading ships attacked without hesitation. Then, as they came into collision, the Carthaginians found that their vessels were invariably held fast by the 'ravens', and the Roman troops swarmed aboard them by means of the gangways and fought them hand-to-hand on deck.[12]

Carthaginians taken by surprise

The Carthaginians were confused by these tactics and lost thirty ships, including the flagship. The remaining vessels, depending on their speed, circled around the Roman fleet hoping to ram them from the other side, but discovered that the corvi could be swung around to meet an attack from any direction. The Carthaginians fled, after losing fifty ships in all.

Failed to cope with the corvi

Significance

The Romans, 'contrary to all expectations, had made good their hopes to win control of the sea, and their determination to continue the war was redoubled'.[13]

Roman confidence enhanced

According to Caven in his book *The Punic Wars*, 'A centuries-old command of the western Mediterranean and a myth of invincibility were destroyed in a single day'.[14]

The invasion of Africa 256–255

The Romans now aimed 'to shift the whole scene of operations to that country [Africa]: they wished to make the Carthaginians feel that the war no longer threatened Sicily, but their own territory'.[15] By striking at Carthage directly, the Romans hoped to dislodge the Carthaginians from Sicily.

Roman decision to attack Africa

The Carthaginians were concerned: they knew that they were vulnerable, since the African population in the territory around Carthage would offer the Romans no resistance if they succeeded in getting ashore. They therefore prepared to fight exclusively at sea.

The Romans, under the command of the consuls M. Atilius Regulus and L. Manlius Vulso, had to prepare for action at sea as well as for a landing in enemy territory; however, they had some serious concerns about the seaborne invasion they were preparing (330 warships and 140 000 men). They realised that they had a considerable area of open sea to cross and that the Carthaginians' ships were the faster, so they devised

The wedge-shaped naval formation adopted by the Romans at the battle of Ecnomus, as described by Polybius

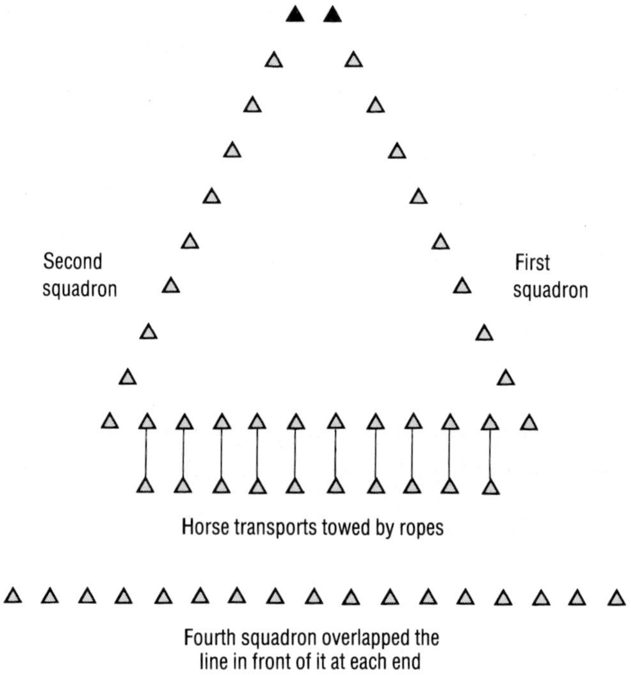

a fleet formation (wedge-shaped, with a strong, compact base and an open point) which was 'effective and easy to maintain but difficult to break up'.[16]

The Battle of Cape Ecnomus

The naval battle off Cape Ecnomus on the southwest coast of Sicily, vividly described by Polybius (I:27–8), could have been the decisive battle of the war, since the Carthaginians withdrew their fleet from Sicilian waters to protect the approaches to Carthage. The Romans, however, made a successful landing further down the African coast near the town of Aspis, which they captured and garrisoned. Regulus remained in Africa with 15 000 troops and 500 cavalry, while the other consul returned home with the fleet.

Romans' initial success in Africa

The countryside around Carthage was plundered and many towns were sacked. A Carthaginian force, sent out to prevent Regulus' marauding expeditions, was defeated. The Romans then captured the city of Tunis, which provided a useful base for operations against the capital and its surroundings.

Critical situation for Carthaginians

The Carthaginians were in a critical situation, having been defeated both at sea and on land. According to Polybius the defeat was due not to lack of bravery on the part of the troops but to the incompetence of their commanders and the fact that the Numidians chose this time to attack as well. 'The inhabitants fled in terror to the capital, where they found nothing but famine and despair, the first being caused by overcrowding and the second by the prospect of a siege'.[17]

The war could have ended at this stage. Regulus invited the Carthaginians to negotiate, because he was concerned that the consul who succeeded him would get the credit and glory for his success. The Carthaginians sent an embassy of their leading citizens to negotiate, but were shocked by the severity of the terms imposed by Regulus. 'They behaved with manly dignity and resolved that they would suffer any extremity and try every resource rather than submit to a settlement which was so ignoble and so unworthy of their past achievements.'[18]

Severe terms imposed by Regulus

Regulus was no diplomat; the Carthaginians decided to fight on, recruiting a large number of troops from Greece among whom was Xanthippus, a Lacedaemonian. He had been brought up under Spartan discipline and saw immediately that the problem facing the Carthaginians was the inexperience of their generals; he was given the task of reorganising and training the Carthaginians in the Spartan manner. He changed their strategy, and in the next confrontation they soundly defeated the Romans and captured Regulus. The Roman survivors made their way to Aspis, where they waited to be rescued.

Carthaginians' decision to fight on

Spartan mercenary leads Carthaginians to victory

Rome's fleets destroyed

A relief expedition of more than 350 ships set sail in 255 to pick up the survivors waiting in Libya, successfully routing a Carthaginian fleet off the Hermaean promontory in Africa and taking the Roman survivors on board. However, after safely crossing the straits to Sicily, the Roman fleet was destroyed in a storm in which only eighty of their ships were saved. The rest were smashed against the rocky headlands and were broken to pieces. 'There is no record in all history of a greater catastrophe having taken place at sea on any one occasion.'[19] Yet the terrible disaster cannot be blamed on bad luck but rather on the ships' commanders, who had been warned repeatedly not to sail along that part of the coastline—especially at that time.

Roman relief fleet destroyed in a storm

Inexperience of Roman commanders

This Roman setback had the following effects:

On the Romans	**On the Carthaginians**
Demonstrating their determination to continue war at all costs, in three months they built yet another fleet (of 220 ships) and sent them to Sicily to besiege the Punic stronghold of Panormus.	Confidently they began to make plans for further operations. More troops and 140 elephants were sent to Sicily, and 200 ships were sent to the stronghold at Lilybaeum.

Carthaginian confidence increased; determination of Romans

Determination of Romans

Yet despite the determination of the Romans and the increased confidence of the Carthaginians, both sides suffered serious reverses soon after.

Second Roman fleet destroyed in storm

The Romans, after their capture of Panormus, made another attempt to raid the coast of Africa. This had no important result but in returning to Italy this fleet also was destroyed by a storm, with the loss of 150 ships and the accompanying transports.

Carthaginians soundly defeated at Panormus

The Carthaginian army, in an attempt to retake Panormus, was cleverly defeated by the Romans (led by their consul for 251, L. Caecilius Metellus) outside the walls of the city; the Carthaginian elephants had been frightened into stampeding among their own soldiers, creating great confusion. This was a severe blow to Carthage, which was now left without an army in Sicily that could challenge Rome in the field. It was now apparent to the Carthaginians that the Romans would make an attempt to take the heavily fortified city of Lilybaeum.

The Roman siege of Lilybaeum and the Battle of Drepana, 250–248

From Polybius' account of the Roman siege of Lilybaeum and the attempted attack on Drepana, it is obvious how important naval power was in any blockade and defence of the Carthaginian strongholds of coastal Sicily.

The importance of sea power in siege of Lilybaeum

Lilybaeum was not only the headquarters of the Carthaginians but was ideally suited as a base for an attack on Africa, being only about 180 kilometres from Carthage. It was heavily fortified with walls and, according to Diodorus, a moat about 27½ metres wide and 18 metres deep. On the seaward side it was protected by a series of lagoons 'demanding great skill and much practice to find the channel through these into the harbour'.[20]

Difficulties faced by both sides

Two Roman consular armies and a fleet of 200 ships (recently brought up to full force) laid siege to Lilybaeum. The Carthaginians 'concentrated their whole effort upon the relief of the city, and prepared to accept any risk or sacrifice to this end'.[21] While the Roman army with alarming speed reduced the walls and towers, the Carthaginians built a new wall behind the demolished one and continually mined the Romans' siege-works. The Roman fleet, anchored off the harbour, was unable to prevent Carthaginian ships from entering the port with reinforcements 10 000 strong. The Carthaginian fleet

> hoisted all sail and running before the wind made straight for the mouth of the harbour, with the men drawn up on the decks armed and ready for action. The Romans were taken unawares by the sudden appearance of the fleet, and they

> were also afraid of being swept by the force of the wind into their enemies' harbour in the midst of a hostile force, and so they made no attempt to bar the entry of the relieving fleet; instead they remained standing out at sea; still half lost in amazement at the audacity of the Carthaginians'.[22]

The arrival of the reinforcements allowed the Carthaginian commander of Lilybaeum to leave the protection of the city and attack the Romans and their siege-works outside the walls. The Romans came very close to losing everything, but held on.

Carthaginian naval experience displayed

Not only was the Roman navy unable to prevent the Carthaginian fleet from leaving the harbour at night, but the naval commanders were also outwitted by the blockade runner, Hannibal 'the Rhodian'. On many occasions he sailed in and out of the harbour in full view of the Romans, but was eventually captured. 'He kept the Carthaginian authorities continually informed of the most urgent news and raised the spirits of the defenders, while at the same time his audacity served to dishearten the Romans.'[23]

Further Roman problems during siege

The Romans suffered just as greatly as the Carthaginians during the siege: their siege engines were set on fire and destroyed; disease and famine further weakened them, and their fleet in the harbour was partly immobilised since many of the rowers and seamen were used on shore as light infantry and sappers. They were able to continue the siege only because of the loyal support of Hiero of Syracuse, who sent them provisions, and the recruitment in 249 of 10 000 fresh rowers for the fleet.

Loyalty of Hiero

One of the Roman consuls for 249 was P. Claudius Pulcher. His instructions were to take part of the fleet besieging Lilybaeum and with the newly recruited rowers to strike at the Carthaginian naval base of Drepana. He hoped to take it by surprise, but the Carthaginians were forewarned and had already taken the initiative. Not only was the Roman fleet forced into shallow water with little room to manoeuvre, but the rowers were inexperienced and the ships were without their corvi, which had been removed the previous season because the ships were intended to mount a blockade, not engage in a naval battle. Also, the Romans thought that the previous sea disasters may have been caused by the fact that the corvi tended to make the ships top-heavy, yet without them the soldiers on board were not effective.

Roman naval defeat at Drepana

The Carthaginians captured ninety-three ships, many of which had run ashore, while approximately twenty-four were sunk. Claudius escaped to Lilybaeum with thirty ships, but was disgraced because of his poor judgment.

Roman tenacity

> Yet despite this catastrophe, such was the determination of the Romans to win the war that they in no way slackened the effort that was now required, to put in hand all the necessary measures to continue the campaign.[24]

A surprise attack on the Roman fleet at Lilybaeum by the Carthaginians from Drepana (setting fire to some and towing others away) caused great consternation in the Roman camp, and the Carthaginians within the city used this diversion to attack the Romans from the landward side.

Large Roman supply convoy sent to Lilybaeum

The Carthaginian fleet then left Lilybaeum in order to intercept a huge convoy of supply ships — and accompanying warships — which had sailed from Ostia to reinforce the blockade and provision the troops at Lilybaeum. It was led by L. Iunius Paullus, who decided to take the southerly route to Lilybaeum to avoid the Carthaginian fleet. The southern coast of Sicily was rugged, with few areas on which to beach ships, and the Carthaginians, informed of the Romans' route, decided to waylay them along this inhospitable coast. Encountering part of the Roman convoy, they did considerable damage to it and then went in search of the main body of ships, which had been keeping close in to the shore. As bad weather was indicated the Carthaginians made for the open sea, but the remaining Roman vessels under Paullus were pounded to pieces on the rocky cliffs during the gale. Polybius describes the destruction as 'being so complete that not even one of the wrecks could be salvaged'.[25] The Romans, 'although they had met with various partial misfortunes before, had never suffered such a total disaster'.[26]

Roman convoy totally destroyed

The significance of these events

Romans abandoned shipbuilding program

- The Romans, having suffered a series of naval disasters since 256, gave up any attempt to carry on further operations at sea. The senate could not ask the allies to supply any more crews at this stage, and the economy could not stand another large shipbuilding program.

Roman determination to continue war

- 'Yet, although both the Roman people and their army at Lilybaeum were deeply disheartened by these reverses, they persisted in their determination to carry on the siege; the government continued without hesitation to send supplies by land, and the troops kept up as close a blockade as they could.'[27]
- The Romans garrisoned and fortified Mount Eryx to the east of Drepana, but without naval forces they could not take the Carthaginian stronghold there or at Lilybaeum.

Failure of Carthaginians to follow up recent successes

- The Carthaginians did not follow up their successes by reinforcing their fleet or their army in Sicily, believing that the Romans would cut their losses and withdraw. They continually failed to understand the tenacity of the Roman people and their leaders.

Hamilcar Barca in Sicily, 247–241

In 247 Hamilcar Barca was appointed Carthaginian admiral and his first action against the Romans was to raid the coast of southern Italy, threatening the naval allies of Rome. The Romans responded by establishing a number of military colonies at strategic points around the coast.

Fortified strategic heights

Since the Roman forces on Mount Eryx threatened Drepana, Hamilcar took his army by sea and fortified a high position behind the city of Panormus, Heircte; from there he was able to harass the Roman forces besieging Drepana and Lilybaeum. For three years he carried out guerilla raids on the surrounding Roman-held territory in addition to continuing his naval attacks on the Italian coastline.

Military operations in Sicily: a stalemate

Hamilcar's fortified position was so strong that the Romans were unable to take it; neither could they starve him out, since they were without a fleet. On the other hand, Hamilcar had insufficient troops to risk a pitched battle with the Roman infantry.

It was a stalemate.

In an attempt to break the stalemate, Hamilcar and his men abandoned Heircte and sailed to Drepana, where they destroyed the Roman garrison on Mount Eryx, cutting off the Roman forces on the summit from their camp below. They made guerilla raids on a number of consular armies, but the situation remained the same.

Hamilcar's guerilla raids

The war had lasted for twenty-three years, and both sides were exhausted. They had used

Hardships suffered by both sides

> every resource, every strategem and every effort . . . endured every kind of hardship and resorted both to pitched battles and every other variety of fighting. In the end the contest was left drawn . . . before either side could overcome the other — and the contest in this theatre lasted another two years — the war was decided by other means and in another place.[28]

A new Roman fleet

For the preceding five years the Romans had not bothered to rebuild their fleet; they had hoped to win the war with their army, but owing to the outstanding leadership of Hamilcar they were failing to achieve any decisive results on land. They decided that the only way to bring the conflict to an end was to build another fleet, 'and for a third time to risk their fortunes upon the sea' in a life-and-death struggle.[29]

Private subscriptions from Romans

Although the Roman treasury was empty, the government was able to persuade the wealthiest citizens to raise the money for the construction of a fleet of 200 warships; the leading families each undertook to build and

Opposite: Rome's naval offensive during the First Punic War

outfit a quinquireme. These loans would be repaid if Rome was able to bring the war to a successful conclusion.

The final battle, 241

Romans blockade Punic strongholds

In 242 the consul C. Lutatius Catulus commanded a fleet of 200 lighter and faster quinquiremes and approximately 700 transports. The Roman fleet blockaded both Drepana and Lilybaeum.

Hamilcar had previously sent his navy back to Carthage, possibly on orders from the government which may have wished to reduce the cost of the war or perhaps to use the crews for wars in Africa. The Carthaginians were unprepared for the Roman naval attacks on their Sicilian strongholds, and faced great difficulty in building new ships and recruiting and training the necessary crews.

Romans intercept Punic supply convoy

In 241, the Carthaginian fleet, weighed down with supplies for the troops at Eryx, was confronted by the Romans off the Aegates Islands. The latter had removed all their heavy equipment, including the corvi, and the ships were more manoeuvrable. The Carthaginian ships were heavy and their crews, who had been enlisted specifically for this emergency, were untrained. The Romans sank fifty enemy ships and captured seventy with their full complement. According to Polybius, the Roman victory was decisive.

The Carthaginians, like the good businessmen they were, decided to cut their losses. They gave Hamilcar complete power to handle the situation, and Hamilcar was not only the greatest general of the war in genius and daring, he also had the good sense to yield to the inevitable.

Hamilcar negotiated peace

While he had even a reasonable chance of success he tried everything, but he knew when he was beaten, and in order to save the men under his command he negotiated peace.

Peace

Refer to Polybius, I: 62–3, III: 27.

These were the final terms of the peace signed between Hamilcar and Lutatius Catulus in 241:

- The Carthaginians were to evacuate Sicily and all the islands between Sicily and Italy.
- Neither side was to attack the allies of the other.

Carthaginian losses

- The Carthaginians were to pay an indemnity of 3200 talents over a period of ten years.

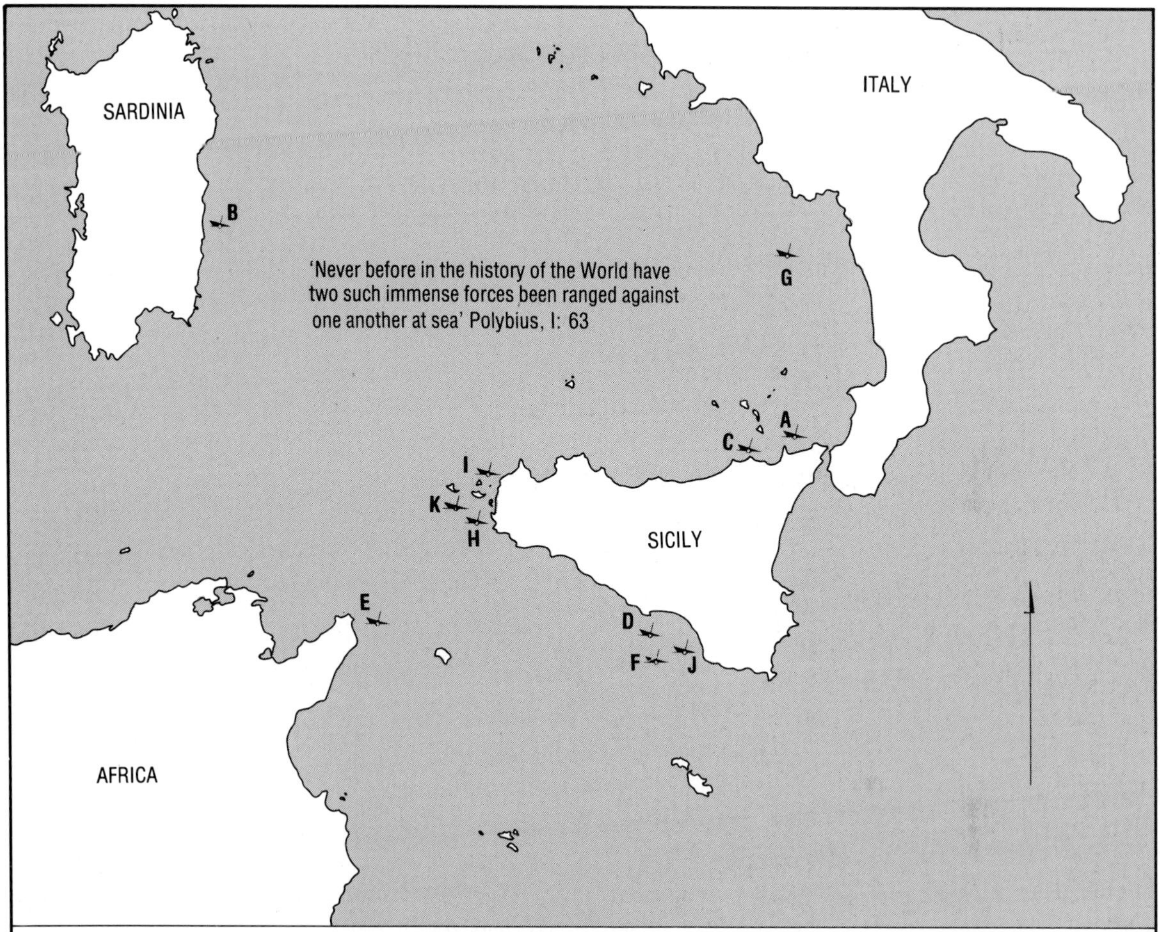

A First Roman victory at Mylae, 260, under C. Duilius. Use of the corvus destroyed the myth of Carthaginian invincibility at sea. Carthage lost fifty ships.
B Roman victory at Sulci in Sardinia, 258. The Romans tricked the Punic commander and had advantage in numbers.
C Roman victory off Tyndaris, 257, under Atilius Regulus. Carthage lost eighteen ships.
D Roman victory at Cape Economus, 256. Roman seaborne invasion to Africa encountered Carthaginians off the south coast of Sicily. Carthage was decisively defeated – the corvus proved its worth. Thirty Punic ships were sunk, sixty-four captured.
E Roman victory off the Hermaean Promontory, 255. A Roman fleet sent to pick up survivors of the African campaign routed the Carthaginian fleet, capturing 114 ships.
F Roman disaster in a storm, 255, off the south coast of Sicily. Fleet returning with survivors from African campaign destroyed.
G Roman disaster, 255. A fleet returning from an unsuccessful raid on the African coast was destroyed in a storm off Cape Palinurus – lost 150 ships.
H Roman setback at Lilybaeum, 250. A fleet of 200 ships blockaded Lilybaeum by sea, but suffered serious losses as crews were used ashore. There were not enough crews to man the ships.
I Roman defeat at Drepana, 249. Consul P. Claudius Pulcher was defeated by Carthaginian tactical skill, with a loss of ninety-three Roman ships.
J Roman disaster off the south coast of Sicily, 249. Two fleets (800 transports and 120 warships) bringing supplies to the Romans besieging Lilybaeum were caught in a storm while anchored off the coast between Camarina and Phintias and were completely destroyed.
K Roman victory – final battle of the war, 241. A new fleet under C. Lutatius Catulus destroyed the enemy fleet which was laden down with supplies. Fifty Carthaginian ships were sunk and seventy captured.

- No Punic ships were to sail in Italian waters and no mercenaries were to be recruited in Italy.
- Carthage was to return all prisoners of war without ransom.

Reasons for the Roman victory

Importance of the corvus

1 The Romans showed extraordinary spirit and audacity in developing a navy, despite their lack of technical skill. The use of the corvus compensated for their inexperience in naval strategy and took the Carthaginians by surprise.

Determination to continue war at all costs

2 The senatorial government of Rome was determined not to surrender or to slacken its efforts, despite many disastrous setbacks. It maintained two consular armies in the field even in the years following disasters, and continued to rebuild its navy and find new crews.

Sacrifice of Roman people

3 The Roman citizens were prepared to sacrifice life and livelihood. They were patriotic and disciplined, and had experienced long years of warfare in Italy.

Loyalty of Italian allies and Hiero

4 Rome's confederacy in Italy was one of allies, not subjects, and the Italian allies remained loyal, providing an inexhaustible supply of manpower for both the army and the navy.

5 Hiero of Syracuse continued to support the Roman war effort in Sicily by providing them with food and supplies.

6 The Romans knew how to learn from their mistakes and to regain the initiative.

Carthaginians lacked initiative and underestimated tenacity of Romans

7 The Carthaginian navy, which had dominated the Mediterranean for hundreds of years, had never really been put to the test. It did not change strategy to deal with the corvus, it did not maintain full strength, and it did not follow up victories.

8 Carthage underestimated Roman resources and determination to continue the war.

Carthaginian trade suffered

9 The war interfered with Carthage's vital trade, leaving it short of money with which to prosecute a long war and maintain full naval strength. It also caused difficulties in paying the Numidian and Libyan mercenaries, who mutinied in the following few years.

Selfishness of Carthaginian nobility

10 The ruling aristocracy in Carthage preferred to follow a continental empire policy and so did not wish to withdraw troops from Africa to re-establish control in Sicily. Despite Hamilcar's daring leadership, the government failed to support his requests for reinforcements. The war in Sicily was not fought with any aggression.

Effects of the war

- Sicily became Rome's first overseas territory, and ways had to be found to administer the province. The cities and towns of Sicily were not incorporated into the Roman confederacy as were the Italian allies, but continued to pay tribute as they had done previously. Some Sicilian towns were exempt from taxation, but the majority of people paid a tithe on their agricultural produce. In 227 two more praetorships were created to administer the provinces of Sicily and Sardinia (the latter being occupied in 238).

Rome's first province

- The conquest of Sicily opened the way for Rome to become an imperial power by drawing the Romans into the wider field of Mediterranean politics.

First step towards an empire

- Many Romans were now aware of the great profits to be made in overseas territories.
- The Romans came into closer contact with the Hellenic culture of the Greek cities of Sicily, particularly Syracuse.
- Sicily became one of Rome's principal suppliers of grain, especially in time of war.

9 Background to the Second Punic War, 239–218

Roman seizure of Sardinia and Corsica

The Barcids in Spain

Hannibal and Saguntum

The causes of the war — from the sources

Controversy over responsibility for second Punic War

BETWEEN 239 and 218 a number of developments occurred involving Carthage and Rome. These events formed the background to the Second Punic War, but the facts concerning them have been interpreted by both ancient and modern historians in a number of different ways. The causes of and responsibility for the war have therefore always been controversial topics, but contributing events include:

Background events

1 the Roman seizure of Sardinia and Corsica
2 Carthaginian expansion in Spain under the Barcids
3 Hannibal's attack on Saguntum

The Mercenary War in Africa and the Roman seizure of Sardinia and Corsica

Carthage unable to pay mercenaries after first war

After the First Punic War the Carthaginian mercenaries were shipped back to Africa, where they expected to be paid and the many promises made to them to be honoured. However, the Carthaginian treasury was low in funds after twenty-three years of war and the payment of the first instalment of the indemnity was due; instead of paying off the mercenaries immediately, the government put them in quarters at an inland town until it should have funds to pay them. These hardened soldiers thought that the Carthaginian government was trying to avoid its obligations, and they took an oath to wage war on Carthage.

They marched on Tunis led by the extremists, Mathos and Spendius, and a war of great savagery was waged until 237. The brutality on both sides can be seen from the following excerpts from Polybius.

Brutality of the war with mercenaries

> [The mutineers] passed a resolution and engaged each other to torture and kill every Carthaginian and send back to the capital, with his hands cut off, every ally of Carthage.[1]

> [Hamilcar] continued to put to the sword those of the enemy who were conquered in the field, while those brought to him as captive prisoners he threw to the elephants to be trampled to death . . .[2]

This was a life-and-death struggle for the Carthaginians, and was finally brought to an end when Hamilcar and Hanno captured Tunis, re-establishing Carthage's control over its African territories.

Romans maintained friendly attitude

During this time (240–237), Rome followed a friendly and even helpful policy towards Carthage by forbidding Romans to trade with the mercenary rebels, sending supplies to Carthage and releasing any Carthaginian prisoners still being held in Italy, and when the Carthaginian garrison in Sardinia invited Rome to take over the island, the Romans refused.

Roman attitude changed in 237

Romans seize Sardinia

In 237, however, at the end of the Mercenary War, the Romans appeared to change their attitude towards Carthage. When that same mutinous garrison—which had meanwhile been driven out of Sardinia by the native inhabitants—once more asked for Rome's intervention, the Roman consul Ti. Sempronius Gracchus seized control of the island.

Great bitterness in Carthage

The Carthaginians, protesting that the Roman action was against the terms of the peace treaty of 241, prepared to reoccupy Sardinia. The Romans regarded this as an act of war and issued an ultimatum which the Carthaginians had no choice but to accept, giving up all further control of Sardinia. 'They deeply resented the injustice, but were powerless to prevent it.'[3] As a further humiliation to the Carthaginians, the Romans 'unjustly extorted' another indemnity of 1200 talents.[4]

Possible Roman motives

The reason for the seizure of Sardinia was probably based on the belief that under the Carthaginians it would pose a permanent threat to Etruria, Latium and Campania. Rome therefore regarded control of the island as essential for the security of Italy, especially if Carthage tried to engage in further war against Rome in order to recover Sicily.

Effect on Carthage's economy

The unjustifiable seizure of Sardinia was deeply resented by the ruling class, and in particular by Hamilcar Barca. The loss of Sardinia so soon after Sicily had a serious effect on the revenues of Carthage and also seriously jeopardised not only the personal profits of the commercial class, but the jobs of craftsmen, labourers and seamen. It was therefore necessary in the national interest for Carthage to embark on a program of overseas expansion.

Carthaginian expansion in Spain

Motives for expansion

Carthage had to find an alternative source of revenue and—perhaps realising that a future conflict with Rome was possible—a way in which to be adequately prepared. If they were to compete on an equal footing with Rome in the future they needed a limitless supply of manpower, resources to pay for that manpower and activities to keep it efficiently employed. The ruling clique in Carthage may also have wished to remove the ambitious and successful Hamilcar Barca, who had become a popular military hero. They may have feared that without a military campaign to occupy him, he might upset domestic politics.

Hamilcar was given a command to re-establish Carthaginian control over Spain and to conquer new territory. He sailed for Gades (Cadiz) in 237 with a force of Libyans, and a large number of elephants; also with him were his son-in-law Hasdrubal and his nine-year-old son Hannibal.

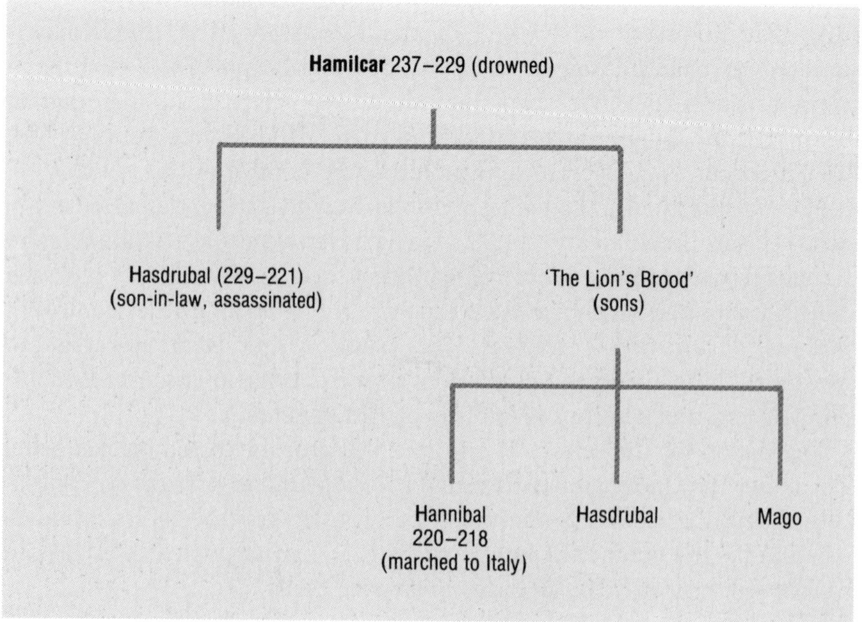

The family of Hamilcar Barca

A coin issued at New Carthage — probably a portrait of Hamilcar Barca

Coins issued at Gades with possible portraits of Hannibal's brothers, Hasdrubal Barca and Mago

Two possible likenesses of Hannibal on coins issued at New Carthage in 220 BC

Since Polybius believed that 'the success of the Carthaginian enterprise in Spain' was one of the causes of the Second Punic War,[5] it is essential to look closely at the motives behind the Barcids' actions in Spain.

- Why was Hamilcar building up Carthaginian power and resources in Spain?
- Why did Hasdrubal sign the Ebro River Treaty with the Romans?
- Why did Hannibal attack Saguntum when he knew it was under the protection of Rome?

Hamilcar Barca

Spanish resources

Spain was rich in timber, minerals (particularly silver), and excellent fighting men, and Hamilcar spent nine years restoring the national prosperity of Carthage by his conquests in the south and east of that country.

Polybius on Hamilcar's motives in Spain

According to Polybius, however, Hamilcar was angered at the outcome of the First Punic War and at subsequent Roman actions, and intended 'using these resources to prepare for a war against Rome';[6] many modern historians also support this view. Gavin de Beer says that Hamilcar developed Spain as a base and a source of manpower and supplies for an invasion of Italy, while Caven also suggests that Hamilcar wanted a base far enough away from Carthage and Rome to prevent either from knowing what was going on.

Dio Cassius on Hamilcar in Spain

On the other hand, Dio Cassius maintains that the Romans sent envoys to investigate what Hamilcar was doing in Spain. They were satisfied by his explanation 'that he was obliged to fight against the Spaniards in order that the money which was still owing to the Romans on the part of the Carthaginians might be paid; for it was impossible to obtain it from any other source.'[7] There is some doubt about Dio's story, however, since Polybius says that Rome had nothing to do with Spain until 226.

War of revenge unsubstantiated by evidence

Even if Dio is incorrect about the Roman embassy (in 331), there is no reliable evidence to suggest that Hamilcar was planning a war of revenge on Rome, as Polybius says. He may have believed that war with Rome was a future possibility, and he may even have hoped that it would occur while he was in command, but he made no obvious move against Rome at this time and the Romans did not appear overly suspicious of Carthage. The other question to consider is this: could Hamilcar have started a war without the Carthaginian government's authority? The question of Hamilcar's motives in expanding Carthaginian power in Spain has been discussed endlessly by ancient and modern historians.

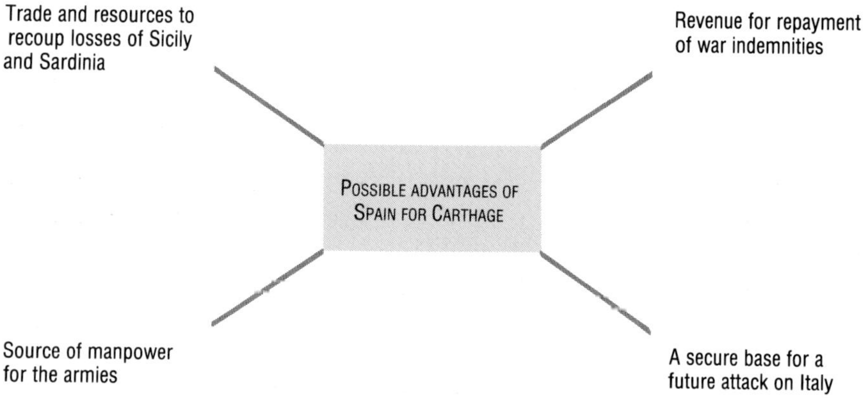
Trade and resources to recoup losses of Sicily and Sardinia
Revenue for repayment of war indemnities
POSSIBLE ADVANTAGES OF SPAIN FOR CARTHAGE
Source of manpower for the armies
A secure base for a future attack on Italy

In 229 Hamilcar was drowned, and command of the Carthaginian forces in Spain passed to his son-in-law, Hasdrubal.

Hasdrubal

Hasdrubal a diplomat

Hasdrubal was a statesman who preferred to use diplomacy rather than arms to carry on the activities begun by Hamilcar. Polybius says that Hasdrubal

> had done much to strengthen the Carthaginian presence in the country, not so much by military achievements as by the friendly relations he had established with the local chieftains.[8]

He founded the city of New Carthage, which served as the Carthaginian headquarters in Spain, and his handling of the province was wise and effective.

In 226 the Romans

> suddenly perceived that Hasdrubal had gone far towards creating a larger and more formidable empire than Carthage had possessed before, and they determined to take a hand in the affairs of Spain.[9]

Roman concern over Punic expansion

They sent an embassy to Spain to conclude an agreement with Hasdrubal.

Why were the Romans so anxious to come to an agreement with Hasdrubal?

Roman reasons for wanting an agreement

- Rome was allied to the city of Massilia, which had two colonies (Rhode and Emporion) on the east coast of Spain, north of the Ebro River. Massilia may have appealed to Rome to protect its interests by imposing some limits on Carthaginian expansion.
- Rome was facing serious threats from the Celts of the Po valley and did not want to be concerned about Carthaginian expansion in Spain.

The Ebro River Treaty, 226

Not a reciprocal agreement

Under this treaty Hasdrubal agreed that 'the Carthaginians shall not cross the Ebro in arms'.[10] However, since this does not appear to have been a reciprocal agreement, why did Hasdrubal sign it?

Hasdrubal's reasons for signing

- It did not impose any serious restrictions on Hasdrubal at this stage, since in 226 Carthage's sphere of influence was nowhere near the Ebro River.
- Although it did not formally recognise the region south of the Ebro as a Carthaginian possession, it did indicate that the Romans had no intention, for the moment, of opposing Hasdrubal's activities there.
- Hasdrubal's position in southern Spain was not so secure that he could have withstood determined Roman interference, and he did not want another episode similar to that in Sardinia.
- He preferred to maintain good relations with Rome, and so agreed to a 'gentle' treaty and a satisfactory boundary. He willingly gave them what they wanted.

The significance of the treaty can be thus summarised:

- Between 225 and 221 Rome was occupied not only with the Celts (Gauls) of Cisalpine Gaul (Po valley), but with the Illyrians across the Adriatic Sea. The Illyrians had been practising piracy on a large scale in the Adriatic and Ionian Seas, causing suffering to the southern Italian cities. The Ebro River Treaty gave the Romans time to deal with these immediate problems rather than concern themselves over Carthaginian expansion.

Treaty did not prevent Roman friendship with Saguntum

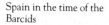

- The treaty did not prevent either Rome or Carthage from having peaceful or friendly relations with other cities on either side of the river. In fact it is believed that at about this time Rome had a pact of friendship with the city of Saguntum, which lay 140 kilometres south of the river. The exact period of Rome's friendship with Saguntum is not known (it could have been as early as 231), but as long as the Romans did not use this friendship to interfere militarily in Carthage's affairs in Spain (and this may have been implied by the Ebro River Treaty), the Carthaginians would raise no objections.
- It was evidence of Hasdrubal's intentions to stay on good relations with Rome.

Hasdrubal was assassinated in 221 by a Celt who had a personal grudge against him.

Spain in the time of the Barcids

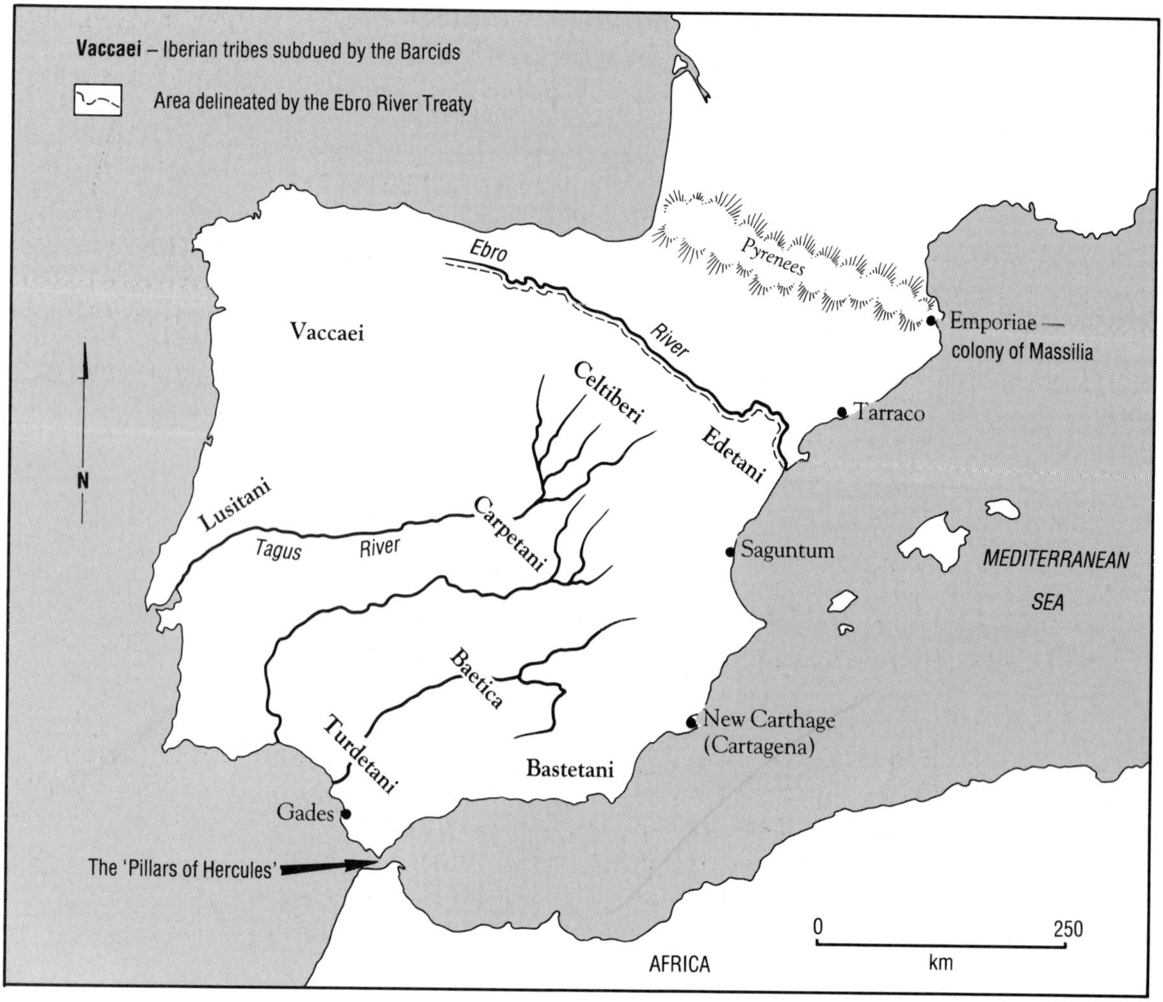

Hannibal

There was no question about Hasdrubal's successor in Spain. According to Livy,

Unanimous choice of Hannibal by army

> The military vote was in favour of the young Hannibal, who was at once escorted to headquarters, where he was unanimously and enthusiastically acclaimed, and there is little doubt that the army's choice was supported by the mass of the people in Carthage.[11]

Hannibal, the eldest of the 'lion's brood', was only twenty-five when he took over the command of the Carthaginian forces in Spain. He was chosen 'not withstanding his youth, because he had already shown that he combined a daring spirit with a quick and fertile brain'.[12]

Beliefs that Hannibal wanted war with Rome

Caven, however, says that the command now passed into the hands of 'an impetuous young man in whom the principal motivating force was a burning desire for military glory', and because of this 'the possibility of war between Carthage and Rome hardened into virtual certainty'.[13]

Polybius and Livy go even further.

> As soon as he took up his command it became clear from the measures which he put in hand that his purpose was to declare war on Rome.[14]

> From the very first day of his command Hannibal acted as if he had definite instructions to take Italy as his sphere of operations and to make war on Rome. Speed was of the essence of his plan.[15]

Not supported by early actions

This belief does not seem to be supported by Hannibal's actions immediately after assuming command. He continued and consolidated the work started by his father and his brother-in-law.

- He laid siege to the capital of the Olcades.
- He carried out operations against the Vaccaei and then moved south to the Tagus River.
- He defeated the Carpetani and eventually brought most of the Iberian peninsula south of the Ebro River under Carthaginian control — except for the city of Saguntum, which was under Roman protection. Hannibal, Polybius said, 'was at great pains to keep his hands off this city for as long as he could'.[16]

Hannibal's long-term objectives unknown

However, since Hannibal did not leave any written accounts we do not really know what his long-term plans were. It is possible that he could have been getting Spain in order before embarking on a war with Rome. Polybius assumes that Hannibal was simply biding his time, waiting for the right moment to start the war, but he gives no proof that war was Hannibal's intention.

Hannibal and Saguntum

The immediate cause of the Second Punic War is generally thought to be Hannibal's attack on Saguntum in 219; Polybius, however, prefers to regard this as the first incident in the war rather than a cause.

The town of Saguntum, 140 kilometres south of the Ebro River, was part of that area of Spain in which, the Romans had indicated, Carthage was free to operate militarily (the Ebro River Treaty, 226). However, the Saguntines had 'some years before Hannibal's time placed themselves under the protection of Rome',[17] probably at the urging of Massilia. It is also possible that the Romans may have seen this as an opportunity to have a 'listening post' in Spain in order to be aware of Carthage's activities. However, they did not pay much attention to the continuing reports coming from Saguntum about the 'growing power of the Carthaginians in Spain'.[18]

Roman pact of friendship with Saguntum

Controversy over Rome's alliance with Saguntum

Many historians both ancient and modern have argued interminably over the question of the legality of this Rome–Saguntum alliance, on the basis of when it was signed—before or after the Ebro River Treaty. If after, did it break the spirit of the treaty? If before, was it automatically annulled by the treaty? In fact the argument does not matter because, as mentioned earlier, the treaty did not deny either side peaceful relations on the other side of the Ebro River. No ancient source indicates that the Carthaginians considered their rights in Spain to have been infringed by Rome's friendship with Saguntum.

Romans' misuse of friendship

Nevertheless, the Carthaginians believed that the Romans misused the friendship when, having been asked to arbitrate in the domestic politics of the city, they put some pro-Carthaginian Saguntines to death and established a pro-Roman party firmly in power. Hannibal regarded this as unjustifiable interference in Spanish affairs, and when the Saguntines (under the protection of Rome) began to quarrel with some of the nearby subjects of Carthage (possibly the Torbeletae), he must have issued an ultimatum to Saguntum to cease its aggressive behaviour. The Romans, who had previously disregarded the alarmist appeals of the Saguntines, sent a delegation in 220–219 to Hannibal, who was wintering in New Carthage.

Hannibal warned by Romans

The Roman envoys warned Hannibal to leave Saguntum alone and, in accordance with Hasdrubal's treaty, not to cross the Ebro River. It is possible that in 220 the Romans thought that Saguntum was north of the river, but it is more likely that it was an extra warning to remind Hannibal that they considered the treaty of 226 to be still in force.

Following this, Hannibal

Instructions from Carthage

> sent home to Carthage asking for instructions on how he was to act, in view of the fact that the Saguntines were relying on their alliance with Rome to commit wrongs against some of the peoples who were subjects of Carthage.[19]

According to Appian, the Carthaginian government gave him the authority to take whatever action he saw fit.

Hannibal blockades Saguntum

Hannibal made immediate preparations to attack Saguntum, and after an eight-months siege the town fell to the Carthaginians. The Romans appear to have done nothing to help the Saguntines during this time.

Why did Hannibal attack Saguntum knowing that it would mean war with Rome?

The anti-Carthaginian view

Those historians who believe that the Second Punic War was a war of revenge on the part of the Barcid family will put forward the argument that this was the moment for which Hannibal had been waiting.

> By picking up this quarrel, Hannibal hoped to force a declaration of war from Rome and throw the onus of the ensuing conflict upon his enemy. If the declaration came from Rome, Carthage would be forced to support him, which it certainly would not do if he invaded Italy on his own initiative, for the Punic aristocracy which lived by trade strongly favoured peace.[20]

According to Polybius Hannibal, by attacking Saguntum,

> would be able to advance in safety towards Italy without leaving an enemy in the rear. Besides these advantages he reckoned that the capture of the city would provide him with ample funds and supplies for his proposed expedition [and the booty would] earn him the goodwill of the Carthaginians at home.[21]

The pro-Hannibal view

For those who hold the view that there is not enough evidence to suggest that Hannibal was planning a war of revenge, it is easy to understand his attitude to the Roman envoys' demands.

He may have been suspicious of Rome's friendship with Saguntum for some time because he would not have forgotten that the First Punic War had started when Messana, which Carthage hoped to gain, had been taken under Roman protection. In 238, Rome's annexation of Sardinia and Corsica had also resulted from Rome's having taken them under her protection.

According to Lazenby,

> if Hannibal had backed down over Saguntum, there can be little doubt that Roman interference in Spain would not have stopped there — it would have been open to any Spanish community which felt itself threatened by Carthage, to seek Roman protection, and this would have spelt the beginning of the end of Carthaginian domination.[22]

Hannibal's preparations after Saguntum

Hannibal's anticipation of war

Saguntum was taken in December 219; Hannibal then dismissed his troops to winter quarters, with orders to report back in the early spring of 218. Even though the Romans had not yet declared war, he wasted no time in making preparations to put into effect his plan to fight a war in Italy if it eventuated. The reasons for his decision to (a) fight in Italy and (b) take the long and difficult route over the Alps are summarised below.

To fight in Italy	*To cross the Alps*
• If he made his stand in Spain he would not be able to protect Africa as well, since the Romans had the resources to fight on a number of different fronts and the persistence to wear the Carthaginians down. By attacking Italy he hoped that he might forestall or prevent an invasion of Spain and Africa. • He hoped to undermine Rome's military and political power by breaking up her confederation of allies. Over half of Rome's manpower was drawn from the allies, and Hannibal's plan was to induce them to desert or remain neutral.	• In 218 Rome was superior in naval power and he could not take the risk of an invasion fleet being intercepted at sea by a larger Roman fleet. • The Gauls of the Po valley, whom the Romans had been fighting for some time, were unsettled and resentful that Rome had established a number of colonies in the area to subdue them. Hannibal hoped to exploit this unrest and gain their support. • It would take Rome by surprise.

His plans had to be carried out in great secrecy, and involved

1 sending envoys to the tribes along his intended route—and particularly to the Gauls of Cisalpine Gaul—to collect military and political information (these envoys had a vast distance to cover—more than 6000 kilometres);

2 taking measures for the security of Spain and Africa.

Information to be collected by envoys				
The nature of the country through which he would pass and obstacles to be overcome	The reception he would get from various Gallic tribes along the way — would they give him men and supplies?	The logistics of feeding his troops and animals during the crossing of the Alps and the Pyrenees	The numbers, fighting capacities and tactics of local populations	Resistance of Gauls to Roman pressure

THE DEFENCE OF SPAIN AND AFRICA

'[Hannibal] adopted the effectual and far-sighted measure of posting soldiers from Spain to Africa and vice versa, helping in this way to cement the loyalty of each province towards the other.'

To Africa
13 850 Spanish infantry
1 200 cavalry
870 slingers from the Balearic Islands
4 000 to garrison Carthage

To Spain
11 580 African foot
2 550 cavalry
500 slingers from the Balearic Islands
21 elephants
50 quinquiremes

'Next he gave instructions to his brother Hasdrubal as how to carry on the administration of Spain, and what preparations to make for the defence of the province against the Romans if he should happen to be absent.'[23]

Rome's reaction to Saguntum

No help from Rome

It appears that the Romans did not expect Carthage to react to their warning about Saguntum so decisively, and it seems that the implied threat which accompanied the warning was meant more as a bluff. The Romans made no attempt to send help to the Saguntines during the eight months of the siege.

Roman ambassadors sent to Carthage

According to Polybius, when news of the fall of Saguntum reached Rome, the senate did not debate whether to go to war or not but appointed ambassadors and sent them immediately to Carthage to demand Hannibal's surrender. It seems highly unlikely, however, that there was no discussion at this point, because the delegation to Carthage did not leave Rome until some time after the fall of Saguntum. The Aemilian and Fabian factions within the senate reacted differently to the crisis: the Aemilian group wanted to vindicate Roman honour by going to war immediately, while the Fabian faction was more cautious, not wanting to become involved in a situation in which the security of Italy was not directly threatened.

Factional differences in the senate

Yet it was probably obvious to everyone that war was inevitable; when the Roman envoys arrived in Carthage they presented the Carthaginian government with the alternatives of surrendering Hannibal or accepting war, but the Carthaginians had already decided to risk war when they supported Hannibal's attack on Saguntum. The Roman envoy, Fabius,

Roman ultimatum

> pointed to the bosom of his toga and declared to the senate [Carthaginian] that in its folds he carried both peace and war, and that he would let fall from it whichever they instructed him to leave. The Carthaginian Suffete answered that he should bring out whichever he thought best, and when the envoy replied that it would be war, many of the Senators shouted at once, 'We accept it!'[24]

Interpreting the causes

Importance of the Second Punic War

The importance of the Second Punic War for the future of the Roman republic cannot be overstated. It launched Rome along the path of imperial conquest and set in motion forces which not only changed the nature of the republic but which, some would say, were responsible for the decline of that republic.

The events leading to the outbreak of war have been outlined, but some of the questions debated by both ancient and modern historians are these:

Possible causes for the outbreak of war

- Was the war inevitable, considering that Rome had now become a world power?
- Was it a war of revenge on the part of the Barcids? Did Hannibal deliberately provoke the war?
- Were the Romans to blame for repeating the bullying tactics that had gained them Sardinia? Did they hope to loosen Carthage's hold on Spain?
- Was the outbreak of war due to each one's inaccurate suspicions of the other — a tragic misunderstanding?

Polybius chief source

Since Polybius is the most important source for this period, most historians have based their arguments on the material included in his history. However, even if Polybius' facts are accurate, his interpretation of those facts need not necessarily be correct. Modern historians using the same facts have been able to develop convincing arguments to support their own particular views. *It is important, therefore, to understand the difference between a fact and an opinion.*

- A *fact* is a statement which has been accepted as true using all available evidence; it is something that has happened, or really was — for example, 'Hannibal attacked Saguntum'.

Facts and opinions

- An *opinion* is a personal view or attitude which is based on limited evidence; there is some evidence supporting it but much is still uncertain — for example, 'Hannibal attacked Saguntum to deliberately provoke a war with Rome', or 'Hannibal had no choice but to attack Saguntum, since the Romans would have used their protection of the town to undermine Carthage's position in Spain'.

It is important, when reading a variety of sources, to be aware of facts and opinions.

The following extracts illustrate the different opinions held by ancient and modern historians about the causes of the Second Punic War.

Polybius

> The first cause, we must recognise, was the anger of Hamilcar, surnamed Barca, the father of Hannibal. His spirit had never been broken by the outcome of the war in Sicily . . . and so he never weakened in his resolve, but waited for his chance to strike again.[25]

Polybius cites three causes

> He passed this hatred for Rome onto his son Hannibal who at nine years of age swore an oath 'that he would never become a friend to the Romans'.[26]

> [The Carthaginians] were further provoked by the affair of Sardinia and the increased indemnity which they had finally been compelled to pay.[27]

> For Hamilcar, the anger provoked by this latest injustice — which all his compatriots now shared — was added to the grievance he already nursed from the past.[28]

> The success of the Carthaginian enterprise in Spain must be regarded as the third cause of the war, for it was the assurance which they drew from this increase in their strength which enabled them to embark on the war with confidence.[29]

Polybius believed that the attack on Saguntum was not a cause of the war but rather the first action of the war, but in attempting to explain the responsibility of the war he later suggests

> If we regard the destruction of Saguntum as the cause of the Hannibalic War, then the Carthaginians must be judged to have been in the wrong in starting the conflict . . . If, on the other hand, we identify the cause of the war with the Roman annexation of Sardinia and with the added indemnity which they extorted from the Carthaginians, then we must certainly agree that the latter had every good reason to embark on the war.[30]

Livy

Livy follows the Roman tradition that the war was caused by the revenge of the house of Barca. This view was meant to play down the extent to which Rome's seizure of Sardinia drove Carthage to war.

> Hamilcar was a proud man and the loss of Sicily and Sardinia was a cruel blow to his pride; he remembered, moreover . . . that Rome, taking advantage of

Livy believed it was a war of revenge

internal troubles in Africa, had tricked Carthage into the loss of Sardinia, and then had added insult to injury by the imposition of a tribute. All this rankled in his mind, and his conduct of affairs during the five years of the war in Africa . . . and subsequently during the nine years he spent in extending Carthaginian influence in Spain, made it clear enough that his ultimate object was an enterprise of far greater moment, and if he had lived the invasion of Italy would have taken place under Hamilcar's leadership, instead of, as actually happened, under Hannibal's.[31]

Modern viewpoints

A variety of modern views

By 221 BC the Romans were victorious against the Gauls . . . after enjoying the benefits of the Ebro River Treaty, Rome began to use Saguntum as a tool to undermine Punic power south of the river and to loosen the hold of Carthage on the enviable wealth of Spain. This does not mean that the Senate contemplated an immediate war. For with the threat of the Gallic invasion removed, it probably reckoned on repeating, if need be, in Spain the successful bullying by which Rome had secured Sardinia.[32]

Their [the Romans] action at Saguntum was little more than a gentle hint to Hannibal to walk warily, but it was enough to fan his smouldering wrath to a blaze. He determined to make it a test case to see whether Rome would abide by her treaty; but he must have foreseen the result. The Barcids had remained true to a defensive policy till they feared, whether with good cause or not, a repetition of the Sardinian question. And this time the Carthaginians refused to bow their necks . . . Hannibal had clearly precipitated a crisis in which the Romans were technically at fault, but from which they could not retreat without loss of prestige. He was thus immediately responsible for a war which neither Rome nor Carthage had deliberately engineered. Yet it is improbable that the two Republics could have lived at peace indefinitely.[33]

The picture that emerges is of a Carthage that had not been planning for war against Rome but was jumpy and suspicious of Roman attitudes to her; and of a Rome which had no plans—at any stage before 218—for war against Carthage but was not quite sure what Carthaginian aims were in building an empire in Spain and felt obliged to punish Carthage after the friend of Rome was captured and destroyed despite a firm warning to leave it alone . . . The two great powers were unable to shed their suspicions of each other, and this led them to put the wrong interpretations on each other's attitude: each was prone to believe the other was more hostile and more disposed to fight than was actually the case.[34]

The Second Punic War, 218–201

10

Hannibal's march to Italy

Hannibal's forces

HANNIBAL left New Carthage some time in June 218 with approximately 90 000 infantry, 12 000 cavalry and thirty-seven elephants. The Romans, unaware of his intentions, obviously intended fighting the war far from Italy, since they assigned Publius Cornelius Scipio to Spain and Tiberius Sempronius Longus to Africa.

Roman war aims

Although the ancient sources give no indication of Roman war aims, Caven suggests that they were probably limited to destroying Hannibal's army in Spain, restoring Saguntum and perhaps setting up a Roman protectorate over central Spain. They probably also included landing an army in Africa to encourage Carthage's subjects to revolt. Even when Hannibal crossed the Ebro River, the Romans still did not seem to have realised that his ultimate objective was Italy.

Punic forces reduced before leaving Spain

Between the Ebro River and the Pyrenees Hannibal lost a considerable number of his troops in heavy fighting; he also left 11 000 with Hanno to control the passes over the Pyrenees, and dismissed approximately 7000 unreliable men. (According to Polybius he left Spain with 50 000 infantry, 9000 cavalry and thirty-seven elephants.)

Hannibal avoided Romans at the Rhone River

When Scipio heard that Hannibal was marching from the Pyrenees towards the Rhone River he believed that he would have time to land his army at the Rhone mouth, allow his men to recover from their sea journey, and then deploy his troops to await Hannibal. He underestimated the speed of Hannibal's march, and only when he missed Hannibal at the Rhone crossing by three days was he aware that the Carthaginian was headed for Italy.

Vital Roman decision

It was then that Scipio made a decision which was to affect the whole course and the eventual outcome of the war. Rather than return to Italy with his whole army, he sent his brother (Cn. Cornelius Scipio, who was accompanying him) on to Spain with the major force, while he returned with only a small escort to take charge of the legions that had been operating against the Gauls in northern Italy. There he would wait for Hannibal and hope to keep him occupied until the return of Sempronius and his legions from Sicily.

Three points demonstrate the significance of this action:

1 'Scipio's decision illustrates the flexibility in strategy which Roman seapower and resources made possible.'[1]

Spain was to become a crucial area of the war

2 By keeping Hasdrubal and the Carthaginians busy in Spain, the Romans would make sure that part of the Carthaginian war effort was directed there rather than to Hannibal in Italy.

3 Roman troops in Spain would make it difficult for reinforcements to get through to Hannibal.

The crossing of the Alps

Consult Polybius and Livy for details of Hannibal's incredible march to Italy. His exact route across the Alps is uncertain, and this has caused much argument, but whichever way he went it was one of the greatest achievements in the history of warfare.

Two possible routes for Hannibal's march across the Alps

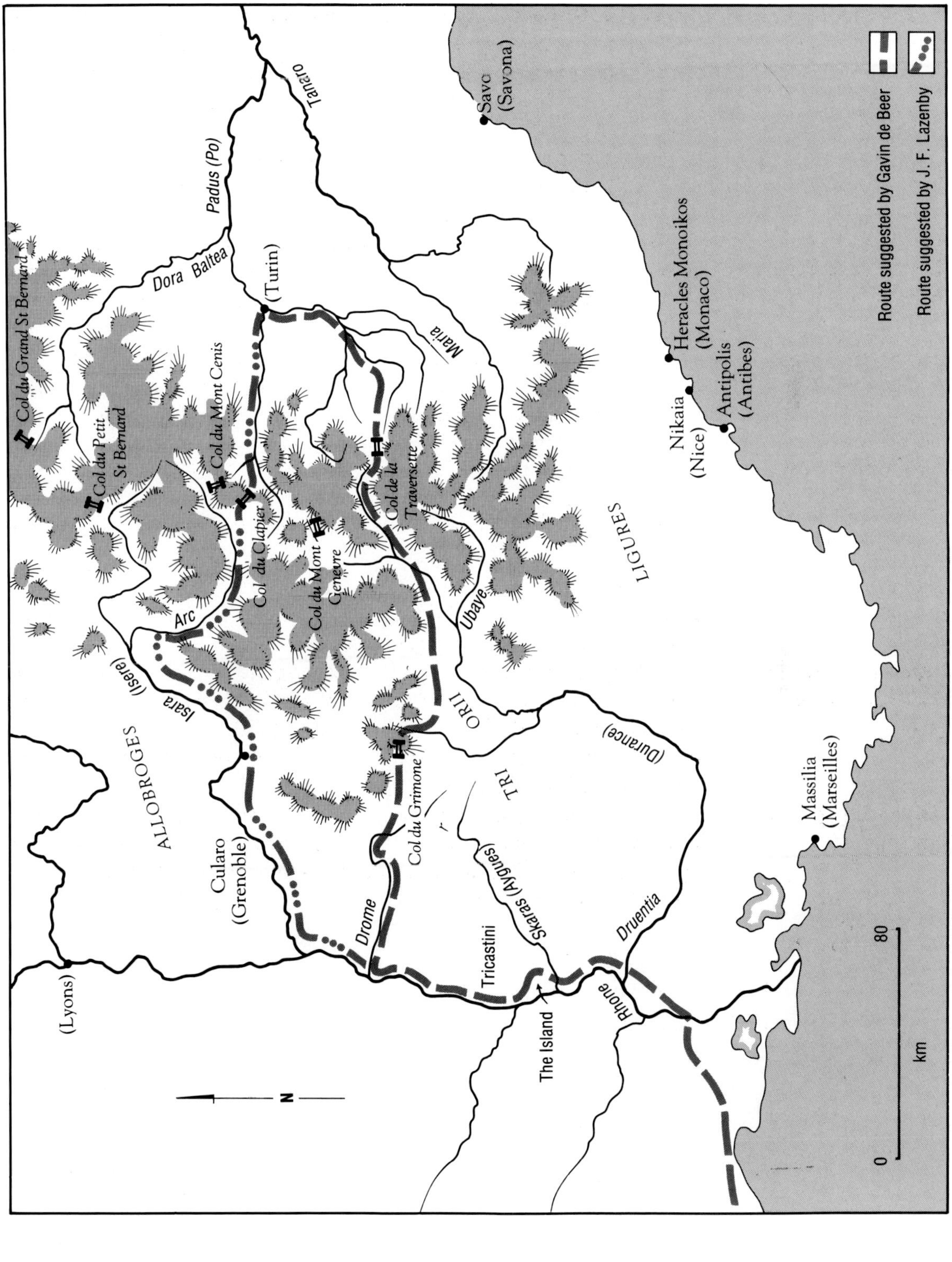
Col du Grand St Bernard
Col du Petit St Bernard
Col du Mont Cenis
Col du Clapier
Col du Mont Genevre
Col de la Traversette
Col du Grimone
Dora Baltea
Padus (Po)
Tanaro
(Turin)
Maria
Arc
Isara (Isere)
Ubaye
ALLOBROGES
LIGURES
ORII
TRI
Cularo (Grenoble)
(Lyons)
Drome
Tricastini
Skaras (Aygues)
Druentia
(Durance)
The Island
Rhone
Savo (Savona)
Heracles Monoikos (Monaco)
Nikaia (Nice)
Antipolis (Antibes)
Massilia (Marseilles)
N
0
80
km
Route suggested by Gavin de Beer
Route suggested by J. F. Lazenby

Hannibal's use of elephants

It is believed that Hannibal left Spain with thirty-seven elephants but lost many of them in the hazardous journey over the Alps. Elephants were used frequently in ancient times, particularly in the armies of eastern rulers. Hannibal hoped to use his to terrorise those native tribes which had never seen them before and to upset the enemy's cavalry by scaring the horses.

The first time the Romans became aware of the use of elephants as the 'tanks' in an army was during Rome's conflict with the Greek adventurer Pyrrhus, about 280. A painted dish of Etruscan origin, found in Campania, shows an Indian elephant — the type used by Pyrrhus — with Macedonian warriors. Other evidence of the same period (coins and terra-cotta figures) show the Indian elephants which were in common use in Syria.

The Carthaginians, however, used the smaller forest elephants from North Africa (obtained in Morocco and around the Atlas Mountains area). These can be seen on the Punic coins minted at the time of Hannibal. The size of the rider on the elephant gives an idea of how small the elephants was (about two metres at the shoulder). In fact they were not very much larger than horses, and were more suitable for crossing mountain ranges. These forest elephants should not be confused with the large African bush elephants.

Both written and archaeological evidence seem to indicate that Hannibal had a least one Indian elephant with him.

After Hannibal's march across the Alps and through the marshes of the Po valley in northern Italy, only one elephant remained. In the second century Cato the Elder referred to this one surviving elephant as Surus, which means 'the Syrian'. The Egyptians captured Indian elephants in Syria, where they were used by rulers such as Antiochus I. Some of these may have reached Carthage.

A bronze coin, found near Lake Trasimene and believed to have been minted about 217 BC, has an Indian elephant on the reverse and a negro head on the obverse. This coin probably represents Hannibal's last surviving elephant, Surus.

Assignment: Hannibal's march

Read particularly the accounts in Polybius and Livy concerning

1 the crossing of the Rhone River (Polybius, III: 42–6; Livy, XXI: 27–8);
2 attacks by Gallic tribes during the ascent of the Alps (Polybius, III: 50–3; Livy, XXI: 32–4);
3 the arrival at the summit (Polybius, III: 54; Livy, XXI: 35);
4 the difficulties of the descent (Polybius, III: 54–6; Livy, XXI: 35–7).

Make a list of the difficulties faced by Hannibal and his troops. Note any differences in the two accounts.

Effects of the crossing on Hannibal's forces

Five months after leaving New Carthage (at about mid-November) Hannibal descended into the territory of the Taurini with his depleted and exhausted army. He had, according to Polybius, lost nearly half his force

> in making his way through the passes while the survivors, because of the ceaseless privations they endured, came in their outward appearance and general condition to look more like beasts than men.[2]

He arrived in Italy with an army of less than 20 000 infantry (12 000 African and 8000 Spanish) and 6000 cavalry (heavily armed Spanish cavalry and lighter, more manoeuvrable Numidian horsemen from Africa). Polybius maintains that his figures come from an inscription (the Lacinian inscription) left by Hannibal himself in southern Italy. The number of elephants that survived the crossing of the Alps is unknown.

The number of Romans and their allies capable of being recruited was more than 700 000 infantry and 70 000 cavalry. (Polybius II: 24 gives details of the resources and forces available to Rome.) It was therefore imperative that Hannibal gain as many allies as possible from among the Gauls and disaffected Roman allies.

After a brief rest the Carthaginians stormed the chief town of the Taurini and Hannibal won the much-needed support of many of the Gauls in the area.

From Ticinis to Cannae

The following map shows (a) the route taken by Hannibal and his forces during the first three years of the war and (b) the sites of major battles during that period.

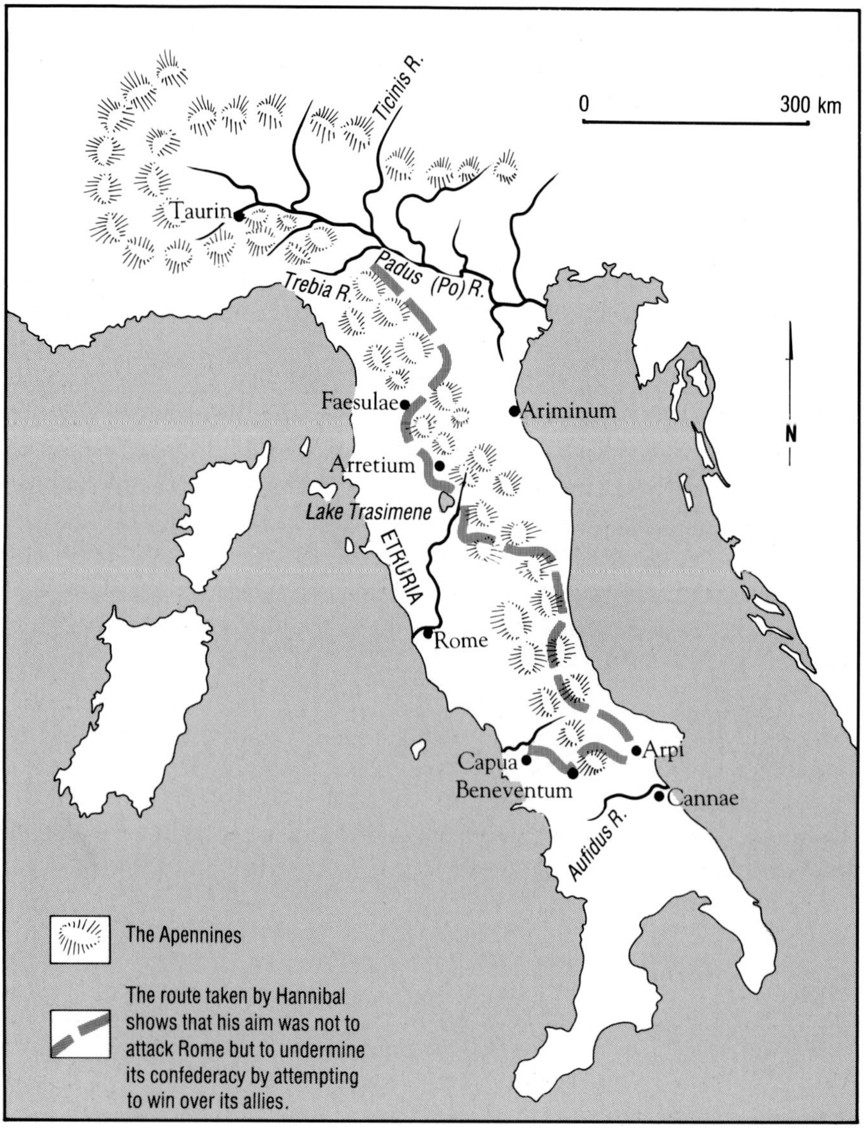

From Ticinis to Cannae, 218–216 BC

Ticinis, 218

The aims of the opponents at Ticinus

The first contact between the Carthaginians and the Romans was somewhere near the Ticinis River, north of the Po. Scipio's aim was to hold Hannibal until the other consular army arrived from Sicily and, more particularly, to prevent the Gallic tribes from joining him. On the other hand, Hannibal needed to 'attempt some action to encourage those [Gauls] who were ready to share in his enterprise'.[3]

A skirmish rather than a battle

This first encounter was simply a cavalry skirmish between 6000 Carthaginian and 2000 Roman horsemen; the Roman spearmen involved retired in terror at the approaching charge of the cavalry for fear of being trampled underfoot. The battle was evenly balanced until the Numidians outflanked the Romans and attacked them from behind. The Romans fled, and during the skirmish Scipio was injured, saved only by his son (the future great Scipio Africanus).

Scipio injured

The significance of Ticinis

Superiority of the Numidians

- It revealed for the first time the superiority of the Carthaginian cavalry, particularly the free-riding Numidians. Hannibal retained this advantage for the sixteen years he was in Italy.
- One view is that it illustrated a favourite tactic of Hannibal—pinning down the enemy's centre while attacking the flanks and rear, a stratagem which he was to use on many occasions.
- The wounded Scipio was unable to take command in their next encounter.

Defection of Gauls to Hannibal

As Hannibal had hoped, many Gauls went over to the Carthaginians, providing them with supplies and sending contingents to supplement Hannibal's troops. The Gauls serving in Scipio's army murdered some of the Romans and joined Hannibal, who

> welcomed them enthusiastically [and] after promising them all fitting rewards, he sent them off to their own cities to tell their compatriots of what they had done and to urge the rest to join him.[4]

Also, a Roman grain store in village of Clastidium was betrayed by its commander to Hannibal.

Trebia, 218

Arrival of Longus from Sicily

After Ticinis, Scipio made camp near the Trebia River. Tiberius Sempronius Longus (the other consul) arrived from Sicily, so doubling the

Opposite: Hannibal's strategy prior to the Battle of Trebia

Roman army, and since Scipio was still wounded Sempronius was 'entitled to handle the situation according to his own judgment'.[5]

Hannibal was camped on the opposite side of the river.

The opponents

Personal motives of Longus

According to Polybius, Ti. Sempronius Longus was 'consumed with the ambition to force a decisive battle' and ignored Scipio's advice to wait before confronting Hannibal.[6] His aim was to deal a blow to Hannibal before Scipio recovered and before he could be replaced by the new consul. He wanted a triumph. 'Since the time he chose for the engagement was dictated not by the facts of the situation but by his personal motives, his judgment was bound to be at fault.'[7] (Polybius' view was bound to be pro-Scipio.)

Longus' judgment dubious

Hannibal's aims at Trebia

Hannibal also was anxious to do battle with the Romans before Scipio recovered, as probably he was aware of Longus' ambition and hoped to exploit it. He also needed a resounding victory to maintain the morale of his men and the enthusiasm and warlike spirit of the Gauls. More important, it was essential that he keep the initiative. Unlike Longus, however, he 'made it a principle never to be drawn into a decisive engagement unless by deliberate choice and certainly not on a casual impulse'.[8] He therefore chose the terrain for the coming battle and carefully laid the trap into which Longus readily fell.

The trap set by Hannibal

The battle

Read Polybius' account of the battle (III: 73–4) which was decisively won by Hannibal. Note the part played in the Roman defeat by each of the following factors:

1 Sempronius' rashness
2 the weather and the flooded river
3 Hannibal's use of each element of his army
- pikemen and slingers
- infantry
- Spanish and Numidian cavalry
- Mago's ambush troops
- elephants

The significance of the Battle of Trebia

Military genius of Hannibal revealed

> The battle of the Trebia illustrates many facets of Hannibal's military genius—his psychological insight into the minds of his opponents, his care for his own men, his willingness to try the unexpected, and his ability to use each element in his forces to the best advantage.[9]

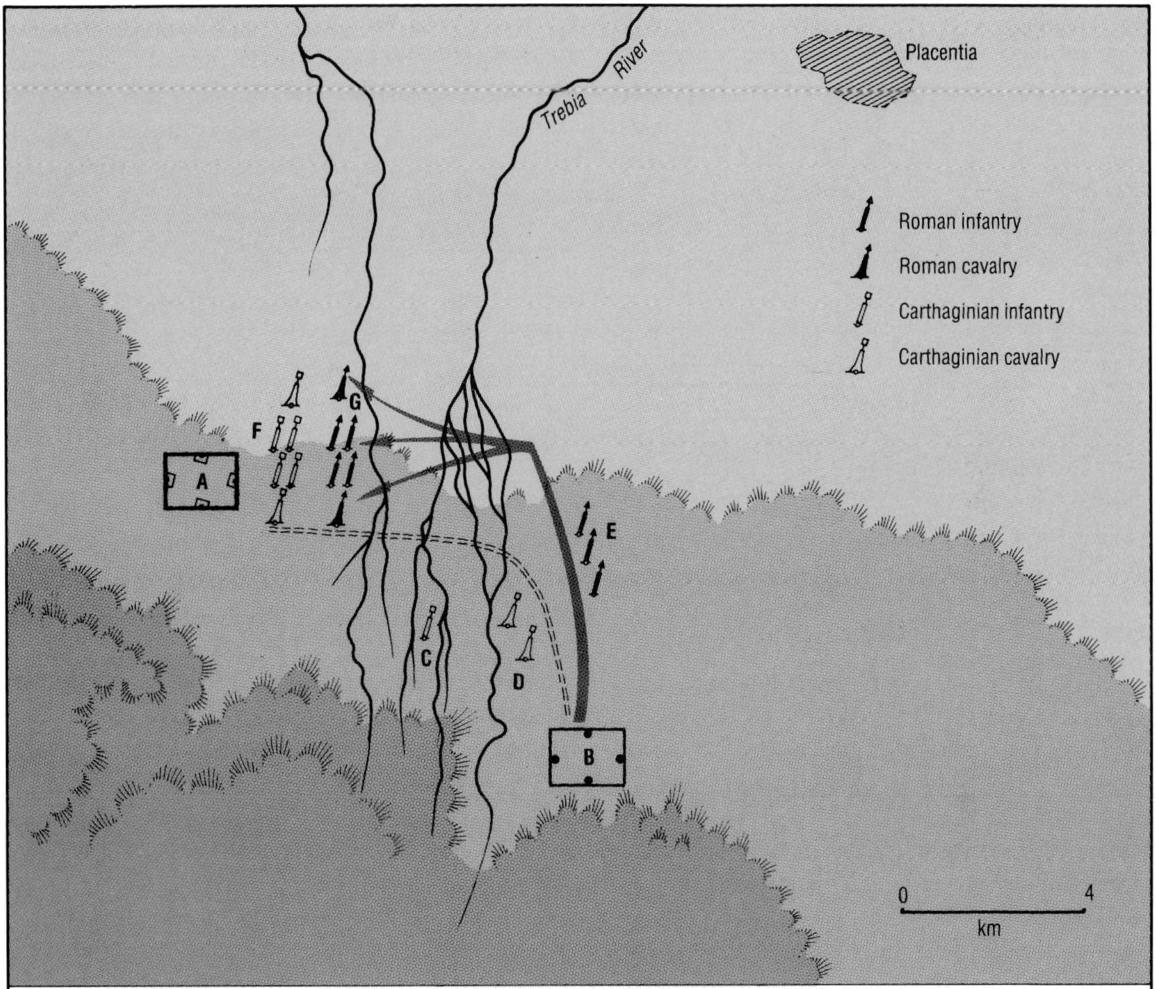

A Hannibal's camp
B Roman camp
C Site of ambush – flat and treeless but crossed by watercourses with high overhanging banks densely overgrown with thorns and brambles which offered concealment (Polybius, III:71).

It was here that Hannibal sent his young brother, Mago, with a detatchment of the most daring horsemen and infantry (2000) with orders to lie in wait for the appropriate moment in the battle.

D At daybreak Hannibal ordered his Numidian cavalry to cross the river, approach the enemy camp and entice the Romans into action before they had been fed or were prepared (III:71).
E The Roman army was ordered to move out and proceeded to cross the swollen Trebia (it was breast-high) with great difficulty – they drew up in battle formation on the left bank. It was a cold, snowy day and they began to suffer from lack of food and the freezing crossing of the river (III:72).
F The Carthaginians had eaten, prepared their horses and arms and covered themselves with oil in front of their fires. Only when Hannibal saw that the Romans had crossed the Trebia did they take up their battle positions.
(i) 20 000 Spaniards, Celts and Africans in a single line with elephants placed in front of the infantry flanks
(ii) Cavalry on the wings (over 10 000)
G The Romans (16 000) and their allies (20 000) marshalled in the usual Roman order (three lines) with 4000 cavalry divided between each wing.

More Gauls supplement Hannibal's forces

The Romans lost approximately 15 000 men, and the previously uncommitted Gauls from the Po valley—many of them horsemen—flocked to support Hannibal. As a result the Romans were now on the defensive, and the senate sent legions to places of strategical importance (Sardinia, Sicily and Tarentum) and fitted out a fleet of sixty quinqueremes. The consuls for 217, C. Flaminius and Cn. Servilius Geminus, began raising troops and established supply depots in Etruria and at Ariminum on the Adriatic coast.

Defensive approach by Rome

Although most of Hannibal's losses had been among the Gauls, his whole army had been adversely affected by the cold, rain and snow, and according to Polybius all except one of his remaining elephants died.

Trasimene, 217

Further difficulties faced by Carthaginians

After wintering in the Po valley, Hannibal marched south and crossed the Appenines into the flooded valley of the Arno River, near Faesulae. The crossing of this marshy countryside adversely affected the whole army: they were marching through water and mud for four days and three nights. Many of the horses went lame and a large number of the pack-animals died. Hannibal, who was supposedly riding the last surviving elephant, had a severe case of ophthalmia and as it was impossible for him to stop and have treatment, he lost the sight in one eye.

Roman preparations to block Hannibal

After resting his men near Faesulae, Hannibal 'collected intelligence about the enemy'.[10] The Roman consuls Flaminius and Servilius waited with their legions at Arretium and Ariminum respectively in order to block his southward march, and the route he chose meant that he was likely to face Flaminius.

The opponents

Bias of sources towards Flaminius

Character of Flaminius

Flaminius received 'bad press' from the later Roman writers, who depicted him as a type of demagogue whose election to the consulship of 217 reflected the people's dissatisfaction with the way the senate was conducting the war. This unfavourable view of a man who had already been consul in 223 and had celebrated a triumph over his defeat of the Insubres (Gauls) was probably put forward by his senatorial opponents (the Fabian faction) after his defeat and death at Trasimene. There is, however, probably some truth in Polybius' belief that he was 'absurdly overconfident in his own resources' and that he was impatient and headstrong.[11] His subsequent actions show this.

Hannibal's plan at Trasimene

Hannibal always made it a practice, if possible, to know something about his opponent's character. He therefore decided to march blatantly past Flaminius' army along the north shore of Lake Trasimene, burning and looting the countryside. He calculated that the Roman general would be lured into an ambush, since he

> would be far too sensitive to the jeers of his rank and file to be able to look on while the country was devastated; at the same time he would be so provoked by the sight that he would follow wherever he was led.[12]

The site of the battle

There is always some controversy about where ancient battles were actually fought or which particular route a commander took; sites as they are today often bear little resemblance to those referred to in the ancient sources. Such an example is Lake Trasimene. The present shoreline at the northern end of the lake is quite different from that which existed in 217.

Controversy over site of battle

According to recent archaeological finds, the site of the ambush may have been the U-shaped valley or basin of Sanguineto. In that area there are a large number of incineration pits and graves and it is believed that the incineration pits, some as deep as 6 metres, contain the ashes of many of the 15 000 Romans who fell there. The graves contain the mutilated skeletons of adult males. In both the *ustrina* (incineration pits) and the graves there were no weapons or equipment, except for a few arrow heads and spear heads. According to Polybius the reason for the lack of arms can be explained by the fact the Hannibal had his men collect all the usable weapons and armour to be used in later battles by his Carthaginians, but J. F. Lazenby, in *Hannibal's War*, says that the cremation pits and graves may have nothing to do with the battle at all.

Archaeological finds at Trasimene

Discrepancies in the sources

The accounts in Livy (XXII:4, 2–7) and Polybius (III:83, 1–4) do not agree concerning the disposition of Hannibal's troops and the beginning of the battle, and therefore their choice of sites differs. Since Livy was no military expert, his vague — and in parts slightly muddled — account may be inaccurate.

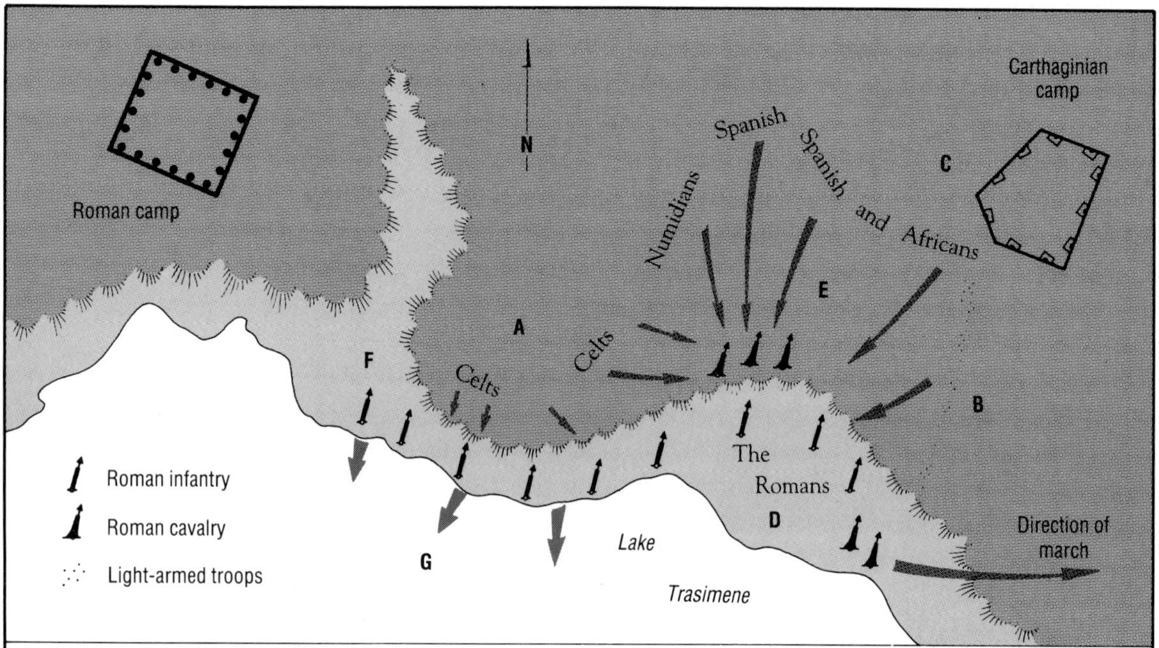

Irrespective of the exact site of the battle, Hannibal set a clever trap for the impulsive Flaminius by placing his troops in the following way:

A The Celts and the cavalry occupied the hills near the entrance to the narrow passage along the shore of the lake.

B The pikemen and slingers (light-armed) were placed under the crest of the slopes in the front of the valley.

C The Spanish and African infantry were placed on the crest of the hill. Flaminius, believing that the Carthaginians were escaping him by marching along the north shore of the lake, decided to follow.

D Leaving their camp in the early morning, the Romans were strung out along the valley, marching through the rising mist and unable to see Hannibal's troops. Flaminius probably believed that the infantry that he could see on the slopes ahead was the rear of Hannibal's army disappearing over the rise, and so hurried to catch up to it.

E Hannibal waited until the head of Flaminius' army was close to his African and Spanish infantry and then gave the word to attack. His men raced down the hillsides shouting and yelling at the shocked Romans in the mist below.

F The Carthaginian cavalry closed the Roman escape route. Not knowing what was happening and unable to organise themselves sufficiently to put up a resistance, the Romans, according to Polybius, were 'unable either to yield to circumstances or to do anything' Polybius, III:84–85. Their training demanded that they stand and fight and this they did for three hours (Livy).

G Those closer to the lake attempted to swim or wade to safety in full armour. Many drowned, but those who did not were cut down by the Carthaginian cavalry which plunged into the lake after them.

Flaminius was killed by a Celt who supposedly recognised him from a previous conflict. Six thousand Romans who escaped were later rounded up by Maharbel.

Servilius, the other consul, three days' march away, lost 4000 of his cavalry at the hands of Maharbel four days later.

Hannibal's strategy at Trasimene

The results and significance of the battle of Lake Trasimene	
For the Romans	*For the Carthaginians*
According to Polybius the Roman losses were 15 000 dead; Livy suggests that 10 000 survived. Rome was left without an effective field army. When the Romans were told that they had been defeated in a great battle, they were extremely anxious, and when they heard later that Servilius' cavalry had also been defeated, the normally cool-headed senators were shaken. They began to put into effect emergency measures. Quintus Fabius was appointed dictator, the city walls were to be repaired, the bridges over the Tiber were to be broken down, crops were burnt and rural populations withdrew to strongly fortified towns. Fabius raised two fresh legions which, with the army of Servilius, gave him a larger and more powerful force than Hannibal, except for cavalry. There was a change in Roman strategy as the conservative, cautious Fabian faction now held a position of predominance in the senate.	Hannibal's losses according to Polybius were 1500; Livy says 2500. Most of these were Gauls. Hannibal kept the Roman prisoners under guard but released the allies and sent them home, reminding them 'that he had not come to fight against the Italians, but on behalf of the Italians against Rome'.[13] Hannibal had annihilated all Roman resistance in the north of Italy and there was no army between him and Rome. The whole peninsula lay open to him. He did not take the direct route to Rome but marched through Umbria and Picenum to Apulia, where he rested his men and animals as well as rearming the men with captured Roman weapons. Despite Hannibal's successes in 218–217, not one member of the Roman confederacy came over to him.

Quintus Fabius and his strategy

Procedure for selecting a dictator

The normal procedure in selecting a dictator was for one of the consuls to nominate a suitably experienced politician. The dictator then nominated his own assistant, the master of the horse. After Trasimene, however, with one consul dead and the other far from Rome, Fabius was elected rather than nominated as was his master of the horse, M. Minucius Rufus.

Factional differences

Fabius (from the Fabii) then found himself with an assistant from the opposing political faction in the senate (the Aemilii/Cornelii), and this was to cause the dictator some problems in carrying out the strategy which he believed would defeat Hannibal.

Roman strategy linked to political factions

It became increasingly apparent as the war progressed that changes in Roman strategy were closely linked with whichever faction had pre-eminence in the senate at the time.

Qualities and experience of Fabius

Polybius says that Fabius was 'a man of great natural gifts, and outstanding for his steadiness of judgment',[14] while Plutarch says that he alone 'possessed a spirit and dignity of character which were equal to the greatness of the office'.[15] He had already been twice consul (233–232 and 228–227), once censor (230) and once dictator (possibly in 221—the exact time is unknown).

The strategy of Fabius and Hannibal	
Fabius	*Hannibal*
To take no risks and fight no pitched battles but to exhaust Hannibal's strength by using delaying tactics. This would make the most of Rome's 'inexhaustible provisions and manpower'.[16] To keep to mountainous positions and attack, where possible, Hannibal's foraging parties — to slowly deplete Hannibal's forces and give his own men renewed confidence.	To use every trick to lure or force the enemy into battle, to exploit his men's superiority in training and to prevent the exhaustion of his inferior numbers and resources. To cause alarm among Rome's allies and to demonstrate that Fabius was abandoning the country to the enemy—'to persuade them to throw off their allegiance to Rome'.[17]

Delaying tactics of Romans

Despite Hannibal's efforts to coax Fabius into battle, the Roman persisted in his delaying tactics and so earned himself the name *cunctator* (delayer). Hannibal decided to cross the peninsula to the fertile plain of Campania. Not only were the cities of Neapolis and Cumae good seaports through which he could possibly make communication with Carthage, but in Capua, the second largest city in Italy, there was an element of discontent among the population which he hoped to exploit.

Hannibal in Campania

Fabius followed Hannibal, but would not be drawn down into the plain. He occupied the main pass through the mountains, hoping to cut off the Carthaginians' fastest return route to Apulia. The Roman army simply looked on from its high position while Hannibal systematically raided and devastated the Campanian countryside.

Concern over Fabius' tactics

Fabius' lack of action was already causing opposition within his own army, particularly from Minucius, his master of the horse. However, he knew that Hannibal would need to get his men back to winter quarters in Apulia, and he believed that he had him blocked in Campania.

Hannibal's plot to outwit Fabius

In this he had totally underestimated Hannibal, who ordered some of his men to attach lighted torches to the horns of 2000 oxen and when it grew dark to drive them over the mountains near the Roman-guarded pass. The Romans keeping watch thought it was Hannibal's army making a forced march over difficult terrain and left the pass unguarded to pursue and intercept them. Hannibal then marched the remainder of his army with its substantial plunder through the pass without opposition. (Refer to Polybius, III: 93–4; Livy, XXII: 15–17.)

Fabius' refusal to change strategy

> Although Fabius was reviled by the populace for his feebleness in allowing the enemy to escape from an apparently hopeless situation, he still refused to depart from his original policy in any respect.[18]

Opposition in Rome to Fabius

Fabius was recalled to Rome in order to perform certain religious functions; he advised Minucius not to do anything rash, but Minucius ignored his warnings and attacked, with partial success, a part of Hannibal's army as it was moving position. This undermined the Fabian faction's policy and it was decided that Fabius should return to the field but share the command equally with Minucius (an unprecedented move). Instead of sharing the command Fabius and Minucius preferred to divide the army, and Hannibal, learning of this, devised a plan to trap Minucius. Minucius duly fell into the trap, and when his men realised that they were surrounded they panicked and fled, only being saved by the approach of Fabius' army.

When Fabius' term of office came to an end the consuls for the previous year resumed command until the elections for 216 were held; these elections were hotly contested. The consuls for the year 216 proved to be Gaius Terentius Varro and Lucius Aemilius Paullus.

Cannae, 216

Another change in Roman strategy

The Romans changed their strategy once again. They decided to increase the size of their army and put an unprecedented eight legions into the field in order to confront Hannibal and end the Carthaginian threat with one blow. Hannibal was camped near a Roman grain depot at Cannae, which he had captured and occupied.

The opponents

Livy's biased view of Varro

Terentius Varro is depicted in the sources in an unflattering light. He is described as the son of a butcher who endeared himself to the people by arrogant speeches and attacks on leading senators, particularly the Fabian group. He had, 'by maligning others, directed the limelight on himself'.[19] He was also regarded as reckless, and devoid of military skill, but boasted that he would bring the war to an end 'on the day he first caught sight of the enemy'.[20]

More objective viewpoint

This view of Varro cannot be totally accepted, for a number of reasons.

1 Although Varro was a 'new man' (novus homo), no son of a butcher would have risen to the position of consul. In order to have achieved his political career (as quaestor, aedile and praetor and now consul) he must have had the support of a powerful section of the nobility.

2 The only 'popular' measure that it is certain he carried out was his support of the recommendation to make Minucius co-dictator with Fabius. He may have been opposed by the Fabian faction, but he was certainly not an enemy of the senate. Its treatment of him after Cannae indicates this.

3 There is also no reason to believe that he and his colleague Aemilius Paullus differed in their strategy and tactics prior to Cannae. It was only later, after the disastrous Roman defeat, that the view arose that Varro and Paullus were at loggerheads; obviously, this was to protect the reputation of the Aemilii: it should be remembered that Polybius' patron in Rome (Scipio Aemilianus) was the grandson of Aemilius Paullus.

The prejudice of Polybius

Qualities and experience of Paullus

Aemilius Paullus was a patrician and an experienced commander. He had already held the consulship in 219, but the normal ten-year interval between successive consulships had been waived to enable Rome to utilise the services of experienced men such as he. Livy puts into the mouth of Paullus the following words: 'Any plan of action sensibly and cautiously carried out would prove successful. Up to the present, recklessness— even apart from its stupidity—had been a failure'.[21]

The traditional view depicts Varro as reckless, arrogant and inexperienced militarily, while seeing Paullus as cautious, sensible and an experienced commander.

The figures for the opposing forces given below are based on Polybius.

Roman army	*Carthaginian army*
40 000 Roman infantry	12 000 Africans
40 000 allied infantry	8 000 Spaniards
2 400 Roman cavalry	25 000 Gauls
3 600 allied cavalry	8 000+ light-armed troops
	4 000 Numidian horsemen
	6 000 Spanish and Gallic cavalry

How many of the Romans actually took to the field (some may have been left in camp) is not known exactly, but it is thought that there were close to 70 000.

Refer to the full account of the battle given by Livy (XXII: 47–9) and Polybius (III: 112–16). The following extract is Livy's description of the battlefield on the following day:

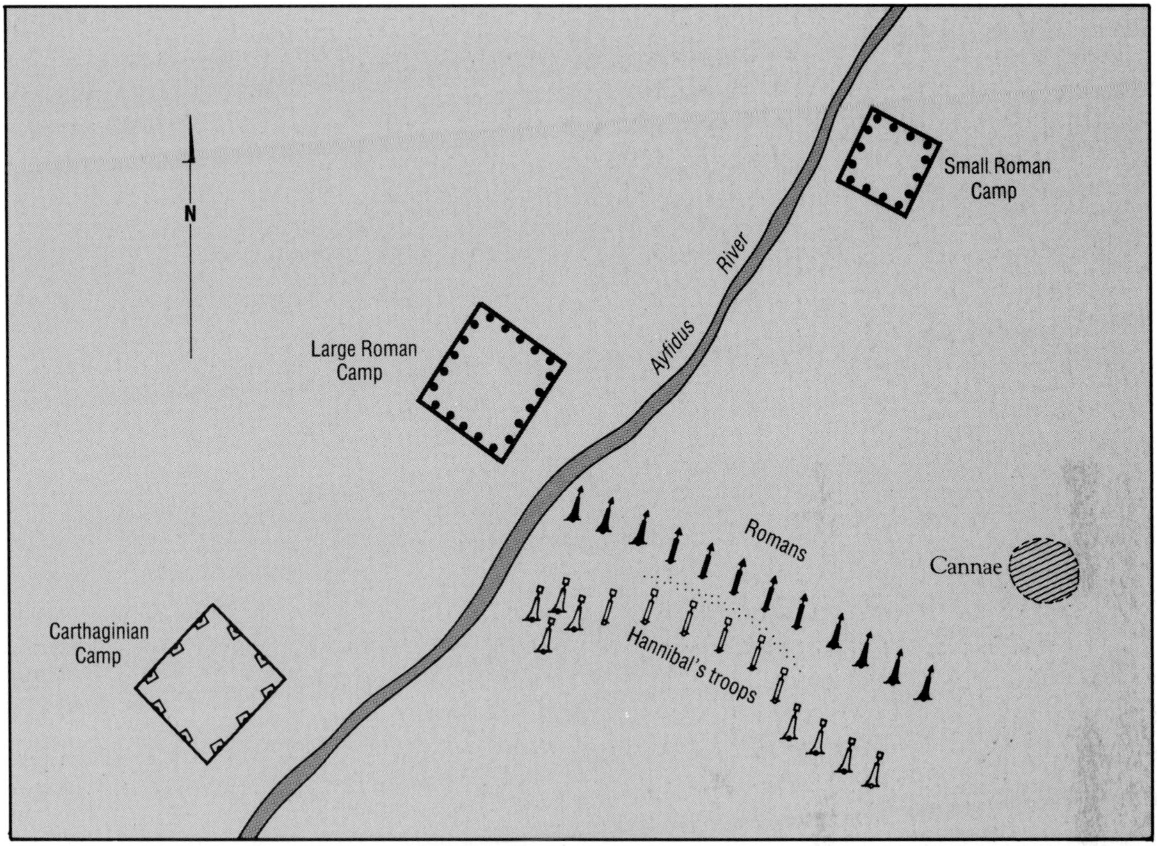

Deployment of troops prior to the Battle of Cannae

At dawn next morning the Carthaginians applied themselves to collecting the spoils and viewing the carnage, which even to an enemy's eye was a shocking spectacle. All over the field Roman soldiers lay dead in their thousands, horse and foot mingled, as the shifting phases of the battle, or the attempt to escape, had brought them together. Here and there wounded men, covered with blood, who had been roused to consciousness by the morning cold, were dispatched by a quick blow as they struggled to rise from amongst the corpses; others were found still alive with the sinews in their thighs and behind their knees sliced through, baring their throats and necks and begging who would to spill what little blood they had left. Some had their heads buried in the ground, having apparently dug themselves holes and by smothering their faces with earth had choked themselves to death. Most strange of all was a Numidian soldier, still living, and lying, with nose and ears horribly lacerated, underneath the body of a Roman who, when his useless hands had been no longer able to grasp his sword, had died in the act of tearing his enemy, in bestial fury, with his teeth.[22]

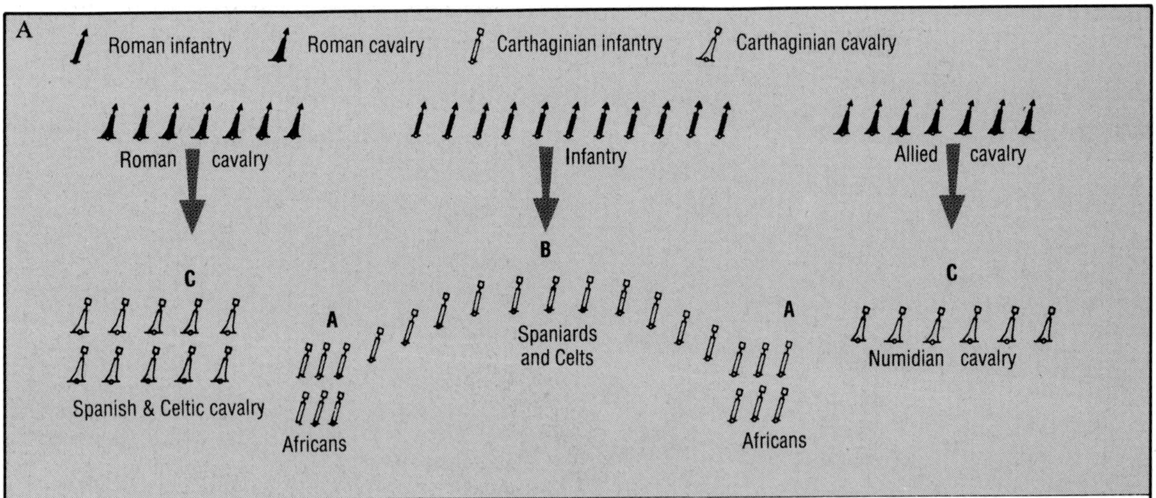

Hannibal hoped to use the strength of the enemy infantry to defeat itself by deliberately provoking it to attack.

A He divided his strong African infantry into two divisions 'to be the jaws of his trap'. They were to remain as a reserve until the right moment.

B He placed his Spaniards and Celts in the centre, but led them forward into a crescent-shaped bulge, thinning their ranks – 'Deliberately tempting the Romans to attack his centre'.

C He did not divide his cavalry equally. His largest force of Spanish and Celtic cavalry he put opposite the smaller Roman cavalry, while his Numidians faced almost equal numbers of allied cavalry.

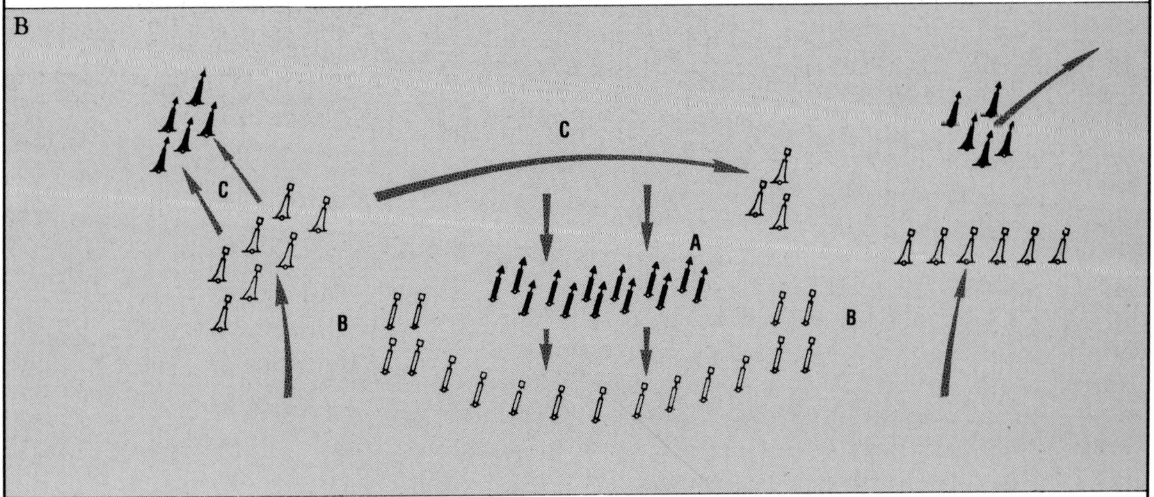

A The Roman infantry gradually pushed the Celts and Spaniards back, breaking the crescent formation. They continued crowding into the centre.

B The African infantry stood firm.

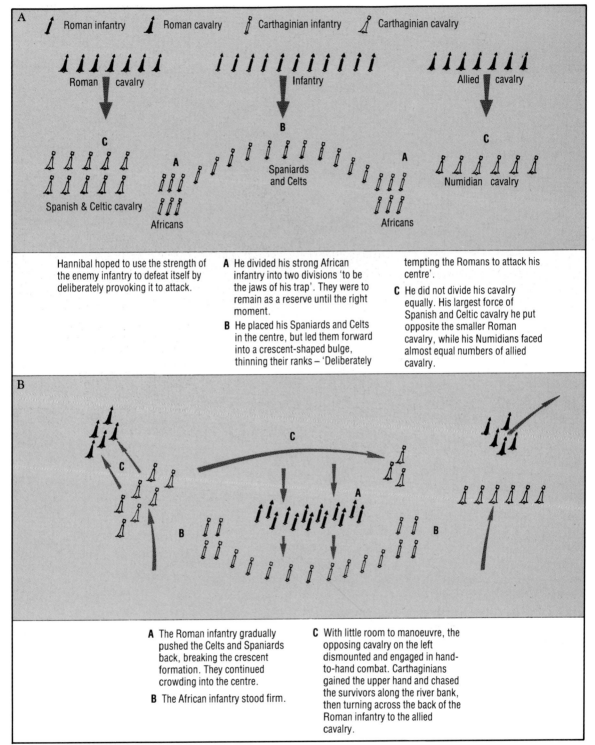

C With little room to manoeuvre, the opposing cavalry on the left dismounted and engaged in hand-to-hand combat. Carthaginians gained the upper hand and chased the survivors along the river bank, then turning across the back of the Roman infantry to the allied cavalry.

First and second phases of the Battle of Cannae

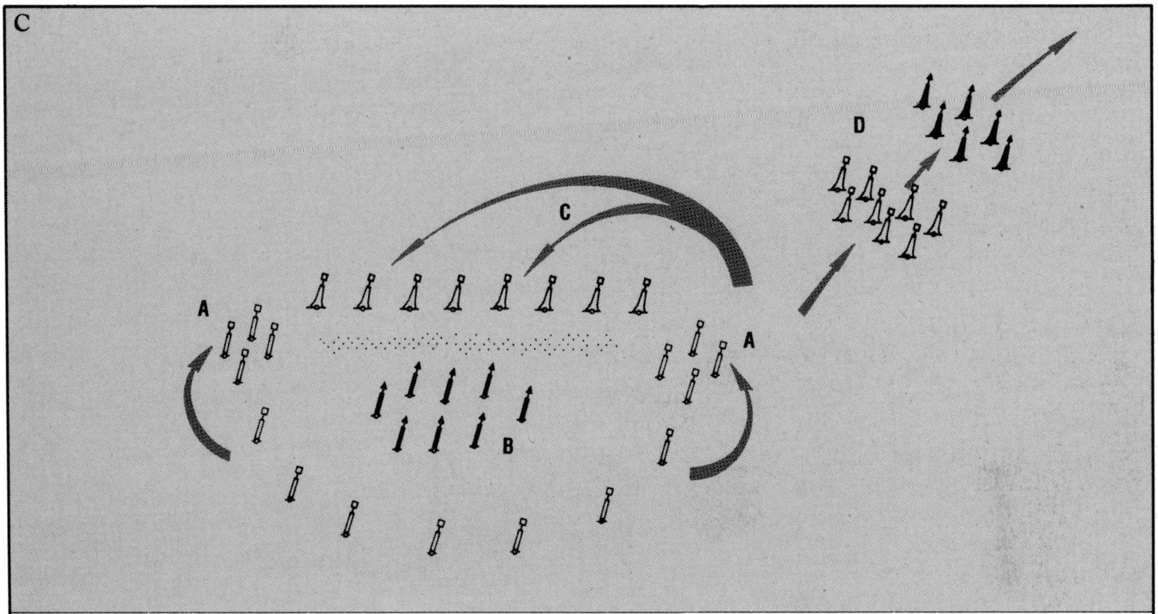

A The Africans on the flanks moved forward and then in perfect discipline turned inwards, facing right and left. They attacked the Roman infantry flanks.

B The Romans, pressing forward, tried desperately to face about to deal with this new threat, but their formation was breaking up.

C Hasdrubal's bridled cavalry closed the 'trap' and the encirclement was complete just as Hannibal had planned it.

D The Numidians chased the allied cavalry from the field.

Third phase of the Battle of Cannae

Losses in the Battle of Cannae*	
Romans	*Hannibal*
47 000 infantry 2 700 cavalry 19 300 prisoners	4000 Gauls 1500 Spaniards 200 cavalry
Many high-ranking officers were killed: Paullus, Servilius, the consuls' quaestors, 29 military tribunes and over 80 men of senatorial rank.	Livy says that Hannibal's losses were 8000.

* Based on Livy, XXII: 49 and Polybius, III: 117.

A sculpture of the Magna Mater, whose worship was introduced into Rome during the crucial years of the Second Punic War

The significance of Cannae

For the Romans

Roman refusal to accept defeat

Roman military power was utterly destroyed at Cannae, but the Romans refused to accept defeat or talk of making peace even when many of their southern allies defected to Hannibal. They also refused to ransom the prisoners held by Hannibal, as to do so would have helped him pay his troops. 'No other nation in the world would have suffered so tremendously a series of disasters and not been overwhelmed.'[23]

Religious reaction in Rome

The series of disasters they had suffered, culminating in Cannae, were regarded by many Romans as punishment by the gods, and so the Sibylline Books were consulted. To placate the gods, a male and a female Gaul and a male and a female Greek were buried alive in the cattle market (Forum Boarium).

War effort directed by senate

The senate now assumed firm control of the war effort, and its members took immediate and effective steps to deal with the crisis. The determination and sacrifice of the Roman people in deciding to continue the war cost them dearly in financial and physical effort, but the decisions taken at this time were responsible for their ultimate victory over Carthage fifteen years later.

- Despite their tremendous losses in manpower and the need to have troops concentrated in Italy, the senate wisely refused to recall their troops from Spain and decided to continue to support the campaign there under the Scipios.

- To rebuild their forces they recruited two more urban legions from young men of seventeen, from 8000 slaves who volunteered (*volones*) and were bought from their owners at public expense, and from 6000 criminals and debtors who were released from gaol. The allies also increased their quota of troops, and by the end of 216 Roman military manpower had been stabilised. In 215 the strength of the Roman army had reached almost a quarter of a million men, and of these twenty legions at least nine were in theatres of war other than Italy (in Spain, Sardinia, Sicily and Cisalpine Gaul).

Drastic measures to increase manpower

- The Romans maintained their naval superiority despite the fact that the fleets in Sicily and Sardinia were in a bad way. Neither the soldiers nor the crews had been paid and there seemed to be no way the money could be obtained. The senate ordered the commanders to use their own initiative to provide for the military and naval personnel in their charge. To supply crews for the fleet in Sicily, a senatorial edict obliged citizens to provide for sailors according to their property rating; senators were subject to the greatest contribution.

Effort involved in maintaining sea power

- To overcome continued financial difficulties, the Romans debased the silver coinage and reduced the weight standard of bronze coins, while the *tributum* (tax paid by Roman citizens) was doubled. However, there was a limit to the amount of revenue that could be raised by direct taxation, and the Romans had to find an alternative solution to the problem of shortage of money. It became the practice for knights and centurions in the army to serve without pay; voluntary contributions of gold, silver and coined bronze were made by senators; and private contractors agreed to supply the army and fleet with supplies at their own expense. (The senate promised to repay them when there was money in the treasury.) 'Thus public business was carried on by means of private funds—so deep was the patriotic sentiment in all classes of society almost without exception.'[24]

Financial strategies

Funding of war effort by individuals

- Rome's war strategy underwent another change as the influence of the Aemilii in the senate waned and the Fabian faction once again directed the war effort. Fabius Maximus' policy of *cunctatio* ('putting off') was accepted as the only way to nullify Hannibal's tactical superiority, even though it had been ridiculed prior to Cannae.

Further change in strategy

For Hannibal

'The year 216 constitutes the high-water mark of Hannibal's military career and Cannae his greatest battle.'[25]

Hannibal's original policy of detatching Rome's allies appeared at last to be working. A number of towns in Apulia (Arpi, Salapia, Herdonia) and

Defection of Rome's allies

Uzentum in Calabria opened their gates to him immediately after Cannae. This was soon followed by the defection of most of the Samnites and the towns of Lucania, all those in Bruttium (except for the Greek cities), the Herpini and, soon after, the wealthy city of Capua in Campania.

Roman loss of Capua

Capua, the second city of the confederacy, was divided by class warfare: the aristocrats were Roman citizens, while the commons did not have the same rights and therefore resented the upper classes, who received support from the Romans; after Cannae, the commons decided to revolt and sent a delegation to Hannibal to conclude a treaty of alliance. This defection of Capua to Hannibal was for him the most important result of Cannae; it encouraged other towns nearby to defect also and gave him a comfortable winter base for his men. It now appeared that he might achieve his original objective.

Problems faced by Hannibal in protecting allies

Yet despite his great success at Cannae, after 216 his fortunes slowly declined and it has been suggested that the revolt of southern Italy against Rome was partly responsible for this. The more allies he gained, the more he had to divide his forces to garrison the newly won areas, and by dividing his forces he made it easier for the Romans to attack: 'He could not hold all of them by garrisons without cutting up his army into numerous small parts . . .';[26] neither could he withdraw the garrisons he had already established without leaving his allies vulnerable. In order to retain these allies, he was obliged to refrain from raiding their territory to feed his army and was unable to force them to provide troops to augment his slowly dwindling numbers. The allies gradually became a liability to Hannibal, as he never had enough troops to protect them all; Livy says that later he was inclined 'to despoil where he could not protect, so that only ruins were left to the enemy'.[27]

Hannibal's dwindling numbers

His veterans (those who had come with him from Spain) had been reduced severely by three years of hard fighting and forced marches. By 215 he desperately needed fresh, experienced troops from Africa or Spain, as the Romans had 45 000 men in Campania. His brother Mago had been dispatched to Carthage to inform the government of his great victory and to bring back reinforcements, but although the Carthaginians promised him considerable forces, they were not immediately available. When they were finally raised they were diverted to Spain (in 215) because Hasdrubal had been defeated by the Scipios. The Carthaginian government revealed where its priorities lay: Hannibal received only a small force brought by Bomilcar.

Lack of support from Carthaginian government

Hannibal's failure to gain a seaport

Hannibal was unable to gain control of a seaport through which to maintain contact with Carthage, and he also appeared to have lost the strategic initiative as he was forced to keep moving around in order to counter the tactics now employed by the Romans and to protect his allies.

Opposite: Expansion of the war beyond Italy, 215–210

Spain

Gnaeus and Publius Scipio had kept Hasdrubal from sending reinforcements to Hannibal. In 215 they took the offensive and defeated Hasdrubal in Ibera. This strengthened Rome's position in Spain and many Spanish tribes revolted from Carthage, which was forced to divert to Spain an army intended for Hannibal

In 212 the Scipios took Saguntum and won a large part of Carthaginian Spain

The Scipios divided their forces in 211 to defeat Hasdrubal and take New Carthage. Both Roman armies were defeated, as they had overstrained their resources. Both Scipios died, and the Romans withdrew to the Ebro River

- The Carthaginians failed to press home their advantage at this time

Italy

By avoiding major engagements and keeping to limited actions, the Roman consuls Fabius, Sempronius Gracchus and Claudius Marcellus successfully prevented Hannibal from keeping control of those towns he had won over

In 212 Hannibal took (by betrayal) the port city of Tarentum, while the Romans began the siege of Capua

Hannibal, unable to do anything to relieve Capua, marched on Rome to divert the Roman troops; this ploy failed

Capua was eventually starved into submission, and surrendered to the Romans in 211

- Hannibal's only chance for ultimate victory in Italy was to gain help from abroad

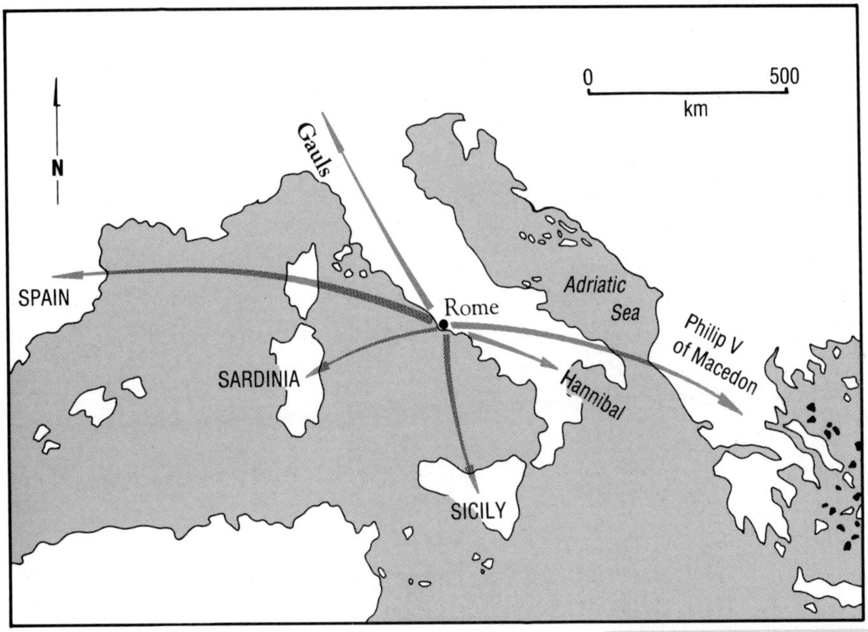

Refer to Polybius, Plutarch and Livy for detailed and vivid descriptions of some of the major incidents, 215–210:

- the betrayal of Tarentum to Hannibal (Polybius, VIII: 24–34; Livy, XXV: 7–11)
- the siege of Syracuse (Polybius VIII: 3–7; Livy, XXIV: 34, XXV: 23–31; Plutarch, *Marcellus*, 14–19)
- the siege and surrender of Capua (Polybius IX: 3–7; Livy, XXVI: 4–16)

Sicily

Hiero, the long-time ally of Rome, died in 215, and this led to intrigue with Carthage to stir up revolt against Rome. There was a general uprising throughout Sicily

In 214 Marcellus invaded Sicily, sacking the town of Leontini with great severity. Syracuse defected to Carthage, but owing to its impregnability the Roman blockade lasted for two and a half years

In 212 Marcellus took Syracuse (which was suffering from plague) because of the treachery of a Spanish mercenary

A Carthaginian relief fleet led by Bomilcar was defeated off Sicily also

- Hannibal was left without a 'bridge' between himself and Carthage

Greece and the Adriatic

The ambitious Philip V of Macedon, hoping to expand his territory by exploiting Rome's weakened position, signed an alliance with Hannibal in 215. This alliance for mutual assistance could have tipped the scales in Hannibal's favour, but the envoys negotiating the alliance were caught by the Romans before it could be implemented.

In 214 the Romans sent a fleet and a military force into the Adriatic and stirred up trouble in Greece on a number of fronts to keep Philip occupied and to prevent him from gaining a base for attack on Italy. This successful campaign was led by Valerius Laevinus

The Roman fleet continued to patrol the Adriatic, to keep Philip in check

- Hannibal was left without a powerful ally

A Latin inscription commemorating Fabius' capture of Tarentum — it is the only surviving inscription containing Hannibal's name

Publius Cornelius Scipio (the younger) in Spain

Scipio's appointment to Spain

In 210 a new Roman army was sent to Spain under the command of the future conqueror of Hannibal, Scipio the younger. He was only twenty-four years of age and had never held a position with imperium (praetor or consul), yet after the death of his father and uncle he put himself forward for the proconsular command of Spain. He was elected unanimously.

His objective in Spain

Scipio had fought at Ticinis at the age of eighteen (and saved his father's life), had possibly been at Trebia and had fought at Cannae. Unlike his father and uncle, he realised that the war in Spain must involve striking directly at Carthage rather than winning over the Spanish tribesmen.

'A man of humane and generous disposition'
'Astute and discreet'
'A reputation for bravery'
'Possessed of a mind which was always concentrated upon the purpose he had in view'
'A man favoured by Fortune who usually succeeded in all his undertakings'
'Strengthened the confidence of the men under his command . . . by instilling into them the faith that his plans were divinely inspired'
'Was careful to refrain from exposing himself to danger when his country's entire hopes rested upon his safety'
'His actions were invariably governed by calculation and foresight'

Polybius' view of Scipio

His first move was to aim at the immediate capture of the headquarters at New Carthage, which would deprive the Carthaginians of their closest port for sea communication with Numidia and Carthage itself. It would also give him a secure base from which to attack southern Spain and gain control over the nearby silver mines.

Scipio's preparations

This was a daring move, but he had collected intelligence and knew that the three Carthaginian commanders were widely dispersed and that none was within ten days' march of New Carthage. He had also studied the plan and site of New Carthage carefully, enabling him to take the great city in a combined land–sea operation (refer to Polybius X: 10–15; Livy XXVI: 43–6).

Benefits gained from its capture

Livy describes the incredible amount of booty taken from the city, particularly the war materials (such as catapults and missiles), the gold and silver, stores of grain, shipbuilding material and sixty-three merchant ships. More important than all of this, however, were the 300 noble Spanish hostages whose later return to their tribes won for Scipio many new allies.

He spent his time in New Carthage retraining his troops to a high pitch of efficiency and equipping them with new weapons. The arms workshops in the city were re-established under Roman control and he opened the mint, which began producing silver coins carrying his own head instead of Hannibal's.

The Battle of Baecula

In 208, near the town of Baecula, Scipio faced Hasdrubal. Scipio had learnt well from Hannibal, and although he used a modified version of the tactics employed at Cannae, he adapted them to suit an attack on higher ground. Hasdrubal was unable to cope with the unorthodox manoeuvres, and rather than wait to suffer total defeat he retreated with about a third of his troops and marched through northern Spain to Italy to bring some relief to Hannibal. Scipio made no attempt to follow him, since he needed to consolidate Rome's control over Spain.

The Battle of Ilipa

He won over many Spanish chieftains and it was not until 206 that he finally faced Hasdrubal's successor (Hasdrubal Gisgo) at Ilipa. Here, using much the same tactics as at Baecula, he won decisively, and 'everyone was talking with boundless delight of the splendour of this achievement, except the one man who had brought it to pass'. 'Already his thoughts were on Africa and Carthage.'[29]

Negotiations with Numidian princes

Scipio realised that the Carthaginians were superior in cavalry (particularly the Numidian horsemen) and that if he fought them in Africa he would need the support of one of the African princes. The young Numidian prince, Masinissa, who had been fighting on the side of the Carthaginians in Spain, had entered into secret negotiations with the Romans after the Battle of Ilipa; Scipio also crossed over to Africa to talk with Syphax, King of the Masaesulii, who agreed to accept the friendship of Rome.

Scipio's return to Italy

By the end of 206 the city of Gades had surrendered to Scipio, and although for the Romans there were to be many years ahead of fighting in Spain, it was completely lost to Carthage. Scipio returned to Rome in 205 to contest the consular elections.

His leadership qualities

Scipio had many qualities that made him a great military leader.

- He possessed personal magnetism — was a leader of men.
- He knew the importance of military intelligence and reconnaissance.
- He had psychological insight, realising the need to 'know the enemy'.
- He had the ability to use topography to his advantage.
- He possessed tenacity of purpose and self-control.
- His actions demonstrated his professionalism.

Events in Italy, 210–205

Difficulties faced by Hannibal after 209

In 210 it appeared that the tide was turning in Rome's favour. Hannibal's failure to save Capua had serious repercussions for him, as many of his allies were now considering returning their allegiance to Rome; those who still supported him had to be protected, or deterred from deserting his cause. Tarentum was recaptured by Fabius in 209; Hannibal's time was spent in forced marches and limited actions, and he was restricted to the south for other reasons also: the Brutii, who made up a large part of his army, were not prepared to engage in long campaigns far from their own territory.

Setbacks for Romans

Yet the Romans did not have everything their own way. The year 208 was rather unfortunate for them: they lost two consuls in an encounter with Hannibal, suffered two minor defeats and had a revolt in Etruria on their hands.

Death of Marcellus

The loss of Marcellus—a general popular with both the army and the people—was serious, as he was a highly competent soldier and leader although he lacked the professionalism of Hannibal. Marcellus had been consul five times, and was admired even by Hannibal. Plutarch says that

Hannibal's display of respect

> Hannibal took little interest in the fate of other soldiers, but when he heard that Marcellus had been killed, he immediately hurried to the spot and stood for a long time by the dead body, admiring its strength and beauty. He uttered not a single boastful word, nor did he show any sign of exultation, such as might be expected of a man who had just rid himself of a formidable enemy... he gave orders that his body should be treated with honour, wrapped in a fine robe, adorned and burned.[30]

Marcus Marcellus, a Roman general admired by Hannibal, who said of him: 'He is the only general who, when victorious, allows no rest, and when we beat him takes none himself'

The Battle of Metaurus, 207

Arrival of Hasdrubal in Italy

Hasdrubal (Hannibal's brother) had left Spain after his defeat by Scipio and arrived in Italy with a small force to which he added recruits from Gaul. The Romans were prepared for his arrival, although not aware of his plans with regard to Hannibal.

Hannibal was hemmed in by six Roman legions and Hasdrubal also was being closely followed as he moved into Italy, but it was imperative that the brothers join forces. Hannibal was forced to wait until he heard from Hasdrubal, but the latter's despatches outlining a possible meeting point and time were intercepted by the Romans and this allowed them to adopt an offensive rather than a defensive approach to the invader. The consul Claudius Nero, who was camped close to Hannibal, left most of his army to keep watch while he, unknown to Hannibal, led a picked force north to join his colleague, M. Livius. When Hasdrubal realised that there were two consuls in the Roman camp he decided to retire until he could make contact with Hannibal, but he was caught and brought to battle on the bank of the Metaurus River.

Roman discovery of the brothers' plan

Hasdrubal forced into battle

Death of Hasdrubal

The battle resulted in a crushing defeat for Hasdrubal (Livy, XXVII: 47–9), who was killed in action. Polybius commends him for having shown great courage throughout his life.

Hannibal's hopes of victory diminished

Nero returned to Apulia and informed Hannibal of his brother's fate by throwing his head into the Carthaginian camp. 'Hannibal under the double blow of so great a public and personal distress exclaimed: "Now, at last, I see the destiny of Carthage plain!"'[31]

The significance of Metaurus

The Romans behaved as if the war was already won, and Hannibal ceased to be of much interest to them for the remainder of his time in Italy. He was forced to retire to the far south and to adopt a defensive strategy for the next four years, waiting to see what happened in other areas of conflict outside Italy.

Sea power in the Second Punic War

Both fleets active throughout the war

As there were no great sea battles in this war some historians have tended to overlook the part played by the Roman navy in the final victory over Carthage, but according to Lazenby, 'If ever there was a silent service it was the Roman navy'.[32] Livy also makes numerous references to the activities of the fleet, which was active in all areas of the war.

Developments in Roman navy after First Punic War

After the First Punic War the Romans, always ready to learn from their past mistakes, developed a faster type of warship (minus the corvus) and had a fleet of over 200 ships in continuous service, which gave crews and commanders valuable experience. One of the most successful of the Roman naval commanders was I. Otacilius Crassus, who was praetor in command of Sicily between 217 and 211. Other notable naval commanders were M. Valerius Laevinus, P. Sulpicius Galba and C. Laelius.

Attitude of Carthaginians to sea power

The Carthaginians, however, after the loss of Sicily, Sardinia and Corsica seemed to be interested only in maintaining a fleet large enough to keep control of the commercial sea-routes between Africa and Spain. They seem to have lost the offensive spirit that had won them control of the western Mediterranean. Not only were they inferior to the Romans in the number and construction of their ships, they were also at a decided disadvantage in regard to recruiting crews.

The map on page 153, together with the extracts from Livy and the references following, makes it very clear how important Rome's control of the sea was during the Second Punic War.

In 215 Hannibal and Philip of Macedon had secretly agreed to join forces against Rome but the Macedonian and Carthaginian envoys carrying the letters were captured at sea.

> Some distance offshore they were seen by the Roman fleet patrolling the Calabrian coast, and Valerius Flaccus ordered out some light vessels to chase them and bring them back. The king's envoys tried for a time to get clear away, but soon found they were being overtaken and gave themselves up.[33]

> [The Romans] promptly initiated discussions on how best to keep the enemy out of Italy by themselves taking the initiative... A decree was issued to the effect that twenty-five new ships should be added to the twenty-five already under the command of Valerius Flaccus. The vessels were got ready and launched, the five which had brought the captured envoys were added to their number, and a fleet of thirty sailed from Ostia for Tarentum. Flaccus received orders to put on board at Tarentum the troops commanded there by Lucius Apustius — they had previously been Varro's men — and with this fleet of fifty sail not only to patrol the Italian coast but also go in search of information about the hostile intentions of Macedon.[34]

> [By 208, the Romans] believed that great naval preparations were going on that year at Carthage and that the enemy intended to cover the coasts in Italy, Sicily and Sardinia with a fleet two hundred strong.

They prepared for a war at sea on a number of fronts:

> Scipio [in Spain] was ordered to send to Sardinia fifty of the eighty ships which he had with him...'

> 'The arrangements for Sicily were... that Laevinus (who also had his command

extended) should have the fleet of seventy ships already stationed at the island and should add to it thirty other vessels which had been at Tarentum the year before. With the fleet of one hundred vessels thus formed he was to raid the African coast, if he judged it advisable.

Sulpicius' command was extended for another year, and his instructions were to hold Macedonia and Greece with the same fleet as before.

Varus, the city praetor, received instructions to refit thirty old warships lying at Ostia and to find crews for twenty new ones, to give him a fleet of fifty vessels for the protection of the coast in the vicinity of Rome.[35]

In the sections cited, Livy refers to naval engagements:

XXII: 19 Spain, 217
XXIII: 32, 34, 41 Sardinia and Africa, 215
XXIII: 34, 38 Southern Italy, 215
XXV: 31 Sicily and Africa, 212
XXVI: 24, 28 Adriatic and Greece, 210
XXVII: 22 Widespread naval arrangements, 208

Exercise

1 Draw up a chart with headings similar to the one below, and by referring to Livy fill in each column.

2 Comment on B. Caven's statement 'that Carthage in effect lost the war in 215'.[36] Write no more than one page.

Roman naval activities between 217 and 208 BC

Date	*Area of activity*	*Type of activity*	*Importance*

Scipio in Africa

Scipio's plan to end war

On his return from Spain Scipio won the consulship for 205, which was a success for the Aemilian faction. Scipio's plan was not only to carry the war to Africa but to finish it off there. He apparently threatened that if the senate opposed his plan, he would put it to the people.

Factional differences within Senate

There was, according to Livy, a bitter debate in the senate between Scipio and Fabius Maximus. Some historians suggest that this was due to a basic difference in how the two groups (Fabii and Aemilii) saw the future of Rome, but it was more a difference in the strategy that would defeat Hannibal and win the war. The decision to give Scipio the consular province of Sicily indicated that there were many in the senate who agreed with him.

Opposing views on strategy to end the war	
Scipio	*Fabius*
The offensive should be taken and Carthage attacked. Rome would never be secure until Carthage was humbled. Carthage's allies were more likely to revolt if the Romans were in Africa. Without allies, Carthage would have no troops. Fighting in Africa would compel Hannibal to return there.	The Romans could not support campaigns in both Italy and Africa. Hannibal was still a threat in Italy and there was the possibility of Mago joining him. Experience showed that invading Africa was risky. Rome should conduct a war of exhaustion and eventually drive Hannibal out of Italy.

Restrictions placed on Scipio

Although the majority in the senate probably agreed with Scipio, they were concerned that he might take it to the people and they wanted an assurance that he would abide by the senate's decision. Eventually it was decided that he should have the province of Sicily, with permission to cross to Africa if he thought that would be in the public interest.

Roman preparations in Sicily

He was not permitted to raise any new troops in Italy, although he could accept volunteers and any help from the allies in providing or equipping ships. It appears that he took 7000 volunteers with him to Sicily, and augmented these with the disgraced remnants from Cannae and with any others he could raise while there. He took thirty warships with him; there were already thirty in Sicily. He spent some time training his army and preparing the invasion force, but although he had sent Laelius across to raid the coast he did not cross over himself until 204.

Carthaginian preparations

This delay gave the Carthaginians time to prepare.

- They sent Mago with an infantry and cavalry force, plus warships, to land on the Ligurian coast (the northwest coast of Italy) and stir up trouble.
- Hasdrubal Gisgo re-established friendly relations with Syphax by marrying his beautiful daughter, Sophinisba, to him. This was a blow to Scipio, who had made an alliance with Syphax in 206 and was relying

on his co-operation in providing experienced cavalry. Scipio was left with only the support of the other Numidian chief, Masinissa, who had been ousted from his kingdom and could not provide as many troops.

- The Carthaginians had also appealed to Philip of Macedon to send help.

Scipio, when he landed in Africa, had hoped to secure the city of Utica as a winter base, but after forty days had failed to take it. As the combined forces of Hasdrubal and Syphax far outnumbered his own, his immediate problem was somehow to overcome this imbalance; both Livy and Polybius describe in detail his plan and success in evening the odds (Livy, XXX: 3–6; Polybius, XIV: 2–5). Scipio led Syphax to believe that he was prepared to consider peace proposals but his envoys, on the pretext of carrying out discussions, were gathering valuable information about the enemy camps which Scipio planned to take by surprise and burn to the ground. He divided his army, sending Masinissa and Laelius to the Numidian camp with half the men while he led the rest to the Carthaginian camp 2 kilometres away. Under cover of night Masinissa fired the Numidian camp and the men, thinking the fire was accidental, rushed out and were cut down as they tried to escape; many were burnt to death. The Carthaginians, seeing the fire, rushed from their camp to help or to watch: unarmed and unsuspecting, they were killed or driven back into their own camp, which was then fired.

Imbalance in numbers remedied by Scipio

Scipio had, at little cost to himself, almost totally annihilated two enemy armies in a single night's work. Hasdrubal and Syphax managed to escape with only a handful of men, but the Carthaginian losses were quickly replaced with fresh recruits.

Roman victory at the Great Plains

Scipio next marched into the Bagradas Valley, and in the Battle of the Great Plains, using a refined version of his tactics at Baecula and Ilipa, he won a complete victory (Livy XXX: 6–9; Polybius, XIV: 8).

Capture of Syphax

Syphax retreated to his capital, Cirta, where he was followed by Laelius and Masinissa. After expelling Syphax from his capital, Masinissa reclaimed his father's kingdom and was later confirmed by Rome as the ruler of Greater and Lesser Numidia. With Syphax' capture, the Carthaginian 'peace party' sued for peace and Scipio, hoping to finish the war before he could be replaced or have to accept help from a colleague, laid down his conditions. The Carthaginians accepted the harsh terms, and an armistice was granted until the Roman senate ratified the agreement; in the interim, the Carthaginians had time to recall Hannibal and Mago.

Armistice and recall of Hannibal

Armistice broken

The Carthaginian request for peace was accepted by Rome, but by then the armistice had already been broken when a Carthaginian fleet attacked a Roman supply convoy. Hannibal had returned with about 15 000 veterans in 203, and now that hostilities were resumed he moved inland to a place called Zama to await reinforcements from a relative of Syphax,

(a)

(b)

Coins depicting the Numidian leaders, (a) Masinissa and (b) Syphax: the reverse of both coins reveals the importance of the horse to the inhabitants of Numidia — their horsemanship played a large part in the early successes of Hannibal in Italy and the success of Scipio at Zama

who was bringing cavalry. Scipio had to link up with Masinissa, who was in the western desert, before he could face Hannibal.

The Battle of Zama, 202

The importance of Zama

According to Livy, this battle was to decide

> whether Rome or Carthage was destined to give laws to the nations, for the prize of victory would be not Italy or Africa but the whole world . . . to decide this great issue, the two most famous generals and the two mightiest armies of the two wealthiest nations in the world advanced to battle, doomed either to crown or to destroy the many triumphs each had won in the past.[37]

The forces

Opposing numbers

The two forces were approximately equal in size (Hannibal may have outnumbered Scipio in infantry, while Scipio outnumbered Hannibal in cavalry). Hannibal had a large force of elephants (about eighty), but his infantry was of a very mixed quality and he was much weaker in cavalry in both numbers and ability. Scipio's infantry was well-trained, and he was reinforced by an extremely strong contingent under Masinissa.

It was Cannae in reverse.

ROMANS

- Scipio did not arrange his cohorts in the usual way but left gaps to allow the enemy elephants to pass through without breaking up his formation. He concealed these gaps initially by occupying them with velites (light-armed skirmishers).
- Laelius with the Italian cavalry was placed on the left wing opposite the Carthaginian cavalry while the Numidians under Masinissa were on the right, opposed to Hannibal's Numidian horsemen.

CARTHAGINIANS

- Even on the admission of Scipio and other military experts, 'Hannibal achieved the distinction of having drawn his line on that day with remarkable skill.' (Polybius, XV: 12, 14)
- 'He massed a large force of elephants and stationed them in front of his army with the express purpose of throwing the enemy into confusion and breaking their ranks.'
- The mercenaries were placed next, in front of the Carthaginians 'in the hope that the enemy would become physically exhausted and their swords lose their edge through the sheer volume of the carnage before the second engagement took place'.
- 'By keeping the Carthaginians hemmed in on both sides, he compelled them to stand and fight.'
- Hannibal put 'the most warlike and the steadiest of his fighting troops (those forces which had been with him in Italy) at some distance in the rear. He intended that they should watch the battle from some distance, leaving their strength and their spirit unimpaired until he could draw upon their martial qualities at the critical moment'.

Deployment of the opposing forces prior to the Battle of Zama

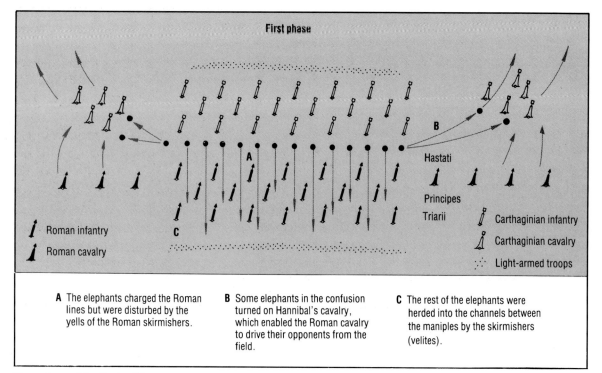

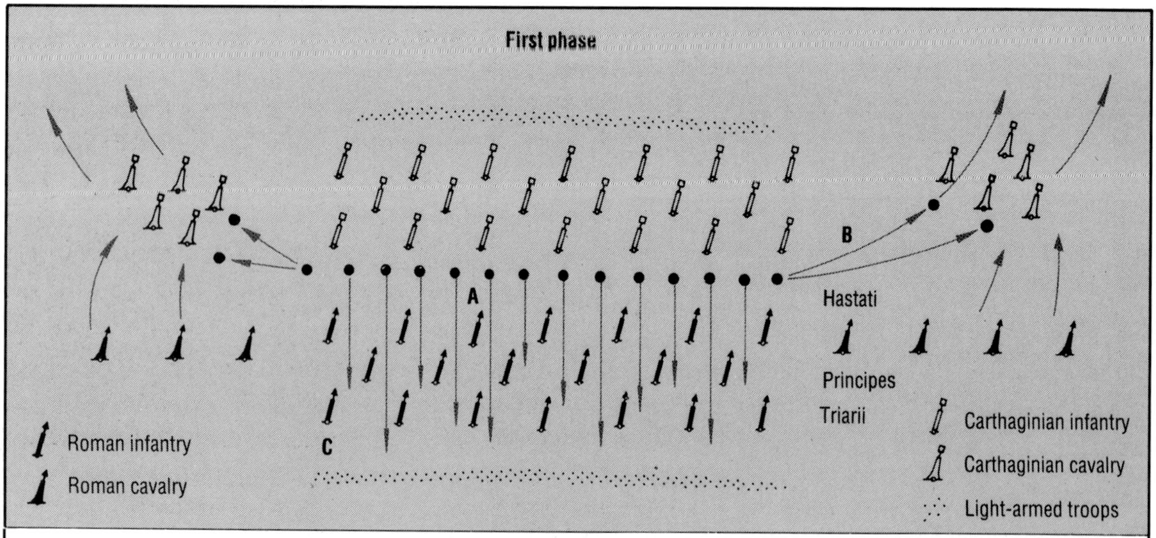

A The elephants charged the Roman lines but were disturbed by the yells of the Roman skirmishers.

B Some elephants in the confusion turned on Hannibal's cavalry, which enabled the Roman cavalry to drive their opponents from the field.

C The rest of the elephants were herded into the channels between the maniples by the skirmishers (velites).

Three phases of the Battle of Zama

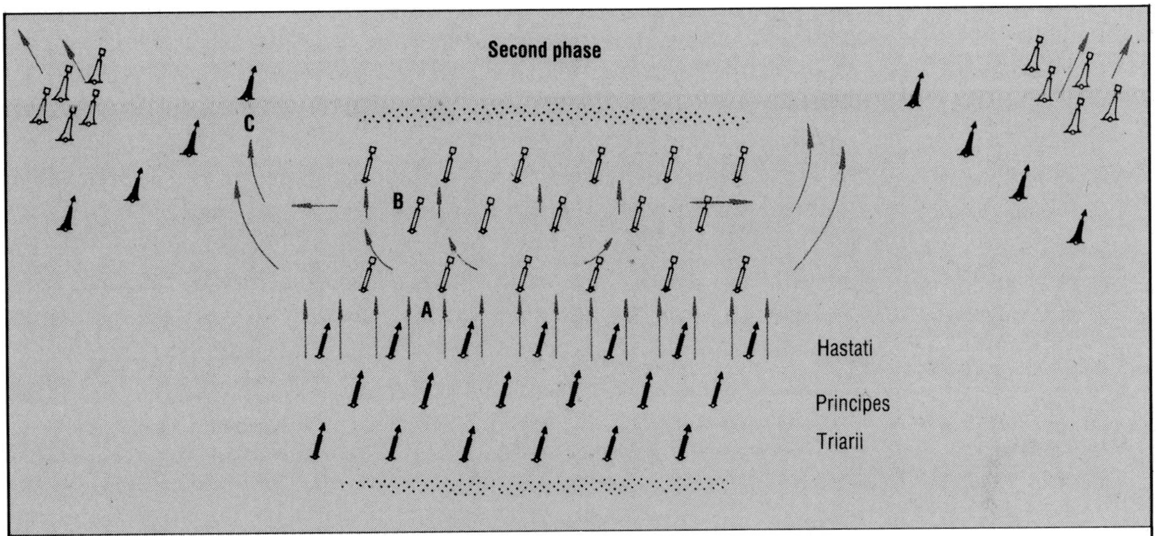

A The Roman hastati (first line) forced Hannibal's mercenaries (Celts and Ligurians) back on to his second line (Carthaginians) who would not let them through the ranks. The infuriated Celts and Ligurians moved around the flanks.
B The Carthaginian second line broke and was forced back on the veterans, who lowered their pikes to stop the fugitives from disrupting their formation.
C Hannibal's front lines were forced out on to the wings of his third line.

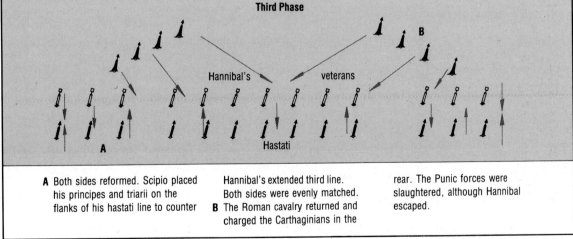

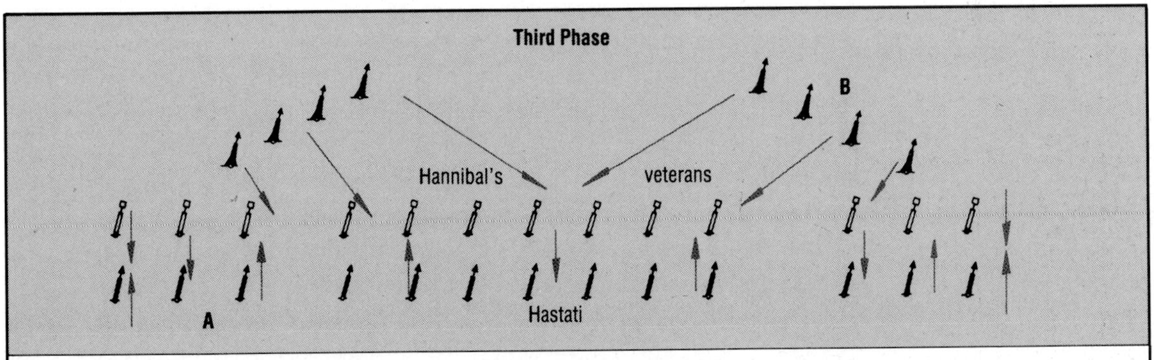

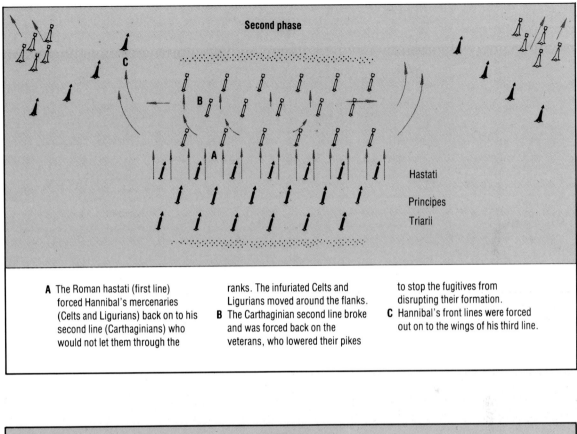

A Both sides reformed. Scipio placed his principes and triarii on the flanks of his hastati line to counter Hannibal's extended third line. Both sides were evenly matched.
B The Roman cavalry returned and charged the Carthaginians in the rear. The Punic forces were slaughtered, although Hannibal escaped.

Results of the battle

Hannibal's advice concerning peace

Hannibal had returned to Carthage thirty-five years after he had left it as a young boy to go to Spain with his father. He immediately advised the Council to accept Roman peace terms as outlined by Scipio.

Peace terms

1 The Carthaginians were to retain their autonomy — to live under their own laws.
2 They were to keep their territory within the 'Phoenician Trenches' and control of their trading centres along the coast, such as Emporia.
3 All their warships except for ten triremes, and all their elephants were to be handed over. Prisoners of war were to be returned.
4 They were to pay an indemnity of 10 000 talents in fifty annual instalments.
5 They were to restore to Masinissa all land and property which had belonged to him or his ancestors.
6 In no circumstances were they permitted to make war on any nation outside Africa, and not on any nation within Africa without Rome's permission.

After the senate ratified Scipio's terms he returned triumphantly to Rome, where he was given the cognomen of *Africanus* after the land he had conquered.

The significance of Zama

Scipio vis-a-vis Hannibal

For seventeen years before the Battle of Zama Rome had produced very few generals who were prepared to face Hannibal in open battle and none who had been able to decisively defeat him. Scipio, although he showed that he had learnt a great deal from Hannibal, was 'no slavish imitator'. His victory reflected 'superior organisation and fighting qualities of his troops' but not superior tactics.[38] Polybius' view that at Zama Hannibal met a better man than himself cannot be justified.

Carthage's dependent position

The peace treaty, although leaving Carthage intact and with wide areas still under its control, reduced it to the position of a dependent ally of Rome; it was vulnerable to any future aggression by its neighbours, and because of this the power which Rome gave to the ambitious Masinissa was to bring Rome and Carthage to war again in another fifty years.

Far-reaching effects of Second Punic War

As a result of Scipio's victory at Zama Rome controlled the western Mediterranean, and there was no power in the east equal to Carthage that could threaten its existence or prevent its future expansion.

The Second Punic War was a turning point in the history of the ancient world. It not only had a profound effect on Rome's economy as well as on its social and cultural life, but it increased the power of the senate and the ruling clique of *nobiles* within it.

A bronze bust, found at Herculaneum, believed to be of P. Cornelius Scipio Africanus

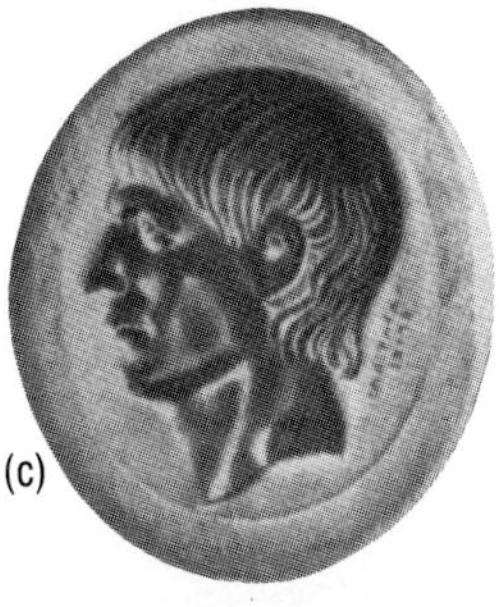

(c)

(a)

(b)

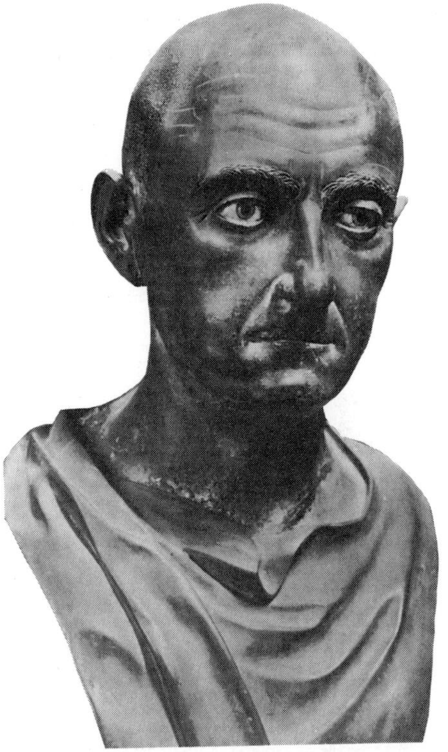

Some probable likenesses of Scipio Africanus: (a) A silver shekel minted at New Carthage; (b) A bronze coin from Apulia; (c) An engraved gold ring bearing a similar likeness to the coin from Apulia; further evidence tends to confirm this — Valerius Maximus related that Scipio's son wore a ring on which was the head of his father

Hannibal

The impact of Hannibal on the Romans

'No other foreigner made such an impact on Roman history or embedded himself so firmly in the national memory' as did Hannibal.[39]

Not only did he remain undefeated in Italy for sixteen years, but he threatened to break up the Roman confederation and he constantly outwitted Rome's best men, which lowered their self-esteem and was an affront to their dignity. According to Livy he 'had filled Italy from the Alps to the Straits of Messana and the provinces of Spain and Gaul with monuments of his tremendous campaign'.[40]

What was this opponent of Rome like?

Material evidence for his appearance

There are a number of marble and bronze busts in existence which are supposed to represent Hannibal because some of the features appear similar to those on the silver coins minted by the Barcids in Spain.

A bronze head found at Volubilis in Morocco and presumed to represent Hannibal

Bust of an older Hannibal

However, according to the historian G. C. Picard, most of them do not provide reliable evidence as to his appearance; the exception is the bronze found at Volubilis in Morocco, which closely resembles a coin from the time of Hannibal's leadership in Spain.

The silver double-shekel, minted about 220, shows a beardless head generally regarded as Hannibal. This bears a striking resemblance to another coin, struck about ten years earlier, of a bearded man believed to be his father, Hamilcar.

Written evidence for his appearance

Livy says that when Hannibal succeeded Hasdrubal in Spain

> the troops received him with unanimous enthusiasm, the old soldiers feeling that in the person of this young man Hamilcar himself was restored to them. In the features and expressions of the son's face they saw the father once again, the same vigour in his look, the same fire in his eyes.[41]

Ancient sources on Hannibal's character

When studying the sources for evidence of Hannibal's character and abilities, it must be remembered that the ancient authors had their own particular bias which was determined by their background, the specific aim of their work, and their sources. Some writers in the Roman tradition, finding nothing to criticise in Hannibal's military achievements, denigrated his personal character. The truth about him can only be gauged by his actions, and even someone as uncritically patriotic as Livy cannot disguise the greatness of Hannibal.

Bias of Polybius and Livy

Polybius and Livy differed in their views of the 'faults' in Hannibal's character.

Polybius

Polybius' admission of difficulties in getting at the truth

Polybius, who attempted to meet a strict criterion of honesty and truthfulness, says that it is 'no easy matter to state the truth either about Hannibal in particular or about other men in general who are engaged in public affairs'.[42] According to him, those aspects of Hannibal's character which created most controversy were 'excessive cruelty and excessive greed'.[43]

Cruelty – a part of war

As far as any cruelty was concerned, Polybius believed that if it did occur it was the result of 'the circumstances he [Hannibal] had to deal with' which 'were at once extraordinary and continually changing'.[44] Cruelty was inseparable from war.

Polybius refutes charges of Hannibal's excessive cruelty

Polybius tends to dismiss the charges of excessive cruelty when they come from the Romans and their allies. He explains that Hannibal's reputation for cruelty originated after Cannae, when he found it difficult to protect all the allied cities that had gone over to him. He was forced to abandon some of the cities as he had not enough troops to garrison them all, and in some cases he removed the Italians to other towns, confiscating their 'property for plunder, and in this way aroused great indignation, so that some peoples accused him of impiety and others of cruelty'[45] There are very few acts of cruelty committed by Hannibal or his army recorded by Polybius in his history. In contrast, he describes the burning by Scipio of the camps of Syphax and Hasdrubal before the Battle of Zama as exceeding 'in horror any event that has hitherto been recorded'.[46]

Prejudice of Polybius' sources

As far as the charge of excessive greed was concerned, Polybius says only that 'the impression which prevailed about him was that to the Carthaginians he was notorious for his love of money'.[47] Polybius seems to be prepared to accept this view because it came from Carthaginian sources, but it must be remembered that the Carthaginians to whom Polybius spoke were those men whose fathers forced Hannibal into exile. Polybius also mentions that

> he heard a more detailed version from Masinissa, who spoke at length on the love of money, which is a general characteristic of the Carthaginians, and which was especially so in the case of Hannibal . . .[48]

Masinissa would not have been a very reliable and unprejudiced witness, since the Romans restored him to the throne of Numidia and gave him a large slice of Carthaginian territory at the end of the Second Punic War.

Livy

Livy: harsher in his condemnation

Livy describes Hannibal's faults as 'inhuman cruelty, a more than Punic perfidy, a total disregard for the truth, honour and religion, of the sanctity of an oath and of all that other men hold sacred'.[49]

In describing the later part of the war, when Hannibal was finding it difficult to protect his allies as well as fight the Romans, Livy says 'The avarice [greed] and cruelty of his temperament inclined him to despoil where he could not protect, so that only ruins might be left to the enemy'.[50] It must be remembered that Hannibal's army had not been reinforced with fresh recruits, his men had been fighting for about fifteen years, and he was forced to keep on the move—factors which combined to make it very difficult for him to keep faith with the allies.

Failure of Livy to substantiate his charges

Despite Livy's accusation of cruelty, he records very few examples of atrocities perpetrated by Hannibal and certainly nothing to compare with Scipio's behaviour before the Battle of Zama (the burning of the camps). In referring to this appalling scene Livy, like Polybius, appears to have admired Scipio for it. In fact, Hannibal was no more cruel or more treacherous than were his contemporaries.

No real evidence of Hannibal's greed

As far as greed is concerned, there is no direct evidence that Hannibal engaged in any practices other than those usually expected of a commander in keeping his men contented and in financing a war. The day following the Battle of Cannae was spent collecting the spoils: 'An enormous quantity of valuable material was taken: Hannibal's men were given the free run of all of it with the exception of horses, men and what silver there was . . .'.[51]

Hannibal's honourable behaviour

Livy's belief that Hannibal had a total disregard for honour is not substantiated by his own account of the honourable treatment accorded the dead Roman commanders (Flaminius, Aemilius Paullus, Sempronius Gracchus and Marcellus) by Hannibal. 'He also wished to honour Flaminius with burial, but though his body was searched for with all diligence, it was never found.'[52]

Of the death of Sempronius Gracchus, Livy says

> . . . Hannibal erected a funeral pyre outside the gates of the Carthaginian camp; his troops in full armour marched past, the Spanish contingents performing dances, each tribe going through its national movements of the body and weapon drill, while Hannibal in person paid honour to the obsequies in all due acts and words.[53]

His reverence for the gods

Livy also accuses Hannibal of having no reverence for the gods and yet records that the Carthaginian travelled from New Carthage to Gades, a distance of approximately 1200 kilometres, to pay homage to his guardian deity, the Tyrian Hercules.

Other characteristics of Hannibal

Greek education

- He was essentially a Hellenistic man. Cornelius Nepos described him as a scholar as well as a soldier. He had learned Greek, and his knowledge of science was revealed when he removed the rocks blocking his way over the Alps with the use of wine and heat.

Extraordinary leadership qualities

- He was a born leader (*hegemonikos*). Hannibal was able to weld together the motley collection of mercenaries in his army so that they never fought among themselves or threatened to mutiny against him or his officers, even though they were frequently without food and money. His men revealed their best fighting qualities under his responsible leadership.

Shared his men's difficulties

- He shared the hardships of his men. Livy says that Hannibal was often seen sharing sentry and picket duty with his men, and sleeping on the ground wrapped in his cloak.

Great endurance

- He had great endurance and was tireless when there was a job to be done. 'Indefatigable both physically and mentally, he could endure with equal ease excessive heat and excessive cold; . . . when his work was done, then, and then only, he rested . . .'.[54]

Courage and coolheadedness

- He was cool-headed in an emergency and was prepared to take dangerous action if it was necessary. Commenting on him even as a young soldier, Livy says that he had more vigour and courage than any of the other officers under Hasdrubal's command, and once he was in a dangerous situation he revealed outstanding tactical ability.

Sense of humour

Use of disguises

- He had a sense of humour. Livy records a number of examples of Hannibal's humour (XXI: 30; XXII: 30; XXIII: 19; XXVII: 16), while Polybius tells the story of Hannibal's attempts to guard against attacks on his life by the Celts by wearing a series of disguises. He

> had a number of wigs made, each of which created the impression of a man of a different age, and these he constantly changed, while at the same time dressing in a style which matched his wig.[55]

Even those who knew him well found it difficult to recognise him.

Upbringing as a soldier

- One of the flaws in his character, according to Caven, was 'his all-consuming ambition to excel in what his father had taught him . . . the terrible game of war, the only worthwhile occupation for a Barca'.[56]
- He was a brilliant general; this is seen particularly in the three years between Ticinis and Cannae, but also in the years in which he was moving around Italy, 215–204. Later in his career he proved that he was a very able administrator as well.

An evaluation, from the sources, of Hannibal as a general

Outstanding generalship for sixteen years

For sixteen years Hannibal remained in Italy at the head of a loyal army and did not suffer one defeat. For the first three years, in a series of brilliant and innovative campaigns (Ticinis, Trebia, Trasimene and Cannae), he annihilated every army that the Romans threw at him. For the remaining thirteen years the Romans did not dare face him in a pitched battle; they were aware of his superiority in generalship, strategy and cavalry and they would not risk another encounter like Cannae. Hannibal, however, survived, marching backwards and forwards across the peninsula, followed and watched by the Roman legions. Polybius seems to think that those last thirteen years are his greatest claim to fame, and Livy expresses a similar view: 'I hardly know whether Hannibal was not more wonderful when Fortune was against him than in his hours of success'.[57] There is no doubt that to have maintained the struggle against the increasing odds required 'great strategic skill, tactical ingenuity and sheer force of personality'.[58]

Aspects of his generalship

Calculated risks

He was prepared to take a calculated risk in order to gain the initiative. Although very few ancient generals would have planned and put into effect Hannibal's march into Italy (considering the distance, the odds to be faced and the weather), Polybius says 'he pursued his plans with sound common sense'.[59] His rapid march to Italy over the Alps gave him the initiative by surprising the Romans and upsetting their plans. His recruitment of Gauls in Cisalpine Gaul enabled him to take northern Italy in two months, and he continued to take the initiative for the next three years.

Took and held initiative

Loyalty of troops

His men, 'a hotch-potch of the riff-raff of all nationalities',[60] showed him the utmost loyalty, and he could make unlimited demands on their courage and endurance. He was able to encourage them and keep up their spirits during the terrible crossing of the Alps, and the struggle through the swamps of northern Italy (when Hannibal lost the sight of one eye) tested their loyalty. Even when all hopes of victory had vanished with the death of Hasdrubal and the destruction of his army, the troops remained staunchly loyal to Hannibal.

Maintained loyalty of his men at all times

Brilliant strategy

He was a master of strategy, able to assess a situation and come up with a solution involving a strategy so daring in its departure from conventional military methods that the early Roman commanders were unable to cope with his tactics. 'Hannibal was always inclined by temperament to favour the unexpected solution'.[61]

Used daring, innovative and appropriate strategies

His ambush at Trasimene was unique, considering the size of his army. It was organised in such a way that the Roman troops and their officers did not understand what was happening. 'In the chaos that reigned not a soldier could recognise his own standard or knew his place in the ranks'.[62]

Trasimene

The disposition of his troops at Cannae, to create a gigantic trap, was brilliant.

Cannae

His escape with his troops from the trap set by Fabius in Campania (using the oxen with lighted branches attached to their horns) showed once again his ability to deceive the enemy.

Fabius' trap

At Zama, his only defeat, he was innovative in the use of his third line of veterans as a reserve. Even though Scipio Africanus adopted and adapted Hannibal's tactics, Polybius considered that it was Scipio's superior army, rather than his skill, that won the day.

Zama

Psychological warfare

Learned his enemies' weaknesses

He was an expert at psychological warfare. He played on his opponents' weaknesses and developed his plans accordingly. Polybius says that 'there is no more precious asset for a general than a knowledge of his opponent's guiding principles and character . . .', and a good commander 'must train his eye upon the weak spots of his opponent's defence, not in his body but in his mind'.[63]

Hannibal was able to use the rashness, excessive audacity, vanity, cautiousness or foolish ambitions of the various Roman commanders for his own benefit—the impulsiveness of Flaminius at Trasimene, the rashness of Minucius, the cautiousness of Fabius and the reckless nature of Varro at Cannae.

Flaminius

According to Polybius, Hannibal learned

> that Flaminius possessed a rare talent for the arts of demagogy and playing to the gallery, but very little for the practical conduct of the war, and yet was absurdly overconfident about his own resources.[64]

Hannibal correctly expected that Flaminius could be easily provoked into battle.

Minucius

Hannibal obtained information about the rivalry between Fabius and Minucius 'and of Municius' ambitious and impulsive nature'. 'He concluded that these factors should work in his favour rather than against him, and he thereupon turned his attention to Minucius.'[65]

Deployment of forces

Utilised each component of his army to the maximum

He had a great ability to make the most of each component of his army—cavalry, heavy infantry, skirmishers, and even his elephants. The cavalry (the 'heavy' cavalry of Spaniards and Celts and the brilliant Numidian horsemen) played a decisive role at Trebia and Cannae. The Spaniards and Celts were used as a striking force because they fought in tight formation, while the Numidians, trained to fight in looser and more manoeuvrable formations, were used by Hannibal in a variety of roles—to screen, cover and harass, and as a holding force. The inferior Roman cavalry could not cope with the Numidians who 'were men of exceptional endurance'.[66]

Numidian cavalry

At Trebia, Hannibal ordered his Numidians to ride up to the enemy's camp and provoke the Romans into following them across the river before they had made their preparations for battle.

Prior to the battle at Cannae, he used his Numidian cavalry to attack the Roman water-carriers, preventing them from drawing water. This action provoked Varro. During the Battle of Cannae, the Numidians 'kept the Roman cavalry effectively out of the battle by drawing them off and attacking them now from one quarter and now from another'. They did not suffer many losses themselves because of 'their peculiar methods of fighting'.[67]

Infantry, skirmishers and elephants

The way Hannibal used his Spaniards, Celts (in the centre) and Africans (on the wings) at Cannae and his skirmishers and elephants at Trebia indicates his ability to use all parts of his army effectively, never throwing away opportunities by asking them to do something of which they were not capable.

Selected site to suit purposes

He chose the site of battle to suit his purposes — the ambush at Trebia along the river with its high overhanging banks covered with dense scrub, the ambush at Trasimene with the narrow defile between the lake and the hills and the flat treeless plain at Cannae which favoured Hannibal's cavalry.

Forced Romans into defensive tactics

His early victories gave him the upper hand and forced the Romans into the defensive 'Fabian' tactics. They were afraid to engage him in open battle.

Why was Rome victorious despite Hannibal's brilliance?

Strength of manpower

Rome had an inexhaustible supply of manpower (Roman citizens, Latin allies and Italian allies) and maintained the loyalty of most of her allies throughout the war. This was the main reason for her victory over Carthage and later control of the Mediterranean region.

Citizens and allies

It has been estimated that in 218 there were approximately 325 000 adult male citizens of whom more than two-thirds would have been available for military service. Those of her Italian allies (socii) who did not as yet have Roman citizenship were still expected to provide contingents of men to fight alongside her legions. These allies were hoping to gain Roman citizenship in the near future.

Increase in number of legions after Cannae

In previous wars Rome's army comprised four legions and an equal number of allies, but Polybius says that for the Battle of Cannae the Romans 'decided to put eight legions into the field, a step which the Romans had never taken before, each legion consisting of 5000 men not counting the allies'.[68] There were already two legions in Spain under the Scipios.

Despite the catastrophe of Cannae Rome had fourteen legions in the field in 215, and within five years of Cannae the number of Roman and allied legions in the various theatres of war (Italy, Spain, Sicily, Sardinia and Gaul) was raised to an unprecedented level of twenty-five. As well as the legionaries, there were the allied troops and those serving at sea. This

Private individuals help pay for troops

effort, however, was not without great sacrifice on the part of Romans and allies alike. Livy records that there were difficulties in finding enough men for the legions and the fleets. In 214 the consuls issued an edict stipulating that people with property over a certain value were to provide for anything from one to seven sailors and take responsibility for their pay for one year. 'This was the first occasion on which a Roman fleet was provided with crews at the expense of private individuals.'[69]

Recruitment after 212

In 212 the consuls were ordered by the senate

> to appoint six commissioners, three to work within fifty miles of Rome and three beyond those limits. Their duty was to inspect all free-born males in every country district, market town and local centre, and to enlist for service any who seemed fit to bear arms even though not yet of military age.[70]

Despite the difficulties after Cannae, there is no evidence that the Romans neglected any of the theatres of war because of lack of men.

Loyalty of Latins and northern allies

Hannibal's efforts to break up the Roman confederation were not really successful. After Trasimene, not a single town in northern or central Italy opened its gates to him. Whether this was due to Rome's policy of granting degrees of citizenship, the similarities between Rome and her Latin allies, the fear of reprisal, the feeling among the Italic people that Hannibal was more of an alien than Rome, or a combination of all these things is unimportant; their loyalty was a major factor in Rome's survival.

Defections among southern allies shortlived

Although many of Rome's southern allies — such as the important cities of Capua and Tarentum — made peace with Hannibal after Cannae, this situation was shortlived. Owing to Roman persistence, most of the south was regained by 209.

Carthaginian manpower limited — sometimes unreliable

It was the pressure of Rome's superior numbers that assured the final result of the Second Punic War. Carthage was unable to call on such a reserve of manpower, despite the size of its empire. Carthaginian citizens were not recruited into the army prior to Scipio's invasion of Africa, and the supply of mercenaries was limited. Even though Hannibal's troops in Italy were staunchly loyal to him, the Spaniards wavered in their support and the Numidians finally allied themselves with Scipio.

Failure of Carthaginian government to reinforce Hannibal

Vital decision to maintain Roman troops in Spain

From the beginning of the war, Rome saw the importance of extending hostilities in Spain and keeping the Carthaginian forces occupied there. This was achieved between 218 and 211 by P. Cornelius Scipio and his brother, Cn. Cornelius Scipio. Although their careers eventually ended in disaster at the hands of Hannibal's brother, Hasdrubal, their campaigns contributed to the Roman victory. They kept Hasdrubal occupied, and prevented him from marching to Italy by defeating him in 215.

Diversion of Carthaginian troops to Spain

The Carthaginian government was forced to divert successive drafts of troops to Spain rather than to Italy.

> Hannibal's brother was on the point of leaving Carthage with reinforcements of 12 000 foot, 1500 horses, twenty elephants and 1000 talents of silver, under an escort of sixty warships; but it was now suggested in certain quarters that he should be diverted with all these forces, naval and military, from Italy to Spain.[71]

The Carthaginians have been criticised for their failure to reinforce Hannibal's troops, but it was vital for them to keep Spain, both as a recruiting ground for troops and for its silver mines.

Inability of Hannibal to recruit Italians

After Cannae, Hannibal could not raise troops from those towns that went over to him. Many of them, such as Capua, demanded that they retain their independence and have the right not to serve in the Carthaginian army against their will.

On one occasion only, in 215, the Carthaginian fleet under Bomilcar successfully landed troops, supplies and elephants at Locri in southern Italy.

No troops from Spain reached Hannibal

The young Scipio (Publius Cornelius Scipio, son of the commander of that name) continued his father's and uncle's work in Spain (209–205); he defeated Hasdrubal at Baecula and accepted the surrender of Spain in 206. Hasdrubal was able to get away with his troops to Italy and hoped to link up with Hannibal, but when he was defeated at the Metaurus River in 207 Hannibal was left without any hope of support.

In 205, Hannibal's brother Mago landed troops in Liguria (in the northwest), where he kept a Roman army occupied, but this did not help Hannibal.

Control of the sea

Although there were no major sea battles in the Second Punic War as there were in the previous conflict between Carthage and Rome, the significance of sea power in the final outcome of the war should not be overlooked.

Carthaginian navy inferior to that of Rome

Not used effectively against Romans

After the First Punic War the Carthaginians did not concentrate on rebuilding their navy, and during the Second Punic War it was inferior in size and used essentially for communications and for transporting supplies and troops between Africa and Spain. It was not used effectively to reinforce Hannibal, to disrupt Roman supply lines, to raid the coastline of Italy or to prevent Scipio from sailing to Africa. In fact, it appears that the Carthaginian navy preferred to avoid any encounter with the Roman fleet.

Only in 213, at Syracuse, did the Carthaginian fleet make any real effort, although the landing of troops and supplies by Bomilcar at Locri and Mago in Liguria indicates that Hannibal could have been given more support by the navy.

Romans transported troops without interference

Rome's possession of Sicily, Sardinia and Corsica and its alliance with Massilia gave it complete control of the western Mediterranean. This allowed the Romans to transport their troops to these areas without any interference and to keep them provisioned. The naval bases of Sicily provided starting points for raids on Africa: Scipio's invasion (204–203) began from Lilybaeum.

Roman navy prevented Philip joining up with Hannibal

A vital contribution of the Roman navy was in preventing Hannibal from gaining the support of Philip V of Macedon after the two had signed an alliance in 215. A Roman fleet of fifty ships patrolled the Adriatic, preventing Philip from carrying out his part of the bargain with Hannibal — 'to cross to Italy with the largest fleet he could raise [perhaps 200 ships], harry the coast, and carry on offensive operations by land and sea to the best of his ability'.[72]

Strong leadership of the senate

Experienced politicians

The senate, especially after Cannae, directed the whole war effort sensibly and successfully since it contained experienced politicians and successful military commanders.

The senate's decision to keep and reinforce the troops in Spain showed its understanding of the importance of the Spanish front, and its continued siege of Capua, when Hannibal marched on Rome, indicated that the senators had no intention of allowing Hannibal to dictate strategy. As well as deciding where the legions and the fleet were to operate and how many troops and ships were to be sent to which theatres of war, they organised supply lines and reinforcements, dealt with their allies, and handled the state's finances.

Prorogation of commands

The senate chose men of proven merit for the chief commands, and in order to allow these men to retain command of the same armies and fleets for long periods, the senate made use of the practice of prorogation (extending commands).

Rival factions 'united' to resist

Although 'rival' factions within the senate determined the changing strategy during the war, there was no group which would have negotiated peace while Hannibal was on Italian soil, or from a position of weakness.

Personal sacrifices of senators

The senators themselves led the way in the self-sacrifice needed after Cannae, and took unusual methods to alleviate the fears of the people at that time. As well as resorting to the primitive practice of human sacrifice, they sent delegations to foreign religious centres, such as Delphi, they consulted the Sibylline Books and they introduced the worship of the Magna Mater.

Popular support

Patriotism and tenacity of Roman people

The Roman people were determined and patriotic. After Cannae, they showed their determination to continue the fight by making great personal sacrifices. The wealthier citizens advanced money to the bankrupt treasury and contributed slaves to the army, while the ordinary soldiers did not press for their pay and all citizens paid a double rate of tribute.

Greatness of Scipio Africanus

Scipio's foresight

In Scipio Africanus, Rome possessed a great military leader. He realised that Spain was the key to the war and it was there that he secured his base, prepared his army and cut off Hannibal's supply lines. He knew, however, that Hannibal had to be defeated not in Italy, but on his own ground in Africa.

Acquisition of a Numidian cavalry

He saw the need for a strong cavalry to equal Hannibal's, so he negotiated with the Numidian chieftains, Masinissa and Syphax. He trained his army to a standard never before reached by Roman troops.

Scipio's training methods

His reform of traditional tactics made the army more flexible and also allowed individual commanders to use their initiative. Each soldier underwent a program of drill and weapon-handling similar to that of the gladiatorial schools.

Adapted Hannibal's methods

Scipio learned from Hannibal's tactics, and employed them against him at Zama.

11 The Third Punic War, 149–146

IN THE FIFTY YEARS after the Second Punic War Rome became involved in events in Macedon, Greece and Asia (see chapter 12). During this time the Roman attitude to overseas possessions and allies gradually hardened, until in the year 146 both Corinth and Carthage were totally destroyed by Roman forces.

The following assignment requires the student to read relevant passages from the sources:

Plutarch, *Cato the Elder* (Makers of Rome), 25–6
Livy, XLII: 23–5, 'Rome and the Mediterranean'
Polybius, XXXVI: 9, 'The Rise of the Roman Empire'
Appian, *The Punic Wars*, 8, 19: 132–5

Several general texts—for instance H. H. Scullard's *A History of the Roman World 753–146 BC*—should be consulted as well as texts specifically on the period, such as A. E. Astin's *Scipio Aemilianus*, chapters 5, 6 and 7, and B. Caven's *The Punic Wars.*

Assignment: The Third Punic War

1 *The period between the wars*
Referring to any major text, draw a timeline from 201 to 146, marking in events relevant to Carthage and its relationship to Masinissa and Rome—for example, the dates of the various commissions sent by Rome to investigate Carthage's complaints against Masinissa.

2 *The background to the Third Punic War*

(a) What was the position of Carthage as a result of the peace treaty signed in 201?

(b) What part did Hannibal play in restoring Carthage's prosperity?

(c) What does Hannibal's exile from Carthage and subsequent death in Asia indicate about certain elements in the Carthaginian and Roman governments at the time?

(d) What was Masinissa's position at the end of the Second Punic War?

(e) How did Masinissa abuse his position in Africa and undermine Carthage?

(f) What was Rome's reaction to Masinissa's activities? Consider the various commissions sent to Africa by Rome (193, 182, 174, 172, 157 and 153) noting particularly the one in 172, mentioned in Livy, and the one in 153 mentioned in Plutarch, *Cato the Elder*, 26.

(g) Describe the part played by Cato in promoting fear and hatred towards Carthage, and note the attitude of Scipio Nasica.

3 *The outbreak of the war*

(a) What action did Carthage take, 151–150, which the Romans believed gave them a cause for war?

(b) To avoid war, the Carthaginians surrendered unconditionally to Rome. By this act of *deditio* they thought they were safe. What does Polybius mean when he says

> But latterly throughout their dealings with the Carthaginians they [the Romans] had practised deceit and fraud, coming forward with one set of proposals at one moment and disguising them at the next, until they deprived the city of all hope of obtaining help from her allies. These methods . . . could only be described in any honest view as something hardly distinguishable from impiety or treachery.
>
> The Carthaginians had committed no irretrievable offence against their opponents, yet the Romans had inflicted penalties which were not only harsh but final, even though the enemy had agreed to accept all their conditions and obey all their commands.[1]

(c) Why did the senate follow Cato's line to destroy Carthage totally when there was no reason to do so?

(d) How did the Carthaginians react to this treachery on the part of Rome?

4 *The war with Carthage and its final destruction*

(a) Explain briefly why the consuls Manilius, Censorinus and Piso were unsuccessful against Carthage in 149 and 148.

(b) In point form, outline the background and the political and military career of Scipio Aemilianus, to 148.

(c) How was Scipio Aemilianus elected to the consulship in 147, when he was ineligible for it?

(d) Very briefly describe Scipio's siege of Carthage and the desperate reactions to it of the Carthaginians.

(e) Read Appian's account of the final destruction of Carthage.

The destruction of Carthage was a result of fear, hatred and a chance to settle old scores once and for all. However, it also reflected a general hardening of attitude towards and impatience with those states which broke treaties and which involved Rome in long and costly wars.

Rome's good name was tarnished by 'the callous and calculating way in which the order [to destroy Carthage] was enforced, together with the nervous bullying which had originally goaded Carthage into retaliating against Masinissa'.[2]

The Romans annexed about 13 000 square kilometres of Carthaginian territory, and formed the province of Africa. By 146 Rome had six provinces, five of which were acquired as a result of the wars with Carthage.

Timeline: The Punic Wars

		Events	*Personalities*
First Punic War	265	Mamertines appeal to Rome for help	Claudius Caudex (R)[1] Hanno (C)[2]
	264	Rome accepts; declaration of war	
	263	Rome's treaty with Hiero of Syracuse	Hiero (Syr)[3]
	262	Rome builds a fleet; first Roman victory at sea in Battle of Mylae	Duilius (R)
	257	Battle of Tyndaris	
	256	Carthaginian naval defeat—Ecnomus Roman invasion of Africa	Atilius Regulus (R) Xanthippus (Sp)[4]
	255	Roman forces under Regulus defeated Roman fleet wrecked off Camerina	
	253	Another Roman fleet lost	
	251	Roman victory at Panormus in Sicily	
	249	Romans defeated at sea off Drepana Another Roman fleet lost in a storm	Claudius Pulcher (R)
	247	Hamilcar Barca appointed to command in Sicily; Hannibal born	Hamilcar Barca (C)

		Events	Personalities
First Punic War	245	Rome abandons sea; numerous losses Punic fleet recalled and decommissioned	
	244	Hamilcar's guerilla warfare in west Sicily	
	243	Rome constructs new fleet by private subscription; Carthage refits fleet	
	242	Lilybaeum captured by Romans	
	241	Romans defeat Carthaginians at Aegates Islands; end of First Punic War	Lutatius Catulus (R)
Interwar period	240	Carthaginian Mercenary War in Africa	Mathos (L)[5]
	238	Roman occupation of Sardinia	
	237	End of Mercenary War Hamilcar commands in Spain Hamilcar builds up Carthaginian resources and power in Spain	Hamilcar Barca (C)
	231	Roman embassy sent to check on Hamilcar	
	229	Death of Hamilcar — succeeded by son-in-law Hasdrubal Hasdrubal establishes the city of New Carthage as Punic headquarters	Hasdrubal (C)
	226	Ebro River Treaty between Rome and Hasdrubal Hasdrubal extends Carthaginian sphere of influence in Spain more by diplomacy than force	
	221	Hasdrubal assassinated — Hannibal (Hamilcar's son) commander in Spain	
	219	Siege and capture of Saguntum by Hannibal	Hannibal (C)
Second Punic War	218	Outbreak of Second Punic War; Hannibal crosses Alps to Italy; Battle of Trebia	
	217	Battle of Lake Trasimene	Flaminius (R) Fabius Maximus (R)

		Events	Personalities
Second Punic War	216	Battle of Cannae — turning point in the war; Capua defects to Hannibal	Terentius Varro (R) Aemilius Paulus (R)
	215	Alliance between Hannibal and Philip V of Macedon	
	214	War spreads to Syracuse	
	212	Hannibal takes Tarentum, Syracuse falls to Rome, Romans begin siege of Capua	
	211	Hannibal marches on Rome; fall of Capua Elder Scipios killed in Spain	Gnaeus Scipio (R) Publius Scipio (R)
	210	Younger Scipio — P. Cornelius Scipio (Africanus) — takes command in Spain	
	209	Scipio captures New Carthage Q. Fabius Maximus recaptures Tarentum	Publius Cornelius Scipio (Africanus) (R)
	208	Battle of Baecula in Spain	
	207	Battle of Metaurus; Hasdrubal killed bringing reinforcements to Hannibal	Hasdrubal (C) Claudius Nero (R)
	206	Further successes for Scipio in Spain Minor operations in Italy	 Claudius Marcellus (R)
	204	Scipio lands in Africa	Masinissa (N)[6]
	203	Battle of the Great Plains; Hannibal withdraws from Italy to Africa	P. Cornelius Scipio (Africanus) (R)
	202	Battle of Zama	
	201	Peace concludes Second Punic War Carthage becomes a client state	Hannibal (C)
		Romans concerned with troubles in Macedon, Greece and the east for next fifty years (see chapter 12)	
Third Punic War	151	Carthage forced to declare war on Masinissa, King of Numidia	Masinissa (N)
	150	Rome accuses Carthage of breaking the peace and declares war	

		Events	*Personalities*
Third Punic War	149	Romans invade Africa and siege of Carthage begins	
		Total blockade of Carthage organised by Scipio Aemilianus	Scipio Aemilianus (R)
	146	Sack and destruction of Carthage, which becomes the Roman province of Africa	

[1] Rome
[2] Carthage
[3] Syracuse
[4] Sparta
[5] Libya
[6] Numidia

12 Rome and the east, 200–146

The wars in Macedonia, Greece and Asia

Changing policies in Rome

By 200 Rome was at war with Macedon

Rome had become a world power in 201 with the defeat of Carthage in the Second Punic War, but the long struggle with Hannibal had left the Roman people tired of war, the treasury empty, Italy devastated, the state with more land than it could develop, and newly acquired provinces to organise. Yet within the space of one year, in 200, Rome became involved in a series of campaigns in Macedonia, Greece and Asia which eventually gave it control of the eastern Mediterranean as well.

Timeline: The wars in the east

214–205	First Macedonian War
200–196	Second Macedonian War
194	Roman evacuation of Greece
192–188	War with Antiochus of Syria
172–168	Third Macedonian War
167	Macedon divided into four independent states
149	Andriscus' attempt to reunite Macedon (Fourth Macedonian War)

147	Macedon a Roman province
146	War between Rome and the Achaean League Corinth destroyed (the same year as Carthage)

Two questions are relevant in regard to this period.

1 Why did Rome embark on a war with Philip V of Macedon in 200?

2 What changes occurred in Rome's policy towards the east between 200 and 146?

Reasons for Rome's war with Philip in 200

Conflict with Philip of Macedon

Rome had been drawn into Greek affairs as early as 214 in the so-called First Macedonian War with Philip V.

While Rome was engaged in a deadly struggle with Hannibal, Philip—ambitious, anxious to expand his influence and suspicious of Rome—concluded an alliance with Hannibal. After sending a fleet into the Adriatic Sea, the Romans made a temporary alliance with the Aetolian League in central Greece and stirred up trouble for Philip, which kept him occupied and unable to help Hannibal.

At this point the Romans did little to help the Greeks; they left them to work out their own future, and made peace with Philip. This was merely a side issue, and although the Romans were watchful of Philip they were not interested in getting involved in the east.

Alliance between Philip and Antiochus

In 202 Philip and Antiochus of Syria made a secret alliance, agreeing to divide up the Asian and European possessions of the Ptolemies of Egypt, since a child had come to the throne there. This threatened the balance of power in the east.

When Philip committed certain atrocities in the Aegean region and

The head of Philip V of Macedon depicted on a silver tetradrachm

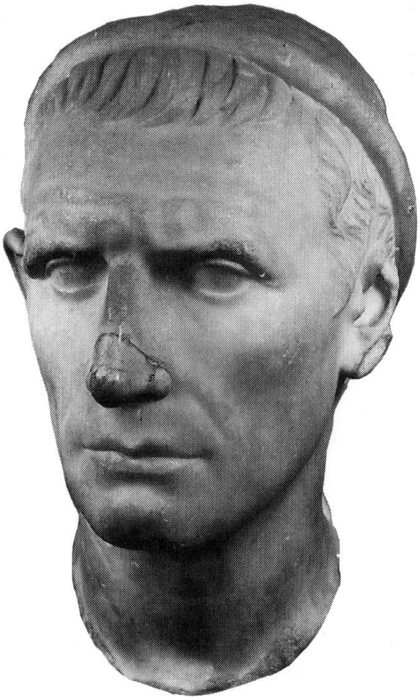

Antiochus, King of Syria

had attacked Athenian territory, Pergamum, Rhodes and Athens appealed to Rome for help. This put Rome in a difficult position, because

Romans' dilemma

- its rules relating to warfare (*ius fetiale*) permitted only wars in which Rome was the injured party or in which its allies (socii) were threatened;
- Philip had kept his peace with Rome and the Romans could not justifiably declare war on him;
- the Roman people did not want war, and rejected the consuls' first call for it.

Rhodes and Pergamum stressed the danger from Antiochus rather than from Philip and suggested that the pact between these two could ultimately be aimed at Italy, using Greece as a base. The Romans would not have forgotten Philip's alliance with Hannibal but the question of the legality of the war had to be considered, and when it was referred to the fetial priests they decided to disregard the distinction between allies by oath (socii) and 'friends' (*amici*). By stretching the fetial law to cover 'friends', the priests put an end to the people's fears and the comitia centuriata voted for a preventative war to be fought in Greece.

A defensive war in Greece

An ultimatum was issued to Philip: he was not to interfere in Greek states in the future and he must pay back Rhodes and Pergamum for any losses incurred. Philip refused.

Battle of Cynocephalae

A Roman force under Titus Quinctius Flamininus, consul for 198 and a staunch philhellene (lover of things Greek), achieved a victory over Philip's phalanx at Cynocephalae in 197, using both force and diplomacy. The leniency of the peace imposed on Philip was due to the Roman fear of Antiochus: Flamininus had received information 'that Antiochus had started from Syria with an army, with the intention of crossing over into Europe',[1] and it would suit the Romans not to incur the hatred of Philip by imposing a harsh peace.

Greek 'freedom' declared by Flamininus

The Roman senate decided on a settlement for the Greek cities, and at the Isthmian Games at Corinth in 196 Flamininus declared Greek freedom.

> The senate and the people of Rome and Titus Quinctius their general, having subjected King Philip and the Macedonians, do hereby order that the following states shall be free, independent and ruled by their own laws.[2]

He then read the list of states.

Roman evacuation of Greece — no annexations

It was two more years, in 194, before Roman troops evacuated Greece, leaving the cities under carefully selected municipal authorities. Livy records that Flamininus called on the Greek leaders 'to work for harmony among themselves; he appealed to all the cities to take counsel together in the interest of unity'. He ended his speech by 'saying that they gained their freedom through the arms of others' and that they should 'guard and preserve it by their own watchfulness, so that the Roman people might be assured that liberty had been given to men who deserved it, and that their boon had been well bestowed'.[3]

The Greeks were 'free' under a Roman protectorate.

Modern scholars ascribe variety of motives to Rome

The ancient sources say very little about the motives behind the senate's decision to fight Philip, but modern historians have suggested a number of reasons, ranging from greed for empire to sentimental philhellenism.

A gold stater showing the head of T. Quinctius Flamininus, the victor at the Battle of Cynocephalae in 197 — this was the first occasion on which a living Roman was shown on a coin

Modern viewpoints

Jerome Carcopino

Carcopino maintains that during the war with Hannibal successful generals —and others—saw the possibilities of conquest and eventually 'led the people into imperialism without their wishing to'.[4] These men used the pretext of Rome's safety to wage war, and although they did not ask for territory for Rome when they were successful, they plundered, and demanded heavy indemnities. Their triumphs (ritual processions awarded to victorious generals) reflected the enormous qualities of wealth that flowed into Rome.

Plutarch's account of the triumph of Aemilius Paullus (see page 193), the victor at the battle of Pydna in 168, leaves no doubt about the rewards gained by the Romans.

Theodor Mommsen

Mommsen says that political, commercial and moral motives induced Rome to go to war with Philip.

1 Rome did not want to have dangerous neighbours; when Philip attempted to increase his power at the expense of Egypt, he had to be stopped.
2 By attempting to subjugate Rhodes and Pergamum, Philip would have upset the trade of Italy and Sicily in the east.
3 Hellenic sympathies were very strong in Rome at that stage, especially with the consul Flamininus.

Tenney Frank

Frank put forward three reasons for Rome's war with Philip.

1 Rome feared and hated Philip but knew that he would have to be faced at some time, since he was daring, forceful and ambitious.
2 Rome wished to be accepted into the 'Aegean concert of powers',[5] as this would gain it prestige and dignity among the civilisations of the old world.
3 Philhellenism was also a factor, since 'never in Rome was enthusiasm for things Greek so outspoken as at this time'.[6]

Ernst Badian

Badian also maintains that Rome feared and hated Philip. There were many Romans who wanted revenge for his act of treachery in allying himself with Hannibal. This aggressive policy was supported by the 'principal Eastern experts', Galba, Tuditanus and Cotta. These man 'knew Philip's weaknesses' and 'had discovered how the Greeks could be turned against him, . . . it was they, moreover who knew that Illyria would only be safe when Macedon had been humbled'.[7]

Maurice Holleaux

Holleaux believes that the Romans 'imagined themselves to be threatened when they were not'—that in fact the relationship between Philip and Antiochus was not aimed at Italy.[8] The senate rushed into the war with Philip because Pergamum and Rhodes, in their own interests, were able to persuade Rome to do it. 'Rome was serving the cause and furthering the interests of Pergamum and Rhodes' in the belief that she was securing her own safety.[9]

Suggested motives for the war – a summary

- Rome feared that Philip in his ambition to expand might attack Italy.
- Strong sympathies were felt towards the Greeks—philhellenism.
- Some members of the ruling class harboured feelings of revenge.
- The balance of power in the east could be upset.
- There were possibilities of rewards from conquest apart from acquired territory.

Rome's changing policy, 200–146

Romans preferred a policy of non-interference

From 200–194 the Romans had followed a policy of championing the Greeks and of non-interference. Their evacuation in 194 indicated that they had no intention of making permanent conquests.

192–189

During this period the policy was of continuing surveillance of Greek activities, but this was unsettled by the expanding activities of Antiochus—aided by Hannibal, in exile in Asia—and by the Aetolian League in Greece.

Romans reluctantly intervened in Greek affairs

The Romans were forced to intervene once more when the Aetolian League began stirring up trouble for them. The League had helped Rome against Philip, and had expected a large slice of Philip's territory when he was defeated.

Resentful of Flamininus' settlement, the League invited Antiochus to occupy Greece as a liberator, but when he accepted the offer he found that few Greeks supported him; he was defeated by a Roman force at Thermopylae and driven from the country. His fleet was beaten in the Aegean and he was pursued to Asia, where he was defeated by Publius and Lucius Scipio. He was forced to sign a peace treaty, by the terms of which he was to confine himself to Syria, to pay a large indemnity and to surrender captured territory, a large part of which was divided between Pergamum and Rhodes.

No desire to be involved in eastern affairs

The Romans evacuated Asia, keeping no territory for themselves as they were anxious to disentangle themselves from eastern affairs. The Aetolian League was crushed, and in 188 the Roman troops left Greece for the second time.

189–168

This was a time of subtle changes.

Romans drawn into continuing Greek quarrels

The Romans had guaranteed Greek independence and adopted a policy of protection towards them. As a result, they were drawn more and more into Greek affairs in order to arbitrate in the continuing Hellenic quarrels. The senate was often slow to act, and when it did its decisions often created further problems because the Romans tended to support those who appealed to their authority, whether or not they were right. As the number of disputes increased, Rome's patience suffered.

Reaction against philhellenic policy

By 187 the philhellenic faction within the senate, led by the Scipios, was suffering from a reaction in Rome; Cato, who disliked things Greek and the corrupting influence of the east on Roman character, was the spokeman for the conservative, anti-Hellenic group. The new sentiment was reflected in the purging in 185 of the Bacchanalia (societies which practised the secret orgiastic rites of the Greek cult of Bacchus) and in attempts to discredit the Scipios by a number of prosecutions. The adverse effect of the east on Roman generals was illustrated by the treatment of Galatia by the consul Manlius, in 189. Without any justification, Manlius crushed Galatia and extorted enormous amounts of booty and plunder.

Macedonian power was revived, first under Philip and then by his eldest son, Perseus, when he succeeded to the throne in 179. Not only did Perseus build up Macedon's resources and prosperity, he also contracted marriage alliances with Syria and Bithynia and began interfering in the Greek cities by supporting anti-Roman factions.

Alarm in Rome at resurgence of Macedonian power

Perseus' activities caused alarm in Rome, and although many complaints about him were unfounded Rome declared war on him in 171 — this was the Third Macedonian War. Lucius Aemilius Paullus was sent to deal with Perseus, whom he defeated in 168 at the Battle of Pydna.

168–149

The year 168 marked an obvious turning point in Rome's policy towards Greece and Macedon.

A hardening of attitude and an increase in brutality

Increasing brutality and awareness of benefits after 168

The Romans still showed no desire to acquire territory in the east — there were no annexations and no direct government, but the senate had been patient long enough. A certain brutality became apparent in its treatment of those who had supported Perseus. It was also obvious that there were many benefits to be gained from conquest.

- Macedon was divided into four independent republics.
- In Aetolia, 500 members of the anti-Roman party were put to death.
- One thousand hostages were sent from Achaea to Rome, among whom was the historian Polybius.
- The most brutal treatment was reserved for Epirus, where Aemilius Paullus ordered his army to plunder seventy cities and demolish their walls:

Hostages taken from Achaea

> early in the morning all the gold and silver was collected; and at the fourth hour the troops were given the signal to plunder the towns. So great was the amount of booty that each cavalryman received 400 denarii in the distribution and each footsoldier 200.[10]

Even more brutal was the treatment of the inhabitants; 150 000 people were sold into slavery, leaving the countryside totally devastated.

Recognition of the benefits that could be gained by conquest

Triumph of Aemilius Paullus

The triumph of Aemilius Paullus (the hero of Pydna), which continued for three days, was evidence of the rewards of conquest. Great wealth began to flow into Rome from this time, and after 168 the Roman people were no longer required to pay the tributum. It has been estimated that between 200 and 146 the value of booty and indemnities from Greece and Macedonia alone amounted to 292 917 344 sesterces.

> The triumph lasted three days. On the first, which was scarcely long enough for the sight, were to be seen the statues, pictures, and collossal images which were taken from the enemy, drawn upon two hundred and fifty chariots. On the second, was carried in a great many wagons, the finest and richest armour of the Macedonians, both of brass and steel, all newly polished and gleaming; . . . after these wagons loaded with armour there followed three thousand men who carried the silver that was coined, in seven hundred and fifty vessels, each of which weighed three talents, and was carried by four men. Others brought silver bowls and drinking horns and flat bowls and wine cups . . . all extraordinary as well for the size as for the thickness of their embossed work.
>
> On the third day . . . first proceeded the trumpeters . . . Next followed the young men wearing tunics with purple borders who led to the sacrifice 120 stalled oxen with gilded horns and heads adorned with ribbons and garlands; and with these were boys that carried basins for libations, of silver and gold.

A coin commemorating the victory of Aemilius Paullus over Perseus at Pydna in 168

Then after these came those carrying the gold coin, which was divided into vessels each holding three talents, like those that contained the silver; the number of the vessels was seventy-seven. These were followed by those that brought the consecrated bowl which Aemilius had caused to be made of ten talents of gold set with precious stones.

[Then there followed the cups of Antigonus and Seleucus and the gold plate from Perseus' table.] Next to these came Perseus' chariot, and, and lying on that this diadem. [Perseus, his family, friends and attendants followed, and] after these were were carried four hundred golden crowns, sent from the cities by embassies to Aemilius in honour of his victory. [Finally came Aemilius himself] magnificently adorned [and his army].[11]

149–146

At this time Rome departed radically from her policy of no annexations and a free Greece.

Macedon annexed as a province

In 149 a pretender to the Macedonian throne, Andriscus, stirred up rebellion and defeated a small Roman force. His career was short-lived; in 148 he was defeated by Caecilius Metellus in the Fourth Macedonian War. The Romans realised that the only way to ensure permanent peace was to annex Macedon as a province under a Roman magistrate. Illyria and Epirus were also part of the province.

The Achaean League had become increasingly anti-Roman because of the hostages Rome had held for fifteen years. When Sparta, a reluctant member of the League, was given permission by Rome to leave it, Roman senators were attacked by a mob in Corinth and the League declared war on Sparta — a war really aimed at Rome.

End of Greek independence

Total destruction of Corinth

Greek independence came to an end in 146 when Metellus and Lucius Mummius defeated the Achaean League and punished Corinth as an example to the rest of Greece. Corinth was sacked — razed to the ground, her inhabitants sold into slavery and her treasures sent to Rome.

At first though the gates were open, Mummius hesitated to enter Corinth, suspecting that some ambush had been laid within the walls. But on the third day after the battle he proceeded to storm Corinth and set it on fire. The majority of those in it were put to the sword by the Romans, but the women and children Mummius sold into slavery. He also sold all the slaves who had been set free and had fought on the side of the Achaeans but had not fallen at once on the field of battle. The most admired votive offerings [offerings to the gods] and works of art were carried off by Mummius; the less valuable he gave to Philopoemen, the general sent by Attalus . . .'[12]

Greece was neither annexed nor organised as a province, but was subject to Rome and placed under the control of the governor of Macedon.

The cruel destruction of Corinth occurred in the same year as the annihilation of Carthage and was the culmination of an increasingly brutal foreign policy which had also been evident from 154 in Rome's campaigns in Spain.

Timeline: Rome's changing attitude and policy towards Greece and Macedon

Prior to 200	Watchful
200–189	Non-interference and freedom for the Greeks Strong philhellenic attitudes Continuing surveillance
189–168	Reluctantly involved in Greek quarrels — acting as arbiter No annexations Some reaction against philhellenic policies
168–149	Hardening of attitude — more selfish and impatient; still no annexations, but an end to philhellenic policies
149–146	Ruthless imperialism: the end of Greek independence the annexation of Macedon the destruction of Corinth

By the year 146 the Romans had added the provinces of Africa (Carthaginian territory) and Macedon and a dependent Greece to their empire. In 133 Attalus III of Pergamum died, leaving his kingdom to the Roman people, and in 129 this became the Roman province of Asia.

Rome's control of the eastern Mediterranean had been won with far less cost than her acquisition of the lands to the west.

13 *The immediate and long-term effects of the wars of expansion*

Changing social and economic conditions

The influence of Greece

Cato the Censor

Supremacy of the senate

Provincial government

DURING THE SECOND CENTURY the traditional Roman way of life underwent considerable change as a result of Rome's wars of expansion in both the western and the eastern Mediterranean. New ideas and practices, and tremendous wealth in the form of booty, taxes and indemnities flowed into Rome and Italy.

Changes in Rome, Italy and provinces

All aspects of Roman urban and rural life were affected to some extent by the foreign influences, particularly from Greece and the Hellenistic cities of the east: the form of land use, the size of properties, food supply, the population structure, employment, family life, living conditions, trade and business, entertainment, religion, education, and even the physical appearance of Roman cities. Life in the provinces changed also as Roman businessmen, traders, soldiers, magistrates and adventurers flocked to the far ends of the Mediterranean.

In their turn these changes created a number of serious problems, but the ruling class, who benefited most from Rome's conquests, were either unaware of or unconcerned about the urgent problems facing other groups in Roman and provincial society.

Sallust, a Roman writer of the first century BC, believed that the problems of his own time began 'when Carthage, Rome's rival in her quest for empire had been annihilated' in 146 and 'every land and sea lay open to her. It was then that fortune turned unkind and confounded all her enterprises'.[1]

Problems arising

According to Sallust it was the influx of incredible wealth into Rome and Italy which was the vital element in all these changes and their associated problems. He maintained that 'wealth and luxury began to undermine earlier standards of public and private conduct'. The oligarchy used its wealth to gain and maintain power and 'had no interest in the plight of the poor, for whom there was destitution at home and debt everywhere'. The provincials 'complained bitterly of the rapacity of Roman officials' and the 'cruel harshness of money lenders' robbed many of their homes and fortunes.[2] Although this was written by Sallust to explain the moral degeneration and political corruption in the middle of the first century, the situation resulted from the failure of the government to deal with the urgent problems which became apparent in the previous century.

A knowledge of this period is vital to an understanding of the series of explosive events which occurred from 133; the following chart is a summary of these changes and the associated problems.

A changing order — economic, social, cultural and political	
Changes	*Problems*
By 133 Rome had seven provinces but still only the institutions of a city-state. Efficient ways had to be found to govern them.	Some greedy governors and their staffs exploited the provincials, which caused discontent and hatred.
Vast amounts of wealth poured into Rome from the provinces: booty, indemnities and taxes, creating a building boom and the abolition of direct taxes for Romans after 167.	Much of this wealth went into the hands of the governing classes, who year by year became wealthier and more powerful at the expense of the poor.
The lifestyle of the upper classes became more luxurious as they spent more and more on houses, food, works of art, jewellery and slaves. Great wealth was lavished on public entertainments.	There was a gradual moral deterioration as wealth led to greed and idleness. The entertainments paid for by the rich became more brutal, adversely affecting the character of the people.

Changes	*Problems*
The increase in wealth allowed the upper classes to invest in land, building up huge estates which were added to by leasing public land (*ager publicus*).	Many small farmers returning from the wars either did not have the money to set themselves up again or did not have the inclination to farm.
Grain from the provinces of Sicily and Sardinia was imported cheaply to feed the growing population. Roman landowners changed to the production of more profitable crops and ranching.	The ruined small farmer who wished to remain on his farm could not sell his grain at competitive prices and did not have the capital or the skill to switch from corn production.
The Italian slave market was flooded with slaves taken during the wars and from the provinces. The more barbaric slaves were used in the mines and on the large estates, while the Greek slaves were employed as teachers, secretaries and doctors.	Slave labour forced free labourers to drift to the cities, seeking employment. Slaves in the mines and on the estates were exploited ruthlessly; runaways turned to robbery and conspiracies — large-scale slave uprisings
Peasants who abandoned or were forced off their land sought a new life in the cities. Some depended on patrons, others found jobs in the building boom, financed by the influx of tribute. Many were crowded in high-rise tenement buildings with few of the basic essentials.	By 138 there was an economic crisis — the building boom ended and grain prices increased. Unemployment created a discontented urban mob who dominated the assembly. Politicians had to take into account the interests of the mob — food and entertainment represented bribery.
The small farmers had formed the backbone of the army, but with their disappearance from the land the numbers available for military duty dropped. Property qualifications for service were lowered.	There was a decline in the morale and discipline in the army and a reluctance to fight in any more foreign wars. Unruly veterans returning from the wars in Spain caused tension.
From 218 (lex Claudia) the senatorial class had not been allowed to engage in commerce. This gave the equites (the wealthiest non-senatorial group — business class) great opportunities to make money in the provinces collecting taxes, banking, money-lending and operating mines. There was a distinction between wealth from land and from commerce.	The equites were wealthy but lacked the prestige of the senatorial class. They began to demand some political influence. Hostility between the two groups became a problem, especially over control of the law courts dealing with extortion in the provinces. The equites advanced themselves at the expense of the provincials.

Changes	*Problems*
The Italian allies had provided troops for Rome's wars and in most cases had remained loyal. Their numbers had declined, their land was devastated and general economic conditions made life difficult for them. The majority desired Roman citizenship, but Rome's attitude had now hardened.	There was increasing discontent among the allies as it became apparent that Rome would refuse them the benefits of full Roman citizenship. War with the allies seemed inevitable, which could lead to a break-up of the Roman confederation.
The senate had become the supreme governing body as a result of its successful handling of Rome's wars in the third and second centuries. It continued to control the magistrates, influence assemblies, and control foreign affairs and finances. It aimed to maintain the status quo (the existing state of affairs).	The senate was dominated by a small clique of wealthy nobles — about 20 families. Their failure to see and resolve the major issues facing Rome led to a challenge to its authority, the introduction of violence into politics and the eventual downfall of the republic.
The cultural influences of the Hellenistic world (Sicily, Greece and the east) changed Roman thought and learning as well as the Romans' attitude to religion.	The traditional Roman way of life (mos maiorum) was corrupted by the less beneficial aspects of Greek life, There was a general deterioration of morals.

Economic and social conditions

The following pages, including extracts from the ancient sources, describe in more detail the economic and social conditions existing in Italy in the second century.

The growth of the latifundia

One of the greatest changes in the economic life of Italy after the Second Punic War was the growth of the huge estates of the nobility. These are often referred to as *latifundia*, and operated on slave labour; many owners of such estates preferred to live in Rome, visiting them from time to time.

Reasons for the growth of the latifundia

Availability of public land

The policy of the Roman government in the past had been to confiscate part of the lands of those Italian people defeated in war and to incorporate it into the Roman state. This public land (ager publicus) was either leased at a nominal rent or left open to occupation by *possessores* (squatters). After the Hannibalic war large areas of land became available because the cities and communities that had sided with Hannibal had some of their land confiscated. The wealthy classes occupied most of the best parts of this land, particularly where it adjoined their own properties, and over a period they built on it and regarded it as their own.

Returning soldiers unable or unwilling to resume independent farming

Much of southern Italy had been devastated by the long occupation of Hannibal, and huge tracts of cheap land became available as returning soldiers were unable or disinclined to start farming again; many of their holdings were run-down and it would have cost them too much to start over again — to provide seed and equipment, for instance. Some failed to return to the land because of the liability of small landowners for military duty; others who did make an attempt to return to farming found that they could not compete with the larger landowners and became hopelessly in debt. These peasant farmers, who had formed the backbone of the Roman legions, either sold their land cheaply or were taken over by their wealthier neighbours. Whole districts became depopulated as the drift to the cities — particularly to Rome — increased.

Lex Claudia

A law (the lex Claudia) forbidding the senatorial class to engage in commerce encouraged them to invest their wealth in land instead.

Slave labour

An abundance of cheap slave labour from Rome's recent conquests encouraged the growth of the large estates, which could be run very profitably with gangs of slaves. Any remaining peasant farmers found it extremely difficult to compete with those employing slave labour, and many were forced to go to the city to seek work.

Appian sums up this situation:

> . . . for the rich, taking possession of the greater part of the undistributed lands and being emboldened by the lapse of time to believe that they would never be dispossessed, absorbing any adjacent strips and their poor neighbours' allotments partly by purchase under persuasion and partly by force, came to cultivate vast tracts instead of single estates, using purchased slaves as agricultural labourers and herdsmen, since free labourers could be drawn from agriculture into the army.[3]

Varied land use

Along with the growth of the large properties went changes in land use. As Italy became more dependent on cheap corn imported from the provinces, wealthy landowners replaced grain production with ranching (beef and wool) and the production of wine and olives. There was a growing interest in scientific farming. Cato, the politician, wrote a manual for running an estate, called *De Agricultura*.

Slavery

The following chart illustrates the reasons for the increase of slavery and its social consequences.

Reasons	*Effects*
It has been estimated that there were approximately 250 000 prisoners of war taken by the Romans in the first half of the second century.	Many of the 'uncivilised' slaves were used in the mines of Spain and Macedon and on the latifundia, where they often worked in chain gangs and were treated extremely harshly. This exploitation led to a number of serious slave uprisings in Sicily and Italy.
The growth of wealth and luxury in Rome increased the demand for household slaves.	The more educated captives, particularly Greeks, were used as personal slaves and as teachers to the sons of the wealthy.
The Romans made Delos into a free port. It became the centre of a very lucrative slave trade.	A decline in free peasantry and the increase in the number of freedmen changed the population structure of Italy.

Appian explains why the number of slaves increased in proportion to the citizen and allied population of Italy, and how the wealthy landowners became even richer owing to the use of slaves.

> ... the ownership of slaves brought them [the large landowners] great gain from the multitude of progeny [offspring], who increased free from danger because they were exempt from military service. Thus certain powerful men became extremely rich and the class of slaves multiplied.[4]

However, some modern scholars question the profitability of slave labour. K. Hopkins, in *Conquerors and Slaves*, believes that the whole slave question is very complex.

Revolt of slaves, 134

Diodorus Siculus (Diodorus of Sicily) gives a graphic account of the slave uprising in 134 in Sicily. This revolt, led by a slave called Eunus, involved over 70 000 slaves and reached the scale of a full war; it was brought to an end by the Romans only with great difficulty. The success of the Sicilian slaves encouraged other slave outbreaks in Rome, Athens and Delos.

> Never had there been such an uprising of slaves as now occurred in Sicily. In it many cities experienced terrible misfortunes, and untold numbers of men, women and children suffered most grievous calamities; and the whole island

> was on the point of falling into the power of the runaways, who set the complete destruction of their masters as the goal of their power.
>
> The Servile War broke out from the following cause. The Sicilians, being grown very rich and elegant in their manner of living, bought up large numbers of slaves. They brought them in droves from the places where they were reared, and immediately branded them with marks on their bodies. Those that were young they used as shepherds, and the others as need required... Oppressed by the grinding toil and beatings, maltreated for the most part beyond all reason, the slaves could endure it no longer. Therefore, meeting together at suitable opportunities they discussed revolt, until at last they put their plan into effect.
>
> ... the evil kept increasing—cities were taken and their inhabitants enslaved, and many armies were cut to pieces by the rebels until the Roman general Rupilius recovered, with difficulty, the major strongholds of the slaves.[5]

The lifestyle of the wealthy

Influx of wealth

As money and other forms of wealth poured into Rome in the second century, changes occurred in the lifestyle of all Romans but particularly the upper classes, who began to surround themselves with all kinds of luxury. Both Sallust and Velleius Paterculus (a historian in the time of Augustus) agree that the love of money and the pursuit of pleasure, idleness and corruption increased at a great rate after Scipio Aemilianus' destruction of Carthage in 146: 'The first Scipio [Africanus] opened the way for the world power of the Romans; the second [Scipio Aemilianus] opened the way for luxury'.[6]

According to Livy, it was not until the Roman army served in Asia that:

Foreign luxury

> the beginnings of foreign luxury were introduced into Rome. These men brought into Rome for the first time bronze couches, costly coverlets, bed curtains, and other fabrics, and—what was considered at that time gorgeous furniture—one-legged tables and sideboards. Banquets were made more attractive by the presence of girls who played on the lute and the harp and by other forms of entertainment, and the banquets began to be prepared with greater care and expense.[7]

Both Plutarch and Polybius give details of the social life of Aemilia and Cornelia, wife and daughter respectively of Scipio Africanus.

> Aemilia used to display great magnificence, whenever she took part in the religious ceremonies of the women. For apart from the richness of her own dress and the decorations of her carriage, all the baskets, cups, and other

> utensils of the sacrifice were of gold or silver . . . while the number of her maids and servants in attendance were correspondingly large.[8]

> Cornelia had many friends and kept a good table that she might show hospitality, for she always had Greek and other literary men about her, and all the reigning kings interchanged gifts with her.[9]

Greek influence

According to Polybius, during the war with Perseus and the Macedonians the Romans very quickly adopted the luxurious habits of the Greeks.

More opulent villas were built incorporating a Greek peristyle and Hellenistic frescoes on the walls, while the old pebble floors were replaced with elaborate floor mosaics. The rooms were furnished with sculpture, paintings and rich furniture either taken from Greece or made in imitation of the original Greek objects.

Sumptuary laws

Banquets in the Greek style, with imported foods and wines, symposia, music and flute-playing dancing girls became common among the upper classes. Judging by the number of sumptuary laws (introduced to curb extravagance and luxury) passed from the beginning of the second century the conservatives, led by Cato (particularly during his term as censor), were concerned at the growing extravagance. These laws, however, were extremely difficult to enforce.

- In 215, as a war measure, the Oppian law was passed — it attempted to restrict the amount of jewellery and luxury clothing a woman could wear. It was repealed in 195 despite the opposition of Cato. According to Livy women protested in the streets for the repeal of this law, and were successful (see page 205).

Detail of a mosaic showing girls in transparent dresses dancing to a flute

- In 184, as censor, Marcus Porcius Cato heavily taxed all luxuries, including the possession of slaves and women's dress and jewellery.
- In 181, with the lex Orchia, the government attempted to restrict the number of guests a person could invite to a party.
- In 161 the lex Fannia limited the amount of money that could be spent on a party or banquet.
- In 125 a man was fined by the censors for building a house that was too expensive.

Ineffective laws

The laws were not successful in curbing the growing luxury among the upper classes, even though Cato and the philhellene Scipio Aemilianus both spoke out against the increasing vices of their day. Scipio, who had adopted all the worthwhile aspects of Greek culture, denounced excessive luxury, foppery, homosexual practices, and singing and dancing by upper-class boys and girls.

According to Sallust, by the middle of the first century

> Riches made the younger generation a prey to luxury, avarice, and pride. Squandering with one hand what they grabbed with the other, they set small value on their own property, while they coveted that of others. [The upper classes] treated their wealth as a mere plaything: . . . shamefully misused it on the first wasteful project that occurred to them. Equally strong was their passion for fornication, guzzling and other forms of sensuality.[10]

The old Roman virtues of dignity, discipline, economy and simplicity seemed to have been replaced with extravagance and self-ingulgence.

Misuse of wealth

As the nobles competed for wealth and popularity they poured more and more money into the public games. This was a form of political bribery, as the growing numbers of unemployed in Rome expected to be entertained on a lavish scale. The aediles (magistrates in charge of public festivals and games) spent fortunes, often borrowing heavily, and were obliged to recoup their expenses when they went abroad to the provinces at a later date.

Ancient historians all agree that the deterioration in the Roman traditional way of life, mos maiorum, began with the influx of wealth from the east in the second century.

The changing status of women

Upper-class women tended to become more independent, and some attempted to free themselves of the old conventions. Divorce became more common. Livy relates a story about women and their reaction to the sumptuary laws and describes how conservative men such as Cato viewed the changing behaviour of women.

Protests by women over sumptuary laws

The Oppian law, which had been passed in 215, was up for discussion in 195. It had forbidden women to wear coloured clothes and to adorn themselves with more than an ounce of gold. The women were anxious to have it repealed and they actively canvassed for the men's votes by appearing in every street that led to the Forum. Cato was outraged by what he considered this shameless behaviour by which women addressed other women's husbands in public and even boldly approached the consuls and other magistrates.

> Citizens of Rome, if each one of us has set himself to retain the rights and the dignity of a husband over his own wife, we should have less trouble with women as a whole sex. As things are, our liberty, overthrown in the home by female indiscipline, is now being crushed and trodden underfoot here too in the Forum.
>
> Our ancestors refused to allow any woman to transact even private business without a guardian to represent her: women have to remain under the control of fathers, brothers or husbands. But we (heaven preserve us!) are now allowing them to even take part in politics, and actually to appear in the Forum... What they are looking for is complete liberty, or rather—if we want to speak the truth—complete licence.[11]

The drift to the cities and the urban mob

Unemployment—poor living conditions

There was a drift from the rural areas of dispossessed farmers, unemployed farm labourers and soldiers who no longer wished to return to the land; in the cities they had to compete for employment with skilled craftsmen and traders, freedmen and slaves. Although there was a building boom in the 140s due to the influx of wealth, this was short-lived, and in the next decade Rome became overcrowded with unemployed.

Living conditions for the lower classes were uncomfortable, as many families shared the same basic accommodation in the high-rise tenement buildings called *insulae*.

Public entertainment

The urban mob had to be kept fed and entertained, and men wishing to seek higher office tended to 'bribe' the people with a variety of entertainments and provision of cheap corn. The six regular festivals increased in duration, and in 186 contests between Greek athletes and wild beast hunts in conjunction with gladiatorial contests were added to the chariot races held at the Circus. When the senate passed a law forbidding the importation of wild animals for shows, the city population demanded its repeal in 170. Gladiatorial contests had been first introduced as private entertainment at funerals in about 264, but as schools of gladiators were established and regular gladiatorial shows were held, the urban population became increasingly brutalised.

Gladiatorial schools

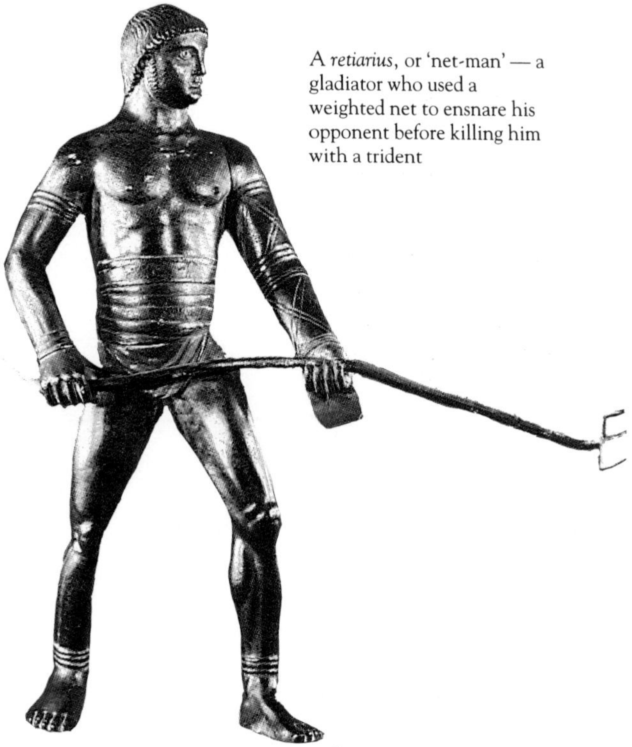

A *retiarius*, or 'net-man' — a gladiator who used a weighted net to ensnare his opponent before killing him with a trident

A Roman charioteer with his team of four horses at the turning point in the Circus Maximus

The growth of the equestrian class (equites)

The Latin word *equites* means 'horsemen'. The equites were originally an elite group of 'knights' whose horses were provided by the state. In the fourth and third centuries, however, as Rome's wars of expansion necessitated more cavalry, the equestrian class was increased by the addition of wealthy men who provided their own horses. Later, the Italian allies provided the cavalry.

Wealthy, non-political business class

By the second century, equites was a term used to describe the wealthy business or capitalist class who did not stand for office or enter the senate; many commercial opportunities for banking, importing and exporting occurred in the newly acquired provinces. The equites also benefited from the lack of a public service, as they were able to contract to carry out public works such as the building of roads and bridges, to supply equipment and food to the army and to collect the state's revenues in the form of taxes, harbour dues and so on. A law preventing senators from engaging in commerce also helped the equites.

The affairs of the government were of very real interest to this group of rich men, since any decision of the senate concerning the letting of contracts and administration in the provinces affected their livelihood. They wanted some political influence, and this eventually brought them into conflict with the senatorial class.

Link with foreign affairs

The following extracts from Polybius and Cicero indicate not only the opportunities available to the equestrian class in the provinces, but also the close link between their activities and Rome's foreign policy.

Polybius, writing at about the middle of the second century, described the system of public contracts.

> All over Italy an immense number of contracts, far too numerous to specify, are awarded by the censors for the construction and repair of public buildings, and besides this the collection of revenues from navigable rivers, harbours, gardens, mines, lands — in a word every transaction which comes under the control of the Roman government — is farmed out to contractors.[12]

Cicero, defending an equestrian called Rabirius Postumus in the courts about a hundred years later (56 BC) says of his client:

> His business interests and contracts were extensive; he held many shares in the farming of public revenues; whole peoples had him for creditor; his transactions covered many provinces; he put himself at the disposal even of kings.[13]

Problems within the army

During the second century Rome was faced with a military crisis. The Roman legions were recruited from those citizens who owned property of a certain value, and it was the small peasant landowner who had formed the backbone of the army. However, with the drift from the land of this group of citizens, many of whom became part of the unemployed urban population, there was a reduction in the number of those with the property qualification necessary for the military levies. Some, tired of fighting in campaigns far away and for long periods, sold their properties to avoid recruitment.

Source of army personnel reduced

Fall in population

The relatively constant fighting against Carthaginians, Macedonians, Greeks and Syrians for over a century had taken its toll; it has been estimated that in the first half of the second century about 94 000 Romans lost their lives in battle and countless more died of disease. The census figures also indicate that there was a decline in the birth rate during this period.

Constant recruitment cause of unrest

As Rome's empire grew the government was forced to raise more legions to maintain control in the provinces, but not only were the numbers eligible for recruitment declining, campaigns in places such as Spain, where fighting was tough, were extremely unpopular. Soldiers who were recruited year after year became disgruntled; there were desertions and attempted mutinies, and this forced many commanders to resort to harsh disciplinary measures. By 140 there were riots in Rome protesting against heavy recruiting.

Discontent among the Italian allies

The position of Rome's Italian allies gave them many causes for complaint.

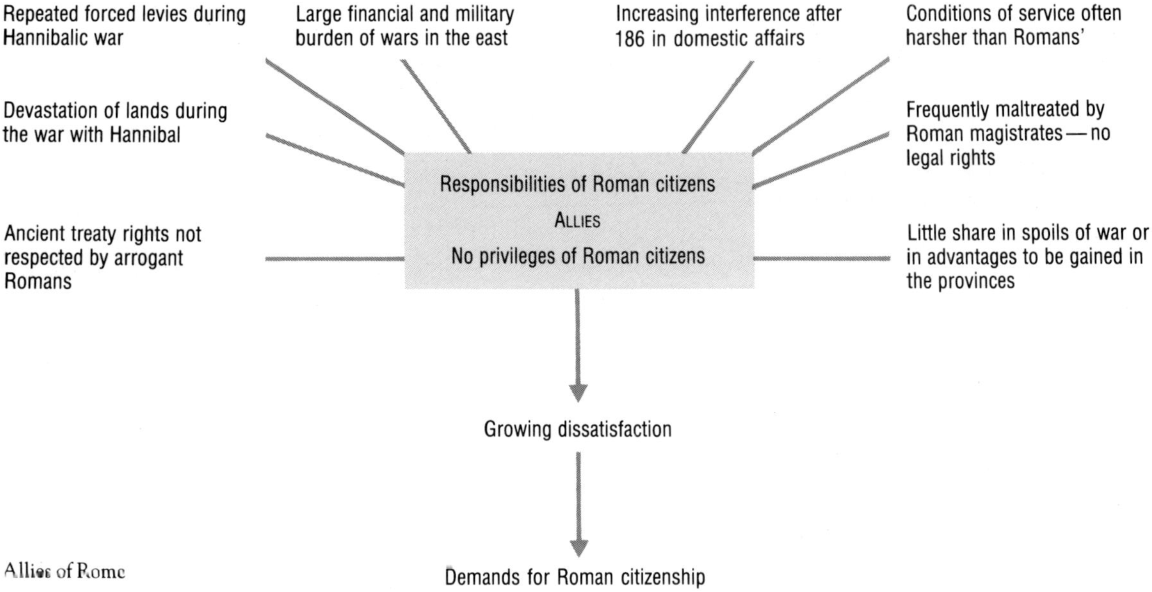
Repeated forced levies during Hannibalic war
Large financial and military burden of wars in the east
Increasing interference after 186 in domestic affairs
Conditions of service often harsher than Romans'
Devastation of lands during the war with Hannibal
Frequently maltreated by Roman magistrates — no legal rights
Responsibilities of Roman citizens
ALLIES
No privileges of Roman citizens
Ancient treaty rights not respected by arrogant Romans
Little share in spoils of war or in advantages to be gained in the provinces
Growing dissatisfaction
Demands for Roman citizenship

Allies of Rome

The Social War

The following extract from Velleius Paterculus was part of his account of the Italic or 'Social' War which broke out in 90 between the Italian allies (socii) and the Romans. It was a result of the continued failure of the senate to deal with the problems mentioned above.

> The fortune of the Italians was as cruel as their cause was just, for they were seeking citizenship in the state whose power they were defending by their arms: every year and in every war they were furnishing a double number of men, both of cavalry and of infantry, and yet were not admitted to the rights of citizens in the state which through their efforts had reached so high a position that it could look down upon men of the same stock and blood as foreigners and aliens.[14]

The influence of Greece and the east on cultural life of Rome in the second century

Changes in traditional Roman way of life

In this century the Romans were exposed to the cultural influences of the Hellenistic world (Sicily, Greece and the eastern Mediterranean). The extent to which the predominantly Greek civilisation influenced the Romans is reflected in the following quotes from Horace and Cicero:

> Captive Greece captivated her barbarous conqueror.[15]

> For it was not a little rivulet that flowed from Greece, but a mighty river of culture and learning.[16]

Twofold reaction from nobility

The reaction to this influence among the nobility was twofold. Plutarch says that most nobles were pleased to see their sons educated in Greek culture: two of these philhellenic nobles were Scipio Africanus and Flamininus. The ultraconservatives, however, were deeply disturbed that the ambitions of the younger generation might be diverted by Greek learning and that the new ideas would undermine the established laws and customs. Led by Marcus Porcius Cato, they launched an anti-Hellenic campaign.

Blend of the best of both cultures

By the end of the second century many Romans had blended their traditional way of life with the more acceptable influences of the Hellenistic world to produce a Graeco-Roman culture, but there were also less beneficial effects on Roman society.

Education

Traditional style	*Greek influence*
Teaching was centred on the home under the personal supervision of the paterfamilias.	Greek-style schools were introduced in which education was largely in the hands of Greek slaves and freedmen.
A young man was taught the traditional Roman values, was introduced to the civil law in memorising the Twelve Tables, and was given extensive physical training.	The chief subjects taught were literature, philosophy, rhetoric, the liberal arts and oratory, which was regarded as the most important.
The young upper-class Roman often served an 'apprenticeship' with a distinguished soldier or statesman.	Some time was usually spent in one of the 'university' cities in Greece or the east, such as Athens or Rhodes.
The education of the son of M. Porcius Cato	*The education of Scipio Aemilianus*
'As soon as he showed signs of understanding, Cato himself took him in his charge and taught him to read, although he had an accomplished slave, Chilo by name, who was a	Aemilius Paullus 'brought up his sons in accordance with the traditional native type of education, as he himself had been brought up, but also, and more zealously, on the Greek pattern.

The education of the son of M. Porcius Cato	*The education of Scipio Aemilianus*
teacher and taught many boys. But he thought it not proper, as he himself said, to have his son reprimanded by a slave, . . . nor would he have him under obligation to a slave for so priceless a thing as education. He himself was his reading teacher, his law teacher, and his athletic trainer, and he taught his son not only how to hurl the javelin, to fight in armour, and to ride a horse, but also to box, to endure both heat and cold and swim through the eddies and billows of the river.' Cato also taught his son Rome's ancient traditions, and never used bad language in his presence. 'Thus, like a beautiful work, Cato moulded and fashioned his son to virtue.'[18]	For the young men were surrounded not only by Greek teachers, scholars and rhetoricians, but also by Greek sculptors, painters, overseers of horses and hounds, and instructors in hunting'.[17] His education in Greek literature and interest in philosophy led to a lifelong friendship with the Greek historian Polybius, and later to his close association with the Stoic philosopher, Panaetius of Rhodes. Scipio gathered around him a group of acquaintances and friends interested in Greek literature and thought, and this so-called 'Scipionic Circle' tried to blend the best aspects of Greek and Roman life.

Oratory and rhetoric

Importance of oratory for a political career

Oratory and rhetoric were important aspects of the 'new' Greek-style education.

In order to develop his skills in oratory a young boy from the upper classes would be taken to a well-known orator, whom he would then accompany on all his public engagements, to the law courts and to the assemblies.

> The more influence a man could wield by his powers of speech, the more readily did he attain to high office, the farther did he, when in office, outstrip his colleagues, the more did he gain favour with the great, authority with the Senate, and name and fame with the common people.[19]

It also helped him if—once in office—he was called on to appear in the law courts.

Roman objections to rhetoric

The study of rhetoric (the art of persuasive speaking—the use of language to create an impression, sometimes sounding exaggerated and insincere) was prohibited in 161 when a senatorial decree was issued preventing rhetoricians (teachers of rhetoric) from living in Rome. A later edict, passed in 92, outlined the conservatives' objections to rhetoricians: they believed that their sons were idling away their days and that the new kind of training was undermining the traditions of their forefathers.

An orator, holding the text of his speech in his left hand

Exercise

1 What was a philhellene?
2 Who were two notable philhellenes of the second century?
3 Who was the leader of the anti-Hellenic movement?
4 What was his attitude to philhellenism?
5 What was the so-called 'Scipionic Circle'?
6 Who were often employed as teachers in Rome in the second century?
7 What was regarded as a necessary education for a Roman boy from the upper classes in the second century? Compare this with the traditional form of education.
8 Why was oratory regarded as an essential skill for a young upper-class Roman male?
9 What is rhetoric?
10 Why did many Romans fear rhetoricians so much that they passed an edict to banish them from Rome in 161?

A Roman mosaic depicting theatrical masks in the Greek style

A bas-relief showing the performance of an early Latin comedy based on Greek New Comedy — the actors are wearing Greek-style masks

Literature

Adoption of Greek literature

The Romans were impressed by all areas of Greek literature and, as Mommsen says, they began to realise their own lack of a rich intellectual life. They adopted Greek literature wholeheartedly, starting with direct translations of Greek works and then adapting them to suit their own needs.

Greek works translated into Latin

Livius Andronicus (c.284–204), a Greek from Tarentum, translated the *Odyssey* of Homer into Latin and based his tragedies on the great fifth-century poets of Athens, especially Sophocles. He really initiated written Latin literature, but he was surpassed by greater writers such as Naevius, Ennius, Plautus and Terence (Terentius) all of whom were greatly influenced by the Greeks. Cato, who is regarded as the father of Latin prose, 'mocked all Greek culture and learning' and expressed the opinion 'that if ever the Romans became infected with the literature of Greece they would lose their empire'.[20]

Cato's objection to Greek literature

Art

Admiration for Greek art

When Marcus Marcellus captured and looted Syracuse in 212–211, he started an enthusiasm for Greek works of art.

> Marcus greatly pleased the common people because he adorned the capital with works of art which possessed the Hellenic grace and charm and truth to

nature... He liked to claim that he had taught the ignorant Romans to admire and honour the glories of Greek art.[21]

Respect for Greek art spread, and after the sack of Corinth in 146 Mummius presented some of the captured art pieces to communities as far afield as Spain. Bronzes from Corinth became display pieces in many Roman houses.

Livy complained that in their enthusiasm for Greek art the Romans destroyed numerous religious and secular (non-religious) buildings. Plutarch records how Marcellus was blamed for teaching Romans to become 'glib connoisseurs of art and artists, so that they idled away the greater part of the day in clever and trivial chatter about aesthetics'.[22]

Greek architects employed by Romans

In this century Greek basilicas and temples arose around the Forum, and the colonnade was first introduced in the wharf area as part of the Emporium. Although most of the architects employed in Rome were Greeks, the Romans—unlike the Greeks—put as much effort into their secular buildings as they did into their religious ones. They copied many Greek works of art, but they were not just imitators. They developed their own realistic form, particularly in the area of portraiture, whereas Greek form had been more idealistic.

Development of Roman portraiture

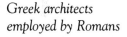

The circular temple in the Forum Boarium (mistakenly called the Temple of Vesta), built in the second century BC in pure Greek style

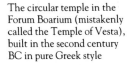

A remarkably realistic bronze portrait bust

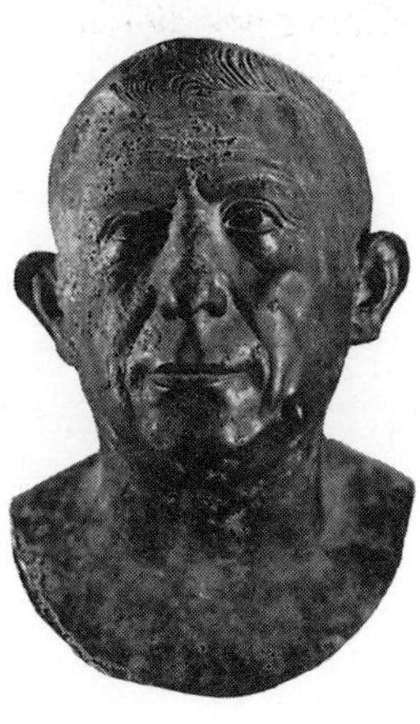

Exercise

1 Read any reliable text and then write several sentences on the influence of the Greeks on the work of the writers Naevius, Ennius, Plautus and Terence.

2 What are the views expressed (see foregoing pages) by Plutarch and Livy on the effect of the enthusiasm for Greek art in the second century?

Religion

Introduction of foreign cults

Roman religion had been greatly influenced by the Greeks of southern Italy from early times through the oracle of the sibyl at Cumae, and Greek gods were adopted and adapted to suit the Roman needs (see chapter 4).

The formal state religion was impersonal and lacked emotion. In times of great fear and anxiety such as the Second Punic War, the people turned their attention to the interpretation of prodigies (unusual happenings) as well as to foreign cults.

The cult of the 'Great Mother'

Towards the end of the Hannibalic war the worship of the 'Great Mother' (*Magna Mater*) of Phrygia was introduced into Rome in response to a saying found in the Sibylline Books. The cult stone was shipped from Asia and placed in a temple specially built in 191 for the Magna Mater: this was the first eastern deity to be officially introduced into Rome. The Roman magistrates did not realise the extreme emotionalism and sensual

A high priest of the Magna Mater (Cybele) with a medallion-studded headdress, a pomegranate (symbol of life) in his right hand, a dish of fruit and phallic pine-cone (symbols of fertility) in his left hand and the magic rattle, drum, flute, cymbals and whip (used in the cult rites) beside him

The headless statue of Cybele, the great mother goddess, near the ancient site of her temple on the Palatine Hill

rites associated with the cult, in which the eunuch priests performed self-mutilation during the ritual dances. Later, Roman citizens were forbidden to take part.

The way was now prepared for the acceptance of mystery cults and wilder rites from the east. These particularly appealed to the lower classes.

The cult of Bacchus

The secret cult of Bacchus (the Greek Dionysus), introduced from southern Italy to Rome in about 186, found a great following among the poorer classes and slaves. Livy describes the orgiastic rites that spread 'like a contagious disease' among men and women alike. 'To the religious content were added the pleasures of wine and feasting' and while under the influence of wine, 'debaucheries of every kind commenced'.

> Men, apparently out of their wits, would utter prophecies with frenzied bodily convulsions: matrons, attired as Bacchantes, with their hair dishevelled and carrying blazing torches, would run down to the Tiber, plunge their torches in and bring them out still alight . . .'

He also describes some of the criminal activities associated with the rites: 'false witnesses and evidence, forged seals and wills . . . also poisonings and murders of kin'.[23]

Official suppression of the Bacchic societies

The senate instructed the consuls to conduct a special inquiry into the Bacchanalia, and authorised them to stamp out the societies. The members

A portion of a large painting on the walls of the Villa of the Mysteries in Pompeii depicting aspects of the sacred ceremonies involved in the worship of Bacchus (Dionysus): a young woman awaits the stroke of the whip of initiation while a Bacchante begins a dance — the painting was probably commissioned by the mistress of the house who had been iniated into the secret cult

of the senate were concerned about the secret nature of these organisations: they feared they might become centres of rebellion or conspiracy against the state. The worship of Bacchus by individuals was not forbidden if they gained permission from the praetor, but the societies were banned. In general the policy of the Roman government towards foreign religious cults was one of tolerance if they were harmless to the state and Roman morality, but if they were thought to be dangerous they were rigidly suppressed.

Exercise

1 What was the first oriental deity introduced into Rome?
2 Why was government support withdrawn soon after?
3 What were the Bacchanalian societies?
4 What reasons did the government have for authorising the consuls to ban them?
5 What was the general religious policy of the Roman government?

Philosophy

Under the impact of Hellenism, Roman society became more individualistic and many members of the educated and ruling class found an outlet for their individuality in one of the branches of Greek philosophy. They continued, however, to use the state religion as a political tool.

Epicureanism

Epicureanism was the first philosophy to appear in Rome but it did not appeal to the Romans of the second century, who distrusted the idea that the object of life was pleasure. The aim of the Epicureans was to withdraw from the problems of political life and and seek pleasure in intellectual reflection. A century later, however, Epicureanism took the form of self-indulgence, and this appealed to the luxury-loving and less serious-minded Romans of the first century. Two Epicurean philosophers were forced to leave Rome in 173, and twelve years later (161) a decree was passed against philosophers and rhetoricians in general, banning them from Rome.

Decree against philosophers

In 155 the three most noted philosophers of the day (Carneades the Academic, Diogenes the Stoic and Critolaus the Peripatetic) came to Rome on a political embassy. According to Plutarch all young Romans who were interested in literature frequented their company and listened to them with wonder and delight. Cato, however, who regarded philosophy

Cato's attitude

with suspicion, urged that a vote should be taken on whether these distinguished men should be required to return to their own cities and teach their own Greek youth, leaving young Romans to pay attention to the Roman laws and magistrates.

Stoicism

Although many practical-minded Romans were distrustful of philosophy, the branch of Greek thought which provided an acceptable guide for life was that of Stoicism: after the arrival of the Stoic Panaetius in Rome about 144 many educated people became interested in it, as it was more suited to the Roman character—they were more able to accept the Stoic view of the relationship between god and man. God was seen as both divine and rational, and man had the same spark of divine reason within him. Stoicism provided the educated Roman with a spiritual, rational and ethical ideal to follow.

Appealed to Romans

Exercise

1 What was the Epicurean philosophy?
2 Why were the Epicureans banished from Rome in 171?
3 Who was Panaetius of Rhodes?
4 Why did Stoicism appeal particularly to the Roman intellectuals?

Students should refer to several major texts. Examples are Scullard's *A History of the Roman World 753–146 BC*, Part 4; appropriate sections from Plutarch's *Lives* (*Marcellus*, *Cato the Elder* and *Aemilius Paullus*) and Livy's *History of Rome*. An excellent book for source material on this work is *Roman Civilisation Sourcebook 1—The Republic* by Lewis and Reinhold.

Profile of Cato 'the Censor', 234–149

Marcus Porcius Cato exhibited all the virtues and vices of a Roman gentleman.

- A novus homo, at some time he held every office from quaestor to consul and in 184 became censor.
- He was conservative; he followed the old ideals and stood out against the tide of change.
- A passionate hater of the Greek culture, he saw it corrupting Roman society and morals—yet even he learned Greek (at the age of eighty).
- He opposed the philhellenic Scipio faction.
- He was patriotic and an uncompromising enemy of Carthage.
- A brave soldier and officer, he served in Africa, Spain and the east.

- He was an enthusiastic farmer of a large estate run with slave labour, but was cruel to his slaves.
- He was an eloquent speaker, and the first author of a history of Rome written in Latin.

The supremacy of the senate in the second century

Roman government oligarchic in practice

In chapter 6 it was seen that legally, the power to make decisions relating to the running of the Roman state was vested in the Roman people, in their assemblies. They elected annual magistrates, passed laws — usually in the tribal but sometimes in the centuriate assemblies — and elected their own representatives (tribunes) whose function it was to protect the interests of the people by vetoing the proposals of the magistrates and the senate, which constitutionally was only an advisory body without legislative or executive powers. In practice, however, the senate was the governing body of Rome throughout the second century. It governed until 133 virtually unchallenged.

Influence and power of the senate

How power and authority was acquired

Senate's power increased during Second Punic War

The crisis caused by the Second Punic War helped the senate's rise to power more than any other single factor. For fourteen years the Romans were forced to cope with a seemingly invincible enemy in their territory. To deal with this situation experience, authority and the ability to calmly make decisions were necessary.

Reasons for senatorial control of state

The average Roman lacked the experience to make decisions in a crisis and many were away fighting for long periods, making it difficult to attend meetings of the assemblies. The senate was made up of ex-magistrates with a vast amount of experience in government; the senators showed real leadership after Cannae. They provided loans, slaves for the army and fleet, food and arms; they lent money to ruined farmers and ended the war successfully, increasing in prestige as a result. The people were prepared to accept their continuing guidance, especially during the wars in Greece and Macedonia when foreign policy was rather complicated.

Once the system was established and a precedent set, it was easy for it to continue.

Influence over magistrates

Magistrates sought senate's advice

Although Roman magistrates were not compelled to seek or follow the senate's advice, in practice they usually submitted all matters of importance to it before taking them to the assemblies. Some reasons were:

1 The senate appointed provincial governors, and since all urban magistrates hoped to gain one of these lucrative posts, they would not antagonise the source of these commands.
2 The senate influenced the assemblies to elect members of its own rank to official positions, and the magistrates were unlikely to do anything against the interests of their own class.
3 The principle of collegiality and veto meant that the senate could always find other magistrates to veto any action by one who showed too much independence or ambition. This applied particularly to the tribunes, who had gradually become tools of the senate. Usually at least one of the ten representatives of the people could be found to veto the actions of his colleagues or of other magistrates.
4 The restriction on re-election to the same office, the regulation of a fixed order of offices (the cursus honorum) and a minimum age for each official position gave the senate the strongest hold over the magistrates (see chapter 6).

Senate's control over magistrates

During the Punic Wars the consuls' and promagistrates' powers had increased dramatically. They were far from home, with control of large armies, and they made decisions which affected the lives of Rome's allies and subjects and influenced the fate of countries. The careers of men like Scipio Africanus, Q. Fabius Maximus and M. Claudius Marcellus are evidence of this. Scipio had command for ten consecutive years through his proconsulships in Spain (210–206) and Africa (204–201), and his consulship in 205. There needed to be a check kept on popular and ambitious magistrates. This was achieved by the lex Villia Annalis of 181.

Lex Villia Annalis

Control over the assemblies

Methods used to control assemblies

1 The senate was able to use magistrates to put to the people only those issues of which it approved.
2 Block-voting methods in both assemblies (tributa and centuriata) favoured the wealthy ruling class (see below).
3 Voters could be bribed by magistrates either directly with money or indirectly by promises to carry out something.
4 State priests, usually chosen from the senatorial class, could declare that omens were unfavourable and so postpone meetings of the assemblies.

The block-voting method in the assemblies	
Comitia tributa (*Assembly of tribes*)	*Comitia centuriata* (*Assembly of centuries*)
The people sat and voted in their tribes, of which there were thirty-five — four urban and thirty-one rural. A majority decision within a tribe became its vote, so this amounted to one tribe–one vote. The urban tribes with their labourers, craftsmen, small businessmen and freed slaves could be outvoted by the rural tribes in which most of the senators, who had large estates, registered themselves. Also, through the votes of their clients they could control the assembly.	The people sat and voted according to their military ranking — that is, according to age, wealth and class. Out of the total number of votes possible, the wealthy first class, which always voted first, controlled a large proportion and only needed a small number of votes from the second class to get a majority on any decision. The poorer classes voted last and had fewer votes.

Powers in the second century

The senate assigned to the consuls and praetors their duties and advised higher magistrates, appointed the promagistrates and allotted them their *provinciae* and controlled the legislative and elective activities of the assemblies through their influence over the magistrates.

Further powers of the senate		
Finances	*Foreign policy*	*Special commissions*
Through the censor, the senate supervised the letting of contracts for state mines, public lands forests, quarries, sale of war booty and the mint.	The senate arranged treaties: although the centuriate assembly had the right to decide between war and peace, the senate controlled them because of its experience. It sent and received embassies.	The senate claimed the right to appoint special commissions with unlimited power to deal with matters concerning the safety of the state.

The senate was not a popularly elected body, but had won its pre-eminent position through long experience, reasonable leadership and devotion to the state.

The ruling oligarchy

Within the body of 300 members there was an exclusive oligarchy of less than twenty families who dominated the highest positions in the state—those with imperium. These men were called nobiles, as they could count a consul among the members of their family. The same family names (for example the Cornelii, Claudii, Aemilii, Valerii and Fabii) recurred frequently in the list of consuls. Although most of these men were dedicated to service to the state, the family's reputation (*fama*), prestige (*dignitas*) and praise (*gloria*) were all important. Their sons were expected further to add to the family honour.

'Nobiles'

In order to achieve this, all the family's resources—finances, political 'friendships' (*amicitiae*) and personal connections built around mutual obligations and favours—were used to launch their sons into politics via an early military or legal career. The institution of *clientela*, whereby the lower classes in Italy and the provinces were closely bound to particular noble families, was the basis of the political power of the nobility.

Prerequisites for a military career

By the first century BC very few Romans who did not belong to these families ever reached consular rank. The few men outside this clique who did become consuls were called 'new men', and achieved this position only if they had at least an equestrian fortune, an aristocratic patron or military or oratorical ability. Only fifteen of these new men are known in the middle and late republic, and most were men of exceptional ability and ambition who were in the right place at the right time. Three such men were Cato the Censor, Marius and Cicero. A new man was very rarely admitted socially to the exclusive circle, although he was often supported for political reasons.

'New men'

Factions (factiones)

Within the oligarchy there were usually a number of political alliances or factions of leading families among whom competition for power was fierce and incessant. They played a significant role in Roman politics.

These factions were built on a complex basis of kinship (blood, marriage and adoption), traditional ties of friendship and co-operation between families, and *beneficia* (patronage of a leading personality or family). They were not always hard-and-fast groups; there was often some overlap between factions and occasionally men found themselves with obligations in more than one direction. Defections from family alliances sometimes occurred because of personal ambition and opportunism.

Bases of factions

Every faction—and every member within it—aimed to reach a position of predominance in the state while preventing opponents from gaining superior power or prestige. There was a continual struggle for

Factional struggles

position, which tended to maintain a kind of balance within politics. This explains why the Roman nobility tended to resist change, since any important reform was likely to bring an increase in prestige and clientela to its sponsors and upset the existing political balance.

At the time of the Second Punic War and during Rome's expansion eastward the Scipionic (Cornelii) and Fabian (Fabii) factions dominated the senate, although other groupings also tried to undermine the influence of Scipio Africanus and his group—one such was the coalition of the Fulvii, Claudii and Servilii before Zama.

Dominant factions in the second century

For a large part of the second century the Roman government's policy veered between the philhellenic tendencies of the Scipios and the anti-Hellenic views of the conservative Fabian group led by Cato, whose patron was L. Valerius Flaccus. Cato and his faction used personal and political scandal and prosecutions against Scipio and his brother Lucius in order to weaken the popularity of the opposing faction and its policy.

By 133 the two leading factions centred around Scipio Aemilianus (Cornelii/Aemilii) and Appius Claudius Pulcher (Claudii). According to A. E. Astin, as a political leader Scipio Aemilianus failed to handle his associates and relatives in a tactful and conciliatory way, with the result that two of his family, Tiberius and Gaius Gracchus, were linked with the faction headed by A. Claudius Pulcher.

Failure of the oligarchy to deal with problems

In the latter part of the second century many senators who had been enjoying the 'fruits' of government and empire had lost some of their prestige, as they failed to deal with the real problems of the state. They became more interested in their large estates, in acquiring wealth and in maintaining their luxurious lifestyle.

Assignment: Roman provincial government at the end of the second century

1 By 129 the Romans had acquired seven provinces around the Mediterranean basin.

On an outline map of the region, mark in and name those seven areas, including the dates on which they were annexed by Rome.

2 Read several accounts of provincial government in recognised modern texts, and make detailed notes on:

(a) the governor
- how he was appointed
- his qualifications
- his term of office
- extension of office
- his powers and responsibilities
- his staff and their duties

(b) the form of government

- lex provinciae
- differences between provinces

(c) taxation
- two forms of taxation
- methods of collection
  - *publicani*
  - tax farming (contract system)
- other sources of revenue

From the time Rome acquired its first province, the opportunities for governors and businessmen to enrich themselves at the expense of the provincials became apparent. After the defeat of Perseus at Pydna in 168 the wealth and possibilities for gain in the provinces were even more obvious. There were many examples in the second century, particularly in Spain, of Roman governors plundering and committing atrocities against the Spanish tribes. By the first century a tour of duty in the provinces was regarded by both the governors and their staff as the quickest way to acquire wealth, and corruption in provincial administration was rife.

Most of the ancient source material available deals with corruption during the first century, the most flagrant example of which occurred during the administration of Gaius Verres in Sicily from 73 to 71. Although this period is beyond the cut-off point for this assignment, it is appropriate to read Cicero's account of his prosecution of Verres in order to see just how unscrupulous some Roman governors were. There is no reason to believe that Verres was unique.

The best reference for this topic is the Penguin edition of Cicero's 'Attack on misgovernment: Against Verres 1' in Cicero, *Selected Works*. Extracts from Cicero's speech can also be found in McDermott and Caldwell's *Readings in the History of the Ancient World* (pp. 287, 289–92) and Lewis and Reinhold's *Roman Civilisation, Sourcebook 1: The Republic* (pp. 358–66, 401–5).

3 From modern texts and the ancient sources make notes on the following:

(a) provincial corruption
- how and why it occurred
- what forms it took
- the attempts to maintain fair government
- the success of these measures

(b) benefits of Roman rule
- the advantages (if any) of Roman rule for provincials
- benefits for Romans

4 Summarise the information you have collected in a chart under the following headings:

Name of province
How and when acquired
Form of taxation
Importance to Rome

Essay topics

1 'The First Punic War was the result of a local incident plus a misunderstanding about the motives of the interested states.'

Comment on this statement, with regard to the causes of the First Punic War in 264.

2 'We shall find that never before in the history of the world have two such immense forces been ranged against one another at sea.' (Polybius, I: 63)

How important was naval power in the First Punic War?

3 How successful was Roman naval policy during the First Punic War?

4 Use the following five extracts from Polybius as a guide to answering the question below:

> Yet it is this fact [building of quinqueremes] which illustrates better than any other the extraordinary spirit and audacity of the Romans' decisions. (I: 20)
>
> Then at last the Carthaginians turned and fled, for they were completely unnerved by these new tactics. (I: 23)
>
> For his part Hiero, once he had placed himself under the protection of the Romans, kept them provided at all times with their essential supplies. (I: 16)
>
> There were no funds in the Treasury to finance the enterprise; but in spite of this, thanks to the patriotism and generosity of the leading citizens, the money was found. (I: 59)
>
> The Carthaginians had assumed that the Romans would never again challenge their naval supremacy and so in their contempt for their opponents, they had neglected their own navy. (I: 61)

Why did the Romans win the First Punic War?

5 'As soon as he took up his command it became clear from the measures which he put into hand that his purpose was to declare war on Rome.' (Polybius, II: 36)

Assess Hannibal's role in the outbreak of the Second Punic War.

6 Account for the outbreak of war between Rome and Carthage in 218. Was Carthage or Rome more to blame? Why?

7 Discuss the importance of the Battles of Trasimene, Cannae, Metaurus and Zama in the Second Punic War.

8 Discuss the role played by the various members of the Scipio family in the Second Punic War. What effect did the Scipionic faction have on the policy of the Roman government throughout the war?

9
> It is impossible to withhold our admiration for Hannibal's leadership, his courage and his ability in the field, when we consider the duration of his campaigns, and take note of the major and minor battles, the sieges, the defections of cities from one side to the other, the difficulties he encountered at various times and in short, the whole scope of his design and its execution. (Polybius, XI: 19)

What aspects of Hannibal's leadership enabled him to remain undefeated in Italy for sixteen years?

10 'Despite the brilliance of Hannibal's triumphs, the principal heroes of the war were the senate, the people of Rome and the Italian allies who stood by them.'

Comment on this statement.

11 Discuss Rome's changing relationship with Macedonia and Greece from 200 to 146.

12 What were the causes of the third conflict between Rome and Carthage which broke out in 149?

13 Discuss the part played by Scipio Aemilianus and Cato in the total destruction of Carthage in 146. What did the decision to do this indicate about Roman foreign policy at this time?

14 What were the major economic, social and cultural changes in Roman life as a result of the Punic Wars and Rome's involvement in Greece and the east?

15 What advantages and disadvantages did Rome derive from her conquests of Greece and the east in the second century BC?

Further reading

Ancient sources

Livy. *Rome and the Mediterranean.*
_____ . *The War with Hannibal.*
Plutarch. *Lives: Aemilius Paullus, Flamininus.*
_____ . *Makers of Rome: Fabius, Marcellus, Cato the Elder.*
Polybius. *The Rise of the Roman Empire.*

Modern sources

Astin, A. A. *Scipio Aemilianus.*
Cary, M. *A History of the Greek World 323–146 BC.*
Caven, B. *The Punic Wars.*
Connolly, P. *Greece and Rome at War.*
De Beer, G. *Hannibal.*
Frank, T. *Roman Imperialism.*
Lazenby, J. F. *Hannibal's War.*
Lewis, N. & Reinhold, M. *Roman Civilisation—Sourcebook 1: The Republic.*
Proctor, D. *Hannibal's March into History.*
Scullard, H. H. *A History of the Roman World, 753–146 BC.*
Wallbank, F. W. *A Historical Commentary on Polybius.*
Warmington, B. H. *Carthage.*

PART

4

The late republic: First phase, 146–78

THE LATE REPUBLIC (146–28)—particularly from the tribunate of Tiberius Sempronius Gracchus in 133—was marked by events which contributed to the decline and eventual overthrow of the Roman republic. Sir Ronald Syme referred to it as the 'Roman revolution'.

It can be divided into two phases:

1 the period from the tribunate of Tiberius Gracchus to the death of Lucius Cornelius Sulla: 133–78;
2 the period from the rise of Gnaeus Pompeius to the end of the civil war between Marcus Antonius and Gaius Octavius: 78–28.

Tiberius and Gaius Gracchus were the first to challenge the whole practice of the constitution by threatening the supremacy of the senate. In their attempts at reform they employed methods which undermined the position of those nobiles who saw the government of Rome as their prerogative. When the oligarchy responded to this apparent attack on their privileges with violence, the first phase of the 'revolution' began.

The senatorial oligarchy reasserted its control over the state after the death of the Gracchi and retained it until the emergence of a new kind of popular leader. Gaius Marius' reorganisation of the army probably did more than anything else to make possible the civil wars which eventually destroyed the republic. By recruiting the legions from volunteers who relied on their generals to reward them at the end of their term of service, Marius introduced a system which replaced loyalty to the state with loyalty to the general. This had disastrous consequences for Rome, since the emergence of a series of ambitious and powerful generals backed by loyal armies became a threat to the very existence of the state. Marius' successive consulships and use of force in politics were also a contributing factor to the destruction of republican institutions.

Lucius Cornelius Sulla tried to restore the power of the senate and to strengthen it so that it could govern unchallenged. However, his own example—of marching on Rome with an army and the ruthless destruction of his opponents—set a dangerous precedent.

The Gracchi 14

Economic, political and social conditions in 133

Tiberius Gracchus

The decade following Tiberius' death

Gaius Gracchus

Significance of the Gracchan tribunates

Sources on Tiberius and Gaius Gracchus

IT IS VERY DIFFICULT to reconstruct an accurate account of the events of this period since anti-Gracchan propaganda infects most of the sources, many of which survive only in fragments such as incomplete inscriptions or scraps of speeches. These miscellaneous pieces of information have to be fitted in to the framework provided by Appian, Plutarch and Cicero, who wrote some time after the events of 133 and 123–122.

Fragmentary sources

Anti-Gracchan sources

There were a number of writers, such as Sempronius Asellio and C. Fannius, who lived at about the time of the Gracchi and wrote about these turbulent years, but only fragments of their work have survived. Their accounts of Tiberius and Gaius Gracchus would not have been sympathetic, since they were members of the intellectual circle that surrounded Scipio Aemilianus.

Cicero

Cicero

The earliest surviving author to mention the Gracchi is Cicero, who wrote nearly three-quarters of a century after the events. Cicero was born in 106 and would have associated with men—some considerably older than himself—who had heard of or taken part in the affairs of the late second and early first centuries. Also, Cicero had access to contemporary historical accounts, public records and published speeches as well as the *annales maximi*, all of which are no longer available to the historian. His references to events and personalities, however, are often coloured by his own conservative prejudice and he says very little about the lower classes of Roman society.

Appian and Plutarch

Appian and Plutarch

The most important sources for this period are Appian's *The Civil Wars*, Bk. 1 (written about the middle of the second century AD) and Plutarch's *Lives of Tiberius and Gaius Gracchus* (written about the end of the second century AD). In the first book of *The Civil Wars* Appian was rather selective in his handling of the issues, while Plutarch was more concerned with character and moral issues than with historical analysis.

Their accounts 'are now generally agreed to be compatible (except for the events that led to Tiberius' death). Most of their differences consist of details supplied by Plutarch but missing in Appian'.[1]

Plutarch

The bias of sources

All sources are biased to some degree, depending on the background, personal experiences and political allegiance of the writer and the period in which he lived. Many of those writing about this period in which the senate was under threat were themselves members of the ruling clique of their day. Some may have had particular axes to grind, in which case there would be some deliberate slanting of the truth or selective treatment of the available material. Some of the anti-Gracchan sources are based on nothing more than malicious gossip.

Background to the tribunates of the Gracchi

The crisis that occurred in 133 was the culmination of a number of economic, social and political problems which had been developing throughout the second century and which, according to Sallust, had worsened after the destruction in 146 of Carthage and Corinth.

Economic, social and military problems

The reasons for the development of these problems, of which the origins lie in the wars of expansion, are treated fully in chapter 12. They are summarised in the following diagrams.

THE MILITARY CRISIS IN THE SECOND CENTURY

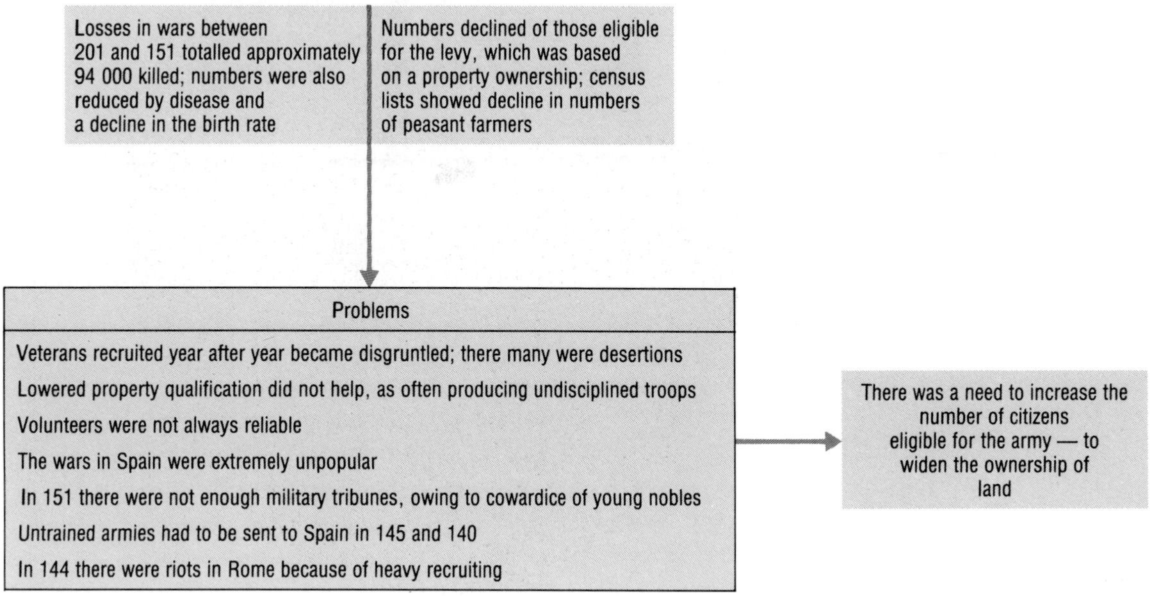
Losses in wars between 201 and 151 totalled approximately 94 000 killed; numbers were also reduced by disease and a decline in the birth rate
Numbers declined of those eligible for the levy, which was based on a property ownership; census lists showed decline in numbers of peasant farmers
Problems
Veterans recruited year after year became disgruntled; there many were desertions
Lowered property qualification did not help, as often producing undisciplined troops
Volunteers were not always reliable
The wars in Spain were extremely unpopular
In 151 there were not enough military tribunes, owing to cowardice of young nobles
Untrained armies had to be sent to Spain in 145 and 140
In 144 there were riots in Rome because of heavy recruiting
There was a need to increase the number of citizens eligible for the army — to widen the ownership of land

Economic and social conditions prior to 133

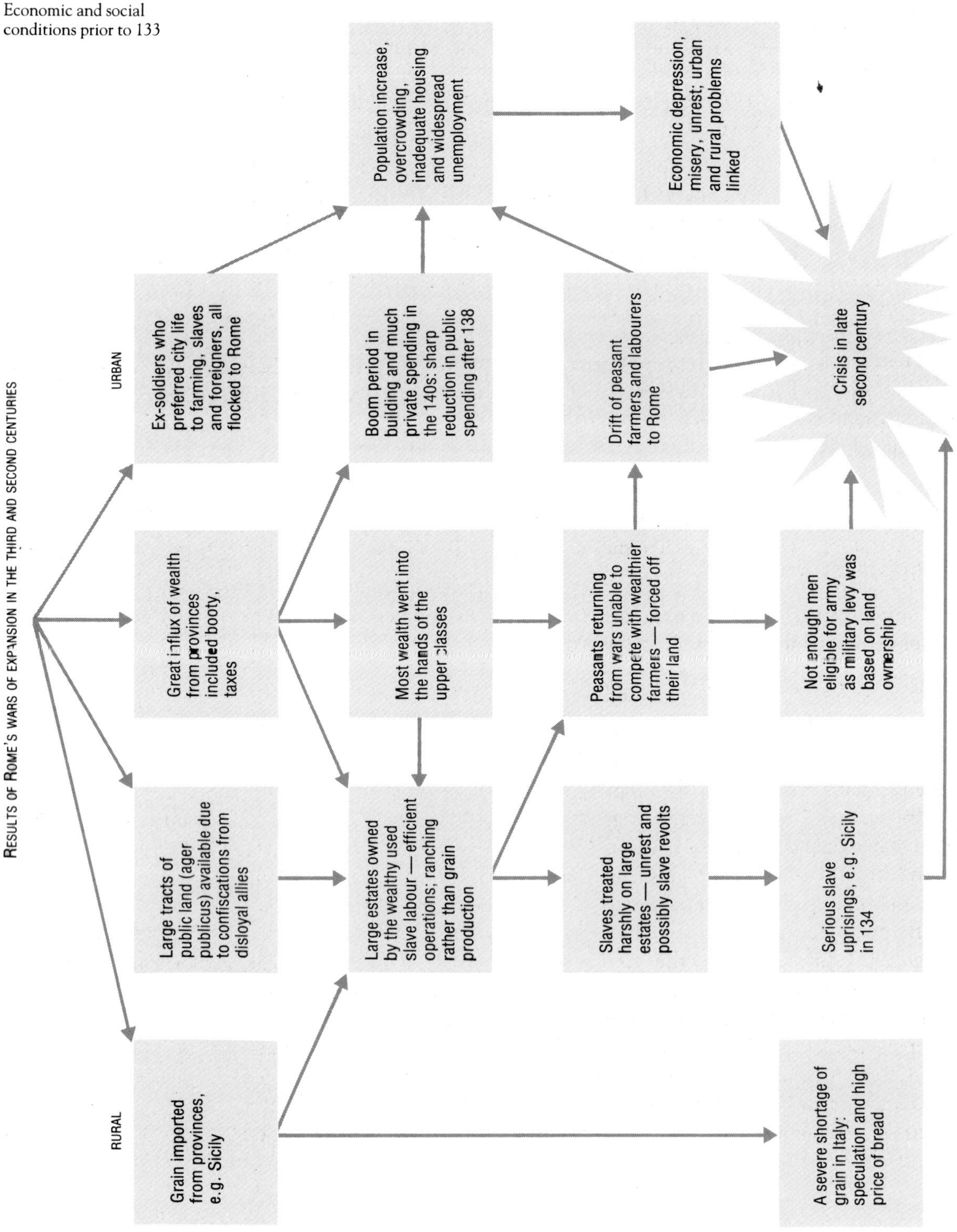
RESULTS OF ROME'S WARS OF EXPANSION IN THE THIRD AND SECOND CENTURIES
URBAN
RURAL
Ex-soldiers who preferred city life to farming, slaves and foreigners, all flocked to Rome
Great influx of wealth from provinces included booty, taxes
Large tracts of public land (ager publicus) available due to confiscations from disloyal allies
Grain imported from provinces, e.g. Sicily
Population increase, overcrowding, inadequate housing and widespread unemployment
Boom period in building and much private spending in the 140s: sharp reduction in public spending after 138
Most wealth went into the hands of the upper classes
Large estates owned by the wealthy used slave labour — efficient operations; ranching rather than grain production
Drift of peasant farmers and labourers to Rome
Peasants returning from wars unable to compete with wealthier farmers — forced off their land
Slaves treated harshly on large estates — unrest and possibly slave revolts
Economic depression, misery, unrest; urban and rural problems linked
Crisis in late second century
Not enough men eligible for army as military levy was based on land ownership
Serious slave uprisings, e.g. Sicily in 134
A severe shortage of grain in Italy: speculation and high price of bread

Political conditions in 133

The failure of the senatorial oligarchy to put the welfare of the republic before its own interests

During and immediately after the Second Punic War the senate, which had assumed control of the state, had shown that it was capable of firm leadership — and with power and responsibility went certain privileges. These had never been questioned while ever the senators appeared to be doing their job, even though they identified the interests of the state with their own. The aristocratic ideal was to serve the state while gaining gloria for the individual and the family.

Abuse of privileges by oligarchy

During the latter part of the second century, however, many members of the ruling clique were enjoying all the privileges of government without dealing with the serious problems that now began to confront the state. As Sallust says,

> One small group of oligarchs had everything in its control alike in peace and war — the treasury, the provinces, public offices, all distinctions and triumphs . . . while the spoils of war were snatched by the generals and shared with a handful of friends.[2]

In other words, they were more concerned with their own material interests and gloria than with the welfare of the republic.

The factional struggles and changing political trends

The two chief factions in the senate in the years immediately before 133 were the Cornelii Scipiones, led by P. Cornelius Scipio Aemilianus, and the Claudii/Sempronii, led by Appius Claudius Pulcher.

Aemilii — predominant faction in 140s

In the late 140s the Scipionic group held most of the top positions in the state: Scipio Aemilianus was censor in 142, Scipio Nasica held the pontificate in 141, C. Servilius Caepio and Q. Pompeius were the consuls for 141 and Q. Servilius Caepio and C. Laelius were the consuls for 140.

Claudian faction dominant in 130s

By the late 130s however, the opposing faction of the Claudii had begun to gain many of the top positions, particularly when Scipio Aemilianus was sent on an inspection tour of the east. Of the six consuls for the period 139–137 five were from the Claudian faction, and in 136 Appius Claudius Pulcher and Quintus Fabius Nobilior were the censors. A. Claudius Pulcher was also made princeps senatus at this time. Between 135 and 133 three of the six consulships also were held by members of this faction, although in 134 Scipio Aemilianus was elected to his second consulship.

Promotion of factional interests

Every faction in the senate was determined to gain a position of predominance at the expense of the opposing ones and would not stand by while another increased its prestige and the number of its clients. Any reform, particularly one dealing with the lower classes, the army or the provinces, would be likely to receive strenuous opposition because of its potential to increase the clients of the faction proposing it.

Methods used to undermine opposition factions

Various methods were used to undermine an opposition faction: prosecutions, public humiliation for military failure, the use of private pressure to remove a tribune's veto, or the use of religion for political advantage. There was also a growing tendency for the various factions to find a way around a hostile senate by appealing to the people.

Challenges to senate prior to Gracchi

By the time of Tiberius Gracchus, the authority of the senate had been challenged on a number of occasions.

- When the arrogant A. Claudius Pulcher was consul in 143, the senate had refused him a triumph for his victory over the Salessi. Instead of accepting this decision, he celebrated one on his own authority.
- Two secret-ballot laws, proposed by tribunes in 139 and 137, were passed in the face of opposition from the majority in the senate.
- The tribal assembly insisted, successfully, that the law should be suspended to enable Scipio Aemilianus to be elected to his second consulship in 134.
- There were even a number of attempts to ignore the tribune's veto.

These challenges created a fuss, but they did not threaten to upset the status quo. However, if the nobiles' customary rights to control the affairs of Rome were seriously challenged they would not relinquish them without a fight, even though their powers had no legal basis.

The crisis of 133

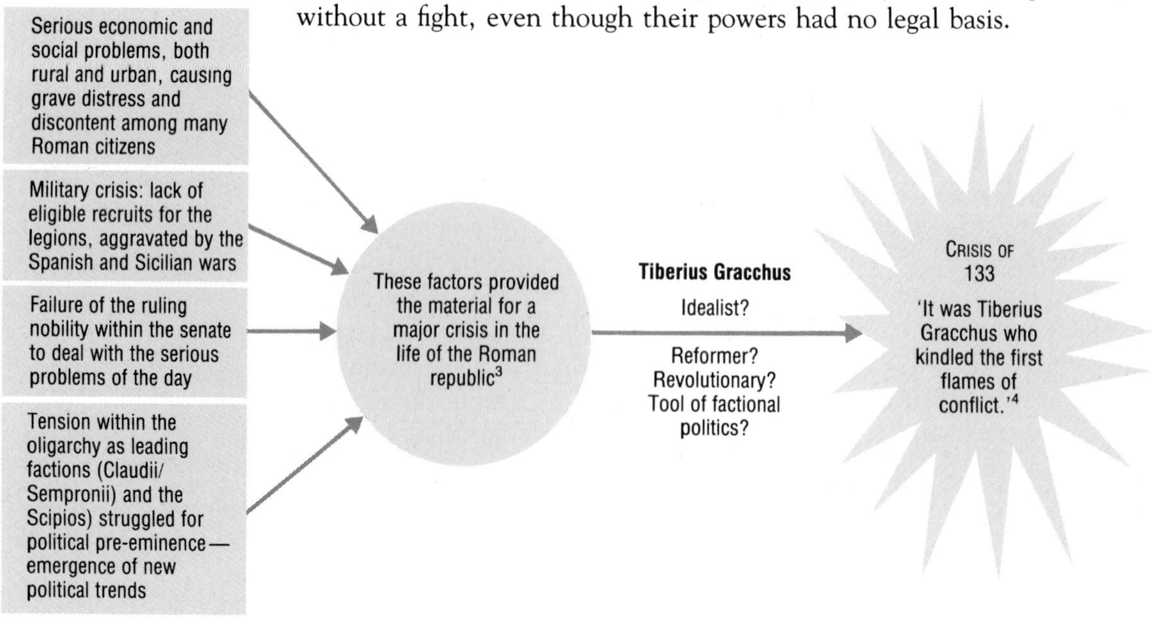
Serious economic and social problems, both rural and urban, causing grave distress and discontent among many Roman citizens
Military crisis: lack of eligible recruits for the legions, aggravated by the Spanish and Sicilian wars
Failure of the ruling nobility within the senate to deal with the serious problems of the day
Tension within the oligarchy as leading factions (Claudii/Sempronii) and the Scipios) struggled for political pre-eminence—emergence of new political trends
These factors provided the material for a major crisis in the life of the Roman republic[3]
Tiberius Gracchus
Idealist?
Reformer?
Revolutionary?
Tool of factional politics?
CRISIS OF 133
'It was Tiberius Gracchus who kindled the first flames of conflict.'[4]

Background and early political career of Tiberius Gracchus

Tiberius' background

Distinguished background

Tiberius Gracchus and his brother Gaius were born into a family whose members had attained the highest positions in Rome. They were expected to follow in the footsteps of their ancestors.

Their father, Tiberius Sempronius Gracchus, was one of the most important and powerful men in Rome in the second century. He was twice consul (177 and 163), censor in 169 and provincial governor of Hither (Nearer) Spain (180–179) and Sardinia and Corsica (163–162); he celebrated a number of triumphs and led important embassies to the east. During this time he built up a very large and powerful clientela, particularly in Spain.

Father — member of Claudian faction

He had started his career under the protection of the Cornelii/Scipiones, but broke with them and became associated with the Claudii for most of his career. His opponents believed he was a political opportunist.

Mother — a Scipio

Tiberius' mother was Cornelia, the daughter of Scipio Africanus. (Despite the fact that the elder Gracchus was an enemy of Scipio and in a rival faction, he married into the Scipionic family after Africanus' death.) Cornelia was a remarkable woman, having once been courted by the King of Egypt. She carefully supervised her children's education, which was a balance of traditional Roman values and the best of Greek learning. The Gracchi probably leaned towards the attitudes of their brother-in-law, Scipio Aemilianus (he had married their sister Sempronia), who was not only a military and political leader in Rome in the mid-second century but was also the focus of a circle of intellectuals.

Greek influence on their education

According to Plutarch the Gracchi were influenced by two Greek thinkers: Blossius of Cumae (a Stoic) and Diophanes of Mitylene (a rhetorician who taught public speaking). To what extent these men influenced the two brothers is not known, but it has been suggested that Blossius may have encouraged Tiberius to become a radical. Diophanes obviously played some part in developing the public-speaking skills that Tiberius — and particularly Gaius — acquired.

Florus — a Roman historian of the late first century AD, who wrote a brief sketch of the history of Rome to 25 BC — described Tiberius as 'a man who easily stood ahead of all others in birth, appearance and eloquence'.[5]

His early political career

Tiberius had been given the honour of being made augur in early adolescence, and in 147 accompanied his brother-in-law Scipio Aemilianus to Carthage. Despite his family connections with the Scipios, like his father he became part of the Claudian faction. He was married to Appius Claudius Pulcher's daughter, while his younger brother Gaius was married to the daughter of another influential member of the same group, P. Licinius Crassus Mucianus.

Tiberius' marriage links with Claudii

Tiberius became quaestor in 137 and was assigned to Hither Spain, where his father had made valuable connections among the Celtiberians. He served under the consul C. Mancinus, whose command against the warlike Iberian tribesmen was no more successful than his immediate predecessors. Roman military action in Spain had been marred by unscrupulous and ambitious commanders, undisciplined and resentful soldiers, and repudiated treaties with the native inhabitants. It may have been while serving there that Tiberius became concerned over the quality of Rome's military manpower.

Career influenced by events in Spain

An incident which some historians believe to have had a significant effect on Tiberius' later political actions occurred while he was in Spain. Mancinus, Tiberius and the Roman army were surrounded by the Numantines (Iberians from the town of Numantia). As they had no hope of escape, they wished to negotiate. Since Tiberius' father had treated the Numantines fairly in 179 and was remembered by them as their protector, they would deal only with Tiberius, who made what he believed was a reasonable agreement. The Numantines freed the Roman army of 20 000, but all their equipment and property was kept as booty.

Numantine Treaty

The senate repudiated the agreement, regarding it as disgraceful. This was a humiliating blow to Tiberius, who saw it as an attack on the prestige and reputation of his family, and to make it worse his brother-in-law Scipio Aemilianus 'seems to have emerged as the dominating figure in the crisis'.[6] Mancinus was blamed for the whole affair, but deep humiliation was felt by Tiberius in being unable to fulfil his *fides* (good faith) with the Numantines.

Tiberius' reaction to senate's repudiation of treaty

The tribunate of Tiberius Gracchus

Tiberius Gracchus, from a distinguished senatorial family, became one of the ten tribunes elected for 133.

Within a few months he had presented a highly controversial bill for land reform to the people's assembly without reference to the senate. He

Overview of Tiberius' tribunate

Families and factions in the late second century

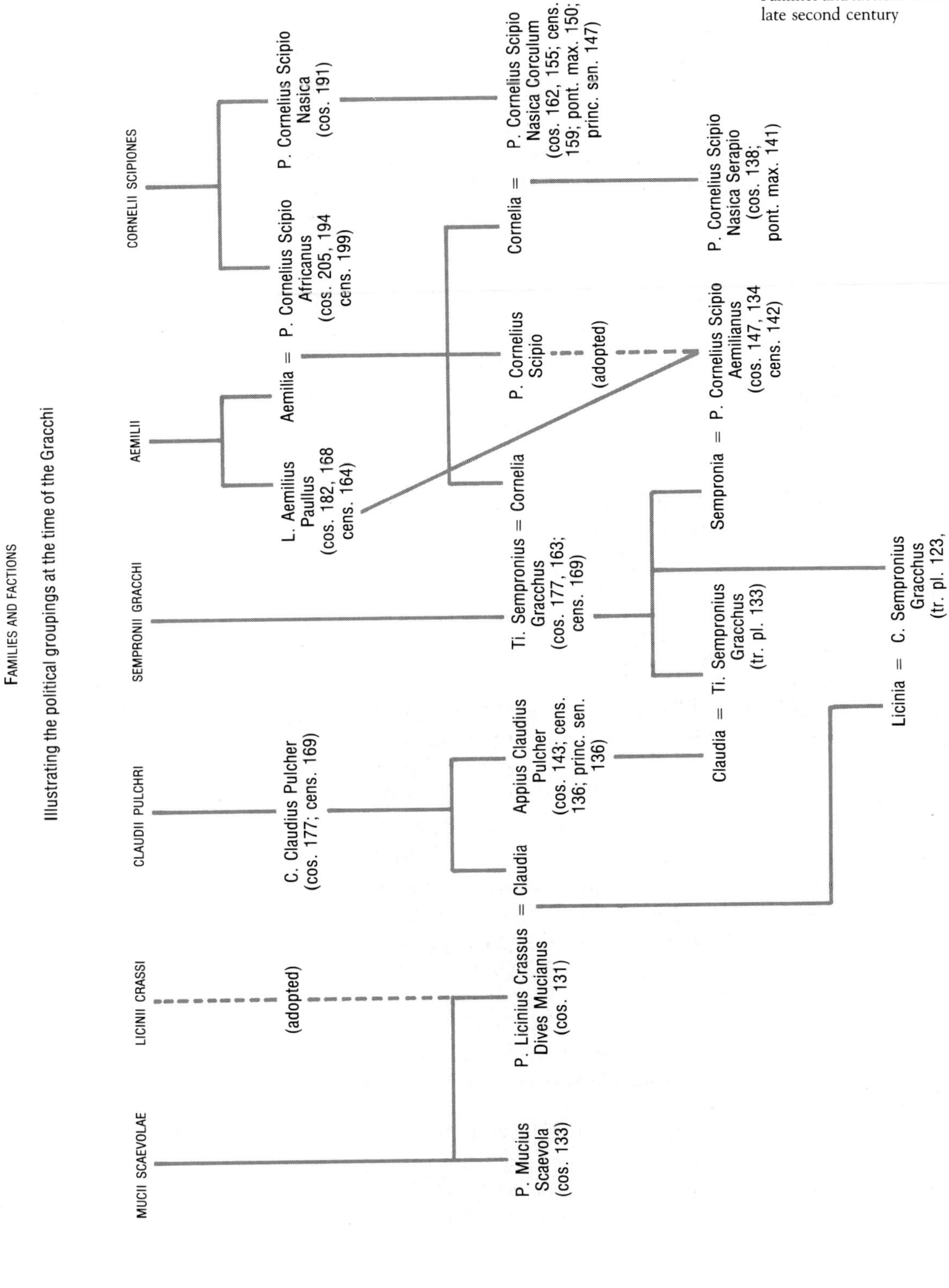

guided it through the assembly and put it into operation in the face of opposition from the majority of the ruling nobility; he overcame the veto of a fellow tribune by having him deposed from office, organised (without consulting the senate) use of the recently acquired treasure from the kingdom of Pergamum to fund his scheme, and attempted to have himself re-elected as tribune for the following year. He was battered to death (as were a considerable number of his supporters) when a riot broke out involving a group of senators led by the pontifex maximus, Scipio Nasica: 'the first bloodshed in the long agony of the Roman Revolution'.[7]

The land bill (lex agraria)

In 133 the young, confident aristocrat, as tribune of the plebeians, proposed an agrarian (land) bill to the people's assembly, without prior consultation with the senate.

Conservative nature of agrarian bill

Although the bill became controversial, there was really nothing in it which was novel or radical. The essence of the plan was that a commission of three people should allocate small holdings of land owned by the state (ager publicus) to landless citizens. The public land involved in the scheme had never been distributed or rented out, but wealthy Romans had occupied large portions of it for farming or for grazing their herds and flocks. (In 367 the Licinian/Sextian law had been passed regulating the amount of public land a person could use, but this had been frequently overlooked.) Tiberius now proposed that the wealthy farmers should surrender some of this land to the state. They were to be permitted to keep 500 *iugera* (about 326 acres) each, and an additional 250 iugera for each of two sons or daughters; they would be compensated for any land they gave up by being allowed to retain the remainder virtually as private property. The poor citizens settled on the land were to be charged a small rental and the allotments would be inalienable (unable to be sold); this was to prevent the wealthy farmers buying up many small holdings to add to their own land, as they had done in the past.

Provisions of lex agraria

A complex issue

This outline has simplified the situation with regard to ager publicus, since the total picture is extremely complicated and there are many debatable aspects. D. C. Earl, in chapter 2 of his book *Tiberius Gracchus — A Study in Politics* deals with the complexities of the *lex agraria.*

Tiberius' associates

Tiberius did not devise the land bill on his own or present it to the senate on a sudden impulse. He was supported and advised by a group of very knowledgeable and influential senators. The bill was carefully planned, as these men were aware that there would be serious opposition to it. Laelius, friend of Scipio Aemilianus, had attempted to introduce a similar land reform in 145 but had been forced to drop it under pressure from the senate. For this action he was given the name Laelius 'the Wise'.

Influential associates of Tiberius

The powerful supporters of Tiberius included two brothers with great legal minds, P. Licinius Crassus Dives Mucianus and P. Mucius Scaevola (consul for 133), as well as Appius Claudius Pulcher, the princeps senatus (this position entitled him to speak first in all senatorial debates). From 143 to 130 these men held between them three consulships, two high priesthoods, a censorship and the position of princeps senatus. There were also close links of marriage between them (see diagram on p. 237). Other influential allies were M. Fulvius Flaccus, C. Papirius Carbo and C. Porcius Cato. Tiberius' supporters in the senate came from five different families of consular standing.

Plan to gain passage of bill

These men would have known what opposition to expect and realised that the only way to secure the passage of this bill was to bypass the senate and go directly to the people. Since legally a tribune was not a true magistrate but was responsible to the people, the bill had more chance of success if a tribune proposed it, and it was obviously easier to present such a reform if the consul for the year was involved in drawing it up and the first speaker in the senate was also sympathetic. The presence of these factors suggest that the program was carefully planned.

The motives behind Tiberius and his associates' attempts at reform

Opinions on Tiberius' motives

Not only do the ancient sources differ considerably in their views about Tiberius' purpose in proposing the lex agraria to the people's assembly, modern scholars also present a large range of opinions. It is interesting to note what motivated Tiberius and his associates to initiate land reform which they knew would generate considerable opposition.

Cicero

Cicero — in company with Velleius Paterculus, Florus and Orosius — suggests that the senate's repudiation of the Numantine Treaty, of which Tiberius was a signatory, motivated him to initiate reform. Two suggestions are usually made concerning this: one, that he wished to regain his good name — to the Roman noble gloria, dignitas and fides were all important; the other, that he wanted revenge on the senate — the reason he took his bill to the assembly.

Bitterness over Numantine Treaty

> For Tiberius Gracchus the scandal of the Numantine Treaty of which he had been a signatory as quaestor of the consul Gaius Mancinus, and the severity of the senate in repudiating that treaty, was a source of outrage and fear: and this matter drove that brave and distinguished man to abandon the responsibility of the senators.[8]

Plutarch

Plutarch outlines a number of motives ascribed to Tiberius by other writers.

Greek teachers encouraged radical politics

> He was encouraged in his plans, as most writers report, by Diophanes the orator and Blossius the philosopher.
>
> Some writers consider that Cornelia was at least partly to blame for Tiberius' death, since she often reproached her sons with the fact that the Romans still referred to her as the mother-in-law of Scipio, but not yet as the mother of the Gracchi.

Jealousy of a rival

> Others maintain that Tiberius was also influenced by his jealousy of a certain Spurius Postumius. This man was of the same age as Tiberius and a close rival as a public speaker . . . it seems likely that he resolved to outdo him by introducing a challenging political program, which would arouse great expectations among the people.[9]

Rural depression, urban unemployment

> While travelling through Etruria on his way to Numantia he saw for himself how the country had been deserted by its native inhabitants, and how those who tilled the soil or tended the flocks were barbarian slaves introduced from abroad: it was this experience which inspired the policy that later brought so many misfortunes upon the two brothers. But it was above all the people themselves who did most to arouse Tiberius' energy and ambitions by inscribing slogans and appeals on porticoes, monuments, and the walls of houses, calling upon him to recover the public land for the poor.[10]

Earl

Some modern historians, such as D. C. Earl, see Tiberius as simply a front man for or pawn of the ruthless Claudian faction, who were using him to break the power of the opposing faction led by Scipio Aemilianus.

Desire to increase clientelae

> In proposing the land reform Tiberius and his associates will not have been unmindful of the possibility of obtaining the political support of the urban plebs and the rural proletariate, of adding these classes, or a section of them, to their clientelae.[11]

Carcopino

Jerome Carcopino maintains that the motivation behind the Claudian faction was

To seize government

> to drive out the dominant faction and seize the reins of government [while Tiberius] was ambitious for the honour of attaching his name to the bill.[12]

Carcopino also suggests that while his associates were political opportunists, Tiberius himself, profoundly influenced by the teachings of Blossius (a socialist) and Diophanes (a supporter of Periclean democracy), introduced the law from a moral obligation.

An extreme view held by some ancient sources, such as Cicero, was that Tiberius' aims were subversive (deliberately undermining the constitution) and that he was aiming at a tyranny. 'He tried to seize a kingdom, indeed he actually reigned for a few months.'[13]

From the preceding extracts, the following motives are attributed to Tiberius and his associates:

1 To gain revenge on the senate.
2 To restore Tiberius' good name.
3 To gain political pre-eminence by introducing a challenging political program.
4 To build up a large clientelae for future support.
5 To fulfil a moral obligation.
6 To undermine the constitution.
7 To break the power of the opposing faction.

Some views slanderous

Some of the motives mentioned above can probably be rejected. Any suggestions that Tiberius intended either introducing a democracy of the Periclean kind or establishing a tyranny are deliberate slanders or based on the failure to distinguish between his original intention and the effects of his tribunate. These motives also attribute to Blossius and Diophanes a far greater influence over Tiberius than was probably the case. The influence of his mother and the humiliating blow he suffered with the senate's rejection of the Numantine Treaty may have had some effect on his determination to achieve political prominence and increase his prestige, but as A. A. Astin points out, his powerful associates would not have been prepared to clash with the other factions simply in order to restore his prestige or dignitas.

No justification for view of revenge

If Tiberius' motives were to seek revenge on the senate by introducing the land reform, surely he would have put forward a more radical bill that would have stripped the wealthy landowners of all their illegally held land. Also, his associates would not have suggested bypassing the senate if they believed his motives were to undermine the constitution and threaten their position within the state.

Advantage of increased clientelae

Obviously Tiberius realised that the land reform would increase his own and the faction's clientelae and that the newly acquired clients would probably vote for him in the future, so giving him political prominence. The frequent mention in the sources of his ambition indicates that he hoped to make some political gain out of the reform; this was certainly a big advantage for him, but it may not have been the main motive.

Sincere reformer

Tiberius' determination to carry the bill through, despite the difficulties, seems to suggest that he was a sincere reformer rather than a politician pushing a policy that was expedient at the time. Plutarch and Appian believed that his actions were a genuine response to a serious agrarian crisis. Appian says:

> What Gracchus had in mind in proposing the measure was not wealth, but an increase of efficient population. Inspired greatly by the usefulness of the work, and believing that nothing more advantageous or admirable could ever happen to Italy, he took no account of the difficulties surrounding it.[14]

The Claudian faction had a history of political opportunism and knew that the land bill, if passed, would bring it considerable political gain at the expense of its rivals; however, this was not incompatible with a genuine desire to find a solution to the serious agrarian problems. It is therefore possible that Tiberius was a genuine reformer backed by a group of like-minded nobles.

According to Astin:

No single motive

> It cannot 'be assumed that there was a single 'real' motive . . . for behind such a major venture it is reasonable to expect a complex of several motives . . . it is more than likely that there was some variation in motive or in the relative importance of different motives among the members of the group.[15]

The declared purpose of the reform

Problems interrelated

Although Appian and Plutarch indicate that the bill was aimed at relieving the crisis on the land, some modern scholars believe that it was a response to an acute urban problem while others suggest that it was aimed at easing the crisis of recruitment in the legions. Yet all these things combined to form basically one problem and Tiberius, perhaps naively, sought to redistribute land-ownership and return to a situation which existed before the Hannibalic war—that is, in which the economy and the army were based on a class of peasant landowners. In this respect, the reform was very conservative.

Opposition to the bill

Opposition from wealthy classes

Plutarch says that the wealthy landowners were bitterly opposed to the reform because they were motivated by greed. Some resented Tiberius personally, while others were opposed to him because of 'party' prejudice. Appian gives details of the landowners' expressions of indignation at the injustice of the proposal, while Cicero maintains that the rich opposed the bill because they 'were being shifted from their long-standing rights of occupation'. He considered that this would cause discord as 'the commonwealth was being robbed of its champions'.[16]

Specific injustices

Some of the specific complaints made by the wealthy landowners were that (a) they would be deprived of buildings and vineyards that had been on the ager publicus for generations, (b) the graves of their ancestors would be disturbed, (c) they had spent their wives' dowries improving the land, (d) some of the ager publicus had formed part of their daughters' dowries and (e) since many had inherited the land with their estate they did not know just exactly which part of it was illegally held.

Although the difficulties and injustices of the bill were exaggerated, most members of the senate — including those who had helped to frame the reform — would probably have suffered some financial loss. These men, however, were aware that there was a serious rural problem and knew that earlier in the century (196, 193, 173 and 167) there had been a number of prosecutions of ranchers for violating the law concerning the use of ager publicus.

Some genuine opponents

There may have been some who opposed the bill because they genuinely believed the scheme was not a suitable way to solve the economic problems, but it is more likely that most were motivated by anger, fear, ambitions, jealousies and calculations of political advantage. Factional jealousies were great at this time, and the supporters and opponents of the bill corresponded very closely to the existing groups. The long-standing rivalry between factions meant that the Cornelii Scipiones, in particular, would not stand by and allow the Claudii to extend their clientelae.

Fear of opposing faction gaining advantages

Most opposition concerned Tiberius' methods

Apart from the two major factional groups, there were probably those whose opposition was not so much about the land reform but about Tiberius' methods of pushing it through. The difficulties involved in the passage and implementation of the bill are shown in the diagram on page 244.

Tiberius' death

Differing accounts of Tiberius' death

It is very difficult to reconstruct the events on the final day of Tiberius' tribunate because the major sources, Appian and Plutarch, not only oversimplify the facts but differ quite considerably in their views of which side was the first to use force. This is understandable, since 'the events themselves were characterised by confusion and disorder'[17] and both sides in the conflict were interested in putting as much blame as possible on their opponents.

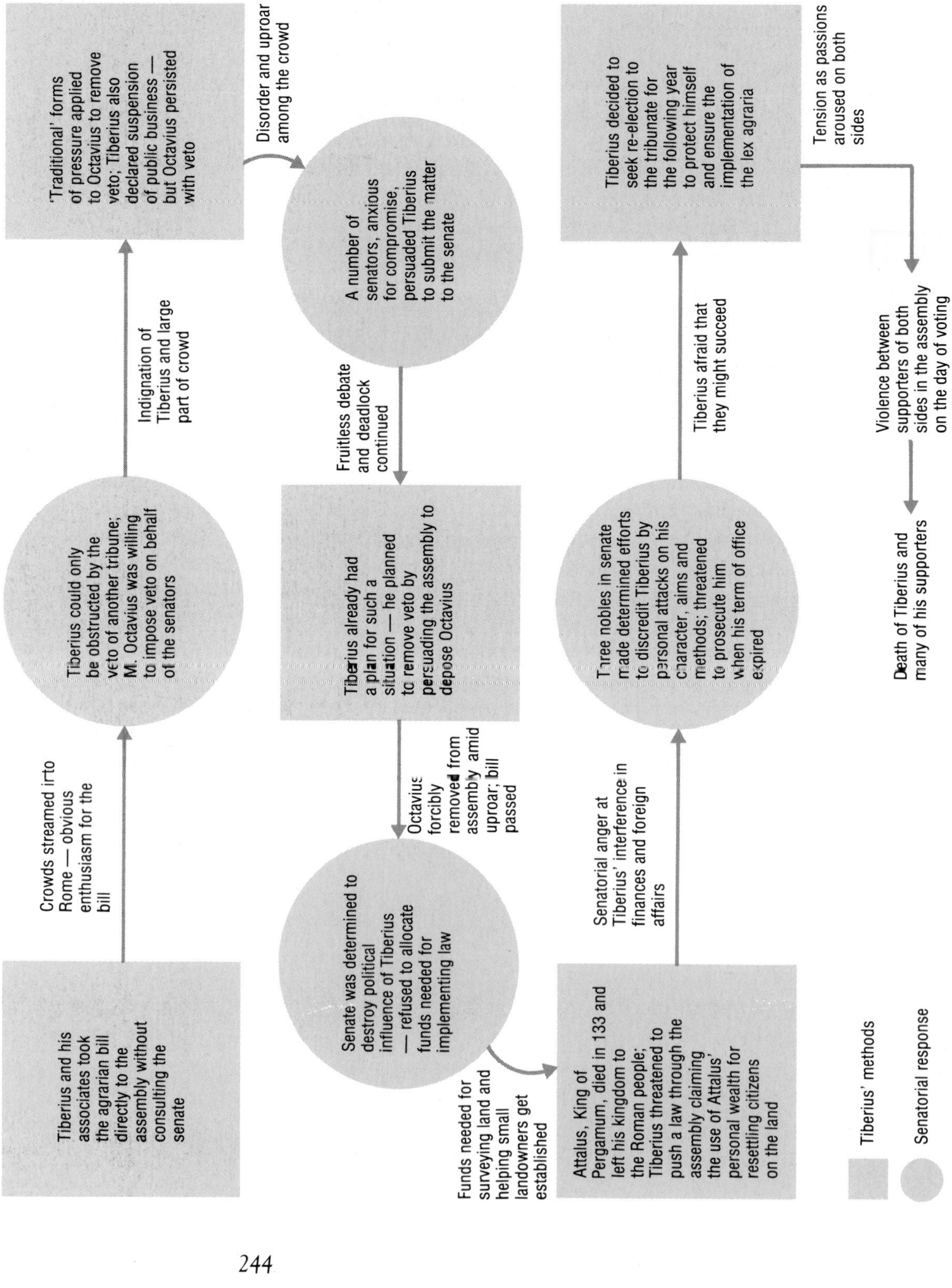
Tiberius and his associates took the agrarian bill directly to the assembly without consulting the senate
Crowds streamed into Rome — obvious enthusiasm for the bill
Tiberius could only be obstructed by the veto of another tribune; M. Octavius was willing to impose veto on behalf of the senators
Indignation of Tiberius and large part of crowd
'Traditional' forms of pressure applied to Octavius to remove veto; Tiberius also declared suspension of public business — but Octavius persisted with veto
Disorder and uproar among the crowd
A number of senators, anxious for compromise, persuaded Tiberius to submit the matter to the senate
Fruitless debate and deadlock continued
Tiberius already had a plan for such a situation — he planned to remove veto by persuading the assembly to depose Octavius
Octavius forcibly removed from assembly amid uproar; bill passed
Senate was determined to destroy political influence of Tiberius — refused to allocate funds needed for implementing law
Funds needed for surveying land and helping small landowners get established
Attalus, King of Pergamum, died in 133 and left his kingdom to the Roman people; Tiberius threatened to push a law through the assembly claiming the use of Attalus' personal wealth for resettling citizens on the land
Senatorial anger at Tiberius' interference in finances and foreign affairs
Three nobles in senate made determined efforts to discredit Tiberius by personal attacks on his character, aims and methods; threatened to prosecute him when his term of office expired
Tiberius afraid that they might succeed
Tiberius decided to seek re-election to the tribunate for the following year to protect himself and ensure the implementation of the lex agraria
Tension as passions aroused on both sides
Violence between supporters of both sides in the assembly on the day of voting
Death of Tiberius and many of his supporters
Tiberius' methods
Senatorial response

Attalus III of Pergamum

A silver denarius commemorating Tiberius Gracchus — the inscription on the reverse includes his family name, Sempronius

Opposite: The land bill — Tiberius' methods and the senate's responses

Exercise

Refer to Appian, *The Civil Wars*, I, 2: 14–17 and Plutarch, *Tiberius Gracchus*, 18–20, and answer the following questions.

1 (a) According to Appian, who started the violence?

(b) Who did Plutarch see as responsible for initiating force?

Illustrate each view by writing out the most appropriate sentences.

2 Is there any evidence in Appian's and Plutarch's accounts to suggest that violence had been *planned* by either side?

3 Using the source material, give a plausible explanation of what could have happened.

The crisis of 133 from the senate's point of view

Nobiles fear of losing traditional privileges

The Roman nobles believed that Tiberius was upsetting the status quo. They were afraid of losing the control over the affairs of Rome that their families had been exercising for generations. The government of Rome was what their lives were all about, and it was this tradition that Tiberius was threatening to destroy.

Senate not concerned initially

When Tiberius failed to consult the senate prior to presenting the bill they probably felt angered, but it was a minor breach of custom and not unprecedented. They could control the situation by using one of the ten tribunes to veto the bill. The de facto control of the tribunate had been one of the main sources of the senate's power throughout the republic.

Deposition of Octavius alarmed Senate

However, when Tiberius convinced the people in their assembly that Octavius should be deposed, the senators saw that their usual method of controlling officials could be bypassed and were afraid that the tribunate could once again threaten the senate as it had in the early days of the republic. When Octavius had to be forcibly removed from the assembly, they argued that this violated the sacrosanctity of the tribune.

The land commission, made up of Tiberius, his brother Gaius and his father-in-law, A. Claudius Pulcher, offended them.

Interference in foreign affaris and finances

Each further development during Tiberius' tribunate added to their fears of losing their traditional authority. When Tiberius proposed that the money from the new province of Asia be used to finance the land redistribution, the senate saw another area of their authority being challenged: here was an unprecedented use of vast sums of money for a program to assist the lower classes. Tiberius was also interfering in foreign affairs when he declared 'that the senate had no right to decide' the destiny of the cities of Pergamum (Attalus' kingdom). When he indicated his plan to submit the question to the people, 'No proposal could have been better calculated to give offence to the senate'.[18]

Methods not deliberately revolutionary

Although Tiberius' actions were not deliberately revolutionary, he appeared to be establishing precedents for direct control by the people in major areas of government, but the urban mob, in the concilium plebis, did not represent the whole Roman people and lacked the knowledge and skill to take over from the senate.

Senate feared the emergence of a permanent leader

Finally, Tiberius' decision to stand for a second tribunate appeared to the senators as an attempt to exert direct influence for a longer period. They may have been afraid of the possibility of a permanent leader of the people emerging, and this may explain why there are so many references in the Latin sources to Tiberius' wishing to seize a crown.

Senatus consultum ultimum

The senate had no provision to deal with a challenge or apparent threat to its authority. The only legal device which could be used was the *senatus consultum ultimum* (final senatorial decree), a safeguard for the state in an emergency, and this could only be issued by a consul. The consul for 133 was Scaevola; he refused to be the first to use force, declaring that he 'would put no citizen to death without a regular trial'.[19]

When the chief priest Scipio Nasica took matters into his own hands and led the senators out towards the Capitol, he probably believed that he was championing 'the liberty of the republic against the domination of Tiberius Gracchus'.[20]

The significance of Tiberius' tribunate

Genuine reformer

The evidence suggests that Tiberius was a genuine reformer who believed that his scheme of partial redistribution of the ager publicus would solve the rural and urban problems facing Rome. His aims were conservative, but in his enthusiasm, impatience or determination to see the reform introduced he adopted methods which, although not deliberately revolutionary, threatened the long-established (traditional) constitutional practices of Rome.

Although he did nothing actually illegal, 'he behaved in a way that was fundamentally irresponsible'[21] because the issues he raised threatened to destroy the balance that existed between the senate, the magistrates and the people. By his use of the tribunate Tiberius had shown a way for ambitious men to use it for their own benefit, and by threatening the position of the governing class he put them on the defensive, so that preserving their privileges became more important than the problems of the state.

Threatened stability of the state

According to Cicero, 'Tiberius Gracchus shattered the stability of the state'.[22]

The decade following Tiberius' death, 132–123

Both sides, shocked by the violence and bloodshed, must have realised that the struggle was not yet over. However, another explosion was avoided by directing the struggle into legal channels. The bodies of Tiberius and his supporters were thrown into the Tiber at night in order to avoid the obvious demonstrations that a public funeral would generate.

132

The consuls P. Rupilius and Popillius Laenas set up a court to try the surviving Gracchans, who were condemned and executed.

Scipio Nasica was sent on a commission to Asia to get him out of the way as he was responsible for violating the sacrosancity of a tribune; he died soon after in Pergamum.

The agrarian commission was allowed to continue and Licinius Crassus replaced Tiberius; with the death of Appius Claudius and Licinius Crassus in 130, it comprised Gaius Gracchus, M. Fulvius Flaccus and C. Papirius Carbo, all of whom remain in office until 122.

131–130

Papirius Carbo introduced a measure to extend the secret ballot to assemblies and to legalise re-election to the tribunate; this was supported by Gaius Gracchus but defeated with the help of Scipio Aemilianus, recently returned from the sacking of Numantia.

129

The interests of Latin and Italian allies were threatened by the work of the land commission—disputes arose over boundaries between ager publicus and allies' land. The allies also complained that the commission violated the rights of the treaty they had with Rome and they sought help from Scipio Aemilianus. He recommended that such cases be handled by the consul, but then the consul conveniently went off to his province—attempted to frustrate the work of the land commission. Scipio lost popularity with the urban mob and just before he was due to make a speech on behalf of the allies, he was found dead (probably, however, a natural death).

127

Gaius Gracchus was elected quaestor.

126

Many allies went to Rome to agitate about their grievances, but a law was passed to prevent non-citizens from living in Rome and to expel those who were already doing so.

125

Fulvius Flaccus, a member of the land commission and consul for 125, proposed a measure to give Roman citizenship to those allies who wished it. Those who preferred to remain independent would have the right of appeal against arbitrary action by Roman magistrates. The senate put pressure on Flaccus to drop the measure, which—had it been accepted—would have saved the Romans political problems for a generation and prevented a disastrous war thirty-five years later.

124

Gaius Gracchus was elected tribune of the plebs for the following year, 123.

Gaius Gracchus

A brief overview

Gaius Gracchus was nine years younger than his brother and only about twenty-one when Tiberius was murdered. Despite the violent nature of his brother's death, Gaius had 'no intention of remaining inactive'[23] and was well known to the Roman people for the part he played in the land commission and for his powers of oratory. He developed a high profile by supporting Carbo's proposal concerning re-election to the tribunate (131–130); he spoke against Penius' act to expel non-Roman citizens living in Rome (126), and he supported Fulvius Flaccus' unsuccessful attempt to give Roman citizenship to the allies (125). He made a name for himself speaking in the courts, and on one occasion, according to Plutarch, 'the force of his eloquence aroused the people to an ecstatic almost frenzied enthusiasm', so that 'the long-dormant fears of the aristocratic party revived once more'.[24]

Ability as a public speaker

He was elected quaestor in 127 and spent the next two years in Sardinia, but when the senate extended the appointment of the consul there Gaius refused to remain in the province any longer. He again used his ability as a public speaker to successfully defend himself against the charge of leaving his post prematurely.

Early political career

When he was elected as a tribune for 123, he 'quickly asserted his predominance over the other tribunes'.[25] He was not only resourceful, determined and imaginative; he had formulated, in the ten years since his brother's death, a clear program of reform. He had also learnt, from his brother's death, that if he were to overcome the senate's opposition and achieve his aims (see chart, p. 252), he would need the support of more than just the peasantry. A coalition with other groups in Roman society would need to be built up.

Election to tribunate

Learned from his brother's mistakes

He introduced and carried out a number of economic, political and judicial reforms in his first tribunate; 'these services won him the wholehearted devotion of the people and they were prepared to do almost anything in the world to show their goodwill'.[26] He was easily re-elected to the tribunate for 122, but opposition from the senate, which had been obvious from the beginning of his political career, grew in intensity throughout that year. This forced him to put forward new proposals to win the people to his side.

Won support of the people initially

Re-elected in 122

Unfortunately Gaius was not prepared for the fickle nature of the people, whose support for him waned when the senate very cleverly used another tribune to counter many of his genuine proposals. The measures

Gaius' genuine proposals undermined by senate

put forward by the tribune M. Livius Drusus on behalf of the senate were, according to Plutarch, 'neither creditable in themselves, nor beneficial to the community, since his [Drusus'] sole object . . . was to outbid his opponent in flattering and gratifying the people'.[27] The people, however, found these proposals attractive, and Gaius was forced to resort to more extreme measures.

Desire to help allies unpopular

His popularity suffered even more when he put forward his proposals for the allies. All classes of Roman citizens (the urban mob, the equites and the senatorial class) selfishly opposed his statesmanlike bill to give franchise to the Latin and Italian allies.

Unfortunately Gaius was away from Rome for some time during 122, supervising the foundation of the new colony of Junonia on the former site of Carthage. His enemies used this opportunity to undermine his position, attack his friend Fulvius Flaccus and spread rumours concerning bad omens associated with the organisation of the colony in Africa.

Senatorial attack on Gaius

Opimius — a bitter opponent

When L. Opimius — a bitter opponent of Gaius and a leading member of the senate — stood for the consulship for 121, he made it known that if he were successful he would repeal Gaius' laws. He hoped to provoke Gaius 'into committing some act of violence which would give him the excuse to destroy him'.[28]

Gaius was not elected to the tribunate for a third term, and this left him vulnerable to attack by his enemies; according to Plutarch he was pressured by his friends into gathering a body of supporters around him. Such a move was unwise as it led to a disturbance on the Capitol between the supporters of both groups, and one of Opimius' servants was killed.

Gaius' bodyguard clashed with senate's supporters

Gaius reproached his supporters for having given their enemies the pretext they had been looking for all this time, while Opimius was triumphant, as if he could now seize a long-awaited opportunity, and he proceeded to urge the people to take revenge.[29]

Gaius' death

Opimius persuaded the senate to take action in order to see that the state suffered no harm at the hands of Gaius and his supporters. For the first time, the emergency decree of the senate — the senatus consultum ultimum — was used. Unfortunately the Gracchans, deciding to resist the combined force of senators and equites, were defeated. Many died, including Gaius and Flaccus, and 3000 of their supporters were later put to death without trial.

Gaius' reform program

His aims

Gaius' objectives difficult to determine

It is obvious from the reforms that Gaius' aims were not contained within a single fixed objective, but what they were is difficult to determine since the order in which his measures were proposed is not really known. Plutarch suggests that he wanted (a) to avenge his brother's death, taking every opportunity to remind the people of what had happened to Tiberius, and (b) to introduce laws that would be popular with the people while undermining the senate's authority. Appian also agrees that he wanted to break the power of the senate.

Obviously Gaius hated the men who had been responsible for his brother's death, but since that had happened ten years earlier it is unlikely that revenge was his chief motivation. He was eager to continue Tiberius' land policy and build on it, developing a broader based program for relieving the suffering of the unemployed and the poor.

To help the poor and unemployed

Since he was a shrewder politician than his brother, he probably realised that only the senate could carry on government at this stage, so it is unlikely that he set out to destroy the senate's power totally; he possibly hoped to reduce some of its powers and privileges. One aim about which there is no doubt, however, was his desire to extend Roman citizenship to the Latin and Italian allies.

To weaken the senate

To help allies

Summary: Possible aims of Gaius' program

1 To avenge his brother's death.
2 To further the agrarian settlements initiated by Tiberius.
3 To relieve the suffering of the urban unemployed and poor.
4 To reduce the power of the ruling nobility.
5 To resolve the increasing discontent of the Latin and Italian allies by offering them Roman citizenship.

According to P. A. Brunt, each of the measures he introduced could be justified as attempting to solve a specific problem, but at the same time he hoped that each would contribute to the success of the rest and to his own power.

To build up a power base

His reforms

Owing to the difficulty of arranging his reforms chronologically, they have often been grouped under headings either according to type (economic, political, judicial) or according to the aims he wished to achieve (to avenge Tiberius' death, to alleviate unemployment and to weaken the senate).

The following chart classifies them under five headings: type, aims, description, results, and long-term significance.

Gaius' program of reforms				
Type	*Aims*	*Description*	*Results*	*Long-term effects or significance*
Judicial	To avenge his brother's death — aimed specifically at Octavius.	Any magistrate deposed from office by the people should be disqualified from further office.	Gaius was persuaded by his mother, Cornelia, to drop the measure.	nil
	To avenge his brother's death by challenging the senate's actions in putting Tiberius' supporters to death without a trial.	Any courts with powers of capital punishment not set up by the people were declared illegal; this was made retrospective.	Popilius, the consul of 132 who had presided over the tribunal which tried and condemned Tiberius' followers, was impeached and exiled.	Reaffirmed the ancient principle that a citizen's life was protected from the summary jurisdiction of a magistrate and was under the protection of the assembled people.
Economic: Land	To continue his brother's work and broaden it to help more unemployed.	Tiberius' agrarian bill was re-enacted, with certain amendments providing for larger allotments so that free labourers could be employed.	Although there was a considerable increase in small-scale farmers, the reform only touched the surface of the problem.	By 120 restrictions on the sale of allotments were removed, which enabled the wealthy to buy back some of their land, and in 118 the Land Commission was abolished. The agrarian problem did not disappear. Later veterans returning from long campaigns expected their commanders to secure land for them.

Type	*Aims*	*Description*	*Results*	*Long-term effects or significance*
Economic: Colonies	To relieve overcrowded cities of poor and unemployed. To continue his brother's policy of rehabilitating the peasantry. To also attract those with capital to establish industries.	The foundation or proposed foundation of colonies in Italy and overseas: by the lex Rubria, a colony called Junonia was proposed for the former site of Carthage. Large allotments with absolute ownership for 6000 settlers were planned. The colony may have been intended to include some Italians as well as Roman citizens.	Colonies were useful in alleviating the crowded conditions in Rome and the plight of the poor. Two colonies were founded in southern Italy: Minervia at Scolacium and Neptunia near Tarentum.	This was the beginning of a new type of colony — urban and commercial. The attempt to establish Junonia was the forerunner of later overseas settlements of Romans under Julius Caesar and his successors.
Economic: Grain	To relieve the growing poverty and hunger of the urban mob. To reduce the annual fluctuations in corn prices. To prevent speculation and private profiteering in grain. To provide employment on building of warehouses. To (perhaps) detach the plebs from their patrons.	Lex Frumentaria: the state was to buy up the grain supplies in bulk to be stored in public warehouses built at Ostia. The government would then sell a monthly ration to Roman citizens at a low price.	These vital grain measures alleviated the hunger of the poor and gave Gaius, for a short time, the support of the urban mob. This measure probably contributed to the mob's selfish refusal to support citizenship for the allies.	'Cheap' grain measures were later perverted by ambitious and unscrupulous politicians into a dole, and used as a form of political bribery. The fact that in the view of the ancient sources such doles demoralised the people was not the fault of Gaius.

Type	*Aims*	*Description*	*Results*	*Long-term effects or significance*
Economic: Roads	To provide employment. To improve communications. To help farmers get grain to markets.	Provision was made for the construction of an extensive system of secondary roads.	Roads which had previously been built for strategic purposes now provided direct communication between fertile areas, and facilitated Italian agriculture.	The roads constructed so carefully under Gaius' supervision became part of the extensive network of Roman roads which served the empire.
Economic: Army	To improve conditions in the army.	Clothing for soldiers was to be provided by the state and youths under 17 were forbidden to enlist.	This measure helped the peasantry, who made up the bulk of the legions.	The measure was the forerunner of further army reforms introduced under Marius c. 104–100.
Economic and political: Provinces	To finance his social reforms. To gain the support of the equites for later legislation. To avoid creating a body of financial officials. To protect provincials in Asia from exploitation by rapacious governors and their staffs.	The contract for the collection of taxes in the province of Asia was auctioned in Rome by the censors. The successful contractors (only rich equites had the capital to bid) paid a lump sum to the government and then collected the taxes plus their profit from the provincials through their agents (publicani).	This reform gave the equites and their agents great opportunities to make enormous profits in the provinces both legally and illegally.	Inadvertently Gaius had helped to increase the injustices and misery suffered by the provincials for many generations, as the equites ruthlessly exploited them.
Judicial and political: Courts	To gain the favour and support of the equites for his legislation concerning the allies. To give the equites a share in government to balance and so	Lex Acilia: the court of extortion for trying corrupt governors was transferred from the senate to the equites. The senatorial juries in the past had been too lenient towards	This gave the equites some political power in the state in keeping with their importance as a class. This reform put the provincial governors	The equites became a third political force in Rome. Within ten years of Gaius' death they allied themselves with either the people or the senate for their own political gain.

Type	*Aims*	*Description*	*Results*	*Long-term effects or significance*
	weaken the powers of the senate. To protect the welfare of the provincials.	corrupt governors, who were members of their own class — recent scandals.	at the mercy of the equites in the courts if they tried to check abuses, so many governors turned a blind eye to the activities of the equites.	The question of control of the law courts became a source of contention for the next fifty years and antagonised relations between the two classes, while the provincials endured further misery.
Political: Provinces	To prevent senators from rewarding their friends with favourable provinces. To improve efficiency in provinces.	A measure which compelled the senate to allocate the provinces prior to the consular elections. Previously the senate decided the provinces after the consul's year of office.	The senate continued to choose the provinces to be allocated, since they knew what was needed in foreign affairs.	In the long term this reform did not improve the efficiency in the provinces, since the people did not always elect the most suitable people to govern in particular provinces.
Political: Allies	To solve a potentially dangerous situation which was embittering political life. To recognise the support and loyalty given by the allies to Rome in times of crisis. To gain the allies' support in his attempts to further weaken the senate.	This was a far-sighted proposal to extend full citizenship to the Latin allies and Latin status to the Italian allies.	This proposal, vetoed by the tribune Livius Drusus, was opposed by most sections of society. The nobility feared that an influx of new voters might disturb their control of the assemblies, while the equites wanted to avoid giving any advantages to their Italian commercial rivals. The Roman plebs had no wish to share the benefits of citizenship — cheap grain and entertainments.	The selfish refusal of the Romans to grant citizenship to the allies embittered the Italians to such an extent that they eventually (90) took matters into their own hands. They won citizenship by waging war on Rome — the Social War, which almost destroyed the Roman state.

Senatorial opposition to Gaius

Gaius' opponents used a number of methods to oppose his legislation and undermine him personally.

1 The senate used another tribune, Livius Drusus, to outbid Gaius for the support of the people in the hope of humiliating and destroying him. Plutarch, in *Gaius Gracchus*, 9, explains how they did this.

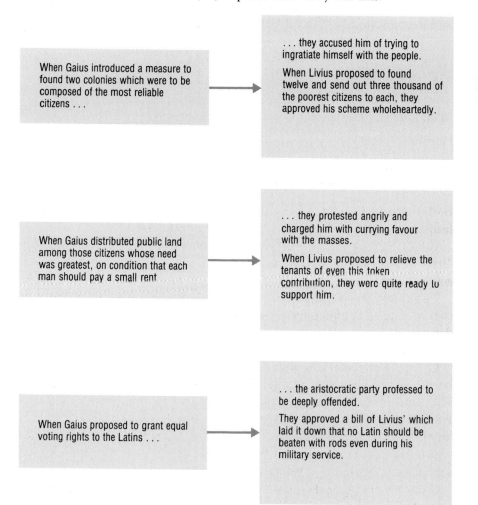

Senatorial opposition to Gaius

When Gaius introduced a measure to found two colonies which were to be composed of the most reliable citizens . . . → . . . they accused him of trying to ingratiate himself with the people.

When Livius proposed to found twelve and send out three thousand of the poorest citizens to each, they approved his scheme wholeheartedly.

When Gaius distributed public land among those citizens whose need was greatest, on condition that each man should pay a small rent → . . . they protested angrily and charged him with currying favour with the masses.

When Livius proposed to relieve the tenants of even this token contribution, they were quite ready to support him.

When Gaius proposed to grant equal voting rights to the Latins . . . → . . . the aristocratic party professed to be deeply offended.

They approved a bill of Livius' which laid it down that no Latin should be beaten with rods even during his military service.

Widespread opposition to franchise bill

2 When Gaius attempted to reintroduce and widen the appeal of his previous franchise bill, people from all over Italy flocked to Rome to support him. Plutarch says that the senate persuaded the consul, Fannius, 'to expel from the city all persons who were not Roman by birth'.[30] Fannius also played on the selfishness of the Roman people to undermine the proposal.

3 While Gaius was away in Africa organising the foundation of the colony of Junonia, his enemies spread rumours about the number of unfavourable portents associated with the new colony. The people were convinced that these indicated the displeasure of the gods with the enterprise.

Unfavourable omens for colony

Drusus also took the opportunity of Gaius' absence from Rome to attack his friend and associate, Fulvius Flaccus. He was accused without any evidence of stirring up trouble among the allies and the hatred which was felt for Flaccus extended to Gaius.

Gaius' friends attacked

4 One of Gaius' most bitter opponents was Opimius, a leading senator who was almost certain to be elected to the consulship for 121. It was generally known that once in office he would attempt to repeal as many of Gaius' laws as possible.

Threats to repeal Gaius' laws

The death of Gaius

Both Plutarch and Appian describe in vivid detail the sequence of events leading up to the death of Gaius and Fulvius Flaccus.

Accounts of the sources on Gaius' death

On the day that the consul Opimius planned to repeal Gaius' laws, the Gracchans and their opponents gathered on the Capitoline Hill. In the general confusion one of Opimius' servants, Quintus Antyllius, was killed.

The assembly was postponed, and Gaius' opponents in the senate used the killing of Antyllius as an excuse to declare that the state was in danger. The following day they formally passed the senatus consultum ultimum.

Opimius instructed the senators and equites to arm themselves and to be ready on the following day. The Gracchans occupied the Aventine Hill, and according to both sources there was an attempt by Gaius and Flaccus to come to an agreement with the senate. Flaccus' son was sent as an envoy to the Senate House twice but was arrested by Opimius, who was anxious to bring the matter to a head. He then led the force of senators and equites against the Gracchans.

Gaius was urged to flee, but with his opponents close behind him he persuaded his slave to cut his throat. Flaccus was captured and put to death. According to Plutarch, Opimius promised that 'anyone who brought him the head of Gaius or Fulvius would be paid its weight in gold'.[31]

Three thousand Gracchans were arrested and put to death without trial.

The senate believed that it had saved the state and restored order, and as evidence of this it instructed Opimius to restore the Temple of Concord in the Forum of Rome.

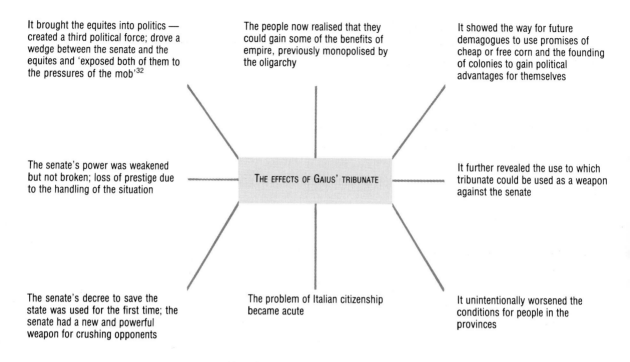

The effects of Gaius' tribunate

- It brought the equites into politics — created a third political force; drove a wedge between the senate and the equites and 'exposed both of them to the pressures of the mob'[32]
- The people now realised that they could gain some of the benefits of empire, previously monopolised by the oligarchy
- It showed the way for future demagogues to use promises of cheap or free corn and the founding of colonies to gain political advantages for themselves
- The senate's power was weakened but not broken; loss of prestige due to the handling of the situation
- It further revealed the use to which tribunate could be used as a weapon against the senate
- The senate's decree to save the state was used for the first time; the senate had a new and powerful weapon for crushing opponents
- The problem of Italian citizenship became acute
- It unintentionally worsened the conditions for people in the provinces

An assessment of the Gracchi

Difficulties involved in assessing the Gracchi

An objective assessment of the Gracchi is very difficult to make, since it relies on the ancient sources (which are biased), on probable motivations and on what might have happened. The following quotes from Sallust and Cicero reveal the difficulties:

> When Tiberius and Gaius Gracchus sought to establish the liberty of the common people and expose the crimes of the oligarchs, the guilty nobles took fright and opposed their proceedings by every means at their disposal.[33]

> But his sons were not approved by reputable people in their lifetime and in death they counted amongst those who were rightly killed. A person therefore who wishes to gain true glory should perform the obligations of justice.[34]

Much-needed reforms thwarted by senate

At the time of the Gracchi reform was long overdue, and the programs put forward by them were genuine attempts to deal with the acute problems of the day. When they were frustrated by the conservatism and selfishness of the oligarchy, they adopted methods which threatened the balance between the senate, the magistrates and people that had existed for a very long time. In this way they could be regarded as revolutionary.

Failure of senate to see changes in society

They probably interpreted the problems too simply. Roman society had changed, but they were in too much of a hurry to implement what they saw as the solutions to problems, while the senate persisted in maintaining the status quo in the face of the changing society. In ignoring tradition the Gracchi were provocative, and the senate had no way to counter the threat to its position except by violence.

Gracchi ignored tradition

Their significance for the future of the republic

The tribunates of Tiberius and Gaius Gracchus marked a turning point in Roman political history.

The tribunate

The tribunate was never intended to bring about change (revolution); it was intended to protect the ordinary citizen from being unjustly treated by the magistrates. However, the Gracchi showed the way that the tribunate could be used as an instrument for change. They had used it to undermine the traditional powers of the senate and revealed the potential for ambitious men to promote their own political careers.

Gracchi used tribunate as an instrument for change

According to R. E. Smith in *The Failure of the Roman Republic*,

> The Gracchi undid the evolution of centuries. It was impossible to guarantee orderly government if one tribune after another, with all the personal differences of policy, could initiate legislation and deal with the highest affairs of the state by bringing the business before a chance gathering of the Roman mob.[35]

The people's assemblies

As a result of the actions of the Gracchi, the Roman people discovered that in their assemblies (the concilium plebis and the comitia tributa) they could wield great power when combined with a tribune. The concilium plebis, however, did not represent the whole Roman people; in fact it came to be associated more and more with the urban mob, people who were 'not equipped for the task of governing an empire'.[36] The tribunates of Tiberius and Gaius Gracchus opened the way for the Roman mob to use its authority selfishly. Those issues which appealed particularly to the urban mob were not necessarily in the interests of all Roman citizens.

After the Gracchi, the assemblies were more than ready to support any aspiring politician who promised them benefits and relief. Since the majority of the senatorial class could only hope to maintain their position by developing policies that would win some degree of 'popular' support, the assemblies became pawns in the struggles for political supremacy.

Assemblies pawns in future political struggles

Optimates and populares

After the Gracchan period, the ruling body (senatorial class) was divided into two groups referred to as *optimates* and *populares*. Cicero said that 'Tiberius Gracchus' tribunate divided one people into two factions'.[37]

Optimates

Optimates comprised the majority of senators and nobiles (those with a consul among their ancestors); they were oligarchs and wished to maintain the status quo as prior to the upheaval of the Gracchan period. Any changes that would adversely affect their authority, prestige and economic interests were opposed. Occasionally they sponsored a 'popular' measure if it would gain some political advantage for their group. The optimates were a powerful, determined and cohesive group who could be utterly ruthless in protecting their interests.

Populares

The populares, also senators, were men of reform, who proposed measures to the people without consulting the senate first. They did not support continuous government by the people, but they did believe that the assembly had the right to decide any issues put before it without prior senatorial approval. Some of the populares after Gaius Gracchus may have been genuine reformers, but many were interested only in political advancement; they did not always present a united front and many of them later became optimates when it suited their careers.

Although Appian says that 'repeatedly the parties came into open conflict',[38] the optimates and populares were not political parties as such, although there was hostility between them which eventually erupted into civil war.

The senatus consultum ultimum (SCU)

SCU used to crush senate's opponents

When 'the Senate passed a decree that Opimius the consul was to see to it that the state took no harm',[39] it sanctioned the use of violence to crush its opponents. The senatus consultum ultimum (last decree of the senate) remained the only method of dealing with political threats throughout the life of the republic.

Violence and civil war

Increasing violence in politics

Roman society had changed, producing great social contrasts and intolerable economic and social abuses. The Gracchi had attempted to solve some of the problems associated with these changes, but many of their reforms left the Roman state and the provinces in a worse situation than before. They brought to a head issues which resulted in increasing violence and civil war.

There was a need for constitutional reform since the machinery of government was still geared to a city-state rather than an empire, but the violent reaction of the senate to the Gracchi inhibited peaceful changes and the Roman republican system was only changed by violent or illegal means.

The decade following the death of Gaius

Optimates regain control, 119–109

In the decade after the death of Gaius Gracchus the optimates regained and maintained their control of the state with only a few challenges; in one instance, L. Opimius was prosecuted by a tribune over the putting to death of the Gracchan supporters without a trial. He was acquitted, and so the use of the senatus consultum ultimum was legitimised.

During this period (119–109) the moderate Caecilii/Metelli family dominated the political scene, holding six consulships (119, 117, 115, 113, 111 and 109). The government was predominantly concerned with foreign affairs in these years, as Rome was threatened by a number of serious developments in the north, in the eastern Mediterranean and in Africa.

Foreign wars become a problem for the senate

Many of the senatorial commanders who led the Roman armies during these campaigns were far from successful, and in fact some were involved in serious military disasters. Others were accused of bribery and corruption in their dealings with foreign rulers, which led to popular agitation against the nobility generally. This applied particularly to the situation in Africa (Numidia), where the Romans became involved in a war with Jugurtha, and in the north against the wandering Germanic tribes, the Cimbri and the Teutones.

The war against Jugurtha

The conflict between Jugurtha and the Romans revealed the incompetence of many of the senatorial commanders, caused a serious break between the senate and the equites and brought to military and political prominence Gaius Marius and the young L. Cornelius Sulla.

Conflicts over succession in Numidia

Numidia under King Masinissa had been an ally of Rome since the end of the Second Punic War. When Masinissa's son, Micipsa, died in 118, the kingdom was left to his two sons, Adherbal and Hiempsal, and a nephew, Jugurtha. The ambitious Jugurtha murdered Hiempsal and defeated Adherbal, who fled to Rome to seek help. Adherbal and envoys sent by Jugurtha presented their respective cases before the senate, which decided that ten Roman commissioners, led by L. Opimius, should divide the kingdom into two parts. Sallust maintains that Jugurtha's envoys in Rome bribed a number of senators, and that once Opimius was in Numidia Jugurtha lavished gifts and promises on him and the other Roman commissioners to gain favours: 'Only a few were above being bought'.[40]

Suspected bribery of Roman officials

The settlement providing for a divided kingdom did not work; Jugurtha, who was energetic and warlike, invaded his 'brother's' kingdom and attacked the capital, Cirta. However, it was here that he made a crucial error: ignoring Rome's warning to raise the siege of Cirta, he took the city, put Adherbal to death and massacred all adult males found in possession of weapons. Such men included a large number of Italian businessmen and traders living in Cirta.

Italian traders massacred in Numidia

The equites were furious at the indiscriminate killing of members of their own class and at the disruption to trade which Jugurtha's activities were creating, and the urban populace were ready to join them in pressuring the reluctant senate to declare war on Jugurtha. They depended on imported grain for their food and were stirred up about the suspected corruption of the nobility.

Equites and people pressure senate for war

L. Calpurnius Bestia was sent to Numidia in 111, although many senators wished to avoid a war in Africa—which was understandable, since the Romans faced greater threats nearer home (the Cimbri on their northern frontier). However, Bestia appeared to come to an arrangement with Jugurtha, and a peace treaty was signed: in return for his surrender and some concessions, Jugurtha was left in control of Numidia. The equites and 'the masses were gravely incensed against him [Bestia]' and the eloquent tribune Gaius Memmius 'did his utmost to inflame the people's feelings', demanding an investigation into the affair.[41]

Further suspicion of optimate corruption

Jugurtha was summoned to Rome under safe conduct to give evidence against any members of the nobility who had accepted bribes from him, but was saved from doing this when a tribune ordered him not to answer the questions put to him by Memmius. Jugurtha, however, sealed his own future. A grandson of Masinissa lived in Rome and was a possible rival to the throne of Numidia; Jugurtha organised his assassination, and when the murderer was caught, and confessed, the senate had no option but to order Jugurtha out of Italy and to prepare for war.

Jugurtha brought to Rome

War unavoidable

The war which followed was under the command of Spurius Postumius Albinus and his brother Aulus. The former achieved nothing and returned to Rome to conduct the elections, while the latter was completely outwitted and humiliated by Jugurtha, who forced the Roman troops to surrender and to evacuate Numidia. This further disgrace prompted a tribune to propose the setting up of a special court of equestrian jurors to inquire into suspected cases of corruption and the conduct of the war. As a result, although no real evidence of corruption was produced Opimius, Bestia and Albinus were exiled.

Unsatisfactory conduct of war by senate

In 109, the command in Numidia was given to Q. Caecilius Metellus, 'who, although an opponent of the popular party, enjoyed an unblemished reputation among all sections of the community'.[42] Under Metellus the war became a full-scale effort, and continued for another five years. (This is treated more fully in chapter 15.)

Metellus appointed to Numidian command

Marius and Sulla

15

The Jugurthine War and Marius' first consulship

Marius' successive consulships

The Social War

The war with Mithridates

The dictatorship and reforms of Sulla

THIS PERIOD (approximately 119–78) corresponds to the military and political careers of Gaius Marius and Lucius Cornelius Sulla—careers that were extraordinary and were closely bound one with the other, Sulla being the young associate (quaestor and legate) of Marius in the wars against Jugurtha and the Germanic tribes, and later his ruthless opponent. The effect of the careers of these two men in causing the eventual downfall of the Roman republic can never be overstated.

Careers of Marius and Sulla linked

Sources for Marius and Sulla

Sallust

Sallust wrote an account of the war in Numidia against Jugurtha, and in it he presents a favourable picture of Marius and an extremely hostile view of senatorial leadership and behaviour. His bias is understandable, however, considering his own political experiences and his friendship with Marius' nephew, Julius Caesar. Sallust's treatment of Sulla appears fair.

Sallust's bias

Plutarch

Plutarch's weaknesses

Although Plutarch's biography of Marius is the most complete account of his life and career, it is also the most unfavourable. As sources, he made extensive use of the memoirs of Sulla and Rutilius Rufus, two of Marius' chief enemies.

Apart from the usual moralising (which is a feature of all of Plutarch's biographies), he seems to have been chiefly interested in Marius' military achievements and some dramatic incidents such as the mass suicide of the Cimbri. The greatest weakness is his failure to emphasise the significance of Marius' military reforms, particularly the changes in military recruitment.

Plutarch certainly used Sulla's memoirs for much of the information in his biography, but he confuses many of the events; his account should therefore be treated with great caution. He does not, unfortunately, bring out the real significance of Sulla's reforms.

Other sources

Military details by Appian

Appian's *The Civil Wars*, Book 1, gives a fairly detailed, continuous account of the careers of both men, particularly their military campaigns. Livy's account of this crucial period in the breakdown of the republic has been lost, and scholars are forced to rely on the brief *Epitomes* (summaries). Fragments from Cicero and writers such as Velleius Paterculus provide additional information.

Modern scholars are as divided in their opinions of these men as are the ancient sources.

The career of Gaius Marius

Although most historians are in agreement about the consequences of Marius' career, the sources — both ancient and modern — differ with respect to his aims.

Diverse views on Marius' aims

Some see him as a *popularis* who in his opposition to the senatorial oligarchy was a true successor of the Gracchi. Others believe he was a military adventurer, aiming at a dictatorship but lacking the necessary political skill. The most common contemporary view is that Marius was an unusual but not unique politician who sought glory and reputation for himself within the traditional constitutional framework. He hoped to be the saviour of his country and to build up a far-flung clientelae which would gain him, a novus homo, the acceptance of the nobility and the prestige normally conferred on a noble.

Gaius Marius, a portrait partly recarved in the 18th century

L. Cornelius Sulla

THE BACKGROUND AND CHARACTERS OF MARIUS AND SULLA, DRAWN FROM THE SOURCES

'As to what Marius looked like, there is a stone statue of him at Ravenna in Gaul which I have seen myself. It agrees well with the rough, bitter character which is supposed to have been his. He was by nature a very virile type.'[1]

Background
Marius was born in Arpinum, southeast of Rome, where he spent all his youth. According to Plutarch, 'His upbringing was rough and unrefined, if compared with the polished ways of cities, but it was temperate and in accordance with the ancient Roman standards of education'.[3]

He did not study Greek literature or attempt to speak Greek, since he was not interested in rhetoric or 'the elegant accomplishments of a man about town'.[5]

Once he reached military age he 'set himself to learn the art of warfare' which hardened him and protected him from 'demoralising influences'.[7]

Character
Sallust sums him up as 'a hard worker, a man of integrity, and an experienced soldier. Indomitable on the battlefield, he was frugal in his private life, proof against the temptations of passion and riches, and covetous only of glory'.[9]

Plutarch agrees with much of Sallust's description, but adds a number of unflattering characteristics — arrogance, a fierce manner and expression, an inability to control his passions when in power and a 'dislike of all who outshone him'.[11]

Marius' later career is summed up by Plutarch in the following way: 'a bloodthirsty and savage old age, shipwrecked by his passions, his ill-timed ambition and his insatiable greed'.[14]

(*Note*: The above illustration is generally believed to be a likeness of Marius, but there is no existing portrait that can with certainty be identified as such.)

'As for his personal appearance, one can get a general idea of it from the statues. But the terribly sharp and dominating glare of his blue eyes was made still more dreadful by the complexion of his face in which the pale skin was covered with angry blotches of red'.[2]

Background
Sulla was born into a patrician family, 'but to a branch of it that had fallen into almost total oblivion because for some generations its members were lacking in energy'.[4]

As a young man he was relatively poor, but was left money by his stepmother and a lover, which made him moderately well-off.

'He had a knowledge of Greek and Latin literature equal to that of the best scholars.'[6]

As a young man he spent his time with 'ballet dancers and comedians and shared their dissolute way of life'. He was 'prone to sexual indulgence'.[8]

Character
Sallust says he was 'eloquent, shrewd, and an accommodating friend. His skill in pretence was such that no one could penetrate the depths of his mind: but he was a generous giver, especially of money'.[10]

Although he spent his leisure time in the pursuit of pleasure he was very ambitious and never let his passions interfere with what he considered his duties to the state.

Plutarch describes his later career as marked by acts of 'butchery' and 'the most disgraceful and shameless sort of passion'.[12] Sallust agrees that Sulla's subsequent conduct filled him with 'feelings of shame and disgust'.[13]

Extraordinary career pattern

The pattern of Marius' career was one of the most extraordinary in Roman history, the more particularly since he was a novus homo. Although he came from a well-to-do family from Arpinum, he had no consular family connections or clients to help promote his career. Sallust says that

> at that time although citizens of low birth had access to other magistracies, the consulship was still preserved by custom for noblemen, who contrived to pass it on from one to another of their number... A self-made man, however distinguished he might be and however admirable his achievements, was invariably considered unworthy of that honour, almost as if he were unclean.[15]

Yet despite the difficulties which he knew he would face, Marius was obsessed with a desire to gain the consulship.

The early career, 133–109

Beginning of military career in Spain

Marius served as a junior officer under Scipio Aemilianus at Numantia in 133, and his outstanding bravery and ready acceptance of discipline attracted Scipio's attention. Plutarch suggests that it was owing to Scipio's acknowledgment of his great natural abilities that Marius began to have high hopes of a political career.

Political patronage of Metelli

Not much is known of his activities until he stood for the tribunate for 119. This was made possible by the patronage of the influential Metelli family, in particular of Q. Caecilius Balearicus (consul for 123)— there was probably a hereditary relationship between the family of Marius (clients) and the Metelli (patrons). According to Plutarch, when Marius was tribune he showed independence and courage in the first instance by proposing a bill which displeased his patron and the rest of the senators and—when asked to present himself to the senate and explain his actions—by threatening to have Metellus and the consul Aurelius Cotta arrested if they cancelled his proposal. The consul failed to get the support of any of the other tribunes, and the senate dropped its objections. This won for Marius the support of the people, who felt that he would not betray their interests in favour of 'conventional feelings of respect'.[16]

Independence revealed as a tribune

During the same tribunate, however, he opposed a law relating to corn distribution that would have favoured the proletariat. This seemed to indicate that he was a man who 'would favour neither [side] at the expense of the general good',[17] but according to Ernst Badian it revealed how little anyone could rely on his loyalty. Was Marius politically naive in alienating important supporters like the Metelli or was he deliberately using every opportunity to promote his own career?

Climb up political ladder difficult

His climb up the political ladder was not easy. He was unsuccessful in gaining the aedileship for 117 and was accused of having used bribery when elected to the praetorship for 115; he scraped in by a narrow margin as last on the list. Although brought to trial for bribery, he was acquitted in a close decision. His praetorship was followed by service in Further Spain as a promagistrate, and during this period he formed close connections with the equites and built up his business interests, perhaps from handling government contracts.

Business ties with equites

In 111 he made a very good political marriage with Julia, who came from the patrician—though impoverished—family of the Caesars. This 'brought him nearer to power',[18] as Julia was an aunt of Julius Caesar.

Political marriage

The Jugurthine War, 109–104, and Marius' first consulship

When Q. Caecilius Metellus was given the command against Jugurtha in 109 he took Marius with him as one of his legates, and this opened a new phase in Marius' career. It gave him not only a chance to reveal his military ability but an opportunity to develop influence and cultivate connections for his advancement to the consulship.

Metellus' legate in Africa

Metellus had won a number of victories over the forces of Jugurtha, but the wily king continued to elude his traps and the war dragged on. In 108 Marius asked Metellus for permission to return to Rome to contest the consular elections; Sallust says that Metellus treated this request with disdain and arrogantly suggested to Marius that he was seeking a position well above his station. '"Do not imagine", he said, "that all aspirations are proper to all men; be content with your lot, and do not ask of the Roman people a favour which they would have every right to refuse you"'. But Marius' desire for the consulship was increased, and 'there was nothing he would not do or say to make himself popular'.[19] His anger at Metellus' offensive behaviour prompted him to aim at undermining his patron's reputation in Numidia.

Aimed at consulship

Enmity of Metellus

Sallust, in *Jugurtha*, chapters 64–5, outlines Marius' attempts to gain support of various groups.

Won support of soldiers, equites and people

- He won the affection of soldiers under his immediate command by indulging them, but also by showing that he was prepared to endure as many hardships as they did.
- The Roman equites serving in the army and the large body of businessmen and traders operating in Utica (a large city in Numidia) were wooed by his criticising Metellus for prolonging the war; they were promised peace if he were in command.
- A pretender to the throne of Numidia, called Gauda, who had been insulted by Metellus, was approached and promised Jugurtha's throne if Marius became consul.
- As the plebs were looking for new men to replace the disgraced nobles,

> the equites and soldiers in Numidia communicated with their friends, families and associates in Rome demanding that the command against Jugurtha be given to Marius—'In this way he secured a large body of supporters who urged his claims to the consulship in the most complimentary terms'.[20]

Marius took the opportunity presented by the situation in Rome and continued pressing Metellus for leave of absence, which was eventually granted. In Rome, the tribunes stirred up the mob and Marius was greeted with great enthusiasm by the people when presented to the assembly, promising either to kill Jugurtha or bring him to Rome alive.

Elected consul by people

Although he was elected to his first consulship (107) with the intention of assuming the command against Jugurtha, there was a problem to be overcome before this could happen. One of Gaius Gracchus' laws stipulated that consular provinces must be allocated prior to the elections, but in this case the senate had already extended Metellus' command in Numidia and assigned the consuls-elect other areas of responsibility. The Roman people would not tolerate the frustration of their wishes by the nobles, so a tribune, Manlius Mancinus, introduced a bill to the assembly conferring the Jugurthine command on Marius. The senate had no choice but to revoke Metellus' command and grant Marius whatever he demanded in the way of soldiers and equipment.

Command against Jugurtha conferred by assembly

The people and the equites had interfered in foreign affairs in order to procure a command for Marius, so beginning his series of unconstitutional consulships.

Recruitment of army from proletariat

Before leaving for Africa in 107, Marius recruited an army—'not, in accordance with traditional custom, from the propertied classes, but accepting any man who volunteered—members of the proletariat for the most part'.[21] According to Badian, this was only the culmination of a process of lowering the property qualification because of increasing shortage of manpower. Whether Marius saw the potential for personal power inherent in this method of enlistment, as Sallust and Badian suggest, or whether he was totally unaware of its importance, is irrelevant. The fact is that it had disastrous consequences—the army was given a 'place of unprecedented power in the political life of Rome'.[22]

Future importance of military power in politics

Marius was a practical soldier, and he knew that the previous practice of recruitment based on property filled the legions with men who were reluctant to leave their farms and businesses. Such recruits were also anxious to be demobilised as soon as possible. Marius opened up the legions to men who in civilian life were probably either unemployed or landless labourers, but who could now make the army a profession and would probably be indifferent to the nature of the cause for which they fought, even if it were for a general's own advancement.

Sulla as Marius' quaestor

Marius' quaestor for the Jugurthine War was Lucius Cornelius Sulla, who had no previous military experience. Although young noblemen previously were expected to have completed at least ten years' military service before contesting public office, by Sulla's day it seems to have been generally accepted that an aspiring politician might stand for the quaestorship provided that he had reached the age of thirty. Both Sallust and Plutarch agree that despite Sulla's lack of military experience, after his arrival in Africa he soon made a good name for himself, but it seems strange that Marius gave Sulla the very important task of raising a large cavalry force in Italy *before* coming to Africa, and once he was there, entrusted him with the administration of the camp. Arthur Keaveney suggests that Marius was shrewd enough to see Sulla's abundant natural talent.

Sulla's natural talent

Difficulties faced by Marius in Africa

Marius had promised the people that he would end the war quickly either by killing Jugurtha or producing him as a prisoner at Rome. However, like Metellus, he soon found that the mountainous, desert country suited his opponents' guerilla warfare and that the only way to defeat Jugurtha was to weaken his hold over his subjects and allies. This was a slow process, and in the following year Marius' command was extended. He did succeed in forcing Jugurtha to take refuge with his father-in-law (Bocchus, King of Mauretania), and it was probably owing to the energy that Marius put into the campaign that persuaded Bocchus to open discussions with the Romans. However, it was Sulla's courage and diplomatic skill as Marius' personal representative that induced Bocchus to betray Jugurtha. Sulla then handed Jugurtha over to Marius, and the war came to an end.

Capture of Jugurtha by Sulla

Beginning of enmity between Marius and Sulla

Although Marius was given the credit for bringing the war to an end and celebrated a triumph on his return to Rome, Plutarch suggests that the surrender of Jugurtha to Sulla made him envious. 'It was this that sowed the first seed of that irreconcilable and bitter hatred between Marius and Sulla which very nearly brought Rome to ruin.'[23] However, Marius continued to employ Sulla in his campaigns.

A silver denarius struck by Sulla's son, depicting Bocchus, King of Mauretania, handing over Jugurtha to Sulla: Jugurtha has his hands tied, and the word 'Felix' (Sulla Felix) can be seen

The campaigns against the Cimbri and Teutones and Marius' successive consulships, 104–101

Problems in north with Germanic tribes

While Marius was fighting in Africa the Cimbri and Teutones, Germanic tribes from the north, continued to threaten Italy. Just as had happened in the war with Jugurtha, the senatorial commanders sent north to deal with them displayed incompetence resulting in a number of major disasters for the Roman armies. The most serious one occurred at Arausio in 105 under the command of Q. Servilius Caepio. This was certainly the worst disaster since Cannae, and produced a panic in Rome.

Illegality of Marius' second consulship

Anger of people at nobility

As the war in Numidia had just finished, the people demanded that the command against the Cimbri and Teutones be given to Marius, and although under the lex Villia Annalis he was ineligible for re-election to the consulship, he was voted in for a second time while still absent in Africa. Plutarch says that 'it was illegal for a man to be elected consul unless he was actually present in Rome' but 'the people would tolerate no opposition'.[24] The people also expressed their anger against the nobility by supporting a law, put forward by the tribune C. Servilius Glaucia, returning control of the law courts to the equites. (Caepio, consul in 106, had deprived the equites of their control of the juries.)

Marius returned to Rome the people's hero and began immediate preparations for a confrontation with the Cimbri and the Teutones, who had for the time being moved away from the north of Italy.

Marius' military reforms

During his second consulship (and at this time Sulla was a legate under him) Marius carried out a major reorganisation of the army which included the continuation of voluntary recruitment, the introduction of new training methods and innovations in organisation and weaponry. Details of these are given in the following chart.

Marius' military reforms		
	Description	*Significance*
Recruitment	Volunteers from among the landless were signed on for an extended period, such as sixteen years.	The army became a career — semi-professional soldiers rather than a citizen militia. The troops depended on their generals to look after them during the campaign (spoils) and after demobilisation (pensions in the form of land).

	Description	*Significance*
Recruitment		Since the state failed to organise any pension scheme, individual commanders were forced to involve themselves in politics to provide for their veterans. Soldiers were thus 'tied' to their generals and this allowed the later development of armies loyal to an individual rather than to the state.
Organisation	The three separate lines based on age and equipment were done away with, as all legionaries now carried the same equipment provided by the state.	
	The legion was divided into ten cohorts of three maniples each. The cohort became the main tactical unit of the army and it was divided into six centuries. A legion's sixty centuries were led by centurions, who were experienced veterans. There were six military tribunes attached to each legion.	The legion became more efficient. Firm leadership was provided for the ordinary soldier by the hardened centurions.
	The silver eagle (*aquila*) was adopted as the special standard of each legion.	The men developed a special loyalty to their legion.
Equipment	A new wooden spear (*pilum*) with a detachable metal head was introduced. The weak wooden nail attaching it would break on impact with an enemy shield.	This prevented the enemy from hurling the javelin back.
	Each soldier carried all his own baggage (cooking utensils, entrenching equipment) as well as weapons. They were referred to as *muli Mariani* (Marius' mules).	The army became more mobile and independent. The troops were able to make camp each night without waiting for the baggage 'train', as was the previous practice.

	Description	Significance
Training and discipline	A new system of drill was introduced, based on the training given in the gladiatorial schools. This had already been used by Rutilius Rufus, consul in 105. Marius lost no opportunity to toughen up his men with forced marches and runs in full equipment, and he never allowed them to become idle: they diverted a river and built a canal while waiting for the Cimbri and Teutones to return.	The discipline imposed and the skills developed made the Roman army 'one of the finest fighting machines of antiquity'.[25]

A representation of one of Marius' soldiers, who were referred to as *muli Mariani* (Marius' mules)

A battle scene from part of a sarcophagus, depicting Germanic warriors fighting Roman legionaries

While ever there was a threat of an invasion by the Cimbri and Teutones, Marius continued to hold the consulship. He was re-elected (in his absence) for a third time in 103, but by the following year the nobles were making a concerted effort to have their own candidates installed. Marius returned to Rome for the consular elections and it was at this time that he first became associated with the popularis L. Appuleius Saturninus —an alliance which eventually proved disastrous for him.

First association of Marius with Saturninus

Saturninus was a young man from a good family of praetorian rank; however, 'he became a popularis out of indignation at the action of the Senate':[26] he had been quaestor in charge of the corn-supply at Ostia, and because of a shortage—which was not his fault—the senate dismissed him and appointed M. Scaurus. This filled him with a bitter hatred for the government, and when elected to the tribunate for 103 he proposed a number of measures that he hoped would help him to get his revenge on the senate and also build up a popular following.

Saturninus' hatred of senate

1 His first attack on the senate took the form of a proposal to prosecute the consuls responsible for the disaster at Arausio in 105 (Caepio and Mallius went into exile). He was also responsible for the introduction of a court to try cases of treason against the Roman people, and since this court would be manned by jurors from the equestrian class it was obviously a bid for their support.

Saturninus' attempts to get support from equites and people

2 In an attempt to obtain the backing of the masses, he put forward a corn bill to reduce the price of grain to one-eighth of that laid down by Gaius Gracchus. This created an uproar in the senate, and tribunes were found to obstruct the bill. When Saturninus ignored their veto, the son of Caepio broke up the meeting of the assembly by force. Whether the bill ever became law is not known, but it had the desired effect for Saturninus—he gained the goodwill of the plebeians.

Land allotments for Marius' veterans

3 Saturninus then secured the support of Marius' Numidian veterans by providing generous land allotments for them in Africa. When the elections for consul were due, he 'called upon the people to elect Marius consul',[27] although Marius pretended he did not want to stand. Marius thus won his fourth consulship, one shared with Lutatius Catulus, who was held in high regard by the nobility.

Marius' fourth consulship

Marius returned to the north just in time, as the Germanic tribes had planned a three-pronged attack on Italy. In 102 Marius annihilated the Teutones at Aquae Sextiae in Transalpine Gaul: the Cimbri, taking a longer route, had not yet arrived. In 101 Marius (in absentia) was voted into the consulship for a fifth time, and when the Cimbri entered Cisalpine Gaul he joined forces with Catulus to face them. The Cimbri were decisively defeated at Vercellae in the Po valley, while a third group, the Tigurini, were forced to retreat into Switzerland under pressure from Sulla. Plutarch says that although Sulla had served as a military tribune on Marius' staff in 103, he transferred to the staff of Catulus because he believed that Marius was blocking his advancement. Plutarch gives a detailed and graphic account of these campaigns in *Marius*, 15–27.

Fifth consulship

Defeat of Cimbri and Teutones

The sixth consulship and the alliance with Saturninus and Glaucia, 100

Marius — the people's hero

With the war against the Cimbri and Teutones successfully concluded Marius returned triumphantly to Rome in 101, the people's hero. However, he now had another group of loyal veterans for whom to provide and this meant that he was either obliged to work for them directly or to use sympathetic magistrates. Of course he also wanted further advancement for himself, and the opportunity to command in other trouble spots in the empire, and to achieve these objectives he sought the consulship for the sixth time; to do this he openly allied himself with the populares, L. Appuleius Saturninus and C. Servilius Glaucia, since he himself was not a politician, had little ability as an orator, and expected the optimates to be united against him.

Political involvement with populares

Dubious character and aims of Glaucia

Saturninus, an able politician, had already gained the support of the masses with his legislation in 103. Glaucia, whom Cicero described as 'the greatest scoundrel since the world began', was 'very clever and crafty and extremely witty. He had the common people in his pocket, and had bound the equestrian order to him through the good turn his law did them'.[28] (He had returned control of the law courts to the equites.) In 102 one of the censors, Metellus Numidicus, had attempted to have Saturninus and Glaucia removed from the senatorial lists on the grounds that they were unsuitable members, but he failed when the other censor (his cousin) would not support him.

Sixth consulship for Marius

Under the arrangement with these two, Marius was to be consul for the sixth time, Glaucia was to be praetor, and Saturninus was to be tribune for the second time. Marius was elected with the help of his veterans, who were in the city after celebrating their triumph. (According to some sources he still had to resort to bribery to win.) Glaucia was elected, but for Saturninus it was more difficult and it seemed that he would lose the election until a rival for the position was fortunately murdered: it has been suggested that some of Marius' veterans were responsible for this.[29]

Violence in elections

Proposed measures for Marius' veterans

Once in office, the three attempted to carry out a program aimed at satisfying the veterans. Bills were introduced to grant allotments of land in Gaul and establish colonies in Sicily, Achaea and Macedonia. Since Marius' army consisted of allied contingents as well as Roman citizens, it was only fair that population for proposed colonies should be recruited in part from the Italian communities. There is evidence to suggest that some of the colonies were to be of Latin status rather than Roman.

Resentment against allied veterans by urban plebs

Although this proposal revealed the value that Marius put on his allied contingents it caused a great deal of opposition and resentment from the city plebs, who forgot the favours that had been done for them in the past. Realising that force might be needed to get the bill passed, Marius brought some of his veterans into the Forum. Also, in anticipation of opposition from the senate the bill included a clause by which senators were required, within five days of it becoming law, to take an oath to abide by its terms; failure to do this would entail exile.

Passage of bill due to veterans' presence

Despite the senate's attempts to obstruct the passage of the bill by means of a veto and a declaration of unfavourable omens, the presence of Marius' veterans made sure that the measure was passed; the subsequent behaviour of Marius, however, is hard to understand. Both Appian and Plutarch give accounts that tend to be unfavourable to him. According to them he at first indicated to the senators that he would not take the oath, and 'Metellus joined him in this declaration and everybody praised the action'.[30] However, when the day came for the oath to be sworn, he told them 'that he was fearful about the people's enthusiasm for the law' and would swear to uphold it 'if it really was a law'.[31] The other senators

Problems over senatorial oath

followed Marius' lead—all except for Metellus, who preferred to stick to his principles and go into exile.

Marius' suspicions of Glaucia and Saturninus

Marius was probably beginning to suspect the political aims of Saturninus and Glaucia and to regret his association with them; it was not long before he broke with his political associates. Their attempts to be re-elected for the following year (99) were marked by illegalities and murder: Saturninus was elected for a third time to the tribunate, but Glaucia illegally became a candidate for the consulship (he was praetor at the time, and according to the lex Villia Annalis an interval of two years was required between magistracies) and when another consular candidate, C. Memmius, appeared likely to win, he was murdered. Livy suggests that Saturninus had him killed, 'fearing him as hostile to his own policies'.[32] Whatever the case, this electoral violence was too much for Marius, who now (having satisfied his veterans) really wanted respectability and acceptance from the nobility and felt that continued support of the demagogues would make his aims unrealisable. The death of Memmius alienated all responsible people and the outraged senate passed the senatus consultum ultimum instructing Marius, as consul, to restore order and arrest his former associates. Saturninus and Glaucia, with some of their associates, had taken refuge on the Capitol, but were forced to surrender when Marius cut off their water supply. To protect them from the violence of the mob Marius locked them in the Senate House until they could be dealt with according to the law, but he was unable to prevent some of the mob from climbing onto the roof and battering them to death with roof tiles. They were 'still wearing the insignia of their offices'.[33]

Illegalities and violence at elections

SCU issued by senate

Marius forced to arrest associates

Murder of Glaucia and Saturninus

The results of the alliance

Marius' reputation blemished

Saturninus' legislation of 100 was probably declared invalid because it had been passed under a threat of force and at the time of unfavourable omens. Marius' popularity with the people suffered as a result of his apparent 'changeable convictions';[34] his reputation was tarnished, and in 98 he set out for the east (Cappadocia and Galatia) on the pretence of undertaking a religious mission to the goddess Cybele. Plutarch maintains that his real purpose was to 'make trouble among the Kings of Asia, and in particular to goad on Mithridates, who was thought to be on the point of making war on Rome', and that Marius believed 'he would then immediately be given the command against him and would be able to delight Rome with the spectacle of more triumphs'.[35]

Marius was elected to the college of augurs in 98–97, during his absence abroad, but although this was a tribute to the influence he still commanded he was distrusted by many senators. At this stage he had no role to play in the state, and all his plans for future activities were systematically blocked throughout the nineties. He therefore spent a number of years in obscurity, until the outbreak of the Social War with the Italian allies.

Temporary retirement from public life

Sulla as praetor and propraetor

While Marius was away in the east Sulla was elected to the praetorship for 97, and when his term had expired he was sent as propraetor to the province of Cilicia. His instructions from the senate were to settle the affairs of neighbouring states that were being disturbed by the actions of Mithridates. He not only achieved a coalition of states opposed to Mithridates, but also concluded an agreement with the Parthians over boundaries; he was the first Roman to make contact with this powerful eastern kingdom. However, these activities of Sulla in the east (96–95) had interfered with Marius' schemes, and his intense jealousy towards his former subordinate now came into the open.

Increased jealousy of Marius for Sulla

The significance of Marius' career

The career of Marius, a plebeian who had risen to the top position in the state through military excellence, weakened the hold of the senatorial aristocracy on Roman politics even more than the Gracchi had done.

1. The people, when they replaced Metellus with Marius, usurped the traditional right of the senate to appoint military leaders and allocate provincial commands.
2. Republican institutions were undermined when the lex Villia Annalis was violated by the election of Marius to five consecutive consulships. This example paved the way for the extraordinary commands later granted to Pompey and Julius Caesar, and made possible a future 'military monarchy'.
3. In throwing open the legions to the plebs on a voluntary basis, Marius converted the Roman army into a professional force of soldiers, providing a career for a large number of the unemployed. With his military reforms he prepared the way for the victories of his more famous successors, Pompey and Caesar.
4. The loyalty of the new recruits was to their commanding officer or general rather than to the senate or the people. The use of Marius' soldiers in the riots of 100 showed that the new-style army could in the future be used to destroy the established order just as easily as to maintain it.
5. The collision between the senate and Marius over land grants for his veterans raised the question of pay and pensions for the army. Had the

senate provided the soldiers with cash or land at the end of their term of service, instead of leaving this to the generals, it might have retained its hold on the Roman army. Instead, it played into the hands of the generals and brought nearer the day when commanders would use the armies as though they were their own private forces. The first civil war in Italy was due to the personal conflict of two military leaders; Marius and Sulla (see page 287).

6 Marius' career illustrated the incredible power that a tribune and a military commander could wield in the state.

7 The opposition of the urban plebs and the senate to Saturninus' proposals for fair treatment for the allied soldier on retirement added to the growing resentment of the allies.

Exercise

By referring to the diagram opposite and the requirements of the lex Villia Annalis, explain the most unusual aspects of Marius' career.

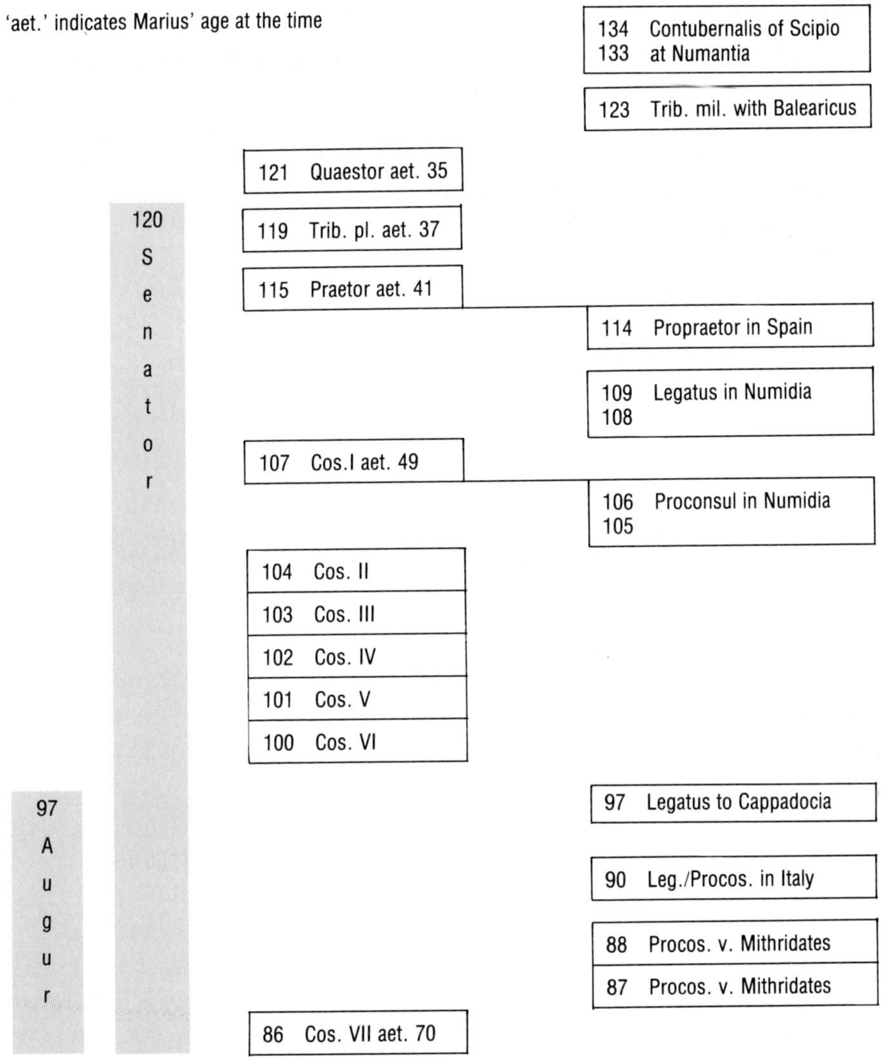

Diagrammatic representation of Marius' career

Assignment: Italian citizenship and the Social War

This assignment is an integral part of the work on Marius and Sulla and must be completed in order to fully understand the subsequent events.

Part A: The background to the war

1 Explain the meaning of the word 'franchise'.
2 Revise the status of Roman citizens, Latin allies and Italian allies (socii).
3 Note the significant part played by the allies in Rome's wars of expansion (264–146), and their general loyalty.
4 Revise earlier unsuccessful proposals concerning the Italian allies, as shown in the chart on page 280.

5 Why were most groups in Roman society (the ordinary people, the equites and the senators) opposed to an extension of Roman citizenship to the allies?
6 What were the main grievances of the allies?

125	Fulvius Flaccus (friend of Gaius Gracchus)	Proposed that all Italian communities should receive full franchise or the right of appeal against Roman magistrates	→ Proposal shelved by the senate
122 121	Gaius Gracchus	Modified form of Flaccus' proposal: allies of Latin status to be given full franchise and others raised to Latin status	→ Defeated by senate with counter-proposals of the tribune Livius Drusus
100	Saturninus	Raised Italian hopes by offering franchise to a select number of Marius' veterans	→ This law declared invalid by senate after his murder

Part B: Events prior to the outbreak of war

Use the extracts given from the ancient sources to answer the following questions in your own words.

1 *The lex Licinia Mucia, 95*

> It is a wicked thing to prohibit non-citizens from entering a town that is not their own and physically expel them from it . . . Of course, it is quite right and proper to forbid anyone who is not a citizen to masquerade as a citizen, as was laid down in the law which those wise consuls Crassus and Scaevola carried. But it is downright uncivilised to bar non-citizens from even entering a town.[36]

> . . . At a time when the peoples of Italy were fired by an enormous appetite for Roman citizenship and for that reason a large number of them were passing themselves off as Roman citizens, it seemed necessary to carry a law to restore everyone to his proper legal status in his own native place. However, so alienated were the leaders of the Italian peoples by this law that it was perhaps the chief cause of the Italian War which broke out three years later.[37]

> . . . the sort of law which L. Licinius Crassus and Q. Mucius Scaevola passed ordering the allies and Latins to go back to their own home towns.[38]

(a) How did this law get its name?
(b) What was the purpose of this law?
(c) What was Cicero's opinion of it?
(d) What effect did it have on the allies?

2 *The tribunate (91) of M. Livius Drusus (the younger)*

The reformer Livius Drusus (the son of Gaius Gracchus' opponent) was honest and well-meaning and had two main objectives: to return the law courts to the senators and to help the Italian allies.

> Subsequently, the tribune Livius Drusus, a man of the most distinguished ancestry, promised at the request of the Italian allies once again to introduce legislation to enfranchise them . . . In order to get the Roman people in the mood to accept this, Drusus sought to win them over with many colonies in Italy and Sicily, long ago promised but never realised. He also attempted to bring together by a

common law the senate and the knights (equites) who at that time were seriously at odds with each other over the courts. Being unable to transfer the courts openly to the senate, he devised the following compromise: to the senators who were then because of the internal troubles scarely three hundred in number he proposed to add an equal number of men chosen from the knights on the criterion of quality and birth, so that the courts should in future be chosen from this whole six hundred body.[39]

Though he was anxious to restore to the senate its old glory and transfer the courts to the senate from the knights . . . in seeking to implement his pro-senatorial program he ran into opposition from the senate itself, which did not understand that his proposals to benefit the people were no more than inducements to get the people to accept his more important proposals in return for the lesser gains they were themselves getting.[40]

The allies of Rome were trying to secure the Roman citizenship. A certain Pompaedius Silo, a soldierly man of the highest standing (he was the leader of the Marsi), was a friend of Drusus, and spent many days at his house.[41]

While working for this [granting of citizenship to the Italians], he had returned one day from the Forum, surrounded by his customary immense and straggling crowd of followers, when he was struck in the forecourt of his own house with a knife . . . With the death of Drusus, the long-burgeoning Italian War broke out.[42]

(a) Explain how Drusus tried to gain the support of the people, the senate and the equites before attempting to champion the cause of Italian citizenship.
(b) Drusus was killed by an unknown assassin before he could help the allies. Suggest reasons why he may have been murdered.
(c) Why did the optimates blame Drusus for starting the Social War?

Part C: The Social War, 91–89

1 Why was it called the Social War?
2 It was a war of secession. What is meant by that?
3 Read an account of the war in one of the modern texts and in Appian's *The Civil Wars*, if available.
4 Draw a map showing the areas involved in the war and the areas which remained loyal.
5 How serious was this war for Rome?
6 Explain the part played by Marius and Sulla.
7 Explain why the lex Iulia was passed in 90. What were its terms and its effect?
8 How important was the supplementary measure (the lex Plautia-Papiria), which was passed in 89?
9 Why was the Italian question (the registration of new citizens in tribes) not yet finally settled?

The career of Sulla, 88–79

His consulship, and the tribunate of Sulpicius Rufus

The events of 88 brought the careers of the ageing Marius (seventy) and the younger Sulla (fifty) into violent collision.

Command in the east granted to Sulla

Sulla had proved his military competence during the Social War and was favoured by the senate. As a result he was elected consul for 88, granted the province of Asia and the command against Mithridates for the following year. (Mithridates, King of Pontus, near the Black Sea, had used Rome's preoccupation with the Social War to extend his territory, threatening the Roman province of Asia.) However, 'Marius, thinking it an easy and very lucrative war, wanted the command [against Mithridates] for himself'.[43] He was, according to Plutarch, 'under the influence of those never-ageing passions, love of distinction and a mania for fame'[44] and was bitter at being overlooked for many years.

Continuing problem of 'new' citizens

The most pressing issue in domestic politics in 88 concerned the failure of the government to register the new citizens (previously the allies) in all thirty-five tribes. (While ever these were registered in a limited number of tribes the 'old' citizens could control the vote in the assembly, since it was taken on a tribal basis.) One of the tribunes for 88 was P. Sulpicius Rufus, a persuasive orator and a friend of the recently murdered Drusus, whose main objective in his tribunate appears to have been to see that the allies received fair treatment. Plutarch and Appian refer to him in very unfavourable terms, but Cicero's view of him seems fairer.

Tribunate of Sulpicius Rufus

Alliance of Sulpicius and Marius for mutual gain

Marius now allied himself with the tribune Sulpicius, and in return for his supporting a measure to distribute the newly enfranchised citizens in all thirty-five tribes Sulpicius was prepared to replace Sulla with Marius as commander in the war against Mithridates. Sulpicius also hoped to gain the support of the equites and the people by two further measures: men who had debts of more than 2000 denarii were to be expelled from the senate, and those exiled for sympathy with the allies were to be recalled. It was obvious that Sulpicius expected a violent reaction to his proposals from the optimates, since he surrounded himself with '3000 swordsmen and went about accompanied by large bands of young men from the moneyed class outside the senate, who were ready for anything and whom he used to call his Anti-senate'.[45]

Bodyguard for Sulpicius

Sulpicius' proposed transfer of command from Sulla to Marius was insulting, since it was a well-deserved reward for Sulla's successful career and Marius, who was well passed the military retiring age, had no claim to the position. As well, Sulpicius had resorted to an illegal method to get his bills passed: he put all his proposals forward as one block measure, a method of legislation that had been declared illegal in 98.

Failure of Sulla to obstruct Sulpicius' legislation

Sulla and his consular colleague, Pompeius Rufus, attempted to prevent the proposals being put to the vote by declaring a suspension of public business. However, this led to violence in the Forum and Sulla fled from Rome to join his army in the south, where it was gathering for the Mithridatic campaign. Sulpicius was then able to have all his proposals passed.

Sulla's march on Rome

Sulla appealed to his army to support him as consul in restoring order, and with six legions behind him he marched on Rome. This was a 'momentous event in Rome's history',[46] since armed troops were not permitted in the city (except to celebrate a triumph) and no commander with imperium was allowed within the ritually consecrated city boundary, the pomerium. Marius and Sulpicius, having no army to support them, fled the city and with twelve others were declared outlaws. Sulpicius was captured and killed but Marius escaped to Africa, where some of his veterans from the Jugurthine War were settled. Plutarch gives a detailed account of his difficult escape from Italy in *Marius*, 35–40.

Populares forced out of Italy

Repeal of Sulpicius' legislation

Sulla had Sulpicius' legislation rescinded. He then attempted to strengthen the senate so that he could take up his command against Mithridates in the knowledge that it would be able to govern without challenge until his return. To achieve this he passed a measure which prevented any business being brought before the people without the prior approval of the senate. He also restricted the activities of the tribunes by passing a law that proposals could only be submitted to the people in the comitia centuriata: tribunes were unable to present legislation in this assembly. Sulla also hoped to have sympathetic consuls elected to office for the following year, but in this he was disappointed. Although one of the consuls for 87 (Cn. Octavius) was a loyal optimate, the other was a man (L. Cornelius Cinna) whom Sulla considered untrustworthy, so he made him swear to abide by the new constitutional arrangements. Sulla then left Italy for his eastern campaign.

Senate strengthened prior to Sulla's departure to east

Politics in Rome during Sulla's absence

Undermining of Sulla's arrangements by Cinna

According to the sources (although these are rather scanty and biased on the subject), Sulla had every reason to distrust Cinna, for 'as soon as he came into office he attempted to undermine the existing order of things'.[47] Here Plutarch is referring to Cinna's attempt to take up the cause of the 'new' Italian citizens and have them registered in all tribes. The other consul, Octavius, followed the optimates' position of restricting them to just a few. This issue once again led to rioting in the Forum; Cinna was driven out of Rome by Octavius and the optimates, and made for Campania. He was deprived of his consulship and declared a public enemy.

Combined forces of Cinna and Marius

Cinna successfully won over the army in Campania and also had a large following of 'new' citizens. The sources indicate that he then sent for Marius and his companions, exiled in Africa, but it is possible that Marius had already returned and was raising an army in Etruria. The two leaders

Rome in hands of populares — 'Marians'

joined forces and followed Sulla's example by marching on Rome, which was inadequately protected by Octavius and Pompeius Strabo; the senate had no choice but to reinstate Cinna as consul and to annul the decree outlawing Marius. When Marius entered the city, he 'laid it waste with murder and looting';[48] for five days he took his revenge on all those who had ever offended him. His 'rage and thirst for blood increased from day to day',[49] and his band of slaves—the Bardyaiae, as they were called—plundered and murdered indiscriminately until Cinna and Q. Sertorius put a stop to them. Plutarch believes that Marius had suffered a breakdown owing to the dangers he had faced during his flight in 88 from Rome.

Marius' revenge

Seventh consulship for Marius and his death

Cinna and Marius were declared consuls for 86, the seventh time for Marius and the second for Cinna. Sulla's laws were repealed, he was declared an outlaw and his property was confiscated. Fortunately for Rome Marius died a short while after assuming office, but Cinna was re-elected in 85 with Cn. Carbo as his colleague. During this time Cinna was finally able to settle the question of the registration of new citizens.

Allied question resolved

The campaign against Mithridates, 87–84

The Mithridatic War is illustrated and summarised on pages 285–6.

Coin portrait of Mithridates VI of Pontus

King Mithridates Eupator (VI)
Adversary of Sulla, Lucullus and Pompey

This portrait deliberately copies the personal appearance of Alexander the Great

Velleius Paterculus describes him as 'ever eager for war, of exceptional bravery, always great in spirit and sometimes in achievement, in strategy a general, in bodily prowess a soldier, in hatred to the Romans, a Hannibal'.[50]

Mithridates 120–63: A summary

- He was extremely ambitious—he gained the throne by murdering his brother and imprisoning his mother.
- He had a forceful character and exceptional physical strength.
- His ability as a general was matched by his diplomacy.
- He was an admirer of Greek culture.
- He possessed characteristics of a Hellenistic monarch and of an oriental despot, but these elements in his personality never really fused.
- He was one of the most powerful rulers in Asia.

Opposite: Sulla's command against Mithridates

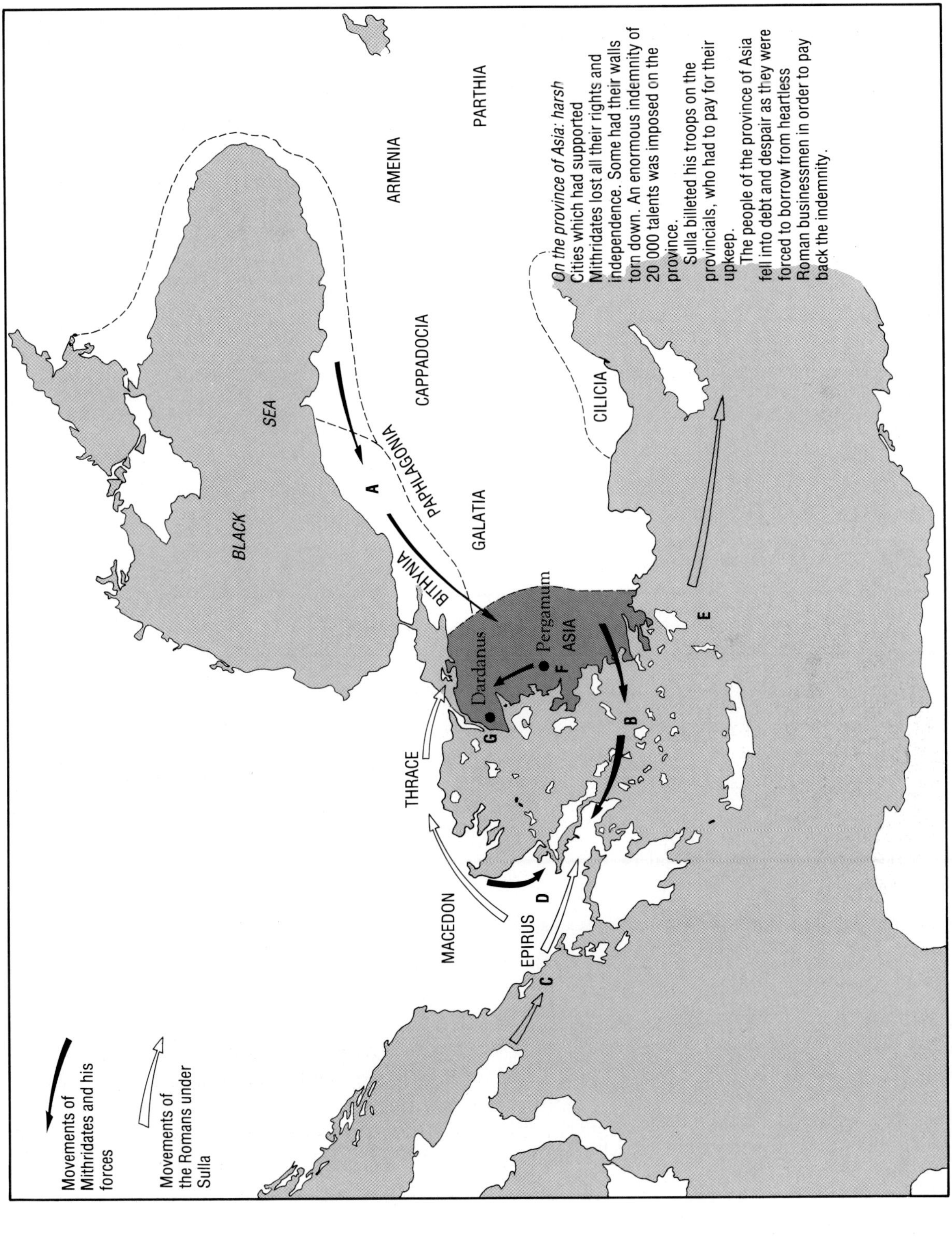

On the province of Asia: harsh
Cities which had supported Mithridates lost all their rights and independence. Some had their walls torn down. An enormous indemnity of 20 000 talents was imposed on the province.
Sulla billeted his troops on the provincials, who had to pay for their upkeep.
The people of the province of Asia fell into debt and despair as they were forced to borrow from heartless Roman businessmen in order to pay back the indemnity.
PARTHIA
ARMENIA
CAPPADOCIA
CILICIA
BLACK
SEA
PAPHLAGONIA
GALATIA
BITHYNIA
A
Pergamum
ASIA
Dardanus
F
G
B
E
THRACE
MACEDON
EPIRUS
D
C
Movements of Mithridates and his forces
Movements of the Romans under Sulla

BACKGROUND

- Mithridates had already expanded his kingdom of Pontus north of the Black Sea.
- In 104 he occupied Galatia, Paphlagonia and Cappadocia. This brought him into conflict with rulers friendly to Rome.
- In 96 Sulla, as governor of Cilicia, reinstated the King of Cappadocia and prevented Mithridates linking up with Tigranes of Armenia.
- At the time of the Social War (91–90), Mithridates and Tigranes (his son-in-law) seized Bithynia and Cappadocia again.
- M. Aquilius was sent to eject Mithridates from Cappadocia and to restore Nicomedes to the throne of Bithynia. Mithridates withdrew without a battle, but then Aquilius encouraged Nicomedes to invade Pontus.

A This provoked Mithridates in 88 to sweep through Bithynia and into the Roman province of Asia, promising freedom to the Greek cities and the cancellation of debts. He took the whole of Asia except for a few towns in the south.

In the hope of getting rid of the Romans permanently, he organised the massacre of approximately 80 000 Italian residents in the province — men, women and children. The readiness with which the Asiatic cities carried out his orders indicated the extent to which they had been exploited by the Romans.

B Mithridates prepared an invasion of Europe when he was invited into Athens by the democratic party to free Greece. He sent his naval force under Archelaus across the Aegean, took Delos and killed the Italian businessmen there, and then occupied southern and central Greece.

C Sulla crossed to Epirus with 30 000 men in 87, took Athens by assault in 86 and forced Archelaus out of the Piraeus.

D Sulla outmanoeuvred a combined force of Mithridates at Chaeronea in central Greece, and soon after defeated another force at Orchomenus.

E Sulla moved slowly through Macedonia to the Dardanelles in 85, and sent his lieutenant, Lucullus, to Phoenicia for help.

F A second Roman force (under Flaccus and Fimbria) was sent out by Sulla's opponent, Cinna, instructed to deal with Mithridates and with secret orders to turn against Sulla. The men refused; Flaccus was killed by Fimbria, who continued to the province of Asia, where he defeated an army of Mithridates. Mithridates escaped from Pergamum, but in 85 was prepared to make peace. Sulla took over the army of Fimbria, who committed suicide.

G At Dardanus, Mithridates accepted Sulla's peace terms. These were lenient in comparison with the settlement imposed on the cities of the province of Asia which had supported Mithridates.

Terms imposed by Sulla	
On Mithridates: lenient	*On the province of Asia: harsh*
All territory conquered in Asia Minor was to be evacuated. The seventy ships of his Aegean fleet were surrendered. A moderate indemnity of 2000 talents was demanded. He retained his position as King of Pontus and was recognised as an ally of Rome. ↓ Mithridates was to continue to be a problem for Rome until the time of Pompey.	Cities which had supported Mithridates lost all their rights and independence. Some had their walls torn down. An enormous indemnity of 20 000 talents was imposed on the province. Sulla billeted his troops on the provincials, who had to pay for their upkeep. ↓ The people of the province of Asia fell into debt and despair as they were forced to borrow from heartless Roman businessmen in order to pay back the indemnity.
Sulla's hurried settlement of the east left great future problems for others to handle, but at the time he was anxious to return to Rome to deal with his opponents.	

Sulla's return and civil war, 83–82

Sulla's warning — Marians' raise troops

Before Sulla left the east he warned the senate, in an official letter, that he was returning to punish those who had committed crimes against him. The small group of populares (the Marians) who had been leading Rome during Sulla's absence began raising an army with the intention of meeting him in Greece rather than in Italy; Cinna and Carbo (consul of 84) gathered the army at Brundisium in preparation for the crossing to Greece. However, the troops refused to go and Cinna was murdered, leaving Carbo as sole consul for the remainder of the year and with the task of raising more troops to face Sulla.

Sulla's return to Italy

Sulla had no trouble gaining reinforcements when he landed in Italy and among them were a number of young men from consular families, two of whom (Gnaeus Pompeius, later Pompey the Great, and M. Licinius Crassus) were to play vital military and political roles in the near future. (The details of the civil war can be read in Appian's *The Civil Wars*, Book 1, 84–94 and Plutarch's *Sulla*, 27–9.)

Civil war

During the war many of the Marians fled to Sicily, Africa and Spain, where Marian governors such as Q. Sertorius still held office. It was imperative for Sulla to secure these provinces and rid them of the opposition, so he sent the young Pompey (24 years old) with special imperium to deal with organised resistance in Sicily and Africa. Pompey's success in putting Carbo to death in Sicily and in defeating Cinna's son-in-law in Africa led him to demand a triumph, which was reluctantly granted by Sulla. The only province in which the Marians held out was in Spain, under the capable leadership of Sertorius.

The emergence of Pompey

After the final battle of the civil war, fought outside Rome's Colline Gate, Sulla entered the city and immediately began to carry out the punishment he had threatened.

Sulla, master of Rome and Italy

The proscriptions of Sulla

'Sulla now devoted himself entirely to the work of butchery.'[51]

In the following extracts, Plutarch and Appian give graphic accounts of the proscriptions of Sulla.

Brutality of the proscriptions

> Then immediately, and without consulting any magistrate, Sulla published a list of eighty men to be condemned. Public opinion was horrified, but after a single day's interval, he published another list containing 220 more names, and next day a third list with the same number of names on it. And in a public speech which he made on the subject he said that he was publishing the names of all those whom he happened to remember: those who escaped his memory for the moment would have their names put up later. He also condemned

anyone who sheltered or attempted to save a person whose name was on the lists. Death was the penalty for such acts of humanity . . . the reward for murder was two talents and this sum was paid to anyone who killed a condemned man . . . Also (and this was considered the greatest injustice of all) he took away all civil rights from the sons and grandsons of those on the lists and confiscated the property of all of them. These lists were published not only in Rome but in every city of Italy.

Many people were killed because of purely personal ill feeling; they had no connection with Sulla in any way, but Sulla, in order to gratify members of his own party, permitted them to be done away with.[52]

. . . he forthwith proscribed about forty senators and 1600 knights (equites). He seems to have been the first to make a formal list of those whom he punished, to offer prizes to assassins and rewards to informers, and to threaten with punishment those who should conceal the proscribed . . . Some of these, taken unawares, were killed where they were caught, in their houses, in the streets, or in the temples . . . Banishment was inflicted upon some and confiscation upon others.

There was much massacre, banishment and confiscation also among those Italians who had obeyed Carbo or Marius . . . These accusations abounded mostly against the rich. When charges against individuals failed Sulla took vengeance on whole communities . . . Among most of them he placed colonies of his troops in order to hold Italy under garrisons, sequestrating their lands and houses and dividing them among his soldiers . . .'[53]

. . . during the period of the proscriptions and of the selling up of confiscated property he [Crassus] again got himself a bad name by demanding gifts and by buying up large estates for low prices. It is said that in Bruttium he actually added a man's name to the proscription lists purely in order to get hold of his property and with no authority from Sulla.[54]

Exercise

1 What is the meaning of 'proscription'?
2 Which particular groups suffered the most from Sulla's proscriptions?
3 What were the penalties laid down for those proscribed?
4 What evidence is there that Sulla was careless about drawing up the lists?
5 Apart from eliminating political opponents, how did he use the proscriptions to provide for his veterans?
6 How was Crassus, one of Sulla's young lieutenants, able to make his fortune during the proscriptions?

Sulla's dictatorship and reforms

Sulla had made himself the master of Rome and Italy with military force and violence, and now he believed that the only way to restore order was to revive the dictatorship. In a letter to the senate he suggested that, since the consuls were dead, it should appoint an interrex. This temporary ruler would introduce into the assembly a bill appointing Sulla as dictator for the purpose of restoring the republic (*reipublicae constituendae*). The dictatorship was to last as long as Sulla thought necessary, and his authority was to be superior to all others and free from any checks. 'Nevertheless by way of keeping up the form of the republic he allowed them to appoint consuls',[55] and when he began his task of regulating the constitution his reforms were passed in the comitia as was the usual practice.

Appointment of Sulla as dictator to restore the republic

Sulla's reform program

Sulla's objective was clear-cut: to re-establish stable and efficient government in Rome.

His aims

1 To strengthen the senate
2 To restrict the powers of the tribunes
3 To curb the independence of regular magistrates
4 To avoid the dangers from proconsuls in the provinces
5 To increase the number of magistrates available for administration and jurisdiction
6 To reorganise the courts and juries

The reforms

1 *The senate*

- The senate was enlarged immediately by 300 new members, predominantly from good equestrian families; it had been depleted by wars, massacres and proscriptions. Sulla anticipated a membership between 500 and 600 in the future.
- Sulla provided for future automatic recruitment from ex-quaestors.
- The senate's approval was necessary before legislation was presented to the people.
- The senate was to continue to decide provincial commands.

2 *The tribunes*

- Tribunes could not propose legislation to the people except those measures sanctioned by the senate.
- Their right of veto was limited.
- They were deprived of their judicial powers.
- Anyone holding the office of tribune was barred from further political office.

3 *Other magistrates*
- Sulla redrafted the lex Villia Annalis whereby the cursus honorum was to be strictly enforced. He set minimum age limits for each office: thirty for quaestors, thirty-nine for praetors and forty-two for consuls.
- A man could not hold the same office twice within a ten-year period.
- Sulla, suspicious of the censors, deprived them of their most important function—drawing up the list of those eligible to sit in the senate.
- The number of quaestors was increased to twenty and of praetors to eight.

4 *Proconsuls in the provinces*
- Sulla regulated the method of appointing provincial governors—the senate still decided on the allocation of the ten provinces.
- Commands in the provinces were to be annual, with extensions in crises.
- A lex de Maiestate (treason law) was passed which forbade governors to leave their provinces, march beyond the frontiers or make war without the permission of the senate and the people of Rome.
- Consular imperium remained superior to that of the provincial governors.

5 *Courts* (quaestiones)
- The number of standing courts was increased to seven, covering all major crimes from treason to forgery.
- The procedures for treating each type of crime were clearly laid down and the penalties for each were fixed—there was no appeal against the verdicts.
- The penalties for electoral bribery were increased.
- Juries were once again recruited from senators, not equites.

6 *Corn distributions*
- Sulla abolished the cheap grain distributions which had been introduced by Gaius Gracchus and continued by others.

The effects and significance of his reforms

1 *The senate*

The increase in the number of senators provided for an adequate supply of jurors for the law courts. The fact that many of the new recruits were from the equestrian class may have been an attempt to bring the two classes closer together and to avoid future opposition from the commercial class. Whatever his motives, the new senators owed their position to him and he could count on their support.

Sulla prevented interference from the censors when he introduced the method of automatic recruitment from ex-quaestors. Since quaestors were elected by the people, the senate was recruited by indirect popular election.

He failed, however, to realise the potential of the new citizens from the Italian communities who could have put fresh blood into the senate. The governing body needed to represent a larger section of Roman society.

Although he strengthened the senate, he did not see that the needs of the republic were changing.

2 *The tribunes*

Sulla virtually destroyed the tribunate, stripping it of those powers with which it had undermined the authority of the senate since the time of the Gracchi. 'Anyone of reputation or birth shunned the office thereafter.'[56] As Velleius Paterculus says, 'he left the tribunician power a shadow without substance'.[57] However, this situation did not last long. By the year 70 the tribunate's powers were fully restored by two of Sulla's own lieutenants (men backed by armies).

3 *Other magistrates*

Although Sulla hoped to prevent ambitious young men from getting to the top too quickly by redrafting the lex Villia Annalis, he failed to achieve this even in his own lifetime. Pompey was only twenty-four when he was given a kind of extraordinary propraetorian imperium in order to lead an army against the Marians in Africa and Sicily. When he returned successfully, he asked the senate for a triumph, but it was not the 'strengthened' senate which eventually granted it, but Sulla, although he had objected at first. In demanding a triumph Pompey was contravening Sulla's own revision of the lex Villia Annalis, for he had not yet held even the quaestorship, the lowest office on the cursus. He was seeking an honour which was usually granted to those outstanding generals who had reached the level of praetor or consul. By granting it, Sulla himself took the first steps in destroying his own work.

4 *Proconsuls in the provinces*

Sulla tried to minimise the dangers from ambitious proconsuls in the provinces by limiting their term of office to one year and by having enough ex-consuls and ex-praetors to become governors. However, it was not from provincial governors that a future threat to the state would come. The greatest failure of Sulla's reforms was in not taking precautions against the abuse of the imperium by those men who would be granted extraordinary commands to deal with the increasing threats to the empire. His own career was an example of a successful takeover of the state by military means. While ever there was no provision for the state to reward veterans with pensions at the time of their discharge, ambitious men with the backing of loyal armies would continue to be a problem, and no amount of strengthening of the senate would help the oligarchy to cope with this. Pompey's career revealed this problem. As a young man returning from his successful campaign against the Marians he did not automatically disband his army, but used the threat of force to gain what he wanted—a triumph. He and others were to use this method many times in the future.

5 *Courts* (quaestiones)

The most lasting reform was in the organisation of the quaestiones which continued to function unchanged well into the principate of Augustus, who supplemented them with two new forms of jurisdiction. However, the question of the composition of the juries continued to be a problem and changed several more times.

6 *Corn distributions*

This change was not long-lasting. Later popular leaders such as Clodius used the offer of free distribution to gain support from the urban mob.

Unexpected retirement

In 79 Sulla unexpectedly resigned from the dictatorship and retired to Campania, where he died the following year.

An evaluation of Sulla's career

Uncommitted at start of career

At the end of his career Sulla appeared to be the leader of the conservative optimates, although at the outset he had not been committed to any faction or program. 'Circumstances and the actions of others had charted his course.'[58] His political career started later than was usual for someone from a patrician background, owing to the poverty and obscurity of his family. As quaestor, legatus and military tribune he was attached to the popularis, Marius, but in 102 he became an associate of the optimate Catulus because he believed that the jealousy of Marius was hindering his career. His successful command as governor of Cilicia, his diplomatic contact with the Parthians and his competent handling of his area of command during the Social War gave him the support of the optimates in his bid for the consulship for 88; if he was still not committed to the optimates, his marriage to Metella strengthened his link with the nobility. When the populares attempted to transfer his Mithridatic command to Marius and he was declared an outlaw while in the east, he was driven into the arms of the conservatives. On his return from the east a number of young men from noble families, and other optimates, came to support him in the civil war. As dictator he was above all factions, but he realised that if political stability were to be achieved he had no choice but to strengthen the senate, although he was probably under no illusions about the selfishness of the oligarchy.

Gradual alignment with optimates

Sulla — an enigma?

Although Sulla is one of the outstanding figures in Roman history, to many of his contemporaries—as to many modern scholars—he was an enigma. He followed a career of self-advancement, reaching a point where his authority was so complete that he had imperium over all magistrates and promagistrates in his position as dictator. He even anticipated the later emperors by keeping a bodyguard and striking coins with his own image. Yet as soon as he had reorganised the government, 'he laid down his dictatorship and gave back to the people the right of electing consuls'.[59] He dismissed the twenty-four lictors and the bodyguard and walked around the Forum as a private citizen.

Motives behind retirement

Julius Caesar found this behaviour strange and naive, but it is unlikely that Sulla ever aimed at a permanent dictatorship and always intended to retire. Appian thought that he retired from public life 'because he was weary of war, weary of power, weary of Rome'.[60]

One modern historian, Carcopino, believes that he did intend to make himself a 'monarch' but lost the support of the nobility, and that when they opposed him he refused to take up arms again and so was forced into retirement. This view has generally been discounted by most scholars.

Another view suggests that he had no strong political convictions, but aimed simply at acquiring great wealth from provincial commands and profitable wars, having no desire to hold office longer than was absolutely necessary. The power he enjoyed gave him the opportunity to reorganise the government in such a way that he could retire to enjoy his wealth free from dangers and anxieties.

Eventual failure of most reforms

Whatever his aims, his reforms were a failure if they were intended to promote political stability. Even before Sulla's death the consul for 78, M. Aemilius Lepidus, proposed measures that would have undermined much of his work, and when the senate attempted to oppose Lepidus he led a rebellion against the government.

P. A. Brunt sums up Sulla's work in the following way:

> Sulla achieved little besides adding to the sum of human misery. His system aggrieved the equites, the urban populace, the dispossessed peasants and the new citizens and made no provision for veterans in the future. Social discontents continued, as the senate remained indifferent to the distress of the poor.[61]
>
> It was the memory of Sulla's example and methods that proved most enduring.[62]

Diagramatic representation of the career of Sulla

L. CORNELIUS SULLA FELIX
n. 138 B.C.

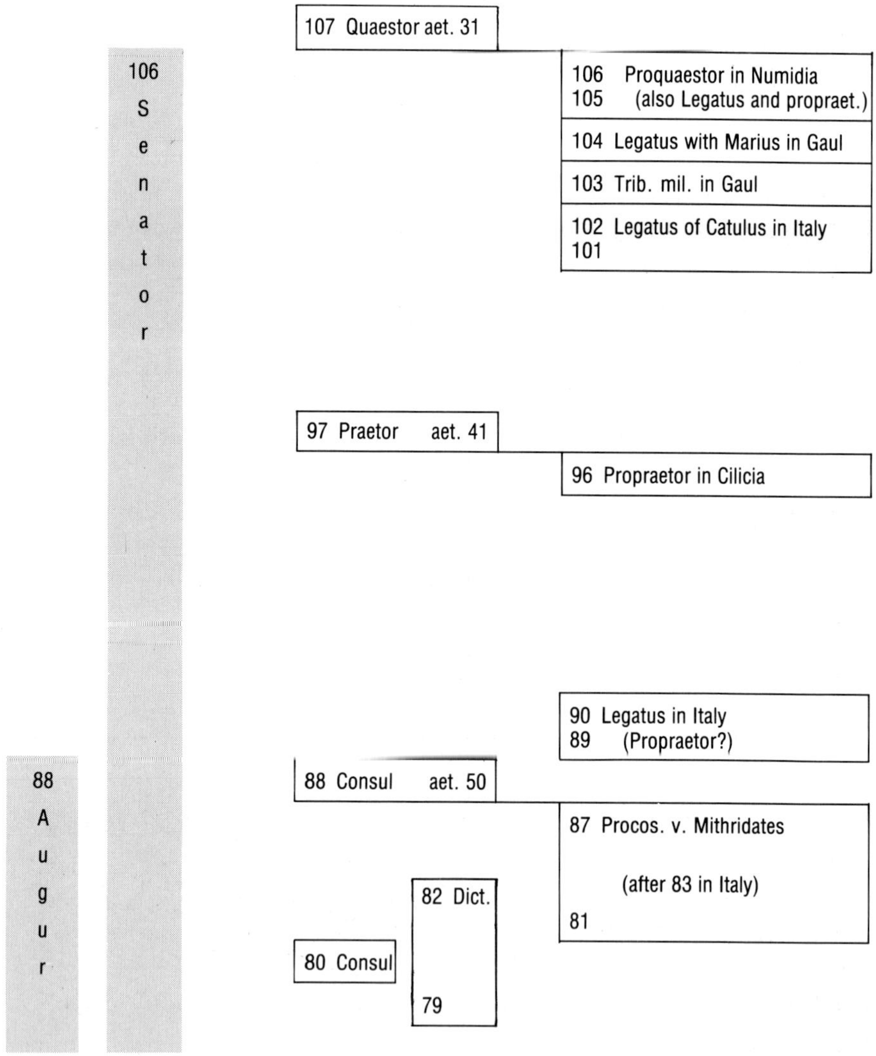

Exercise

1 What is noticeable about Sulla's career prior to 107? How does it differ from the usual career pattern?

2 What aspects of his career after 97 are unusual?

Timeline: The careers of Marius and Sulla

Marius		*Sulla*
Born into a good equestrian family from Arpinum	c.155	
	138	Born into a poor but patrician family
Serves with distinction under Scipio Aemilianus at Numantia	134 133	
Elected as quaestor	121	
Gains tribunate under the patronage of the Metelli	119	
Gains the praetorship	115	
Promagistrate in Spain	114	
Marries Julia (aunt of Julius Caesar)	111	
Serves as legate under Q. Caecilius Metellus in Numidia	109 108	
Elected consul — given command against Jugurtha in Numidia	107	Elected quaestor, with no previous military experience; accompanies Marius of Africa
Jugurtha betrayed and captured; Marius returns to Rome a popular hero; jealous of Sulla	106 105	Plays a major role in arranging the surrender of Jugurtha; beginning of rivalry with Marius
Elected to second consulship in absentia to fight Cimbri and Teutones in the north	104	Legate with Marius in Gaul
Elected to third consulship in absentia — first association with Saturninus	103	Military tribune in Gaul
Re-elected consul	102	Legate of Catulus in Italy

Marius		*Sulla*
Re-elected consul; defeats Cimbri at Vercellae	101	Defeats Tigurini
Sixth consulship given in honour of military leadership	100	
Alliance with demagogues Saturninus and Glaucia; SCU issued owing to violence; Marius' reputation suffers	99	
Goes to Cappadocia	98	
Elected augur while absent in Asia	97	Elected praetor
Sulla's activities in east increase his jealousy	96 95	Propraetor in Cilicia and Asia; settles affairs, receives Parthian embassy, negotiates treaty of friendship
Social War — legate in Italy	90	Social War — legate in Italy
Fights in the north		Fights in the south against Samnites; marries Caecilia Metella
Desires command against Mithridates; tribune Sulpicius Rufus transfers the command to him from Sulla, leading to violence; sentenced to death, flees to Africa	88	Elected consul, aged 50, with help of Metelli; given command against Mithridates; violence in Rome; flees south, returns with an army and captures Rome; Sulpicius and Marius outlawed
Sulla's opponents (populares) seize control in Italy; Marius returns from Africa — seventh consulship, with Cinna; Sulla declared an outlaw	87 87	Proconsular command against Mithridates; overcomes attempts by populares to remove him from command
Death		

Marius		*Sulla*
Populares (Marians) prepare for Sulla's return	84	Settles Greek and Asiatic affairs
	83	Returns from the east
Civil war against Sulla; Marians flee to Spain and Africa	82	Civil War against Marius — captures Rome, carries out proscriptions (death lists of Marians)
	81	As dictator to 'restore the
	80	constitution' — reforms
	79	Retires to country estate
	78	Death

Note: The shaded sections indicate the periods in which the two careers clashed.

Essay topics

1 How did the Roman senate acquire and maintain its position of supremacy within the state during the second century BC?

2 How did the Romans administer their provinces by the end of the second century? What advantages and disadvantages did the provincials experience under Roman administration?

3 What were the motives of Tiberius Gracchus in proposing the lex agraria of 133? How did his actions threaten the long-established authority of the senate?

4 'Tiberius Gracchus undid the evolution of centuries' (R. E. Smith).
Comment on this statement.

5 What problems was Gaius Gracchus attempting to solve during his tribunates of 123–122? How successful was he?

6 What were the long-term social and political results of the work of Gaius Gracchus?

7 The tragedy of the Gracchi 'lay in the methods they adopted rather than the ends they sought' (R. E. Smith).
How accurate is this assessment of the work of the Gracchi?

8 Discuss the significance of the army in the career of Gaius Marius.

9 'The pattern of Marius' career was one of the most extraordinary in Roman history.' Explain this comment.

10 Outline the changes that Marius introduced into the Roman army. What was their long-term significance?

11 Explain how the career of Marius weakened the hold of the senatorial aristocracy on Roman politics even more than did the careers of the Gracchi.

12 Why did the Italian allies declare war on Rome in the year 90? To what extent were their grievances solved by the Social War, 90–88?

13 Discuss Sulla's use of military means to extend his political influence.

14 What were the aims of the legislative measures introduced by Sulla during his dictatorship?

15 How was the tribunate of the plebs used by individuals for their own advancement during the period 133–78?

Further reading

Ancient sources

Appian. *The Civil Wars.*
Plutarch. *The Fall of the Roman Republic: Marius and Sulla.*
——— . *Makers of Rome: Tiberius Gracchus and Gaius Gracchus.*
Sallust. *The Jugurthine War.*

Modern sources

Adcock, F. E. *Roman Political Ideas and Practice.*
Astin, A. A. *Scipio Aemilianus.*
Badian, E. *Foreign Clientelae, 264–70 BC.*
——— . *Lucius Sulla—the Deadly Reformer.*
Brunt, P. A. *Social Conflicts in the Roman Republic.*
Earl, D. C. *The Moral and Political Tradition of Rome.*
Gruen, E. S. *Roman Politics and the Criminal Courts, 149–78.*
Kagen, D. *Problems in Ancient History*, vol. 2: *The Roman World.*
Last, H. *Cambridge Ancient History*, vol. 9: *Marius and Sulla.*
Scullard, H. H. *From the Gracchi to Nero.*
Smith, R. E. *The Failure of the Roman Republic.*
Syme, R. *The Roman Revolution.*
——— . *Tiberius Gracchus—a Study in Politics.*

PART

5

The late republic: Second phase, 78–28

SULLA'S ATTEMPT to restore the senate to the position of power it had prior to the Gracchan tribunates was a failure, and the next fifty years were marked by the attempts of powerful individuals and senatorial factions to gain predominance in the state. The civil wars fought during this period were not confined to Italy alone, but ranged across the full extent of the Roman empire as the generals mobilised their provincial clients as well as their supporters in Italy.

The end of the civil war between Pompey (leading the senatorial forces) and Caesar, which lasted from 49 to 46, was a significant stage in the transition from republic to empire. It was obvious to Julius Caesar, who emerged from the civil war as the unchallenged leader of Rome, that the days of senatorial government were over. However, that most Romans were not yet ready to accept one-man rule is evident by his assassination in 44 by a group of his peers, including former friends.

Caesar's assassination did not lead to the restoration of republican government as his murderers had hoped. Instead, the Roman world was once again drawn into a destructive war between Octavian, Caesar's heir, and Mark Antony. After more than a decade of fighting Octavian (later called Augustus) triumphed, and the gradual process of rule by the first citizen (*princeps*) began: the days of the republic were over and the period of the principate had begun.

The rise of Pompey and the period of his eastern commands, 78–61 16

GNAEUS POMPEIUS MAGNUS (Pompey the Great) dominated the Roman state for approximately three decades (83–48) and during this time his 'pursuit of glory, as they say, always took an unlikely or an unusual course'.[1] His rise to power was spectacular and rapid, and throughout his career he was granted the most extraordinary powers by the senate and the people in order to save the state from internal or external threats.

There are four clearly defined stages in Pompey's career, which was closely linked to the careers of Marcus Licinius Crassus, Gaius Julius Caesar and Marcus Tullius Cicero. A timeline on page 368 places in juxtaposition the political life of the four in the years 83–43.

Sources for the period

The sources given here apply both to this chapter and to the one following, 'From the First Triumvirate to the death of Caesar, 60–44'. There is more contemporary information about this period in Roman history than about any other.

Cicero

Cicero, whose life and political career spanned the last phase of the republic, was a prolific writer. He participated in and observed the intense political struggles between individuals and factions that eventually shattered the republic.

The use of Cicero's letters

Over 800 of his letters to friends, family and leading politicians survive, and since most were never intended for publication they appear to be an honest reflection of his feelings and opinions at the time of writing. His views sometimes appear to change from week to week and month to month, but this should not be regarded as dishonesty on Cicero's part. The rapidly changing political and social scene put certain pressures on him, and although at times he was in a dilemma, he continued to defend the republican institutions against authoritarian rule. Cicero's relationship with Pompey and Caesar is clearly revealed in his letters.

Cicero's speeches

On the other hand, his speeches—many of which required great courage to deliver—were intended for publication, and when studying them it is wise to take into account his audience and his purpose in making them.

Caesar's commentaries on the Gallic and civil wars

Caesar's style

The word *commentarius* implied something like a memoir or a report. During his campaigns in Gaul and throughout most of the civil war Caesar wrote reports of his actions in 'plain' but well-expressed Latin. His style and language were highly praised by Cicero. Unfortunately, both accounts were incomplete and were finished by others with less writing ability.

The purpose of Caesar's commentaries

His commentaries were meant not only to inform his reader but to justify his actions and to present himself and the course he took in the best possible light. Although the *Gallic War* may have been written to help him in his candidature for the consulship of 49 and the *Civil War* may have been intended to win over some of his opponents, there is not as much deliberate misrepresentation as some modern writers indicate. There are, however, sections of the works which are not entirely accurate, and some setbacks he suffered have been left out.

The accounts of his campaigns reveal his ability as a general and have been used as textbooks to demonstrate the art of warfare.

Sallust

Sallust took an active part in Roman politics until Caesar's death and then chose a new career — writing history.

His public career covered the turbulent years from 55 to 44, during which time he was a supporter of Caesar in the rivalry with Pompey; in 50, his association with Caesar and the populares made him an ideal target for the censors, who expelled him from the senate. Although the accusation of immorality and sacrilege sounds plausible enough, it was probably a political move. His later writing reveals a marked dislike for the oligarchy.

He held military commands under Caesar during the civil war and in 49, when Caesar became dictator for the first time, Sallust was reinstated in the senate. He then served as a governor of Africa in 46, and seems to have enriched himself at the provincials' expense. Sallust described his retirement from politics in the following way: 'After suffering manifold perils and hardships, peace of mind at last returned to me, and I decided that I must bid farewell to politics'.[2]

He devoted the next eleven years to writing history. His major work was a history of Rome in which he proposed to explain the whole process of national collapse; however, only fragments of this survive. Two short monographs, 'The Jugurthine War' and 'The Catilinarian Conspiracy', have survived intact and are valuable for two reasons: first, his anti-conservative viewpoint, although a reflection of the disappointments in his own career, provides historians and scholars with a different slant from that of the predominantly pro-conservative writers of the period; second, unlike Livy and Cicero he reveals an appreciation of the Roman and Italian poor and the discontent that prevailed in the first century BC.

Sallust's anti-conservative background

Sallust presents his characters vividly and treats the various incidents dramatically, but is not always historically accurate.

Plutarch

Weaknesses in Plutarch

Plutarch's biographies of Pompey, Crassus, Caesar and Cicero (as well as of Sertorius, Brutus and Antony) provide fascinating and valuable details of the latter part of the first century. His main failure is his inability to appreciate fully the complex nature of Roman politics and the changing balance of power in the 60s and 50s.

Although he gives an insight into Pompey's need for popular approval and his sensitivity to criticism, he fails to pay much attention to his relations with the optimates in the 50s. In the life of Caesar he assumes that Caesar planned to overthrow the republic from the beginning. He did not seem to understand either Caesar's reliance on others before 59 or the fact that had the optimates not been so short-sighted, his career after 59 might have taken a different direction.

Suetonius (Gaius Suetonius Tranquillus)

Suetonius, who lived during the first and second centuries AD, wrote *The Twelve Caesars*, which starts with the life of Julius Caesar.

The use of Suetonius

His account of the first sixteen years of Caesar's life is missing, but the work is full of fascinating (sometimes scandalous) and vivid anecdotes. Suetonius' writing is important, as he had access to public documents, letters, biographies and other archival material, but he was uncritical in his use of sources. He also did not hesitate to report backstairs gossip.

Other sources

Velleius Paterculus (c.19 BC–after AD 30), in his *Roman Histories*, includes some interesting biographical material; Lucan (Marcus Annaeus Lucanus, AD 39–65) wrote an epic poem about the civil war called *Pharsalia*; Appian (c.AD 160) was chiefly concerned with wars, and Dio Cassius (early third century AD) seems to have used Livy's account of the age of Caesar (which is lost) as his main source.

Archaeological material available

Inscriptions, buildings, works of art and coins—particularly those relating to Caesar's constitutional position—supplement the vast amount of written material extant for this period.

Pompey's spectacular rise to power and the breakdown of the Sullan constitution

Pompey and Sulla, 83–78

In 83 the 23-year-old Pompey raised a 'private' army—on his own initiative—to aid Sulla. This was a feat in itself, but then he was granted propraetorian imperium in order to command such a force under Sulla. Not only was he far below the requisite age, but he had never held any public office. Sulla was apparently so impressed with the young man that on one occasion he hailed him as 'imperator', even though Pompey was not entitled to be addressed in this fashion. Later Sulla thought enough of him to give him his stepdaughter, Aemilia, in marriage. This was an indication of the future direction of Pompey's career.

Pompey's early relations with Sulla

Pompey continued to hold the imperium of a propraetor for a further two years while he waged a successful campaign against the Marians in Sicily and Africa.

Pompey's demand for a triumph

On his return to Italy, Sulla is supposed to have addressed him as 'magnus' (great), a cognomen which Pompey continued to use from that time, but when Pompey demanded a triumph for his success over the

Marians Sulla refused, since such a request was against his own restatement of the lex Villia Annalis. Here was a young man with no previous political or military experience, at the head of his own army (which he had not yet disbanded), requesting an honour that was usually the high point of a long career. However, Sulla angrily and reluctantly gave in to the request when Pompey suggested 'that more people worship the rising than the setting sun, implying that while his power was on the increase that of Sulla was growing less and less'.[3]

Sulla's concern over Pompey's ambition

Sulla undermined his own reform of the constitution by permitting Pompey his triumph. He became even more concerned when he saw how quickly Pompey's reputation was growing. 'Acting in direct opposition to Sulla's wishes, Pompey had got M. Aemilius Lepidus elected to the consulship'[4] by using his own popularity to win votes for him. Sulla's fears about Lepidus were borne out when as consul in 78 Lepidus outlined a program that was directly opposed to Sulla's work: he proposed to renew the sale of cheap corn, to restore the former powers of the tribunes, to restore the land to those farmers dispossessed by Sulla and to recall the Marian exiles. He failed, however, to achieve these measures.

Lepidus' program

In the same year, Sulla died.

The revolt of Lepidus, 77

In 77, when he was proconsul of Gaul, Lepidus raised an army and prepared to march on Rome with his legate, Brutus. The senate passed the senatus consultum ultimum, declaring him a public enemy. Plutarch states that events 'seemed to call for Pompey', who quickly decided which side to support. 'He attached himself to the cause of the nobility',[5] and the senate reluctantly granted him propraetorian imperium once again, to help Lutatius Catulus.

Pompey's support of optimates

Catulus defeated Lepidus, who fled to Sardinia where he died soon after. Brutus, besieged at Mutina by Pompey, surrendered to him but was killed. Led by M. Perpena, many of Lepidus' supporters escaped to Spain, where they joined the outstanding Roman rebel leader, Sertorius.

Defeat of Lepidus

Pompey now saw an opportunity to enhance his gloria. He delayed disbanding his army — despite Catulus' order to do so — in the hope of persuading the senate to send him to Spain to help Q. Metellus against Sertorius, and when the two consuls for that year (77) showed a reluctance to face Sertorius they played into Pompey's hands. The senate had no choice but to grant yet another 'illegal' (in terms of the constitution) command to Pompey, this time with proconsular imperium.

Pompey's illegal command in Spain

The campaign against Sertorius in Spain, 77–72

Sertorius' popularity in Spain

Sertorius was a popularis who had fought with the Marians against Sulla. He was chosen as governor of Hither Spain during the civil war, and when he arrived in his province he found the Spanish tribesmen bitterly resentful of Roman administration there. Sertorius 'set himself to win them over by entering into personal dealings with the chiefs and by reducing the taxes imposed on the people'.[6] However, the action that earned him the most gratitude from the Spanish tribesmen was 'his decision to cease billeting his soldiers upon them. . .'[7]

Leader of Spanish tribes

When Sulla captured Rome after defeating the Marians in Italy, he sent an army to Spain to deal with Sertorius. Sertorius fled to Africa to join other Marian commanders, but in 80 returned to Spain at the request of the Lusitanians (a Spanish tribe), who wanted him to become their leader. Plutarch says that 'he took control of their affairs as general with absolute powers' and 'brought the neighbouring parts of Spain under their control'.[8] The various tribes accepted his authority because he was moderate and efficient.

Sertorius against Sulla's government

He triumphed time and again over the senatorial generals (such as Metellus) who were sent against him because he made extensive preparations, transformed the undisciplined Spanish tribesmen into a formidable army, and employed guerilla tactics. He maintained that he was not fighting against the Romans but against Sulla's illegal government; although he made contact with the pirates around the Mediterranean coastline and through them negotiated with Mithridates, he would not support Mithridates' seizure of the Roman province of Asia.

Established alternative government in Spain

As more Roman troops joined his cause, he organised an alternative Roman government with a 'senate', praetors and quaestors, but 'he longed to return home from exile'.[9]

Pompey's arrival in Spain

Pompey, with proconsular imperium (for which he was ineligible), arrived in Spain in 76 to help Metellus, but lost two major battles against Sertorius—near Lauro in 76 and near the Sucro River in 75; the combined forces of Pompey and Metellus fought an indecisive battle with Sertorius near Saguntum. Pompey was running short of supplies and warned the senate that the war could spread to Italy if it did not send him reinforcements. He subsequently received two more legions, which allowed him to maintain the pressure on Sertorius, who was having difficulty in maintaining the number and the loyalty of his Spanish allies; it is believed that he became much harsher in his treatment of them.

Many of the Romans who had joined Sertorius after Lepidus' revolt became envious of him and 'foolishly resentful of his authority'.[10] Perpena encouraged these attitudes, since he was ambitious for the supreme command himself, and formed a conspiracy to murder Sertorius which was carried out in 72 at a banquet organised by Perpena.

Sertorius' death

Perpena himself did not last long; he was defeated and executed by Pompey in 71, and this brought the war to an end. Pompey's treatment of Sertorius' Spanish allies was fair and humane, while he granted Roman citizenship to those who had supported him.

Pompey's humane settlement

Pompey was given the credit for the victory, although it is doubtful whether without Sertorius' murder he would have been successful. His favourable reputation in Spain was due more to his diplomatic and organisational skill, as well as his liberal attitude to the Spaniards.

The slave uprising in Italy led by Spartacus, 73–71

In 73, while Pompey was in Spain, a serious uprising of gladiators and slaves occurred in Italy. It was led by the Thracian gladiator Spartacus, and gained momentum after a number of early successes in which the rebels managed to get hold of weapons.

Early successes of Spartacus

> The situation had become dangerous enough to inspire real fear, and as a result both consuls were sent out to deal with what was considered a major war and a most difficult one to fight.[11]

When both consuls were defeated by the rebels, an efficient commander was sought to take charge of the government's forces; M. Licinius Crassus, the praetor of 73, was given either propraetorian or proconsular imperium in 72 to take supreme command of the war. Crassus as a young man had, like Pompey, came forward to help Sulla and in fact had been responsible for Sulla's victory at the Colline Gate of Rome in 82.

Appointment of Crassus

Plutarch (*Crassus*, 10–11) gives a full account of the rebellion and Crassus' successes in the south. From this it appears that Crassus at one point thought the danger was so serious that he wrote to the senate asking them to recall Pompey from Spain and Lucullus from Thrace. He regretted this, however, and 'made all the haste he could to finish the war before these generals arrived'[12] since it was likely that they would gain the credit for ending the war. In three engagements in which he risked his life Crassus defeated Spartacus' divided forces. Spartacus, surrounded by enemies, fought until the very end; later, approximately 6000 of his supporters were crucified along the Appian Way.

Crassus' successes

Pompey had arrived from Spain in 71 and was officially associated with Crassus in the command. Although Crassus had done all the work, 'fortune somehow or other managed to give Pompey a share' when he prevented 5000 fugitives from escaping to the north.[13] In a despatch to the senate he wrote 'that while Crassus had certainly defeated the

Pompey as Crassus' colleague

gladiators in a pitched battle, he himself had finished the war off utterly and entirely'.[14] Not only would Crassus have been upset by this boastful claim, his jealousy of Pompey would have increased also when he had to settle for the lesser honour of an ovation while Pompey was awarded his second triumph.

Decision to stand for consulship in 70

Although the two were not friends, they both wanted the consulship for 70 and so sometime in 71 they agreed to campaign together. For Crassus this was obviously the next step in his career, as he had held the praetorship (73) and propraetorship (72–1). Pompey, on the other hand, was seven years too young, had never held any magistracy and was not even a senator.

Threat of force by Pompey

Both men waited with their armies outside Rome. Pompey claimed that he was waiting to be awarded a triumph, but it appeared that he was also coercing the senate into granting him a dispensation from the provisions of the revised lex Annalis of Sulla; a decree was passed by the senate exempting him from the usual age provision (42 years old for a consul) and experience of subconsular offices. Pompey was granted his triumph and Crassus his ovation.

The joint consulship of Pompey and Crassus, 70

Although both Pompey and Crassus had been Sulla's lieutenants, once they were elected to the consulship they proceeded to destroy what was left of his constitution.

Plans to restore tribune's powers

Pompey's career up to this point had contravened Sulla's redrafted lex Annalis, by which the cursus honorum was to be rigidly enforced, and prior to his election he had obviously indicated his intention to restore the legislative powers of the tribunes.

Sulla had previously deprived the tribunes of their legislative powers and had also debarred them from further office. The latter restriction had been removed in 75 by a law of the consul C. Aurelius Cotta, but the Roman people wanted to see all powers returned to the tribunes. Pompey

Benefits for Pompey

> thought himself extremely lucky to have the opportunity of passing this particular measure, since if some other statesman had anticipated him in this, he could never have found an equally good way of expressing his thanks to the people for the goodwill which they had shown him.[15]

In addition, he would have been aware of the future possibilities of using a tribune to promote his career. Pompey and Crassus had also won power by promising drastic reform of the senatorial juries, which had proved to be extremely corrupt.

Licinio/Pompeian reforms, 70 BC

There were three important pieces of legislation passed during this joint consulship. Two were undertaken in their own names and were referred to as the Licinio/Pompeian laws. They were

- the restoration to the tribunate of the legislative powers and the right of veto, thus completing what the lex Aurelia of 75 had begun;
- the revival of the censorship, which had been suspended under Sulla. The censors immediately revised the senatorial list and removed sixty-four senators, enrolling instead new senators — who would undoubtedly show their appreciation to Pompey in the future.

The third important piece of legislation concerned the composition of the law courts, which at this time were made up exclusively of senators. L. Aurelius Cotta, brother of the consul of 75, proposed that in future the courts should be composed of equal numbers of senators, equites and the *tribuni aerarii*, a group just below the equites in wealth. Since this third group had similar interests to the equites, together they would be able to keep the senatorial jurors in check.

The prosecution of Verres by Cicero

Prior to the reform of the law courts, however, a scandal occurred which involved the prosecution of the governor of Sicily, Gaius Verres, for the most blatant misgovernment and extortion.

Importance of Verres' trial

The trial of Verres was significant.

- He had powerful optimate friends — such as Q. Hortensius, the most distinguished orator of his day — and therefore expected to be acquitted, as many before him had been. But since the senatorial juries had proved to be so corrupt, it was not just Verres who was on trial, but the whole Roman senate.
- The trial was a turning point in the career of M. Tullius Cicero, who was the man selected by the Sicilians to prosecute Verres. Cicero was already a successful lawyer and had Sicilian clients of his own as a result of his fairness during his quaestorship in 75 in Sicily. He was sympathetic to the equites, as he came from the same background and believed they had some right to be on the extortion juries. However, as he pointed out to the senatorial jury, 'I am eager to remove your bad reputation — which is as much mine as yours'.[16] He genuinely believed that the stability of the state was bound up with its judicial decisions.

Verres' prosecution

During the year Verres' friends made every effort to frustrate Cicero and to delay the trial until the following year, when one of their associates would be the presiding judge (praetor). Cicero outwitted them and produced so much damning evidence, which he had personally collected from Sicily, that Verres went into voluntary exile before the verdict was given. He was condemned in his absence and a fine two and a half times the amount he extorted was imposed. The fact that the senatorial jury condemned Verres may have been partly due to their fear of being replaced in the courts, as the question of reform had already been discussed. Cicero's speeches against Verres (particularly his second speech) are important reading for this topic and can be found in the Penguin edition of Cicero, *Selected Works*.

The reforms that Sulla had implemented to bring stability to the state had been unrealistic, and by 70 (within ten years of his seizure of power) almost all his measures had been altered, replaced or undermined—the chief agent in this being Pompey. One that was not altered, however, was the increase in the number of quaestors to twenty, and with twenty quastors but only two consuls holding office the competition for consulship was intensified. This effect, unforeseen by Sulla, was to prove disastrous to the republic.

Gnaeus Pompeius Magnus
(Pompey the Great)

The period of Pompey's extraordinary commands in the east and the activities of Crassus, Caesar and Cicero, 69–61

Pompey's temporary retirement from public life

At the end of their consulship neither Pompey nor Crassus took up the usual provincia, possibly because the proconsular commands available did not offer sufficient opportunity to enhance their reputations. This was more likely to have been true of Pompey, who had already had a spectacular career.

Pompey's spectacular retirement

Plutarch says that 'Crassus now went back to the way of life which he had adopted from the beginning of his career',[17] while Pompey in retirement stressed his availability for one of the commands against the two most serious threats to Rome at this time—the pirate menace in the Mediterranean and Mithridates of Pontus. These serious problems were being handled with varying degrees of success by Q. Caecilius Metellus (piracy in Crete) and L. Lucullus (command against Mithridates).

The early career of Caesar

Julius Caesar emerged in the years 69–61 as a political force to be considered, although on account of his relationship to Marius (who was married to Caesar's aunt) he had not gone unnoticed in the previous decade. At the age of nineteen Caesar had defied Sulla's demand that he should divorce his wife Cornelia, the daughter of the popularis Cinna. Caesar left Rome for the east and for a few years served on the staff of the governors of Asia and Cilicia. He became friendly with the king of Bithynia and won a Civic Crown for gallantry. On Sulla's death he returned to Rome for a short time during which he prosecuted a number of notable people in the courts, and then returned to the east to study oratory at Rhodes. While in the east he was captured by pirates and later intervened in the war against Mithridates. When he returned to Rome in 73 he took the seat of his mother's cousin (Cotta) on the board of priests, and supported Pompey's move to restore the tribunes' powers.

Caesar's quaestorship

By 69 he was eligible to stand for the quaestorship, and for the next ten years his career followed the standard pattern of the cursus honorum. Despite this, the optimates were nervous about him because he had refused to break with the tradition of Marius. Suetonius records a statement made earlier by Sulla, that 'There are many Mariuses in this fellow Caesar'.[18]

Links with Marius

During his quaestorship his aunt (Julia) died, and he used the occasion of the public funeral to express his anti-conservative attitude. He carried effigies of Marius and his son in the funeral procession even though this had been expressly forbidden by an earlier order of Sulla, and he traced his pedigree back to the legendary kings of Rome. When Cornelia died not long after, Caesar exploited the occasion to refer to her father, Cinna, and his association with Marius.

As quaestor Caesar went to Spain, and on his way home through Cisalpine Gaul he exploited the unrest felt by the people on the far side of the Po River because of their lack of full Roman citizenship.

The optimates were already suspicious of him.

Piracy and the lex Gabinia

Piracy had been a problem in the eastern Mediterranean for a long time. Strong naval powers like Rhodes, which had kept piracy in check, had been weakened or destroyed by Rome during the Second Macedonian War and since Rome no longer had any serious rival in the region, the government made no real effort to patrol the seas and coastlines.

Strength of Mediterranean pirates

The pirates became bolder, operating out of strongholds in Cilicia and Crete. With well-organised fleets they raided and plundered the length and breadth of the Mediterranean, including the coastline of Italy. Plutarch maintains that they had 1000 ships in service, equipped with expert crews and pilots. They not only captured cities, demanding ransoms, and sacked and plundered religious sanctuaries, but they would 'even march inland up the Roman roads from the sea, plundering the country and sacking the country houses on their way'.[19] As well as disrupting regular commerce they operated a lucrative slave trade, kidnapping and then selling the captives at the slave market on Delos. The Roman government at first turned a blind eye to their activities, since wealthy Roman landowners employing slave labour on their large estates made a profit out of the pirates' trade.

Failure of early attempts against pirates

Eventually the problem became so serious that the government was forced to do something about it. In 78, Servilius Vatia successfully dislodged them from their strongholds in Cilicia, but they simply relocated in Crete. In 74 M. Antonius was given special imperium and invaded Crete, achieving very little before he was killed. Q. Caecilius Metellus in 69 reduced Crete and annexed it as a Roman province, but the dislodged pirates simply moved elsewhere.

By 67 the Roman corn trade was so seriously threatened that the people were faced with famine. It was this situation which prompted one of the tribunes for that year, Aulus Gabinius, to propose that an extraordinary command be created to 'drive the pirates off the seas'.[20] Since Gabinius was a friend of Pompey it was obviously intended for him, and this would give Pompey the opportunity he had been waiting for to increase his prestige further.

Tribunate of Gabinius

Gabinius proposed that a man of consular rank be given a three-year imperium to operate anywhere in the Mediterranean and in all Roman provinces up to fifty miles inland. He was to have the authority to nominate his legates, to take as much money as he needed from the treasury and from the tax officials, and to recruit troops and sailors for the large fleet that would be necessary (probably 200 ships).

Gabinius' proposals

When the provisions of the bill were read out to the people in the assembly they were received with great enthusiasm, but in the senate only Julius Caesar spoke in favour of the bill. The highly respected and distinguished Q. Lutatius Catulus opposed it, and addressed the people in the assembly about the dangers of granting such extraordinary powers to one man. Although they listened with great respect, the people voted for the lex Gabinia, granting Pompey even greater powers: 500 ships, 120 000 troops and 5000 cavalry, and 'twenty-four men who had been in command of armies or held the office of praetor were chosen by him out of the senate to act as his lieutenants and in addition he had two quaestors'.[21]

Senatorial opposition

Lex Gabinia passed by the people

Pompey lived up to the people's expectations. He divided the Mediterranean and adjacent coasts into thirteen areas, each patrolled by a commander with a fleet. His plan was to first clear the western Mediterranean, from the Pillars of Hercules to Sicily. Commanding a small number of ships (about sixty) himself, Pompey drove the pirates out of each area into the arms of his legates. 'The dispersal of his forces throughout the sea enabled him to surround entire fleets of pirate ships which he hunted down and brought into harbour';[22] within forty days he had cleared the pirates from the entire western half of the Mediterranean Sea. When he moved into the eastern half, some who were operating at a great distance from their bases gave themselves up and were treated humanely by him, but the majority fled to their fortresses near the Taurus mountains (Cilicia), where they left their families and property while preparing to face Pompey. At Coracesium in Cilicia they were defeated at sea and their stronghold was besieged. Their surrender marked the end of the war, which had been completed in less than three months. This was an incredible feat.

Pompey's brilliant organisation

Removal of pirates in three months

Pompey did not put his captives to death, but devised a plan of resettlement based on the belief that if they were transferred to another

Resettlement scheme

place to live and given the opportunity to live in cities and cultivate the land, they 'might lose their savage and intractable qualities'.[23] Some settled in the half-populated cities of Cilicia and were given citizenship, while a large number were given land in Achaea in Greece, which was very underpopulated.

Mithridates and the lex Manilia

Mithridates' attack on Roman territory

Mithridates used Rome's preoccupation with Sertorius, Spartacus and the pirates to begin building up his power and resources once again see p. 284 for Sulla's campaign against him). He formed an alliance with his son-in-law, Tigranes of Armenia, who had become the most powerful ruler in the east with the capture of Cappadocia, Syria and part of Cilicia. With Tigranes' support, Mithridates felt confident enough to attack Rome's province of Bithynia.

Successes of Lucullus

L. Lucullus had been granted the provinces of Cilicia and Asia as well as the overall command in 74 of the war against Mithridates. Lucullus was a master tactician, and by the end of 70 he had deprived Mithridates of all his conquests and a large part of his army, and had taken control of his kingdom of Pontus. Mithridates had taken refuge with Tigranes, who refused to give him up, so Lucullus invaded Armenia although the senate had not given him permission to do so. He defeated Tigranes (who escaped), took his capital of Tigranocerta, and in 68 defeated the combined forces of Mithridates and Tigranes in central Armenia. At this point his troops, alienated by his harsh discipline and refusal to allow them to plunder, mutinied and refused to go any further. Lucullus was forced to remain inactive while Mithridates recovered much of his kingdom.

Opposition to Lucullus

Lucullus knew that Asia would never be safe while Mithridates remained free, yet he was being criticised not only by his men but by powerful interests in Rome for prolonging the war for his own benefit. He had incurred the hatred of the equites by reorganising the finances of the cities of Asia and alleviating the burden of debt caused by the excessive payments the provincials were forced to make to Roman bankers and tax-collectors. His treatment of the provincials was fair, but the business class in Rome called for his replacement. They were supported by the people and by those populares who denounced Lucullus for not bringing the war to a quick end. Even the optimates were not happy with the way he had invaded Armenia without the senate's permission.

Pompey's desire for Mithridatic command

Pompey, with over two and a half years of his imperium left, was lingering in the east, having completed the resettlement of the pirates. If Lucullus was to be replaced Pompey was the obvious choice, and it appears that Pompey had been hoping to have the Mithridatic command for some time.

Pompey's success against the pirates had benefited traders, businessmen and the people; there was not likely to be as much opposition from the senate to an extension of his command in 66 as there had been the previous year. In fact, when the tribune Gaius Manilius proposed the legislation to give Pompey the command against Mithridates as well as control of Cilicia, Bithynia and Pontus, only Catulus and Hortensius spoke publicly against it. Catulus probably put forward the same arguments as he had the year before.

Proposals of tribune Manilius

Julius Caesar and Cicero spoke in favour of the bill. Although Cicero did not generally approve of tribunician legislation, he needed to be associated with Pompey's interests if he were to campaign successfully for the consulship in a few years' time. He was a novus homo, and would need the votes of Pompey's supporters.

Support from Caesar and Cicero for Pompey

When the bill was passed, Pompey was in Cilicia and is reported to have said, 'How sad it makes me, this constant succession of labours! Really I would rather be one of those people whom no one has heard about . . .'.[24] Even his close friends found this play-acting unacceptable, since they knew of his hatred for Lucullus and 'his natural passion for distinction and love of power . . .'.[25] According to Plutarch,

> Lucullus was being robbed of the glory which he had earned by his achievements and was being replaced by someone who would merely reap the honour of triumph rather than undertake the difficulties of war.[26]

Contemporary opinions: Catulus and Cicero

The following extracts from Dio Cassius and Cicero give two reactions to the proposals of the tribunes Gabinius and Manilius in 67 and 66 regarding the extraordinary commands against the pirates and Mithridates.

1 A speech before the Roman people given by the *princeps senatus* Quintus Catulus in 67 expresses the views of the optimates on extraordinary commands.

> . . . I, for my part, assert first and foremost that it is not proper to entrust to any one man so many positions of command one after another. This has not only been forbidden by the laws, but has been found by experience to be most perilous. What made Marius what he became was practically nothing else than being entrusted with so many wars in the shortest space of time and being made consul six times in the briefest period; and similarly Sulla became what he was because he held command of the armies so many years in succession and later was appointed dictator . . . For it does not lie in human nature for a person — I speak not alone of the young but of the mature as well — after holding positions of authority for a long period to be willing to abide by ancestral customs. Now I do not say this in any disparagement of Pompey, but because it does not appear ever to have been of advantage to you in any way, and in particular because it is not permitted by the laws . . .

Second, there is the consideration that so long as consuls and praetors and those serving in their places are receiving their offices and commands conformably to the law it is in no wise fitting, nor yet advantageous, for you to overlook them and introduce some new office. To what end, indeed, do you elect the annual officials, if you are going to make no use of them for such occasions? . . . How can you fail to arouse the enmity of these and all the rest who have a purpose to enter public life at all, if you overthrow the ancient offices, and entrust nothing to those elected by law, but assign some strange and hitherto unheard-of command to a private individual?[27]

2 An extract follows from a speech by Cicero in 66 on the proposal of the tribune Manilius to transfer the command against Mithridates to Pompey.

The war under discussion, then, is so necessary that it cannot be avoided and so important that it requires the utmost care. But you are in the happy position of being able to entrust its conduct to a commander whose remarkable military knowledge is only equalled by his extraordinary personal gifts, outstanding prestige and pre-eminent good fortune. It is inconceivable then, gentlemen, that you should hestitate to utilise, for the preservation and greater glory of our country, this exceptional blessing . . . [and it is a] remarkably fortunate coincidence that he is actually on the spot with an army of his own: which moreover he can supplement by taking over the forces of other commanders.

Cicero then discusses the objections raised by the opponents to the bill.

Innovations, it is objected, must not be made contrary to the precedents and principles of our ancestors. I will refrain from pointing out, in reply, that whereas our ancestors respected tradition when Rome was at peace, they were invariably guided by expediency in time of war, constantly meeting new emergencies by fresh devices.

He continues by first pointing out the unusual nature of the commands of Scipio and Marius and then reminding his listeners of Pompey's exceptional career to date.

And finally, let us pass on to Gnaeus Pompeius himself. Here is the man for whom Quintus Catulus objects that no new precedent ought to be established. But just consider how many new precedents have already been created in his favour—with Catulus' full approval. That someone of extreme youthfulness, who held no public office, should raise an army in a time of national crisis was a complete innovation. Yet that is what Pompeius did. For the same young man to be made its commander was equally novel. However, that is what he became. That he should succeed so triumphantly in the enterprise was equally unparalleled. Nevertheless, such was his achievement. It was wholly contrary to custom that a youth of very tender years, who was far below the minimum age even for admission to the senate, should be given a command and an army, allocated a sphere of action comprising Sicily and Africa . . .

> ... For a Roman knight to be awarded a Triumph was unheard of.
>
> ... it was totally unprecedented when two eminent and gallant consuls were available, for a Roman knight to be sent out with consular powers to wage a grave and terrible war. All the same, he was sent.
>
> It was equally without parallel, again, that he should be exempted from the laws by a resolution of the senate, and elected to a consulship actually before he had the legal right to hold any office at all. And that he, not yet a senator but only a knight, should celebrate a triumph, not once but twice, might seem incredible. If you count up every single departure from precedent since the very beginning of Roman history, they add up to a smaller total than those which have been lavished on the career of this single man. And all these remarkable and revolutionary innovations ... were brought about as a result of enactments by distinguished national leaders — of whom Quintus Catulus was one.[28]

Cicero stresses that it is important that the optimates, who granted these exceptional powers to Pompey in the recent past, should not show their disapproval of the present position of Pompey simply because it is the Roman people who are making the decision. After all, he is the only man capable of the task.

Exercise

1. What are the two arguments put forward by Catulus to illustrate his objections to extraordinary commands?
2. Suggest another reason for the opposition of Catulus and the optimates to Pompey's being given any more exceptional commands.
3. What arguments does Cicero use to refute Catulus' and Hortensius' objections to the lex Manilia?
4. What does Cicero say about Roman government policy?
5. List the exceptional steps in Pompey's career mentioned by Cicero.
6. What do you consider to be Cicero's underlying motive in this speech supporting the lex Manilia?

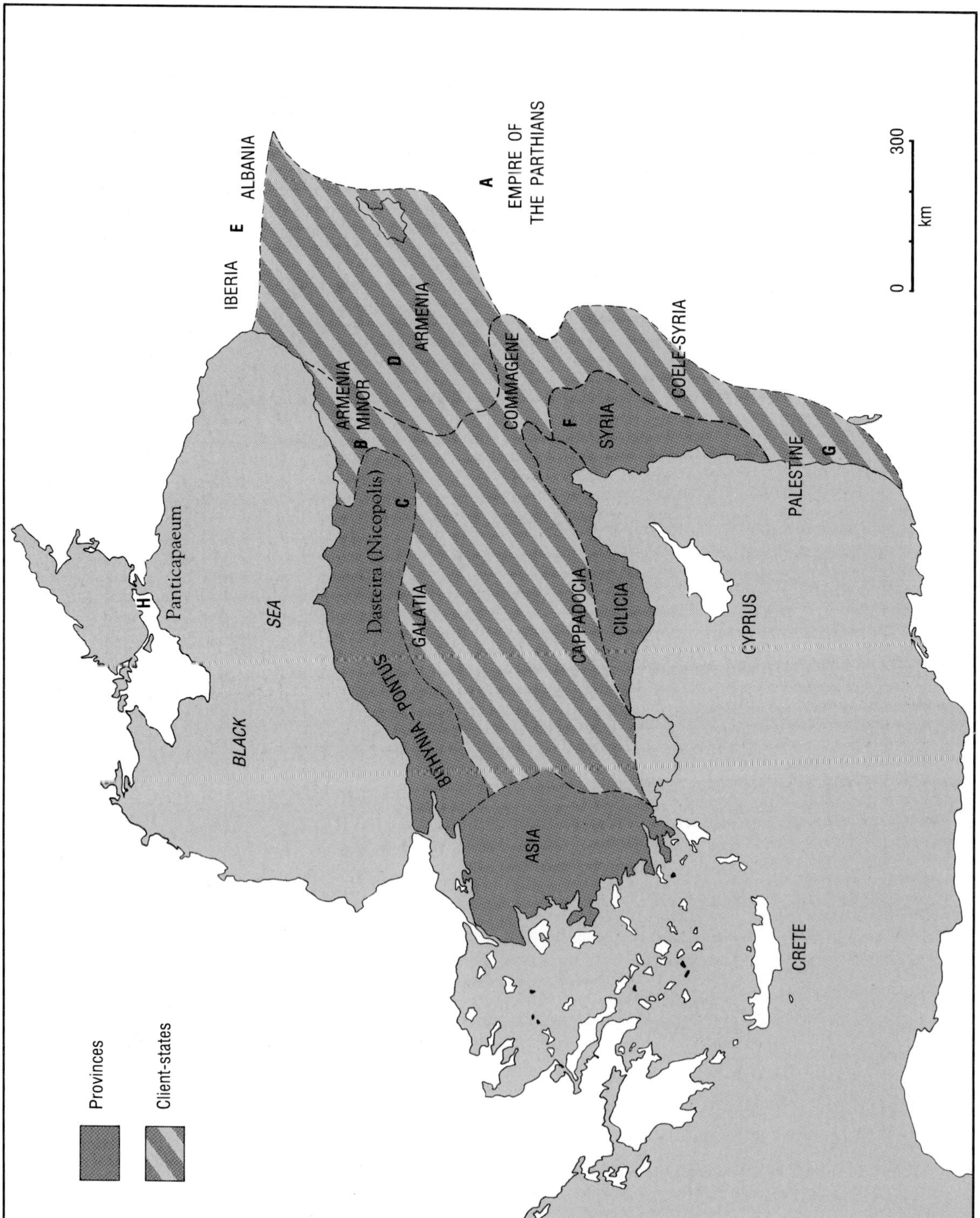
Provinces
Client-states
BLACK
SEA
Panticapaeum
H
IBERIA
E
ALBANIA
A
EMPIRE OF
THE PARTHIANS
ARMENIA
D
ARMENIA
MINOR
B
Dasteira (Nicopolis)
C
BITHYNIA–PONTUS
GALATIA
CAPPADOCIA
CILICIA
COMMAGENE
F
SYRIA
COELE-SYRIA
PALESTINE
G
ASIA
CYPRUS
CRETE
0
300
km

A Pompey persuaded Phraates, King of Parthia, to distract Tigranes of Armenia so that he could attack Mithridates.
B In 66, Pompey and 50 000 men surrounded Mithridates at Dasteira, totally destroying his army. Mithridates escaped to the Crimea where he proceeded to raise another army intending to march via the Danube and attack Italy from the North.
C Pompey renamed Dasteira, Nicopolis, to celebrate his victory over Mithridates.
D Pompey turned towards Armenia —Tigranes submitted to him.
E In 65 Pompey turned north to the Caucasus Mountains where he campaigned against the Albanians and marched through the territory of the Iberians to the Black Sea to catch up with Mithridates. As his way was blocked by physical barriers, he retraced his steps to Pontus. He hoped that Mithridates could be kept in check by Roman naval power for the time being.
F In 64 he moved into Syria, which was in a state of anarchy due to the feuds of the Seleucid princes. Pompey restored order.
G In 63 he entered Palestine which was in a state of civil war—two Jewish brothers were quarrelling over the succession and both claimants referred the problem to Pompey. He decided in favour of the elder brother, Hyrcanus, but was forced to lay siege to Jerusalem for three months.
H While in Jerusalem in 63, Pompey received word that Mithridates, who was at Panticapaeum, was dead: faced with a rebellion led by his son, Pharnaces, he had requested one of his slaves to put an end to his life.

Opposite: Pompey's eastern settlement, 63 BC

Pompey's eastern settlement

Lucullus' successes benefited Pompey

Although Pompey was a competent soldier, his military achievements in the east were based on the hard campaigning carried out by Lucullus in the previous six years. Lucullus had reduced the resources of both Mithridates and Tigranes, so that they presented no real opposition to Pompey's troops. It was also fortunate for Pompey that in 63 Mithridates died.

What Pompey's settlement of the east once again revealed was his outstanding ability as an organiser, administrator and diplomat.

New provinces in the East

1 He created an almost continuous ring of provinces around the coastline from the southern shore of the Black Sea to the Levant (Syria and Palestine). He added western Pontus to Bithynia to create the province of Bithynia/Pontus; he annexed the territory of the Seleucids and added to it parts of Judaea to form the province of Syria, and he enlarged the already existing province of Cilicia.

City-building

2 He united the area under Roman control by fostering the growth of cities of the Hellenistic type. These were to make administration and taxation easier; they were administrated by local authorities and had considerable autonomy.

Client-states

3 In order to protect the Roman provinces from future threats from the powerful kingdom of Parthia, east of the Euphrates River, Pompey organised and promoted a large number of client-states (of which the chief ones are mentioned below). These states were independent, but

maintained friendly relations with Rome since many of their rulers owed their position and some of their territory to Pompey.

- Tigranes was left in possession of Armenia and also received part of western Mesopotamia. This decision to divide western Mesopotamia between Tigranes and King Phraates III of Parthia sowed the seeds for future trouble: Phraates had believed that the whole of the disputed area up the Euphrates River would be recovered for Parthia, since he had helped Pompey in 66.
- Pharnaces, the son of Mithridates, was permitted to keep his father's European possessions.
- Hyrcanus of Judaea was deprived of the title of king and was made high priest of Judaea, which came under the control of the governor of Syria.
- Galatia, under Deiotarus, received eastern Pontus.
- Other states included Cappadocia, Armenia Minor, Commagene and Coele-Syria.

The benefits of Pompey's eastern settlement

For Rome	*For the provincials*	*For Pompey*
Added to and consolidated Rome's empire and sphere of influence. Added 480 million sesterces in war spoils to the Roman treasury. Raised Rome's annual revenue from tribute by 70 per cent.	The east received peace and security for the future. Pompey became a patron for the provincials in their dealings with Rome.	Pompey increased his overseas clientelae from whom he would be able to find support in case of civil war.

Attempts by Crassus and Caesar to gain power in Pompey's absence

Concern about Pompey's return

During Pompey's absence in the east Crassus became increasingly jealous of his former colleague's military triumphs and apprehensive about his return. He was not alone in his anxiety. The optimates were also fearful of the possibility of Pompey's return to Rome as a second Sulla.

Crassus used wealth to gain support

Crassus was extremely influential with both politicians and businessmen owing to the skilful use of his incredible wealth. He made loans to both

During his aedileship, Caesar filled the Comitium, the Forum, its adjacent basilicas, and the Capitol itself with a display of the material which he meant to use in his public shows, building temporary colonnades for the purpose. He exhibited wild-beast hunts and stage-plays . . . Caesar also put on a gladiatorial show, but had collected so immense a troop of combatants that his terrified political opponents rushed a bill through the House, limiting the number of gladiators that anyone might keep in Rome . . . (Suetonius, Julius Caesar, 10)

A terra-cotta plaque showing a wild-animal hunt in an amphitheatre

Working relationship between Crassus and Caesar

optimates and popular leaders who in their scramble for position and prestige often fell into debt and ruin, and he also had considerable influence in equestrian circles because of his investments. He had used his wealth to help Caesar gain the aedileship for 65, since political advancement was an expensive business; Caesar won great popularity as a result of the lavish public games he presented, but was left with an overwhelming debt to Crassus.

Yet Crassus realised that despite the number of influential people in his debt, it would take more than wealth to achieve his ends. With the support of Julius Caesar, he attempted to build up a power base both at home and abroad in order to put himself in a bargaining position when Pompey returned. The two were often involved in behind-the-scene activities.

Crassus' attempts to gain power	
Scheme	*Result*
To turn the first Catilinarian conspiracy to good account When the consuls elected for 65 were declared ineligible because of the bribery of electors, L. Sergius Catilina attempted to become a candidate for the consulship. His candidature was refused, as	Crassus, although not involved in the plot, used his wealth and position as censor to hush the whole

Scheme	*Result*
he was awaiting trial for extortion in the province of Africa. He and the two other ineligible men devised a plot to kill the new consuls, but the plot failed.	thing up. He thought these men might prove useful at some later stage.
To build up power in Spain Crassus used his influence as a creditor of many senators and as censor to press the senate to send Calpurnius Piso (involved in the plot above) as governor of Hither Spain. His aim may have been to control the province through Piso.	Piso was vicious and incompetent and was killed by the native inhabitants.
To gain support in Gaul As censor, Crassus proposed full citizenship to the Transpadine Gauls (on the far side of the River Po), perhaps hoping that this would provide a future recruiting ground for troops.	Catulus, his colleague in the censorship, blocked it.
To annex Egypt Claiming that the father of the previous king of Egypt had bequeathed his kingdom to Rome, Crassus put up a tribune to propose its annexation. This was supported by the people and the equites because of Egypt's great resources. Crassus would have gained great popularity if the proposal had been successful.	The optimates, led by Catulus, were determined in their opposition. Cicero made a speech against it, as he was supposedly 'protecting' the interests of Pompey.
To support Catiline's second attempt at consulship Crassus supported the candidature of Catiline and Antonius for 63, seeing them as potential tools for the future.	The optimates, determined to prevent their election, were forced to support the novus homo, Cicero. Catiline failed again.
To get control of available public land in Italy and provinces Aware that Pompey would need land for his veterans when he returned, Crassus used the tribune Servilius Rullus to propose a land bill providing for a commission to purchase and dispose of public land. As a commissioner, he would have the upper hand.	Cicero spoke against the proposal and it was withdrawn.

Marcus Tullius Cicero

Cicero's consulship and the Catilinarian conspiracy, 63

Importance of political friends

In 63 Cicero offered himself as a candidate for the consulship. As a novus homo in politics, Cicero was aware of the importance of amici: it was imperative for him not only to have the support of influential politicians, but also to become as widely known as possible among his fellow citizens in Rome and in the townships of Italy. The author of a pamphlet called *A Short Guide to Electioneering* (possibly Cicero's brother Quintus) gave the following advice:

> Search out and discover men in every area; get to know them, visit them, strengthen their loyalty, make sure that in their vicinity they are campaigning for you, and pleading your cause as though they themselves were the candidate.[29]

Candidates for 63

Cicero had the advantage of a fine reputation in the law courts and many friends and associates who were indebted to him as a lawyer and public speaker, although some of the optimates (Catulus, Hortensius, Metellus and Lucullus) were cool towards him as a result of his speech in support of the lex Manilia. He became a candidate for the consulship of 63 with Lucius Sergius Catilina (Catiline), a man of noble family but doubtful reputation, and Gaius Antonius Hybrida. On account of Catiline's reckless nature and chequered past, the conservatives preferred to support Cicero's candidature in spite of his being a novus homo. Cicero was elected overwhelmingly, and his colleague was Antonius. This was a great achievement for someone of Cicero's background, and he pointed this fact out in a speech to the people in the assembly.

> I am the first 'new man', after a very long interval, almost more remote than our times can remember, whom you have made consul; that position which the nobility held secured by guards and fortified in every way, you have broken open, and have shown your desire that it should in future be open to merit, allowing me to take the lead.[30]

Early speeches of Cicero as consul

At this time Cicero made three speeches — together known under the title 'On the Agrarian Law' — in which he strenuously argued against the proposal of the tribune Rullus (backed by Crassus) to allocate land and establish colonies in Italy and the provinces. Cicero represented the law as against the interests of Pompey, away in the east. During one of these speeches he warned against anyone attempting to gain office by means of violence and revolution while he was consul, but in fact that was exactly what he had to face later in the year. Catiline, having missed out at the elections in 64, decided to campaign once again in 63 (for the following year).

Character of Catiline

Catiline has been depicted by Sallust and Cicero as a monster guilty of murder and every kind of immoral conduct (Sallust, *The Conspiracy of Catiline*, pp. 184–5). Cicero, in his speech against Catiline, said;

> For imagine every type of criminality and wickedness that you can think of; he has been behind them all. In the whole of Italy there is not one single poisoner, gladiator, robber, assassin, parricide, will-forger, cheat, glutton, wastrel, adulterer, prostitute, corrupter of youth, or youth who has been corrupted, indeed any nasty individual of any kind whatever, who would not be obliged to admit he had been Catilina's intimate.[31]

However, Catiline's early career does not quite match the versions of his character that appear in the ancient sources. Lutatius Catulus spoke in his defence in 73 and he had the support of many *consulars* (ex-consuls) at his extortion trial in 65; Cicero thought of defending him at this trial and in 63 even considered allying himself with Catiline in the elections.

Catiline certainly had talent, charm, energy and leadership qualities, but he was reckless, ambitious and in serious debt. He was not alone in this, since all nobles aspired to a public career and many of them were generally in debt by the time they reached the praetorship; the less successful often became bankrupt, unable to repay their debts to the moneylenders or financiers. The sources indicate that public and private debts had never been greater in Rome and Italy than at this time, creating widespread poverty and misery; this serious economic situation was partly the result of the civil war between Marius and Sulla, the slave revolt under Spartacus, the disruption to trade by the pirates and the enormous cost of the war against Mithridates, but Sallust maintains that greed and ambition among the upper classes also contributed to the situation.

Public and private debt widespread

In his election campaign in 63 Catiline made promises that if elected he would cancel all debts. As a result, he won a large following from all those who were disadvantaged—from bankrupt nobles to the urban poor. Unfortunately he also attracted the criminal element, 'who poured into Rome till it was like a sewer', and the dissolute youth of the capital, who preferred 'an idle life to thankless toil'.[32]

Catiline's promise to cancel debts

Cicero, in an attempt to warn the people against Catiline, conducted the elections wearing a cuirass (breastplate) under his toga and with a bodyguard of supporters around him; Catiline, for the second time, failed to be elected. Up to this point Catiline had used constitutional methods to satisfy his political ambitions but these were now abandoned in favour of extreme measures. 'Open war was now his only resource',[33] and he conspired to overthrow the government—there were many others in Roman society who were also anxious for a new regime.

Catiline's failure to be elected

According to Sallust, Catiline sent his agent Manlius north to organise troops and keep them ready to march on Rome. Catiline himself remained in the city with the other conspirators, 'plotting by stealth against the lives of the consuls, organising acts of arson and occupying strategic points with armed men'.[34] When Cicero received news that the army was to march on Rome and carry out a massacre, he told the senate and the senatus consultum ultimum was passed. This gave Cicero the right to make military preparations, but Catiline—against whom there was no real proof at this stage—continued to take his seat in the senate, carrying out a war of nerves with Cicero.

Catiline's conspiracy

The conspirators hired assassins to kill Cicero, but he was warned and was well-protected. He then made a number of stirring speeches in the senate and the assembly, pointing out that what Catiline was planning was far worse than all the other acts of violence between 88 and 77. He maintained that Marius, Sulla, Cinna and Lepidus had wanted only to be the leading figures in the state, while Catiline aimed to burn the city and

Cicero's Catilinarian speeches

destroy the republic. In fact, Catiline and his associates had exactly the same ambitions as the other Romans who resorted to civil war.

Catiline denied everything in the senate but was shouted down; very shortly afterwards he left to join Manlius and the army, leaving Lentulus, one of the praetors and a leading conspirator, in charge in Rome.

Proof of conspiracy provided

The senate outlawed Catiline, and when evidence was brought to Cicero in the form of letters written by the conspirators to Catiline urging him to hurry his advance on Rome, the others involved were arrested and admitted their part in the conspiracy.

> The disclosure of the plot produced a 'volte-face' in public opinion. The common people, who at first, in their desire for a new regime, had been only too eager for war, now cursed Catiline's scheme and praised Cicero to the skies.[35]

Debate in senate on punishment of conspirators

For two days there was a debate in the senate concerning the punishment to be imposed on the self-confessed traitors. The majority of senators who spoke supported the death penalty, but Julius Caesar was courageous enough to point out that they were all Roman citizens and that execution without a trial was illegal. Romans threatened with execution were entitled to appeal to the assembly. Caesar therefore suggested that they should be imprisoned for life in various Italian towns. His argument was very convincing (Sallust, 50–1), but the young Marcus Porcius Cato, in a determined speech against Caesar, turned the decision in favour of the death penalty. The execution, described in Plutarch's *Cicero*, 22, was supervised by Cicero himself.

When news reached Catiline's camp of the death of Lentulus and the others, many of his followers deserted, but Catiline—with the 'hard core' who stood by him—made a courageous and determined stand against the government forces led by Antonius. They were all killed.

Catiline's death

At the end of his consulship, Cicero pronounced 'I swear . . . in very truth that I have saved my country and maintained her supremacy'.[36] Cato also glorified Cicero's consulship in a speech to the people, who 'voted him the greatest honours that had ever been conferred and called him father of the fatherland. Cicero was the first it seems to receive this title'.[37]

Cicero–'Father of his country'

The importance of the Catilinarian conspiracy

Sources exaggerate Catiline's importance

Cicero (in his letters and speeches) and Sallust (in his monograph) appear to have exaggerated Catiline's place in history. Sallust described the conspiracy as worth writing about because it was 'fraught with unprecedented dangers to Rome',[38] while Cicero described in vivid detail what would have happened had he not saved his country: a city 'suddenly plunged into all-engulfing flames . . . corpses of unburied citizens lying in miserable heaps . . . the panic flight of girls and boys, the rape of Vestal

Virgins'.[39] Not only did Cicero exaggerate the danger to the state, he also continued to praise himself and magnify his achievements.

> One could attend neither the senate nor a public meeting, nor a session of the law courts without having to listen to endless repetitions of the story of Catiline and Lentulus. He went on to fill his books and writings with these praises of himself . . .[40]

If Sallust's moralising and Cicero's vanity can be overlooked, the whole episode falls into clearer perspective. Catiline was no more dangerous than many others who tried to rally discontented elements in society against the oligarchy.

Before Cicero's term of office had come to an end a number of people attacked him for what he had done — executing Roman citizens without a trial. One of these was the tribune Metellus Nepos, who was a supporter of Pompey: he forbade Cicero to make the customary speech to the people at the end of his consulship. Cicero's friends and associates were concerned that he might suffer in the future as a result of his actions, and Q. Metellus Celer wrote to him early in 62, 'seeing that your procedure in these matters has been marked neither by reasonableness, nor by the clemency of our ancestors, nobody need be surprised if you all live to regret it'.[41] Cicero was later sent into exile (58) for his actions in 63 (see p. 340).

Future danger for Cicero

During his consulship Cicero developed a political ideal, referred to later as the *concordia ordinum* (harmony of the orders). He had been impressed with the way the senatorial and equestrian orders had worked together for the safety of Rome during the Catilinarian conspiracy. He outlined his hope for the future in his fourth speech against Catiline.

Concordia ordinum

> If this harmony, brought about in my consulship, can survive for ever in the Republic, then we shall never again see the state torn by Civil War and strife.[42]

His plan for the future also depended on Pompey, who he hoped would return to Rome and lead the united senatorial and equestrian orders with Cicero as his chief adviser on political matters. He outlined this in a letter to Pompey in which he compared Pompey to Scipio Africanus and himself to Laelius, Scipio's friend and adviser.

Cicero was disappointed that Pompey's letter in return included no recognition of his achievement in 63, yet Pompey's coolness is not surprising since he had just won unprecedented victories in the east, established peace, added more provinces and a large number of allies to Rome's empire, and increased Rome's wealth from treasure and revenue. Suppressing the conspiracy of Catiline hardly measured up to these achievements.

Cicero disappointed with Pompey

The Bona Dea scandal

Clodius' trial for sacrilege

In 62 a young aristocrat, P. Clodius Pulcher, had committed sacrilege by dressing up as a woman and secretly attending a gathering of the all-female cult of the Bona Dea (good goddess). It is believed that at the time he was having an affair with Caesar's wife, Pomponia; Caesar divorced her. Clodius was brought to trial for sacrilege, and despite Cicero's expertise in breaking his alibi he was acquitted because of massive bribery of the jurors by Crassus. Not only did Cicero incur the lasting hatred of Clodius for his part in the trial (see p. 340), but the susbequent inquiry into the bribery of the jurors created further hostility between the equites and optimates (Plutarch, *Caesar*, 9–10).

The Bona Dea (Good Goddess), whose cult was introduced from the Greek cities of southern Italy during the third century BC

The return of Pompey

Concern over Pompey's return

The optimates were deeply concerned about Pompey's return. Some thought that he would 'lead his army against the city and make sure of absolute power for himself' [43] However, it was not in Pompey's nature to seize a military dictatorship; his desire was always to be popular — to be given power, not to seize it. He disbanded his army on landing in Italy, discharging his veterans to their cities until the celebration of his triumph. Unarmed and accompanied only by a few close friends he returned to Rome, remaining outside the city until his triumph, which 'was on such a scale that, although two separate days were devoted to it, the time was still not long enough . . . '.[44] Plutarch gives a vivid description of the spectacle in *Pompey*.[45]

Cicero, who had great hopes for Pompey after his return, reveals his disappointment in several letters to his friend Atticus in early 61, believing that Pompey's outward signs of friendship hid the fact that he was jealous.

The position of Pompey, Crassus and Caesar in 61–60

Pompey

Pompey's need for optimate support

Although Pompey was now the pre-eminent man in Rome, he wanted and needed the backing of the optimates in order to gain land for his veterans and to have his innumerable arrangements in the east ratified. By disbanding his army he had diffused the tension in Rome and proved to the optimates that he had no intention of overthrowing the government, but the majority in the senate were still suspicious of him and some were even openly hostile.

Opposition to Pompey

From the time he returned he had been continually frustrated by Metellus Celer, Cato and Lucullus.

Metellus	*Cato*	*Lucullus*
Pompey had alienated Metellus Celer because he had divorced his wife, Mucia, who was Metellus' half-sister. Mucia 'had been living a very loose life'[46] while Pompey was away in the east. The divorce was to have political repercussions for Pompey, as Metellus was the consul designate for 60.	Pompey hoped to remarry into the family of Cato, who was the optimates' spokesman at this time. However, Cato refused Pompey's offer of marriage to one of his nieces because (according to Plutarch) he thought that it was 'a form of bribery and the whole scheme an attempt to corrupt him . . . '.[42] Cato was a staunch conservative, and distrusted Pompey's motives.	Lucullus, who had been treated badly by Pompey in Asia, was encouraged to take a more active role in politics now that Pompey was back in Rome and 'he plunged straight into the fray',[48] attacking Pompey's arrangements in the east.

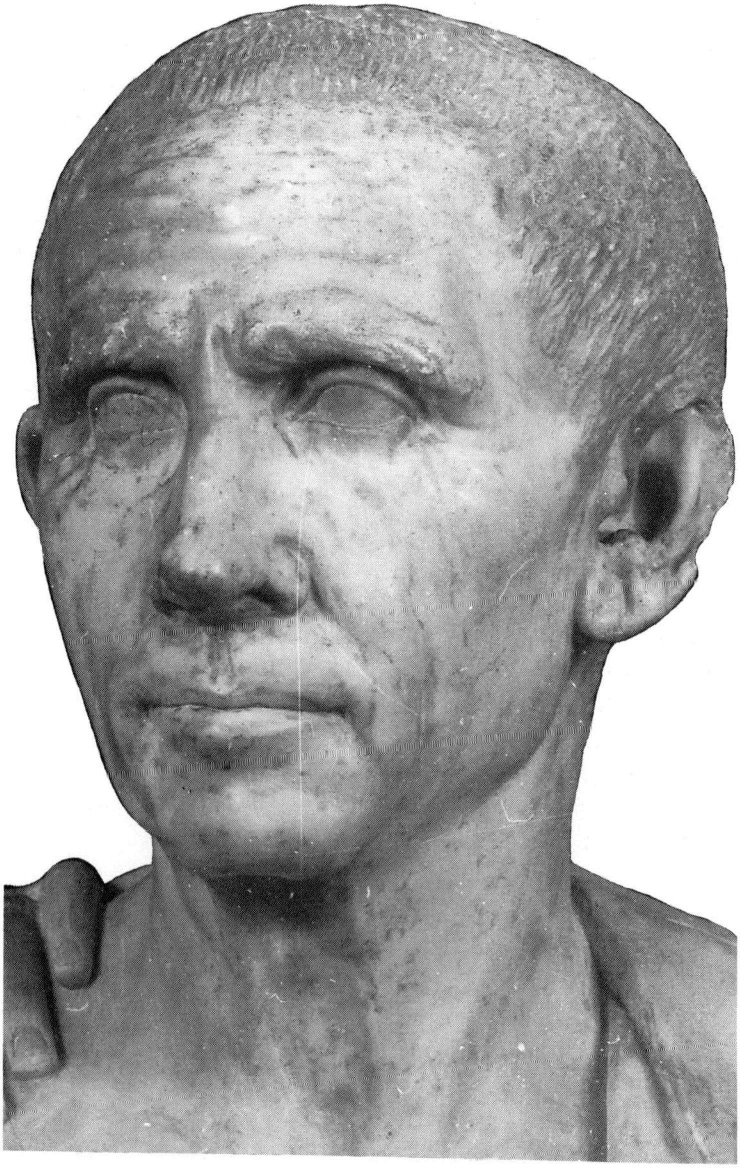

M. Porcius Cato, the optimate who was one of the chief opponents of Caesar (the authenticity of this likeness is now in doubt — there is evidently no existing portrait of Cato that can with certainty be identified as such)

Continued obstruction

Despite all the money he had spent in getting his nominees elected to the consulship (Piso, 61, and Afranius, 60), the opposition of Cato and his associates had blocked Pompey's attempts to get the land for his veterans. Lucullus had also persuaded the senate to scrutinise and discuss in detail every item in Pompey's eastern settlement, which Pompey had hoped would be ratified en bloc. Pompey was forced to seek help from the populares; he turned to a tribune, L. Flavius, to introduce an agrarian bill, but the other consul, Metellus Celer, opposed it.

Pompey's loss of prestige

Not only had the optimates rebuffed him personally by rejecting his marriage proposals, they had also discredited him by preventing him from honouring his promises to his veterans. His prestige suffered severely.

Crassus

Crassus as spokesman for equites

Crassus was also frustrated in 61 by the optimates. He had become the spokesman for the equestrian tax farmers who had contracted to collect the taxes from the province of Asia. This group of businessmen had not anticipated the economic disruption to Asia due to the Mithridatic War, but soon realised that far from making their usual huge profit, they would barely recover their costs. Instead of accepting their losses they requested the senate, through Crassus, to grant them a rebate.

Equites request tax rebate

Crassus may have had financial interests in the matter or he may have been attempting to increase his influence. Whatever his motives, the request was outrageous and the optimates refused to consider any concessions. Supported by Cato, Metellus Celer spoke firmly against it but Cicero, who thought that the request was immoral, supported it because he was anxious to preserve the unity which he naively believed existed between the senate and the equites.

Crassus and his equestrian friends were also offended by the inquiry into the bribery of jurors in the notorious Bona Dea trial.

Cato and the optimates maintained their opposition to the requests of Pompey and Crassus, and by mid 61 both the land bill of Flavius and the question of the Asian taxes had been dropped.

Caesar

Caesar's hopes for consulship of 59

Caesar, who had been in Spain as a propraetor during 61, hoped to return to Rome in 60 and stand for the consulship for the following year. Since he would be unable to celebrate his triumph and appear in Rome to hand in his nomination for consulship in person, he wrote to the senate requesting to be allowed to stand in absentia.

Cato and the optimates refused his request, hoping to force him to abandon his bid for the consulship. They believed that Caesar would never give up the honour of a triumph—but that is exactly what he did, and arrived in Rome in time to enter his nomination.

Optimates' attempts to block Caesar

Prior to the election, as was the usual practice, the senate had decided on the provinces to be allocated to the consuls of 59; for Caesar, if elected, this was to be the administration of the forests and cattle tracks of Italy (*silvae callesque*). Whether or not this was a deliberate attempt to deprive him of an important provincial post, it would never satisfy anyone as ambitious as Caesar.

Caesar's decision to seek support

Caesar now saw the possibilities for exploiting the difficulties that Pompey and Crassus were having with the optimates. He needed powerful supporters in order to be elected, particularly since Cato and his associates put all their resources behind one of his competitors, Bibulus (Cato's son-in-law). Caesar had supported Pompey in the past (concerning lex Gabinia and lex Manilia) and had worked with Crassus before; he therefore hoped that they would support him now.

Pompey's decision to join Caesar

Since Pompey's use of ineffective consuls (Piso and Afranius) and a tribune (Flavius) had failed to get him what he wanted, he had no alternative but to back Caesar, regardless of the possible consequences,

> if he was not to recede into insignificance, have his credit with the veterans and the common people destroyed, his godlike stature in the provinces and the Kingdoms of the East undermined and his self-respect in shreds.[49]

Crassus had short-term objectives which Caesar could satisfy as consul, but he also needed to safeguard himself in the long term against Pompey, and a political coalition with Caesar would achieve this.

From the First Triumvirate to the death of Caesar, 60–44

17

THIS PERIOD is marked by the political alliance between Pompey, Caesar and Crassus which was formed to further their own ends in the face of opposition from the optimates. Almost from the beginning the so-called First Triumvirate was put under pressure from those—for instance, Cicero—who wished to see its destruction and from ambitious men such as Clodius, who fought for their share of political power. Intrigue, gang warfare, street violence, massive bribery, and murder were commonplace.

The rivalry between Pompey and Caesar for supremacy within the state eventually led to a civil war (49–44) which involved the whole Roman empire, since these men had established enormous provincial clientelae during their years of extraordinary commands. Caesar's pre-eminence as a result of his victory over the Pompey-led senatorial forces was cut short by his assassination, but his death did not result in a return to the old republican form of government as his assassins and Cicero had hoped would happen. A second civil war between Antony (Caesar's lieutenant) and Octavian (Caesar's heir) eventually led to the establishment of one-man rule.

The 'First Triumvirate'—the coalition of Pompey, Crassus and Caesar, 60–53

'Triumvirate' a misnomer

The agreement of Pompey, Crassus and Caesar to work together for their own ends has been misleadingly called the 'First Triumvirate' by modern historians. A triumvirate was a legally established body, whereas the alliance between Pompey, Crassus and Caesar was not official and for some time remained secret. The exact date of its formation is not known, but it is believed that there were still some negotiations going on well after Caesar's election to the consulship.

Reconcialiation of Pompey and Crassus needed

To increase the political effectiveness of the coalition, Caesar had to reconcile Pompey and Crassus. They had never really been on good terms, and even during their first consulship in 70 there had only been an uneasy co-operation. Caesar's appeal for the three of them to work together was accepted, although it is doubtful if the other two thought beyond the short-term satisfaction of their own needs.

Strength of Triumvirate

A coalition of this kind was not unusual in Rome. Political friendships or partnerships (amicitiae) were normal in Roman politics. There were two aspects of this one, however, which made it different: the combined power of the three men—who between them had prestige, wealth, popularity with the people, the support of the equites and armed force if necessary (veterans)—and the dramatic repercussions of their failure to sustain the alliance.

Many historians, both ancient and modern, trace the civil war in 49 between Pompey and Caesar back to the formation of the triumvirate.

Scullard maintains that

> Its formation was a turning point in the history of the Free State, and it was, as both Cicero and Cato recognised, the ultimate origin of the Civil War of 49 BC.[1]

Plutarch comments that

Views of Triumvirate as origin of Civil War

> the first disaster and the worst had been, not the quarrel and split between Caesar and Pompey, but the friendship and harmony that had existed between them.[2]

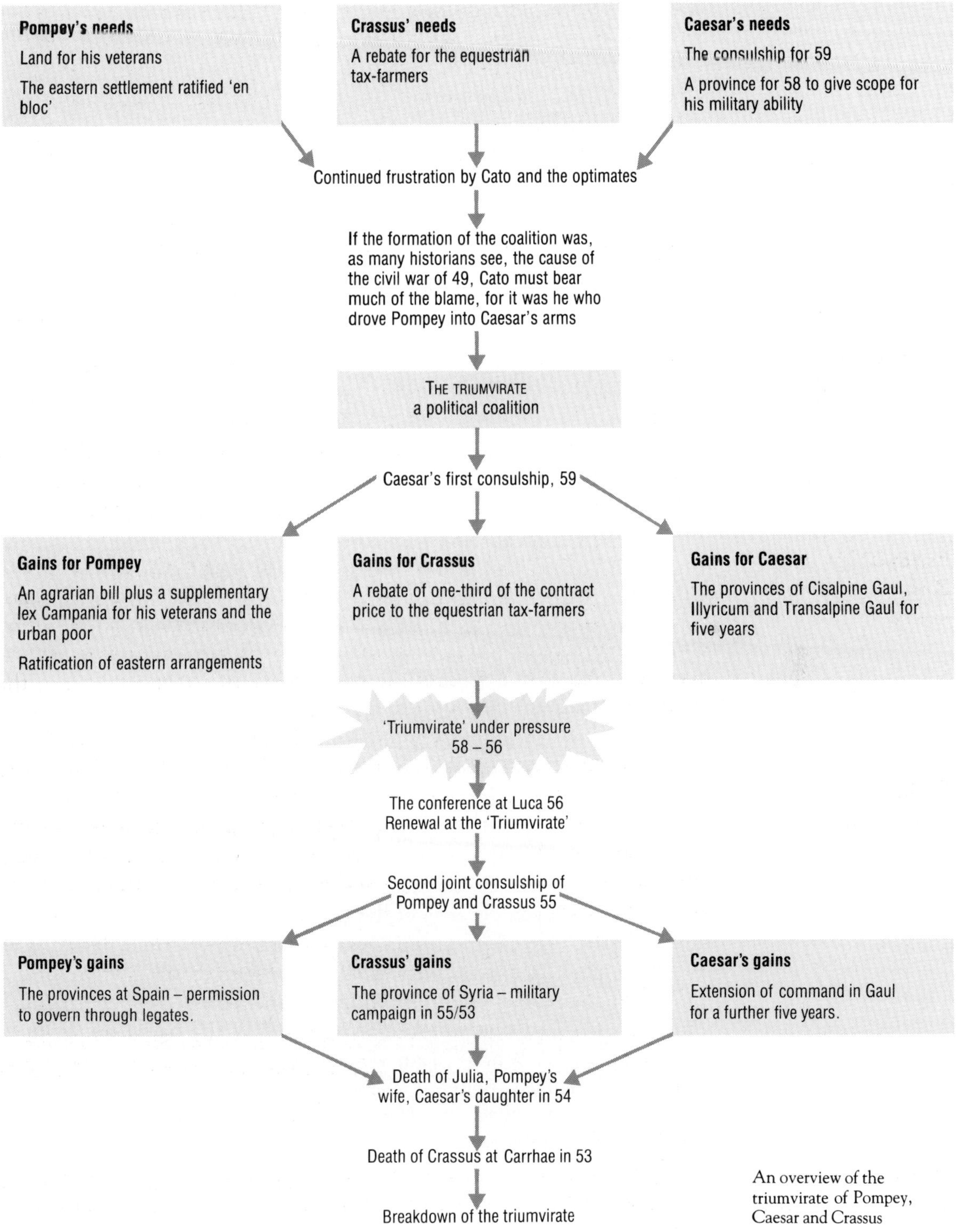
Pompey's needs
Land for his veterans
The eastern settlement ratified 'en bloc'
Crassus' needs
A rebate for the equestrian tax-farmers
Caesar's needs
The consulship for 59
A province for 58 to give scope for his military ability
Continued frustration by Cato and the optimates
If the formation of the coalition was, as many historians see, the cause of the civil war of 49, Cato must bear much of the blame, for it was he who drove Pompey into Caesar's arms
THE TRIUMVIRATE
a political coalition
Caesar's first consulship, 59
Gains for Pompey
An agrarian bill plus a supplementary lex Campania for his veterans and the urban poor
Ratification of eastern arrangements
Gains for Crassus
A rebate of one-third of the contract price to the equestrian tax-farmers
Gains for Caesar
The provinces of Cisalpine Gaul, Illyricum and Transalpine Gaul for five years
'Triumvirate' under pressure
58 – 56
The conference at Luca 56
Renewal at the 'Triumvirate'
Second joint consulship of
Pompey and Crassus 55
Pompey's gains
The provinces at Spain – permission to govern through legates.
Crassus' gains
The province of Syria – military campaign in 55/53
Caesar's gains
Extension of command in Gaul for a further five years.
Death of Julia, Pompey's
wife, Caesar's daughter in 54
Death of Crassus at Carrhae in 53
Breakdown of the triumvirate

An overview of the triumvirate of Pompey, Caesar and Crassus

Cicero was reported as having said

> Oh Pompey, I wish you had either never formed an alliance with Caesar or never broken it.[3]

Velleius Paterculus believed

> its results were to bring ruin to the city, the world, and even, at different times, to each of the three men.[4]

If the formation of the coalition in 60 was the cause of the civil war in 49, then Cato must bear much of the blame, for he and the optimates 'drove Pompeius into Caesar's arms'.[5]

Caesar's first consulship, 59

Caesar, the popularis, was elected with the individual backing of Pompey and Crassus. His colleague in the consulship was the conservative Calpurnius Bibulus, Cato's son-in-law.

Opposition to Caesar's legislation

Caesar wasted no time in preparing his program of legislation, but he realised the difficulties ahead. The senate was hostile towards him, his colleague's purpose was to check his actions, it was obvious that Cato would continue to oppose him, and many of the tribunes were ready to fight for the nobles.

He adopted a conciliatory attitude at first by treating Bibulus with courtesy and consulting the senate. A moderate bill to provide for Pompey's veterans was presented to the senate, and Caesar indicated that he was willing to accept amendments if the objections were reasonable.

Use of force by triumvirs

The senate spurned his offer of compromise; he was met with prolonged and systematic obstruction, so he presented his land bill to the assembly. Bibulus vetoed the bill and when Caesar asked him publicly to withdraw the veto, he refused. Caesar then realised that he would only be able to carry the bill in open defiance of the law, and would have to resort to the threat of force. He called on Pompey and Crassus, who had remained in the background, to express their approval. According to Plutarch, Caesar 'brought Pompey out openly in front of the people on the speaker's platform and asked him whether he approved of the new laws. Pompey said that he did'.[6] When Caesar went further and asked him if he would defend the people's rights if their opponents used force, Pompey is supposed to have replied, 'if it is a question of swords, [he] could produce a sword and a shield as well'.[7] It is unlikely that Plutarch is strictly correct when he says that Pompey 'filled the city with his soldiers and held everyone down by force';[8] it is more likely that some of his veterans (who were private citizens at this point) were brought into the Forum. Some

Marble bust of Julius Caesar

> Caesar is said to have been tall, fair and well-built, with a rather broad face and keen, dark-brown eyes. His health was sound apart from sudden comas and a tendency to nightmares, which troubled him towards the end of his life; but he twice had epileptic fits while on campaign. He was something of a dandy, always keeping his head carefully trimmed and shaved, and has been accused of having certain other hairy parts of his body depilated with tweezers. His baldness was a disfigurement which his enemies harped upon, much to his exasperation, but he used to comb the thin strands of hair forward from his poll, and of all the honours voted him by the Senate and the People, none pleased him so much as the privilege of wearing a laurel wreath on all occasions — he constantly took advantage of it. (Suetonius, *Julius Caesar*, 45)

rioting supposedly occurred during which Bibulus, Cato and Lucullus were threatened. Bibulus

> was set upon by the crowd who broke the fasces of his lictors in pieces; someone emptied a basket of dung over Bibulus' head; and two of the tribunes who were escorting him were wounded.[9]

The threat of force was a very strong factor in preventing the triumvirs' opponents from resorting to violence themselves. According to Dio

Cassius, when Bibulus realised that he could not prevent the agrarian law from being passed by any of the normal methods, he proclaimed that the remaining days of the year were to be regarded as a 'sacred period': this meant that it was legally impossible for the people even to meet in an assembly. Although this was an unusual method to employ, it was probably constitutionally correct; Caesar, however, ignored it and declared the bill passed. Bibulus withdrew to his house for the remainder of his term of office and declared that he would be watching the sky for unfavourable omens (taking the auspices) — this had the effect of making the rest of Caesar's legislation technically invalid. Suetonius says that Caesar governed alone, and did very much as he pleased.

Illegal legislation of Caesar

The land destined for Pompey's veterans and some of the urban plebs was to be purchased with funds from Pompey's eastern conquests. (The senators reluctantly swore an oath to abide by the provisions of the bill.) Caesar later introduced a second, harsher land law (lex Campania), which provided for the last public lands in Italy (in Campania) to be divided into 20 000 allotments and distributed predominantly to the urban poor. This land was an important source of Roman revenue and previous attempts to distribute it had created violent opposition.

Provisions of Caesar's land bills

Pompey's uneasiness with Caesar's methods

Pompey appeared to be upset with the way the land bill was passed. The use of violence and the fact that he had committed himself openly in the Forum had exposed him to the hostility of the people. Cicero, in a letter to Atticus, described Pompey's position at this stage.

> Pompey has fenced so far with the important questions. When asked, he said that he agreed with Caesar's laws. But what about his methods? 'Caesar must answer that for himself', he replied.[19]

Caesar and Pompey linked by marriage

In order to assure himself of Pompey's loyalty Caesar arranged for him to marry his daughter, Julia. No matter how much Pompey may have wanted to disassociate himself from the illegalities of Caesar's legislation, he could not abandon the coalition at this point, for fear of losing what he had already gained. He agreed to the marriage link.

Further legislation satisfies Pompey and Crassus

Caesar honoured the rest of his promises to Pompey and Crassus by using the tribune Vatinius. Pompey's eastern settlement was ratified en bloc and the equestrians received a rebate of one-third of their tax contract.

Caesar's Gallic provinces

Vatinius also worked on Caesar's behalf. He proposed to the assembly that Caesar be given Cisalpine Gaul and Illyricum as his province for the following year, with imperium for five years and an army of three legions. This was to replace the silvae callesque, which had been nominated as the province for the consuls of 59; unfavourable omens were announced, but Vatinius ignored them and the measure was passed. Caesar could now raise an army and keep it near Rome. Later, on the death of the governor of Transalpine Gaul, the senate added this vital part of Gaul to Caesar's province and an additional legion was added to the army under his command.

Other legislation of 59

Also during 59 the coalition supported an appeal from a German chief to be recognised as a 'Friend of Rome', and arranged for the recognition of Ptolemy Auletes as the king of Egypt — Ptolemy promised to pay a huge fee. A more statesmanlike measure was passed to prevent exploitation by Roman governors in the provinces: a limit was put on what governors and their staffs could requisition from the provincials, and the acceptance of gifts was restricted. Strict accounts had to be kept also. Another measure provided that all senatorial resolutions had to be published.

Caesar continued to legislate throughout 59 without any thought for the constitution, and used the threat of force to suppress any opposition. The initial alarm felt by the optimates when they learned of the coalition's existence turned to fear. Cicero voiced the opinion of many people when he told Atticus that he was afraid 'that they may find it necessary to use terror'.[11] Resentment against the three increased, and Cato predicted in the senate what he believed the future would bring to Rome and to Pompey. Bibulus issued abusive edicts from his home, and there were demonstrations against the partners at gladiatorial shows and at the theatre. Cicero pointed out to Atticus that these 'popular politicians have taught even quiet folk to hiss'.[12] Caesar received no applause when he entered the theatre, and the actors ridiculed Pompey to the delight of the whole audience. Although this reaction concerned Caesar, Pompey was the main target of the opposition's attack: they probably regarded him as the most influential member of the coalition and the one most likely to be humiliated and hurt by the criticism. Pompey had always wanted acceptance and respect.

Open opposition to triumvirs

Attacks on Pompey

Cicero's hopes of triumvirate breakdown

Cicero, who had refused to join the coalition in 60, regarded it as an infamous and disgraceful alliance 'and uniformly odious to all sorts and classes and ages of men . . .'.[13] However, because of his 'friendship' with Pompey he did not fight what they were doing, but continued to hope that the triumvirate would break up; he believed that this would be a possibility once Pompey had got what he wanted, because Pompey did not like being unpopular. If anyone could persuade Pompey to break with the others it would be the persuasive Cicero, and Caesar, realising this, offered Cicero a post on his staff during his governorship of Gaul. This second offer to join the group Cicero also refused.

Caesar's safeguards for 58

Caesar wanted to make sure that Rome was in safe hands before leaving in 58 for his province. The triumvirs secured the election of favourable candidates to the consulship of 58 — L. Calpurnius Piso and A. Gabinius, but Caesar also needed a friendly tribune to keep an eye on Pompey while he was away and to remove Cicero and Cato, the most outspoken opponents of the triumvirate, from Rome.

In 59 P. Clodius Pulcher, a patrician by birth, changed his status to that of a plebeian with the help of Caesar (as pontifex maximus), so that he could be elected to the tribunate for 58; he was motivated by hatred for Cicero, against whom he wanted revenge. (Clodius had been charged with sacrilege and involved in the notorious Bona Dea trial. Cicero had broken his alibi, making his prosecution certain, but he was acquitted after the blatant bribery of the jury by Crassus.)

Clodius' threats to Cicero

Towards the end of 59 Cicero realised the danger he faced from Clodius, confiding to Atticus that 'he's definitely an enemy, and there's trouble in store of such a kind that I only hope that you can come at once'.[14] Cicero wanted to believe that Pompey would prevent Clodius from attacking him, but admitted to Atticus that he was not convinced of Pompey's support.

Caesar's departure for Gaul

Caesar did not depart for his province until after Clodius had removed Cicero and Cato from the political scene in the following year.

The significance of Caesar's consulship

Illegality

- Caesar's use of force and his failure to pay any attention to his colleague's legal methods of blocking legislation made his measures technically illegal. His opponents now had a legitimate excuse to threaten him with prosecution as soon as he became a private citizen. This made it imperative that Caesar retain the imperium of either a consul or a proconsul in the future.
- Caesar's lex Campania created more resentment than any other aspect of his legislation.

Pompey's loss of popularity

- For Pompey, a man used to glory, the loss of popularity with the people and the optimates was humiliating. He was extremely vulnerable to public opinion.

Weakness in the coalition

- Cracks in the coalition were obvious from the beginning. The aims of Pompey and Crassus were short-term, and once they had been satisfied it became difficult to hide their enmity towards one another, especially after Caesar left Italy. (The course of Caesar's campaigns in Gaul is treated on pp. 348–54.)

The tribunate of Clodius and the exile of Cicero, 58

Clodius' popular measures

During his tribunate Clodius proposed a number of measures to gain popularity with the urban masses. These included the distribution of free corn (a blatant corn-dole, which was later used to bribe the people), the abolition of the use of omens in order to stop public business (Bibulus had used this against Caesar) and legalisation of *collegia* (clubs or associations). This last measure led to the organisation of gangs of thugs under the guise of political clubs; during the next few years rival political gangs undermined law and order in Rome.

Clodius' bill to prosecute Cicero

The triumvirs had tried on several occasions to make offers to Cicero in order to keep him from speaking out against them, but he had refused any office or honour. He therefore had to be removed from Rome. Clodius introduced a bill to banish any magistrate who had put to death a citizen without trial; this was aimed at Cicero (he had put the Catilinarian conspirators to death in 63), although he was not mentioned by name. When the bill was passed Cicero, believing himself to be in danger of prosecution,

> put on mourning and, with his hair long and unkempt, went about the city approaching the people as a suppliant. However, he could not enter a single street without being accosted by Clodius with a band of insolent ruffians round him . . .'[15]

Pompey's failure to support Cicero

Cicero appealed to Pompey for help, believing that his past actions on Pompey's behalf would gain him his protection. Pompey, however, told Cicero that as a private citizen he did not have any influence over Clodius. This was probably true, but Pompey was not too sympathetic at this stage—Cicero had declined an offer of a position on Caesar's staff, which would have removed him from the dangerous situation he now faced. Also, as Plutarch points out, Pompey 'was Caesar's son-in-law, and at Caesar's request he proved false to the obligations of the past'.[16] This desertion by Pompey upset Cicero greatly; however, it was not only Pompey who deserted him, but many of his aristocratic friends also.

Cicero's exile

On the advice of friends Cicero left Rome, and after his departure Clodius passed a law officially exiling him and preventing him from living less than 650 kilometres from Rome. His property was confiscated and put up for auction by Clodius, who also burned down his country villas and his house in Rome. Cicero crossed over to Greece and spent most of his time in Macedonia; from his letters to his family and friends it was obvious that he was a shattered man and 'remained for most of the time miserable and disconsolate, keeping his eyes fixed, like a distressed lover, on Italy'.[17]

Cato's special mission to Cyprus

Clodius removed Cato from Rome by arranging that he be sent on a special mission to Cyprus to supervise its annexation (it later became part of the province of Cilicia); this interfered with part of Pompey's settlement of the east, and Pompey became increasingly suspicious of Clodius when he made further changes to the eastern arrangements. He replaced Pompey's appointee to the high priesthood of the Magna Mater (in Galatia) and also freed Tigranes, whom Pompey had brought to Rome as a hostage. These were just the first of a series of public humiliations of Pompey by Clodius, and it has been suggested that Crassus may have been behind them. Clodius and his gang attacked Pompey verbally, which upset him greatly since he 'was quite unused to hearing any ill spoken of him and in this sort of warfare he had no experience at all'.[18] When Clodius instigated a plot to make Pompey believe that his life was threatened, the latter did not show himself in public for the remainder of Clodius' tribunate.

Clodius' attacks on Pompey

During the second half of 58 Cicero's friends, led by Atticus, used all their influence to have Clodius' law against Cicero repealed.

Significance of Clodius' tribunate

- His corn dole won over the urban masses, and the legalisation of the collegia made it possible to build up a gang of ruffians with which to terrorise his opponents when he was out of office. For the next few years there was constant gang warfare in the streets of Rome.
- The question of Cicero's exile revealed Pompey's hypocrisy.
- Cato, who had always been an outspoken opponent of exceptional commands, would find it difficult in future to speak against them since he had accepted one himself.

The triumvirate under pressure, 58–56

After Caesar left for Gaul, the triumvirate was subjected to a considerable amount of pressure from a number of areas, as can be seen in the diagram opposite.

Crassus' hostility to Pompey

Pompey and Crassus had always been hostile to one another, and once they had achieved their immediate objectives the tension between the two became even more obvious. Clodius carried out a vicious campaign against Pompey—which Crassus was probably backing—and many of the optimates were pleased to see Pompey's discomfort. The constant public humiliations he suffered at the hands of Clodius, together with his belief that his life was in danger, forced Pompey to use a rival gang of ruffians under the leadership of T. Annius Milo. Gang warfare between Clodius and Milo throughout this period highlighted the conflict between Pompey and Crassus.

Move to have Cicero recalled

The increase in Clodius' attacks also prompted Pompey to support a bill for Cicero's recall from exile. He did not want to upset Caesar over this move, so sent one of the tribunes for 57 to get his approval, which was given only grudgingly. During 57 the movement for Cicero's recall gained in momentum and Clodius, although now out of office, used violence and rioting to stop the bill, but Pompey summoned men from his own estates,

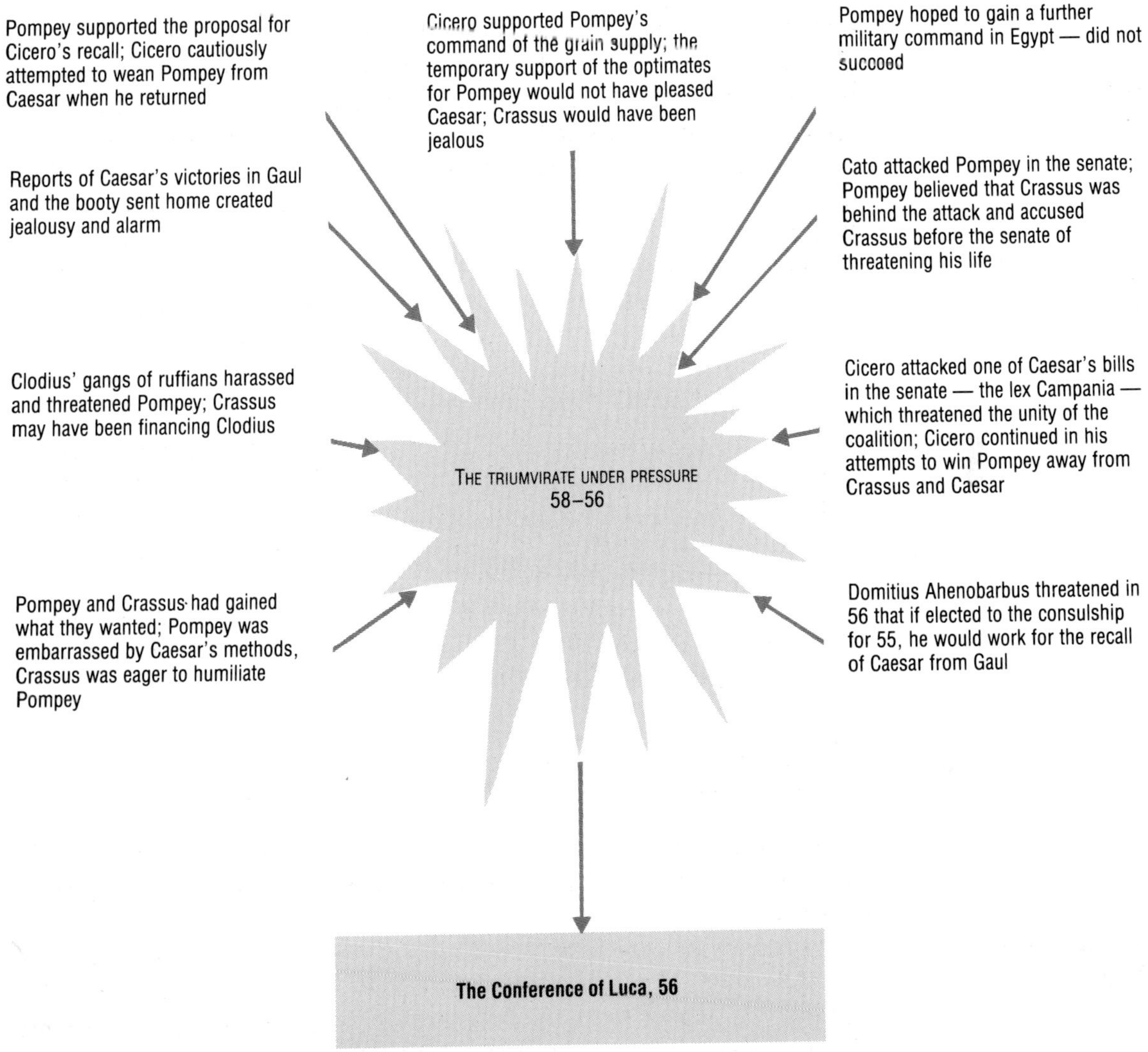
Pompey supported the proposal for Cicero's recall; Cicero cautiously attempted to wean Pompey from Caesar when he returned
Cicero supported Pompey's command of the grain supply; the temporary support of the optimates for Pompey would not have pleased Caesar; Crassus would have been jealous
Pompey hoped to gain a further military command in Egypt — did not succeed
Reports of Caesar's victories in Gaul and the booty sent home created jealousy and alarm
Cato attacked Pompey in the senate; Pompey believed that Crassus was behind the attack and accused Crassus before the senate of threatening his life
Clodius' gangs of ruffians harassed and threatened Pompey; Crassus may have been financing Clodius
Cicero attacked one of Caesar's bills in the senate — the lex Campania — which threatened the unity of the coalition; Cicero continued in his attempts to win Pompey away from Crassus and Caesar
THE TRIUMVIRATE UNDER PRESSURE 58–56
Pompey and Crassus had gained what they wanted; Pompey was embarrassed by Caesar's methods, Crassus was eager to humiliate Pompey
Domitius Ahenobarbus threatened in 56 that if elected to the consulship for 55, he would work for the recall of Caesar from Gaul
The Conference of Luca, 56

and from those areas in which he had great influence, to come to Rome to voice their opinions and vote on the issue. The bill was passed and Cicero returned to Rome like a triumphant general. He wrote to his friend Atticus,

> . . . when I reached the Porta Capena I found the steps of the temples thronged by the common people who welcomed me with vociferous applause. Like numbers and applause followed me to the Capitol.[19]

Pressure from Cicero

Cicero now helped to further undermine the triumvirate by speaking in favour of the appointment of Pompey to a special command. There had been riots outside the senate, the people complaining about the critical shortage of corn and its high price. They demanded that Pompey be

Pompey's special command — grain supply

appointed to take charge of the grain supplies. Cicero spoke in favour of the appointment of Pompey as Curator of the Grain Supply, and a bill was drafted by the two consuls giving him fifteen legates and total control of 'all ports and trading centres, with authority to arrange the distribution of foodstuffs'[20] for five years. A tribune, Messius, brought forward an alternative proposal which would have given Pompey even greater imperium and the control of an army, but since the opposition to this was widespread Pompey declared that he was in favour of the consuls' bill. He may have been testing public opinion, to see whether he could be given greater powers.

Pompey's organisational ability made him the perfect choice for co-ordinating the efforts of his fifteen legates over a wide area, and

> with good fortune assisting his own daring and energy, he filled the sea with ships and the markets with grain. In fact he provided so much of it that there was a surplus left over for the use of the people outside Italy.[21]

Concern of Crassus and Caesar

This appointment, which Plutarch suggests 'made Pompey once again virtually the master of all Roman possessions by sea and land',[22] would not have pleased Crassus and Caesar. Even though it was a non-military command, it served as good propaganda since Pompey was working for the welfare of the masses. He may have begun to wonder whether the triumvirate was of any benefit to him now that he had recovered a large part of the prestige and power he had lost during 58.

Controversy over Egyptian monarchy

Further strain was put on the coalition when the question was raised of restoring the former king of Egypt, Ptolemy Auletes, to the throne. Ptolemy, who been helped to the throne by the triumvirs during Caesar's consulship in 59, was unacceptable to his people and was deposed; he now requested that Pompey be appointed to restore him once again. Cicero urged Pompey to disassociate himself from the whole question, as the powerful optimates were totally opposed to such an appointment, as was Cicero himself. Crassus also, eager to spoil Pompey's chances, encouraged further humiliating verbal attacks on him by Clodius and his gang. Pompey finally decided to drop the whole matter — it had lost him considerable support and his relationship with Crassus had never been worse.

Relations between Pompey and Crassus worsen

Cicero's proposed attacks on Caesar's land bill

Cicero, in an attempt to finally break the unity of the coalition and to repair the rift between Pompey and the optimates, revived the question of Caesar's lex Campania which had been resented more than any other aspect of his legislation in 59. If Pompey did not object to Caesar's law being repealed or modified, he might benefit in two ways. Campania was a valuable source of revenue and Pompey needed funds from the senate to carry out his task as grain controller; Cicero also hoped that Pompey would win back some of the senatorial support he had recently lost, while any discussion of repealing the lex Campania would be a major threat to Caesar.

Further threats to Caesar

There was a further threat to Caesar when a candidate for the consulship for 55, L. Domitius Ahenobarbus, declared that if he were elected for the following year he would immediately initiate a move to have Caesar recalled from Gaul.

The coalition appeared to be breaking apart.

Triumvirs' need to renew alliance

Despite the part played by Crassus in Clodius' attacks on Pompey over the preceding three years, he was not anxious for the triumvirate to end at this point; he wanted an appointment which would give him the same sort of prestige as that enjoyed by Pompey and Caesar. It was also imperative for Caesar that the alliance between the three men continue, as he had not completed his conquest of Gaul and to be recalled to Rome at this stage could be disastrous for his career. For Pompey, there was no guarantee that the optimates would accept him if he broke from the coalition, and Clodius and Crassus would certainly have continued to harass him. He would have also alienated Caesar. For the moment it was in the best interests of Pompey to renew his political association with Crassus and Caesar.

The Conference of Luca in 56 — the renewal of the triumvirate

Caesar had spent the winter at Ravenna in Cisalpine Gaul, and Crassus now travelled north to inform him of the latest threats to the coalition, particularly of the interference by Cicero. Caesar needed to sort out the situation before he returned to campaigning in Transalpine Gaul and before Pompey sailed for Sardinia in his capacity as Curator of the Grain Supply.

Caesar moved to Luca, the town in his province nearest to Rome, where the three men are supposed to have discussed the future of the triumvirate. There is some doubt as to whether Crassus went with Caesar (Plutarch and Suetonius imply that he did) from Ravenna to Luca to meet Pompey, who had been accompanied there by 120 senators, but whether Crassus was there or not is unimportant, as the decisions made at Luca provided for a public reconciliation between Crassus and Pompey and strengthened the position of all three.

Plans for the future made at Luca

It was agreed that Pompey and Crassus would stand for their second joint consulship in the following year and that they would then look after their own proconsular futures and gain an extension for Caesar's command in Gaul. It was also to be impressed on Cicero that there was to be no discussion of the lex Campania or of Caesar's recall. Crassus was to disassociate himself from Clodius and try to persuade him to stop his attacks on Pompey.

The second joint consulship of Pompey and Crassus, 55

Election difficulties for Pompey and Crassus

Despite their decision to stand for the consulship, Pompey and Crassus were aware that it would not be an easy matter to be elected in the normal manner. They had many powerful enemies, one of which was a rival candidate, Domitius Ahenobarbus. He had to be prevented from standing, since he made it clear that if he were elected he would raise the question of Caesar's recall.

Appointment of interrex

Pompey and Crassus could not afford to risk standing at a normal election and so planned not only to delay submitting their nominations, but also to prevent the consuls for 56 holding the elections until the end of their term. They resorted to all means of obstruction, including violence, and by the end of the year no elections had been held. This meant that as there were no longer any consuls in office to conduct elections, the procedure of appointing an *interrex* would have to be used. (An interrex, appointed from the ranks of the patricians, had five days in which to conduct the elections; if he failed to do so within that period another interrex was selected, and so on.) An interrex, friendly to Pompey, was duly appointed and proposed only two candidates for the elections. The two triumvirs were elected, but only after considerable violence during which Domitius Ahenobarbus was wounded. The elections for praetors and aediles were also accompanied by massive bribery and violence.

Violence at elections for 55

Proconsular commands for Pompey and Crassus

C. Trebonius, a tribune, was used to gain for Pompey and Crassus valuable proconsular commands. Crassus was awarded the province of Syria, which he hoped would give him the opportunity to invade Parthia and win military glory, although this was not mentioned in his appointment. Pompey was granted the two Spains, but was permitted to stay in the vicinity of Rome and govern his provinces by proxy, through his legates. His command of the corn supply was a convenient excuse for remaining near Rome, but in fact he was able to keep an eye on the situation in the city. Both these proconsular commands were for a period of five years and entitled Pompey and Crassus to make war and peace without prior reference to the senate and the people. Crassus did not wait until the end of his consulship before going off to his province of Syria.

Caesar's command in Gaul extended

Once the two men had gained what they wanted, they secured the passage of a law extending Caesar's command in Gaul for a further five years — until the end of 50 or the beginning of the following year.

It was during his term of office that Pompey dedicated the first permanent stone theatre in Rome in the Campus Martius, where he gave lavish but brutal games. Caesar also outlined plans in 55 for his own impressive building program, which included an extension to the Forum. This became the Julian Forum, eventually dedicated in 46 (see chapter 20).

The breakdown of the triumvirate

Pompey's position of strength in 54

Pompey in Italy, with the imperium associated with his corn commission and his control over the Spanish provinces, was in a stronger position than either Crassus or Caesar, both of whom were subjected during 54 to a number of attacks.

Death of Julia

In the second half of 54 Julia, Pompey's wife (Caesar's daughter), died in childbirth and although this did not immediately affect the coalition, it offered an opportunity for Pompey to link himself with another powerful senatorial family if he wished to draw away from Caesar.

Growing anarchy

More significant than Julia's death for the future of the triumvirate was the critical situation in Rome. Growing anarchy in 54 delayed the elections for the following year, and Plutarch indicates that there was a 'collapse of good government in Rome'.[23] All the candidates for 53 were awaiting prosecution for corruption, and it seemed unlikely that the elections would be held before the end of the year. In fact there were no consuls for the first half of 53; there were even rumours of a possible dictatorship. A political crisis seemed to be developing, and Pompey was in a good position to take advantage of any situation which might call for the appointment of someone with exceptional powers.

Death of Crassus

In the middle of 53 news reached Rome of the defeat of the Roman army by the Parthians and the death of Crassus at Carrhae. The political repercussions were great now 'that fortune had, as it were, removed from the ring the third competitor . . .'.[24] Crassus' death did not mean that civil war between Pompey and Caesar was now inevitable, as Plutarch suggests, but the danger of a serious split was more likely.

Caesar's marriage offers to Pompey refused

The situation worried Caesar, and he hoped to bind Pompey to him by another marriage alliance. He offered his great-niece Octavia to Pompey, and even suggested divorcing his own wife in order to marry Pompey's daughter. Pompey refused the offer, possibly to keep his options open so that later he could move towards the optimates; in fact, in 52 he married Cornelia, the daughter of Q. Caecilius Metellus Pius Scipio Nasica. Although he had shifted his position slightly towards the optimates, he had no wish to break with Caesar at this point, preferring to maintain a position between the two.

Caesar's campaigns in Gaul 58–50

In 58 Caesar took command of Cisalpine Gaul and Illyricum with three legions for a period of five years. To this command was later added Transalpine Gaul (Gallia Narbonensis) with an additional legion. This command imparted several advantages.

In Cisalpine Gaul:

- The Po valley was a good recruiting ground for troops.
- It would be a future source of strength, since Caesar had won clients in 65 there by proposing full Roman citizenship.

Gaul at the time of Caesar's conquest

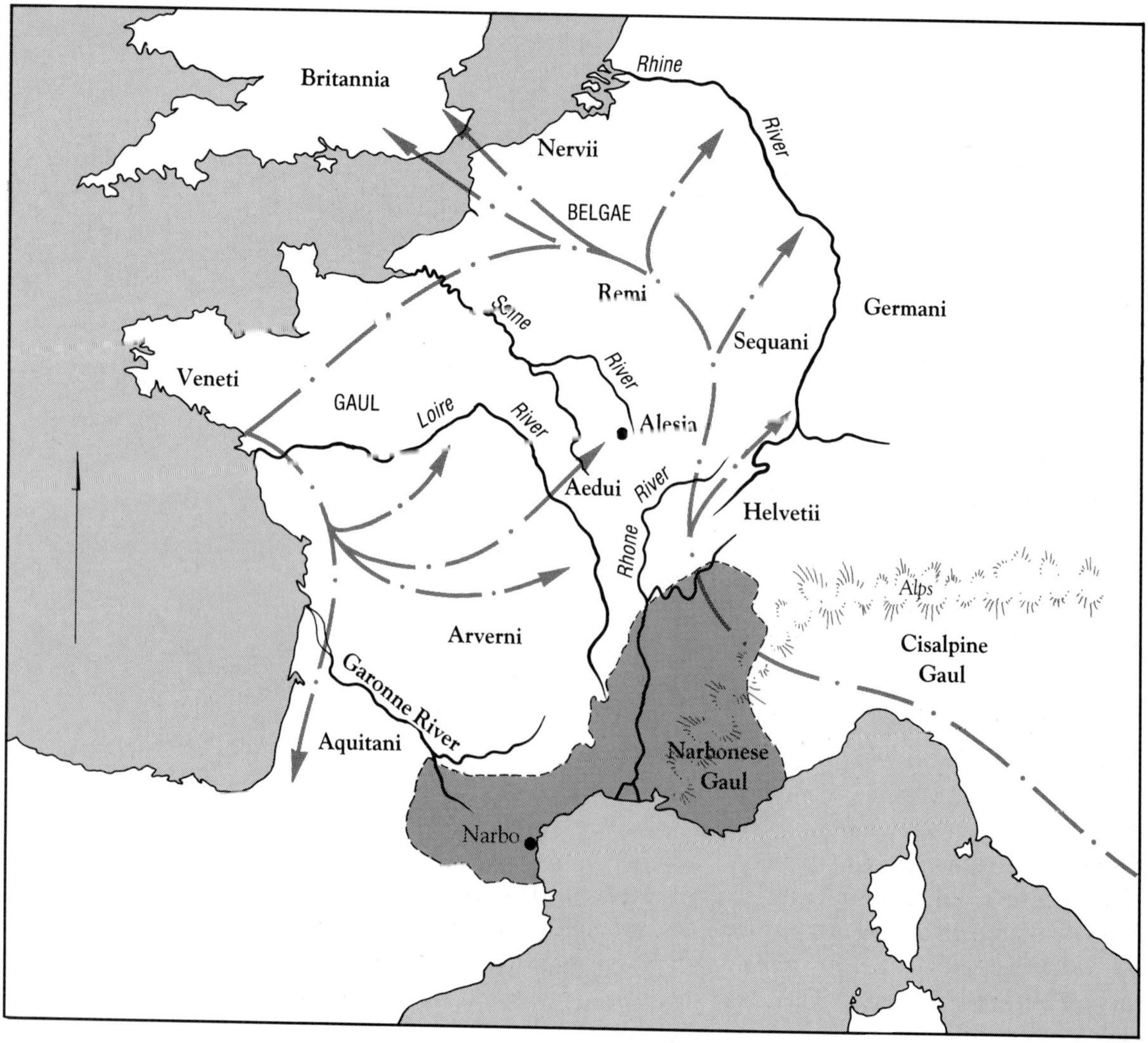

- Its proximity to Rome would allow Caesar keep an eye on what was going on in the capital.

In Transalpine Gaul (Narbonese Gaul):

- Disturbances among the Gauls outside the Roman province would give Caesar opportunities to win military glory for himself and to extend Rome's influence.
- There was the possibility of acquiring great wealth, which Caesar needed for his future career.

The length of the command (five years, later extended for a further five) assured him of immunity for a long time from attempts to prosecute him for the unconstitutional acts committed during his consulship.

The map at left illustrates the course of Caesar's campaigns in Gaul.

58–56

The defeat of the Helvetii and Suebi

The Helvetii from northern Switzerland were seeking new homes in Gaul; 400 000 intended migrating westwards by passing through the northern corner of the Roman province. When Caesar prevented this they entered at the Jura Mountains, plundering the countryside of the Aedui and Sequani. The Aedui were allies of Rome, even though their territory was outside the Roman province. Caesar provoked a war, followed and defeated the Helvetii at Bibracte, and forced them to return to their homeland.

The Suebi, Germans from across the Rhine, had been used by the Sequani in a conflict with the Aedui but had refused to leave, and in 59 the Romans had recognised the Suebi chieftain, Ariovistus, as a Friend of the Roman People. However, he had begun to expand at the expense of the Aedui and the Sequani. When negotiations between Caesar and Ariovistus broke down, Caesar saw another opportunity for a spectacular campaign. He drove the Germans beyond the Rhine.

Caesar's return to Gaul

Caesar returned to Cisalpine Gaul for the winter in order to administer his province, but left troops stationed in the area of the Sequani as he believed they could be a future problem. He was also concerned that if he withdrew his troops to Narbonese Gaul, the Germans might cross the Rhine again.

Sujugation of the Belgae

The Belgian Gauls comprised a large group of tribes north of the Seine and the Marne rivers. An armed force was preparing an attempt to expel the Romans. Caesar took the offensive on the pretext of protecting the southernmost Belgian tribe, the Remi, who had submitted to the Romans earlier. Most of the tribes gave way as he approached, and after defeating the strongest tribe, the Nervii, the peoples of Normandy and Brittany yielded to Caesar's legates.

Dissension in the triumvirate

Caesar needed more time to complete his work in Gaul, but events in Rome were causing a rift between Pompey and Crassus and the optimates were attempting to cause a break between Caesar and Pompey. In 56 the three triumvirs met just inside Cisalpine Gaul at Luca (see p. 345) to renew their coalition, and in the following year Caesar's command in Gaul was extended for a further five years.

Revolt of the Veneti

In the winter of 56 the Veneti revolted and attacked the Roman garrisons. Caesar built a fleet at the mouth of the Loire River and defeated the rebellious Veneti. In 56 the Aquitani were defeated by Publius Crassus (the son of Caesar's political partner).

Results and importance of the period 58–56

- Caesar's reputation was enhanced.
- The Romans were now practically the masters of all Gaul and Caesar had become the champion and protector of the Gallic people.

A statuette of a dying Gaul

A Roman legionary plundering a Gallic village

- It appears that Caesar now intended either to annex the whole area or to set up a group of client states, as Pompey had done in the east.
- The large amount of booty sent back to Rome created great excitement.
- Although Pompey proposed a long thanksgiving to Caesar, it is likely that he may have felt some jealousy about his successes.

55–54

Caesar crosses the Rhine

In the winter of 55 two German tribes crossed the Rhine into Gaul. Caesar arrested the German peace envoys and exterminated the two tribes, including the women and children. He then carried out a spectacular bridging of the Rhine River. His engineers built a bridge 280 metres long by 12 metres wide, crossed the river in order to indicate the strength and power of Rome, then returned and destroyed the bridge.

Invasion of Britain

The lively trade between Britain and Gaul may have given Caesar an exaggerated idea of Britain's potentialities—prospects for booty or tribute. In 55 he only carried out reconnaissance, but in 54 he crossed the channel again, defeated King Cassivellaunus (the commander-in-chief of the Britons) and crossed the Thames River, taking the capital of the king. Caesar received the submission of the tribes in the southeast and may have been given hostages and promises of tribute; he then returned to Gaul.

Results and importance of the period 55–54

- Caesar's harsh treatment of the Germans compared with his leniency towards the Gauls was denounced in the senate by Cato, but nothing came of this as Caesar could argue that it was necessary to make an example of the invaders. In fact, the Germans did not disturb Gaul again.
- His spectacular excursion into unexplored territory excited the Romans and enhanced his reputation.
- His crossing to Britain was only an exploit and had no permanent results, but it created great interest in Rome and opened the way for future trade. It was a hundred years before Britain became Roman.

54–51

Eburones' attack

Caesar suffered a major setback when an independent Belgic tribe, the Eburones, organised a surprise attack on the Roman garrison at Aduatucas, annihilating one and a half legions. Caesar's rapid action crushed this revolt, but discontent among the Gauls spread.

Problems in Rome

Caesar was also concerned with events in Rome, since it appeared that Pompey was being placed in a situation where he had to make a choice between the optimates and Caesar.

Events in Rome may have encouraged the discontented Gauls to get rid of the Romans, since it was obvious that the Romans were intent on permanent annexation of Gaul.

Vercingetorix of the Arverni

A serious uprising occurred in 52 under the leadership of a young noble of the Arverni tribe, Vercingetorix. He had fought with Caesar as a cavalry officer, but now used his organising talents to unite the Gauls. The revolt spread and Caesar was forced to divide his forces. The situation became extremely critical for Caesar, who used a cavalry of Germans from across the Rhine. Even the Aedui (long-time allies of Rome) joined the revolt, and at one point the capital of the Narbonese province was threatened.

After a series of Roman victories, Vercingetorex and his troops were besieged in a fortress on the plateau of Alesia and were eventually starved into submission.

The Gauls were by no means pacified, and Caesar spent 51–50 subduing remnants of the rebels and organising the government of the province.

Coin showing the head of the Gallic chief, Vercingetorix

In his Gallic commentaries, Caesar describes Vercingetorix thus:

'Vercingetorix, a very powerful young Arvernian, whose father, Celtillus, had held suzerainty over all Gaul . . . had no difficulty in exciting their [his father's retainers] passions, and the news of what was afoot soon brought others out in arms . . . He was proclaimed king by his adherents, and sent embassies in every direction adjuring the tribes to keep faith . . . Himself a man of boundless energy, he terrorised waiverers with the rigours of an Iron discipline. Serious cases of disaffection were punished by torture and death at the stake, or even for a minor fault he would cut off a man's ears or gouge out one of his eyes and send him home to serve as a warning to others of the severe chastisement meted out to offenders.' (*Conquest of Gaul*, VII: 4)

A description of the siege works at Alesia, where Vercingetorix was blockaded.

'He dug a trench twenty feet wide, which, having perpendicular sides, was as broad at the bottom as at the top. The other works were kept some six hundred and fifty yards behind this trench, to protect them from surprise attacks . . . At this distance, therefore, Caesar dug two trenches of equal depth, each fifteen feet wide, and filled the inner one with water diverted from the streams. Behind the trenches a palisaded rampart twelve feet high was erected, strengthened by a battlemented breastwork, with large forked branches projecting where it joined the rampart . . . Towers were placed at intervals of a hundred and thirty yards along the entire circuit of fortifications . . . tree trunks or very stout boughs were cut and their tops stripped of bark and sharpened; they were then fixed in long trenches dug five feet deep, with their lower ends made fast to one another to prevent their being pulled up and the branches projecting. There were five rows in each trench, touching one another and interlaced and anyone who went among them was likely to impale himself on the sharp points . . . In front of them, arranged in diagonal rows forming quincunxes, were pits three feet deep, tapering gradually towards the bottom, in which were embedded smooth logs as thick as a man's thigh with the ends sharpened and charred, and projecting only three inches above the ground. To keep the logs firmly in position, earth was thrown into the pits and trodden down to a depth of one foot, the rest of the cavity being filled with twigs and brushwood to hide the trap. These were planted in groups, each containing eight rows three feet apart . . . In front of these again were blocks of wood a foot long with iron hooks fixed in them . . . these were right sunk into the ground and strewn thickly everywhere.

'When these defences were completed, Caesar constructed a similar line of fortications facing outwards instead of inwards.'
(*Conquest of Gaul*, VII: 72–4)

A model of Caesar's siege works at Alesia

Results and importance of the period 54–51

- The Gallic War, which had lasted for more than eight years, was over: in thirty pitched battles Caesar is believed to have captured a million men, killed more than a million (1 192 000) and captured more than 800 towns. The enormous amount of plunder taken during eight years left the Gauls financially exhausted.
- Caesar now adopted a conciliatory policy, after years of what he considered necessary brutality. He realised that he might need a supportive Gaul in any future conflict with the optimates.
- The conquered territory was called Gallia Comata (Long-Haired Gaul) and was organised with the minimum of supervision from the Roman governor of Narbonese Gaul. The tribes retained their own organisation and collected the moderate tribute imposed.

The importance of the conquest of Gaul		
For Caesar	*For the Romans*	*For the Gauls*
He built up a great military reputation to equal that of Pompey and had the support of a devoted army. It provided him with the wealth needed to buy political supporters in Rome. He had the support of Gaul during the subsequent civil war.	It increased Rome's strength by adding to it an area twice the size of Italy, with a greater population than Spain and offering vast resources.	It promised future peace and protection from the Germans. It opened the land of the Gauls to Roman civilisation.

The Roman successes in Gaul were partly due to
1 the lack of unity, discipline and determination among the Gauls;
2 the German cavalry employed by Caesar during the great revolt led by Vercingetorix;
3 Caesar's genius in military tactics and strategy, swift action and superb leadership; and
4 the leniency shown by Caesar in his organisation of Gaul.

Events leading to civil war between Pompey and Caesar, 52–49

Anarchy in Rome: Clodius and Milo

The lawlessness of 53 (bribery and violence), which had again prevented the election of consuls, intensified in the following year and it was obvious to Pompey that he could exploit the situation for his own benefit.

Clodius and Milo clash — death of Clodius

Annius Milo, who had been useful to Pompey in the past, was one of the candidates for the consulship; Clodius was standing for the praetorship. The long-standing enmity between these two men erupted in a clash between them (and their supporters) on the Appian Way in January 52. Clodius was wounded and carried to a tavern where, on the orders of Milo, he was killed. His body was taken to Rome and placed in the Curia (Senate House) to be cremated, but the blaze of the funeral pyre burnt out of control and the Senate House was destroyed. Clodius' wife stirred up the mob, and the houses of Milo and the interrex, Lepidus, were raided. In this critical situation the senate issued the senatus consultum ultimum, giving Pompey the authority to raise troops and restore order since he was the only one with imperium, there being no consuls.

Optimates propose Pompey as sole consul

For another month a series of *interreges* failed to hold any elections, and demands increased for Pompey to be appointed as dictator to restore order. To prevent this happening, the optimates Calpurnius Bibulus and Cato proposed a compromise whereby Pompey was to be appointed as consul without a colleague. The example of Sulla was too fresh in their memories even to contemplate a dictatorship, whereas a sole consul would still be subject to certain restrictions, such as the tribunician veto. It was also expected that once Pompey had dealt with the emergency he would arrange for the election of a colleague, making the return to normal government easier.

Pompey's sole-consulship, 52

Exceptional nature of command

This sole-consulship was another in the series of extraordinary positions held by Pompey during his career. Despite the fact that a ten-year interval was normally required between consulships, it was only three years since his previous one. The most exceptional feature of this appointment, however, was that it was proposed by the conservatives and yet was a most unconstitutional position.

Pompey's legislation in 52

Once installed in this irregular office, Pompey proceeded to pass three pieces of legislation, two of which were important for his future relations with Caesar:

- a law against public violence
- a law stipulating a five-year interval between urban magistracies and provincial commands
- a law demanding that candidates must appear in person at elections

It was under the first of these, designed to control public violence, that Milo was prosecuted. Milo's trial caused considerable disturbances in Rome, and Pompey was forced to bring troops into the Forum to maintain order. It has also been suggested that Pompey may now have seen Milo as a potential rival and wanted his conviction, and that the troops in the Forum were to make sure of this. Despite Cicero's defence, Milo was condemned for Clodius' death and sent into exile.

The other two laws were to have an effect on Caesar's position although they were not deliberately devised by Pompey to undermine him.

Caesar's plans for the future

Caesar hoped to extend his command in Gaul until 49, when he could stand in absentia for the consulship of the following year. In this way he would be able to step from a proconsulship into a consulship, and the following year into another proconsular command. While he had the imperium associated with these positions he would be immune from prosecution for the illegal acts he had committed in 59 during his first consulship.

Effect of Pompey's laws on Caesar

The second of Pompey's laws was intended to 'make urban office less tempting as a passport to extortion abroad',[25] but it was to affect Caesar. Under the previous system, a provincial command was allocated before the election of the consuls, who would not take up their commands until after their year in office. This meant that there could be eighteen months' notice given to a governor concerning his replacement. Under Pompey's new law, a successor could be nominated straightaway and set out for his new province immediately. This meant that Caesar could be replaced immediately his command came to an end, and between his proconsulship and his election to a second consulship there would be an interval during which he could be prosecuted. Also, the new law could adversely affect Caesar after his consulship (if elected) of 48. He would have hoped to go straight into another proconsular command, avoiding prosecution once again, but under the new system there was to be a five-year interval between consulship and proconsulship.

The third law made Caesar very suspicious of Pompey's motives. Caesar's plans to avoid prosecution also depended on being able to stand for the consulship in absentia, while still in Gaul. In 52 a bill had been sponsored by all ten tribunes granting him this right, but Pompey now decreed that all candidates must appear in person at the elections. Caesar's supporters pointed out the inconsistency of this with the law of the ten tribunes, and Pompey added a clause exempting Caesar.

Pompey took a colleague for remainder of year

For the last five months of the year Pompey took Metellus Scipio, his new father-in-law, as his colleague. He also put himself in a strong position by having his command over the two Spains extended for a further five years, but he did nothing more for Caesar.

Pompey's position between Caesar and optimates

In 52 Pompey maintained a position somewhere between Caesar and the optimates. Caesar had been made aware that his political survival depended on Pompey's support and the senate was aware that it needed Pompey to preserve law and order. This was a position of power which Pompey enjoyed, but it was not to last. Caesar's enemies would not be deterred from their efforts to have him recalled as soon as possible, which would upset the balance and force Pompey to commit himself openly to one side or the other.

The aims of Pompey, Caesar and the optimates in 51

The chart presents the conflicting interests which gave rise to political manoeuvres against Caesar.

Optimates	*Pompey*	*Caesar*
The optimates wanted Caesar to return early from his command in Gaul so that they could prosecute him for illegal legislation passed in 59 during his consulship.	Pompey wanted to keep the balance between Caesar and the optimates. He wanted to make sure that Caesar did not become his equal.	Caesar wanted his command in Gaul extended until he could stand (in absentia) for the consulship of 48; he would then be able to leave Rome again in 47 as a proconsul, thus avoiding prosecution.

Political manoeuvres by the optimates and Pompey

1 M. Marcellus (cos. 51) agitated early in 51 to remove Caesar from his command in Gaul. This was illegal, since it would have disregarded the law that Pompey and Crassus passed on Caesar's behalf in 55. Pompey objected to Marcellus' proposal.
2 Marcellus humiliated Caesar by flogging some Transpadane Gauls whom Caesar had treated as citizens.
3 Pompey indicated that it would be legitimate to discuss Caesar's recall after 1 March 50.
4 Curio, a young noble, became tribune for 50. He struck a bargain with Caesar: to work on his behalf in return for Caesar's paying off his enormous debts. He vetoed any discussion of Caesar's replacement throughout 50, but suggested that both Pompey and Caesar give up their extraordinary commands.
5 Pompey would not accept this proposal as he had no intention of giving up his Spanish command. He made a counter-proposal that Caesar should leave his province on 13 November.
6 Curio vetoed this as Caesar was no longer prepared to accept Pompey's superiority. He once again proposed that both men give up their commands in order to preserve the balance of power in the state and reduce the tension.
7 The threat of a war in Syria led the senate to decree that Caesar and Pompey sacrifice a legion each to be sent to the east. Pompey asked

for the return of the legion he had previously lent Caesar. Caesar therefore was weakened by the loss of two legions, while Pompey lost none. When the emergency in the east failed to eventuate the legions were kept in Italy, which strengthened Pompey's position.

8 In December Curio again urged that a vote be taken on the proposal that both men resign their commands. The vote in the senate resulted in 370 for Curio's proposal and twenty-two against. However, C. Marcellus (cos. 50) dismissed the senate and spread rumours that Caesar was marching on Rome. He placed a sword in Pompey's hands and demanded that he undertake the defence of the state as well as levy troops. Pompey agreed, and by so doing openly committed himself to the optimates.

9 Curio left to join Caesar at the end of 50, but Marcus Antonius (Antony) and Cassius, tribunes for 49, continued to work on Caesar's behalf. Antony attempted to read a letter from Caesar which again suggested that the commanders should give up their powers simultaneously. He pointed out that it was unreasonable to expect him to make concessions while Pompey retained his power, and he threatened civil war if Pompey did not comply.

10 Although the moderates in the senate were angered at the tone of the letter, they still wanted peace. However, Lentulus, the consul for 49, declared that he would override the senate if they tried to adopt a policy of conciliation with Caesar.

11 Scipio Metellus proposed a motion that Caesar should dismiss his army by a certain date or be declared an enemy of the state.

12 The tribunes Antony and Cassius vetoed this, and Cicero made further attempts at conciliation.

13 Cato, Lentulus and Scipio, the hard-line reactionaries, refused any conciliatory offers and the SCU was passed. The tribunes were warned that if they interfered their safety could not be guaranteed.

14 The tribunes fled to Caesar.

15 Pompey confidently assumed command of the Roman forces in Italy.

16 Caesar crossed the frontier at the River Rubicon, and by so doing committed Rome to civil war.

A coin portrait of Pompey, struck by his son after his father's death

The extraordinary nature of Pompey's career

Although Pompey lived for approximately another year (his part in the civil war and his death in Egypt in 48 are discussed on pp. 378–9), it is appropriate to evaluate his outstanding career at this point. The following charts, source material exercises and point summaries analyse the years from 83 to 49, and a timeline sets the course of his career beside the careers of Crassus, Cicero and Caesar.

Exercise

Cn. Pompeius Cn. f. Sex. m. Magnus (Pompey the Great) (born 106 BC)

Propr. 83–79 (*Italy* 83–82, *Sicily* 82–80, *Africa* 80–79), *Propr.* vs Lepidus 77, *Procos.* Nearer Spain vs Sertorius 77–71 Cos. 70 *Procos* with imperius procons. infinitum vs *pirates* 67–, vs *Mithridates* 66–61, *XX vir* (and V vir) land commission 59–, *Curator annonae* with cons. imperium 57–52, *Cos. II* 55, *Procos.* Spain 54–49, *Cos. III* 52, *Procos.* vs Caesar 49, probably with imperium maius 48, *Augur* before 61–48.[26]

1 At what ages did Pompey hold the various offices between 83 and 70?
2 Did the offices he held follow the accepted pattern? Explain.
3 There were four periods in his career during which he held a series of great commands. Give the dates for these.
4 What positions did he hold concurrently (at the same time) in 55, 54 and 52?
5 List the reasons why each step in Pompey's career departed from the accepted pattern.
6 Compare Pompey's early career with that of Caesar (shown below). What was notable about Caesar's career until 59?

C. Iulius C. f. C. n. Caesar (Julius Caesar) (born 100 BC)

Leg. Envoy 81, *Leg. Lieut.* 73–72, *Tr. Mil.* 71, *Q* 69–68, *Aed. Cur.* 65, *Iud. Quaest.* 64, II *vir perduell.* 63, *Pr.* 62, Promag. (? *Procos.*) Farther Spain 61–60, *Cos.* 59, *Procos.* Cisalpine Gaul, Transalpine Gaul and Illyrium 58–49, Dict. I 49, Cos. II 48, Dict. II 48–47, Cos. III 46, Dict. III 46–45, Cos. IV 45, Dict. IV 45–44, Cos. V 44, Dict. perpet 44. *Pont.* 73–44, *Pont.* Max. 63–44, *Augur* ca. 47–44 *Flamen. Dial.* (nominated, but not inaugurated) 87–82?[27]

A summary of the exceptional or extraordinary aspects of Pompey's military and political career

	Appointments/achievements	*Exceptional aspects*
83–78	At twenty-three raised troops to fight Sulla Given propraetorian commands against the Marians in Spain and Africa Hailed as imperator by Sulla Awarded a triumph by Sulla	Extreme youth, when three legions were raised on his own initiative Qualifying magistracy never held — illegal according to the constitution Too young for these appointments according to the cursus honorum Was not even a senator Sulla traditionally incorrect to hail him as imperator Award of two triumphs when not even a member of the senate
77–71	Granted propraetorian command by senate to assist Catulus against Lepidus Appointed by the senate to proconsular command against Sertorius in Spain Spartacus' final defeat accomplished; awarded his second triumph	

	Appointments/achievements	Exceptional aspects
70	Elected to first consulship with Crassus	Seven years too young for consulship — no qualifying subconsular offices held Use of intimidation (threats of force) to gain special dispensation from the senate to stand in absentia, and exemption from the age provision Refusal to take the usual provincia — did not go to a province after his year as consul
67–62	Voted by the people to a command for three years against pirates (lex Gabinia) Voted by people to a command against Mithridates	Voted *imperium infinitum* with sweeping powers over the whole Mediterranean and provinces for 50 miles inland, with unlimited funds, men and ships, and twenty-four legates — super province Powers extended — given permission to make war or peace on his own initiative
57	By a consular bill, appointed Controller of the Corn Supply for five years	Imperium overlapped all others although not a military appointment; authorised to administer the Mediterranean with fifteen legates
55	Elected to second consulship with Crassus	Election achieved only by resorting to the procedure of appointing an interrex to conduct elections; imperium of Controller of the Grain Supply retained
54	Granted proconsular command of Spain for five years	Province of Spain governed through legates — stayed in Rome
52	Appointed by the senate as sole consul — no colleague	Appointment against all principles of republican government, i.e. collegiality (having a colleague) Position conterred by previous opponents — interrex procedure used again owing to violence; further break with tradition as specifically named by senate the as the person to be appointed — usually choice was from a list of names Technically illegal — only three years since last consulship instead of the required ten; also, proconsular imperium for Spain still held so appointment made in absentia — could not cross the pomerium; command of Spain renewed for a further five years at this point
49	Appointed to command against Caesar	Proconsular imperium with control over all military forces in Italy

Pompey's changing relationship with the senate and the optimates

It was Pompey's ambition to reach a position of pre-eminence within the state and so he took the opportunities which would advance his career regardless of whether it meant siding with the optimates or the populares. The optimates feared and distrusted him, but were forced to use him at the beginning and at the end of his career. They never totally accepted him, even when their survival depended on it.

Pompey's frequent change of sides

1 Pompey was not born into the privileged class and his father, Gnaeus Pompeius Strabo, left a bad reputation behind him. When Pompey threw in his lot with Sulla against the Marians he appeared to be supporting the optimates, but they could not forget that he was not really one of them.

Supported Sulla

2 He showed a lack of judgment when he supported Lepidus for the consulship of 78 while Sulla was still alive. Lepidus was a Marian, advocating a policy hostile to Sulla's constitution.

Supported popularis Lepidus

3 When Lepidus was declared a public enemy in 77 Pompey gave his support to the optimates, who rashly granted him propraetorian imperium to fight against Lepidus. The senate was also reluctantly forced to give in to Pompey's suggestion to help Metellus in Spain against Sertorius. They nervously granted him proconsular imperium, although he was ineligible, because there were no other suitable or willing generals to take on the task. The senate's distrust of him was increased since he had used the threat of force (by not disbanding his army) to gain the command against Sertorius.

Gave support to optimates in 77 to gain further commands

4 After his victory in Spain, he requested that the senate give him permission to bring his army into Italy and help Crassus against the slave leader, Spartacus. The people intervened in this and demanded that he be made Crassus' colleague. When he claimed he had ended the war against Spartacus, the senate saw through this propaganda and realised his preoccupation with his own advancement. However, they still granted him a triumph.

The people made him Crassus' colleague

5 By 71 the senate distrusted him even more, but because of his threat of force he was elected to an illegal consulship with Crassus for 70. He was granted a special dispensation from the lex Villia Annalis, since the senate feared another Sullan revolution.

Senate waived lex Annalis for Pompey in 71

6 The joint consulship of Pompey and Crassus in 70 was a great blow to the optimates, since the two men proceeded to further destroy the Sullan constitution. They restored the tribunes' powers, purged the senate of its extremists and took away the monopoly of the law courts

Consulship in 70 undermined optimates' position

from the senate. By these measures they secured the support of the equites and the people.

Followed Marius' example to gain commands

7 Pompey now began to follow Marius' example of looking for tribunician support for further military commands. The optimates objected to the extraordinary commands proposed by the tribunes Gabinius and Manilius in 67 and 66, which were obviously designed with Pompey in mind. They particularly opposed the transfer of the command against Mithridates from their own representative, Lucullus, to Pompey. Their objections were overruled by the people and the equites, and Pompey was given powers unprecedented in Roman history.

Granted his extraordinary commands by people

8 His spectacular successes in the east, both militarily and in organising a permanent settlement of the region, made him a popular hero and increased the numbers of his clients (his veterans and the eastern provincials). The optimates' hostility and fear increased as the time for his return from the east drew nearer; they were apprehensive as to how he would use his great power and popularity.

Rejected by optimates on return from the east

9 Pompey acted constitutionally on his return and disbanded his army, assuming that his predominance in the state would carry all before him. The optimates, however, relieved of immediate fear of him, continued to rebuff him politically for the next two years. This made it impossible for him to honour his responsibility to his veterans and the people of the eastern provinces.

Joined populares, Caesar and Crassus, in 60

10 By 60 he was alienated from the optimates and was forced to align himself with Caesar and Crassus in the secret agreement referred to as the First Triumvirate. When the existence of this alliance became known it created a great deal of fear and anger among the optimates, since these three men between them had power, wealth, status, and support from the people and the equites. However, Pompey became increasingly embarrassed by the methods used by Caesar to secure the passage of a land bill, and felt guilty that the group had forced Cicero into exile. When Clodius commenced a humiliating series of attacks on Pompey, he began to regret his part in the triumvirate.

Attempt at reconciliation with optimates in 58–57

11 After Caesar's departure for Gaul, Pompey made a shrewd political move by supporting the recall of Cicero from exile—perhaps in the hope that he would be reconciled with the optimates. In gratitude, Cicero proposed that Pompey be put in charge of the Roman grain supply, which involved proconsular imperium for five years.

Renewed alliance with Crassus and Caesar in 56

12 By 56 Pompey's position was somewhere between Caesar and the optimates; this suited him, because he could take the best of both sides. As usual, he was still fully occupied with his own advancement. He was not yet ready to break with Caesar, and met with him at Luca to renew the triumvirate and get what he wanted—another consulship, followed by a further military command.

13 Two events now changed the direction of his career: the death of his wife (Julia, Caesar's daughter) and of Crassus at Carrhae in the east. Caesar could do no more for Pompey, so he refused to renew the marriage alliance and chose rather to marry into the Scipio family. Pompey was moving towards the optimates, although they still did not really trust him.

Breakdown of alliance — moved towards optimates

14 In the next few years gang warfare raged in Rome and political anarchy forced the optimates to rely on Pompey to restore order. The senate passed a bill, supported by Cato, making Pompey sole consul (52). His greatest political aim had been fulfilled: the radical republicans had been forced to submit themselves to his care. Pompey used this third consulship to put himself in a very strong position in regard to Caesar.

Appointed sole consul by optimates in 52

15 The optimates began a political struggle with Caesar while he was still in Gaul. Pompey's position was ambiguous at this stage, as he had not yet openly committed himself to the optimates. As Caesar was manoeuvred into a more and more difficult situation by the small core of hard-liners among the optimates, Pompey made his decision to side with them. They had asked him to protect the state against Caesar and he led the republican forces in the civil war. Had Caesar been defeated and Pompey not lost his life, it is more than likely that the optimates would have dropped Pompey once the war was over.

Led senatorial forces against Caesar 49

An evaluation of Pompey

Pompey was ambitious, but he did not wish to rule Rome as a dictator. His aim at all times was to be the man to whom the senate and the Roman people turned every time there was a military or administrative crisis. He wanted to be the man of the hour, the republic's hero, and in between these crises he expected to be given the highest possible respect (particularly from the optimates), to which he believed his achievements entitled him.

Desire to be needed by people and optimates

All Roman nobiles desired pre-eminence, but the 'trouble with Pompeius [was that] he didn't want anyone to be his equal in dignity'.[28] These words by Caesar are repeated by Lucan in his poem *Pharsalia* when he compares Pompey with Caesar—Pompey could tolerate no equal in power and esteem and Caesar no superior. According to Velleius Paterculus,

Would tolerate no equal

> When Pompey was in civilian life he behaved very moderately except when he feared he might be facing a peer and he was free of all vices unless you counted the greatest one that in a free state . . . he should be indignant that anyone should be seen to be an equal to him in dignity.[29]

Pompey wanted glory rather than power.

Unusual career

'His pursuit of glory, as they say, always took an unusual course',[30] seeking to dramatise himself to the public. His political career began at the top and at far below the required age, the methods of his appointments were exceptional, the usual relationship between magistracies and provincial commands did not exist until late in his career, and he held almost continuous imperium (twelve promagistracies, as compared with Caesar's two).

Career marked by moderation

His desire for power was tempered by an innate moderation. He wanted his appointments to appear constitutional—to be granted legally by the senate and/or the people—but he did not mind how far the constitution was stretched for him; he received twelve grants of imperium of which only one followed the normal constitutional pattern. In other words, he

> was willing to violate the spirit of the constitution if he could observe the letter of it and was ready to profit by illegality if someone else would take the responsibility.[31]

An opportunist

Pompey was an opportunist. He deliberately avoided binding commitments and preferred to keep his options open. In the course of his career he changed sides eleven times. (whereas Caesar was an unbending popularis) and married five times. It was this aspect of Pompey that Cicero failed to understand; he constantly questioned Pompey's credibility and was often unable to understand what he was up to. Cicero tried to pin Pompey down after the events of 63, but Pompey wanted to keep his options open.

Exploited violence for his own benefit

Pompey always benefited from violence. He came to the fore during the civil war between Marius and Sulla, he used the street violence of the fifties (between the gangs of Clodius and Milo) for his own benefit (sole consulship, 52), and he ended his career in command of the republican forces opposing Caesar in a civil war.

Threatened the use of force

He never seized power by force, but often played on the fear of the senate and the people that he could and might use force to gain what he wanted. On defeating the Marians in Africa, in order to gain a triumph he directly disobeyed Sulla's instructions in 81 to discharge five of his six legions; when ordered by the consul Catulus to disband his army after defeating Lepidus, he delayed, suggesting that he should be sent to Spain to help Metellus against Sertorius; in 71, when he wished to stand for the consulship for 70 with Crassus, he again delayed disbanding his army on the excuse that he was awaiting a triumph. In each of these cases he gained what he wanted, showing that he had a certain amount of political cunning.

A competent soldier

Cicero believed that Pompey was a great soldier and a poor politician, and many modern viewpoints tend to agree with this. However, a closer look at his career reveals that this is too simple an evaluation. In most of his commands there was not much actual campaigning; he often simply completed what other commanders' hard work had achieved. There were only two occasions on which he was faced with a serious military opponent (Sertorius in Spain and Caesar in the civil war), and without Sertorius' murder and Mithridates' death he might not have been so successful in Spain and the east. Pompey was not a great soldier, but rather a good manager and a clever organiser of campaigns; he also had great diplomatic skill and took a liberal and humane attitude in all his post-campaign settlements.

A brilliant organiser

His military career appeared to be great since he always made sure that any military successes were of political benefit (his great proconsular appointments were also political appointments). His was a new type of political career, one in which he showed that it was possible to get the great military commands without holding the requisite magistracies, and then applying them to get the political appointments. His unorthodox political techniques were not appreciated by Cicero.

His career a paradox

His extraordinary career embodied everything that the oligarchy opposed and yet they were responsible for granting him many of his exceptional appointments. He was a catalyst in the breakdown of the republic, and yet his friendship was eagerly sought by the conservative Cicero and he died in 48 leading the republicans. His whole career was a paradox.

Cicero's views of Pompey

The following extracts from Cicero's correspondence and speeches (66–49) should be read closely; they will be referred to in the exercise that follows.

> *1 On the command of Gnaeus Pompeius (in support of the Manilian law)*, 66
> ... Gnaeus Pompeius is in the unique position of not only exceeding all his contemporaries in merit but even eclipsing every figure recorded from the past... The ideal general... should possess four qualities—military knowledge, talent, prestige and luck. In knowledge of military affairs Pompey has never been surpassed... The abilities of Gnaeus Pompeius are too vast for any words to do them justice... The talents a general needs are numerous... meticulous organisation, courage in danger, painstaking execution, prompt action, foresight in planning. In each and every one of those qualities Pompeius excels all other generals we have ever seen or heard of... such gifts need to be accompanied and supported by a variety of other notable talents... a general needs to possess complete integrity. He must be a man of moderation in all that he does. He has to be trustworthy; he has to be accessible, intelligent and civilised as well. Let me now review these characteristics

as they are found in Gnaeus Pompeius. Gentlemen, he has them all—in the highest possible degree.[32]

2 Letters from Cicero to Atticus, January and February 61

As to that friend [Pompey] . . . he professes the highest regard for me and makes a parade of warm affection, praising on the surface while below it, but not so far below that it's difficult to see, he's jealous. Awkward, tortuous, politically paltry, shabby, timid, disingenuous—but I shall go into more detail on another occasion.[33]

I have already given you a description of Pompey's first public speech—of no comfort to the poor or interest to the rascals; on the other hand the rich were not pleased and the honest men were not edified.[34]

3 Letters from Cicero to Atticus, May and July 59

What our friend Gnaeus is up to now I simply do not know . . . seeing that he's allowed himself to be pushed even to this length. Hitherto he has quibbled, taking the line that he approves of Caesar's legislation but that Caesar must take responsibility for his procedure.[35]

My beloved Pompey, to my great sorrow, has been the author of his own downfall.[36]

So there is our poor friend [Pompey], unused to disrepute, his whole career passed in a blaze of admiration and glory, now physically disfigured and broken in spirit, at his wits' end for what to do. He sees the precipice if he goes on and the stigma of a turncoat if he turns back . . . See now how soft-hearted I am. I could not keep back my tears when I saw him addressing a public meeting on the 25th about Bibulus' edicts . . . How humble and abject he was then, what a sorry figure he cut in his own eyes, to say nothing of his audience! What a sight![37]

4 Letter from Cicero to Atticus, late July 59

Clodius is hostile. Pompey continues to assure that he will do nothing against me. It would be dangerous for me to believe that, and I am getting ready to defend myself.[38]

5 Letter from Cicero to Lentulus Spinther, 54

But the leading man in Rome was Cn. Pompeius. The power and glory he enjoyed had been earned by state services of the highest importance and by the most signal military achievements. From early manhood I had rejoiced in his success, and as Praetor and Consul came forward to promote it. On his side, he had individually helped me with his influence and voice in the senate.[39]

6 Letter from Cicero to Atticus, February 49

Our friend Pompey's proceedings have throughout been destitute alike of wisdom and of courage, and I may add, contrary throughout to my advice and influence. I say nothing of ancient history—his building up and aggrandising and arming against the state, his backing the violent and unconstitutional passage of Caesar's laws, his addition of Transalpine Gaul to Caesar's command, his marriage to Caesar's daughter, his appearance as Augur at P. Clodius' adoption, his greater concern for my restoration than for the prevention of my banishment, his prolongation of Caesar's tenure, his consistent support during Caesar's absence, his pressure (even during his third consulship, after he had taken up the role of champion of the constitution) on the ten tribunes to propose their law enabling Caesar to stand 'in absentia', a privilege which he confirmed after a fashion by a law of his own, his opposition to Consul M. Marcellus when he tried to fix the Kalends of March as the term of Caesar's command in Gaul — to say nothing of all this, what could be more undignified or more disorderly than this withdrawal from the capital or rather this disgraceful flight in which we are now involved?[40]

Exercise

1 Explain briefly to what events Cicero is referring in the extracts 1,2,3,4 and 6.
2 Explain the great difference in Cicero's views of Pompey in 66 and in 49.
3 List all the qualities, both good and bad, that Cicero attributes to Pompey in these extracts.
4 By referring to the information provided in the previous chapters on Pompey's career, comment on the accuracy of Cicero's view of Pompey as (a) a general, (b) a politician.
5 From these extracts, provide evidence to show that Pompey was an opportunist.

Timeline: The four stages of the career of Pompey seen in relation to Crassus, Caesar and Cicero

Background		*Pompey*	*Crassus*
		• Born 106 • His father, Cn. Pompeius Strabo, cos. 89, was bitterly hated by his troops • Served with his father against Cinna • Went into hiding from Cinna and Carbo • After his father's death was tried for misappropriation of funds, but acquitted	• Born 115 • Father, cos. 97 • Took part in the Social War as a military tribune • Father committed suicide when followers of Marius and Cinna seized Rome • Inherited family fortune • Went into hiding until Sulla's return from the east
First phase, 83–70 Rapid rise to power and breakdown of Sullan constitution	83	Pompey recruits forces to help Sulla — 23 years old; defeats the Marians in the north	Joins with Sulla during Civil War; seeks revenge for father's and brother's deaths
	82	Military command against the remainder of the Marian troops in Sicily	Valuable assistance to Sulla at the Battle of the Colline Gate; during Sulla's proscriptions, buys up confiscated property and sells later at public auction, amassing an incredible fortune
	81		
	80	Military command against Marians Africa Celebrates a triumph, although not even a senator	Disappears from military affairs until 74 Begins to speculate in other men's careers
	79		
	78	Appointed by senate to the command against Lepidus	
	77	Appointed by senate to the command in Spain againt Sertorius, with proconsular imperium	
	76	In Spain	
	75	In Spain; suffers a number of setbacks at hands of Sertorius	
	74		Praetor 74–?73
	73		Serious slave uprising led by Spartacus spreads throughout Italy; granted command by senate

Caesar	*Cicero*
• Born 100 • From an ancient patrician family undistinguished until Caesar's aunt married Marius • Grew up during Social War and violence associated with Marius' later career • Family were populares	• Born 106 • Had no aristocratic connections • A distinguished student; spent much of youth listening to speakers in law courts • At seventeen spent short time in army during Social War • Studied in Rome with Greek scholars, developing public speaking
In danger of losing life owing to Marian connections and marriage to Cinna's daughter Leaves for the east; on governor's staff in Asia and Cilicia An envoy to King Nicomedes of Bithynia Returns to Rome Goes to Rhodes to study Co-opted to the college of priests	First famous case: defence of Roscius, which displeases Sulla; wins the case but leaves Rome to study in Asia and Rhodes Elected to the quaestorship; serves in Sicily, gaining a good reputation Enters senate and for next five years builds reputation as a lawyer

Background		*Pompey*	*Crassus*
	72	Sertorius murdered by one of his own lieutenants (Perpena); war brought to an end by Pompey	
	71	Returns from Spain and rounds up the remnants of the slave revolt led by Spartacus; celebrates his second triumph	Successfully brings slave uprising to an end; awarded an ovation
	70	Joint consulship with Crassus (Pompey ineligble according to Sullan constitution); full powers restored to tribunes	Joint consulship with Pompey — an uneasy co-operation
Second phase, 69–61 Period of extra-ordinary commands in the east	69	Does not take up provincial command after consulship; retires to private life to await worthwhile command	Does not take up proconsular command after consulship with Pompey
	68		Busy with financial interests
	67	Lex Gabinia; is given great powers by assembly to suppress widespread piracy in Mediterranean	Departure of Pompey to the east gives freedom to build up a personal power base
	66	Lex Manilia; appointed to eastern command against Mithridates — enormous powers	
	65		Supports bill to annex Egypt (failed); as censor, proposes citizenship for Cisalpine Gaul; becomes creditor to Caesar
	64	In the east	Possibly supports Catiline's early candidature for consulships; checked in attempt to set up a land commission to control distribution of public land
	63	Settlement of the east on death of Mithridates	Conspiracy of Catiline; severs ties with this former associate
	62	Returns to Italy; disbands army	
	61	Rebuffed by senate; attempts to get land for veterans and to get eastern arrangement ratified are blocked	Attempts to help a company of tax-gatherers rejected by senate

Caesar	*Cicero*
Supports the popular measures put forward by Pompey and Crassus to change Sulla's reforms	Famous prosecution of Verres, notorious governor of Sicily; beginning of climb up the political ladder
Becomes quaestor (69 or 68) and serves in Spain	Elected aedile; his continued appearance in courts helps to maintain a high profile
Supports Gabinius' proposal for Pompey's command against the pirates	
Supports Manilius' proposal for Pompey's command against Mithridates	Elected praetor; speaks in favour of Manilius' proposal to give Pompey command against Mithridates
Gains the aedileship, helped by Crassus' wealth; supports Crassus in various intrigues to gain power while Pompey absent; support Catiline's early attempts to gain consulship	Loses support of powerful nobles by speaking in favour of a law against electoral bribery Needs support for future — attempts to look after Pompey's interests while he is away in the east
Elected as chief priest (pontifex maximus); Crassus' money helps defeat two more senior candidates	Elected consul — new man; speaks against proposed setting up of land commission — against interests of Pompey; carries out the SCU against the Catilinarian conspirators, put to death without trial
Elected praetor; Bona Dea scandal involving Clodius, Caesar and Cicero	
Governorship of Further Spain; Crassus pays off creditors to enable him to go to his province	Aims at a *concordia ordinum* (harmony between senators and equites); seeks Pompey's approval

Background		*Pompey*	*Crassus*
Third phase, 60–53 The triumvirate (Pompey, Crassus and Caesar)	60	Secret agreement between Pompey, Crassus and Caesar to work for their own ends — referred to as the First Triumvirate	Backs Caesar in candidacy for the consulship — reconciliation with Pompey Formation of the triumvirate
	59	Uses veterans to help Caesar, as consul, get land for veterans and ratification of eastern settlement	Caesar satisfies demand re the tax-gatherers
	58	Clodius' tribunate — Pompey does not prevent Cicero's exile	
	57	Attacked by Clodius Urges Cicero's recall Granted a five-year imperium as Curator of the Grain Supply	May have been behind Clodius' attacks on Pompey
	56	Disunity between Pompey and Crassus — Caesar in Gaul Meets Caesar at Luca — renews coalition	Meets with Caesar and Pompey at Luca to renew coalition
	55	Second joint consulship with Crassus — agreement to extend Caesar's command in Gaul	Second joint consulship with Pompey Leaves Rome for province of Syria — Parthian war Military operations in Mesopotamia
	54	Awarded command of Spain for five years — remains in Italy raising troops Violence in Rome; death of Julia, his wife and Caesar's daughter	
	53	Anarchy in Rome; breakdown of triumvirate with Crassus' death	Killed at Carrhae (a trap) End of the triumvirate
Fourth phase, 52–48 Break with Caesar, and the civil war	52	Anarchy in Rome due to gang warfare; appointed sole consul to restore order	
	51	Strengthens position in relation to Caesar; optimates hope to recall Caesar from Gaul to prosecute him; not committed	
	50	Sides with optimates against Caesar	

Caesar	*Cicero*
Returns from Spain. Stands for consulship with individual backing of Pompey and Crassus; first triumvirate formed	Unaware of secret alliance between Pompey, Caesar and Crassus, believes he can influence Pompey
First consulship; honoured promises to Crassus and Pompey; illegal actions Gains Cisalpine and Transalpine Gaul for 58	Refuses to join coalition and speaks against Caesar's land law
Leaves for Gaul after using Clodius to get rid of Cato and Cicero	Decree of banishment against him (Clodius); exile in Greece
Campaigns in Gaul	Pompey supports a move for his recall Triumphant return to Rome; supports a proposal for special command for Pompey to deal with food crisis
Campaigns in Gaul; conference at Luca with Pompey and Crassus to renew triumvirate	Attempts to break up triumvirate
During consulship of Pompey and Crassus command in Gaul is extended for further five years; crosses to Britain	Makes strong attack on Caesar's illegal acts while consul
Second expedition to Britain; death of daughter, Julia	Retires from politics for a time, writing
Death of Crassus, end of the triumvirate	
Revolt of Vercingetorix in Gaul Optimates threaten to recall him early from Gaul	Governor of Cilicia — fair and honest governor
Capture of Vercingetorix	On friendly terms with Caesar, but in dilemma as Pompey and Caesar begin to fall out
Uses tribune Curio on his behalf in Rome to reach compromise	

Background		Pompey	Crassus
	49	Given command of republican forces when Caesar crosses Rubicon — civil war Crosses to Greece with troops	
	48	Defeated by Caesar at Pharsalus — flees to Egypt, where is murdered	
	44		

The last years of Caesar's career, 49–44

His motives for crossing the Rubicon

The four extracts discussed below come from Suetonius' *Julius Caesar*, 30, and express a number of possible motives for Caesar's crossing of the Rubicon.

> . . . He [Caesar] was resolved to invade Italy if force were used against the tribunes of the people who had vetoed the senate's decree disbanding his army by a given date. Force was, in effect, used, and the tribunes fled towards Cisalpine Gaul, which became Caesar's pretexts for launching the Civil War.

Caesar	*Cicero*
Uses Mark Antony as tribune in Rome Optimates outmanoeuvre him — declared an outlaw; crosses Rubicon — civil war	Disapproves of Pompey's flight from Italy
Defeats Pompey at Pharsalus; appointed dictator and consul; in Egypt, Syria Civil war continues against republican forces in Africa and Spain — Battles of Thapsus and Munda; end of civil war Reforms and reconstruction	Hesitates in his support; eventually joins Pompey and republicans in Greece Reconciled with Caesar after Pompey's death Spends most of his time writing
Dictator for life (*Dictator perpetuus*) Assassinated 15 March (Ides of March)	Not informed of conspiracy against Caesar; reconciled to his death — hoped for return to the old republic; Second Triumvirate (Antony, Octavian and Lepidus) Antony seeks revenge for his *Philippics* (speeches against Antony); proscribed by the triumvirs and killed

Protection of tribunes — a pretext

Comment: Suetonius' opinion is that Caesar used the protection of rights of the tribunes as a pretext for war. Plutarch says much the same thing. When the consul Lentulus drove the tribunes out of Rome in disgrace, it 'gave Caesar the best possible excuse for taking action and supplied him with excellent material for propaganda among his troops'.[41] He presented the tribunes Antony and Cassius to his troops in the slaves' disguise which they were allegedly forced to adopt in order to escape. Appian says that Caesar excited his soldiers by informing them that 'distinguished men like these, who had dared to say a word for them, had been thus driven out with ignominy'.[42] This was also aimed at whipping up popular opinion in Rome.

Some modern scholars maintain that the so-called flight of the tribunes was 'staged' by Caesar because he was being systematically outmanoeuvred by his political opponents. Cicero maintained that the tribunes were not driven out, and that it was a pretence.

Caesar's later threats to a number of tribunes (Plutarch, *Caesar*, 35, 61) indicate that he was not particularly concerned about their sacrosanctity, and tend to confirm Suetonius' view.

> Additional motives are suspected, however: Pompey's comment was that because Caesar had insufficient capital to carry out his grandiose schemes or give the people all that they had been encouraged to expect on his return, he chose to create an atmosphere of political confusion.

Caesar's financial difficulties

Comment: There may be some truth in Pompey's view. Caesar had been sending back to Rome vast quantities of gold and silver and other spoils of war, which had been used to build up support for himself while he was away. By 51–50 he was

> in a most lavish way making available to public figures in Rome the wealth which he had won in Gaul. He paid the enormous debts of the tribune Curio, and he gave the consul Paullus fifteen hundred talents with which he added to the beauty of the forum by building the famous Basilica . . .[43]

He was very generous with his troops. When Pompey asked for the return of the legion he had lent Caesar, he sent the soldiers back with a present of 250 drachmas each. Caesar has also doubled every soldier's pay (Suetonius, 26), and according to Suetonius he had promised every man a gratuity.

When he occupied Rome in 49 he broke into the Treasury, as he was in desperate need of funds. It is therefore possible that Caesar did not have the money needed to fulfil his promises to his men and to guarantee his own protection if he were forced to return to Rome as a private citizen. He knew that he would be prosecuted for the illegal acts of his consulship and could only avoid being condemned by the use of massive amounts of money in the right places. There seems to be some substance in what Pompey believed.

> Another view is that he dreaded having to account for the irregularities of his first consulship . . . [and] he said in these very words: 'They would have condemned me regardless of all my victories — me, Gaius Caesar — had I not appealed to my army for help'.

Fear of impeachment

Comment: This extract gives a clue to Caesar's real reason for crossing the Rubicon. He believed that his political enemies would have impeached him for breaking the law during his first consulship and that he would have been condemned, despite everything that he had achieved, and sent into exile. This was one of the normal hazards of Roman political life — it was not the penalty that Caesar feared, but the indignity of it. He was concerned with his honour and reputation, and all Roman nobles would have understood when he said,

> Prestige had always been of prime importance to me, even outweighing life itself; it pained me to see the privilege conferred on me by the Roman people being insultingly wrested from me by my enemies.[44]

Real reason — to defend his honour

He was even prepared to give up the right which the people had granted him — standing for the consulship in absentia — if Pompey would agree to general demobilisation. When his final attempts at negotiation were ignored, he appealed to his troops to defend his reputation. He later reiterated his feelings when he pointed out that

> I alone have been denied the right always accorded to all commanders — that is, the right of coming home, after successful campaigns, with some honour, or at least without disgrace, and disbanding one's army.[45]

> It has also been suggested that constant exercise of power gave Caesar a love of it; and that, after weighing his enemies' strength against his own, he took his chance of fulfilling his youthful dreams of making a bid for the monarchy: Cicero seems to have come to a similar conclusion.

Comment: Although Caesar was ambitious, and like all Roman nobles wanted personal supremacy, there is no evidence that he ever aimed at becoming a king or that he initiated a civil war to gain a crown.

A bid for the monarchy — no evidence

Caesar crossed the Rubicon on the pretext of protecting the sacrosanctity of the tribunes, but his real reason was to defend his own honour and reputation.

Responsibility for the war

There is no doubt that by crossing the Rubicon — the stream that separated Italy from Cisalpine Gaul — Caesar committed treason and was legally responsible for the civil war. However, the evidence seems to suggest that he did not want to fight such a war, but rather hoped for a quick political capitulation by his enemies, followed by his election to the consulship of 48.

Pompey's main aim in the late fifties seems to have been to make sure that Caesar did not become his equal, but to do this without resorting to civil war. His refusal to accept Curio's compromise proposal indicates that he intended to continue standing alone on the pinnacle of power. Pompey accepted the demands of the hard-core optimates to raise troops and save the state because he believed that this would force Caesar to make a peaceful settlement; a back-down by Caesar would have maintained Pompey's supremacy over him. It appears that Pompey did not want civil war, either.

Most of the senators were eager to prevent a conflict between the two men, but the small group of optimates, long-time enemies of Caesar, were not interested in any appeasement or compromise. They wanted to destroy Caesar and this could only be done by war, so they forced the issue to prevent any wavering by the rest of the senate and to prevent Pompey from making a compromise with Caesar.

Assignment: The civil war, 49–45

Find the following places on a map of the Mediterranean region: Ariminum, Corfinium, Brundisium, Dyrrhachium, Pharsalus, Alexandria, Zela, Thapsus, Utica and Munda.

Read a brief account of the civil war in any reliable modern text and refer, if possible, to the following ancient sources:

Plutarch, *Pompey*, 59–80; *Caesar*, 32–56, *Cicero*, 37–9.
Suetonius, *Julius Caesar*, 34–9, 52, 75.
Caesar, Civil War, III: 82, 83, 96, 107–8; *The African War*, 80–8.
Cicero, *Ad Atticum* (Letters to Atticus); *Ad Familiares* (Letters to Friends).

1 *Caesar in Italy and Pompey's departure for Greece*

Pompey and the optimates were taken by surprise by the speed of Caesar's movements once he had crossed the Rubicon. They evacuated Rome (to Capua), since Pompey's army was not yet ready to face Caesar. Pompey's plans were further upset when the proconsul L. Domitius Ahenobarbus failed in an attempt to intercept Caesar at Corfinium, and surrendered with three legions. Pompey then made the decision to evacuate Italy and headed for the port of Brundisium. Before he left for Greece with his army and the majority of senators, Caesar made several attempts to arrange a personal interview with him, but this Pompey refused.

Caesar did not follow Pompey immediately, but returned to Rome. In order to get the funds he needed to carry on the war, he broke into the Treasury.

Cicero was in a dilemma. He did not accompany Pompey and the rest of the senators to Greece, and his letters during this period reflect his distressed state of mind (Cicero to Atticus, 18–19 February 49). Plutarch says that 'He did not know which way to turn'.[46] He was being urged to join Caesar, but felt obliged to continue in his support of Pompey even though he disapproved of his actions. After three months of hesitation he sailed for Greece, but was unhappy with the situation he found there.

(a) What were Caesar's peace proposals to Pompey before he left Italy? How did Pompey and the optimates react?
(b) What were Pompey's reasons for leaving Italy? Refer to Plutarch, *Pompey*, 62, 64.
(c) Read the three extracts below and comment on Cicero's feelings about Pompey's strategy and departure from Italy.

> I really don't know what I am doing or going to do, I am so confounded by the

> rashness of this crazy proceeding of ours . . . What our Gnaeus [Pompey] has decided or is deciding I don't know, cooped up there in the country towns in a daze. If he makes a stand in Italy we shall all be with him, but if he leaves, it's a matter for consideration. So far anyhow, unless I am out of my mind, there has been nothing but folly and recklessness.[47]

> My whole mind is fixed in expectation of news from Brundisium. If Caesar has found our Gnaeus there, there is a faint hope of peace, but if he has crossed over beforehand, there is the fear of a deadly war.[48]

> What a disgrace – and, consequently, what misery . . . Pompey cherished Caesar, suddenly became afraid of him, refused all peace terms, failed to prepare for war, evacuated Rome, culpably lost Picenum, got himself tied up in Apulia, and then went off to Greece without getting in touch with us or letting us know anything about his unprecedented plan upon which so much depended.'[49]

(d) Why did Caesar fail to follow Pompey and the optimates across the Adriatic immediately? Refer to Plutarch, *Pompey*, 62; *Caesar*, 35.

(e) What was the significance of Caesar's threat against the tribune Caecilius Metellus when the latter tried to prevent him from breaking into the Treasury? Consider this in the light of Caesar's excuse for crossing the Rubicon.

2 *The war in Greece*

Before following Pompey to Greece, Caesar decided to secure Spain by driving out Pompey's commanders, Afranius and Varro. 'He would then march against Pompey without leaving any enemy forces behind his back'.[50] He also sent his own commanders to take control of the grain supplies of Sardinia and Sicily.

Caesar eventually crossed the Adriatic in early 48 after being elected consul for that year. Near Dyrrhachium, Pompey's base for naval operations, Caesar attempted a blockade of the Pompeians, but he failed to maintain it and moved inland to Thessaly. Pompey 'quietly followed in the enemy's tracks',[51] as he was not anxious to expose his men at this stage to the more experienced troops of Caesar. However, he allowed himself to be pressured by the optimates into adopting a course which he knew was not the best. The two Roman forces met in battle on the plain of Pharsalus.

(a) What is Plutarch's view of Pompey's generalship at this point? (Refer to Plutarch, *Pompey*, 67.)

(b) What evidence is there from Caesar's *Civil War*, III: 83 and III: 96 that the Pompeians expected a decisive victory at Pharsalus?

(c) Comment on Plutarch's statement 'that Pompey's greatest mistake and Caesar's cleverest move was in having this battle fought so far away from any naval engagement'.[52]

(d) Why did Caesar not mention the Battle of Pharsalus in any official statement, or celebrate it in a triumph?

(e) How did he make use of his victory to create propaganda for himself? (Refer to Caesar, *Civil War*, III: 98; Plutarch, *Caesar*, 48.)

(f) Why did Pompey flee to Egypt after his defeat at Pharsalus?

(g) Read Plutarch, *Pompey*, 77–80 and Caesar, *Civil War*, III: 104 for an account of Pompey's death in Egypt.

(h) Comment on Cicero's reaction to Pompey's death.

A portrait of Cleopatra

> I never had any doubts how Pompey would end. People everywhere had so completely lost faith in his chances of success that it seemed likely that this would happen wherever he tried to land. I can't help feeling sorry he's dead. I know that he was an honest, decent and upright man.[53]

3 *Caesar in Egypt and Asia*

For over a year after Pharsalus, Caesar was involved in two campaigns (Egypt and Asia) which bore little relationship to the civil war. Michael Grant describes Caesar's stay in Egypt as 'an interlude between the war with Pompey and the war against his sons and supporters'.[54]

Caesar had followed Pompey to Egypt to prevent him from gathering new forces and renewing the war, but once there he became involved in the dynastic intrigues of the court of Ptolemy XII and his sister/wife, Cleopatra. Although Plutarch suggests that the war in Egypt was 'brought on by Caesar's passion for Cleopatra',[55] his prolonged stay was not due to his infatuation with her.

In the summer of 47 he returned to Rome via Syria and Asia Minor. During his short stay in this area he reorganised the provincial administration and dealt with Pharnaces, the son of Mithridates, at the Battle of Zela. Pharnaces had taken advantage of the confusion caused by the civil war to gain several successes at Rome's expense.

Caesar returned to Rome just in time to settle a mutiny by the veterans he had sent home after Pharsalus.

(a) Explain why Caesar felt a certain obligation to act as arbiter in the Egyptian dynastic quarrels. (Refer to Caesar, *Civil War*, III: 107–8.)

(b) Why did it take so long to come to a satisfactory arrangement?

(c) The profile at left is one impression of Cleopatra. She was ambitious, desiring to revive the glory of Egypt under her rule, and by using her charm, intelligence and determination was able to captivate Caesar. He eventually settled the affairs of Egypt by arranging for her to govern jointly with her younger brother. Her older brother and opponent had been killed fighting against Caesar. (Refer to Suetonius, *Julius Caesar*, 52.)

(d) Caesar sent a message to Rome in 47 which was later exhibited in his triumph. To what did the words *'Veni, vedi, vici'* *refer?*

4 *Caesar in Africa*

At the end of 47 Caesar sailed to Africa, where the remants of the Pompeians had gathered under Metellus Scipio, Afranius,

Labienus, Cato and Pompey's two sons. Their forces were augmented by four legions offered by King Juba of Numidia.

Caesar faced the Pompeians at Thapsus. During the pursuit of the enemy, his troops got out of hand, and the death toll was higher than at Pharsalus. All the Pompeian leaders — except Labienus and Pompey's sons, who escaped to Spain — lost their lives. Cato committed suicide at Utica.

Caesar returned to Rome and 'celebrated four triumphs in one month with a few days' interval between them . . . These triumphs were the Gallic — the first and most magnificent — the Alexandrian, the Pontic, the African . . .'.[56]

He had spent only short periods in Rome between the campaigns of the civil war, but during these brief stays he carried out a number of reforms, initiated the construction of many great buildings, was appointed dictator for various periods and accepted honours and powers.

(a) Refer to Caesar, *The African War*, 80–6, 88; and Plutarch, *Caesar*, 54.

(b) Refer to Suetonius, *Julius Caesar*, 37–9, for a description of Caesar's triumphs and the spectacular public shows which followed.

5 *Caesar in Spain*

Caesar had celebrated his triumphs in the belief that the war was over. However, in 45 he was forced to campaign in Spain against the sons of Pompey. The Battle of Munda was one of his hardest battles, and although Sextus Pompeius escaped to cause further trouble for Rome, no other Pompeian officer survived. 'This was Caesar's last war.'[57]

(a) Explain why 'the triumph which he held for it [Munda] displeased the Romans more than anything else he had done'.[58]

(b) Explain what Suetonius meant when he said, 'Nobody can deny that during the civil war, and after, he behaved with wonderful restraint and clemency'.[59]

6 *Caesar as general*

The civil war had been fought over the entire Mediterranean and was noteworthy for the decisive nature of Caesar's victories. It had proved his legions to be the greatest infantry of ancient times and himself to be one of the world's greatest generals.

(a) Read Suetonius, *Julius Caesar*, 57–70, and make a list of Caesar's qualities as a soldier and leader of men. Add to this list from Plutarch, *Caesar*, 15–17, 26–7.

Caesar returned to Rome to be acclaimed and honoured as no other Roman had ever been, and as dictator he carried out a huge amount of administrative and legislative reform and initiated vast building programs.

Caesar's autocratic position

The extent of Caesar's power is summarised in the chart on page 385.

Accepted dictatorship in stages

While the civil war was in progress (49–45) Caesar's position became more and more autocratic, and he settled into the dictatorship in stages.

In 49, he was appointed dictator by the praetor Lepidus, but this he resigned after eleven days when he was elected to the consulship for 48; this appears to have been an attempt to reconstruct normal government. After the Battle of Pharsalus he was appointed dictator for one year,

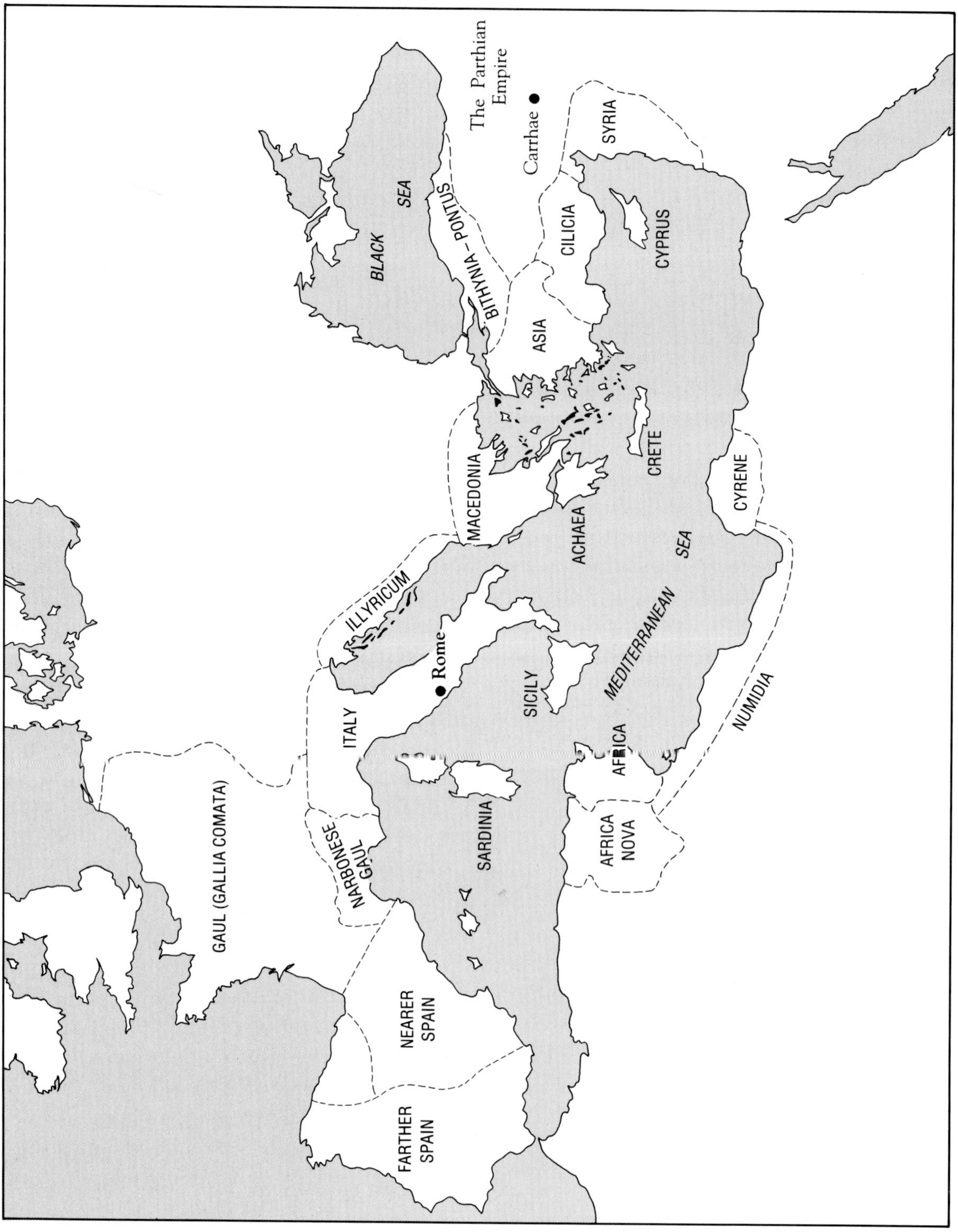
The Parthian Empire
Carrhae
SYRIA
BLACK SEA
BITHYNIA–PONTUS
CILICIA
CYPRUS
ASIA
MACEDONIA
CRETE
CYRENE
ACHAEA
SEA
ILLYRICUM
MEDITERRANEAN
Rome
SICILY
ITALY
AFRICA
NUMIDIA
SARDINIA
AFRICA NOVA
NARBONESE GAUL
GAUL (GALLIA COMATA)
NEARER SPAIN
FARTHER SPAIN

apparently to deal with the emergency situation. In 46, after his victorious command in Africa, his appointment as dictator for ten years indicated that he was looking at a more permanent form of autocracy; however, he held the consulship in 46 and 45 as well, which may have been intended to disguise his rise to power.

Opposite: The Roman Empire at the death of Julius Caesar in 44 BC

During this time he accepted offices and honours from a subservient senate, throwing a veil of legality over his position.

Nobility's hopes for a return to republican government

After the republicans' defeat at Munda, Caesar was in complete control of the Roman world and the nobility were hoping for normalisation of government. Up to this point they may have clung to the belief that Caesar did not intend to hold power forever and so felt able to tolerate his dictatorship as a temporary necessity. After the civil war, however, it became obvious that he had no intention of giving up his position and going back to the old republican form of government, which to them meant the oligarchic rule of their own clique.

Caesar's intention to retain absolute control

In 44, during his fifth consulship (sole-consulship), he took the title of dictator 'for life', which revealed his intention to retain absolute authority. This position was a contradiction in terms, since a dictator was appointed only to deal with an immediate crisis. 'Never before had Rome endured a dictator who set no limit to his dictatorship.'[60]

At this time his head began to appear on Roman coins, several bearing the inscription *Dict. Perpetuo.* Since portraits of great men only appeared on coins after their death, the depiction of a live Caesar must have indicated that he regarded himself as being like no other man.

Belief that he wanted to become king

This may have led to the belief that he intended going even further and assuming the title of *rex* (king). However, although he believed that the senate-controlled republic was finished, and probably thought that some form of autocratic control was needed, there is no real evidence that he intended establishing a monarchy.

Rumours spread in 44 that he intended making himself king, and a number of incidents—the meaning of which is unclear—may have been attempts by his opponents to embarrass him. Since all Roman noblemen sought personal supremacy, it was usual practice to suggest that one's rivals were aiming for a crown. Cicero refers to both Pompey and Caesar in this way.

Caesar already had the powers of a king without having assumed the title which all Romans hated. Although Mommsen maintains that from the beginning Caesar planned to take the crown of Rome, the actual title he took is unimportant. As Gelzer said, 'Caesar had only one unshakeable principle—he would not let go of the power he had won'.[61]

Resentment of nobility as their ambitions were frustrated

Although his future plans for the government of Rome are unknown, his behaviour at that time was enough to create widespread unpopularity and growing hostility towards him. 'Caesar's unconcealed intention to retain absolute authority antagonised everybody of any importance.'[62] Since the members of the ruling class of Rome considered themselves the equals of Caesar, they resented being treated as the tools of an autocrat. His position, which placed him far above the constitution, not only reduced all other magistrates to the status of mere servants but deprived them of the right to compete for the highest offices of the state. He appeared to be totally indifferent to their feelings, humiliating them personally and affronting them by his contempt of all constitutional forms. Their legitimate political ambitions were frustrated, and their need for dignity overlooked.

'Incompetent as many of them were, they were not willing to . . . submit to political impotence leading quite obviously to political extinction.'[63]

Coins issued to honour Caesar, bearing the following inscriptions: (a) *Parens patriae*; (b) *Caesar imper.*; (c) *Caesar dict. quart*; (d) *Clementia Caesar*; (e) *Caesar dict. perpetuo*; (f) *Divus Iulius*

Exercise

Refer to the preceding text, and to Suetonius, *Julius Caesar*, 45, 75, 76, 88 and Plutarch, *Caesar*, 57, 67, 69.

Examine the six coins carefully. Write out the inscription on each one and explain what it means.

1 What is the earliest possible date for any of these coins?
2 What is the meaning of the veil over Caesar's head, the laurel wreath, the temple, the comet.

Caesar's autocratic position	
Powers	*Honours*
Dictatorship was held for varying intervals: 49 – 11 days 48 – 1 year 46 – ten years 44 – life All other offices were secondary to this, as it raised him above the veto of the tribunes and the imperium of all other magistrates. He was able to dominate the senate, magistrates and people. Consulships were held in 48, 46, 45 (sole-consulship) and 44; these positions disguised his rise to power. The position of prefect of public morals (*praefectura morum*) gave him from 46 the powers of a censor. Tribunician sacrosanctity was granted in 45. Caesar could not have the authority of a tribune since he was a patrician, but he was eligible to sit with the tribunes on public occasions. He had been chief priest (pontifex maximus) since 63; in 47 he was elected to all other priestly colleges, including that of the augurs. This gave him great influence over the state's religion. Other powers not associated with any office were the right to speak first in the senate, the right to nominate Roman and provincial magistrates, the sole right to command armies, and control over all public money. The climax of all these powers was that advance agreement was given to all his future acts and all magistrates were to take an oath to uphold them.	After Munda (45), he was hailed as *parens patriae* (which can be interpreted as 'father of the state'). At the games which he celebrated after Munda, his statue was carried with that of Victory. The month of Quinctilis was renamed Iulius (July). Statues of him were placed in the Temple of Quirinus and near the statues of the kings of Rome, his chariot was set up opposite the Temple of Jupiter, and an ivory statue was carried with those of the gods in festive processions. He was entitled to build a house with a pediment resembling a temple. He was permitted the use of a gilded chair; he wore the triumphal robe and was entitled to wear a laurel crown on special occasions. From 49 to 46 he bore the title *imperator*, given to victorious generals. After the end of the civil war, the senate may have granted its use as a permanent honour in peacetime. In 44 his head appeared on Roman coins. A temple was erected to his clemency. A new college of priests was established, called the Julian Luperci, and a priest (*flamen*) was appointed in his honour.
'Never before had a Roman citizen allowed himself to receive the honours and marks of distinction normally reserved for the gods.'[64]	

The following extracts from Suetonius illustrate some aspects of Caesar's autocratic position and the behaviour which caused offence to a large number of members of the senatorial class.

> Not only did he accept excessive honours, such as life-consulship, a life-dictatorship, a perpetual Censorship, the title 'Imperator' put before his name and the title of 'Father of his Country' appended to it . . . but took other honours, which as a mere mortal, he should have refused.[65]

> He showed equal scorn of traditional precedent by choosing magistrates several years ahead, decorating ten former praetors with the emblems of the consular rank, and admitting to the Senate men of foreign birth.[66]

> . . public statements which reveal a similar presumption: that the Republic was nothing — a mere name without form or substance; . . . and that, now his own word was law, people ought to be more careful how they approached him.[67]

> What made the Romans hate him so bitterly was that when, one day, the entire senate, armed with an imposing list of honours that they had just voted him, came to where he sat in front of the Temple of Mother Venus, he did not rise to greet them.[68]

> This open insult to the senate was emphasised by an even worse example of his arrogance. As he returned to Rome . . . a member of the crowd set a laurel wreath, bound with a royal white fillet, on the head of his statue. Two tribunes of the people . . . ordered the fillet to be removed at once and the offender imprisoned. But Caesar reprimanded and summarily deposed them both.[69]

Exercise

Use the preceding information to comment, in about one page, on Suetonius' statement: 'Yet other deeds and sayings of Caesar's may be set to the debit account, and justify the conclusion that he deserved assassination'.[70]

Caesar's reforms

The information contained in the following text is detailed in the chart on page 388.

Variety of Caesar's legislation

Although between 49 and 44 Caesar spent very little time in Rome, during his brief appearances he initiated a large number of legislative and administrative reforms. He had an eye for efficiency, and when he saw obvious abuses in the system he did not hesitate to remove them as quickly as possible. He pushed through a large number of senatorial decrees and laws dealing with such things as the reorganisation of the local government of Italian towns; the length of tenure of provincial governors; the reduction in the number of Romans receiving free grain supplies; penalties for criminal offences; the ratio of free labourers to slaves on large estates; traffic congestion in the Forum; the composition of the law courts; reform of the calendar and the restriction of luxury displayed by the nobility.

Much left for others to complete

Some legislation was simply a tidying-up process, while other reforms had more far-reaching effects. Much of what he started and planned was left for others to complete or implement, particularly in regard to his building and engineering program. Like many great men, he wanted to leave a permanent reminder of himself in the form of public buildings, and his greatest monument was the Julian Forum (an annexe of the Roman Forum), in the centre of which was the Temple of Venus Genetrix (Mother) from whom Caesar claimed to be descended.

Caesar started the effective Romanisation of the Empire

His most important initiative—the founding of colonies outside Italy and the extension of Roman citizenship to provincials—was linked to his need to provide for the vast number of veterans. Since the amount of land in Italy was limited, he was forced to established colonies (some new settlements and some incorporating already-existing native towns) in Spain, Gaul, North Africa and the east. Most of these colonies included vast numbers of the unemployed and poor from Rome as well as his veterans, so in this way Caesar began the process of breaking down the distinction between Romans and provincials (the Romanisation of the empire). He had always shown an interest in extending Roman citizenship to worthy individuals and communities, and he continued this process. He even added new members to the senate from among the most influential of the Romanised Gauls.

Opponents not impressed

Caesar's reforms did not impress his opponents. No matter how moderate they were or how much they may have benefited the people of Rome, Italy and the provinces, the conservatives resented his actions. Even his reform of the calendar offended those who were jealous of his power. Cicero's reply to a comment that a certain constellation would rise the next day was, 'No doubt it has been ordered to do so',[71] implying that even the stars were under his control, as was everything else.

Caesar's reforms
Franchise In 49 Caesar granted franchise to Transpadane Gaul. He enfranchised a Gallic legion en masse and granted full Roman citizenship to certain provincial towns, such as Lisbon and Cadiz (Gades).
Colonisation He promoted overseas colonies for his veterans and urban poor in places such as Carthage and Corinth, which owed their rebirth to him. Other colonies founded or planned included Hispalis and Tarraco in Spain, Sinope in the east and Cirta in Africa. Colonies had either Roman or Latin status. With Caesar, the effective Romanisation of the empire began: this was his most statesmanlike reform.
Italians His lex Julia Municipalis provided a uniform system of local government for all towns in Italy possessing the franchise. The affairs of each town were managed by a locally elected senate and magistrates.
Finance He replenished the public treasury by penalties extracted from obstinate rebels after the Battle of Munda, and by 'benevolences' from vassal kings. He struck the first gold coins.
Provinces He replaced the tithe system of taxation in Sicily and Asia with a fixed land tax, in order to reduce the middleman. He tried to assure just government by limiting the tenure of governors. He enrolled prominent provincials — Gauls and Spaniards — in the senate. (This was a very unpopular measure in Rome.)
Magistrates The senate's numbers were brought up to 900, quaestors were increased from twenty to forty, aediles from four to six, and praetors from eight to sixteen.
Army He paid his soldiers handsome bounties and pensions and raised their pay from 120 to 225 denarii a year
Public works He began to extend the Forum and to pave it — the Julian Forum. The Basilica Julia was unfinished, and he planned a vast library. He also had plans to drain the Pontine Marshes (south of Rome), improve the city's drainage, deepen the harbour at Ostia, build a new road over the Apennine Mountains and cut a canal at the Isthmus of Corinth.

Caesar's reforms

Masses
He reduced the number in receipt of the corn dole by half and drafted the surplus to his new colonies.
At least one-third of the labourers working on the large estates had to be free men, not slaves.

Calendar
He employed a Greek mathematician from Alexandria (Sosigenes) to reform the Roman calendar. The resultant Julian calendar (with one important modification) is still in use today.

Law/judiciary
The *tribuni aerarii*, who had served in the courts since 70, were excluded from them. The courts were now composed of equal numbers of senators and equites. Penalties for criminal offenses were increased.

Miscellaneous
He suppressed all private clubs and collegia except guilds of craftsmen and Jewish synagogues. He passed measures to relieve debt and to protect creditors from incurring heavy losses. Laws against luxury were instituted.

For further details refer to Suetonius, Julius Caesar, 38–44; Plutarch, *Caesar*, 37, 51, 52, 55, 58, 59; Lewis & Reinhold, *Roman Civilisation — the Republic*, pp. 408–12, 416–28.

Caesar's plans for the immediate future

As early as 46 Caesar made references to his death. This was possibly due to his recent bouts of illness. He suffered from epilepsy, and during the last years of his life he was plagued with headaches and fainting attacks.

Caesar's thoughts for the future — his will

When he returned from Munda in 45 he began to give some thought to his future and it was at about his time that he drew up his will, which left most of his extremely valuable estate to his grandnephew, Gaius Octavius (later Augustus). The young Octavius (seventeen years old), who had served Caesar in Spain, had already impressed him with his outstanding talents, but there was nothing in his will to indicate that he saw Octavius as a successor to his position in the state or in fact that he had any idea what the future of the Roman state would be after his death.

No evidence for a grand scheme for the future

One of his closest friends, Gaius Matius, indicated that Caesar had given no real thought to any alternative form of Roman government, even though he believed that the republic, which his opponents wanted restored, was finished. He had probably not worked out any long-lasting solution for bringing about much-needed political stability. His mind was on other things.

Caesar had spent most of the years since his first consulship (59) campaigning throughout the empire, and he may have found life in the capital rather suffocating after life in camp. He therefore made plans to leave Rome once again, to fight another great war.

Plans for a campaign against the Parthians

> Caesar was born to do great things and to seek constantly for distinction. His many successes, so far from encouraging him to rest and to enjoy the fruits of all his labours, only served to kindle in him fresh confidence for the future, filling his mind with projects of still greater actions and with a passion for new glory, as though he had run through his stock of the old. His feelings can best be described by saying that he was competing with himself, as though he were someone else, and was struggling to make the future excel the past. He had made his plans and preparations for an expedition against the Parthians.[72]

A war against Parthia could be justified on two grounds. Nine years earlier the Romans had suffered a humiliating defeat at the hands of the Parthians at Carrhae, where Crassus had lost both his life and the legionary eagles. Caesar could now use the pretext of avenging Crassus' death. Also, a governor sent out to Syria by Caesar had been prevented from taking up his appointment because of a raid on the province by the Parthians.

An enormous army of sixteen legions was already being recruited, and Caesar planned to leave Rome about the middle of March 44.

The assassination of Caesar

There were many Romans who found Caesar's despotism unacceptable, and the possibility of a perpetual dictator ruling Rome from the east (the war against Parthia could occupy Caesar for years) could not be endured. A group of sixty leading Romans, who had formed a conspiracy to assassinate him, decided to strike on 15 March (the Ides of March), three days before his departure for the east.

Caesar unconcerned over threats of his life

To what extent Caesar was aware of the offence caused by his growing autocracy is unknown. He certainly treated rumours of attempts against his life and pronouncements of unfavourable omens with disdain, by dismissing his Spanish bodyguard. He may have hoped that an oath sworn by the senators to protect his life — and also his tribunician inviolability — were enough to safeguard him against violence.

Cassius — leader of plot to kill Caesar

The instigator of the plot was one of the praetors, Gaius Cassius Longinus, a stern, proud man who had come over to Caesar's side after Pharsalus. The figurehead of the conspiracy, however, was the intense Marcus Brutus, who had also benefited from Caesar's clemency after Pharsalus. Although Brutus had served on Caesar's staff, and his mother

Brutus' motives

Marcus Junius Brutus

(Servilia) was Caesar's lover, Cato was his uncle, and after Cato's death Brutus married his daughter Porcia. These relationships may have created something of a dilemma for him; Cassius, however, exploited his obsession with his ancestors, Lucius Brutus and Servilius Ahala, both of whom had been responsible for freeing Rome of a hated king and tyrant.

Another of the leading conspirators was Decimus Junius Brutus Albinus, a relative of M. Brutus. Decimus Brutus had been with Caesar all along and was even mentioned in his will; he must have found Caesar's excessive power unbearable. There was obviously a variety of motives guiding the individual conspirators, but they all believed that with the death of Caesar, the republic would be restored to its old form.

This was a gross miscalculation.

Cicero not included

Cicero was not informed of the plot, since the conspirators believed that he would find it difficult to hold his tongue, even though he would probably have supported their action at this time.

Caesar's murder in 44

Suetonius describes the actual murder of Caesar, which took place in the Senate House. When the conspirators surrounded him as though to pay their respects, one of their number pretended to ask him a question, and grabbed hold of his shoulder.

> 'This is violence!' Caesar cried, and at that moment, as he turned away, one of the Casca brothers with a sweep of his dagger stabbed him just below the throat . . . he was leaping away when another dagger blow stopped him. Confronted by a ring of drawn daggers, he drew the top of his gown over his face, and at the same time ungirded the lower part, letting it fall to his feet so that he would die with both legs decently covered. Twenty-three dagger thrusts went home as he stood there . . .[73]

Plutarch maintains that he fell at the foot of the statue of Pompey, which was covered with blood 'so that one might have thought that Pompey himself was presiding over this act of vengeance against his enemy'.[74]

Coin commemorating the assassination of Julius Caesar, issued in 43–42

1 EID. MAR indicates the date of Caesar's death, the Ides of March (15 March 44).
2 The *pileus* (a type of felt cap worn by freed slaves) is a symbol of liberty, which the assassins believed they were restoring.
3 The daggers represent the weapons used to kill Caesar.

Caesar's death mask

Upper-class Romans had moulded wax masks made of their relatives immediately after their deaths. The mask was used for a number of purposes.

1 It was worn by someone in the funeral procession and a cast of it was carried before the body. After the funeral it was placed in the entrance hall of the man's home, with the masks of his ancestors.
2 It was used as a model for later marble or bronze portrait busts.

An evaluation of Julius Caesar	
He was ambitious for glory like all Roman nobles, but until his first consulship in 59 his career followed the standard military and political requirements of the cursus. He was also a committed popularis and did not veer from that position during his career.	He realised that the old republican form of government was finished and made no attempt to hide his opinion, often arrogantly bypassing traditional practices. He either failed to realise or did not care that his autocratic power and behaviour gave offence to many leading Romans.
He was an outstanding soldier and military leader. He actually liked fighting, was a brilliant tactician and was admired by his men. Although he was ruthless at times, 'he was not naturally vindictive'.[75] His clemency towards his enemies is well-documented.	He had little interest in religion, although he made an efficient pontifex maximus. The only goddess he associated with was Venus, from whom he claimed the Caesars were descended. 'Religious scruples never deterred him for a moment.'[76]
His practical good sense gave him a flair for administrative efficiency and he made and carried out decisions swiftly — often too quickly in the view of his opponents.	He was a highly intelligent and cultured man. Cicero 'confessed that he knew no more eloquent speaker than Caesar'.[77] Cicero also admired Caesar's writing style: 'his memoirs are cleanly, directly and gracefully composed'.[78]
He introduced a number of statesman-like measures during his career, such as the extension of Roman citizenship. However, he had no great ideals about benefiting his fellow man, and if he had any overall plan for the future of the empire, it died with him.	He was devoted to his dependants and consistently affectionate to his friends, but 'his affairs with women are commonly described as numerous and extravagant'.[79]

Caesar Imperator

18 From republic to principate, 44–28

Antony's bid for power

Octavian— heir to Caesar

The Second Triumvirate

The Battle of Actium

THIS CHAPTER covers the years from the death of Julius Caesar to the principate (rule of the first citizen) of his adopted son, Octavian—or as he was to be called from 27, Augustus.

Sources on Octavian's early career

The written sources used by historians for this period are very similar to those for the following section, and are described in greater detail on pages 417–21. There are, however, several which deal specifically with Octavian's early career and the formal arrangement between Antony, Octavian and Lepidus that was known as the Second Triumvirate.

Cicero, Plutarch, Appian

Cicero's speeches against Antony—called the 'Philippics'—are a very useful reference for the year immediately following Caesar's assassination, while Plutarch's lives of Brutus and Antony cover the years 44 to 30. Appian's *Civil Wars* provide a reasonably reliable account of the major events to 36.

Augustus' Memoirs

Of Augustus' own writings the *Res Gestae*, a record of his achievements, is the most complete and valuable (it is analysed in the following chapter). He also wrote his *Memoirs*, in thirteen books, but of these only twenty fragments survive. They would have been extremely valuable to the historian, even though they covered his career only as far as the Cantabrian war in 26; they appear to have been intended for his peers (unlike the *Res Gestae*, which was written for a wider public) and they were full of the names of competitors and enemies who do not appear in the other work. However, although so few of these fragments survive today, they were available to other writers until late antiquity and there are references to them in such sources as Suetonius, Plutarch, Dio Cassius, Appian and Nicolaus of Damascus.

Marcus Antonius' reaction to Caesar's assassination

Caesar's political heirs

Since Caesar held both the consulship and the dictatorship at the time of his death, his political heirs were Marcus Antonius (Antony, his colleague in the consulship) and Marcus Aemilius Lepidus, his master of the horse (assistant to the dictator).

> There was a noble dignity about Antony's appearance. His beard was full grown, his forehead broad, his nose aquiline, and these features combined to give him a certain bold and masculine look which is found in the statues and portraits of Hercules.[1]

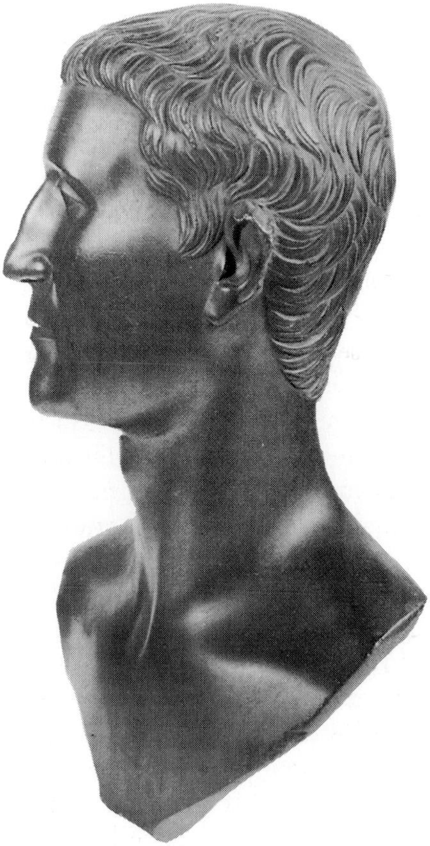

Marcus Antonius (Mark Antony)

Antony's abilities

Despite his youthful reputation for extravagance and riotous living, Antony had proved to be a capable, courageous, popular and energetic leader of men. He had served Caesar well during the civil war and in 44 was rewarded with the consulship.

Antony's initial actions avert further trouble

In the period immediately following Caesar's murder Antony quickly took the initiative. He gained the support of Lepidus and his troops and obtained possession of Caesar's money and papers from Calpurnia. He arranged a meeting of the senate, at which a compromise was reached—the assassins were granted an amnesty and those of them who were eligible to take up provincial commands were permitted to do so. In return it was agreed that all Caesar's measures would remain unchanged, his will would be read in public and his body would be buried with all the usual honours. According to Plutarch the senate passed a 'vote of thanks to Antony for having averted the outbreak of a civil war'[2] and for resolving 'an exceptionally difficult and confused situation in a most prudent and statesmanlike fashion'.[3]

Disappointment at contents of Caesar's will

When the will was read Antony was extremely disappointed; he had not expected Caesar to adopt a young, obscure relative (Gaius Octavius, his grandnephew) as his son and make him the heir to three-quarters of his estate. Nevertheless, at this stage Antony would not have considered the 18-year-old Octavius a political rival for leadership of the Caesarians.

Cassius' objections to a public funeral

Cassius, one of the assassins, had strenuously opposed the public reading of the will and his fears were borne out when it was revealed that Caesar had also bequeathed 75 denarii to every member of the Roman plebs (those who received the corn dole) and the general use of his gardens beyond the Tiber. 'A great wave of affection for Caesar and a powerful sense of his loss swept over the people.'[4]

Reaction of the mob at Caesar's funeral

Even more serious in its effect on the conspirators was the reaction of the people to the funeral oration delivered by Antony over the body of Caesar. Here again Cassius had urged against allowing Antony this customary privilege, but Brutus had agreed to it. Plutarch maintained that in this Brutus 'committed a fatal blunder',[5] for when the Romans were shown Caesar's bloodstained toga with the gashes made by the daggers, they 'almost lost control of their emotions'.[6] Serious rioting broke out, and the conspirators fled from the city.

Although Antony was left in complete control of Rome he continued to behave, as Cicero said, in a way that 'gave the state a mighty proof that he wanted our country to be free'.[7] He proposed many excellent measures

Abolition of the dictatorship

to the senate, gaining their confidence. According to Cicero the most admirable step he took was his proposal to abolish the dictatorship: 'The dictatorship, which had come to usurp virtually monarchical powers, was completely eliminated from the Roman constitution'.[8] He also continued to conciliate the conspirators by referring to them in public with respect, allowing Decimus Brutus and Trebonius to go to their provinces and providing an exemption for Brutus and Cassius from their duties as praetors: according to the law, a praetor was not allowed to be away from Rome for more than ten nights, but Brutus and Cassius had fled from the city after Caesar's funeral. In fact, they never returned.

Further compromise with assassins

If the majority of senators thought that the republic would be restored by Caesar's death and by Antony's initial actions, they soon became aware that this was unlikely. As he skilfully strengthened his position in the state, Antony began to show every sign that he intended keeping full control.

Antony's attempts to maintain control

To maintain his leadership of the Caesarians he had first checked the power of Lepidus by making him Caesar's successor as pontifex maximus and persuading him to leave for his province in Spain. He also provided land for Caesar's veterans in Campania, personally supervising settlements there, and when he returned to Rome he was accompanied by armed supporters for himself.

He had acquired Caesar's documents, some of which he is supposed to have forged in order to gain benefits for himself such as the appointment of magistrates and the recall from exile of men he favoured. According to Cicero, Antony brought forward 'countless memoranda' and 'numerous alleged examples of Caesar's handwriting', some of which were sold 'as openly as though these were programs of gladiatorial shows'.[9]

Possible forgery of documents

Antony had originally been assigned the province of Macedonia for the following year, but he wished to keep control of Italy and could do this if he had Cisalpine and Transalpine Gaul as his province. He therefore secured a law transferring these provinces from Decimus Brutus to himself while retaining the right to command the Macedonian legions, which contravened the arrangements made by Caesar; he also extended the commands for proconsuls, which was a violation of another of Caesar's laws. Cicero accused Antony of suppressing Caesar's laws—'good laws, too—in order to upset the constitution. He lengthened the tenures of provincial governorships. Instead of protecting Caesar's acts, as he should have, he annulled them: those relating to national and private affairs alike'.[10]

Transfer of Gaul from Decimus Brutus to himself

Plutarch believed that Brutus had made a serious error in judgment when he failed to kill Antony at the same time as Caesar, and Cicero agreed with this sentiment when he said, in letters to Atticus a month after the assassination, ''Twas a fine deed but half done',[11] and 'the recovery of freedom did not mean the revival of free government'.[12]

This was the situation in Rome when the young Octavius appeared to claim his inheritance.

Gaius Octavius (Octavian), Caesar's heir

Family background

Gaius Octavius was born in 63, the year of Cicero's consulship, into a wealthy and respected family (the Octavii) from the countryside south of Rome. His mother, Atia, was the niece of Julius Caesar and his father, Gaius Octavius, had reached the position of praetor and governor of Macedonia before his death when Octavius was four years old. Atia subsequently married the aristocratic L. Marcius Philippus (cos. 56) who proved to be a good stepfather to Octavius and his sisters, providing the young boy with a solid if rather old-fashioned education.

Early promotion

When Octavius was eleven he was granted the honour of giving a speech at the funeral of his grandmother, Julia, and undoubtedly he would have recalled the impressive ancestry of the Iulii (Julians). Caesar, impressed with the boy's abilities, had him elected to the college of pontiffs and allowed him to take part in his African triumph when Octavius was only sixteen. Caesar also made use of a recent law (lex Cassia) to have the youth enrolled into the previously hereditary aristocracy, the patricians.

Recurrent illnesses

Octavius had always been a delicate boy and was to suffer recurrent bouts of illness throughout his life. Sickness prevented him from accompanying Caesar to Spain in 46, but he followed soon after 'with a small escort, along roads held by the enemy, after a shipwreck, too, and in a state of semi-convalescence'.[13] Caesar was very impressed with the youth's initiative and enterprise; it was soon after this episode that he made his will in favour of Octavius, although the young man was not aware of it.

Impressed Caesar

Preparation for Parthian campaign

In preparation for his planned campaign against the Parthians, Caesar appointed Octavius to his staff (as his magister equitum) and sent him to Macedonia to complete his education and also to receive military training. Octavius took with him a school friend, Marcus Vipsanius Agrippa, who until his death in 12 BC was to remain Octavius' loyal friend and supporter. It was while in Macedonia that Octavius heard of Caesar's murder.

Octavian's attempts to secure his inheritance

Octavius did not learn that he was Caesar's adopted son and heir until he returned to Italy. Then, despite the fact that his parents urged him not to accept the inheritance because of the dangers involved, he not only decided to accept but changed his name to Gaius Julius Caesar Octavianus.

Need to avenge his 'father's' death

He now had two aims: to carry out his sacred duty to avenge his father's death, and to prove himself worthy of such a father and if possible surpass his achievements.

Portrait of the young Octavian

Cicero's feelings towards Octavian

As he moved through Italy Caesar's veterans and friends welcomed him, but Octavian (now referred to in this way to avoid confusion with his father) was shrewd enough to know that he would have to move cautiously and discreetly to achieve his ends. Cicero, who met him at this time, did not trust him, and in a letter to Atticus expressed the fear he had for his friends who had killed Caesar: '. . .there are too many around him. They threaten death to our friends and call the present state of affairs intolerable'.[14]

Hostile reception from Antony

Octavian did not expect the cold and hostile reception he received, on his arrival in Rome, from his adoptive father's best friend. Antony blocked Octavian's attempt to have his adoption made legally valid and refused to hand over Caesar's money — most of which had in fact already been spent. Octavian, however, was obliged to honour his father's legacy and so was forced to borrow money as well as to sell off some of his own property in order to pay the 75 denarii to each person as instructed by Caesar. This won him great popularity, and when he followed it up with games (honouring Venus Genetrix) at his own expense, his standing with the people increased further. An incident that occurred on the day of the games, and which Octavian recorded in his memoirs, added to his prestige with the common people.

Comet — 'soul of Caesar'

> On those very days of my games, the comet was seen for seven days in the region of heaven which is under the Great Bear. It would rise at the eleventh hour of the day and was evident to all on earth. The common people believed that the comet signified the soul of Caesar being received into the divinities of the immortal gods, to whose name his was added, with a distinguished likeness of his head consecrated by us soon afterwards in the Forum [see coin illustrated on p. 384].[15]

Antony's behaviour towards Octavian probably was not due to his belief that the young man was a serious political rival for leadership of the Caesarians; it was more likely 'that Antonius had been irritated at Caesar's favouritism towards an obscure young relative and acted out of bad temper'.[16] If this was indeed the case, Antony had seriously underestimated Octavian.

Octavian's temporary collaboration with the republicans

The political situation in Rome at this time was unstable.

Republicans		*Caesarians*	
Brutus and **Cassius** left for the east (Syria and Macedonia) to raise troops and naval forces.	**Cicero** returned to Rome to lead the senate against Antony; gave a series of Philippics attacking Antony as a would-be tyrant.	**Antony** deprived Decimus Brutus of his Gallic province, but Brutus refused to leave Cisalpine Gaul. Antony laid siege to Brutus at Mutina.	**Octavian**, rebuffed by Antony, appealed to Caesar's veterans in Campania and seduced two of Antony's legions.

Antony was threatening the safety of the state by attacking Decimus Brutus at Mutina, and Cicero urged active support for Brutus. However, the republicans had no troops in Italy whereas Octavian on his own initiative and at his own expense had raised a considerable army from among Caesar's veterans. Two of Antony's Macedonian legions had also gone over to Octavian.

Cicero's attempt to use Octavian

Cicero, who had indicated his lack of trust in Octavian when the latter arrived in Italy soon after Caesar's death, now praised him. He also urged the senate to confer on him propraetorian imperium in order to assist the consuls Hirtius and Pansa against Antony.

> Look at young Gaius Caesar [Octavian]—he's scarcely more than a lad but he has raised a devoted army of those veterans of Caesar's who have never known defeat: we did not ask him to do it, we did not expect it, we did not even hope for it because it seemed impossible. His is an astonishing, I might say superhuman, quality of mind and spirit; . . . we must give him our formal support, so that his defence of the res publica may be not just his own private enterprise but a commission from us.[17]

Cicero overlooks Octavian's illegal activities

Cicero may not have trusted Octavian in January 43 any more than he had in April 44, but he had decided to use the young man for the republican cause and to 'try to keep him on the right side by honours and compliments and loudly affirm his loyalty to the republic'.[18] What Octavian had done was wholly illegal, but Cicero was prepared to overlook this in the interests of the safety of the republic and to legalise his position by the grant of propraetorian imperium. Brutus was upset by Cicero's actions, even though they were done in the interests of the republic: '. . . what he has done is to encourage, not check, the ambition and desire for power of this youth',[19] and indeed at the beginning of his *Res Gestae*, Octavian (Augustus) announces his acquisition of the imperium, which he was to hold until his death.

Octavian gains imperium

> On that account the senate passed decrees in my honour enrolling me in its order in the consulship of Gaius Pansa and Aulus Hirtius, assigning me the right to give my opinion among the consulars and giving me imperium. It ordered me as propraetor to provide in concert with the consuls that the republic should come to no harm.[20]

Cicero was naive if he believed that the senate could use this youth and then later put him aside when the threat of Antony no longer existed.

Antony defeated

The senate ordered Antony to leave Cisalpine Gaul; when he refused, the consuls and Octavian marched against him. Antony was soundly defeated in two engagements and fled to Transalpine Gaul; both consuls were killed, which left Octavian in sole command.

Octavian's first consulship

Republicans' attempt to discard Octavian

The senate and Cicero now made a serious mistake. Assuming that they were free from the immediate threat of Antony (whom they declared a public enemy), they attempted to discard Octavian. They awarded Decimus Brutus a triumph and appointed him to the command against Antony, and in addition to this attempt to set Octavian aside the senate granted supreme command of the eastern provinces to M. Brutus and Cassius, his father's murderers.

Octavian's interests lie with Antony

Antony's position had been strengthened by the addition of Lepidus and other commanders from Spain and Gaul, but Octavian realised that if Antony were defeated the party who supported his father's assassins would gain control of the state, which would make it difficult for him to honour his duty to take vengeance on them. Realising that his best interests therefore lay with the Caesarian party, he refused to co-operate with Decimus Brutus against Antony in Transalpine Gaul and also refused to surrender his legions. What he wanted was the consulship, as this would help him to gain a leading position in the Caesarian party. As he was only twenty, this was an outrageous demand and Cicero vigorously opposed it.

Octavian demands consulship

While Octavian was refusing to move against Antony, hoping that the senate would accede to his demands for the consulship, the republican cause in Gaul collapsed. Decimus Brutus was deserted by his legions and was killed trying to escape to Macedonia.

Senate's rejection — Octavian seizes control

The senate and Cicero continued to reject Octavian's demands, so he sent a deputation of 400 centurions to Rome to demand that their commander be given the consulship. When this also was resisted, Octavian marched on Rome with his legions, seized the treasury in order to pay his troops and made arrangements for the consular elections. When he and his cousin Quintus Pedius were elected (43), they revoked the decree outlawing Antony, legalised Octavian's adoption and set up a court to try Caesar's assassins, who were condemned in their absence.

Octavian had thus achieved his immediate objectives, but now had to make preparations to meet Marcus Brutus and Cassius in battle.

The Second Triumvirate 43–33: Antony, Lepidus and Octavian

Octavian had obviously been in communication with Antony and Lepidus, and a meeting was arranged between them during which there was a reconciliation and some hard bargaining about their immediate futures. They then marched on Rome.

Formation of the triumvirate

Difference between First and Second Triumvirates

The so-called First Triumvirate between Caesar, Pompey and Crassus was originally a secret arrangement between three men who were never officially recognised as triumvirs. The Second Triumvirate, on the other hand, came into existence in 43 by means of a tribune's law, proposed by P. Titius and passed in the tribal assembly on 27 November.

The Second Triumvirate	
Members:	Antony, Lepidus and Octavian
Official title:	*Triumviri Reipublicae Constituendae*
Length of appointment:	Five years
Purpose of alliance:	To set the state in order and to attack the republican armies of Brutus and Cassius in the east
Powers of triumvirs:	Absolute — the powers of a dictator without the name The right to nominate all magistrates in advance
Territory controlled:	Antony — Transalpine and Cisalpine Gaul Lepidus — Narbonese Gaul and Spain Octavian — Africa, Sicily and Sardinia
First task undertaken:	A savage campaign of proscription similar to that carried out by Sulla
Purpose of proscriptions:	To confiscate estates in order to have money and land for their troops To destroy their enemies — Caesar had shown that clemency did not pay
Results of proscriptions:	Death of 300 senators, including Cicero (see following section), and 2000 equites Escaped republicans joined Sextus Pompeius
Further activities:	Julius Caesar officially deified Lepidus appointed consul for 42 Preparations made for Antony and Octavian to face Brutus and Cassius in Macedonia

The proscription of Cicero

Refer to the First and Second Philippics in Cicero, *Selected Political Speeches* and *Selected Works*, and Plutarch, *Cicero*, 47–9.

Cicero's Philippics

In the light of the speeches made by Cicero against Antony (they were called 'Philippics' by Cicero himself, after the speeches by the Athenian Demosthenes against Philip of Macedon), it is not surprising that his name was included among those proscribed by the triumvirs. His attempts to restore the republic cost him his life. When he was caught by the triumvirs' agents attempting to escape from his country estate, his throat was cut and on Antony's orders his head and hands were removed and taken to Rome. There they were 'fastened up over the ships' rams on the public platform in the Forum. It was a sight to make the Romans shudder'.[21] It is also believed that Antony's wife, Fulvia, who previously had been married to Clodius, pierced Cicero's tongue with a hairpin.

Cicero proscribed

The Battle of Philippi, 42

Refer to Plutarch, *Antony*, 22, and *Brutus*, 38–52.

Death of Brutus and Cassius

Brutus and Cassius, who had gained control over the eastern provinces, marched west with their nineteen legions and took up a position at Philippi in Macedonia to face Antony and Octavian, who had control of twenty-eight legions. In two engagements about three weeks apart the republicans were defeated; both Cassius and Brutus took their own lives. Antony was given the credit for the victories, as Octavian was ill and took little part in the action.

Results of the republican defeat

End of republican cause

1 The defeat marked the effective end of the republican party as most of the leaders had died fighting. Those who escaped fled to join Sextus Pompeius (the son of Pompey), who was to remain a problem for Octavian and Antony until his death in 36.

2 Octavian had finally avenged the murder of his father, Julius Caesar.

Empire divided between triumvirs

3 In a signed agreement, the triumvirs divided the empire between them.
- Antony had control of all Gaul except for Cisalpine Gaul, which became part of Italy. He was also to take the majority of the legions and proceed to the east to settle the provinces and raise money to pay the troops.
- Octavian received Spain, Sardinia and Africa and was to return to Italy to settle huge numbers of veterans. He was also to deal with Sextus Pompeius, who had seized Sicily.
- Lepidus was ignored for the time being, as the others suspected him of intriguing with Sextus Pompeius. He was later given Africa.

Lepidus a minor partner

Lepidus' position within the triumvirate was that of a minor partner. A. H. M. Jones believes that he allowed himself to be ordered about by the others because although he had all the attributes and material possessions of a great noble, 'under them there was only a lay figure. He lacked the ruthless qualities needed for success, or indeed survival, in these troublous times'.[22]

Activities of the triumvirs after Philippi

The events of the years after the battle are given in diagrammatic form.

Philippi

↓

The empire was divided, 42.

Octavian in the west	*Lepidus in Africa*	*Antony in the east*
Octavian returned to Italy to settle veterans — he hoped to increase his prestige and build up a huge body of clients. Land shortage forced him to confiscate the land of eighteen towns — a huge outcry resulted. Rome and Italy were threatened with famine as Sextus Pompeius, based in Sicily, prevented the grain ships from reaching Italy. Antony's brother (cos. 42) and wife (Fulvia) were hostile to Octavian and raised six legions against him, but he laid siege to them at Perusia, where they were starved into submission 41–40. Antony's legates in Gaul went over to Octavian, who now commanded most of the west except Africa and Sicily.	Lepidus did not occupy his province until the following year.	Antony extracted money from the provincials of Asia Minor and Syria. He arbitrated in dynastic disputes, establishing rulers according to their loyalty to Rome. He met with Cleopatra at Tarsus and accepted an invitation to winter in Alexandria. He wanted some of the wealth of the Ptolemies, while she needed his help to gain control of Egypt. Antony was probably unaware of the war between Octavian and his brother and wife until it was over. Antony decided to return to Italy in 40, but was prevented from landing at Brundisium by Octavian's troops. Civil war appeared imminent.

Treaty of Brundisium, 40

↓

The triumvirs were reconciled; Antony was to marry Octavia, Octavian's sister (Fulvia had died), and a further division of the empire was carried out.

<table>
<tr><td>Octavian controlled all the provinces west of Illyricum except Africa.

Italy was shared.</td><td>Lepidus retained Africa.

Italy was shared.</td><td>Antony controlled all the provinces eastwards from Macedonia and Cyrenaica.

Italy was shared.</td></tr>
<tr><td colspan="3">The Treaty of Misenum, 39
↓
Sextus Pompeius demanded a share in the control of the empire, since he had occupied Sicily and Sardinia and could interfere with the corn trade. He was given control of Sicily, Sardinia, Corsica and Achaea as proconsul for five years.</td></tr>
<tr><td>War broke out with Pompeius when one of his freedmen handed over Sardinia, Corsica and a naval force to Octavian.

Octavian was unsuccessful against Pompeius in Sicily and asked Lepidus and Antony for help.

He was forced to rely on his trusted friend, Agrippa, to supervise construction of a fleet and training of the crews.

He married Livia (see p. 443).</td><td>Lepidus ignored Octavian's plea.</td><td>Antony made his base in Athens and used his legates to carry out a war against the Parthians, who had overrun Syria and Asia Minor; his men successfully drove the Parthians beyond the Euphrates.

He arrived at Brundisium to bring help to Octavian, but when the latter failed to appear, Antony returned to Greece, condemning him for breaking the treaty with Pompeius.</td></tr>
<tr><td colspan="3">A conference at Tarentum, 37
↓
Octavian wanted ships from Antony for his war against Sextus Pompeius; Antony wanted 20 000 soldiers from Octavian for his war against the Parthians. An agreement was made, but Octavian did not fulfil his part. Lepidus was persuaded to help Octavian and the triumvirate was renewed for a further five years.</td></tr>
<tr><td>In Sicily Octavian (with Agrippa and Lepidus) attacked Pompeius, who was finally defeated by Agrippa in a naval battle and fled to the east, where he was killed by one of Antony's officers.

Octavian took over Lepidus'</td><td>Lepidus tried to take over Sicily, but his men mutinied.

He was deposed from the</td><td>Antony sent Octavia to Rome and went to Syria to organise his Parthian campaign.

He summoned Cleopatra to Antioch; whether he married her then is not known, but he recognised his children by her and</td></tr>
</table>

<table>
<tr>
<td>troops and also those of Pompeius.

He dealt with Lepidus, sent one of his men to occupy Africa, demobilised 20 000 veterans out of the forty legions he now commanded, and returned to Rome after settling Sicily.

At the start of the war against Pompeius Octavian had adopted a new name: Imperator Caesar divi filius (Commander Caesar, the son of the god).

On his return to Rome he was granted a number of honours, among which was the sacrosanctity of a tribune. He also had a golden statue in the Forum inscribed, emphasising his restoration of security and prosperity to the west.

In 35 and 34 he conducted two campaigns in Illyricum to gain military prestige and keep his troops busy. He secured the northeast frontier and a safe route from Italy to Macedonia.

He had bound the Roman people to him by clearing the west of the 'pirate' Sextus Pompeius, safeguarding the north and, through friends such as Agrippa, providing the Roman people with a regular food supply and (with the building of aqueducts) good water.</td>
<td>triumvirate but permitted to remain as pontifex maximus.

He lived under guard in an Italian town.</td>
<td>gave her (and them) Cyrenaica, Cyprus, parts of Crete, parts of Syria and the area of Jericho, plus some other smaller areas, together representing almost all the old Ptolemaic kingdom at its greatest extent.

He then left for his Parthian campaign.

Antony marched into Armenia with 60 000 troops but failed in his attempt against Parthia, losing 22 000 men.

Two years later (34) he invaded Armenia and annexed it.

He returned to Alexandria in 34 and celebrated a triumph at which he and Cleopatra, who was dressed as Isis, sat on gold thrones.

Cleopatra and her son by Caesar (Ptolemy Caesar) were declared Queen and King of Kings and controlled Egypt and Cyprus, while her three children by Antony were to share Armenia, Media, Syria, Phoenicia, Cilicia and Cyrenaica. These arrangements were referred to as the 'Donations of Alexandria'.

Antony's behaviour in the east between 36–34 can perhaps be explained by the fact that he fell totally under the spell of Cleopatra, whose main aim was to restore the old Ptolemaic kingdom.</td>
</tr>
<tr>
<td colspan="3">The end of the triumvirate, 33
↓
The triumvirate was due to end officially in December 33. The removal of Lepidus had</td>
</tr>
</table>

weakened it, but it was Antony's treatment of Octavia (in recognising Cleopatra as his wife) which severed the alliance. Octavian gave up the title of triumvir at the end of 33; Antony kept it as though still in office. War between the two was inevitable.

In the war of propaganda which followed, Octavian had the upper hand since he was in Rome and had close contact with the people of Italy.

When the inhabitants of the Italian towns and cities swore an oath of allegiance to Octavian and his descendants and a pledge to support him against his private enemies, the provincials of Sicily, Sardinia, Africa, Spain and Gaul followed suit.

The consuls for 32 were Antony's friends, and made a speech in his favour in the senate.

They opposed Octavian's demands to read Antony's latest despatches, since they knew what the reaction would be to his 'donations' to Cleopatra and her children.

When Octavian entered the senate with an armed guard, the consuls and pro-Antony senators fled to join Antony

Antony sent notification of his formal divorce of Octavia.

When the contents of Antony's will (which Octavian had taken from the Vestal Virgins) became known, war was declared on Cleopatra. Apart from the recognition of Ptolemy Caesar as the true son of Julius Caesar and the extravagant legacies to Antony and Cleopatra's children, the aspect that most horrified the Romans was his instruction to send his body to Alexandria to be buried, if he should die in Rome.

The victory of Octavian over Antony and Cleopatra

Oath of loyalty to Octavian

It is possible that Octavian continued to hold the powers of a triumvir after 33; he also had tribunician sacrosanctity (from 36) and was to be consul again in 31. However, it was the oath of loyalty sworn to him by Roman senators, Italian municipalities and the western provinces that he used as the basis of his authority for the following years.

During the winter of 33–32 both sides prepared for war, using the most extreme propaganda against each other.

Portrait of Livia, whom Octavian took away from her husband, Tiberius Nero, when she was three months pregnant

The Battle of Actium, 31

Support of Cleopatra

Antony had gathered his forces at Ephesus; they included one of the greatest fleets ever assembled. Plutarch says that it numbered over 500 ships, of which Cleopatra had contributed sixty. She also is supposed to have contributed 20 000 talents and vast supplies of grain, and despite several attempts by his Roman supporters to persuade him to leave her behind, Antony acceded to her demands to accompany the fleet. He moved his forces to western Greece, occupying the promontory of Actium.

Octavian's strategy

Octavian crossed the Adriatic with a smaller force and occupied an area just north of Actium from where his troops could prevent access by Antony to the best routes to the east. Agrippa not only blockaded Antony's fleet in the Bay of Actium, but in a number of brilliant naval raids secured various strategic ports in Greece, cutting off Antony's supplies and communication.

Antony and Cleopatra's plan

Antony's troops were weakened by hunger and malaria and many leading Romans and client-kings deserted him, particularly angered by Cleopatra's influence over him. The blockade had to be broken, and it is believed that he and Cleopatra had a plan to risk everything on a naval battle and try to break out with as many ships and legionaries as possible, making for Egypt. Apparently, however, the plan was not communicated to the bulk of the fleet or to the army. During the engagement—which was no real contest—Cleopatra, with her royal squadron of sixty ships 'was suddenly seen to hoist sail and make through the very midst of the battle. They had been stationed astern of the heavy ships, and so threw their whole formation into disorder as they plunged through'.[23] Once out of danger she waited for Antony and his small number of ships, leaving the remainder of the fleet to be captured or to surrender to Octavian. Cleopatra and Antony sailed back to Alexandria while Antony's troops, stationed in Greece, gave themselves up to Octavian.

Escape of Antony and Cleopatra

The results of Actium

1 Octavian was hailed as imperator for the sixth time.

Demobilisation of many troops

2 Agrippa was sent to Italy to demobilise and settle the men in both Octavian's and Antony's army who had served for a long time. They, however, began to make insistent demands for their promised payments; they were becoming restless. Octavian had to return briefly to Italy to reassure them with part payment until he could gain the treasure of Egypt.

Octavian in Egypt — Antony's death

3 In 30, Octavian invaded Egypt. Antony, deserted by his troops on Octavian's arrival in Alexandria, committed suicide, believing that Cleopatra was already dead. (Refer to Plutarch, *Antony*, 76–7.)

Death of Cleopatra

4 Cleopatra, unable to win Octavian over and realising that he would never allow her to retain independent rule of Egypt for her dynasty, also committed suicide. Plutarch (*Antony*, 85–6) gives a number of accounts of her death, which is generally believed to have been caused by the bite of an asp. Cleopatra's death ended the 300-year-old Ptolemaic kingdom of Egypt.

Fate of Cleopatra's children

5 Octavian treated most of Antony's Roman supporters leniently, and although he had both Ptolemy Caesar (son of Julius Caesar) and Antony's eldest son by Fulvia killed, he was merciful to the rest of Cleopatra's children. They were brought up by Octavia as her own.

6 Egypt was annexed to Rome but was to remain the personal domain of Octavian (and of later Roman emperors), administered for him by an equestrian prefect.

The wealth of Egypt

7 The vast treasure of the Ptolemies was used by Octavian to pay the expenses of his various campaigns, to enhance his triumph and to provide for the adornment of Rome.

8 Before returning to Rome, Octavian spent some time establishing his authority over the eastern provinces and client kingdoms. Apart from the Donations, which were cancelled, most of Antony's arrangements were allowed to remain.

Octavian's return to Rome and the restoration of order and confidence, 29–28

A century of political upheaval, civil wars, proscriptions, economic devastation, oppressive taxation and continued exactions from the once-rich eastern provinces—now on the verge of bankruptcy—had come to an end, and in January 29 the gates of the Temple of Janus, which remained open while ever the country was not at peace, were closed for the first time in two hundred years.

Temple of Janus closed

Before Octavian returned to Rome, the senate voted him extravagant honours as the saviour of the state and ordered that in future prayers and libations should be made to him by the people and priests. On his return in August 29 he celebrated a splendid, three-day triumph for his victories in Illyricum, at Actium and over Egypt.

Octavian's triumph

His immediate tasks when he returned from the east were

1 to restore order and confidence throughout the Roman world;
2 to normalise his own position within the state, since at that time it was a temporary and exceptional one.

The first task occupied him for two years, 29–27; the second was achieved in 27, when he laid aside the extraordinary powers he had held since 43 (see diagram, p. 412).

Essay topics

1 How did the early career of Pompey, to 70 BC, contribute to the breakdown of Sulla's legislation?

2 What methods did Pompey use to advance his career in the period to 62?

3 Explain what motivated Pompey, Crassus and Caesar to form the so-called First Triumvirate in 60? How was this alliance put under pressure from its inception? What factors eventually led to its breakdown?

4 'His pursuit of glory, as they say, always took an unlikely or an unusual course' (Plutarch, Pompey, 14).
Discuss the exceptional nature of Pompey's career from 78 to 52.

5 What were Pompey's political aims? Account for his changing relationship with the senate and the optimates.

6 'Caesar was a committed popularis and did not veer from that position during his career.'
Comment on this statement by referring to particular events in his career to 49.

7 What was Cicero's relationship with Pompey between 67 and 49?

8 How significant were the following events in Cicero's political career?
The trial of Verres, 74
The conspiracy of Catiline, 63
The tribunate of Clodius, 58
The outbreak of civil war, 49

Creation of financial stability

He scrupulously paid off all his own debts and ignored the debts of others

He attempted to help rehabilitate senators who had suffered financially

Peace and stability brought financial confidence and the interest rate was reduced by two-thirds

Indication that peace was to continue

The Temple of Janus was closed

He reduced sixty legions to twenty-eight

He settled 120 000 veterans in colonies in Italy and overseas with their pensions paid in full, himself paying cash for the land provided

No acceptance of exceptional honours or powers

He held the consulship on equal terms with his colleague and for the first time in twenty years the consuls spent their full term in Rome

He avoided the office of censor because of its previous control over the senate, but carried out a census as a consul with censorial powers

OCTAVIAN'S RESTORATION OF ORDER AND CONFIDENCE, 29–28

No vengeance in the form of proscriptions exacted against enemies

He annulled all the illegal acts of the triumvirate, which amounted to a kind of amnesty for those proscribed in 43 and an end to the injustices suffered by their families

Use of propaganda to promote the new era of peace

Since 40 BC writers such as Virgil had been promising a 'golden age' of peace and stability — fourth poem in Virgil's *Eclogues*

Emphasis on interest in traditional and conservative activities

He became an augur with the right to appoint members of the priestly colleges; he took this task seriously and re-established religious rites and ceremonies that had been neglected

He attempted to restore respect for the senate by removing unworthy members and expecting those who remained to take their tasks seriously

Provision of diversions and employment for the people

He spent lavishly on games and other forms of entertainment and used the traditional hand-outs of grain to keep the people happy initially ('bread and circuses')

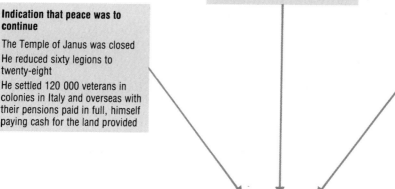

He began the building program (including roads, temples and basilicas) which was to continue throughout his principate; this provided employment

The political dominance of Antony, 44–43

9 What were the problems in Roman society as shown by Sallust in the Catilinarian conspiracy?

10 What use did Pompey and Caesar make of the tribunate between 70 and 49 to advance their careers?

11 To what extent was Caesar responsible for the civil war of 49?

12 How did Caesar's reforms, introduced during his dictatorship, benefit the people of Rome, Italy and the provinces?

13 'Never before had a Roman citizen allowed himself to receive the honours and marks of distinction normally reserved for the gods.'
Why was Caesar assassinated?

14 What circumstances led to the formation of the Second Triumvirate in 43? In what way did it differ from the first? Explain how Octavian, one of the triumvirs, gained complete control of the state by the year 30?

Further reading

Ancient sources

Appian. *The Civil Wars.*
Caesar. *The Civil War.*
_____ . *The Conquest of Gaul.*
Cicero. *Letters to Atticus.*
_____ . *Letters to his Friends.*
_____ . *Selected Political Speeches.*
_____ . *Selected Works.*
Plutarch. *The Fall of the Roman Republic: Crassus, Pompey, Caesar, Cicero.*
_____ . *Makers of Rome: Sertorius, Brutus, Mark Antony.*
Suetonius. *Julius Caesar.*

Modern sources

Adcock, F. E. *Caesar's Dictatorship*, Cambridge Ancient History, vol. 9.
Brunt, P. A. *Social Conflicts in the Roman Republic.*
Carter, J. M. *The Battle of Actium.*
Gelzer, M. *Caesar: Politician and Statesman.*
Grant, M. *Julius Caesar.*
Gruen, E. S. *The Last Generation of the Roman Republic, 78–44.*
Kagan, D. *The Roman World*, Problems in Ancient History, vol. 2.
Rawson, B. *Politics of Friendship.*
Seager, R. *Pompey: A Political Biography.*
Syme, R. *The Roman Revolution.*
Taylor, L. R. *Party Politics in the Age of Caesar.*

PART

6

Augustus and the Julio-Claudians, 28 BC–AD 68

IN 27 BC Octavian, who had disposed of all his rivals and re-established peace in the Roman world, laid aside his extraordinary powers and transferred them to the control of the senate and people of Rome. Although he believed that centralised power in the hands of one man (himself) was the only solution in the circumstances, he preferred to have supreme power granted to him constitutionally. From 27, Octavian not only became princeps (first citizen) but adopted the name 'Augustus', and it is from this date that the new political order referred to as the 'principate' (rule of the first citizen) came into effect. Augustus, as commander of the imperial army, was the master of the state but by compromise and constructive statesmanship from 27 to AD 14 he brought peace, order and good government to the Roman world.

Although the principate was not hereditary, Augustus probably hoped that his personal heir would assume his public position and responsibilities on his death. Augustus had hoped that a Julian (direct descendant of himself as the 'son' of Julius Caesar) would succeed him, but it was his adopted son Tiberius (a Claudian) who eventually became princeps.

The Julio-Claudian dynasty (Tiberius, Gaius, Claudius and Nero), which reigned from AD 14 to 68, revealed the basic weakness of the principate—it depended for its success on the person of the princeps. During this period the imperial court became the scene of intrigues and violence as the Julio-Claudian women, praetorian prefects and imperial freedmen vied for positions of power and influence over each successive emperor. However, despite the suspicious and grim nature of Tiberius, the madness of Gaius, the infirmities of Claudius and the vanity and tyranny of Nero, the Roman Empire remained generally peaceful, prosperous and well-governed.

The principate of Augustus, 27 BC–AD 14 19

The *Res Gestae*

Augustus' position and titles

Augustus' relationship with the senate, the equites and the people

Religion and morality

Legal and financial reforms

Roman and provincial administration

The army and the frontier policy

Literature as propaganda

The question of succession

Evaluation of Augustus

Sources for the period

Augustus' own material

THE BEST MATERIAL for this period is that written by Augustus himself and includes the official record of his schievements (the *Res Gestae*), fragments of his *Memoirs*, extracts from his private correspondence, and his edicts, decrees and funeral eulogies. Apart from the *Res Gestae*, which appears to have survived largely intact, only fragments of the others are found in such sources as Suetonius, Dio Cassius and Plutarch.

As well as the material written by Augustus, there are archaeological and epigraphic remains that throw light on his reign—his Forum, the eulogistic inscriptions on the bases of the statues of great men which stood there, and his Altar of Peace.

The Res Gestae

What is the Res Gestae?

> The achievements of the Divine Augustus, by which he brought the world under the empire of the Roman people, and of the expenses which he bore for the state and people of Rome.[1]

The work was composed by Augustus over a period of time; it was intended to be read in the senate after his death and subsequently to be engraved upon the bronze tablets attached to the pillars of his Mausoleum in the Campus Martius.

In thus enumerating his achievements Augustus was following the usual custom of influential Romans, who caused to be inscribed on their tombstones a list of the regular magistracies held by them, any distinctive tributes paid to them by the people, and a particular example of their leadership.

What was the purpose of the Res Gestae?

Its immediate purpose was to direct discussion in the senate after his death to the particular themes he had selected, but more important was the intention to prescribe what people in the future would think of him.

How was the work preserved?

Suetonius mentions that among Augustus' documents deposited with the Vestal Virgins was a 'record of his reign which he wished to have engraved on bronze pillars and placed at the entrance to his Mausoleum'.[2] Although a shell of the Mausoleum still exists today the pillars have long since disappeared, but copies of the inscription were made in both Latin and Greek and set up on the walls of many provincial temples to Rome and Augustus. The copy available to historians today was found on a temple in Ancyra (modern Ankara) in the province of Galatia (modern Turkey), and although there were a few gaps in the Latin version, the Greek text is complete.

Particular features of the Res Gestae

- Since the document was intended to be inscribed, its text is simple and concise with not a word too many. It avoids superlatives, descriptive adjectives and adverbs.
- Most honorific inscriptions and eulogies were brief, but the *Res Gestae* comprises 300 lines in all. Obviously Augustus had a very long public career and had much more to record than other influential Romans. No-one had ever held so many offices for so long, nor had anyone before him given the Roman people so many benefits.
- Many eulogies emphasised the dead man's clan, family, father and ancestors, as well as his heirs. Augustus did not mention any of his family except where they were linked with him in his public honours or affairs. Nothing is said about his natural family; they were not greatly distinguished, and he was aware that to emphasise his connection with Julius Caesar would not win him universal support. As far as his heirs were concerned, he was rather unfortunate in that most of them died before him. He claimed that his fame rested on the fact that he honoured and benefited not just his own family but rather the whole Roman people. His use of the title *Pater Patriae* (Father of the Country) in the *Res Gestae*, in his Forum, on coins and in official documents emphasises this.
- At no point does he mention his enemies (Antony, Brutus, Cassius, Lepidus or Sextus Pompeius) by name. Antony is referred to as part of 'a faction', Brutus and Cassius are called 'the murderers of my father', Lepidus is described as his 'colleague who is still alive' and Sextus Pompeius as a pirate.[3]
- Since the *Res Gestae* was meant to be inscribed in Rome, it emphasises those things that he did for the people of Rome particularly and only mentions the provinces when describing his conquests.
- It was natural for Augustus to want to present to posterity a favourable view of his reign, and in order to achieve this he omitted certain pieces of information and so deliberately slanted his account. 'Not only does the document omit those things which Augustus probably wished forgotten, but it is also not a complete enumeration of his achievements.'[4] He fails to explain his foreign policy, mentions only part of his legislation, ignores altogether his reforms of the administration and disregards some of the old religious customs he revived.
- He goes to a great deal of trouble to insist that he did not accept any individual position or honour which was unrepublican in character, and throughout the work he plays down his imperium and stresses his tribunician powers. Yet although he maintained that he had no more official power than other magistrates, it must have been obvious to all

Romans that no other man had held so many positions and powers simultaneously and for so long.

The main divisions within the document

Sections 1–14 outline the magistracies (*honores*) and special tributes awarded to Augustus. These reveal the extent of the Roman people's trust in him.

Sections 15–25 list the expenses (*impensae*) that he incurred for the Roman people. The fact that he paid for so much was the reason they trusted him.

Sections 26–33 outline the military and diplomatic achievements (*res gestae*) by which he 'brought the world under the empire of the Roman people'.[5] This was to emphasise to the people the extent to which they were dependent on him for their security.

Sections 34–35 represent the culmination of the whole document. Here he points out his greatest achievement, qualities for posterity to imitate (*exempla virtutis*), and his relationship (*Pater Patriae*) with the people of Rome.

Later in this chapter there is an exercise on each of these divisions of the *Res Gestae*.

Other sources

Velleius Paterculus

An admirer of Augustus

Paterculus (born 19 BC) was a contemporary of Augustus and Tiberius and wrote a brief history of Rome from the destruction of Troy to AD 30, in two books. As an ardent admirer of Augustus, he devotes half a book to him. His chief interest was in military affairs, as he had served as a military tribune in Thrace and Macedonia and under Gaius Caesar in the east. During the Pannonian revolt in AD 6 he was sent to help Tiberius and subsequently served as his legate in Pannonia. He reached the position of praetor in AD 15 (the year after Augustus' death).

Although his history is rather naive, and typical of other contemporary writers in its excessive praise of Augustus, it is particularly useful for the wars in the north and as a balance to the work of Tacitus on Augustus and Tiberius.

Tacitus

Unfavourable view of Augustus

Tacitus, who lived about AD 55–120, wrote his famous *Annals* from the end of Augustus' reign to the death of Nero. Since his work applies more to the reigns of the emperors, Tiberius, Claudius and Nero, it is looked at in more detail in the introduction to the section on the Julio-Claudians. His account is not favourable to the principate in general, nor to Augustus in particular.

Suetonius

Suetonius revealed character of Augustus

Born towards the end of the first century AD, Suetonius reached the position of secretary to Emperor Hadrian, which enabled him to have access to the imperial archives. His *Lives of the Twelve Caesars* (from Julius Caesar to Domitian) is a valuable source of information for the first century, although some of it is unreliable and based on court gossip. He does not follow a chronological order and was not particularly interested in military matters, but his personal anecdotes reveal a great deal about the characters of the emperors and it is obvious that he had access to Augustus' *Memoirs* and correspondence, as well as being familiar with earlier historians.

Dio Cassius

Dio Cassius — only surviving full-length account

Dio Cassius, born about AD 150 in Bithynia, went to Rome in 180 and served in various capacities under the emperors Commodus, Caracalla, Septimius and Alexander Severus. He wrote eighty books on the history of Rome from the arrival of Aeneas in Italy to AD 229, but only those dealing with the period from 68 BC to AD 47 have survived intact. His work is the only surviving full-length account of Augustus' reign but since it was written over 200 years after the events it describes, it must be treated with care. He tends to interpret some of the events of Augustus' day in terms of what things were like in his own time, but he seems to have been aware of the administrative and constitutional organisation of the empire in the preceding centuries. Without his work, modern historians would know very little about the constitutional changes that occurred in 23 and 19 BC, and he is a good source for the lists of powers and honours conferred on Augustus throughout his reign.

Augustus' constitutional position, honours and titles

After his defeat of Antony and Cleopatra, Augustus returned from the east and spent several years restoring order and confidence among the people. However, at this time he had to give up the extraordinary and temporary powers he had held as a triumvir and establish a new position for himself within the state.

Factors that influenced Augustus' actions in 27

He believed that the safety and wellbeing of the state depended on him personally. The senate had failed in the preceding century to change its methods of government and had been unable to prevent ambitious commanders and their armies from seizing control. Further civil war and anarchy had to be avoided, and this could only be achieved if he kept control of the armed forces, so preventing the rise of military rivals.

On the other hand, because of his conservative temperament he preferred constitutional government rather than military monarchy, and in order to avoid the fate of his adoptive father, Julius Caesar, he had to remain sensitive to the needs of his peers in the nobility. Although he was overwhelmingly popular with the mass of the people, he had to avoid any hostility from the senatorial order.

It is believed that he consulted with his friends and supporters about his position, and at the beginning of 27 he renounced all his powers. 'I transferred the republic from my power to the dominion of the senate and the people of Rome.'[6]

Augustus' constitutional position, 31–19

31–27

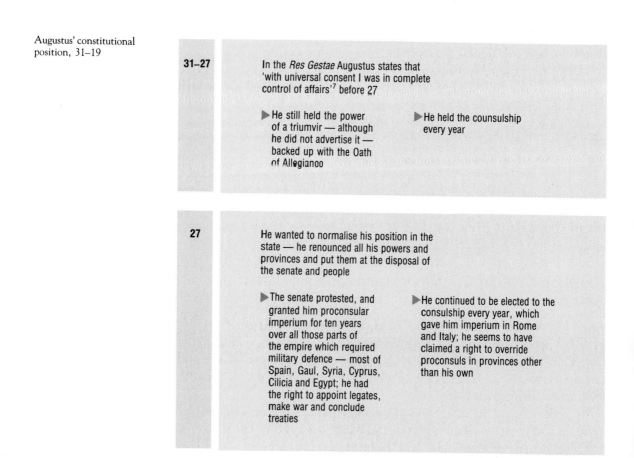

In the *Res Gestae* Augustus states that 'with universal consent I was in complete control of affairs'[7] before 27

- He still held the power of a triumvir — although he did not advertise it — backed up with the Oath of Allegiance
- He held the counsulship every year

27

He wanted to normalise his position in the state — he renounced all his powers and provinces and put them at the disposal of the senate and people

- The senate protested, and granted him proconsular imperium for ten years over all those parts of the empire which required military defence — most of Spain, Gaul, Syria, Cyprus, Cilicia and Egypt; he had the right to appoint legates, make war and conclude treaties
- He continued to be elected to the consulship every year, which gave him imperium in Rome and Italy; he seems to have claimed a right to override proconsuls in provinces other than his own

23

Between 27 and 24 he was away in his provinces, but in 23 two events occurred which made him reconsider his constitutional position

A serious conspiracy was organised against him by Varro Murena and Fannius Caepio, highlighting senatorial resentment of his continuing consulships, which limited their ambitions

He became desperately ill and believed he was about to die; this may have encouraged him to give up the consulship with its tiring day-to-day business — at least it was a convenient excuse

He resigned the consulship in 23 but was compensated for the loss of his consular imperium in two ways

- His proconsular imperium was recognised as superior (maius): although it was restricted by a time limit (renewed when necessary), there was virtually no other limitation on his imperium; his control of the army through his proconsular power was the basis of his exceptional position within the empire, but he chose to play this down and disguise it by emphasising the tribunician power
- He was granted tribunician power for life without a colleague unless he co-opted one, which gave him the right to legislate in the assembly, to summon the senate and put motions to it, to veto and to officially help citizens who were oppressed by magistrates; although he had little need to use this power, the tribunicia potestas came to be officially regarded as the legal basis of his power and was used to date his 'reign'

22–19

In 23 his imperium applied only to the provinces and lapsed when he entered Rome, and to compensate him for this he was granted the imperium of a consul and the various outward signs of this power between 22 and 19; he refused the offer of a dictatorship, of the consulship for life and of censorship during this period. 'The dictatorship was offered to me by both the senate and the people in my absence . . . but I refused it . . . At that time the consulship was also offered to me, to be held each year for the rest of my life, and I refused it'[8]

- The imperium of a consul without holding the position of consul gave him jurisdiction in Rome and Italy
- He had the right to sit on a curule chair between the consuls in the senate, to be attended by twelve lictors, and to summon the senate and put the first business before it

His constitutional powers were complete: other titles and honours were given to him after this date (see pp. 426, 428), but they did not alter this; the real powers — his maius imperium as a proconsul and his consular imperium — are not emphasised in the *Res Gestae*, while his tribunician power is, appearing on every inscription and being used to give honour to the one with whom Augustus chose to share it from time to time

'On five occasions, of my own initiative, I asked for and received from the senate a colleague in that power.'[9]

Did Augustus 'restore the republic' in 27?

Interpretations of res publica restituta

Some modern and ancient sources make reference to the so-called 'restoration of the republic' by Augustus in 27. They seem to indicate that when he claimed to have transferred the republic from his control to that of the senate and people (Res Gestae), he meant that he restored a system of government that had existed in the past. According to E. A. Judge, Augustus' words should rather be interpreted as meaning that he handed back control of the 'commonwealth' or 'country' (*res publica*) after having held extraordinary powers by 'universal consent'.

Contemporary view — Paterculus

For example, Velleius Paterculus wrote,

> After twenty years the civil wars were ended . . . their force was restored to the laws, authority to the courts, its majesty to the senate; the rule of the magistrates was restored to its old form.'[10]

Another contemporary of Augustus also refers to the anniversary of the day when 'every province was given back to our own people'.[11]

View of Suetonius

Suetonius believed that

> Twice Augustus seriously thought of restoring the republican system: immediately after the fall of Antony . . . and again when he could not shake off an exhausting illness . . . On reconsideration, however, he decided that to divide the responsibilities of government among several hands would be to jeopardise not only his own life, but national security; so he did not do so.[12]

Opinion of Tacitus

Tacitus, writing towards the end of the first century AD, did not believe that Augustus had restored the republic. 'Then he gradually pushed ahead and absorbed the functions of the senate, the officials, and even the law.'[13] Tacitus maintains that the position of Augustus was monarchical.

Dio Cassius — 'a pretence'

Dio Cassius, more than two hundred years later, believed that Augustus' attempt to 'restore the republic' was mere pretence. It is his view that has influenced many modern writers to subscribe to a 'facade' theory — that Augustus pretended to restore the republic by building up an elaborate facade behind which he hid his real powers while gradually establishing another form of government, the principate. However, it is in the article called 'Res Publica Restituta — a Modern Illusion', that E. A. Judge says that there is no evidence that Augustus ever claimed to have 'restored the republic', but that, in fact, his words should be taken to mean that after having himself held, with universal approval, extraordinary powers as princeps he returned control of the res publica to the senate and the people. Judge believes it is not likely that

Influence on modern views

An alternative modern view

so realistic a devotee of self-display as Augustus would have wanted or needed to lurk behind anything, or that the Roman people would have expected him to do so, or would have been taken in if he had.[14]

Exercise: The Res Gestae — *tributes and magistracies*

In the *Res Gestae* Augustus follows the usual Roman custom of enumerating his magistracies (honores) and the many special tributes conferred on him. Self-praise was a normal feature of Roman public life, and it was expected that a man's achievements should be outlined at his funeral and later inscribed on his sarcophagus or tomb.

1 Draw up a chart of two columns under the headings 'Magistracies' and 'Services for which they were conferred'. Read sections 1–7 in the *Res Gestae* and fill in the appropriate details.

2 On a number of occasions Augustus omits certain information and is highly selective in his choice of what is included, so that although his statements are not inaccurate they do not give all the facts.

From your previous work on the early years of Augustus' career, explain why sections 1, 3.1 and 7.1 do not give the complete picture and are therefore misleading.

3 Make a list of the special tributes conferred on Augustus mentioned in sections 9–14 and 34–35.

Shown here and on the following page are portions of the Ara Pacis (Altar of Peace) which was erected in the Campus Martius between 13 and 9 BC to celebrate the return of Augustus from his long absence in Gaul; the monument consisted of an altar surrounded by a square marble wall on which was carved a frieze of figures symbolising the ideals of Augustus

The broken east wall shows a woman with two babies, representing Mother Earth of Italy, with fruit in her lap and animals at her feet — symbols of contentment and abundance

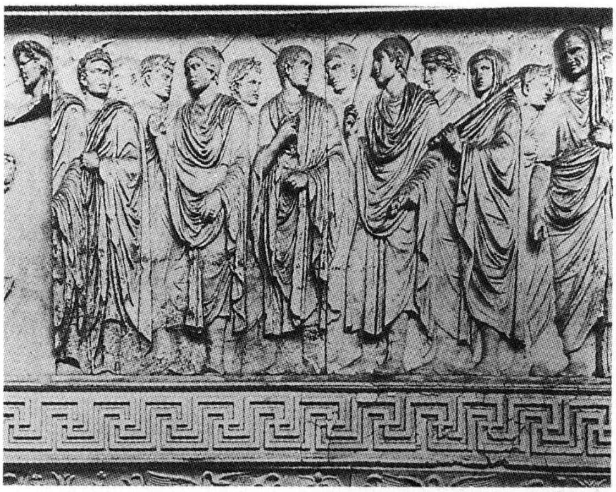

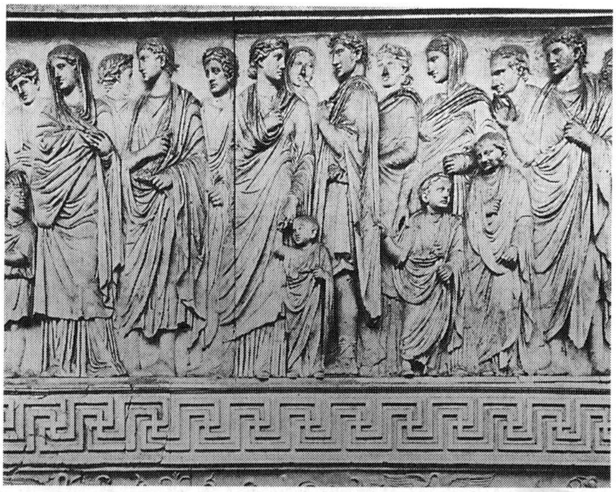

The south wall depicts a procession of Augustus and his family with members of the priestly colleges: this illustrates the importance he placed on religion and the family, and may also have symbolised his dynastic hopes — the figures appear to be realistic portarits

The north wall shows senators, magistrates and people following the procession of Augustus; another representation on the monument includes Aeneas arriving in Italy

The significance of Augustus' titles

Titles found in inscriptions

Augustus held the consulship thirteen times in the first century BC (43, 33, 31–23, 5, 2); he held the tribunicia potestas for thirty-seven years from 23 BC, and the maius imperium was renewed every five years from 23 BC — in 18, 13 and 8 BC and in AD 3 and 13. He was also granted additional titles, and by AD 14 those appearing on inscriptions were

Coin representing Augustus as 'pater patriae' (father of his country), an honour that was granted to him in 2 BC

usually shown as Pontifex Maximus, Consul XIII, Tribunicia Potestate XXXVII, Imperator XXI and Pater Patriae. However, since none of these was really suitable for everyday use, the title Princeps was adopted.

Title	*Date*	*Significance*	*Reference in the sources*
Imperator	43	This was first conferred as a temporary military title.	'I was twenty-one times saluted as imperator.'[15]
	30	Officially a praenomen, owing to its military nature Augustus did not use this in Rome or Italy — only in the eastern provinces.	
Princeps senatus	28	After Augustus had revised the list of senators for the first time, his name was placed at the head of the senatorial list and this entitled him to be the first to give his opinion in the senate.	'Up to the time of writing I have been princeps senatus for forty years.'[16]

Title	*Date*	*Significance*	*Reference in the sources*
Augustus	27	This was conferred by the senate. It increased his dignity since it meant 'one to be revered', but it did not add to his power.	'Later he adopted . . . the title Augustus after a motion to that effect had been introduced by Munatius Plancus. Some senators wished him to be called Romulus, as the second founder of the city; but Plancus had his way. He argued that "Augustus" was both a more original and honourable title, since sanctuaries and all places consecrated by the augurs are known as "august".'[17]
Princeps	27	This was short for *princeps civitatis* and meant 'first citizen'. It had been used to describe leading men of the republic, and implied authority but not power.	'While I was the leading citizen, the senate resolved that it should be shut on three occasions.'[18]
Pontifex maximus	12	Augustus succeeded Lepidus, on his death, as the head of the priesthoods and the state religion, through which he had control of political and judicial procedure.	'I declined to be made pontifex maximus in the place of my colleague who was still alive when the people offered me this priesthood . . . Some years later . . . I received this priesthood . . . and such concourse poured in from the whole of Italy to my election as has never been recorded at Rome before that time.'[19]
Pater patriae	2	This title had been held by Cicero. It meant 'Father of the Country' and was the title which Augustus inscribed on the monument set in the middle of his new forum, which was opened in this year. He regarded this as the high point of his career.	'In my thirteenth consulship the senate, the equestrian order and the whole people of Rome gave me the title of Father of my Country, and resolved that this should be incribed in the porch of my house and in the Curia Julia and in the Forum Augustum below the chariot . . .'[20] 'Fathers of the Senate, I have at last achieved my highest ambition. What more can I ask of the immortal gods than that they permit me to enjoy your approval until my dying day.'[21]

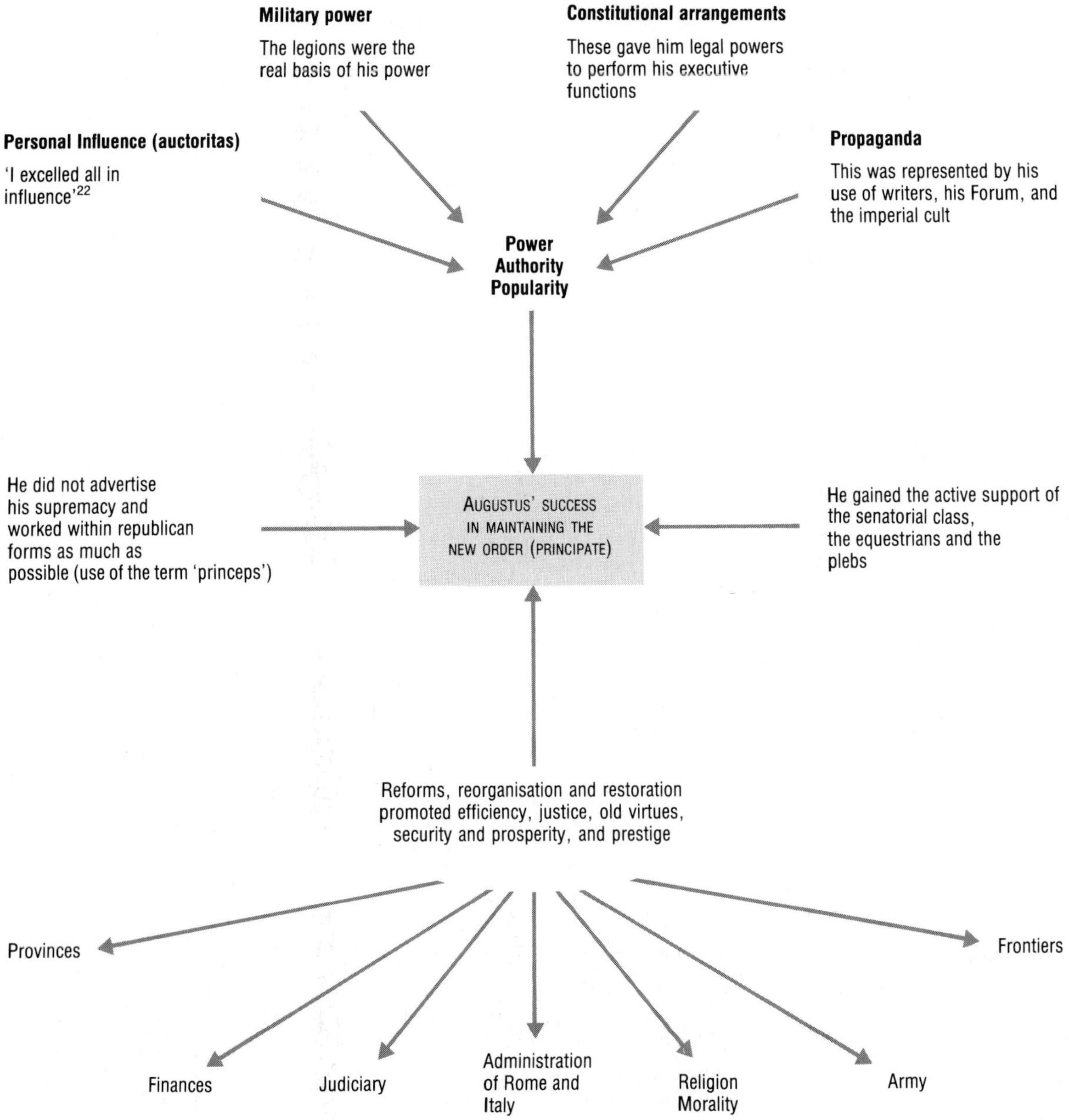
Military power
The legions were the real basis of his power
Constitutional arrangements
These gave him legal powers to perform his executive functions
Personal Influence (auctoritas)
'I excelled all in influence'[22]
Propaganda
This was represented by his use of writers, his Forum, and the imperial cult
Power
Authority
Popularity
He did not advertise his supremacy and worked within republican forms as much as possible (use of the term 'princeps')
Augustus' success in maintaining the new order (principate)
He gained the active support of the senatorial class, the equestrians and the plebs
Reforms, reorganisation and restoration promoted efficiency, justice, old virtues, security and prosperity, and prestige
Provinces
Frontiers
Finances
Judiciary
Administration of Rome and Italy
Religion
Morality
Army

The senate and the magistrates under Augustus

Three factors influenced Augustus in his relationship with the senate. The experiences of Julius Caesar, his own conservative inclinations and his need for co-operation in the running of the empire.

Influence of Julius Caesar on Augustus

He had learnt from Julius Caesar's mistakes. Towards the end of Caesar's career he had shown his lack of respect for the senate quite openly, and had also blocked the ambitions of prominent men by holding so many of the top positions himself, particularly the dictatorship. Augustus, however, attempted to reconcile the senate to his regime by restoring its dignity and making it a more worthy body than it had been in the last years of the republic. He also realised that the traditional desire of the members of the senatorial order to compete for the highest positions in the state could not be frustrated.

Attempts to retain republican forms

Augustus was a conservative, and where possible he preferred to maintain republican forms as long as they were efficient. Where change was needed he showed political tact, so that he avoided offending the upper classes. He wanted it to be said that the senate was performing its ancient functions.

Its members still held the annual magistracies and chief military positions; they retained control of the treasury, administered the more peaceful provinces, voted honours to Augustus and in theory had the right to choose the new princeps and either honour or condemn him after his death.

Enormous administrative task

The administration of the empire was an enormous task. Maecenas, one of Augustus' most trusted friends, expressed the view that

> The cause of our troubles is the multitude of our population and the magnitude of the business of our government: for the population embraces men of every kind, in respect both of race and endowment and both their tempers and their desires are manifold: and the business of the State has become so vast that it can be administered only with the greatest difficulty.[23]

Work (not power) shared with senate

Augustus therefore needed to share the workload with the senators, and they co-operated in running the empire, dividing legislative, executive and judicial functions between them. There was never a division of power, however, since Augustus alone had control of the armed forces and he was also able to influence most areas of administration controlled by the senate.

Augustus' relationship with the senate and magistrates

Revision of the senatorial roll

Removal of unsuitable members

Augustus attempted to raise the tone of the senate by removing the large number of disreputable characters who had

> secured admission after Caesar's death through influence or bribery. The sight of this sad and ill-assorted rabble decided Augustus to restore the order to its former size and repute by two new acts of enrolment.[24]

Although Suetonius mentions two revisions of the senatorial rolls, (probably the ones held in 28 and 18), there is believed to have been another held in 11 BC. Augustus hoped to reduce the numbers from 1000 to the Sullan figure of 600, but only 150 men were expelled; a further fifty who resigned were allowed to keep the trappings of the senatorial order. In the subsequent revision he hoped further to reduce the number to 300 by encouraging the senators themselves to select those members who they considered should be removed. When he detected corruption, however, he made the choice himself, and managed only to reduce the 800 to 600.

Number reduced to 600

Qualification for membership

The qualification for membership of the senatorial order was by birth — in special cases, by imperial grant. Although Augustus encouraged the hereditary nature of the class by allowing the sons of members to attend the senate when they came of age, and to wear the tunic with the broad purple stripe (*laticlave*), he also added other worthy men to the senatorial rolls himself: those favoured by him to join the senatorial order were from the equestrian class. Augustus also laid down a monetary qualification of one million sesterces for entry into the order — this was usually in the form of landed wealth. He personally assisted some worthy families without the required capital qualification to remain within the class.

Augustus favoured entry of equestrians

Monetary qualification

Restoration of dignity and responsibility

Augustus attempted to make each sitting of the senate more dignified by ruling that the senators should offer wine and incense before taking their places. Also — to encourage a more serious attitude to their duties — he increased the fines for non-attendance and forbade senators to leave Italy without permission. According to Suetonius, during critical debates Augustus ignored the usual custom of calling on speakers in order of seniority, but chose them at random.

Members encouraged to take more interest

> This was intended to make all present take an alert interest in proceedings and feel responsible for constructive thought, instead of merely rising to remark: 'I agree with the last speaker'.[25]

Fewer sessions

To allow senators to discharge their duties with less inconvenience, Augustus reduced the sessions to two a month and established the quorum necessary for different kinds of business. A senate committee composed of himself, the consuls, one from each of the colleges of magistrates and fifteen senators (chosen by lot every six months) prepared business to be submitted to the senate.

Removed inconveniences

Competition encouraged

Retained the prestige of the consulship

Augustus retained the glamour of the consulship, which was the stepping stone to achieving the proconsulships of the important provinces of Asia and Africa; it opened the way for the more outstanding and experienced to become *legati propraetore* of imperial provinces, and to command armies. Ex-consuls also directed boards of senators, appointed to look after specific administrative areas such as the supervision of grain and water supplies, highways and roads, and public works. Augustus used them to hear appeals from the provinces and to listen to the requests of foreign envoys in matters which did not require the princeps and senate's attention.

Shortened tenure of consuls

Consulship opened to 'new men'

In order to give more senators the chance to attain the consulship and more families the opportunity to become noble, as well as to increase the number of ex-consuls for administration, Augustus shortened the length of consulship from one year to six months after 5 BC. This enabled two pairs of consuls—*consules ordinarii* (the first pair of the year) and *consules suffecti* (the later pair)—to be elected. Augustus also opened the consulship to more 'new men'.

Increased responsibility for praetors

Praetorships still competitive

Competition for the position of praetor was still keen under Augustus, since propraetors were selected for military commands and as governors of some senatorial provinces. Augustus increased their functions. Not only were praetors still in charge of urban jurisdiction—two were appointed to manage the state treasury, and three ex-praetors were in charge of the military treasury. After 22 they also took over from the aediles the organisation of games and festivals.

Quaestorship

Opportunities for experience

Aediles' loss of functions

The quaestorship retained its importance as the prerequisite for entry into the senate. It also provided an opportunity for young members of the senatorial order to gain experience in administration, since six quaestors served in the provinces and the rest assisted the consuls and Augustus. Since the aediles lost most of their traditional functions (the corn supply and the giving of the games in 22, water supply in 11 and fire control in AD 6), Augustus found it difficult to fill these positions. The same situation existed with regard to tribunes, since in effect they no longer had the ability to propose legislation or to use the veto.

The following chart summarises the relative legislative, executive and judicial functions and powers of the senate and Augustus.

	The senate	*Augustus*
Legislative functions	The senate gradually developed into a legislative body — its senatus consulta became law.	
	A senate committee prepared material for presentation to the whole senate. The initiative and advice often came from Augustus, who was a member, and it was unlikely that the committee would submit something of which he disapproved. After AD 13 the committee included members who were not senators and was able to pass resolutions which became law.	Augustus could legislate by using his tribunician power to present measures to the people. However, he normally did it in other ways — through edicts, judicial decisions, replies to petitions and instructions to officials.
Executive functions	The senate controlled the peaceful provinces.	
	Augustus could interfere, if he thought it necessary, by virtue of his maius imperium. He also reallocated provinces to the senate as conditions changed.	He was responsible for those provinces which needed a military presence. Egypt was the princeps' personal domain.
	The senate and the annual magistrates were in charge of many of the public services.	
	Augustus began to interfere more and more. The candidates which he personally recommended were generally elected; later, prefects nominated by him were in charge of most departments.	Augustus avoided taking over departments of the administration of Rome himself and entrusted them to senatorial commissioners, but he did employ talented equites. In Italy, his personal force, the Praetorian Guard, provided the garrison.
	The senate was in charge of the state treasury and had the right to mint copper and bronze coins in Rome.	
	Augustus could control even this area of the senate's administration, since he occasionally supplemented funds in the treasury with his own personal wealth. He was also able to draw from the provincial *fisci*.	He kept departmental chests in his provinces from which he drew his expenses and indirectly controlled the military treasury. He alone had the power to mint gold and silver coins.
	The senate had no control over foreign affairs except to occasionally exchange greetings with foreign embassies.	
		Augustus had the power to negotiate with client-kings, to sign treaties and to decide between war and peace, since he had the real power in the state.

	The senate	*Augustus*
Judicial functions	The senate, sitting with the two consuls, formed one of two new criminal courts (see also p. 445). This tried important political cases and those involving senators and other prominent people. Augustus could attend and exercise his authority, since voting was open. However, the senate was more independent in judicial functions than in other areas.	Augustus in council formed another court of criminal justice. Those cases which came before him were wider in scope than those which the senatorial court handled. 'Appeals to Caesar' against capital punishment decided by a magistrate increased in frequency.

The equestrian order, the plebs and the freedmen

Augustus and the equestrian order

Reorganisation of equestrian order

Throughout the period of the late republic there had been a certain amount of hostility between the senate and the equites, particularly with regard to the control of the courts. Augustus attempted to prevent further clashes by finding positions in the new regime for the equites which would not compete with the interests of the senatorial class. He also aimed to reorganise the equestrian order so that it was not just a class of wealthy men but was filled with able individuals, some of whom would be recruited from the more worthwhile and successful lower classes, such as the veteran centurions.

Positions available for equites

The administration of Rome, Italy and the provinces was shared by the senate and the princeps. This meant that there were many new posts created which had never been part of the republican government, some of which involved performing duties for Augustus. Members of the senate would have been offended if he had asked them to carry out such duties, since they were regarded as his equals. So began the civil service which, although in its infancy, provided Augustus with the opportunity to employ talented equites who had vast experience in banking, tax collecting and business.

Revived military aspect

Augustus wanted to also revive the ancient link between the equestrian order and the military (they had originated as a class of knights). Not only did this revive republican traditions, it also emphasised the fact that if young ambitious members of this class wished to pursue an administrative career they would first have to undergo real military service.

Qualifications for membership

Membership of the equestrian order not only was restricted to those of honourable character with a census rating of at least 4 000 000 sesterces; it also depended on the approval of the princeps. Admission was controlled completely by Augustus, who carried out periodical revision of the rolls. Membership entitled equites to wear a tunic with a narrow purple stripe (*angusticlave*), to occupy the first fourteen rows in the theatre, to wear a gold ring and to sit on the jury courts. A member was also presented with a horse at the public expense, and Augustus revived the old annual march-past of knights and their horses before the consuls. It now took place before Augustus on 15 July, and included only those knights under thirty-five.

The diagram below shows the steps that could be followed by ambitious and talented equites. However, under Augustus there does not appear to have been a regular pattern of promotion.

Possible career path for a member of the equestrian order under Augustus

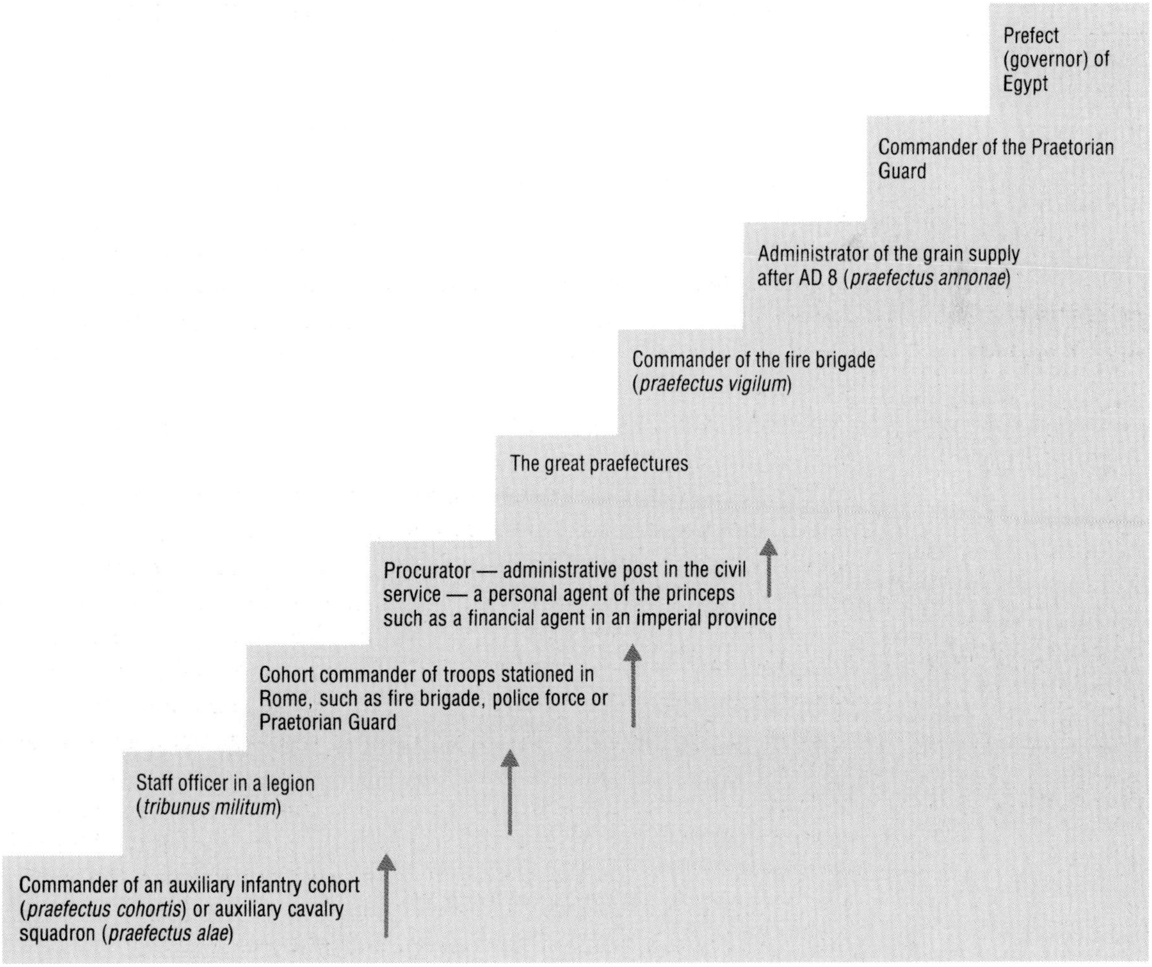

The plebs and the freedmen

> Augustus seems to have regarded the Roman plebs with the same contemptuous indulgence as most upper-class Romans. He made no attempt to carry on his adoptive father's radical policy of sending them out to colonies . . . but kept them quiet with games and money distributions.[26]

Social legislation reflected unemployment

As there was no real industry in Rome, there were large numbers of unemployed Roman citizens who found it difficult to survive. However, even those with a trade or those employed as labourers still suffered from food shortages, and it had become an important part of social legislation to provide grain doles and free games to keep them relatively contented. The government alone could not provide enough; it was up to wealthy individuals to supplement the state's contributions. The idea of patronage had existed throughout the republic and had provided the nobles with dependants who supported them politically.

Recipients of corn dole reduced in number

At the time of Augustus about two-thirds of the *plebs urbana* (urban mob) were recipients of the grain dole (sometimes referred to as the *urbs frumentaria*); he had reduced the number eligible for the ration of 5 modii a month from 250 000 to approximately 200 000, not all of whom were unemployed idlers. According to Suetonius,

> Augustus revised the roll of citizens, ward by ward; and tried to obviate the frequent interruptions of their trade and businesses which the public grain-distribution entailed, by handing out tickets, three times a year, valid for a four months' supply; but was implored to resume the former custom of monthly distributions, and consented.[27]

Personal donations by Augustus to plebs

The provision of grain doles was a great drain on the treasury and Augustus, like other wealthy nobles, himself made frequent cash donations to the plebs as well as providing grain from his own granary in times of serious shortages. He outlines some of these in the *Res Gestae* 15, 1–2; 18.

> . . . and once again in my tenth consulship I paid out 400 sesterces as largesse to each man from my own patrimony, and in my eleventh consulship I bought grain with my own money and distributed twelve rations apiece, and in the twelfth year of my tribunician power I gave every man 400 sesterces for the third time. These largesses of mine never reached fewer than 250 000 persons. In the eighteenth year of my tribunician power and my twelfth consulship I gave 240 sesterces apiece to 320 000 members of the urban plebs.[28]

Political implications of donations

It is interesting to note that his donations seem to correspond to politically important events in his reign. This is pointed out in the commentary by Brunt and Moore on the *Res Gestae*; for example, his donations of 23 seem to coincide with his changed constitutional position in that year, and his distributions in 5 and 2 BC correspond to the introduction of his 'sons' to official life. However, Suetonius cites a number of examples to 'show that he did all this not to win popularity but to improve public welfare'.[29]

Unfortunately, these handouts by both government and individuals encouraged a large number of the Roman plebs to attempt to survive solely on public and private charity. According to Suetonius, on one occasion Augustus, in response to citizens' demand for largesse, 'issued a proclamation in which he called them a pack of shameless rascals and added that though he intended to make them a money present, he would now tighten his purse-strings'.[30]

Augustus' attitude to those seeking 'hand-outs'

Suetonius maintains that no Roman magistrate had ever 'provided so many, so different, or such splendid public shows' as had Augustus.[31] They included gladiatorial games and beast hunts in the Forum, the amphitheatre and the Circus; athletic competitions in the Campus Martius; plays presented in various city districts; and even a mock sea battle, for which he excavated an artificial lake beside the Tiber River, approximately 600 metres long by 200 metres wide (refer to Suetonius, 43–5, and the *Res Gestae*, 22–3). Many of these spectacles were presented in his own name and the names of various family members, while twenty-three were given on behalf of other magistrates who were unable to afford the expense or else were absent from Rome.

Games and shows provided

As well as providing free grain and shows, Augustus helped many of the plebs to gain steady work through his extensive building program, and they regarded him as their benefactor. They were particularly bound to him by virtue of his tribunician power, which he stressed throughout the *Res Gestae*.

Employment opportunities

The plebs were gradually excluded from any meaningful part in political life; the popular assemblies were still held, but their legislative function eventually faded away and their election of magistrates was influenced by Augustus' 'recommendation' of candidates. However, in the past the nobles had been able to control the assemblies, particularly through their clients, so the replacement of an oligarchy with a princeps did not really make any difference to them politically.

Gradual loss of legislative powers

Freedmen (libertini)

Freedmen, referred to as libertini, were former slaves freed by their masters for a variety of reasons; those manumitted (freed) were usually the most trusted and intelligent. Although there was a tax on manumission, and other discriminatory legislation was passed by Augustus to restrict their numbers, the proportion of freedmen to free-born (*ingenui*) was rather high in Rome.

Manumission restrictions

Once manumitted, they took the citizenship of their former masters, but even so were not regarded as fully privileged Roman citizens.

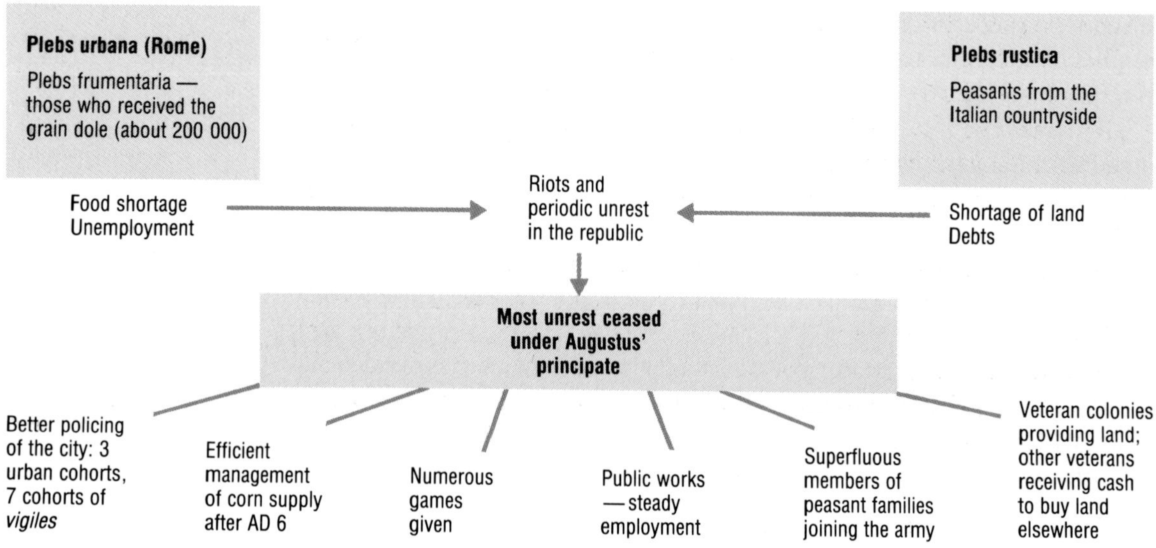

The Roman plebs

Status of freedmen	
Disadvantages	*Advantages*
They continued to owe their former masters certain obligations — were unable to take any legal action against them. They were unable to hold any magistracy. They were forbidden to serve as priests of any of the old Roman gods. They could not serve as soldiers in the Praetorian Guard, legions or urban cohorts. Since a freedman was expected to wear a special cap, they were easily recognisable and therefore suffered a certain stigma socially. They were forbidden to intermarry with the senatorial class.	The ex-master continued to protect a freedman's legal interest. They were admitted to guilds, which they often organised. They were permitted to intermarry with the free-born, and their children were ingenui. They could serve in the vigiles. They monopolised the priesthoods of the non-Roman deities, and after 7 BC became wardmasters for the supervision of the worship of the Lares. They played a prominent part in the cult of Rome and Augustus — were elected as *Seviri Augustales* to promote Caesar-worship. They could obtain free-born status by the presentation of the Gold Ring by Augustus. This made them eligible to reach equestrian status.

Careers available for freedmen

- They could be artisans, messengers for magistrates, attendants, clerks and shopkeepers.
- Many remained in the households of their former masters, performing secretarial jobs or running their estates.
- Some became extremely wealthy and successful in business, particularly those who were formerly from eastern lands such as Syria.
- The more fortunate were those who were part of Augustus' household. His personal freedmen (*liberti Caesaris*) were used to manage his private affairs, particularly finance. As it was very difficult to distinguish between the princeps' private and public affairs, these men became influential civil servants and their power in the courts of Augustus' successors increased.

Religion and morality under Augustus

The extracts quoted in this diagram give some indication of the decadence of Roman society in the last years of the republic.

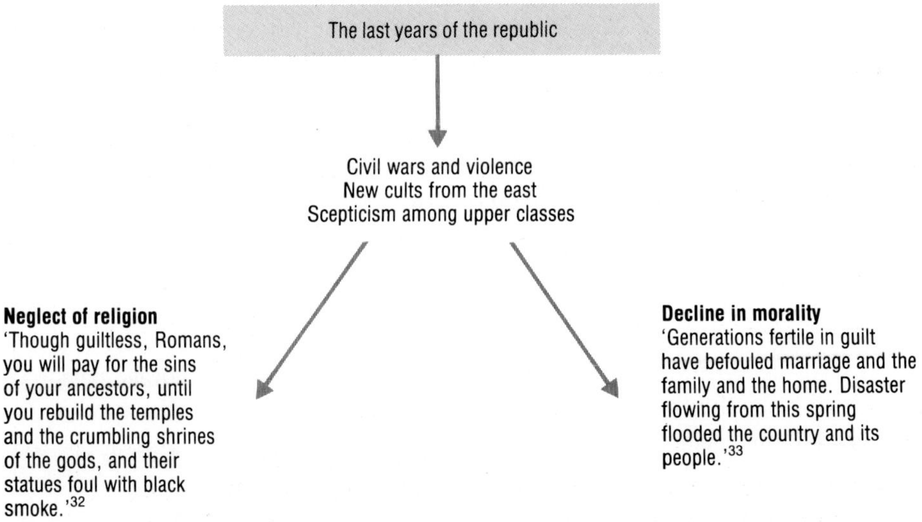

The last years of the republic
Civil wars and violence
New cults from the east
Scepticism among upper classes
Neglect of religion
'Though guiltless, Romans, you will pay for the sins of your ancestors, until you rebuild the temples and the crumbling shrines of the gods, and their statues foul with black smoke.'[32]
Decline in morality
'Generations fertile in guilt have befouled marriage and the family and the home. Disaster flowing from this spring flooded the country and its people.'[33]

Augustus' religious policy

Augustus' religious policy reflected his genuine conservative inclinations as well as his political acumen.

Reasons for revival of ancient customs

He believed that it was necessary to return to the old Roman virtues in order to strengthen his new regime and bring about permanent improvement, and one way of achieving this was to revive some of the old religious practices. Not only would this gain him the support of the pious conservatives and those people who believed that their past problems were due to negligence of the gods, but it would unite his new order with the old and both of them with himself.

As the founder of this new era, he hoped to glorify himself and the Julian family, and promote loyalty and unity within the empire.

The Secular Games

Purpose of the Games

The Secular Games, celebrated in 17 to mark the beginning of the new 'Golden Age', was the greatest religious festival celebrated during Augustus' reign. It acclaimed the restoration of peace, prosperity and the traditional virtues of the Romans. From this time it became obvious that Augustus was promoting particularly those gods which had links with the Julian family (Venus, Mars and Apollo).

The cult of Caesar-worship

Growth of Caesar-worship

This religious shift was reinforced by the growth of Caesar-worship after 12 BC, which took the form of the cults of 'Rome and Augustus' and 'Rome and the Deified Julius' in the provinces.

Hellenistic practices

In the Hellenic kingdoms of the east it was common practice to worship a ruler as a god, but this was essentially an expression of loyalty and respect rather than an act of devotion. From the time Rome became the dominant force in the east, temples had been built to Rome (the personification of Rome) and also to successful generals. It was natural then that the provincials should wish to show their gratitude to and respect for Augustus as the one responsible for restoring peace and prosperity.

Combined practices of east and west

Augustus could see the need for a common practice that would unite all the provinces in loyalty to Rome, but eastern customs would not be readily accepted in the west and he could not officially encourage personal worship of himself—particularly by Roman citizens in the provinces. He adopted a compromise, which combined the eastern worship of the ruler with the Roman reverence for dead ancestors.

Spread of the cult of Rome and Augustus

He could quite legitimately suggest that the fortunes of the imperial house were closely bound to those of the state, so his name was linked with that of Rome. The worship of Rome and Augustus spread among the provincials in the east, and after 12 BC provincials in the west also adopted the cult, which was controlled and organised by a council of delegates from major cities and areas within a province. Each year the council elected a high priest from among the upper classes, and this high priesthood was the greatest honour a provincial could receive. Annual festivals and games were also held.

The Temple of Rome and Augustus at Pola, built around AD 2–14

Cult of Rome and the Deified Julius

Roman citizens in the provinces did not worship Rome and Augustus, but—in keeping with their custom of reverence for dead ancestors—instead worshipped 'Rome and the Deified Julius'.

Municipal cults in Italy

Augustus, however, faced a bigger problem in Italy, where he could not condone worship of the imperial family or of himself, but here municipal cults of the Genius Augusti developed and were associated with the worship of the Lares.

The diagram on the page following presents eight aspects of the changes brought about by Augustus.

1

He revived priestly colleges (paying particular attention to the Vestals), defunct brotherhoods (*Arvai*), festivals (*Lupercalia*) and appointments (*flamen dialis*); he created new patrician families from which to recruit members to the colleges

He became a member of each college himself and the head of religion, as pontifex maximus, in 12 BC

2

He built new temples to Jupiter Feretrius, Jupiter the Thunderer, Quirinus, Minerva, the Great Mother, Apollo, Divine Julius and Mars the Avenger

Many of these emphasised his link with the Julian clan and its divine nature; others glorified his own achievements

3

He encouraged the worship of deities associated with the common people (the Lares guarded crossroads and the home) and divided the city into 265 areas, each with its shrine and wardmasters

He associated the worship of the Genius of Augustus (the spirit of his family and fortune) with the worship of the Lares; the people regarded him as their guardian

4

He repaired temples and shrines throughout Rome and Italy which had fallen into disrepair

In his sixth consulship he restored 82 temples in the city of Rome alone

5

He made official the worship of deities which had emerged during the civil war: Fortune, Peace, Mercury

He associated his name with them, so that they were worshipped as Fortuna Augusta, Pax Augusta and Mercurius Augusta

6

He suppressed the worship of some of the more alien cults (such as Druidism) and restricted some for Romans but not for provincials; the worship of Isis and Serapis was banned within the sacred boundary of Rome, but he was tolerant towards the Jews

He approved of some and was himself initiated into the Eleusinian Mysteries

7

Unofficial municipal cults grew up in Italy, centred around Augustus; a new college of priests drawn from freedmen was formed (Severi Augustales)

He discouraged the worship of himself by Roman citizens, as this was contrary to the principle principate

8

He allowed the worship of Rome and Augustus in the provinces, where temples were built to the personification of Rome and the imperial family (see p. 586 for details on the imperial cult of the Caesars)

He did not encourage worship of himself individually, but linked himself with Rome in order to create loyalty to the empire

Morality and Augustus' social legislation

Decline in morality among upper classes

Standards of morality among the Roman upper classes had declined, and Augustus appeared to be genuinely concerned about the breakdown of marriage and family life. Marriage was often taken lightly, with adultery becoming not only tolerated but even fashionable, and divorce common. Many people remained unmarried, and many of those who did marry appeared to have an aversion to taking on the responsibilities of children. These classes also indulged in excessive luxury, spending enormous sums of money on clothes, jewellery, houses and food. Augustus hoped to raise the general level of morality by supplementing his religious policy with social legislation, and in his efforts he was supported by the poets Horace and Ovid.

Augustus' family situation

The attitude of Augustus seems strange when one considers his own early behaviour and that of his daughter, Julia. Augustus married three times, taking his last wife, Livia, from her husband (Tiberius Nero) when she was pregnant with her second child; from his three marriages he had only one child, and she was notorious for her sexual immorality. He also forced his stepson Tiberius to divorce the wife he loved (Vipsania) and marry Julia. However, from the time Augustus married Livia (36 BC) until his death (AD 14) he seems to have been a devoted and faithful husband. The gossip related in Suetonius 68–71 can be discounted.

Used tribunician powers to legislate on morality

Using his tribunician power, Augustus pushed through the Julian Laws of 18 BC which were concerned with public morality as well as with criminal jurisdiction, but he found that to improve morals by legislation was much harder than to improve the criminal code; he seems to have been unaware of the long-term conditions that were responsible for the moral relaxation of his own day. Continued opposition to many of his regulations—especially from the equestrians—forced some adjustments to them in AD 9 (lex Papia Poppaea).

Laws on marriage, children, divorce, adultery and luxury

- He tried to limit excessive luxury through a sumptuary law, but as with previous attempts, this was a failure.
- He attempted to protect marriage by regulating sexual relations and divorce. A man had to divorce his wife before he could take any action against her for suspected adultery. Punishments for guilty parties were severe: they were sent to different islands and large parts of their estates were confiscated. A man also was punished if he married an adulterous woman or failed to divorce an adulterous wife.
- He tried to encourage marriage and the rearing of children by setting age limits on marriage (twenty-five for men, twenty for women), by imposing penalties on unmarried people (who were not permitted to accept inheritances or legacies except from close relatives) and by

Opposite: Religious changes under Augustus, here depicted as pontifex maximus

giving rewards to men and women with children (preference was given to family men in elections and allocation of provinces).

Although these laws generally failed to achieve his objectives, Augustus banished both his daughter Julia and his granddaughter Julia because of their promiscuity.

Exile of Augustus' daughter and granddaughter for immorality

> His satisfaction with the success of his family and its training was, however, suddenly dashed by Fortune. He came to the conclusion that the Elder and the Younger Julia had both been indulging in every sort of vice; and banished them.[34]

His daughter's adulteries broke his spirit; he found it harder to deal with his family's disgraces than with their deaths. According to Suetonius, he 'kept Julia for five years on a prison island before moving her to the mainland', and would not allow her any wine, luxury or male company. 'Nothing would persuade him to forgive his daughter.'[35]

Laws generally ineffective

An indication of the ineffectiveness of the laws is the fact that the two consuls (Papius and Poppaeus) who proposed the adjustments to the Julian laws in AD 9 were themselves unmarried, as were Augustus' supporters, the poets Horace and Virgil.

Judicial changes

Supervised judicial system closely

Augustus' desire for just and efficient administration was reflected in his close personal supervision of all areas of the judicial system. The changes he instituted minimised corruption, speeded up justice and reversed many poor decisions.

Reforms of existing system

The public jury courts (for criminal cases), which were now to be drawn from the equites, continued as they had under the republic but no longer dealt with notorious cases. Augustus added a court for dealing with cases of adultery, increased the number of jurymen available and paid great attention to those selected on the panels. Trial procedures were improved, and to increase the speed at which justice was dispensed he increased the number of days on which cases could be heard. Usually a governor charged with mismanagement of his province was prosecuted in the court of extortion, but Augustus initiated a speedier process for settling cases that only concerned restitution of property to a provincial: a jury of five men was expected to give a verdict within thirty days. Civil cases were still heard before magistrates — usually the praetors.

Changes in provincial justice

There appear to have been some changes in procedure in the provinces, although the evidence is by no means conclusive for the time of Augustus. Under the republic, a governor (with his consilium) exercised judicial authority but was forbidden to carry out a capital sentence on a Roman citizen; this could be done only in Rome. There seems to be evidence (criminal courts functioned in the province of Cyrenaica from 6 BC) that a new type of criminal court, manned by Roman citizens in the provinces, was introduced to deal with crimes similar to those handled by the public courts in Rome. This change was probably meant to overcome the often arbitrary punishments handed out by governors to provincials, and to allow the prosecution of Romans living in the provinces. There were still cases that were handled by the governors, but an individual had the right of appeal to Caesar against the governor's decision.

Two new high courts

The major changes that occurred in the judicial field under Augustus were the addition of two new high courts and the vast extension of the procedure of appeal.

The new criminal courts were

Senatorial court

- the *senatorial court*, which consisted of the consuls using the senate as their consilium (group of expert advisers): this court dealt with political cases such as treason and those which involved senators and their wives or other people of prominence;

Imperial court

- the *imperial court*, which consisted of Augustus and his unofficial group of advisers: this court seems to have dealt with a wider range of cases—there are examples of Augustus deciding cases of parricide, forgery (Suetonius, *Augustus*, 33) and murder.

Both courts functioned on a voluntary basis, with the accused requesting either the consul or the princeps to take the case. This request could be refused; however, according to Suetonius,

> Augustus proved assiduous in his administration of justice, once remaining in court until nightfall; and, if he happened to be unwell, would have his litter carried up to the tribunal. Sometimes he even judged cases from his sick-bed in his house. As a judge he was both conscientious and lenient.[36]

Appeal to Caesar

A system of appeal against the decisions of magistrates in Rome, Italy and the provinces became very common, and usually went to Augustus (an appeal to Caesar).

Augustus' financial arrangements

State of the public finances

The control of the state's finances had been in the hands of the senate, but by the end of the civil war the public finances were in chaos. The treasury was temporarily bankrupt, there was no fair or efficient taxation system, no budget and no reliable census records. Augustus' aims were to stabilise conditions after the civil war, to secure sufficient revenue to run a huge empire, and to control and carefully scrutinise all sources of income.

Augustus' financial aims

Imperial expenses

The revenue needed to run the empire was enormous. The greatest expense was the army; not only did the troops have to be paid, but they had to be provided with pensions at the end of their service. Another drain on the public finances was the provision of grain at reduced prices (and often free) in times of scarcity. Public works, public religion, police, fire protection, and shows for the people also required the expenditure of vast sums of money.

Need for regulation of revenue

Augustus needed to develop a new systematic regulation of revenue over which he had either direct or indirect control (see chart, p. 448). As in other areas of administration he was careful to preserve an appearance of constitutionalism, and only slowly — and in some cases indirectly — did he assume control of the imperial finances. His power as princeps depended on this. Augustus' control over the state came not only from expenditure of public money, but from the lavish use of his own personal wealth (patrimony).

The use of Augustus' personal wealth

The importance that he placed on this aspect of his financial administration can be deduced from sections 15–24 of the *Res Gestae* in which he outlines the donations made from his personal wealth to the state and military treasury, to discharged soldiers, to the Roman plebs and for buildings, games and shows in Rome. However, he selects only the most outstanding examples of his generosity to the people of Rome and Italy and does not include any gifts to the provinces (except in section 24) or to individuals.

He did not mention the occasions on which he used public money, since he would have gained no credit from that.

Exercise: The Res Gestae — *expenditure*

The following table gives the section numbers for Augustus' personal expenditure.

Money and grain contributions to the urban plebs	15:1, 2, 4; 18
Payments to his veterans	15:3; 16:2
Payments for land for his veterans	16:1
Assistance to the state treasury (*aerarium Saturni*)	17:1, 2
Payment into the military treasury (*aerarium militare*)	17:2
Building and restoration of temples	19:1, 2; 20:4

Religious dedications	21:2
Public works	19.1; 20.1, 20.3, 20.5; 21.1
Games and shows	22:1, 2, 3; 23
Remittances to Italian municipia	21:3
Gifts to provincial cities	24

Read the relevant sections and note the following:

1 the number of times he distributed largesses and the scale of them;
2 the size of the individual donations;
3 the recipients;
4 the sources of his funds.

Size of donations by Augustus

The author of the appendix to the *Res Gestae* believed that 'The amount of the money that he gave to the treasury or to the Roman plebs or to discharged soldiers was 2 400 000 000 sesterces'.[37] This figure is higher than the total mentioned in Augustus' account and so seems to indicate that he had not brought the figures up to date.

The appendix goes on to enumerate all the buildings—both religious and secular—that he built or restored at great cost, and finishes with the statement:

Expenditures

> The expenditure that he devoted to dramatic shows, to gladiatorial exhibitions and athletes and hunts and the sea battle, and the money granted to colonies, municipia, towns destroyed by earthquake and fire or to individual friends and senators whose property qualification he made up, was beyond counting.[38]

According to Suetonius, Augustus

Amount left in his will

> left a bequest of 400 000 gold pieces to the Roman commons in general; 35 000 to the two tribes with which he had family connections, ten to every Praetorian guardsman, five to every member of the city cohort; three to every legionary soldier.[39]

In addition to other large legacies to friends, he left his heirs 1 500 000 gold pieces.

The sources of Augustus' income

The word *fiscus* is sometimes used in reference to Augustus' funds (the various fisci in the imperial provinces and his private patrimony), but although in running the empire Augustus may not have drawn any distinction between these sources, he certainly did when it came to his accounting, and he also made a clear distinction in his references in the *Res Gestae*.

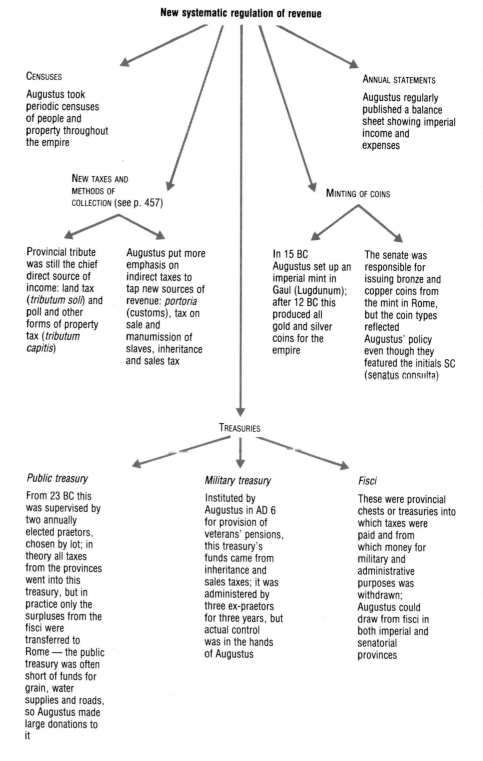

Regulation of revenue under Augustus

New systematic regulation of revenue

Censuses

Augustus took periodic censuses of people and property throughout the empire

Annual statements

Augustus regularly published a balance sheet showing imperial income and expenses

New taxes and methods of collection (see p. 457)

Provincial tribute was still the chief direct source of income: land tax (*tributum soli*) and poll and other forms of property tax (*tributum capitis*)

Augustus put more emphasis on indirect taxes to tap new sources of revenue: *portoria* (customs), tax on sale and manumission of slaves, inheritance and sales tax

Minting of coins

In 15 BC Augustus set up an imperial mint in Gaul (Lugdunum); after 12 BC this produced all gold and silver coins for the empire

The senate was responsible for issuing bronze and copper coins from the mint in Rome, but the coin types reflected Augustus' policy even though they featured the initials SC (senatus consulta)

Treasuries

Public treasury

From 23 BC this was supervised by two annually elected praetors, chosen by lot; in theory all taxes from the provinces went into this treasury, but in practice only the surpluses from the fisci were transferred to Rome — the public treasury was often short of funds for grain, water supplies and roads, so Augustus made large donations to it

Military treasury

Instituted by Augustus in AD 6 for provision of veterans' pensions, this treasury's funds came from inheritance and sales taxes; it was administered by three ex-praetors for three years, but actual control was in the hands of Augustus

Fisci

These were provincial chests or treasuries into which taxes were paid and from which money for military and administrative purposes was withdrawn; Augustus could draw from fisci in both imperial and senatorial provinces

His personal wealth came from

- inheritances from his natural father (Gaius Octavius) and his adoptive father (Julius Caesar);
- property confiscated during the proscriptions;
- the treasures of the Ptolemies of Egypt;
- booty from various wars;
- legacies from friends such as Marcellus, Maecenas, Agrippa and other prominent Romans.

Augustus' building program

Purpose of building program

Augustus' building program was intended not only to provide for the obvious needs of the people but also to promote the prestige of the empire and to glorify his own and his family's name. His new Forum Augustum also was designed to make a statement about the nature of his leadership (see pp. 502–4 for details on the contruction and propaganda value of this forum).

Some of the temples and public works were built in his name and some in the names of others. Agrippa and Tiberius were responsible for a large number of constructions, as were other leading citizens whom Augustus

Present remains of the Theatre of Marcellus, built by Augustus in memory of his son-in-law, who died in 23 BC

The Pantheon as it stands today: the original was built by Agrippa, Augustus' loyal friend and son-in-law; the domed rotunda was added by Hadrian

encouraged 'to embellish the city . . . according to their means'.[40] He also called upon men 'who had won triumphs to spend their prize money on putting other main roads into good condition'.[41]

Building materials

The traditional building materials of volcanic tufa, travertine and Roman bricks were still used, but Augustus made extensive use of the white marble from the quarries of Carrara and the various coloured marbles from the Mediterranean area.

Exercise: The Res Gestae *— public works and buildings*

Use the information in sections 19–21 and the appendix, as well as Suetonius, *Augustus*, 29–30, and draw up a chart showing the public works and temples for which Augustus and others were responsible. If possible, include information concerning the reasons for particular constructions.

	Public works	*Temples*	*Reasons*
Augustus			
Others (e.g. Agrippa)			

The administration of Rome — a summary

Aware that the city was architecturally unworthy of her position as capital of the Roman Empire, besides being vulnerable to fire and river floods, Augustus so improved her appearance that he could justifiably boast: 'I found Rome built of bricks; I leave her clothed in marble'. He also used as much foresight as could have possibly been provided in guarding against future disasters.[42]

Augustus' aims

1 To make the city worthy of its imperial position
2 To create jobs for the unemployed
3 To provide a regular supply of cheap grain
4 To provide an adequate water supply
5 To provide a system for policing the city
6 To prevent the danger of frequent fires
7 To relieve Rome from periodic flooding
8 To foster a civic spirit and local patriotism

Augustus' methods

1, 2 He embarked on an ambitious building program which included temples, basilicas, theatres, baths, libraries, granaries, warehouses,

An Augustan coin, dated 27–20, depicting ears of corn; Augustus took control of the corn supply in Rome in 22

aqueducts and a new forum. This provided employment for both skilled and unskilled workers.

3 After a serious famine a 22 BC, he took over control of the grain supply from the aediles and later established an equestrian office of Curator of the Grain Supply.

4 Prior to 12 BC he relied totally on Agrippa to build and maintain the aqueducts, reservoirs and collection basins. Agrippa kept his own gang of 240 slaves for this purpose, and on his death in 12 BC he left the slaves to Augustus, who gave them to the state and established a permanent water board in the charge of three water curators (senators).

5 He established three urban cohorts (semi-military) of 1500 men each, under the control of a consular prefect, as a special police force. If more help was needed to quell major disturbances, the Praetorian Guard could be called in. For day-to-day policing Rome was divided into 265 wards, each with four magistrates.

6 He took measures to prevent the Tiber flooding the city, 'cleared the Tiber channel which had been choked with an accumulation of rubbish and narrowed by projecting houses'.[43] This provided only temporary relief, and in AD 15 a permanent board under a consular was set up.

7 He organised a fire brigade of 600 slaves under the control of an aedile, but this proved ineffective. In AD 6 he formed seven cohorts of freedmen into the vigiles, under an equestrian prefect. Rome had been divided into fourteen districts, and each cohort of vigiles watched over two of them.

8 He promoted civic pride by setting up 265 wards, each with its own annual magistrates (see p. 586 for reference to local worship of Lares and the Genius of Augustus).

The administration of Italy

Improvements in administration

Augustus did not ignore the administration of the peninsula. Italy was divided into eleven districts, and within these areas safe and easy travel was ensured by the building and repair of roads as well as the control of brigandage and the strict regulation of slave gangs. In 27 he repaired the Via Flaminia and its bridges at his own expense, and in 20 set up a board of senators of praetorian rank to supervise the building and repair of highways throughout Italy. The twenty-eight colonies of veterans which he had established in Italy helped to lay the foundations for a revival of prosperity.

The provinces under the principate

The division of the empire between princeps and senate

Augustus' maius imperium

In 27 BC Augustus was granted a ten-year commission to administer the provinces of Spain, Gaul and Syria with proconsular imperium. In 23 his imperium was officially recognised as superior to that of all other proconsuls — maius imperium. The provinces that he was 'invited' to control in 27 were those which required huge standing armies.

Augustus kept military power in his hands

Augustus realised that the senate had failed in the past to curb ambitious commanders with large, loyal armies. In order to keep such men in their place and avoid a recurrence of civil wars — and also to maintain his own pre-eminence — he would need to make sure that most of Rome's military power remained in his hands at all times. The empire was therefore divided into two provincial groups: those provinces which had been under Roman rule for a long time and were relatively peaceful and those which had recently been subdued or were more unruly and barbaric. The more peaceful and civilised were the public provinces, administered by the senate (senatorial provinces) while the 'armed' provinces were under the control of Augustus (imperial provinces).

Division of provinces

Later changes in provincial responsibility

Some of the senatorial provinces also needed the presence of military forces, and Augustus' maius imperium entitled him to interfere in their affairs if necessary. However, as conditions changed within the empire, so the division of provincial responsibility changed: when an 'armed' province became more settled and troops were no longer needed, Augustus transferred it to the control of senate. All newly acquired territory came automatically under the control of Augustus.

The division of the empire in AD 14 (the date of Augustus' death) was somewhat different from that of 27 BC (see pp. 454–5).

Exercise

1 Carefully compare the maps overleaf and draw up a chart (as shown at right) listing the imperial and senatorial provinces in 27 BC and in AD 14.

Imperial		*Senatorial*	
27 BC	AD 14	27 BC	AD 14

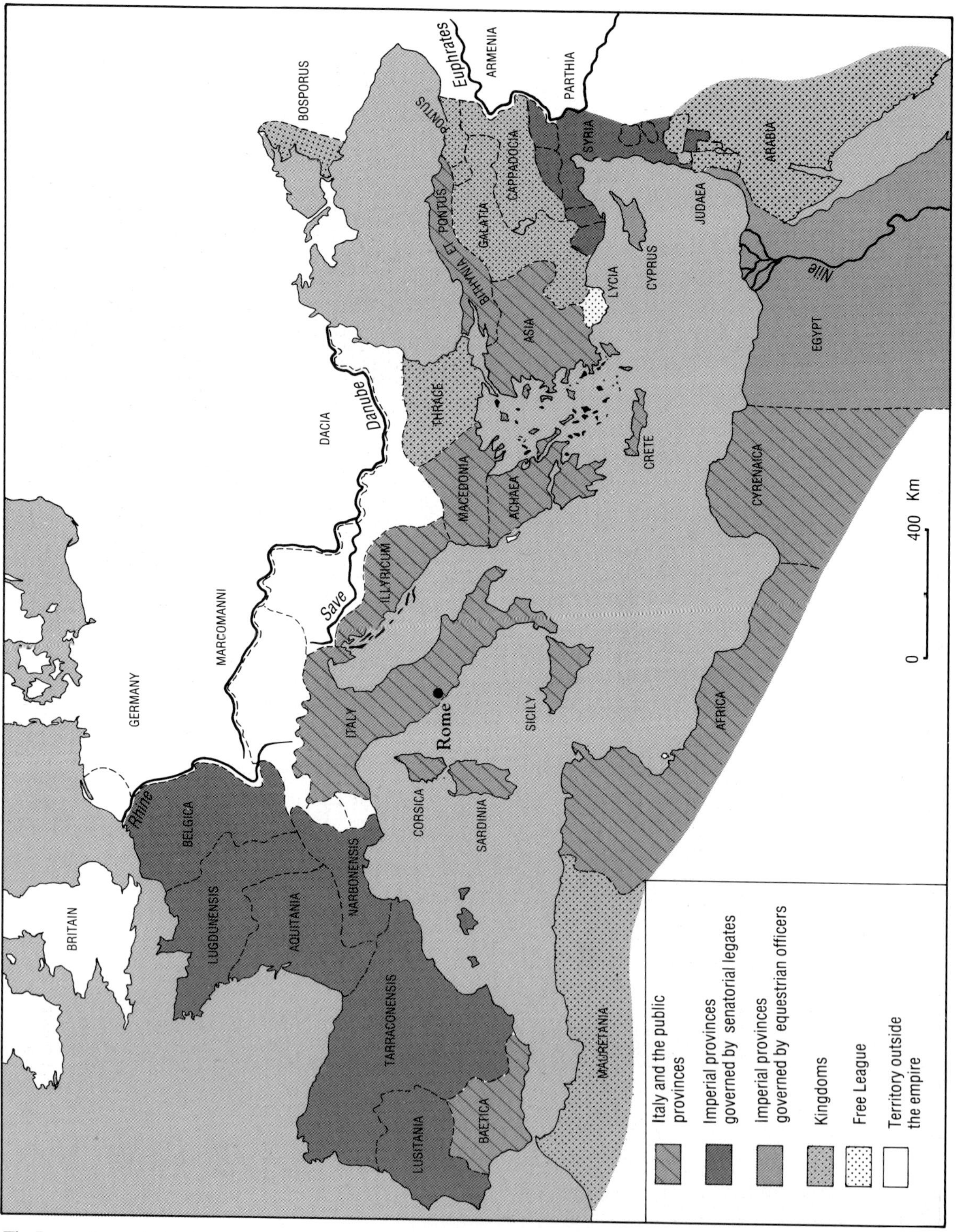
BOSPORUS
PONTUS
Euphrates
ARMENIA
PARTHIA
SYRIA
ARABIA
CAPPADOCIA
GALATIA
BITHYNIA ET PONTUS
JUDAEA
CYPRUS
LYCIA
Nile
ASIA
EGYPT
THRACE
DACIA
Danube
CRETE
MACEDONIA
ACHAEA
CYRENAICA
ILLYRICUM
Save
MARCOMANNI
GERMANY
ITALY
Rome
SICILY
AFRICA
CORSICA
SARDINIA
Rhine
BELGICA
NARBONENSIS
LUGDUNENSIS
AQUITANIA
BRITAIN
TARRACONENSIS
MAURETANIA
LUSITANIA
BAETICA
0
400 Km
Italy and the public provinces
Imperial provinces governed by senatorial legates
Imperial provinces governed by equestrian officers
Kingdoms
Free League
Territory outside the empire

The Roman Empire in 27 BC

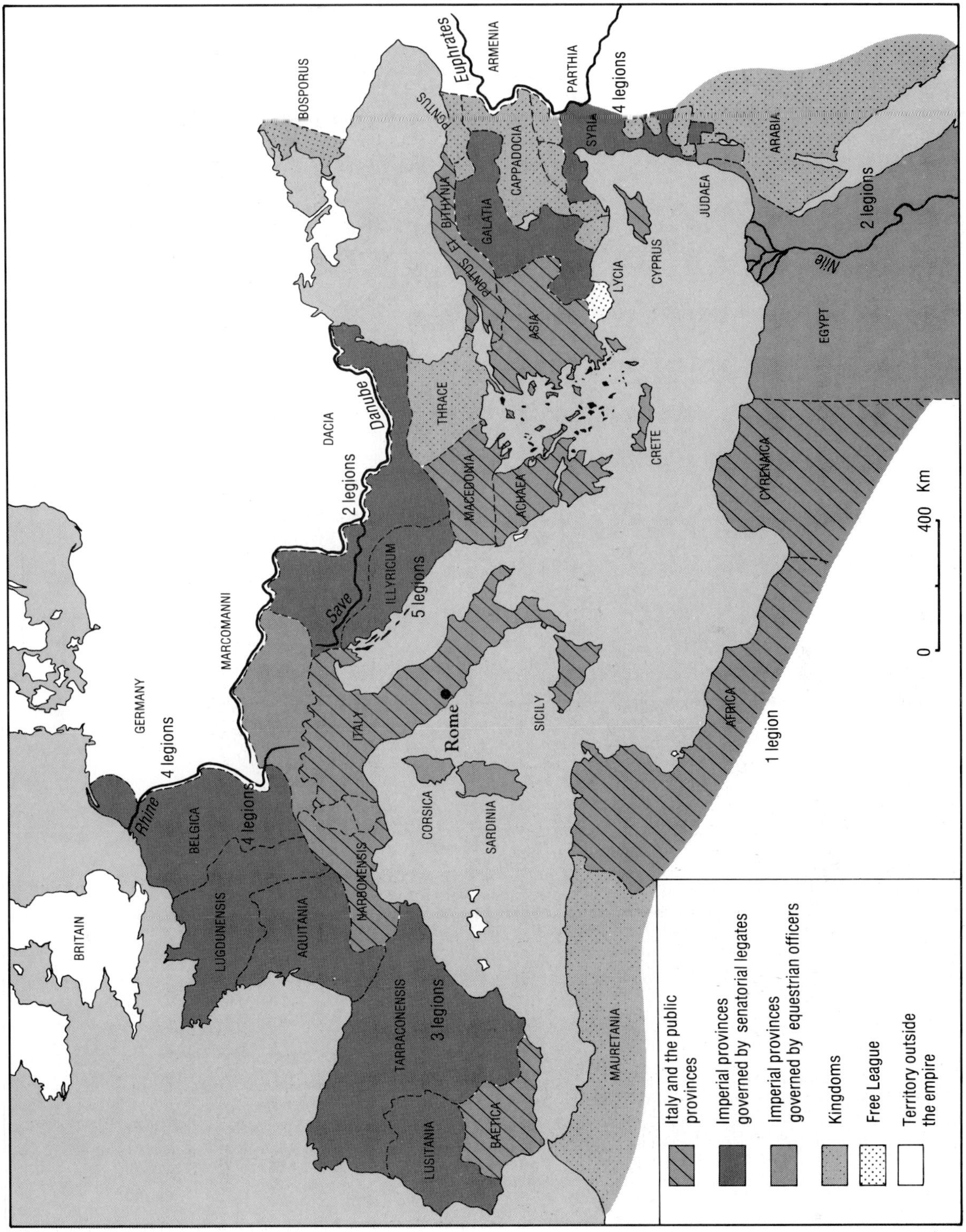

The Roman Empire in AD 14

2 Which of the original imperial provinces were transferred to the senate by AD 14 and which of the early senatorial provinces came under the control of Augustus by AD 14?
3 What additions were made to the empire between 27 BC and AD 14? In which two areas did these occur?
4 From the maps, what can be deduced about Augustus' frontier policy?

Reform of provincial administration

Aspects of this administrative reform are summed up in the following illustration.

PAX ROMANA

With peace came an end to the billeting of Roman troops in the provinces and the massive financial and material exactions demanded of the provincials

Improvements in provincial administration

A more equitable taxation system based on a series of censuses

Greater care in selection and control of governors

Greater responsibility given to local communities

An inscription from the provincials of Asia in 9 BC expresses their gratitude to Augustus

'Whereas the divine providence that guides our life has displayed its zeal and benevolence by ordaining for our life the most perfect good, bringing to us Augustus, whom it has filled with virtue for the benefit of mankind, employing him as a saviour for us and our descendants, him who has put an end to wars and adorned peace . . .'[44]

There were scores of such inscriptions

Vast building programs were carried out in the provinces, financed in many cases by the wealthy inhabitants whose prosperity had increased owing to the peaceful conditions that prevailed; they dedicated theatres, baths, aqueducts and other amenities — grateful provincials also dedicated temples to 'Rome and Augustus'

A fairer system of taxation

Taxation reforms based on censuses

Augustus conducted a number of provincial censuses during his principate in order to gain a clearer idea of the resources of the empire. These provided the basis of the formulation of a much fairer taxation system, an extension of that which had been started under Julius Caesar.

By accurately assessing the wealth of the provincials (land and other property was registered in detail), Augustus was able to increase the total revenue without causing any hardship. In most cases the system of contractors was abolished, and since the amount required was known well in advance it was collected by the local authorities. Where the hated publicani were still used, they were much more strictly controlled.

Imperial and senatorial provinces differed in their methods of collection, while the province of Egypt did not follow the system of either.

Type of taxation	
Direct	*Indirect*
Tributum soli — a tax on land and fixed property Tributum capitis — a poll tax, which included a tax on property other than land	Portoria — 5% on goods crossing certain frontiers, the empire being divided into nine districts Tax on the sale (2–4%) and manumission (5%) of slaves Death duties paid by Roman citizens in the provinces Grain needed for a governor and his staff

Tax collection	
Imperial provinces	*Senatorial provinces*
Direct taxes were collected by an imperial procurator of equestrian status independent of the governor. Indirect tax collection was done by contractors who were carefully scrutinised.	A quaestor was in charge of collection, but he still used publicani. Moreover, Augustus subjected all financial operations to careful control and scrutiny.

Greater care in the choice and control of governors

	Governors in imperial and senatorial provinces			
	Recruited from	*Official title*	*Method of appointment*	*Length of office*
Imperial	Ex-consuls, Ex-praetors	Legati propraetore	By Augustus from the best men available — legati may already have been governors of senatorial provinces.	Normally three years, or as long as Augustus liked.
Imperial	Equestrian class	Praefecti	As above.	As above.
Senatorial	Ex-consuls	Proconsuls	Assigned by lot ten years after holding the consulship.	Officially one year, but sometimes longer.
Senatorial	Ex-praetors	Proconsuls	Assigned by lot five years after holding the praetorship.	As above.

The standard of governors gradually improved, although A. H. M. Jones says that it is impossible to say to what extent this occurred. Although they tended to be drawn from men of proven administrative ability, Jones says

> that there is no reason to believe that the character of the Roman nobility changed suddenly for the better after 27 BC. They were still grossly extravagant and looked to their provinces to pay their debts and re-establish their fortunes. The civil war had not made them any less brutal.[45]

Stricter control over governors

However, certain of Augustus' reforms made sure that they were much more strictly controlled and that there was a greater probability of conviction if they were brought to trial.

Salaries and allowances

During the republican period a governor received an annual grant from the senate to cover his expenses, which included paying his troops and his staff and requisitioning supplies. He received no salary but could organise the accounts so that he made a profit, and could demand certain payments from the provincials. Those under his control also extorted money from the provincials.

Provided with salaries rather than grants

Under Augustus, governors were given a large but fixed salary and were provided with travel allowances; this reduced the need to plunder the provinces. There was a marked improvement in their staff and also in their assistants. The gradual development of a regular civil service meant that a large body of experienced officials became available to assist governors; they no longer needed to depend on the advice and support of private contractors and their representatives, the publicani. The provinces under Augustus' direct control probably had the better officials, as he was able to select whomever he wanted.

Improved communication

Courier service

This control over the activities of governors was facilitated by a vast improvement in communications between Rome and the provinces. An improved and extended imperial courier service, based on relays of post-horses at regular intervals along the main roads of the empire, allowed Augustus to get more frequent and reliable reports from the provinces.

Imperial procurators

Careful supervision of the governors was carried out by Augustus' procurators, who handled the financial affairs of the provinces and acted almost as provincial spies. These officials, independent of the governors, often moved between provinces. Occasionally Augustus used his maius imperium to send his procurators into senatorial provinces as well as those under his immediate direction.

Provincial councils

Check on governors

The provincial concilia (councils), which were organised to conduct the worship of Rome and Augustus, played a part in controlling the activities of governors. They were composed of representatives from each of the provincial cities or major communities, and although their chief functions were to elect a high priest and to conduct sacrifices and games, they also became forums for the discussion of matters which various communities had in common. This could involve complaints about the behaviour of a governor or about any legislation introduced by him which they felt was not in the interests of the province, and when a governor's term of office came to an end they might organise his prosecution. Under the Julio-Claudian emperors these concilia had the right to go directly to the emperor or the senate with their complaints.

Judicial punishment

Prosecution of corrupt governors

The punishment of incompetent or corrupt governors and officials was carried out much more quickly than under the republic. An offender in an imperial province was recalled immediately and punished by the princeps; an offending official in a senatorial province was brought to trial before the senate rather than in the public courts. Although available evidence is not reliable, it is possible that Augustus introduced this practice, which was common in the reign of Tiberius. The senate tended to be lenient to its own members, but it is believed that Augustus may have attended their sessions to make sure that corrupt ex-governors received severe punishment.

Greater responsibility given to local communities

Administration through autonomous communities

Rome's administration of the provinces was carried out through the independent and self-governing local communities. By encouraging local responsibility, the Romans benefited in three ways: they could concentrate on maintaining peace and protecting the frontiers, Roman officials received greater co-operation from the provincials, and loyalty to Rome was assured.

Spread of urbanisation

The Romans encouraged urbanisation since this was the easiest way for Roman civilisation to spread, and as life in the provinces was easier for a Roman citizen than for a non-citizen, citizenship was eagerly sought. Cities varied in status according to the degrees of citizenship their inhabitants enjoyed.

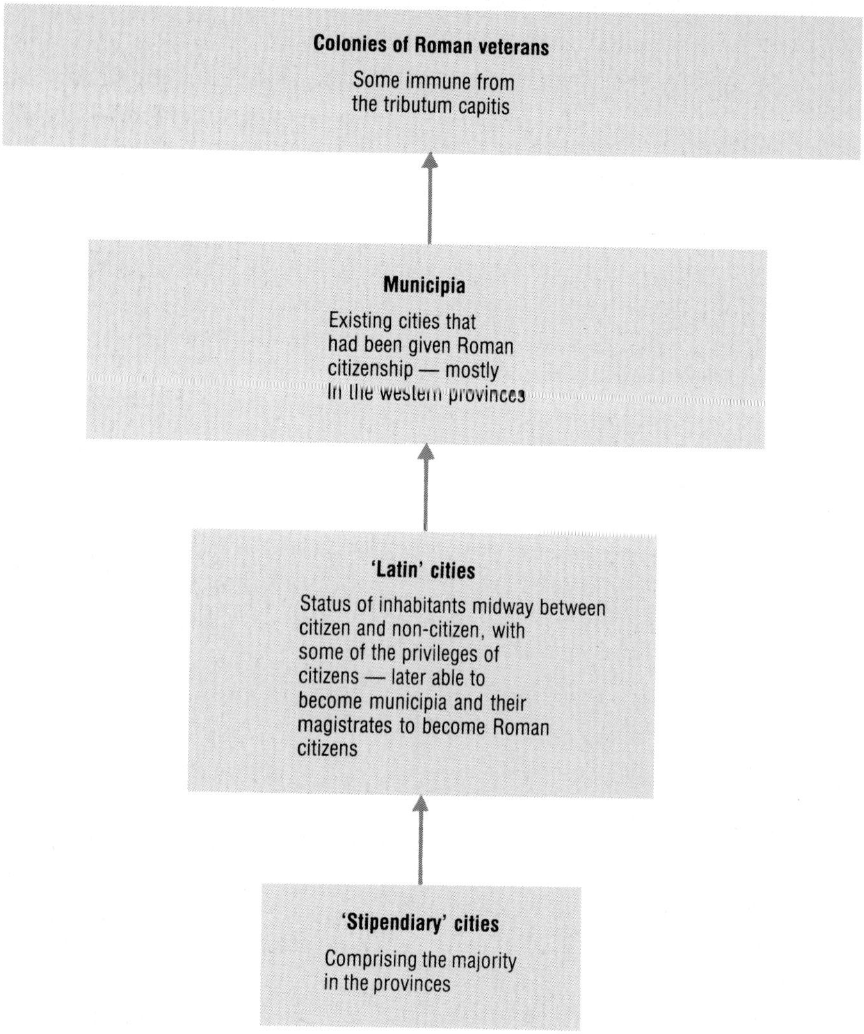
Colonies of Roman veterans
Some immune from the tributum capitis
Municipia
Existing cities that had been given Roman citizenship — mostly in the western provinces
'Latin' cities
Status of inhabitants midway between citizen and non-citizen, with some of the privileges of citizens — later able to become municipia and their magistrates to become Roman citizens
'Stipendiary' cities
Comprising the majority in the provinces

Hierarchical arrangement of provincial cities

The province of Egypt — a special case

After the death of Cleopatra and Antony Egypt was annexed to the Roman empire, but it was never administered as a regular province. Its position was exceptional.

- Augustus kept it under very close control, although it was never regarded as part of the princeps' personal property. *Princeps' private domain*
- It was governed by an equestrian officer or prefect, its three legions were commanded by equestrian prefects rather than senatorial legates, and all subordinate officers were equestrian also. The equestrian prefects were granted imperium like that of a proconsul. *Equestrian prefect as governor*
- No senators or influential equites were permitted to enter Egypt without the express permission of the princeps, as it was a vital source of grain for Rome and Italy and was strategically important in the eastern Mediterranean. *Entry restricted*
- Unlike other provinces, Egypt was not composed of a number of self-governing communities which managed their own local affairs and collected taxes. Alexandria was the only large centre and under the Ptolemies it had lost its right to govern itself; Augustus continued this practice. The whole country was run from Alexandria by a complex, centralised bureaucracy. All officials who assisted the prefect bore Ptolemaic titles, *Centralised bureaucracy*
- The Egyptians were expected to meet a set grain quota each year, providing at least one-third of Rome's needs, and male Egyptians between sixteen and sixty were expected to pay a poll-tax. The communities in Alexandria (Greeks, Jews, Romans and Egyptians) did not share the burden of taxation equally. *Yearly grain quota*

Although Augustus was more conservative than Julius Caesar had been about extending Roman citizenship to the provincials, he was interested in their welfare and continued Caesar's constructive policy. Their appreciation of his bringing peace and prosperity can be gauged by the large number of provincial inscriptions honouring him and referring to him as their benefactor and saviour. *Gratitude of provincials*

The Roman army under Augustus

The republican army was in great need of reform because *Reasons for army reforms*

1 there was no real standing army to man the vast frontier regions of the empire;
2 the burden of military service rested too much on the Italians;

3 there was no provision for the regular pay of soldiers;
4 troops depended on their commanders to make arrangements for their rewards at the end of their service;
5 loyalty of the troops was to their generals rather than to the state.

In order to bring the army under the control of the state, and to maintain his own position, Augustus, as first citizen (princeps), kept control of the armed forces through his maius imperium. He then carried out a gradual reform which only reached its final form about AD 5.

Augustus as Imperator addressing his troops — his breastplate displays the return of the Roman standards taken by the Parthians from Crassus thirty years before

Demobilisation

Reduction in size of army

His immediate task was to reduce the army to an effective size. This he did in two major demobilisations: one in 30 and the other in 14. The sixty legions involved in the civil war between himself (as Octavian) and Antony were reduced to twenty-eight, and when three legions were lost in the Varian disaster in AD 9 they were not replaced; this left a standing army of twenty-five legions. Each legion was given a number and a title, as were the auxilia. The three legions lost in AD 9 were the 17th, 18th and 19th.

Settlement of veterans

In the *Res Gestae* Augustus states that he settled more than 300 000 veterans in colonies, but there is some confusion about which soldiers this statement applies to since he also settled some of Antony's men in 41–40 and others in 36. P. A. Brunt suggests that Augustus discharged 160 000 troops before 29 and 140 000 after that date.

Veteran colonies

The soldiers discharged in 30 and 14 were settled in veteran colonies in Italy and the provinces.

> I founded colonies of soldiers in Africa, Sicily, Macedonia, both Spanish provinces, Achaea, Asia, Syria, Gallia Narbonensis and Pisidia. Italy too has twenty-eight colonies founded by my authority, which were densely populated in my lifetime.[46]

Some of the colonies mentioned in his list were established for the protection of unruly areas rather than for veterans.

Augustus says he paid a total of 860 000 000 sesterces to the towns from whom he bought the land, but in the *Res Gestae* he does not mention the settlements that were founded on confiscated land or for which he did not personally cover the cost.

Cash rewards for some veterans

The veterans settled between 7 and 2 BC were given cash rewards rather than land, and as there was not enough public money to cover this cost Augustus provided it from his own income. In the *Res Gestae* he explains: 'I paid monetary rewards to soldiers whom I settled in their home towns after completion of their service, and on this account I expended about 400 000 000 sesterces'.[47]

Terms of service

Fixed terms

Augustus introduced a fixed term of service for Praetorians, legionaries and auxiliary troops, and this was gradually lengthened. In 13 BC Praetorians served for twelve years and legionaries for sixteen years, but these terms were extended to sixteen and twenty years respectively about

AD 6, when the new military treasury was established; auxiliaries usually served for twenty-five years. Roman citizens and provincials could now make the army a lifetime career.

Eventual complaints

Towards the end of Augustus' reign, however, many soldiers complained about being kept in service for thirty years or more, and these grievances resulted in a number of serious mutinies (see Tacitus, *Annals*, 1:17).

Financial support by the state

For the first thirty years of his rule Augustus bore the financial burden of veteran settlements himself, but by AD 6 he could not continue to do this. He established a military treasury (*aerarium militare*) from which the pensions due to retired soldiers were paid. The funds in the military treasury came from two taxes—a 1 per cent sales tax and a 5 per cent inheritance tax—but Augustus added 170 000 000 sesterces from his own income. This development meant that the troops were no longer financially dependent on their generals and removed the connection between soldier and general that had proved so disastrous to the republic. Since the state now provided veterans' gratuities, their loyalty tended to be to the government.

Military treasury established

Removed link between general and soldiers

Restriction on marriage by soldiers

It is believed that Augustus forbade soldiers to marry. This, however, was a practice which apparently did not create much hardship since it was largely ignored, with soldiers taking foreign wives. The children of such unions were illegitimate, but since they were usually brought up in camp they followed their fathers into the army and thereby obtained Roman citizenship.

Peacetime activities

In peacetime the legionaries were used for building roads, canals, aqueducts and bridges, and fortifying frontier posts.

Provincial troops

Recruitment of provincials

Under Augustus it became increasingly necessary to use the manpower of the provinces to supplement the legions; these auxiliary troops were generally recruited from the more warlike peoples of the northern and western provinces. Although their exact number in Augustus' day is unknown, it is probable that their strength was equal to that of the legions. They probably served in the area from which they were enlisted, since they would have first-hand knowledge of conditions and of enemy fighting techniques.

By showing his trust in the provincial troops and rewarding them and their families with Roman citizenship on discharge, Augustus fostered loyalty to the empire.

The Praetorian Guard

The troops who protected Italy were not legionaries or auxiliaries, but Praetorian Guardsmen. The Praetorian Guard, organised by Augustus in 28 BC, was composed of nine cohorts of picked soldiers whose conditions of service were superior to those of the ordinary legionary. Yet although the Praetorians were regarded as the princeps' personal bodyguard, Augustus in fact had a select body of German troops to undertake that task. The troops of the Praetorian Guard did not usually take part in campaigns unless the princeps went on active service. Three of the nine cohorts were stationed in or near Rome, while the remaining six were distributed in a number of Italian towns.

Urban cohorts

Augustus also organised three semi-military urban cohorts, whose main function was to police the city.

Sea power

Naval bases

Naval bases were maintained at Misenum and Ravenna in Italy, Forum Iulii in Gallia Narbonensis, Alexandria in Egypt and Seleucia in Syria. There were also flotillas on the Rhine and Danube rivers. The sailors in the fleets were free provincials and served for twenty-five years, while the commanders were equestrian prefects.

	The army under Augustus		
	Legions	*Auxilia*	*Praetorians*
Recruitment	Roman citizens and provincials given Roman citizenship on enlistment; the western legions recruited chiefly from Italy	Non-citizens from the more warlike provinces (armed, imperial provinces)	Citizen soldiers selected exclusively from Italy
Strength	28 legions — 25 after AD 9; legions of 5500–6000 men, with 120 cavalry to each legion	About 150 000, made up of cohorts of 500; cavalry was an important part of auxilia	Nine cohorts of 1000 each

	Legions	*Auxilia*	*Praetorians*
Commanders	Senatorial legati (legati legionis — usually ex-praetors); military tribunes were staff officers and the 60 centurions per legion professional soldiers who had risen from the ranks	Praefecti cohortis — Roman citizens of equestrian rank; the centurions also were Roman citizens	Two Praetorian prefects
Length of service after AD 5	20 years	25 years	16 years
Pay	225 denarii a year	unsure	750 denarii a year
Location	On or near the borders in the imperial provinces, in large camps that developed into permanent bases	Usually guarding the areas between the legions' camps — often stationed in the areas from which they were recruited	Quartered in various Italian towns; several cohorts may have been in or near Rome
Retirement	Land allotments or cash; 3000 denarii on discharge (after AD 5)	Roman citizenship granted on discharge to soldier and family	5000 denarii on retirement

The army as a cultural force

From the time of Augustus, the Roman army played an important part as a cultural force: it formed a common bond between the heterogeneous population of the empire. The language used in communication between the soldiers themselves and between those in authority and those in the ranks was Latin; the culture of camp life tended to be that of Rome, and Roman citizenship was extended through the army. All these factors contributed to the Romanisation of the empire.

Augustus' frontier policy

The diagram following encapsulates Augustus' view of the issues involved in the maintenance of peace and security.

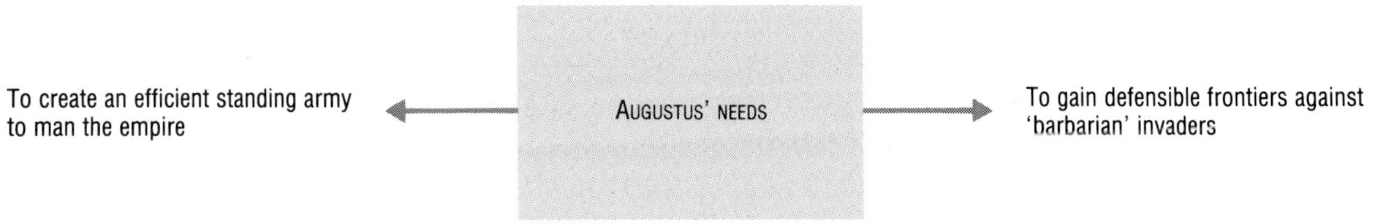

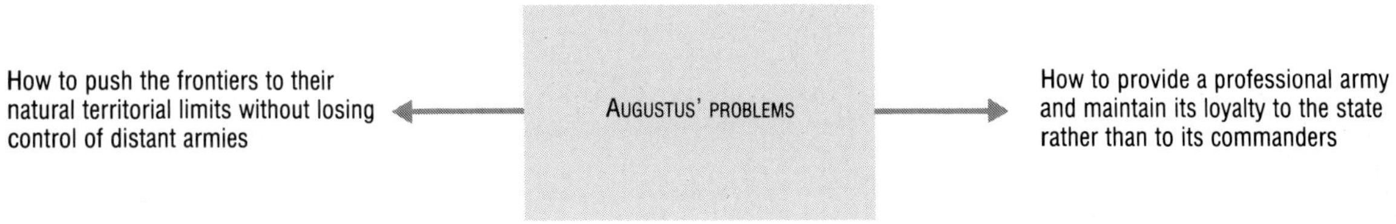

Change in frontier policy after AD 9

Although Augustus was not an outstanding general like his 'father', Julius Caesar, he was responsible for adding a great deal of territory to the empire (see maps, pp. 454–5); there is evidence to suggest that in the earlier stages of the principate he pursued an imperialistic policy. It was only after the annihilation of three legions in Germany in AD 9 and the realisation that Armenia could not be annexed outright that Augustus was content to follow a defensive policy. His aims were

Aims

1 to consolidate those areas within the empire which were not yet pacified or organised;
2 to abandon the haphazard expansion of the republic and to extend the empire to its natural and most defensible boundaries;
3 to follow a general policy of non-aggression in the east, if possible.

Consolidation of territory at both ends of the Mediterranean

Spain subdued

Northern Spain had not been subdued, and it took the Romans seven years (26–19) to do this. Augustus himself took to the field in 26, but it was his trusted friend Agrippa who eventually suppressed the warlike tribes. At some stage (27 or 16) Farther Spain was divided into the two provinces of Baetica and Lusitania, while Nearer Spain became known as Tarraconensis.

Organisation of Gaul completed

Gallia Comata had not been completely organised since the time of Julius Caesar. Between 27 and 13 the province was divided into three districts for ease of administration: Belgica, Aquitania and Lugdunensis; a census was taken in 27 and a system of roads, developed by Agrippa, radiated from the chief city of Lugdunum.

Galatia annexed — Syria strenghtened

In the east, Augustus annexed Galatia as a Roman province on the death in 25 of its client-king, Amyntas. He also added part of Cilicia to Syria in order to strengthen that vital province. Judaea, under Herod the Great, was enlarged by the addition of Ituraea, but on Herod's death in 4 BC Augustus divided the kingdom between his three sons. One of them, however, proved to be such a poor ruler that Augustus exiled him and annexed his portion, which became the imperial province of Judaea. The Jews were treated very generously by the Roman authorities, who allowed them many privileges such as exemption from military duty.

Imperial province of Judaea created

Egypt–Ethiopian frontier fixed

The only frontier in Egypt that required attention was in the south. Several disputes with Ethiopia over the Roman selection of the First Cataract as its southernmost border occurred in 29 and 22 BC, but in 21 the Queen of Ethiopia and the Romans established a military zone between their territories which removed any further trouble.

Juba — client-king of Mauretania

The province of Africa was relatively peaceful, although there was intermittent fighting on the frontiers with the tribes to the south and from across the border in Mauretania. In 25 Augustus established Juba — son of the last king of Numidia — on the throne of Mauretania as a client-king. Juba had been brought up in Rome and had married the daughter of Antony and Cleopatra.

The extension of the frontiers in the north

The frontiers of most concern to Augustus were in the north, where Germanic and other 'barbarians' threatened Gaul and Italy.

The Alpine districts and the Danube

Need for a strong frontier in Danube

Augustus wanted to establish a strong natural frontier between the Alps and the Black Sea, and he relied to a large extent on members of his own family (Tiberius, Drusus and Agrippa) to achieve this.

Raetia and Noricum added

- In 16–15 Tiberius and Drusus (his stepsons) combined in a campaign to conquer the territory north of the Alps as far as the Danube River. This area was organised into two districts called Raetia (modern Switzerland) and Noricum (the modern Tyrol area of Austria).

Alpine province added

- The Maritime Alpine districts between Gaul and the Italian peninsula were unconquered until 14, when they were incorporated into a small province called Alpes Maritimae, governed by a prefect of equestrian rank.

Control of middle and lower Danube Valley

- Since the provinces of Illyricum and Macedonia were frequently attacked by tribes in the middle and lower Danube valley, it was essential for Augustus to gain control of this territory. The Pannonians were subdued between 13 and 9 first by Agrippa and then by Tiberius.

The Gemma Augusta, carved in onyx about AD 10, shows Augustus seated with the goddess Roma and being crowned with the symbol of the civilised world; it commemorated the victory of Tiberius, Augustus' stepson, over the Pannonians — he is seen getting down from his chariot, while in the lower section the Romans are shown with their prisoners and erecting a trophy

Moesia, further east, had been defeated in 29 and added to Macedonia, but in AD 6 it was organised as a province. A Thracian uprising was suppressed between 11 and 9 BC, but Thrace was left under the control of native rulers.

Later uprisings south of Danube

Although Rome's northern frontier now followed the Danube River, in AD 6 an extremely serious uprising occurred among the Pannonians and Dalmatians south of the Danube. It took Tiberius three years to restore order in Illyricum.

The Rhine and the Elbe

Plans to make the Elbe River the northern frontier

The Rhine frontier in the northwest, which had been established by Julius Caesar during his Gallic campaigns, was the most dangerous of the empire's boundaries. Parts of Gaul were still restless and in 29, 17–16 and 12 the Germanic tribes beyond the Rhine had made several raids into the Roman province. Since Gaul was a vital part of the empire, Augustus hoped to campaign against the Germans and push the Roman frontier as far as the Elbe River. Another consideration that probably influenced Augustus to expand as far as the Elbe was that an Elbe–Danube frontier would be shorter, and would therefore require fewer troops to man it.[48]

Drusus killed in Germany
Tiberius extends Roman territory

Between 12 and 9 Augustus' stepson Drusus subdued various Germanic tribes and eventually reached the Elbe before he was tragically killed in a fall from his horse. His brother, Tiberius, continued his work and attempted to extend the frontier even further by conquering the territory between the Elbe and the Danube, but the successful campaign was cut short in AD 6 when Tiberius was forced to deal with serious revolts that had broken out in Illyricum among the Pannonians and Dalmatians.

Varus' disaster

The German tribes between the Rhine and the Elbe remained subdued until in AD 9 the command of the Rhine was entrusted to P. Quinctilius Varus, whose lack of tact and insolence towards the Germans—particularly the Cherusci—and his attempts to introduce stricter measures led to a combined attack on the Romans in which the 20 000 men of the 17th, 18th and 19th legions were wiped out in the Teutoberg Forest. Varus committed suicide.

Tiberius was once again sent to deal with the general revolt, and after several successful campaigns beyond the Rhine he withdrew to the original Roman frontier and secured the Rhine fortifications. The lost German territory was never regained. After AD 9, Augustus' frontier policy became more defensive.

General policy of non-aggression in the east

The powerful kingdom of Parthia was the major threat to the Roman territories in the east.

Need to regain Roman prestige in east

Many Romans expected Augustus to campaign across the Euphrates in order to regain Roman prestige after the disasters suffered in 53 by Crassus and in 36 by Antony. However, Augustus behaved prudently towards Parthia and attempted to avenge Rome's previous losses by using diplomacy rather than force—by promoting rivalries within the kingdom, creating suspicions among the smaller neighbouring kingdoms and disseminating propaganda.

Armenia important to Rome

Armenia, on the eastern side of the Euphrates, was the key to the future relationship between Rome and Parthia. The Romans considered that control over Armenia was essential: it would act as a buffer against an attack by Parthia and it was the main link between the Roman provinces of Asia and Syria and the Far East. Augustus was faced with a dilemma. Direct annexation of Armenia would require troops to be taken from the province of Syria, which the Romans could not risk—it would provoke Parthia and would involve Rome in further military commitments as far as the Tigris River. On the other hand, to leave Armenia to the Parthians would advertise Rome's weakness to Parthia and result in loss of prestige for Augustus. The only solution was to put a Roman nominee on the throne of Armenia.

An opportunity to do this presented itself when dynastic problems broke out in both Parthia (where there was a pretender to the throne) and Armenia (where the people wanted the king to be replaced by his brother Tigranes, who had been in Rome for ten years). In 20 BC Tiberius joined Augustus in the east, advanced into Armenia, installed Tigranes on the throne and negotiated with the Parthians for the return of the Roman standards ('eagles') lost by Crassus at Carrhae. This satisfied public opinion in Rome and was of great propaganda value for Augustus.

Roman standards returned by Parthia

With the Parthian king sending his sons to live in Rome for a time, Augustus had achieved a diplomatic coup and peace was maintained in the area until the death of Tigranes in 6 BC. When the Parthians achieved influence in Armenia again about AD 1, Augustus sent his grandson Gaius to negotiate with the new king of Parthia. As well as employing diplomacy, he strengthened the imperial province of Syria and developed a chain of client-kingdoms along the eastern frontier, which saved the cost in money and manpower of stationing Roman troops there.

Augustus' diplomacy kept the peace with Parthia

Syria protected by client-kingdoms

The only act of aggression carried out by Augustus in the east was against the ancient kingdom of Sheba (Sabaea) which was located in the south-west of the Arabian peninsula (modern Yemen); the Sabaeans monopolised the trade between India and Egypt and Syria. The Roman expedition in 25 BC was led by the Prefect of Egypt and achieved little more than the establishment of friendly relations with the Sabaeans.

Arabian campaign

Exercise: The Res Gestae *— imperial achievements*

The term 'res gestae' refers specifically to the deeds by which Augustus subdued the world to the rule of the Roman people; these are enumerated in sections 25–33. There is very little reference to actual fighting, since Augustus was 'far more concerned with political themes such as peace, security and prestige'.[49]

1 Read carefully the sections cited above and list Augustus' deeds under these headings:
   (a) Activities for which Augustus gained prestige
   (b) Activities by which the frontiers were secured
   (c) Deeds by which peace was restored or maintained
2 Using the information in the general part of the text, outline any major aspects of Augustus' frontier policy that he does not mention in his list of achievements.
3 Compare the statement of Suetonius that Augustus 'made no war on any people without unjust and necessary reasons'[50] with the statement in section 26:3 of the *Res Gestae*.
4 Suetonius said that 'Augustus commanded armies in only two foreign wars... The remainder of his foreign wars were conducted by his lieutenants'.[51] Who does Augustus recognise, in the *Res Gestae*, as having contributed to his great successes?

Latin literature and its propaganda value for the principate

Patronage in the arts

Patronage of the arts was an important aspect of Roman life, and it applied equally to literature. Poets and historians gave readings from their works in the homes of their wealthy patrons, who often provided the writers with material security. Maecenas, the good friend of Augustus, was one such patron of literature, and

> Augustus gave all possible encouragement to intellectuals: he would politely and patiently attend readings not only of their poems and historical works, but of their speeches and dialogues;[52]

Augustus obviously realised the propaganda value of writers, but there was no need for him to pressure these men into expressing their approval of the new regime from which they gained their inspiration, since most of them were sincere supporters of it.

Virgil, Horace and Livy

Augustus was fortunate that three men of genius were his literary friends. The poets Virgil and Horace were introduced to him by Maecenas, and the historian Livy became a teacher in the imperial household.

Common themes in their works

Virgil and Horace began their writing in the triumviral period, and were grateful for the restoration of peace. Their poetry expresses their love of the Italian countryside, praises the old Roman virtues and ancestral customs and reflects the ideals and hopes of the new age. Livy expresses the same sentiment in prose.

Ovid

There were other notable writers of this period, such as Ovid, Tibullus and Sextus Propertius, and although they were not as great as Virgil, Horace and Livy, all contributed to the so-called Golden Age.

The following chart gives a summary of the lives and major works of Virgil, Horace, Ovid and Livy, and is in turn followed by extracts from Virgil's *Eclogues* and *Aeneid*, and the *Odes* of Horace.

A portrait of the poet Horace

Name	*Dates*	*Background*	*Major works*	*Propaganda aspects*
Virgil (Publius Vergilius Maro)	76–19 BC	He was born in Mantua in northern Italy, but lost his farm as a result of the confiscations and veteran settlements after Philippi. He was reimbursed by Maecenas and later lived on an estate in Naples that he received from Augustus. Well-educated despite his humble background, he was influenced by the Epicureans and particularly by the Stoics. He was retiring, sensitive and religious, and disliked city life.	The *Eclogues* or *Bucolics* are poems reflecting his great love of the Italian countryside. The theme of Italian agriculture in the *Georgics* was supposedly suggested to him by Maecenas. The *Aeneid* was Virgil's masterpiece. It tells how the Trojan prince Aeneas, guided by his mother, Venus, led a band of escapees from burning Troy to settle in Latium. Aeneas' son, lulus, married a Latin princess and founded the Julian family.	Virgil showed that the ancient virtues which Augustus was anxious to revive flourished in the simple rural life of Italy. In the fourth poem of the *Eclogues*, written in 40 BC, he prophesied a new era that would 'herald the end of war'. In the *Aeneid* Virgil represented Aeneas as the ideal Roman who exhibits virtues such as a sense of duty, loyalty and piety. He predicted the future greatness of Rome and alluded to Augustus and the Julian family.
Horace (Quintus Horatius Flaccus)	65–8 BC	He was the son of a freedman from Apulia, but received the best education in Rome and studied philosophy in Athens. In 44 he joined Brutus, who was defeated at Philippi. He lost his farm in the resettlement, so went to Rome to become a clerk to the quaestors. Virgil was impressed with his poetic talent and introduced him to Maecenas, who later provided him with a large estate in the Sabine hills.	The *Satires* and *Epistles* of Horace attack many of the evils and weaknesses of Augustan society and are valuable as brief sketches of social manners and customs. Horace wrote the *Carmen Saeculare*, which was sung by a chorus of youths and girls at the Secular Games celebrated by Augustus in 17 BC. This ceremony ushered in the new age of peace and prosperity. His most famous works were his lyric *Odes*, written in four books at two stages, 30–23 and 17–13. Apart	The *Carmen Saeculare*, written by someone who had fought at Philippi against Augustus and who was now eulogising the New Age, indicated that old differences were settled. In the first six odes of Book III and in Book IV, the *Roman Odes*, Horace supported Augustus' religious and moral reforms and made reference to the restoration of order and discipline; he glorified the empire, and Augustus and his family.

Name	*Dates*	*Background*	*Major works*	*Propaganda aspects*
			from such themes as the simple life, frugality, wine and love, he includes odes to Augustus, Tiberius and Drusus.	
Ovid (Publius Ovidius Naso)	43 BC–AD 17	He came from a wealthy equestrian family, was educated in Rome and Athens, and did not have need of a patron since he was a member of the high society of the capital. He was married three times and in AD 8 was banished by Augustus to Tomi on the Black Sea. Ovid's erotic verse caused Augustus displeasure, since he was trying to curb the lax lifestyle of the upper classes. Ovid may have also been involved in the scandalous behaviour of Augustus' granddaughter, Julia.	Ovids's love elegies include *Amores*, *Remedia Amoris* and *Ars Amatoria*, and although frivolous, they are humorous. It was the *Ars Amatoria* (on the art of seduction) which showed the futility of Augustus' moral legislation. His *Fasti* was a calendar of Roman festivals dedicated to Augustus.	Although much of Ovid's work reflected the immorality of high society and did not support the official policy of Augustus, he did attempt in his *Fasti* to promote patriotism, religion and respect for the past. In his *Metamorphoses* he ended by predicting a divine future for Augustus.
Livy (Titus Livius)	59 BC–AD 17	He was born of well-to-do parents at Patavium, where he remained until he was about thirty; he then moved to Rome. He gained the friendship of Augustus and taught Claudius, encouraging his interest in history.	Livy's great work was his *History of the Roman Republic*, which covered 700 years from the founding of Rome to the death of Drusus in AD 9. It comprised 142 books.	Livy contributed to Augustus' policy of patriotic and religious revival by aiming to show the past greatness of Rome and the virtues that great men — and the Roman people in general — exhibited during their history.

Virgil

Now is come the last age of the Cumaean prophecy: the great cycle of periods is born anew . . . now from high heaven a new generation comes down. Yet do

> thou at that boy's birth, in whom the iron race shall begin to cease, and the golden to arise over all the world, Holy Lucina, be gracious; now thine own Apollo reigns. And in thy consulate, in thine, O Pollio, shall this glorious age enter, and the great months begin their march: under thy rule what traces of our guilt yet remain, vanishing shall free earth for ever from Alarm. *Eclogues*, 4.[53]

> A day will come in the lapse of cycles, when the house of Assaracus shall lay Phthia and famed Mycenae in bondage, and reign over conquered Argos. From the fair line of Troy a Caesar shall arise, who shall limit his empire with ocean, his glory with the firmament, Julius, inheritor of great lulus' name . . . then shall war cease, and the iron ages soften. The dreadful steel-clenched gates of War shall be shut fast. *Aeneid*, 1:257–96.[54]

In this extract Virgil describes a divine shield made for Aeneas, with scenes from Roman history culminating in Augustus' conquest of Antony.

> But Caesar rode into the city of Rome in triple triumph, and dedicated his vowed offering to the gods to stand for ever, three hundred stately shrines all about the city. The streets were loud with gladness, games and cheering. *Aeneid*, 8:626–728[55]

> It is your task, Roman, to rule nations with your power; these will be your arts; to enforce the maintenance of peace, to spare those who submit, and crush with war the proud. *Aeneid*, 6:851–3.[56]

Horace

> Thy reign restores rich friuts to the countryside,
> Augustus; brings back safe to our Capitol
> Crassus's long-lost standards, ripped from
> Arrogant Parthia's temple pillars;
>
> Keeps Janus' temple empty of warfare and
> Shuts tight the gates there; bridles the runaway
> Beast, Licence, strayed far off the true road;
> Banishes vice and recalls the ancient
>
> Rules whereby Rome's name, Italy's majesty,
> Fame, strength and empire spread from the uttermost
> West, where the sun goes down at evening,
> East to the shores of his rising.
>
> While Caesar [Augustus] stands guard, peace is assured, the peace
> No power can break — not civil dissension or
> Brute force or wrath, that weapon forger,
> Misery-maker for warring cities. *Odes*, IV:15[57]

Exercise

Refer to a variety of sources, including the *Res Gestae*, and comment on each of the following references from Horace:

- 'brings back . . . Crassus's long-lost standards'
- 'Keeps Janus' temple empty of warfare'
- 'Banishes vice and recalls the ancient rules'
- 'empire spread from the uttermost west, where the sun goes down . . . east to the shores of its rising'
- 'peace is assured'

The question of succession

Reasons for Augustus' preoccupation with succession

Augustus appears to have been preoccupied with the question of succession. This was natural for a number of reasons:

- The Roman nobility were concerned with the inheritance of political prestige. In order to maintain the good name of a family, sons were expected to follow in their fathers' footsteps and equal or surpass their achievements.
- Augustus had no natural son (only one daughter, Julia). He therefore needed to secure one through adoption if the prestige he had won was to be maintained by his family.
- His recurring ill-health spurred him on in his arrangements to secure an heir. In 23 BC he was apparently close to death.
- His extremely long life — despite his illnesses — meant that several of his chosen successors died before him.
- The principate could not be inherited but there were those during Augustus' lifetime who believed that some provision should be made for its transference when he died. There is evidence to suggest that Augustus found this difficult to reconcile with his insistence that the Roman state had not changed and with his belief that each leader should win power in open competition and according to merit; however, he remembered the disastrous rivalry that had occurred on the death of Julius Caesar, and he may have hoped that his authority would ensure the public succession of his private heir.

Methods used by Augustus to endorse his 'sons'

Augustus used the device of associating members of his family with him in the tribunician power and taking them as colleagues through a grant of imperium in order to endorse them.

Augustus' attempts to find a successor			
Name	*Relationship to Augustus*	*Political promotion*	*Outcome*
Marcellus	Nephew, married to Julia in 25	Permission to take all offices ten years before the legal age Elected aedile at 18	Died 23 BC
Agrippa	Loyal friend, forced to marry the widowed Julia in 21 BC	Granted proconsular imperium and powers of a tribune in 18 BC for five years Powers renewed in 13 BC	Intended as regent for children adopted by Augustus in 17 Died 12 BC
Tiberius	Stepson (elder son of Livia) Forced to divorce Vipsania and marry Julia, whom he hated, in 11 BC	Permission to take offices five years ahead of legal age in 24; praetorian rank in 19; given important Illyricum campaign Received tribunician power for five years in 6 BC	Intended as regent for Agrippa's sons, Gaius and Lucius Caesar Retired to Rhodes in 6 BC until AD 2
Gaius and Lucius Caesar	Grandsons of Augustus, adopted as his sons in 17 BC	Entered public life, aged 15, in 5 and 2 BC respectively Attended senate at 15, made priests and each proclaimed *princeps iuventutis* To be consuls at 20 Groomed as Augustus' successors	Gaius: went to the east in 1 BC; died AD 4 in Lycia Lucius: died AD 2
Tiberius	Adopted as Augustus' son in AD 4 (at the same time as Augustus' other grandson, Agrippa Postumus, who was exiled in AD 7)	Received tribunician potestas for ten years, renewed in AD 13 for life Reluctantly accepted by Augustus as possible successor	Although having a son of his own, was made to adopt Germanicus, son of his dead brother Drusus

Attempts to find Julian successors

Augustus always attempted to ensure the ultimate succession of someone with Julian blood, but was eventually forced to rely on Tiberius—a Claudian—as the only one with sufficient experience, since other members of the family were still too young. (The lineage of the Julian and Claudian families is described in chapter 21, 'The Julio-Claudian dynasty'.) Germanicus, whom Tiberius was obliged to put ahead of his own son, although technically a Claudian had Julian blood and was married to Agrippina, the daughter of Julia and Agrippa.

Augustus' opinion of Tiberius

It is generally thought that Augustus was not fond of Tiberius, although some of his correspondence seems to contradict this opinion. Suetonius believed

> that Augustus weighed Tiberius' good qualities against the bad, and decided that the good tipped the scale; he had publicly sworn that his adoption of Tiberius was in the national interest, and had often referred to him as an outstanding general and the only one capable of defending Rome against her enemies.[58]

On the other hand Tacitus, in his usual fashion of damning the principate and Tiberius, says

> His appointment of Tiberius as his successor was due neither to personal affection nor to regard for the national interests. Thoroughly aware of Tiberius' cruelty and arrogance, he intended to heighten his own glory by the contrast with one so inferior.[59]

The death of Augustus

Augustus buried in his Mausoleum

Augustus died in August AD 14—about a month short of his seventy-eighth birthday—and was given two eulogies, by Tiberius and his son Drusus. His body was carried by a group of senators to a funeral pyre on the Campus Martius, where it was burned; his ashes were placed in the family Mausoleum, built in 28 BC.

Documents read in the senate

Four documents which had been entrusted to the Vestal Virgins for safekeeping were now handed over and read in the senate. According to Suetonius, they were his will (naming Tiberius and Livia as heirs to the major part of his estate), instructions regarding his funeral, a statement of the military and financial condition of the empire, and 'a record of his reign which he wished to have engraved on bronze and posted to the entrance to the Mausoleum'—the *Res Gestae*.[60]

An evaluation of Augustus

Bias in the sources

It is very hard to get an accurate picture of Augustus, since the evidence is biased. There are the hostile republican accounts of his earlier career, the extravagant praise of his contemporary, Velleius Peterculus, the personal anecdotes and gossip of Suetonius and the sinister insinuations made by Tacitus. Added to these are his own forms of propaganda as expressed in the *Res Gestae* and his Forum Augustum. The following extracts are evidence of this bias.

Present remains of the Mausoleum of Augustus

. . . Thereafter men could hope for nothing from the gods, the gods could give nothing to men, nothing could be the object of prayer and the gift of good fortune, which Augustus did not bestow upon the Republic and upon the world after his return from the city.[61]

He seduced the army with bonuses, and his cheap food policy was successful bait for civilians. Indeed he attracted everybody's goodwill by the enjoyable gifts of peace. Then he gradually pushed ahead and absorbed the functions of the senate, the officials, and even the law. Opposition did not exist. War or judicial murder had disposed of all men of spirit.[62]

In my fifth consulship I gave 1000 sesterces out of booty to every one of the colonists drawn from my soldiers: about 120 000 men in the colonies received this largesse at the time of my triumph.[63]

I did not decline in the great dearth of corn to undertake the charge of the corn-supply, which I so administered that within a few days I delivered the whole city from apprehension and immediate danger at my own cost and by my own efforts.[64]

. . . After I had extinguished civil wars, and at a time when with universal consent I was in complete control of affairs, I transferred the republic from my power to the dominion of the senate and people of Rome . . . After this time I excelled all others in influence, although I possessed no more official power than others who were my colleagues in the several magistracies.[65]

Tacitus' view of the principate of Augustus

Tacitus' negative view

Tacitus, who attempts to outline the vices associated with one-man rule throughout his *Annals*, begins with the last years of the principate of Augustus; his attitude to it becomes very clear when he uses terms such as 'a nation's enslavement' and 'suppression of the old order'.[66]

After Augustus' funeral 'there was much discussion of Augustus himself . . . intelligent people praised or criticised him in varying terms'.[67] Tacitus outlines the arguments for and against the principate, but gives twice as much space to those which are critical and allows the accusers to refute the Augustan supporters, but not vice versa.

The following chart lists the points of view of both sides.

Arguments in favour	*Arguments against*
Augustus was *driven* to civil war by *filial duty* and a national emergency. He made many *concessions* to the other triumvirs. 'The *only cure* for the distracted country had been *government by one man*' because of Antony's self-indulgence and Lepidus' laziness. He *did not make himself dictator* to restore order. The frontiers of the empire were taken as far as *natural boundaries*. Armies, fleets and provinces were *interrelated*. 'Roman citizens were *protected by law*.' Provincials were *fairly treated*. Rome was *beautified*. *Force was spared* to 'preserve *peace for the majority*'.	'Filial duty and national crisis were *merely pretexts*.' His real motive '*was lust for power*'. He raised an army '*by bribery, pretended* to support Sextus Pompeius' and *usurped* the rank of praetor. He *instigated* the killing of at least one of the consuls Pansa and Hirtius, and '*took over* both their armies'. He *forced* 'the senate to make him consul'. He *turned the army against* the state. 'His *judicial murders* and land distributions were *distasteful*' to those who carried them out. He *cheated* Sextus Pompeius and Lepidus. Antony paid *with his life* for his friendship with Octavian. A *bloodstained peace* was followed by further *disasters and assassinations*. 'He had *abducted* the wife of Tiberius Claudius Nero' while she was pregnant.

Arguments in favour	*Arguments against*
	His friend, Vedius Pollio, was involved in *debauchery*. 'Livia was a *real catastrophe* to the nation, as a mother and to the Caesars as a stepmother.' He '*superseded the worship of the gods*' by having himself worshipped as a god by priests. He appointed Tiberius as his successor because he hoped that his adopted son's cruelty and arrogance '*would heighten his own glory by the contrast with one so inferior*'.

Augustus' personal qualities according to Suetonius

Possessing a sense of duty to and affection for his family (*Augustus*, 10,61,62,64,65,87; *Tiberius*, 21; *Claudius*, 4; *Gaius*, 8)

Religious, superstitious, cautious and conservative (*Augustus*, 31, 34, 37, 38, 53, 90–3, 95–6)

Affectionate as a friend, with an ability to inspire loyalty; kind; strict with dependants (*Augustus* 57, 60, 66, 67)

Frugal and old-fashioned (*Augustus*, 40, 64, 72–7)

Generous and lenient in later life (*Augustus*, 31, 41, 42, 43)

Ruthless, self-seeking and cunning when young (*Augustus*, 13, 27)

Interested in the arts — writing and speaking (*Augustus*, 84–9, 101)

Fun-loving, with a sense of humour; fond of gambling (*Augustus*, 45, 53, 71, 99)

Augustus' personal qualities

The qualities which the sources attribute to Augustus in the early part of his career — vengefulness, ruthlessness, cunning and brutality — seem as he matured to have been replaced by greater clemency, tolerance, responsibility, and a single-minded devotion to the welfare of the empire.

Although he lacked the brilliance of Julius Ceasar (yet some scholars question this), he was an excellent administrator who aimed at efficiency and fairness; innovative and generous where necessary, he was conservative and cautious when appropriate and he exercised great political tact. Suetonius maintained that he took 'great trouble to prevent his political system from causing any individual distress'.[68] The reorganisation of the empire and the maintenance of peace for forty years are the mark of a great statesman.

Although in his outline of the particular achievements for which he wanted to be remembered — the *Res Gestae* — there are some aspects which are not entirely accurate, his real services to the state were more far-reaching than his bare summary indicates.

Suetonius records an edict published by Augustus in which he sets out his aim.

> May I be privileged to build firm and lasting foundations for the Government of the State. May I also achieve the reward to which I aspire: that of being known as the author of the best possible Constitution, and of carrying with me, when I die, the hope that these foundations, which I have established for the State will abide secure.

Suetonius believed that 'the results were almost as good as his intentions'.[69]

How Augustus saw his own place in Rome's history

Qualities stressed in the Res Gestae

In section 34 of the *Res Gestae* Augustus outlines the qualities for which he claimed honour: enterprise (leadership), clemency, justice and piety, and for these he was awarded the title of 'Father of his Country' in 2 BC.

Augustus' view expressed in his Forum

In the Forum Augustum, which was opened in that year, he had the opportunity to display publicly what he considered his place in Rome's history to be. The statue of Augustus riding in a chariot, underneath Which was the inscription 'Father of his Country', stood in the middle of the Forum. On one side were statues of his family, with Aeneas in the centre, and on the other side Romulus stood among those leaders who had made Rome great. Beneath each statue was an inscription which included some feat of statecraft for which the great man had become known as the leader of his age. As Romans wandered up and down the porticoes they would have clearly understood how Augustus saw himself as a leader. (The Forum is described in more detail in the following chapter.)

Timeline: The principate of Augustus

Rome		*Provinces and frontiers*
	BC	
Transfer of control of the republic to the people and the senate Augustus cos. VII; takes the name 'Augustus'	27	Augustus becomes proconsul of all armed provinces
Augustus cos. VIII–IX	26	Consolidation of provinces and frontiers Galatia annexed Expedition to Arabia Ethiopian War
Augustus returns to Rome, cos. X Senate votes exceptional honours to Marcellus and Tiberius Conspiracy in Rome	24	
Augustus resigns his eleventh consulship; receives tribunician powers (now or earlier, in 30) and *maius imperium* Death of Marcellus, Augustus' son-in-law	23	Cyprus and Narbonensis transferred from Augustus' control to the senate
Augustus refuses dictatorship and censorship	22	Augustus in the east
Agrippa marries Julia	21	
	20	Parthians surrender Crassus' standards Tiberius installs a king in Armenia
Augustus receives the imperium of a consul	19	Augustus returns to Rome from the east
Agrippa becomes a colleague with Augustus in tribunician	18	

Rome		*Provinces and frontiers*
	BC	
and proconsular power for five years Second purge of senate Julian laws on marriage, divorce, extravagance		
Augustus adopts Gaius and Lucius Caesar, Julia's sons Holds Secular Games	17	
	16	Augustus in Gaul and Agrippa in the east Tiberius and Drusus begin their conquests in the north Noricum annexed
	15	Annexation of Raetia and the Alpine areas
Agrippa's powers renewed	13	
Death of Lepidus — Augustus becomes pontifex maximus Death of Agrippa	12	Campaigns of Drusus and Tiberius in Germany and Pannonia
Tiberius marries Julia Augustus sets up a permanent water board	11	Illyricum transferred to Augustus from senate
	9	Death of Drusus, Augustus' younger stepson in Germany
Death of Maecenas	8	Campaigns of Tiberius in Germany
Tiberius receives tribunicia potestas for five years Tiberius retires to Rhodes in voluntary exile	6	Subjugation of Alpine people completed
Augustus, cos. XII, to introduce Gaius Caesar to public life	5	

Rome		*Provinces and frontiers*
	BC	
	4	Death of Herod the Great
Augustus, cos. XIII, to introduce Lucius Caesar to public life Augustus acclaimed pater patriae Exile of Julia and legislation restricting manumission of slaves	2	
	1	Gaius Caesar in the east
	AD	
	1	Gaius Caesar, cos. I
Tiberius returns from Rhodes	2	Death of Lucius Caesar at Massilia
Augustus adopts Tiberius, who gains tribunician power for ten years Augustus adopts Agrippa Postumus Fourth purge of the senate	4	Death of Gaius Caesar in Lycia
Military treasury established	6	Revolt in Pannonia and Dalmatia Annexation of Judaea Transfer of Sardinia to Augustus' control
Adjustments to Julian laws — lex Papia-Poppaea	9	Annihilation of Varus' three legions in Germany
Tiberius' tribunician powers renewed	13	
Death of Augustus	14	Augustus' third census

20 The forums of Rome in the time of Augustus

The Roman Forum

The Forum of Julius Caesar

The Forum of Augustus

The Roman Forum

THE ROMAN FORUM was the political, commercial, religious and social centre of the Roman republic and later of the great Roman Empire.

Centre of Roman life

All decisions of importance concerning the government of the Roman people, their allies and provincials were made in the buildings surrounding this small, open rectangle (approximately 100 by 70 metres), and it witnessed most of the important events in the history of Rome.

Activities held in the Forum

The life of the entire city was concentrated there, and all the city roads converged on it. Magistrates, future political candidates and lawyers addressed the citizens from its many rostrums and basilicas; elections and political assemblies were held in its comitia and curia; vital public notices were posted there; triumphant generals passed through it along the Via Sacra as they wound their way up the Capitoline Hill; triumphal banquets were given there; great processions passed through it; funeral orations were given there in honour of the dead; sacrifices and prayers were offered in its many temples and shrines; even gladiatorial games were held there with the people seated on temporary wooden stands erected in front of the *tabernae* (shops), and bankers, money lenders, silversmiths, food sellers and other businessmen carried on their busy trade in the arcades of the great basilicas.

In addition to respectable people occupied with every sort of business, there were idlers and riffraff of every description hanging about the Forum. The Roman comic playwright, Plautus, who lived in the second century BC, wittily described some of these.

People to be found there

Perjurers, those who 'swear through thick and thin', could be found at the Comitium or the law courts, while 'a lying boaster' would be 'not far from Cloacina's altar'. One would find rich, married spendthrifts and 'stale harlots ready for any bargain' at the exchange, while club stewards were always at the fish markets. In the lower Forum citizens of good reputation and wealth would stroll about, but in the middle Forum, near the canal, were the showy set, and 'above the Lake, malevolent and foul-mouthed fellows' spent their time slandering others without cause. Near the Old Shops (*Tabernae Veteres*) were those 'who lend out money, or borrow it, on usury' and behind the Temple of Castor were people who could not be trusted at all. Men who were prepared to sell themselves were found in the Tuscan quarter—that is, around the Vicus Tuscus, and in the Velabrum were the bakers, butchers, the haruspex or any others who were 'dedicated to vice'.[1]

The development of the Forum

Origin

Below the Palatine Hill, where the earliest settlements were made, was a marshy valley crossed by small streams and frequently flooded by the Tiber River. This swampy area, originally a cemetery, was the site of the future *Forum Romanum*. As the settlements on the hills grew, the flat areas at their base became markets, such as the cattle market (the *Forum Boarium*) at the bottom of the Palatine Hill and the fruit market (the *Forum Holitorium*) at the bottom of the Capitoline Hill.

The Etruscans

Development under the Tarquins

During the rule of the Etruscan kings (the Tarquins) Rome underwent a building boom, and it was at this time that the Forum was drained and paved. The Etruscans' knowledge of drainage and building is revealed in the Cloaca Maxima (great drain) which kept the Forum dry and emptied into the Tiber, which it continues to do to this day. It was originally left open. Associated with the Cloaca Maxima land reclamation project was a shrine to Venus Cloacina, of which a round marble rim can still be seen.

In the northeast of the Forum was the Comitium, a place where the people assembled, and in the southeast corner was the building (Regia) that contained the chief priest's records and the sanctuary of Vesta, where

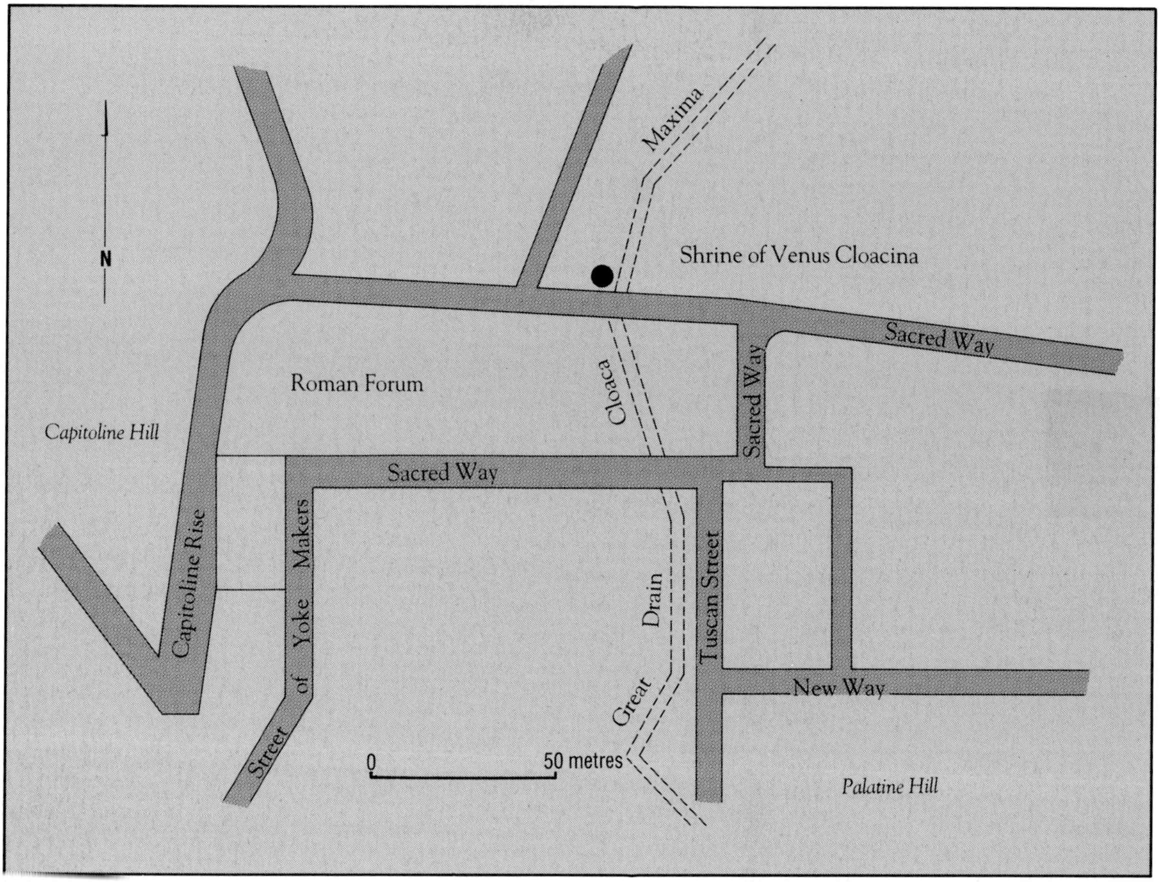

A plan of the early Forum showing the location of the Cloaca Maxima

the ritual devoted to the sacred fire was carried out. This was one of the most ancient rituals, and the earliest temple was probably a round hut thatched with straw. The worship continued until well past AD 300 and the temple, with its associated House of the Vestals, underwent many changes.

The early republic

Buildings of the early republic

During the early republic (sixth to third centuries BC) the number of buildings in the Forum increased, but these were made only of tufa (volcanic stone) and given a single coat of stucco with painted terracotta decorations. Some of the temples constructed during this period were the Temple of Janus (c.500 BC), the Temple of Saturn (c.498 BC), the Temple of Castor and Pollux (c.484 BC) and the Temple of Concord (367 BC).

The Laws of the Twelve Tables were attached to the speakers' platforms (the *rostra*) and the Curia Hostilia was built to house the senate.

Left: Present remains of the Temple of Vesta

A marble relief of a Temple of Vesta, probably that of Augustus on the Palatine Hill

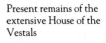

Below left: Statue of a Vestal from the House of the Vestals

Present remains of the extensive House of the Vestals

Present remains of the great Temple of Saturn

All that remains of the Temple of Castor and Pollux

Greek influence

Forum reflected increase in wealth from Rome's overseas expansion

At the end of the Second Punic War Rome came into closer contact with the Hellenistic world of Greece and the east, and the increase in the urban population and the influx of great wealth was reflected in the construction of numerous basilicas: the Porcia (built by Cato the Censor in 184 BC); the Basilica Aemilia (built by the Aemilian family in 179 BC); the Basilica Sempronia (built by Ti. Sempronius Gracchus, father of the Gracchi, in 170 BC) and the Basilica Opimia (built by Lucius Opimius after the murder of his enemy Gaius Gracchus in 121 BC). These large, rectangular halls catered for all the activities that were normally held outside, such as business transactions, discussions about lawsuits, hearings by magistrates, financial operations, and retailers selling their wares. The old stalls and shops were incorporated into the arcades of the basilicas.

Travertine (limestone) began to replace the tufa stone in building works and paving, while the invention of concrete revolutionised Roman architecture. Some of the older temples (such as the Temple of Concord) were restored and enlarged.

Part of a decorative frieze from the Basilica Aemilia

The Senate House (Curia): the original building burned down during the cremation of Clodius and was rebuilt by Julius Caesar, but the present structure is a late second-century construction

The great vaulted gallery inside the Tabularium (Record Office)

Remains of the 'new Rostra', which was the main platform for public speaking in the Forum

The later republic

Buildings as a form of propaganda in late republic

From the last years of the republic (during the mid-first century BC) the buildings in the Forum became the tools of propaganda; they were a form of political persuasion, and this can be seen in the choice of their location, their sculptured decorations and their inscriptions. A limited number of men asserted their power by the monuments they created in this most public of places. Sulla, Caesar and Augustus each left his mark on the Forum as well as elsewhere in Rome.

Sulla redesigned and reconstructed much of the Forum after a destructive fire during the civil war had destroyed the Capitoline Temple. In this reconstruction he made much use of marble. He redesigned and enlarged the Curia Hostilius (Senate House) when he increased the number of senators after the proscriptions. However, the building that was his greatest monument was the Tabularium, or Record Office. This was one of the most important buildings in Rome, and in its design Sulla introduced an architectural innovation: he used whole rows of arches superimposed one on another.

Building by Julius Caesar

Julius Caesar, in his building program, took over the most strategic points in the Forum. The Speakers' Rostra (the main platform for public speaking) was moved from its old site in front of the Senate House to the centre of the north side of the Forum. Caesar retained the bronze 'beaks' (taken from captured ships) which decorated the old Rostra and also added a column on which were displayed the 'beaks' taken by Gaius Duillius in Rome's first naval victory (against the Carthaginians in 460 BC).

Caesar demolished the old Curia (Senate House) and built a new and larger one called, after himself, the Curia Iulia, and on the site of the Basilica Sempronia and the old shops he began work on the Basilica Iulia. He intended this building to house all the law courts.

Besides altering the old Forum, Julius Caesar created an even more magnificent one close by. This was the first of a series of imperial forums (see p. 500).

The period of Augustus

After the death of Julius Caesar and the civil war between Octavian (Augustus) and Antony, Augustus brought peace to the Romans and ushered in the so-called 'golden age'. His building program reflected two of his political goals: he wanted to make his new form of government (the principate) acceptable by basing it on the restoration of the ancient republican traditions as well as on the great deeds of the Julian clan.

Below and right: Remains of the enormous Basilica Iulia, begun by Julius Caesar and completed by Augustus

A reconstruction of the Basilica Iulia

The restored shrine of Juturna

Additions by Augustus

He built a temple to Julius Caesar at the very spot on which the dictator's body had been cremated, and a statue of the deified Julius (Divus Iulius), with a star upon its head, was placed in the temple. According to Suetonius, Caesar's 'immediate deification, formally decreed, was more than a mere official decree since it reflected public conviction'.[2] The platform of this temple was used for impressive funerals, such as that of Augustus.

Augustus also had the Forum repaved in travertine, completed the five-aisled Basilica Iulia and the Curia Iulia, moved the residence of the chief priest, built a new temple to the cult of Juturna around the Juturna spring, and added a courtyard to the Senate House. As well, he sumptuously restored the Basilica Aemilia after it was destroyed in a fire in AD 14, incorporating in it a chapel to his grandsons, Gaius and Lucius. According to Pliny the Elder, this was now one of the three most beautiful buildings in the world.

In his *Res Gestae*, Augustus wrote:

> I completed the Forum Julium and the basilica between the Temples of Castor and Saturn, works begun and almost finished by my father, and when the same basilica was destroyed by fire, I began to rebuild it on an enlarged site, to be dedicated in the name of my sons.[3]

Use of marble under Augustus

At the time of Augustus the whole of the Forum glowed with many coloured marbles, including the brilliant white marble from Carrara. However, public buildings were still built of brick with a facing of marble.

Like Caesar, Augustus built another Forum that was even larger and more spectacular than that of his predecessor.

Need to expand beyond the Forum

By the latter part of the first century BC, the buildings of the Forum Romanum could no longer hold the activities of the growing city; its commercial and administrative centre needed to be expanded. However, Julius Caesar and Augustus did not stop at expanding and improving the old forum, but created even more magnificent forums in their own names.

Plan of the Forum at the time of Augustus' death, AD 14

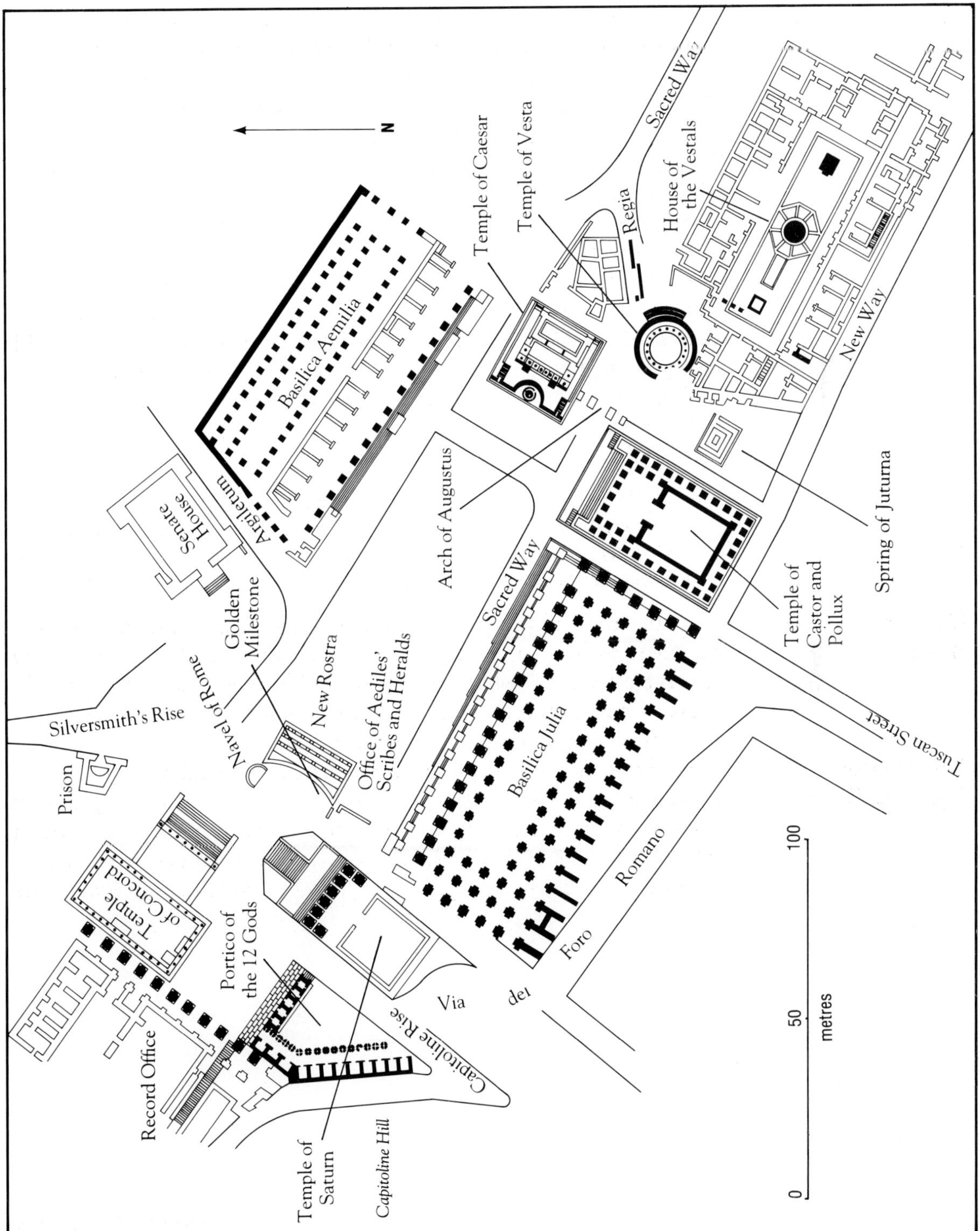
N
Sacred Way
Temple of Caesar
Temple of Vesta
Regia
House of the Vestals
New Way
Basilica Aemilia
Argiletum
Senate House
Arch of Augustus
Spring of Juturna
Temple of Castor and Pollux
Sacred Way
Golden Milestone
Navel of Rome
New Rostra
Office of Aediles' Scribes and Heralds
Basilica Julia
Tuscan Street
Silversmith's Rise
Prison
Temple of Concord
Portico of the 12 Gods
Via del Foro Romano
Capitoline Rise
Record Office
Temple of Saturn
Capitoline Hill
0
50
100
metres

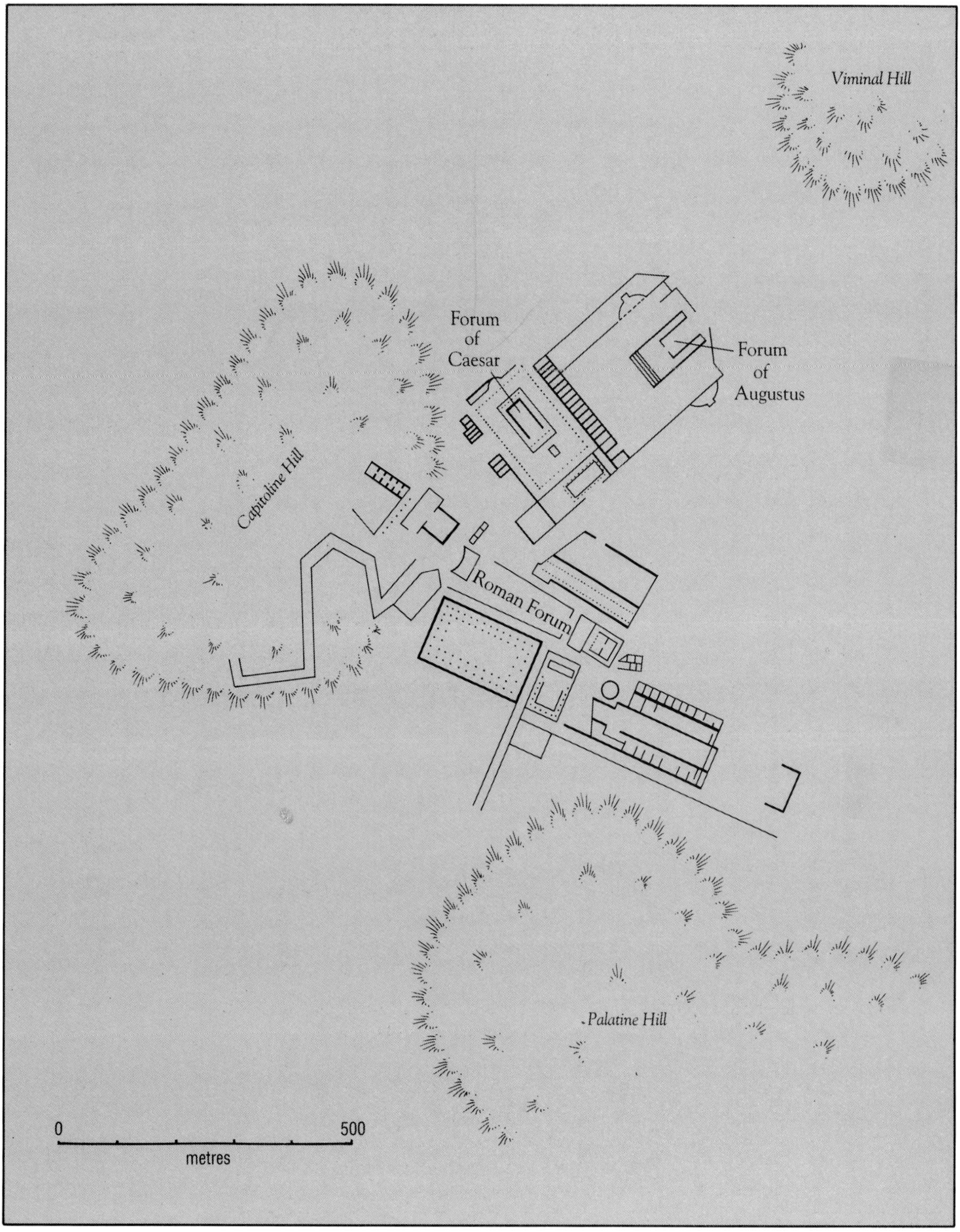
Viminal Hill
Forum of Caesar
Forum of Augustus
Capitoline Hill
Roman Forum
Palatine Hill
0
500
metres

Opposite: Plan showing the relative locations of the forums of Julius Caesar and Augustus

	Some important features of the Roman Forum at the time of Augustus	
	Features	*Purpose*
Government & business buildings	The Curia	The meeting place of the senate
	The Rostra	The speakers' platform for addressing the crowd
	The Tabularium	A storage place for national archives (records) — possibly also served as an annexe of the Treasury.
	The Basilica Aemilia	Primarily a business centre — for financial operations such as banking, commercial transactions, business interviews and offices performed by a variety of magistrates
	The Basilica Iulia	A place of law courts
Temples and shrines	The Temple of Vesta	The place in which the sacred fire, symbol of Rome's continuity, was kept alight at all times by the Vestal Virgins
	The House of the Vestals	The living quarters of the six Vestal Virgins — also housed public and private documents, such as wills, which could be left there for safekeeping
	The Regia	The holy place where the pontifex maximus (chief priest) carried out his official duties
	The Temple of Janus	The symbolic entrance to the Forum (Janus) was associated with the door of a house or a town gate) — its doors were open in time of war and closed only in time of peace
	The Temple of Saturn	Dedicated to an ancient Italian god Saturn — a festival (originally agricultural), the Saturnalia, was held every December; also the headquarters of the Aerarium or State Treasury, and a storehouse for the bronze tablets on which the state's laws were inscribed

	Features	Purpose
Temples and shrines	The Temple of Castor and Pollux	Dedicated to the divine twins, referred to as the Dioscuri, who were supposed to have come to the aid of the Romans in a battle against the Etruscans and Latins at Lake Regillus in 499 BC — the worship of Castor and Pollux was associated with the social order of the knights; copies of treaties on bronze were placed around its walls, and not only were its vaults used as safe-deposit boxes, it was also used as an office for testing weights and measures
	The Temple of Julius Caesar	Built to honour the first mortal elevated to the rank of a god
	The Temple of Concord	A symbol of unity, built at the end of the conflict between the patricians and plebeians and subsequently twice rebuilt — once by Opimius, to try to encourage harmony after the death of Gaius Gracchus, and the second time by Tiberius to show harmony in the imperial family; the senate often met there

The Forum of Julius Caesar

Julius Caesar began his forum in 48 BC, but it was completed by his adopted son, Augustus. It was inspired by the agorae of the Greeks and by ancient Etruscan temples.

Plan of the forum of Julius Caesar

A porticoed colonnade in the Hellenistic style enclosed three sides of a rectangular area, while on the fourth side was a magnificent temple dedicated to Venus Genetrix (his divine ancestor) and built against the flanks of the Capitoline Hill. Caesar claimed to be descended from Iulus (also called Ascanius) the son of Aeneas, who was born from the union of Venus and Anchises.

In this new seat of political power Caesar set the seal of divinity on his power, which had been won by force.

The Forum of Julius Caesar

Remains of the Temple of Venus Genetrix in the Forum of Julius Caesar

The Forum of Augustus

Augustus built another forum, even larger than that of his 'father'. Not only did it fulfil a real need in a city whose population increased day by day, it was also a wonderful piece of political propaganda. It expressed his political goals and placed his leadership of the Roman world in the context of his mythical and divine ancestors and those men who had helped to make Rome great.

The purpose of Augustus' forum

Suetonius gives Augustus' reasons for building the new forum:

> He built his Forum because the two already in existence could not deal with the recent increase in the number of lawsuits caused by a corresponding increase in population . . . Augustus had vowed to build the Temple of Mars during the Philippi campaign of Vengeance against Julius Caesar's assassins.[4]

The forum was inaugurated in AD 2, the year in which he was awarded the title 'pater patriae' (father of his country) and some forty years after his vow to dedicate a temple to Mars the Avenger if he defeated Cassius and Brutus. The delay was due to the fact that the unknown owner of the land refused to sell it to him and he preferred to wait until he could buy it legally rather than gain it by force. 'I built the Temple of Mars the Avenger and the Forum Augustum on private ground from the proceeds of booty.'[5]

The present remains of the Forum of Augustus, showing part of the great Temple of Mars Ultor

When reading the following description, refer to the numbered diagram on page 505.

The Forum as a whole (a) formed a forecourt for (b) the Temple of Mars Ultor (the Avenger), which was backed up against a huge stone wall (c) separating it from the heavily populated lower-class district of Rome. The temple podium (d) rose behind a large stairway, built of tufa stone with a finishing coat of marble (e). The temple was encircled on three sides by twenty-four columns of Carrara marble (f), three of which have been put back into place.

Two porticoes (h) with large *exedrae* (i) formed the long sides of the forum. The exedrae were marked off from the porticoes by a row of columns (j) and on the inside wall of each exedra were two rows of niches. The lower row had seven niches on either side of a large central one (k), while the upper row had an equal number of smaller niches. At the end of the western portico, in a huge square hall, was a colossus of Augustus (l). The two exedrae contained statues of Aeneas and Romulus (m).

Beside the statue of Mars in the temple, there were statues of Venus and the Divine Julius (g).

The intercolumns of the porticoes surrounding the main square contained niches in which were placed statues of illustrious Romans. On one side were the statues of Augustus' own family, with Aeneas in the centre, and on the other (on either side of Romulus) were those of the leading men of other families who had made Rome great. Beneath each statue were inscriptions (*elogia*) outlining the particular deed which made the man a great leader.

> On the one side he sees Aeneas laden with his precious burden, and so many ancestors of Julian nobility. On the other he sees Ilia's son bearing on his shoulders the arms of the [conquered] general, and the splendid records of action [inscribed] beneath the [statues of the] men arranged in order.[6]

> Next to the Immortals, Augustus most honoured the memory of those citizens who had raised the Roman people from small beginnings to their present glory; which was why he . . . raised statues to them, wearing triumphal dress, in the twin colonnades of his Forum. Then he proclaimed: 'This has been done to make my fellow citizens insist that both I while I live, and my successors, shall not fall below the standards set by great men of old'.[7]

In the centre of the forum was a statue of Augustus, riding in a chariot, bearing the title 'father of his country'(n).

> In my thirteenth consulship the Senate, the equestrian order and the whole people of Rome gave me the title of Father of my Country, and resolved that this should be inscribed . . . in the Forum Augustum below the chariot which had been set there in my honour by decree of the Senate.[8]

The following is a list of the heroes of the past whose statues stood in the niches in the porticoes of the forum:

Brutus	Marcellus
Regillensis	Africanus
Val. Maximus	Cethegus
Cossus	Cato
Camillus	Asiaticus
Torquatus	Paullus
Corvus	Gracchus
Cursor	Aemilianus
Decius Mus	Mummius
Caecus	Numidicus
Fabricius	Marius
Regulus	Sulla
Duillus	Lucullus
Cuncator	Pompey

The inscriptions beneath each statue were meant to teach a lesson. These men were chosen not simply because they were military heroes, but because they had performed some deed (of statecraft) which had elevated them above the level of what was expected of a magistrate, such as taking the initiative in saving the people of Rome. Augustus was pointing out what made each man a leader in his day, and by linking them with himself he was making a statement about his own leadership. By expressing what he considered to be the model of leadership, he urged the Roman people to apply the standard to their future leaders.

The Forum is as much a form of propaganda as the *Res Gestae*. It reveals Augustus as:

- victorious general
- bringer of peace and the new Golden Age
- reviver of the traditional way of life

It is a statement about his place in Roman history and the model of leadership that the Roman people should look for in future leaders.

It was meant to legitimise the principate by stressing the restoration of ancient Roman traditions on the one hand and the charismatic deeds of the Julian gens on the other. It was the Augustan Compromise.

Plan of the Forum of Augustus

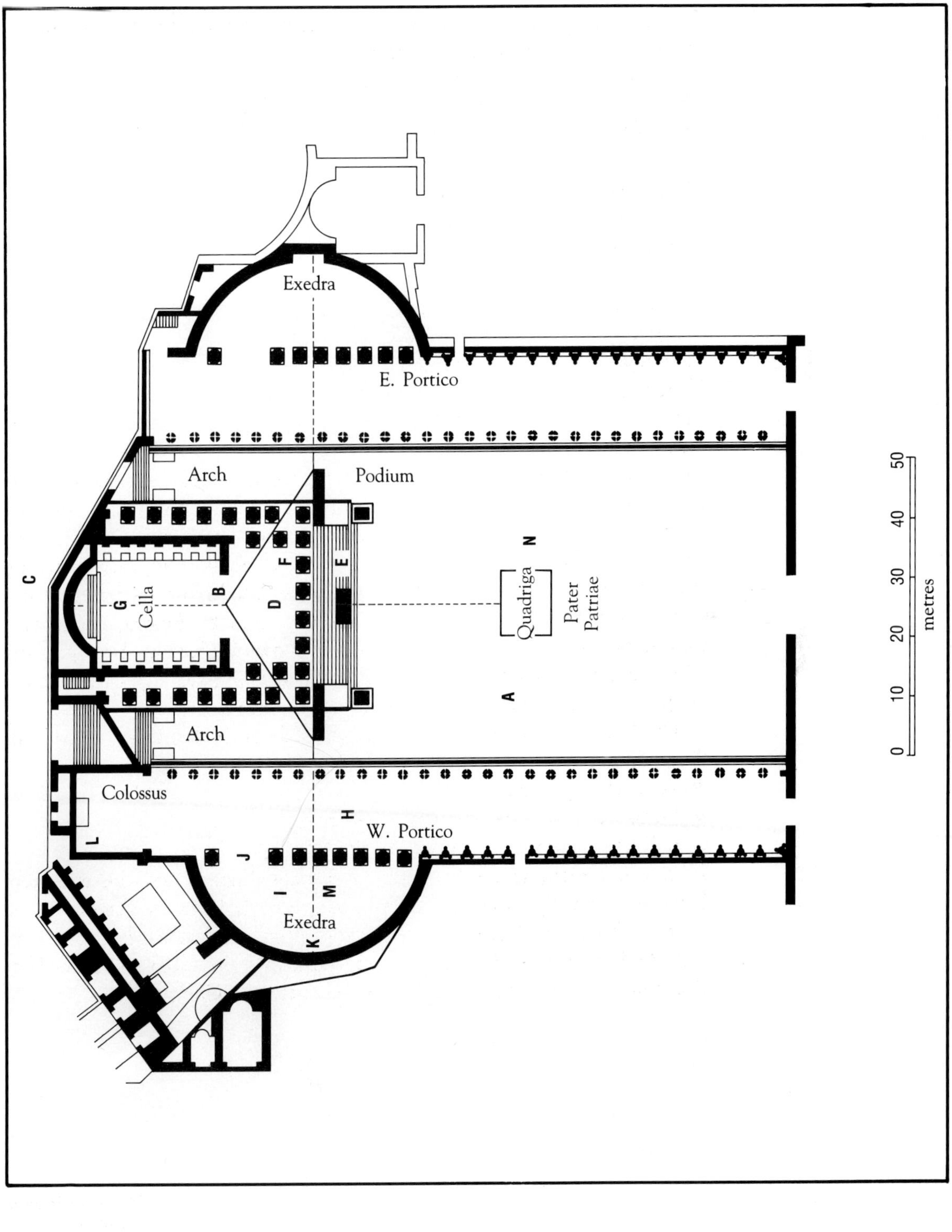

Exedra
E. Portico
Arch
Podium
Cella
Quadriga
Pater Patriae
Arch
Colossus
W. Portico
Exedra
A
B
C
D
E
F
G
H
I
J
K
L
M
N
0 10 20 30 40 50
metres

Portion of the steps leading to the Temple of Mars Ultor

The Julio-Claudian dynasty, AD 14–68

21

Julians and Claudians

THE EMPERORS who followed Augustus (Tiberius, Gaius, Claudius and Nero) are referred to as the Julio-Claudians. The direct descendants of Augustus (who was adopted into the family of Julius Caesar) were referred to as Julian, while those descended from Livia and her first husband, Tiberius Claudius Nero, were regarded as Claudian.

The principate of Augustus could not be legally inherited; he could only have a private heir. However, members of the Roman ruling classes had always been concerned with the transmission of family power from one generation to the next, and Augustus could hope that the authority of his own position would ensure the public succession of his private heir. For forty years he continually engineered situations intended to provide a possible successor within his own family.

Augustus' attempts to ensure public succession for his heir

He ruthlessly arranged political marriages for his female relations, including the daughters of his sister Octavia and Mark Antony. The importance of the women of the imperial house and the complexity of the relationships between the Julian and Claudian gens can be seen from the genealogical table below, although only a part of the overall picture can be seen here. Apart from political marriages, there were forced divorces, adoptions, early deaths and murders which contributed to this complex

Julio-Claudian history one of intrigue and bloodshed

manipulation. Much of the history of the Julio-Claudian dynasty was marked by bloodshed and intrigue, and one of the reasons for this was absence of an accepted rule of succession established within the imperial family. An increasingly important element in the succession was the support given by the Praetorian Guard and its prefects.

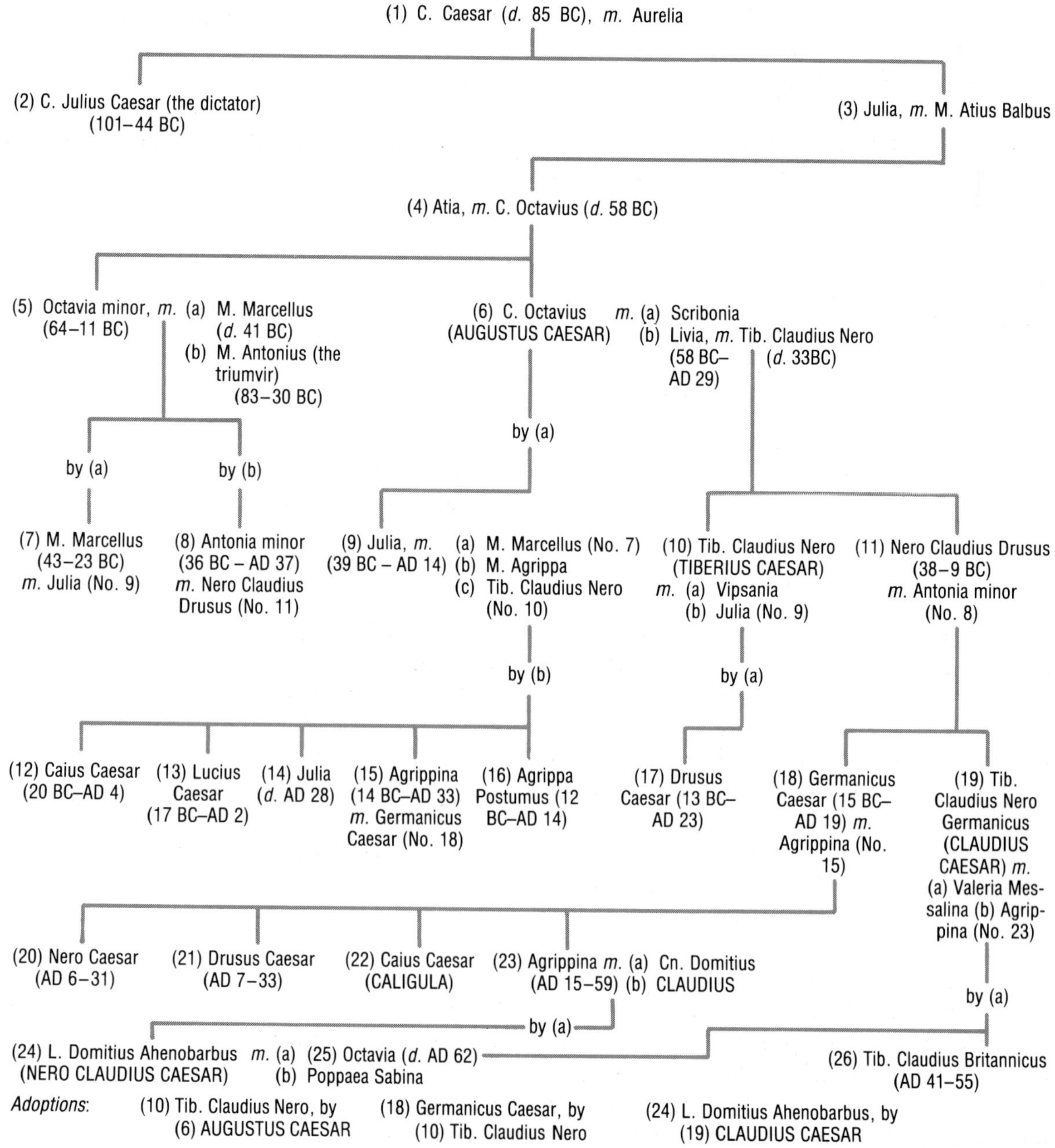

Exercise

1 Name the three men that Augustus' daughter, Julia, was forced to marry.
2 What was the relationship of Germanicus to Augustus and to Tiberius?
3 List the women descended directly from Augustus. Which ones were the mothers of future emperors?
4 What was the exact relationship of each of the emperors Tiberius, Gaius (Caligula), Claudius and Nero to Augustus? Which ones were Julian (descended directly from Augustus) and which were Claudian?
5 What was the relationship between Gaius and Claudius and between Claudius and Nero?
6 Explain why Agrippina the Younger would have wanted to murder Britannicus (he was killed in AD 55).

Sources for the period

Tacitus

Tacitus' *Annals* is the most important written source for this period, but it should be supplemented with the records of other writers such as Suetonius and Dio Cassius as well as with evidence supplied by archaeological remains, papyri, coins and art.

Background and political career

Tacitus under Emperor Domitian

Tacitus was born about AD 56 in either Cisalpine Gaul or Narbonensis. As an upper-class provincial, he received a good basic Roman education and was particularly interested in oratory. He moved to Rome and became a member of the senate at the time of the emperor Domitian (81–96). Domitian's reign was marked by tyranny; most high officials feared for their lives and although Tacitus survived this tyranny, many of his friends and aquaintances did not. It is possible that he himself had to carry out some very onerous tasks. In 97, during the reign of Nerva, Tacitus became consul, and from 112 to 113 he was the governor of Asia.

Literary works

Agricola is a semi-biographical account of his father-in-law, Agricola, who was governor of Britain in 77–78.

Germania is a study of central Europe from which historians have gained a great deal of knowledge of Germanic civilisation.

The *Histories* were written about the period from the death of Nero in 68 to the year 96, but only about one-third of this account has survived.

The *Annals* trace the history of the Julio-Claudian emperors from Augustus (only the very last part of his reign) to the death of Nero. Not all of it has survived: the missing parts include two years of Tiberius' reign, the whole of the four-year reign of Gaius, half the reign of Claudius and the last two years of the life of Nero.

The effect of his background and political career on the composition of the Annals

Influence of his background on his writing

- His first-hand experience with Domitian, who admired Tiberius, influenced his attitude to the principate generally and to Tiberius in particular. He outlines the evils associated with one-man rule, and spends six books building up a picture of Tiberius as the arch tyrant.
- As an orator and an expert in rhetoric he knew how to use vocal propaganda, and this was utilised in his written work frequently as the 'damning asides'. This was an effective method by which he was able to influence the reader to accept his views of a particular character.
- His provincial background and his time as governor of Asia made him particularly interested in the details of provincial administration and rebellions.
- Because of his position as senator, consul and governor and his personal contact with emperors, he had vast inside information on the machinery of government.

Historiography and its influence on Tacitus

Ancient historiography

The following diagram shows the main aspects of historiography (the art of history writing) that influenced Tacitus in his choice of theme and in the structure and style of his work.

History was a branch of literature

It was meant to be read aloud to an audience

It was judged by the rules of poetry

Historians always claimed to tell the truth, but did not need to cite their sources

Historiography: the art of history writing

Historians always claimed to be impartial, but were selective in their choice of material

History was meant to teach a moral lesson

Economic factors were generally ignored

Supernatural or unusual forces were used to explain events

These features of ancient history writing meant that it was important to write in a highly descriptive, dramatic, emotional and persuasive way, and to tell a good story that would also present a moral lesson. Tacitus achieved all of these things.

His aim

Tacitus claimed that 'a historian's foremost duty is to ensure that merit is recorded, and to confront evil words and deeds with the fear of posterity's denunciation'.[1] His aim in the *Annals* was to expose the evils of the principate under the Julio-Claudians and to show its degeneration into tyranny. He hoped that his readers would learn a lesson from the experiences of those in the past. So Tacitus wrote with a moral purpose.

Facts generally accurate, interpretations not always so

He also made the customary claim that in order to carry out his duty he would write in an impartial way since he had no reason either to fear the consequences or to benefit from what he recorded. Unfortunately, he does not live up to his claim to be free of bias. Although his facts are generally believed to be accurate, his interpretation of them is often invidious. In order to persuade his readers to support his own convictions about the principate in general and Tiberius in particular, he used a number of clever devices.

His methods

One of his most successful methods of creating prejudice is the 'damning aside', represented in the following extracts by the words in italic type.

The 'damning aside'

> Tiberius said 'a state which could rely on so many distinguished personages ought not to concentrate the supreme power in the hands of one man—the task of government would be more easily carried out by the combined efforts of a greater number'. *But grand sentiments of this kind sounded unconvincing.*[2]

> Tiberius refused the title 'Father of his country'. He also declined the senate's proposal that obedience should be sworn to his enactments... *Nevertheless he did not convince people of his Republicanism.*[3]

> In the name of Germanicus, the emperor distributed three hundred sesterces a head to the population, and proposed to serve personally as his fellow-consul. *But people did not believe his affection was sincere.*[4]

Innuendoes

He also created prejudice by making sinister innuendoes and attributing false motives to actions.

> In deference to public opinion, Tiberius wanted to seem the person chosen by the State—*instead of one who had wormed his way in by an old man's adoption and intrigues of the old man's wife.* Afterwards it was understood that Tiberius had pretended to be hesitant for another reason too, *in order to detect what leading men were thinking. Every word, every look he twisted into some criminal significance—and stored them up in his his memory.*[5]

Tiberius wanted to use Germanicus' diplomatic skills in the east (Armenian troubles), but Tacitus says that Tiberius wanted '*to find honourable excuses for the young man's elimination*'.[6]

He says of the failure of Tiberius and his mother to make a public appearance after Germanicus' death:

> Either they considered open mourning beneath their dignity, *or they feared that the public gaze would detect insincerity on their faces.*[7]

Tacitus often gives two points of view but allows more space to the one which verifies his convictions, and he uses rumours to good effect even when discounting them as untrue.

> In describing Drusus' death I have followed the most numerous and reputable authorities. *But I should also record a contemporary rumour strong enough to remain current today.*

He then gives a detailed description of the rumour, but finishes by saying '*This was wildly rumoured. But it is not backed by any reliable authority—and it can be confidently refuted*'.[8]

Emphasised negative aspects

Tacitus chose his material carefully in order to emphasise the negative and oppressive aspects of the principate, such as

- the intrigues of Livia;
- the sinister nature and frequency of the treason trials under Tiberius;
- the evil influence of Sejanus and the persecution of Agrippina;
- the weakness of Claudius under the influence of his wives and freedmen;
- the murder of Nero's mother;
- the depraved behaviour of Nero and Tigellinus;
- the conspiracies against Nero and the assassinations of the nobility; and
- the utter servility of the senate throughout the Julio-Claudian period.

Some positive aspects

When he does mention some positive or favourable aspect, the reader is so conditioned by the prejudice he has already created that the constructive features of each of the reigns are almost overlooked.

He also restricts the drama of his history almost exclusively to Rome and the court of the emperors. He barely mentions the fortunes of the millions of provincials who benefited from the general peace and prosperity of the period.

Although Tacitus can be criticised for some of his judgments, his facts—where they can be verified by other written and archaeological sources—are accurate. He was a brilliant literary artist, and his account of this significant period in Roman history is vivid and searching. The *Annals* is the only full and connected history of this period that has survived, and most of our understanding of the Julio-Claudians comes from it.

Tiberius

Tiberius' accession

Augustus' hopes for a successor from among his direct descendants had been frustrated by the early deaths of his grandsons Lucius and Gaius Caesar. The favourite of his two stepsons, Drusus, had also died and so Tiberius Claudius Nero, the surviving stepson, had been adopted as Augustus' son in AD 4. He took the name Tiberius Caesar Augustus, was granted civil and military authority and the powers of a tribune, and was 'displayed to all the armies'. He had been a loyal and efficient deputy to Augustus before and after his adoption and had achieved great military and diplomatic successes along the northern frontiers and in the east.

Loyal deputy to Augustus

Portrait head of Tiberius: Tiberius was, according to Suetonius, above average height, strong, well-built and with a handsome, fresh-complexioned face — he grew his hair long at the back, walked with a stiff gait and his head poked forward; he maintained a stern silence, but when he spoke it was with great deliberation[9]

Since Tiberius was Augustus' designated successor, it was expected that on the death of his 'father' he would have his powers conferred on him by the senate, although they were entitled to choose someone else.

Principate conferred on him by senate

The consuls, followed by the commander of the Praetorian Guard, the senate, the knights and the people, swore allegiance to Tiberius, and the senate conferred the principate on him.

Hesitation on accession

Despite the fact that he had the necessary experience and training to become princeps, Tiberius appeared to be genuinely reluctant to assume the position and 'showed signs of hesitation when he addressed the senate'.[10] Tacitus maintains that he was being hypocritical and was testing the attitude of the leading men. At no time does Tacitus consider that his motives were sincere.

There are a number of possible reasons for Tiberius' hesitation in accepting the powers of princeps.

Possible reasons for hesitation

1 As 'There was no fixed or even generally recognised rule of succession within the imperial family',[11] Tiberius may have wanted to give the senate the freedom to set a precedent for transferring power in the future. As Tacitus says, Tiberius wanted to appear to have been chosen and called by the state, not to have 'wormed his way in by an old man's adoption, and intrigues of the old man's wife'.[12]
2 E. T. Salmon says: 'It may be that in this as in so much else, he was simply following Augustus' example; the scene in AD 14 is strikingly reminiscent of the scene in 27 BC'.[13]
3 Tiberius was fifty-five when Augustus died, and he already knew 'what hard hazardous work it was to rule the empire'.[14] Not only was he not a Julian, but he was reserved by nature and may have doubted his ability to handle the senate with the same tact as Augustus. Once before he had retired from public life (to Rhodes for seven years) as a protest.

Tiberius eventually accepted the powers of the princeps, 'exhausted by the general outcry and individual entreaties' of the senators. According to Suetonius, even when he finally accepted the position he hinted that he might resign at a later date: '. . . until I grow so old that you may be good enough to grant me a respite'.[15]

The first incidents of Tiberius' reign

The murder of Agrippa Postumus

Tacitus maintained that 'the new reign's first crime was the assassination of Agrippa Postumus',[16] who was the grandson of Augustus and the youngest child of Julia and Agrippa. He had been adopted by Augustus as his son at the same time as Tiberius (AD 4) because at that time the princeps still hoped that a member of the Julian clan would succeed him.

A silver cup depicting Tiberius in his triumphal chariot

However, in AD 7 Augustus had been forced by his vulgar and brutal behaviour to banish him to a prison island, where he remained until the death of the princeps. He was murdered by the staff officer who guarded him, supposedly on written instructions from Tiberius. According to Suetonius, 'Tiberius revealed Augustus' death only after getting rid of young Agrippa Postumus'.[17]

Exercise

1 Read Tacitus, pp. 34–5, and Suetonius' *Tiberius*, 22, and suggest others who may have been responsible for Agrippa Postumus' death.

2 Explain the comment that 'in view of the circumstances, the decision to execute Agrippa Postumus, while cruel and unjust, was certainly prudent'.[18]

The mutinies on the frontiers

Troops use change of emperor to protest

Immediately after Tiberius' accession two serious mutinies occurred—among the troops in Pannonia (on the Danube) and in Lower Germany (on the Rhine). Although these outbreaks were not personal protests against Tiberius, a change of emperor gave the troops the opportunity to show their dissatisfaction with existing conditions in the army and their concern about future terms of service.

Tacitus maintains, however, that there were those among the troops in Germany who hoped that their supreme commander, Germanicus (Tiberius' nephew and adopted son), would 'put himself at the disposal of the forces' and allow himself to be declared emperor.[19]

Grievances of the troops

Problems among troops in Germany and Pannonia

Tacitus outlines the grievances of the Pannonian troops and adds that the regular brigades in Lower Germany mutinied 'for all the same reasons'.[20]

Length of service

The usual term of service (twenty years) was often prolonged, so that 'old men, mutilated by wounds' were 'serving their thirtieth or fortieth year',[21] and even after discharge many soldiers were kept on as reserves.

Pay

The pay of two and a half sesterces a day, or approximately 900 sesterces a year (225 denarii), was not considered enough by the soldiers since about two-thirds of it was deducted for clothes, weapons and equipment. They also complained about 'the high cost of exemptions from duty'.[22]

Conditions

They complained about the savagery of the company commanders, the floggings, the drudgery of service, the severe winters, and being 'dragged off to some remote country and "settled" in some waterlogged swamp or untilled mountainside'.[23] It has been suggested that the insubordination was partly due to the numbers of ex-slaves who had been recruited into the army in AD 6–9, after the Pannonian revolt and the Varian disaster.

The progress of the mutinies

Pannonia

Demands

According to Tacitus, the members of the regular army in Pannonia under the command of Q. Junius Blaesus were encouraged to mutiny by a private soldier, Percennius, who had been a professional applause-leader in the theatre and knew how to excite crowds. He urged them to demand payment of four sesterces a day, a sixteen-year term of service and a cash payment on retirement.

The commander, Blaesus, appealed to them to refrain from using violent and insubordinate measures to get what they wanted from the new emperor but rather to send delegates to request the sixteen-year term. When Blaesus' own son was sent to Rome, the troops became more peaceful. However, a detachment of troops who had been building roads and bridges heard of the mutiny in the camp and rioted, looting the nearby villages and abusing their company commanders. When they returned to camp, the mutiny broke out anew and quickly gained momentum; new leaders inflamed the troops, who killed a number of senior officers.

The emperor's son, Drusus, sent to handle the crisis

Tiberius sent his son, Drusus, to Pannonia, with two battalions of the Praetorian Guard plus the pick of his own German bodyguard. Accompanying Drusus and acting as his adviser was L. Aelius Sejanus, joint commander of the Guard. Tiberius gave Drusus no firm instructions, but directed him 'to act as the circumstances required'.[24]

Marble statue of Tiberius' son, Drusus

Drusus addressed the mutineers and read to them a letter from Tiberius, who referred to them as his comrades and promised them that as soon as he was over the shock of Augustus' death he would put their claims to the senate. In the meantime, Drusus was to grant them any concession that could be awarded without the necessity of senatorial debate. When the soldiers' spokesman put forward their demands, Drusus reminded them that 'the senate and the Emperor must have their say'.[25] The hostility of the men could have resulted in a further outbreak of rioting had it not been for an unexpected eclipse of the moon and Drusus' clever handling of the situation. He played on their superstitions and fears that the waning moon was an omen indicating that their crimes would bring endless hardships. He had trusted officers suggest to the men that it was unwise to treat the emperor's son with hostility, and that their behaviour would not gain them their reforms.

Drusus plays on superstitions of the soldiers

Mutiny quelled

The following day Drusus addressed the men again, and although not a 'practised orator, he spoke with natural dignity'.[26] He criticised their previous behaviour, but promised them a fair and merciful hearing from his father if discipline was restored. They pleaded for his pardon, and a delegation was sent to Tiberius. However, Drusus thought it necessary to execute the leaders of the mutiny while superstition still had a hold on the men.

Lower Germany

Germanicus supreme commander of Rhine armies

Supreme command of the legions of Upper and Lower Germany was in the hands of Germanicus, who at the time of the death of Augustus and the mutiny of the army of Lower Germany was making property assessments in Gaul. A. Caecina Severus, general of the mutinous troops, was unable to handle the situation as the frenzied men attacked and killed their company commanders.

More serious threat

This mutiny was far more serious than the outbreak in Pannonia, since the numbers involved were greater and there was the possibility of the revolt spreading to the troops of Upper Germany and the Rhine frontier being abandoned, leaving Roman territory open to invasion.

When Germanicus arrived at the camp, the mutinous troops 'assailed him with all manner of complaints'[27] and demanded that he end 'this crushing service' and pay them the legacies left by Augustus. They also added that if he wanted the throne, they would support him. His theatrical response to the latter suggestion included pulling a sword from his belt and lifting it as if to stab himself in the chest, 'shouting that death was better than disloyalty'.[28]

Germanicus' dramatic response to troops' demands

Although Tacitus attempts to depict Germanicus' handling of the mutiny in a very favourable light by playing down the negative aspects and devoting much more space to him than to Drusus, he cannot hide the fact that Germanicus did not show any evidence of great leadership in this situation. Germanicus decided to make some concessions in the name of the emperor, but they 'were hastily improvised',[29] and when a senatorial delegation arrived from Rome the men were afraid that the concessions 'which they had won by mutinous methods would be cancelled by the senatorial delegation'.[30] The troops abused the members of the delegation, particularly the high-ranking Plancus, whom they planned to kill. Although Germanicus quelled the riot, Tacitus admits that he was criticised for failing to call in the loyal troops from Upper Germany instead of instigating 'releases and payments and mild measures'.[31]

Hasty concessions granted

Criticisms of Germanicus' handling of the mutiny

There was also general criticism of Germanicus for endangering the life of his pregnant wife, Agrippina, and his young son Gaius (Caligula—'little boots') by keeping them in the camp during the mutiny. Agrippina accompanied him on military campaigns as the model wife and also as a representative of the Julian family. Tacitus depicts her as the equal of her husband when she refused to leave the camp, reminding Germanicus 'that she was of the blood of the divine Augustus and would live up to it, whatever the danger'.[32]

Tacitus' description of Germanicus' tearful farewell to his family; the men's shame at what was happening; Germanicus' outbursts against them and his invoking of the spirit of Augustus to 'wash clean this stain';[33] their petition for mercy, and his failure to intervene in the butchering of the ringleaders, gives the reader the impression of rather weak leadership and undignified behaviour.

On the other hand, Germanicus had shown his loyalty to Tiberius who 'was glad the mutiny had been put down. But he was not pleased that Germanicus had courted the army's goodwill by money payments and accelerated discharges'.[34] According to Tacitus, Tiberius granted the troops in Pannonia the same concessions as those awarded to the troops in Germany.

Tiberius justified his actions

The emperor, also according to Tacitus, had been criticised for endangering the state by sending 'two half-grown boys'[35] to control the mutinies instead of going himself. However, Tiberius felt it would be more dangerous for him to leave the capital at this stage and that it was important to 'keep intact his imperial dignity'[36] by dealing through his sons. It allowed Germanicus and Drusus to refer some of the points in question to him: if there were any reactions against them, he would be responsible for making the final decisions. This would be preferable to the emperor appearing at the camps and being treated contemptuously by the mutineers.

Exercise

Compare the ways in which Drusus and Germanicus respectively handled the mutinies in Pannonia and Lower Germany.

Tiberius' relationship with Germanicus

Germanicus, the son of Tiberius' popular brother, Drusus (who had died in 9 BC), was adopted by Tiberius on the instigation of Augustus, even though Tiberius had a natural son of his own called Drusus.

Germanicus in the sources

The sources paint a glowing but not altogether accurate picture of Germanicus and his wife, Agrippina. According to Suetonius, 'Germanicus is everywhere described as having been of outstanding physical and moral excellence'.[37] Tacitus maintains that had he lived 'he would have equalled Alexander [the Great] in military renown as easily as he outdid him in clemency, self-control and every other good quality'.[38] Also in Tacitus' *Annals*, Agrippina emerges as the most admirable and striking of the imperial women.

There is no doubt that Germanicus was immensely popular with the Roman people and the army, was a loyal and competent commander and was a good diplomat. His popularity was probably due to his family lineage—he was partly Julian, and his wife was the granddaughter of Augustus. However, Tacitus' excessive praise of Germanicus is not substantiated by a careful reading of the *Annals*. There is no evidence that he was a brilliant military commander of the calibre of Alexander, and his actions while in the east show a certain amount of irresponsibility and arrogance. Tacitus' motive is describing him in such a favourable light was to blacken the character of Tiberius by contrast.

Germanicus' campaigns across the Rhine

Once Germanicus had quelled the mutiny among the troops of Lower Germany, he embarked on a number of campaigns across the Rhine without the authority of Tiberius. His aim was probably twofold. Tacitus indicates that it was to restore discipline in the army, as 'there was still a savage feeling among the troops—and a desire to make up for their lunacy by attacking the enemy'.[39] A second motive was possibly the desire to emulate and complete the work of his father, Drusus, by conquering and extending the border to the Elbe River, even though this was against the policy dictated by Augustus and followed closely by Tiberius.

Three campaigns — minor successes, substantial losses

His three successive German campaigns in the years 14 to 16 were not major successes and were costly in manpower and supplies. His first foray across the Rhine was against the Marsi, who had been celebrating a festival and were still in a state of 'uncontrolled drunken prostration'.[40] The helpless and unsuspecting Germans were slaughtered, and no compassion was shown by reason of age or sex.

In the following year, after preliminary successes against the Chatti, Germanicus aimed to avenge the disaster suffered by Varus six years before. He advanced against the Cherusci and their formidable leader, Arminius, gaining some territory, and then buried the remains of the three Roman legions destroyed in the Teutoberg Forest in AD 9, 'laying the first turf of the funeral mound as a heartfelt tribute'.[41] However, Arminius almost caught Germanicus and his men in a trap similar to the one that defeated Varus. The battle which resulted was indecisive; Arminius and his Germans were far from subdued and Germanicus had made only temporary gains. In AD 16 he campaigned once again, having constructed a huge fleet to transport his troops by sea and river into Arminius' territory. In two battles he had only minor successes, and in withdrawing he suffered serious losses of men, ships and supplies in stormy seas.

Recalled to Rome by Tiberius

Germanicus believed that one more campaigning season would end the war with the Germans. However, Tiberius (who had given him a certain amount of leeway, since he was his heir and popular with the army) instructed him to return to Rome. Tacitus attributes motives of jealousy to Tiberius, but the wars had been costly and provocative. More important, from the point of view of Tiberius, the activities of Germanicus contravened the policy of Augustus to maintain a strong frontier on the Rhine. Tiberius also preferred diplomacy to force, and he pointed out to Germanicus in a letter that in the nine times he had been sent into Germany by Augustus, he had 'achieved less by force than by diplomacy'.[42]

Diplomatic mission to the east

On his return to Rome, Germanicus was offered a second consulship—with Tiberius as his colleague—and a diplomatic mission to the east to install a pro-Roman on the throne of Armenia. Tacitus maintains that Tiberius was attempting to find an honourable way to eliminate Germanicus, but Tiberius would have been aware of the need for the heir apparent to familiarise himself with the eastern situation, particularly with regard to Parthia. After all, Tiberius had been sent there himself by Augustus.

Appointment of Piso to Syria

Although Tiberius wished to use Germanicus' diplomatic skills, he was aware that his adopted son was anxious to seek personal glory. He therefore arranged for Calpurnius Piso to take over the province of Syria in order to assist and keep an eye on Germanicus even though the emperor's son had maius imperium (control over all governors and commanders) in the east.

Germanicus' breaches of protocol

Germanicus successfully carried out his task with regard to Armenia and negotiated with the Parthians, but during his 'tour' of the east he breached protocol on a number of occasions and it seems that Tiberius may have had some justification in sending Piso as a 'watchdog'. Germanicus' most serious mistake was in flouting the imperial edict regarding Egypt: no senator was permitted to enter Egypt without the emperor's personal approval. Germanicus went there to look at the antiquities, walking 'about without guards, in sandalled feet and Greek clothes imitating Scipio Africanus . . .'.[43] He committed another breach of protocol by releasing grains from the public granaries without Tiberius' assent, thereby lowering the price of corn, and he had his image cast on silver coins. Whether his behaviour was simply impulsive or was the result of arrogance is not certain, but he does appear to have been seeking personal advancement. 'Tiberius criticised Germanicus mildly for his clothes and deportment, but reprimanded him severely for infringing a ruling of Augustus by entering Alexandria without the Emperor's permission.'[44]

Hostility between Piso and Germanicus

Unfortunately, Tiberius had shown lack of judgment in his selection of Piso, who chose to interpret his task to check on Germanicus and report back to Tiberius as the right to cancel or reverse Germanicus' instructions. He also refused to provide Germanicus with troops. The relationship between the two men deteriorated and was not helped by the animosity of their respective wives, Agrippina and Plancina.

When Germanicus ordered Piso out of the province, Piso retaliated by attempting to stir up the Syrian troops against Germanicus. Not long after Piso's departure from his province, Germanicus became ill, and died.

Death of Germanicus

Tacitus records that on his deathbed Germanicus accused Piso and Plancina of poisoning him, and warned Agrippina 'to forget her pride, submit to cruel fortune, and, back in Rome, to avoid provoking those stronger than herself by competing for their power'.[45] Privately, he warned her of the danger from Tiberius.

At Germanicus' funeral in Antioch there were many words spoken about his fine character. It is here that Tacitus compares Germanicus favourably with Alexander the Great.

Piso re-enters Syria

On the death of Germanicus Piso had been superseded in his province, but he attempted to re-establish control of Syria by force. When he failed he sailed for Italy, preceded by Agrippina, who accused him and Plancina of murdering her husband on the instructions of Tiberius. Tacitus says that she had returned quickly to Rome with Germanicus' ashes, 'impatient of anything that postponed revenge'.[46]

Agrippina's accusations

Germanicus' popularity

Germanicus' great popularity throughout the empire is obvious from the honours bestowed on him postumously and the triumphal arches, statues and flattering inscriptions set up in Rome, Syria and along the Rhine. Tiberius incurred the hostility of many by his failure to appear at the funeral ceremonies held in Rome, and by his call for moderation in mourning.

No evidence of murder by Piso

There is no evidence for believing that either Piso or Tiberius had anything to do with Germanicus' death, and Tacitus admits that it was 'uncertain if the body showed signs of poisoning'.[47] However, any investigation into the affair was certain to cause problems for Tiberius. 'He anticipated malevolence among senators and others',[48] so referred the case to the senate and requested that they 'offer the accused every opportunity of producing evidence which may establish his innocence or Germanicus' unfairness, if there was any'.[49] He also asked them not to take into account his own grief or the slanders invented against him.

Piso's trial and death

Piso was aquitted on the charge of poisoning Germanicus, but in anticipation of his condemnation for misconduct in his province, he committed suicide.

Hostility of Agrippina towards Tiberius

Agrippina continued to believe that Tiberius had been responsible in some way for her husband's death and was openly hostile towards him for the next nine years. She ignored Germanicus' warning not to provoke those in power, and worked for the succession of her sons by building up a 'party' of supporters.

Tacitus portrays Germanicus as a brilliant and virtuous hero whose early death deprived the Roman world of a genius of the stature of Alexander. However, although in doing so he was reflecting the popular legend that had grown up about Germanicus in his own day, he used the 'noble' Germanicus as a contrast to the suspicious, hypocritical, deceptive 'arch tyrant', Tiberius.

The influence of Sejanus on Tiberius

After the death of Germanicus, Tiberius planned to promote his own son, Drusus, to secure the succession for him. In 21 Drusus became consul for the second time, and in the following year he was granted the tribunician authority. This not only embittered the faction loyal to Germanicus, but did not suit the plans of the capable prefect of the Praetorian Guard, L. Aelius Sejanus, who had become Tiberius' trusted adviser.

Tiberius' trusted adviser

Sejanus had been joint commander of the Guard with his father, and had served Augustus; he had accompanied Drusus to Pannonia during the revolts of AD 14, and from AD 17 he was sole prefect of the Guard. According to Tacitus he was the only one to whom Tiberius could speak 'freely and unguardedly',[50] and Tiberius referred to him as 'the partner of my labours'.[51]

Sejanus' ambition

However, Sejanus 'concealed behind a carefully modest exterior an unbounded lust for power',[52] and he had already taken some steps to realise his ambitions. In 23, he concentrated the normally scattered battalions of the Praetorian Guard into one camp just outside Rome on the pretext that this arrangement would minimise discipline problems and be more effective in an emergency. His real reasons were to increase the Guard's power and to intimidate the citizens.

Since Drusus suspected Sejanus' designs and resented his influence over his father, he had to be removed. However, to do this would not ensure Sejanus' rise to power, as there was 'a well-stocked imperial house',[53] including grown-up grandchildren.

Seduction of Livilla and death of Drusus

Sejanus planned to remove these individuals at intervals. It appears that Livilla, Drusus' unprincipled wife, was seduced by Sejanus and promised marriage and the throne if she poisoned her husband. Drusus died suddenly in 23, and Tiberius never really recovered from his grief at this death. According to Tacitus this was a turning point in the reign of Tiberius, as he became more morose and came to depend on Sejanus to an even greater extent.

Court intrigue

Sejanus was now at the centre of court intrigue since the imperial widows, Livia, Livilla and Agrippina, were jealous of each other, each constantly planning to undermine the others. Livia sided with Livilla against the bitter and outspoken Agrippina, who did not hide her hatred for Tiberius, whom she blamed for Germanicus' death. Agrippina also attempted to advance the interests of her children, Nero and Drusus Caesar. When it became apparent that these great-grandchildren of Augustus were in line to succeed Tiberius, Sejanus planned to undermine the influence of their mother by playing off Livia and Livilla against her. 'These ladies were to notify Tiberius that Agrippina, proud of her large family and relying on her popularity, had designs on the throne.'[54]

Sejanus' plans for Agrippina

Agrippina's 'party'

Tired of Agrippina's outspokenness and urged on by Sejanus, Tiberius was determined to crush Agrippina's 'party' and there were many charges brought by the *delatores* (informers) against her friends and supporters.

Tiberius refuses to give Livilla in marriage to Sejanus

Tacitus says that Sejanus, under pressure from Livilla, now applied to Tiberius for permission to marry her, but Tiberius was not in favour of this proposal. He believed that such a marriage would intensify Agrippina's ill feeling and would split the imperial house in two, since the two widows were already rivals and his grandsons were torn between them. He also pointed out that it would create jealousy among the more distinguished men in the senate. However, he later allowed Sejanus to become betrothed to Livilla's daughter.

Tiberius' retirement to Capri

Tiberius now made a serious mistake. Weary of the plotting factions and the hostility at court, he retired to the island of Capri. Tacitus says that this was done on the urging of Sejanus, who 'foresaw many advantages in this. He himself would control access to the Emperor — as well as most of his correspondence, since it would be transmitted by the Guardsmen' and he felt that the ageing monarch 'would soon be readier to delegate governmental functions'.[55] He therefore encouraged the emperor to leave the capital. There is no evidence of truth in Tacitus' other suggestions—that Tiberius may have retired there to satisfy his perversions, or to escape the bullying of his mother or the hard day-to-day administration of the empire. In fact, his government from Capri was as efficient as ever, although his removal from Rome did allow Sejanus a free rein with his intrigues. An incident which further increased Sejanus' power over Tiberius occurred at this time: Tiberius, Sejanus and a number of servants were dining in a natural cavern when a rock-fall threatened the emperor's life and, it is said, Sejanus protected Tiberius from the falling boulders. From that time, 'Tiberius believed him disinterested and listened trustingly to his advice, however disastrous'.[56]

Emperor's life saved by Sejanus

It was now a time of great tension for the members of the senate and for anybody with links with the family of Germanicus. Sejanus played Agrippina's sons off against each other; he encouraged the ambition and jealousy of Drusus Caesar against his elder brother, Nero Caesar. However, it was not until the death of Livia (the Augusta) in 29 that Tiberius and Sejanus were able to remove Agrippina. According to Tacitus, 'While the Augusta had lived there was still a moderating influence, for Tiberius had retained a deep-seated deference for his mother. Sejanus, too, had not ventured to outbid her parental authority'.[57] Soon after Livia's death, Tiberius sent a letter to the senate charging Agrippina with 'insubordinate language and disobedient spirit' and Nero with 'homosexual indecency',[58] and they were banished to barren islands. Drusus Caesar was imprisoned in Rome. Nero is believed to have been driven to suicide; Drusus was apparently executed in 33, the year of Agrippina's death.

Death of Livia guaranteed the ruin of Agrippina

The position of Sejanus now appeared secure. He had control of the Praetorian Guard and the senate, was engaged to the granddaughter of Tiberius, was granted proconsular imperium and was honoured with statues and Games. However, when it became apparent that Tiberius was promoting Gaius, the youngest son of Agrippina, Sejanus plotted to kill him. Tiberius was warned by Antonia (mother of Germanicus) and carefully arranged Sejanus' downfall, although he continued to make promises of further honours to the unsuspecting prefect. Naevius Sutorius Macro, the Prefect of the Vigiles, was sent to Rome to take command of the Praetorian Guard, and a letter from Tiberius was read in the senate denouncing Sejanus as a traitor. He was arrested, taken to prison and executed immediately, and for over a year the supporters of Sejanus were prosecuted.

Sejanus' ambitions revealed to Tiberius

Sejanus' arrest and death

When Sejanus' ex-wife informed Tiberius that Livilla and Sejanus had been responsible for his son's death, Tiberius became even more embittered and suspicious, taking a much harsher attitude to accusations of treason. It

Executions increased in number

is this period which Tacitus refers to as the Reign of Terror. Although his account is undoubtedly exaggerated, some innocent people did lose their lives as a result of the increasing accusations made by the despicable delatores.

Tiberius, who remained at Capri until his death in AD 37 at the age of seventy-eight, continued to administer the empire through dispatches but often hesitated in making important decisions, and the senate became even more dependent on him.

A commemorative coin for Agrippina the Elder, wife of Germanicus and mother of Gaius (Caligula)

Exercise: Livia

Read Tacitus, I, pp. 33, 34, 39, 52, 120; IV: 72, p. 193, and IV: 76, pp. 195–6.

1 Describe the portrait of Livia drawn by Tacitus.

2 Which aspect of her personality does he emphasise?

3 Read any reliable modern text on the subject. From this reading, explain to what extent Tacitus' view is accurate.

Tacitus' view of Agrippina the Elder

While in Germany during the mutinies 'she scorned the proposal' that Germanicus should send her away, 'reminding him that she was the blood of the divine Augustus and would live up to it'[59]

During the war with the Germans, 'this great-hearted woman acted as a Commander. She herself dispensed clothes to needy soldiers and dressed the wounds . . . She stood at the bridge-head to thank and congratulate the returning column[60]

After Germanicus' death, Agrippina 'was exhausted by grief and unwell but impatient of anything that postponed revenge'[61]

After Germanicus' funeral, the people called her 'the glory of her country . . . the only true descendant of Augustus, the unmatched model of traditional behaviour'[62]

Sejanus found it difficult to attack her, as her virtue made her unassailable; however, her insubordination to Tiberius gave Sejanus an excuse to undermine her[63]

'Agrippina knew no feminine weaknesses. Intolerant of rivalry, thirsting for power, she had a man's preoccupations'[65]

The trial of many of her friends and family led 'Agrippina, always violent', to verbally attack Tiberius: 'I, born of his sacred blood [Augustus] am his incarnation'; 'Agrippina, resentful as ever, became physically ill'[64]

Tiberius and the senate

If Augustus' principate was to continue to appear legitimate, it was necessary for Tiberius to rule with the full co-operation of the senate. R. Syme maintains that he was genuine when he professed, at the beginning of his reign, his intention to govern as a true princeps.

Need for senatorial support

Tiberius needed the senate's help. Running the empire was an enormous task; it was not until the time of Claudius that a centralised bureaucracy handled most of the business of empire. Also, Tiberius preferred to have an independent body helping him, since he appears to have been genuinely hesitant about the responsibility.

Tiberius' attempts at co-ruling with the senate

Guaranteed traditional rights

Like Augustus, Tiberius attempted to uphold the traditional rights of the senate as well as treat it with dignity and as a partner in running the empire. Even Tacitus admits that this was the case before the death of Drusus in 23.

> In the first place public business—and the most important private business—was transacted in the senate. Among its chief men, there was freedom of discussion; their lapses into servility were arrested by the emperor himself. His conferments of office took into consideration birth, military distinction, and civilian eminence, and the choice manifestly fell on the worthiest men. The consuls and praetors maintained their prestige. The lesser offices, too, each exercised their proper authority. Moreover, the treason court excepted, the laws were duly enforced.[66]

Consulted the senate

Tiberius genuinely sought its aid, sometimes on matters which were not its concern.

> . . . asking for advice in every matter that concerned the national revenue, the allocation of monopolies, and the construction or repair of public buildings. He actually consulted them about the drafting or disbanding of troops, the stationing of legions and auxiliaries, the extension of military commands, the choice of generals to conduct particular campaigns and how to answer particular letters from foreign potentates.[67]

Showed respect to consuls

He showed courtesy and respect when addressing not only individual senators but the House as a whole, and stood in the presence of the consuls. 'Tiberius made a habit of always allowing the consuls the initiative, as though the Republic still existed.'[68]

Avoided giving offence

Any titles which the nobility might find offensive, such as 'imperator' and 'father of his country', he avoided; he refused to have a month called after him or any temples constructed in his honour, and he discouraged flattery.

> He vetoed all bills for the dedication of temples and priests to his divinity, and reserved the right to sanction even the setting up of his statues and busts . . .
> . . . Such was his hatred of flatterers that he refused to let senators approach his litter, whether in greeting or on business; . . . [and] if anyone, either in conversation or a speech, spoke of him in too fulsome terms, Tiberius would interrupt and sternly correct the phrase.[69]

Widened range of duties

He enlarged and developed some of the senate's duties. Under him the senate became practically the only legislative body after AD 14, as he transferred the election of magistrates to it from the people's assembly. Although he followed Augustus' example of commending candidates for election, he did it on a smaller scale and competition in the senate for official positions became a real contest, without the opportunity for electoral bribery that had occurred in the assembly. Tiberius never overrode the normal electoral system.

Increased responsibilities

Under Tiberius the senate became the chief criminal court, particularly for treason trials. In theory it retained wide powers over the provinces and the State Treasury, and had increased administrative duties.

Supported worthy men

He was anxious to retain worthy men in the senate, and if any had fallen on hard times he was inclined to help them financially as in the case of Celer, to whom he awarded one million sesterces. He would not, however, assist those senators whose poverty was due to their own extravagance. He objected strongly when a young nobleman, Marcus Hortensius, who had been given one million sesterces by Augustus to marry and have a family, asked for assistance from the floor of the senate.

> If every poor man is to come here . . . and start requesting money for his children, the applicants will never be satisfied and the nation's finances will collapse. When our ancestors authorised senators to digress sometimes from their subject-matter and raise matters of public importance when it was their turn to speak, this was not to enable us to promote our own private interests and personal finances.[70]

When this speech was received with silence, Tiberius announced that he would give each of Hortensius' children 200 000 sesterces.

Encouraged participation in decision making

Tiberius invited the senate to discuss provincial petitions from delegations of Ephesians and Magnesians, and from many other cities. Tacitus points out, however, that 'the extensive material and local rivalries proved wearisome',[71] and the senate asked the consuls to carry out investigations for them and then report back. Tiberius also sent a letter to the senators 'blaming them (by implication) for referring all their difficulties to him';[72] he was referring to their indecision about the choice of a governor for the province of Africa. They had requested Tiberius to make the choice; when he suggested two names, Lepidus and Blaesus, the senate (according to Tacitus) chose Blaesus, since he was Sejanus' uncle.

Encouraged independence

He encouraged the senate to be independent, and on a few occasions it did overrule him. Suetonius says that 'If decrees were passed in defiance of his wishes, he abstained from complaint', and once, when a motion was being voted on, 'he went into a minority lobby and not a soul followed him'.[73]

Complained of servility and subservience

However, generally the senators were subservient. Tacitus had complained that in Augustus' reign 'opposition did not exist' and that the senate was filled with men 'who found that slavish obedience was the way to succeed politically . . .'.[74] This servility increased under Tiberius, and according to Tacitus 'all ex-consuls, most ex-praetors, even many junior senators competed with each other's offensively sycophantic proposals'.[75] Tiberius complained each time he left the Senate House that the senators were 'men fit to be slaves'.[76] Syme maintains that Tiberius was thirty years out of touch in his expectations of an independent senate, 'for he had seldom seen the senate since his praetorship in 16 BC, and 'forgot (or tried to forget) how far that body had been corrupted and debased by Caesar Augustus'.[77]

Reasons for the senate's increasing subservience

Tiberius' character appeared threatening

- It is possible that in the earlier part of his reign Tiberius' reserved temperament and hesitant attitude unnerved the senators, who never really knew what he was thinking; Tacitus refers often to the cryptic way in which Tiberius spoke. Senators apparently preferred not to take chances by speaking their minds. In fact, Tiberius generally respected those who spoke openly and frankly but was unable to impart this to the senate, because of his manner.

Free speech/treason

- Because there was no clear definition of the crime of treason, the distinction between free speech and treason was unclear. Senators were not prepared to take up contentious issues. As treason trials appeared to become more frequent, sycophancy increased.

Fear of Sejanus

- Senators feared the power wielded by Sejanus as commander of the Praetorian Guard, and his influence over Tiberius.

Individuals showed some independence

When Tiberius retired to Capri, Sejanus interfered in public business, influencing the decisions of both Tiberius and the senate. He also began a series of prosecutions of senators who had shown any friendship to the family of Germanicus. Senators, afraid for their own safety,

Excessive flattery

> sought relief in flattery. Though assembled to consider some unrelated business, they voted the erection of altars to Mercy and Friendship—the latter to be flanked by statues of Tiberius and Sejanus.[78]

The once proud senators also begged that Tiberius or Sejanus make an appearance in Rome, but when neither did senators and knights flocked to Campania, 'anxiously regarding Sejanus'.[79] They waited for days for an interview, but were denied access to him and returned to Rome.

After the downfall of Sejanus Tiberius did not return to Rome, but continued to rule the empire from Capri. His early hopes of sharing the work with the senate had been disappointed, and he became increasingly impatient with its lack of independence.

There had been some individual cases of independent behaviour in the senate, such as that of the distinguished lawyer, Marcus Antistius Labeo. However, 'Labeo's incorruptible independence' won him no imperial favours, and in fact his political career suffered as a result—'Labeo stopped short at the praetorship'.[80] Another senator who was not afraid to say what he believed in front of Tiberius was Aulua Cremutius Cordus, who was accused of praising Brutus in his *History* and of referring to Cassius as the 'last of the Romans'. He defended himself bravely, pointing out that Julius Caesar and Augustus did not condemn other writers for their words but 'endured them and let them be'.[81] However, when he had concluded his defence and left the senate, he committed suicide. Tacitus suggests that this was because condemnation appeared certain, since the prosecutors were dependants of Sejanus and Tiberius' face was grim as he listened to the defence. By subsequently ordering Cremutius' books to be burnt, the senate once again showed the depths to which it had sunk.

Treason (maiestas) trials

Treason trials form a sinister part of Tacitus' account of the reign of Tiberius, his purpose being to show the gradual degeneration of the reign into tyranny.

The law of treason

Definition of treason

Treason was one of the earliest crimes subject to Roman law, but the definition of the crime of treason (*maiestas*) was never precise. For instance, Cicero believed that it was an attack on the dignity, greatness or power of the people or of those to whom the people had given power. Tacitus defined it as 'official misconduct damaging the Roman state, such as betrayal of an army or incitement to sedition'.[82] Augustus redefined the law, and it came to be interpreted as any offence or insult offered to the princeps in deed, writing or speech. However, Augustus was hesitant about invoking the law.

Tiberius' respect for the laws

When in AD 15 Tiberius was asked by a praetor, Q. Pompeius Macer, 'whether cases under the treason law were to receive attention', he replied that 'the laws must take their course'.[83] Since no precedent had been set by Augustus, the cases which came before the senate in the time of Tiberius tended to be test cases.

Delatores

Position of delatores in Roman society

Rome had no public prosecutor; information was brought to the authorities, the senate and emperor, by private individuals. If a charge of treason brought by these informers (delatores) was upheld, they were awarded at least one-quarter of the property confiscated from the guilty person. The remaining three-quarters went into the treasury. This encouraged the growing 'class' of delatores to lie, bribe and manufacture evidence in order to secure the conviction of wealthy men. It also enabled ambitious Romans to eliminate their rivals. 'It was an odious system, destructive of the very fabric of society.'[84]

Types of delatores

Some delatores were like Romanius Hispo, who in AD 15 brought charges against M. Granius Marcellus, governor of Bithynia. He was 'needy, obscure and restless', and set a precedent 'which enabled imitators to exchange beggary for wealth'.[85] Many were senators, such as Bruttedius Niger, whom Tacitus described as

> a highly cultured man who, if he had gone straight, would have attained great eminence. But impatience spurred him to outstrip first his equals, then his superiors—and finally his own former ambitions.[86]

Example of methods used by delatores

Four ex-praetors, ambitious for the consulship, planned the downfall of Titius Sabinus, a respectable man whose only crime was that he was a loyal friend to the family of Germanicus; this case is an example of the despicable methods to which many delatores resorted. Lucanius Latiaris, Marcus Porcius Cato, Petilius Rufus and Marcus Opsius realised that the only access to the consulship was through Sejanus, 'and only crimes secured Sejanus' goodwill'.[87] By pretending friendship with Sabinus, Latiaris tricked him into revealing his feelings for Germanicus' family and his attitude towards Sejanus: three other senators hid in a space between the wall and ceiling of a room in order to overhear the incriminating evidence. Tacitus described this as a sordid trick. This method of collecting evidence threw conspicuous Romans into a 'state of unprecedented agitation and terror'.[88] People became secretive, avoiding conversations and encounters with close friends and family as well as with strangers.

According to Tacitus 'there was no alleviation of the accusers, who became more formidable and vicious every day'.[89]

Charges

Many frivolous charges

Many of the charges were trivial and ridiculous, such as the accusations made against a Roman knight, Falanius. He was charged with allowing a comic actor — who was also a male prostitute — to assist in the worship of Augustus and with selling a statue of Augustus as part of some garden furniture.

M. Scribonius Libo Drusus, a member of a prominent Roman family, was accused of subversive plotting because he placed too much confidence in astrological predictions. He was also charged with consulting a fortune-teller to find out 'if he would be rich enough to pave the Via Appia with money as far as Brundisium'.[90] Tacitus admitted that the charges were preposterous and pointless, but he cited this case because he believed 'it initiated an evil which for many years corroded public life'.[91] Other charges were easy to make and difficult to disprove, such as Hispo's allegations that Marcellus had told scandalous stories about Tiberius.

Treason linked with other offences

Often the charge of treason was linked with other offences as in the case of Appuleia Varilla, a member of the imperial family (grandniece of Augustus). She was charged with treason for insulting Tiberius, his mother (Livia) and the deified Augustus, as well as for committing adultery.

There were, of course, genuine cases of treason such as Piso's attempt to re-enter his province of Syria by force, and there were those condemned for real conspiracies against Tiberius.

Condemnations

Number and frequency of treason trials exaggerated

Tacitus attempted to create in the minds of his readers the impression that the number and frequency of treason trials increased as Tiberius' reign progressed. He builds up a picture of continuous prosecutions, culminating in the so-called Reign of Terror (after 33) during which many innocent men perished.

However, a careful study of Tacitus' account reveals that during Tiberius' reign of almost twenty-three years no more than fifty-two people were charged with treason, and of these thirty were never executed. Of the twelve who were put to death, Tiberius is supposed to have ordered the execution of eight; an overzealous senate was responsible for the four apparently innocent victims. Many of those charged with treason and other offences chose to commit suicide rather than wait for the senate's verdict. In the case of treason, if the accused killed himself his family was allowed to retain its property, apart from the quarter awarded to the informer.

Many suicided before trial

Tiberius' dismissal of trivial charges

In the first part of his reign Tiberius dismissed many cases which he considered ridiculous and intervened in others to pardon the accused or to lessen the sentence. He made it very clear that he did not consider insulting remarks about himself or his mother as treasonable, but that disrespectful comments about the divine Augustus should be punished.

When Tiberius heard the accusations against Falanius, he wrote to the consuls that 'Augustus had not been voted divine honours in order to ruin Roman citizens' and 'to include the latter's statues in sales of houses or gardens was not sacrilegious'.[92] On the suicide of Libo, the emperor commented that he 'would have interceded for his life if he had not so hastily killed himself'.[93] When Marcellus was charged with recounting 'the most repulsive features in the Emperor's character',[94] Tiberius 'voted for aquittal on the treason counts'.[95] In the case of Appuleia Varilla, he 'insisted on a distinction between disrespectul remarks about Augustus—for which she should be condemned—and about himself, on which he desired no enquiry to be held'.[96] He also requested that any words spoken against his mother should not be the subject of a charge. In fact, 'he released Appuleia from liability under the treason law'.[97]

Prosecutions increased after death of Sejanus

Tiberius did try at first to check the abuse of the law of treason by insisting that trials be fair and technically legal; later in his reign, as actual conspiracies against him increased and Sejanus played on his suspicions, the number of treason cases grew. After the death of Sejanus prosecutions against his friends continued for a year, but there were never the wholesale executions suggested by Tacitus, and his statement that 'at Rome the massacre was continuous'[98] is exaggerated. Tacitus actually recorded numerous deaths during this period, but some were from natural causes or were executions for other offences, while many were suicides.

Law of maiestas widened under Tiberius

Although the problem of the interpretation of the maiestas law was a legacy of Augustus and the delatores had long been an accepted part of the administration of justice, Tiberius does have to take responsibility for widening the law of treason, for failing to check the excessive activities of the informers in the latter part of his reign and for allowing so much power to the unscrupulous and ambitious Sejanus. The last years of his reign were marked by extreme tension and fear among the upper classes of Rome.

Tiberius' frontier and provincial policies

Tiberius' government of the empire was carried out with real statesmanship. Even Tacitus admits this.

The frontier policy

Augustus' frontier policy followed

Tiberius followed Augustus' advice to avoid an extension of the empire beyond its present frontiers except where it was necessary for security, such as in the east. He strengthened the eastern frontiers by 'astute diplomacy without warfare'[99] and limited annexations of client-kingdoms, which Augustus had implied was acceptable once they were sufficiently Romanised. Tiberius paid particular attention to improving the discipline of the troops on the frontiers and to maintaining economy in the forces after the initial mutinies in Germany and Pannonia.

The Rhine

The northern frontier was maintained at the Rhine after Germanicus' attempts to extend it to the Elbe were curtailed by Tiberius. His belief that the rebellious tribes beyond the Rhine could be 'left to their own internal disturbances'[100] was justified when some years later, after the Romans had gone, national rivalries turned the German tribes led by Maroboduus and Arminius against each other.

The Danube

Tiberius used a number of methods of secure the Danube frontier. He hired a native leader to use the Suebi and Marcomanni to keep watch on the Upper Danube. He strengthened the middle Danube region by combining the previous senatorial provinces of Achaea and Macedonia with Moesia under the competent imperial legate, Poppaeus Sabinus, who was left in charge of this large province for twenty years. The Lower Danube area had been divided by Augustus between two Thracian kings. As a result of trouble between them, during which one was killed, Tiberius replaced them and appointed a Roman resident to supervise the new kings. There was intermittent trouble in this area until 46, when it was finally organised as a province.

The east

Germanicus was sent to the east in AD 17 to settle the question of kingship in Armenia, where he appointed Ataxias III to the throne. The client-kingdoms of Cappadocia and Commagene were annexed, and Cilicia was added to Syria. Later, Tiberius installed a new king of Parthia.

Africa

The only serious frontier trouble spot for Tiberius was in Africa. Tacfarinas, a Numidian and once a member of the Roman army, was conversant with Roman military tactics. He carried out successful guerrilla raids on the province of Africa for seven years (17–23). In 21, Junius Blaesus was put in command and succeeded in breaking the back of the insurrection, and in two years peace returned to the province.

A coin minted about AD 22 to commemorate the help given by Tiberius to the people of Asia Minor after an earthquake

Provincial policy

Tiberius recognised Rome's responsibility for the welfare of provincials, and would tolerate no abuses by governors or the Roman business class.

The following chart illustrates the main features of his administration.

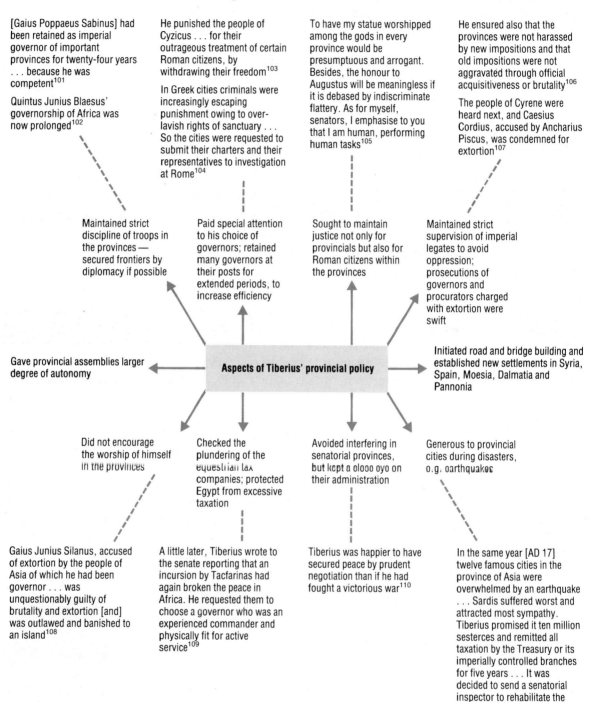

Aspects of Tiberius' provincial policy

Maintained strict discipline of troops in the provinces — secured frontiers by diplomacy if possible

[Gaius Poppaeus Sabinus] had been retained as imperial governor of important provinces for twenty-four years . . . because he was competent[101]

Quintus Junius Blaesus' governorship of Africa was now prolonged[102]

Paid special attention to his choice of governors; retained many governors at their posts for extended periods, to increase efficiency

He punished the people of Cyzicus . . . for their outrageous treatment of certain Roman citizens, by withdrawing their freedom[103]

In Greek cities criminals were increasingly escaping punishment owing to over-lavish rights of sanctuary . . . So the cities were requested to submit their charters and their representatives to investigation at Rome[104]

Sought to maintain justice not only for provincials but also for Roman citizens within the provinces

To have my statue worshipped among the gods in every province would be presumptuous and arrogant. Besides, the honour to Augustus will be meaningless if it is debased by indiscriminate flattery. As for myself, senators, I emphasise to you that I am human, performing human tasks[105]

Maintained strict supervision of imperial legates to avoid oppression; prosecutions of governors and procurators charged with extortion were swift

He ensured also that the provinces were not harassed by new impositions and that old impositions were not aggravated through official acquisitiveness or brutality[106]

The people of Cyrene were heard next, and Caesius Cordius, accused by Ancharius Piscus, was condemned for extortion[107]

Gave provincial assemblies larger degree of autonomy

Initiated road and bridge building and established new settlements in Syria, Spain, Moesia, Dalmatia and Pannonia

Did not encourage the worship of himself in the provinces

Gaius Junius Silanus, accused of extortion by the people of Asia of which he had been governor . . . was unquestionably guilty of brutality and extortion [and] was outlawed and banished to an island[108]

Checked the plundering of the equestrian tax companies; protected Egypt from excessive taxation

A little later, Tiberius wrote to the senate reporting that an incursion by Tacfarinas had again broken the peace in Africa. He requested them to choose a governor who was an experienced commander and physically fit for active service[109]

Avoided interfering in senatorial provinces, but kept a close eye on their administration

Tiberius was happier to have secured peace by prudent negotiation than if he had fought a victorious war[110]

Generous to provincial cities during disasters, e.g. earthquakes

In the same year [AD 17] twelve famous cities in the province of Asia were overwhelmed by an earthquake . . . Sardis suffered worst and attracted most sympathy. Tiberius promised it ten million sesterces and remitted all taxation by the Treasury or its imperially controlled branches for five years . . . It was decided to send a senatorial inspector to rehabilitate the sufferers[111]

Despite Tiberius' efforts to govern the provinces fairly and equably and to promote peace and prosperity, there were a number of problems.

Rebellion in Gaul

As well as the trouble in Africa, there was a brief rebellion in Gaul in AD 21 which, according to Tacitus, was due to the burden of debt owed to Roman creditors. An added grievance may have been due to Tiberius' attempt to curb the Druids.

Criticism over extended governorships

Tiberius' policy of leaving governors in office for long periods in order to benefit the provincials fell down when he made a poor judgment about a governor. For example, ten years was too long for Pontius Pilatus (26–36), who was the governor of Judaea at the time of Christ's crucifixion. He made a number of serious mistakes, provoking the inhabitants unnecessarily, and it took the governor of Syria, Vitellius, to conciliate the Jews after Pilatus was sent to Rome to stand trial.

Senate's resentment

The senate resented his guidance and control in the provinces, and were particularly affronted when he encroached on the senatorial sphere by refusing to permit a change of proconsuls for Asia and Africa and keeping the same men there for six years.

Exercise

With reference to the following pages in Tacitus, which relate to Tiberius' provincial and frontier policies, answer the questions that follow.

- 43–60: mutinies in Lower Germany and Pannonia
- 61–73, 193–4: German campaigns of Germanicus and the loss of Frisia
- 139–41: rebellion in Gaul
- 138: disturbances in Thrace
- 103, 129–30, 154–5, 168–70: war in Africa
- 98, 215–19: relations with Parthia and the east

1. What are the reasons given by Tacitus for the outbreak of rebellions in Gaul and Thrace in AD 21?
2. Who was Tacfarinas? What fighting methods did he use? How did Junius Blaesus break the back of the Numidian war?
3. Explain how Tiberius used 'astute diplomacy without warfare'[112] and the services of Lucius Vitellius, governor of Syria, to establish Rome's nominee on the throne of Parthia.

An evaluation of Tiberius and his reign

The Tacitean Tiberius

Tacitus' treatment of Tiberius appears excessively harsh and he has often been criticised for 'rewriting another tyrant' because 'he was unable to shake off the memory of the last years under Domitian'.[113] However,

Syme says that this is too simple an explanation of his bias against Tiberius. The tradition which survived about Tiberius—and which is reflected not only in Tacitus, but also in Suetonius and Dio Cassius—was uniformly hostile. Syme maintains that Tacitus faithfully recorded the documentary evidence, but could not refrain 'from adding his own commentary and reconstruction in generous measure in order to heighten the colours and shape the outlines'.[114] Tacitus' Tiberius therefore appears to be

> composed of layers. [There is] the Tiberius of history . . . there is the Tiberius of the hostile senatorial tradition . . . This composite has been endowed by Tacitus with some of the features and colours of Domitian. As a further refinement it has been modelled on those archetypal tyrants to be found in the philosophers and tragic poets.[115]

Although there are discrepancies between the facts recorded by Tacitus and his interpretation of them, it is possible from a careful reading of the *Annals* and the other ancient sources to arrive at a more realistic picture of 'the Republican princeps to whom destiny awarded the inheritance of Caesar Augustus'.[116] In building up his picture of Tiberius, Tacitus 'disclosed more than he intended' and 'certain features of the Tacitean Tiberius, detestable on a superficial view, carried praise, not blame'.[117]

Tacitus believed, as did many of the ancients, that man's nature never changed and that although it could be suppressed or disguised for a time, it would eventually come to the surface. Therefore, if Tiberius ended his reign as an evil man, he must have always had evil tendencies. Tacitus outlined what he considered to have been the various stages through which Tiberius' character was revealed.

Stages in the revelation of Tiberius' character

> His character, too, had its different stages. While he was a private citizen or holding commands under Augustus, his life was blameless; and so was his reputation. While Germanicus and Drusus still lived, he concealed his real self, cunningly affecting virtuous qualities. However, until his mother died there was good in Tiberius as well as evil. Again, as long as he favoured (or feared) Sejanus, the cruelty of Tiberius was detested but his perversions unrevealed. Then fear vanished, and with it shame. Thereafter he expressed only his own personality—by unrestrained infamy.[118]

Tacitus has described Tiberius as cryptic, secretive, cloaking his thoughts, keeping his true motives hidden, repressing his feelings, deceptive, dissembling, hypocritical, insincere, crafty, resentful, cruel, grim, terrifying, arrogant, morose, hesitant and secretly sensual.

In order to understand his character and behaviour it is necessary to study the predicaments in which he found himself with regard to his family, his environment and his career, and to remember that he was fifty-five when became emperor.

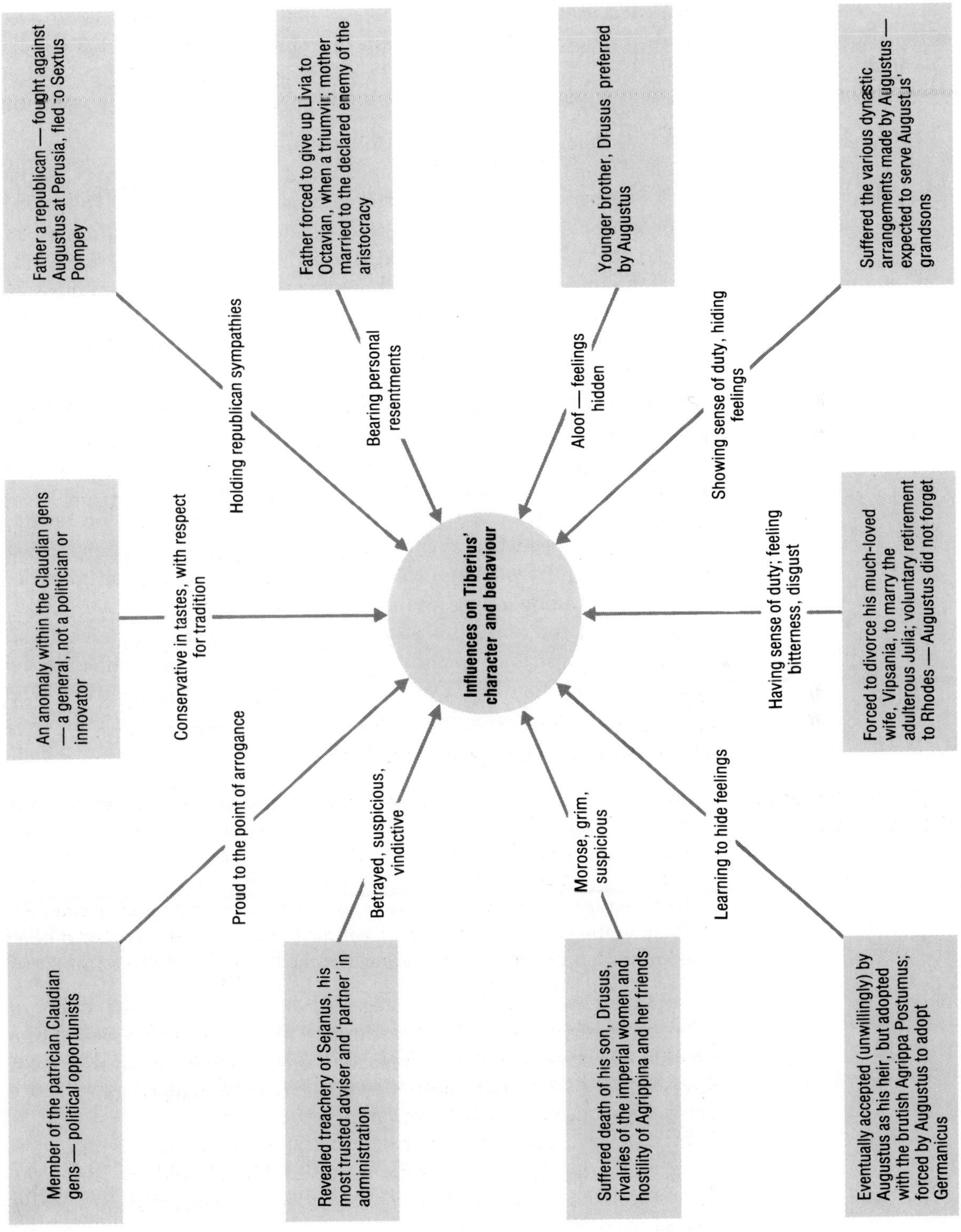
Influences on Tiberius' character and behaviour
Father a republican — fought against Augustus at Perusia, fled to Sextus Pompey
Holding republican sympathies
Father forced to give up Livia to Octavian, when a triumvir; mother married to the declared enemy of the aristocracy
Bearing personal resentments
Younger brother, Drusus preferred by Augustus
Aloof — feelings hidden
Suffered the various dynastic arrangements made by Augustus — expected to serve Augustus' grandsons
Showing sense of duty, hiding feelings
An anomaly within the Claudian gens — a general, not a politician or innovator
Conservative in tastes, with respect for tradition
Forced to divorce his much-loved wife, Vipsania, to marry the adulterous Julia; voluntary retirement to Rhodes — Augustus did not forget
Having sense of duty; feeling bitterness, disgust
Member of the patrician Claudian gens — political opportunists
Proud to the point of arrogance
Revealed treachery of Sejanus, his most trusted adviser and 'partner' in administration
Betrayed, suspicious, vindictive
Suffered death of his son, Drusus, rivalries of the imperial women and hostility of Agrippina and her friends
Morose, grim, suspicious
Eventually accepted (unwillingly) by Augustus as his heir, but adopted with the brutish Agrippa Postumus; forced by Augustus to adopt Germanicus
Learning to hide feelings

Negative attributes

Dissimulation

Hypocrisy and deceit

Tacitus accused Tiberius of hypocrisy and deceit. This criticism encompasses many of the other descriptions of him — as dissembling, secretive, hiding his thoughts and motives, and so on.

Considering the number of humiliations suffered by Tiberius at the hands of Augustus, it is not surprising that an old-fashioned and proud aristocrat would learn to hide his feelings and thoughts. His firm sense of duty to the state and to his adoptive father forced him to behave as though nothing had happened and to carry on in his official capacity.

His hesitation in assuming the power of princeps, interpreted by the senate as hypocrisy, may have been genuinely intended to give the senate the opportunity of setting a precedent for future imperial appointments. On the other hand, he may not have felt capable of running the empire single-handedly.

Once in office, his genuine intention to govern as a true princeps and to allow free debate meant that he had to be careful about expressing his own thoughts and feelings, in case they unduly influenced the senate. This was illustrated when a senator asked him: 'Caesar, will you vote first or last? If first, I shall have your lead to follow; if last, I am afraid of inadvertently voting against you'.[119]

Also, when the senate sat as a court it was necessary for Tiberius to conceal his own attitude towards the people involved. For example, in the case of M. Scribonius Libo Drusus, charged with subversive plotting, 'The Emperor, without altering his expression, read out the accusation and its signatures in a toneless voice calculated neither to aggravate not to extenuate the charges'.[120]

There were, however, occasions when Tiberius' statements and behaviour did smack of hypocrisy. He continually promised to visit the provinces and the armies but never did, and after Drusus' death,

> by reverting to empty discredited talk about restoring the Republic and handing the government to the consuls or others, he undermined the belief even in what he had said sincerely and truthfully.[121]

According to Tacitus, Tiberius regarded dissimulation, or the ability to 'cloak his thoughts', as his greatest virtue. Although Tacitus criticised him for this characteristic, he in fact built up a picture of Tiberius as a successful ruler who survived for a very long time by dissimulation.

Vindictiveness

Vindictiveness was another charge made by Tacitus against Tiberius. This was associated with the bitter resentment that developed during his marriage to Julia and as a result of the hostility of Agrippina, the death of Drusus and the treachery of Sejanus.

Examples

Tiberius ordered the execution of Sempronius Gracchus. He had been the lover of Julia when she was married to Agrippa, and when she 'was transferred to Tiberius this persistent adulterer made her defiant and unfriendly to her new husband'.[122] He had been exiled to an African island, but when Tiberius became emperor he sent soldiers to kill him.

Tiberius also hated Gaius Asinius Gallus, who had married Vipsania, Tiberius' first wife, when Tiberius had been forced against his will to divorce her and marry Julia. Gallus' behaviour in the senate on a number of occasions provoked the anger of Tiberius. According to Dio Cassius, he was arrested in AD 30 (possibly as an associate of Sejanus) and imprisoned for three years. 'He died of starvation—whether self-inflicted or forcible was undiscovered.'[123] Tacitus records that after Agrippina's death in the following year, Tiberius claimed that she had committed adultery with Gallus, so slandering both of them.

In his biography, Tiberius maintained that Sejanus had been killed for persecuting Nero and Drusus, yet after Sejanus' death Tiberius did not lessen the suffering of the imprisoned Agrippina and Drusus. Even after their deaths he attacked them, slandering Agrippina and reciting publicly a record 'of the prince's daily doings and sayings' while confined. He had had agents 'noting every look and groan and even private mutterings' of Drusus.[124]

It would have been strange if Tiberius had been unaffected by the revelation that his most trusted friend and adviser had been plotting against him and was responsible for his only son's death. Tiberius' natural suspicion of people was intensified and it was to be expected that Sejanus' friends and relatives would suffer, although his treatment of Sejanus' children, according to Tacitus, was unnecessary and excessively brutal. Tiberius' vengeance against those involved with Sejanus was understandable, but unfortunately there was little attempt to distinguish between those directly involved with him and those who were simply political aquaintances. There were certainly innocent victims at this time, but the 'continuous massacres' approved by an emperor 'frenzied with bloodshed' (as described by Tacitus) were exaggerated. Many committed suicide out of fear, because they believed that Tiberius disliked them. Scullard points out that it is highly unlikely that Tiberius emerged as a bloodthirsty tyrant after maintaining 'a mask of virtue for nearly seventy years'.[125]

Not a bloodthirsty tyrant

Grimness of manner

Tacitus also criticises Tiberius for his grim and morose manner, referring to his 'natural glumness'.[126] Suetonius supports this view and records that

Augustus so 'disliked Tiberius' dour manner as to interrupt his own careless chatter when he entered . . . '.[127] Considering the influences of his early years, it is not surprising that Tiberius should have grown up rather serious and morose. Neither is it surprising that his grimness, along with suspicion, should have increased with the years.

Vices unsubstantiated

No evidence for sensual perversions

The accusations of Tacitus and Suetonius regarding Tiberius' sensual vices while on Capri cannot be substantiated by first-class evidence. Tacitus believed that Tiberius' criminal lusts were uncontrollable, and 'worthy of an oriental despot'.[128]

Positive qualities

A more careful reading of the *Annals* reveals that Tiberius had many good qualities. He had a firm sense of the duty of a ruler, he behaved stoically at times of personal grief, he respected tradition, he was not deceived by pretence, he was frugal, courteous, slow to anger, and unperturbed by personal abuse; he hated excessive flattery and servility, believed in advancement for merit, respected those who spoke their minds and preferred to use diplomacy rather than force.

Tacitus admits that Tiberius not only efficiently administered the state but 'ensured also that the provinces were not harassed by new impositions and that old impositions were not aggravated through official acquisitiveness or brutality'.[129]

It is possible to discern the historic Tiberius from the narrative of Tacitus. Although some of the modern attempts to cleanse his character have perhaps gone too far, F. B. Marsh and M. P. Charlesworth have successfully rehabilitated his character and achievements.

He was unpopular in Rome and was feared and hated by most of the senators. This was partly due to the faults in his character such as bluntness and lack of personal charm, to his naturally serious and morose nature, his insecurity and suspicion, and his cryptic way of speaking. Also, some of his policies did not endear him to the urban mob (cutting down on public expenditure) or the nobility (extension of tenure for imperial officials). The increase in the maiestas trials and his retirement to Capri contributed most to the general condemnation of him.

Although he lacked brilliance, he had been a very successful military commander, was an extremely efficient administrator and was regarded highly by the provincials. He wisely continued the policies of Augustus, which gave the Roman world peace and prosperity for over twenty years.

R. Syme makes an interesting evaluation of Tiberius when he says:

A 'victim of Augustus'?

> Compelled to honour the precedents set by Augustus everywhere, Tiberius was hampered in thought and deed by his own past, and by the oppressive memory of Augustus . . . Tiberius was the victim of Augustus.[130]

The strengths and weaknesses of Tiberius' reign	
Strengths	*Weaknesses*
Continuance of Augustus' arrangements as much as possible	Servility of senators — little co-rule, dependence on Tiberius
Excellent civil administration: • Alleviated food shortages • Maintained law and order in the city through the city prefect • Gave substantial relief to help victims of an amphitheatre tragedy and a fire on the Aventine • Supervised carefully the empire's revenue • Cut down public expenses — erected few public buildings and reduced gladiatorial shows • Took measures to safeguard the countryside from brigandage • Reduced sales tax • Chose officials carefully	Treason trials and growing numbers of delatores Crisis as a result of Germanicus' death Influence of Sejanus and elimination of members of imperial family Retirement of Tiberius to Capri — alienation of senate Vengeance taken on Sejanus' supporters Gaius given no training for public life — contributed to the difficulties of his reign Praetorian Guard conscious of increased power — repercussions for future influence on succession
Attempt to work with senate: • Took no exceptional honours • Upheld traditional rights • Treated it with respect • Consulted it • Extended its administrative and legal functions	
Provincial and frontier policies: • Maintained peace and prosperity • Settled disputes in provinces fairly • Gave extensive tax relief after earthquake damage • Built roads and bridges • Built public buildings in provinces • Chose best men wherever possible • Maintained thorough discipline, loyalty and efficiency in armies	

The question of succession and the death of Tiberius

Tiberius' hesitation

Tiberius had hesitated over making a decision about the succession, although within the imperial family there were three possible candidates: Tiberius Gemellus, Gaius and Claudius. Tacitus said that 'Tiberius feared that to nominate a successor outside the imperial house might bring contempt and humiliation upon Augustus' memory'.[131]

Tiberius had made his grandson, Tiberius Gemellus, joint heir with his grandnephew, Gaius. Gemellus, however, was still too young, although Tiberius may have hoped to live long enough for the boy to succeed him.

Gaius on Capri

On the other hand, Gaius (the remaining and youngest son of Germanicus) was 'in the prime of early manhood'[132] and had been taken to live on Capri with Tiberius when he was nineteen. Although he had been given no training by Tiberius to assume greater responsibility, he had won the support of Macro, the prefect of the Praetorian Guard who had succeeded Sejanus; Macro had been cultivating Gaius' friendship since he had been on Capri. The other candidate, Claudius, was already middle-aged and 'his weakmindedness was an objection'.[133]

Supposed part of Macro in Tiberius' death

When it appeared that Tiberius was dying, Macro organised the sending of messages to provincial governors and generals and was supposed to have helped Gaius to hasten the death of Tiberius by ordering him to be smothered. Tiberius died in March AD 37, when seventy-eight.

Gaius (Caligula)

Gaius' accession

Tacitus had already indicated what was likely to happen if Gaius were to succeed Tiberius. The prospect of Gaius' accession to the throne was enough to make a leading Roman, Lucius Arruntius, commit suicide. Arruntius predicted:

A grim prediction

> If Tiberius, in spite of all his experience, has been transformed and deranged by absolute power, will Gaius do any better? Almost a boy, wholly ignorant, with a criminal upbringing, guided by Macro—the man chosen to suppress Sejanus, though Macro is the worse man of the two and responsible for more terrible crimes and national suffering. I forsee even grimmer slavery ahead.[135]

Tiberius showed that he also was aware of the faults in Gaius' character when he declared that 'he has Sulla's vices without his virtues'.[136]

Declared emperor by Macro

However, Macro declared Gaius to be emperor, and according to Suetonius, 'Gaius' accession seemed like a dream come true'[137] since he was the son of the popular Germanicus. When he arrived in Rome the senate was unanimous in its conferment on him of absolute power, and it also declared Tiberius' will, in which he had made his grandson joint heir with Gaius, invalid.

Coin portrait of Gaius (Caligula): Gaius was tall, pale, with a poorly built and hairy body, spindly legs and an almost totally bald head, which upset him greatly; he was both mentally and physically sick, suffering from epilepsy and insomnia[134]

Gaius and the senate

The senate had grown inceasingly servile and dependent on Tiberius, but during the reign of Gaius it was treated with absolute contempt.

For a brief period after his accession, Gaius wisely attempted to conciliate the senatorial nobility; this was apparently on the advice of his grandmother, Antonia. He put an end to the activities of informers (delatores) and the treason trials, honoured his uncle, Claudius, by choosing him as his colleague in the consulship, and recalled those senators exiled under Tiberius.

Effect of his illness in 37

However, sometime in 37 he suffered a serious illness and when he recovered, according to Suetonius, Gaius the emperor was replaced by Gaius the monster. His attitude to the senate changed radically as he moved more and more towards despotism, 'doing away with the pretence that he was merely the chief executive of a republic'.[138] In fact, he insisted on being treated as a god, basing his belief on the divine right of the Julian family.

He made no effort to hide his contempt for the senate and dispensed with its services generally as well as publicly humiliating individual senators. Suetonius maintains that he

Senators humiliated

> made some of the highest officials run for miles beside his chariot, dressed in their gowns; or wait in short linen tunics at the head or foot of his dining couch.[139]

He deposed two consuls who forgot to announce his birthday and he had a sick ex-praetor executed because he asked for an extension of sick leave. The members of the senate were abused for having been friends of Sejanus or as informers against his mother and brothers.

He held the consulship in every year except 38; renewed the laws of treason, and encouraged informers so that he could use condemnations to confiscate the property of wealthy senators; ended the senate's right to mint coinage in Rome; handed back to the people the election of magistrates, and executed any senator who offered him advice.

Gaius' frontier and provincial policy

Gaius reversed Augustus' policy—particularly with regard to Parthia—and rewarded 'friends' with client-kingdoms, hoping to bind them to him personally. He was autocratic, provocative and erratic in his foreign policy, and his treatment of the Jews in particular 'revealed the havoc an irresponsible ruler might create'.[140]

The Rhine

Gaius went to the Rhine frontier himself, since he needed the support of the army. He used the pretext that he wished to strengthen the frontiers, but in fact he was concerned that one of the Rhine commanders, Aemilius Lepidus, was in league with two of Gaius' sisters in a conspiracy. Sulpicius Galba, a future Roman emperor, was given command of the Upper Rhine. Gaius' objectives in Germany were unclear.

Britain

Whether Gaius seriously considered invading Britain or not, his army refused to make the crossing; he announced its annexation even though no military action had been taken. Refer to Suetonius, *Gaius*, 43–8.

Africa

Gaius' actions in Africa were very provocative. He deposed Mauretania's client-king (Ptolemy) and ordered him to commit suicide in preparation for its annexation, but its people resisted.

The senatorial governor in Africa was reduced to the status of a civil authority, and handed over his troops to an imperial legate.

The east

In the east, he restored some friendly kings and princes to their former thrones and found kingdoms for others he favoured: he restored Commagene to Antiochus, provided kingdoms for the three sons of a Thracian prince since they had been raised in Rome with him, and gave to his friend Herod Agrippa the territories belonging to his uncles. This created major disorders in that part of the world.

Gaius was anti-Semitic and his policy towards the Jews was to lead to future discontent. The Greeks and Jews in the Egyptian city of Alexandria were hostile towards each other — the Greeks were angry that the Romans had granted the Jews a large degree of autonomy. They not only refused them local citizenship but sent a deputation to Gaius to demand that the Jews be forced to display statues of the emperor in the synagogues in Alexandria and also in Jerusalem. Gaius supported their request, but fortunately died before it could be carried out.

Gaius weakened Rome's position in the east by reversing Augustus' policy of strengthening the frontiers against Parthia. By removing the King of Armenia from his throne, he gave Parthia the opportunity to regain influence in Armenia.

Gaius' 'madness' and death

Suetonius details the numerous acts of cruelty, tyranny and extravagance carried out by Gaius after the illness which supposedly changed his personality and behaviour. However, Tacitus says that Tiberius was well aware of the evil nature of Gaius from an early age, and Suetonius agrees that even in the early days on Capri 'Caligula could not control his natural brutality'[141] and enjoyed watching executions and tortures.

Natural brutality

In his insistence on being treated as a god, he went to great lengths to see that his directions were carried out. He replaced the heads on many famous Greek statues with his own likeness; converted the shrine of the 'heavenly twins', Castor and Pollux, into the vestibule of his newly extended palace, and would be seen standing beside the gods; established a priesthood to supervise the worship of himself, and connected his palace to the Capitol by a bridge over the Temple of Augustus in order to share the home of the Capitoline Jupiter.

Demands to be treated as a god

His cruelty knew no bounds and was not restricted to senators, knights and the people; it extended to members of his own family. He had Tiberius Gemellus killed because he appeared to have taken an antidote for poison, and he forced his father-in-law to cut his throat because he did not follow the imperial ship to sea during a storm. His unkind treatment of his grandmother, Antonia, is supposed to have speeded up her death. He 'preserved his uncle Claudius mainly as a butt for practical jokes'.[142]

Cruelty to all classes

Gaius enjoyed organising lingering ways to make people die, and not only watched these executions himself but also forced parents to watch the deaths of their sons. He devised methods of provoking the people at gladiatorial shows, closed the granaries so that they would go hungry, and enjoyed creating panic, so that large numbers died.

He was promiscuous, and supposedly committed incest with his sisters. His criminal activities focused particularly on devising 'wickedly ingenious methods of raising funds by false accusations, auctions and taxes'[143] when he found himself bankrupt due to his extravagant lifestyle.

Criminal activities

His assassination

Since Gaius had alienated most groups in Roman society, it was not surprising that there were several plots to assassinate him. Suetonius says that 'His frantic and reckless behaviour roused murderous thoughts in certain minds',[144] and in 41, at the age of 29, he was murdered at the Palatine Games by a tribune of the Praetorian Guard (Cassius Chaerea).

Killed by Praetorians

The conspirators had no particular person in mind to replace him as emperor, but most senators were determined to restore the republic.

Claudius

Claudius' accession

Coin portrait of Claudius: According to Suetonius, Claudius was well-built and tall with a fine head of white hair, but owing to a weakness in his knees he sometimes stumbled when walking; if he became excited or angry he slobbered at the mouth, his nose ran, he stammered and his face twitched — when he was particularly stressed, 'his head would toss from side to side'[145]

A coin showing Claudius in the camp of the Praetorian Guard, who made him emperor despite the senate

When Gaius lost the support of the Praetorian Guard and was killed in 41, Claudius was supposedly found hiding in the palace by some of the guardsmen. They carried him off to their barracks, where he was pressed to accept the imperial power from them. After his initial fear, and encouraged by his friend Herod Agrippa, he accepted the position of emperor and bound himself to the Praetorian Guard with a donative of 15 000 sesterces each. Claudius never forgot his debt to the Praetorians, and repeated this payment annually. This was the first time — but was not to be the last — that the Praetorian Guard interfered in the succession and that the position of emperor was 'bought' in the Praetorian camp.

The senators, unaware of the situation, were discussing a successor to Gaius when the Guards forced Claudius on them. After a certain resistance, they conferred the imperial title on him; he was fifty-one years old at the time.

Although Claudius' physical problems (he may have suffered from polio as a child) made him awkward and unstable on his feet, he was certainly not the fool which many of the ancient sources indicated. As he was growing up, he was made aware of his inferiority within the imperial family and so devoted his time to his studies. He spoke and wrote in Greek and became increasingly interested in history, which he studied under the guidance of the great Livy. He began a history of Rome while still a boy.

Augustus and Livia were concerned about his future. Suetonius quotes a letter from Augustus to his wife, outlining his worries.

> . . . The question is whether he has — shall I say? — full command of his five senses. If so I see nothing against sending him through the same degrees of office as his brother; the public . . . must not be given a chance of laughing at him and us. I fear that we shall find ourselves in constant trouble if the question of his fitness to officiate in this or that capacity keeps cropping up. We should therefore decide in advance whether he can or cannot be trusted with offices of state generally.[146]

Held some minor positions

Claudius remained relatively obscure at court and it has been suggested that he survived the conspiracies and intrigues by playing the fool. However, he did hold several official positions under Augustus, Tiberius and Gaius: he presided at Games, was given a seat in the College of Augurs and the insignia of a consul, and was made colleague with Gaius in the consulship.

A further letter from Augustus to Livia expresses surprise at Claudius' ability to make a public speech.

> . . . I'll be damned if your grandson Tiberius Claudius hasn't given me a pleasant surprise! How on earth anyone who talks so confusedly can nevertheless speak so well in public — with such clearness, saying all that needs to be said — I simply do not understand.[147]

He was therefore not totally without ability when he was thrust into the position of emperor, and on assuming power, he made every effort to associate himself with the Julian house and to appeal to all groups in Roman society.

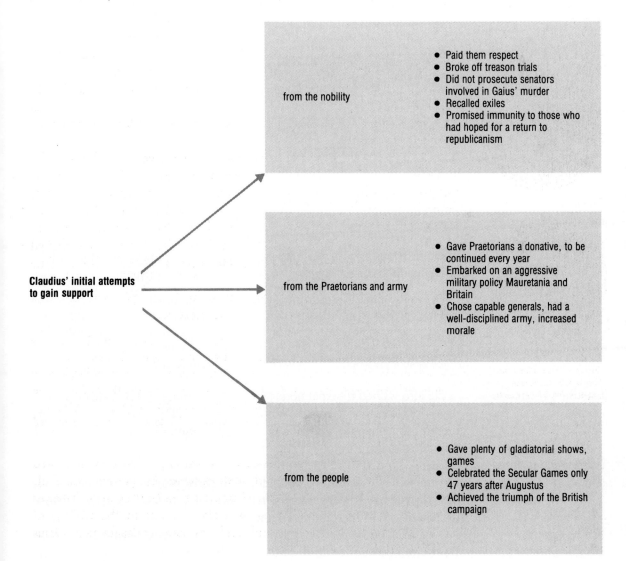

Claudius' initial attempts to gain support

- from the nobility
  - Paid them respect
  - Broke off treason trials
  - Did not prosecute senators involved in Gaius' murder
  - Recalled exiles
  - Promised immunity to those who had hoped for a return to republicanism
- from the Praetorians and army
  - Gave Praetorians a donative, to be continued every year
  - Embarked on an aggressive military policy Mauretania and Britain
  - Chose capable generals, had a well-disciplined army, increased morale
- from the people
  - Gave plenty of gladiatorial shows, games
  - Celebrated the Secular Games only 47 years after Augustus
  - Achieved the triumph of the British campaign

Claudius, the senate and the civil service

Claudius and the senate

Saw need for change

Claudius was aware that the principate needed to be modified, since the definition of imperial and senatorial authority was very vague and the business of running the empire had become more complex. However, he was conservative and — like Augustus — he knew that any move towards a centralised autocracy would have to be achieved slowly.

Encouraged serious debate

Also like Augustus, he showed great respect for the senate and attempted to increase its prestige. He encouraged the senators to debate and to vote seriously, and in his own speeches he argued with moderation and recognised the senate's point of view.

> If these proposals are approved by you, show your assent at once plainly and sincerely. If, however, you do not approve them then find some other remedies, but here in this temple now, or if you wish to take a longer time for consideration, take it so long as you recollect that wherever you meet you should produce an opinion of your own. For it is extremely unfitting, conscript fathers, to the high dignity of this order that at this meeting one man only . . . should make a speech . . . and the rest utter one word only, 'Agreed', and then after leaving the House remark 'There we've given our opinion'.[148]

Provincials added to the senate

Claudius revised the membership of the senate in order to recruit the best political talent. He strengthened it by adding new patrician families and by extending senatorial privileges to the Aedui (Gauls). This latter measure aroused the senate's anger, but the argument put forward by Claudius in favour of it revealed his statesmanlike attitude.

> Senators, however ancient any institution seems, once upon a time it was new! First, plebeians joined patricians in office. Next, Latins were added. Then came men from other Italian peoples. The innovation now proposed will, in its turn, one day be old: what we seek to justify by precedents today will itself become a precedent.[149]

Expulsion of senators

He also wished to expel notoriously bad senators, and he became censor in order to carry this out. However, rather than use the old severe method, he gave those concerned the opportunity to voluntarily renounce senatorial rank and so avoid humiliation.

Fairness in provincial allocation

In 44 he returned the provinces of Achaea and Macedonia to the senate — they had been converted into imperial provinces by Tiberius. He also distributed the newly acquired imperial provinces equally between legates of senatorial and imperial rank.

Senate's rights regarding elections and coinage

The election of magistrates was returned to the senate (Gaius having transferred them once again to the assembly), and many senatorial decrees were issued during his reign. He recognised the senate's right to mint copper coinage, but although during his reign coins with the senate's mark increased in number, Claudius' head never appeared on them.

However, despite his apparent show of respect and his desire for the senate's co-operation, he established a new system which he himself dominated. He encroached on the various spheres of senatorial privilege by setting up an imperial civil service (see p. 552). The senate began to lose its importance as a partner in the government as Claudius set up special departments staffed by his own personal freedmen, who were answerable to him. This centralised bureaucracy was established to 'obtain administrative efficiency, not to humble the senate and the urban magistrates'[150] or to increase Claudius' autocratic power.

Civil service established

The proud senatorial aristocracy became embittered as they watched the emperor entrust confidential tasks to the group of freedmen belonging to his household. A new governing class was being created from men who stood outside the Roman tradition and represented the interests of the emperor.

Senatorial bitterness

The senate was weakened in other ways:

Further encroachment on senate's privileges

- The treasury (Aerarium) came to a greater extent under Claudius' control when he replaced its praetors with quaestors chosen by himself and holding their positions for three years.
- In 53, jurisdiction of financial cases in the senatorial provinces was transferred from the proconsuls (governors) to Claudius' own personal procurators. This meant that the fisci (provincial treasuries) were freed from the control of the senate.
- Claudius spent much time in the law courts hearing criminal cases. Theoretically he had the right to do this, but it had previously been handed over to the senate. He expanded his own court so that the senate would not be forced to condemn its own members if they were charged with criminal offences; Claudius is supposed to have executed thirty-five senators during his reign. The members of the senate were particularly bitter about these prosecutions, since they believed that they were due to the influence exerted on Claudius by his freedmen and his wives.
- On at least one occasion — and perhaps more — Claudius nominated the governor of a senatorial province. Dio Cassius records the appointment of Galba to the province of Africa.

The senate resented particularly the gradual encroachment on its rights by Claudius and the apparent power wielded by his freedmen. However, this did not stop it from voting honours and wealth for Narcissus and Pallas, Claudius' most influential freedmen. Such was the subservience of the senators that they passed a copious and effusive decree rewarding Pallas for his diligence and fidelity as 'guardian of the emperor's property'.[151] Pliny comments with disgust that these senators were slaves themselves.

Claudius' civil service and the influence of his freedmen

In order to increase administrative efficiency, Claudius developed specialised departments each under the control of one of his freedmen, most of whom were well-educated Greeks or Orientals.

Status and importance of freedmen

Narcissus was a kind of secretary-general (*ab epistulis*) to Claudius, handling the huge amount of correspondence (letters, resolutions, reports and so on) in Greek and Latin which passed between the emperor and Roman officials and provincials in all parts of the empire.

Pallas was the head of the financial department (*a rationibus*), and supervised the revenues which flowed into the imperial provincial fisci. These included money from the emperor's personal estates and from the imperial provinces.

Callistus was the legal secretary (*a libellis*) whose duty was to attend to all petitions and requests to the emperor, to deal with judicial inquiries and to see that all papers on cases to come before the emperor were prepared.

Polybius was the privy seal and librarian (*a studiis*), providing Claudius with material for speeches and edicts as well as acting as his literary adviser.

Numerous other freedmen were employed in the bureaucracy, but these were the chief officers of the state. They became very powerful, and retained great influence with Claudius; the sources indicate that he became the tool of these freedmen, making no independent decisions. He did seek their advice, but was quite capable of challenging their opinions and usually made decisions based on administrative efficiency. Although the charges of favouritism, nepotism and corruption could be justified, these men were loyal and efficient ministers.

The development of this bureaucracy angered the senatorial and equestrian classes because Augustus and Tiberius had sought their advisers from among these two groups, whereas Claudius relied on foreigners who owed their allegiance to him.

Tacitus' attitude towards freedmen

Tacitus felt nothing but contempt for these freedmen, referring to them constantly as ex-slaves. They were involved in all the intrigues of the imperial court. Callistus had been associated with the conspiracy which resulted in the death of Gaius; Narcissus had been responsible for the death of Messalina's stepfather (Gaius Appius Junius Silanus); Narcissus informed Claudius of Messalina's misconduct, and ordered her execution; Pallas, Callistus and Narcissus each promoted a different candidate for Claudius' fourth wife; Pallas, as the successful backer—and later lover—of Agrippina, devoted himself to the promotion of her son, the future Nero, at the expense of Claudius' own son Britannicus, and Narcissus supported Britannicus against the intrigues of Agrippina and Pallas (see assignment, p. 560).

Involvement in court intrigue

Honours and rewards given to freedmen

These men were not only honoured and rewarded by Claudius and the senate, but acquired immense wealth; Suetonius outlines some of the honours Claudius' awarded his favourites. Posides, a eunuch, was given the same honour as soldiers who had fought in the British campaign (a headless spear). Felix was made governor of Judaea, while Harpocras rode through the streets of Rome and was permitted to give entertainments as if he were a member of the equestrian order.

> . . . Claudius had an even higher regard for Polybius, his literary mentor, who often walked between the two Consuls. But his firmest devotion was reserved for Narcissus, his secretary, and Pallas, his treasurer, whom he encouraged the senate to honour with large gifts of money and the insignia of quaestors and praetors as well.[152]

Senatorial decree of praise for Pallas

Tacitus and Pliny both record with disgust the decree of the senate — later inscribed on a monument — honouring Pallas 'For his fidelity and loyalty towards his patrons', whereby he was awarded 'the insignia of praetorian rank together with 15 000 000 sesterces, of which he accepted the honour alone'.[153] Tacitus adds further that he was thanked for letting 'himself be regarded as one of the emperor's servants'[154] although he came from a long line of Arcadian kings. Tacitus was particularly critical of the senate for loading 'praises of old-world frugality on a man who had once been a slave and was now worth three hundred million sesterces'.[155] Narcissus, whom Tacitus accused of greed and extravagance, owned a large estate in Egypt.

Acquired great wealth

These men were able to acquire riches by both legitimate and illegitimate means. Suetonius relates the story that when 'one day Claudius complained how little cash was left in the imperial treasury, someone answered neatly that he would have heaps of pocket money if only his two freedmen took him into partnership'.[156]

The imperial freedmen were generally capable and intelligent advisers and civil servants in Claudius' administration, but they wielded great power through patronage and intrigue and promoted their own interests wherever possible.

Some aspects of Claudius' administration

Although the literary sources have tended to emphasise the negative side of Claudius' reign, he showed sound political judgment and a capacity for serious and sustained work. Despite his lack of training for the position, he developed into an efficient administrator. Many of the changes he introduced were made during his censorship of 47 and 48.

Public works	Religion	Finances	Justice
Public utilities and great engineering feats	*Attempt to follow Augustus' policy to restore some of the old religions*	*Greater concentration of finances in the hands of the emperor*	*Great interest in judicial matters — a large amount of time spent in the courts*
Extensive road-building in Italy and the provinces, e.g. Via Claudia Augusta from Altinum to the Danube Completion of two aqueducts — the Aqua Claudia was a huge, double-arched aqueduct carrying water to the hills of Rome Construction of a new harbour and lighthouse at Ostia, north of the Tiber mouth, which had silted up; the harbour was surrounded with huge walls Excavation of a 3-mile tunnel to drain the flood waters from the Fucine Lake and reclaim agricultural land, employing 30 000 men for 11 years but not completely successful Help in securing food supply by encouraging non-Romans to build ships and insuring ships and cargoes against storm damage	Celebration of the Secular Games only 47 years after Augustus Reorganisation of a college of 60 haruspices for ancient Etruscan auguries Explusion of astrologers from Rome Suppression of Druidism in Gaul greater than that of Tiberius Attempt to curb the practice in Rome of some foreign cults (Jews denied the right to worship in synagogues) although tolerant of many Extension of the pomerium (sacred boundary of Rome) to include the Campus Martius Prohibition of worship of himself in temples in the provinces	Closer supervision of imperial treasury by department of the financial secretary, Pallas Procurators created to look after the emperor's personal estates and revenue as well as to supervise the inheritance tax Increased control by imperial procurators in senatorial provinces Greater control of the state treasury (Aerarium) by appointment of quaestors to administer it	Many legal abuses removed and legal business speeded up Introduction of many minor laws, including legislation against • unruly behaviour in the theatre • harsh treatment of debtors • purchase and demolition of buildings for profit • loans being made to a son in the expectation of his father's death • disclaiming of sick slaves by masters (if slaves recovered, they were given their freedom) Frequent judgment of cases previously heard by the senate, causing opposition

Further references to Claudius' administration can be found in Suetonius' *Claudius*, 20 (public works), 21 (games and shows), 22, 25 (religion), and 23, 25 (legal issues); and in Tacitus' *Annals*, p. 237 (laws), pp. 236–7, 238, 275 (religion), and pp. 277–8 (public works).

A Roman relief of the port of Ostia, where Claudius constructed a new harbour

Claudius' frontier and provincial policies

Claudius' foreign policy tended to follow that of Julius Caesar rather than of Augustus — expansion and assimilation. His reign was one of military achievements, since he desired to be known as 'extender of the empire'. He extended the frontiers if he thought it appropriate, and believed that direct Roman rule was preferable to client-kingdoms — he added five provinces. Like Julius Caesar, he was interested in raising the status of the provincials by encouraging Romanisation and extending Roman citizenship or Latin rights to both individuals and groups. He was responsible for founding many colonies, was always interested in good provincial administration and made it possible for more provincials to enter the senate.

The Rhine frontier and Gaul

Although Claudius did not basically change Tiberius' policy towards the Rhine and Germany, he did extend the Roman frontier to the mouth of the Rhine; Corbulo carried this out for him. He believed that Gaul would never be completely Romanised while Britain remained independent, and this was one of his reasons for its annexation. Apart from establishing colonies at Triers and Cologne, he granted Roman and Latin citizenship to many Gallic tribes.

Britain

There were many reasons why Claudius wanted to annex Britain, but the most crucial was his belief that a successful British conquest would strengthen his regime and increase his popularity. He had read the Roman people accurately. Fifty thousand troops crossed the Channel in 43, and Claudius followed with reinforcements. When Camulodunum (Colchester) was taken he returned to Rome, leaving the legions to subdue further territory. Caractacus, a famous British leader, was captured but was spared by Claudius, and by 54 most of England (not Wales) south of a line drawn east to west through Lincoln was under Roman control. A number of client-kingdoms, including the Regni and the Iceni, continued to exist. Although the city of Camulodunum became the centre of Caesar-worship, it was the growing port city of Londinium (London), which became the headquarters of the imperial governor.

North Africa

At the beginning of his reign Claudius had to deal with the rebellion in Mauretania, which was a legacy of Gaius. He annexed it and divided it into two provinces, Tingitana and Caesariensis.

He attempted to curb the anti-Semitism of the Greeks of Alexandria and to insist that the Jews refrain from making demands for local citizenship.

Southeast Europe and the Danube area

Claudius returned control of Achaea and Macedonia once more to the senate, while Noricum, on the northern Danube frontier, was governed by an equestrian procurator.

The east

In the east Claudius not only annexed and organised new provinces (Lycia in 43 and Thrace in 46), he reversed Gaius' arrangements for Judaea (44), returned Commagene to its former ruler, enlarged Syria with the addition of Ituraea and spread Roman influence around the Black Sea. Gaius' weak policy towards Parthia had been very damaging, and Claudius strengthened Armenia after 49 when a Roman nominee, Mithridates, was placed on the throne. He also promoted internal strife in Parthia in order to keep the Parthians occupied.

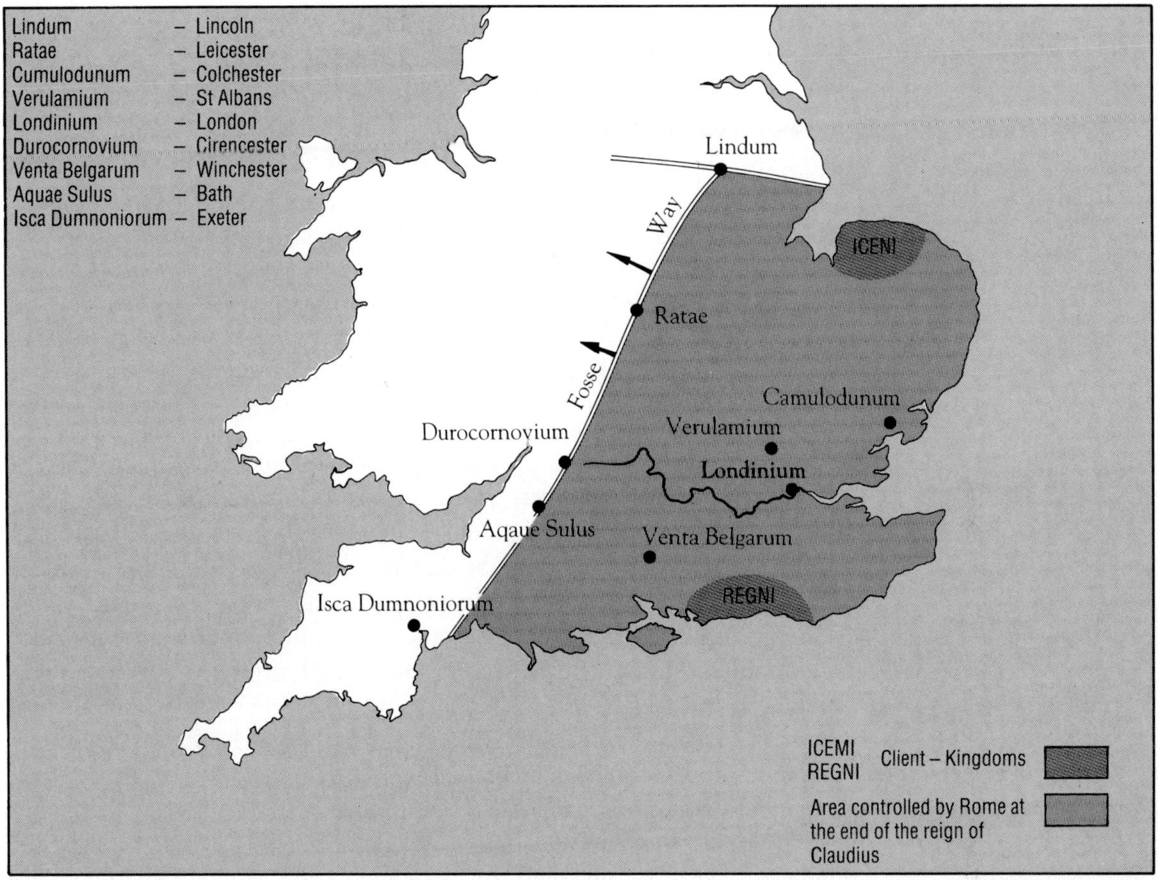

The extent of Roman control in Britain at the end of the reign of Claudius, AD 54

Page references in Tacitus to Claudius' provincial and frontier policy are as follows:

The east (Armenia, Parthia and the Jews): 234–6, 255–6, 258, 271–5, 276

The Rhine, Germany and Gaul: 238–41, 263–4

Crimean Bosphorus: 258–60

Britain: 264–8

Claudius' attitude to enlisting provincials in the senate: 243–4

Suetonius describes Claudius' treatment of individual provincial peoples in *Claudius*, 25.

Exercise

1 What military actions did the general Domitius Corbulo take along the Rhine during the reign of Claudius?

2 Who was Caractacus? How significant for Rome were his actions in the years 41–50?

The influence of Messalina and Agrippina

Most of the ancient sources depict Claudius as submissive to his wives and totally unaware of what was going on in his own household. Their influence of him and his ignorance of their behaviour are probably exaggerated, but there is no doubt that his third wife, Messalina, and his fourth, Agrippina, wielded considerable power at court.

Valeria Messalina was of Julian stock, related to Augustus on both sides of her family, and for this reason Gaius had arranged for his uncle Claudius to marry her. She was fourteen at the time and Claudius was over thirty years her senior. Although she bore him two children, Britannicus and Octavia, it is not surprising that she was concerned with gratifying her passions with other men. She was not only sexually depraved, but also insanely jealous of possible female rivals. Through her influence over Claudius and his freedmen, she gained whatever she wanted and eliminated those who stood in her way.

Nature of Messalina

Prosecutions of rivals

She organised the destruction of Poppaea Sabina, one of her rivals, and acquired the lavish gardens of Decimus Valerius Asiaticus, Poppaea's lover. 'Agents were suborned to threaten Poppaea with imprisonment, and thus terrorise her into suicide',[157] and Asiaticus was brought to trial on the pretext of corrupting the army; he also committed suicide. She became more virulent, and 'was only distracted from launching prosecutions and prosecutors by a new and almost maniacal love affair'[150] with the young, handsome, intelligent nobleman, Gaius Silius, who was consul-elect. She made no secret of the relationship, visiting him at his home, clinging to him in public and showering him with wealth and distinctions. When in 48 they decided to publicly marry while Claudius was at Ostia, thus committing bigamy, the 'imperial household shuddered'.[159]

'Marriage' to Gaius Silius

Claudius' freedmen feared that it was a senatorial conspiracy to put Silius on the throne and they 'had everything to fear from a new emperor'.[160] Tacitus describes the discussion between the freedmen

Narcissus, Callistus and Pallas regarding the actions they should take to put an end to Messalina's scandalous behaviour or to inform Claudius. Pallas and Callistus were loath to do anything which might endanger their own positions, but Narcissus decided to denounce her without any warning. He approached two of Claudius' mistresses and bribed them into acting as informers. After their denunciations, Narcissus urged Claudius to take immediate action—otherwise Messalina's new husband would control Rome. However, even after confirmation of the story was given to him by the controller of the grain supply and the commander of the Guard, Claudius was hesitant. He was urged to go immediately to the Guards' camp to secure their support.

Narcissus took control in the destruction of Messalina

In order to make sure that Claudius would arrive safely at Rome from Ostia, Narcissus took over command of the Guard for the day and accompanied the emperor in his carriage. He presented Claudius with a document listing all of Messalina's immoralities, and when she appeared with the two children on the outskirts of Rome to meet him, Narcissus had them removed. After taking Claudius to the home of Silius which was full of heirlooms of the imperial family, he conducted him to the Guards' camp, where Silius and others involved with Messalina were condemned.

Messalina planned an appeal to Claudius, and according to Tacitus, 'if Narcissus had not speedily caused her death, the fatal blow would have rebounded on her accuser',[161] since Claudius' anger appeared to be cooling. Narcissus gave orders (supposedly from Claudius) to officers of the Guard to kill her. The senate decreed that all statues of her and inscriptions bearing her name were to be removed, and they awarded Narcissus an honorary quaestorship.

The repercussions of her death

Tacitus ends this episode in his *Annals* with the ominous statement: 'the vengeance on Messalina was just. But its consequences were grim'.[162] He was referring to the convulsions that occurred in the imperial household with the rise to power of Agrippina, Claudius' fourth wife.

Agrippina II, Claudius' niece, had kept a low profile while Messalina was alive; she had already been persecuted by Messalina, and she feared for her son, Lucius Domitius Ahenobarbus (the future emperor, Nero). Agrippina was a widow, and on Messalina's death wasted no time in securing support—particularly from the freedman Pallas—for her marriage to Claudius and promotion for her son at the expense of Messalina's son, Britannicus.

According to the sources Agrippina completely dominated Claudius in the last years of his life, behaving as if she were a partner in his rule.

Strengths and weaknesses of Claudius' reign	
Strengths	*Weaknesses*
He was an efficient and humane administrator. His social legislation illustrates his belief that it was his duty to look after the welfare of the people and to protect the weaker members of society such as women, slaves and minors. This was a preoccupation with him whether he was in the law courts or initiating policies. He provided public utilities, entertainments and justice, and he won the loyalty of the common people.	The creation of a centralised bureaucracy caused problems. Claudius' freedmen wielded great power as he delegated more and more state business to them. They were able to enrich themselves and secure the condemnation of anyone they wanted removed on even the flimsiest of evidence. The formation of the civil service deprived the senatorial and equestrian orders of much of their previous responsibilities, which created hostility towards Claudius.
His policy of assimilation was far-sighted, whether in the provinces (liberal extension of citizenship and encouragement of Romanisation through colonies) or by injecting new talent — the Aedui (Gauls) — into the senate. He was highly appreciated by the provincials.	His debauched and ambitious wives were responsible for the elimination of many influential people and the promotion of others of their choice. His weakness was shown when he allowed Agrippina practically equal status with himself.
His successful military campaigns (Britain) gave him the support of the army. He also promoted the Praetorian Guard.	

Assignment: Agrippina the Younger — mother of Nero

Refer to Tacitus. Relevant page numbers are given throughout the assignment.

Part 1

1 At the age of twenty-five Agrippina II, the daughter of Agrippina I and Germanicus, was left a widow with one son, Lucius Domitius Ahenobarbus. With the death of Messalina, she lost no time in taking her place as Claudius' fourth wife. According to Suetonius she had been accustomed to every kind of immorality by her brother Gaius, the previous emperor; the fact that Claudius was her uncle, and that such a marriage would be regarded as incestuous, did not deter her.
- Who supported Agrippina as a possible wife for Claudius?
- Explain how the difficulties facing the marriage of Claudius and Agrippina were overcome. (pp. 252–4)

2 Tacitus describes the change that occurred from the time of Agrippina's marriage: 'the country was transformed'. (p. 255)
- How does Tacitus describe her character?

3 Agrippina immediately began to implement her plan to promote her son (Domitius) by removing the fiancé of Claudius' daughter, Octavia, and securing Octavia's engagement to Domitius. She recalled the philosopher and writer Seneca from exile to be her son's tutor, and then proceeded to eliminate her enemies and confiscate their property.
- How did she arrange for her son's adoption by Claudius in AD 50? Who assisted her in her plans? (pp. 262–3)
- What were the implications of this? (p. 263)

4 Agrippina now asserted 'her partnership in the empire her ancestors had won'.
- Give two examples of her increased status. (pp. 267, 270)

5 Partnership in rule was not, however, the limit of Agrippina's ambition. When Narcissus was away from Rome recovering from an illness, Agrippina seized the chance to murder Claudius and proclaim Domitius emperor (Nero).
- According to Tacitus, how did Agrippina murder Claudius? (pp. 281–3)

Once Nero was proclaimed emperor, Agrippina gave Claudius a funeral 'modelled on that of the divine Augustus' (p. 283). Like Augustus, he also was accorded divine honours.

Part 2 of the assignment follows on page 562.

Nero

The accession of Nero

Nero's ultimate accession to the principate was due to the intrigues of his mother, Agrippina the Younger, in the years preceding Claudius' death. On the sudden death of Claudius, his natural children were detained in the palace while Nero appeared outside with Burrus, commander of the Praetorian Guard. Nero was then taken to the Praetorian barracks where he was hailed as imperator, having made a promise to pay each guardsman 15 000 sesterces. Only then did he appear at the Senate House to receive the appropriate powers and honours.

Proclaimed emperor by Praetorians

As in the case of Gaius when Tiberius' will was declared invalid, so now the senate suppressed the will of Claudius — probably because it implied the equality of Nero and Britannicus. In the following year (55) Britannicus was poisoned, to remove the possibility of a Claudian conspiracy against Nero.

Bust of Nero: Nero was of average height with blond hair which he always had set in rows of curls — he was 'pretty rather than handsome', although his stomach protruded and his legs were spindly; Suetonius says that his body smelt and he was shameless in his manner of dress, often giving audiences in his silk dressing gown and slippers — yet despite his indulgent lifestyle, he was healthy[163]

Assignment: Agrippina the Younger — mother of Nero

Part 2

1 After his accession Agrippina started to lose control over Nero, who found his overbearing mother intolerable. His friends 'urged him to beware of the tricks of this always terrible and now insincere woman'. (p. 289)

- How was Agrippina's position undermined from the beginning of Nero's reign? (pp. 288–9)

2 Agrippina now seemed to 'be looking around for a Party, and a leader for it'. (p. 292)

- To what methods did she resort in order to maintain her supremacy?

3 Nero decided to kill his mother. Although 'everyone longed for the mother's domination to end no one believed that her son's hatred would go as far as murder' (p. 313). When her murder was finally arranged, it was bungled. Agrippina died courageously.

- Describe, in half a page, how her death was arranged.

4 In a letter to the senate Nero justified his mother's murder, accusing her of many crimes.

- What were these crimes? (p. 318)

After his mother's death 'he plunged into the wildest improprieties, which vestiges of respect for his mother had hitherto not indeed repressed, but at least impeded'. (p. 319)

A coin issued in the early part of Nero's reign showing the young emperor with his mother, Agrippina the Younger; it clearly indicates Agrippina's position at this stage

Nero's early years

Agrippina, Nero's mother, 'devoted herself to scheming for her son . . .' (p. 253)

Agrippina secured Seneca's recall from exile, as she 'had designs on him as a distinguished tutor for her young son . . .' and 'he was believed to be devoted to her in gratitude for her favours' (p. 255)

Agrippina had Claudius remove the commanders of the Praetorian Guard in 51; 'The command was transferred to Sextus Afranius Burrus . . . who was fully aware whose initiative was behind his appointment' (p. 270)

By 55, 'Agrippina was gradually losing control over Nero' (p. 288)

First phase of Nero's reign, 54–61

The 'quinquennium Neronis', 56–61

Annaeus Seneca, philosopher and tutor, influenced Nero from 49 to 62; Seneca's strength was 'in amiable high principles and his tuition of Nero in public speaking' (p. 284)

'These two men, with a unanimity rare among partners in power were by different methods equally influential' (p. 284)
'They collaborated in controlling the Emperor's adolescence. Their policy was to direct his deviations from virtue into licensed channels of indulgence' (p. 284)

Afranius Burrus, commander of the Praetorian Guard, influenced Nero's career from 51 to 61; 'Burrus' strength lay in soldierly efficiency and seriousness of character . . .' (p. 284)

'The death of Burrus caused great public distress' (p. 336) It 'undermined the influence of Seneca . . . now Nero listened to more disreputable advisers' (p. 337)

INFLUENCES ON NERO

Second phase of Nero's reign, 62–68

Poppaea sowed seeds of suspicion in the mind of Nero about Seneca

Poppaea, mistress — later wife — of Nero, influenced him from 58 to 66. 'Poppaea obtained access to Nero and established her ascendancy. First she used flirtatious wiles, pretending to be unable to resist her passion for Nero's looks. Then as the emperor fell in love with her she became more haughty . . .' (p. 307)

'Poppaea and Tigellinus, ultimate counsellors of the Emperor's brutalities' (p. 375)

Ofonius Tigellinus, prefect of the Praetorian Guards, influenced Nero from 62 to 67; Tigellinus was appointed on the death of Burrus because 'Nero found his unending immoralities and evil reputation fascinating'; 'Tigellinus was influential with the Emperor, in whose private debaucheries he participated' (pp. 336–7)

An overview of Nero's reign, 54–68

The first phase

After the murder of Agrippina, Nero was under the wise guidance of Seneca and Burrus from 56 to 61. This period has been referred to as the 'quinquennium Neronis', the five-year period of Nero's reign which was generally marked by peace, prosperity, internal order and protection of the frontiers.

The welfare of Rome and Italy was considered.

- Sufficient grain was assured by the appointment of an excellent prefect of the grain supply in the person of Faenius Rufus.
- Claudius' aqueduct system was extended and his harbour developments at Ostia were completed.
- Provisions were made for better accommodation and greater order at Games.
- Nero twice distributed 400 sesterces each to the people.
- Justice was carefully supervised and a law was passed allowing slaves to bring to the city prefect any complaints they had against their masters.
- Nero replenished the bankrupt treasury with 40 000 000 sesterces of his own money, and replaced the quaestors in charge of the treasury with imperial prefects.
- To check the serious depopulation of Italy, and to provide for the army, colonies were established at Capua, Nuceria, Puteoli and various other sites between 57 and 60.

Sound domestic and foreign policy under Seneca and Burrus

The economic welfare of the provinces was promoted—Seneca had extensive financial interests.

- Governors charged with extortion were punished more readily. Of twelve governors tried for maladministration during the first seven years of Nero's reign, over half were condemned.
- An edict of 57 prevented governors from organising wild-beast and gladiatorial displays in their provinces.
- The activities of the publicani were curbed even further.
- Substantial aid was given to the Campanian cities (including Pompeii) which suffered an earthquake in AD 63.
- An attempt to stimulate trade throughout the empire by abolishing harbour dues (establishing free trade) was a good scheme, but was blocked by the senate because there were practical difficulties in its implementation.

The second phase

Influence of Poppaea and Tigellinus

The reasonable government of Nero under the guidance of Seneca and Burrus was replaced from 62 to 68 with a tyranny. Seneca and Burrus had aquiesced to Nero's murder of Agrippina in 59, but they soon lost control over him as he was encouraged by Poppaea—his mistress, and later his wife—to rule alone. She created suspicions in Nero's mind about Seneca and he retired after Burrus died in 62. Tigellinus, the coarse and vicious prefect of the vigiles, was appointed as one of the Praetorian prefects. He encouraged Nero in his cruelty and debauchery.

- Nero's artistic interests and passion for things Greek were given free rein. He was no longer content to perform in private, but was eager to display his talents in public.

Extravagance and debauchery

- His extravagant spending on the rebuilding of Rome after the Great Fire in 64, the construction of his Golden Palace, and the numerous parties and banquets at which all sorts of vices were indulged forced him to look for more ways of raising funds.
- To finance his every whim, he forced the people of Italy and the provinces to pay more taxes, sold off many of the works of art from Greece, put wealthy people to death in order to confiscate their property, and debased the coinage.
- He employed a large number of Greek and Oriental freedmen in positions of power—for example, Felix, the procurator of Judaea.

A coin showing Nero and Poppaea as the sun god and goddess

- Under the influence of Poppaea, who wished to replace Octavia as his wife, he accused Octavia of adultery and sterility, banished her, and later had her murdered. Other members of the imperial family were also eliminated, including Tiberius' grandson Rubellius Plautus, Claudius' son-in-law Sulla, and a descendant of Augustus, Junius Silanus.

Cruelty

- After the Great Fire he embarked on such a ferocious attack on the Christians, whom he used as scapegoats, that the Roman citizens were eventually sickened by his brutality.
- As a result of the attempted plot against his life in 65 (the conspiracy of Piso), he used Tigellinus to carry out savage reprisals which decimated the ranks of the old nobility.
- Nero had never bothered too much about the troops or visited their camps, and they began to hate him as much as did the nobility and the Roman mob. He ordered the famous general Corbulo and the commanders of Upper and Lower Germany to commit suicide.
- By the last six years of his reign, Nero had alienated all classes of Romans.

Nero—artist and philhellene

From early childhood Nero had shown an interest in artistic activities and in riding, and as he matured his great loves became singing to his own accompaniment on the lyre and chariot racing. He believed that chariot

Early interests in artistic pursuits tolerated

racing 'was an accomplishment of ancient kings and leaders',[164] while singing was sacred to Apollo. These activities were tolerated within the imperial court, away from the public eye, but Nero craved applause and desired the popularity and adulation that professional performers were accorded. He admired all things Greek, but this admiration did not stop with acceptance of all aspects of Greek culture. He wanted to become a popular performer on the stage and in the circus, in a Greek environment.

Alienation of upper classes

His artistic and athletic desires alienated most groups in Roman society except the urban mob; they were enthusiastic about an emperor who enjoyed the same entertainments as themselves. The nobility and equites were shocked, offended and repelled by his undignified behaviour in public.

1 At first his performances were semiprivate, with a few specially invited spectators.
2 He then instituted 'Youth Games' (*Ludi Iuvenales*) comprising musical and theatrical performances in Latin and Greek, and held in his own gardens. This gave him the chance to perform, and it was the first occasion on which men of senatorial and equestrian rank took part.
3 A corps of young, wealthy Romans was formed in order to enthusiastically applaud Nero's performances. They were called 'Augustiani', and were trained in rhythmic applause.
4 He instituted the 'Neronia' (five-yearly contest), which lasted several days and included competitions in poetry, rhetoric, music and athletics. He encouraged the well-educated classes in Rome to enter.

Nero's performances become more public

5 In 64, he made his first really public appearance in a Greek environment. He performed as singer and musician on the stage in Naples (a Greek city).

Tour of and performances in Greece

6 He believed, however, that the Greeks in their own country were the only ones who would really appreciate his vast talents, so in 66 he set out for Greece. He remained there for a year, intending to extend his tour to the east. During this one year the Greeks held all four Games — Olympic, Isthmian, Pythian and Nemean — so that Nero could take part, and win all the prizes. He was awarded winner's honours in contests in which he failed, or in some cases did not even enter.

A certain degree of megalomania was revealed when in 67 he repeated the proclamation of Flamininus (196 BC) at the Isthmian Games.

Reward for the Greeks

> Men of Hellas, I give you an unlooked for gift — if indeed anything may not be hoped for from one of my greatness of mind — a gift so great, you were incapable of asking for it. All Greeks inhabiting Achaea and the land called till now the Peloponnese receive freedom and immunity from taxes, something which not all of you enjoyed even in your happiest days.[165]

The Great Fire, AD 64

In July 64 one of the most famous incidents of Nero's principate occurred —a great fire, which burned for over a week. It had serious consequences for Nero and the people of Rome as well as for a group of 'notoriously depraved' people with 'antisocial tendencies',[166] called Christians.

Although fires were common in Rome owing to the overcrowded and poorly built insulae (tenements), this was 'the most terrible and destructive fire which Rome had ever experienced'.[167]

Fires common in Rome

Origin

The fire began in shops selling inflammable materials in the Circus Maximus area, and was fanned by a wind so that it quickly spread through the narrow streets of timber tenements and up the hills.

The extent of the damage

Only four of the fourteen regions of Rome escaped damage, while three were completely destroyed. Although the Forum, the Capitol and part of the Palatine were not damaged, many ancient shrines, public buildings, palaces, temples, mansions and tenements were burnt to the ground. 'Among the losses too were . . . Greek artistic masterpieces, and authentic records of old Roman genius'.[168]

Many inscriptions and records lost

Accidental or deliberate?

Tacitus says that 'whether it was accidental or caused by a criminal act on the part of the emperor is uncertain—both versions have supporters'.[169] However, he then adds that Nero was at Antium and only 'returned to Rome when the fire was approaching the mansion he had built . . .'[170]

Most other sources, including Suetonius and Dio Cassius, preferred to believe that Nero was responsible and in fact record that he sang of the Sack of Troy while he watched the city burn. Despite the lack of any evidence of his responsibility, rumours soon spread among the panicking people that his agents had been caught in the act of lighting the fire. It was believed that Nero wanted 'to found a new city to be called after himself'.[171] This view was reinforced when a new outbreak started on the estate of Tigellinus.

No evidence of Nero's responsibility

Nero's temporary relief measures

He opened his own gardens, the Field of Mars and public buildings for the homeless; emergency housing was built, food supplies were brought in from Ostia and surrounding towns, and the price of corn was reduced considerably.

Persecution of the Christians

Christians as scapegoats

In an attempt to appease the gods the Sibylline Books were consulted and various rites carried out, but 'neither human resources, nor imperial munificence, nor appeasement of the gods, eliminated sinister suspicions that the fire had been instigated'.[172] Nero desperately needed someone to blame (a scapegoat) and he chose the Christians, whom Suetonius described as 'a sect professing a new and mischievous belief'.[173] Tacitus said that they were punished by Nero not so much for starting the fire, but for their 'degraded and shameful practices'[174] (the words and symbols used in the communion — the 'body and blood of Christ').

Those who admitted to being Christians were arrested, and informed on others. Their punishments were brutal — they were torn to pieces by dogs, crucified or made into human torches and ignited after dark to create a spectacle. Such unnecessary brutality moved even the urban mob to pity the victims.

Rebuilding Rome

The fire gave Nero the opportunity not only to rebuild Rome but to construct an enormous and lavish palace for himself, called the Domus Aurea (Golden House).

New building regulations

In rebuilding the burnt section of the city, he combined practicality with beauty. A proportion of each newly constructed house had to be of fireproof stone; streets were broadened; frontages were aligned; no semi-detached houses were allowed; heights were restricted; houses were built around courtyards with protective colonnades in the front and with firefighting equipment readily available. A better water supply was provided also.

His new Golden House was so large that it extended from the Palatine to the Esquiline Hill. The following extracts from Tacitus and Suetonius refer to the origin of Christianity and Nero's Golden House.

> ... the notoriously depraved Christians (as they were popularly called). Their originator, Christ, had been executed in Tiberius' reign by the governor of Judaea, Pontius Pilatus. But in spite of this temporary setback the deadly superstition had broken out afresh, not only in Judaea (where the mischief had started) but even in Rome.[175]

The 'Golden House'

> The entrance hall was large enough to contain a huge statue of himself, 120 feet high; and the pillared arcade ran for a whole mile. An enormous pool, like a sea, was surrounded by buildings made to resemble cities, and by a landscape garden consisting of ploughed fields, vineyards, pastures and woodlands... Parts of the house were overlaid with gold and studded with precious stones and mother-of-pearl. All the dining-rooms had ceilings of fretted ivory, the panels of which could slide back and let a rain of flowers or of perfume from

Remains of the circular dining-room of Nero's Golden House, which had a revolving dome representing the sky

hidden sprinklers shower upon his guests. The main dining-room was circular, and its roof revolved, day and night, in time with the sky. Sea water or sulphur water was always on tap in the baths.[176]

Nero's frontier and provincial policies

Little interest in the provinces

It appears that Nero had very little interest in the provinces apart from Greece, which interested him because of the artistic accomplishments of its people. He had no real interest in his troops and never visited them, and his only involvement in the provinces seems to have been his choice of governors for those which were armed. Some areas were fortunate to experience good government, while others suffered from incompetent administrators—as is evidenced by the outbreaks of revolt. He reversed Claudius' policy with regard to client-kingdoms.

The Rhine and the west

There appeared to be no problems along the Rhine frontier, but although nothing much is recorded of events in the western provinces, it was from this area that the movement to eliminate Nero came.

Britain

Revolt of Boudicca

A dangerous situation arose in Britain with the uprising of Boudicca of the Iceni. The Iceni were victims of the Roman tax collectors and money-lenders, and Boudicca (widow of King Prasutagus) and her daughters were treated outrageously by the Romans. They were flogged and raped. Boudicca gained the support of other discontented British tribes, and serious revolt spread through the southeast. Despite the efforts of the Roman governor, Suetonius Paulinus, the towns of Colchester, St Albans and London were threatened and over 70 000 people were killed. Reinforcements from Rome eventually enabled Suetonius to put down this serious threat to Roman control of Britain.

Southeast Europe, the Danube, and North Africa

In 67, Nero responded to a flattering delegation from Greece (Achaea) by freeing this province from the authority of the governor of Macedonia and granting it immunity from taxation. To compensate for the loss of the province, he gave the senate Sardinia. The Danube frontier caused no trouble at this time.

There is very little information on affairs in Africa during Nero's reign.

The east

Nero faced his greatest dangers in the east.

Parthia

The Roman nominee on the throne of Armenia was replaced by the Parthian king's brother. Nero was advised to use force in Armenia, and the Roman commander, Corbulo, crossed the Euphrates River in 57 and captured Tigranocerta. When the new king of Armenia fled to join his brother in Parthia, Corbulo placed Tigranes on the throne, and this move provoked the Parthians. The king of Parthia made sure that the Roman province of Syria was prevented from sending help to the Romans, and Corbulo began negotiations. However, Nero decided to annex Armenia.

This was unsuccessful, since the Roman commander, Paetus, was defeated by the Parthians and Armenia was once more under their control. The Romans and Parthians reached a form of compromise—Tiridates (the brother of the Parthian king) was restored to the throne, but the Parthians agreed to allow the Romans to install him as king and he was crowned in a ceremony in Rome. This marked the beginning of approximately fifty years of peace between Parthia and Rome.

Judaea

Another trouble spot was the province of Judaea. The Jews were always difficult to govern, and the post of governor was not popular. There was continued strife between Jews and Greeks, Jews and Christians, and the two Jewish sects, the Pharisees and the Sadducees. The Jewish desire for national independence, misgovernment by the Roman officials in Judaea between 62 and 64, and the Roman preoccupation with Armenia and Parthia led to rebellion in 66. In the following year Jerusalem was heavily fortified by the Jews and Josephus raised a force of 60 000, with which he defended Galilee. The future Roman emperor, Vespasian, was given the command against the Jews and in 67 and 68 he gradually overran the country; the death of Nero interrupted his task. It was not until the following year that Jerusalem was finally captured, after a herioc defence. Vespasian's son, Titus, totally destroyed the city.

Page references in Tacitus to Nero's provincial and frontier policy are as follows:

Campaigns in Britain: 327–31

Campaigns in the east 345–53

Suetonius refers to these campaigns in *Nero*, 39.

Exercise

1 What was Tacitus' view of Corbulo as a general and diplomat in dealing with the problem of Armenia and Parthia during the reign of Nero?

2 According to Tacitus, why did Boudicca lead a revolt of British tribes against the Romans in 66?

Nero and the senate

In a speech to the senate on his accession, the young Nero outlined his future policy. He promised to put an end to further encroachment on the senate's authority. Criminal cases concerning Italy and the provinces were to be tried once again in the senatorial court and there was to be an end to the interference of freedmen in state affairs.

Early relations with senate reasonable

> 'I will not judge every kind of case myself', he said, 'and give too free rein to the influence of a few individuals by hearing prosecutors and defendants behind closed doors. From my house, bribery and favouritism will be excluded. I will keep personal and State affairs separate. The senate is to preserve its ancient functions. By applying to the consuls, people from Italy and the senatorial provinces may have access to its tribunals. I myself will look after the armies under my control'.[177]

Any charges brought by delatores were dismissed. 'He refused to allow the prosecution of . . . a junior senator, Carinas Celer, who was accused by a slave.'[178]

He rejected offers to erect gold and silver statues of himself, refused to accept the title of 'Father of his country', and exempted his colleague in the consulship from 'swearing allegiance, like the other officials, to the Emperor's acts. The senate praised this vigorously'.[179] Promises of clemency were made in many speeches, and he 'showed leniency by readmitting to the senate Plautius Lateranus, who had been expelled for adultery with Messalina'.[180]

With 'the high-minded guidance' of Seneca, Nero's relationship with the senate was reasonable. There were even times when the senate was independent enough to block proposals put forward by the emperor himself, such as Nero's suggestion of introducing free trade throughout the empire.

Some independent voices in the senate — Thrasea Paetus

Individual senators spoke out; one such was the Stoic, Thrasea Paetus, who was very influential in the early years of Nero's principate and was open about his dislike of many of the adulatory decrees passed by the senate. Tacitus says that it was his practice 'to pass over flatteries in silence or with curt agreement',[181] but when a decree of thanksgiving for Nero's escape from his mother was being discussed, Thrasea left the Senate House, 'thereby endangering himself'.[182] However, when the treason law was revived in 62 and the praetor Antistius Sosanius was charged with writing verse satirising the emperor, 'Thrasea's independence made others less servile'.[183] He had argued against the death sentence, and the rest of the senate — despite Nero's anger — supported him. In the following year, Nero forbade Thrasea to accompany other senators to Antium to celebrate the birth of Nero's daughter Claudia, and as a form of protest Thrasea withdrew from public life for three years.

Adulatory decrees

Adulatory senatorial decrees reached 'new depths of sycophancy or abasement'[184] after Burrus' death and Seneca's retirement. Nero was under the influence of his mistress, Poppaea, who organised false charges against his wife, Octavia. As a result, Octavia was divorced, banished and later killed, and the senate celebrated the murder with a decree of thanksgiving. Two years after Poppaea's marriage to Nero she died while pregnant (supposedly from a kick from Nero), and the senate deified her and her daughter.

With the help of the low-born Praetorian perfect Tigellinus, whose cruelty and debauched activities offended all dignified Romans, Nero's artistic activities and extravagances increased. He needed massive funds, but had already drained the treasury and deprived the senate of its right to mint copper coins; he therefore now took advantage of any opportunity to confiscate the property of senators. Dissatisfaction with Nero among senators increased, until in 65 it culminated in a serious conspiracy against his life.

Opposition to Nero increased

Conspiracy of Piso

A plot involving forty-one senators was formed to assassinate Nero and replace him with C. Calpurnius Piso, a member of one of the remaining republican families; Piso himself was not the originator of the conspiracy, which included such people as Lucan (the poet), Faenius Rufus (one of the two Praetorian prefects) and the consul-designate, Plautius Lateranus. There were also a number of officers of the Guards involved. Individual motives for joining the conspiracy varied, but most were probably disgusted with Nero's criminal record, his abolition of the senate's rights and, more particularly, the way in which he had lowered the tone of the imperial position. However, the plot was discovered and many distinguished senators, innocent or guilty, were executed or forced to commit suicide. Many of the deaths followed the same pattern: guardsmen would be sent with Nero's order to commit suicide, at which the accused would 'open his veins'. Among those who died were Seneca (although 'Nero had no proof of Seneca's complicity'),[185] his nephew Lucan, the consul M. Junius Vestinus Atticus (against whom there was no charge) and the consul-designate, Lateranus. As a result of the conspiracy and the growing fear of Nero for his life, there were nineteen deaths and many exiles. 'After the massacre of so many distinguished men, Nero finally coveted the destruction of Virtue herself by killing Thrasea and Marcius Barea Soranus. He had long hated them both.'[186] They had not been actively involved in the plot, but were outspoken against Nero.

Executions

Tyranny

In the remaining years of his reign, Nero's informers were everywhere; wealthy and prominent senators were not safe from Tigellinus, on whose authority leading Romans could be destroyed without even the pretence of a trial. Some years of this tyrannical power almost annihilated the senatorial class — which Suetonius maintained was Nero's avowed purpose. 'Often he [Nero] hinted broadly that it was not his intention to spare the remaining senators, but would one day wipe out the entire Senatorial Order'.[187]

The revolt of Vindex and Galba and the downfall of Nero

While Nero was in Greece opposition against him grew not only in Rome, but in the western provinces particularly.

Discontent in the western provinces

Julius Vindex was the governor of Gallia Lugdunensis, and with the support of other governors planned to rebel against Nero. When the proposed uprising became known Vindex suggested to the governor of Tarraconensis (Spain), Sulpicius Galba, that he accept the leadership of the revolt. Vindex was defeated by the governor of Upper Germany, and committed suicide, but Galba — the veteran aristocrat — declared himself 'Legate of the Senate and Roman People'. His own troops hailed him as imperator, other commanders joined him, and he followed the practice of Claudius in offering the Praetorian Guard 30 000 sesterces per man. Tigellinus had deserted Nero; he was now without the support of the Praetorian Guard which, with the senate, recognised Galba as emperor and declared Nero a public enemy.

Galba declared emperor by army

Suicide of Nero

Nero had alienated the upper class and had neglected the army, and for an emperor to survive under these conditions was difficult. He fled from Rome and hid in the home of one of his freedmen, but chose to commit suicide rather than wait for the soldiers to arrest him.

His death at the age of only thirty-one brought to an end the supremacy of the Julian and Claudian gens.

Tacitus sums up the response to Nero's death in his *Histories*.

> The senators were happy and at once used their new freedom of speech more freely since they had an emperor who was still absent; the most important of the knights were next to the senators in feeling satisfaction; the respectable part of the people, attached to the powerful families, and the clients and freedmen of the condemned and exiled, were full of hope. But the base plebs, addicted to the circus and the theatre, and the worst of the slaves, and those who had wasted their money and were maintained by the emperor, to his own disgrace, were resentful and open to rumour. The Praetorians, long accustomed to their oath to the Caesars, had been led to depose Nero by diplomacy and pressure rather than their own wish.[188]

Timeline: The Julio-Claudians — Tiberius to Nero, AD 14–68

Tiberius	14	Tiberius succeeds Augustus as princeps; mutinies break out among troops in Lower Germany and Pannonia
	15	Germanicus' campaigns against the Germans
	16	Germanicus recalled by Tiberius and sent on a diplomatic mission to the east
	18	Conflict between Germanicus and Piso in the east
	19	Death of Germanicus in the east; Agrippina blames Tiberius
	21	Tacfarinas causes trouble in the province of Africa
	22	Sejanus, the Praetorian prefect, begins his rise to power
	23	Murder of Drusus (Tiberius' son) by Sejanus
	24	Opposition of Agrippina and her supporters to Tiberius continues to grow
	26	Tiberius retires to Capri, from where he administered the empire by corresponding daily with the senate
	27	Sejanus now virtually in charge; in the following years, many of Germanicus' family, friends and supporters are exiled or killed
	29	Death of Livia
	31	Execution of Sejanus after Tiberius becomes aware of his ambitions and treachery Tiberius keeps Germanicus' youngest son (Gaius) with him on Capri and rules the empire from there
	37	Tiberius' death and the succession of Gaius (Caligula)
Gaius	37	Gaius goes to the Rhine frontier—a suspected conspiracy involving members of after recovery his reign is despotic — he believes himself a god
	38	Tiberius' grandson (Tiberius Gemellus) killed on orders of Gaius
	39	Gaius goes to the Rhine frontier — a suspected conspiracy involving members of his own family
	40	Troops refuse to invade Britain — Gaius returns to Rome Provocative attitude towards the Jews
	41	Assassinated by a group of Praetorian guardsmen
Claudius	41	Claudius proclaimed emperor by Praetorian Guard; is already married to his third wife, Messalina
	42	Suppresses the revolt in Mauretania and begins his conquest of Britain
	43	Extends the empire: annexation of Britain and Lycia

Claudius	44	Annexes Judaea
	46	Annexes Thrace
	47	Becomes censor
	48	Aedui (Gauls) granted admission to the senate The sexually depraved Messalina executed on Claudius' orders
	49	Marries Agrippina the Younger, the mother of Nero Nero betrothed to Claudius' daughter, Octavia
	50	Nero adopted by Claudius — a rival to Claudius' real son, Britannicus
	51	Nero named Princeps Iuventutis.
	52	Marriage of Nero and Octavia
	54	Death of Claudius, possibly at the hands of Agrippina
Nero	54	Agrippina conspires to have all possible rivals killed
	55	Britannicus killed by Nero (poisoned)
	56	Agrippina's influence wanes — Burrus and Seneca guide Nero; the next five years generally marked by good government
	58	The Parthian War
	59	Agrippina murdered by Nero's men
	60	Rebellion of Boudicca of the Iceni and other British tribes
	62	Death of Burrus and murder of Octavia
	63	Settlement of the Parthian/Armenian problem
	64	The Great Fire of Rome
	65	The so-called conspiracy of Piso to kill Nero Death of Seneca
	66	Nero sees himself as a god and visits Greece — enters artistic and athletic competitions A great rebellion breaks out among the Jews, centred around a violent group called the Zealots
	67	Nero grants Greece its 'freedom' The Jewish War continues
	68	The revolt of Vindex in Gaul and Galba in Spain Nero flees from Rome and commits suicide

Life in an imperial city in the first century AD

22

Pompeii, Herculaneum and Ostia

Religion

Commerce and politics

Public facilities

Housing

Abundant archaeological evidence

THE WELL-PRESERVED remains of three imperial cities—Pompeii, Herculaneum and Ostia—have provided historians with abundant material with which to establish what life was like for all classes of Roman citizens living in flourishing centres outside Rome. This takes the form of houses, apartment blocks, shops, craftsmen's workshops, warehouses, paved streets, drainage systems, temples, shrines, necropoleis, basilicas, artifacts and furniture, mosaics, wall paintings, formal inscriptions and everyday graffiti.

Pompeii, Herculaneum and Ostia

The manner in which Pompeii and Herculaneum were destroyed (the eruption of Vesuvius in AD 79) allowed these two Campanian cities to remain just as they were the first century AD. Ostia, on the other hand, which declined gradually owing to the decadence of the administration in the second half of the fourth century AD and the spread of malaria, was subjected to much restoration, remodelling and adaptation during the late empire, so that it is harder to gain a clear idea of the city as it was in the first century.

This archaeological and epigraphic material can be supplemented by written sources, such as Pliny the Younger and Tacitus.

Pompeii and Herculaneum

Early history and destruction

Pompeii and Herculaneum became allies of Rome after the Romans defeated the Samnites in the early third century BC. It was not until after the Social War (the war of the Italian allies against Rome) that they were forced to surrender to Sulla and became part of the Roman state. Pompeii was a Roman colony, with much of its land confiscated and given to Sulla's veterans; this created bad feeling for some time.

The archaeological evidence (the streets, the number and style of houses, the number of shops and the political graffiti) indicates that Pompeii was a wealthy, bustling, lively commercial centre, while Herculaneum was a quieter seaside resort for cultured Romans who were attracted to the mild climate of Campania.

Cast of a human figure found in excavating the city of Pompeii

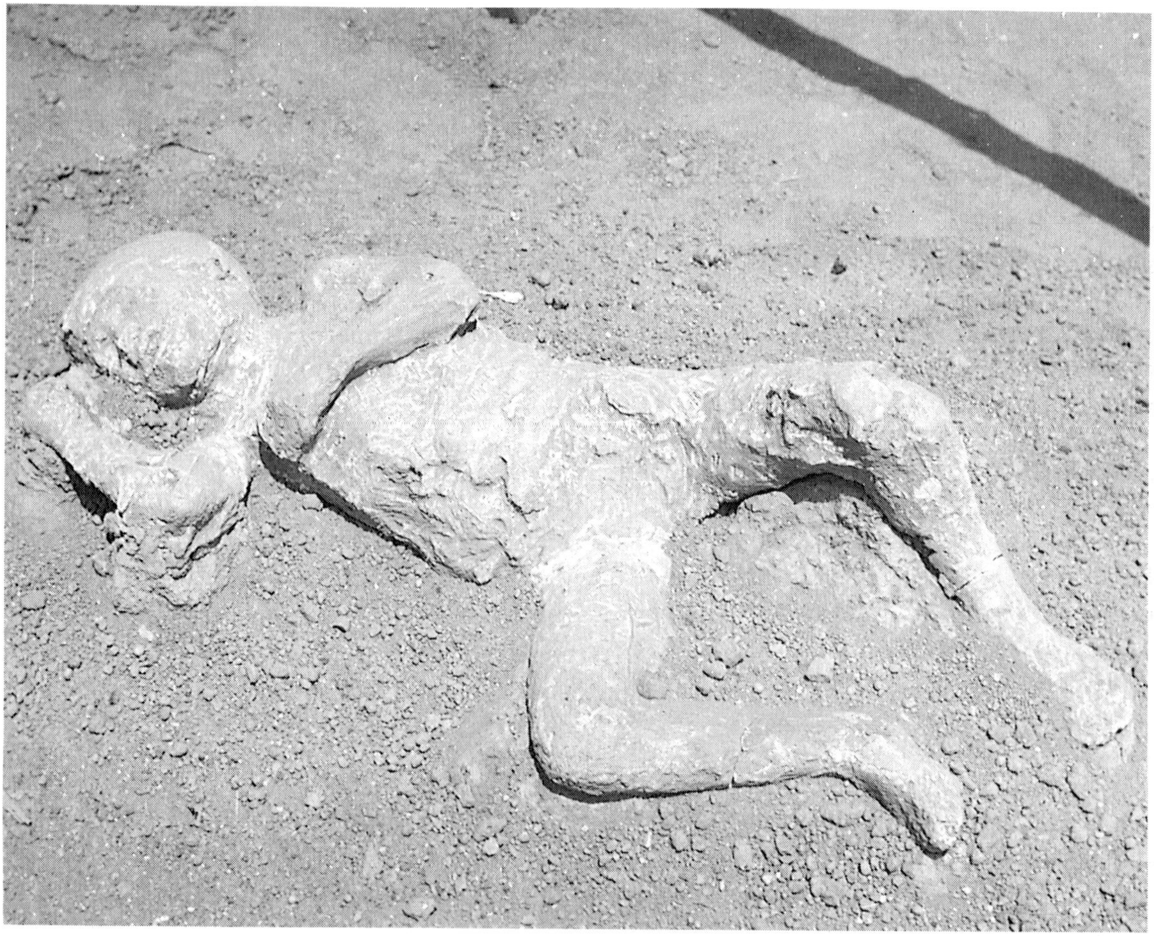

When Vesuvius erupted in 79 Pompeii was covered with thick layers of *lapilli* (pumice) and ashes, in places eight metres thick, and many of the people were suffocated by the poisonous gases that penetrated every part of the city. Herculaneum, on the other hand, was destroyed by a layer of lava and mud which in parts of the city was twenty metres thick.

Ostia

Origin of Ostia

Ostia was Portus Romae (the port of Rome), established at the mouth of the Tiber River sometime in the sixth century BC. It was originally a fortified citadel for a garrison stationed there to defend navigation of the Tiber, but it developed rapidly into a flourishing commercial and port city, especially after Rome acquired an overseas empire. It had enormous warehouses (*horrea*), and shipyards where warships, cargo ships and river barges were constructed; the Roman fleet was stationed there. Wealthy merchants and maritime contractors built huge homes, while employees and sailors lived in multistoreyed apartments (insulae).

Ostia at its height

In the second half of the first century AD, when Pompeii and Herculaneum ceased to exist, Ostia was at its height. Claudius, who took a real interest in the social and religious life of the city, set up facilities for fire protection, public security and traffic control. When the river mouth silted up, he built a new port for the city by digging inland along the coast. Caligula gave Ostia a lead pipeline which distributed water to the city, while Nero used the rubble from the Great Fire to reclaim the swamp areas inland from Ostia. Trajan later added to the harbour with new wharves and a canal, while a building boom took place under Hadrian.

Ostia, which was neither grandiose nor sumptuous, in the view of many archaeologists represents the most complete example of a Roman city of the imperial age.

From the excavations at Pompeii, Herculaneum and Ostia, the following can be deduced:

1 attitudes to religion—public and household worship, popular cults imported from the east, the cult of the emperor and burial practices;
2 commercial and political life—shops, taverns and markets, workshops, mills, granaries and warehouses, corporations, forums, municipal buildings and elections;
3 public facilities, housing and entertainment—public baths and toilets, drainage and water supplies, streets, villas and apartments, theatres, stadiums and gymnasiums.

Religion

State religion and household cults

In both Pompeii and Ostia the chief temple of the city was the Capitolium —dedicated to Jupiter, Juno and Minerva—located adjacent to the forum, the political and religious centre. Temples to other deities such as Apollo, Venus, Mercury, Hercules and the goddess Roma were also found scattered throughout the cities. In Ostia, associations of people with the same profession—such as naval carpenters or masons—had their own temples, called *collegiate temples*. In private homes the cult of the Lares was predominant, being worshipped at a small shrine called a *lararium*.

Details from the lararium (opposite): the man in the toga represents the genius of the family and the dancing figures on both sides are the Lares; the snake personifies the spirit of the household

A household shrine (*lararium*)

The remains of a lararium in an apartment block in Ostia

Religions from the east

'New' religions from the east

The conquest of Greece and the east brought with it the cults of the Hellenistic world, including the Dionysian, Eleusinian and Orphic mysteries and the cults of Cybele, Isis, Osiris and Mithras. These oriental cults satisfied an emotional need in the people which the traditional religion did not. Judaism was also practised in Italy in the first century, and there is evidence of Christianity.

Hellenistic religion

Dionysiac mysteries

The mysteries of the Dionysiac rites (worship of Dionysus or Bacchus) had spread rapidly despite the senate's attempt to abolish them. The best evidence for the worship of Dionysus in Pompeii is found in the Villa of the Mysteries, where a triclinium (dining room) had all its walls painted with vivid scenes from the Dionysiac secret rites. The mistress of the house was probably initiated into the sect herself, satisfying her need for spirituality.

Cult of Magna Mater

The worship of Cybele — the Great Mother (Magna Mater) — from Phrygia had been established in Italy since the end of the Second Punic

War, but it received new recognition under Augustus and increased in popularity in the first century AD. Associated with the Cybele was her companion, Attis, who sacrificed his virility to her; those who wished to become priests of Cybele castrated themselves during mystic rites. There were numerous shrines in Ostia dedicated to Magna Mater as well as to Attis, Isis, Serapis and Mithras, since people poured into the port city from every corner of the Mediterranean bringing their customs and religions with them. The importance of the Temple of the Magna Mater in Herculaneum can be gauged by the fact that after the earthquake of 63 AD the Emperor Vespasian paid for its restoration himself.

Egyptian religion

The cult of Isis

The Egyptian cult of Isis and her partner Serapis became increasingly popular from the time of Sulla to that of Nero, and her temples were

A painted scene of a sacrifice to Isis: the head priest holds a bowl, probably containing water from the Nile, while an attendant performs a sacrifice on an Egyptian horned altar

Remains of the Temple of Isis in Pompeii, one of the most important sanctuaries in the city

widespread. The cult's initiation rites and daily ritual appealed particularly to women, although there were male adherents also. Isis came to be seen as the universal mother who cleansed and comforted her followers with the promise of deliverance from death, and of immortality. There were many services held throughout the day, accompanied by songs and the *sistrum* (a musical instrument). Those undergoing initiation were expected to take part in a representation of the death and return to life of Osiris (whom Isis had restored to life).

The Temple of Isis in Pompeii, one of the most important sanctuaries in the city, was restored immediately after the earthquake in 63 AD. This temple contained—as well as the statue of the goddess—the images of Horus and Anubis (two other Egyptian gods). A statue of Osiris with a panther was found beside the sanctuary, and in the sacred enclosure was a small, vaulted underground room in which was stored the Nile water used for sacred washing. Behind the Temple there were some large rooms, the biggest of which was the *ecclesiasterion* (hall) for the secret meetings of the initiates. The walls of this room and of the sacrarium beside it were decorated with frescoes of cult motifs referring to Isis, Serapis and Osiris. There is also a *sacellum* (chapel) dedicated to Isis, Serapis and Anubis in a private home in Pompeii — the House of the Gilded Cupids.

Mithraism

Worship of Mithras

The Persian religion of Mithras is believed to have appeared in the west in about 70 BC and was exclusively a man's religion, especially popular among the soldiers of the legions; it spread from camp to camp and among the civilian population of Italy. It emphasised the battle of the forces of light and truth against evil and darkness, and Mithras became the male counterpart to Isis. It was the religion most resembling Christianity, and

A marble statue (from Ostia) of Mithra slaying a bull

its ritual — conducted by a special priesthood — included baptism and the use of holy water and consecrated bread and wine. The number seven was also important.

Evidence of the widespread worship of Mithras is seen in Ostia, where there were about sixteen *mithraea* (places dedicated to Mithras). One of the best preserved is called the Mithraeum of the Seven Spheres: the long, rectangular room was divided into three parts — two podia for holding the participants in the rites, a corridor leading to the sacrificial altar, and the place where the image of the god stood. The floor was decorated with seven semicircles in progressive order going towards the altar; these symbolised the seven phases needed to be passed through in order to reach truth. The number seven is represented in almost all of Ostia's mithraea.

One of the strangest of them was in the Baths of Mithras. This place of worship was made out of one of the baths' disused underground cisterns, and its light came through a small trapdoor in the vault. In this mithraeum was found a beautiful marble group representing the god killing a bull.

Judaism

The Roman attitude towards the Jews was generally tolerant and for a long time they did not distinguish between Judaism and Christianity — regarding the latter as simply another sect.

Evidence

There is ample evidence of the presence of Jewish communities in Ostia, where there was a synagogue, while many graffiti in Pompeii testify to their presence there.

Christianity

Birth and death of Christ

Jesus Christ was born during the reign of Augustus and was crucified in the latter part of the reign of Tiberius, in AD 29, 30 or 33. His interpretation of the Mosaic law caused opposition from the Jewish authorities, and their court (the Sanhedrin) handed him over to the Roman procurator of Judaea, Pontius Pilatus. Pilate, finding no reason to put Jesus to death, handed him back to the Jewish authorities as he feared political repercussions and was afraid of the reaction of the mob.

The spread of Christianity

The number of supporters of Jesus increased as a result of the ministry of Paul of Tarsus, a Roman citizen who had converted to Christianity. The Jewish authorities, afraid of his teachings, caused disturbances wherever he went. The governor of Achaea, the procurators of Judaea and King Herod Agrippa II refused to find him guilty on the trumped-up charges of the Jews, who then accused him of treason. Paul appealed to Caesar, and was taken to Rome; at the time of his arrival in the city there was already a small community of Christians, although the average Roman knew very little about them. However, after Nero's persecution of the Christians as scapegoats for the Great Fire, the Romans recognised them as a group separate from the Jews.

There is reasonable evidence to support the view that there were Christians also in Pompeii.

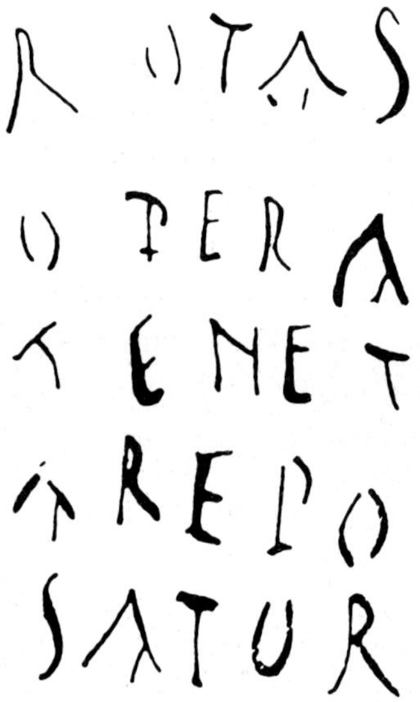

A cryptogram of the Lord's Prayer (*Paternoster* — 'Our Father') found in the large Palaestra in Pompeii; this appears to be the best evidence of the presence of Christians in the city before the volcanic eruption in AD 79

The imperial cult

'Genius' of Augustus

The cult of the emperor's 'genius' was first introduced during the time of Augustus. The genius was regarded as the divine part of man, and to worship the genius of the princeps was a form of homage. (After Augustus, more obvious steps towards deification were taken by emperors such as Caligula and Nero.) Augustus established a new religious college of freedmen (those who had once been slaves) called the Augustales, who supervised the cult of the emperor. The emperor's name was also often associated with the worship of Fortuna and Roma.

The Sanctuary of the Household Gods at Pompeii, dedicated at the time of Nero to the protectors of the city, featured in its central apse the statue of the Genius of Augustus alongside ten young dancers representing the Lares. This reflected the practice implemented in other parts of Rome and Italy where Augustus had the shrines at crossroads replaced with new statues of the Lares — known as the Lares Augusti — between which was the image of his own genius.

Recent excavations at Herculaneum have brought to light the Collegium Augustalium, dedicated to the imperial cult. Ostia also had its political-

Remains of the Temple of Rome and Augustus in Ostia

religious college of Augustales, in the ruins of which were found statues representing members of the imperial household, as well as a Temple of Rome and Augustus.

The Temple of Fortuna Augusta in Pompeii was built by a private person who held high office during the Augustan age. It was built on his own property and reveals the link between religion and politics, as it obviously celebrated some important event and was a way of repaying an imperial favour. At the same time, it would have encouraged the deification of the emperor.

In Pompeii, the so-called Edifice of Eumachia was dedicated by a priestess (Eumachia) and her son to 'the Concordia and the Pietas Augusta', and in the niches were statues of Aeneas, Romulus, Caesar and Augustus. This was obviously a dedication celebration to the Julian clan. There is also evidence of the cult of the genius of the emperor in the unfinished Temple of Vespasian.

Burial customs

Decoration of tombs

The great necropoleis of Pompeii and Ostia, built outside the city walls, include tombs of all sizes, shapes and decoration. Some were built to house urns containing the ashes of the dead person, while others were constructed for the interment of many bodies. Frescoes of animals, birds and flowers decorated the walls, while mosaics covered the floors. The marble sarcophagi were decorated with bas-reliefs depicting scenes from ancient Greek myths, while tablets and tombstones were inscribed with the virtues or outstanding actions of the deceased.

The lower classes — for instance, tradesmen — wanted to be remembered for the quality of their work and their tombs often had terra-cotta panels illustrating details of the deceased's former activity.

Even cheaper ways were found to bury the poor. Many of them were simply buried under tiles, with perhaps a bowl or vase which had belonged to them.

Commercial and political life

Buildings around the Forum

Facing on to the Civil Forum of Pompeii were some of the most important buildings related to the economic and political life of the city (as well as its religious life).

Municipal buildings

The Municipal buildings (three large rooms on the south side of the Forum) are believed to have been used for meetings of the eighty to a

Election notices written on the walls of private houses in Pompeii

hundred members of the local council (*Ordo Decurionum*), as headquarters of the *duovirs* (council members who were elected for life), and for storage of the city's archives.

Comitium

The Comitium, with its numerous doors, made the entrances and exits of the voters easier, and a podium was used by the magistrate presiding over elections. Election propaganda was painted on the walls of houses.

Court

The Basilica was not only a business centre, but was also the Court of Justice.

Market

The Macellum (market) had a counter running around three sides of it for the sale of fish, meat and vegetables; the courtyard had a portico decorated with paintings depicting the foodstuffs that were sold there.

On the long side of the Forum was the weighing station, *mensa ponderaria*—a slab with nine cavities of different sizes, which corresponded to an equal number of measures. The cavities were perforated in the bottom to allow the products being measured to fall through.

The Macellum (market) in Pompeii

The *mensa ponderaria* (weighing station) — a slab with nine cavities equal to the correct measures that Pompeian merchants were expected to use

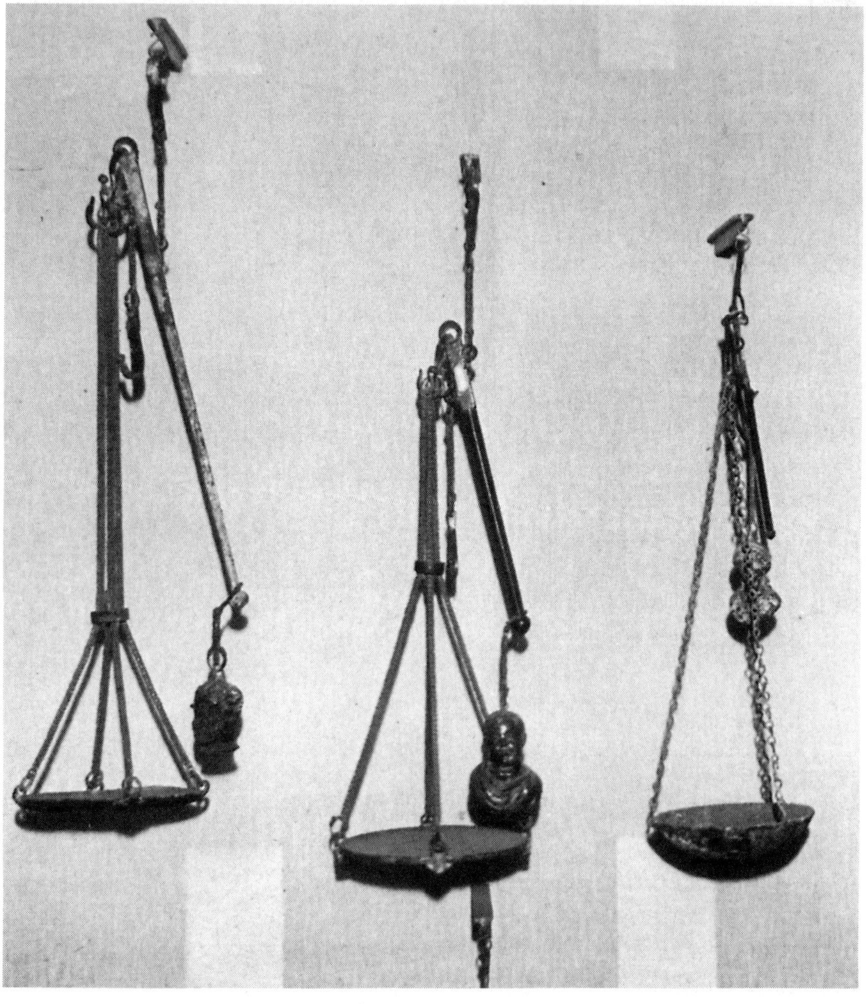

Balances and weights used by merchants

The Forum of the Corporations in Ostia

Grain store

Adjacent to the weighing station was the horreum, for storing grain. The Edifice of Eumachia may have been the headquarters of the guild of *fullones* (the washers and dyers of fabrics), and also possibly a wool store.

Forums

Similarly, the Forum (and the Forum of the Corporations) at Ostia were surrounded by political, business and religious buildings. The Forum of the Corporations contained over fifty offices in which all business connected with maritime affairs was conducted, and the mosaic inscriptions publicised the various activities.

Shops and taverns

Plan of shops

Shops were scattered along most streets. At the entrance to a shop was a selling counter, often of brick, while shelves on the walls held the merchandise; another room at the back served as a storeroom. In Herculaneum one of the tabernae (shops) is so well preserved that the counter with *dolia*, the ovens, the shelves for amphoras of wine, the loft where provisions were stored and the owner's furnishings are still intact.

A shop in Herculaneum — perhaps a wine shop, with living quarters upstairs

Variety of eating and drinking establishments

Taverns (such as the Tavern of the Peacock and the Tavern of Alexander of the Marine Gate in Ostia) and eating houses were full of clients at all hours of the day and night, and were the meeting places of gamblers and young men. The *thermopolia* (dining areas) in Pompeii, Herculaneum and Ostia were the more luxurious eating places, where hot drinks and food were served and where in a more comfortable back room clients could linger in a pleasant atmosphere.

A bar with holes in the marble counter, where clay jars were possibly kept or perhaps where food was kept hot

A *thermopolium*, a place for dining

Workshops and warehouses

Aspects of commercial life

There were many workshops where craftsmen such as potters, glassmakers and silversmiths produced and sold their products. In other premises there were specialist industries such as dyeworks, tanneries, laundries (*fullonicae*), and mills and bakeries. The Fullonica Stephani is one of the most important places where washing and ironing were done in Pompeii.

The mills and bakeries still have their millwheels in place. These were used to make flour, and were turned by both human and animal power. It is still possible to see the hoofprints of the donkeys that turned the millstones in Ostia.

A bakery in Pompeii, with central oven and millstones

Bread found in an oven when Pompeii was excavated 2000 years after its destruction

Millstones in a bakery in Herculaneum

A large basin in a laundry/dye shop (*fullonica*)

Horrea were enormous warehouses one or more storeys high, with enormous rooms capable of holding tons of wares. They were scattered all over the city of Ostia, which was the emporium of Rome. The Great Horrea, built between the reigns of Claudius and Nero, was majestic in size and had spaces under the floors to prevent the humidity from spoiling the grain.

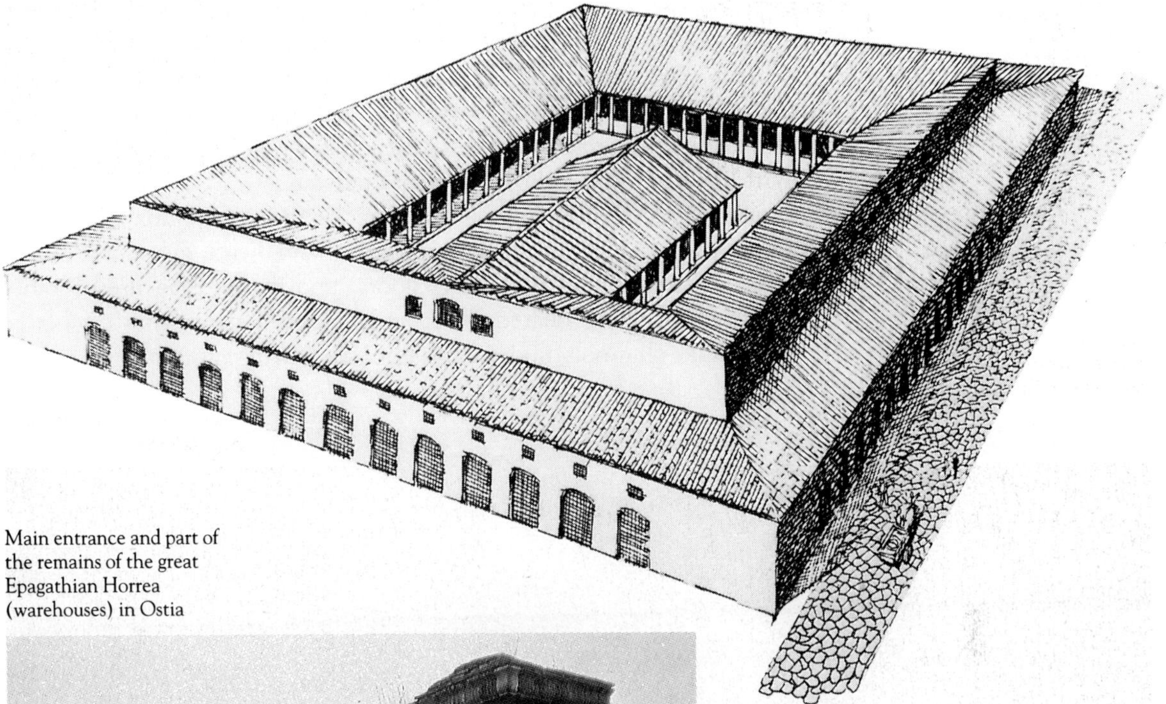

Reconstructed horrea

Main entrance and part of the remains of the great Epagathian Horrea (warehouses) in Ostia

Public facilities, housing and entertainment

Public facilities

Municipal baths

Public baths (*thermae*) and toilets (*foricae*) were an important feature of all Roman towns and cities, many of which had several thermae. There was usually one complex close to the Forum (the Forum Baths) as in Pompeii, Herculaneum and Ostia, but also — depending on the size of the city — others scattered throughout the suburban areas. Excavations at Ostia have revealed eighteen thermae, some of which belonged to corporations of merchants, seamen and various types of craftsmen.

Plan of bath houses

Thermae were usually arranged in two sections, one male and one female, with separate entrances but using the same heating system. Wood-fed furnaces were located below the floors, and in the area used for hot baths (*calidarium*) these heated water and produced steam that circulated through special channels underneath the floor (*hypocaustum*) and in the

The Forum Baths in Pompeii

Inside the suburban baths in Herculaneum

Mosaic floors in the Baths of Neptune in Ostia

walls (*concameration*). The water was kept at a constant temperature. Besides the room for hot baths, there was also a room with a cold-water pool (*frigidarium*), a room for resting, heated with hot air and warm tubs, a dressing room (*apodyterium*) where the bathers could change and hang their clothes, and a public toilet. Underneath the complex enormous cisterns collected water from the aqueduct, and there were underground passages for the attendants' use in lighting the boilers and changing the pool water.

The baths as a meeting place

Associated with the baths in a large complex there were decorated rooms (with stuccoed ceilings, mosaic floors and niches containing terracotta statues) reserved for people to meet in and perhaps even to discuss business. Some thermae were well-lit, with large windows, and as Seneca comments in a letter to a friend,

> people regard baths as fit for moths if they have not been so arranged that they receive the sun all day long through the widest of windows, if men cannot bathe and get a coat of tan at the same time, and if they cannot look out from their bath-tubs over stretches of land and sea.[1]

An open courtyard (*palaestra*), surrounded by porticoes, was used for sporting practice.

Found in the vicinity of the baths were many *ampullae* (terra-cotta or glass bottles containing ointments and perfumed oils), and statues or mosaics of athletes.

Public toilets

Foricae were public toilets. Rarely have any toilets been found in private homes or apartments, but in thermae, apartment blocks and public buildings there was usually a room set aside for the purpose. It would contain long, marble benches fitted with holes, and could accommodate many people at one time. The lack of privacy did not create any uneasiness.

Water collection and distribution

Providing water to a city population was always a problem. Originally, public and private wells — sometimes as deep as forty metres — were used. In the better homes, an *impluvium* — a basin in the floor of the atrium (vestibule) — caught rainwater, which collected in an underground reservoir.

After the Serinum Aqueduct was built, water in Pompeii was carried to the Water Tower, erected at the highest point of the city. From this, drainage pipes supplied water to public fountains on the streets and private fountains in the courtyards of some apartment blocks, as well as to the wealthiest homes.

Although there were drainage and sewage pipes in the public areas (such as under streets) and in the more luxurious villas, they were not installed everywhere; it was not unusual for people in apartment blocks to

The *forica* (public toilet) in Ostia

A lead pipe in the atrium of a private home in Herculaneum

Above left: Drainage holes under pavements in Herculaneum

Pavement in a street

Pedestrian crossing blocks

simply throw their liquid waste out of the windows into the streets below.

Streets and pavements

The streets were relatively narrow, but were paved; they had raised footpaths, and stepping stones at crossings, and were well-drained.

Housing

In the first century AD in Pompeii, Herculaneum and Ostia there were basically three types of housing.

The domus

The *domus* was usually single-storeyed (as in Pompeii), but sometimes two-storeyed with terraces, loggias, hanging gardens and alcoves (as in Herculaneum). Herculaneum was on the sea, and so the villas of the rich were built to make the most of the panorama. The burial of Herculaneum by lava (rather than by burning ashes, as in Pompeii) allowed the timber of the upper storeys to be preserved.

Plan of a domus

A domus was built around an atrium and a *peristylium* (portico with gardens and fountains—*vividarium*). In the atrium was the lararium

The stuccoed exterior of the House of the Ceii in Pompeii

A painting from a villa, depicting a number of tall buildings in a Roman town

The peristyle and garden in the House of the Vetii in Pompeii

Above left: The atrium of a domus with the *compluvium* (for allowing in light and air) and the *impluvium* (for catching water)

A two-storeyed peristyle in Pompeii

(the shrine of the Lares). In some of the poorer houses this was reduced to a tiny niche, or a painting. The impluvium was a tiled basin to catch rainwater from the opening in the roof of the atrium.

The two largest rooms in the house were the living room (*tablinum*) and the dining room (triclinium). In the latter, diners reclined on couches which were arranged in a horseshore shape; these couches were the most important and handsomest pieces of furniture in the house, and each one could seat three people.

The other rooms in the domus were usually small—*cubiculae* (bedroom), *alae* (open halls), *penaria* (larders for keeping food), and servants' quarters—because the men spent little time at home and even the women had the freedom to engage in activities outside the home.

Furnishings and decoration

Furniture for the most part was built into the structure—wall niches, shelves and cupboards. The main decoration of the house was provided by wall paintings and mosaics; there were many styles of wall painting, but the most common subjects featured in the houses of Pompeii, Herculaneum and Ostia were stories from Greek mythology, gardens, flowers, birds, animals, sea creatures, oriental landscapes and masks. Illusionary effects were created by painting architectural features onto the wall.

Mosaic floor in the House of the Tragic Poet in Pompeii

Mosaic floor in the House of the Dioscuri in Ostia

A delicate wall painting from the House of the Floating Venus in Pompeii

The remains of a bed in a house in Herculaneum

Fresco of an upper-class woman seated on a bronze chair, playing the cithara

Wealthy Pompeians flaunted their riches, and this is seen in the size and decoration of houses such as that of the Vetii, the House of the Faun and the Villa of the Mysteries.

Many of these homes had tabernae (shops) facing onto the street. As the population grew, a great number of the single-family residences were divided into many rental apartments.

Craftsmen's houses

Shopkeepers, craftsmen and poorer merchants lived above their workshops, as they had no room to expand on the ground floor. At Herculaneum

Two-storeyed houses in Herculaneum, including workshops

it is still possible to see a shopkeeper's wares on the ground floor and his charred bed on the mezzanine, a few metres above the floor, reached by a ladder or staircase.

Insulae

Apartment blocks

The most common form of housing at the end of the republican period was the insulae — block-long, multistoreyed apartment buildings set around courtyards. Along the ground floor were shops and shopkeepers' premises, while on the courtyard side were more comfortable and elegant apartments, some with balconies and galleries.

Since the individual units did not have water and sanitary equipment, facilities such as a fountain, a bath, a toilet and often a dyer and cleaner's shop were found on the ground floor.

Vast numbers of these insulae were found to have been in Ostia at the time of the early empire.

Remains of high-rise apartment blocks (*insulae*) in Ostia

A reconstructed *insula*

Entertainment

Theatres

Pantomime and mime

Although tragedies and comedies were performed in the theatres, the most successful types of performance were pantomime and mime. Pantomime involved masked dancers portraying the action of some mythological story, while mime shows were spiced with realistic violence, and elements of horror and licentiousness.

The stages of these first-century theatres had permanent scenery, three-storeys high and decorated with columns, niches and statues. Pompeii had two theatres (the small and the large theatre) located near the most important city gate. In the same area was the sports field (palaestra) and the gladiators' barracks. The most imposing building in Ostia Antica today is the theatre, which was built in the consulship of Agrippa in AD 12 (the time of Augustus).

The theatre in Ostia

Above right: The large theatre in Pompeii

Masks outside the theatre in Ostia

A tragic actor's mask from Pompeii

Amphitheatres

Enthusiasm for gladiatorial combats

There was great popular enthusiasm for the gladiatorial combats and wild-animal hunts performed in the arenas. These were savage and cruel, and usually ended in a bloodbath; overexcitement and cheering often became frenzied, and could lead to the outbreak of brawls and hooliganism. A famous and bloody riot occurred in 59 between the people of Pompeii and their neighbours of Nuceria; this battle so shocked the Romans that the Emperor Nero closed the Pompeian amphitheatre for over ten years—Tacitus commented on this in the *Annals*.[2] Pompeii's amphitheatre is the oldest example that is still perfectly preserved; it is conveniently located near two of the city's gates—to serve those people coming in from the outlying areas. It had a capacity of 15 000, and there are numerous examples of graffiti announcing the events or praising successful gladiators and popular idols.

The Gladiators' Barracks and Gladiators' School are recognised by the numerous graffiti (150 on the columns of the porticoes of their barracks) and the arms, helmets, embroidered uniforms and shackles found on the site.

Aerial view of the amphitheatre in Pompeii

Graffito from the amphitheatre in Pompeii referring to the fight in AD 59: 'Hail O Capuans who won a single battle for us, but perished in it with the Nucerians'

Above right: A painting representing a blood battle in amphitheatre in Pompeii between the people of Pompeii and those of Nuceria, in AD 59

Graffiti from Pompeii and Ostia

A terra-cotta relief of bestiarii (those who fought with wild beasts at public shows) fighting with a lion and a lioness

A gladiator's parade helmet

The palaestra

Sports arena

The palaestra was a place where men could train and play sports. It was usually a large, open area surrounded by shady porticoes and trees, with sometimes an open-air swimming pool (*natatio*) in the centre. The Large Palaestra in Pompeii was built in the Augustan age, when the earlier, Samnite Palaestra became too small for the city's youth. It was so large (the pool itself was 766 square metres) that archaelogists believe it was used also for mustering troops, for holding markets, and as a gathering place for the enormous crowds waiting to enter the nearby amphitheatre. There was also a Collegium Juvenum (Young Men's Sports Association); this boasted an official doctor, whose professional instruments were found there.

The Palaestra in Pompeii

Essay topics

1 What was Augustus' constitutional position in 23 BC? Show how in organising the new system of government (the principate) he took account of the failure of Julius Caesar.

2 What benefits did the Augustan principate bring to the people of Rome and the empire? In your answer, refer to archaeological and written evidence from the Augustan Age.

3 Discuss the relationship of Augustus with the senate and the equestrian order.

4 What changes did Augustus bring about in one of the following?
   (a) organisation of the provinces and the army
   (b) religious practices and law and order

5 How full an account of Augustus' achievements is the *Res Gestae*?

6 To what extent does Tacitus' treatment of Augustus support his claim to impartiality?

7 From the description of the archaeological remains of the forum of Augustus, outline its main features. What can be learned from the remains about Augustus' motives in building his forum?

8 What buildings existed in the Roman Forum at the time of Augustus? What purpose did they serve?

9 'The weakness of the principate was its dependence for success on the person of the princeps.' Discuss this statement in relation to any two of the Julio-Claudians.

10 How accurate is Tacitus' view of the treason trials during the reign of Tiberius?

11 Discuss the comment by Suetonius: 'So much for the Emperor; the rest of this history must deal with the Monster'.

12 Discuss the frontier policies of Tiberius and of Claudius. To what extent did they follow the policy of Augustus?

13 How important was the Praetorian Guard and its commanders during the reigns of any two of the Julio-Claudians?

14 What changes did Claudius introduce in the government and administration of Rome and the empire?

15 What was the relationship of each of the Julio-Claudian emperors with the senate?

16 To what extent were Claudius and Nero influenced by the advice of others?

17 To what extent were Nero's artistic and sporting activities responsible for his downfall? Were there any other contributing factors?

Further reading

Ancient sources

Augustus. *Res Gestae*, ed. P. A. Brunt & J. M. Moore.
Suetonius. *The Twelve Caesars*.
Tacitus. *Annals of Imperial Rome*.
Virgil. *Aeneid*.

Modern sources

Balsdon, J. P. V. D. *The Emperor Gaius.*
Charlesworth, M. P. *The Augustan Empire 44 BC–AD 70.* Cambridge Ancient History, vol. 10.
Carcopino, J. *Daily Life in Ancient Rome.*
Dudley, D. R. *The World of Tacitus.*
Garzetti, A. *From Tiberius to the Antonines*, AD 14–192.
Grant, M. *The Roman Forum.*
_____ . *Roman History from Coins.*
_____ . *Roman Readings.*
Kagan, D. *The Roman World*, Problems in Ancient History, vol. 2.
Levick, B. *Tiberius the Politician.*
Lewis, N. & Reinhold, M. *Roman Civilisation Sourcebook II: The Empire.*
Paoli, U. E. *Rome: Its People, Life and Customs.*
Romanelli, P. *The Roman Forum.*
Salmon, E. T. *A History of the Roman World, 30 BC–AD 138.*
Scramuzza, V. M. *The Emperor Claudius.*
Strong, D. E. *Roman Art.*
Warmington, B. H. *Nero: Reality and Legend.*

Notes to the text

Full details of all works cited appear in the Bibliography, p. 632.

All references to Polybius' work are from *The Rise of the Roman Empire*, with the exception of those otherwise noted in chapter 9.

Chapter 1: The evidence

1. Livy, *History of Rome*, VI, i: 1–3.
2. E. H. Warmington, p. 451.
3. ibid., pp. 3–5.
4. ibid.
5. ibid., pp. 287–9.
6. ibid., pp. 291–3.
7. ibid., p. 177.
8. ibid.
9. ibid., pp. 291–3.

Chapter 4: Roman society in the early republic

1. Twelve Tables, Table VIII, in Lewis & Reinhold, *The Republic*, p. 107.
2. Dionysius of Halicarnassus, II. lxvii, in Lewis & Reinhold, op. cit., pp. 135–6.
3. Livy , *History of Rome*, IV. 44, II, in Grant, *The Roman Forum*, p. 67.

Chapter 5: Conquest and organisation

1. Dionysius of Halicarnassus, VI. xcv. 1–3, in Lewis & Reinhold, op. cit., p. 85.
2. Polybius, II: 18.
3. Livy , *History of Rome*, V. xlviii. 8–9, in Lewis & Reinhold, op. cit., p. 76.
4. Plutarch, *Pyrrhus*, 21.

Chapter 6: The plebeian struggle for equality

1. Plutarch, *Cato the Elder*, 16.
2. Broughton, *Magistrates of the Roman Republic*, pp. 330–1.

Chapter 7: Background to the wars of expansion

1. Polybius, I: 12.
2. Caven, p. 5.
3. Polybius, Introduction, p. 15.
4. ibid., I: 1.
5. ibid., I: 14.
6. ibid., XVI: 14.
7. Livy, *The Early History of Rome*, I: Preface.
8. Polybius, III: 24.

Chapter 8: The First Punic War

1. Polybius, I: 12.
2. ibid., I: 13.
3. Caven, p. 15.
4. Polybius, I: 10.
5. Caven, p. 5.
6. Polybius, I: 11.
7. ibid., I: 20.
8. ibid.
9. ibid.
10. ibid.
11. ibid., I: 23.
12. ibid.
13. ibid., I: 24.
14. Caven, p. 30.

15. Polybius, I: 26.
16. ibid.
17. ibid. I: 31.
18. ibid.
19. ibid., I: 37.
20. ibid., I: 42.
21. ibid., I: 41
22. ibid., I: 44.
23. ibid., I: 46.
24. ibid., I: 52.
25. ibid., I: 54
26. ibid., I: 55.
27. ibid.
28. ibid., I: 58.
29. ibid., I: 59.

Chapter 9: Background to Second Punic War

1. Polybius, *Histories*, p. 219.
2. ibid., p. 221.
3. Polybius, III: 10.
4. ibid, III: 15.
5. ibid, III: 11.
6. ibid, III: 10.
7. Dio Cassius, fragment 48.
8. Polybius, II: 36.
9. ibid., II: 13.
10. ibid., III: 29.
11. Livy, *The War with Hannibal*, XXI: 3.
12. Polybius, II: 36.
13. Caven, p. 85.
14. Polybius, II. 36.
15. Livy, op. cit., XXI: 5.
16. Polybius, III: 14.
17. ibid., III: 30.
18. ibid., III: 15.
19. ibid.
20. Frank, pp. 119–26, in Kagan, pp. 115–19.
21. Polybius, III: 17.
22. Lazenby, p. 27.
23. Polybius, III: 33.
24. ibid.
25. ibid., 9.
26. ibid., 11.
27. ibid., 13.
28. ibid., 10.
29. ibid.
30. ibid., 30.
31. Livy, *The War with Hannibal*, XXI: 1–2.
32. B. L. Hallward, *Hannibal's Invasion of Italy*, in Kagan, pp. 119–23.
33. Scullard, *History of the Roman World*, pp. 181–5.
34. Hoyos, p. 10.

Chapter 10: The Second Punic War

1. Lazenby, p. 52.
2. Polybius, III: 60.
3. ibid.
4. ibid., 67.
5. ibid., 70.
6. ibid.
7. ibid.
8. ibid., 69.
9. Lazenby, p. 58.
10. Polybius, III: 80.
11. ibid.
12. ibid., 81.
13. ibid., 85.
14. ibid., 87.
15. Plutarch, *Fabius Maximus*, 3.
16. Polybius, III: 89.
17. ibid., 90.
18. ibid., 94.
19. Livy, *The War with Hannibal*, XXII: 33.
20. ibid., 38.
21. ibid.
22. ibid., 51.
23. ibid., 54.
24. ibid., XXIII: 48.
25. Caven, p. 140.
26. Livy, op. cit, XXVI: 38.
27. ibid.
28. Polybius, X: 2–3.
29. Livy, op. cit., XXVIII: 17.

30. Plutarch, *Marcellus*, 30.
31. Livy, op. cit. XXVII: 51.
32. Lazenby, p.235.
33. Livy, op. cit., XXIII: 34.
34. ibid., 38.
35. ibid., XXVII: 23.
36. Caven, p. 155.
37. Livy, op. cit., XXX: 32.
38. Lazenby, p. 226.
39. Caven, p. 85.
40. Livy, op. cit., XXX: 28.
41. ibid., XXI: 2.
42. Polybius, IX: 22.
43. ibid.
44. ibid., 24.
45. ibid., 26.
46. ibid.
47. ibid., 25.
48. Livy, op. cit., XXI: 4.
49. ibid., XXVI: 38.
50. ibid., XIV: 2–3.
51. ibid., XXII: 52.
52. ibid., 7.
53. ibid., XXV: 17.
54. ibid., XXI: 4.
55. Polybius, III: 78.
56. Caven, p. 86.
57. Livy, op. cit., XXVIII: 12.
58. Lazenby, p. 256.
59. Polybius, II: 48.
60. Livy, op. cit., XXVIII: 12.
61. Polybius, III: 78.
62. Livy, op. cit., XXII: 5.
63. Polybius, III: 81.
64. ibid., 80.
65. ibid., 104.
66. ibid., 71.
67. ibid., 116.
68. ibid., 107.
69. Livy, op. cit., XXIV: 11.
70. ibid., XXV: 5.
71. ibid., XXIII: 32.
72. ibid., 33.

Chapter 11: The Third Punic War

1. Polybius, XXXVI: 9.
2. Scullard, *A History of the Roman World*, p. 308.

Chapter 12: Rome and the east

1. Polybius, XVIII: 39.
2. Livy, *Rome and the Mediterranean*, XXXIII, in Kagan, p. 135.
3. Livy, op. cit., XXXIV: 49.
4. Carcopino, 'Points de vue sur l'impérialisme romain', in Kagan, pp. 148–9.
5. Frank, in Kagan, pp. 151–4.
6. ibid.
7. Badian, pp. 62–9.
8. Holleaux, M. in *Cambridge Ancient History*, vol. 8, pp. 156–60.
9. ibid.
10. Livy, op. cit., XLV: 34.
11. Plutarch, *Aemilius Paullus*, 32–4, in Lewis & Reinhold, *The Republic*, p. 218.
12. Pausanias, *Description of Greece*, VII.xvi.7–10, in Lewis & Reinhold, op. cit., p. 198.

Chapter 13: The immediate and long-term effects of the wars

1. Sallust, *The Conspiracy of Catiline*, p. 181.
2. ibid., pp. 186, 190–1, 206.
3. Appian, I.i.7, in Lewis & Reinhold, *The Republic*, p. 228.
4. ibid.
5. Diodorus Siculus, Historical Library XXXIV, *Fragments*, in Lewis & Reinhold, op. cit., p. 231.
6. Velleius Paterculus, II.i.1–2, in Lewis & Reinhold, op. cit., p. 457.
7. Livy, *History of Rome*, XXXIX: 6, in Lewis & Reinhold, op. cit., p. 456.
8. Polybius, XXXI: 26.
9. Plutarch, *Gaius Gracchus*, 19.

10. Sallust, op. cit., p. 183.
11. Livy, *Rome and the Mediterranean*, XXXIV: 108.
12. Polybius, VI: 17.
13. Cicero, 'In defence of Rabirius Postumus', in Lewis & Reinhold, op. cit., p. 451.
14. Velleius Paterculus, in Lewis & Reinhold, op. cit., p. 265.
15. Horace, *Epodes*, 2, 1, 156, Loeb Classical Library, Heinemann, London.
16. Cicero, *De re publica*, 2, 19, 34, trans. Clinton W. Keyes, Loeb Classical Library.
17. Plutarch, *Aemilius Paullus*, 6.
18. Plutarch, *Cato the Elder*, 20.
19. Tacitus, 'Dialogue on oratory', in Lewis & Reinhold, op. cit., p. 499.
20. Plutarch, *Cato the Elder*, 23.
21. Plutarch, *Marcellus*, 21.
22. ibid.
23. Livy, *Rome and the Mediterranean*, XXXIX: 8, 13.

Chapter 14: The Gracchi

1. Bernstein, p. 232.
2. Astin, p. 189.
3. Florus, II: 2.
4. Sallust, *The Jugurthine War*, p. 78.
5. Astin, p. 190.
6. Florus, II: 2.
7. Astin, p. 179.
8. Cicero, 'De haruspicum responsis', in Macquarie University, School of History extracts, *Latin Sources on Tiberius Gracchus*, reprinted from Loeb Classical Library.
9. Plutarch, *Tiberius Gracchus*, 8.
10. Earl, *Tiberius Gracchus*, p. 40.
11. Carcopino, 'La république de 133 à 44', in Kagan, pp. 195–6.
12. Cicero, 'De amicitia', 12.41, in Macquarie University, op. cit.
13. Plutarch, *Tiberius Gracchus*, 8.
14. Appian, I: 1.11.
15. Astin, p. 194.
16. Cicero, 'Pro Sestio', 48.103, in Macquarie University, op. cit.
17. Astin, p. 219.
18. Plutarch, *Tiberius Gracchus*, 14.
19. ibid., 19.
20. Cicero, 'Brutus', 58.212, in Macquarie University, op. cit.
21. Smith, in Kagan, p. 197.
22. Cicero, 'De haruspicum responsis', 19.41, in Macquarie University, op. cit.
23. Plutarch, *Gaius Gracchus*, 1.
24. ibid.
25. ibid., 3.
26. ibid., 8.
27. ibid., 9.
28. ibid., 13.
29. ibid.
30. ibid., 12.
31. ibid., 17.
32. Smith, in Kagan, p. 199.
33. Sallust; *The Jugurthine War*, p. 78.
34. Cicero, 'De officiis', II: 12.43, in *Orations*, Loeb Classical Library , vol. 11.
35. Smith, in Kagan, p. 199.
36. Last, 'Gaius Gracchus', in Kagan, p. 183.
37. Cicero, 'De re publica', I: 19.31, in *Philosophical Treatises*, Loeb Classical Library, vol. 21.
38. Appian, I: Introduction, 2.
39. Cicero, *Selected Political Speeches*, I: 4.
40. Sallust, op. cit., p. 53.
41. ibid., p. 65.
42. ibid., p. 80.

Chapter 15: Marius and Sulla

1. Plutarch, *Marius*, 2.
2. Plutarch, *Sulla*, 2.
3. Plutarch, *Marius*, 3.
4. Sallust, *The Jugurthine War*, p. 131.
5. ibid., p. 99.
6. ibid., p. 131.
7. ibid., p. 99.
8. Plutarch, *Sulla*, 2.

9. Sallust, op. cit., p. 99.
10. ibid., p. 131.
11. Plutarch, *Marius*, 33.
12. Plutarch, *Sulla*, 31, 35.
13. Sallust, op. cit., p. 131.
14. Plutarch, *Marius*, 2.
15. Sallust, op. cit., p. 100.
16. Plutarch, *Marius*, 4.
17. ibid.
18. ibid., 6.
19. Sallust, op. cit., p. 100.
20. ibid., p. 102.
21. ibid., p. 122.
22. Last, p. 229.
23. Plutarch, *Marius*, 10.
24. ibid., 12.
25. Scullard, *From the Gracchi to Nero*, p. 56.
26. Cicero, 'De haruspicum responsis', 43, in *Orations*, Loeb Classical Library , vol. 9.
27. Plutarch, *Marius*, 14.
28. Cicero, 'Brutus', 224, in *Rhetorical Treatises*, Loeb Classical Library , vol. 5.
29. 'Epitome of Livy', in Stockton, p. 98.
30. Appian, I: 30.
31. Plutarch, *Marius*, 29.
32. 'Epitome', op. cit., p. 103.
33. Appian, I: 32.
34. 'Epitome', op. cit., p. 103.
35. Plutarch, *Marius*, 31.
36. Cicero, 'De officiis', 3.47, in *Philosophical Treatises*, Loeb Classical Library , vol. 21.
37. Asconius, 'Commentary on Cicero's "Pro Cornelia"', in Clark's *Oxford Text of Asconius*, A. C. Clark, Oxford, 1907, p. 67.
38. Bobbiensis Scholiast on Cicero's 'Pro Sestio', in Thomas Strong (ed.), *Ciceronis Orationum Scholiastae*, 1912, repr. Hildesheim, 1964.
39. Appian, I: 35.
40. Velleius Paterculus, II.13–15.
41. Plutarch, *Cato the Younger*, 2.
42. Velleius Paterculus, II.13–15.
43. Appian, I: 55.
44. Plutarch, Sulla, 7.
45. ibid., 8.
46. Scullard, *From the Gracchi to Nero*, p. 69.
47. Plutarch, *Sulla*, 10.
48. Florus, 79–80.
49. Plutarch, *Marius*, 43.
50. Velleius Paterculus, II.18.1–3.
51. Plutarch, *Sulla*, 31.
52. ibid.
53. Appian, I: 95–6.
54. Plutarch, *Crassus*, 6.
55. Appian, I: 100.
56. ibid.
57. Velleius Paterculus, II.30.
58. Stockton, in Kagan, 1st edn, p. 266.
59. Plutarch, *Sulla*, 34.
60. Appian, I: 104.
61. Brunt, p. 111.
62. ibid.

Chapter 16: The rise of Pompey

1. Sallust, *The Conspiracy of Catiline*, p. 177.
2. Plutarch, *Pompey*, 14.
3. ibid.
4. ibid., 15.
5. ibid., 16.
6. Plutarch, *Sertorius*, 6.
7. ibid.
8. ibid., 11.
9. ibid., 22.
10. ibid., 25.
11. Plutarch, *Crassus*, 9.
12. ibid., 11.
13. Plutarch, *Pompey*, 21.
14. ibid.
15. ibid.
16. Cicero, 'Against Verres 1', in *Selected Works*, p. 37.
17. Plutarch, *Pompey*, 23.
18. Suetonius, 'Julius Caesar', 1.
19. Plutarch, *Pompey*, 24.
20. ibid., 25.
21. ibid., 26.

22. ibid.
23. ibid., 28.
24. ibid., 30.
25. ibid.
26. ibid., 36.
27. Dio Cassius, 33–6.
28. Cicero, 'De imperio Cn. Pompeii, in *Selected Political Speeches*, 49–63.
29. D. Taylor, p. 25.
30. Cicero, 'The Second Speech on the agrarian law against Rullus', in *Orations*, Loeb Classical Library , vol. 6, p. 371.
31. Cicero, 'Against Lucius Sergius Catalina', in *Selected Political Speeches*, p. 97.
32. Sallust, *The Conspiracy of Catiline*, p. 204.
33. ibid., p. 194.
34. ibid., p. 195.
35. ibid., p. 212.
36. Plutarch, *Cicero*, 23.
37. ibid.
38. Sallust, op. cit., p. 177.
39. Cicero, 'Against Lucius Sergius Catilina, op. cit., p. 137.
40. Plutarch, *Cicero*, 24.
41. Cicero, *Letters to his Friends*, pp. 321–3.
42. Cicero, 'Against Lucius Sergius Catilina', op. cit., 4th speech.
43. Plutarch, *Pompey*, 13.
44. ibid., 45.
45. ibid.
46. ibid., 42.
47. ibid., 44.
48. ibid., 46.
49. Seager, *Pompey*, p. 82.

Chapter 17: From the First Triumvirate to the death of Caesar

1. Scullard, *From the Gracchi to Nero*, p. 118.
2. Plutarch, *Pompey*, 47.
3. Cicero, 'Orationes Philippicae', 2.23–4, in Rawson, p. 182.
4. Velleius Paterculus, II: 44, in D. Taylor, p. 42.
5. Seager, *Pompey*, p. 82.
6. Plutarch, *Pompey*, 47.
7. Plutarch, *Caesar*, 14.
8. Plutarch, *Pompey*, 48.
9. ibid.
10. Cicero, *Letters to Atticus*, 2.16, in D. Taylor, p. 44.
11. ibid., 2.19, in *Selected Letters*, p. 56.
12. ibid.
13. ibid.
14. ibid., in D. Taylor, p. 46.
15. Plutarch, *Cicero*, 30.
16. ibid., 31.
17. ibid., 32.
18. Plutarch, *Pompey*, 49.
19. Cicero, op. cit., 4.1, in *Selected Letters*, p. 68.
20. Plutarch, *Pompey*, 49.
21. ibid., 50.
22. ibid., 49.
23. Plutarch, *Caesar*, 28.
24. Plutarch, *Pompey*, 53.
25. Seager, *Pompey*, p. 148.
26. Broughton, vol. 2, p. 603.
27. ibid., p. 574.
28. Caesar, *The Civil War*, 4: 1–4.
29. Velleius Paterculus, II: ch.29.
30. Plutarch, *Pompey*, 14.
31. Marsh, p. 241.
32. Cicero, *Selected Political Speeches*, pp. 48–53.
33. Cicero, *Selected Letters*, p. 39.
34. ibid., p. 40.
35. ibid., p. 53.
36. ibid., p. 56.
37. ibid., p. 58.
38. ibid., p. 59.
39. ibid., p. 100.
40. ibid., p. 145.
41. Plutarch, *Caesar*, 31.
42. Appian, II: V.33.
43. Plutarch, *Caesar*, 39.
44. Caesar, *The Civil War*, 1.9.

45. ibid., 1.85.
46. Plutarch, *Cicero*, 37.
47. Cicero, *Selected Letters*, p. 140.
48. ibid., p. 148.
49. Cicero, *Selected Works*, pp. 78–9.
50. Plutarch, *Caesar*, 36.
51. Plutarch, *Pompey*, 67.
52. ibid., 76.
53. Cicero, *Letters to Atticus*, 11.6, in D. Taylor, p. 74.
54. Grant, *Julius Caesar*, p. 173.
55. Plutarch, *Caesar*, 48.
56. Suetonius, 'Julius Caesar', 37.
57. Plutarch, *Caesar*, 56.
58. ibid.
59. Suetonius, 'Julius Caesar', 75.
60. Cowell, p. 256.
61. Gelzer, *Caesar*, p. 276.
62. Cowell, p. 262.
63. ibid., p. 261.
64. ibid., p. 256.
65. Suetonius, 'Julius Caesar', 76.
66. ibid.
67. ibid., 77.
68. ibid., 78.
69. ibid., 79.
70. ibid., 76.
71. Plutarch, *Caesar*, 59.
72. ibid., 58.
73. Suetonius, 'Julius Caesar', 82.
74. Plutarch, *Caesar*, 66.
75. Suetonius, 'Julius Caesar', 73.
76. ibid., 50.
77. ibid., 55.
78. ibid., 56.
79. ibid., 50.

Chapter 18: From republic to principate

1. Plutarch, *Mark Antony*, 4.
2. Plutarch, *Brutus*, 19.
3. Plutarch, *Mark Antony*, 14.
4. Plutarch, *Brutus*, 20.
5. ibid.
6. ibid.
7. Cicero, 'First Philippic', in *Selected Political Speeches*, p. 298.
8. ibid.
9. Cicero, 'Second Philippic', in *Selected Works*, p. 143.
10. ibid., p. 149.
11. Cicero, *Selected Letters*, p. 197.
12. Cicero, 'Letter to Atticus', in *Selected Works*, p. 91.
13. Suetonius, 'Augustus', 8.
14. Cicero, 'To Atticus', in *Selected Letters*, p. 198.
15. Pliny, *Natural History*, II: 93, in extracts compiled by the School of History, Philosophy and Politics, Macquarie University, Sydney, NSW.
16. Jones, p. 14.
17. Cicero, 'Third Philippic', in Judge, p. 111.
18. Jones, p. 18.
19. Cicero, 'To Brutus', in D. Taylor, p. 86.
20. Brunt & Moore, I: 2–3, p. 19.
21. Plutarch, *Cicero*, 49.
22. Jones, p. 26.
23. Plutarch, *Mark Antony*, 66.

Chapter 19: The principate of Augustus

1. Augustus, in Brunt & Moore, p. 19.
2. Suetonius, 'Augustus', 101.
3. Augustus, 1.1, 2; 25.1.
4. Augustus, in Brunt & Moore, p. 4.
5. ibid., p.19.
6. Augustus, 34.
7. ibid., 34, 1.
8. ibid., 34.
9. ibid., 5, 1–3.
10. ibid., 6, 2.
11. Velleius Paterculus, II: 89.
12. Ovid, *Fasti*, I, 589, in Brunt & Moore, p. 91.
13. Suetonius, 'Augustus', 28.
14. Tacitus, *Annals*, p. 32.

15. Judge, pp. 172–3: 'Res publica restituta — a modern illusion'.
16. Augustus, 4, in Brunt & Moore, p. 19.
17. ibid., 7.2, p. 21.
18. Suetonius, 'Augustus', 7.
19. Augustus, 13, in Brunt & Moore, p. 25.
20. ibid., 10.2, p. 23.
21. ibid., 35, p. 37.
22. Suetonius, 'Augustus', 58.
23. Augustus, 34, in Brunt & Moore, p. 37.
24. Suetonius, 'Augustus', 35.
25. ibid.
26. Dio Cassius, LII.15, in Salmon, p. 2.
27. Jones, p. 141.
28. Suetonius, 'Augustus', 40.
29. Augustus, 15, 1–2, in Brunt & Moore, p. 25.
30. Suetonius, 'Augustus', 42.
31. ibid.
32. ibid., 43.
33. Horace, *Odes*, III.6, in Jones, p. 147.
34. ibid., p. 148.
35. Suetonius, 'Augustus', 65.
36. ibid.
37. ibid., 33.
38. ibid., 28.
39. ibid., 29.
40. ibid., 30.
41 Augustus, in Brunt & Moore, p. 37.
42. ibid.
43. Suetonius, 'Augustus', 101.
44. Jones, p. 94.
45. ibid., p. 99
46. Augustus, 28.
47. ibid, 16.
48. Salmon, p. 109.
49. The papers of the Macquarie Continuing Education Conference for Ancient History Teachers, 1979, p. 158.
50. Suetonius, 'Augustus', 20.
51. ibid., p. 89
52. Virgil, *Eclogues*, 4 in McDermott & Caldwell, p. 332.
53. Virgil, *Aeneid*, 1.257–96, op. cit., p. 334.
54. ibid., 8.626–728, pp. 334–6.
55. Virgil, *Aeneid*, 6.851–3, trans. H. R. Fairclough, Loeb Classical Library, vol. 1.
56. Horace, 'Odes', IV.5, in *Odes and Epodes*, trans. C. E. Bennett, Loeb Classical Library.
57. Suetonius, 'Tiberius', 21.
58. Tacitus, *Annals*, p. 39.
59. Suetonius, 'Augustus', 101.
60. Velleius Paterculus, II, 89, in Jones, p. 17.
61. Tacitus, *Annals*, p. 32.
62. Augustus, 15.3, in Brunt & Moore, p. 25.
63. ibid., 5.2, p. 21.
64. ibid., 34.1; 34.3, pp. 35, 37.
65. Tacitus, *Annals*, p. 37.
66. ibid.
67. Suetonius, 'Augustus', 28.
68. ibid.
69. ibid.

Chapter 20: The forums of Rome in the time of Augustus

1. Plautus, *Curculio*, 470, trans, Paul Nixon, Loeb Classical Library, 1917.
2. Suetonius, 'Julius Caesar, 88.
3. Augustus, 20.3, in Brunt & Moore, p. 29.
4. Suetonius, 'Augustus', 29.
5. Augustus, 21.1, in Brunt & Moore, p. 29.
6. Ovid, *Fasti*, V.563–6, in 'Eulogistic Inscriptions of the Augustan Forum, article in the papers of the Macquarie Continuing Education for Ancient History Teachers, 1980, pp. 1–26.
7. Suetonius, 'Augustus', 31.
8. Augustus, 35.1.

Chapter 21: The Julio-Claudian dynasty

1. Tacitus, *Annals*, p. 150.
2. ibid., p. 39.
3. ibid., p. 73.
4. ibid., p. 97.

5. ibid., p. 36.
6. ibid., p. 97.
7. ibid., p. 120.
8. ibid., p. 162.
9. Suetonius, 'Tiberius', 68.
10. Tacitus, *Annals*, p. 33.
11. ibid., p. 36.
12. B. H. Warmington, *Nero: Reality and Legend*, p. 11.
13. Salmon, p. 123.
14. Tacitus, *Annals*, p. 39.
15. Suetonius, 'Tiberius', 24.
16. Tacitus, *Annals*, p. 34.
17. Syme, *Tacitus*, vol. 1, p. 427.
18. Salmon, p. 126.
19. Tacitus, *Annals*, p. 50.
20. ibid.
21. ibid., p. 43.
22. ibid., pp. 52–3.
23. ibid., p. 44.
24. ibid., p. 47.
25. ibid., p. 48.
26. ibid., p. 49.
27. ibid., p. 52.
28. ibid., p. 53.
29. ibid., p. 54.
30. ibid., p. 55.
31. ibid.
32. ibid., pp. 55–6.
33. ibid., p. 57.
34. ibid., p. 62.
35. ibid., p. 58.
36. ibid., p. 59.
37. Suetonius, 'Gaius', 3.
38. Tacitus, *Annals*, p. 113.
39. ibid., p. 61.
40. ibid.
41. ibid., p. 68.
42. ibid., p. 89.
43. ibid., p. 110.
44. ibid.
45. ibid., p. 113.
46. ibid., p. 114.
47. ibid., p. 113.
48. ibid., p. 123.
49. ibid., p. 124.
50. ibid., p. 157.
51. ibid., p. 158.
52. ibid., p. 157.
53. ibid., p. 158.
54. ibid., p. 163.
55. ibid., p. 178.
56. ibid., p. 187.
57. ibid., p. 196.
58. ibid.
59. ibid., p. 55.
60. ibid., p. 71.
61. ibid., p. 114.
62. ibid., p. 121.
63. ibid., p. 163.
64. ibid., p. 183.
65. ibid., p. 212.
66. ibid., p. 160.
67. Suetonius, 'Tiberius', 30.
68. Tacitus, *Annals*, p. 35.
69. Suetonius, 'Tiberius', 26–7.
70. Tacitus, *Annals*, p. 95.
71. ibid., p. 149.
72. ibid., p. 137.
73. Suetonius, 'Tiberius', 31.
74. Tacitus, *Annals*, p. 32.
75. ibid., p. 150.
76. ibid.
77. Syme, *Tacitus*, vol. 1, p. 427.
78. Tacitus, *Annals*, p. 194.
79. ibid.
80. ibid., p. 155.
81. ibid., p. 174.
82. ibid., p. 73.
83. ibid.
84. Dudley, p. 112.
85. Tacitus, *Annals*, p. 74.
86. ibid., p. 151.
87. ibid., p. 191.
88. ibid.
89. ibid., p. 189.

90. ibid., p. 91.
91. ibid., p. 90.
92. ibid., p. 74.
93. ibid., p. 92.
94. ibid., p. 74.
95. ibid., p. 75.
96. ibid., p. 102.
97. ibid.
98. ibid., p. 214.
99. ibid., p. 216.
100. ibid., p. 89.
101. ibid., p. 220.
102. ibid., p. 147.
103. Suetonius, 'Tiberius', 37.
104. Tacitus, *Annals*, p. 148.
105. ibid., p. 175.
106. ibid., p. 160.
107. ibid., p. 150.
108. ibid., pp. 150–1.
109. ibid., p. 135.
110. ibid., p. 108.
111. ibid., p. 101.
112. ibid., p. 216.
113. Syme, *Tacitus*, vol. 1, p. 422.
114. ibid., p. 421.
115. Dudley, p. 118.
116. Syme, *Tacitus*, vol. 1, p. 436.
117. ibid., p. 429.
118. Tacitus, *Annals*, p. 227.
119. ibid., p. 75.
120. ibid., p. 91.
121. ibid., pp. 161–2.
122. ibid., p. 63.
123. ibid., p. 211.
124. ibid.
125. Scullard, *From the Gracchi to Nero*, p. 292.
126. Tacitus, *Annals*, p. 75.
127. Suetonius, 'Tiberius', 21.
128. Tacitus, *Annals*, p. 200.
129. ibid., p. 160.
130. Syme, *Tacitus*, vol. 1, p. 428.
131. Tacitus, *Annals*, p. 224.
132. ibid.
133. ibid.
134. Suetonius, 'Gaius', 50.
135. Tacitus, *Annals*, p. 225.
136. ibid., p. 224.
137. Suetonius, 'Gaius', 13.
138. ibid., 22.
139. ibid., 26.
140. Syme, vol. 1, p. 439.
141. Suetonius, 'Gaius', 11.
142. ibid., 23.
143. Suetonius, 'Gaius', 38.
144. ibid., 56.
145. Suetonius, 'Claudius', 30.
146. ibid., 4.
147. ibid.
148. Berlin Papyrus, No. 611, col. 3, lines 10–12, in Lewis & Reinhold, *The Empire*, p. 119.
149. Tacitus, *Annals*, p. 244.
150. Salmon, p. 168.
151. Pliny, 'Letters', VIII: 6, in Lewis & Reinhold, op. cit., p. 119.
152. ibid. Suetonius, 'Claudius', 28.
153. Pliny, op. cit.
154. Tacitus, *Annals*, p. 276.
155. ibid.
156. Suetonius, 'Claudius', 28.
157. Tacitus, *Annals*, p. 232.
158. ibid., p. 237.
159. ibid., p. 246.
160. ibid.
161. ibid., p. 250.
162. ibid., p. 251.
163. Suetonius, 'Nero', 51.
164. Tacitus, *Annals*, p. 320.
165. B. H. Warmington, *Nero: Reality and Legend*, p. 117 (taken from an inscription found in Acraephia in Boeotia).
166. Tacitus, *Annals*, p. 365.
167. ibid., p. 362.
168. ibid., p. 364.
169. ibid., p. 362.
170. ibid., p. 363.

171. ibid.
172. ibid., p. 365.
173. Suetonius, 'Nero', 16.
174. Tacitus, *Annals*, p. 365.
175. ibid.
176. Suetonius, 'Nero', 31.
177. Tacitus, *Annals*, p. 286.
178. ibid., p. 288.
179. ibid.
180. ibid.
181. ibid., p. 318.
182. ibid.
183. ibid., p. 335.
184. ibid., p. 343.
185. ibid., p. 375.
186. ibid., p. 390.
187. Suetonius, 'Nero', 37.
188. Tacitus, *Histories*, I: 4–5, in B. H. Warmington, *Nero*, p. 166.

Chapter 22: Life in an imperial city

1. Seneca, *Epistulae Morales*, (Ep. Mor.), LXXXVI, 8, trans. R. M. Gummere, Loeb Classical Library, vol. 5, Letters LXVI–XCII.
2. Tacitus, *Annals*, pp. 321–2.

Glossary

Most of the listed words are Latin; some are commonly used, anglicised versions of Latin words and some are Greek. All are defined here according to their usage in this text; translations are not necessarily literal.

a libellis legal secretary (one of the chief officials in the imperial civil service of the Emperor Claudius)

a rationibus head of the financial department in the imperial civil service

a studiis privy seal — librarian in the imperial civil service

ab epistulis secretary-general in the imperial civil service

aedile a Roman magistrate whose duties included maintaining the city of Rome (streets, traffic, markets etc.) and arranging public festivals and games

aerarium militare military treasury established by Augustus in AD 6 to provide for veterans

aerarium Saturni the state treasury of Rome, housed in the Temple of Saturn

ager publicus public land in Italy which had been confiscated from a conquered enemy

ager Romanus land comprising the Roman state

agnomen an additional surname added to the *praenomen* (personal name), *nomen* (clan name) and *cognomen* (family name) to indicate a great victory, an adoption or a special attribute

alae wings — referring originally to the contingents of allies on the flanks of a Roman legion and later more specifically to the cavalry units

amici friends

amicitia friendship

ampullae terra-cotta or glass bottles containing ointments or perfumed oils

angusticlave a narrow purple stripe on the tunics worn by members of the equestrian order (at the time of Augustus)

annales maximi the year-by-year arrangement in eighty books) of official events of the state — elections, commands, and civic, provincial and religious business organised by the *pontifex maximus* P. Mucius Scaevola in 131–130 BC

apodyterium a dressing room in the public baths

aquila an eagle — generally referring to the standard carried by a Roman legion into battle (after the time of Marius), which featured an eagle

as a large copper coin of small monetary value, usually bearing the head of Janus on one side and the prow of a ship on the other
atrium the vestibule or open central room in a Roman house
auctoritas great authority, influence and prestige
augur a priest whose duty it was to observe and interpret signs (auspices) in order to determine the will of the gods on all important occasions
aula the hall of a Roman house
auspicium the right of taking the auspices
auxilia the auxiliary Roman army created by Augustus: contingents of cavalry and light infantry raised from non-Roman provincials and attached to individual legions — also used for garrison duty in the provinces
beneficia benefits received by a client from his patron
bestiarii men who fought wild animals in the arena
calidarium area used for hot baths
censi assessments made according to property for division of people into military classes
century a division of the Roman army led by a centurion
cliens a client or dependant — a free man who entrusted himself to another and received protection in return
clientelae a body of clients
cognomen the family name
collegia official title for the four great priestly colleges — also referred to associations of men practising the same craft or trade (guilds)
comitia assembly of the Roman people summoned in groups by a magistrate
comitia centuriata assembly of the Roman people sitting and voting in their military centuries
comitia curiata assembly of the Roman people sitting and voting in their parishes (*curiae*)
comitia tributa assembly of the Roman people sitting and voting in their tribes
comitium an open place of assembly
commentarii notebooks, memoirs, personal diaries
commercium the right to enter into a business contract enforceable in Roman courts
concilium general name for any assembly or gathering — often used to denote the plebeian assembly, *concilium plebis*
concilium plebis assembly of plebeians only
concordia ordinum harmony of the orders — a concept promoted by Cicero in 63 BC which envisaged a working together of the senatorial and equestrian orders for the benefit of the state
concameration channels in the walls of public baths through which steam circulated
connubium the right to contract a legal marriage with a member of another state without forfeiting inheritance or paternity rights
conscripti patrician and elected plebeian members of the senate
consilium a body of advisers — the *consilium principis*, the body of advisers summoned by the emperor, was like a privy council

consulars those who had held the consulship

consules ordinarii consuls (from the time of Augustus) who held office for only the first part of a year — that is, those entering office on the first of January; these consuls gave their names to the years

consules suffecti consuls (from the time of Augustus) who held office for the second part of the year

corvus a raven — the name given to a device comprising a grappling spike and a boarding platform, attached to Roman ships during the First Punic War as a means to overcome Rome's inferiority at sea

cubiculum a bedroom in a Roman house

cursus honorum the 'ladder of office' that an aspiring politician was expected to climb: it comprised the official positions of *quaestor, aedile* (optional), *praetor* and *consul*, with age limits for each and set periods between the holding of consecutive positions by one person

curulis curule or official — describing the special magistrates permitted to sit on the curule chair: a curule aedile was the patrician aedile

deditio surrender or capitulation

delatores informers

dignitas prestige

divination foreseeing the future

dolia large wine jars

dominium lordship or absolute ownership

domus a Roman house — usually a town house

dromos (Gr.) passage-like entrance

duovir magistrate elected for life to the local council in Pompeii

ecclesiasterion (Gr.) hall for secret meetings, perhaps of initiates in the mysteries

eulogia (Gr.) an inscription recording details of a distinguished man's career

exedra a semicircular recess or niche in a wall, which projects

fasces a bundle of rods enclosing an axe (its blade projecting) and carried by lictors — symbol of imperium

fasti consulares annual lists of consuls

Fetiales priests who were in charge of the rituals for declaring war and concluding treaties

fides good faith

fiscus a provincial chest or treasury

flamen one of the fifteen priests who made up the college of pontiffs; each flamen was assigned to the cult of one particular god

foedus a special treaty defining the relations of individual communities with Rome

forica a public toilet

frigidarium a room with a cold-water pool

fullones washers and dyers of fabrics

fullonicae laundries

gens (gentes)	clan(s)
gravitas	seriousness about life
haruspex	a priest who inspected the entrails of sacrificial animals, observed the meaning of natural phenomena and prodigies, and interpreted their meaning
hastati	the first line (young men) in the early republican army
horrea	large warehouses
hypocaustum	special channels under the floors of public baths through which steam circulated
imperium	supreme authority, including the right to flog or execute, held by consuls, praetors and dictators
impulvium	a basin in the floor of the atrium for collecting rainwater
ingenui	free-born Romans (as compared with freedmen)
insula	a high-rise apartment building
intercessio	the right of a magistrate to veto a motion carried by another magistrate
interrex	a patrician appointed by the senate to exercise provisional authority for five days if for some reason (death or resignation) there were no consuls; the office was held only until new consuls were elected
iugera	a measure of land
ius fetiale	sacred rules and regulations to do with declaring war and making treaties
lapilli	small, round fragments of lava ejected from a volcano during an eruption
lararium	a small shrine in a private home where the Lares were worshipped
laticlave	purple stripe on the tunic of a Roman senator
legati legionis	commanders of a legion and *auxilia*, normally of praetorian rank, in the first centuries AD
legati propraetore	governor (from the time of Augustus) of a province where there was more than one legion — sometimes appointed to carry out special work for the emperor
lex (leges)	law(s)
libertini	freedmen (former slaves)
lictor	one of the attendants of magistrates with imperium — carried the *fasces* (symbols of the magistrates' power)
Ludi Iuvenales	Youth Games — sometimes referred to as the Juvenalia
maiestas	treason
maius imperium	imperium greater than all others
magister equitum	master of the horse — assistant to the dictator
maniple	a tactical unit of a legion
manus	complete disciplinary control
mensa ponderaria	weighing table (weighing station)
mithraea	shrines dedicated to the worship of Mithras
mos maiorum	ancestral custom
muli Mariani	Marius' mules — soldiers from the time of Marius' military reforms who carried all their needs (weapons, food, entrenching tools)

municipia communities that had received partial Roman citizenship
natatio swimming
necropoleis (Gr.) literally, 'cities of the dead' — cemeteries containing streets lined with tombs
nefastus literally, 'forbidden' — describing days in the calendar on which certain types of public business could not be carried out
nomen clan name
novus homo literally, 'new man' — the first in a family to reach the consulship
optimates 'best men' — a term coming into use after the time of the Gracchi (late second century BC) and referring to the majority of the members of the senatorial oligarchy, who wished to maintain the status quo whereby that body controlled the Roman state
optimo iure full Roman citizenship, with private and public rights
palaestra an open courtyard surrounded with porticoes and used as a training field
pater patriae father of the country
patres fathers or elders — members of the senate in the early republic
patria potestas paternal authority
patrocinium patronage
penaria larders
peristylum portico with gardens and fountains
phalanx a compact body of heavy-armed infantry in battle formation — consisting of a series of parallel columns of men standing close one behind the other, sixteen lines deep, with overlapping shields
pietas sense of duty to the gods, one's parents and one's country
plebs common people, lower classes
pomerium sacred boundary around Rome which no Roman in arms was permitted to cross except for the purpose of a triumph
pontifex maximus chief priest
populares a minority in the senate (as opposed to the optimates) who sought to gain the support of the people's assembly in their desire for reform of self-advancement
portoria taxes on goods entering or leaving harbours and crossing borders
praefectus alae cavalry prefect
praefectus annonae prefect of the grain supply
praefectus cohortus prefect of a cohort
praefectus vigilum prefect of the watch (fire brigade)
praenomen personal name
praetor a Roman magistrate whose chief duties were judicial
praetor peregrinus a judge concerned with cases involving foreigners
praetor urbanus supreme civil judge of Rome
princeps civitatis first citizen
princeps iuventutis title given to the heirs of Augustus and his successors
princeps senatus the senator whose name headed the senatorial lists and who was entitled to speak first in the senate

principes	second line in the early republican army, composed of men in their prime
proletarii	citizens without sufficient property to be classified in one of the five property classes on which the early army was based
provincia	sphere of action or duty — province
provocatio	the right of appeal against a capital charge or act of a magistrate
publicani	tax collectors
quaestor	a Roman magistrate whose duties were chiefly financial (superintended the public treasury, acted as a paymaster in the army and supervised the collection of taxes in the provinces)
sacellum	chapel
sacrarium	shrine
Salii	priests connected with the worship of Mars and Quirinus
sella curulis	a special chair of office reserved for higher (curule) magistrates
senatus consulta	decrees of the senate — advice of the senate to the magistrates
senatus consultum ultimum	an emergency decree of the senate, usually interpreted as authorising the consuls to use every means to save the state
silvae callesque	a type of forestry commission
sine suffragio	without a vote
sistrum	a musical instrument — a type of cymbal
socii	Roman allies within Italy
suffetes	chief Carthaginian magistrates
tabernae	shops
tablinum	living room in a Roman house
thermae	public baths
thermopolium	public dining place serving hot drinks
toga praetexta	gown bordered with purple
triarii	the third line in the early republican army, comprising older and more experienced men and usually operating as a reserve
tribuni aerarii	exact status unknown, but probably men of considerable property — perhaps just below the equestrian class in assessment
tribuni plebis	tribunes of the plebeians
tribunus militum	a military tribune
tributum capitis	poll tax
tributum soli	a tax on land and fixed property
triclinium	dining room in a Roman house
tumulus	bell-shaped mound — domed tomb of the Etruscans
urbs	city
urbs frumentaria	citizens eligible for corn hand-outs
velites	light-armed skirmishers in the army, composed of the youngest and poorest citizens
vigiles	a body of freedmen, organised by Augustus in seven cohorts to act as the fire brigade of Rome — sometimes performing military functions
vividarium	a place of gardens and fountains in a Roman house
volones	volunteers

Bibliography

Ancient sources

Appian. *The Civil Wars*, trans. Horace White (*Appian's Roman History*, vol. 3). Loeb Classical Library, Heinemann, London, 1958.

Augustus. *Res Gestae Divi Augusti*, ed. P. A. Brunt & J. M. Moore. Oxford University Press, Oxford, 1967.

Caesar. *The Civil War, together with the Alexandrian War, the African War and the Spanish War*, trans. Jane F. Mitchell. Penguin, Harmondsworth, 1976.

——. *The Conquest of Gaul*, trans. S. A. Handford. Penguin Classics, Harmondsworth, 1982.

Cicero. *Letters to Atticus*, trans. E. O. Winstedt. Loeb Classical Library, Heinemann, London, 1980.

——. *Letters to his Friends*, trans. W. Glynn Williams. Loeb Classical Library, Heinemann, London, 1979.

——. *Selected Letters*, trans. D. R. Shackleton Bailey. Penguin Classics, Harmondsworth, 1982.

——. *Selected Political Speeches*, trans. Michael Grant. Penguin Classics, Harmondsworth, 1981.

——. *Selected Works*, trans. Michael Grant. Penguin Classics, Harmondsworth, 1967.

Dio Cassius. *History of Rome*, trans. E. Cary. Loeb Classical Library, Heinemann, London, 1927.

Dionysius of Halicarnassus. *Roman Antiquities*, trans. E. Cary. Loeb Classical Library, Heinemann, London, 1947.

Florus. *Epitome of Roman History*, trans. E. S. Forster. Loeb Classical Library, Heinemann, London, 1929.

Livy. *The History of Rome from its Foundations*, vol. 3 (bks III–IV), trans. B. O. Foster; vol. 4 (bks VI–X), trans. J. P. V. D. Balsdon, Loeb Classical Library, Heinemann, London, 1926.

——. *The Early History of Rome*, trans. Aubrey de Sélincourt (*History of Rome*, bks I–V). Penguin Classics, Harmondsworth, 1986.

——. *Rome and Italy*, trans. Betty Radice (*History of Rome*, bks VI–X). Penguin Classics, Harmondsworth, 1982.
——. *Rome and the Mediterranean*, trans. Henry Bettenson (*History of Rome*, bks. XXXI–XLV). Penguin Classics, Harmondsworth, 1983.
——. *The War with Hannibal*, trans. Aubrey de Sélincourt (*History of Rome*, bks XXI–XXX). Penguin Classics, Harmondsworth, 1972.
Plutarch. *The Age of Alexander (Pyrrhus)*, trans. Ian Scott-Kilvert. Penguin Classics, Harmondsworth, 1973.
——. *Fall of the Roman Republic (Marius, Sulla, Crassus, Pompey, Caesar, Cicero)*, trans. Rex Warner. Penguin Classics, Harmondsworth, 1974.
——. *Lives (Aemilius Paullus, Cato the Younger)*, trans. Bernadotte Perrin. Loeb Classical Library, Heinemann, London, 1921.
——. *Makers of Rome (Fabius Maximus, Marcellus, Cato the Elder, Tiberius Gracchus, Gaius Gracchus, Sertorius, Brutus, Mark Antony)*, trans. Ian Scott-Kilvert. Penguin Classics, Harmondsworth, 1986.
Polybius. *The Histories*, vols 1–6, trans. W. R. Paton. Loeb Classical Library, Heinemann, London, 1922.
——. *The Rise of the Roman Empire*, trans. Ian Scott-Kilvert. Penguin Classics, Harmondsworth, 1982.
Sallust. *The Jugurthine War* and *The Conspiracy of Catiline*, trans. S. A. Handford. Penguin Classics, Harmondsworth, 1975.
Suetonius. *The Twelve Caesars*, trans. Robert Graves. Penguin Classics, Harmondsworth, 1979; ill. edn, 1986.
Tacitus. *The Annals of Imperial Rome*, trans. Michael Grant. Penguin Classics, Harmondsworth, 1981.
——. *The Histories*, trans. Kenneth Wellesley. Penguin Classics, Harmondsworth, 1964.
Velleius Paterculus. *Compendium of Roman History*, trans. F. W. Shipley. Loeb Classical Library, Heinemann, London, 1924.
Virgil. *The Aeneid*, trans. W. F. Jackson Knight. Penguin, Harmondsworth, 1971.

Modern sources

Adcock, F. E. *Roman Political Ideas and Practice*. Ann Arbor Paperbacks, University of Michigan Press, Ann Arbor, 1967.
——. 'Caesar's Dictatorship', in *Cambridge Ancient History, vol. 9. Cambridge University Press, 1932.*
Armstrong, D. Horace. Yale University Press, New Haven, 1986.
Astin, A. E. *Scipio Aemilianus*. Clarendon Press, Oxford, 1967.
Badian, E. *Foreign Clientelae, 264–70 BC*. Clarendon Press, Oxford, 1958.

Balsdon, J. P. V. D. *The Emperor Gaius*. Greenwood Press, Wesport, Conn., 1977.
Bernstein. A. H. *Tiberius Gracchus — Tradition and Apostasy*. Cornell University Press, Ithaca, NY, 1978.
Bloch, R. *The Etruscans*. Thames & Hudson, London, 1961.
——. *The Origins of Rome*. Thames & Hudson, London, 1960.
Boren, H. C. *The Gracchi*. Twayne Publishers, NY, 1969.
Broughton, T. R. S. *Magistrates of the Roman Republic*. 2 vols, with supplements. American Philological Society, NY, 1952.
Brunt, P. A. *Social Conflicts in the Roman Republic*. Chatto & Windus, London, 1978.
——. & Moore, J. M. (eds). *Res Gestae Divi Augusti*. Oxford University Press, Oxford, 1967.
Cambridge Ancient History, vols 8, 9, 10, eds S. A. Cook, F. E. Adcock & M. P. Charlesworth. Cambridge University Press, 1932, 1934.
Carter, J. M. *The Battle of Actium*. Hamish Hamilton, London, 1970.
Cary, M. A *History of the Greek World 323–146*. Methuen, London, 1951.
Carcopino, J. *Daily Life in Ancient Rome*. Penguin, Harmondsworth, 1941.
Caven, B. *The Punic Wars*. St Martin's Press, NY, 1980.
Charlesworth, M. P. *The Roman Empire*. Oxford University Press, London, 1968.
Connolly, P. *Greece and Rome at War*. Macdonald, London, 1981.
Cowell, F. R. *Cicero and the Roman Republic*. Pelican Books, Penguin, Harmondsworth, 1964.
De Beer, G. *Hannibal — the Struggle for Power*. Thames & Hudson, London, 1969.
Dudley, D. R. *The World of Tacitus*. Camelot Press, London, 1968.
Earl, D. C. The Moral and Political Tradition of Rome. Thames & Hudson, London, 1967.
——. *Tiberius Gracchus — a Study in Politics*. Berchem, Latomus Revue d'Etudes Latines, Bruxelles, 1963.
Frank, T. *Roman Imperialism*. Macmillan Co, NY, 1914.
Garzetti, A. *From Tiberius to the Antonines, AD 14–192*. Methuen, London, 1974.
Gelzer, M. *Caesar: Politician and Statesman*. 6th edn. Blackwell, Oxford, 1968.
——. *Pompeius*. 2nd edn. S. Bruckmann, Munich, 1949.
Grant, M. *Julius Caesar*. Chancellor Press, London, 1969.
——. *The Roman Forum*. Hamlyn, London, 1974.
——. *Roman History from Coins*. Cambridge University Press, Cambridge, 1958.
——. *Roman Readings*. Penguin, Harmondsworth, 1967.

Gruen, E. S. *The Last Generation of the Roman Republic, 78–44*. University of California Press, Berkeley, 1974.

——. *Roman Politics and the Criminal Courts, 149–78*. Harvard University Press, Cambridge. Mass., 1968.

Hoyos, D. *Hannibal and Rome: The Outbreak of the Second Punic War*. History Teachers Association, NSW, 1975.

Jones, A. H. M. *Augustus*. Chatto & Windus, London, 1970.

Judge, E. E. *Augustus and Roman History: Documents and Papers for Students' Use*. School of History, Philosophy & Politics, Macquarie University, Sydney, 1983.

Kagan, D. *The Roman World*. Problems in Ancient History, vol. 2. 2nd edn. Macmillan Co., NY, 1975.

Last, H. 'Marius and Sulla', in *Cambridge Ancient History*, vol. 9. Cambridge University Press, 1932.

Lazenby, J. F. *Hannibal's War*. Aris & Phillips, Warminster, 1978.

Levick, B. *Tiberius the Politician*. Croom Helm, Beckenham, 1986.

Lewis, N. & Reinhold, M. *Roman Civilisation, Sourcebook I: The Republic; Sourcebook II: The Empire*. Harper & Row, London, 1966.

Lintott, A. W. *Violence in Republican Rome*. Clarendon Press, Oxford, 1968.

McDermott, W. C. & Caldwell, W. E. *Readings in the History of the Ancient World*. 2nd edn. Holt, Reinhart & Winston, NY, 1970.

Marsh, F. B. *A History of the Roman World 146–30 BC*. 3rd edn. Methuen, London, 1964.

Ogilvie, R. M. *The Romans and their Gods in the Age of Augustus*. Chatto & Windus, London, 1969.

Paoli, U. E. *Rome — its People, Life and Customs*. Longmans, Harlow, 1964.

Proctor, D. *Hannibal's March into History*. Oxford University Press, London, 1971.

Rawson, B. *The Politics of Friendship*. Sydney University Press, Sydney, 1978.

Romanelli, P. *The Roman Forum*. Instituto Poligrafico delo Stato, Rome, 1955.

Salmon, E. T. *A History of the Roman World 30 BC-AD 138*. 5th edn. Methuen, London, 1966.

Scramuzza, V. M. *The Emperor Claudius*. Harvard University Press, Cambridge, Mass., 1940.

Scullard, H. H. *From the Gracchi to Nero*. Methuen, London, 1979.

——. *A History of the Roman World 753–146 BC*. Methuen, London, 1964.

——. *Scipio Africanus: Soldier and Politician*. Thames & Hudson, 1970.

Seager, R. *Pompey — a Political Biography*. Blackwell, Oxford, 1979.

____. *Tiberius*. University of California Press, Berkeley, 1972.
Smith, R. E. *The Failure of the Roman Republic*. Cambridge University Press, 1955.
Stockton, D. *From the Gracchi to Sulla*. Sources for Roman History, 133–80 BC, trans., ed. Stockton. London Association of Classical Teachers, Brasenose College, Oxford, 1981.
Strong, D. E. *Roman Art*. Penguin, Harmondsworth, 1988.
Syme, R. *The Roman Revolution*. Clarendon Press, Oxford, 1951.
____. Tacitus. 2 vols. Clarendon Press, Oxford, 1958.
Taylor, D. *Cicero and Rome*. Macmillan Education, London, 1978.
Taylor, L. R. *Party Politics in the Age of Caesar*. University of California Press, Berkeley, 1949.
Walbank, F. W. *A Historical Commentary on Polybius*. 3 vols. Clarendon Press, Oxford, 1975–79.
Warmington, B. H. *Carthage*. Praeger, NY, 1960.
____. *Nero: Reality and Legend*. Chatto & Windus, London, 1969.
Warmington, E. H. *Remains of Old Latin Archaic Inscriptions*, vol. 4. Heinemann, London, 1940–79.

Acknowledgments

The publisher's thanks are due to the following for permission to reproduce copyright photographs:

Accademia Etrusca di Cortona; Archivi Alinari, Rome; Ashmolean Museum, Oxford; Bibliothèque Nationale, Paris; Emmett Bright; The British Museum; Carcavallo, Rome; Deutsches Archaeologisches Institut, Rome; Fototeca Unione, American Academy, Rome; Photographie Giraudon, Paris; Hirmer Fotoarchiv, Munich; Hulton Picture Company, London; Kingston Lacy (S. F. James) Dorset; Kunsthistorisches Museum, Vienna; Mansell Collection, London; Mansell/Alinari; Mansell/Anderson; Metropolitan Museum of Art, New York; Musei Capitolini, Rome; Musée du Louvre; Museo Nazionale di Napoli; Museo Archeologico di Palermo; Museo Civico di Piacenza; Museum of Roman Civilisation, Rome; Musée des Antiquités Nationales, St Germain-en-Laye; Museo delle Terme, Rome; Museum de Antiquities, Turin; Musei Vaticani; Museo Nazionale Etrusco di Villa Guilia; Les Editions Nagel, Geneva; Ny Carlsberg Glyptotek, Copenhagen; Rabat Museum; Réunion des Musées Nationaux, Paris; Roger-Viollet, Paris; Mrs Olive Smith; Staatliche Antikensammlungen und Glyptothek, Munich; Photo Tanjug; Weidenfeld & Nicholson, London.

Every effort has been made to trace and acknowledge copyright, but in some instances this has not been possible.

Index

Page numbers in italic type indicate illustrations; numbers followed by 'm' indicate maps.